CW01034935

Comparative International Commercial Arbitration

About the Authors

Julian D M Lew
Solicitor, Queen's Counsel (England and Wales). Attorney-at-Law (New York).
Partner and head of international arbitration practice group, Herbert Smith.
Visiting Professor and Head, School of International Arbitration,
Centre for Commercial Law Studies, Queen Mary, University of London.

Loukas A Mistelis
Advocate (Athens Bar).
Clive Schmitthoff Senior Lecturer in International Commercial Law,
School of International Arbitration, Centre for Commercial Law Studies,
Queen Mary, University of London.

Stefan M Kröll
Rechtsanwalt.
Senior Research Fellow, Law Centre for European and International
Cooperation (RIZ), University of Cologne.

Comparative International Commercial Arbitration

by

Julian D M Lew QC
LLB (Hons) Lond; Doc Spéc Dr Int'l (Louvain), FCIArb

Loukas A Mistelis
LLB (Athens) MLE (Hannover) Dr juris (Hannover), MCIArb

Stefan M Kröll
LLM (Lond) Dr juris (Köln)

Wolters Kluwer
Law & Business

A C.I.P. Catalogue record for this book is available from the Library of Congress.

ISBN 90 411 1568 4

Published by Kluwer Law International,
P.O. Box 85889, 2508 CN The Hague, The Netherlands.
sales@kluwerlaw.com
http://www.kluwerlaw.com

Sold and distributed in North, Central and South America
by Aspen Publishers, Inc.
7201 McKinney Circle, Frederick, MD 21704, USA.

Sold and distributed in all other countries
by Turpin Distribution Services Limited,
Blackhorse Road, Letchworth, Herts,
SG6 1HN, United Kingdom.

Printed on acid-free paper

All Rights Reserved
© 2003 Kluwer Law International

No part of this work may be reproduced, stored in a retrieval system, or transmitted in any form or by any means, electronic, mechanical, photocopying, microfilming, recording or otherwise, without written permission from the Publisher, with the exception of any material supplied specifically for the purpose of being entered and executed on a computer system, for exclusive use by the purchaser of the work.

Printed in the Netherlands.

FOREWORD

This book has been long in gestation. Originally conceived as a textbook for students on the London University and other postgraduate international commercial arbitration programmes it has developed to a significantly deeper study. It is now a work that it is hoped will be a guide and assistance to lawyers practising in the area of international arbitration. We hope that it will be useful also to the student and lawyer involved occasionally with international dispute settlement.

International arbitration is essentially a private, comparative and international mechanism. No two arbitrations are the same. There are few absolutes. There are no fixed rules or procedures. Any factual variation will invariably result in a significant change in the context and structure of the arbitration. The matrix which affects every arbitration varies depending upon the arbitration agreement, the procedure agreed by the parties, the nationality of the parties, the make-up of the tribunal, the applicable arbitration rules, the substantive applicable law or rules, the subject-matter of the dispute, the mandatory law of the place of arbitration and the permissive law where everything else is silent.

All of these factors are directly controlled by party autonomy. The choice of arbitration by the parties and their decision as to how, where and what the procedure should be is the decisive factor in every case. The simple agreement of the parties to refer disputes to arbitration is a positive rejection of the national courts and in many cases strict national law procedure. The right of parties to determine all aspects of the arbitration is unquestioned. Accordingly, party autonomy has the greatest control on international commercial arbitration.

The effect of party autonomy is a major reason why arbitration has achieved world-wide acceptance as the favoured and principal mechanism for resolving disputes arising out of international commercial transactions. Party autonomy also has been the main influence on the development of truly transnational rules and practices for international arbitration. These rules and practices have crossed the barriers of legal systems and national laws. There are accordingly few determinative answers in arbitration.

The principal factor outside party autonomy that has directly influenced international arbitration practice and law has been the New York Convention on the Recognition and Enforcement of Foreign Arbitral Awards 1958. This Convention is the backbone to the acceptance of international arbitration by the business world. It sets down simply the obligation of states to recognise and give effect to the agreement of parties to refer their disputes to arbitration in preference to a national court jurisdiction. If one party commences court proceedings in defiance of a valid arbitration agreement the national court should stay its proceedings and send the parties to arbitration.

The New York Convention also established the system to ensure the maximum possibility for the simple enforceability of arbitration awards. Over 130 countries are presently party to the New York Convention. The most significant effect of the New York Convention has been the harmonisation of the approach to enforcement of awards through the application of the New York Convention principles in national laws and courts. Whilst there remain countries whose courts do not always follow the spirit and letter of the New York Convention, they are rare exceptions. In the main arbitration awards made in one country will be recognised and enforced in any other state party to the New York Convention.

International arbitration has become independent from national laws and courts in practice and legally. Parties and arbitrators do, in the main, conduct proceedings in a rarefied non-national or international legal environment. Whilst there may, in some cases, be influences from national law on the procedure, this can be controlled by the parties, the arbitrators and international practice. Experienced arbitration lawyers and the major international arbitration institutions have recognised national procedural laws are generally irrelevant and inapplicable. These international practices are acknowledged and upheld by arbitration awards being recognised and enforced under the New York Convention.

The plethora of other international instruments, such as the Algiers Accords, bilateral investment treaties, North American Free Trade Association and the Energy Charter Treaty, further evidence the recognition of arbitration as an autonomous process. The *lex mercatoria*, as evidenced in part in the UNIDROIT Principles of International Commercial Contracts and the Vienna Convention on International Sale of Goods, is naturally applicable by international arbitration tribunals. This again is testament to the autonomous character of the international arbitration process.

The UNCITRAL Model Law on International Commercial Arbitration has reduced to legal formality much that transpires in practice. It reflects a common denominator of laws applicable to international arbitration. It is a compromise which has stripped out national characteristics and contains provisions acceptable to most systems. Many of its provisions are general and it is left to arbitration tribunals and national courts to interpret them. The Model Law has been adopted in over 30 jurisdictions. Decisions of an international tribunal or national court concerning the terms of the Model Law will influence how other tribunals or courts will interpret and apply the same provisions.

This book addresses all these issues and seeks to reflect international arbitration practice, *i.e.* what parties and arbitrators do, how arbitration is conducted, and the principles pertaining to the arbitration agreement, the formation, role and functions of arbitration tribunal, and the importance and effect of the arbitration award. These practices are illustrated by published international awards, the international instruments and arbitration rules, and some national court decisions. At every stage of the arbitration process there remains a conceptual legal conflict between the inherent international and autonomous character of arbitration and the national laws of the parties and the place of arbitration. These issues are reviewed with particular reference to national constitutional and regulatory systems, the effect of mandatory laws of connected states, European and international law including international human rights instruments.

As with any project of this kind there are many individuals who have supported, cajoled, encouraged and assisted in its completion. In particular, my secretary at Herbert Smith, Martina Gamberoni, has typed and retyped many drafts and revisions of the text, and prepared the camera ready script. My assistant at Herbert Smith, Norah Gallagher, has co-ordinated the editorial of the project, with additions and footnotes added by each of the authors, and has taken the editorial role to help with consistency and objective clarity. Gui Conde e Silva, a research student at the School of International Arbitration, Centre for Commercial law Studies, Queen Mary, has assisted with editing the book and the footnotes, and prepared the lists of abbreviations, laws, conventions, cases and awards and the general index. Our publisher, Gwen de Vries, has shown patience as deadlines have passed. Her encouragement and support are much appreciated.

Responsibility for the content and views in this book are those of its three authors. Its merits will be judged by those who use this book.

Julian D M Lew
March 2003

SUMMARY TABLE OF CONTENTS

Table of Contents

TABLE OF ABBREVIATIONS

INSTITUTIONS, ORGANISATIONS AND RULES

The Institution may import the Rules

AAA	American Arbitration Association
AIA	Italian Arbitration Association
ASA	Swiss Arbitration Association
CAMCA	Commercial Arbitration and Mediation Centre for the Americas
CCPIT	China Council for the Promotion of International Trade
CEPANI	Belgian Centre for Arbitration and Mediation
CIETAC	China International Economic and Trade Arbitration Commission
CMEA	Council for Mutual Economic Assistance (Eastern Europe) (COMECON)
CMI	Comité Maritime International
CPR Institute for Dispute Resolution	Center for Public Resources Institute for Dispute Resolution
CRCICA	Cairo Regional Centre For International Commercial Arbitration
CRT	Claims Resolution Tribunal for Dormant Accounts in Switzerland
DIS	Deutsche Institution für Schiedsgerichtsbarkeit
EC	European Community
ECAFE	United Nations Economic Commission for Asia and the Far East
ECOSOC	United Nations Economic and Social Council
EDF	European Development Fund
EEC	European Economic Community
EU	European Union
FALCA	Fast and Low Cost Arbitration (LMAA)
FIDIC	Fédération Internationale des Ingénieurs-Conseils
GAFTA	Grain and Feed Trade Association

Geneva	Chamber of Commerce and Industry of Geneva Arbitration Centre
HKIAC	Hong Kong International Arbitration Centre
IACAC	Inter-American Commercial Arbitration Commission
IBA	International Bar Association
ICA	Indian Council of Arbitration
ICAC	Moscow International Commercial Arbitration Court
ICANN	Internet Corporation for Assigned Names and Numbers
ICC	International Chamber of Commerce
ICCA	International Council for Commercial Arbitration
ICDR	American Arbitration Association International Center for Dispute Resolution
ICHEIC	International Commission on Holocaust Era Insurance Claims
ICSID	International Centre for the Settlement of Investment Disputes
IFCAI	International Federation of Commercial Arbitration Institutions
JCAA	Japan Commercial Arbitration Association
Korea	Korean Commercial Arbitration Association
Kuala Lumpur	Kuala Lumpur Regional Centre for Arbitration
LCIA	London Court of International Arbitration
LMAA	London Maritime Arbitration Association
LME	London Metal Exchange
MERCOSUR	Common Market of the Southern Cone pursuant to the Treaty of Asunción of 26 March 1991
MIGA	Multilateral Investment Guarantee Agency
NAI	Netherlands Arbitration Institute
NOFOTA	Netherlands Oil, Fats and Oilseeds Trade Association

OECD	Organisation for Economic Co-operation and Development
OHADA	Organization for the Harmonization of Business Law in Africa
PCA	Permanent Court of Arbitration (The Hague)
SCC	Stockholm Chamber of Commerce Arbitration Institute
SIAC	Singapore International Arbitration Centre
UNCC	United Nations Compensation Commission
UNCITRAL	United Nations Commission for International Trade Law
UNECE	United Nations Economic Commission for Europe
UNIDROIT	International Institute for the Unification of Private Law
Venice	Venice Arbitration Court Rules 1998
Vienna	Austrian Federal Economic Chamber in Vienna
WIPO	World Intellectual Property Organisation
Zurich	Zurich Chamber of Commerce

General Abbreviations

AC	Law Reports, House of Lords (Appeal Cases)
ADRLJ	Arbitration and Dispute Resolution Law Journal
All ER	All England Law Reports
ALR	Australian Law Reports
Am J Comp L	American Journal of Comparative Law
Am J Int'l L	American Journal of International Law
Am Rev Int'l Arb	American Review of International Arbitration
Am U Int'l L Rev	American University International Law Review
Ann IDI	Annuaire de l'Institut de droit international

Arb Int	Arbitration International
Arbitration	Arbitration, Journal of the Chartered Institute of Arbitrators
ASA Bulletin	Swiss Arbitration Association Bulletin
Asian DR	Asian Dispute Review
ATF	Arrêts du Tribunal Fédéral Suisse
Betriebs-Berater	Der Betriebs-Berater (German journal)
BGB	Bürgerliches Gesetzbuch (German Civil Code)
BGE	Entscheidungen des schweizerischen Bundesgerichts
BGHZ	Sammlung der Entscheidungen des Bundesgerichtshofs in Zivilsachen
Boston U Int'l L J	Boston University International Law Journal
BT-Drs	Bundestags-Drucksache
BverfGE	Entscheidungen des Bundesverfassungsgerichts
BYBIL	British Yearbook of International Law
CA	Court of Appeal of England and Wales
Case W Res J Int'l L	Case Western Reserve Journal of International Law
CC	Code civil, codice civile, civil code
CCI	Chamber of Commerce and Industry of the Russian Federation
CCP	Code of Civil Procedure
ChD	Chancery Division
CIF	Cost, insurance, freight
CISG	United Nations Convention on the International Sale Goods
CLR	Commonwealth Law Reports
Clunet	Journal de droit international
Columbia J Transnat'l L	Columbia Journal of Transnational Law
Con LR	Construction Law Reports
CPR	Civil Procedure Rules (England)
Croat Arbit Yearb	Croatian Arbitration Yearbook

DAC	Departmental Advisory Committee
Décisions et rapports	Décisions et rapports of the European Court of Human Right
DIS-Materialien	DIS collection of materials on arbitration
Disp Res J	Dispute Resolution Journal
DLR	Dominion Law Reports
ECHR	European Convention on Human Rights
ECJ	Court of Justice of the European Communities
ECR	Report of Cases before the Court of Justice of the European Communities
EDNY	Eastern District of New York
EHRR	European Human Rights Reports
EJCL	Electronic Journal of Comparative Law
ER	English Reports
European Convention	European Convention on International Commercial Arbitration 1961(Geneva).
European Comm HR	European Commission of Human Rights
European Ct HR	European Court of Human Rights
EWCA Civ	Neutral citation for England and Wales Court of Appeal civil division decisions
EWiR	Entscheidungen zum Wirtschaftsrecht
F 2d	The Federal Reporter Second Series
F 3d	The Federal Reporter Third Series
FAA	United States Federal Arbitration Act
Fair Empl Prac Cas	Fair Employment Practice Cases
FOB	Free on board
FS	Festschrift
F Supp	Federal Supplement
GDR	German Democratic Republic
Geo Wash J Int'l L & Eco	George Washington University Journal of International Law and Economics
Hastings Int'l & Comp L Rev	Hastings International and Comparative Law Review
HKHC	Hong Kong High Court

HKLJ	Hong Kong Law Journal
HL	House of Lords
IBA Rules	IBA Rules on the taking of Evidence in International Commercial Arbitration, 1999
ICC Bulletin	International Chamber of Commerce International Court of Arbitration Bulletin
ICLQ	International and Comparative Law Quarterly.
ICSID Rev-FILJ	ICSID Review – Foreign Investment Law Journal
IECL	International Encyclopedia of Comparative Law
INCOTERMS	ICC International Commercial Terms
Int ALR	International Arbitration Law Review
Int'l Bus Law	International Business Lawyer
Int'l Fin L Rev	International Financial Law Review
Int'l Law	International Lawyer
ILM	International Legal Materials
ILR	International Law Reports
IPRax	Praxis des internationalen Privat- und Verfahrensrechts
IPRspr	Die deutsche Rechtsprechung auf dem Gebiete des internationalen Privatrechts im Jahre ...
Iran-US CTR	Iran-US Claims Tribunal Reports
JBL	Journal of Business Law
J Int'l Arb	Journal of International Arbitration.
Journal des Tribunaux	(Belgian) Journal des Tribunaux
Juris-Classeur Proc Civ	Juris-Classeur (procedure civile)
KTS	Konkurs-Treuhand und Schiedsgerichtswesen
Law & Policy in Int'l Bus	Law & Policy in International Business
Lloyd's Rep	Lloyd's Law Reports
Lloyd's MCLQ	Lloyd's Maritime and Commercial Law Quarterly
LNTS	League of Nations Treaty Series
Louisiana L Rev	Louisiana Law Review

Mealey's IAR	Mealey's International Arbitration Reports
Minn L Rev	Minnesota Law Review
Model Law	UNCITRAL Model Law on International Commercial Arbitration adopted 21 June 1985
MR	Master of the Rolls
NCPC	French Code of Civil Procedure (Nouveau Code de Procedure Civile)
NE	North East Reporter
Ned Jur	Nederlands Jurisprudentie
New L J	New Law Journal
New York Convention	1958 New York Convention on the Recognition and Enforcement of Foreign Arbitral Awards
NJW	Neue Juristische Wochenschrift.
NSWLR	New South Wales Law Reports
NW J Int'l L & Bus	Northwestern Journal of International Law and Business
NYAD	New York Appellate Division
NYLJ	New York Law Journal
NY L Sch J Int'l & Comp L	New York Law School Journal of International and Comparative Law
OJ	Official Journal of the European Communities
PC	Privy Council
PIL	(Swiss) Private International Law
QBD	Queen's Bench Division
RabelsZ	Rabels Zeitschrift für ausländisches und internationales Privatrecht
RCADI	Recueil des Cours de l'Académie de Droit International de la Haye / Collected Courses of the Hague Academy of International Law
RDAI/IBLJ	Revue de droit des affaires internationales / International Business Law Journal
Rev Arb	Revue de l'arbitrage
Rev crit dip	Revue critique de droit international privé

RHDI	Revue hellénique de droit international
Riv Arb	Rivista dell' Arbitrato
RIW	Recht der Internationalen Wirtschaft
Rome Convention	EC (Rome) Convention on the Law Applicable to Contractual Obligations 1980
RPS	Recht und Praxis der Schiedsgerichtsbarkeit
Rutgers L Rev	Rutgers Law Review
SchiedsVZ	Zeitschrift für Schiedsverfahren
SchwZIER	Schweizeriche Zeitschrift für internationales und europäisches Recht
S Ct	Supreme Court of the United States
SDNY	Southern District of New York
SLT	Scots Law Times Reports
Texas Int'l LJ	Texas International Law Journal
Tulane L Rev	Tulane Law Review
UCC	Uniform Commercial Code
U Cin L Rev	University of Cincinnati Law Review
UCP 500	Uniform Customs and Practices relating to Documentary Credits – ICC publication no 500
U Ill L Rev	University of Illinois Law Review
UKPC	Neutral citation for decisions of the Privy Council
U Miami Inter-Am L Rev	University of Miami Inter-American Law Review
UNCITRAL Notes	UNCITRAL Notes on Organizing Arbitral Proceedings
UNTS	United Nations Treaty Series
USSR	Union of Soviet Socialist Republics
Vanderbilt L Rev	Vanderbilt Law Review
WAMR	World Arbitration and Mediation Report
Washington Convention	Washington Convention on the Settlement of Investment Disputes between States and Nationals of other States 1965

WIPO Expedited Rules	WIPO Expedited Rules
WL	Westlaw
WLR	The Weekly Law Reports
WM	Wertpapier-Mitteilungen
WTAM	World Trade and Arbitration Materials
WuB	Entscheidungssammlung zum Wirtschafts- und Bankrecht
Yale LJ	Yale Law Journal
YBCA	Yearbook of Commercial Arbitration
ZBB	Zeitschrift für Bankrecht und Bankwirtschaft
ZfRV	Zeitschrift für Rechtsvergleichung
ZIP	Zeitschrift für Wirtschaftsrecht und Insolvenzpraxis
ZPO	German Code of Civil Procedure (ZPO)
ZVglRwiss	Zeitschrift für vergleichende Rechstwissenschaften

Chapter 1

ARBITRATION AS A DISPUTE SETTLEMENT MECHANISM

1-1 International arbitration is a specially established mechanism for the final and binding determination of disputes, concerning a contractual or other relationship with an international element, by independent arbitrators, in accordance with procedures, structures and substantive legal or non-legal standards chosen directly or indirectly by the parties.

1-2 Disputes are an inevitable occurrence in many international commercial transactions. Different commercial and legal expectations, cultural approaches, political ramifications and geographic situations are all sources for disagreement and dispute between contracting parties. Genuine differences can concern the meaning of contract terms, the legal implications for a contract, and the respective rights and obligations of the parties. Sometimes parties agree to perform a contract where performance is just not possible. Extraneous factors and human frailties, whether through mismanagement or over-expectation, will also interfere with contractual performance. A major area of dispute is failure to pay moneys due under a contract: this may be because of an inability to pay or a wish not to pay and therefore one party is seeking an excuse or a justification to refuse to pay all or part of the contract price.

1-3 Where these disputes arise and they cannot be resolved by negotiation, they will need to be resolved in accordance with a legal process. This process should have the confidence of the parties or at least be in a forum that is acceptable to the parties. In these circumstances, parties to international commercial contracts frequently look to arbitration as a private, independent and neutral system.

1-4 This chapter deals with (1) the meaning of arbitration, its definition, advantages, disadvantages, and its fundamental characteristics, (2) what arbitration is not, and (3) other alternative dispute resolution mechanisms.

1. What is Arbitration?

1.1. Definitions of Arbitration

1-5 The various attempts to define arbitration have sought to reflect the evolving general understanding and essential legal forms of arbitration. For example:

- *Shorter Oxford English Dictionary:* "Uncontrolled decision"; "The settlement of a question at issue by one to whom the parties agree to refer their claims in order to obtain an equitable decision."[1]
- *David:* "Arbitration is a device whereby the settlement of a question, which is of interest for two or more persons, is entrusted to one or more other persons – the arbitrator or arbitrators – who derive their powers from a private agreement, not from the authorities of a State, and who are to proceed and decide the case on the basis of such an agreement."[2]
- *Words and phrases judicially defined*: "The reference of a dispute or difference between not less than two parties for determination, after hearing both sides in a judicial manner, by a person or persons other than a court of competent jurisdiction."[3]

---

1 *The Shorter Oxford English Dictionary* (3rd ed, 1969).

2 David, *Arbitration in International Trade*, 5.

3 Saunders (ed), *Words and Phrases Legally Defined* (3rd ed, Butterworths 1988), 105.

- *Halsbury's Laws of England*: "The process by which a dispute or difference between two or more parties as to their mutual legal rights and liabilities is referred to and determined judicially and with binding effect by the application of law by one or more persons (the arbitral tribunal) instead of by a court of law."[4]

- *Domke "Commercial Arbitration"*: "[A] process by which parties voluntarily refer their disputes to an impartial third person, an arbitrator, selected by them for a decision based on the evidence and arguments to be presented before the arbitration tribunal. The parties agree in advance that the arbitrator's determination, the award, will be accepted as final and binding upon them."[5]

1-6 As arbitration is a dynamic dispute resolution mechanism varying according to law and international practice, national laws do not attempt a final definition.[6] Although it does not provide a definition, the English Arbitration Act 1996 did set out clear statements of principle of what was expected from arbitration. Section 1 provides

> (a) the object of arbitration is to obtain the fair resolution of disputes by an impartial tribunal without unnecessary delay or expense;
>
> (b) the parties should be free to agree how their disputes are resolved, subject only to such safeguards as are necessary in the public interest.

1.2. Fundamental Features of Arbitration

1-7 What is clear is that there are four fundamental features of arbitration:

- An alternative to national court;
- A private mechanism for dispute resolution;
- Selected and controlled by the parties;
- Final and binding determination of parties' rights and obligations.

---

4 Halsbury's *Laws of England* (4th ed, Butterworths 1991), para 601, 332.

5 Domke, *Arbitration*, 1.

6 By contrast some national laws define arbitration agreements. See, *e.g.*, Model Law, Article 7.

(a) An alternative to national courts

1-8 The most obvious *fora* for all disputes are national courts. They exist and are maintained by the state to provide a dispute settlement service for parties. It is a manifestation of state power and the responsibility of the state to ensure that courts exist, that appropriately qualified judges are appointed, that there are procedural rules to regulate the basis of jurisdiction and the conduct of cases before the court.

1-9 Arbitration is not a national court procedure. When parties agree to arbitration they remove their relationships and disputes from the jurisdiction of national courts. There are many reasons for parties to decide that their disputes should be resolved other than in the national courts; in reality, parties regularly agree to arbitration instead of the courts.

(b) A private mechanism for dispute resolution

1-10 Just as national courts are public, arbitration is generally private. In the same way as every contract between parties is a private matter between them, so too the arbitration agreement is private between the parties. Accordingly, when a dispute arises it is to be resolved in the private dispute resolution system agreed between the parties, subject to certain safeguards. Having selected arbitration, the intention is for the arbitrators to determine the dispute and the entitlements and obligations of the parties in respect of the issues raised.

(c) Selected and controlled by the parties

1-11 The principal characteristic of arbitration is that it is chosen by the parties. However fulsome or simple the arbitration agreement, the parties have ultimate control of *their* dispute resolution system. Party autonomy is the ultimate power determining the form, structure, system and other details of the arbitration. In the main, national arbitration law seeks only to give effect to, supplement, and support the agreement of the parties for their disputes to be resolved by arbitration. Most laws are largely permissive and aim to support and enforce the agreement to arbitrate, rather than to intervene. Only where the parties are silent as to some aspect of the arbitration process will national laws impose their provisions.

(d) Final and binding determination of parties' rights and obligations

1-12 As the chosen alternative to a national court, the decision of the parties is for arbitrators to resolve the dispute finally. The parties have accepted that not only will arbitration be the form of dispute settlement, but also that they will accept and give effect to the arbitration award. Implied with the agreement to arbitrate is the acceptance that the strict rules of procedure and rights of appeal of a national court are excluded, subject to very limited, but essential, protections. The decision of the arbitrators is final and binding on the parties. This is both a contractual commitment of the parties and the effect of the applicable law.

1.3. Arbitration Compared with National Courts

1-13 National courts have, or are at least perceived to have, an inherent national prejudice. Judges are drawn from that nationality. They do not necessarily have the knowledge of, or ability to handle, disputes arising from international business transactions or even disputes between parties from different countries, *i.e.* with conflicting legal, cultural, political and ethical systems. The procedure followed in national courts is in accordance with the laws set down by that state. National courts are generally open to the public; any one can enter to watch and listen to the proceedings.

1-14 A principal factor differentiating a national court from an arbitration tribunal is the rigidity of national court procedures. Whichever court one goes to, inevitably, there are civil procedural rules or codes or precedent as to the way in which cases are conducted. The procedural rules or code lay down the basis for the courts' jurisdiction, the circumstances in which an action can be brought, which particular national court has jurisdiction over a particular type of dispute, how to initiate proceedings, what documents must be filed, the rights of reply and how the case, generally, should be conducted. There are little or no areas on which the judge can, in his discretion, even with the agreement of the parties, move away from the strictures of the civil procedure rules or code.

1-15 By contrast, the form, structure and procedure of every arbitration is different and will vary according to the characteristics of the case. The arbitrations may be under different rules, with different national or international laws applying, with one or three arbitrators and one or more claimants or respondents. In international arbitration, even the variants of the position of the arbitration tribunal can affect and influence how the arbitration will proceed. It is for these reasons that for many types of international commercial arrangements, arbitration is the preferred mechanism for dispute resolution.

1-16 *Flexible procedure:* With parties of different origins and from different parts of the world, with arbitrations being conducted under different legal systems and arbitration rules, with arbitrators coming from various jurisdictions, there can be no rigid arbitration procedure. A special procedure is needed for each arbitration. Due to the private nature of arbitration and that it is established by agreement of the parties, the procedure can be fixed by the parties and arbitrators to meet the characteristics of each case.

1-17 All of the major international arbitration rules give authority and power to the arbitrators to determine the procedure that they consider appropriate, subject always to party autonomy. For example, Article 15 ICC Rules provides

> The proceedings before the Arbitral Tribunal shall be governed by these Rules, and, where these Rules are silent, by any rules which the parties or, failing them, the Arbitral Tribunal may settle on, whether or not reference is thereby made to the rules of procedure of a national law to be applied to the arbitration.[7]

1-18 National laws contain similar provisions. Section 34(1) English Arbitration Act 1996 provides that it is

> ... for the tribunal to decide all procedural and evidential matters, subject to the right of the parties to agree any matter.[8]

1-19 *Suitability for international transactions*: Contracting parties from one country are generally unwilling to submit to the national courts of the other party or to any national courts. Justifiable or not, there is often a distrust of foreign courts, as well as a question as to their suitability for certain types of international contracts. The neutrality and independence of the arbitration process, established within the context of a neutral venue, and not belonging to any national system, is a real attraction for the parties for international arbitration as a system to resolve disputes arising from international transactions. As parties are drawn from jurisdictions across the world, with very different legal, political, cultural and ethical systems, arbitration provides a forum in which all of these interests can be protected and respected, whilst determining the most appropriate way to resolve the dispute between the parties.

---

7 See also, *e.g*,. AAA ICDR Rules Article 16(1); LCIA Article 14(2); NAI Arbitration Rules Article 23(2); UNCITRAL Arbitration Rules Article 15(1); WIPO Arbitration Rules Article 38(a).

8 See, *e.g.*, Belgium, Judicial Code Article 1693; Germany, ZPO section 1042; Italy, CCP Article 816; Netherlands, CCP Article 1036; Sweden, Arbitration Act section 21; Switzerland, PIL Article 182; Model Law Article 19.

1-20 *Final and binding:* As a general rule the decisions of arbitrators are to be final and binding. There are no or very limited grounds on which arbitrators' awards can be appealed to the courts on the basis that the arbitrators' conclusions are wrong. Equally, the grounds upon which the decisions of arbitrators can be challenged and set aside are limited to where the arbitrators have either exceeded the jurisdictional authority in the arbitration agreement or have committed some serious breach of natural justice.

1-21 *Easy enforcement*: Both domestic and international arbitration awards should be easily enforceable. In many countries, a domestic award can be enforced in the same way and as simply as a national court judgment. There is no review of the decision of the arbitrators and how they reached that conclusion. The legal system recognises that the parties have decided that arbitrators should make the final determination of their dispute as an alternative to the national court. The law therefore gives effect to the intention of the parties and enforces the award just as it would a national judgment.

1-22 In the international arena arbitration awards are more easily enforceable than national court judgments. As a result of the New York Convention there are now more than 130 countries which have accepted the obligation to give effect to arbitration awards made in other countries which are party to the New York Convention. There are limited grounds to refuse enforcement. This is far more effective than the enforcement of foreign judgments which are dependent on bilateral conventions (with limited exceptions, for example, within Europe where EC Regulation 44/2001 and the Brussels and Lugano Conventions apply).

1-23 *Neutrality*: By contrast to the perceived partiality of a national court, an arbitration tribunal is thought to be neutral. It can be established with its seat in a country with which neither party has any connection; arbitrators can be selected from different countries and with different nationalities, and the tribunal is independent of direct national influence. This neutrality gives arbitration an independence and a loyalty primarily to the parties. The neutrality also enables the tribunal to function in a non-national way reflecting the need for international developments.

1-24 This is also of particular importance where parties from different parts of the world would like to have an arbitrator on the tribunal who understands their background and thinking, and the circumstances and situations from which they come. It is often possible to balance a tribunal by selecting arbitrators with different skills and knowledge as well as experience and background.

1-25 *Expert arbitrators*: Particularly for disputes that arise out of specialist industries or where there is a particular characteristic of the dispute, parties are able to select arbitrators with expert knowledge. Whilst, generally, arbitrators are not expected to use their relevant background experience for the purpose of making decisions (that is a function for an expert determination), having specific knowledge and an understanding of the subject-matter will often give increased confidence in the arbitration process.

1-26 *Confidentiality*: Due to the private nature of arbitration, many consider that arbitration is also a confidential process. As a result, what proceeds in the arbitration will not only be kept private between the parties but will remain absolutely confidential. This means that the existence of the arbitration, the subject matter, the evidence, the documents that are prepared for and exchanged in the arbitration, and the arbitrators' awards cannot be divulged to third parties. It also means that only parties to the arbitration, their legal representatives and those who are specifically authorised by each party, can attend the arbitration hearing. Each of those individuals are considered to be subject to the duty of confidentiality on behalf of the party they are representing.

1-27 Whilst the legal effectiveness of this confidentiality is in dispute, it is clearly a concept that many consider to be a fundamental and important advantage to arbitration.[9]

1-28 *Expedition*: It is often assumed that arbitration is, or at least should be, quicker than national courts. In theory and in many cases this is so. Due to party autonomy, the fact that arbitrators can be selected, and as each case stands on its own, there is no backlog of cases. In many countries, the national courts have such a long backlog that it can be years before a hearing date can be obtained. If the parties are agreed, they can seek the involvement of an arbitrator at very short notice; if they are able to present their cases to the arbitrator within a short period, the whole matter can be resolved with great expedition.

---

[9] See expert reports by Bond, Boyd, Lew and Smit in 11 *Arb Int* 231 (1995), in the case of *Esso Australia Resources Ltd and others v The Hon Sidney James Plowman, The Minister for Energy and Minerals and others*, 183 Commonwealth Law Reports 10 (1995). See also Collins, "Privacy and Confidentiality in Arbitration Proceedings", 11 *Arb Int* 321 (1995); Neill, "Confidentiality in Arbitration", 12 *Arb Int* 287 (1996); Fortier, "The Occasional Unwarranted Assumption of Confidentiality", 15 *Arb Int* 131 (1999). See *also* Supreme Court of Sweden, 27 October 2000, *Bulgarian Foreign Trade Bank Limited v AI Trade Finance Inc*, 13(1) WTAM 147 (2001); *Associated Electric & Gas Insurance Services Ltd v European Reinsurance Company of Zurich* [2003] UKPC 11 (PC, 29 January 2003).

1-29 However, in reality, major complicated international arbitrations frequently continue for lengthy periods. Nonetheless, in most such cases, they are still resolved more quickly than in national courts. Under the English Arbitration Act 1996 there is an obligation on arbitrators to ensure that there is no unnecessary delay in the conduct of the arbitration.[10]

1-30 *Cost:* Due to the inherent advantages discussed above, in principle arbitration should be less expensive than national courts. Again, in theory, this may be the case, but in practice it is not always so. Where arbitrations can be held quickly and the awards issued with little or no delay, the costs may be significantly reduced in contrast to those of a lengthy court procedure. However, for complicated international arbitrations, particularly before three arbitrators, this may not always be the case as in addition to the costs of the lawyers, the parties will also have to pay the significant fees of the arbitrators.

2. What Arbitration Is Not

1-31 It is important to be clear what arbitration is not:

- It is not a national court procedure;
- It is not an expert determination;
- It is not a mediation;
- It is not any of the alternative dispute systems discussed below.

3. Other Alternative Dispute Resolution Mechanisms[11]

1-32 Essentially there are two forms of dispute resolution: one which imposes a decision and determines issues definitively, *e.g.* expert determinations and baseball arbitrations; the other provides the basis to help the parties reach an

---

10 Section 33(1)(b). See also ICC Rules Article 24(1).

11 See generally Brown & Marriott, *ADR Principles and Practice* (2d ed, Sweet & Maxwell 1999); Bernstein, *Handbook*, 585-601; Stipanowich & Kneckell, *Commercial Arbitration*; Hoellering, "Comments on the Growing Inter-Action of Arbitration and Mediation", in van den Berg, *ICCA Congress Series no 8*, 121-124; Mackie, Miles & Marsh, *Commercial Disputes Resolution - an ADR Practice Guide* (2nd ed, Butterworths 2000); Freeman, *Alternative Dispute Resolution* (Dartmouth 1995); Nolan-Haley, *Alternative Dispute Resolution in a Nutshell* (2d ed, West 2001); Carroll & Mackie, *International Mediation - The Art of Business Diplomacy* (Kluwer 2000); Mistelis, "ADR in England and Wales", 13 *Am Rev Int'l Arb* 167 (2002); de Boisseson, "Thoughts on the Future of ADR in Europe: A Critical Approach", 15(4) *Arb Int* 349 (1999).

agreed solution or settlement, *i.e.* negotiation, mediation/conciliation, mini-trial, executive appraisal, neutral listener, early neutral or expert evaluation.

3.1. Definitive Determination

1-33 There are various mechanisms to achieve a final determination of the dispute by the intervention of a third party who imposes a decision. Once the mechanism is agreed upon neither party can unilaterally withdraw from the process. The parties can still settle the dispute themselves but if not, then a binding determination will be made which, in principle, is enforceable through the courts.

1-34 *Expert determination:*[12] This is the referral of a dispute to an independent third party to resolve by using his own expertise. It is particularly useful for resolving valuation disputes, *e.g.* intellectual property, technical issues, accounting disputes and earn-outs under company accounts. It can be cheaper and quicker than arbitration as the expert can conduct his own investigations without relying upon, or waiting for, information to be provided by the parties. A decision of an expert cannot be directly enforced in the same way as an arbitration award. There is no appeal from the decision of an expert. Unlike an arbitrator, an expert can be sued for negligence. The main difference between expert determination and arbitration is that the expert can use his own knowledge to reach his conclusions and is not required to give reasons for his decision.

1-35 In civil law systems experts are frequently retained to determine the subject matter of the contract such as the price of sale agreements. The Italian Civil Code[13] distinguishes two cases. First, if in the contract the parties do not specify that the third person should make his determination entirely upon his own discretion and the determination is clearly wrong or unfair, then the parties can appeal to the court for the expert's decision to be set aside. In these cases the party seeking to challenge the decision must prove, for instance, that the opinion of the expert is manifestly wrong or illogical. If the court decides that the determination is wrong or unfair then the court itself makes this determination. If, on the other hand, the parties specify expressly that they wish to rely totally on the discretion of the third person, and his decision is final, then the expert determination is binding as a contract and it can only be challenged on the

---

[12] See Kendall, *Expert Determination* (3rd ed, Sweet & Maxwell 2001).

[13] Article 1349.

ground of bad faith of the third person. The contract is void if the third person cannot for some reason determine the subject matter of the agreement and the parties do not agree to substitute the third person.[14]

1-36 It is also generally recognised that the parties can agree an *expertise-arbitrage*[15] whereby they appoint an expert to determine technical disputes and to evaluate assets or damage.[16] The expert is empowered by the agreement reached by the parties and his decision is binding as a contract. It is doubtful that this expert's determination can be considered a binding decision even if the decision of the expert on the technical issue would settle the dispute.[17]

1-37 Parties can submit a dispute to the ICC's International Centre for Expertise to obtain an expert opinion as to contractual compliance or adjustments in performance in cases of great technical complexity.[18] This Centre, established in 1976, co-operates with several professional organisations to obtain advice on an *ad hoc* basis taking into consideration the specific characteristics of each case. The expert is empowered to make findings within the limits set by the request for expertise, after giving the parties an opportunity to make submissions. Article 8 of the ICC Rules for Expertise provides that "the findings or recommendations of the expert shall not be binding upon the parties." Therefore the results of the technical expert will be binding only if the parties have made an express stipulation to that effect and in this case it is not clear if and how the determination of the expert can be challenged.

1-38 The ICC International Centre operates under the 2003 ICC Rules for Expertise. It deals with technical, financial or other questions calling for specialised knowledge. The expert's intervention can help the parties to resolve questions amicably or simply to establish certain facts. Recent cases concern assessing, for instance, the operational capacity of a product unit, the corrosion of materials, the financial audit of a company during a take-over and the revaluation of a contract price.[19]

---

14 See similarly France, NCPC Article 1592; Germany, BGB sections 317-319. See also Kröll, *Ergänzung und Anpassung von Verträgen durch Schiedsgerichte* (Haymanns 1998), 248 *et seq.*

15 *Schiedsgutachten* in German, *arbitraggio* in Italian, *bindend advies* in Dutch.

16 Fouchard Gaillard Goldman *on International Commercial Arbitration*, para 26. See also Berger, *International Economic Arbitration*, 73 *et seq.*

17 Fouchard Gaillard Goldman *on International Commercial Arbitration*, para 25.

18 Craig, Park, Paulsson, *ICC Arbitration*, 701-705.

19 <www.iccwbo.org.drs.english. Expertise/all_topics.asp>.

1-39 *Adjudication*:[20] This involves the binding, but not necessarily final, resolution of disputes on an expedited basis. It acts as a form of interim dispute resolution, although its effect may often be to dispose of disputes without further proceedings. In the UK it is required by statute for all contracts involving the carrying out of construction operations.[21] However, it is also commonly included in contracts for construction or engineering work elsewhere, where it may also be referred to a Dispute Adjudication Board or a Dispute Review Board.[22]

1-40 The adjudicator is required to reach his decision in a specified, short period of time. Under UK statute this is only 28 days from the reference of the dispute to him, extendable only by agreement of the parties or by up to 14 days with the agreement only of the referring party. Frequently, in large infrastructure projects a time for adjudication is expressly provided for in the agreement. Critically, once the adjudicator has made his decision it is binding on the parties and is immediately enforceable. However, it cannot be enforced as an award but must be sued upon for enforcement.

1-41 Whether or not a decision is enforced, unless the contract expressly provides that the adjudicator's decision is also final, the parties may have the dispute re-heard in its entirety by whatever ultimate dispute resolution method they have chosen, whether arbitration or national courts. The ultimate tribunal is in no way bound by the adjudicator's decision and it re-hears the dispute afresh, rather than reviewing or hearing an appeal from the adjudicator's decision. If the ultimate tribunal comes to a different conclusion to the adjudicator's decision, its judgment or award will replace the decision, with money being repaid if necessary.

1-42 *Rent-a-judge or private judging*: This is a court-annexed or private ADR process. It is available where statutes or local court rules permit court referral of cases to neutral third parties, usually retired judges, for formal trials. The procedure followed by the retired judge or neutral is usually akin to that in a

---

20 See Stevenson Chapman, *Construction Adjudication* (Jordan 1999); McInnis, *The New Engineering Contract* (Thomas Talford 2001), 545-552; Seppala, "The New FIDIC Provision for a Dispute Adjudication Board", 8 *RDAI/IBL* 967 (1997); Morris, "Adjudication as Operated on the Construction of the Dartford River Crossing (The Queen Elizabeth II Bridge)", 60 *Arbitration* 13 (1994).

21 Housing Grants, Construction and Regeneration Act 1996. See also Davies, "Section 9 of the English Arbitration Act 1996 and Section 108 of the Housing Grants, Construction and Regeneration Act 1996: A Conflict Waiting to be Exploited", 13 *Arb Int* 411 (1997).

22 See, *e.g.*, *FIDIC Conditions of Contract for Construction* 1999 (1st ed), clause 20(4); *FIDIC Conditions of Contract for EPC/Turnkey Projects* 1999 (1st ed), clause 20(4).

common court trial. The decision of the neutral is referred to the competent court, and is considered to be a judgment of the court. Generally the parties' rights to appellate review and enforcement of the decision are the same as if the judgment had been entered into by a court. It is also possible where parties wish to expedite or avoid the delay of the courts. It is especially common in the United States and appropriate primarily for domestic matters.

1-43 *Baseball arbitration*: This is also known as final or last offer or pendulum arbitration. This process involves the parties narrowing the risk themselves by the claims and admissions made and it ties the hand of the arbitrators as to the extent of the awards they can make. Following its submission in a binding arbitration, each party also submits its best offer to the tribunal in a sealed envelope. The tribunal's responsibility is to choose the best offer which comes nearest to its own assessment. The arbitrators do not have to make assessments as to the correct level of damages, but rather which party is nearer to the mark, and that is the amount awarded. The effect of this procedure is to compel the parties to narrow their demands because an over-stated claim will almost certainly result in the award going to the other side. Final offer arbitration is potentially unfair unless all parties have essentially equal access to the basic facts. This technique is also known as "baseball" arbitration because it is used in the negotiation of professional athletes' contracts in the US.

3.2. Mechanisms Requiring Parties' Agreement for Resolution of Dispute

1-44 *Negotiation*: Straightforward negotiations between the parties or their advisors are always the most obvious but not the easiest way of reaching a consensus and to compromise the controversy. Negotiation is the most flexible, informal, and party-directed method; it is the closest to the parties' circumstances and control, and can be geared to each party's own concerns. Parties choose location, timing, agenda, subject matter and participants. Negotiation should normally be the first approach at resolution of any dispute. However, negotiations may fail because of previous poor relations, intransigent positions of the parties, neither party being prepared to "lose face" and the fact that a party cannot be pressured against its wishes from adopting an unreasonable position.

1-45 *Mediation/conciliation*: Mediation is a process whereby a mediator, *i.e.* a neutral third party, works with the parties to resolve their dispute by agreement, rather than imposing a solution. It is sometimes known as conciliation. Historically, and because of the slightly different methods applied in mediation and conciliation in public international law, they were perceived as different processes. Consequently mediation sometimes refers to a method where a mediator has a more proactive role (evaluative mediation) and conciliation sometimes refers to a method where a conciliator has a more facilitating mediator role (facilitative mediation).

1-46 Mediation can be more effective than simple negotiations. This is because the mediator works with the parties to effect a compromise, either by suggesting grounds of agreement or forcing them to recognise weaknesses in their cases. The mediator may, if required, evaluate the merits of the parties' cases in a non-binding manner. However, the mediator cannot make a binding adjudicatory decision. The parties can obtain any remedy they wish; the only limits are on what they can agree. This differs from the position in litigation, arbitration and expert determination, where the court or tribunal is limited to remedies available at law.

1-47 *Mediation/arbitration* (med-arb):[23] This can happen where parties agree that if mediation does not result in a negotiated settlement, the dispute will be resolved by arbitration and the mediator is converted into an arbitrator. In this process, there is initially facilitative mediation (*i.e.* the mediator does not evaluate the strength of the parties' cases) followed by binding arbitration. This is a normal situation in arbitrations in China. What is unique in this situation is that the mediator is converted into an arbitrator, in order to make a determinative decision if the mediation fails.

1-48 The idea of the same individual acting as both a mediator and then an arbitrator gives serious misgivings. In view of the confidential and prejudicial information relied on during the mediation process, it is generally considered that the mediator would be compromised to then convert himself into an arbitrator to make a decision on the merits. In these circumstances many parties would not be fully open and frank with the mediator for fear of being prejudiced at the arbitration stage.

1-49 *Mini-trial/executive appraisal*: In mini-trials, voluntary court-style procedures are adopted which involve the parties presenting a summarised version of their case (including calling evidence and making submissions) before a tribunal. The tribunal may ask questions and comment on evidence and arguments. The tribunal can be a neutral advisor who, following the presentation,

---

[23] See Hill, "MED-ARB: New Coke or Swatch?", 13 *Arb Int* 105 (1997); Motiwal, "Alternative Dispute Resolution in India", 15(2) *J Int'l Arb* 117 (1998).

advises the parties on how he sees the strengths and weaknesses of their case. Where the tribunal consists of neutrals, it can render a non-binding decision, which is intended as an aid to the parties' further negotiation toward settlement.

1-50 Alternatively, the tribunal can consist of senior executives of the companies in dispute perhaps with a neutral chairman, who use the mini-trial as a springboard for settlement discussions (executive appraisal). Parties to a mini-trial may agree that the neutral advisor will not act as an arbitrator or mediator.

1-51 A mini-trial aims at facilitating a prompt and cost effective resolution of a complex litigation case concerning mixed questions of fact and law. Its goal is to keep the problem on a purely commercial basis, to narrow the area of controversy, to dispose of collateral issues, and to encourage a fair and equitable settlement.

1-52 *Neutral listener arrangements*: In this case, each party submits its best offer in settlement to a neutral third party. This "neutral listener" informs the parties whether their offers are either substantially similar or within a range which looks negotiable. With the agreement of the parties, the neutral listener may try to assist them to bridge the gap.

1-53 *Early neutral evaluation/expert evaluation/non-binding appraisal*: Parties present their cases in the early stages of a dispute to a neutral evaluator. The evaluator, following an oral presentation by each party, confidentially assesses the arguments and submissions. The assessment is not binding on the parties. No records of assessment are kept and the evaluation is considered "off the record". The aim is to demonstrate to each party the strengths and weaknesses of its case. This is intended to help parties to settle their differences by subsequent negotiation or perhaps with an independent mediator.

1-54 All of the above mechanisms require the parties to conclude the settlement agreement between themselves. These procedures aim to bring the parties closer, to understand the respective position of the other side, and to help the parties see the weaknesses of their own case. This should, in principle, with or without the assistance of a third party, enable the parties to agree the terms for the settlement of their differences. If no agreement is possible, the parties can resort to arbitration or the courts for the determination of their dispute.

Chapter 2

REGULATORY FRAMEWORK FOR ARBITRATION

2-1 For arbitration to exist and succeed there must be a regulatory framework which controls the legal status and effectiveness of arbitration in a national and international legal environment. This regulatory framework must give effect to the agreement to arbitrate, the organisation of the arbitration process and the finality and enforceability of the arbitration award.

2-2 Arbitration is the alternative jurisdiction to national courts which are specifically established by the state to apply and uphold the law and determine all forms of dispute. Arbitration is also the jurisdiction selected by the parties in preference to national courts. Parties may have many reasons for this selection. However, the extent to which parties can refer their disputes to arbitration is inevitably a matter to be regulated by the law. In recent years this has been through both national and international law.[1]

---

1 This issue gave rise to the extensive debate about the legal nature of arbitration, *i.e.* contractual, jurisdictional, hybrid or *sui iuris*.

2-3 This chapter reviews (1) the historical development of international arbitration, (2) the adoption of the New York Convention, (3) the influence of international arbitration rules and practice, (4) the UNCITRAL Model Law and the adoption of new arbitration laws in many jurisdictions, and (5) the effect of this regulatory web on international commercial arbitration.

1. Historical Development of International Arbitration

2-4 For centuries arbitration has been accepted by the commercial world as a preferred or at least an appropriate system for dispute resolution of international trade disputes. The law has lagged behind in recognising and giving effect to the decisions of arbitrators. Most arbitrations were held on an *ad hoc* basis and despite rather than with support of the law. Even in England, for long a centre for international commercial arbitration due to its pivotal position as the centre for shipping, insurance, commodity and financing businesses, arbitration was closely controlled by the English courts.

2-5 During this period there was significant national court intervention in the arbitration process, including reviewing the substantive decisions of the arbitrators. By corollary, there was no international regulation of arbitration. This invariably meant that the enforcement of awards was dealt with differently in every country which took account of not only its own national law on the recognition of foreign awards but also other political factors which might have been relevant.

2-6 In the late 19th century and at the beginning of the 20th century, the development of modern international arbitration practice began. However it was based on national laws. The approach of these national laws was directly reflective of the attitude of most national courts. The law and the courts were reluctant to recognise that the commercial world was agreeing to arbitration as part of their business decisions.

2-7 However arbitration was considered an exception to and an erosion of national courts' jurisdiction. The courts saw arbitration as a rival. Most importantly, although states agreed to recognise and enforce the arbitration agreements and awards, they wanted to closely supervise the arbitration process. This meant that arbitration, from its commencement, throughout the procedure and including recognition of the award, was strictly regulated in national laws. Although not all aspects of arbitration laws were considered mandatory, there was only little room for party autonomy.

2-8 The development of national arbitration laws to the current regulation of international commercial arbitration has been evidenced in many legal systems.[2] The earliest law dedicated to arbitration in England was in 1698. In France, the subject of arbitration was first included in the Code of Civil Procedure 1806. In the United States the first federal arbitration legislation was the Federal Arbitration Act 1925.

2. International Regulation of Arbitration

2.1. Early Efforts to Support International Arbitration

2-9 As world trade expanded, the need to create a mechanism for international recognition and enforcement of both arbitration agreements and awards in relation to international commercial agreements was of paramount importance. To facilitate arbitration, two Hague Conventions were concluded in 1899 and in 1907[3], both entitled The Hague Convention for the Pacific Settlement of International Disputes. These Conventions created the Permanent Court of Arbitration which still exists and functions today.

2-10 The world's business community established the International Chamber of Commerce (ICC) in 1919. This institution has been and remains the voice of the international business community. In 1923 the ICC created its Court of International Arbitration to provide the framework for an independent and neutral arbitration system for the determination of commercial disputes between parties from different countries. Since the early 1920s the ICC has been a major driving force in the promotion of both arbitration as a mechanism for the resolution of

---

2 See generally Roebuck, "A short history of arbitration", in Kaplan, *Hong Kong and China Arbitration*, xxxiii-lxv; "The myth of judicial jealousy", 10 *Arb Int* 395 (1994); Roebuck, "Sources for the history of arbitration", 14 *Arb Int* 237 (1998); Robert, *L'Arbitrage*, 4-6, Fouchard Gaillard Goldman *on International Commercial Arbitration*, paras 131-135; Monnier, "Le role de la Suisse dans l'histoire de l'arbitrage de droit international public", *Recueil de Travaux Suisses*, 3-14; Bucher, *Arbitrage International en Suisse,* 18-21; Bucher and Tschanz, *International Arbitration in Switzerland,* 20–25.

3 The Convention for the Pacific Settlement of Disputes, adopted 29 July 1899, was one of the most important results of the First International Peace Conference held in The Hague in 1899. This resolved "to promote by their best efforts friendly settlement of international disputes" and therefore sought to establish a "permanent institution of a tribunal of arbitration, accessible to all." These aims were furthered by the (second) Convention for the Pacific Settlement of Disputes, adopted at the Second International Peace Conference on 18 October 1907.

international commercial disputes and the need for international regulations to uphold and support the arbitration process.

2.2. The Geneva Conventions 1923 and 1927

2-11 The ICC was directly involved in the promotion and adoption of the 1923 Geneva Protocol on Arbitration Clauses[4] and the 1927 Geneva Convention on the Execution of Foreign Awards.[5] These instruments were collectively aimed at international recognition of arbitration agreements and awards. In those days, the mechanisms brought by those instruments were considered successful, but their operation was not problem-free.[6]

2-12 The main problem was the recognition of awards and is known as the problem of double *exequatur*. For a foreign award to be enforced in the national jurisdiction, it was generally necessary to demonstrate that the award had become final in the country where it was rendered. This often required some form of confirmatory order or permission from the court in the country where the award was rendered. Often such court would review the award and a losing party would use the opportunity to challenge the arbitration tribunal's findings or conclusions in the award, and the procedure according to which the arbitration was conducted. Furthermore, the successful party had the burden of proof in the country where it was seeking enforcement, that the conditions for enforcement set out in the 1927 Convention were satisfied. In addition, the enforcing party had to show that the constitution of a tribunal and the arbitration process had conformed with the law of the place of arbitration.

2-13 The Geneva Protocol and the Geneva Convention have been almost entirely superseded by the New York Convention.

2.3. The New York Convention

2-14 The major catalyst for the development of an international arbitration regime was the adoption of the New York Convention on the Recognition and Enforcement of Foreign Arbitral Awards 1958. As will be seen throughout this

---

4 As of December 2002, 39 states had ratified this Convention.

5 As of December 2002, 33 states had ratified this Convention.

6 See generally Lorenzen, "Commercial Arbitration – International and Interstate Aspects", 43 *Yale LJ* 716 (1934).

book the New York Convention continues to set the standard requirements for a successful international arbitration process.

2-15 With the expansion of international trade after World War II the ICC took the initiative to develop a new convention that would obviate the problems and could replace the Geneva Conventions.

2-16 In 1953, the ICC prepared a draft convention entitled Enforcement of International Arbitral Awards - Report and Preliminary Draft Convention.[7] The aim was to "greatly increase the efficiency of international commercial arbitration, by ensuring a rapid enforcement of arbitration awards rendered in accordance with the will of the parties."[8] In the eyes of the promoters of the Preliminary Draft, international enforcement of arbitration awards could only be attained "by giving full value to the autonomy of the [parties'] will ...." This effectively proposed arbitration not governed by a national law. The idea, however, did not attract enough international support.

2-17 The United Nations, through its Economic and Social Council (ECOSOC), took the lead in the review of the ICC draft convention. It then prepared its own draft convention in terms closer to the Geneva Convention than the ICC draft. The ECOSOC draft together with the ICC draft were considered at a conference in New York in 1958. A compromise text was adopted as the New York Convention. The Convention provides for international recognition of arbitration agreements and awards by national courts.

2-18 The New York Convention replaced the two Geneva Conventions although there remain countries party to those Conventions. More significantly, today and for the past 30 years, the New York Convention is the cornerstone of international commercial arbitration. The Convention established an international regime to be adopted in national laws which facilitates the recognition and enforcement of both arbitration agreements and awards.

2-19 The success of the Convention is well illustrated by three factors. First, over 130 countries are party to the Convention. There are few private law conventions that have achieved such a wide international acceptance.[9]

---

7 Reprinted in 9(1) *ICC Bulletin* 32 (1998) 35-36.

8 *Ibid*, 32.

9 See, *e.g.*, the United Nations Convention on Contracts for the International Sale of Goods 1980 ratified by more than 60 countries and the work of the Hague Conference on Private International Law. UNCITRAL currently has a membership of 60 states as of 21 January 2003.

2-20 Secondly, for the purpose of interpreting and applying the New York Convention, it is now common for the courts of one country to look to the decisions of other foreign national courts to see how specific provisions have been interpreted and applied. Whilst these national court decisions are not automatically binding, such applications of the common rules of the New York Convention have had a direct influence on the development of international arbitration practice and law, which is increasingly of significant influence on parties, arbitrators, and national courts, regardless of nationality.

2-21 Thirdly, and this follows from the above two points, it is now generally accepted that agreements to arbitrate and arbitration awards will be enforced by the courts of most countries which are party to the New York Convention. Upholding arbitration agreements and awards is an absolute prerequisite if international arbitration is to succeed and the New York Convention has provided the framework for this success.[10]

2.4. Other Arbitration Conventions

2-22 The New York Convention was followed by a series of bilateral and multilateral Conventions.[11] They had varied purposes and were directed generally to different areas of international business. None of these conventions, with the exception of the ICSID Convention, have achieved anything like the level of success of the New York Convention.

2-23 *The European Convention on International Commercial Arbitration 1961*[12]: This Convention, concluded during the cold war period, was aimed at promoting east-west trade. It was developed by the United Nations Economic Commission for Europe. It covers general issues of parties' rights to submit to arbitration, who can be an arbitrator, how arbitration proceedings should be

---

[10] A review of the New York Convention is being undertaken at the United Nations following the conference in 1998 to celebrate the 40th anniversary of the Convention. One of the topics being considered is how the orders or directions of arbitrators, especially concerning interim measures of protection or relief, could be made enforceable through national courts in countries other than the place of arbitration.

[11] See, *e.g.*, Treaty for Conciliation, Judicial Settlement and Arbitration between United Kingdom and Northern Ireland and Switzerland 1965; and The Convention between France and Spain 1969 on the Recognition and Enforcement of Judicial and Arbitral Decisions and Authentic Acts. Many of these treaties deal with trade, investments and judicial assistance.

[12] See, *e.g.*, Benjamin, "The European Convention on International Commercial Arbitration", *BYBIL* 478 (1961), and Hascher, "European Convention on International Commercial Arbitration of 1961", XX *YBCA* 1006 (1995).

organised, how to determine the applicable law, and the setting aside and challenge of awards. Although it is still in operation it never really achieved real international recognition. In fact, the number of countries which have acceded to the Convention has recently been increased.[13]

2-24 *The Washington Convention on the Settlement of Investment Disputes between States and Nationals of other States* was promoted by the World Bank 1965: In the late 1950s and 1960s many of the former colonial countries achieved their independence and were looking to take over ownership and control of major concessions owned by foreign companies. This Convention created the International Centre for the Settlement of Investment Disputes (ICSID) which has jurisdiction over legal disputes arising from investments between a contracting state and a national of another contracting state. It was hoped that by the developing countries accepting ICSID jurisdiction this would give investors confidence to continue with and make further investments in such countries. The Washington Convention has been ratified by over 130 countries.[14]

2-25 *The European Convention Providing a Uniform Law on Arbitration 1966*: This Convention was developed through the Council of Europe and was aimed at providing a uniform national and international arbitration law. It was signed by Austria and Belgium and ratified only by the latter. It has never come into force.

2-26 *The Convention on the Settlement by Arbitration of Civil Law Disputes Resulting From Economic Scientific and Technical Co-operation of 1972*: This Convention had real influence and effect during the existence of the Soviet dominated trading block in eastern and central Europe. It came into force under the auspices of the Council for Mutual Economic Assistance (Comecon) and provided for arbitration to resolve disputes between trading entities from the countries members of Comecon. Following the demise of the Soviet Union and the disintegration of Comecon this Convention no longer has any real purpose or reason to exist.[15]

---

[13] As of December 2002, the Convention had been signed and ratified by 29 states.

[14] <www.worldbank.org/ICSID>.

[15] The Secretariat of the COMECON in Moscow officially ceased to function on 1 January 1991. In the light of this fact the only way to denounce the Convention is bilaterally. Poland and Hungary terminated their participation in the agreement in 1994 and the Czech Republic gave a notice of termination in 1995. Only the Russian Federation is still a member of the Convention. See further Keglevic, "Arbitration in Central Europe", 9 *Croat Arbit Yearb 79* (2002), 81-3.

2-27 *The Inter-American Convention on International Commercial Arbitration of 1975*: It is based on the New York Convention and is primarily concerned with the recognition and enforcement of arbitration agreements and awards but it is territorially restricted to the area of America.[16]

2-28 *The MERCOSUR Agreement on International Commercial Arbitration of 1998*: Mercosur was created by the Treaty of Asuncion in March 1991.[17] The Mercosur Agreement on International Commercial Arbitration was signed on 23 July 1998 but only Argentina has ratified it to date.[18] The Agreement is a complete code of arbitration the object of which is "the regulation of arbitration as an alternative private means for the solution of disputes arising from international commercial contracts between natural or legal persons of private law." It covers situations where there is an arbitration agreement made by entities located or domiciled in more than one member state or if there is a contract with an objective connection, whether legal or economic, with a Mercosur state.

2-29 *The Amman Arab Convention on Commercial Arbitration* was concluded in 1987. Its purpose was to establish "unified Arab Rules on commercial arbitrations." It established the Arab Centre for Commercial Arbitration as a permanent organization which provides an arbitration service in accordance with the rules in the Convention.[19]

2-30 *The 1993 Treaty establishing OHADA*, the Organization for the harmonization of business law in Africa, effected co-operation also in the area of arbitration. Following this mandate on 11 March 1999 the OHADA Council of Ministers adopted a uniform law on arbitration, repealing all contrary provisions in national legislation of its member states. The Treaty (which entered into effect in 1995) also established a "Joint court of Justice and Arbitration" which plays the dual role of an arbitration institution and a court empowered to review awards. The new regime applies to both domestic and international arbitration.[20]

---

16 This Convention has been ratified by Argentina, Bolivia, Brazil, Chile, Colombia, Costa Rica, Dominican Republic, Ecuador, El Salvador, Guatemala, Honduras, Nicaragua, Panama, Paraguay, Peru, United States, Uruguay and Venezuela.

17 Argentina, Bolivia, Brazil, Chile, Paraguay and Uruguay have signed the Treaty.

18 As of December 2002.

19 This Convention has been ratified by 14 Arab countries including Algeria, Iraq, Jordan, Lebanon, Libya, Morocco, Sudan, Syria and Tunisia.

20 See <http://www.ohada.com/textes.php?categorie=658> See also Meyer, *OHADA – Droit de arbitrage* (Bruylant 2002); Fouchard, *L'OHADA et les perspectives de l'arbitrage en Afrique* (Bruylant 2002); Feneon, "The OHADA Treaty. Paving the Way Towards a New Legal System

3. INFLUENCE OF INTERNATIONAL ARBITRATION INSTRUMENTS AND PRACTICE

2-31 With the many different legal procedures and systems which existed, international arbitrators and the lawyers representing parties had to show flexibility in determining the procedures to follow. The arrangements for appointment, challenge and removal of arbitrators, the procedure for the conduct of the arbitration, and the form and content of awards, varied between legal systems. As arbitration became more popular common standard practices developed. Arbitrators were prepared to look away from national law to international practice and to the development of procedures on a specific basis for each case.

2-32 As international arbitration increased and the influence and benefits of the New York Convention became apparent new arbitration institutions began to emerge, each with its own arbitration rules and procedures. Each offered arbitration services influenced by its own national environment. The established arbitration institutions like the ICC, and the London Maritime Arbitration Association (LMAA) and the commodity institutions in England, whilst fixed with their rules, were aware of the need to develop new and more flexible procedures.

3.1. The UNECE and UNECAFE Arbitration Rules

2-33 A major influence in the 1960s, following its success with the New York Convention, was the United Nations. Through its Economic Commissions for Europe and for Asia and the Far East it developed special arbitration rules and procedures for arbitrations involving parties from and taking place in eastern and western Europe (UNECE) and in the large and emerging economies of Asia and the Far East (ECAFE). These Rules were almost identical in content which was due in large part to the common attitudes of specialists of the day as to how international arbitration practice should be conducted. These Rules were used in many cases but never achieved international recognition in circumstances where institutional arbitration was inappropriate.[21] They have been superseded by the UNCITRAL Arbitration Rules.

---

in French Speaking Africa?", 3(3) *Int ALR* N43 (2000); Leboulanger, "L'arbitrage et l'harmonisation du droit des affaires en Afrique", *Rev Arb* 541 (1999).

[21] On these rules see, respectively, Benjamin, "New Arbitration Rules for Use in International Trade", in Sanders (ed), *International Commercial Arbitration*, vol III, 361; and Sanders,

3.2. The UNCITRAL Arbitration Rules

2-34 In the early 1970s there was an increasing need for a neutral set of arbitration rules suitable for use in *ad hoc* arbitrations. Once again it was under the auspices of the United Nations that special arbitration rules were prepared, this time by the Commission on International Trade Law ("UNCITRAL"). The UNCITRAL Rules for *ad hoc* arbitration were "intended to be acceptable in both capitalist and socialist, in developed and developing countries and in common law as well as civil law jurisdictions."[22] This is because the Rules have a "truly universal origin, in particular their parallel creation in six languages (Arabic, Chinese, English, French, Russian and Spanish) by experts representing all regions of the world as well as the various legal and economic systems."[23]

2-35 The UNCITRAL Rules have achieved international recognition and are widely used. They are autonomous and suitable for use in almost every kind of arbitration and in every part of the world. Although originally developed for *ad hoc* arbitration they have now been adopted by many arbitration institutions[24] either for their general rules or for optional use.[25]

2-36 The UNCITRAL Rules deal with every aspect of arbitration from the formation of the tribunal to rendering an award. They were intended to provide the guidelines and flexibility for the smooth operation of arbitration proceedings. When approved, these Rules reflected what the drafters believed were the accepted and desired independent standards for use in international arbitration. Today these Rules are in fact reflective of what actually transpires in international arbitration practice and provide a milestone for review in many arbitrations under other systems.

2-37 Apart from the very wide acceptance and use of the UNCITRAL Rules generally, perhaps the most significant use has been their adoption, in slightly modified form, by the Iran-US Claims Tribunal. The publication of over 800

"ECAFE Rules for International Commercial Arbitration", in Sanders (ed), *Liber Amicorum Martin Domke*, 252.

22 Sanders, "Commentary on UNCITRAL Arbitration Rules", II *YBCA* 172 (1977) 173.

23 Herrmann, "UNCITRAL's Basic Contribution to the International Arbitration Culture in International Dispute Resolution: Towards an International Arbitration Culture", in van den Berg (ed), *ICCA's Congress Series no 8* (1996), 49, 50.

24 See, *e.g.*, Kuala Lumpur Regional Centre for Arbitration, the Cairo Regional Centre for International Commercial Arbitration, the Hong Kong International Arbitration Centre, and the Spanish Court of Arbitration.

25 See, *e.g.*, the American Arbitration Association, the London Court of International Arbitration and the Inter-American Commercial Arbitration Commission.

awards and decisions of the Iran-US Claims Tribunal has provided a jurisprudence on which parties in international arbitrations, either under the UNCITRAL Rules or in international arbitrations generally, can rely. This has contributed to the development of a common standard for the conduct and procedure of international commercial arbitrations.

3.3. The UNCITRAL Model Law and the Development of Modern Arbitration Laws in many Jurisdictions

2-38 As a result of the successful operation of the New York Convention and the development of established arbitration practice, the differences between national arbitration laws became only too apparent. There were essentially three different situations.

2-39 In some countries the courts still sought to control and supervise arbitrations taking place in their jurisdictions. Other countries sought rather to provide support for the arbitration process whilst refusing to intervene or interfere in the process itself, as opposed to strict supervision of the arbitration process.[26] This can be called a minimalist approach to international commercial arbitration. This last development recognised the fundamental influence of party autonomy in international arbitration, which effectively required very limited interference with a party's will. The third group of countries had either old and out of date arbitration laws or no arbitration laws at all.

2-40 It became increasingly clear that some uniformity was needed to reflect the commonly accepted standards for international arbitration. The benchmark event in this respect was the introduction of the UNCITRAL Model Law of 1985. The concepts of party autonomy and the supportive role of courts to the arbitration process are the basis of the Model Law. The Model Law harmonised and modernised[27] the issues it touches upon and represents a step forward along with the New York Convention and the UNCITRAL Rules.[28] What is equally

---

[26] Goldman, "The Complementary Roles of Judges and Arbitrators in Ensuring that International Commercial Arbitration is Effective", in *60 Years of ICC Arbitration*, 257.

[27] Blessing, *Introduction to Arbitration*, para 277.

[28] This is particularly so in England where the Arbitration Act 1996 expressly did not follow the UNCITRAL Model Law but was directly influenced in many ways by it. Although the 1989 Report of the Departmental Advisory Committee on Arbitration Law recommended against the adoption of the UNCITRAL Model Law, when preparing the Arbitration Act 1996 the DAC paid "at every stage ...very close regard " to the Model Law and the content and structure of the Act owe a great deal to the Model Law.

important is the jurisdictions where new legislation has been influenced by the Model Law.[29]

2-41 The minimalist approach and the primacy of the principle of party autonomy, as embodied in the Model Law, have now been recognised in all modern arbitration laws. They reshape the scope of courts' powers in respect of assistance and supervision. The scope of court assistance is generally confined to the appointment and removal of arbitrators, the grant of provisional relief and the collection of evidence. The supervisory powers of a court are limited generally to the challenge to jurisdiction, removal of arbitrators, and appeal from, setting aside and enforcement of arbitration awards. In addition, no derogation is allowed from the due process requirements and there is a limit in each jurisdiction to matters which are arbitrable.

4. Effect of the Regulatory Web

2-42 Wherever the parties are from and whatever form and place of arbitration is selected, every arbitration will be situated within and subject to some legal and regulatory systems. In most international arbitrations, there will be an overlap between two or more of these systems, *e.g.* the law of the place of arbitration and the arbitration rules. The effectiveness of the arbitration and the enforceability of the arbitration award will depend on the relevant law and rules being respected.

2-43 As will be seen throughout this study, in every arbitration there is an underlying national law, normally that of the place of arbitration, which regulate and controls the arbitration. It will be tempered by international arbitration practice and the rules of arbitration, institutional or *ad hoc*, which the parties may have selected to govern their arbitration. An inevitable question is which shall prevail where the two are in conflict.

2-44 As illustrated by the table below, the regulatory web for international arbitration is hierarchical involving elements of party autonomy, the chosen arbitration rules, international arbitration practice, the applicable arbitration laws as well as the relevant international arbitration conventions. Party autonomy is the primary source of the arbitration and the procedure. The arbitration will be governed by what the parties have agreed in the arbitration agreement (1), subject to the limits provided by mandatory rules (5). The agreement may either directly specify the rules and procedures to follow (1) or do so indirectly by selecting the

[29] For a current list of countries which have adopted the Model Law see <www.uncitral.org>.

applicable arbitration rules (2). For example, the parties can either directly fix the number of arbitrators, or do so indirectly by choosing rules which specify the number of arbitrators, *e.g.* the UNCITRAL Rules.

The Regulatory Web

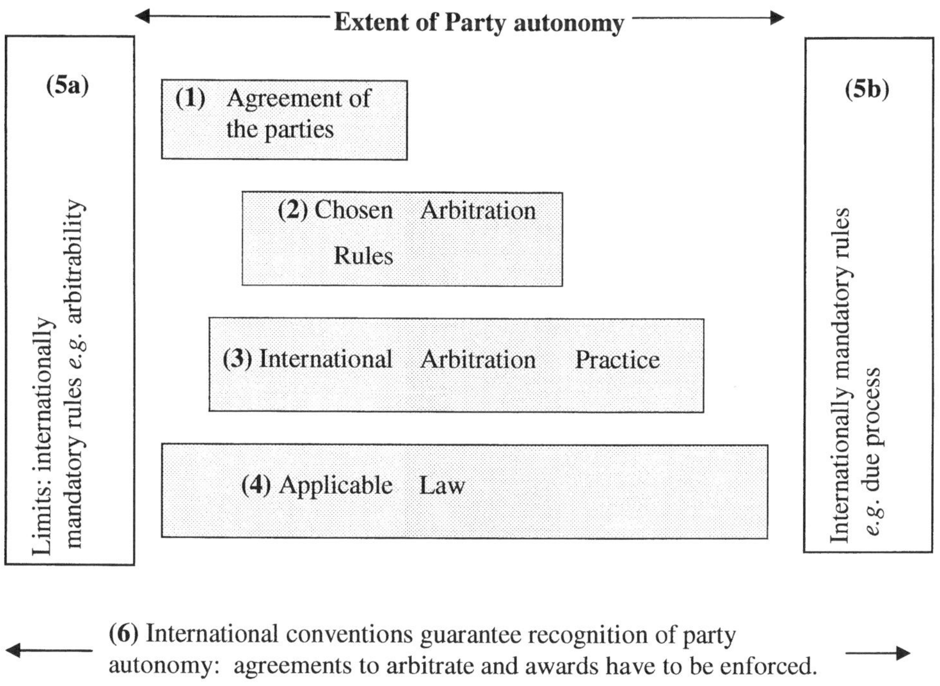

2-45 The agreement of the parties (1) will prevail over the provisions in the chosen arbitration rules (2) which in turn prevail over international arbitration practice (3) and the applicable law (4). In this hierarchy the norms of a lower stage are superseded by those of a higher stage and are only applicable where there is no regulation in any of the preceding stages. By corollary, in the absence of agreement as to specific rules or arbitration rules it is the applicable law (4) that will govern the arbitration.

2-46 International arbitration practice (3) comes into play at all stages, not only as a separate source but also to interpret the arbitration agreement, the chosen arbitration and the applicable national law. The international conventions (6) form part of the applicable law and aim to ensure that arbitration agreements and awards are enforced. In so doing, they uphold party autonomy as the backbone of the regulatory web. The shape of the web changes over time with the international arbitration practice influencing the contents of the applicable arbitration rules and the law.

2-47 The regulatory web is constrained at both sides by relevant mandatory rules. These impact, at the outset, on the types of issues that can be submitted to arbitration (5a) and ultimately the effectiveness and enforceability of the arbitration award (5b).

2-48 There are few mandatory requirements in national arbitration laws.[30] Most arbitration laws are permissive allowing the parties a wide degree of discretion in deciding how their arbitration should be organised and conducted. The selection, intentional or inadvertent, of a particular arbitration system will demonstrate the parties' intention and will generally be respected. Ultimately, just as the decision to submit disputes to arbitration is based on the parties' choice, so too the applicable rules will be determined according to the wishes of the parties.

2-49 Where there are complications and uncertainties, these should be resolved by national courts and arbitrators in accordance with international arbitration practice, as illustrated and recorded in the international arbitration instruments, including the New York Convention, the UNCITRAL Rules and the Model Law. The overriding factors must be the importance of the will of the parties and the absolute essential to achieve an effective and enforceable arbitration award. Hence the importance of the criteria set out as fundamental to the validity of an award in Article V of the New York Convention.

---

[30] *E.g.*, Schedule 1 England, Arbitration Act provides that 25 of the 110 provisions in the Act are mandatory and cannot be excluded or avoided by the parties in arbitrations which have their seat in England.

Chapter 3

FORMS OF ARBITRATION

3-1 Arbitration is the generic term for a form of binding dispute resolution outside the national court system. It is equally so for domestic and international arbitration. In every case the question for the parties and their lawyers is which type of arbitration, in what circumstances and under what structure.

3-2 There are different kinds and forms of arbitration. In every situation it is essential for parties to determine which type of arbitration is appropriate or relevant for each case. There may be implications for the choice of arbitration from national law, relevant international instruments, the agreement of the parties and the applicable arbitration rules. This is important because of the legal regimes that will apply, the extent to which the parties are able to control the arbitration process and the ultimate enforceability of the award of the tribunal. For this reason, the decision for disputes to be submitted to arbitration and which form of arbitration must always be carefully considered.

3-3 This chapter reviews (1) the principal forms of arbitration, (2) *ad hoc* arbitration and (3) the general structure of institutional arbitration. It considers the circumstances in which each of these forms may be appropriate and some of the best known institutions. It also considers, briefly, some special purpose arbitration institutions, which whilst differently structured, also provide a form of arbitration even though not based on a specific arbitration agreement.

1. The Principal Forms of Arbitration

3-4 There are two basic forms or types of arbitration: *ad hoc* and institutional.[1] Both of these forms are based on the parties' agreement: it is a choice that the parties must make when selecting arbitration.

3-5 *Ad hoc* arbitration is where the arbitration mechanism is established specifically for the particular agreement or dispute. Where parties are silent and have not selected an institutional arbitration, the arbitration will be *ad hoc*. When agreeing on *ad hoc* arbitration the parties often also agree on the arrangements for initiating the procedure, selecting the arbitrators and determining the procedural rules. When the parties fail to agree on these issues, *e.g.* they have agreed only "arbitration" or "arbitration in [a nominated city]", usually default provisions of the law of the place of arbitration will be applicable.

3-6 Institutional arbitration is where parties submit their disputes to an arbitration procedure, which is conducted under the auspices of or administered or directed by an existing institution. There are a large number of institutions of different kinds. These institutions aim to provide an arbitration service specifically, or within the context of their overall activities and objectives, and due to their infrastructure will in some cases assist with the running of the arbitration.

1 See, *e.g.*, Aksen, "Ad Hoc Versus Institutional Arbitration", 2(1) *ICC Bulletin* 8 (1991).

3-7 Due to the lack of accurate statistical information, no one really knows how many arbitrations take place in any year, and whether there is more *ad hoc* or institutional arbitration. Some of the institutions publish the number of arbitrations that they have in a year.[2]

3-8 There is no definitive report on the number of *ad hoc* arbitrations that take place around the world every year. The International Federation of Commercial Arbitration Institutions published the following table[3] which suggests there are over 2000 arbitrations a year under the auspices of the better known arbitration institutions.

Institution	**1992**	**1994**	**1996**	**1998**	**1999**	**2000**	**2001**
AAA – ICDR	204	187	226	387	453	510	649
CIETAC	267	829	778	645	609	543	731
DIS	20	30	31	42	32	62	58
HKIAC	185	150	197	240	257	298	307
ICC	337	384	433	466	529	541	566
JCAA	5	4	8	14	12	10	17
LCIA	21	39	37	70	56	81	71
SIAC	7	22	25	67	67	55	56
Stockholm Institute	44	74	75	92	104	73	74
Vienna	47	64	45	46	37	55	33

2. *AD HOC* ARBITRATION

2.1. *Characteristics of ad hoc Arbitration*

3-9 The essential characteristic of *ad hoc* arbitration is that it is independent of all institutions. The arbitration system selected or provided for in the agreement does not exist except in the context of the dispute between the parties.

2 The ICC publishes its annual statistics in the spring issue of the Bulletin of the International Court of Arbitration. The LCIA, Stockholm Institute, HKIAC, SIAC and CIETAC all periodically issue details of the number of arbitrations commenced.

3 Source: IFCAI and HKIAC. See also <www.hkiac.org/en_statistics.html> (last visited in December 2002).

The arbitration system is activated if a dispute arises between the parties and one of them calls for arbitration or otherwise initiates the procedure in accordance with the terms of the arbitration agreement or, where appropriate, by some subsidiary rules that have been selected to apply to the arbitration.

3-10 Accordingly, whilst every arbitration institution has its own characteristics and therefore mechanisms for establishing and controlling the arbitration process, with *ad hoc* arbitration, there are none of these procedures. For this reason, in *ad hoc* arbitration the parties have the maximum degree of flexibility to agree and specify those aspects of the procedure that they wish, subject to any mandatory law in the place of arbitration.[4] This would include how the arbitrators are to be appointed, how many arbitrators there should be, the procedure to be followed, the arrangements for the presentation of evidence and how the arbitration should be pleaded. The parties can also agree on the timetable for the arbitration and any other special requirements to reflect the specific characteristics of the contract in dispute.

2.2. Regulating ad hoc Arbitration

3-11 One relatively simple way to regulate an *ad hoc* arbitration is with the express selection, in the arbitration agreement, of appropriate arbitration rules. Such rules will generally provide for all or most of the above matters. Particularly popular for international arbitration are the UNCITRAL Rules.[5] Although initially intended for use in non-institutional arbitration it is now also used in some institutional arbitrations.[6]

3-12 The one exception where there may be the involvement of an institution in an *ad hoc* arbitration is with respect to the appointment of the arbitrators. On occasion, where parties are unable to agree, they can select an appointing authority which has responsibility for selecting and appointing the arbitrator. Several of the major arbitration institutions provide a service of this kind.[7]

3-13 In the absence of any agreement on the rules to apply, the parties and in turn the arbitrators appointed will generally look to the *lex arbitri*, the law

---

4 See, *e.g.*, Model Law Article 19.

5 Other rules which can be selected include the CPR Institute for Dispute Resolution (formerly the Centre for Public Resources) and the PCA Rules.

6 See, *e.g.*, HKIAC and CRCICA.

7 See, *e.g.*, the PCA and the LCIA.

governing the arbitration, to determine how the arbitration should be organised.[8] This carries a double-edged risk: is the law of the place suitable and arbitration-friendly generally, and specifically for the contract or dispute, *e.g.* for the granting of interim relief by the arbitrators or by the court in support of the arbitration process? This uncertainty will always remain where the parties are unable to agree on a specific procedural structure or a set of rules to govern.

2.3. Advantages of ad hoc Arbitration

3-14 *Ad hoc* arbitration is generally favoured where the parties are unable to agree on the arbitration institution. There are many reasons why particular institutions may or may not be acceptable to parties. Where parties have opposing views as to which institution to choose, *ad hoc* arbitration is often the compromise. From a more positive position, the parties may feel that *ad hoc* arbitration is preferable for their specific case. Parties can also favour *ad hoc* arbitration where they wish to have control of the procedure and the mechanism rather than to be subjected to institutional administration or control.

3-15 A popular reason for *ad hoc* arbitration is that one party is a state or state-entity or parastatal. Sovereign entities are often reluctant to submit to the authority of any institution, regardless of its standing; to do so would be to devalue or deny its sovereignty. This is due to a perceived partiality or non-neutrality of certain institutions or the place where the institution is located. Whilst this concern is totally unjustified, some states prefer to create a totally independent *ad hoc* mechanism, through which they can ensure the maximum degree of non-nationality and the least embarrassment to their sovereignty.

3-16 A perceived but not necessarily correct advantage of *ad hoc* arbitration is that, because the parties control the process, it can be less expensive than institutional arbitration. In fact this depends in each case and on how the institution charges for its arbitration services.

3. General Structure of Institutional Arbitration

3-17 The first issue for parties to a contract is to select the institution appropriate for their particular contract or dispute. Most frequently, the

---

8 See, *e.g.*, Model Law Article 19, which empowers the Tribunal, in the absence of an agreement between the parties, to conduct the arbitration in "such manner as it considers appropriate".

institution is chosen by default because one of the parties makes a suggestion and the other one knows nothing else. Alternatively, the choice may be based on the fact that an institution is well known in a particular geographic or industrial area. However, this is an important decision that should be made at the outset of the contractual discussions and requires careful consideration.

3.1. Characteristics of Institutional Arbitration

3-18 Every arbitration institution has its own special characteristics. It is essential that parties are aware and take account of these.[9] It is tied in with an understanding of the special requirements of different arbitration systems and rules. For example, how many arbitrators should there be? Different rules will make different provisions; in the absence of agreement by the parties some favour one, *e.g.* the LCIA; others favour three, *e.g.* the Stockholm Institute. There are similarly differences in other areas including: the right of the parties to select, nominate and appoint arbitrators; the degree of independence and neutrality required of arbitrators; the power of arbitrators to control the proceedings and in particular, to make orders concerning interim relief; and how the costs of the arbitration, especially the arbitrators' fees, are calculated.

3-19 Important differences also include the level of administration of the institution. For example, the ICC is heavily administered with the terms of reference, fixing of times for the making of the award and scrutiny procedures being fundamental to the system. By contrast, after the appointment of the tribunal, the LCIA limits its administration to dealing with challenges to the arbitrators and to interceding to agree, collect and pay the fees of the arbitrators.

3.2. Advantages of Institutional Arbitration[10]

3-20 A strongly perceived advantage of institutional arbitration is the cachet behind the name of the institution. Accordingly, especially in countries where there is political interference or where the courts and law are not always arbitration-friendly, parties consider it beneficial when seeking to enforce an award which was issued by, or which carries the name of, an internationally

---

9 See, *e.g.*, Simpson, Thacher & Bartlett (eds), *International Arbitration Rules*.

10 See, Slate II, "International Arbitration: Do Institutions Make a Difference?" 31 *Wake Forest Law Review* 41 (1996).

respected institution. Whilst there are doubts as to the value of such cachet, *i.e.* ultimately being able to have an arbitration award issued under the name of that institution, it is still often considered to be helpful.

3-21 Another advantage of institutional arbitration is the fact that there is a "comfort" element in its existence. There have been many cases under the rules of each institution, and every year it has a continuing number of new arbitrations. This provides an obvious comfort as the parties know that the institution has experience in the way it establishes the tribunal and arranges for the award to be issued. On the other hand, just like in a court, each arbitration has to be looked at individually. One should never forget that it is the specific arbitrators who make the decisions on both procedural and substantive issues rather than the arbitration institution. Arbitrators are, of course, independent from the institution itself.

3-22 Through the structure of the institutions, there is often someone to turn to for assistance. For example, the ICC has a large secretariat comprising numerous counsel who, on a day to day basis, are responsible for the administration of a caseload of arbitrations. Accordingly, both arbitrators and parties are free to seek the advice of the ICC counsel as to how to take matters forward or overcome a difficult impasse. It is also a convenient way to ensure that the arbitrators are aware of the needs and concerns of the parties where they are not necessarily addressing the arbitrators directly. This is particularly so where arbitration awards have taken longer to be issued than should have been the case.

3-23 An important advantage of institutional arbitration is that it avoids the discomfort of the parties and the arbitrators discussing, agreeing and fixing their remuneration. Most institutions have a mechanism for collecting from the parties the money from which the arbitrators will be paid and without directly involving the arbitrators. This means that the arbitrators are able to maintain a certain level of material detachment. This has the very definitive advantage of allowing the arbitrators to focus solely on the substance of the case rather than discuss with the parties a matter that is personal to them.

3.3. International Arbitration Institutions

3-24 There are many international arbitration institutions.[11] In recent years there has been a plethora of new institutions created all around the world. In

[11] For a comprehensive collection/or list of the major arbitration institutions see <www.internationaladr.org>.

addition to the traditional and long existing institutions very many countries and major commercial centres have established organisations offering arbitration services.

3-25 A distinction can be made between arbitration institutions created by private law means and those established by an instrument of public international law. Following this division we refer to what are perhaps the most frequently discussed and used arbitration institutions.

(a) Private international institutions

3-26 *International Chamber of Commerce, International Court of Arbitration*:[12] The ICC is the most widely used and accepted international arbitration institution. It handles disputes arising out of all kinds of cases. Established in 1923 it has had well over 10,000 cases. In the year 2001 over 560 new international arbitrations were filed with the ICC. These cases concerned 1492 parties from 116 different countries on five continents.

3-27 *London Court of International Arbitration*:[13] The LCIA is the oldest arbitration institution having been established in 1893. It was then known as the London Chamber of Arbitration. It was restructured in the early 1980s and has since developed an annual caseload in excess of 80 new arbitrations.

3-28 *American Arbitration Association:*[14] The AAA has been providing dispute resolution services for nearly 75 years. This institution undoubtedly has the largest arbitration caseload with almost 200,000 cases per year, over 640 of which were international in character in the year 2001. It also has specialist rules including rules for international, commercial, construction and patent disputes. The International Centre for Dispute Resolution (ICDR) administers international cases. The ICDR was established in 1996 as a separate division of the AAA. It has specialised administrative staff in New York and in May 2001 ICDR opened its first European office in Dublin. The ICDR International Arbitration Rules are modelled on the UNCITRAL Rules.

3-29 *Arbitration Institute of the Stockholm Chamber of Commerce*:[15] The Stockholm Institute became prominent as a neutral institution during the cold war

---

12 <www.iccwbo.org/index_court.asp>.

13 <www.lcia-arbitration.com>.

14 <www.adr.org>.

15 <www.chamber.se/arbitration/english/index.html>.

when the AAA and the Soviet Foreign Trade Arbitration Commission agreed that contracts between American and Soviet entities should be submitted to the Swedish tribunal.[16] Since then contracts between former Soviet and western parties frequently provide for arbitration at the Stockholm Institute. Even after the fall of the Soviet empire it is still frequently used for commercial contracts involving parties from the west and from Russia or the other former Soviet Republics. It also has a good reputation for the resolution of disputes where one of the parties is a state or state entity. 74 new cases were filed with the Stockholm Institute in 2001.

3-30 *China International Economic Trade Arbitration Commission:*[17] CIETAC is the largest arbitration institution in the Peoples Republic of China. It is organised under the auspices of the China Council for the Promotion of International Trade (CCPIT). To this extent it is controlled and influenced by the Chinese government. The CCPIT is a powerful force for trade with China and CIETAC is invariably insisted upon by Chinese contracting parties. It had in excess of 700 international cases filed in the year 2001. The hearings are short and, unless otherwise agreed, in Chinese.

3-31 *Hong Kong International Arbitration Centre:*[18] The HKIAC was established in the early 1980s to provide an independent arbitration forum in the Far East and Asia for settling international commercial disputes of all kinds. Over 300 new cases were filed in 2001.

3-32 *Singapore International Arbitration Centre:*[19] In recent years the SIAC has developed a reputation as an acceptable neutral venue in Asia for both Chinese and Europeans. It is often acceptable to PRC commercial entities and to

---

16 See the 1977 US/USSR Optional Clause Agreement, reproduced with background correspondence as Appendix 5 in SCC (ed), *Arbitration in Sweden*, 203. On 24 March 1992 representatives of the AAA, the Russian Chamber of Commerce and Industry, and the Stockholm Chamber of Commerce announced the signing of the 1992 Optional Clause Agreement (which closely mirrors the 1977 Optional Clause Agreement). The 1992 Agreement is set out in Appendix 7 of Hober, "Enforcing Foreign Arbitral Awards against Russian Entities", in Arbitration Institute of the Stockholm Chamber of Commerce (ed), *Swedish and International Arbitration* (Stockholm 1993) 4(4) *WAMR* 82 (1993), 4(5) *WAMR* 122 (1993); 4(6) *WAMR* 150 (1993).

17 See, *e.g.*, the Shenzhen Sub-Commission of CIETAC <www.cietac.org.cn/ENGLISH/E_index.html>.

18 <www.hkiac.org>.

19 <www.siac.org.sg/main.html>.

businesses from the West. Over 50 new international cases were filed in the year 2001.

3-33 *Cairo Regional Centre for International Commercial Arbitration:*[20] Established in the mid 1980s, this was intended to be a neutral venue in the Middle East, with an understanding of the needs and concerns for parties in the Arab world. It was also intended that it would appoint arbitrators from the Arab world where appropriate, something which it was alleged the western arbitration institutions did only rarely. The Cairo Centre had a sister institution in Kuala Lumpur.[21] The Cairo Regional Centre has an increasing caseload and is regularly used by western and Arab parties. Over 50 cases were filed in the year 2001.

3-34 *World Intellectual Property Organization, Arbitration and Mediation Centre:*[22] This specialist intellectual property organisation created an arbitration and mediation service in the early 1990s. Its rules were prepared and developed with the assistance of a group of experts in international arbitration and intellectual property disputes. The arbitration (and mediation) facilities offered by WIPO are aimed specifically at resolution of disputes involving intellectual property. The Centre is also internationally recognised as the leading institution in the area resolution of domain names disputes, where it handled over 1,500 cases in the year 2001.

(b) Industry focused and commodity institutions[23]

3-35 There are many specialised arbitration institutions, for example:

- Grain and Feed Trade Association (GAFTA)[24]
- Refined Sugar Association (RSA)
- Federation of Oils, Seeds and Fats Association (FOSFA)[25]
- London Metal Exchange (LME)[26]
- London Maritime Arbitration Association (LMAA)[27]
- The Association of Food Distributors, Inc., of New York
- The Bremen Cotton Exchange in Germany (Baumwollbörse)[28]

---

20 <www.crcica.org.eg>.

21 <www.klrca.org>.

22 <www.arbiter.wipo.int/center/index.html>.

23 See, *e.g.*, Johnson, *Commodity Arbitration*.

24 <www.gafta.com>.

25 <www.fosfa.org>.

26 <www.lme.co.uk>.

27 <www.lmaa.org>.

- Hamburg Freundliche Arbitrage
- Piraeus Commodities-Exchange
- Japan Shipping Exchange.[29]

(c) Public international law institutions

3-36 *Permanent Court of Arbitration:*[30] The PCA was established by the Hague Conventions for Pacific Settlement of International Disputes of 1899 and 1907 to promote peace through peaceful resolution of international disputes. Disputes between two states or a state and a private party may be referred to the PCA. Although not many disputes have been referred to the PCA (40 since 1902), it provides excellent facilities and is flexible in respect of applicable arbitration rules. Parties may opt for optional rules of the PCA or for UNCITRAL Rules.

3-37 *International Centre for Settlement of Investment Disputes:*[31] Established in 1965 by the Washington Convention, ICSID has jurisdiction over legal investment disputes arising directly from a contract between a contracting state and a foreign investor from another contracting state, provided both parties have agreed to arbitration which is normally done in the investment contract. Under the Washington Convention ICSID awards are simple to enforce as a public international obligation of the countries party to the Convention. Over 100 arbitrations have been commenced under the ICSID Rules and fourteen new cases were filed in 2001.

3-38 *Additional Facility Rules*: ICSID also administers disputes arising out of investment contracts where a state party, or the state where the investor comes from, is not a party to the ICSID Convention. ICSID has administered eleven cases under those Rules to date. The only disadvantage is that the ICSID Convention is not applicable to arbitration under these Additional Facility Rules so that enforcement is not a direct obligation. However, enforcement remains possible in the normal way under the New York Convention or other applicable bilateral or multilateral conventions.

---

28 <www.baumwollboerse.de>.

29 <www.jseinc.org/en/tomac/index.htm>.

30 <www.pca-cpa.org>.

31 <www.worldbank.org/icsid>.

3.4. Special Purpose Institutions

3-39 From time to time, special standing tribunals are established to undertake resolution of certain types of dispute. For example, a number of claims commissions or claims tribunals have been set up in order to deal with the legal and economic consequences of nationalizations, revolutions, wars or other events affecting a large number of parties in the same way. These tribunals are usually a form of non-national arbitration. Parties who have a claim falling within the declared jurisdiction of such a tribunal have the right to submit their claims to those tribunals. Normally national courts will not have or accept jurisdiction over such claims.

3-40 This type of tribunal will generally have been established by an international convention or some other international instrument. The parties against whom specific claims are made accept that the designated tribunal has the responsibility and authority to determine such claims. In general the creation of these claims commissions is part of an overall settlement of the underlying political disputes between the states involved.

3-41 These special purpose tribunals have made a significant contribution towards the development of international arbitration because of the substantive law and procedural questions raised, and also the sheer volume of cases involved. There is generally no formal arbitration agreement between the claimants and the parties against whom claims are brought in this type of tribunal. This is not strictly necessary because of the nature of the tribunal and the basis of the jurisdiction. Furthermore, the instrument under which the tribunal is established will provide a mechanism of enforcement if necessary. In any event, as the parties against whom claims are made have accepted the jurisdiction of the tribunal in advance, the effect of a party submitting a formal claim would be to create an agreement giving jurisdiction to the tribunal. This would be a form of acceptance of the standing offer of arbitration. The award of the tribunal should therefore be enforceable under the New York Convention in the normal way.

(a) Iran-US Claims Tribunal

3-42 There was enormous political hostility and tension in 1979 between Iran and the US due mainly to the detention of the US citizens in Iran when the Iranian revolution was underway. Before the Iranian Revolution, Iran and the US had an annual bilateral trade of approximately US$6 billion.[32] Not only had American nationals made very significant investments in Iran, but Iran had also held investments of billions of dollars in the US and other Western countries. In the wake of the American embassy hostage crisis and based upon rumours that Iran was intending to withdraw its money from the US, the US government froze all Iranian assets in the US. In addition to their actions in the US, US nationals also brought claims elsewhere and attached Iranian property in several countries. The tension was significantly reduced by a settlement agreement known as the "Algiers Accords."[33] The Iran-US Claims Tribunal was established in accordance with the Claims Settlement Agreement within the Algiers Accords which ended the American embassy hostage crisis.

3-43 In the Algiers Accords, brokered by the Government in Algeria, Iran and the US agreed that all claims arising out of the Iranian revolution between nationals of both states should be decided by the Iran-US Claims Tribunal. The hundreds of commercial lawsuits pending in the US relating to Iran were suspended by presidential order. Furthermore, the parties agreed that in return for releasing Iranian frozen assets in the US, one billion US dollars would be deposited in an escrow account placed under the control of the tribunal. This account was to be topped up periodically by Iran and was at the disposal of the tribunal to satisfy awards rendered in favour of US nationals. The administrative expenses of the tribunal were to be borne by both states jointly. The tribunal, which is based in The Hague, is composed of nine members and was officially established in 1981. Iran and the US appointed three members each. The three remaining third country or neutral arbitrators are appointed according to the UNCITRAL Rules by agreement of the state appointed arbitrators. The President of the tribunal is one of the third country arbitrators. The tribunal's activities are conducted according to a slightly amended version of the UNCITRAL Rules.

3-44 The tribunal is divided into three chambers composed of one arbitrator from each group. Those chambers hear most of the tribunal's caseload. The full tribunal of nine at its regular meetings deals primarily with cases concerning the interpretation of the Accords and official disputes between the parties relating to contracts for the sale and purchase of goods and services. Other types of cases

---

32 See Carbonneau, *Arbitration,* 852.

33 See 20 *ILM* 224 (1981) for the Declaration and related documents. For commentary, see, *e.g.* Brower and Brueschke, *Iran-United States Claims Tribunal*; Khan, *The Iran-United States Claims Tribunal*; Lillich (ed), *The Iran-United States Claims Tribunal 1981-83*; Westberg, *Case Law of the Iran-United States Claims Tribunal.*

can, however, be referred to the full tribunal if they involve important questions of law and there is a possibility of divergent opinions from the different chambers.

3-45 The private claims, which are by far the largest group, are divided into claims under and over US$ 250,000. While large claims are to be presented by the parties themselves, small claims are, for reasons of procedural economy, presented by the governments and have largely been subject to a lump sum settlement between the two States.[34] The breadth of private claims range from expropriation of property, breach of contractual obligations, non-payment of debts, outstanding salaries, and claims for medical and educational expenses of Iranian nationals in the US.

3-46 The jurisdiction of the tribunal is limited to disputes between nationals of Iran and the US under Article II of the Algiers Accords. Parties from other countries had no right to have their disputes resulting from the Iranian revolution decided by the tribunal or even profit from the facilitated procedure of executing awards available to the tribunal. They must bring claims against Iran in their local courts with all the problems of execution in Iran. The tribunal's decisions are to a large extent published and have given rise to a body of international jurisprudence. They have had an important influence on many aspects of the practice and development of international commercial arbitration in the past 20 years. There have been almost 5,000 cases filed with the Iran-US Claims Tribunal.

(b) United Nations Compensation Commission

3-47 The United Nations Compensation Commission (UNCC) is a subsidiary organ of the United Nations Security Council based in Geneva. It was established by the Security Council in 1991 to process claims and pay compensation for losses resulting from Iraq's invasion and occupation of Kuwait. Compensation is payable to successful claimants from a special fund that receives a percentage of the proceeds from sales of Iraqi oil.

3-48 The Security Council established Iraq's legal responsibility for such losses in its Resolution 687 of 3 April 1991, which states in pertinent part

---

[34] Brower, "The Lessons from the Iran-U.S. Claims Tribunal applied to Claims against Iraq", in Lillich (ed), *The Iran-United States Claims Tribunal 1981-83*, 19.

> Iraq ... is liable under international law for any direct loss, damage, including environmental damage and the depletion of natural resources, or injury to foreign Governments, nationals and corporations, as a result of Iraq's unlawful invasion and occupation of Kuwait.

3-49 Resolution 687 (1991) is one of the most complex and far-reaching decisions ever taken by the Security Council. It was adopted under Chapter VII of the UN Charter, which concerns action with respect to threats to the peace, breaches of the peace and acts of aggression.

3-50 The UNCC structure includes a Governing Council, a Secretariat and panels of commissioners. Operations are conducted by the Secretariat which also prepares the cases to be decided by the panels of commissioners. Their reports and recommendations, however, require approval by the Governing Council. Despite its function to resolve claims against Iraq, the UNCC

> ... is not a court or an arbitral tribunal before which the parties appear; it is a political organ that performs an essentially fact-finding function of examining claims, verifying their validity, evaluating losses, assessing payments and resolving disputed claims.[35]

3-51 The character of the UNCC is influenced by the fact that the general liability of Iraq for all direct losses resulting from its invasion of Kuwait has already been determined.[36]

3-52 Over 2,500,000 claims with an asserted value of greater than US$ 176 billion have been filed with the UNCC. Those claims range from issues of personal injury and death, evacuation and environmental damages, to ordinary commercial claims. Due to the volume of claims it was necessary to adopt procedures to decide the claims within a reasonable period of time. Those procedures deviate considerably from the classical approaches usually adopted by courts and arbitration tribunals. The procedure followed is set out in the

---

35 Report of the Secretary-General Pursuant to Paragraph 19 of the Security Council Resolution 687, UN Doc S/22559 (1991), para 20; see also Alzamora, "The UN Compensation Commission: An Overview", in Lillich (ed), *The Iran-United States Claims Tribunal 1981-83*, 8. For the differences between the UNCC and the Iran-US Claims Tribunal, see Brower, "The Lessons from the Iran-U.S. Claims Tribunal applied to Claims against Iraq", in Lillich (ed), *ibid*, 15 et seq.

36 Resolution 687, paragraph 16.

Provisional Rules for Claims Procedure adopted by the Governing Council in 1992.[37]

3-53 In general all claims had to be submitted by governments on behalf of their nationals or residents on standardised claims forms. The Secretariat makes a preliminary assessment on whether the claims meet the formal requirements (Article 14) and reports to the Governing Council on the claims received and the legal and factual issues raised (Article 16). Payments are not made to the individual claimants but to the relevant government which then distributes the payment on the basis of Governing Council guidelines. The compensatory decision of the UNCC does not qualify as an arbitration award and cannot be enforced under the New York Convention. Therefore the UNCC does not bar a party from pursuing its claim to a national court or arbitration tribunal and then to enforce them against other available assets of Iraq.[38]

(c) The Claims Resolution Tribunal for Dormant Accounts in Switzerland[39]

3-54 The Claims Resolution Tribunal for Dormant Accounts in Switzerland (CRT) was set up in 1998 by the Independent Claims Resolution Foundation set up by the Swiss Bankers Association. It is a claims resolution process in respect of accounts in Swiss banks, particularly since before and after the World War II.[40] The CRT is an independent tribunal based in Zurich under the supervision of the Swiss Bankers Association and the Independent Committee of Eminent Persons, created by agreement between the Swiss Bankers Association and the World Jewish Restitution Organisation.[41] The claims resolution process itself is carried out by the Independent Claims Resolution Foundation.

3-55 The CRT may hear claims concerning accounts opened by non-Swiss nationals or residents, which have been dormant since 9 May 1945 and details of which were published by the Swiss Bankers Association in 1997 and 1999. Both the claimant and the bank concerned must enter a claims resolution agreement

---

[37] Decision 10, Provisional Rules for Claims Procedures, S/AC.26/1992/10 (1992), reproduced in Lillich (ed), *The Iran-United States Claims Tribunal 1981-83*, Appendix C, 427. For a detailed review of the procedure see Gibson, "Using Computers to Evaluate Claims at the United Nations Compensation Commission", 13 *Arb Int* 167 (1997) 172.

[38] <www.uncc.ch> (last visited November 2002).

[39] See <www.crt.ch/menu.html>.

[40] See, generally, Karrer (ed), "The Claims Resolution Process on Dormant Accounts in Switzerland", *ASA Special Series*, 13 (2000).

[41] Riemer, von Segesser and von der Crone, "Schiedsgericht für nachrichtenlose Konten in der Schweiz", *ASA Bulletin* 252 (1998); Blessing, *Introduction to Arbitration*, para 108.

(*i.e.* arbitration agreement) before a claim is submitted to the tribunal. The CRT is composed of a secretariat, a chairman, a vice chairman and up to fifteen other members and deals with those claims where the alleged ownership is contested by the bank holding the account or several persons who claim to be entitled. The jurisdiction of the CRT rests on a submission by the Swiss banks and the choice of the claimant to pursue its rights by means of the CRT and not through the state courts. The procedure is based on the "Rules of Procedure for the Claims Resolution Process"[42] agreed upon by the Board of Trustees of the sponsoring foundation and the "Internal Rules of the Claims Resolution Tribunal".

3-56 Claims rejected by the banks are submitted to an initial screening procedure before a sole arbitrator who decides whether or not sufficient proof has been submitted by the claimant which would justify the release of the name of the bank and the amount held in the dormant account. Given the problems created by the destruction of evidence during the war, a relaxed standard of proof applies in the tribunal. According to Article 22 CRT Rules of Procedure, the claimant only has to make a plausible case that he is entitled to the dormant account. The law applicable to the merits of the claim is usually Swiss law in so far as the relationship between the original holder of the account and the bank is concerned. Since the publication of two lists of dormant account by the Swiss Banker Association in 1997 32,000 claims have been filed with the CRT.[43]

(d) International Commission on Holocaust Era Insurance Claims[44]

3-57 The ICHEIC was established in 2000 by several European insurance companies, US insurance regulators and the State of Israel. The aim of this body is to consider claims by holocaust survivors and their families to recover under unpaid insurance policies. The ICHEIC has its seat in London.

3-58 There is a two year period for the filing of claims to be considered by the Commission. As the insurance companies have accepted the jurisdiction of the ICHEIC its decisions should be final. The jurisdiction over claimants only comes about when the claim is filed; this is an acceptance by conduct of the Commission decision. These decisions will have the effect of an arbitration award and will be enforceable under the New York Convention.

---

42 Published in *ASA Bulletin* 258 (1998).

43 Blessing, *Introduction to Arbitration*, para 113. See <www.crt-ii.org>.

44 <www.icheic.org>.

3.5. Online Dispute Resolution[45] *Institutions*

3-59 There are a number of companies and organizations offering on line dispute resolution services. Services offered range from negotiating the amount of a settlement to full mediation or arbitration.[46] There are no universally accepted rules currently governing on line resolution procedures.[47] There are international dispute resolution procedures specifically for the determination of domain name disputes.[48]

---

[45] See, *e.g.*, Katsch and Rivkin, *Online Dispute Resolution*; Rule, *Online Dispute Resolution for Business* (Jossey-Bass 2002).

[46] See, *e.g.*, WIPO Domain Name Dispute Resolution Service Center, e-Resolution Integrity Online Organisation, ICANN Non-Profit Corporation.

[47] WIPO has adapted its standard arbitration rules to suit the on line arena, primarily to allow on line secure filing of documents and real time correspondence between the parties.

[48] See: i) Uniform Domain Name Dispute Resolution Policy adopted by the Internet Corporation for Assigned Names and Numbers (ICANN) on 26 August 1999, www.icann.org/udrp/udrp-policy-24pct99.htm (last visited 30 September 2002); ii) "Rules for Uniform Domain Name Dispute Resolution Policy" adopted by the Internet Corporation for Assigned Names and Numbers (ICANN) on 24 October 1999, www.icann.org/udrp/udrp-policy-24oct99.htm; iii) WIPO Arbitration and Mediation Center Supplemental rules for Uniform Domain Name Dispute Resolution Policy" in effect as 1 December 1999 on <www.arbiter.wipo.int/domains/rules/supplemental.html> (last visited 30 September 2002).

Chapter 4

ESSENTIAL CHARACTERISTICS OF INTERNATIONAL COMMERCIAL ARBITRATION

4-1 The characteristics of arbitration discussed above equally apply to all types of arbitration, irrespective of subject matter and whether or not domestic or international. This chapter is concerned with what makes an arbitration (1) commercial (2) international[1], and (3) the debate on transnational and delocalised arbitration.

---

1 Domestic arbitration is regulated in almost every legal system. Some countries additionally have specific legislation relating to particular types of arbitration disputes, *e.g.* employment, securities, maritime or they may require disputes of a certain kind to be resolved exclusively by arbitration. For examples of statutory arbitration or *arbitrage forcé*, see Bermuda, Arbitration Act (Labour Relations) section 43(1); England, Arbitration Act sections 95-97; Rubino-Sammartano, *International Arbitration*, 25-28.

Chapter 4

1. The Meaning of "Commercial"

1.1. Importance of the Definition of "Commercial"

4-2 While the term "commercial" or "economic"[2] adds little to the description of "international arbitration" it has become the accepted term due to its consistent use by lawyers from civil law countries.[3] The term "economic" is generally considered to be wider than the term "commercial".[4] The addition of "economic" adds little to the scope of arbitration, but it can also be misleading. As the term "international economic law" has specific connotations[5], the traditional and established term "international commercial arbitration" is preferred. The qualification "commercial" is used in the broadest sense and is not without consequences.

4-3 Historically, the unqualified term "international arbitration" has been used for public international law arbitration with the participation of one or more states. Public international law arbitrations, due to state participation and state sovereignty implications, are often subject to different rules. Arbitrations involving investments by parties from one country in another and disputes concerning energy-related issues frequently involve international law issues. While these types of arbitration possess characteristics of both commercial and public international arbitration, in recent years the commercial arbitration elements have outweighed the public international law arbitration elements. Also, disputes which are labelled by American lawyers as trade disputes in the context of the WTO[6] or NAFTA[7] and related to public law regulation of trade qualify as commercial disputes.

---

2 The attribute "economic" is rarely given to international arbitration. The scope of international economic arbitration is, in principle, identical to the scope of international commercial arbitration. See Berger, *International Economic Arbitration*, which effectively covers what is referred to elsewhere as international commercial arbitration.

3 See, *e.g.*, Redfern and Hunter, *International Commercial Arbitration*, paras 1-27.

4 See Berger, *International Economic Arbitration*, 67-69.

5 See, *e.g.*, the *Journal of International Economic Law* which deals with international economic integration as well as WTO issues. Also relevant textbooks and university courses address international economic integration, WTO, TRIPS, GATT, GATS and related issues.

6 See Qureshi, *The World Trade Organization—Implementing International Trade Norms* (Manchester University Press 1996). For the WTO Settlement of Disputes mechanism see, *e.g*,. Petersmann, *The GATT/WTO Settlement System* (Kluwer Law International 1997); Palmeter and Mavroidis, *Dispute Settlement in the World Trade Organization—Practice and Procedure*

4-4 It may be important to label an arbitration as "commercial" because commercial law is often subject to a distinct set of flexible rules. For instance, disputes involving consumers may be subject to stricter consumer protection rules[8] concerning the negotiation, formation and validity of an arbitration agreement. While the added protection may be justified in consumer transactions, with the rationale of protecting the allegedly weaker party, it is in most cases unjustified and unwelcome in commercial transactions.

4-5 It may be difficult to define a commercial dispute, as many jurisdictions have their own definition of commercial law and commercial disputes. Some disputes are deemed commercial due to the fact that commercial persons are involved[9] whereas other disputes are deemed commercial irrespective of the persons involved.[10] In international commercial arbitration, it is important to characterise the nature of the underlying transaction and whether or not the relevant dispute is commercial; the involvement of commercial persons may be of relevance but should not be the guiding principle. For instance, states, their ministries and agencies may be involved in a commercial activity although they do not qualify, strictly speaking, as a commercial person.

4-6 Most civil law countries will have a commercial law code. Commercial law has developed on the basis of special legislation, scholarly commentaries and relevant case law. While it may be argued that in civil law countries it may not always be clear what is commercial, local lawyers can easily identify a commercial transaction. Similarly, in common law jurisdictions where distinctions between the various areas of law are less formal, it is possible to identify commercial transactions. In the US the Uniform Commercial Code

---

(Kluwer Law International 1999); Pescatore, Davey and Lowenfeld, *Handbook of WTO/GATT Dispute Settlement* (Transnational and Kluwer Law International 1997); Komuro, "The WTO Dispute Settlement Mechanism Coverage and Procedures of the WTO Understanding", 12(3) *J Int'l Arb* 81 (1995).

7 See, *e.g.*, Soloway, "NAFTA's Chapter 11", 16(2) *J Int'l Arb* 1 (1999); Anderson, "Prioritizing an Agenda for Trade Dispute Settlement in North America", 12(4) *J Int'l Arb* 113 (1995).

8 See, *e.g.*, EC Directive 93/13 of 5 April 1993 on Unfair Contracts Terms in Consumer Contracts, OJ 1993 L 95, 29, which on the basis of Article 3 and Annex point (g) significantly restricts the effectiveness of arbitration clauses in consumer contracts. See also England, Arbitration Act sections 89-92; see also Germany, ZPO section 1031(5) where a special form is required.

9 See, *e.g.*, the subjective criterion (definition of merchant) codified in the German Commercial Code, sections 1 *et seq.*

10 See, *e.g.*, the objective criterion (definition of "*acte de commerce*") codified in the French *Code de Commerce*.

delimits a non exclusive set of commercial transactions.[11] In England delimitation of commercial law can be found in legislation, in scholarly writings[12], and in the Civil Procedure Rules which set out the jurisdiction of the Commercial Court with respect to commercial disputes.[13]

4-7 This book uses an autonomous concept of commercial transactions closely following the Model Law. It includes disputes with state parties and does not distinguish between civil and commercial arbitration as in some national legal systems.[14]

1.2. "Commercial" in the UNCITRAL Model Law and Model Law Countries

4-8 The Model Law describes "commercial" in a footnote

> The term "commercial" should be given a wide interpretation so as to cover matters arising from all relationships of a commercial nature, whether contractual or not. Relationships of a commercial nature include, but are not limited to, the following transactions: any trade transaction for the supply or exchange of goods or services; distribution agreement; commercial representation or agency; factoring; leasing; construction of works; consulting; engineering; licensing; investment; financing; banking; insurance; exploitation agreement or concession; joint venture and other forms of industrial or business co-operation; carriage of goods or passengers by air, sea, rail or road.

4-9 Despite its presence in a footnote, this definition is an integral part of the Model Law. The drafters of the Model Law wanted to produce an inclusive and open-ended description of the term commercial. The intention was to have a definition which can be used, in particular, by states which do not have a distinctive body of commercial law so that the Model Law would be applicable to all aspects of international business.

---

[11] The Uniform Commercial Code is the model law prepared by the American Law Institute and, with some amendments, it has been adopted by all US states. See White and Summers, *Uniform Commercial Code* (5th ed, West 1999).

[12] See, *e.g.*, Goode, *Commercial Law* (2d ed, Penguin 1995); *Schmitthoff's Export Trade* (10th ed, Sweet and Maxwell 2000).

[13] See English Civil Procedure Rules, Part 49 together with the English Commercial Court Practice Direction and the Commercial Court's Guide.

[14] See, *e.g.*, French domestic arbitration law; Fouchard Gaillard Goldman *on International Commercial Arbitration*, para 64.

4-10 Some countries which adopted the Model Law incorporated the text of the footnote into a section of the law;[15] other jurisdictions simply reproduced the text in a schedule.[16] India has opted for an expressly Indian characterisation of commercial disputes[17] while other countries have for various reasons not included the definition when adopting the Model Law.[18]

4-11 The decision of the drafters of the Model Law to include an open-ended definition of "commercial" is well justified, especially when read together with reference to international proceedings. The intention is to have a scope of application which is flexible enough to meet the needs of the international business community and which will facilitate the widest possible application of the Model Law. The drafters managed to avoid doctrinal traps and to focus on the nature of the transaction rather than the persons involved.[19]

---

15 See, *e.g.*, Canada, British Columbia International Commercial Arbitration Act 1986 Article 1(6); Bulgaria, Law on International Commercial Arbitration 2001 Article 1(2); Cyprus, International Commercial Arbitration Law no 110/1987 sections 2(4) and (5). Similarly, Egypt, Law no 27 of 1994 Promulgating the Law concerning Arbitration in Civil and Commercial Matters Article 2; Ireland, Arbitration (International Commercial) Act 1998 Article 3(1); Nigeria, Arbitration and Conciliation Act 1990 Article 57(1); Oman, Law of Arbitration in Civil and Commercial Matters 1997 Article 2; Russian Federation, Law on International Commercial Arbitration 1993 Article 1(2); Ukraine, Law on Commercial Arbitration 1994 Article 1(2) and Article 2.

16 See, *e.g.*, Australia, Bahrain, Bermuda, Canada, Malta, Singapore.

17 See India, Arbitration Ordinance section 2(1)(f):

> 'international commercial arbitration' means an arbitration relating to disputes arising out of legal relationships, whether contractual or not, considered as commercial under the law in force in India and where at least one of the parties is -
> (i) an individual who is a national of, or habitually resident in any country other than India; or
> (ii) a body corporate which is incorporated in any country other than India; or
> (iii) a company or an association or a body of individuals whose central management and control is exercised in any country other than India; or
> (iv) the Government of a foreign country.

18 See, *e.g.*, Germany, Greece, Hong Kong, Hungary, Iran, Libya, Zimbabwe. Kaplan, "The Hong Kong Arbitration Ordinance, Some Features and Recent Amendments", 1 *Am Rev Int'l Arb* 25 (1990) 29, justifies the Hong Kong decision to delete the reference to "commercial" with the argument that the delimitation is incompatible with the nature of common law.

19 See UN Doc A/40/17, para 22; Holtzmann and Neuhaus, *Model Law*, 33.

1.3. "Commercial" in National Legislation

4-12 While a number of jurisdictions, which have not enacted the Model Law, make references to commercial arbitration or commercial transactions[20], almost none appears to define "commercial" in the context of arbitration. This silence is often deemed an implied reference to the concept of commercial law and commercial transactions as developed in the national (domestic) law.

4-13 The 1925 US Federal Arbitration Act definition is much narrower than that of the Model Law and is now outdated. It sees international commerce as a maritime and shipping transaction and the word "commerce" adds only the international character of the transaction or the legal relationship; "commerce" appears almost synonymous to "cross-border." Section 1 FAA provides

> COMMERCE" DEFINED; EXCEPTIONS TO OPERATION OF TITLE
> "Maritime transaction", as herein defined, means charter parties, bills of lading of water carriers, agreements relating to wharfage, supplies furnished vessels or repairs to vessels, collisions, or any other matters in foreign commerce which, if the subject of controversy, would be embraced within admiralty jurisdiction; "commerce", as herein defined, means commerce among the several States or with foreign nations, or in any Territory of the United States or in the District of Columbia, or between any such Territory and another, or between any such Territory and any State or foreign nation, or between the District of Columbia and any State or Territory or foreign nation, but nothing herein contained shall apply to contracts of employment of seamen, railroad employees, or any other class of workers engaged in foreign or interstate commerce.

1.4. "Commercial" in Arbitration Rules

4-14 Few arbitration rules define commercial disputes or commercial transactions. The rationale behind this decision is the intention to make it possible to accept any dispute that the parties wish to submit to the arbitration institution. Definitions of "commercial" can be found in Article 2 CIETAC Rules. Commercial disputes that can be resolved by arbitration under the 2001 CIETAC Rules Article 2 include disputes between an enterprise with foreign investment and another Chinese legal or physical person, or economic organisation or arising from project financing, invitation to tender, bidding,

---

[20] See Finland, Arbitration Act 1992 section 2. The French NCPC Article 1492 refers to "international commercial interests".

construction and other activities conducted by Chinese legal or physical persons and/or other economic organisations through utilising the capital, technology or service from foreign countries, international organisations or from the Honk Kong SAR, Macao and Taiwan regions.[21] The Rules attempt to combine "international" with "commercial" and to provide for the maximum scope of application. In most cases international is used as synonymous for commercial.

1.5. "Commercial" in International Conventions

4-15 International arbitration conventions also refer to the commercial nature of transactions. They do not necessarily limit their scope to commercial disputes. Most of them, however, operate only for commercial transactions.

4-16 The New York Convention allows for a distinction to be made between commercial and non-commercial arbitration. This is reflected in Article 1(3), which contains what is known as the commercial reservation

> When signing, ratifying or acceding to this Convention ..., any State may ... declare that it will apply the Convention only to differences arising out of legal relationships, whether contractual or not, which are considered as commercial under the national law of the State making such declaration.

4-17 The commercial reservation was inserted because at the New York Conference of 1958 it was believed that, without this clause, it would be impossible for certain civil law countries, which distinguish between commercial and non-commercial transactions, to adhere to the Convention. About one third of the contracting states have made use of this commercial reservation.

4-18 The New York Convention suggests that "commercial" should be characterised on the basis of national law. In practice, national courts tend to

---

[21] CIETAC Rules Articles 2(3) and (4); see also for another definition paragraph 1(2) 1995 Rules of the Moscow International Commercial Arbitration Court (ICAC). It provides that matters which may be referred to the ICAC include disputes arising from contractual or other civil-law relationships in the course of foreign trade and other forms of international economic affairs between enterprises with foreign investment, international associations and organizations set up in the territory of the Russian Federation and from purchase and sale (delivery) of goods, contracts of service and labour, exchange of goods and/or services, carriage of goods and passengers, commercial representation or agency, leasing, scientific-technical exchange, exchange with other results of intellectual activity, construction of industrial and other objects, licensing operations, investment, crediting and settlement operations, insurance, joint ventures and other forms of industrial and business co-operation.

interpret the scope of "commercial" broadly. However there is some Indian case law which interprets the term "commercial" narrowly by holding that it means "commercial under a provision of Indian law in force." Accordingly Indian courts have held that neither the construction of a factory accompanied with transfer of technology[22] nor a contract of technical know-how to be of commercial nature.[23] Similarly, the Tunisian Cour de cassation refused to consider as commercial a contract concerning a town-planning programme drawn by architects.[24]

4-19 The more liberal approach can be seen in the US which excludes from the scope of the New York Convention only matters arising out of legal relationships, whether contractual or not, which are not considered as commercial under the national law of the US.[25] International employment contracts have been considered to be a commercial legal relationship.[26]

4-20 Due to the uncertainty that the commercial reservation may create, France, which originally expressed a reservation, has withdrawn its commercial reservation. It is expected that other countries may follow.

4-21 The European Convention on International Commercial Arbitration did not contain a specific definition of commercial. It adopted a general definition with a reference in Article I(1)(a)

> to arbitration agreements concluded for the purpose of settling disputes arising from international trade.

4-22 In a case related to this provision of the European Convention, an arbitration tribunal held that the term has to be effected independently of notions

---

22 See commentary by van den Berg, VIII *YBCA* 341 (1983).

23 See *RM Investment & Trading Co Pvt Limited (India) v Boeing Company and another (US)*, (1994) 1 Supreme Court Journal 657, (1997) XXII YBCA 710 (Supreme Court of India, 10 February 1994).

24 Tunisian Cour de cassation, 10 November 1993, *Taieb Haddad and Hans Barett v Société d'Investissement Kal*, XXIII YBCA 770 (1998).

25 US Reservation on Accession to the New York Convention (took effect 29 December 1970). It is understood that personal, matrimonial and domestic employment matters are not of a commercial nature.

26 See *Paragraph International Inc (Nova Scotia, Canada) and Prograph Inc (US) and Pictorius Incorporated (Nova Scotia, Canada) and Philip Cox and Paul Davies v Ralph Barhydt (US)*, 928 F Supp 983, XXII YBCA 901 (1998) (ND Cal 1996).

of domestic law and that economic contracts concluded by a state may fall under the Convention definition.[27]

4-23 The 1987 Amman Arab Convention on Commercial Arbitration also contains no clear definition of commercial transactions. Article 2 provides only that the Convention will apply

> ... to commercial disputes between natural or legal persons of any nationality, linked by commercial transactions with one of the contracting States or one of its nationals, or which have their main headquarters in one of these States.

4-24 To the extent that most Arab states have harmonised commercial and civil law practices, the absence of a definition should not normally create any problems.

4-25 Similarly, the Inter-American Convention on International Commercial Arbitration[28] states in Article 1

> An agreement in which the parties undertake to submit to arbitral decision any differences that may arise or have arisen between them with respect to a commercial transaction is valid. ...

4-26 When the ambit of a "commercial transaction" is to be ascertained, regard should be given to the international character of a convention and the need to promote uniformity. Accordingly, only an autonomous and comparative interpretation and characterisation is appropriate.

2. The Meaning of "International"

4-27 The international or domestic character of commercial arbitration may result in the application of a different set of rules. Several legal systems have special rules for domestic and international arbitration.[29] Other systems opt for a unified regulation.[30] What makes arbitration an international one? What are the

---

27 See Interim Award of 18 November 1983 in *ad hoc* arbitration *Erick Benteler KG and Helmut Benteler KG (both FR Germany) v Belgian State and SA ABC (Belgium)*, Journal des Tribunaux 230 (1984), X YBCA 37 (1985), Rev Arb 339 (1989).

28 Panama Convention, signed 30 January 1975.

29 See, *e.g.*, Australia, Bermuda, Canada and also in the US where the Federal Arbitration Act only applies to international and interstate arbitration.

30 See, *e.g.*, France, England and the US. It has been suggested that the introduction of an International Commercial Arbitration Act in the US would make clear that the protective review standards appropriate for domestic disputes would not affect cross-border arbitration. It would

criteria employed for such a classification? The international or domestic character of commercial arbitration is not to be confused with the domestic or foreign character of awards for which different regimes for their enforcement exist.

2.1. Relevant Criteria

4-28 There are three ways of establishing the international character of an arbitration. An arbitration may be international because (a) its subject matter or its procedure[31] or its organisation is international; or (b) the parties involved are connected with different jurisdictions; or (c) there is a combination of both.

(a) The objective criterion: Dispute with foreign element or of international character

4-29 The objective criterion focuses on the subject matter of the dispute and the international or national character of the underlying transaction. Hence, the international commercial interests, or the cross-border element of the underlying contract, or the fact that the dispute is referred to a genuinely international arbitration institution, such as the ICC, the LCIA or ICSID, would be sufficient for the arbitration to qualify as international.

4-30 The objective criterion is found most simply in French law. Article 1492 of the French Code of Civil Procedure reads

> An arbitration is international if it implicates international commercial interests.[32]

4-31 There is a significant body of French case law relating to the concept of international transaction.[33] The French courts have taken a liberal approach in

---

also clarify the relationship between federal and state arbitration law: see Park, "Duty and Discretion in International Arbitration", 93 *Am J Int'l L* 805 (1999) 822-3. See also Mantakou, "The Concept of International Arbitration: An "Endangered Species"?", 50 *RHDI* 139 (1997) who contends that international arbitration free from restrictions imposed on domestic arbitration is nowadays a seriously endangered species. It also suggested that the traditional distinction between domestic and international arbitration is no longer useful.

31 See Fouchard, "Quand un arbitrage est-il international?", *Rev Arb* 59 (1970) 64.

32 An almost verbatim approach is found in Portuguese law. See Portugal, Law no 31/86 Article 33. See also Tunisia, Arbitration Code 1993 Article 48(1)(d) (alternative criterion).

33 See, *e.g.*, Cour de cassation, 21 May 1997; *Renault v V 2000 (formerly Jaguar France)*, Rev Arb 537 (1997); Cour d'appel de Paris, 14 March 1989, *Murgue Seigle v Coflexip*, Rev Arb 355 (1991); Cour d'appel de Paris, 8 December 1988, *Chantiers Modernes v CMGC*, Rev Arb 111 (1989); Cour d'appel de Paris, 26 April 1985, *Aranella v Italo-Equadoriana*, Rev Arb 311

order to delimit the purely economic definition of international arbitration: an arbitration is international if it results from a dispute involving the economies of more than one country. More specifically it was held by the Paris Court of Appeal that

> the international nature of an arbitration must be determined according to the economic reality of the process during which it arises. In this respect, all that is required is that the economic transaction should entail a transfer of goods, services or funds across national boundaries, while the nationality of the parties, the law applicable to the contract or the arbitration, and the place of arbitration are irrelevant.[34]

4-32 The approach of the French courts has been consistent and has effectively promoted international commercial arbitration. The Romanian Code of Civil Procedure takes a more classical conflict of laws approach in Article 369

> ... an arbitration taking place in Romania shall be considered international if it has arisen out of a private law relation having a foreign element.

4-33 An inherent drawback relates to the definition of "international commercial interests" while the term "foreign element" seems to be less problematic and is adequately wide.

(b) The subjective criterion: Diversity of nationality/place of business of parties

4-34 According to the subjective criterion the focus is on the different nationality or domicile or place of business of the parties to the arbitration agreement. It follows that parties, individuals or companies, should come from different jurisdictions. The subjective criterion was employed by previous English arbitration laws.[35] It is currently applied in Article 176(1) of the Swiss Private International Law Act

---

(1985). For a more detailed discussion see Fouchard Gaillard Goldman *on International Commercial Arbitration*, paras 114-126, current law, and paras 108-113 for the pre-1981 case law. See also Delaume, "What is an International Contract? An American and a Gallic Dilemma," 28 *ICLQ* 258 (1979).

[34] Cour d'appel de Paris, 14 March 1989, *Murgue Seigle v Coflexip*, Rev Arb 355 (1991). For translation of the extract, see Fouchard Gaillard Goldman, *on International Commercial Arbitration*, paras 120-121. This definition was confirmed by the Cour de cassation, 21 May 1997, *Renault v V 2000 (formerly Jaguar France)*, Rev Arb 537 (1997).

[35] See England, Arbitration Act 1975 section 1(4)(a)(b) and Arbitration Act 1979 section 3(7)(a)(b). The 1996 Arbitration Act included a provision (section 85) which distinguished between domestic and international arbitration but it was not brought into effect.

> The provisions of this chapter shall apply to any arbitration if the seat of the arbitral tribunal is in Switzerland and if, at the time when the arbitration agreement was concluded, at least one of the parties had neither its domicile nor its habitual residence in Switzerland.

4-35 The subjective criterion may significantly restrict the scope of international arbitration.[36] An illustration of the potential pitfall can be seen in the example of a distributorship agreement. Two companies from the same country enter into a distributorship agreement according to which, one of them receives world-wide distributorship rights of the other company's products. Disputes arising out of such an agreement would be domestic under Swiss law if both companies have their seat in Switzerland.[37] In contrast such a dispute is international under French law.[38]

(c) The modern combined criterion: The Model Law approach and other national legal systems

4-36 A third approach combines both the subjective and objective criteria. The new tendency towards a combined criterion can be found in the Model Law. According to Article 1(3)

> An arbitration is international if:
> a. the parties to an arbitration agreement have, at the time of the conclusion of that agreement, their places of business in different States; or
> b. one of the following places is situated outside the State in which the parties have their places of business:
> (i) the place of arbitration if determined in, or pursuant to, the arbitration agreement
> (ii) any place where a substantial part of the obligations of the commercial relationship is to be performed or the place with which the subject-matter of the dispute is most closely connected; or
> c. the parties have expressly agreed that the subject-matter of the arbitration agreement relates to more than one country.

---

36 See Mantakou, "The Concept of International Arbitration: An "Endangered Species"?", 50 *RHDI* 142 (1997).

37 See Blessing, *Introduction to Arbitration*, para 472.

38 See Cour d'appel de Paris, 25 November 1993, *Paco Rabanne Parfums v Les Maisons Paco Rabanne*, Rev Arb 730 (1994).

4-37 The Model Law creates a flexible and effective system for the determination of the international character of arbitration. Its approach consists of alternative criteria and also includes a conflict of laws rule for the connection of legal entities with a particular legal system.[39] Article 1(3)(c) has been criticised as too broad as it allows the parties to a dispute to internationalise it without apparent reason or any foreign link. Accordingly, some countries[40] when adopting the Model Law omitted this final case of internationality. Other countries have added as a default criterion the French approach.[41] While yet other countries, such as Hong Kong,[42] offer the parties to arbitration the option of submitting their dispute to domestic or international arbitration law.

4-38 Another successful merger of the subjective with the objective criteria[43] can be found in the 1994 reform of Article 832 Italian Code of Civil Procedure

> If at the date of signing the arbitration clause or submission to arbitration at least one of the parties has its domicile (*residenza*) or principal place of business (*sede effettiva*) abroad, or if a substantial part (*parte rilevante*) of the obligations arising out of the relationship to which the dispute refers must be performed abroad, the provisions of Chapters I to V of this Title shall apply to arbitration in so far as they are not derogated from by this Chapter.
>
> The provisions of international treaties shall in any case be applicable.

4-39 Section 202 US Federal Arbitration Act gives the definition of the arbitration agreement or arbitration award falling under the New York Convention. While the nationality test is used for the purposes of the New York

---

39 Model Law Article 1(4) provides that

> if a party has more than one place of business, the place of business is that which has the closest relationship to the arbitration agreement;
>
> if a party does not have a place of business, reference is to be made to his habitual residence.

40 See, *e.g.*, Hungarian Act LXXI 1994 section 47. See also Canada, Ontario International Commercial Arbitration Act section 2(3), RSO 1990 c. 1-9.

41 See, *e.g.*, Tunisia, Arbitration Code Article 48.

42 Arbitration Ordinance sections 2L and 2M. Singapore, International Arbitration Act section 15; for a detailed discussion on its application in practice see Hsu, "Section 15 of the Singapore International Arbitration Act – What are the options?, 2 *IntALR* 17 (1999).

43 See Bernardini, "L'arbitrage en Italie après la récente réforme", *Rev Arb* 479 (1994) 483.

Convention,[44] the case law of the US Supreme Court introduces objective criteria.[45] This cohabitation functions effectively.

2.2. Nationality of Arbitration: "International" Arbitration in International Conventions

4-40 Only the European Convention attempts a definition of an international arbitration when it is setting out its scope of application. In Article I(1)(a) it states

> 1. This Convention shall apply:
>
> (a) to arbitration agreements concluded for the purpose of settling disputes arising from international trade between physical or legal persons having, when concluding the agreement, their habitual place of residence or their seat in different Contracting States; . . .

4-41 Both the objective (a "dispute arising from international trade" and the subjective criteria ("between . . . persons . . . in different contracting States") are present. They are to be applied cumulatively. Unfortunately, the second criterion may prevent some arbitrations which are international (in respect of subject matter) from falling within the scope of the Convention.

4-42 The New York Convention confines its application to foreign awards, but makes no attempt to provide a definition of international arbitration.

4-43 The rapid development of international commercial arbitration has forced national legal systems not only to tolerate international commercial arbitration, but also to provide for favourable, legal regimes within which it can flourish. It has been rightly suggested that in the 1980s and the 1990s we have experienced a period of competition amongst legislators and judiciary; they all tried to attract more international arbitrations.[46]

4-44 The two main effects of this competition were the modernization and liberalization of arbitration regimes and the transfer of the favourable treatment

---

44 US, FAA section 202.

45 See *Scherk v Alberto Culver*, 417 US 506, 94 S Ct 2449 (1974) 2455; the judgment introduces three non-restrictive criteria to assist in the characterisation of an agreement as international.

46 See, *e.g.*, Berger, *International Economic Arbitration*, 1-13;

of international arbitration onto the domestic level.[47] This was also reflected in the new trend for unified regulation of international and domestic arbitrations.[48] The Dutch legislator opted for a unified system with the argument "what is good for international arbitration is also good for domestic arbitration."[49] The same approach to a single arbitration act was taken in Sweden, Germany and other countries. In England, although different systems were anticipated in the Arbitration Act, the domestic rules were not put into effect.[50] The modern unified arbitration systems minimise the importance of the distinction of the national and international arbitration.

4-45 An undisputed significant role towards unification and internationalisation of international commercial arbitration is ascribed to the success of the Model Law. It appears that a unified regulatory model, which is often referred to as monism, is the emerging trend.[51] The internationalisation of international arbitration appears to be well established and welcome.[52] There is

---

[47] This trend is best seen in US cases: *Moses H Cone Memorial Hospital v Mercury Construction Corp*, 460 US 1 (S Ct 1983); *Southland Corp v Keating*, 465 US 1, 104 S Ct 852, 79 L Ed 2d 1 (S Ct 1984); *Dean Witter Reynolds, Inc v Byrd*, 470 US 213, 105 S Ct 1238, 84 L Ed 2d 158 (S Ct 1985). For these three cases (the new trilogy) see Carbonneau, "L'arbitrage en droit americaine", *Rev Arb* 3 (1988) 14-20. See also *Shearson/American Express, Inc v McMahon*, 482 US 220, 107 S Ct 2332, 96 LEd 2d 185 (S Ct 1987), XIII YBCA 165 (1988); *Ofelia Rodriguez de Quijas and others v Shearson/American Express, Inc*, 490 US 477 (S Ct 1989), XV YBCA 141 (1990). See also Mantakou, "The Concept of International Arbitration: An "Endangered Species"?", 50 *RHDI* 148 (1997).

[48] See, *e.g.*, Bulgaria, Canada (Quebec, and arguably also at the federal level), Egypt, Finland, Germany, Hong Kong, Netherlands, Spain, Sweden. The dualist approach, *i.e.*, special law for international arbitration, can be seen, *e.g.*, in the US States which adopted the Model Law (California, Connecticut, Oregon and Texas), France, Italy, Peru, Portugal, Tunisia, and Switzerland.

[49] See van den Berg, "Netherlands, A Special Report", in *Resolving Disputes* (International Financial Law Review 1991), 40.

[50] It was found to be discriminatory to have two different systems. This argument was supported by the EC obligation for non-discrimination and was highlighted in *Philip Alexander Securities and Futures v Werner Bamberger and others* (1996), XXII YBCA 872 (1997) (English Court of Appeal).

[51] Berger, *International Commercial Arbitration*, 746-748, however, suggests that it is desirable to have separate regulation of domestic and international arbitration.

[52] See Lew, "Internationalization – the Answer to Unification", *Proceedings of the Fifth ICCA Conference* (Kluwer 1976); Philip, "A Century of Internationalization of International Arbitration: An Overview"; Hunter, Marriott and Veeder (eds), *Internationalization of International Arbitration*, 25-35; Lalive, "The Internationalization of International Arbitration: Some Observations", *ibid*, 49-58; Böckstiegel, "The Internationalization of International Arbitration: Looking Ahead to the Next Ten Years", *ibid*, 71-83; Shackleton, "The Internationalization of English Arbitration Law", 11(1) *ICC Bulletin* 16 (2000).

an element of the doctrinal monism-dualism debate, as well as the apparent internationalisation of international commercial arbitration, which should be recognised from the outset: there is a gradual convergence of national arbitration systems, greatly enhanced by modern arbitration laws, the revised international and institutional arbitration rules and the increased acceptance of party autonomy, which can be found in the vast majority of international commercial contracts.

3. Transnational and Delocalised Arbitration

4-46 It follows from the nationality of arbitration discussion that even international arbitration normally operates within the constraints of a national legal system. However, it should not be the case that an arbitration is national because of the applicable legal regime. Rather, the applicable legal regime should be the consequence of the fact that the arbitration is international. Some legal systems may not have a developed concept of international arbitration and therefore only distinguish between national and foreign arbitration.

4-47 The nationality of arbitration retains an important role to the extent that the place of arbitration is of significance. For instance, a number of laws provide that a country's procedural rules apply automatically to an arbitration held on its territory subject to the express will of the parties and the rules selected to govern the arbitration.[53] Other jurisdictions follow this position but adopt a different set of rules for international arbitrations.[54]

4-48 However, the importance of the seat of arbitration has been challenged on several grounds. In particular

- The choice of seat is often a matter of convenience;
- The choice of seat is often determined not by the parties but by the arbitration institution they have selected;
- The choice of seat is often governed by the desire for neutrality;
- The role of the arbitration tribunal is transitory and the seat has no necessary connection with the dispute.[55]

---

53 See, *e.g.*, England, Arbitration Act section 2; Germany, ZPO section 1025.

54 See, e.g., Switzerland, PIL Article 176 and Model Law.

55 See the comprehensive summary in Goode, "The Role of Lex Loci Arbitri in International Commercial Arbitration", *17 Arb Int* 19 (2000) 32-33.

4-49 In light of the emancipation of arbitration from national laws and the above arguments there is a school of thought that international arbitration can be delocalised. Delocalised arbitration is detached completely from the law of the place of arbitration to the extent that there is no need for support by local courts, *e.g.*, for enforcement purposes.[56] In support of arbitration proceedings detached from national law, it is argued that "it is both pointless and misleading to create a link between the arbitrator and some national law just in case ... one of the parties wishes to resort to the courts."[57] Also, in support of detached proceedings is the international business community that has successfully carried on arbitration proceedings detached from national legal systems.[58]

4-50 There are a number of illustrations of this trend. For example, parties may choose procedural law other than the law of the seat of arbitration.[59] Further a tribunal may decide not to follow any particular national law but to conduct the proceedings under general principles of procedure. This could be expressed in the UNCITRAL Rules or the UNCITRAL Notes on Organising Arbitral Proceedings or international rules prepared by one of the international institutions, such as the ICC or the IBA. In most cases the application of national arbitration law is unnecessary. A tribunal may conduct proceedings in accordance with the arbitration agreement on general rules or, if one of the parties is a sovereign state, the arbitration tribunal may also have the option of conducting the proceedings based on principles of public international law. In such cases, it is suggested that the tribunal could render an award unattached to any legal system, making it a so-called floating award.[60]

4-51 Additional support for delocalisation is drawn from a series of cases[61] in which French or other courts held that setting aside or suspension of an award by

---

[56] See the discussion in Nakamura, "The Place of Arbitration in International Arbitration - Its Fictitious Character and Lex Arbitri", 15(10) *Mealey's IAR* 23 (2000); Rubins, "The Arbitral Seat Is No Fiction: A Brief Reply to Tatsuya Nakamura's Commentary, 'The Place of Arbitration in International Arbitration- Its Fictitious Nature and Lex Arbitri'", 16(1) *Mealey's IAR* 23 (2001).

[57] See Lew, *Applicable Law*, 253.

[58] *Ibid.*

[59] Mayer, "The Trend Towards Delocalisation in the Last 100 Years", in Hunter, Marriott and Veeder (eds), *Internationalisation of International Arbitration*, 37.

[60] See Paulsson, "Delocalisation of International Commercial Arbitration: When and Why It Matters", 32 ICLQ 53-61 (1983); Paulsson, "Arbitration Unbound: Award Detached from the Law of its Country of Origin", 30 ICLQ 358 (1981).

[61] See Cour de cassation, 9 October 1984, *Pabalk Ticaret Limited Sirketi v Norsolor SA*, 112 Clunet 679 (1985), with comment by Kahn, 681, Rev Arb 432 (1985) with note by Goldman, 24

a court at the place of arbitration did not deprive the party obtaining the award of its right to enforce it in France. The French decisions relied on the fact that French law does not contain the restriction of Article V(1)(e) New York Convention.[62]

4-52 Sports arbitration, in particular in the context of Olympic games, is another example of delocalised arbitration. The International Olympic Committee Tribunal for Sports has a "fictional" place of arbitration in Lausanne, Switzerland, irrespective of the actual place of arbitration, in Athens, Sydney or Nagano.[63]

4-53 Further, the emerging electronic online arbitration, including fully online arbitration as well as asynchronous offline arbitration with use of electronic media,[64] may be delocalised. In such arbitrations there are no physical hearings; the tribunals may have no physical or legal seat. Consequently, the creation of new substantive rules has been suggested since it has been considered problematic to link online arbitration with a particular legal system.[65] An alternative to further regulation is the wider acceptance of party autonomy or the acceptance of delocalised and denationalised arbitration.

ILM 360 (1985) with note Gaillard, XI YBCA 484 (1986); Cour de cassation, 10 March 1993, *Polish Ocean Line v Jolasry,* Rev Arb 258 (1993), with note Hascher, 265, XIX YBCA 662 (1994); Cour de cassation, 23 March 1994, *Hilmarton Ltd v Omnium de traitement et de valorisation - OTV*, Rev Arb 327 (1994), XX YBCA 663 (1995); Cour d'appel de Paris, 14 January 1997, *The Arab Republic of Egypt v Chromalloy Aeroservices Inc*, Rev Arb 395 (1997), 12(4) Mealey's IAR B-1 (1997), XXII YBCA 691 (1997).

62 The US decision *Chromalloy Aeroservices Inc v The Arab Republic of Egypt*, 939 F Supp 907 (DDC 1996) was criticised. See Petrochilos, 49 ICLQ 856 (2000); Schwartz, "A Comment on Chromalloy Hilmarton, à l'américaine", 14(2) *J Int'l Arb* 125 (1997).

63 See Kaufmann-Kohler, *Arbitration at the Olympics*, 3, 22, 80.

64 See, *e.g.*, Katsch and Rifkin, *Online Dispute Resolution,* Rule, *Online Dispute Resolution for Business* (Jossey Bass 2002).

65 See, *e.g.*, Schneider and Kuner. "Dispute Resolution in International Electronic Commerce", 14(3) *J Int'l Arb* 5 (1997); Arsic, "International Commercial Arbitration on the Internet - Has the Future Come Too Early?", 14(3) *J Int'l Arb* 209 (1997); Hill, "The Internet, Electronic Commerce and Dispute Resolution: Comments", 14(4) *J Int'l Arb* 103 (1997); Kaufmann-Kohler, "Le lieu de l'arbitrage à l'aune de la mondialisation - Réflexions à propos de deux formes récentes d'arbitrage", *Rev Arb* 517 (1998); Kessedjian and Cahn, "Dispute Resolution On-Line", 32 *Int'l Law* 977 (1998); Donahey, "Dispute Resolution in Cyberspace", 15(4) *J Int'l Arb* 127 (1998); Hill, "On-line Arbitration: Issues and Solutions", 15(2) *Arb Int* 199 (1999). See also the contributions by Gélinas, Hill, Antaki, Horning and Schneider, "Electronic Means for Dispute Resolution: Extending the Use of Modern Information Technologies", in Davis (ed), *Improving International Arbitration,* 51. See also Goodman-Everard, "Arbitration in Cyberspace — an Off-line, Low-tech Guide for Compucowards", 14(3) *Arb Int* 345 (1998).

4-54 The main argument against delocalised arbitration is that arbitration cannot operate in a legal vacuum. At the very least, ultimately, the parties will expect the law to recognise and give effect to the tribunal's award. There are other areas where the support of the courts may be needed, *e.g.*, to uphold and enforce the agreement to arbitrate, to appoint or remove arbitrators, and for interim relief in support of the arbitration process. National courts are always asked to support or intervene for these purposes. This is why arbitration cannot be fully delocalised from the national law.[66]

4-55 In fact, delocalised arbitration is not an extra-legal arbitration; it is a self-regulatory arbitration. Delocalisation relates usually to the arbitration process or to the award. While the emancipation from the procedural law of the place of arbitration is now accepted, the enforcement of delocalised awards appears to be problematic; ultimately, the enforcement is controlled by national courts. However, at least French and US courts[67] have enforced delocalised awards.[68] Belgium[69] and Switzerland have given foreign parties the option to contract out of any judicial review in limited circumstances.[70]

4-56 Another widely used expression relates to transnational[71] or a-national arbitration. Transnational arbitration law has been described as

> a theoretical ideal which posits that international arbitration, at least as regards certain types of arbitral institution arbitration, is a self-contained judicial system, by its very nature separate from national systems of law, and indeed antithetical to

---

[66] See Park, "The Lex Loci Arbitri and International Commercial Arbitration", 32 ICLQ 21 (1983); Boyd, "The Role of National Law and the National Courts of England", in Lew, *Contemporary Problems*, 149 *et seq*.

[67] See, *e.g.*, Cour de cassation, 23 March 1994, *Société Hilmarton Ltd v Société Omnium de traitement et de valorisation (OTV)*, 121 Clunet 701 (1994); *In re Chromalloy Aeroservices Inc and The Arab Republic of Egypt*, 939 F Supp 907 (DDC 1996), 35 ILM 1359 (1996); XXII YBCA 1001 (1997) 1004; Cour d'appel de Paris, 14 January 1997, *République arabe d'Egypte v Chromalloy Aeroservices*, Rev Arb 395 (1997), XXII YBCA 691 (1997).

[68] Also, in the context of the Iran-US Claims Tribunals, the US Courts enforced anational awards under the New York Convention. See, *e.g.*, *Ministry of Defense of the Islamic Republic of Iran v Gould*, 887 F 2d 1357 (9th Cir 1989), cert denied, 110 S Ct 1319 (1990); *Iran Aircraft Industries and Iran Helicopter and Renewal Company v A VCO Corporation*, 980 F 2d 141 (2d Cir 1992).

[69] See Belgium, Judicial Code Article 1717(3).

[70] See Switzerland, PIL Article 192; Swiss Tribunal Fédéral, 21 December 1992, *Groupement d'Entreprises Fougerolle et consorts*, BGE 118 I b, 562, 568.

[71] See Lord Mustill in *SA Coppée Lavalin NV et al v Ken-Ren Chemicals and Fertilizers Ltd (in liquidation in Kenya)* [1994] 2 WLR 631, 640.

them. If the ideal is fully realised national courts will not feature in the law and practice of international arbitration at all.

4-57 As major international contracts are often very long and regulatory, and to the extent that a number of disputes can be resolved with extra-legal standards, a-national arbitration[72] with full self-regulation has found acceptance.[73] Transnational and a-national arbitration denotes also the application of *lex mercatoria* or transnational commercial law. There are a significant number of arbitration awards which apply or make references to the rules of transnational commercial law. It has also been suggested that international commercial arbitration is autonomous. Due to the involvement of international law firms and a number of distinguished arbitrators, one can now speak of the construction of a transnational legal order relating to the settlement of international commercial disputes.[74]

4-58 One obstacle to the development of denationalised arbitration, however, is lack of uniformity in national arbitration rules. This difficulty might be overcome by an international convention which ensures that proceedings conducted outside the national legal system will be recognised and floating awards will be enforced. In the interim it suffices if international conventions or national laws confirm the parties' right to choose the law that governs the arbitration. The European and ICSID Conventions provide implicitly for the recognition and enforcement of floating awards, but the case may be complicated under the New York Convention. However, while the New York Convention focuses on the place where the award was rendered (a functional equivalent of the place of arbitration), a choice of law by the parties in favour of a foreign law to govern the arbitration will remedy the problem sufficiently.

4-59 It is, however, possible that the whole doctrine of denationalised awards and proceedings will eventually become redundant as a result of increased and indirect unification of arbitration procedural law achieved through the emergence of the Model Law.[75] Delocalisation can only function provided that quasi

---

72 Smit, "A-national arbitration", 63 *Tulane L Rev* 62 (1989).

73 See Arfazadeh, "New Perspectives in South East Asia and Delocalized Arbitration in Kuala Lumpur" 8(4) *J Int'l Arb* 103 (1991); Pradhan, "Kuala Lumpur, Regional Centre for Arbitration: Arbitral Awards", 2 *Malayan Law Journal* (1994) cxxiv *et seq.*

74 See Dezalay and Garth, *Dealing in Virtue*; Appelbaum and Felstiner (ed), *Rules and Networks: The Legal Culture of Global Business Transactions* (Hart Publishing 2002).

75 Lionnet, "Should the Procedural Law Applicable to International Arbitration be Denationalised or Unified? The Answer of the UNCITRAL Model Law", 8(3) *J Int'l Arb* 5 (1991).

autonomous international procedural rules emerge.[76] This is limited delocalisation and covers the aspect of delocalisation where there is no need to rely on local courts and where parties voluntarily enforce the awards. While proceedings can effectively be delocalised, awards normally acquire a nationality at the time of enforcement.

[76] See Lazareff, "International Arbitration: Towards a Common Procedural Approach", in Frommel and Rider (eds), *Conflicting Legal Cultures*, 31; Lowenfeld, "International Arbitration as an Omelette: What Goes into the Mix", in Frommel and Rider (eds), *ibid*, 19.

Chapter 5

JURIDICAL NATURE OF ARBITRATION

5-1 This chapter focuses on three fundamentally interrelated questions (1) What is the juridical nature of arbitration? (2) What is the constitutional position of arbitration in a national legal system? Is it a private procedure guaranteed by the state? Can state courts compel parties to arbitration? (3) How does the international or national protection of human rights relate to this private system for the settlement of disputes?

1. JURIDICAL NATURE OF ARBITRATION

5-2 What is the legal nature of arbitration? As a private, non-national system of dispute settlement, is it subject to legal regulation? If so, to what legal order: a national law (which?), an international law or a mixture of the two? Alternatively, is arbitration, as a creation of the parties, subject only to their regulation (party autonomy)? In short, how does arbitration fit, if at all, into a clearly defined system of state justice?

5-3 These questions, triggered by French case law,[1] have been the subject of mainly academic discourse,[2] in particular, in the first half of the 20th century. It has been argued that, in theory, the attitude of national legal systems to arbitration proceedings (*e.g.* whether to uphold arbitration agreements, or to assist with the appointment and removal of arbitrators) and the award (*e.g.* whether or not to enforce the award), depends on the legal character of arbitration.[3] The legal nature of arbitration allegedly holds the key to the identification of the legal and non-legal yardsticks available to arbitrators in international trade disputes.[4] It inevitably deals with jurisdictional consequences resulting from party autonomy.

5-4 Four theories have been suggested with respect to the juridical nature of arbitration. These are known as the jurisdictional, contractual, mixed or hybrid, and autonomous theories. Each purports to describe how the legal system relates to the arbitration mechanism.

5-5 No one viewpoint has received universal support in theory or practice. Even at a regional level, states treat the juridical nature of arbitration in a different manner.[5] While some have suggested that this discussion is an academic

---

1 Cour d'appel Paris, 10 December 1901, *Del Drago*, 29 Clunet 314 (1902); Cour de cassation, 27 July 1937, *Roses*, Dalloz I, 25. See also more recently Supreme Court of Colombia, 21 March 1991, *Rev Arb* 720 (1991).

2 See, *e.g.*, Klein, *l'arbitrage en droit international prive*, 181-182, 203; Rubellin-Devichi, *L'arbitrage: nature juridique*; Jarrosson, *La notion d'arbitrage*; Kassis, *Problèmes de base*, Tome I; Sauser-Hall, "L'arbitrage en droit international privé", 44 I *AnnIDI* 469 (1952) 516-528, 47 II *AnnIDI* 394 (1957); Carabiber, "L'evolution de L'arbitrage commercial international", 1 *RCADI* 148 (1960); Mann, "Lex Facit Arbitrum", in Sanders (ed), *Liber Amicorum Martin Domke*, 157-183; Loquin, "Arbitrage - Définition - Nature Juridique - Distinction avec d'autres institutions - Avantages et inconvénients", 1005 *Juris-Classeur Proc Civ* para 1 (1997); Fouchard, *L'arbitrage*, 320-21; Lew, *Applicable Law*, paras 63-81; Samuel, *Jurisdictional Problems*, 31-32; Schlosser, *Internationale Schiedsgerichtsbarkeit*, paras 40 *et seq*; Koussoulis, *Main Issues on Arbitration*, 1-7; Fouchard Gaillard Goldman *on International Commercial Arbitration*, paras 9-57.

3 Wilner, "Determining the Law Governing Performance in International Commercial Arbitration: A Comparative Study", 19 *Rutgers L Rev* 646 (1965) 650-652.

4 Lew, *Applicable Law*, 51; Mann, footnote 2 above, 157-183; Samuel, footnote 2 above, 31-32; Briseño Sierra, "The Juridical Nature of Private Arbitration. Its Projection Image and Practice", XI *YBCA* 602 (1986).

5 In relation to Latin America Siqueiros, "Comment on Latin America", Sanders (ed), *ICCA Congress Series no 3*, 165-168, states that "while some countries like Brazil and Peru still maintain in their legal thinking that arbitration is a process of judicial nature rather than a contractual one, others, like Chile, Mexico and Panama have shown a more liberal opening to international commercial arbitration."

"tempest in a teapot",[6] it has few practical ramifications. In particular, these theories show how the international arbitration process, with extensive detachment but with some recognition and support required from the national legal system, can be explained in the light of the sovereignty and control of the national legal order.

5-6 For example, the determination of the jurisdictional or non-jurisdictional nature of arbitration may have effect in the compensation for counsel's fees for the successful party, failing express agreement between the parties. In a partial award of 21 March 1996 and final award of 21 June 1996 between a claimant (seller) from Hong Kong and a defendant (buyer) from Germany, the arbitration tribunal with its seat in Hamburg found[7]

> [34] ... compensation for counsel's fees might not be necessary in arbitrations which are less juridical in nature, like quality arbitration or *Schiedsgutachten*; ...
>
> [35] On the contrary, the compensation for counsel's fees is indicated where the arbitral tribunal is exclusively comprised of lawyers, who decide on complicated legal issues and substantial claims. This is the case here. Apart from the chairman, who was appointed by the Chamber of Commerce, the parties also have chosen lawyers as arbitrators. The subject matter of the dispute was a series of undecided issues concerning the application of the CISG.[8]

5-7 Therefore, one needs to consider these major theories and their effect on contemporary international arbitration practice. These theories ignore or at least do not fully accord with what happens in the real world of international commercial arbitration. When considering reported awards and cases, there is some support for all theories. In 1937, an author wrote synthesising the three older theories in the following terms

> According to the first - which distinguishes between the submission to arbitration and the award - [the award] is compared to a judgment rendered by the ordinary courts; according to the second - which considers the submission to arbitration and the award as two phases of the same agreement: the arbitration agreement - the

---

[6] Carbonneau, *Arbitration*, 624.

[7] Hamburg Chamber of Commerce, partial award of 21 March 1996 and final award of 21 June 1996, *claimant (seller, Hong Kong) v defendant (buyer, Germany)*, XXII YBCA 35 (1997). Also published in German (original language) in 6 *Rechtsprechung Kaufmännischer Schiedsgerichte*, E 5b no 84 (partial award) and B 5 no 21 (final award).

[8] Other issues include the powers of arbitrators, control or supervision by the courts and immunity of arbitrators.

award has a contractual character and cannot be compared to a judgment; the third - which can be considered an intermediary [between the two] - considers an award subject to the ordinary courts to the extent that it requires their preliminary order (*exequatur*).[9]

5-8 It follows that the legal quality of the award was the focal point of that discussion. This criterion has supporters up to the present time.[10] Recently, the Croatian Constitutional Court dealt with two constitutional complaints[11] requesting the annulment of arbitration awards rendered by the arbitration tribunals of the Permanent Arbitration Court at the Croatian Chamber of Commerce in Zagreb, without prior initiation of setting aside procedures. The Court dismissed both complaints and discussed in passing the legal nature of arbitration and arbitration awards. Judge Momcinovic invoked that an arbitration award is an "act of delegated jurisdiction" which has the same effect as a final judgment of a court of law.[12]

1.1. The Jurisdictional Theory[13]

5-9 The jurisdictional theory relies on the state power to control and regulate arbitrations which take place within its jurisdiction.

5-10 The interpretation and application of the law and the determination of disputes is a sovereign function normally exercised by national courts established

---

[9] Bernard, *L'arbitrage voluntaire*, para 469. Translation in Lew, *Applicable Law*, para 64.

[10] See, *e.g.*, Bajons, "Enforcing Annulled Arbitral Awards - A Comparative View", 7 *Croat Arbit Yearb* 55 (2000) 59-60.

[11] Constitutional Complaint in case U 410/95 and Constitutional Complaint in case U 488/96. See Triva, "Arbitration and Public Policy: Constitutional Complaint as Means for Setting Aside Arbitral Awards", 7 *Croat Arbit Yearb* 115 (2000) 116-123.

[12] See further the discussion in Triva, *ibid*, 7 *Croat Arbit Yearb* 115 (2000) 125-126.

[13] For the justification of this theory see Lainé, "De l'exécution en France des sentences arbitrales étrangères", 26 *Clunet* 641 (1899); Pillet, *Traité pratique de droit international privé*, Tome II (Sirey 1924), para 659; Bartin, *Principes de droit international privé*, Tome I (Domat-Montchrestien 1930), paras 217-8; Niboyet, *Traité de droit international privé français,* Tome VI (Sirey 1950), paras 1983-95; Mann, "Lex Facit Arbitrum", in Sanders (ed), *Liber Amicorum Martin Domke*, 158 *et seq.* Discussions of the jurisdictional theory and its effect also in Balladore-Pallieri, "L'arbitrage privé dans les rapports internationaux", 51 *RCADI* 295 (1935); Bernard, *l'arbitrage voluntaire*, para 470-72; Klein, *L'arbitrage en droit international prive,,* paras 105-12; Sauser-Hall, "L'arbitrage en droit international privé", 44 *AnnIDI* 520 (1952); Fouchard, *L'arbitrage*, paras 16-18; Rubellin-Devichi, *L'arbitrage: nature juridique*, paras 6, 151-157 Lew, *Applicable Law*, paras 65-68; Kassis, *Problèmes de base*, 37-54.

by the state for that purpose. Parties can only submit to arbitration to the extent expressly allowed or accepted implicitly by the law of the place of arbitration.[14] According to the jurisdictional theory, the state allows within its territory privately administered justice systems (delegated justice or parallel justice) by way of assignment or tolerance. This follows from the legal effect which a state and its legal system attaches to an arbitration agreement and to an arbitration award. Consequently, arbitrators exercise a public function.[15]

5-11 The jurisdictional theory is based on the quasi-judicial role of the arbitrator, as an alternative to the local judge and with the acceptance of the local law. The increasing "judicialisation" of arbitration has been also addressed in scholarly writings.[16] It is beyond doubt that arbitrators resolve disputes and that their decisions are final and binding. In the absence of the agreement to arbitrate, these disputes would be referred for determination in the national courts. The jurisdictional theory is summarised as follows

> It follows that the arbitrator, like the judge, draws his power and authority from the local law; hence the arbitrator is considered to closely resemble a judge. [...] The only difference between judge and arbitrator is that the former derives his nomination and authority directly from the sovereign, whilst the latter derives his authority from the sovereign but his nomination is a matter for the parties.[17]

5-12 A major effect of the jurisdictional theory can be seen in the famous *Del Drago* judgment where it was rightly pointed out that an award (like a judgment) is not self-executing. If not voluntarily given effect to by the parties it will have to be enforced by the courts. So at least at the stage of enforcement it becomes evident that the jurisdictional theory stands only with the support of state courts.

---

[14] Mann, "Lex Facit Arbitrum", in Sanders (ed), *Liber Amicorum Martin Domke*, 162. For a complete picture of the debate on the relevance of the law of the seat of arbitration, see Paulsson, "The extent of independence of international arbitration from the law of the situs", in Lew (ed), *Contemporary Problems*, 141-148; Boyd, "The role of national law and national courts in England", in Lew (ed), *Contemporary Problems*, 149-163.

[15] See further Carabiber, "L'evolution de L'arbitrage commercial international", 1 *RCADI* 148 (1960) 148-50; Samuel, *Jurisdictional Problems*, 55-56. On the judicial role of arbitrators see *Sutcliffe v Thackrah* [1974] AC 727 (HL). See also Triva, "Arbitration and Public Policy: Constitutional Complaint as Means for Setting Aside Arbitral Awards", 7 *Croat Arbit Yearb* 115 (2000) 116-125 with reference to Croatian law and comparative remarks.

[16] See Lillich & Brower (eds), *International Arbitration*; Fouchard Gaillard Goldman, *on International Commercial Arbitration*, paras 12-43.

[17] Lew, *Applicable Law*, para 66.

In *Del Drago*[18], the Paris Court of Appeal declared a foreign arbitration award equal or equivalent to a foreign judgment, highlighting the jurisdictional character of the award. The judgment managed to initiate discussion about the legal nature of arbitration.

5-13 The classical argument in favour of the jurisdictional theory was followed by the Supreme Court of Colombia in 1991[19] with the consequence that a statute, which had allowed foreign nationals to act as arbitrators in Colombia, was declared unconstitutional.[20] The issue has been addressed and resolved internationally in Article III European Convention, Article 11(1) Model Law and the overwhelming acceptance of party autonomy.[21] However, it is remarkable that, even in the late 20th century, the hard core of the jurisdictional theory was the subject of discussion by international and national legislators.

5-14 A clear illustration of the jurisdictional theory in modern arbitration law can be found in the discussion about the neutrality and impartiality of arbitrators.[22] The English Court of Appeal concluded in *AT & T Corporation and another v Saudi Cable Company* (*per* Lord Woolf, MR) that

> the test under English Law for apparent or unconscious bias in an arbitrator is the same as that for all those who make judicial decisions and is that to be found in the opinion of Lord Goff of Chieveley in *R v Gough* [1993] AC 646.[23]

5-15 The jurisdictional theory in practice, however, can most clearly be seen in countries where arbitration institutions are attached to the national chambers of

---

[18] Cour d'appel Paris, 10 December 1901, *Clunet* 314 (1902),. See also discussion in Rubellin-Devichi, *L'arbitrage: nature juridique*, 10-11; Schlosser, *Internationale Schiedsgerichtsbarkeit*, para 41.

[19] Decision of 21 March 1991, *Rev Arb* 720 (1991). See note by Garro, "The Colombia Supreme Court Holds Unconstitutional the Participation of Foreign Arbitrators Under the New Arbitration Law", 1 *Am Rev Int'l Arb* 594 (1990).

[20] As a direct result the Arbitration Act Article 8 was amended to the effect that foreign nationals can act as arbitrators in Colombia only in international commercial arbitrations. This problem had also arisen in other countries.

[21] In Greece, for instance, the law changed in the early 1970s to fully comply with the European Convention. See Koussoulis, *Main Issues on Arbitration*, 2-3.

[22] See Kerameus, "La fonction jurisdictionelle de l'arbitre dans la jurisprudence hellénique récente", in *Studia Iuridica III* (Sakkoulas 1995), 269; Cour d'appel Paris, 2 June 1989, *Rev Arb* 87 (1991) 91; Cour d'appel Paris, 6 April 1990, *Rev Arb* 880 (1990) 885; Cour d'appel Paris, 28 June 1991, *Rev Arb* 568 (1992) 570.

[23] [2000] 2 Lloyd's Rep 127. In the same direction see Liebscher, "Fair Trial and Challenge of Awards in International Arbitration", 6 *Croat Arbit Yearb* 83 (1999) 85-90.

commerce and retain a close connection with the state. Arbitration is the officially favoured system for resolving international trade disputes. Such arbitration systems exist in several former socialist countries and in some emerging markets. The jurisdictional theory can also be seen clearly in a number of legal issues relating to the arbitration process, such as the immunity of arbitrators, *i.e.* to the extent that arbitrators are often treated in law as if they were judges. Furthermore, it can be seen in the power of a tribunal to carry on proceedings even in the event of default of one party and the fact that the arbitration decisions are final and binding.

1.2. The Contractual Theory[24]

5-16 The second theory emphasises that arbitration has a contractual character. It has its origins in and depends, for its existence and continuity, on the parties' agreement. The supporters of this theory deny the primacy or control of the state in arbitration and argue that the very essence of arbitration is that it is "created by the will and consent of the parties."[25]

5-17 The French Cour de cassation in *Roses*[26] formulated the ratio of the contractual theory: "Arbitral awards which rely on an arbitration agreement, constitute a unit with it and share with it its contractual character."[27] Without subscribing to the idea that the arbitration award is a contract made by the arbitrators who act as proxies of the parties, the Cour de cassation stated emphatically that arbitration has a contractual starting point and that the award is, in principle, of contractual nature too.

5-18 The real basis for the contractual theory is the fact that the whole arbitration process is based on contractual arrangements. Both the agreement and

---

[24] See Balladore-Pallieri, 51 *RCADI* 291 (1935-I); Bernard, *L'arbitrage volontaire*, paras 473, 481-483; Klein, *L'arbitrage en droit international prive*, para 106; Klein, "Autonomie de la volonté et l'arbitrage", 47 *Rev crit dip* 255 (1958). See also discussions in Sauser-Hall, "L'arbitrage en droit international privé", 44 I *Ann IDI.* 516 (1952); Fouchard, *L'arbitrage*, 18-21; Rubellin-Devichi, *L'arbitrage: nature juridique*, paras 5, 7, 110; Lew, *Applicable Law*, 54-57; Kassis, *Problèmes de base*, paras 55-107; Fouchard Gaillard Goldman *on International Commercial Arbitration*, paras 44-57.

[25] See US judgment, *Reily v Russel*, 34 Mo 524 (1864) 528.

[26] Cour de cassation, 27 July 1937, *Roses v Moller et Cie*, I Dalloz 25 (1938). See also discussion in Klein, 47 *Rev crit dip* 255 (1958) 255-256; Rubellin-Devichi, *L'arbitrage: nature juridique*, 12-13, 36; Schlosser, *Internationale Schiedsgerichtsbarkeit*, para 41.

[27] See Samuel, *Jurisdictional Problems*, 36.

the award reflect the contractual character of arbitration. The origin of every arbitration is a contract. The parties agree to submit their disputes to arbitration; the state has no influence or control over this decision. If parties do not voluntarily honour the award, it may be enforced as a contract.[28]

5-19 For some scholars though, the arbitration award is not a contract but a mere joint act (*Gesamtakt*). According to others, the arbitration proceedings and the award comprise only "a group of private contractual acts."[29]

5-20 In any event, modern or traditional versions of the contractual theory make a case for arbitration as an illustration of freedom of contract and an almost unlimited party autonomy, *i.e.* a private justice system.[30]

5-21 Some suggest that we are now in "the era of arbitration without contractual relationships."[31] This can be illustrated in the "unilateral commencement of proceedings" provided for in the 1965 ICSID Convention,[32] as well as in certain bilateral treaties and national investment laws, the 1992 North American Free Trade Agreement (NAFTA)[33] and the 1994 Energy Charter Treaty.[34] However, the resolution of a dispute by private judges without the

---

[28] Lew, *Applicable Law*, para 73. See also Klein, *l'arbitrage en droit international prive*, para 115. Two recent cases of the Italian Supreme Court held that the award has a contractual nature and the underlying arbitration can have no jurisdictional nature; this had the connotation that an award in domestic Italian arbitration may have no *res judicata* effect. See Italy, Corte di cassazione, 3 August 2000, *Comune di Cinisello Balsamo v AEM, Rivista di diritto processuale* (Riv dir proc) 254 (2001), Riv arb 699 (2000); and Corte di cassazione, 27 November 2001, *Aeroporto di Roma v Ministero dei Transporti*, Riv dir proc 238 (2002). For a critical discussion of the cases see Ricci, La crise de larbitrage jurisdictionnel en Italie, *Rev Arb* 857 (2002).

[29] See Samuel, *Jurisdictional Problems*, 39-44; Bernard, *L'arbitrage voluntaire*, para 473.

[30] See David, *L'arbitrage*, para 85.

[31] Werner, "The Trade Explosion and Some Likely Effects on International Arbitration", 14(2) *J Int'l Arb* 5 (1997).

[32] See, *e.g.*, ICSID case no ARB/87/3, *Asian Agricultural Products (AAPL) v Republic of Sri Lanka*, 27 June 2000, 30 ILM 577 (1991); XVII YBCA 106 (1992); ICSID case no ARB/93/1, *American Manufacturing & Trading Inc v Republic of Zaire*, 21 February 1997, 125 Clunet 243 (1998), XXII YBCA 60 (1997), 36 ILM 1531; ICSID case no ARB/96/3, *Fedax NV v The Republic of Venezuela*, 126 Clunet 298 (1999).

[33] NAFTA is ratified by Canada, Mexico and the United States. Chapter 11B allows an investor from one contracting state to submit disputes against another contracting state to arbitration if the investor considers that the state has violated its rights under NAFTA. See Horlick and Marti, "NAFTA Chapter 11B - A Private Right of Action to Enforce Market Access through Investments", 14(1) *J Int'l Arb* 43 (1997).

[34] Article 26 allows the private investor to submit the dispute, at its discretion, either to ICSID or to an *ad hoc* tribunal applying the UNCITRAL Rules, or to the Arbitration Institute of

parties' consent is not arbitration. In the above cases, there is no arbitration agreement in the traditional sense. The arbitrators' jurisdiction stems from the initial consent of the state or public entity (expressed in the signing of the treaty) and the subsequent consent of the claimant, who accepts the arbitrator's jurisdiction by starting the arbitration. Consequently, the attempt to emancipate arbitration from a state justice system is clear and unavoidable.

1.3. The Mixed or Hybrid Theory[35]

5-22 The fundamental points of the contractual theory, *i.e.* "the contractual character of the arbitral award" and the role of arbitrators as parties' representatives or proxies, were subject to fundamental criticism. For instance, it can be argued that the consensual nature of arbitration is instrumental in initiating arbitration proceedings; after proceedings have commenced, the parties have only limited autonomy and the arbitration tribunal is empowered to make important decisions. Nevertheless, the contractual theory has been instrumental in the development of modern arbitration.

5-23 Attempts were made to bridge the two schools of thought. In spite of their apparent diametrically opposing views, the jurisdictional and contractual theories can be reconciled. Arbitration requires and depends upon elements from both the jurisdictional and the contractual viewpoints; it contains elements of both private and public law; it has procedural and contractual features. It is not surprising that a compromise theory claiming arbitration to have a mixed or hybrid character should have been developed.

5-24 The theory was developed by Professor Sauser-Hall in his report to the Institut de Droit International in 1952.[36] He argued that arbitration could not be

---

Stockholm Chamber of Commerce. See also Wälde, *The Energy Charter Treaty* (Kluwer 1996); Wälde, "Investment Arbitration Under the Energy Charter Treaty – From Dispute Settlement to Treaty Implementation", 12(4) *Arb Int* 429 (1996).

35 See Sauser-Hall, "L'arbitrage en droit international privé", 44-I *Ann IDI* 469 (1952); developed further in 47-II *Ann IDI* 394 (1957); Marmo, "Gli arbitrati stranieri e nazionali con elementi di estraneitá", 23 *Annuario di diritto comparato e di studi legislativi* 34 (1946); Motulsky, "Note on judgment of Cour d'appel de Paris, 9 December 1955", 45 *Rev crit dip* 523 (1956); Carabiber, 99 *RCADI* 119 (1960-I) 141-160; Robert, "De la place de la loi dans l'arbitrage", in *Liber Amicorum Martin Domke*, 226; Robert, *Arbitrage*, para 210. See also discussion in Fouchard, *L'arbitrage*, paras 18-21; Rubellin-Devichi, *L'arbitrage: nature juridique*, paras 9, 111, 112; Lew, *Applicable Law*, paras 74-77.

36 44-I *Ann IDI* 469 (1952); developed further in 47-II *Ann IDI* 394 (1957).

beyond every legal system: there had to be some law which could determine the validity of submission to arbitration and the enforceability of the award. Equally he acknowledged that each arbitration has its origin in a private contract, and the arbitrators selected and the rules to govern the arbitration procedure depend primarily on the parties agreement. Thus he maintained the contractual and jurisdictional elements of arbitration to be "indissoluably intertwined."[37]

5-25 Accordingly, it is accepted that arbitrators are decision-makers and perform a quasi-judicial function without exercising any (state) judicial power, as there is no act of delegation of state power: they resolve disputes and their decisions may be given state judicial power at the time and place of enforcement. Hence, the arbitration function is equivalent to the function of a judge, but not of a particular state's judge. While a judge is vested in principle with state power, the arbitrator's decision is only in effect vested with the same power. This was recognised by the European Court of Justice in *Nordsee v Reederei*[38] where it stated that only state courts exercise state power.[39]

5-26 The mixed or hybrid theory has become the dominant world-wide theory as elements of both the jurisdictional and the contractual theory are found in modern law and practice of international commercial arbitration. According to the mixed theory we have a private justice system created by contract. It is also common that such a hybrid system exists *de facto*. This can be seen in cohabitation of the jurisdictional approach of the New York Convention with the contractual approach of French law.[40] Thus, both the contractual origin and the jurisdictional function have an important influence on arbitration.[41] An effect of the hybrid or mixed theory is to acknowledge the strong, though not overwhelming, connection between arbitration and the place where the tribunal has its seat.[42]

---

[37] *Ibid*, 47-II *Ann IDI* (1957) 399.

[38] Judgment of 23 March 1982, ECR 1095 (1982).

[39] See also Greece, Efeteion Athens, case 6839/1986, 27 *Helleniki Dikaiossyni* (Hell Dni) 1489 (1986); Greece, Areios Pagos, case 1509/1982, 31 *Nomiko Vima* (NoB) 1355 (1983). See also Germany, Bundesgerichtshof, 15 May 1986, BGHZ 98, 70.

[40] See, *e.g.*, Bajons, 7 *Croat Arbit Yearb* 55 (2000) 59-60.

[41] See Fragistas, "Arbitrage étranger et arbitrage international en droit privé", *Rev crit dip* 1 (1960) 2-3; Oppetit, "Justice étatique et justice arbitrale", *Études offertes à P Bellet* (Litec 1991), 415, 420, 424; Schlosser, *Internationale Schiedsgerichtsbarkeit*, para 41.

[42] Lew, *Applicable Law*, para 77.

*1.4. The Autonomous (*sui juris*) Theory*[43]

5-27 The most recently developed theory presumes that arbitration evolves in an emancipated regime and, hence, is of an autonomous character. It was originally developed in 1965 by Rubellin-Devichi.[44] She argued that the character of arbitration could, in fact and in law, be determined by looking at its use and purpose. In this light, arbitration cannot be classified as purely contractual or jurisdictional; equally it is not an "institution mixte".

5-28 The autonomous theory looks to arbitration *per se*, what it does, what it aims to do, how and why it functions in the way it does. It recognises that the relevant laws have developed to help to facilitate the smooth working of arbitration.

5-29 Arbitration cannot work in the context of the ideologies established in the context of private international law; it does not need to fit in internationalist or nationalist-positivist views. It can eventually operate outside the constraints of positive law or national legal systems. Thus, the autonomous theory is an enlightened development of the mixed theory. However, it has the added dimension of being in tune with the modern forms of non-national, transnational and delocalised arbitration, as it does not attach too much value to the seat of arbitration and its law.

5-30 International arbitration has developed because parties sought a flexible, non-national system for the regulation of their commercial disputes. They wanted their agreement to arbitrate to be respected and enforced; they envisaged fair procedures, fashioned according to the characteristics of the particular case but not copying any national procedural system; they expected the arbitrators would be impartial and fair; they believed the ultimate award would be final and binding, and they presumed that it would be easily enforceable. Arbitration, organised the way they considered it appropriate, is how the parties have decided to determine disputes between them. National criteria are of little significance to the international commercial community, as national public policy and mandatory law has little influence on the day to day conduct of the international arbitration process.

---

43 See Rubellin-Devichi, *L'arbitrage: nature juridique*; See also Lew, *Applicable Law*, paras 78-81; Samuel, *Jurisdictional Problems*, 67-73.

44 Rubellin-Devichi, *ibid*, 17-18.

5-31 International commercial arbitration is a fact of life. It is used by the international business world because it can be, and has been, tailored for their particular needs. In its course, arbitration practice has been the catalyst for the development of new and less parochial national arbitration laws, and truly international instruments to regulate what happens in practice. It is the practice of arbitration rather than national considerations that now controls the arbitration framework.[45] To meet the needs and expectations of the parties national and international laws have been amended. It is the process and its users, rather than the national interest and the law, that has determined the changes to international arbitration practice.

5-32 This is well illustrated by the Geneva Conventions 1923-1927 and the New York Convention 1958 aimed at enforcing arbitration agreements and awards. It was equally the impetus for the UNCITRAL and its monumental contributions through its Arbitration Rules and the Model Law. The very significant liberalisation of many national laws, independently and by the adoption of the Model Law, is a further illustration of the law seeking to keep up with the autonomous and continuing development of international commercial arbitration practice.

5-33 The autonomous theory is a refined mixed theory which develops the regime to reflect the market place. It acknowledges jurisdictional and contractual elements in the arbitration regime, but shifts the focus from the control that the law of seat of arbitration *may* exercise and the autonomy of parties to the business and legal level where parties agree to and participate in the arbitration process. This theory which prevails today will inevitably dominate arbitration in the years to come.

2. Interplay of International Commercial Arbitration and National Legal System

5-34 By opting for arbitration, parties to a dispute effectively waive their constitutional rights to have their dispute heard by a national court. An important question is whether the constitutional guarantees, which relate to the state justice system, are applicable to arbitration proceedings? Is there actually a fundamental

---

[45] Lew, *Applicable Law*, para 80.

right of parties to submit to arbitration?[46] Are the fundamental principles of arbitration regulated by the constitution, especially with respect to states which have a clearly defined constitutional system? It is also important to establish which constitutional law may be relevant. To the extent that arbitration may be effectively delocalised, or indeed that the chosen seat is coincidental and neutral, constitutional issues appear to be less important or often difficult to localise. Is it sufficient to apply generally accepted constitutional standards? Are there any such standards and how do they affect the arbitration agreement, parties, and arbitrators?

2.1. Relationship between Arbitration and State Justice System

5-35 There is in many cases a constitutional[47] or legal obligation for state courts to supervise and assist arbitration within their jurisdiction.[48] This is expressed in three general principles:

- In most systems the existence of a valid arbitration agreement is a constitutional prerequisite for the commencement and validity of arbitration proceedings;
- State courts can interfere if arbitration tribunals are dealing with matters which are declared to be non-arbitrable; and
- Arbitration, as a constitutionally guaranteed adjudication method, is subject to some fundamental rules (fair hearing / due process[49], neutrality and impartiality of arbitrators[50]) which also apply to state courts.

---

46 This question is answered in the affirmative by Delvolvé, "The Fundamental Right to Arbitration", in Hunter, Marriott and Veeder (eds), *Internationalisation of International Arbitration*, 141. See also Cour d'appel Paris, 29 March and 8 November 2001, *NIOC v State of Israel*, 17(6) Mealey's IAR B-1 (2002).

47 The Italian Constitutional Court accepted a reference from an arbitration tribunal hearing a domestic case to decide on the constitutionality of a provision of an Italian statute. In passing the court stated clearly that since arbitrators perform *de facto* a judicial function, they must refer any constitutional issue to the Constitutional Court. It also implied that the Constitutional Court would accept in the future similar references as it sees arbitration as a separate jurisdiction of the judicial system. See Corte Costituzionale, 22 November 2001, no 376. Pres. Ruperto; rel. Marini. Available at <www.diritto.it>.

48 See the example of the evolution of arbitration in France in von Mehren, "International Commercial Arbitration: The Contribution of the French Jurisprudence", 46 *Louisiana L Rev* 1048 (1986).

5-36 This view can be restated as a question: is it possible to oust court jurisdiction by concluding a valid arbitration agreement, or is there a constitutional right to arbitration as is the case with state jurisdiction?

5-37 In *Hi-Fert Pty Ltd (Australia) and Cargill Fertilizer Inc v Kiukiang Maritime Carriers and Western Bulk Carriers (Australia) Ltd*, the Federal Court of Australia[51] had to decide the constitutionality of section 7 International Arbitration Act 1974. Simply, the legal issue was whether arbitrators in London were capable of dealing with matters falling under the Australian Trade Practices Act. In that way a matter of arbitrability was classified as a constitutional issue. The "constitutional issues" in common law-context read as follows

> Ouster of federal court jurisdiction (…)
>
> [12] The common law doctrine that the jurisdiction of the court should not be ousted is based on public policy that the access of citizens to the courts should be preserved. This public policy as applied by the courts overrides the intentions of the contracting parties who insist on such a provision in their contract. However, the principle is not one which is concerned to delimit the power of the legislature. The principle does not, and indeed cannot, prevent the legislature from permitting specified types of dispute or differences to be referred to and determined by arbitration where certain conditions are satisfied. The public policy embodied in the common law contractual principle of non-ouster is subject to, and must give way to, express contrary provisions such as Sect. 7.[52]
>
> (…)

---

[49] See Carbonneau, "Arbitral Justice: The Demise of Due Process in American law", 70 *Tulane L Rev* 1945 (1996); Kessedjian, "Principe de la contradiction et arbitrage", *Rev Arb* 381 (1995).

[50] *AT & T and Another v Saudi Cable Company*, [2000] 2 Lloyd's Rep 127 (CA).

[51] XXIII YBCA 606 (1998).

[52] *Ibid*, 612. The pertinent part of Section 7, entitled "Enforcement of Foreign Arbitration Agreements", provides:

(2) … , where:

(a) proceedings instituted by a party to an arbitration agreement to which this section applies against another party to the agreement are pending in a court; and

(b) the proceedings involve the determination of a matter that, in pursuance of the agreement, is capable of settlement by arbitration; on the application of a party to the agreement, the court shall, by order, upon such conditions (if any) as it thinks fit, stay the proceedings or so much of the proceedings as involves the determination of that matter, as the case may be, and refer the parties to arbitration in respect of that matter.

Extract from *Int'l Handbook on Comm Arb* Suppl 13 September 1992 Australia: Annex II, International Arbitration Act 1974, Reprinted as of 31 January 1992.

> [18] The effect of Sect. 7 is that a general common law discretion, which the court might otherwise have exercised in relation to the grant or refusal of the stay, is not available. This does not constitute an intrusion by the legislature into the area of judicial power, nor can it properly be said to be an assumption of judicial power. The Section simply enables the agreement of the parties as to resolution of their potential disputes to be implemented. Furthermore, the determinations that the court must make as to the application of Sect. 7 involve the exercise of judicial power.

5-38 This was also the main issue in the US case of *Kulukundis Shipping Co v Amtorg Trading Corp* concerning various national constitutional provisions as well as some international conventions. *Kulukundis* pertinently describes the relationship between arbitration and the state justice system in the US

> the agreement to arbitrate was not illegal, since suit could be maintained for its breach ... The United States Arbitration Act of 1925 was sustained as constitutional ... The purpose of that Act was deliberately to alter the judicial atmosphere previously existing ... In the light of the clear intention of Congress, it is our obligation to shake off the old judicial hostility to arbitration.[53]

5-39 In continental European legal systems the attitude was different. Arbitration is deeply rooted in Ancient Greek and Roman laws and since the French Revolution, arbitration was considered a *droit naturel.* Moreover the French Constitution of 1791[54] and the Constitution of Year III (Article 210)[55] proclaimed the constitutional right of citizens to resort to arbitration. A similar provision could be found in the Greek constitution of 1827 (Article 139), which however was omitted in subsequent amendments. By the beginning of the 20th century, arbitration was a well-established procedure in Europe and accepted by the national courts.[56]

---

53 126 F 2d 978 (2d Cir 1942).

54 "Le droit des citoyens de terminer définitevement leurs contestations par la voie de l'arbitrage, ne peut recevoir aucune atteinte par les acts du Pouvoir législatif." (The legislative power [Parliament] cannot by any means hinder the right of the citizens to settle their disputes by means of arbitration). Title III, Chap V, Article 5, Constitution of 3 September 1791.

55 "Il ne peut être porté aucune atteinte au droit de faire prononcer sur les différends par les arbitres du choix des parties", Constitution, 22 August 1795.

56 For more details see Böckstiegel, "The Role of National Courts in the Development of an Arbitration Culture", in van den Berg (ed), *ICCA Congress Series no 8*, 219. See also Roebuck, "Sources for the History of Arbitration: A Bibliographical Introduction", 14(3) *Arb Int* 237 (1998).

5-40 At the international level the constitutionality of arbitration was established in legal provisions which codified the basic contractual and economic freedom as an economic rather than as a fundamental right.[57] Moreover, it has been reiterated quite often that decision-making power is not and should not be synonymous to judicial power. Clearly, decision-making power or power to adjudicate is a "neutral term". In any event, a closer look at modern constitutions provides evidence for the submission that arbitration is in full conformity with them. State courts remain in the background as the forum of ultimate resort and thus the state privilege to adjudicate disputes is not an exclusive one.

2.2. Arbitration Agreement as a Constitutional Prerequisite

5-41 Many modern constitutions and international human rights treaties provide for the right to have one's case heard before a state court and promulgate the concept of a "natural judge". For example, Article 8 of the Universal Declaration of Human Rights (1948) provided

> Everyone has the right to an effective remedy by the competent national tribunals for acts violating the fundamental rights granted him by the constitution or by law.

5-42 In several constitutions similar provisions were included.[58] These provisions guarantee legal protection before the courts as a human right. In such a constitutional framework arbitration is, in principle, in conformity with the constitution if agreed to voluntarily.[59] However, a great deal of flexibility is left

---

[57] See Schwab and Gottwald, "Verfassung und Zivilprozeß", in *Effektiver Rechtsschutz und verfassungsmäßige Ordnung* 1 (1983) 43 with comparative references. See also discussion about juridical nature and constitutionality of arbitration in Geimer, *Schiedgerichtsbarkeit und Verfassung,* Lecture at the Conference of the Wissenschaftliche Vereinigung für Internationales Verfahrensrecht, Zurich, 15 October 1993, 37.

[58] See, *e.g.*, German Basic Law (1949) Articles 92(1) and 101(1) and (2); Constitution of Japan (1994) Article 32; Constitution of the Russian Federation (1993) Article 47(1); Federal Constitution of the Swiss Confederation (1999) Articles 29a and 30.

[59] This is, *e.g.*, the dominant opinion in Brazil where it was found that the 1996 Arbitration Act is in conformity with Art XXXV of the Constitution ("No law may exclude from review by the Judiciary any injury or threat to a right"). See Wald, Schellenberg and Rosenn, "Some Controversial Aspects of the New Brazilian Arbitration Law", 31 *U Miami Inter-Am L Rev* 223 (2000). See also Greek Constitution Article 8.

with state courts which may[60] or may not stay proceedings when arbitration proceedings are already ongoing or where there is a valid arbitration agreement.

5-43 It is possible that constitutions, such as those of the Russian Federation, Japan and some Latin American states may cause problems in domestic arbitrations when a claim for the protection of human rights is raised.[61] This may also be a problem in consumer and employment arbitration. One should not automatically assume that arbitration may not be compelled in domestic cases where one party is apparently weaker.[62] State courts should compel parties to arbitration when the parties agree to arbitrate in a manner acceptable by law.

5-44 The Greek constitution is an illustration of modern standards where the constitutional text makes positive reference to the rights of persons to waive or oust the jurisdiction of national courts. Article 8 Greek Constitution (1975/1986/2001) provides

> No person shall be deprived of the judge assigned to him by law against *his will.* [Emphasis added]

5-45 Article 20(1) provides

> Every person shall be entitled to receive legal protection by the courts and may plead before them his views concerning his rights or interests, as specified by law.

5-46 Certain constitutional aspects were raised in a recent case before the Brazilian Supreme Court. It involved the constitutional validity of Articles 6 and 7 of the 1996 Brazilian Arbitration Law. These provisions permit the courts to compel the parties to go to arbitration even if the parties have failed to provide for the appointment of arbitrators, applicable procedural rules, or have failed to agree upon a specific submission to arbitration. To do this a Brazilian court would issue a judgment that operates as a specific submission to arbitration. In effect, the Brazilian Arbitration Law permits the courts to fill in the components of the arbitration process that the parties left blank.

---

60 Courts stayed proceedings and ordered arbitration in, *e.g.*, *Bauhinia Corp v China National Machinery & Equipment Import & Export Corp*, 819 F 2d 247 (9th Cir CA); *Filanto SpA v Chilewich International Corp*, 789 F Supp 1229 (US DCt, SDNY), confirmed in 984 F 2d 58 (2d Cir CA).

61 Several voices suggest that it should not be possible for state courts to compel parties to arbitration since courts are the natural forum for settlement of disputes.

62 *E.g.*, US courts have compelled parties to arbitration: *Monica Snow v BE & K Construction Company*, 84 Fair Empl Prac Cas (BNA) 1260, 17 IER Cases 170, 126 F Supp 2d 5.

5-47 Sepulveda Pertence, former President of the Supreme Court, declared these provisions of the Arbitration Law unconstitutional in a case involving a contract that contained no arbitration clause.[63] Nevertheless the parties subsequently agreed to submit this particular dispute to arbitration in Spain.[64] This decision was a curious anachronism, which, if it had been sustained by the full Supreme Court, would have assured that arbitration would not be widely used in Brazil.[65] Members of the Supreme Court requested the opportunity to peruse the proceedings. By a majority of 7:4 the Supreme Court held Brazil's arbitration law could finally apply unhindered by the shadow of a constitutional challenge. The Supreme Court confirmed that the authority granted to the courts to sign the submission agreement was implied in an arbitration clause contractually agreed and did not breach the constitutional right to have disputes heard by state courts.

5-48 In 1999, Mauricio Correa of the Brazilian Supreme Court, in a case[66] involving a contract containing a clause agreeing to arbitrate under the Liverpool Cotton Association Limited, took the opportunity to express disagreement with the reasoning of Pertence and to determine incidentally that the new Brazilian Arbitration Law is constitutional. Furthermore, Brazil ratified the New York Convention in 2002.

5-49 There should not be a problem with international commercial cases and where there is a well-drafted arbitration agreement and no apparent national interest. The critical provisions may generate problems in cases where the parties have not been able to agree to arbitrate in a form that conforms with domestic or international practice.

5-50 This issue was also considered by the Swiss Supreme Court in 1987.[67] The case arose from a joint venture agreement which provided for any dispute to

---

[63] Supremo Tribunal Federal, 10 October 1996, Case no 5206-7, *MBV Commercial & Export Management Establishment v Agravado: Resil Industria e Comercio Ltda*, reprinted in Lima, *Curso de Introdução a Arbitragem* (1999), 335. Although Judge Pertence was followed by three other judges, the remaining four judges all voted in favour of the constitutionality of the new law, the last vote being handed down in December 2001.

[64] *Ibid.*

[65] Schellenberg and Rosenn, "Some Controversial Aspects of the New Brazilian Arbitration Law", 31 *U Miami Inter-Am L Rev* 223 (2000).

[66] Supremo Tribunal Federal No 5847-1, 20 May 1999, *Aiglon Dublin Ltd v Teka Teelagem Kuenrich SA*, unpublished.

[67] *Ali and Fahd Shobokshi and General Agencies Corporation (Saudi Arabia) v Saiecom SA and Nicola Rivelli* (Switzerland), XV YBCA 505 (1990), 109 La Semaine Judiciaire 230 (1987).

be resolved by arbitration in Geneva under the ICC Rules. After a dispute arose and the claimant started arbitration proceedings, the respondents objected to the constitution of the arbitration tribunal. They argued that the parties were bound by three contracts, only one of which contained an arbitration clause. However, the ICC Court of Arbitration decided to constitute the arbitration tribunal and to designate Geneva as the place of arbitration. Respondents brought an action before the Court of First Instance in Geneva seeking a declaration that the arbitration clause in the contract was non-existent and that the ICC arbitration proceedings were null and void and in breach of Article 58 of the Swiss Constitution. The Court of First Instance dismissed the petition.

5-51 Relying on the New York Convention the Supreme Court affirmed the decisions of the lower courts dismissing the petition reasoning as follows

> ... By restricting its examination to the prima facie existence of an arbitration clause, the Court of Appeal did not violate the principle according to which the defendant must be brought to court before his natural judge [i.e., the judge of the domicile of the defendant], thereby violating Art. 58 of the Constitution. The Court of Appeal has in no way violated a constitutional or legal rule of jurisdiction.
>
> Claimants' objections based on the denial of justice are of no importance. They merge into the pleas concerning the violation of the New York Convention and Article 58 of the Constitution. Consequently, they will have to be rejected together with these claims.[68]

5-52 These provisions simply classify contracts involving the state or state entities as administrative contracts which cannot be submitted to arbitration at all, or only with specific authority. Most national arbitration laws take a robust approach where the state or state entity has agreed to arbitration.[69]

5-53 Questions relating to the conformity of an arbitration agreement with the constitution of a given state also arise in the context of proceedings which involve state parties. In the ICC interim award in case no 7263 of 1994[70] the respondent invoked possible violations of the constitution of a given state. The tribunal, however, held that the respondent was not entitled to invoke such violations and that the tribunal lacked authority to make such decision on the

---

68 *Ibid*, 507.

69 Silva-Romero, "ICC Arbitration and State Contracts", 13(1) *ICC Bulletin* 34 (2002) 39-41.

70 *Case between Country X's Ministry of Defence and a US Contractor*, XXII YBCA 92 (1997).

basis of a constitutional text. Nevertheless, the tribunal stated in pertinent part, in its award that

> [23] In the field of international commercial arbitration, similar provisions are embodied in international instruments such as Article 2 of the 1961 Geneva Convention and in national law such as Article 177(2) of the Swiss PILA. The limitations imposed by said rules refer to states and public bodies as defendants; the latter cannot avail themselves of the incapacity and lack of authorization deriving from their national laws.[71]

3. Human Rights and Arbitration

5-54 Whilst there has been little academic discussion[72] about the human rights implications for international commercial arbitration, the European Commission[73] and the European Court of Human Rights as well as national courts have already delivered several judgments in the last 20 years.

5-55 It was generally considered that human rights had little or no relevance to international arbitration. This was because arbitration was used by the international business community to resolve disputes in international commercial transactions. The parties did not need the protection of human rights regimes and they were presumed to be adequately protected by the obligation of due process which is upheld through the New York Convention. Furthermore, as the parties agreed to submit to arbitration, they had effectively waived their rights of protection in the courts. This view was strongly supported by the fact that the human rights instruments make no reference to arbitration.

5-56 There are two essential questions which should be addressed. First, what is the effect of human rights obligations now enshrined in the law in many countries on the conduct of international commercial arbitration? Second, what

---

[71] *Ibid*, 98.

[72] See, *e.g.*, Jarrosson, "L'arbitrage et la convention européenne des droits de l'homme", *Rev Arb* 573, 1989; Ambrose, "Arbitration and the Human Rights Act", [2000] *LMCLQ* 468; Mourre, "Le droit français de l'arbitrage international face à la Convention européenne des droits de l'homme", *Gazette du Palais*, Vendredi 1er (2 December 2000) 16-29; Ribbing, "International Arbitration: The Human Rights Perspective", 4 *Am Rev Int Arb* 537 (1993).

[73] The European Commission of Human Rights no longer exists as a result of Protocol no 11, European Convention of Human Rights on Procedural Reforms. It came into force on 1 November 1998 giving the Commission one year to deal with cases declared admissible before the Protocol entered into force. The decisions of the Commission are still useful authority.

is the relationship between due process and human rights in the context of international arbitration?

3.1. The Application of Human Rights Law to Arbitration

5-57 The 1950 European Convention on Human Rights has since been ratified by all members of the Council of Europe. The ECHR is incorporated in national law by an implementing act or an act of ratification. The ECHR provides for a comprehensive system of human rights protection and most states have agreed to allow individual petitions to the European Commission and the European Court of Human Rights. This is possible only after the exhaustion of local remedies. Irrespective of the individual petition, the ECHR when implemented and ratified provides also for protection before state courts as well as judicial review of domestic legislation.

5-58 Neither the ECHR nor its *travaux préparatoires* make express reference to arbitration, the question is whether the ECHR may be directly or indirectly applicable, or may be a source of inspiration for arbitration tribunals. The provision of the ECHR which affects international arbitration is Article 6(1). This provides

> In the determination of his civil rights and obligations or of any criminal charge against him, everyone is entitled to a fair and public hearing within a reasonable time by an independent and impartial tribunal established by law. Judgment shall be pronounced publicly but the press and public may be excluded from all or part of the trial in the interest of morals, public order and national security in a democratic society ....

5-59 The purpose of this provision is to ensure that every party to court proceedings will have a fair and public opportunity to put forward its case and defend itself. The public character of the proceedings, in particular in criminal proceedings, was to ensure that unfairness, dishonesty or corruption on the part of judges cannot be hidden. By contrast, arbitration is a private process and is generally intended to be confidential. This is in direct contradiction to the public nature of hearings required under the ECHR.[74]

5-60 The question of the relationship between arbitration and ECHR was considered by the European Commission of Human Rights in *X v Federal*

---

[74] See Houghton, "Does Arbitration infringe your Human Rights?", *Asian DR* 76 (2001).

Republic of Germany.[75] In this case the Commission considered an arbitration clause included in a standard contract of employment concluded by a German teacher employed by a German school in Spain. The clause provided for arbitration before a qualified representative of the German Foreign Ministry. When a dispute arose, the teacher brought an action before the Spanish courts which assumed jurisdiction and found the arbitration clause to be void. The German courts did not recognise the Spanish decisions and the German teacher made a request before the European Commission of Human Rights claiming that his rights under Article 6(1) had been infringed. The Commission declined the request and considered the agreement to submit to arbitration to be a question of renunciation of rights under the ECHR.

5-61 In the 1983 case of *Bramelid and Malmstrom v Sweden*[76], the Commission again considered the relationship between arbitration and the ECHR. Swedish company law permitted a company owning more that 90% of the shares in another company to purchase the remaining 10% for a value which would, in the event of any dispute, be decided by arbitration. After a valuation was made in this case, the minority shareholders petitioned to the European Commission of Human Rights claiming that their rights under Article 6(1) had been infringed. The complaint was that all the minority shareholders had been forced to choose the same arbitrator while the purchasing company had been able to choose its own arbitrator.

5-62 The Commission distinguished voluntary from compulsory arbitration.[77] It upheld the complaint on the basis that the parties had been forced to arbitrate. However, it also stated that in principle there is no problem under Article 6 when one is dealing with voluntary arbitration. This conclusion is welcome as the right to arbitrate is guaranteed in all ECHR states, often as part of the obligation undertaken with the ratification of the New York Convention. Were arbitration not to be compatible with the ECHR, the two international conventions would be in conflict.[78]

---

[75] 5 March 1962, 5 *Annuaire de la Convention Européenne des droits de l'homme* (1962) Rec 8, 68.

[76] 38 *Décisions et rapports* 18 (1983).

[77] See also *Lithgow and others v United Kingdom*, 8 July 1986, Series A, no 102. The consent of parties to arbitration is paramount: European Ct HR, 9 December 1994, *Raffineries grecques Stran et Stratis Andreadis v Grèce*, Rev Arb 283 (1996).

[78] In a similar case before the Cour de cassation, 7 January 1992, *Siemens AG and BKMI Industrienlagen GmbH v Dutco Construction Company (Dubai)*, Rev Arb 470 (1992), with note

5-63 The position of state courts in relation to arbitration has been considered by the European Court and the European Commission of Human Rights in a number of cases.[79] It was consistently held that arbitration agreements are not in principle contrary to Article 6 of the ECHR, as the aim pursued is legitimate and the means employed to achieve the aim is proportionate. Accordingly an agreement of the parties to arbitrate, which at the same time renounces the jurisdiction of the courts, is binding on them and makes the award enforceable.[80]

5-64 The only responsibility a state has with respect to an arbitration taking place on its territory is to ensure that the support provided for arbitration proceedings by the state courts complies with the guarantees set out in Article 6. In *KR v Switzerland*,[81] the European Court of Human Rights confirmed that while the state was not responsible for the actions of arbitrators, it was responsible for the way in which state courts are called to intervene in arbitration.

5-65 The case law of the European Commission and European Court of Human Rights leave a number of issues unanswered. For instance, the issue as to whether the ECHR *must* be considered by an arbitration tribunal is still open. National courts have expressed views to the affirmative.[82] To the extent that

---

by Bellet, 473; Clunet 712 (1992), with the conclusions of the Attorney General, 713-726 and note Jarosson, 726, the French court decided that the equality of parties in the appointment of arbitrators is a matter of public policy and can only be waived after the dispute has arisen.

79 See, *e.g.*, European Comm HR, 13 July 1990, *Axelsson and Ors v Sweden*, 65 DR 99.

80 See, *e.g.*, European Comm HR, 2 December 1991, *Jakob Boss Söhne KG v Federal Republic of Germany*; European Comm HR, 2 December 1991, *Firma Heinz Schiebler KG v Federal Republic of Germany*; European Ct HR, 23 February 1999, *Suovaniemi and Ors v Finland*; European Ct HR, 25 May 1998, *Guido Pastore v Italy*.

81 European Ct HR, 4 March 1987, and Cour d'appel Paris, 15 September 1998, *Société Cubic Defense Systems Inc v Chambre de commerce internationale*, Rev Arb (1999), 103, the complaint was relating to delays in arbitration. See also European Comm HR, 27 November 1996, *Norsdtröm-Janzon v The Netherlands*, D.R. 87-B, 112, where the complaint was based upon the fact that an arbitral award had been rendered by a three-man tribunal, one of whose members has at one point rendered legal advice to the other side. The complaint was rejected by the Netherlands Supreme Court and the European Comm HR declined to intervene.

82 Corte di Appello Milan, 4 December 1992, *Allsop Automatic Inc v Tecnoski snc*, 30 Rivista di diritto internazionale privato e processuale 873 (1994), XXII YBCA 725 (1997) para 4

> The issue which remains to be settled in the present case, and which is raised by the respondent, is whether the award, which is only to be reviewed formally, is consistent with public policy. We must say that, where this consistency is to be examined, reference must be made to the so-called international public policy, being a "body of universal principles shared by nations of similar civilization, aiming at the protection of fundamental human rights, often embodied in international declarations or conventions.

human rights protection constitutes a core part of international or national public policy, human rights aspects must be considered by the tribunal. Arbitrators may also invoke human rights as part of general principles of law but not as part of law not pleaded and proven by the parties, to the extent that the principle *jura novit curia, i.e.* that the arbitrators know the law and are under an obligation to assert the law, is not generally acceptable in international commercial arbitration. In some cases, human rights protection will also be relevant as part of the law applicable to the merits of the dispute, to the extent that parties plead and prove the relevant provisions or that the tribunal adopts inquisitorial proceedings.

5-66 The European Court of Human Rights' decision in *McGonnell v United Kingdom*[83] may have implications for the selection of arbitrators. The applicant brought a planning application before the courts of Guernsey. It was refused by the Bailiff and seven Jurats. The Bailiff of Guernsey in his judicial capacity is the senior judge of the Royal Court and also exercises some legislative powers. The applicant argued violation of Article 6 ECHR before the European Court of Human Rights on the basis that there was too close a connection between the Bailiff's judicial role and his functions in legislative and executive government, such that he no longer had the necessary capacities of independence and impartiality. The European Court of Human Rights unanimously found a violation of Article 6(1).

5-67 This decision gives rise to interesting questions. Would an arbitrator be excluded under this principle because he was a member of a committee that was involved in the development of the relevant law with which the issue in dispute was concerned? Would an arbitrator likewise be excluded if he were a retired judge of a member of a supreme court?[84] Undoubtedly the European Court of Human Rights will elaborate the rationale of *McGonnell* in the future.

See also Austrian Oberster Gerichtshof, 4 December 1994 4 Ob 1542/94, *Respondent in arbitral proceedings v Arbitral tribunal*, XXII YBCA 263 (1997) para 5

> An injunction may be issued in case of an imminent breach of a right guaranteed by the European Convention on Human Rights, provided that (...) the injunction must appear to be necessary for the prevention of imminent acts of violence or the avoidance of an imminent irreversible damage. It has not even been alleged by the claimant that such dangers were imminent.

[83] Decision of 8 February 2000, *McGonnell v United Kingdom*, 30 EHRR 289.

[84] This may be particularly so for a member of the UK House of Lords who has both a judicial and a legislative function.

3.2. "Due Process" and Arbitration

5-68 Regardless of the procedure and the law chosen, it is undisputed that the arbitration tribunal shall guarantee a number of principles that constitute the procedural "*magna carta of arbitration.*" What are these fundamental standards of international commercial arbitration and where are they to be found? In fact they are the constitutional cornerstones of arbitration proceedings - due process, fairness and the application of the appropriate law or other standard to the substance of the dispute. The *magna carta* of arbitration has two main principles:

- due process and fair hearing; and
- independence and impartiality of arbitrators

5-69 The first main principle of due process and fair hearing is not only guaranteed in Article 6(1) ECHR but is also safeguarded in most arbitration laws[85] and, in particular, in Article V(1)(b) of the New York Convention. Consequently, all parties shall be treated with equality and each party shall be given a full or at least reasonable opportunity to present his case. The principle of fair trial will effectively imply that:

- each party is given a reasonable opportunity to put his case and to deal with that of his opponent;
- delays will be avoided by fixing appropriate short periods for written submissions and oral arguments;
- exercising maximum discretion when deciding as to the admissibility of evidence[86];
- the arbitration tribunal treats parties equally and fairly.

5-70 The principle of due process and fair hearing will be considered and respected by tribunals even without an express reference to or direct application of the ECHR.

---

[85] See, *e.g.*, Model Law Article 18; Belgium, Judicial Code Article 1694(1); England, Arbitration Act section 33(1)(a); Swiss PIL Article 182(3).

[86] See, *e.g.*, *Dombo Beheer BV v The Netherlands* [1993] EHRR 213. The plaintiff company had sought to prove an oral agreement made between its former managing director and the branch manager of the defendant bank. The Dutch court permitted the branch manager to testify but refused to hear the former managing director as a competent witness, a ruling subsequently upheld by the Dutch Supreme Court. The European Court of Human Rights found that the decisions violated ECHR Article 6(1).

5-71 The fundamental principle of independence and impartiality of arbitrators is recognised in international commercial arbitration and is regulated by all major arbitration institution rules and laws. The question relating to the ECHR is whether, after the arbitration procedure has been completed and an award was rendered, the courts in any national jurisdiction should review the questions of conflict of interest of arbitrators. Having done so, the issue can be reviewed by the European Court of Human Rights.

5-72 There are two cases[87] where these issues arose. In both instances the European Court declined to get involved on the basis that these issues had been determined in accordance with the applicable arbitration rules and courts.

5-73 The English Commercial Court has held that when exercising its supervisory role over arbitration proceedings it is not immune from the tentacles of the Human Rights Act 1998. A corporate body is protected by the Human Rights Act and can invoke Article 6 where it may be a victim of action incompatible with due process. The particular issue that arose was whether the judge, in refusing to give permission to appeal to the High Court from a reasoned award, has a duty to state his reasons in full for that refusal. It was decided that a decision refusing leave is not challengeable as being devoid of appropriate and relevant reasoning.[88]

5-74 While arbitration tribunals should be inspired by human rights legislation, strict direct application of human rights law will be inappropriate.[89] First, normally human rights legislation is addressed to states. Secondly, Article 6 ECHR, for instance, speaks of public hearings, while it is universally accepted that arbitration hearings are private and usually confidential. While the ECHR

---

87 European Comm HR, 27 November 1996, *Norsdtröm-Janzon v The Netherlands*, DR. 87-B, 112; the complaint was rejected by the Netherlands Supreme Court and the European Comm HR declined to intervene; European Ct HR, 23 February 1999, *Osmo Suovaniemi and Others v Finland*; the complaint was dismissed by the Finnish courts and European Court HR.

88 *In the Matter of an Arbitration Mousaka Inc (Applicant) v Golden Seagull Maritine Inc and Golden Seabird Maritime Inc (Respondents)*, (2001) WL 825138 (QBD), [2001] 2 Lloyd's Rep 657, [2001] 2 All ER (Comm) 794. See also *Fence Gate Ltd v NEL Construction Ltd* [2001] All ER (D) 214, para 28 and *North Range Shipping Ltd v Seatrans Shipping Corp* [2002] EWCA Civ 405 (14 March 2002, CA).

89 Belgium, Court of Appeals, 8 October 2002, *Ferrera v SA AG 1824 & SA AG Belgium*, unreported

has no direct application[90] to arbitration it does have an indirect influence on both arbitrators and arbitration institutions.

[90] For arguments to the contrary see Matscher, "L'arbitrage et la Convention, article 6 (suite)", in Pettiti, Decaux, Imbert, *La Convention européenne des droits de l'homme. Commentaire article par article* (Economica 1995), 281 *et seq*; Moitry, "Right to a Fair Trial and the European Convention on Human Rights: Some Remarks on the République de Guinée Case", 6(2) *J Int'l Arb* 115 (1989).

Chapter 6

ARBITRATION AGREEMENTS – AUTONOMY AND APPLICABLE LAW

6-1 The arbitration agreement is the foundation of almost every arbitration. There can be no arbitration between parties which have not agreed to arbitrate their disputes.[1] The contractual nature of arbitration requires the consent of each party for an arbitration to happen. State courts derive their jurisdiction either from statutory provisions or a jurisdiction agreement. In contrast, the arbitration

[1] An exception are the rare cases of statutory arbitration.

tribunal's jurisdiction is based solely on an agreement between two or more parties to submit their existing or future disputes to arbitration.

6-2 An arbitration agreement fulfils a number of different functions. First, it evidences the consent of the parties to submit their disputes to arbitration. Second, it establishes the jurisdiction and authority of the tribunal over that of the courts. Third, it is the basic source of the power of the arbitrators. The parties can in their arbitration agreement extend or limit the powers ordinarily conferred upon arbitration tribunals according to the applicable national law. In addition, the arbitration agreement establishes an obligation for the parties to arbitrate. Arbitration agreements therefore have both a contractual and a jurisdictional character. It is contractual by virtue of the required agreement of the parties. It is jurisdictional by virtue of conferring jurisdiction upon the arbitration tribunal.[2]

6-3 Arbitration agreements can take different forms. They may be pages long, trying to address every conceivable issue at the time of drafting, or may be very short simply providing for "Arbitration, if any, by I.C.C. rules in London"[3] or "Arbitration: Hamburg West Germany"[4] and nevertheless be enforced by the courts.[5] They may have been specifically drafted for the particular contract or be standard clauses. They may be contained in a separate document or at least a separate clause in the contract or can be tied in to the choice of applicable law and a wider dispute resolution provision.

6-4 The differences in form often depend on whether the agreements deal with future disputes or existing disputes. This latter type of arbitration agreements, despite being contained in a separate document, generally tends to be longer. The parties know the nature and circumstances of their dispute and in some cases the tribunal to which they wish to refer the dispute. They often try to devise special rules for certain procedural issues and agree on tailor-made

---

2 Lew, "The Law Applicable to the Form and Substance of the Arbitration Clause", in van den Berg (ed), *ICCA Congress series no 9*, 114 *et seq*; see also the classification by the German Bundesgerichtshof, 30 January 1957, *BGHZ* 23, 198, 200.

3 *Mangistaumunaigaz Oil Production Association v United World Trade Inc*, [1995] 1 *Lloyd's Rep* 619; for a nearly identical clause see *Arab African Energy Corp Ltd v Olieprodukten Nederland BV* [1983] 2 *Lloyd's Rep* 419.

4 Award of the Arbitration Court of the German Coffee Association, XIX *YBCA* 48 (1994).

5 See, *e.g.*, Corte d'Appello Genoa, 3 February 1990, *Della Sanara Kustvaart - Bevrachting & Overslagbedrijf BV v Fallimento Cap Giovanni Coppola srl*, XVII YBCA 542 (1992) 543 (General Average/arbitration, if any, in London in the usual manner); for further examples see *Chitty on Contracts* Vol I (28th ed, Sweet & Maxwell 1999), para 16-014; Schlosser, *Internationale Schiedsgerichtsbarkeit*, 320.

procedures. Historically these so called submission agreements[6] were the only type of arbitration agreements enforceable in a number of countries.[7]

6-5 In modern practice arbitration agreements dealing with future disputes prevail by far. [8] It is often difficult to negotiate a submission agreement once a dispute has arisen. In addition Article II(1) New York Convention imposes on all Contracting States an obligation to recognise agreements "under which the parties undertake to submit to arbitration all or any differences which have arisen or *which may arise*." Where the distinction between the two types of arbitration agreements is kept in the national laws it is mainly for form purposes.[9]

6-6 This chapter describes (1) the extent and effect of the autonomy of the arbitration agreement, (2) the general considerations affecting the law applicable to the arbitration agreement, (3) the law governing the formal validity of the arbitration agreement, (4) the law governing the capacity of the parties to enter into an arbitration agreement and (5) the law governing the substantive validity.

1. AUTONOMY OF THE ARBITRATION AGREEMENT

6-7 It is generally self-evident that a submission agreement concluded after the main contract is an autonomous agreement. It is contained in a separate document, has an existence of its own, has a specific object, and may be governed by a different law. Although it relates to the main contract - it could relate to several contracts - it is concerned only with the dispute between the parties and that it should be resolved by arbitration. Performance of the submission agreement is completely independent from performance of the substantive commercial obligations under the main contract.

---

6 Known in French as a *compromis*.

7 Sanders, *Quo Vadis Arbitration?*, 154; Herrmann, "The Arbitration Agreement as the Foundation of Arbitration and Its Recognition by the Courts", in van den Berg (ed), *ICCA Congress series no 6*, 42 *et seq*; David, *Arbitration in International Trade*, para 216 *et seq*; Nehring Getto, "The New Brazilian Arbitration Law", in ICC (ed), *International Commercial Arbitration in Latin America*, 11.

8 Known in French as a *clause compromissoire.*

9 See, *e.g.*, France, NCPC Article 1442 *et seq* (arbitration clause), Article 1447 *et seq* (submission agreement). See Lew, "The Law Applicable to the Form and Substance of the Arbitration Clause", *ICCA Congress series no 9*, 114, 115 *et seq*; however, in Brazil submission agreements even after their recognition by the Arbitration Act of 1996 gave rise to discussion in relation to their constitutional validity; see Barral and Prazeres, "Trends of Arbitration in Brazil", 15(7) *Mealey's IAR* 22 (2000) 26-27.

6-8 Most arbitration agreements are, however, contained in an arbitration clause inserted in the main contract. It is primarily in these cases where the autonomy of the arbitration clause is an issue, *i.e.*, the interaction between the status of the main contract and the jurisdiction of the arbitrator. What happens if the main contract is deemed to be void or illegal? What is the effect of the arbitration clause after the termination of the main contract? This is the realm of the "doctrine of separability". Further, the autonomy of the arbitration agreement has a bearing on the question of whether the law governing the rest of the contract also extends to the arbitration agreement.[10]

1.1. Separability of the Arbitration Agreement

6-9 The doctrine of separability recognises the arbitration clause in a main contract as a separate contract, independent and distinct from the main contract.[11] The essence of the doctrine is that the validity of an arbitration clause is not bound to that of the main contract and vice versa. Therefore the illegality or termination of the main contract does not affect the jurisdiction of an arbitration tribunal based on an arbitration clause contained in that contract. The obligation to resolve all disputes by arbitration continues even if the main obligation or indeed the contract expires or is vitiated.

6-10 Separability protects the integrity of the agreement to arbitrate and plays an important role in ensuring that the parties intention to submit disputes is not easily defeated. In this way it also protects the jurisdiction of the arbitration tribunal. While the doctrine of competence-competence empowers the tribunal to decide on its own jurisdiction, the doctrine of separability ensures that it can decide on the merits.

6-11 In disputes arising out of contractual relationships parties may allege the termination, invalidity or non-existence of the underlying contract. If the arbitration clause was deemed to be simply a part of the contract these claims would directly affect the jurisdiction of the arbitration tribunal. Where the allegations are justified, the arbitration clause would share the fate of the main

---

[10] In this respect the notion of autonomy is also sometimes used in a slightly different but misleading sense to describe an alleged autonomy of the arbitration agreement from any national law. This is an application of a substantive rule of the French law on international arbitration.

[11] For the development of the doctrine see Samuel, "Separability of arbitration clauses – some awkward questions about the law on contracts, conflict of laws and the administration of justice", 9 *ADRLJ* 36 (2000).

contract, so that it could no longer form the basis of the tribunals's jurisdiction. Consequently the tribunal could not decide on the merits but just decline jurisdiction with the result that disputes as to the existence or validity of the main contract would have to be referred to the state courts.

6-12 This would be contrary to what the parties had agreed in their arbitration agreement. Where the agreement provides that *any* or *all* disputes arising out of a contractual relationship should be referred to arbitration this also covers disputes as to the existence, validity and termination of the contract. If allegations of the non-existence, invalidity or termination automatically affect the jurisdiction of the tribunal they would be a powerful tool in the hands of parties who want to defeat an agreed submission to arbitration. Separability extends the effect of the arbitration clause to cover the subsequent termination of the main contract but also to claims that the main contract is void *ab initio* or never came into existence.

6-13 The operation of the doctrine of separability as well as its limitations are well illustrated in the decision of the Bermuda Court of Appeal in *Sojuznefteexport v Joc Oil.*[12] Sojuznefteexport sought to enforce an award rendered in its favour in Bermuda. Joc Oil tried to resist enforcement alleging *inter alia* that the arbitration agreement was invalid since the contract in which it was included did not comply with the mandatory signature requirements for foreign trade transactions under the applicable Russian law. The court dealt first with the issue of whether these signature requirements also extended to the arbitration agreement since in that case the arbitration agreement as such would already have been invalid.[13] It rejected that assertion and the court then dealt with the issue of whether the arbitration agreement was tainted by the invalidity of the main contract in which it was included. The court held that this was not the case since Russian law considered the arbitration agreement to be a separate contract

---

[12] *Sojuznefteexport (SNE) v Joc Oil Ltd*, (1990) XV YBCA 384, 407 *et seq* (Bermuda Court of Appeal, 7 July 1989).

[13] *Ibid*, para 39

> It would appear that logically the question of whether the arbitration clause is itself a 'transaction in foreign trade' within the meaning of the 1935 Signature Decree (as Joc Oil contends) so as to require the signatures of two authorized persons should be considered before one embarks upon an examination of the doctrine of Separability, for if Joc Oil is right in their contention, and there is no valid arbitration agreement and that is an end of the matter and the question of the existence of the doctrine of Separability in Soviet law would become an academic issue.

which is generally valid irrespective of the invalidity of the main contract. Concerning the limitation of the doctrine of separability the court held

> [47] There are two qualifications on the doctrine of separability which are generally accepted. The first is ... the case where the existence of the contract itself is contested. If the question arises whether the parties have indeed concluded a contract containing an arbitration clause, the jurisdiction of the arbitrator is put in question. If there is no contract at all, the legal basis of the arbitrator's powers which reside in the arbitration clause found in the contract "is also missing".
>
> ...
>
> [49] The second qualification arises when the attack is not upon the principal agreement but upon the validity of the arbitration clause itself - whether, for instance, it conformed to the requirements for conclusion of a valid arbitration agreement under the proper law of the agreement or whether it is, for example, itself vitiated by fraud. Here, while the arbitral tribunal is competent to pass upon that question, it is, as a rule not competent to pass upon it with definitive effect. [References omitted]

6-14 This quote makes clear that the effect of separability is limited to preventing the fate of the main contract *automatically* affecting the arbitration agreement. The agreement may, however, be tainted by the same defects. While that is not so common in cases of voidness or termination this will often apply in cases where a party alleges that a contract was never concluded or that the parties were still in the process of negotiation. This will often be true also for the arbitration agreement.[14]

6-15 However, even in those cases the doctrine of separablity requires that the question whether the parties consented to the arbitration agreement has to be determined separately from whether they agreed on the main contract. There might be cases where although the main contract never came into existence the parties agreed on arbitration so that all disputes arising out of work done under the non-existing contract have to go to arbitration.[15]

---

[14] Samuel, "Separability of arbitration clauses", 9 *ADRLJ* 36 (2000) 45; see also *Sandvik AB v Advent International Corp*, 15(7) Mealey's IAR 4 (2000), XXVI YBCA 961 (2001) 968 *et seq* (3rd Cir); for a case where not only the main contract was repudiated but also the arbitration agreement see the decision by the English Court of Appeal in *John Downing v Al Tameer Establishment, Shaikh Khalid Al Ibrahim* [2002] All ER (Comm) 545.

[15] Shackleton, "Arbitration without a contract", 17(9) *Mealey's IAR* 25 (2002).

6-16 The doctrine of separability is now embedded in most modern arbitration laws. Since it relates to the jurisdiction of the arbitrator it is often treated in conjunction with the general power of the arbitrators to rule on their jurisdiction. The Model Law provides in Article 16(1)

> The arbitral tribunal may rule on its own jurisdiction, including any objections with respect to the existence or validity of the arbitration agreement. For that purpose, an arbitration clause which forms part of a contract shall be treated as an agreement independent of the other terms of the contract. A decision by the arbitral tribunal that the contract is null and void shall not entail *ipso jure* the invalidity of the arbitration clause.

6-17 The same applies not only to other Model Law countries[16] but also in other jurisdictions[17] including those which previously were reluctant to fully recognise the doctrine.[18]

6-18 Separability is also provided for in the arbitration rules of the major institutions. Article 6(4) of the ICC Rules[19] provides

> Unless otherwise agreed, the Arbitral Tribunal shall not cease to have jurisdiction by reason of any claim that the contract is null and void or allegation that it is non-existent provided that the Arbitral Tribunal upholds the validity of the arbitration agreement. The Arbitral Tribunal shall continue to have jurisdiction to determine the respective rights of the parties and to adjudicate upon their claims and pleas even though the contract itself may be non-existent or null and void.

---

16 See, *e.g.*, Germany, ZPO section 1040(1); Egypt, Arbitration Law Article 23; Tunisia, Arbitration Code Article 61(1); Algeria, Code of Civil Procedure Article 458bis 1(4); for further references see Sanders, *Quo Vadis Arbitration?*, 172 *et seq*; for an application of the provisions see *Sojuznefteexport (SNE) v Joc Oil Ltd*, (1990) XV YBCA 384 (Bermuda Court of Appeal, 7 July 1989); Canada, *Brian Harper v Kvaerner Fjellstrand Shipping AS*, (1993) XVIII YBCA 358 (BC Supreme Court, 13 September 1991).

17 Switzerland, PIL Article 178(3); Netherlands, CCP Article 1053; Sweden, Arbitration Act section 3; China, Arbitration Law section 19(1).

18 England Arbitration Act section 7. Previously the doctrine was only fully recognised in 1993, in *Harbour Assurance Co Ltd v Kansa General International Insurance Co Ltd*, [1993] 1 Lloyd's Rep 455. See Gross, "Separability Comes of Age in England: Harbour v Kansa and clause 3 of the Draft Bill", 11 *Arb Int* 85 (1995); Samuel, "Separability of arbitration clauses – some awkward questions about the law on contracts, conflict of laws and the administration of justice", 9 *ADRLJ* 36 (2000) 37 *et seq*; for a comparable development in India see the decision by the Delhi High Court, *Brawn Laboratories Ltd v Fittydent International GmbH et al*, XXVI YBCA 783 (2001), 786, para 623 (DHC July 1999).

19 The ICC first recognised the doctrine of separability in its 1955 Arbitration Rules.

6-19 Express provisions to the same effect can also be found in other institutional rules[20] and in Article 21(2) UNCITRAL Rules.

6-20 Even where the applicable law or chosen rules do not provide for the principle courts have recognized it. The US Supreme Court, for example, long before separability found its way into the codifications of national arbitration laws held in *Prima Paint v Flood & Conklin*, a landmark decision for the development of the doctrine[21]

> Except where the parties otherwise intend, arbitration clauses as a matter of federal law are 'separable' from the contract in which they are embedded, and where no claim is made that fraud was directed to the arbitration clause itself, a broad arbitration clause will be held to encompass arbitration of the claim that the contract itself was induced by fraud.[22]

6-21 Decisions to the same effect can be found in France[23] and a number of other jurisdictions including those countries where the arbitration law now provides for separability but the courts already recognized the doctrine before its statutory recognition.[24] Full acceptance of the doctrine is still outstanding, for example, in certain Arab countries.[25]

6-22 In the light of this widespread recognition the doctrine of separability can be considered as one of the true transnational rules of international commercial arbitration, even if it is not expressly mentioned in the different international conventions.[26]

---

[20] See *e.g.*, LCIA Article 23; AAA ICDR Article 15.

[21] *Prima Paint Corp v Flood & Conklin Mfg Co* 388 US 395 (1967). For the evolution of separability in US case law see: Peterson, "International Arbitration Agreements in United States Courts", 55 *Disp Res J* 44 (2000) 80-82.

[22] *Ibid*, 402.

[23] Cour de cassation, 7 May 1963, *Ets Raymond Gosset v Carapelli,* 91 Clunet 82 (1964); Cour d'appel Paris, 7 December 1994, *Société V 2000 v Société Project XJ 220 ITD et autre*, Rev Arb 245 (1996); for further references see Fouchard Gaillard Goldman *on International Commercial Arbitration*, para 391.

[24] For further references see Samuel, "Separability of arbitration clauses", 9 *ADRLJ* 36 (2000) 38 *et seq*; see also the comprehensive comparative analysis by the Bermuda Court of Appeal, *Sojuznefteexport (SNE) v Joc Oil Ltd*, (1990) XV YBCA 384, 407 *et seq* (Bermuda Court of Appeal, 7 July 1989).

[25] See, *e.g.*, Turck, "Saudi Arabia", *ICCA Handbook*, 4; El Ahdab, *Arbitration with the Arab Countries,* 610.

[26] Berger, *International Economic Arbitration*, 121; Fouchard Gaillard Goldman *on International Commercial Arbitration*, para 398.

1.2. Effect of Autonomy on the Determination of the Applicable Law

6-23 Another consequence of the autonomy of the arbitration agreement is that it may be governed by a different law to the main contract. The considerations relevant for determining the applicable law for the main contract are different from those involved in choosing the law governing the arbitration agreement.[27] This is particularly evident in the role of the place of arbitration as a connecting factor where the parties have not chosen any law. While it has little influence on the law applicable to the main contract, this connecting factor has important implications for the arbitration agreement;[28] the law and courts of the place of arbitration will have authority and a supervisory role over the proceedings. Where the actual existence of an arbitration agreement is challenged and in the absence of an otherwise clearly applicable law, it is the law of the place of arbitration which determines the standards against which the existence of the arbitration agreement has to be verified.

6-24 While these differences are widely recognised when the contract does not contain a choice of law clause, the situation is different if the parties have chosen a law to govern the main contract. In such situations there is a strong tendency to regard the choice of the law as equally applicable to the arbitration agreement unless there is agreement to the contrary.[29] There are different considerations applicable to both agreements and rarely will the parties think of the law applicable to the arbitration agreement when making a choice of law for the main contract. Accordingly, there may be cases where a different law will govern, for

---

[27] Interim Award in ICC case no 4131 of 1982, *Dow Chemical France et al v Isover Saint Gobain*, IX YBCA 131 (1984) 133 *et seq*; ICC case no 4504, 113 *Clunet* 1118 (1986) 1119; ICC case no 5730 of 1988, 117 *Clunet* 1029 (1990) 1034; Berger, *International Economic Arbitration*, 158; van den Berg, *New York Arbitration Convention*, 293.

[28] Article V(1)(a) New York Convention which determines that unless the parties have chosen a law applicable to the arbitration agreement it is the law of the place of arbitration according to which the arbitration agreement has to be valid; see also Model Law, Article 36(1)(a)(i).

[29] That is the prevailing view in England; see Russell *on Arbitration*, para 2-094; Merkin, *Arbitration Act*, 180; Dicey & Morris, *The Conflict of Laws* (12th ed, Sweet & Maxwell 1993), 577; but see also *XL Insurance Ltd v Owens Corning*, (2001) XXVI YBCA 869, 878 *et seq* deviating from this approach; for Germany see Bundesgerichtshof, 28 November 1963, *BGHZ* 40, 320, 323; Bundesgerichtshof, 12 December 1976, *RIW* 449 (1976); Oberlandesgericht Hamburg, 22 September 1978, V *YBCA* 262 (1980) 264; from the arbitration practice see NOFOTA award, 5 September 1977, IV *YBCA* 218 (1979) 219; ICC case no 2626, 105 *Clunet* 980 (1978) 981; ICC case no 6840, 119 *Clunet* 1030 (1992) 1032; ICC case no 6379 of 1990, XVII *YBCA* 212 (1992) 215.

example where under the law governing the main contract the arbitration agreement would be invalid.[30]

2. LAW GOVERNING THE ARBITRATION AGREEMENT

6-25 The law applicable to the various aspects of the arbitration agreement has received considerable attention both in academic discussion and in practice. Despite a certain harmonisation achieved through the adoption of the Model Law in various countries the question of the law applicable to the arbitration agreement has not lost its importance. As long as national laws differ as to the formal and substantive requirements for the validity of the arbitration agreement it may be a question of the applicable law whether or not a dispute can and must be referred to arbitration.[31]

6-26 How the law applicable to the various aspects of the arbitration agreement is to be determined is far from clear. Nine different approaches have been identified in arbitration practice as to how to determine the applicable law.[32] Those differences result from a number of facts

- There are various, often closely related factors which might affect the existence and validity of the arbitration agreement, all of which may be submitted to different laws.
- The issue of the existence of a valid arbitration agreement may arise in different fora and at different stages of the proceedings.
- Furthermore, the scope and applicability of some of the potentially relevant provisions, in particular those of the New York Convention, are not clear. This can aggravate the complex interplay between the international conventions and the national laws.

---

30 See, *e.g.*, the decision by the Swiss Tribunal Fédéral, 21 March 1995, XXII *YBCA* 800 (1997) 803.

31 This is particularly true if under one of the potentially applicable laws the agreement would be invalid as was the case for example in ICC case no 6379 of 1990, XVII *YBCA* 212 (1992); therefore the issue is not primarily of an academic interest, as suggested by Blessing, "The Law Applicable to the Arbitration Clause and Arbitrability", in van den Berg (ed), *ICCA Congress series no 9*, 169, 171.

32 Blessing, *ibid*, 169.

2.1. Multiplicity of Applicable Rules

6-27 In considering the law applicable to the arbitration agreement it is necessary to distinguish between the various aspects of its existence and validity. That becomes particularly obvious in the European Convention, one of the few legal instruments which contains a special rule dealing with the law applicable to the arbitration agreement. Article VI provides in pertinent part

> In taking a decision concerning the existence or the validity of an arbitration agreement, courts of Contracting States shall examine the validity of such agreement with reference to the capacity of the parties, under the law applicable to them, and with reference to other questions;
> (a) under the law to which the parties have subjected their arbitration agreement;
> (b) failing any indication thereon, under the law of the country in which the award is to be made;
> (c) failing any indication as to the law to which the parties have subjected the agreement, and where at the time when the question is raised in the court of the country in which the award is to be made cannot be determined, under the competent law by virtue of the rules of conflict of the court seized of the dispute.
> The courts may also refuse recognition of the Arbitration Agreement if under the law of their country the dispute is not capable of settlement by arbitration.

6-28 In addition to these three specific conflict of laws rules in Article VI, the Convention contains in Article VII(2) a separate substantive conflict of laws rule dealing with the form requirements.

2.2. Different Stages where the Issue Arises

6-29 The existence and validity of an arbitration agreement, including the law governing these questions, may be an issue in national courts and the arbitration tribunal at different stages of the proceedings. Where and when these questions arise may have a bearing on the determination of the law governing them.[33]

6-30 National courts may have to deal with this question when

- one party starts proceedings on the merits in a court and the other party asks for a referral to arbitration on the basis of a valid arbitration clause;

---

[33] Hanotiau, "The Law Applicable to Arbitrability", in van den Berg (ed), *ICCA Congress series no 9*, 146, 153 *et seq* in relation to the law governing the arbitrability of a dispute.

- when interim measures of relief or protection are sought in support of arbitration proceedings;
- one party applies to the court for the appointment of an arbitrator because the other party has failed or refused to participate in the establishment of the arbitration tribunal;[34] and
- at the post award stage in proceedings to have an award set aside or annulled, or enforced.

6-31 At all stages different considerations may be relevant in relation to the determination of the applicable law and result in the application of different conflict rules. For example, once an award has been rendered the expenses and time incurred are a much stronger argument for an approach favouring the validity of an arbitration agreement than if the existence of an arbitration agreement is questioned before arbitration proceedings have started.[35] Or it may be felt that the exigencies of the New York Convention require the application of different rules as to the necessary form at the enforcement stage.

6-32 In principle, the inconsistencies which can result from the application of different rules at various stages may justify a unified rule for all stages. The application of different criteria at the pre-award and post-award stage entails the danger that the validity of an arbitration agreement might be treated differently by the courts of the same country depending on the stage the question is asked. For example, a court could be bound to refer the parties to arbitration but

[34] In those proceedings the court may be asked to determine the validity of the arbitration agreement if it is challenged by the defendant as happened for example in a case before the German Bayerisches Oberstes Landesgericht, 28 February 2000, 4Z *Sch* 13/99, 1 *RPS* (2000) 15 where the court refused to appoint an arbitrator since in its view the arbitration clause was void for uncertainty; often, however, the courts at this stage limit themselves to verifying the *prima facie* existence of the arbitration agreement without entering into full proceedings.

[35] See, *e.g.*, Bernardini,"Achieving Effectiveness in the Law Applicable to the Arbitration Clause", *ICCA Congress series no 9*, 197, 200 according to whom the courts when faced with the question whether a dispute should be referred to arbitration have to rely on their *lex fori*, since the issue is whether their jurisdiction was validly excluded, while at the enforcement stage they have to apply the law referred to in Article V(1)(a) New York Convention (law chosen by the parties or law of the place of arbitration); see also *Meadows Indemnity Co Ltd v Baccala & Shoop Insurance Services Inc*, XVII YBCA 686 (1992) 689 (EDNY, 29 March 1991); Cour d'appel Brussels, 4 October 1985, *Company M v M SA*, XIV YBCA 618 (1989) 619.

nevertheless set aside or refuse to enforce the award for lack of a valid arbitration agreement.[36]

6-33 Where the question of the law governing the arbitration agreement is raised before an arbitration tribunal an additional issue may be triggered. State courts generally rely on the conflict of laws rules contained in their national law. By contrast an arbitration tribunal has no "*lex fori*" providing the necessary conflict rules. It is not part of the judicial system of the place of arbitration and is not the guardian of state public policy.[37] The consequence is that different approaches have been used by arbitrators in selecting and applying the relevant conflict rules.

2.3. International Conventions and National Arbitration Laws

6-34 Often the law applicable to the various aspects of the arbitration agreement depends on rules contained in international conventions. While the European Convention[38] defines clearly which arbitration agreements fall within its scope of application this is not the case with the New York Convention.[39] It is primarily concerned with the recognition and enforcement of awards. Therefore, it defines its scope only in relation to awards and does not contain any special criteria as to what arbitration agreements fall under the Convention. The absence of any qualifying criteria, however, is not the result of a conscious decision of the drafters of the New York Convention to regulate all arbitration agreements without limitation. It is the outcome of the drafting history. Article II, which deals with the enforcement of arbitration agreements, was included at the last minute without specifying clearly the exact scope of application of its terms.[40] Therefore its scope in relation to arbitration agreements has to be deduced from

---

36 See criticism of the application of different conflict of laws rules in the decision of the Swiss Tribunal Fédéral, 21 March 1995, XXII *YBCA* 800 (1997).

37 Lew, "The Law Applicable to the Form and Substance of the Arbitration Clause", *ICCA Congress series no 9*, 114, 136; Hanotiau, "The Law Applicable to Arbitrability", *ICCA Congress series no 9*, 146, 158.

38 Article I(1)(a) provides that the Convention applies to arbitration agreements concluded for the purpose of settling disputes arising from international trade between physical or legal persons having, when concluding the agreement, their habitual place of residence or their seat in different contracting states.

39 See the study prepared by the UNCITRAL Secretariat for the drafting of the Model Law, Secretariat Study on the New York Convention, A/CN9/168 (20 April 1979), para 16 *et seq*, reproduced in Holtzmann & Neuhaus, *Model Law*, 307 *et seq*.

40 See van den Berg, *New York Arbitration Convention*, 56.

the provisions defining it in relation to awards and the underlying rationale of the New York Convention.

6-35 In determining the scope of the New York Convention in relation to arbitration agreements two different approaches have been adopted. First, Article II only applies to those arbitration agreements which will probably lead to an award covered by the Convention, *i.e.* where the arbitration is to be in a different contracting state irrespective of the country where the parties are resident. By contrast, agreements providing for arbitration in the state itself or in a non-contracting state would usually not be covered.[41]

6-36 Second, any international element is sufficient to bring an arbitration agreement within the ambit of the New York Convention. That can either be the place of arbitration in a third country or the parties having their principal places of business in different countries.[42] In *Corcoran v AIG Inc*[43] the Supreme Court of New York applied the New York Convention to an agreement providing for arbitration within the US because some of the parties involved were of a foreign nationality. It justified this wide interpretation of the Convention's scope of application with the intention of the drafters of the Convention to facilitate arbitration in international transactions.[44]

3. Law Applicable to Formal Validity

6-37 The formal validity of the arbitration agreement is generally regulated directly in most Conventions and national laws by a substantive rule of private international law.[45] Such a substantive rule facilitates the determination of the

---

[41] Reithmann and Martiny, *Internationales Vertragsrecht* (5th ed, Schmidt 1996), para 2332 *et seq*; the situation is also different if in those cases the ensuing awards would be considered to be foreign awards in the sense of the second alternative of Article I(1) New York Convention.

[42] Van den Berg, *New York Convention*, 61 *et seq.*

[43] *James P Corcoran v AIG Multi-line Syndicate, Inc, et al*, XV YBCA 586 (1990) (SCtNY 1989); see also the extensive discussion on the applicability of the New York Convention to arbitration agreements in *Smith Enron Cogeneration Limited Partnership, Inc et al v Smith Cogeneration International, Inc*, XXV YBCA 1088 (2000) paras 2-12 (2d Cir).

[44] See also Austria, Oberster Gerichtshof, 17 November 1974, I *YBCA* 183 (1976) 183; Switzerland, Tribunal Fédéral, 7 February 1984, *Tradax Export SA v Amoco Iran Oil Company*, XI YBCA 532 (1986) 533.

[45] See New York Convention Article II; European Convention 1961 Article I(2)(a); Model Law Article 7; Germany, ZPO section 1031; England, Arbitration Act section 5; Netherlands, CCP Article 1021; Switzerland, PIL Article 178.

law applicable to formal validity but by no means solves all problems. As the various substantive conflict rules differ as to the required form it has to be determined which rule is actually applicable. This process raises questions as to:

- The relationship between the form requirements contained in the international conventions and the often wider provisions in the national arbitration laws;
- The scope of application of the substantive rules contained in the national arbitration laws, in particular the Model Law; and
- The rules relevant for an arbitration tribunal in determining the formal validity of an arbitration agreement.

3.1. Article II New York Convention and the Different National Form Requirements

6-38 The New York Convention contains a uniform substantive rule on the form of arbitration agreements. Article II(1)[46] requires the agreements to be in writing. According to the definition in Article II(2) this covers agreements "signed by the parties or contained in an exchange of letters or telegrams."

6-39 It is now generally accepted that the New York Convention sets a maximum standard: arbitration clauses cannot be submitted to stricter requirements under national law.[47] Therefore, any arbitration agreement which fulfils the form requirement of Article II(2) New York Convention must be enforced by the courts of a contracting state, regardless of any stricter form

---

[46] Article II(1) provides

> Each Contracting State shall recognize an agreement in writing under which the parties undertake to submit to arbitration all or any differences which have arisen or which may arise between them in respect of a defined legal relationship, whether contractual or not, which are considered as commercial under the national law of the State making such declaration.

[47] Friedland, "US Courts' Misapplication of the "Agreement in Writing" Requirement for Enforcement of an Arbitration Agreement under the New York Convention", 15(5) *Mealey's IAR* 21 (1998) 25; Alvarez, "Article II(2) of the New York Convention and the Courts", *ICCA Congress series no 9*, 67, 69 *et seq.*

requirements of the national arbitration law which existed, for example, for a long time in Italian law.[48]

6-40 An interesting question is whether this also covers the special form requirements existing in a number of countries for arbitration agreements in consumer contracts.[49] Unless the Contracting State when signing the New York Convention has declared that it will only apply the Convention to commercial transactions it should in general also apply to arbitration agreements in consumer contracts. Consequently, Article II would exclude reliance on stricter form requirements for such arbitration agreements subject to arbitrability.[50]

6-41 However, national arbitration laws often adopt a more permissive definition of "writing" than the New York Convention. Accordingly an arbitration agreement which does not meet the form requirement of Article II may satisfy the more lenient form requirements of the applicable national law.[51] In such a situation the question as to the relationship of the different form requirements arises.

6-42 It is not clear whether Article II(2) is also the teste to b applied for enforcement of the award under the New York Convention.[52]

6-43 To attain the intended harmonising effect in respect of enforcement of arbitration agreements under the New York Convention, acknowledgement of such a minimum standard would be necessary.[53] As a consequence parties to an arbitration agreement which meets the more lenient form requirements of a national law but not that of the New York Convention may not be able to rely on

---

[48] Before the enactment of Law no 25, 5 January 1994, several Italian courts declared null and void arbitration agreements reached by an exchange of faxes. Article 2 of Law no 25 clarifies that "written form" includes all agreements reached by fax.

[49] See, *e.g.*, Germany, ZPO section 1031(5) which requires that the agreement must be contained in a separate document, signed by the consumer.

[50] For example, a German court could not rely on the fact that an arbitration agreement did not meet the special form requirement in ZPO section 1031(5) (separate document/signed by the consumer) to assume jurisdiction, as long as the agreement fulfils the form requirements of Article II(2). By contrast the German court would be required under Article II(3) to refer the parties to arbitration.

[51] See, *e.g,*, Italy CCP Article 807 requiring the arbitration agreement to be in writing on the sanction of nullity. See for further examples van Houtte, "Consent to Arbitration Through Agreement to Printed Contracts: The Continental Experience", 16 *Arb Int* 1 (2000) 7 *et seq.*

[52] Articles IV(1)(6) and V(1)(a).

[53] For a summary of the discussion see Di Pietro and Platte, *Enforcement of International Arbitration Awards,* 81.

the provisions of the New York Convention to enforce the arbitration agreement or an award based on it.[54]

6-44 Parties could only enforce the agreement under the provisions of the national law where appropriate. The most favourable treatment clause in Article VII New York Convention allows parties to rely on the more favourable provision of national laws and treaties.[55] In those cases, however, enforcement is not based on the New York Convention but on local law which in practice can make a considerable difference.[56] For example, parties to an oral agreement which refers to a document containing an arbitration clause will be able to resist court proceedings in England; an English court could not assume jurisdiction by referring to the non-fulfilment of the form requirements of the New York Convention. Since the agreement fulfils the form requirements of Section 5(3) Arbitration Act 1996 the courts would refer the parties to arbitration. By contrast no such obligation would exist for an Italian court.[57] Since the agreement does not meet the form requirement of Article II(2) New York Convention nor of the Italian arbitration law the court could assume jurisdiction.

---

54 See Germany, Oberlandesgericht, Schleswig, 30 March 2000, 46 *RIW* 706 (2000) 707; Switzerland, Obergericht Basle, 5 July 1994, *DIETF v RF AG*, XXI YBCA 685 (1996) 688; Friedland, "US Courts' Misapplication of the "Agreement in Writing" Requirement for Enforcement of an Arbitration Agreement under the New York Convention", 15(5) *Mealey's IAR* 21 (1998) 25; van den Berg, *New York Arbitration Convention*, 179 *et seq*, who has, however, questioned that view in a more recent keynote address at the ICCA Congress in Paris; van den Berg, "The Application of the New York Convention by Courts", *ICCA Congress series no 9*, 25, 32. For a different view see Herrmann, "Does the World Need Additional Uniform Legislation on Arbitration? The 1998 Freshfields Lecture", 15 *Arb Int* 211 (1999) 217; Fouchard Gaillard Goldman *on International Commercial Arbitration*, para 271. The situation may also be different under the European Convention which in its definition of the term 'arbitration agreement' in Article I(2)(a) explicitly includes agreements which do not fulfil the writing requirement set out in the provision but are valid according to the law of the states involved.

55 A more favourable provision can be found in the European Convention 1961 Article I(2)(a) according to which more lenient national form requirements also fulfil the form requirement of the Convention itself; see, *e.g.*, Oberlandesgericht Hamburg, 22 September 1978, V *YBCA* 262 (1980) 263 *et seq.*

56 In the US the question on which provisions a court relies for the enforcement of an agreement may have consequences on which courts have jurisdiction, federal courts or state courts.

57 Italy, CCP Articles 807 and 833 concerning international arbitration.

3.2. Scope of Article 7 Model Law and Comparable Provisions

6-45 Problems as to the law applicable to formal validity may also arise under the Model Law. According to the wording of Article 1(2) most provisions of the Model Law, including Article 7 governing the form requirement are applicable only if the place of arbitration is in the territory of the state. If the arbitration agreement provides for arbitration abroad, courts in Model Law countries are faced with the difficult question of which law governs the issue of formal validity. Is it the law at the place of arbitration? Article II New York Convention? Or is Article 7, despite the clear wording of Article I(2), the relevant rule?

6-46 A German court, for example, could be faced with this question when asked to determine the formal validity of an arbitration agreement providing for arbitration in France. According to the wording of section 1025 ZPO,[58] the rules regulating the form of arbitration agreements[59] would not be applicable, since the place of arbitration is not in Germany. The ZPO is, however, silent as to which standard should be applied to determine whether a matter has to be referred to arbitration. To do so only if the arbitration agreement meets the requirements of Article II(2) New York Convention would lead to the result that arbitration agreements providing for arbitration abroad would be submitted to stricter form requirements than those providing for arbitration in Germany. This would be inappropriate where the German interest in the case is minimal.

6-47 The other option would be to determine the formal validity of the arbitration agreement by reference to the law of the place of arbitration, *i.e.* in the above example, French law which allows for oral agreements for international arbitrations.[60] However, this would make it easy for a party to circumvent the writing requirement under German law. The principle of territoriality enshrined in the Model Law is an argument in favour of relying on the place of arbitration. The prevailing tendency in state practice is, however, that each state wants to determine for itself under which circumstances the jurisdiction of its courts can be excluded, *i.e.*, whether or not a written agreement is required.

---

[58] Model Law Article 1(2).

[59] Germany, ZPO section 1032.

[60] De Boisséson, *Le droit français de l'arbitrage,* 477; for a different view see Lörcher, *Das Internationale Handelsschiedsverfahren in Frankreich* (Carl Heymanns 1996), 47.

3.3. Laws to be Applied by Arbitrator

6-48 When the issue of formal validity arises in proceedings before an arbitration tribunal which different substantive rules should the arbitrators apply. It is often assumed that an arbitrator should measure the formal validity of the arbitration agreement against the standard contained in Article II New York Convention.[61] The provisions of the New York Convention, however, are only directly binding on the courts in the Member States and not on the arbitration tribunal.[62] Nevertheless, there are good reasons why an arbitration tribunal should base its decision on the New York Convention. The widespread applicability of the Convention and that enforcement under the Convention is only possible if the form requirement is met are strong arguments in favour of the application of Article II. Thus, taking into account this fact the arbitrator should render an enforceable award.[63]

6-49 If, however, the arbitration agreement does not meet the form requirements of Article II but does satisfy the more lenient requirements of the law at the seat of arbitration, the tribunal should assume jurisdiction to give effect to the parties agreement. At that early stage it cannot be decided with any certainty whether and where enforcement will be necessary. Enforcement may be possible either in the country where the award was rendered or in a country which recognises that form of arbitration agreement.

4. LAW APPLICABLE TO CAPACITY OF THE PARTIES

6-50 Few arbitration laws deal directly with the issue of what law governs the capacity of the parties to enter into an arbitration agreement. One exception is Article VI European Convention according to which the issue is governed by the "law applicable to the parties." The New York Convention and most national arbitration laws address the issue within the context of enforcement or setting aside an award. According to Article V(1)(a) recognition and enforcement of an award can be refused if the parties to the agreement were "under the law

---

61 Cour d'appel Paris, 20 January 1987, *Bonmar Oil NV v Entreprise Tunisienne d'Activités*, XIII YBCA 466 (1988) 469.

62 ICC case no 5730 of 1988, 117 *Clunet* 1029 (1990) 1033; see also critical comment by Loquin, 114 *Clunet* 934 (1987) to the above mentioned *Bonmar* decision of the Paris Court of Appeal.

63 See van den Berg, *New York Arbitration Convention*, 189 *et seq* with further references; the obligation to render an enforceable award is expressly mentioned in some arbitration rules such as the ICC Rules Article 35.

applicable to them", under some incapacity.[64] Comparable provisions can be found in a number of national arbitration laws.[65]

6-51 These provisions do not define how the law applicable to the parties' capacity is determined. Therefore, what law is applicable has to be determined in accordance with the general conflict of laws provisions. These generally consider either a party's nationality, place of incorporation, main place of business, domicile or residence to be the relevant connecting factors.

5. Law Applicable to Substantive Validity of the Arbitration Agreement

6-52 There are different approaches to determining the law applicable to all other issues of the agreement in the various legal instruments and international practice. Some laws take a traditional conflict of laws approach; others contain specific substantive conflict rules. French arbitration law aims to determine the validity of the arbitration agreement on the basis of the parties' intent without any reference to a national law.

5.1. Traditional Conflict of Laws Approaches

6-53 The New York Convention as well as most national arbitration laws contain no special provisions dealing with the law applicable to the various aspects of the arbitration agreement. They do, however, deal with the issue in the annulment and enforcement context where the lack of a valid arbitration agreement in general constitutes a defence against an application to set aside or enforce an award.

6-54 Article V(1)(a) New York Convention provides that enforcement may be refused where the arbitration

---

[64] While Article 34(2)(a)(i) Model Law only refers to incapacity but not to the law governing the issue, enactments of the Model Law such as Article 1059(2)(1)(a) German ZPO contain a reference to the "law applicable to the parties."

[65] See Hong Kong, Arbitration Ordinance section 44(2)(a). Some laws just declare the provisions of the New York Convention applicable. See, *e.g.*, Switzerland, PIL Article 194; Germany, ZPO section 1061(1); Model Law Article 36(1)(a)(i) only mentions incapacity as a ground for refusing enforcement without indicating which law is to govern that issue.

> … agreement is not valid under the law to which the *parties have subjected it* or, failing any indication thereon, under the law of the *country where the award was made*. [Emphasis added]

6-55 Comparable provisions can be found in most national arbitration laws, including Article 36(1)(a)(i) Model Law. Though these provisions address the issue only from the perspective of the annulment or enforcement judge, there is a strong argument in favour of applying the same criteria at the pre-award stage.[66] The application of different criteria at the pre-award stage could entail the danger of divergent decisions. Accordingly, an arbitration agreement considered valid if challenged at the outset, could be set aside because the agreement does not meet the requirements of the law chosen or the law of the place of arbitration. It cannot, however, be excluded that there will be decisions going the other way, applying different criteria at the pre-award stage than those set out for the enforcement stage.[67]

6-56 No such uncertainty exists under the few laws which contain a provision determining the law applicable to the arbitration agreement. The Swedish Arbitration Act is a rare example of this second approach. Section 48 provides

> Where an arbitration agreement has an international connection, the agreement shall be governed by the law agreed upon by the parties. Where the parties have not reached such an agreement, the arbitration agreement shall be governed by the law of the country in which, by virtue of the agreement, the proceedings have taken place or shall take place. The first paragraph shall not apply to the issue of whether a party was authorised to enter into an arbitration agreement or was duly represented.[68]

6-57 This approach has a considerable advantage in comparison to the indirect rules contained in most other laws. It ensures that Swedish courts will apply the

---

66 In favour of such an approach see, *e.g.*, Corte d'Appello Genoa, 3 February 1990, *Della Sanara Kustvaart - Bevrachting & Overslagbedrijf BV v Fallimento Cap Giovanni Coppola srl*, XVII YBCA 542 (1992) 543.

67 See, *e.g.*, the US decision in *Meadows Indemnity Co Ltd v Baccala & Shoop Insurance Services Inc*, XVII YBCA 686 (1992) 689 (EDNY, 29 March 1991); Belgian decision, Cour d'appel Brussels, 4 October 1985, *Company M v M SA*, XIV YBCA 618 (1989) 619.

68 For a detailed analysis of the provision see Hober, "Arbitration Reform in Sweden", 17 *Arb Int* 351 (2001) 355; see also Article 7 Mercosur. A comparable provision, which even determines what is to happen where the parties have not determined the place of arbitration, can be found in Article VI European Convention 1961.

same criteria to determine the applicable law, irrespective of whether the question arises at pre or post award stage.

6-58 In general these provisions, whether they deal with the issue of the applicable law directly or only from the perspective of the annulment or enforcement court, submit the law applicable to the arbitration agreement to the same two criteria: the law chosen by the parties and in the absence of such a choice the law of the place of arbitration.

6-59 In practice it is rare that the parties have expressly chosen the law applicable to the arbitration agreement. However, frequently a choice made in relation to the law governing the merits can be interpreted to apply also to the arbitration agreement.[69] The choice of arbitration rules is of little help in determining the law applicable to the arbitration agreement. Most arbitration rules presuppose the existence of a valid arbitration agreement but do not contain any substantive rules governing the issue. In fact, the rules are activated only if there is a *prima facie* arbitration agreement. Only the WIPO Rules contain a conflict of laws provision on how to determine the law applicable to the arbitration agreement. Other rules contain provisions only dealing with the law applicable to the merits.[70] Article 59(c) WIPO Rules provides

> An Arbitration Agreement shall be regarded as effective if it conforms to the requirements concerning form, existence, validity and scope of either the law or rules of law applicable in accordance with paragraph (a) [law chosen by the parties], or the law applicable in accordance with paragraph (b) [law of the place of arbitration].

6-60 This article is subject to further interpretation. It basically repeats the criteria found in most national laws and the New York Convention but does not

---

[69] See from the arbitration practice NOFOTA award, 5 September 1977, IV *YBCA* 218 (1979) 219; ICC case no 2626, 105 *Clunet* 980 (1978) 981; ICC case no 6840, 119 *Clunet* 1030 (1992) 1032; ICC case no 6379, XVII *YBCA* 212 (1992) 215; see also for Germany: Bundesgerichtshof, 28 November 1963, 40 *BGHZ* 320, 323; Bundesgerichtshof 12 December 1976, *RIW* 449 (1976); Oberlandesgericht Hamburg, 22 September 1978, V *YBCA* 262 (1980) 264; for English cases see Russell *on Arbitration*, para 2-094; Merkin, *Arbitration Act*, 180 and *ABB Lummus Global Ltd v Keppel Fels Ltd* [1999] 2 Lloyd's Rep 24; *Sonatrach Petroleum Corp v Ferrell International Ltd* [2002] 1 All ER (Comm) 627.

[70] It is not uncommon however that those rules are also applied in determining the law applicable to the arbitration agreement. Since the rules in general do not provide for a specific connecting factor but give the arbitrator the discretion to decide which conflict of laws rule or which law to apply the consequences of that misapplication are not of greater relevance.

contain a choice of the applicable law. Consequently it is then the law at the place of arbitration which governs the arbitration agreement.

6-61 A good example for the reasoning applied where the parties have not determined the law applicable to the arbitration agreement is provided by the decision of the Dutch Court of Appeal in The Hague in *Owerri v Dielle*.[71] In this case concerning the enforcement of a foreign award the arbitration agreement did not meet the form requirements of the New York Convention so enforcement had to be sought under the more favourable Dutch law. According to Article 1076(1)(A)(a) Netherlands Code of Civil Procedure recognition can be denied if "a valid arbitration agreement under the law applicable thereto is lacking." Relying on the relevant Dutch conflict of laws rules the court had to determine which law was the most closely connected with the arbitration agreement. It held

> [9] The court is of the opinion, as opposed to Dielle, that the closest connection is with English law. The connecting factor is to be found in the place of arbitration and is in conformity with Art. V(1)(a) New York Convention which states that the validity of the arbitration agreement, in absence of a choice of law, has to be determined according to the law of the country where the award was made. This rule can be considered as a general rule of private international law as a result of the broad international influence of the Convention and in addition it has been recognized and adopted by the Dutch legislator, as appears from Art. 1073 CCP.
> [10] Furthermore it is usual to make a connection with the so-called lex fori of the arbitrators. Here it is an issue of the recognition and enforcement of the awards made in London and the related question whether the arbitrators could base their jurisdiction upon a valid arbitration agreement. This question is to be decided according to procedural arbitration law of the place of arbitration, London, in accordance with the arbitral clause (Art. 30) in the FOSFA conditions and the Rules of Arbitration, to which Art. 30 refers. Therefore it must be concluded that English law is applicable.
> [11] Needless to say, parties, in general, would prefer - excluding special circumstances which do not arise in this case - to submit the validity of the arbitration clause to the same law to which they submitted the main agreement of which the arbitration clause forms a part. According to Art. 28 of the FOSFA Conditions, English law is applicable. An indication can also be found here -

---

[71] Gerechtshof, The Hague, 4 August 1993, *Owerri Commercial Inc v Dielle Srl*, XIX YBCA 703 (1994).

although not sufficient in itself - that the question should be decided according to English law.[72]

6-62 Under the New York Convention and similar laws in the absence of a choice of law provision the place of arbitration, where it has been chosen by the parties, may be the strongest connecting factor to the arbitration agreement. It is the place where the arbitration agreement is to be performed and where the existence of the agreement might be tested in setting aside procedures.[73]

5.2. Substantive Rule of Private International Law

6-63 Swiss arbitration law contains a rare example of a substantive rule on the validity of an arbitration agreement. This approach avoids the pitfalls of the conflict of laws analysing the categorisation of the arbitration agreement and the idiosyncrasies of the applicable national private international law rules. It considers it to be sufficient if the arbitration agreement fulfils the requirements of either the law governing the main contract or Swiss law. Article 178(2) PIL provides

> As regards its substance, an arbitration agreement shall be valid if it conforms either to the law chosen by the parties, or to the law governing the subject-matter of the dispute, in particular the law governing the main contract, or it conforms to Swiss law.

6-64 This Swiss rule goes further than any of the traditional conflict of laws approaches in upholding the validity of an arbitration agreement. Generally, an agreement which does not fulfil the requirements of the chosen law is invariably invalid. By contrast, Swiss courts will enforce an agreement considered to be valid under Swiss law or the law governing the main contract. Accordingly, there may be an issue on enforcement under the New York Convention since the invalidity of an arbitration agreement according to the law chosen by the parties can justify refusal of enforcement.

---

[72] *Ibid*, 706. For an application of the conflict rule contained in Article V(1)(a) see the decision of the Swiss Tribunal Fédéral, 21 March 1995, XXII *YBCA* 800 (1997) 804 *et seq.*

[73] Some decisions have treated the express choice of a place of arbitration by the parties as an implied choice of the law applicable to the arbitration agreement: Arrondissementsrechtbank Rotterdam, 28 September 1995, *Petrasol BV v Stolt Spur Inc*, XXII YBCA 762 (1997) 765. See also *XL Insurance Ltd v Owens Corning,* (2001) XXVI YBCA 869, 883.

5.3. French Approach

6-65 A substantive rule approach can be found in the French arbitration law. It was developed by the Cour de cassation in the *Dalico*[74] decision in 1993. The case arose out of a contract for the construction of a water supply between the Libyan municipal authority and a Danish contractor. The contract, submitted to Libyan law, provided that the general conditions of contract, supplemented or amended by an annex, were considered to be an integral part of the contract. The Danish contractor started arbitration proceedings on the basis of an arbitration clause contained in the annex which was not signed by the parties. The Libyan respondent challenged the jurisdiction of the arbitration tribunal, alleging that under Libyan law the arbitration clause was invalid. The arbitrator rejected that plea and the Libyan party applied to the French courts to have the award set aside. The Court of Appeal rejected the application finding that both parties consented to arbitration without determining which law was applicable to the arbitration agreement. The Cour de cassation upheld that decision finding that

> ... according to a substantive rule of international arbitration law the arbitration clause is legally independent from the main contract in which it is included or which refers to it and, provided that no mandatory provision of French law or international ordre public is affected, that its existence and its validity depends only on the common intention of the parties, without it being necessary to make reference to a national law.[75]

6-66 This approach has been followed in other French decisions and is supported in the literature.[76] Taking into account the international character of arbitration, the validity should be determined independently from the provisions of any national law. In addition to the limits imposed by international public policy only the mandatory provision of French law remain applicable. In this respect the French courts stopped short of a complete delocalisation of the arbitration agreement.

---

74 French Cour de cassation, 20 December 1993, *Comité populaire de la municipalité de Khoms El Mergeb v Dalico Contractors,* 121 Clunet 432 (1994).

75 Authors' translation.

76 See, *e.g.*, Cour de cassation, 21 May 1997, *Renault v V 2000 (formerly Jaguar France)*, Rev Arb 537 (1997), with note Gaillard; Cour d' appel Paris, 25 November 1999, *SA Burkinabe des ciments et matériaux v société des ciments d'Abidjan*, Rev Arb 165 (2001) 168 in relation to the rules governing the assignment of the arbitration clause; Cour de cassation, 5 January 1999, *Banque Worms v Bellot*, Rev Arb 85 (2000) 86. For the development of the rule and its reception in France see Fouchard Gaillard Goldman *on International Commercial Arbitration*, paras 435 *et seq.*

5.4. International Arbitration Practice

6-67 A comparable if not greater divergence of approach exists in reported arbitration practice.[77] This is partly due to two additional problems faced by arbitration tribunals in determining the applicable law: the lack of a directly applicable conflict rules, and the tribunal's obligation to render a valid award.

6-68 In many cases a traditional conflict of laws approach is adopted and there is wide consent that the primary factor in determining the applicable law is party autonomy. The differences relate primarily to the relevant connecting factors where the parties have not chosen the law applicable to the arbitration agreement. The factors employed in these cases include the place where the arbitration agreement was concluded, the law governing the main contract, the law of the probable place of enforcement, and a combination of some of those factors.[78]

6-69 In most cases tribunals relying on Article V(1)(a) New York Convention, consider the place of arbitration as the relevant factor to determine the applicable law, if no choice has been made by the parties.[79] A typical example is the interim award in ICC Case 6149.[80] The dispute concerned three sales contracts between a Korean seller and a Jordanian buyer which provided for arbitration under the ICC rules. The defendant challenged the jurisdiction of the arbitration tribunal alleging that the arbitration clause was not valid according to a mandatory provision of Jordanian law. The tribunal decided that this provision was not applicable since the validity of the arbitration agreement was governed by a different law. In determining that law it held

> Pursuant to [the then] Art. 13(3) of the ICC Rules of Conciliation and Arbitration, failing any indication by the parties as to the applicable law, the arbitrator shall apply the law designated as the proper law by the rule of conflict which he deems appropriate. If, according to the second doctrine, the proper law of the three arbitration agreements could not necessarily be derived from the proper law of the three sales contracts themselves, the only other rule of conflicts of laws whose

---

77 Blessing, "The Law Applicable to the Arbitration Clause and Arbitrability", *ICCA Congress series no 9*, 169, 171 *et seq* set out not less than nine different approaches used in international arbitration practice to determine the law applicable to the arbitration agreement.

78 Others factors employed are the origin of the parties and the proper law of the arbitration agreement.

79 Lew, "The Law Applicable to the Form and Substance of the Arbitration Clause", *ICCA Congress series no 9*, 114, 126 *et seq*; Bernardini,"Achieving Effectiveness in the Law Applicable to the Arbitration Clause", van den Berg (ed) *ICCA Congress series no 9*, 197, 201.

80 Interim Award in ICC case no 6149 of 1990, XX *YBCA* 41 (1995).

> application would seem appropriate in the sense of the above-mentioned Art. 13(3), would be the application of the law where the arbitration takes place and where the award is rendered.
> This conclusion would be supported also by Art. V(1)(a) of the ...[1958 New York] Convention which has been ratified by the Republic of Korea, Jordan, France and Iraq. According to the said Art. V, the validity of the arbitration agreement has to be determined 'under the law of the country where the award was made'.[81]

6-70 The reason for such an approach is primarily the often claimed duty to render an enforceable award. So for example, in ICC Case 5485[82] the tribunal in determining the applicable law held

> Whereas Art. 26 [now Article 35] of the ICC Rules of Arbitration establishes that the arbitrators shall make every effort to make sure that the award is enforceable at law. As the place of this arbitration is the city of Paris (France), the Tribunal has examined French law (Nouveau Code de Procédure Civile, Arts. 1492 to 1497) and have concluded that said law contains nothing which is in conflict with the full validity and effectiveness of the arbitration clause in dispute. Again, the parties have sustained nothing to the contrary.[83]

6-71 Determining the validity of an arbitration agreement by reference to the same rules as the courts at the place of arbitration may reduce the risk of rendering an award which is unenforceable or susceptible to challenges. Enforcement can normally be resisted if the award has been set aside in the country where it was rendered. In those annulment procedures at the place of arbitration the courts base their findings on the existence of a valid arbitration agreement on their own law, *i.e.* the law of the place of arbitration. If an arbitrator has determined the validity of the agreement under a different law it is possible that the courts could decide in annulment proceedings that the agreement was invalid under the law of the place of arbitration.

6-72 By contrast, under Article V(1)(a) New York Convention Contracting States are bound to recognise awards based on agreements which are valid or enforceable according to the law of the place of arbitration. This supports the

---

81 *Ibid*, 44 *et seq*; see also ICC case no 5721 of 1990, 117 *Clunet* 1019 (1990) 1021; ICC case no 4504, 113 *Clunet* 1118 (1986) 1119; ICC case no 5485 of 1987, XIV *YBCA* 156 (1989) 160 *et seq*; Preliminary Award in ICC case no 5505 of 1987, XIII *YBCA* 110 (1988) 116 *et seq*; Interim Award in ICC case no 4145, XII *YBCA* 97 (1987); ICC case no 4392, 110 *Clunet* 907 (1983); ICC case no 4472, 111 *Clunet* 946 (1984) 947.

82 ICC case no 5485 of 1987, XIV *YBCA* 156 (1989).

83 *Ibid*, para 15.

presumption that that law is applicable to the arbitration agreement. Furthermore where the law of the place of arbitration and any other law applied by the tribunal come to a different result regarding the validity of the agreement the parties may be unable to rely on the supportive powers of the local courts. Before such local courts grant interim relief, support the taking of evidence or order other measures in support of an arbitration, they may seek to decide the existence of a valid arbitration agreement according to the rules applicable to them.[84]

6-73 In arbitration practice there is also a trend to detach the question of the existence of a valid arbitration agreement from any national law and to determine it by reference to the parties' intent and general principles applicable to international arbitration. A well known example of this approach is the preliminary award in *Dow Chemical v Isover Saint Gobain*.[85] The case arose out of a contract submitted to French law and providing for arbitration under ICC Rules. The contract was only signed by one member of the Dow Chemical Group, rather than by all claimants which all belonged to the group. The respondent challenged the jurisdiction of the tribunal in relation to the parties who had not signed the contract arguing that the scope and validity of the arbitration agreement should be governed by the law applicable to the contract. The tribunal in an interim award on jurisdiction rejected those objections. It decided that, under the chosen ICC Rules, since the arbitration agreement was a separate agreement, the tribunal could decide on its own jurisdiction without being bound to apply a specific law. Determining the law governing the arbitration clause the tribunal held

> Considering that the tribunal shall, accordingly, determine the scope and effect of the arbitration clauses in question, and thereby reach its decision regarding jurisdiction, by reference to the common intent of the parties to these proceedings, such as it appears from the circumstances that surround the conclusion and characterize the performance and later the termination of the contracts in which they appear. In doing so, the tribunal, following, in particular, French case law relating to international arbitration should also take into account, usages conforming to the needs of international commerce, in particular, in the presence of a group of companies.

---

[84] See, *e.g.*, the German decision of the Bayerisches Oberlandesgericht, 28 February 2000, 4Z *Sch* 13/99, 1 *RPS* 15 (2000) where an application to appoint an arbitrator was denied, since the court considered the arbitration clause to be void for uncertainty.

[85] Interim Award in ICC case no 4131 of 1982, *Dow Chemical France et al v Isover Saint Gobain*, IX YBCA 131 (1984).

> Considering that in conformity with the 'General rule' set forth in Article 31 (1955 version) and Article 26 of the 'Arbitration' Section of the ICC Rules, the tribunal will however make every effort to make sure that the award is enforceable at law. To this end, it will assure itself that the solution it adopts is compatible with international public policy, in particular, in France.[86]

6-74 This approach based solely on the intention of the parties and the limits of public policy has found support in some of the literature. It is based on the idea that the arbitrators have no institutional reason to apply the conflict of laws rules or substantive rules of a given country and should therefore rely on a substantive rule of international arbitration.[87]

---

[86] *Ibid*, 134; see also ICC case no 5721, 117 *Clunet* 1019 (1990) 1023; ICC case no 2375, 103 *Clunet* 973 (1976) 973 *et seq.*

[87] Fouchard Gaillard Goldman *on International Commercial Arbitration*, para 443 *et seq*, who argue that such an approach would lead to more predictable results and avoid the pitfalls of the conflict of laws approach; Blessing, "The Law Applicable to the Arbitration Clause and Arbitrability", van den Berg (ed), *ICCA Congress series no 9*, 169, 174.

Chapter 7

ARBITRATION AGREEMENTS – VALIDITY AND INTERPRETATION

7-1 An arbitration agreement is the expression of the intent of the parties to withdraw their disputes from a national court system and to submit them to arbitration. The arbitration agreement will deliver the intended results if it is enforceable. Only if it was validly entered into and covers the dispute in question will courts deny jurisdiction.

7-2 The special procedural effects of the arbitration agreement find their expression primarily in the limitation to the admissibility of such agreements, known as arbitrability. Certain types of disputes cannot be referred to arbitration but are reserved for the exclusive jurisdiction of state courts. In addition the procedural effects have lead in most countries to form requirements and influenced the means of enforcement of the agreement.

7-3 Despite its procedural effects, the arbitration agreement is primarily a substantive contract by which the parties agree to refer their disputes to arbitration instead of the state courts. This implies that for the agreement to come into existence the requirements for the conclusion of a contract must be fulfilled. The parties must have agreed the extent of the referral to arbitration and there should be no factors present which may vitiate their consent under general contract law. Furthermore, the parties must have had capacity to enter into an arbitration agreement. In this respect the arbitration agreement is a contract like any other contract.

7-4 This chapter deals with (1) the formal validity of the arbitration agreement, (2) the capacity of the parties to enter into an arbitration agreement, (3) its substantive validity, (4) its scope and interpretation, (5) the effects and the enforcement of arbitration agreements, and (6) its termination and the waiver of the right to arbitrate.

1. Formal Validity of the Arbitration Agreement

7-5 The formal validity of an arbitration agreement is closely related to the issue of whether the party actually consented to arbitration. The formal requirements are intended to ensure that the parties actually agreed on arbitration. Consequently questions as to the fulfilment of the form requirements and the necessary consent are often interwoven and treated jointly. However, there are cases where national courts despite an agreement to arbitrate have accepted jurisdiction over a dispute because the arbitration agreement did not fulfil the necessary form requirements.[1]

7-6 Most international conventions and national arbitration laws contain substantive conflict of laws provisions in relation to form requirements. Few national laws allow for an oral arbitration agreement.[2] However, the majority of

---

1 Corte di cassazione, 28 October 1993, *Robobar Ltd v Finncold sas*, XX YBCA 739 (1995) 740; Germany, Bayerisches Oberstes Landesgericht, 12 December 2002, 4 *Z Sch* 16/02.

2 French law is an exception with regard to international arbitration. See Cour d'appel Paris, 8 June 1995, *Sarl Centro Stoccaggio Grani v SA Granit*, Rev Arb 89 (1997); Fouchard Gaillard

arbitration laws, including the Model Law, in line with the international conventions, require arbitration agreements to be either in writing or at least to be evidenced in writing.[3] This is now also the case in the new German and Dutch laws, which traditionally allowed for oral agreements.[4]

1.1. Form Requirement: Function and Criticism

7-7 The rationale underlying the writing requirement has two aspects. First, in light of the legal consequences connected with the conclusion of an arbitration agreement the writing requirement is intended to ensure that the parties actually agreed on arbitration. As the agreement to arbitrate may lead to renunciation by the parties of their constitutional right to have their disputes decided in court, the written form aims to prevent the agreement going unnoticed. Second, writing provides a record of the agreement which helps to prove the existence and the content of an arbitration agreement in subsequent proceedings.[5] In fact under the New York Convention enforcement of the arbitration agreement and any award requires a written arbitration agreement. The drafters of the Model Law did not want to set up form requirements in conflict with the New York Convention.[6]

7-8 Form requirements sometimes do not always reflect business practice. While in certain areas of trade parties often rely on oral agreements, strict form requirements can defeat an agreement to arbitrate, the existence of which is beyond doubt. It has been criticised correctly that the parties can orally agree a

---

Goldman *on International Commercial Arbitration*, paras 608 *et seq*. In England, common law still recognises an oral arbitration agreement but it cannot be enforced under the Arbitration Act; see Merkin, *Arbitration Act*, 27.

3 Model Law Article 7(2); for other Model Law countries see Sanders, *Quo Vadis Arbitration?*, 101, 155; Austria, CCP Article 577(3); China, Arbitration Law Article 16; England, Arbitration Act section 5; France, NCPC Articles 1443, 1449 (for domestic arbitration); US, FAA section 2; for a more complete list see Alvarez, "Article II(2) of the New York Convention and the Courts", *ICCA Congress series no* 9, 67, 68; see also survey of national laws in preparation for the Model Law: First Secretariat Note, A/CN9/207, paras 40 *et seq*.

4 See for Germany, ZPO section 1027(2) pre-1998 version, Schlosser, *Internationale Schiedsgerichtsbarkeit*, 261 para 360; for Netherlands see van den Berg, van Delden, Snijders, *Netherlands Arbitration Law*, 36 para 4-8-2.

5 ICC case no 5832, 115 *Clunet* 1198 (1988) 1202; Herrmann, "The Arbitration Agreement as the Foundation of Arbitration and Its Recognition by the Courts", *ICCA Congress series no 6*, 41, 44; Reiner, "The Form of the Agent's Power to Sign an Arbitration Agreement and Article II(2) of the New York Convention", *ICCA Congress series no 9*, 82, 85 *et seq*.

6 See First Working Group Report, A/CN9/216, para 23; Commission Report, A/40/17, paras 85 *et seq*.

multi-million dollar contract which will be considered to be valid but for the arbitration clause.[7] The arbitration agreement would be invalid irrespective of whether it can be established that the parties actually agreed on arbitration. A party can enforce the substantive provisions of a contract while being able to walk away from the agreement to arbitrate concluded at the same time.

7-9 There is no justification to submit arbitration agreements to stricter form requirements than other contractual provisions. Arbitration is no longer considered a dangerous waiver of substantial rights. In fact the selection of arbitration is not an exclusion of the national forum but rather the natural forum for international disputes.[8] Form requirements do not necessarily promote legal certainty; they are often the source of additional disputes. For these reasons the writing requirements in most national laws and under the New York Convention have been liberally interpreted.

7-10 This all supports the complete abolition of the "in-writing" requirement[9] or at least the submission of the issue of formal validity to a substantive rule of international arbitration.[10] In any event, the writing requirement should be interpreted dynamically in the light of modern means of communication. Arbitration clauses included in contracts negotiated and concluded by e-mail should be accepted as fulfilling the writing requirement in line with the general development that contracts which require written form but are concluded by e-mail are valid.[11]

---

7 Kaplan, "Is the Need for Writing as Expressed in the New York Convention and the Model Law Out of Step with Commercial Practice?", 12 *Arb Int* 27 (1996) 30 *et seq*; Herrmann, "The Arbitration Agreement as the Foundation of Arbitration and Its Recognition by the Courts", *ICCA Congress series no 6*, 41, 46; Blessing, *Introduction to Arbitration*, para 486.

8 Lionnet, "Rechtspolitische Bedeutung der Schiedsgerichtsbarkeit", in Berger, Ebke, Elsing, Grossfeld & Kuehne (ed), *Festschrift für Otto Sandrock* (Recht und Wirtschaft 2000), 603, 606.

9 Herrmann, "Does the World Need Additional Uniform Legislation on Arbitration? The 1998 Freshfields Lecture", 15 *Arb Int* 211 (1999) 216; Herrmann, "The Arbitration Agreement as the Foundation of Arbitration and Its Recognition by the Courts", *ICCA Congress series no 6*, 41, 45 *et seq*; Sanders, *Quo Vadis Arbitration?*, 157 *et seq*.

10 Blessing, "The Laws Applicable to the Arbitration Clause and Arbitrability", *ICCA Congress series no 9*, 169, 172.

11 The UNCITRAL Model Law on Electronic Commerce Article 6 provides that where the law requires information to be in writing, that requirement is met by a data message if the information contained is accessible so as to be useable for subsequent reference. Many countries with a developed e-commerce practice consider electronic and data messages to be equivalent to written documents. There are also US cases which upheld the validity of arbitration agreements which form part of an online contract. See *Lieschke v RealNetworks, Inc*, no 99C 7274, 99C

1.2. Different International and National Rules

7-11 Despite significant harmonisation, national laws differ considerably as to what satisfies the requirement of a written agreement. This is partly due to the different times at which various rules were drafted. The New York Convention, for example, adopted in 1958, contains a very narrow definition of "writing". Article II(2) provides

> The term "agreement in writing" shall include an arbitral clause in a contract or an arbitration agreement, signed by the parties or contained in an exchange of letters or telegrams.[12]

7-12 The drafters of the Convention did not foresee the revolution in telecommunication technology. Telefax and e-mail were not thought of in 1958. Furthermore the "exchange" requirement has created uncertainties and diverging views.[13]

7-13 The Model Law contains a broader functional definition of the "agreement in writing" in Article 7(2)

> The arbitration agreement shall be in writing. An agreement is in writing if it is contained in a document signed by the parties or in an exchange of letters, telex, telegrams or *other means of telecommunication which provide a record of the agreement*, or in an exchange of statements of claim and defence in which the existence of an agreement is alleged by one party and not denied by another. The reference in a contract to a document containing an arbitration clause constitutes an arbitration agreement provided that the contract is in writing and the reference is such as to make that clause part of the contract. [Emphasis added.]

7380, 2000 WL, XXV YBCA 530 (2000) (ND Ill, 2000), where the arbitration clause was held to be binding on the parties; on the other hand in *Brower v Gateway 2000 Inc*, 676 NYS 2d 569 (NYAD 1998), where the contract was formed, the particular term relating to arbitration was unconscionable and, at least in part, unenforceable. See, however, the misguided, Norway, Hålogaland Court of Appeal, 16 August 1999, *Charterer (Norway) v Shipowner (Russian Federation)*, XXVII YBCA 519 (2002) where enforcement of an award was refused because the arbitration agreement was contained in e-mails.

12 A wider provision is included in the European Convention Article I(2)(a); it refers to an arbitration agreement contained in communications by teleprinters; see Hascher, "European Convention on International Commercial Arbitration of 1961", XX *YBCA* 1006 (1995) 1014.

13 See van den Berg, *New York Convention*, 190 *et seq*, and the various court decisions reported in the *YBCA*. See also Wang, "International Judicial Practice and the Written Form Requirement for International Arbitration Agreements", 10 *Pacific Rim Law and Policy Journal* 375 (2001).

7-14 This provision recognises modern means of telecommunication and can accommodate future developments. The writing requirement will be satisfied provided the means of communications provides a record of the agreement.[14] However, the Model Law still requires an exchange of documents, more or less as evidence of consent. It is doubtful whether a tacit or oral acceptance of a written purchase order or confirmation letter would be valid. The same applies to orally concluded contracts referring to written general conditions, certain brokers' notes, bills of lading or other instruments granting rights to non-signing third parties.[15] The last sentence of Article 7(2) is intended to satisfy the writing requirement when there is reference in a written contract to a separate written arbitration agreement, such as general terms and conditions sent in previous or possibly subsequent communications. An open question remains whether there is an affirmative duty to accept or reject the clause.[16]

7-15 The German Law extended the "in writing" requirement of the Model Law in several respects. Section 1031(2)-(4) ZPO provides

> (2) The form requirement of subsection 1 shall be deemed to have been complied with if the arbitration agreement is contained in a document transmitted from one party to the other party or by a third party to both parties and - if no objection was raised in good time - the contents of such document are considered to be part of the contract in accordance with common usage.
> (3) The reference in a contract complying with the form requirements of subsection 1 or 2 to a document containing an arbitration clause constitutes an arbitration agreement provided that the reference is such as to make that clause part of the contract.
>
> (4) An arbitration agreement is also concluded by the issuance of a bill of lading, if the latter contains an express reference to an arbitration clause in a charter party.

7-16 Section 1031(4) addresses a well known problem under the New York Convention. Section 1031(2) takes account of the German practice, that the absence of an objection in certain circumstances is a tacit consent. Contrary to the Model Law a written assent by both parties is no longer required; it is

---

[14] Holtzmann & Neuhaus, *Model Law,* 262 *et seq.*

[15] *Ibid*, 261; Herrmann, "Does the World Need Additional Uniform Legislation on Arbitration? The 1998 Freshfields Lecture", 15 *Arb Int* 211 (1999) 214 *et seq.* For the unsatisfactory consequences which may result from that see the Hong Kong case *Small v Goldroyce*, [1994] 2 HKC 526.

[16] See UNCITRAL Working Group II (Arbitration and Conciliation), *Preparation of uniform provisions on written form for arbitration agreements*, UN Document A/CN9/WGII/WP118.

sufficient that the arbitration agreement is evidenced in writing. German law imposes an affirmative duty to reject the clause on the party which does not wish to be bound by it.

7-17 The problematic requirement of an exchange of documents has also been discarded in other non-Model Law jurisdictions. For example, article 178(1) Swiss PIL provides

> As regards its form, an arbitration agreement shall be valid if made in writing, by telegram, telex, telecopier or any other means of communication which permits it to be evidenced by a text.

7-18 The English Arbitration Act 1996 even recognises certain categories of oral arbitration agreements. Section 5 provides in pertinent part

> (2) There is an agreement in writing-
> (a) if the agreement is made in writing (whether or not it is signed by the parties),
> (b) if the agreement is made by exchange of communications in writing, or
> (c) if the agreement is evidenced in writing.
> (3) Where parties agree otherwise than in writing by reference to terms which are in writing, they make an agreement in writing.
> (4) An agreement is evidenced in writing if an agreement made otherwise than in writing is recorded by one of the parties, or by a third party, with the authority of the parties to the agreement.

1.3. Interpretation of the Writing Requirement by Courts and Arbitration Tribunals[17]

7-19 National differences are also reflected in the judicial interpretation of the writing requirement pursuant to Article II(2) New York Convention. Indeed adjustments are necessitated by business and technological developments, such as electronic and digital telecommunication which were unknown when the Convention was drafted. The Geneva Court of Appeal, for example, held in 1983

> It is clear that by treating an arbitration clause contained in an exchange of telegrams as an 'agreement in writing', Article II New York Convention

[17] The writing requirement for arbitration agreements is currently being reviewed by an UNCITRAL working group considering a redraft of Article 7 Model Law and an interpretive instrument relating to Article II(2) New York Convention. See UNCITRAL Working Group II (Arbitration and Conciliation), *Preparation of uniform provisions on written form for arbitration agreements*, UN Document A/CN9/WGII/WP118.

> contemplates in a general way the transmission by telecommunication of messages which are reproduced in a lasting format. In this respect a telex produces messages whose senders and receivers can be identified in a better manner than was the case for the traditional telegrams.[18]

7-20 What adjustments should be made to the requirement of an assent in writing by all parties differs from country to country. The approach taken by national courts to Article II(2) often reflects the general attitude of the courts towards arbitration. The general problem and conflicting interests involved were illustrated by the Swiss Tribunal Fédéral in *Tradax Export v Amoco Iranian Oil Company.*[19] It dealt with the question whether or not a generic reference in the written communications to general conditions is sufficient or if the reference must specifically mention the arbitration clause. The court held that Article II(2) New York Convention

> ... has to be interpreted in accordance with its object, and with a view to the interests it is clearly designed to protect. The purpose of the Convention is to facilitate the resolution of disputes through arbitration, taking particular account of the needs of international commerce; nonetheless, the requirement of writing prescribed in Article II of the Convention has the effect of protecting the parties concerned from entering into ill-thought-out commitments involving the renunciation of the right of access to normal courts and judges. From the standpoint of the interests at stake, the validity of an arbitration clause has to be evaluated in the light of the circumstances of the particular case. This being so, regard should be had to such considerations as whether it was entered into by seasoned businessmen, or by people with little experience; in the same way, a different degree of awareness is required of the signatories depending on whether the contract refers back to the provisions of another contract which is deemed to be known to them, or to general conditions which may or may not be known to them.[20]

7-21 The above case related to bills of lading signed by both parties. The Swiss Federal Tribunal decided that a general reference to a separate document containing an arbitration clause was sufficient to constitute an "arbitral clause in

---

[18] Cour de justice Canton de Genève, 14 April 1983, *Carbomin SA v Ekton Corporation*, XII YBCA 502 (1987); see also Corte di appello Napoli, 17 March 1979, VII *YBCA* 297 (1982); Austria, Oberster Gerichtshof, 17 November 1971, I *YBCA* 183 (1976).

[19] Tribunal Fédéral, 7 February 1984, *Tradax Export SA (Panama) v Amoco Iran Oil Company (US),* XI YBCA 532 (1986).

[20] *Ibid*, para 10; see also Obergericht Basel, 5 July 1994, XXI *YBCA* 685 (1996).

a contract signed by both parties" in the sense of Article II(2).[21] Courts in other countries have come to the same conclusion that no specific reference to the arbitration clause is required.[22]

7-22 The main differences relate to the interpretation of the second alternative form requirement, *i.e.* the exchange of documents. Problems do arise where only one party has clearly consented in writing to arbitration. The typical examples are purchase orders or letters of confirmation with an arbitration clause upon which the other party acts without sending a written reply.

7-23 A restrictive interpretation can be found in the judgment of the Italian Supreme Court in *Robobar v Finncold* in 1993[23]. The contract concerned the supply of refrigerating units by Finncold to Robobar for the manufacture of refrigerators. The purchase confirmations sent by Robobar contained a clause providing for arbitration but Finncold never replied to them. Two years later Robobar suspended payments alleging bad quality of the units. In the proceedings for payment and damages brought by Finncold in the Italian courts, Robobar tried to rely on the arbitration clause. The Court held that the Italian courts had jurisdiction since the arbitration clause lacked formal validity. Article II recognises as valid an arbitration clause contained in a document signed by the parties or in an exchange of letters or telegrams. None of these formalities were met in the *Robabar* case.[24]

7-24 A wide interpretation of Article II(2) was adopted by the US courts in *Sphere Drake Insurance v Marine Towing.*[25] A contract for marine insurance provided for arbitration in London. After the broker procured the policy but before it was delivered to the insured party and signed the insured vessel sank. In an action for coverage in the US courts the insured party argued that the

---

21 See for the same ruling in relation to the second alternative, the exchange of documents, Switzerland, Tribunal Fédéral, 12 January 1989, XV *YBCA 509* (1990).

22 France, Cour de cassation, 9 November 1993, *Bomar Oil NV v ETAP - l'Entreprise Tunisienne d'Activités Pétrolières,* XX YBCA 660 (1995); Spain, Tribunal Supremo, 30 January 1986, *X v Y,* XIII YBCA 512 (1988). Specific reference was required in *Tryff Hansa v Equitas* [1998] 2 Lloyd's Rep 439 and in another case cited by Merkin, *Arbitration Act,* 30.

23 Corte di cassazione, 28 October 1993, no 10704/93, *Robobar Ltd v Finncold sas,* XX YBCA 739 (1995). See also: Corte di cassazione, 18 September 1978, no 4167, *Gaetano Butera v Pietro e Romano Pagnan,* IV YBCA 296 (1979) 299 *et seq*; see also the German decision by the Landgericht München, 20 June 1978, V *YBCA* 260 (1980) 261; and the Hong Kong case *Small v Goldroyce* [1994] 2 HKC 526.

24 In Robabar, *ibid,* 740,741, the clause was contained in Robabar's confirmation letters. Finncold did not appear to have agreed by letter or telegram.

25 *Sphere Drake Insurance Plc v Marine Towing, Inc,* 16 F 3d 666, 669 (5th Cir 1994).

arbitration agreement did not fulfil the requirements of Article II(2) since it neither signed the contract nor was there an exchange of correspondence. The Court of Appeal for the Fifth Circuit held that there was no requirement for signature or exchange of documents if the arbitration clause is part of a contract.[26]

7-25 The *Sphere Drake* interpretation applies intent over form. It does not follow the legislative history or a strict textual interpretation of Article II(2): the New York Convention requires signature or exchange of documents for arbitration agreements and clauses.

7-26 This is also the understanding prevailing in most countries.[27] The Swiss Federal Tribunal in *Compagnie de Navigation et Transport v MSC*[28] expressed the opinion that abolishing or at least relaxing of the signature requirement may become an issue as

> ... with the development of modern means of communication, unsigned written documents have an increasing importance and diffusion, that the need for a signature inevitably diminishes, especially in international commerce, and that the different treatment reserved to signed and unsigned documents is under discussion.[29]

7-27 Abolishing the express language of Article II(2) is a matter for future legislative action. However, it is generally accepted that the New York Convention may be interpreted in the light of wider provisions in national laws.[30] This will not be helpful in all cases where national laws contain the requirement of an "exchange" of written communications which is at the heart of the problem. This restriction of Article II(2) may be overcome if it is interpreted dynamically

---

26 See however *Sen Mar Inc v Tiger Petroleum Corp*, 774 F Supp 879, 882 (SDNY 1991) which requires that an arbitration clause be found in a signed document or an exchange of letters to be enforceable; see also *Kahn Lucas Lancaster, Inc v Lark International Ltd*, 956 F Supp 1131 XXIII YBCA 1029 (1998) 1036 (SDNY 1997) rev'd 186 F 3d 210 (2d Cir 1999).

27 For other cases and an overview of arguments see Friedland, "US Courts' Misapplication of the "Agreement in Writing" Requirement for Enforcement of an Arbitration Agreement under the New York Convention", 15(5) *Mealey's IAR* 21 (1998) 28 *et seq*; van den Berg, *New York Convention*, 191 *et seq.*

28 Swiss Tribunal Fédéral, 16 January 1995, *Compagnie de Navigation et Transport SA v MSC (Mediterranean Shipping Company)*, XXI YBCA 690 (1996).

29 *Ibid*, 697 para 12.

30 The Swiss Federal Tribunal in *Compagnie de Navigation et Transport v MSC*, *ibid*, interpreted the New York Convention in the light of the wider Article 7 Model Law.

in accordance with laws which have abolished the requirement that both parties must consent in writing.[31]

7-28 If a contract containing the arbitration clause is signed only by one party, the question is whether it is necessary to find another document containing the written consent of the other party. It is widely accepted that this second document does not have to be signed. The signature requirement only applies to the first alternative of Article II(2) but not to the second, the exchange of documents.[32]

7-29 In bills of lading and other three party situations it frequently happens that the third party signs a document or engages in written communications. In such cases it may be possible to attribute those written communications to the party which has not expressly consented to arbitration in writing. The third party may be considered to have acted as an agent or a broker when consenting in writing.[33]

7-30 Where the consent of both parties to the arbitration clause was clear, despite the non-fulfilment of formal requirements, courts have resorted to considerations of good faith and estoppel to uphold the arbitration agreement. The Swiss Federal Tribunal in *Compagnie de Navigation et Transport v MSC* stated[34]

> ... in particular situations, a certain behaviour can replace compliance with a formal requirement according to the rules of good faith. This is exactly the case here. The parties, which have a long standing business relationship, base it in fact on general conditions containing, at Art. 2, the arbitration clause at issue. Further, the shipper itself has filled in the bill of lading before returning it to the carrier, which signed it. Leaving aside the fact that this procedure is not different from an exchange of declarations by telex or similar documents, the carrier had the right to believe in good faith that the shipper, its business partner since several years, approved of the

---

31 Alvarez, "Article II(2) of the New York Convention and the Courts", *ICCA Congress series no 9*, 67, 81; for a very wide interpretation see also Rechtbank Rotterdam, 26 June 1970, *Israel Chemicals & Phosphates Ltd v NV Algemene Oliehandel,* I YBCA 195 (1976).

32 Switzerland, Tribunal Fédéral, 5 November 1985, *Tracomin CA v Sudan Oil Seeds Co Ltd,* XII YBCA 511 (1987); Obergericht Basel, 5 July 1994, *DIETF Ltd v RF AG,* XXI YBCA 685 (1996); see also Di Pietro and Platte, *Enforcement of International Arbitration Awards,* 70.

33 See, *e.g.*, Swiss Tribunal Fédéral, 7 February 1984, *Tradax Export SA (Panama) v Amoco Iran Oil Company (US),* XI YBCA 532 (1986).

34 Swiss Tribunal Federal, 16 January 1995, *Compagnie de Navigation et Transport SA v MSC (Mediterranean Shipping Company),* XXI YBCA 690 (1996) 698 para 13.

contractual documents which it had filled in itself, including the general conditions on the back, among which the arbitration clause. [References omitted] [35]

7-31 Another issue which has given rise to divergent views is whether the form requirements applicable to the arbitration agreement also extend to the authority of an agent to enter into such an agreement. For example, Article 216 Greek Civil Code requires that the evidence of authority of an agent always has to comply with the same form as the main agreement to be signed by the agent.[36] Even where no such provision exists it has often been required that the authority of any agent entering into an arbitration agreement be evidenced in writing.[37] With the relaxation of the protective element in the form requirements there are, however, good reasons to allow oral conferrals of power on an agent, especially where the agent is authorised to enter into the contract on behalf of the principal.[38]

7-32 An UNCITRAL working group is currently working on a new draft of Article 7 Model Law as well as an interpretative instrument relating to Article II(2) New York Convention.[39] The discussion in the working group takes account of most problems and seeks legislative solutions.

2. Capacity of the Parties to Enter into an Arbitration Agreement

7-33 The capacity of parties to enter into an arbitration agreement is governed by the law applicable to the parties. The general rule is that any natural or legal person who has the capacity to enter into a valid contract also has the capacity to conclude a valid arbitration agreement.[40] Except for restrictions aimed at protecting consumers, national laws rarely impose restrictions on the capacity to enter into arbitration agreements. In state controlled economies there may be a

---

[35] There are decisions where for reasons of legal certainty it has been impossible to overcome the lack of form in the arbitration agreements. See, *e.g.*, ICC case no 5832, 115 *Clunet* 1198 (1988) 1202; *Aughton Ltd v MF Kent Services Ltd*, (1991) 31 Con LR 60 (CA).

[36] See also Italy, CCP Article 1392.

[37] See ICC case no 5832, 115 *Clunet* 1198 (1988) 1199 (Austrian Law); Areios Pagos, 14 January 1977, IV *YBCA* 269 (1979); Landgericht Hamburg, 16 March 1977, III *YBCA* 274 (1978).

[38] See ICC case no 5730 of 1988, 117 *Clunet* 1029 (1990) 1036; Reiner, "The Form of the Agent´s Power to Sign an Arbitration Agreement and Article II (2) of the New York Convention", *ICCA Congress series no 9*, 82, 88 *et seq.*

[39] See UN Document A/CN9/WGH/WP118.

[40] See, *e.g.*, Belgium, Judicial Code Article 1676(2)(1).

lack of capacity where the necessary foreign trade licence is missing.[41] A frequent challenge is that the person who signed the contract for one of the parties was not properly authorised.[42]

3. Substantive Validity of the Arbitration Agreement

7-34 An arbitration agreement must fulfil the ordinary requirements for the conclusion of a contract. The parties must have agreed on arbitration and their agreement must not be vitiated by related external factors.

3.1. Agreement between the Parties

7-35 Consent to arbitration is easy to establish if the arbitration clause is contained in a contract negotiated between and signed by the parties. In practice, however, many contracts are concluded by reference to general conditions. The arbitration clause may not have been the object of specific attention by the parties, since they generally conditions or any other document containing the arbitration clause may not be attached to the contract itself. The parties may conclude a contract without reference to an arbitration clause but in the context of a series of contracts which include an arbitration agreement.

7-36 Questions as to consent to arbitration may arise if claims are brought by or against parties who are not expressed to be a party to the contract containing the arbitration agreement. This could be where such party is closely involved with the implementation or performance of the contract or where the contract and arbitration agreement have been assigned to a third party. In these cases the central issue is whether under general principles of contract law the arbitration agreement can be extended to a non-signatory. In US law these principles include "(1) incorporation by reference; (2) assumption; (3) agency; (4) veil-piercing/alter ego; and (5) estoppel."[43]

---

[41] See decision of the German Bundesgerichtshof, 23 April 1998, XXIVb *YBCA* 928 (1999) where an arbitration clause was held invalid because the Yugoslav party did not have the required foreign trade permission and therefore lacked capacity to enter into an arbitration agreement.

[42] See, *e.g.*, ICC case no 6850, XXIII *YBCA* 37 (1998); Court of Cassation Dubai, 25 June 1994, *Int ALR* N-62 (1998), where the person agreeing to the arbitration clause was acting under a power of attorney which the Court held did not cover the submission to arbitration.

[43] *Thomson-CSF, SA v American Arbitration Ass'n*, 64 F 3d 773, 776 (2d Cir 1995); see also *Smith Enron Cogeneration Ltd Partnership, Inc et al v Smith Cogeneration International Inc (Brit*

(a) Reference to standard terms and conditions

7-37 It is generally accepted that an arbitration clause can be included in general conditions.[44] If these standard terms and conditions are on the reverse side of a document usually a generic reference to the conditions is sufficient to incorporate the arbitration clause in the contract. No special reference to the arbitration clause is required to assume that the parties consented to arbitration.

7-38 The situation is more complex where the general conditions and the arbitration agreement are contained in a separate document. The prevailing view is that provided the document is available to both parties at the time of contracting a valid arbitration agreement exists.[45] There are, however court decisions which require a specific reference to the arbitration agreement contained in the general conditions[46] and that the arbitration clause is conspicuous.[47]

7-39 If the parties have a long standing relationship based on the general conditions of one side it is unnecessary for the general conditions to be referred to in each new contract. As long as no objection is raised it is sufficient that the other side has received the general conditions at an earlier stage.[48]

7-40 Arbitration agreements may also be incorporated by reference to other documents, including earlier contracts between the parties. The question has been

---

Virgin Islands), XXV YBCA 641 (2000); *Choctaw Generation Ltd Partnership v American Home Assurance Company*, 17(1) Mealey's IAR C-1 (2002) (2d Cir 2001).

44 In domestic consumer contracts the inclusion of an arbitration agreement in standard conditions may be invalid according to the legislation on unfair contract terms; see, *e.g.*, the German decision, Bundesgerichtshof, 10 October 1991, XIX *YBCA* 200 (1994) 202 *et seq.* See also Drahozal, "Unfair" Arbitration Clauses, *U Ill L Rev* 695 (2001) 696 *et seq*, reporting on the non enforcement of such arbitration clauses in the US for consumer protection reasons.

45 See, *e.g.*, *Progressive Casualty Insurance Company (US) et al v CA Reaseguradora Nacional de Venezuela*, XIX YBCA 825 (1994) (2d Cir, 6 April 1993) with further references.

46 *Concordia Agritrading Pte Ltd v Cornelder Hoogewerff Pte Ltd*, 3 Int ALR N-42 (2000) (Singapore High Court, 13 October 1999).

47 See, *e.g.*, *Brower v Gateway 2000 Inc*, 676, NYS 2d 569 (NYAD 1998), where a particular term relating to arbitration was unconscionable and, at least in part, unenforceable. This is particularly relevant in relation to consumer contracts.

48 See Oberlandesgericht Schleswig, 30 March 2000, 46 *RIW* 706 (2000) 707. See further the Belgian cases referred to in van Houtte, "Consent to Arbitration Through Agreement to Printed Contracts: The Continental Experience", 16 *Arb Int* 1 (2000) 10 *et seq.*

how specific the reference must be. The prevailing view seems to be that a general reference is sufficient.[49]

7-41 The reference may be to a contract between only one of the parties and a third party. This is typically the case where an arbitration clause in a charterparty is included in a bill of lading. There are divergent views as to whether a general reference to the charterparty is sufficient to incorporate the arbitration agreement. According to US courts broadly worded arbitration clauses not restricted to the immediate parties can be included in the bill of lading by a mere general reference.[50]

7-42 In other countries the prevailing view seems to be that a specific reference is required. The position in England was summarised by Lord Justice Bingham (as he then was) in *The Federal Bulker*

> ...it is clear that an arbitration clause is not directly germane to the shipment carriage and delivery of goods. ... It is, therefore, not incorporated by general words in the bill of lading. If it is to be incorporated, it must either be by express words in the bill of lading itself...or by express words in the charterparty itself...If it is desired to bring in an arbitration clause, it must be done explicitly in one document or the other.[51]

7-43 Similarly, the German ZPO section 1031(4) provides that a specific reference to the arbitration clause in the charterparty makes it part of the bill of lading. Once there is such a specific reference it is irrelevant that the wording of

---

[49] See *Macon (BVI) Investment Holding Co Ltd v Heng Holdings SEA (PTE) Ltd*, (2000) 3 Int ALR N-54 (Singapore High Court, 28 December 1999), where a general reference to joint venture agreement containing arbitration clause sufficient to incorporate it in a supplement agreement. However, see *Concordia Agritrading Pte Ltd v Cornelder Hoogewerff (Singapore) Pte Ltd*, (2000) 3 Int ALR N-42 (Singapore High Court, 13 October 1999).

[50] *Compania Espanola de Petroleos SA v Nereus Shipping SA* 527 F 2d 966, 973 (2d Cir 1975); see also for the same problem in the insurance/reinsurance area *Progressive Casualty Ins Co v CA Reaseguradora Nacional de Venezuela*, XIX YBCA 825 (1994) 833, para 24, 991 F 2d 42 (2d Cir 1993); see also Philippines Supreme Court, 26 April 1990, *National Union Fire Insurance Company of Pittsburgh et al v Stolt-Nielson Philippines, Inc*, XXVII YBCA 524 (2002).

[51] *Federal Bulk Carriers Inc v C Itoh & Co Ltd, The "Federal Bulker"* [1989] 1 Lloyd's Rep 103, 108; see also *The "Delos"* [2001] 1 Lloyd's Rep 703. The same view is taken by Canadian and Italian courts; see *Thyssen Canada Ltd v Mariana Maritime SA*, (2001) 1(1) Arbitration Monthly 5 (Federal Court of Appeal of Canada, March 2000); Corte di cassazione, 22 December 2000, *Granitalia v Agenzia Marittima Sorrentina*, XXVII YBCA 506 (2002).

the clause in the charterparty only refers to the original parties. The same applies in English law.[52]

(b) Related agreements

7-44 Consent to arbitration may also exist if a contract does not contain an arbitration clause but forms part of a contractual network which includes an arbitration agreement. This happens where parties enter into a framework agreement, containing an arbitration clause, governing their future relationship within which they conclude a number of separate contracts.[53]

7-45 An arbitration agreement may also exist if the contract is part of a series of contracts between the same parties the majority of which consistently contain arbitration clauses.[54] This depends on the facts of the case. In ICC Case 7154[55] three out of four ship repair contracts contained an arbitration clause, a tribunal sitting in Geneva in relation to the fourth contract denied jurisdiction because Article 178 PIL required an express reference to the other contracts.

7-46 The arbitration clause in the main contract may also extend to follow up or repeat contracts concluded in close connection and in support of a main contract. This is usually a question of interpretation; this may be the case if the

---

[52] *The Rena K* [1978] 1 *Lloyd's Rep* 545; *The Nerano* [1996] 1 Lloyd's Rep 1. Under US law, however, the wording of the arbitration clause was considered to be an obstacle to inclusion by reference; see *Steel* Corp *v Mississippi Valley Barge Line Co*, 351 F 2d 503, 506 (2d Cir 1965); *Continental UK Ltd v Anagel Confidence Compania Naviera SA*, 658 F Supp 809, 814-815 (SDNY 1987).

[53] See, *e.g.*, Cour d'appel Paris, 31 May 2001, *UNI-KOD sarl v Quralkali*, XXVI YBCA 1136 (2001) 1138: arbitration agreement in joint venture covers contracts concluded between members in the implementation of the joint venture; *JJ Ryan & Sons, Inc v Rhône Poulenc Textile, SA et al*, 863 F 2d 315, XV YBCA 543 (1990) 547 *et seq* (4th Cir 1988): arbitration agreement in exclusive distributorship agreement covered all contracts concluded under the agreement; in Germany, Oberlandesgericht Schleswig, 19 October 2000, 16 *Sch* 1/00: arbitration agreement in framework agreement for the sale of cabbage covers all sales executed under the agreement; Raeschke-Kessler and Berger, *Recht und Praxis*, para 276.

[54] David, *Arbitration in International Trade*, para 227; Raeschke-Kessler and Berger, *Recht und Praxis*, para 277; Cour d'appel Paris, 25 March 1983, *Société Sorvia v Weinstein International Disc Corp*, Rev Arb 363 (1984) 365; see also *A & B v C & D* [1982] Lloyd's Rep 166. For the opposite case where the lack of an arbitration agreement in one contract led to an interpretation of a connected contract which struck out an arbitration agreement see *MH Alshaya Company WLL v RETEK Information Systems* (2000) WL 33116470.

[55] ICC case no 7154, 121 *Clunet* 1059 (1994).

subsequent agreements amend or complete the main contract[56] but not where the additional contracts go beyond the implementation of the main contract.[57]

7-47 In general no consent to arbitration can be assumed if third parties are involved. Therefore the arbitration clause contained in a construction contract with the general contractor does not usually cover the general contractor's contract with the subcontractor.[58]

7-48 The same applies in relation to bank guarantees or letters of credit issued on the basis of a contract containing an arbitration clause. It cannot be assumed that the bank has consented to arbitration on the basis of the underlying contract if the guarantee or the letter of credit does not provide for arbitration.[59] However, in *Choctaw Generation v American Home Assurance* the US Court of Appeal for the Second Circuit held that a signatory to an arbitration clause may be bound under the doctrine of estoppel to arbitrate claims against the bank, where the issues "the nonsignatory is seeking to resolve in arbitration are intertwined with the agreement the estopped party has signed."[60]

7-49 An arbitration agreement may exceptionally exist by virtue of trade usages in a certain industry. In the light of the writing requirement such an option is primarily limited to countries which do not require any strict form for arbitration agreements.[61]

---

56 *Maxum Foundation, Inc v Salus Corp*, 779 F 2d 974, 978 (4th Cir 1985); *Hart Enterprises Int, Inc v Anhui Provincial Import & Export Corp*, 888 F Supp 587-591, XXI YBCA 767 (1996) (SDNY 1995).

57 See ICC case no 8420, XXV *YBCA* 328 (2000) 338-340.

58 Under US law this may be so even where the subcontract contains a reference to the main contract, the arbitration clause of which is, however, in its wording limited to the original parties. See the decision in *Intertec Contracting A/S et al v Turner Steiner International SA*, XXVI YBCA 949 (2001) 955, para 15-21, 34 (SDNY 2000, 2d Cir 2001).

59 *Grundstatt v Ritt*, 106 F 3d 201 (7th Cir 1997).

60 *Choctaw Generation Ltd Partnership v American Home Assurance Company*, 17(1) Mealey's IAR C-1 (2002) C-2 (2d Cir 2001); see also *JA Jones, Inc et al v The Bank of Tokyo-Mitsubishi Ltd et al*, XXV YBCA 902 (2000) 904 (EDNC 1999); for the application of the doctrine of equitable estoppel in other cases see *International Paper Company v Schwabedissen Maschinen & Anlagen GmbH*, XXV YBCA 1146 (2000) 1149-1150.

61 See, *e.g.*, Bundesgerichtshof, 3 December 1992, XX *YBCA* 666 (1995) 668 para 5, with note Berger, *DZWiR* 466 (1993); see also *Chelsea Square Textiles Inc et al v Bombay Dyeing and Manufacturing Company Ltd*, 189 F 3d 289, XXV YBCA 1035 (2000) (2d Cir 1999): illegible arbitration clause becomes part of contract as trade usage; David, *Arbitration in International Trade*, para 226.

(c) Consent by third parties

7-50 Questions of consent also arise if an arbitration clause is to be extended to third parties which have not signed the contract or have signed it in a different capacity. In ICC Case 5721,[62] the person who had signed an arbitration agreement in his capacity as a managing director of a company was personally made respondent in an arbitration. The tribunal found that the legal entity was the normal business vehicle, and refused jurisdiction over the director. The tribunal stated the following principle

> A tribunal should be reluctant to extend the arbitration clause to a director who has acted as such. The extension requires that the legal person is nothing but a business instrument of the natural person in such a way that one can transfer the contract and obligations entered into by the former to the latter. The presumptions listed below do not permit to reach an absolute certainty in this respect. [63]

7-51 The certainty required has been found in a number of cases where the arbitration clause was extended to parent[64] and subsidiary[65] companies from the same group which had not signed the arbitration agreement. The underlying argument, where a parent or subsidiary company plays an active role in the conclusion and performance of the contract, is that the agreement is with the group and not with a single member of the group. In such cases it would be contrary to good faith and economic reality to treat the companies of a group as separate legal entities.[66] This argument has also been extended to the relations

---

[62] ICC case no 5721 (1990), 117 *Clunet* 1019 (1990).

[63] *Ibid*, 1021: authors' translation. See generally Blessing, "The Law Applicable to the Arbitration Clause and Arbitrability", *ICCA Congress series no 9*, 169, 177. See also another example from the US, *First Options of Chicago, Inc v Kaplan, et uxor and MK Investments, Inc*, 115 S Ct 1920; 131 L Ed 2d 985 (1995), 1995 US LEXIS 3463, XXII YBCA 278 (1997).

[64] *JJ Ryan & Sons v Rhone Poulenc Textile, S A*, 863 F 2d 315, 320-321, XV YBCA 543 (1990) (4th Cir 1988); Interim Award in ICC case no 4131 of 1982, *Dow Chemical France et al v Isover Saint Gobain* , IX YBCA 131 (1984) 133 *et seq*; see also ICC case no 5730 (1988), 117 *Clunet* 1029 (1990), where the corporate veil was pierced to reach the owner of the company personally; for further references see Blessing, "The Law Applicable to the Arbitration Clause and Arbitrability", *ICCA Congress series no 9*, 169, 175 *et seq*.

[65] ICC case no 2375, 103 *Clunet* 973 (1976); denied in ICC case no 4504, 113 *Clunet* 1118 (1986) 1119 *et seq*; for further references see Blessing, "The Law Applicable to the Arbitration Clause and Arbitrability", *ICCA Congress series no 9*, 169, 175.

[66] Interim award in ICC case no 4131 (1982), *Dow Chemical France et al v Isover Saint Gobain*, IX YBCA 131 (1984) 134 *et seq*; ICC case no 6519, 118 *Clunet* 1065 (1991) 1066 *et seq*; ICC case no 1434, 103 *Clunet* 978 (1976) 979; ICC case no 2375, 103 *Clunet* 973 (1976) 974; Cour d'appel Paris, 30 November 1988, *Société Korsnas Marma v Société Durand-Auzias*, Rev Arb 692 (1989) 694.

between a state and its oil and trading company.[67] Such an extension is justified if the applicable company law allows the corporate veil to be lifted or the companies have created an appearance of or been presented as having the power of agency for another company.[68]

(d) Assignment

7-52 Parties are generally free to assign their contractual rights to a third party.[69] Where those rights are covered by an arbitration agreement the prevailing view in international arbitration is that the assignee automatically becomes a party to the arbitration agreement. Courts in various countries, such as France,[70] England,[71] Sweden[72] and Germany,[73] have consistently held that the assignee can

---

67 This was rejected in Cour d'appel Paris, 16 June 1988, *Société Swiss Oil v Société Petrogap et Republique du Gabon*, Rev Arb 309 (1989) 314.

68 Raeschke-Kessler and Berger, *Recht und Praxis*, para 301 *et seq*; ICC case no 6519, 118 *Clunet* 1065 (1991) 1067; ICC case no 4381, 113 *Clunet* 1102 (1986); ICC case no 5730 (1988), 117 *Clunet* 1029 (1990) 1030; *ad hoc* award, 15 September 1989, *E v Z, ICA Z and Société M*, ASA Bulletin 270 (1990) 272; *ad hoc* award, 1991, *ASA Bulletin* 202 (1992) 215; for US law see *Rhône Poulenc and Resin Intermediates SAS et al v EI Du Pont de Nemours and Company*, XXVII YBCA 779 (2002) 781 *et seq*.

69 See Kötz, in *IECL*, Vol VII, Chapter 13, para 60 *et seq*; Girsberger and Hausmaninger, "Assignment of Rights and Agreement to Arbitrate", 8 *Arb Int* 121 (1992); see also discussion on validity of assignment in Iran-US Claims Tribunal award in case no 255 (176-255-3), 26 April 1985, *DIC of Delaware, Inc et v Tehran Redevelopment Corp, The Government of The Islamic Republic of Iran*, XI YBCA 332 (1986) 333-335.

70 Cour de cassation, 5 January 1999, *Banque Worms v Bellot*, Rev Arb 85 (2000) 86; Cour de cassation, 8 February 2000, *Société Taurus Films v Les Film du Jeudi*, Rev Arb 280 (2000); Cour d'appel Paris, 25 November 1999, *SA Burkinabe des ciments et matériaux v société des ciments d'Abidjan*, Rev Arb 165 (2001) 168; but see the decision in Cour d'appel Paris, 26 May 1992, *Société Guyapêche v Abba Import Aktiebolag*, Rev Arb 624 (1993) 626, where the assignment of single rights was held not to entail the assignment of the arbitration clause.

71 *Shayler v Woolf* [1946] Ch 320; *Schiffahrtsgesellschaft Detlev Von Appen GmbH v Voest Alpine Intertrading* [1997] 2 Lloyd's Rep 279; this follows also from English Arbitration Act section 82(2) which states that "a party to an arbitration agreement includes any person claiming under or through a party to the agreement."

72 Supreme Court of Sweden, 15 October 1997, case no Ö 3174/95, *MS Emja Braack Schiffahrts KG v Wärtsila Diesel Aktiebolag*, XXIV YBCA 317 (1999), Swedish original in *Nytt Jurisdixkt Arkiv* 866 (1997), French translation in *Rev Arb* 431 (1998).

73 Bundesgerichtshof, 18 December 1975, *WM* 331 (1976); Bundesgerichtshof, 5 May 1977, *BGHZ* 68, 356; Bundesgerichtshof, 28 May 1979, *NJW* 2567 (1979); Bundesgerichtshof, 20 March 1980, *BGHZ* 77, 32; Hanseatisches Oberlandesgericht, 17 February 1989, XV *YBCA* 455 (1990) para 11-14; Schlosser, *Internationale Schiedsgerichtsbarkeit*, 326; Raeschke-Kessler and Berger, *Recht und Praxis*, 93.

sue and be sued under the arbitration agreement.[74] The Cour d'appel Paris went as far as considering it a general principle of arbitration law.[75]

7-53 The reason for this automatic assignment is that arbitration agreements are not personal covenants[76] but form part of the economic value of the assigned substantive right.[77] Furthermore, as the Court of Appeal of New York stated in *Hosiery Mfg Corp v Goldston* arbitration contracts would be of no value if either party could escape by assigning a claim subject to arbitration between the original parties to a third party.[78] Otherwise it would be possible for a party to circumvent the arbitration agreement by assigning the main claim.

7-54 However, there are cases where tribunals and courts have rejected the idea of an automatic transfer of the arbitration agreement.[79] An express approval by the assignee or the original debtor was a precondition for the transfer of the right to arbitrate.

7-55 No automatic transfer takes place when the parties have excluded an assignment of the arbitration agreement. Non-assignment clauses in relation to the substantive right are often considered to exclude any assignment of the

---

[74] See also for Swiss law, Tribunal Fédèral, 9 May 2001, *Nextron Holding SA v Watkins International SA*, 5 IntALR N-15 (2002); Tribunal Fédèral, 16 October 2001, *Societé X v Societé O*, ATF 128 III 50 where the assignment was denied since the parties excluded assignments; for a recent clarification of Chinese arbitration law by the PRC Supreme Court, 16 August 2000, *CNIEC Henan Corporation v Liaoning Bohai Nonferrous Metals I/E Ltd*, 4 Int ALR N-11 (2001); for further cases see Girsberger and Hausmaninger, "Assignment of Rights and Agreement to Arbitrate", 8 *Arb Int* 121 (1992) 123-136.

[75] Cour d'appel Paris, 25 November 1999, *SA Burkinabe des ciments et matériaux v société des ciments d'Abidjan*, Rev Arb 165 (2001) 168; see also *Banque de Paris et des Pays-Bas v Amoco Oil Company*, 573 F Supp 1464 (SDNY 1983) 1469 which considered it to be a basic principle of case law.

[76] *Shayler v Woolf* [1946] Ch 320, 324; Swedish Supreme Court, 15 October 1997, *MS Emja Braack Schiffahrts KG v Wärtsila Diesel Aktiebolag*, XXIV YBCA 317 (1999).

[77] See France, Cour d'appel Paris, 28 January 1998, *CCC v Filmkunst*, Rev Arb 567 (1988); Germany, Bundesgerichtshof, 2 March 1978, *NJW* 1585 (1978) 1586.

[78] (1924) 143 NE 779, 780; 238 NY 2d 22.

[79] The Foreign Trade Arbitration Commission at the USSR Chamber of Commerce and Industry, award in case no 109/1980, 9 July 1984, *All-Union Foreign Trade Association "Sojuznefteexport" (USSR) v Joc Oil Ltd (Bermuda)*, XVIII YBCA 92 (1993) para 17. For further US cases see Girsberger and Hausmaninger, "Assignment of Rights and Agreement to Arbitrate", 8 *Arb Int* 121 (1992) 124 referring to *Kaufman v William Iselin & Co, Inc* 143 NE 780 and *Lachmar v Trunklin LNG Co*, 753 F 2d 8 (CA 2d Cir, 1985).

arbitration agreement as well.[80] An exclusion may exist where the agreement to arbitrate is entered into on the basis of a special personal relationship. Furthermore the assignment should not lead to a deterioration of the original debtors position. That would be the case, for example, where due to the financial situation of the assignee the reimbursement for costs may be endangered.

7-56 An automatic transfer may also be excluded when the assignment takes place while arbitration proceedings are already pending. Under English law, for example, the assignee does not automatically become a party to those proceedings; a notification to the other party and the arbitrators is required.[81] This may be of particular importance where the original party no longer exists. If the necessary notifications are not made in time, the tribunal may lose jurisdiction as one of the parties has been dissolved. Any award rendered in such a situation will be null and void.[82]

7-57 The extent to which the assignor remains bound by the arbitration agreement is primarily an issue of interpreting the arbitration agreement. On the basis of an arbitration agreement contained in the shareholders' agreement arbitration proceedings could be initiated against a shareholder who had left the company, where the dispute related to a breach of contract in connection with leaving the company.[83]

3.2. Other Factors Affecting the Validity of the Agreement

7-58 An arbitration agreement might be invalid for other reasons, such as misrepresentation in relation to the arbitration agreement, or the dissolution of the chosen institution. Other factors which might affect the validity of the arbitration agreement are ambiguity,[84] mistakes as to the relationship between an

---

80 See, *e.g.*, Swiss Tribunal Fédéral, 9 April 1991, 8(2) *J Int'l Arb* 21 (1991); Tribunal Fédéral, 16 October 2001, *Societé X v Societé O*, ATF 128 III 50; *United States v Panhandle Eastern Corp*, 672 F Supp 149 (D Del 1987): assignee not deemed to be bound to the arbitration clause because the assignment contract excluded any transfer of obligations to the assignee; see for English law *Bawejem Ltd v MC Fabrications* [1999] 1 All ER (Comm) 377.

81 Merkin, *Arbitration Act*, para 2-33, 2-37; *Montedipe SpA v JTP-RO Jugotantier* [1990] 2 Lloyd's Rep 11; *Charles M Willie & Co (Shipping) Ltd v Ocean Laser Shipping Ltd, The Smaro* [1999] 1 Lloyd's Rep 225, 241-243; *Baytur SA v Finagro Holdings SA* [1992] QB 610.

82 *Baytur SA v Finagro Holdings SA* [1992] QB 610.

83 See German Bundesgerichtshof, 1 August 2002, III *ZB* 66/01.

84 See, *e.g.*, *Hissan Trading Co Ltd v Orkin Shipping Corp*, (1994) XIX YBCA 273 (High Court of Hong Kong, 8 September 1992)

arbitrator and the parties,[85] the insolvency of the parties, the exclusion of statutory rights or remedies[86] and the lack of arbitrability. Where a contract is invalid due to illegality, as a result of the doctrine of separability the arbitration agreement will remain valid.[87]

4. Scope and Interpretation of the Arbitration Agreement

7-59 Invariably, where an issue arises concerning the validity, existence or scope of the arbitration agreement, the court or tribunal will have to interpret the parties' intention. If this is not possible the arbitration agreement may be void for uncertainty or contradiction.

7-60 Arbitration agreements are in general submitted to the same type of rules of interpretation as all other contracts. All relevant circumstances have to be taken into account. Declarations should be interpreted in good faith and the parties' conduct, both at the time of contracting and subsequently, considered. If the arbitration agreement is based on the standard conditions of one party the other party can rely on existing uncertainties as to the scope of the arbitration agreement to resist applications for referral to arbitration or to resist court proceedings.

7-61 In older decisions the jurisdictional effect of arbitration agreements sometimes led to a restrictive interpretation. They were seen as a renunciation of the constitutional right to have a dispute decided by the courts.[88] In today's arbitration-friendly climate the opposite view prevails. In particular, the US courts have consistently held that arbitration agreements must be interpreted in favour of arbitration. In *Mitsubishi v Soler* the Supreme Court stated

> questions of arbitrability [jurisdiction] must be addressed with a healthy regard for the federal policy favouring arbitration ... The Arbitration Act establishes that, as a

---

[85] See Cour de cassation, *Consorts Ury v SA Galeries Lafayette*, 13 April 1972, Rev Arb 235 (1975).

[86] See, in relation to the exclusion of punitive damages, the US decisions in *Graham Oil Co v ARCO Products*, 43 F 3d 1244, 1249 (9th Cir 1994); in relation to costs *Perez v Globe Airport Sec Services, Inc*, 253 F 3d 1280, 1285 (11th Cir 2001).

[87] See, *e.g.*, the decision by the Court for the Southern District of New York, *Bleship Navigation Inc v Sealift Inc*, XXI YBCA 799 (1996) where the arbitration clause in a charter party violation the US embargo against Cuba was held to be valid despite the illegality of the main contract. On this issue see also the decision by the English High Court in *Westacre Investment v Jugoimport-SDPR Holdings Co Ltd et al* (1998) XXIII YBCA 836, 859.

[88] See, *e.g.*, ICC case no 4392, 110 *Clunet* 907 (1983) 908.

matter of federal law, any doubts concerning the scope of arbitrable issues should be resolved in favour of arbitration, whether the problem at hand is the construction of the contract language itself or an allegation of waiver, delay, or defense to arbitrability.[89]

7-62 Comparable views can be found in most countries which have adopted a pro-arbitration policy.[90] This rule can apply only once it has been ascertained that the parties actually agreed on arbitration. In cases where the main issue is whether the parties agreed to arbitration at all there is no justification for such an interpretive rule in favour of arbitration. Though it is the primary mode of dispute settlement in international business every party has a legitimate and a constitutional right to choose to have its rights determined by the courts.[91]

4.1. Disputes covered by the Arbitration Agreement

7-63 Most arbitration agreements are broadly worded. The ICC model clause for example covers "All disputes arising out of or in connection with the present contract." It is generally recognised that this wording covers all differences and claims arising from a given contractual relationship and even to non-contractual and tortious claims. In *Kaverit Ltd v Kone Corp*[92] the Alberta Court of Appeal defined the ambit of such clauses

---

89 *Mitsubishi Motors* Corp *v Soler Chrysler Plymouth Inc*, 473 US 614, 105 S Ct 3346, 3355 *et seq* (1985); see also *Remy Amerique, Inc v Touzet Distribution, SARL*, XIX YBCA 820 (1994) 823 (SDNY, 16 March 1993).

90 Karrer and Kälin-Nauer, "Is there a Favor Jurisdictionis Arbitri? - Standards of Review of Arbitral Jurisdiction Decisions in Switzerland", 13(3) *J Int'l Arb* 3 (1996) 31; Raeschke-Kessler and Berger, *Recht und Praxis*, para 282 *et seq*; but see the decision of the Italian Corte di cassazione, 10 March 2000, *Krauss Maffei Verfahrenstechnik GmbH et al v Bristol Myers Squibb*, XXVI YBCA 816 (2001) 821 para 11 according to which a restrictive interpretation must be preferred.

91 Generally critical to an in interpretation in favor of arbitration Fouchard Gaillard Goldman *on International Commercial Arbitration*, para 481; Schlosser, *Internationale Schiedsgerichtsbarkeit*, 320; see also the award on jurisdiction in *Amco Asia* Corp *and others v Republic of Indonesia*, 23 ILM 351 (1984) 359 *et seq*; compare further the decision in *Ashville Investment Ltd v Elmer Contractors Ltd* [1988] *3* WLR 867, 873.

92 *Kaverit Steel and Crane Ltd et al v Kone Corporation et al*, (1994) XIX YBCA 643 (Alberta Court of Appeal, 16 January 1992).

> A dispute meets the test set by the submission if either claimant or defendant relies on the existence of a contractual obligation as a necessary element to create the claim, or to defeat it.[93]

7-64 Narrower formulations, particularly in common law jurisdictions, have been interpreted not to cover *all* disputes arising out of a contractual relationship. Tort and other non-contractual claims have been held not to arise "under" a contract.[94] The same applies to disputes concerning the formation of the contract or the pre-contractual phase.[95] In a worst case scenario a party may be forced to bring part of its claim in arbitration and the other part, not covered by the clause, in a state court.

7-65 This is illustrated in the decision of the Australian Supreme Court in *Hi-Ferty Pty Ltd v Kiukiang Maritime Carriers.* This case concerned a contract for the shipment of fertilizer from the US to Australia. When the Australian Quarantine Inspection Service denied unloading for contamination the claimant initiated court proceedings for negligence, breach of contract and a violation of section 52 Australian Trade Practice Act in respect of misleading and deceptive conduct. The defendant challenged the jurisdiction of the court invoking an arbitration clause which provided for arbitration in London. The Supreme Court held that only the claims for breach of contract were covered by the arbitration clause and had to be arbitrated in London. The other pre-contractual and non-contractual claims did not "arise from the charter" and therefore could be determined by the Australian courts.[96]

7-66 This situation is undeniably cumbersome and may cause unfair results. Accordingly there is a strong tendency to favour a broad interpretation of

---

93 *Ibid*, 648.

94 See the US decisions in *In re Kinoshita & Co*, 287 F 2d 951 (1961); *Mediterranean Enters v Ssangyong Corp*, 708 F 2d 1458 (9th Cir 1984); *Tracer Research* Corp *v National Environment Services Co*, 42 F 3d 1292, 1295 (9th Cir 1994); *Gerling Global Reinsurance Co v ACE Property & Casualty Insurance*, 17(8) Mealey's IAR 7 (2002); see also the discussion by the English courts *Government of Gibraltar v Kenney and Another* [1956] 2 QB 410; *The Playa Larga* [1983] 2 *Lloyd's Rep* 171. See also: Working Group on the ICC Standard Arbitration Clause, Final Report, 3 March 1992, ICC Doc no 420/318 Rev 16; Nakamura, "The Distinction between 'Narrow' and 'Broad' Arbitration Clauses under the Federal Arbitration Act - Still problematic in the United States", 17(8) *Mealey's IAR* 20 (2002).

95 *Michele Amoruso et Figli v Fisheries Development*, 499 F Supp 1074 (SDNY 1980).

96 *Hi-Ferty Pty Ltd et al v Kiukiang Maritime Carriers Inc et al*, (1999) 159 ALR 142, 12(7) Mealey's IAR C-1 (1997) (Federal Court of Australia); excerpts also in XXIII *YBCA* 606 (1998) which do not, however, include the relevant part.

arbitration clauses. This is in line with the general principle of interpretation stated by the ICSID tribunal in *Amco v Indonesia* that

> any convention, including conventions to arbitrate, should be construed in good faith, that is to say by taking into account the consequences of their commitments the parties may be considered as having reasonably and legitimately envisaged.[97]

7-67 In the absence of clear intention to the contrary "it would be illogical to suppose that the parties would have wanted a "split" jurisdiction."[98] Therefore arbitration agreements without an express limitation should in general be interpreted to cover all claims in connection with a contract, irrespective of whether they are claims in contract, in tort or of statutory nature.

4.2. Set-off and Counterclaims

7-68 In many cases a respondent party will seek to introduce a counterclaim or raise a set-off against the claim. Generally this is admissible provided the counterclaim or set-off relates to the same contract as the main claim.[99] The difficult problem is where a respondent wishes to counterclaim or raise a set-off arising under a different contract between the same parties. In this situation the counterclaim or set-off is not covered by the arbitration agreement. Therefore, the arbitration tribunal does not have jurisdiction to deal with the counterclaims and set-off claims.[100]

7-69 The situation may be different if the contracts underlying the main claims and on which the counterclaims and set-off are based are closely related and form part of the same economic venture. For example, set-off was allowed between a contract of sale and loan contract, where the loan was to finance the sale.[101] In an ICC case arbitrators allowed a set-off between claims arising under

---

97 Decision on Jurisdiction, *Amco Asia* Corp *and others v Republic of Indonesia*, 23 ILM 351 (1984) 359 *et seq.*

98 Landgericht Hamburg, 20 April 1977, IV *YBCA* 261 (1979); *Ashville Investment Ltd v Elmer Contractors Ltd* [1989] QB 488, 517: "very slow to attribute to a reasonable party an intention that there should in any foreseeable eventuality be two sets of proceedings"; see also *Ethiopian Oilseeds & Pulses Export* Corp *v Rio del Mar Foods Inc*, [1990] 1 Lloyd's Rep 86, 97: presumption against having two sets of proceedings arising from a particular transaction.

99 See, *e.g.*, UNCITRAL Rules Article 19(3); Berger, "Set-Off in International Economic Arbitration", 15 *Arb Int* 53 (1999) 64-65.

100 Berger, "Die Aufrechnung im Internationalen Schiedsverfahren", 44 *RIW* 426 (1998) 427 *et seq.*

101 See an award rendered under the auspices of the Court of Arbitration at the Chamber of Commerce and Industry in Sofia, 1 October 1980, case no 60/1980, XII *YBCA* 84 (1987).

a joint venture and a contract for the purchase of equipment for that joint venture, even though both contracts contained arbitration clauses referring to different institutions. The tribunal treated both contracts as an economic and legal unity, since the purchase agreement only settled details, the basics of which had already been fixed in the joint venture contract.[102] In general, however, the existence of a separate arbitration or choice of forum clause is considered to exclude the possibility of a set-off.[103]

7-70 A set-off of a claim from a different contract is also possible if the chosen arbitration rules allow a set-off to be raised. For example, Article 27 Zurich Chamber of Commerce Rules provides

> The Arbitral Tribunal also has jurisdiction over a set-off defense if the claim that is set off does not fall under the arbitration clause, and even if there exists another arbitration clause or jurisdiction for that claim.[104]

4.3. Defective Arbitration Clauses

7-71 As a general rule courts and tribunals seek to interpret arbitration clauses positively. Defective or pathological arbitration clauses[105] give rise to uncertainty and different views as to the meaning of the particular clause.

7-72 Some arbitration clauses use permissive language, for instance merely providing the parties with an option to choose arbitration. The Ontario Court of Appeal held that a clause which provided that "the parties may refer any dispute to arbitration" was a binding arbitration agreement. It held that this manifested an intention to arbitrate and it stayed the court proceedings.[106] In every case the court or arbitrators take a positive view in determining the parties' intention.

---

[102] ICC case no 5971, *ASA Bulletin* 728 (1995); in favour of such a wide approach see also Reiner, "Aufrechnung trotz (Fehlens einer) Schiedsvereinbarung nach österreichischem Recht", in Mayer, von Schlabrendorff, Spiegelfeld and Welser (ed), *Recht in Österreich und Europa – Festschrift, FS Karl Hempel* (Manz 1997), 119.

[103] Berger, "Set-Off in International Economic Arbitration", 15 *Arb Int* 53 (1999) 74-79.

[104] See further Blessing, "The Law Applicable to the Arbitration Clause and Arbitrability", *ICCA Congress series* no 9, 169, 180 *et seq*.

[105] The notion goes back to a seminal article by Eisemann, "La clause d'arbitrage pathologique", in *Commercial Arbitration Essays in Memoriam Eugenio Minoli* (UTET 1974) 129 *et seq*; see also Schmitthoff, "Defective Arbitration Clauses", *JBL* 9 (1975).

[106] *Canadian National Railway Co v Lovat Tunnel Equipment Inc*, 3 Int ALR N-5 (2000), 174 DLR (4th) 385 (Ontario Court of Appeal, 8 July 1999); but see the US decision in *Hoogovens*

7-73 Ambiguity also can arise where it is not conclusive from the arbitration clause whether the parties actually agreed on arbitration or some other form of dispute resolution such as expert determination. It is not necessary that the clause uses the term arbitration or expressly states that the decision rendered should be final and binding.[107] Where the clause provided that any dispute "shall be referred to a Queen's Counsel of the English Bar" the English Court of Appeal held that any agreement which refers "disputes to a person other than the court who is to resolve the dispute in a manner binding on the parties to the agreement" would constitute an arbitration agreement.[108]

7-74 Disputes arise where the contract contains a conflicting dispute resolution provision, for example one choice of forum clause and one arbitration clause. It may be possible through rules of construction to determine which jurisdiction is appropriate for a specific dispute. Where one clause is contained in the general conditions while the other is typewritten into the contract, the latter as a specially agreed provision will generally prevail. It also may be that the parties intended to have the choice between two options, which is preferable to holding the clause void for uncertainty.[109]

7-75 A typical defect is the incorrect reference to the institution under the rules of which an arbitration should take place. There have been references to the "Official chamber of commerce in Paris"[110], the "Arbitration Court at the Swiss

---

Ijmuiden Verkoopkantoor BV v MV Sea Cattleya and others, 852 Fed Supp 6, XXII YBCA 881 (1997) (SDNY 1994), where a clause providing for "General Average and arbitration to be settled in the Netherlands" was interpreted as determining only the situs if the parties agreed on arbitration; for further examples see Craig, Park & Paulsson, *ICC Arbitration*, para 9-02.

[107] See also partial award in ICC case 9759 reported by Grigera Naon, "Choice of Law Problems in International Arbitration", 289 *RCADI* 88 (2001).

[108] *David Wilson Homes Ltd v Survey Services Ltd and Others*, [2001] 1 All ER 449.

[109] Arbitration Court, Japan Shipping Exchange, interlocutory award, 1 September 1981, *MS "Sun River"*, 11 *YBCA* 193 (1986) 194 where a clause referring the disputes to "The Korean Commercial Arbitration Association, Seoul, Korea" *and* "The Japan Shipping Exchange, *Inc*, Japan" was interpreted to give the claimant the choice between the two institutions (and = or); see also partial award ICC case 6000 reported by Grigera Naon, "Choice of Law Problems in International Arbitration", 289 *RCADI* 87 (2001); *William Company v Chu Kong Agency Co Ltd et al*, (1994) XIX YBCA 274 (HCHK 17 February 1993). For a case where the clause was held to be void see *Hissan Trading Co Ltd v Orkin Shipping Corp* (1994) XIX YBCA 274, (HCHK 8 September 1992); see also the very restrictive Swiss decision by the Cour civil, Canton de Vaud, 30 March 1993, *Nokia-Maillefer SA v Mazzer*, 13(1) ASA Bulletin 64 (1995).

[110] Reference to the ICC, Tribunal de Grande Instance Paris, 13 December 1988, *Société Asland v Société European Energy Corporation*, Rev Arb 521 (1990); Cour d'appel Paris, 24 March 1994, *Société Deko v Dingler et société Meva*, Rev Arb 514 (1994) (Chamber of Commerce of

Chamber for Foreign Trade in Geneva"[111] or "International trade arbitration organization in Zurich."[112] While these clauses refer to non existing institutions they show clearly that the parties intended to submit their disputes to arbitration. For this reason courts and tribunals are reluctant to consider these clauses void for uncertainty. In general the reference to a particular city, the type of dispute or industry sector involved have allowed the courts to identify the chosen institution.[113] Only in exceptional cases where it was not possible to ascertain which institutional rules should govern the arbitration have tribunals found such agreements invalid.[114]

7-76 Arbitration agreements which refer to the International Chamber of Commerce in some city are generally interpreted as referring to ICC arbitration with the place of arbitration in the specified city. Difficulties can arise where the clause uses an ambiguous title of the institution.[115] Where there is a well known

---

Paris = ICC); for an overview of clauses considered to be referring to the ICC see Davis, "Pathological Clauses: Frédéric Eisemann's Still Vital Criteria", 7 *Arb Int* 365 (1991).

[111] Reference to the Chamber of Commerce and Industry of Geneva; Interlocutory award in case no 117, 29 November 1996, 15(3) *ASA Bulletin* 534 (1997); see also Chamber of Commerce and Industry of Geneva, Interlocutory award, 30 June 1987, 15(1) *ASA Bulletin* 122 (1997) (Arbitration Court in Geneva working beside the Swiss Chamber of Commerce).

[112] Zurich Chamber of Commerce, preliminary award, 25 November 1994, XXII *YBCA* 211 (1997), 14(2) *ASA Bulletin* 303 (1996).

[113] See also Cour d'appel Paris, 14 February 1985, *Société Tuvomon v Société Amaltex*, Rev Arb 325 (1987) (Tribunal of the Chamber of Commerce of Paris = Paris Arbitration Chamber); Cour de cassation, 14 December 1983, *Epoux Convert v Société Droga*, Rev Arb 483 (1984) 484 (Belgrade Chamber of Commerce = Foreign Trade Arbitration Court at the Economic Chamber of Yugoslavia); PRC Supreme People's Court, 16 August 2000, *CNIEC Henan Corporation v Liaoning Bohai Nonferrous Metals I/E*, 4 Int ALR N-11 (2001) (Arbitration: FTAC of China = CIETAC Arbitration);

[114] See, *e.g.*, Germany, Bayerisches Oberstes Landesgericht, 28 February 2000, 4 Z SchH 13/99, 1 *RPS* 15 (2000) (not clear which of two different Chambers of Commerce, none of which provided arbitration services, was meant); France, Cour d'appel Versailles, 3 October 1991, *Ltd Capital Rice Co v SARL Michel Come*, Rev Arb 654 (1992) (Arbitrage eventual: Chambre arbitrale Londres); Lebanon, Cour de cassation, 27 April 1987, *Rev Arb* 723 (1988) ("Chamber of Commerce in Bucarest or Arbitration Commission at the International Chamber of Commerce in Paris"); Scotland, Court of Session (Outer House), 15 May 2001, *Bruce v Kordula and others*, 4 Int ALR N-6 (2002).

[115] Oberlandesgericht Dresden, 5 December 1994, XXII *YBCA* 266 (1997); for other examples see ICC case no 5946, XVI *YBCA* 97 (1991) (International Chamber of Commerce in Geneva); Eisemann, "La clause d'arbitrage pathologique", in *Commercial Arbitration Essays in Memoriam Eugenio Minoli* (UTET 1974), 129 *et seq*; Davis, "Pathological Clauses: Frédéric Eisemann's Still Vital Criteria", 7 *Arb Int* 365 (1991); Hochbaum, *Mißglückte Internationale Schiedsvereinbarungen* (Recht und Wirtschaft 1995), 57; Hochbaum, "Pathological Arbitration

local arbitration institution at the designated place and it is unclear which institution has been selected, a court or tribunal may be able to resolve the difficulty by the name of the institution's rules.[116]

7-77 Courts have generally made considerable efforts to give effect to the parties' agreement to arbitrate.[117] An extreme case in this respect is the decision of the High Court of Hong Kong in *Lucky-Goldstar v Ng Moo Kee Engineering*.[118] The arbitration agreement provided for arbitration in a "3rd country, under the rule of the 3rd country and in accordance with the rules of procedure of the International Commercial Arbitration Association." Though no country was specified the judge considered the clause to be valid

> I believe that the correct approach in this case is to satisfy myself that the parties have clearly expressed the intention to arbitrate any dispute which may arise under this contract. I am so satisfied.... As to the reference to the non-existent arbitration institution and rules, I believe that the correct approach is simply to ignore it. I can give no effect to it and I reject all reference to it so as to be able to give effect to the clear intention of the parties.

7-78 The designation of a non existent appointing authority has also given rise to problems in practice. There are decisions which have considered these clauses

---

Clauses in German Courts. German Courts Interpret Arbitration Clauses Wrong Designation of the Seat of an Arbitral Institution", 11(1) *Mealey's IAR* 20 (1996).

[116] ICC case no 5294, XIV *YBCA* 137 (1989) 139 (International Chamber of Commerce, Zurich); ICC case no 4472, 111 *Clunet* 946 (1984) 947 (International Chamber of Commerce, Zurich); the same applies for Geneva where the Chamber of Commerce and Industry also has its own arbitration rules; see ICC case no 7290, XXIII *YBCA* 80 (1998) 81; ICC case no 4023, 111 *Clunet* 950 (1984); ICC case no 3460, 108 *Clunet* 939 (1981); for the invalidity of such clauses see the German decision, Oberlandesgericht Hamm, 15 November 1994, XXII *YBCA* 707 (1997), German original at 41 *RIW* 681 (1995).

[117] Kammergericht Berlin, 15 October 1999, 3 *Int ALR* N-30 (2000), German original at 1 *RPS* 13 (2000); see also Cour de cassation, 14 December 1983, *Epoux Convert v Société Droga*, Rev Arb 483 (1984) 484 (Belgrade Chamber of Commerce = Foreign Trade Arbitration Court at the Economic Chamber of Yugoslavia); Cour d'appel de Paris, 14 February 1985, *Société Tuvomon v Société Amaltex*, Rev Arb 325 (1987) (Tribunal of the Chamber of Commerce of Paris = Paris Arbitration Chamber); PRC Supreme People's Court, 16 August 2000, *CNIEC Henan Corporation v Liaoning Bohai Nonferrous Metals I/E*, 4 Int ALR N-11 (2001) (Arbitration: FTAC of China = CIETAC Arbitration); See also Davis, "Pathological Clauses: Frédéric Eisemann's Still Vital Criteria", 7 *Arb Int* 365 (1991).

[118] *Lucky-Goldstar International (HK) Ltd v Ng Moo Kee Engineering Ltd*, excerpts published in [1993] 2 HKLR, 73; case summary in XX YBCA 280 (1995); see also *HZI Research Center, Inc (US) v Sun Instruments Japan Co, Inc (Japan)*, XXI YBCA 830 (1996).

to be void.[119] It is often possible to rely on provisions of the applicable rules or law which provide for a fall back mechanism in cases where the appointment procedure agreed upon by the parties fails. A wide interpretation of the relevant provisions will generally cover the ineffective appointment procedures.

7-79 Another defect which has given rise to dispute is badly drafted pre-arbitration stages in multi-tier dispute resolution clauses. For example, in a contract between a Swedish licensor and a Chinese manufacturer the dispute resolution clause provided that where the parties were unable to reach an amicable settlement the party wishing to proceed to arbitration had to submit "documentary evidence" of a breach of contract to be issued by the AAA or the China Council for Promotion of International Trade. The claimant started arbitration proceedings without having gone through this process and the respondent tried to rely on the non-fulfilment of the precondition to resist arbitration. The tribunal held that it had jurisdiction since the agreed pre-arbitration stage was unworkable. It was not clear what types of documents were required and the two named institutions would not issue these documents.[120]

7-80 Arbitration agreements may also become defective through subsequent events, such as the dissolution of the named institution. That happened in the aftermath of the German unification where the Arbitration Court attached to the Chamber of Foreign Trade of the GDR was dissolved. It raised questions as to the effect and future of arbitration clauses in favour of this institution. The German Bundesgerichtshof held these arbitration agreements to be inoperative. It considered the difference between the privately organised Berlin Arbitration Courts and the state controlled Arbitration Court at the Chamber of Foreign Trade, with its special features affecting the composition of the tribunal, to be too great to assume that the parties consented to arbitration before the Berlin Arbitration Court.[121] The opposite conclusion was reached by the Austrian

---

[119] Cour d'appel Grenoble, 24 January 1996, *Société Harper Robinson v Société internationale de maintenance e de realisation industrielles (SIMRI)*, 124 Clunet 115 (1997).

[120] Stockholm Institute, interim award of 17 July 1992, XXII *YBCA* 197 (1997) 201.

[121] Bundesgerichtshof, 20 January 1994, *BGHZ* 7, 11 *et seq*; Bundesgerichtshof, February 1995, *WM* 1198 (1995) 1201; see also Rechtbank van Koophandel Brussels, 6 May 1993, *Pierreux NV (Belgium) v Transportmaschinen Handelshaus GmbH (Germany),* XXII YBCA 631 (1997); for a different view see Kirchner and Marriot, "International Arbitration in the Aftermath of Socialism - The Example of the Berlin Court of Arbitration", 10(1) *J Int'l Arb* 5 (1991).

Supreme Court in relation the dissolved Court of Arbitration at the USSR Chamber of Commerce and Industry.[122]

5. Effect and Enforcement of the Arbitration Agreement

7-81 The direct effect of a valid arbitration agreement is to confer jurisdiction on the arbitration tribunal to decide the dispute between the parties.[123] By corollary it is a contractual obligation of the parties to have their disputes submitted to arbitration. The arbitration agreement vests the arbitrators either expressly, or through the rules chosen or the law which governs the arbitration, with all powers necessary for this task.

7-82 According to Article II(3) New York Convention and comparable provisions in the national laws[124] the existence of a valid arbitration agreement prevents courts from entertaining jurisdiction when faced with an action on the merits. Unless the arbitration agreement is "null and void, inoperative or incapable of being performed" a court should refer the parties to arbitration. Under some laws, the courts do not even have jurisdiction to decide on the validity of the arbitration agreement before the arbitrators have ruled on the issue.[125]

7-83 It is this indirect effect of the arbitration agreement which plays the central role in its enforcement. It is not really practical to enforce an arbitration agreement in the same way as an ordinary contract. Damages is not an appropriate remedy as it is hard, if not impossible, to quantify the damages which result from the referral of a dispute to state courts.[126]

---

[122] Oberster Gerichtshof, 30 November 1994, XXII *YBCA* 628 (1997), German original in 41 *RIW*, (1995) 773, considering the newly formed Court of Arbitration at the Chamber of Commerce and Industry of the Russian Federation to be the legitimate successor; see also Cour d'appel Paris, 25 March 1999, *SA Caviar Petrossian v Société OAO Vneshintorg*, 127 Clunet 66 (2000) with note Kahn, where the parties, however, had confirmed the jurisdiction of the tribunal.

[123] Lew, "The Law Applicable to the Form and Substance of the Arbitration Clause", *ICCA Congress series no 9*, 114, 125.

[124] See, *e.g.*, Model Law Article 8; England, Arbitration Act section 9; Switzerland, PIL Article 7; France, NCPC Article 1458; Germany, ZPO section 1032.

[125] See, *e.g.*, France, NCPC Article 1458.

[126] See *Schiffahrtsgesellschaft Detlev Von Appen GmbH v Voest Alpine Intertrading GmbH*, [1997] 2 Lloyd's Rep 279 (CA); for one of the rare cases where damages for the breach of an arbitration agreement were granted see the decision of the arbitral tribunal reported by, Wessel and North Cohen, "In tune with *Mantovani:* the "Novel" case of damages for Breach of an arbitration

7-84 Specific performance is also not an appropriate remedy. It is not practical to force a party to take part in arbitration proceedings, appoint its arbitrator and to cooperate in the conduct of the proceedings. However, the US Federal Arbitration Act provides for an action to compel a reluctant party to go to arbitration.[127] A party that does not follow the order of the court to go to arbitration will be in contempt of court. While this may be sufficient to ensure a minimum participation of the party concerned it is doubtful whether the ensuing arbitration proceedings will lead to the originally anticipated type of dispute resolution.

7-85 Enforcement of arbitration agreements against reluctant parties must be done indirectly. A claimant trying to breach the arbitration agreement by initiating court proceedings is prevented from doing so by the courts' obligation to stay such proceedings. The claimant can either commence an arbitration or not pursue its claim at all as, if a stay is granted, there is no third option of having the issue dealt with by the courts.[128] There is no other legal course of action open to it. In some countries it may be possible to apply for an antisuit injunction ordering a claimant who initiated court proceedings in breach of the arbitration to desist from taking any further step in the proceedings.[129]

7-86 The respondent's obligation to participate in an arbitration is also enforced indirectly. If it does not participate, it may be faced with a binding and enforceable default award.[130]

---

agreement", 4 *Int ALR* 65 (2001) 68: Legal costs of Chinese proceedings brought in breach of arbitration agreement were awarded as damages; see also *Mantovani v Caparelli SpA*, [1980] 1 Lloyd's Rep 375.

[127] See FAA sections 4, 206, 303; *Filanto, SpA v Chilewich Int'l Corp*, 789 F Supp 1229, XVIII YBCA 530 (1993) para 31 (SDNY 1992); Samuel, "Arbitration Statutes in England and the US", 8 *ADRLJ* 2 (1999) 11, has described this provision as a "curious throwback" to section 1 of the English 1698 Act, where the "rule of court" was needed to exclude the free revocability of an arbitration agreement; see also Born, *International Commercial Arbitration*, 381-395.

[128] Russell *on Arbitration*, 7-002; Herrmann, "The Arbitration Agreement as the Foundation of Arbitration and Its Recognition by the Courts", *ICCA Congress series no 6*, 41, 43; see also Lord Mustill in *Channel Tunnel Group Ltd v Balfour Beatty Construction Ltd and Others*, [1993] 1 Lloyd's Rep 291, 301.

[129] This option exists in particular in common law countries; See, *e.g.*, US, *Smith Enron Cogeneration Ltd Partnership, Inc v Smith Cogeneration International Inc*, XXV YBCA 1088 (2000) paras 30 *et seq* (2d Cir); England, *Aggeliki Charis Compania Maritima SA v Pagnan SpA (The Angelic Grace)*, [1995] 1 Lloyd's Rep 87, 96.

[130] Model Law Article 25; England, Arbitration Act section 41; US, FAA section 4; Netherlands, CCP Article 1040.

6. TERMINATION AND WAIVER OF THE RIGHT TO ARBITRATE

7-87 Parties can agree to terminate or waive the arbitration agreement and have their disputes decided by the courts. This can be done by agreement or by not objecting to the jurisdiction of the court in which proceedings are brought. In general, the right to rely on the arbitration agreement is lost once a party has taken the first step in court proceedings without objecting to the court's jurisdiction. Article 8(1) Model Law provides

> A court before which an action is brought in a matter which is the subject of an arbitration agreement shall, *if a party so requests not later than when submitting his first statement on the substance of the dispute*, refer the parties to arbitration unless it finds that the agreement is null and void, inoperative or incapable of being performed. [Emphasis added][131]

7-88 In interpreting the German version of this provision[132] the Bundesgerichtshof held that the time limit for raising a defence to court proceedings on the basis of an arbitration agreement is not affected by shorter time limits set by the courts for answering a claim.[133] In this case the defendant had not raised any defence within the time limit set by the court for answering the claim brought against him but had invoked the existence of an arbitration agreement before making any statements on the merits. The Supreme Court held that section 1032 ZPO was the only relevant provision.

7-89 What constitutes a "statement on the substance of the dispute" or "a step in the proceedings" has given rise to considerable case law. Lord Denning held in *Eagle Star Insurance v Yuval Insurance* that, to constitute a "step in the proceedings" depriving a party of its recourse to arbitration, the action of this party

---

[131] English Arbitration Act section 9(3) provides that no right to apply for a stay to court proceedings exists after a party "has taken any step in those proceedings to answer the substantive claim."

[132] Section 1032 ZPO modified Model Law Article 8 so that the relevant event is not the "first statement on the substance of the dispute but the "beginning of the oral hearing on the substance of the dispute."

[133] Bundesgerichtshof, 10 May 2001, III *ZR* 262/00. For an English summary and comment see Kröll, "German Supreme Court: Missed Deadline Does Not Bar Defendant from Invoking Existence of Arbitration Clause", 17(4) *Mealey's IAR* 25 (2002).

> must be one which impliedly affirms the correctness of the proceedings and the willingness of the [party] to go along with a determination by the Courts of law instead of arbitration.[134]

7-90 Consequently a step is generally taken when the defendant answers the substantive claim. It does not matter whether that answer is in accordance with the procedural rules or not.[135] Any conduct of a party which indicates its intention to abandon its right to arbitration and has the effect of invoking the jurisdiction of the court will be considered a step in the proceedings. This is not the case with an application to have a default judgment set aside which does not constitute a step in the action.[136]

7-91 The English Court of Appeal held that where the defendant challenged the jurisdiction of the court but applied for a summary judgment in the case, the arbitration agreement should be upheld. The application for a stay led to

> ...the result that a step which would otherwise be a step in the proceedings, namely the application for summary judgment, is not so treated.[137]

7-92 The right to arbitrate may be waived if a party, after an unsuccessful challenge to the court's jurisdiction, defends on the merits.[138] In these cases where a court assumes jurisdiction despite a challenge a party is faced with a difficult choice. It can either allow the court proceedings go undefended on the merits and pursue its claims by arbitration, which is a risky strategy, or it can defend itself in front of the state courts and thereby waive its right to arbitration.

---

[134] *Eagle Star Insurance Co Ltd v Yuval Insurance Co Ltd*, 1 Lloyd's Rep 357, 361; see also *Capital Trust Investment Ltd v Radio Design TJ AB and others* [2002] All ER (Comm) 514 paras 56 *et seq.*

[135] *London Central and Suburban Developments Ltd v Gary Banger*, 8 ADRLJ 119 (1999) 122 *et seq.* In Malaysia there are conflicting decision as to whether the entrance of an unconditional appearance can already be considered as a step in the proceedings; for an overview see Nathan, "Section 6 of the Malaysian Arbitration Act 1952", 4 *Int ALR* N-35 (2001).

[136] *Patel v Patel* [1999] 1 All ER 923.

[137] *Capital Trust Investment Ltd v Radio Design TJ AB and others* [2002] All ER (Comm) 514, 530 para 60.

[138] *Marc Rich & Co AG v Societa Italiana Impianti PA (The "Atlantic Emperor" No 2)*, [1992] 1 Lloyd's Rep 624 (CA), where an injunction to restrain Impianti to pursue proceedings in Italy was denied, since it was held that Marc Rich had waived its right to arbitration by pleading on the merits in the Italian proceedings after its challenge to the jurisdiction of the Italian courts had been rejected by the Corte di cassazione.

7-93 Several national laws[139] and the Model Law recognise that an application to a court for interim relief cannot be considered a waiver of the right to arbitrate. However, if the request for relief goes beyond the preservation of evidence or the maintenance of the *status quo* it may be considered a waiver. US courts have held on several occasions that a party cannot invoke its right to arbitration after having initiated or participated in pre-trial discovery proceedings.[140]

7-94 The inaction of a party to commence arbitration proceedings for a certain time may also be seen as a waiver of the right to arbitrate or a frustration of the arbitration agreement.[141] In general, however, the mere inaction of a party is not sufficient to constitute a waiver.[142]

7-95 US courts have consistently held that given the strong policy in favour of arbitration in the Federal Arbitration Act and the New York Convention no waiver should be assumed in the absence of clear and unambiguous language. Ambiguities are generally resolved in favour of the right to arbitrate so that, for example, a service of suit clause, does not operate as a waiver of the right to arbitrate.[143] In cases where litigation had already been started a waiver was only assumed when the party seeking to enforce the arbitration agreement had substantially invoked the judicial process to the other parties detriment.[144]

7-96 In *Downing v Al Tameer*[145] the English Court was faced with the situation that one party denied the existence of any contractual relationship with the other party. The case concerned an alleged contract for the joint exploitation of a patent to separate crude oil from water. The dispute resolution clause provided that the parties should try to settle disputes amicably and, should that

---

139 *See, e.g.*, Netherlands, CCP Article 1022(2); Germany, ZPO section 1033; European Convention Article VI(4).

140 *See PPG Industries, Inc v Webster Auto Parts, Inc*, 128 F 3d 103 (2d Cir 1997); *SATCOM International Group plc v ORBCOMM International Partners, LP*, XXV YBCA 949 (2000) 955, para 11, 49 F 2d 331 (SDNY 1999).

141 *Terminix Co v Carroll*, 953 SW 2d 537 (Tex Ct App 1997).

142 See *Multiplex Construction Pty Ltd v Suscindy Management Pty Ltd*, [2000] NSWSC 484 (Supreme Court New South Wales); see also *Consorcio Rive SA de CV v Briggs of Cancun Inc et al*, 16(5) Mealey's IAR C 1 (2001) C 5-6 (District Court for the Eastern District of Louisiana).

143 *Suter v Munich Reinsurance Co*, 15(8) Mealey's IAR B 1 (2000) B 6-9 (3rd Cir 2000).

144 *Certain Underwriters at Lloyd's et al v Bristol-Myers Squibb Co et al*, XXV YBCA 968 (2000) para 22-41 (9th District, Texas Court of Appeals).

145 *John Downing v Al Tameer Establishment, Shaikh Khalid Al Ibrahim* [2002] All ER (Comm) 545.

fail, for arbitration. In pre-action correspondence the defendant always denied having concluded any binding agreement with the claimant. When the claimant initiated court proceedings in England the defendant applied for a stay relying on the arbitration clause contained in the alleged contract.

7-97 The Court of Appeal rejected this application on the basis that the arbitration agreement had been repudiated by the defendant's constant denial of the existence of any contractual relationship. It held that by alleging that there is no contract between the parties "prior to the issue and service of proceedings, the defendants were plainly evincing an intention not to be bound by the agreement to arbitrate." This repudiatory breach of the agreement to arbitrate was accepted by the claimant when it initiated court proceedings.

7-98 The consequence of this decision is that a party who alleges that it is not bound by an agreement risks loosing any right to rely on the arbitration agreement. If this party wants to reserve the right to arbitrate it must say so clearly when contesting the existence of the contract.

Chapter 8

DRAFTING OF THE ARBITRATION AGREEMENT

8-1 The arbitration agreement is the key factor to the existence of every arbitration. If parties wish to go to arbitration they must express this intent clearly and unambiguously. To be valid, the agreement should also be evidenced in writing and signed to ensure its validity according to the applicable law. In the absence of a clear and valid agreement there can be no arbitration; the national courts will retain their normal jurisdiction.

8-2 In practice too little attention is given to the drafting of the arbitration agreement. The arbitration clause is frequently included late in contract negotiations, sometimes as a boilerplate clause or as an afterthought, without debate or consideration of the specific needs of the case. Consequently numerous arbitration clauses are ambiguous as to what process has been chosen and how it is to be organised. Though courts generally undertake considerable efforts to give effect to the parties intention to go to arbitration this may not always be possible. Where the invalidity of an arbitration agreement results in proceedings in a country with an ill-functioning judicial system, it may be of little importance whether the rest of the contract is well drafted.

8-3 Ambiguous or defective arbitration agreements can lead to lengthy litigation challenging jurisdiction both at the outset and when enforcement of the award is sought. An arbitration agreement should not only result in granting jurisdiction to the tribunal and excluding jurisdiction of the courts, but it should also lead to a procedure "leading under the best conditions of efficiency and rapidity to the rendering of an award that is susceptible of judicial enforcement."[1] Lengthy disputes as to the validity and content of the arbitration agreement may therefore defeat one of its primary functions. Hence the importance of drafting an arbitration agreement with precision and clarity.

8-4 Drafting an arbitration agreement should follow the same rules as drafting generally: clarity and simplicity often lead to the least ambiguity. There are differences between common law and civil law drafting. Common lawyers generally try to cover every eventuality, hoping the wording will extend to unseen or unexpected situations, and if not that a court or tribunal will imply a term by analogy to what is provided expressly in the agreement. Civil lawyers by contrast rely on and expect the law to regulate the situation; they deal only with specific issues which are covered in the contract itself.

8-5 The arbitration agreement is different to a normal contract because it relates to a specific procedure.[2] Whilst some lawyers draft lengthy special form arbitration provisions, this is not generally necessary. There are developed procedures and practices in international commercial arbitration followed by institutions and arbitrators. They relate to the appointment of arbitrators, the

---

1 Davis, "Pathological Clauses: Frédéric Eisemann's Still Vital Criteria", 7 *Arb Int* 365 (1991) 366.

2 On the subject of drafting arbitration agreements see: Friedland, *Arbitration Clauses*; Paulsson, Rawding, Reed and Schwartz, *The Freshfields Guide to Arbitration and ADR*; Park, *International Forum Selection*, chapter IV; Bond, "How to Draft an Arbitration Clause" 6(2) *J Int'l Arb* 65 (1989); Born, *International Arbitration and Forum Selection Agreements*; Gélinas, "Arbitration Clauses: Achieving Effectiveness", van den Berg (ed), *ICCA Congress series no 9*, 47; Lew, "Arbitration Agreements: Form and Character", in Sarčević (ed), *Essays*, 55.

conduct of the arbitration, and the form of the award. Accordingly, provided the governing law or applicable arbitration rules are identified it is not necessary to specifically provide for all of these issues. Even such minimal clauses as "Arbitration, if any, by I.C.C. rules in London"[3] will be enforceable in practice.

8-6 Before drafting a fundamental but simple choice must be made: *ad hoc* arbitration or institutional arbitration. There are slightly different needs for agreements providing for *ad hoc* or institutional arbitration. With *ad hoc* clauses nothing can be taken for granted. If required, the arbitration will commence and be conducted outside any formal structure. Hence it is preferable that the parties create some structure for the arbitration in the arbitration agreement. In the absence of a clear statement, the law of the place of arbitration will normally apply. In institutional arbitration the task can be fairly easy. All institutions have recommended arbitration clauses. In some circumstances the institution's rules and practices can be adapted to the specific needs of the parties.

8-7 There is a general concept that should be remembered when drafting an arbitration agreement. Even when incorporated in the substantive contract, the arbitration agreement is a separate and stand alone contract. It will apply to claims and disputes of all kinds including whether the main contract is illegal or has been vitiated by some supervening event. The arbitration agreement also survives the performance and termination of the main contract. Furthermore, there are few if any implications for the main contract from the form and content of the arbitration agreement.

8-8 This chapter considers (1) the essential ingredients which should be contained in every arbitration agreement, (2) other relevant considerations to the arbitration agreement, (3) special factors relevant to *ad hoc* arbitration, (4) multiparty arbitration agreements, and (5) multi-tiered dispute resolution provisions.

1. Essential Ingredients of an Arbitration Agreement

8-9 There are three essentials for an effective arbitration agreement: the agreement to arbitrate, the scope of the arbitration agreement and the finality of the award.

---

3 *Mangistaumunaigaz Oil Production Association v United World Trade Inc*, [1995] 1 Lloyd's Rep 619; for a nearly identical clause see *Arab African Energy Corp Ltd v Olieprodukten Nederland BV*, [1983] 2 Lloyd's Rep 419.

1.1. The Agreement to Arbitrate

8-10 The arbitration agreement must simply express the parties' intention to arbitrate instead of going to a national court. The agreement should make clear that arbitration is the only forum in which disputes between the parties are to be resolved. Ambiguity, such as for example referring to an "expert" when opting for arbitration or additionally including a choice of forum clause, should be avoided.

8-11 Occasionally an arbitration agreement may allow one or both parties the choice whether to go to arbitration or have the dispute decided by state courts. The underlying rationale of such a provision is to give a party the option to apply in appropriate cases for summary judgment in state courts. The lack of summary procedures in arbitration have raised the fear in banks and financial institutions that without an option to apply for summary judgment in court recalcitrant debtors may abuse arbitration to resist clearly justified demands for payment.

8-12 In particular where only one party, in general the one with the greater bargaining power, has the right to chose between arbitration and litigation there might be problems with the enforceability of the arbitration agreement in some systems.[4] In the US this matter is not settled though at least in commercial contracts there seems to be a trend in favour of their validity.[5] The Federal Supreme Court of Germany considered this type of clause to be valid even if contained in standard terms of business.[6]

1.2. Scope of the Arbitration Agreement

8-13 The agreement must identify what disputes should be referred to arbitration: is it all or only specific disputes arising out of the particular contractual relationship between the parties? In general it is advisable to refer all disputes to arbitration instead of having a bifurcated clause. Broad wording should be used to link the disputes and the contract. Accordingly, the model

4 In Mexico such arbitration clauses are not considered valid: see Article 567 Código Federal de Procedimientos Civiles.

5 *Doctor's Assoc v Distajo,* 66 F 3d 438, 451 (2d Cir 1995). For further references see Kröll, "Schiedsverfahren bei Finanzgeschäften – Mehr Chancen als Risiken", *ZBB* 1999, 367, 378; Niddam, "Unilateral arbitration clauses in commercial arbitration", [1997] *ADRLJ* 147, 159 *et seq*; Drahozal, "Unfair Arbitration Clauses", *U Ill L Rev* 695 (2001).

6 Bundesgerichtshof, 24 September 1998 *ZIP* 1998, 2065 with note Kröll, *WuB* VII A § 1025 1-99. For the same position under English law see *Pittalis v Sherefettin* [1986] QB 868; Russell *on arbitration*, para 2-045.

clauses recommended by the various institutions refer to "all"[7] or "any dispute"[8], "all disputes, controversies and differences" [9] or just generally "disputes, controversies or claims."[10] The reference to "each dispute" or "a dispute" could be interpreted to mean each dispute should be the subject of a separate arbitration.

8-14 In identifying the link between the dispute and the contract, clauses may be used such as "arising from / arising out of or in connection with"[11] or "arising out of or relating to or in connection with"[12]. Clearly the terms "relating to" and "in connection with" are wider than "arising out of" a particular contract. The wider language may allow a tribunal to deal with a peripheral agreement which relates to but is separate from the main agreement in which the arbitration agreement is contained even though it is not expressly or directly covered in that main agreement.

8-15 Narrower language will result in certain disputes falling outside the scope of the arbitration clause. Accordingly, claims in tort or other non-contractual claims have been held not to arise under "an agreement" and not to be covered by an arbitration clause.[13] This could result in a party being forced to bring one part of a claim in an arbitration and another in a state court. For this reason, language should be used which identifies the generic issues between the parties, *e.g.* "disputes arising out of or in connection with this contract, including any question regarding its existence, validity or termination." [14] This may facilitate set-off and counterclaims being addressed in the same arbitration.

8-16 It should also be made clear that the disputes are in respect of a particular contract or contracts. An agreement to submit future disputes between the parties

---

7 See ICC recommended arbitration clause.

8 Found in the LCIA, ICSID, SIAC and HKIAC recommended clauses.

9 See, *e.g.*, standard clause of the Japanese Commercial Arbitration Association.

10 See similarly "dispute, controversy or claim" in AAA ICDR, HKIAC, WIPO, SCC Clauses.

11 See, *e.g.*, standard clause of LCIA, SIAC, HKIAC.

12 See, *e.g.*, standard clause of ICC.

13 See Working Group on the ICC Standard Arbitration Clause, Final Report of 3 March 1992, Doc N1111o 420/318. See also *Fillite (Runcorn) Ltd v Aqua-Lift (a firm)* (1989) 45 BLR 27. See also *Empresa Exportadora de Azucar v Industria Azucaera Nacional SA (The Playa Larga)* [1983] 2 Lloyd's Rep 171.

14 LCIA standard clause.

to arbitration without reference to any contractual relationship between the parties may be void for uncertainty.[15]

8-17 Clear express wording should be used if parties want to entrust the arbitration tribunal with the task of gap filling and adaptation of the contract, given the creative as opposed to judicial nature of this task.[16]

1.3. Finality of Awards

8-18 One stop dispute resolution is an advantage of arbitration. Most national laws allow no or only limited rights of appeal against an award. Parties do not wish to be tied up in the national courts on appeal to challenge the arbitrators' conclusions or to delay the effect of the tribunal's decision indefinitely where one party wishes to avoid the determination of the tribunal. For this reason, while it should be self evident and implied in the arbitration agreement, arbitration clauses frequently contain the words "finally settled"[17] or "resolved"[18] by arbitration.

8-19 Where under the law of the place of arbitration there is an appeal mechanism against the decision of the arbitration tribunal, the parties may wish to exclude this right of appeal. The English court has held that the wording of the standard ICC clause was sufficient to manifest the parties' intention to exclude the right of appeal against the award under section 3(1) Arbitration Act 1979.[19]

2. Other Relevant Considerations

8-20 Lawyers often consider and seek to cover many other relevant issues in the arbitration agreement. These include: for institutional arbitration, which institution; the place of arbitration; the number of arbitrators; the method of appointment and qualification of the arbitrators; the language of the arbitration;

---

[15] This was not the case in *Navigazione Alta Italia SpA v Concordia Maritime Chartering AB (The "Stena Pacifica")* [1990] 2 Lloyd's Rep 234.

[16] That applies irrespective of the fact that under some laws standard arbitration agreements may also empower the courts to fill gaps and adapt contracts; see Kröll, *Ergänzung und Anpassung von Verträgen durch Schiedsgerichte*, 104 *et seq*, 165 *et seq*.

[17] See, *e.g.*, recommended arbitration clauses of ICC and Japan Commercial Arbitration Association.

[18] See, *e.g.*, recommended arbitration clauses of LCIA and SIAC.

[19] *Marine Contractors Inc v Shell Petroleum Company of Nigeria* [1984] 2 Lloyd's Rep 77.

the procedure to be followed; the applicable rules to determine the issues in dispute; timetable for the award; and several other less common issues.

2.1. The Institution Chosen

8-21 There are significant differences among the various arbitration institutions.[20] In selecting the institution the content of the rules is a key factor for consideration. Parties should consider the extent to which the institution will supervise or administer the process, the number of arbitrators, how they are appointed including the existence of a panel of arbitrators, the involvement in the institution of local state organs, whether the arbitrators are to decide as *amiables compositeurs* or *ex aequo et bono* and the arrangements for payment to the institution and the tribunal.

8-22 In a perfect world the drafters of arbitration agreements would know and take into account all these differences and would choose the most appropriate rules for the disputes likely to arise in the future. In practice, however, this is not always the case. The nomination of an institution can lead to disputes as to the existence of that institution[21], or where the wrong name of the chosen institution is used, *e.g.*, the London International Arbitration Chamber, the International Arbitration Court, or the Faculty of Arbiters[22] may be void for uncertainty.[23]

8-23 It is advisable that parties use the model clause recommended by the arbitration institution chosen. It has been prepared by the institution, taking account of its experience and challenges to the clause, with the help of arbitration experts and is widely recognised.[24] Some institutions also suggest parties consider and agree on other issues which can be added to the arbitration agreement. This is illustrated by the following clause recommended by the LCIA.

---

20 For an overview on the rules of major institutions see Chao and Schurz, "International Arbitration: Selecting the Proper Forum", 17(2) *Mealey's IAR* 41 (2002).

21 That happened in the wake of the German unification when the East Berlin Court of Arbitration was dissolved; see the decision of the Bundesgerichtshof, 9 February 1995, *RPS* 2/1995, 17.

22 *Bruce v Kordula*, 2001 SLT 983.

23 See also the clause underlying the decision of the German Bundesgerichtshof, 2 December 1982, *NJW* 1983, 1267 where it was not clear which of the two institutional arbitrations in Hamburg was meant. For institutional arbitration Article IV(5) of the European Convention provides in some cases for a means to remedy such unclear clauses.

24 Parties may wish to state which version of the institution's arbitration rules should apply to accommodate any updates and amendments to such rules.

> Any dispute controversy or claim arising out of or relating to this contract regarding its existence, validity or termination, shall be referred to and finally resolved by arbitration under the LCIA Rules, which Rules are deemed to be incorporated by reference into this clause.
>
> The number of arbitrators shall be [*one / three*].
>
> The place of arbitration shall be [*City and / or Country*].
>
> The language to be used in the arbitral proceedings shall be [ ].
>
> The governing law of the contract shall be the substantive law of [ ].[25]

2.2. The Seat of the Arbitration

8-24 The choice of the place or seat of arbitration is one of the key issues in drafting an arbitration agreement.[26] First, it may influence which law governs the arbitration. Second, it has a bearing on the issue which courts can exercise supervisory and supportive powers in relation to the arbitration. Third, the place of arbitration determines the nationality of the award which is relevant for the ultimate enforcement of the award.

8-25 For these reasons parties should check that the arbitration law and its application by the courts of the place of arbitration are supportive to the arbitration process. It is also important that the place of arbitration is in a state party to the New York Convention. Non-legal factors such as available facilities, transportation, accommodation and telecommunication also influence the choice of place of arbitration.[27]

8-26 If the parties cannot or do not agree on the place of the arbitration the decision will be taken by the institution[28] or the tribunal.[29]

8-27 The seat of the arbitration must be distinguished from the place where the actual hearings take place. It may not be convenient for legal and practical reasons for the hearings to be held at the seat of the arbitration. For the

---

[25] See, similarly, the recommended UNCITRAL arbitration clause.

[26] Gélinas "Arbitration Clauses achieving Effectiveness", van den Berg (ed), *ICC Congress Series no 9*, 57.

[27] Jarvin "Leading Arbitration Seats: A (mostly European) Comparative View" in Frommel and Rider (eds), *Conflicting Legal Cultures*, 39. Crook "Leading Arbitration Seats in the Far East" in Frommel and Rider (eds), *Conflicting Legal Cultures,* 62.

[28] See, *e.g.*, ICC Rules, Article 14(1).

[29] See, *e.g.*, UNCITRAL Rules, Article 16.

avoidance of doubt parties can agree that hearings may be held elsewhere than at the place of arbitration. This is important if they subsequently wish to hold hearings in another country where, *e.g.*, most of the witnesses and the evidence are located. Equally witnesses may be unable or unwilling to travel to the place of the arbitration or a site visit may be appropriate.

2.3. Number, Method of Selection and Qualifications of Arbitrators

8-28 Agreements on the number of arbitrators are fairly common. With rare exceptions this means one or three arbitrators.[30] An odd number should be agreed to avoid deadlocks and to fulfil statutory requirements in some states. In deciding on the number of arbitrators, parties should consider cost, speed, expertise and consistency as well as their legal background.

8-29 The major advantage of three arbitrators in bi-party arbitrations is that each party can appoint one arbitrator. This may be important in cases involving parties from different legal and cultural backgrounds, and with different expectations as to procedure. Having the right to choose their own arbitrator often has the psychological effect that a party feels assured that its position will be fully considered by the tribunal. Furthermore, the multiplication of expertise and the interchange of views with co-arbitrators make a fundamentally mistaken approach to the case less likely. However, a three member tribunal will lead to a triplication of the arbitrators fees and, more often than not, to additional delays.

8-30 If the parties do not provide the number of arbitrators this will be determined by the applicable arbitration rules or law. This may be fixed or allow the number of arbitrators to be determined after the dispute has arisen in order to reflect the amount in dispute and the legal questions involved.

8-31 It is inadvisable to nominate a specific individual as an arbitrator in the agreement in respect of future disputes. If a dispute arises this individual may not be available, may have a conflict of interest or may not be the right person for the specific dispute. By contrast, in a submission to arbitration it is normal to name the arbitrators directly and to confirm their acceptance before the submission is signed.

8-32 The arbitration agreement may also provide how the arbitrators are to be appointed and what should occur if one party fails to make an appointment. This

[30] *E.g.*, a full tribunal of the Iran-US Claims Tribunal has nine judges and the Arbitral Tribunal under Annex VII of the United National Convention on the Law of the Sea has five arbitrators.

function is taken up by the institution involved so no nomination of an appointing authority is necessary. To expedite appointment of the tribunal and prevent delaying tactics, parties can submit the primary appointment mechanisms to time limits after the expiry of which appointment will be made by the institution or appointing authority.

8-33 Parties may also include specifications as to the arbitrators' qualifications. These often refer to either special technical knowledge, professional qualifications, language abilities or nationality. Though these specifications may be useful in some cases, they risk limiting the choice of arbitrators if a dispute occurs which was not anticipated when the requirements were drafted and for which other qualifications are appropriate.

2.4. Language of the Arbitration

8-34 Parties have the right to choose the language in which the arbitration should be conducted. If no such choice is made the institutional rules in general leave the language to the discretion of the arbitrators.[31] In most cases the arbitration is conducted in the language of the contract. If parties want the arbitration to be conducted in a certain language, but also that documents or witness statements be admitted in a different language, they should specify so in the arbitration agreement.[32]

2.5. Procedure to be followed

8-35 Parties and their lawyers often expect the procedure to mirror that in the legal system from which they come. This is not the case in international arbitration. Procedure is normally specifically determined as agreed by the parties or, in the absence of agreement, fixed by the tribunal.

8-36 Specifically, parties may wish to regulate in advance whether the arbitration shall be on documents only or if there should be a hearing as well. The parties can agree how many submissions there should be, whether witness or documentary evidence is to be filed at the same time, and the timetable for these submissions. Particularly important is the right to include or exclude common

---

[31] See, *e.g.*, ICC Rules, Article 15(3); UNCITRAL Rules, Article 17; AAA ICDR Rules, Article 14.

[32] Gélinas "Arbitration Clauses achieving Effectiveness", van den Berg (ed), *ICC Congress Series no 9*, para 28, 58 *et seq.*

law style cross examination and discovery. This is especially necessary where parties agree the arbitration be conducted within a short time period or by a fast track process.

2.6. Applicable Substantive Rules

8-37 In every international arbitration there is an issue as to what rules the tribunal should apply to determine the substantive rights and obligations of the parties. Where there is an express choice of law to govern the contract this will be recognised and applied by the arbitrators. The choice of law provision should be separate from the arbitration clause but is frequently considered and agreed at the same time.

8-38 There are situations where the parties want to submit their contract to, or expect the tribunal to apply, rules of a non-national law or some non-legal standard. This includes choice of law clauses providing for the *lex mercatoria* or generally accepted principles, or even legal rules common to the countries from which the parties come.[33] Although it is not always easy to identify the rules of these chosen systems, arbitrators will seek to apply them as agreed by the parties.

8-39 Just as parties exercise their autonomy to select arbitration in preference to national courts, so too they can and should provide the rules according to which the dispute should be resolved. In addition to legal rules, the arbitration agreement may provide for the arbitrators to decide issues between the parties as *amiables compositeurs* or *ex aequo et bono.*

2.7. Timetable for the award

8-40 To expedite determination of their differences parties can also establish a timetable for the issue of the award. As the parties are, directly or indirectly, paying the arbitrators they can require that the arbitrators conclude their deliberations and make their award within a reasonable time after the exchange of submissions and the hearings have been completed. Arbitrators will generally know the issues and evidence very well at this stage of the case and should be able to complete the award if they devote the time necessary. Many arbitrators are busy with other commitments, have new cases and wish to return to their

---

[33] See, *e.g., Channel Tunnel Group Ltd v Balfour Beatty Construction Ltd and Others* [1993] AC 334.

homes. Once the arbitrators have moved on to other issues they may begin to forget the details which in turn will add to the delay in the proceedings.

8-41 Normally this type of provision would require the arbitrators to make their award within, for example, 30 days of the end of the hearing.[34] The risks with this type of requirement is that the arbitrators may fail to make the award within the time period. This can happen for justifiable reasons: an arbitrator can become ill or otherwise indisposed or have other reasons to prevent the award being made within the specified time. Accordingly, if parties impose a timetable they ought to build a mechanism for extending the period, *e.g.* with the parties agreement or limited to a specific period.[35] The real risk of missing the deadline is the effect on the arbitration agreement. The arbitrators will no longer have any authority, the parties may then have no place for their dispute to be determined and will have wasted the money spent on the arbitration.

2.8. Enter Judgment on the Award

8-42 In agreements involving United States parties it is not uncommon to see a provision for the award to be entered as a judgment in a court.[36] The purpose is to agree the conversion of the award into a court judgment, to facilitate enforcement of the award. The use of this type of provision is based on the wording in Section 9 Federal Arbitration Act that

> If the parties in their agreement have agreed that a judgment of the court shall be entered upon the award made pursuant to the arbitration, and shall specify the court, then at any time within one year after the award is made any party to the arbitration may apply to the court so specified for an order confirming the award, and thereupon the court must grant such an order unless the award is vacated.[37]

---

[34] This is expressly provided under AAA ICDR Article 43.

[35] The ICC Rules require the award to be made within two months of the close of the procedure: Article 24. However, the ICC Court can extend this period to ensure that an effective award can be made.

[36] See Friedland, *Arbitration Clauses*, 75-76, which suggests entry of judgment clauses should be included where the arbitration has its place or the award may need to be enforced in the United States.

[37] See *Cortes Byrd Chipps, Inc v Bill Harbert Construction Co,* 529 US 193 (2000) for a discussion of the permissive character of the Federal Arbitration Act's venue provisions.

8-43 This type of provision is probably unnecessary for arbitration awards made outside the United States. These awards are enforceable under the New York Convention.[38]

2.9. Costs of the Arbitration

8-44 While in some systems each party bears its own costs, in other systems the costs are borne according to the degree of winning and losing. Parties can agree how costs are to be apportioned, for example by providing that each will pay the fees of the arbitrator they have appointed regardless of who succeeds in the arbitration. This can avoid unpleasant surprises and helps to assess the costs risk involved in a dispute.[39] This may be appropriate where a party from a developing country is unable or unwilling to pay arbitrators' fees at the same level as the party from the developed country. This can result in an inequality between the arbitrators and should be very carefully considered. Furthermore, the parties may also regulate that certain costs may be borne by a non-cooperative party or a party causing delay.

2.10. Confidentiality

8-45 Parties who want to ensure confidentiality should regulate that in their arbitration agreement. Without an explicit agreement between the parties there will be no binding obligation of confidentiality under most arbitration laws. The Swedish Supreme Court, for example, held that in the absence of an agreement providing for confidentiality a party can publish the award.[40] In any event absolute confidentiality is very difficult to ensure due to the many parties that need to know, and the possibility of court proceedings in support of the arbitration.

2.11. Waiver of Sovereign Immunity

8-46 In arbitration agreements with state parties another issue to consider is a waiver of sovereign immunity. Such clauses help to avoid discussions about

---

38 United States, FAA section 210.

39 For the dangers which may be associated with an agreement on costs see the US decision in *Constantin Mayard-Paul v Mega Life & Health Insurance*, 17(1) Mealey's IAR 14 (2002).

40 See Swedish Supreme Court, 27 October 2000, 51(11) *Mealey's IAR*, B 1; see also Lew, "Expert Report in Esso/BHP v Plowman", 11 *Arb Int* (1995) 283.

whether or not states can rely on their sovereign immunity. It is important to make sure that the state party also waives its immunity in relation to the enforcement and execution of the award. Otherwise the waiver may only affect immunity from adjudication.

3. *AD HOC* ARBITRATIONS

8-47 Most of the issues discussed above are equally relevant to agreements providing for *ad hoc* arbitration. As there are no clear rules applicable (as is the case with institutional arbitration), the agreement should provide for the appointment of the arbitrators and the procedures to follow. If the arbitration agreement is silent then the rules of the applicable law will be applied to these issues. This will be invariably the law of the place of arbitration if one has been agreed. The provisions of the law governing the arbitration may not be appropriate unless very carefully chosen.

8-48 To avoid the uncertainties of the law of the place of arbitration it is advisable, wherever possible, to specify in the arbitration agreement the rules to apply or how the arbitrators are to be appointed and the procedure to follow. This is effectively done when the arbitration is stated to be subject to the UNCITRAL Rules.

8-49 The model arbitration clause in the UNCITRAL Rules provides

> Any dispute, controversy or claim arising out of or relating to this contract, or the breach, termination or invalidity thereof, shall be settled by arbitration in accordance with the UNCITRAL Arbitration Rules as at present in force.
>
> Note – Parties may wish to consider adding:
>
> (a) The appointing authority shall be … (name of institution or person);
>
> (b) The number of arbitrators shall be … (one or three);
>
> (c) The place of arbitration shall be … (town or country);
>
> (d) The language(s) to be used in the arbitral proceedings shall be …

8-50 The UNCITRAL Rules are the most widely used and were specifically drafted for *ad hoc* arbitration. Other rules for non-administered arbitrations are the rules of the CPR Centre for Dispute Resolution[41] and the Permanent Court of

---

41 <www.cpradr.or>.

Arbitration Optional Rules for Arbitrating Disputes Between Two Parties of Which Only One is a State.[42]

8-51 The most important element in connection with appointing the tribunal is agreeing an appropriate "appointing authority". This is in case the parties cannot agree on a sole arbitrator or chairman of the tribunal, or if one party fails to make an appointment at the outset or if the arbitrator it nominated ceases to be able to act. The appointing authority can be an arbitration institution, such as the LCIA or the SIAC, or some professional body, *e.g.* Bar Association, Royal Institute of British Architects.

8-52 Parties should always check that the body it wishes to act as appointing authority can and will do so. Some institutions or offices do not have the knowledge to select competent arbitrators and may be concerned about liability when doing so. They may also not be allowed under their authority to make appointments.

8-53 A frequently chosen appointing authority is the Secretary General of the Permanent Court of Arbitration. The Secretary General also has the role of choosing the appointing authority under the UNCITRAL Rules.[43] In this capacity the PCA will normally choose an arbitration institution appropriate for the case, or might even act as the appointing authority itself.

8-54 Where parties do not specify the rules of procedure to follow, the chosen arbitration rules may provide a framework in which they can be developed. Parties can also adopt the IBA Rules on Taking Evidence in International Commercial Arbitration to regulate the procedure in the arbitration or to supplement the specific procedural arrangements agreed by the parties. They present internationally accepted procedural rules which can regulate how and to what extent evidence is to be submitted.

4. Multiparty Arbitrations

8-55 Where there are more than two parties to a contract, the arbitration agreement should anticipate a dispute involving more than two parties. This may arise where the position of the parties is polarised, *e.g.* two of the parties are contracting from the same perspective, such as two investors, or with a genuinely tri-partite or more situation. These situations can give rise to additional

---

42 <www.pca-cpa.org/BD/Istateeng.htm>.

43 See Article 7(2)(b).

complications, especially with respect to the appointment of arbitrators and ensuring the procedure to be followed allows all the parties a fair opportunity to present its case. These can be regulated in the arbitration agreement.

8-56 Multiparty arrangements arise typically in joint venture agreements where two or more parties establish the joint venture, a new and separate party in itself. When a dispute arises, especially if it involves the actions or rights of the joint venture, or the interpretation of the corporate instruments of the joint venture, it will often be necessary for the joint venture to be party to the arbitration. In this way it will be bound by the award. The joint venture will generally need separate legal representation and may have a different perspective to both parties on the issues in dispute.

8-57 Another example is a consortium agreement, where several parties join together in common purpose to contract with another party. The consortium agreement, and the arbitration clause that is in it, binds all of the consortium members equally. This is usual in certain financial transactions. In such a contract it is necessary to ensure that even though the lead member of the consortium might alone be party to an arbitration agreement with the other party, all the consortium members are bound by the arbitration agreement and the arbitrator's award. There may however be situations where one needs to protect the rights of individual consortium members including allowing participation in the arbitration.

8-58 For the appointment of arbitrators in multiparty situations, the preferred mechanism is for the multiple claimants or multiple respondents to each nominate one arbitrator, and then for the chairman to be appointed either by agreement of all the parties (which will invariably be impossible) or by an independent appointing authority. The alternative is for all of the arbitrators to be appointed by the appointing authority. This is the solution adopted by the ICC and the LCIA after the *Dutco* case.[44] It is impractical for each party to appoint one arbitrator, even with just three parties to the arbitration, because this may result in an unwieldy number of arbitrators. More importantly, it could lead to an imbalance in the tribunal if there were more respondents than claimants. In this type of scenario parties should clearly provide how the tribunal is to be appointed. If they are to use an appointing authority, they should specify the essential qualifications sought in the arbitrators.

[44] ICC Rules, Article 10; LCIA Article 8; Cour de cassation, 7 January 1992, *Siemens AG and BKMI Industrienlagen GmbH v Dutco Construction Company (Dubai)*, Rev Arb 470 (1992).

8-59 The more complicated problem is how to manage the procedure. In a two party arbitration, there is a sequence of claimant and respondent in written and oral submissions. With three parties, it may not be appropriate for both claimants or both respondents to make submissions at the same time. Equally, at the hearing, it will be necessary for each party to have its own representation and time to present its case. Invariably even the multiple claimants and respondents will not have a common position and may well be adverse to one another. It is difficult to determine in advance exactly what the procedure should be. Therefore it is generally appropriate to leave issues for the tribunal to deal with after the case arises unless the nature of the case is such as to leave the situation clear.

8-60 A typical example is a three sided contract between the supplier of goods, the purchaser of goods and the bank which provides a trading facility to its client and equally a guarantee to the client's supplier. If an issue arises concerning liability, the purchaser might well argue that the goods were defective and therefore payment was not due. The issue is when the bank should become involved in the arbitration to defend its position in the event that liability is upheld by the tribunal. This should be regulated in the arbitration agreement, either by allowing the bank to intervene as a party at any time but to allow full information on the passage of the arbitration, or to provide for a subsequent arbitration to determine the bank's liability separately unless the arbitration award is to automatically bind the bank or guarantor.

8-61 One further issue which may need to be regulated is sub-contractors, especially in construction contracts. This occurs where the main contractor wishes to involve a sub-contractor in an arbitration because aspects of the sub-contract, *e.g.* quality of work, prorogation, pricing, are in issue in the arbitration between employer and contractor. To save time and expense it may well be appropriate to join the sub-contract, or to consolidate separate proceedings between the contractor and the sub-contractor. This can only be done if agreed at the time or specifically provided for in the arbitration agreement. In the latter case the right of the contractor to require the sub-contractor to join the arbitration with the employer must be clearly stated. In this case, where the sub-contractor has a separate position to the contractor, it is necessary to ensure procedural equality for the sub-contractor including its right to see the submissions, evidence and other documents relied on by the employer. The contractor may be unwilling to agree this because it can find itself the "jam in the sandwich", squeezed and accused by employer and sub-contractor.

5. Multi-Tiered Dispute Resolution

8-62 In many contractual arrangements it may be appropriate to explore the possibility of a negotiated settlement, or at least a cooling-off period of time, before the parties can resort to court or arbitration. Accordingly, to maximise opportunity to resolve matters amicably without a full blown arbitration, a step by step dispute resolution system can be established. The parties accordingly provide for different mechanisms to assist with the resolution of the issues which divide them, and to prevent the escalation of the dispute too quickly.

8-63 Frequently, when a dispute arises between the parties their positions become entrenched and it becomes difficult for them to resolve the issues themselves. Accordingly, in many cases rather than end up directly before an arbitration tribunal, it may be appropriate to require the parties to meet and undertake a certain minimum level of negotiation with a view to settlement. This provides the opportunity to negotiate freely and pragmatically without the immediate threat of arbitration proceedings. When providing for negotiations in this way, it is generally advisable to allow a specified window of time before arbitration can be commenced.

8-64 In certain types of contract, it may be appropriate to refer matters to a joint special purpose committee. This is particularly the case where there is a joint venture or research and development contract where there will be invariably a scientific or a finance committee with overriding review and decision making authority for commercial issues affecting the contract. This committee, and in some cases ultimately an individual such as the chief executive officer or chief scientist of one of the parties, may have the final say on the issue, including the right to terminate the contract. In such a case the dispute resolution provision should determine when the relevant committee or chief executive officer or scientist should become involved and the timetable for decisions to be made.

8-65 Another mechanism for dispute resolution is to seek the involvement of an outside third party to assist with settlement discussions. Normally this would be a form of mediation where the third party would seek to understand the parties' respective positions and help in their negotiation. Often a mediator would explain to the parties, and challenge, the strengths and weaknesses of their respective cases which could lead to a more realistic approach in negotiation. The dispute resolution provision should clearly provide the form of mediation and the rules according to which it will be conducted. It is also advisable to have a window of time during which the mediation should be started and completed, at least if it is to block the commencement of any arbitration proceedings.

8-66 This is equally appropriate for any other form of third party assisted settlement such as a mini-trial or senior executive appraisal. It is important to remember that in all of these cases settlement is only possible if the parties agree. The third party does not have the power to impose any settlement on the parties.

8-67 Increasingly important in recent years are dispute resolution boards standing ready to make expeditious decisions where a dispute arises in the course of an ongoing contract relationship. The idea is for a mechanism to resolve the parties differences at least until the main contract is concluded. The adjudicator makes a decision on how a dispute should be resolved in the short term. This issue may be brought up again when the contract is completed and arbitration proceedings can finally resolve all outstanding differences. The dispute resolution clause should make clear the extent to which, if at all, matters dealt with by an adjudicator or dispute resolution board can be referred subsequently to arbitration.

8-68 Multi-tier dispute resolution provisions are becoming more frequent. An example of such a clause can be seen in the *Channel Tunnel* case[45]

> Settlement of Disputes
>
> (1) If any dispute or differences shall arise between the Employer and the Contractor during the progress of the Works ... , then ... such dispute or difference shall at the instance of either the Employer or the Contractor in the first place be referred in writing to and be settled by a Panel of three persons (acting as independent experts but not as arbitrators) who shall unless otherwise agreed by both the Employer and the Contractor within a period of 90 days after being requested in writing by either party to do so, and after such investigation as the Panel think fit, state their decision in writing and give notice of the same to the Employer and the Contractor. ...
>
> (2) The Contractor shall in every case continue to proceed with the Works with all due diligence and the Contractor and the Employer shall both give effect forthwith to every such decision of the Panel ... unless and until the same shall be revised by arbitration as hereinafter provided. ...

8-69 This clause required an attempt to resolve disputes by reference to a Panel. If either party was not satisfied it could have the decision of the Panel reviewed and revised by arbitration. Such a clause can only operate if well defined and reasonable time-limits for the completion of each stage of dispute

---

[45] Excerpts from Clause 67 of the Channel Tunnel contract, *Channel Tunnel Group v Balfour Beatty Ltd* [1993] 1 All ER 664, 672 a-e.

resolution are clearly set out; otherwise the parties may be involved in too lengthy and uncertain a process.

8-70 Careful drafting makes such a multi-step dispute resolution agreement effective and enforceable. This is however difficult to assess if the ADR stage is expressed to be in the form of "good faith negotiations." This question was considered in *Halifax Financial Services Ltd v Intuitive Systems Ltd.*[46] There a contract for software design included a provision that in the event of any dispute arising, the parties "would meet in good faith and attempt to resolve the dispute without recourse to legal proceedings." The clause further provided for structured negotiations with the assistance of a neutral or a mediator. McKinnon J considered that this clause was "nearly an immediately effective agreement to arbitrate, albeit not quite"[47] as in *Channel Tunnel.*[48] The decision in *Halifax Financial Services* has been correctly criticised as unduly traditional (and dated) and not in accordance with the accepted approach of the courts both in England and in other jurisdictions of giving effect to dispute resolution mechanisms agreed by the parties.[49]

8-71 It is only after these various stages in a multi-tiered dispute resolution clause have been passed that parties will resort to arbitration. There may be reasons to allow certain parts of this multi-tier process to continue simultaneously with arbitration proceedings. The difficulty of course is that once arbitration proceedings start positions can become further entrenched and settlement becomes significantly more difficult.

8-72 With all of these dispute resolution mechanisms, there are always certain exceptions allowing the parties to go directly to the arbitration or even to the courts. This would certainly be the case where interim relief of some sort is required. This must be carefully considered and should be expressly stated in the dispute resolution clause. It would typically provide that parties will retain the right to seek interim relief from an appropriate court or arbitration tribunal. There are also certain other issues which may be the subject for an expert determination.

---

[46] [1999] 1 All ER 303. See also the note Olatawura, Okanunle, "Managing Multi-Layered Dispute Resolution Under the Arbitration Act 1996 - Smashing Bricks of Intention", 4(3) *Int ALR* 70 (2001).

[47] [1999] 1 All ER 303.

[48] [1993] 1 All ER 664, 678 *per* Lord Mustill.

[49] Brown & Marriott, *ADR Principles and Practice* (2d ed, Sweet & Maxwell 1999), para 6-064.

8-73 Another issue to be covered is to stay the statute of limitations or prescription period during the various stages of the dispute resolution mechanism. The alternative is to allow the arbitration to be started and to run simultaneously with the other prior dispute resolution mechanisms.

Chapter 9

ARBITRABILITY

9-1 Arbitrability is one of the issues where the contractual and jurisdictional natures of international commercial arbitration meet head on.[1] It involves the simple question of what types of issues can and cannot be submitted to arbitration. Party autonomy espouses the right of parties to submit any dispute to arbitration. It is the parties' right to opt out of the normal national court jurisdiction.

9-2 National laws often impose restrictions or limitations on what matters can be referred to and resolved by arbitration. For example, states or state entities may not be allowed to enter into arbitration agreements at all or may require a special authorisation to do so. This is "subjective arbitrability." More

1 See also the definition by Carbonneau and Janson, "Cartesian Logic and Frontier Politics: French and American Concepts of Arbitrability", 2 *Tul J Int'l & Comp L* 193 (1994) 194 according to which arbitrability "determines the point at which the exercise of contractual freedom ends and the public mission of adjudication begins."

important than the restrictions relating to the parties are limitations based on the subject matter in issue. This is "objective arbitrability."[2] Certain disputes may involve such sensitive public policy issues that it is felt that they should only be dealt with by the judicial authority of state courts. An obvious example is criminal law which is generally the domain of the national courts.

9-3 These disputes are not capable of settlement by arbitration. This restriction on party autonomy is justified to the extent that arbitrability is a manifestation of national or international public policy. Consequently, arbitration agreements covering those matters will, in general, not be considered valid, will not establish the jurisdiction of the arbitrators and the subsequent award may not be enforced.

9-4 In the US the term "arbitrability" is often used in a wider sense covering the whole issue of the tribunal's jurisdiction.[3] In line with the prevailing international understanding, this chapter only deals with the restrictions imposed on the parties' freedom to submit certain types of disputes to arbitration. Specifically this chapter discusses (1) the law applicable to questions of arbitrability, (2) the limitations imposed in different countries, and (3) whether arbitration tribunals have the right and duty to deal with the issue of arbitrability on their own initiative.

1. Law Applicable to Questions of Arbitrability

9-5 Determination of the law governing arbitrability is of considerable importance. Despite the generally prevailing tendency to increase the scope of arbitrable disputes national laws frequently differ from each other. A number of disputes which are not arbitrable under the law of one country are arbitrable in another country where the interests involved are considered to be less important.

9-6 The approach to bribery is an example of existing differences. In many countries, whilst bribery is a vitiating factor in all contracts, it can be considered

---

[2] For distinction between subjective and objective arbitrability see Fouchard Gaillard Goldman *on International Commercial Arbitration*, para 533; Kirry, "Arbitrability: Current Trends in Europe", 12 *Arb Int* 373 (1996) 381 *et seq.*

[3] See, *e.g.*, *First Options of Chicago v Manuel Kaplan et and MK Investment, Inc*, 115 S Ct 1920, 1943 (1995); *Smith Enron Cogeneration Limited Partnership, Inc et al v Smith Cogeneration International, Inc*, XXV YBCA 1088 (2000) para 28 (2d Cir); see also Carbonneau and Janson, "Cartesian Logic and Frontier Politics: French and American Concepts of Arbitrability", 2 *Tul J Int'l & Comp L* 193 (1994) 194.

by arbitrators. In other countries not only is bribery illegal but also to preclude it from being legitimised, by a commercial or consultancy arrangement, if allegations of bribery are raised they cannot be considered by arbitrators. Consequently, in some countries, consultancy contracts relating to public procurement are not arbitrable because of the prevalence of excessive commissions considered to be bribes.[4]

9-7 The law governing the arbitrability of a dispute may depend on where and at what stage of the proceedings the question arises. Tribunals may apply different criteria than courts in determining this law and the criteria applied by courts at the post-award stage may differ from those at the pre-award stage.

1.1. International Conventions

9-8 Under the various conventions the obligations of national courts to enforce arbitration agreements and awards only exist where the dispute is arbitrable. Therefore these conventions generally regulate which law governs arbitrability. If a dispute is arbitrable according to *this* law courts may not rely on non-arbitrability of the dispute under a different law to refuse enforcement of the arbitration agreement or award.

9-9 The New York Convention provides for the law of arbitrability only from the perspective of enforcement. It requires the enforcing court to look to its own law to determine whether the dispute is arbitrable. Article V(2)(a) provides

> Recognition and enforcement of an arbitral award may also be refused if the competent authority in the country where recognition and enforcement is sought finds that:
>
> The subject matter of the difference is not capable of settlement by arbitration *under the law of that country*...[5] [Emphasis added.]

9-10 In contrast to this clear rule at the enforcement stage the New York Convention does not contain a rule as to what law governs the question of

---

[4] Another example are disputes arising out of the termination of exclusive distributorships. They are not arbitrable under some laws such as Belgian Law: see Tribunal de Commerce Brussels, 20 September 1999, *Matermaco SA v PPM Cranes Inc et al*, XXV YBCA 673 (2000) 675, while their arbitrability poses no question under most other laws such as *e.g.* US law (*JJ Ryan & Sons, Inc v Rhône Poulenc Textile, SA et al*, XV YBCA 549 (1990) (4th Cir); for further examples see Bortolotti, "International Commercial Agency Agreements and ICC Arbitration", 12(1) *ICC Bulletin* 48 (2001) 50 *et seq.*

[5] An identical provision is contained in Inter-American Convention Article 5(2)(a).

arbitrability at the pre-award stage. For example, when a party challenges the jurisdiction of a court invoking the existence of an arbitration clause. Article II(1) only states that arbitration agreements have to be recognised so that courts have to deny jurisdiction under Article II(3) unless the dispute is not capable of settlement by arbitration. According to which law the dispute has to be capable of settlement by arbitration, however, is not expressly provided for and has given rise to a number of divergent views in national court practices.

9-11 It is not uncommon that courts support the application of different criteria depending on whether the question arises at the referral stage or at the enforcement stage. This is well illustrated by a 1986 Belgian case involving an exclusive distributorship between a Swiss and a Belgian party.[6] The contract was submitted to Swiss law and contained an arbitration clause. The Belgian party started court proceedings in Belgium relying on a provision of Belgian law that disputes arising out of distributorship contracts were not arbitrable. The Swiss party asked for the dispute to be referred to arbitration. The application was granted by the Court of Appeal in Brussels which held that

> the arbitrability of a dispute must be ascertained according to different criteria, depending on whether the question arises when deciding on the validity of the arbitration agreement or when deciding on the recognition and enforcement of the arbitral award.
>
> In the first case, the arbitrability is ascertained according to the law which applies to the validity of the arbitration agreement and ..... its object. It is therefore the law of autonomy which provides the solution to the issue of arbitrability.
>
> An arbitrator or court faced with this issue must first determine which law applies to the arbitration agreement and then ascertain whether, according to this law, the specific dispute is capable of settlement by arbitration. [...]
>
> Within the framework of the New York Convention, the expression 'concerning a subject matter capable of settlement by arbitration' Article II(1) does not affect the applicability of the law designated by the uniform solution of conflict of laws for deciding on the arbitrability of the dispute at the level of the arbitration agreement.
>
> According to the New York Convention, the arbitrability of the dispute under the law of the forum must be taken into consideration only at the stage of recognition and enforcement of the award and not when examining the validity of the arbitration agreement. This rule can be explained by the consideration that the

6 Cour d'appel Brussels, 4 October 1985, *Company M v M SA*, XIV YBCA 618 (1989).

> arbitral award will, in the majority of cases, be executed without the intervention of an enforcement court ....[7] [References omitted.]

9-12 An interesting approach was also adopted by the US District Court for the Eastern District of New York in *Meadows Indemnity v Baccala & Shoop Insurance Services*.[8] The claimant initiated court proceedings in the US, despite an arbitration agreement, alleging that the dispute in question was not arbitrable under the law of Guernsey, where it was incorporated and where an award would have to be enforced. The court had to decide whether to enforce the arbitration agreement under Article II New York Convention or whether the claim was not arbitrable. It treated Article II as a substantive rule, providing for an autonomous international concept of arbitrability. The court held that

> reference to the domestic laws of only one country, even the country where enforcement of the arbitral award will be sought, does not resolve whether a claim is 'capable of settlement by arbitration' under Article II(1) of the Convention.
> The determination of whether a type of claim is 'not capable of settlement by arbitration' under Article II(1) must be made on an international scale, with reference to the laws of the countries party to the Convention. The purpose of the Convention, to encourage the enforcement of commercial arbitration agreements, and the federal policy in favour of arbitral dispute resolution require that the subject matter exception of Article II(1) is extremely narrow.[9] [references omitted]

9-13 However, in the majority of cases courts have determined the question of arbitrability at the pre-award stage according to their own national law.[10] While this is frequently done without any conflict of laws analysis[11] courts which have reviewed the issue properly have in general applied Article V(2)(a) New York Convention. This approach and the underlying rationale of applying the national law are well illustrated by two Italian cases.

---

7 *Ibid*, 619.

8 *Meadows Indemnity Co Ltd v Baccala & Shoop Insurance Services Inc*, 760 F Supp 1036-1045, XVII YBCA 686 (1992) (EDNY 1991). For further examples see Born, *International Commercial Arbitration*, 244.

9 XVII *YBCA* 686 (1992) 690. To give the notion "capable of being referred to arbitration" in Article II an autonomous meaning based not on one law goes a step further than admitting that under the national law a broader concept of "arbitrability" exists for international claims. The latter is still a concept of a national law not dependent on foreign laws.

10 See, *e.g.*, Belgium, Tribunal de Commerce, Brussels, 20 September 1999, *Matermaco SA v PPM Cranes Inc et al*, XXV YBCA 673 (2000) 675; Switzerland, Tribunal Fédéral, 28 April 1992, XVIII *YBCA* 143 (1993) 146.

11 In relation to US practice see Born, *International Commercial Arbitration*, 244.

9-14 In *Fincantieri v Iraq*[12] the Court of Appeal in Genoa was faced with the question whether disputes as to the effects of the United Nations embargo against Iraq were arbitrable. Dealing with the question of the applicable law the court held that

> The answer must be sought in Italian law, according to the jurisprudential principle that, when an objection for foreign arbitration is raised in court proceedings concerning a contractual dispute, the arbitrability of the dispute must be ascertained according to Italian law as this question directly affects jurisdiction, and the court seized of the action can only deny jurisdiction on the basis of its own legal system. This also corresponds to the principles expressed in Arts. II and V of the [New York Convention]. Hence, the answer to the question [of arbitrability] can only be that the dispute was not arbitrable due to [Italian embargo legislation].[13]

9-15 In a case concerning the arbitrability of EC competition law the Bologna Court of First Instance based its reasoning not on the jurisdictional nature of arbitration but on other arguments. The court held that

> Art. II(3) of the said Convention provides that jurisdiction must be denied if the arbitration clause is null and void, inoperative or incapable of being performed, and that this review can only take place in light of the national law.
>
> This principle becomes even clearer if Art. II(3) is read in conjunction with Art. V(2)(a) of the same Convention, which subordinates the efficacy of the arbitral award to the requirement that its subject matter be capable of settlement by arbitration, according to the law of the State where recognition and enforcement are sought.
>
> This provision not only applies to the field which it directly regulates (the efficacy of an arbitral award already rendered); it also applies when the court obtains its own jurisdiction in the presence of an arbitration clause or agreement for international arbitration. It would be totally useless to recognize the jurisdiction of the arbitrator

---

[12] Corte di Appello Genoa, 7 May 1994, *Fincantieri - Cantieri Navali Italiani SpA and Oto Melara SpA v Ministry of Defence, Armament and Supply Directorate of Iraq, Republic of Iraq*, 4 Riv Arb 505 (1994), XXI YBCA 594 (1996).

[13] *Ibid*, XXI *YBCA* 594 (1996) 13; for further examples see Corte di cassazione, 27 April 1979, no 2429, *Compagnia Generale Construzioni CIGECO SpA v Piersanti*, VI YBCA 229 (1981) 230; *Mitsubishi Motors Corp v Soler Chrysler Plymouth Inc*, 473 US 614, 105 S Ct 3346, 3360 Fn 21 (1985) (US Supreme Court, 2 July 1985).

> if the award, when rendered, could in no way be enforced in the legal system of the court which has jurisdiction.[14]

9-16 The practice of national courts determining arbitrability according to their own law is also supported by Article VI(2) European Convention. This provides in its pertinent part

> The courts may also refuse recognition of the arbitration agreement if under the law of their country the dispute is not capable of settlement by arbitration.

9-17 Like Article V New York Convention, Article VI(2) European Convention clearly distinguishes between the law applicable to the issue of arbitrability and the law governing the validity of the arbitration agreement. While the latter is primarily submitted to the parties choice and in the absence of a choice to the law of the place of arbitration, each national court determines the arbitrability of a dispute according to its own law.[15] This distinction and the perception that arbitrability is an issue of the general validity of the arbitration agreement has lead to the view that the dispute must be arbitrable according to both the law governing the arbitration agreement and the law of the deciding court.[16]

9-18 However, such an interpretation of the relevant provision is unnecessarily restrictive and not in line with the general tendency to favour arbitration. Though arbitrability is often considered to be a requirement for the validity of the arbitration agreement it is primarily a question of jurisdiction. Therefore the better view is that the law applicable to the question of arbitrability in court proceedings should be governed exclusively by the provisions of the law of the national court which determines the case.[17] That is also the way in which

---

[14] 18 July 1987, XVII *YBCA* 534 (1992); the decision was later reversed since it considered disputes relating to EC competition law not to be arbitrable, see Corte di Appello Bologna, 21 December 1991, XVIII *YBCA* 422 (1993).

[15] Arfazadeh, "Arbitrability under the New York Convention: The *Lex Fori* Revisited", 17 *Arb Int* 73 (2001) 80.

[16] For that view see Bertheau, *Das New Yorker Abkommen vom 10 Juni 1958 über die Anerkennung und Vollstreckung ausländischer Schiedssprüche* (Wintherthur 1965) 38 *et seq*; von Hülsen, *Die Gültigkeit von internationalen Schiedsvereinbarungen* (Schweitzer 1973) 135 *et seq*; Sandrock/ Kornmeier, *Handbuch der Internationalen Vertragsgestaltung,* Vol 2 (Verlag Recht und Wirtschaft 1980) para 210; see also Article 44 of the draft Japanese Arbitration law according to which the arbitration agreement is only valid if it fulfils the requirements of both, the law of Japan and the law applicable to the arbitration agreement.

[17] Reithmann Martiny, *Internationales Vertragsrecht* (5th ed, Schmidt 1996), para 2380; see also Arfazadeh, "Arbitrability under the New York Convention: The *Lex Fori* Revisited", 17 *Arb Int* 73 (2001) 76 *et seq*.

Article V(2)(a) New York Convention should be interpreted when the issue is the enforcement of an arbitration agreement at the pre-award stage.[18] Each country determines for itself which disputes it considers to be arbitrable.

1.2. National Arbitration Laws

9-19 The different national arbitration rules do not regulate which law governs the question of arbitrability. Rather they determine directly which disputes are arbitrable. While in common law countries this approach can traditionally be found in case law, various civil law countries have attempted to legislate the law applicable to arbitrability.

9-20 In civil law countries two different approaches can be distinguished. The first relies primarily on substantive criteria which are completely self sufficient. For example Swiss PIL Article 177 provides

1. Any dispute involving property can be the subject-matter of an arbitration.
2. If a party to the arbitration agreement is a state or an enterprise held, or an organisation controlled by it, it cannot rely on its own law in order to contest its capacity to be a party to an arbitration or the arbitrability of a dispute covered by the arbitration agreement.[19]

9-21 This approach is based on a broad notion of arbitrability defined by the national legislator. Complex conflict of laws questions may only arise for few claims involving no economic interest in the sense of the broad notion given to this concept.[20]

9-22 The second approach generally relies on the parties' power to dispose of the rights involved in the dispute or to reach a compromise. This requires a

---

[18] Due to the fact that in the enforcement-situation for which the provision is drafted the law referred to is that of the place of enforcement it is sometimes seen as a referral to the law of the place of enforcement; see Hanotiau, "The Law Applicable to Arbitrability", van den Berg (ed), *ICCA Congress series no 9*, 146, 163.

[19] See also Germany, ZPO section 1030(1). This is a change from the previous German law which was based on the first approach.

[20] See the decision of the Swiss Tribunal Fédéral, 23 June 1992, *Fincantieri - Cantieri Navali Italiani SpA and Oto Melara SpA v M and arbitration tribunal,* XX YBCA 766 (1995) para 4; (French Original ATF/BGE 118 (1992) II 353, 356) according to which the notion covered "any claims that have pecuniary value for the parties, whether assets or liabilities, in other words rights which present, for at least one of the parties, an interest that can be assessed in monetary terms".

conflict of laws analysis. An example of this approach is Article 1676(1) Belgian Judicial Code which provides

> Any dispute which has arisen or may arise out of a specific legal relationship and in respect of which it is permissible to compromise may be the subject of an arbitration agreement.[21]

9-23 Other examples of this approach, with certain elements of the first approach, can be found in French and Italian arbitration laws. These require that the parties have the right to dispose of the dispute, but also expressly exclude arbitrability of certain disputes. Article 806 Italian Code of Civil Procedure provides

> The parties may have arbitrators settle the disputes arising between them, excepting those provided for in Arts. 409 [individual labour disputes] and 442 [social security and obligatory medical aid], those regarding issues of personal status and marital separation and those others that cannot be the subject of a compromise. [22]

9-24 Similarly the French Civil Code provides

> Article 2059
> Any person may submit to arbitration the rights of which he has full disposition.
> Article 2060
> Matters regarding the civil status or capacity of a person, relating to divorce or legal separation, or disputes concerning public collectives and public establishment and generally concerning all matters involving public policy may not be submitted to arbitration.
> However, certain industrial and commercial public entities may be authorised by decree to enter into arbitration agreements.[23]

9-25 There are two ways to determine whether parties can settle the specific legal relationship. One is by reference to the substantive law of the seat of arbitration.[24] In practice this question is generally submitted by the conflict of

---

[21] See also Netherlands, CCP Article 1020(3).

[22] According to Article 1966 Civil Code the parties can compromise when they have the capacity to dispose of the rights. For an application of these provisions and the relevance of mandatory provisions in this context see Chamber of National and International Arbitration of Milan, Final award, 23 September 1997, XXIII *YBCA* 93 (1998).

[23] See also Japan, Code of Civil Procedure 1890, Article 786.

[24] For such an approach see ICC case no 4604, X *YBCA* 973 (1985) 975, French original in Jarvin Derains Arnaldez, *ICC Awards 1986-1990*, 545 *et seq*; see also Corte di Appello, Genoa, 7 May 1994, *Fincantieri - Cantieri Navali Italiani SpA and Oto Melara SpA v Ministry of Defence, Armament and Supply Directorate of Iraq, Republic of Iraq*, XXI YBCA 594 (1996). The case

laws of the seat of the arbitration to the law applicable to the relevant legal relationship.[25] The result of the necessary conflict of laws analysis may be that the question of arbitrability is to be determined by a different law.

9-26 A completely different approach is foreseen in the 1989 draft Japanese arbitration law. It favours a more rigid double arbitrability test provision which provides

> An arbitration agreement is valid only when it relates to matters which are arbitrable under both the applicable law governing the arbitration agreement and the law of Japan.

1.3. Arbitration Practice

9-27 Additional problems arise when a tribunal has to determine the arbitrability of a dispute. Article V New York Convention and Article VI European Convention are primarily directed to courts and not to tribunals. It is unclear to what extent these conventions and national laws bind an international arbitration tribunal.

9-28 Consequently the practice of arbitration tribunals concerning the issue of arbitrability varies considerably. Eight different approaches in arbitration practice and scholarly writing relating to the law applicable have been suggested

1. The national law of the parties, or of one of them.
2. The law applicable to the contract as such (lex causae).
3. The law at the seat of the arbitral tribunal (lex loci arbitri).
4. The law of the country whose ordinary courts would be competent to handle the dispute in the absence of an arbitration clause.
5. The law of the country in which it is most likely that enforcement of the award will have to be sought.
6. The law governing the arbitration clause (or arbitration agreement).
7. A combination of laws which may be contemplated under 1.–6. above.
8. Common and fundamental principles of law, applying thus a denationalised approach.[26]

---

relates to embargo legislation and arbitrability and the Italian court applied *lex fori* to determine the arbitrability question.

[25] For those problems in connection with intellectual property rights see Blessing, "Arbitrability of Intellectual Property Disputes", 12 *Arb Int* 191 (1996).

9-29 In the majority of cases, however, tribunals determine the arbitrability of a dispute on the basis of the provisions of the place of arbitration.[27] However, in some cases arbitrators have avoided a definitive decision where the disputes were arbitrable according to all possibly applicable laws.[28]

9-30 There is an alternative view which maintains that as they are not organs of a particular legal order arbitration tribunals should determine arbitrability on the basis of a genuinely international public policy.[29] Whilst this view is intellectually convincing it may lead to unwanted practical consequences in cases where the law of the place of arbitration contains a narrower concept of arbitrability than the "genuinely international public policy". In those cases necessary measures of support from the courts of the place of arbitration may not be available and the award may be open to challenge.

9-31 To ensure enforceability arbitration tribunals should generally determine arbitrability with specific reference to the law of the place of arbitration. If a dispute is not arbitrable according to the relevant rules contained in that law, the award will be open to setting aside procedures in that country, and may also exclude its enforcement in another country. This is the case for provisions relating to *ordre public*,[30] and for all rules declaring certain disputes not to be arbitrable.

---

[26] See Blessing, "Arbitrability of Intellectual Property Disputes", 12 *Arb Int* 191 (1996), 192 and Lew; "Intellectual Property Disputes and Arbitration, Final Report of the Commission on International Arbitration", 9 *ICC Bulletin* 37 (1998) 41 *et seq*.

[27] See, *e.g.*, ICC case no 6162, *Consultant v Egyptian Local Authority*, XVII YBCA 153 (1992); ICC case no 4604, X *YBCA* 973 (1985) 975, French original in Jarvin Derains Arnaldez, *ICC Awards 1986-1990*, 545; Partial Award ICC case no 8420, XXV *YBCA* 328 (2000), 330 *et seq*. In favour of such an approach see also ICC case no 6149 XX *YBCA* 41(1995) 144.

[28] ICC case no 6719, Arnaldez Derains Hascher, *ICC Awards 1991-1995*, 567, 568 *et seq*; ICC case no 6149 Arnaldez Derains Hascher, *ICC Awards 1991-1995*, 315, 318; for the tendency of ICC tribunals to ascertain the arbitrability of a dispute according to all laws concerned, see Schwartz, "The Domain of Arbitration and Issues of Arbitrability: The view from the ICC", *ICSID Rev-FILJ* 17 (1994) 27.

[29] Fouchard Gaillard Goldman *on International Commercial Arbitration*, para 559.

[30] For a comparable view see Arfazadeh, "Arbitrability under the New York Convention: The *Lex Fori* Revisited", 17 *Arb Int* 73 (2001) 79; Hanotiau, "The Law Applicable to Arbitrability", *ICCA Congress series no 9*, 146, 158, wants to limit the applicability of the law of the place of arbitration to those cases involving public policy.

9-32 The lack of arbitrability is codified in Article 34(2) Model Law and in most other laws as a separate reason for annulment besides public policy[31] although arguably arbitrability is an illustration of public policy. Irrespective of their public policy character any conflict with the provisions on arbitrability may lead to the threat of annulment proceedings. In this context the tribunal has to ensure that the rule providing for non-arbitrability is actually applicable to the case at issue. A number of the relevant rules are only applicable to domestic arbitration; accordingly the fewer connections the dispute has with a country the greater is the likelihood that the considerations underlying the rules are not applicable to the case.[32]

9-33 Some authors argue that a tribunal should additionally consider arbitrability according to the law of the probable enforcement state.[33] This is on the basis that enforcement of an award can be resisted if the dispute is not arbitrable according to the law of the state of enforcement.[34] Nevertheless tribunals have been reluctant to deny jurisdiction on the basis that the dispute is not arbitrable under the law of the possible place of enforcement or even another interested country.[35] The probable place of enforcement is often uncertain and not the only place of enforcement. Most awards are complied with voluntarily. Where enforcement may not be possible in the country originally envisaged assets may be available in a different country.

9-34 Irrespective of the approach a tribunal adopts there is always the threat of court proceedings unless the dispute is arbitrable according to the laws of all courts which would have jurisdiction but for the arbitration agreement. If not a recalcitrant party can always bring proceedings in the court where the dispute is considered not to be arbitrable and therefore is not obliged under Article II New York Convention to deny jurisdiction.

---

[31] For example Germany, ZPO section 1059(2) no 2a; Hungary, Arbitration Law section 54; India, Arbitration Ordinance 1996 section 34.

[32] See Craig Park Paulsson, *ICC Arbitration*, para 5-07 with reference to a number of court decisions where rules restraining arbitrability in the domestic context were considered to be not applicable to international cases.

[33] Fouchard Gaillard Goldman *on International Commercial Arbitration*, para 559; see also ICC Rules Article 35; for a detailed discussion of whether an arbitration tribunal having its seat in Geneva should take into account the provisions of the *lex causae*, see Partial Award ICC case no 8420, XXV *YBCA* 328 (2000) 330 *et seq.*

[34] See New York Convention, Article V(2)(a); Model Law, Article 36(1)(b)(i).

[35] See, *e.g.*, ICC case no 2476, 104 *Clunet* 936 (1977) 937; ICC case no 4604, X *YBCA* 973 (1985) 975, French original in Jarvin Derains Arnaldez, *ICC Awards 1986-1990*, 545 *et seq.*

2. SUBSTANTIVE RULES ON OBJECTIVE ARBITRABILITY

9-35 Every national law determines which types of disputes are the exclusive domain of national courts and which can be referred to arbitration. This differs from state to state reflecting the political, social and economic prerogatives of the state, as well as its general attitude towards arbitration. It involves a balancing of the mainly domestic importance of reserving certain matters for exclusive decision of courts with the more general public interest of promoting trade and commerce through an effective means of dispute settlement.[36] Therefore the decision may be different in cases arising in a purely national context from that in relation to international transaction.

9-36 In *Mitsubishi v Soler* the US Supreme Court held that in an international context the ambit of arbitration may be wider than in a national context.[37] Though the case only dealt with US law, the decision describes what is now the prevailing view.[38] The case also evidences a second general trend: the increase in the types of disputes which can be referred to international arbitration.[39] While originally arbitration was often limited to claims arising directly out of a contract, gradually more and more claims based on statutes, for example regulating important parts of the national economy in the public interest, have become arbitrable. In *Mitsubishi v Soler* the court declared antitrust disputes to be arbitrable which in *American Safety Equipment Corp v J P Maguire & Co*[40] were still held not to be arbitrable in a domestic context.

---

36 For a description of the relevant issues in the balancing process in the context of arbitrability of disputes involving allegations of bribery see the decision of the English Commercial Court, 19 December 1997, *Westacre Investments Inc v Jugoimport-SPDR Ltd* [1998] 2 Lloyd's Rep 111, 129.

37 *Mitsubishi Motors Corp v Soler Chrysler Plymouth Inc,* 473 US 614, 105 S Ct 3346, 3355 *et seq* (1985).

38 See the study undertaken by UNCITRAL in preparation for the Model Law, Secretariat Study on the New York Convention, A/CN9/168 (20 April 1979), para 45; Kaplan, "A Case by Case Examination of Whether National Courts Apply Different Standards When Assisting Arbitral Proceedings and Enforcing Awards in International Cases as Contrasting with Domestic Disputes. Is There a Worldwide Trend towards Supporting an International Arbitration Culture", van den Berg (ed), *ICCA Congress series no 8*, 191; for the French law see Fouchard Gaillard Goldman *on International Commercial Arbitration*, para 560.

39 For this trend in the European context see Kirry, "Arbitrability: Current Trends in Europe", 12 *Arb Int* 373 (1996) 374-379; for a critical comment see Carbonneau and Janson, "Cartesian Logic and Frontier Politics: French and American Concepts of Arbitrability", 2 *Tul J Int'l & Comp L* 193 (1994).

40 *American Safety Equipment Corp v JP Maguire & Co,* 391 F 2d 821, 826 *et seq* (2d Cir 1968).

9-37 Although in general limits on arbitrability of disputes arise from public policy only few laws make express reference to the notion of "public policy".[41] Not only is the notion often too vague to give clear guidance but in the contemporary arbitration friendly environment not every rule of public policy justifies reserving the disputes involved for determination by state courts.[42] Therefore, despite the underlying public policy consideration, different criteria are adopted in determining arbitrability.

9-38 Some national laws refer to very broad notions such as "disputes involving economic interest"[43] or "dispute involving property."[44] Other national laws rely on the narrower concept of "capability of the parties to reach an agreement."[45]

9-39 The Model Law does not contain any definition of which disputes are arbitrable. Quite to the contrary Article 1(5) Model Law provides that it is not intended to affect other laws of the state which preclude certain disputes being submitted to arbitration. In implementing the Model Law national legislators are completely free to determine which disputes are arbitrable and which are not. This may be done expressly where arbitrability of certain disputes are excluded by statute. The exclusion may also result from conferring exclusive jurisdiction on specialised tribunals[46] or national courts.[47]

9-40 The express exclusion of certain disputes from arbitration is well illustrated in German law. For example, former section 28 Securities Exchange Act (BörsG) provided that arbitration agreements in contracts for transactions on a German securities exchange were only valid when the customer was a registered businessperson (Vollkaufmann) or a company or businessperson established outside of Germany. Disputes with other private parties could not be referred to arbitration.[48]

---

41 See, *e.g.*, France, NCPC Article 2060.

42 See Kirry, "Arbitrability: Current Trends in Europe", 12 *Arb Int* 373 (1996) 374-379.

43 Germany, ZPO section 1030(1).

44 Switzerland, PIL Article 177.

45 Belgium, Judicial Code Article 1676(1).

46 For an overview of the importance of the "exclusive jurisdiction" criterion and other criteria see Lazic, *Insolvency Proceedings*, 146-158.

47 See, *e.g.*, EC Regulation 44/2001 Article 22.

48 Replaced by 37h WpHG. Further examples are Germany, ZPO section 1030(2) (rent of housing), BGB section 1822(12) (Representation of a child); see also France, NCPC Article

9-41 The differences between the various approaches are, however, diminishing with the gradual enlargement of the scope of arbitration in most countries. The areas where traditionally problems of arbitrability have arisen are anti-trust and competition, securities transactions, insolvency, intellectual property rights, illegality and fraud, bribery and corruption, and investments in natural resources.

2.1. Antitrust and Competition Laws

9-42 Antitrust and competition legislation involve important issues of national or regional economic policy, given the influence they may have on the market structure. The US, Europe and a number of other developed countries have regulations forbidding agreements and practices which restrict competition, lead to a dominant position or can be considered to be an abuse of a such position. Violations of those prohibitions usually result in the illegality of an agreement or practice and may give rise to actions for damages.

9-43 Article 81 EC Treaty, for example, provides that agreements which restrict competition and have an effect on the Community market are forbidden and are void unless entitled to exemption under Article 81(3). Unless by the terms of the agreement a block exemption applies, these exemptions can only be granted by the European Commission after notification and review. However, it is generally recognised that most other issues in relation to competition law are considered to be arbitrable. This has been decided in a number of cases where a party trying to resist contractual claims invoked the illegality of the agreement for alleged infringements of competition law.[49] This has found indirect approval by the ECJ in the *Eco Swiss v Benetton* case, though the case only dealt with the enforcement of an award.[50] It is accepted that under EC law private enforcement of competition remedies is permissible.[51]

2060; Belgium, Judicial Code section 1678(2) (exclusion of labour disputes). Jordan, Law no 35 of 1983 section 2 (disputes relating to bills of lading).

[49] Italy, Corte di Appello Bologna, 21 December 1991 no 1786, *SpA Coveme v CFI – Compagnie Francaise des Isolants SA*, XVIII YBCA 422 (1993) 425 *et seq*; Switzerland, Tribunal Fédéral, 28 April 1992, *V SpA v G SA*, XVIII YBCA 143 (1993) 148; Hanotiau, "The Law Applicable to Arbitrability", van den Berg (ed), *ICCA Congress series no 9*, 146, 161.

[50] ECJ, 1 June 1999, Case 126/97, *Eco Swiss China Time Ltd v Benetton International NV* [1999] ECR I 3055.

[51] See Idot, "Arbitrage et Droit Communautaire" *RDAI/IBLJ* 561 (1996); Hanotiau, "Arbitration and European Competition Law", in *Arbitration and European Law* (Bruylant 1997), 31-64;

9-44 This European approach has been largely influenced by the prevailing opinion in the US case law for antitrust disputes involving claims based on the Sherman Act. The Supreme Court decision in *Mitsubishi v Soler* considered the control at post-award stage to be sufficient to safeguard the national interests underlying the antitrust legislation.[52]

9-45 In this case, the Puerto Rican distributor had entered into a distributor agreement with Chrysler International (CISA), according to which it was to sell automobiles produced by Mitsubishi Motors, a Japanese car manufacturer, a joint venture between CISA and Mitsubishi Heavy Industries. The distributorship agreement required Soler to buy a certain amount of cars from Mitsubishi per year, and provided that any disputes should be resolved by arbitration in Japan under the rules of the Japan Commercial Arbitration Association. After a period of successful selling Soler was unable to maintain the required sales volumes. It requested permission from CISA to sell cars outside the designated area but this was refused. Soler brought an action in the District Court of Puerto Rico for breach of the US Sherman Act and other competition laws. CISA sought a stay of the court proceedings and an order to compel Soler to arbitrate in Japan.

9-46 The Supreme Court determined that the issues were arbitable and compelled the parties to go to arbitration in Japan, under the JCAA Rules, in accordance with the Agreement. Only at the enforcement stage would the Court review the anti-trust issue. The Court stated

> The importance of the private damages remedy, ... does not compel the conclusion that it may not be sought outside an American court. Notwithstanding its important incidental policing function, the treble-damages cause of action conferred on private parties by Sect. 4 of the Clayton Act, ... and pursued by Soler ... seeks primarily to enable an injured competitor to gain compensation for that injury.
> 'Sect. 4... is in essence a remedial provision. It provides treble damages to '[a]ny person who shall be injured in his business or property by reason of anything forbidden in the antitrust laws....' Of course, treble damages also play an important role in penalizing wrongdoers and deterring wrongdoing, as we also have frequently observed.... It nevertheless is true that the treble-damages provision, which makes awards available only to injured parties, and measures the awards by a multiple of the injury actually proved, is designed primarily as a remedy.'

Abdelgawad, *Arbitrage et Droit de la Concurrence*; Komninos, "Arbitration and the Modernisation of European Competition Law Enforcement", 24(2) *World Competition* 211 (2001).

52 *Mitsubishi Motors Corp v Soler Chrysler Plymouth Inc,* 473 US 614, 105 S Ct 3346 (1985).

> There is no reason to assume at the outset of the dispute that international arbitration will not provide an adequate mechanism. To be sure, the international arbitral tribunal owes no prior allegiance to the legal norms of particular States; hence, it has no direct obligation to vindicate their statutory dictates. The tribunal, however, is bound to effectuate the intentions of the parties. Where the parties have agreed that the arbitral body is to decide a defined set of claims which includes, as in these cases, those arising from the application of American antitrust law, the tribunal therefore should be bound to decide that dispute in accord with the national law giving rise to the claim. And so long as the prospective litigant effectively may vindicate its statutory cause of action in the arbitral forum, the statute will continue to serve both its remedial and deterrent function.[53] [References omitted]

9-47 Though the result is convincing the argument is flawed by the fact that it presupposes enforcement will take place in the US. If the losing party has assets in another country the award may be enforced there without US courts having a chance to intervene to safeguard the public interest protected by the Sherman Act.[54] Though any award violating US competition law may not be enforceable in the US it may be enforceable in other countries.

2.2 Securities Transactions

9-48 In the area of securities transactions national laws seek to protect the market but also often grant special protection to customers. Certain transactions may not be enforceable or customers are given special statutory rights to recover damages incurred. For example, the US Securities Act 1933 and the Securities Exchange Act 1934 grant special statutory rights to customers. All agreements which have the effect of limiting those rights granted are declared void. These rules were considered to prevent the arbitrability of all or certain disputes in relation to securities transactions.

9-49 In particular in the US the arbitrability of securities transactions has undergone considerable change over the years. The history of judicial hostility towards securities arbitration can be traced to the *Wilko v Swan* decision of

---

[53] See also the US Supreme Court decision in relation to the protection granted under the Carriage of Goods by Sea Act, *Vimar Seguros y Reaseguros, SA v M/V SKY REEFER, her Engines, etc, et al,* 115 S Ct 2322 1995, 132 L Ed 2d 462 where a comparable reasoning was adopted.

[54] See contrasting views of Werner, "A Swiss Comment on Mitsubishi", 3(4) *J Int'l Arb* 81 (1986), and Jarvin, "Mitsubishi ICC comment", 4(1) *J Int'l Arb* 87 (1987).

1953.[55] There the US Supreme Court held that claims under the Securities Act 1933 were not capable of being resolved by arbitration and had to be referred to the courts, as arbitration offered the parties less protection of their statutory rights than the courts.

9-50 Since then the legal position has shifted completely. First in 1974 in *Scherk v Alberto-Culver Co*[56] the Supreme Court recognised the arbitrability of federal securities claims with an international element. The case involved a cross-border transaction between a German citizen and a US company containing an arbitration clause. As the Court emphasised, the international nature of the agreement was the essential difference between *Wilko* and *Scherk*. While purely domestic claims could not be arbitrated, an international element could make the dispute arbitrable. Indeed, the Supreme Court acknowledged that

> a parochial refusal by the courts of one country to enforce an international arbitration agreement [...] would damage the fabric of international commerce and trade and imperil the willingness and ability of businessmen to enter into international commercial agreement.[57]

9-51 In 1987, in *Shearson v McMahon,*[58] the Supreme Court extended that position to claims under the Securities Exchange Act in purely domestic transactions. Finally two years later, in 1989, in *Rodriquez de Quijas v Shearson/American Express Inc,*[59] the *Wilko* rationale was overruled, and all federal securities claims were declared arbitrable regardless of the nature of the transaction. In that case, the plaintiffs had opened a brokerage account with American Express and their agreement incorporated a standard pre-dispute arbitration clause. The Supreme Court no longer regarded arbitration as falling short in protecting investors' rights, due to the Securities Exchange Commission supervision, and stated that

> [...] arbitration agreements [...] should not be prohibited under the Securities Act, since they, like the provision for concurrent jurisdiction, serve to advance the objective of allowing buyers of securities a broader right to select the forum for resolving disputes, whether it be judicial or otherwise.[60]

---

[55] *Wilko v Swan*, 346 US 427 (1953).

[56] 417 US 506 (1974).

[57] *Ibid.*

[58] *Shearson/American Express Inc et al v McMahon et al*, 482 US 220 (1987).

[59] 490 US 477 (1989).

[60] *Ibid*, 482-483.

9-52 The Court recognised that *Wilko* was pervaded by

> the old judicial hostility to arbitration [...] and it would be undesirable for the decisions in *Wilko* and *McMahon* to continue to exist side by side.[61]

9-53 Since the *Rodriquez* decision there has been an "explosion" of securities arbitration.[62] Brokerage firms in the US now regularly require investors to sign in their consumer accounts agreements to the effect that any dispute is to be settled by arbitration, generally under the stock exchange or self-regulatory body of which the broker is member, such as the National Association of Securities Dealers and the New York Stock Exchange.

9-54 The positive impact of arbitration in the securities area is nowadays evidenced by the fact that most self-regulatory organizations such as the New York Stock Exchange (NYSE), the National Association of Securities Dealers (NASD), the American Stock Exchange (Amex) and the Commodity Exchange administer arbitration services. This trend is not a prerogative of the United States only, as a number of European stock exchanges have established their own arbitration bodies and structures, which adopt specially tailored arbitral procedures and clearly defined rules for settling securities disputes.[63] There is a rapid growth as it can be seen by the recent NASD Dispute Resolution Inc (NASD-DR)[64] and NASDAQ Europe[65] Arbitration Rules.

---

61 *Ibid*, 484.

62 Park, "Arbitration in Banking and Finance", 17 *Annual Review of Banking Law* 213 (1998) 232; Kröll, "Schiedsverfahren bei Finanzgeschäften – Mehr Chancen als Risiken", *ZBB* 376 (1999) 376 *et seq*.

63 *E.g.* Austria and Hungary. For further details see the Eleventh Report of the Securities Industry Conference on Arbitration (July 2001) available at <www.nyse.com/pdfs/SICA2001.pdf>.

64 See NASD Code of Arbitration Procedure. The NASD DR operates the largest dispute resolution forum in the US, handling roughly 80% of all the arbitration cases in this sector.

65 The NASDAQ Stock Market announced in March 2001 that it had agreed to acquire a majority shareholding in EASDAQ market, the pan-European market formed by a consortium of US and European Banks which, thus, will be restructured in a truly pan-European and globally linked exchange called NASDAQ Europe. The NASDAQ Europe, substantially a subsidiary of the NASDAQ Stock Market, is completely independent from any national market place. The market operates on a pan-European basis, with a unified infrastructure including a single Rule Book, a single membership, a dedicated trading platform and settlement. See NASDAQ Europe Rule Book, May 2001, 11 *et seq*, approved by the Belgian Minister of Finance on 11 May 2001 and entered into effect on 8 June 2001, following its publication in the Belgian State Gazette.

2.3. Insolvency Law

9-55 The arbitrability of disputes with an insolvent party has been an issue in a number of cases in various countries.[66] In this respect one has to distinguish between the "pure" bankruptcy issues, such as appointment of an administrator, opening of proceedings and other issues. It is beyond doubt that the "pure" bankruptcy issues are generally not arbitrable.[67] Their purpose is not so much the settlement of disputes between the parties but they are more proceedings for the collective execution or reorganization of the debtor.

9-56 Most cases, however, are not concerned with such "pure" bankruptcy issues but with standard monetary claims against or by an insolvent party. In these cases the question arises whether disputes which are clearly arbitrable as such lose their arbitrability due to the insolvency of one party. The reason for this is that separate arbitration proceedings might conflict with the policies of the national insolvency laws. In order to centralise all claims and to enable the assets of a debtor to be dispersed in an equitable, orderly and systematic manner the national laws often provide for suspension of individual actions, dispossession of the debtor and an exclusive jurisdiction of a particular court.[68]

9-57 The conflict is well described by the Bankruptcy Court of Massachussetts which held in *SONATRACH v Distrigas* that

> there will be occasions where a dispute involving both the Bankruptcy Code, ..., and the Arbitration Act, ..., presents a conflict of near polar extremes: bankruptcy policy exerts an inexorable pull towards centralization while arbitration policy advocates a decentralized approach towards dispute resolution.[69]

9-58 The court came to the conclusion that the strong policy of the Federal Arbitration Act favouring arbitration in international cases overrode the policies underlying the bankruptcy law. The main argument was that the type of dispute

---

66 For a detailed account see Lazic, *Insolvency Proceedings*, 1 *et seq*; Westbrook, "The Coming Encounter: International Arbitration and Bankruptcy", 67 *Minn L Rev* 595 (1983); Newman and Burrows, "Enforcement of Arbitration Provisions in Bankruptcy", *NYLJ* 3 (June 18/1992); Mantilla-Serrano, "International Arbitration and Insolvency Proceedings", 11 *Arb Int* 51 (1995); Fouchard, "Arbitrage et faillité", *Rev Arb* 471 (1998).

67 Lazic, *Insolvency Proceedings*, 156-157.

68 See for an overview of the various techniques employed by the national laws of England, France, Germany, Netherlands and the US, Lazic, *Insolvency Proceedings*, 15 *et seq.*

69 See *Société Nationale Algerienne Pour La Recherche, La Production, Le Transport, La Transformation et La Commercialisation des Hydrocarbures v Distrigas Corp*, 80 BR 606, 610 (D Mass 1987).

involved, *i.e.* the determination of damages arising out of the termination of a contract, did not implicate any major bankruptcy issue.

9-59 The importance of the type of dispute for its arbitrability becomes even more apparent in a recent decision of the Court of Appeal for the Second Circuit.[70] In taking up the distinction in the Bankruptcy Code between "core matters" and "non-core matters", the Court in denying the arbitrability of the claim in dispute held in relation to the balancing of interest and potential conflict between the FAA and the Bankruptcy Code

> Such a conflict is lessened in non-core proceedings which are unlikely to present a conflict sufficient to override by implication the presumption in favor of arbitration. ... Core proceedings implicate more pressing bankruptcy concerns, but even a determination that a proceeding is core will not automatically give the bankruptcy court discretion to stay arbitration. Certainly not all core bankruptcy proceedings are premised on provisions of the Code that inherently conflict with the Federal Arbitration Act; nor would arbitration of such proceedings necessarily jeopardize the objectives of the Bankruptcy Code.' .... However, there are circumstances in which a bankruptcy court may stay arbitration, and in this case the bankruptcy court was correct that it had discretion to do so.
>
> In exercising its discretion over whether, in core proceedings, arbitration provisions ought to be denied effect, the bankruptcy court must still carefully determine whether any underlying purpose of the Bankruptcy Code would be adversely affected by enforcing an arbitration clause. ... The Arbitration Act as interpreted by the Supreme Court dictates that an arbitration clause should be enforced unless [doing so] would seriously jeopardize the objectives of the Code.
>
> In the instant case, the declaratory judgment proceedings are integral to the bankruptcy court's ability to preserve and equitably distribute the Trust's assets. Furthermore, as we have previously pointed out, the bankruptcy court is the preferable venue in which to handle mass tort actions involving claims against an insolvent debtor.... The need for a centralized proceeding is further augmented by the complex factual scenario, involving multiple claims, policies and insurers.[71] [References omitted.]

---

[70] *United States Lines, Inc et al (US) v American Steamship Owners Mutual Protection and Indemnity Association, Inc, et al (US), In re United States Lines*, XXV YBCA 1057 (2000) (2d Cir, 1 November 1999).

[71] *Ibid*, para 14-16.

9-60 In the light of the test promulgated by the Court of Appeal for the Second Circuit the distinction between "core matters" and "non core matters" becomes relevant. Disputes relating to the latter are probably with very few exceptions arbitrable while the opposite is true for "core matters".

9-61 Comparable distinctions underlie the question of arbitrability in other countries, with the effect that the majority of contractual disputes against the insolvent debtor are probably considered to be arbitrable. In France, for example, the exclusive jurisdiction of the Commercial Court in Article 174 of the Bankruptcy Law[72] only covers "pure" bankruptcy issues.[73] The same applies to Italy.[74]

9-62 By contrast under Dutch law only non-monetary claims against the estate are arbitrable while claims for payment have to be settled by the special *renvoi procedure* if they are contested in bankruptcy.[75]

9-63 Under German law the insolvency of one party does not in general affect the arbitrability of a dispute. Claims against the estate have to be filed in bankruptcy and if contested are then arbitrable. Only enforcement actions are barred by the insolvency of the debtor, which do not include actions to have an award declared enforceable.[76] A more serious threat to arbitration than the issue of arbitrability, however, in connection with the insolvency of one party derives from the wide interpretation by German courts of the notion of "inoperability" of the arbitration clause. German courts have consistently held that an arbitration agreement becomes inoperable if one of the parties lacks the necessary funds for arbitration proceedings,[77] which might be the case when a company is insolvent.

---

72 Decree no 85-1388 of 27 December 1985.

73 Cour de cassation, 19 May 1987, *Rev Arb* 142 (1988); Lazic, *Insolvency Proceedings*, 162 with further references.

74 Tribunale Lodi, 13 February 1991, *Adda Officine Elettromeccaniche e Meccaniche et al v Alsthom Atlantique SA et al,* XXI YBCA 580 (1996) para 6.

75 See the Dutch Bankruptcy Act (Faillissementsrecht) Article 122; see also Lazic, *Insolvency Proceedings*, 164-165; for an overview of the legal situation in Hong Kong: Soo, "Impact of Insolvency on Hong Kong Arbitration", 3 *Int ALR* 103 (2000).

76 See Oberlandesgericht Dresden, 25 September 1998, 11 *Sch* 0001/98, unpublished.

77 See Bundesgerichtshof, 14 September 2000, *BB* 2330 (2000) with further references.

2.4. Intellectual Property Rights

9-64 Intellectual property rights derive from legal protection granted by a sovereign power, which affords the beneficiary certain exclusive rights to use and to exploit the intellectual property in question. Their existence often requires the registration with a governmental or quasi governmental agency which alone can grant, amend or revoke these rights and determine their scope. It is this involvement and the effect decisions concerning the existence of an intellectual property right have on third parties which have lead to the non-arbitrability of these disputes in some countries. For example, in the European Union disputes directly affecting the existence or validity of a registered intellectual property right are still not considered to be arbitrable.[78] By contrast in Switzerland where the law contains a comparable definition of arbitrability the opposite is true: arbitration awards are recognised by the Swiss Patent and Trade Mark Office as a basis for revoking the registration of a patent.[79]

9-65 Fewer problems concerning arbitrability arise if the dispute is not about the validity of an intellectual property right but involves contracts concluded in the exercise of a such a right. Disputes as to validity, effect and royalties due under licensing agreements, contracts for the transfer of property rights, or research and development agreements intended to lead to intellectual property rights are generally considered to be arbitrable. They usually do not have a direct effect on third parties.[80]

9-66 Two legal systems which accept the arbitrability of almost all intellectual property disputes are Switzerland[81] and the US.[82] Most other countries do not

---

[78] See generally EC Regulation 44/2001 Article 22(4) which confers exclusive jurisdiction on certain national courts in relation to the registration and validity of patents and trademarks. For Germany, in particular, see Simms, "Arbitrability of Intellectual Property Disputes in Germany", 15 *Arb Int* 193 (1999) 196; for a different view see Raeschke-Kessler and Berger, *Schiedsverfahren*, para 186 *et seq*.

[79] Blessing, "Arbitrability of Intellectual Property Disputes", 12 *Arb Int* 191 (1996) 200.

[80] See, *e.g.*, the decisions on French law by the Cour d'appel Paris, 24 March 1994, *Société Deko v G Dingler et Société Meva*, Rev Arb 513 (1994) 518 and ICC case no 6709, 119 *Clunet* 998 (1992) 1000, which held that claims that do not involve the validity of a patent but just the breach of contract are arbitrable under French law irrespective of Article 68 of the law on patents. For a detailed account on the situation in different countries see Lew, "Intellectual Property Disputes and Arbitration, Final Report of the Commission on International Arbitration", 9(1) *ICC Bulletin* 37 (1998) 41 *et seq*; for references to US cases see Born, *International Commercial Arbitration*, 281.

[81] AAA case no 13T-117-0636-85, 15 September 1987, *IBM Corp v Fujitsu Ltd*, 4(4) J Int'l Arb 153 (1987), XIII YBCA 24 (1988).

exclude intellectual property rights as a whole from the jurisdiction of arbitration tribunals but usually draw a distinction between those rights which have to be registered, *i.e.* patents and trade marks, and those which exist independently of any such formality, such as copyright. With regard to the former category, most jurisdictions will only permit an award which takes effect between the parties. However, most related issues such as ownership, infringement, transfer or violation of the patent can be freely arbitrated in all major jurisdictions. In respect of intellectual property rights which are not subject to registration, such as copyright, arbitrability appears to be internationally accepted. The general acceptance of the arbitrability of intellectual property disputes is reflected in the arbitration system under the World Intellectual Property Organisation Rules.

9-67 A hybrid system has been established for the non judicial settlement of domain name disputes. Domain names which are akin to trademarks are subject to registration under the Uniform Domain Name Dispute Resolution Policy (UDRP) of the Internet Corporation for Assigned Names and Numbers (ICANN).[83] The procedure deals with the issue of abusive domain name registrations. While it is arguable whether the UDRP system is an arbitration system, the point remains that disputes about domain names may be referred to arbitration.

2.5. Illegality and Fraud

9-68 Allegations of illegality and fraud have always raised serious problems as to the arbitrability of a dispute.[84] In conjunction with the acceptance of the doctrine of separability it has become increasingly accepted that allegations of illegality of the main contract do not necessarily lead to the non-arbitrability of the dispute. This is only where the provisions which lead to illegality are of such kind that they require the dispute to be decided by state courts.

---

[82] An example of an arbitration tribunal ruling on the validity of a patent *inter partes* without affecting its registration is ICC case no 6097, 2 *ICC Bulletin* 75 (1993). See also to that effect in the US, Plant, "Binding Arbitration of US Patents", 10(3) *J Int'l Arb* 79 (1993).

[83] See <www.icann.org>. See also Davis, "The New New Thing: Uniform Domain-Name Dispute Resolution Policy of the Internet Corporation for Assigned Names and Number", 17(3) *J Int'l Arb* 115 (2000).

[84] The discussion focused less on "arbitrability", and more on the existence of a valid arbitration clause, which is a question of separability of an arbitration clause; see, *e.g.*, *Heyman v Darwins Ltd* [1942] AC 356.

9-69 One type of provisions which has led to divergent views in this context are United Nations embargoes. In connection with the Iraq embargo legislation Italian and Swiss courts came to opposing conclusions as to the arbitrability of the dispute.

9-70 In the Italian case[85] Fincantieri and other Italian providers of army technology had entered into contracts with agencies of the Republic of Iraq for the supply of corvettes for the Iraqi Navy. After the invasion in Kuwait an embargo was declared by the United Nations Security Council followed by similar legislation by the European Union and Italy which made any dealings with Iraq illegal. At that time, most of the corvettes had not yet been built or delivered.

9-71 The Italian parties commenced proceedings against Iraq in the Court of First Instance of Genoa, alleging frustration of contract and seeking termination and damages. The Iraqi parties objected to the court's jurisdiction and maintained that the dispute should have been referred to arbitration as provided for in the contracts. The Italian parties replied that only arbitrable matters may be referred to arbitration and that the dispute concerned matters which would have been arbitrable before the embargo legislation was issued but were no longer so. They maintained that arbitrability must be ascertained under Italian law and relied on Article 806 Code of Civil Procedure. This provided that only disputes concerning rights of which the parties may freely dispose may be referred to arbitration. They alleged that, due to the embargo legislation, the parties could not freely dispose of the contractual rights at issue.

9-72 The Court of Appeal ruled that Italian courts had jurisdiction over the case as the dispute was not arbitrable under the applicable Italian and European embargo legislation. In connection with the EC Regulation 3541/1992 it held that

> ... Art. 21 of this Regulation forbids [parties] to meet or take any measure to meet Iraqi requests to perform in any way under contracts or transactions falling under Resolution no. 686/1990 .... Art. 1.2 explains that 'request' means a request made in or out of court, before or after the date of entry into force of the Rule; that 'transaction'... generically means negotiation, and that this provision, in the light of its ratio, must be interpreted in the sense that it forbids not only meeting a request but also any (voluntary) act aiming at meeting it. This *jus superveniens* is worth

---

[85] Corte di Appello Genoa, 7 May 1994, *Fincantieri - Cantieri Navali Italiani SpA and Oto Melara SpA v Ministry of Defence, Armament and Supply Directorate of Iraq, Republic of Iraq*, XXI YBCA 594 (1996).

> mentioning: even where the answer given above to the question of jurisdiction were uncertain under the legislation in force at the time of commencing this action, [this EC Rule] would make the arbitral clause null and void and grant the Italian courts jurisdiction to hear the case.
> This solution finds no obstacle in the fact that the main claim aimed at terminating the contracts, not obtaining performance under them. Also in this case, referral of the dispute to the arbitrators could have affected... rights which international and national embargo legislation had made *indisponibili*. .... Further, as a set-off had been claimed, in case termination were granted, between the Iraqi parties' credits for advance payments made and their allegedly higher debts, the arbitration could have led to meeting [Iraqi requests] in violation of the said supranational legislation. Also, an hypothetical arbitral award against the claimants, denying termination of the contract, would have recognized the continuing validity of the contracts, thereby affecting, in a contrary but similar manner, *diritti indisponibili*. [86]

9-73 The Swiss Supreme Court came to the opposite conclusion in a dispute involving the Italian party and its agent for the sales to Iraq.[87] The agent had initiated arbitration proceedings for outstanding payments under the agency contract. In a preliminary award the arbitration tribunal held that despite the embargo legislation it had jurisdiction. An action for the annulment of the award went to the Swiss Supreme Court which rejected the claim that the dispute involved was not arbitrable. The court held that generally the only condition for the arbitrability of disputes according to Swiss law was that it was a dispute in relation to property. Public policy considerations included in the embargo could only lead to non-arbitrability if they required the submission of disputes to the state courts and not only the non-enforcement of the substantive contract. The court held that

> the arbitrability of the dispute does not depend on the material existence of the claim. Thus, it cannot be denied for the only reason that mandatory provisions of law or a given material public policy make the claim null and void or its execution impossible; it could be denied only as far as the claims are concerned which should have been heard exclusively by a State court, according to provisions of law which were to be taken into consideration for reasons of public policy.
> [11] This is not at all the case here. The commercial measures taken against the Republic of Iraq raise indeed the issue of the validity of the contracts concluded

---

[86] *Ibid.*

[87] Tribunal Fédéral, 23 June 1992, *Fincantieri - Cantieri Navali Italiani SpA and Oto Melara SpA v M and arbitration tribunal,* XX YBCA 766 (1995) paras 10, 11.

> before these measures were taken, or the issue of the subsequent impossibility to perform under said contracts. It does not seem, however, and [Fincantieri and Oto Melara] in any case do not prove, that all this must lead us to find that the claims arising out of these contracts are not arbitrable, and even more that the claims arising out of related contracts, like the agency contract on which M. bases his claims, are not arbitrable.

9-74 In the US it has long been recognised that a tribunal has jurisdiction to hear a dispute concerning a contract which has allegedly been induced by fraud. In *Prima Paint Corporation v Flood & Conklin Mfg Co* the Supreme Court was faced with the question of whether a claim of fraud in inducement of an entire contract was arbitrable under an ordinary arbitration clause providing for reference of "any controversy or claim arising out or relating to agreement or breach thereof". The court held that under the Federal Arbitration Act the claim should be referred to arbitration, in the absence of any evidence that contracting parties intended to withhold that issue from arbitration.[88]

2.6. Bribery and Corruption

9-75 Bribery and corruption have been at the heart of several famous arbitrations arising out of contracts for consultancy and related services in the acquisition of contracts of public procurement. The usual situation has been that a party who wants to resist claims for payment of fees or commission alleges that the agreement was actually one for the payment of bribes and is therefore void, negating the arbitration agreement as well.

9-76 In 1963, in ICC case 1110, Judge Lagergren concluded that a dispute relating to bribery was not arbitrable. After determining that he had to enquire into his jurisdiction *ex officio*, despite a different view by the parties, Judge Lagergren held that neither French law, as the law of the place of arbitration, nor Argentine law, as the law governing the contract, would allow the dispute to be arbitrated. He continued[89]

---

[88] 87 S Ct 1801, 18 L Ed 2d 1270.

[89] ICC case no 1110, published by Wetter, "Issues of Corruption before the International Arbitral Tribunals: The Authentic Text and True Meaning of Judge Gunner Lagergren's 1963 Award in ICC Case no 1110", 10 *Arb Int* 277 (1994); but see a case where the arbitrability of allegations of fraud was denied, Supreme Court of Pakistan, 14 June 2000, *The Hub Power Company Ltd (HUBCO) v Pakistan WAPDA and Federation of Pakistan*, 15(7) Mealey's IAR A1 (2000).

> ... Finally, it cannot be contested that there exists a general principle of law recognised by civilised nations that contracts which seriously violate bonos mores or international public policy are invalid or at least unenforceable and that they cannot be sanctioned by courts or arbitrators. This principle is especially apt for use before international arbitration tribunals that lack a 'law of the forum' in the ordinary sense of the term.
> After weighing all the evidence I am convinced that a case such as this, involving such gross violations of good morals and international public policy, can have no countenance in any court either in the Argentine or in France or, for that matter, in any other civilised country, nor in any arbitral tribunal. Thus, jurisdiction must be declined in this case. It follows from the foregoing, that in concluding that I have no jurisdiction, guidance has been sought from general principles denying arbitrators to entertain disputes of this nature rather than from any national rules on arbitrability. Parties who ally themselves in an enterprise of the present nature must realise that they have forfeited any right to ask for the assistance of the machinery of justice (national courts or arbitral tribunals) in settling their disputes.[90]

9-77 According to Judge Lagergren's view credible allegations of bribery not only affect the main contract but also make the dispute non-arbitrable. Therefore the arbitration tribunal lacks jurisdiction to hear the dispute and investigate the truth of those allegations of bribery.

9-78 A decision by the Supreme Court of Pakistan followed the view of Judge Lagergren. In *HUBCO v WAPDA*[91] the dispute arose out of a contract for the purchase of power from a plant constructed and run by the claimant. The Pakistani defendant alleged that several amendments to the original agreement leading to higher prices were obtained by fraud and bribing government officials. The Pakistani Court held that mere allegation of corruption and fraud were insufficient to make disputes not arbitrable. By contrast where *prima facie* evidence of such practices exist, public policy matters are raised which require findings about the alleged criminality, the dispute cannot therefore be referred to arbitration. The Supreme Court held

---

[90] ICC case no 1110, *Argentine engineer v British company*, 3 Arb Int 282 (1987) with note Wetter, "Issues of Corruption before the International Arbitral Tribunals: The Authentic Text and True Meaning of Judge Gunner Lagergren's 1963 Award in ICC Case no 1110", 10 *Arb Int* 277 (1994), XXI *YBCA* 47 (1996).

[91] Supreme Court of Pakistan, 14 June 2000, *The Hub Power Company Ltd (HUBCO) v Pakistan WAPDA and Federation of Pakistan*, 15(7) Mealey's IAR A1 (2000).

> The allegations of corruption in support of which the above mentioned circumstances do provide *prima facie* basis for further probe into matter judicially and, if proved, would render these documents [*i.e.* the amendments of the original contract] as void; therefore, we are of the considered view that according to the public policy such matters, which require finding about alleged criminality, are not referable to Arbitration[92]

9-79 The underlying rationale is that due to the criminal element involved those issues should be left to the state courts. These have greater means of investigation and can better serve the public interest in prosecuting those acts.

9-80 However, the now prevailing view in international arbitration practice, in particular in Europe, supports the arbitrability of disputes involving allegations of corruption and bribery. Relying on the doctrine of separability arbitration tribunals and courts have come to the conclusion that the arbitration agreement as such is generally not tainted by alleged corruption which only affects the main contract.[93] Despite the international public policy implications it is felt that the tribunal should be allowed to decide whether or not there was bribery or corruption involved. National courts retain control over contracts involving bribery and corruption at the enforcement stage since awards which uphold such contracts would be contrary to public policy.

9-81 This is clearly stated in the award and the various court decisions in the *Westacre v Jugoimport* case which arose out of a consultancy agreement between Westacre Investments, Inc and Jugoimport – SDPR Holding Co Ltd. and Beogradsk Banka (the old Directorate). Westacre had agreed to assist Jugoimports in relation to orders to be placed by the Kuwait Ministry of Defence (KMD) for M-84 tanks. In return Westacre was to receive a substantial percentage of the value of the contracts. The contract was submitted to Swiss Law and provided for ICC arbitration in Geneva. After the old Directorate had secured an order from the KMD it gave Westacre written notification that it was terminating their contract because it was in violation of a circular of the KMD which prohibited the use of agents or intermediaries. Westacre started arbitration

---

92 *Ibid*, A17. In support of such an approach see also Sornarajah, *The Settlement of Foreign Investment Disputes*, 184.

93 See Switzerland, Tribunal Fédéral, *ATF* 119 II, 380, 385; England, *Westacre Investments Inc v Jugoimport-SPDR Ltd*, [1999] 2 Lloyd's Rep 65; [1999] 1 All ER (Comm) 865 (CA); Rosell and Prager, "Illicit Commissions and International Arbitration: The Question of Proof", 15 *Arb Int* 329 (1999) 330.

proceedings for the unpaid monies. The arbitrators awarded Westacre approximately US$ 50 million plus interest.

9-82 The arbitration tribunal held that the consultancy agreement was not invalid: there was no infringement of *bona mores*. Furthermore, it had not been established that the KMD Circular was part of the mandatory law of Kuwait, as distinct from a term of the M-84 contract or that it belonged to international public policy. They also held that the respondent had failed to establish that the consultancy agreement was null on grounds that the parties were to procure a contract with the Kuwait Government by illicit means. Accordingly, the consultancy agreement did not violate international public policy. Lobbying by private enterprises to obtain public contracts was not, as such, an illegal activity and contracts to carry out such activities were not illegal.[94]

9-83 The arbitration tribunal made a strong case for the separability of the arbitration agreements and the function of illegality as a defence that renders an agreement void, as well as the adversarial nature of the proceedings which limit significantly, if not extinguish, the inquisitorial role of the tribunal. More importantly, the tribunal expressed a confident opinion that it was entitled to discuss an allegation of bribery.

9-84 The defendants sought to have the award annulled before the Swiss Supreme Court claiming that Westacre was a shell for a member of the Kuwaiti Government. The Swiss court sought information from the arbitrators as to whether this information had been provided during the arbitration. The arbitrators reported that the claim had not been made before them and that in the arbitration proceedings the Directorate had sought to play down the role of the government official it now claimed was behind Westacre. Despite the new evidence, the Swiss court refused to go behind the facts as found by the arbitration tribunal and dismissed this claim in 1995.[95] The claimants had also applied to have the award enforced in Kuwait and in May 1994, without challenge from the respondents, the Kuwaiti court enforced the award.[96]

9-85 Later in 1995, Westacre applied to enforce the award in England. Through affidavit, the respondents presented more evidence of their claim that Westacre was merely a shell for the Kuwaiti government official, including that

---

[94] Westacre award excerpt in [1999] 1 *All ER (Comm)* 865, 869 d-h.

[95] The Swiss decision is reported in XXI *YBCA* 172 (1996).

[96] XXIII *YBCA* 836 (1998) 837-8.

Westacre was run by the son-in-law of the government official in question. The main issue before the English courts was whether the facts should be re-opened to consider the new evidence on the grounds that it may show that the contract violated English public policy. The Court of Appeal refused to reopen the facts holding "that the public policy of sustaining international arbitration awards on the facts of this case outweighs the public policy in discouraging international commercial corruption."[97]

9-86 At the heart of these divergent approaches lies the different weight accorded to the various public policy issues involved in those disputes. There is a clear conflict between the public policies of sustaining the parties' agreement to arbitrate all their disputes, and not enforcing illegal contracts. Allowing arbitration tribunals to deal with disputes involving allegations of bribery does not generally lead to the enforcement of illegal contracts. Arbitration tribunals have refused to enforce such contracts where bribery or corruption was proved.[98] Where tribunals have gone wrong and have issued awards, which have upheld illegal practices, courts have refused to enforce those awards.[99]

9-87 Nevertheless there might be cases which could lead to the enforcement of illegal contracts. Under the existing system courts do not go behind the facts established by the arbitrator unless the basic rules of ascertaining the facts have been violated. They decide on the basis of the facts established by the arbitrator whether the award violates public policy. In these circumstances errors of fact may lead in certain cases to the enforcement of illegal contracts. In England this threat is considered to be so minor that predominant weight is given to the public policy of sustaining the parties' agreement to arbitrate their disputes.[100] In Pakistan it is the other way round.[101]

9-88 It appears that international arbitrators are capable of turning national courts, through the enforcement process, into pawns in the execution of contracts

---

97 *Westacre Investments Inc v Jugoimport-SDPR Holding Co Ltd and others* [1998] 4 All ER 570 (QBD), [1999] 1 All ER (Comm) 865 (CA).

98 See, *e.g.*, ICC case no 3913, 111 *Clunet* 920 (1984); ICC case no 3916 (1982), 111 *Clunet* 930 (1984).

99 See, *e.g.*, *Soleimany v Soleimany* [1998] 3 WLR 811 (CA).

100 See also *Westacre Investments Inc v Jugoimport-SPDR Ltd* [1998] 2 Lloyd's Rep 111, 129 (QBD, 19 December 1997).

101 The same result is sometimes reached by adopting a very restrictive interpretation of the arbitration agreement according to which the parties never intended to submit disputes involving allegations of corruption to the tribunal.

based on egregious illegality. However, it would also be inappropriate to submit a foreign investor in a HUBCO-WAPDA situation to the national courts. In such investment contracts it is unlikely that the foreign investor could obtain a fair chance to present its case that no corruption was involved, in particular, if the people in power have changed. Therefore the solution in those cases cannot be to declare the dispute non-arbitrable but to make sure that no errors of fact arise which could lead to the enforcement of agreements tainted by corruption.

9-89 Objectively the Westacre position may be disturbing. Its effect is to allow an arbitration award effected by illegality to be upheld by a national court simply because illegality was not proven during the arbitration process. There should be no reason why, if new evidence becomes available, a court should not review the award at the time of enforcement. If precluded from doing so, national courts would be the instrument through which contracts that are clearly illegal and contrary to public policy would be legitimised.

2.7. Investment Contracts relating to Infrastructure and Natural Resources

9-90 It has been argued that certain types of investment contracts are not arbitrable[102] since they involved issues of sovereignty over natural resources or other issues of *ius cogens.*[103] Arbitrators should not pronounce on the validity of sovereign actions by a state. This view was rejected by a high profile arbitration tribunal in 1982. The state party challenged the jurisdiction of the arbitration tribunal on the basis that it could not decide on the validity of the decision of the government to renounce the exploitation of natural resources. The arbitrators rejected that view and held that

> one must distinguish the governmental decision itself which, ... escapes as such the considerations of the Arbitral Tribunal and is thus not "arbitrable", from the financial consequences of this decision in relation to the disputed Contract. While the Arbitral Tribunal was invited by the claimants' Request for Arbitration to declare that the claimants have a right to certain payments claimed, and which were claimed to be due under the disputed Contract, which ABC, following the decision

---

[102] Some even argue that these disputes are not covered by the arbitration agreement since state parties only want to submit true commercial disputes but not those involving the exercise of national sovereignty; see Sornarajah, *The Settlement of Foreign Investment Disputes*, 186 *et seq.*

[103] See, *e.g.*, the argument raised by the state party in Award of April 1982 in *ad hoc* arbitration, *Company Z and others v State Organization ABC,* VIII YBCA 94 (1983) 111; see also Sornarajah, *The Settlement of Foreign Investment Disputes*, 186 *et seq.*

> of the Utopian Government, decided not to pursue, the said Tribunal is not invited to "deny the consequences" of the political decision not to have recourse to the exploitation of natural resources. On the contrary, to the extent that the claim put forward by the claimants is based on non-performance resulting from the Government's decision [...] it may be said that the Request for Arbitration invites the Tribunal to "draw the consequences", in a contractual and purely financial context, of the said decision, and not to deny them.[104]

9-91 The distinction drawn by the tribunal seems to be sensible. On the one hand the tribunal does not have to determine the validity of the states exercise of sovereign power. On the other hand it gives the private party the required protection which it might not get in the courts of the host state. To declare these types of disputes relating to the financial effects of measures of nationalization non-arbitrable would allow the state to walk away from the arbitration clause in cases where the private investors are most vulnerable to state interference. If a state agrees to arbitrate these disputes it should be bound by its commitments.

9-92 As a result some countries have adopted a different approach. For example, Turkey which traditionally held concession contracts not to be arbitrable changed its law to allow for arbitration in these types of contracts.[105] There are, however, still a number of countries where this is not the case.[106]

3. Duty to Deal with the Lack of Arbitrability *ex Officio*

9-93 In the majority of cases the non-arbitrability of a dispute is raised by one party seeking to preclude arbitration. It may prefer to have the dispute decided by the courts. There are, however, cases where none of the parties invokes the lack of arbitrability. They may either not have realised it or may have an interest in having their dispute settled in private. For example, parties to contracts involving bribery or certain illegal conduct may accept the need for their dispute to be resolved but may not want the relevant authorities to be informed about their

---

[104] Award of April 1982 in *ad hoc* arbitration, *ABC* , VIII YBCA 94 (1983) 112-113.

[105] See Kroeger, Kautz, Acikel, "Turkey Revisited: Developments in Energy Project Arbitration in the context of Bilateral Investment Treaties and ICSID", 14(9) Mealey's IAR (1999).

[106] See, *e.g.*, the decisions of the Lebanese Conseil d'Etat, 17 July 2001, *Etat Libanais v Société FTML* and *Etat Libanais v Libancell,* Rev Arb 855 (2001), where on the basis of the old French doctrine of the non-arbitrability of administrative contracts, arbitration clauses contained in BOT contracts were considered to be invalid. The court held, however, that under a bilateral investment treaty ICSID arbitration might have been possible.

contract which will invariably be the case if the dispute is dealt with in the courts. In such cases the question arises whether the arbitration tribunal has the right itself to raise the issue of arbitrability even though the parties do not challenge the jurisdiction of the tribunal.

9-94 This was done by Judge Lagergren in ICC case 1110.[107]After studying the pleadings filed by the parties and oral and written witness statements, the sole arbitrator raised the question of his jurisdiction *ex officio*, to entertain the subject matter of the case, and stated

> In this respect both parties affirmed the binding effect of their contractual undertakings and my competence to consider and decide their case in accordance with the terms of reference. However, in the presence of a contract in dispute of the nature set out hereafter, condemned by public policy decency and morality, I cannot in the interest of due administration of justice avoid examining the question of jurisdiction on my own motion.[108]

9-95 It is worth noting that under the New York Convention recognition and enforcement of an award may be refused *ex officio* if the competent authority in the country where recognition and enforcement is sought finds that (a) the subject matter of the difference is not capable of settlement by arbitration under the law of that country, or (b) the recognition or enforcement of the award would be contrary to the public policy of that country.[109]

9-96 One could argue that arbitration tribunals are not part of any national judicial system and therefore do not owe any allegiance to a particular state. As long as the parties want to have their dispute decided by arbitration the tribunal should do so irrespective of the fact that its award may later be set aside for lack of arbitrability. The duty towards the parties to render an enforceable award only exists as long as the parties have not renounced it.

9-97 However, the preferred view is that an arbitration tribunal should on its own initiative deny jurisdiction if the dispute is not arbitrable on the basis of the facts submitted by the parties. This is not contrary to the principle of *"ne ultra petita"*, *i.e.*, not raising an issuing outside the arbitrators' authority[110] but is the

---

[107] ICC case no 1110, *Argentine engineer v British company*, 3 Arb Int 282 (1987) with note Wetter, 10 *Arb Int* 277 (1994), XXI *YBCA* 47 (1996).

[108] *Ibid.*

[109] Article V(2); see also Model Law, Articles 34(2)(b), 36(1)(b).

[110] New York Convention, Article V(1)(c).

result of an application of the law to the facts.[111] Though the parties are in general free to decide which provisions the tribunal should apply this freedom does not extend to avoiding the mandatory rules governing the issue of arbitrability. By declaring certain disputes not arbitrable the legislator has removed these from the disposal of the parties. Accordingly, the arbitration tribunal, despite being a creation of the parties, not only owes a duty to the parties but also the public. The success of arbitration as a recognised dispute settlement mechanism is also due to the fact that arbitration is not abused to circumvent the policy of states in areas which are considered to be so crucial that they are reserved for adjudication by courts.

9-98 The non-arbitrability of a dispute might also exclude any further court support during and after the arbitration. A party that agreed to arbitrate a non-arbitrable dispute might later change its mind when an award has been rendered in favour of the other party and refuse voluntary enforcement. It is at least doubtful whether in an action to set aside courts would consider that party from being estopped from raising the lack of arbitrability defence given the importance of the matter.

[111] For an example of applying provisions not pleaded by the parties *ex officio* in the context of European competition law see ICC case no 7539, 123 *Clunet* 1030 (1996) 1033.

Chapter 10

SELECTION AND APPOINTMENT OF ARBITRATORS BY PARTIES AND INSTITUTIONS

10-1 "The arbitrator is the *sine qua non* of the arbitral process. The process cannot rise above the quality of the arbitrator."[1] This statement describes the key role the arbitrator plays in every arbitration. To a large extent the realisation of the advantages of arbitration depends on the person appointed as arbitrator.[2] Since arbitration is based on a contract the parties are in principle free to choose their arbitrator. They can appoint any person with legal capacity to act as

[1] Von Mehren, "Concluding Remarks", in ICC (ed), *The Status of the Arbitrator*, 129.

[2] See Dezalay and Garth, *Dealing in Virtue*, 8; Sanders, *Quo Vadis Arbitration?*, 224.

arbitrator. The diversity in the subject matter of potential disputes makes it impossible to identify the perfect arbitrator for all cases. There are, however, a number of issues the parties should consider in making their choice as certain qualifications are useful in the majority of cases. The parties or specific rules of law governing the arbitration may even determine conditions for any appointment.

10-2 Unlike state courts, arbitration tribunals are in general not permanent institutions with a given legal status. They have to be constituted for every case. Only after the arbitrators have been appointed will there be a body with jurisdiction to decide a dispute or to order provisional measures. In this respect the actual arbitration tribunal must be distinguished from the arbitration institution under the auspices of which the arbitration may be conducted and which is a pre-existing organisation of a certain permanence. Though the institution administers and in some cases supervises the arbitration proceedings it does not decide the disputes between the parties. This task is reserved to the actual arbitration tribunal specifically appointed for the particular dispute.

10-3 This non-existence of a permanent organisation which is immediately available for deciding the parties' disputes is at the same time one of the great strengths of arbitration as well as one of its weaknesses.

10-4 On the one hand it is a major advantage of arbitration that the parties can submit the settlement of their dispute to a tribunal of their choice. They do not have to rely on an appointee of the state as in a national court, where they have no influence on who is dealing with their dispute. The parties can appoint persons in whom they have confidence, and who have the necessary legal and technical expertise for the determination of the particular dispute. They can decide whether their dispute should be decided by a tribunal of one or more arbitrators, and how those arbitrators are appointed.

10-5 On the other hand the lack of a permanent organization means that there is no competent authority to decide a dispute until the arbitration tribunal is formed. The appointment of the arbitrators can take some time while immediate action may be required to preserve the rights of a party. Parties may refuse to co-operate in the appointment process and try to prevent the creation of the tribunal or at least delay the proceedings. A party may also try to misuse the freedom of appointment to gain procedural advantages by appointing a biased arbitrator.

10-6 Since the constitution of the tribunal is indispensable for every arbitration, all arbitration rules and national laws, contain detailed provisions dealing with the appointment of arbitrators. Furthermore, they often regulate what is to happen if, before rendering an award, the tribunal becomes incomplete, *e.g.*, one of the arbitrators dies, becomes incapacitated or just refuses to co-operate with the other arbitrators.

10-7 This chapter considers the composition of the arbitration tribunal. It deals with (1) the number of arbitrators, (2) the selection of arbitrators, (3) responsibility for their appointment, (4) the procedures for appointing the tribunal, and (5) the limits on the parties' freedom to decide on the appointment process.

1. NUMBER OF ARBITRATORS

10-8 The first question is whether there should be one or more arbitrators. In general the number of arbitrators can be determined by the parties. The Model Law, for example, provides in Article 10(1) that "The parties are free to determine the numbers of arbitrators."

10-9 Similar provisions can be found in most other arbitration laws.[3] However, some laws limit the parties' freedom to agree on an even number of arbitrators.[4]

10-10 In the majority of cases parties make use of their right to determine the numbers of arbitrators either in their arbitration agreement or after the dispute has arisen. Where this is not the case it will be determined in accordance with the chosen arbitration rules or, if no rules have been agreed, on the basis of the applicable law. In practice most arbitration tribunals are composed either of a sole arbitrator or three arbitrators. Other numbers of arbitrators are extremely rare in international arbitration since they are invariably impractical and unsuitable for most cases. Therefore the fall-back provisions in the different arbitration rules and laws provide either for one or for three arbitrators. As a rule of thumb it can be said that in common law countries there exists a certain preference for a sole

---

[3] See, *e.g.*, England, Arbitration Act section 15(1); Switzerland, PIL Article 179(1); Sweden, Arbitration Act section 12; Austria, CCP section 580; Netherlands, CCP Article 1026(2); the various arbitration rules often contain comparable provisions; see only WIPO Rules Article 14(1); AAA ICDR Rules Article 5.

[4] See, *e.g.*, Netherlands, CCP Article 1026(2); similarly Egypt, Law no 27 of 1994, Article 15(2); Washington Convention Article 37(2)(a).

arbitrator while in civil law countries a three member tribunal is the preferred method.[5]

1.1. Sole Arbitrator

10-11 Sole arbitrators have the major advantage of costing less than a three member tribunal. The parties only have to pay for one arbitrator instead of three. This is an important consideration in small and medium sized cases.[6] A sole arbitrator is potentially faster than a three member tribunal. It is not necessary to co-ordinate the busy schedules of three arbitrators to find time for a hearing and there is no danger of a party appointed arbitrator trying to delay the proceedings.[7] More importantly, a sole arbitrator will undoubtedly avoid the natural tendency of a tribunal with arbitrators appointed by the parties to reach a compromise solution. The sole arbitrator is beholden to no one and renders a decision without regard to who the parties are.

10-12 A number of arbitration rules and laws, in particular in common law countries, provide that if the parties have not agreed on the number of arbitrators a sole arbitrator is to be appointed.

10-13 In institutional rules this is often only a presumption from which the institution may deviate where it is appropriate. The ICC Rules, for example, provide in Article 8(2)

> Where the parties have not agreed upon the number of arbitrators, the Court shall appoint a sole arbitrator, save where it appears to the Court that the dispute is such as to warrant the appointment of three arbitrators.

10-14 Few rules contain guidelines as to when, in deviation from the general rule, a three member tribunal should be appointed.[8] In most cases the amount in

---

5 Bernstein's *Handbook*, 47 para 2-143.

6 There are cases where the agreement provides for a sole arbitrator, despite the existence of substantial amounts in dispute, complicated legal and factual issues or even multiple parties. See, e.g., *Andersen Consulting v Arthur Andersen and Andersen Worldwide*, 10(4) Am Rev Int Arb 437 (1999).

7 Derains and Schwartz, *ICC Rules*, 134.

8 AAA ICDR Rules Article 5; see also Netherlands Arbitration Institute, Article 12(2) which provides

> The Administrator shall determine that the number of arbitrators be one or three, taking into account the preference of the parties, the amount of the claim and of the counterclaim, if any, and the complexity of the case.

dispute will be an important factor. The decision in favour of appointing a sole arbitrator is strongly influenced by the higher cost which is less an argument if the amount in dispute is high. Other factors which will be taken into consideration are the nature and complexity of the claim, the number of parties involved and the parties' preferences.[9]

10-15 By contrast, no such flexibility exists under most arbitration laws which provide for the appointment of a sole arbitrator if the parties have not agreed on the number of arbitrators. The English Arbitration Act for example provides in section 15(3)

> If there is no agreement as to the number of arbitrators, the tribunal shall consist of a sole arbitrator.[10]

10-16 In addition to following the former English law, the drafters were of the opinion that parties should only be burdened with the extra-costs involved in a three member tribunal if they agreed on such a tribunal. Furthermore, they thought that a sole arbitrator may be able to overcome the difficulties existing if more than two parties are involved.[11]

10-17 A comparable flexibility in relation to the number of arbitrators is found in the Netherlands arbitration law. Instead of providing for a fixed number, the number of arbitrators is determined by the President of the District Court if the parties cannot agree on it.[12] In deciding whether a sole arbitrator or a three member tribunal is more appropriate the President of the District court can take into account the particular circumstances of each case.

1.2. Three Member Tribunals

10-18 The main advantages of three arbitrator tribunals are

- the arbitrators can discuss the case with each other which may improve the quality of the award and limit the possibility of erratic or eccentric

---

9 See Derains and Schwartz, *ICC Rules*, 133 *et seq.*

10 See also Scotland, Arbitration Act Article 10(2); India, Arbitration Act First Schedule para 1; Singapore, International Arbitration Act section 15(3); Mexico, Code of Civil Procedure Article 1426; United States, FAA section 5; California, Arbitration Act section 1297-101; Florida, Arbitration Act section 648-09.

11 DAC Report on the Arbitration Bill, February 1996, para 79.

12 Article 1026(2).

awards. It also reduces the risk of an arbitrator completely misunderstanding the case;

- in cases involving sophisticated scientific or technical issues, it is possible to have within the tribunal one or more arbitrators with the required scientific or technical knowledge;
- where parties come from different cultural or legal backgrounds the presence of an arbitrator with a similar background appointed by a party can be very reassuring for that party. It may make the arbitration and the award of a tribunal more acceptable to the parties. Not only may an arbitrator with such a background be helpful in understanding the case put forward but it is reassuring for the appointing party that its arguments will be considered by the tribunal during its deliberations.

10-19 The major drawbacks of a three member tribunal are potentially the higher costs and increased delay. If arbitrators with busy schedules are chosen it may be difficult to convene meetings, arrange hearings or reach an agreement on the award. A party appointed arbitrator may use delaying tactics such as refusing to co-operate or unilaterally resigning in the middle of the proceedings.[13] Furthermore, there may be problems within the tribunal if one of the arbitrators is violating the confidentiality of the tribunal's deliberations.

10-20 Nevertheless, a number of institutional arbitration rules, such as CIETAC and DIS,[14] as well as the UNCITRAL Rules, provide for a three member tribunal if the parties have not agreed differently. In general these rules do not allow for any discretion. For example, Article 5 UNCITRAL Rules provides

> If the parties have not previously agreed on the number of arbitrators (*i.e.* one or three), and if within fifteen days after the receipt by the respondent of the notice of arbitration the parties have not agreed that there shall be only one arbitrator, three arbitrators shall be appointed.

10-21 When the parties have selected any of these rules to be applicable the institution cannot appoint a sole arbitrator without the parties' consent even if a one member tribunal is more appropriate. If the institution did so without any prior consent of the parties the award rendered would be open to appeal under

---

13 See, *e.g.*, ICC case no 5017, *Ivan Milutinovic PIM v Deutsche Babcock AG*, reported in detail in Schwebel, "The Validity of an Arbitral Award rendered by a Truncated Tribunal", *ICC Bulletin* 19 (1995) 22 *et seq*, where the refusal of the party appointed arbitrator to co-operate led to an award by a truncated tribunal which was annulled by the Swiss Courts and required the commencement of new arbitration proceedings.

14 See CIETAC Rules Article 24; DIS Rules section 3(1); CRCICA Rules Rule 5.

Article V(1)(d) New York Convention: the tribunal rendering the award would not be the one the parties contracted for by submitting to arbitration under those rules.

10-22 The Stockholm Chamber of Commerce is an exception to this rule. Article 16(1) SCC Rules contains a presumption in favour of a three member tribunal but allows the institution a discretion to appoint a sole arbitrator where appropriate. A more limited discretion in deciding whether a sole arbitrator or a three member tribunal is to be appointed is foreseen in the International Arbitration Rules of the Zurich Chamber of Commerce. According to Article 10 the discretion of the President of the Zurich Chamber of Commerce to decide on the number of arbitrators is limited to disputes where the amount in dispute does not exceed SFr 1,000,000 and no more than two parties are involved. In all other cases a three member tribunal has to be appointed.

10-23 No such discretion exists under the national arbitration laws which anticipate a three member tribunal, as is the case of the Model Law and most laws in civil law countries.[15] The drafters of the Model Law were of the opinion that three member tribunals were the most common configuration in international trade. Parties who preferred, for time and cost reasons, a sole arbitrator would expressly provide for such in their arbitration agreement.[16] In addition, since the Model Law was drafted for international arbitration which often involves parties from different countries it seems sensible to have a three member tribunal as the general rule if the parties cannot agree otherwise. Furthermore, the absence of an experienced institution which can decide whether a sole arbitrator or a three member tribunal is more appropriate in a particular case, justifies having a rule which does not leave any place for arguments.

1.3. Even Number of Arbitrators and Umpires

10-24 Even numbers of arbitrators are very rare in international arbitration since they always entail the danger of a deadlock if the arbitrators cannot agree. A certain exception is the *umpire* system in England and a number of other common law countries.[17] In addition to the two party appointed arbitrators, an

---

[15] See, *e.g.*, Model Law Article 10(2); Germany, ZPO section 1034(1); Belgium, Judicial Code Article 1681(3).

[16] 7th Secretariat Note, A/CN9/264 (24 March 1985) Article 10, para 3; see also Holtzmann and Neuhaus, *Model Law*, 349.

[17] England, Arbitration Act section 21; see also Bermuda Arbitration Act section 13; Victoria (Australia) Commercial Arbitration Act 1984 section 16, no 10167.

umpire is appointed. Unlike the chairman of a tribunal who necessarily is involved in rendering the award, the umpire usually only steps in if the party appointed arbitrators cannot agree on an award. Then the award is not rendered by all three arbitrators but only by the umpire as a kind of sole arbitrator.[18]

10-25 Outside the umpire system the threat of a deadlock has led to some national laws including provisions prohibiting arbitration tribunals with an even numbers of arbitrators. The Egyptian Arbitration Act, for example, provides in Article 15(2) "the Tribunal must, on pain of nullity, be composed of an odd number."[19] Since the Act does not provide for a mechanism of how to arrive at an odd number of arbitrators in these situations, arbitration clauses providing for an even number of arbitrators will probably be invalid under Egyptian law.[20]

10-26 To avoid such a result other arbitration laws which do not allow for an even number of arbitrators, such as Article 1026(3) Netherlands Code of Civil Procedure, provide in those situations for the appointment of an additional arbitrator.[21] Where the law does not expressly do so, as in India, the courts apply the default provisions for cases where the parties have not agreed on an appointment procedure.[22] In comparison to the Egyptian solution, this has the advantage of interfering to a lesser extent with the parties' intention to arbitrate while at the same time avoiding the threat of deadlocks. One can presume that most parties to an arbitration agreement with an even number of arbitrators

[18] Mustill and Boyd, *Commercial Arbitration*, 8; Merkin, *Arbitration Act*, 58.

[19] Though comparable provisions can be found in the laws of a number of other Arab states, Muslim law as such does not require an even number; see El-Ahdab, *Arab Arbitration*, 39; see also for Spain Cremades, "National Report Spain", in *ICCA Handbook*, 9.

[20] See, however, the decision of the Cour d'appel Paris, 24 February 1994, *Ministry of Public Works (Tunisia) v Société Bec Frères (France)*, XXII YBCA 682 (1997) paras 14-16, French original in *Rev Arb* 275 (1995) with note Gaudemet, 285, where the court held, in relation to a comparable situation under Tunisian law which also requires an odd number of arbitrators, that the appointment of a third arbitrator by the two other arbitrators, despite an agreement providing only for a two member tribunal, would not prevent the enforcement of the award in France.

[21] "If the parties have agreed on an even number of arbitrators, the arbitrators shall appoint an additional arbitrator who shall act as the chairman of the arbitral tribunal"; see also Italy, CCP Article 809(3); Belgium, Judicial Code Article 1681; in France the mandatory appointment of an additional arbitrator foreseen in Article 1454 NCPC is limited to domestic arbitration; for the validity of arbitration agreements providing for an even number of arbitrators under French law see Cour de cassation, 25 March 1999, *ITM France v Société Sodexma,* Rev Arb 807 (1999).

[22] See *MMTC Limited (India) v Sterlite Industries (India) Ltd (India)*, (1997) XXII YBCA 273 (Supreme Court of India, 18 November 1996, no 12736/1996). The court held that, although Indian Law did not allow for an even number of arbitrators, arbitration agreements providing for such a number are not invalid, since the rules relating to the appointment of the tribunal do not affect the validity of the arbitration agreement.

would prefer to arbitrate in front of a three member tribunal than to litigate in state courts, which would be the effect of the Egyptian rule.

10-27 The English Arbitration Act does not make the appointment of an additional arbitrator compulsory. It provides only for a rebuttable presumption in favour of having an uneven number of arbitrators. Section 15(2) provides

> Unless otherwise agreed by the parties, an agreement that the number of arbitrators shall be two or any other even number shall be understood as requiring the appointment of an additional arbitrator as chairman of the tribunal.

10-28 In other common law countries the presumption is in favour of the appointment of an umpire rather than a chairman.[23] This is in line with the old English tradition of having two arbitrators and an umpire. This can also be found in various types of contracts, in particular in shipping and insurance.[24]

1.4. Five or more Arbitrators

10-29 The decision making process in tribunals with five or more members is cumbersome and expensive. Co-ordinating the busy schedule of five or more arbitrators, who all have to be paid for by the parties, involves considerable administrative effort and inevitable delays. Therefore, tribunals with more than three arbitrators are only appropriate in very exceptional circumstance where the number or type of parties involved and the amount in dispute justify such efforts.[25] The few examples in practice often have some kind of state involvement and relate to questions of public international law. For example, the full tribunal of the Iran-US Claims Tribunal is composed of nine arbitrators.[26]

---

[23] Bermuda, Arbitration Act 1986 section 13; New Zealand, Arbitration Act 1996 section 19(3)(a); Victoria (Australia), Commercial Arbitration Act 1984 section 12; see also Merkin, *Arbitration Act*, 49.

[24] See, *e.g.*, the arbitration clause underlying the decision of the Federal Court of Australia in *Hi-Fert Pty Limited et al v Kiukiang Maritime Carriers et al*, XXIII YBCA 606 (1998).

[25] Redfern and Hunter, *International Commercial Arbitration*, para 4-14; for further examples of mainly appeal tribunals with five members in specialised commodity arbitration see Berger, *International Economic Arbitration*, 205.

[26] Algiers Declaration Article 3(1); see also the Franco-Tunisian Arbitral Tribunal, 24 *ILR* 770 (1957).

2. Selection of Arbitrators

10-30 The quality of arbitration proceedings depends to a large extent on the quality and the skill of the arbitrators chosen. The same dispute which might be resolved in a speedy, satisfactory and cost effective way by a strong and well chosen tribunal might turn into a lengthy, hard fought arbitration in the hand of a weak tribunal, leading to an award which is open to challenge and anti-enforcement actions. For this reason the choice of arbitrators is one if not the crucial part of every arbitration.[27] The question for the parties is how to identify suitable arbitrators.

10-31 An element arising from the parties' right to select is the fact that they are paying for the services of the arbitrators. It is essential that arbitrators remember they are being paid for their services which include not only professional skill and judgment, but also independence and impartiality, efficiency and expedition. By meeting and talking to potential arbitrators before nomination or appointment parties have an opportunity to appraise the arbitrators' approach on these issues.

2.1 Interviewing Potential Arbitrators

10-32 Given the importance of the appointment parties increasingly seek to interview potential arbitrators. Beyond the mere data which can be derived from a written *curriculum vitae* they may wish to know more about the arbitrators personally so that they are able to assess their attitudes and personality. There is a difference with respect to the sole arbitrator or chairman of the tribunal and the party appointed arbitrator. Interviews of potential sole arbitrators or chairmen should and are generally only held with both parties present.

10-33 The criteria for selecting party appointed arbitrators are often personal to the appointing party. In such a situation the borderline between a justified quest for information and an objectionable *ex parte* communication about the case is very slim and easy to transgress. To make an informed decision whether an

---

[27] See the case of *Andersen Consulting v Arthur Andersen and Andersen Worldwide*, 10(4) Am Rev Int Arb 459 (1999), where the successful selection of a sole arbitrator resulted in the swift and smooth resolution of a dispute involving more than 140 members of the Andersen Organisation within two and a half years; see also the Libyan Producers Agreement Arbitration, where the screening process for the appointment of three arbitrators took more than two years; see Medalie, "The Libyan Producers Agreement Arbitration: Developing Innovative Procedures in an Complex Multiparty Arbitration", 7(2) *J Int'l Arb* 7 (1990).

arbitrator has the required knowledge and experience, and to assess the arbitrator's attitude to certain issues, the party as well as the arbitrator need at least general information about the case. To deal with that problem arbitrators have developed different approaches.

10-34 Some arbitrators refuse to communicate *ex parte* with the parties beyond supplying certain relevant information such as their *curriculum vitae*, fees and availability. They do, however, seek from the parties information about the case so that they can determine conflict of interests, their own suitability and availability, *e.g.* if hearings are necessary. Others agree to be interviewed and be informed about the case in greater detail as long as a transcript of the interview is made available to the other side and the co-arbitrators.[28]

10-35 The AAA ICDR Rules addresses this specific point stating where *ex parte* communications with arbitrators are acceptable. Article 7(2) provides

> No party or anyone acting on its behalf shall have any ex parte communication relating to the case with any arbitrator, or with any candidate for appointment as party-appointed arbitrator except to advise the candidate of the general nature of the controversy and of the anticipated proceedings and to discuss the candidate's qualifications, availability or independence in relation to the parties, or to discuss the suitability of candidates for selection as a third arbitrator where the parties or party-designated arbitrators are to participate in that selection. No party or anyone acting on its behalf shall have any ex parte communication relating to the case with any candidate for presiding arbitrator.

10-36 The IBA Rules of Ethics also allow for *ex parte* contacts as long as the parties' enquiries are designed to determine the arbitrator's "suitability and availability for the appointment and provided that the merits of the case are not discussed."[29] Independent of what approach is taken, to avoid any appearance of improper behaviour and conspiracy, the other side should be informed about any meetings or general briefings. Meetings should preferably not take place at the party's office but at the arbitrator's office or neutral place.

10-37 Where the party appointed arbitrators have the responsibility of selecting the chairman, it is generally accepted that parties may communicate with the arbitrator they have appointed to make known the type of arbitrator they would like to see appointed. This is a basic entitlement of the parties to prevent an

---

[28] See the approach adopted by G Aksen as described in Bernstein's *Handbook*, 50, para 2-153.

[29] Rule 5(1); see, on this issue, Carter, "Rights and Obligations of the Arbitrator", *Arbitration* 170 (1997) 172.

arbitrator who, for some reason, is totally unacceptable being appointed as the chairman. The parties are paying for the process and should not have an arbitrator in whom one of them has no confidence or has had a bad experience in the past, or whose views are considered inappropriate for this case. It is a fine line between not allowing a party a veto but giving it the right to tell the arbitrator it has appointed that a particular arbitrator, or type of individual, is unacceptable. To overcome this potential difficulty, some party appointed arbitrators either ask for or give their appointing party a list of acceptable potential arbitrators or criteria which can be shared with the other party appointed arbitrator. This is an instance where party autonomy does control. Once the chairman has been appointed the avenue for unilateral discussion between a party and its appointed arbitrator is generally closed.[30]

2.2 Qualifications

10-38 An important issue in the selection process is the professional and commercial background of the arbitrator. Disputes about charter-parties require completely different experience and knowledge than financial transaction disputes. In international commercial arbitration it is usual that at least one member of the tribunal is a lawyer or a person with sufficient knowledge about arbitration law and practice. Even simple disputes may, in an international context, lead to difficult problems of procedure or conflict of laws. These problems are generally better handled by a lawyer than by a lay person with expertise in another area.

10-39 In a three member tribunal it is often possible to have the legal as well as the technical expertise within the tribunal. In those situations preferably the chairman should be a lawyer with the two party appointed arbitrators having the necessary non-legal expertise. The chairman will primarily be in charge of the conduct of the proceedings and therefore should have some knowledge of the relevant arbitration law.[31] It is important that the sole arbitrator or chairman has the ability to conduct the proceedings properly as any misconduct or irregularity in the arbitration proceedings may lead to delay, deprive a party of a fair chance to present its case or result in an unenforceable award.

[30] See Lowenfeld, "The Party-Appointed Arbitrator in International Controversies: some Reflections", 11(11) *Mealey's IAR* 29 (1996); Bishop and Reed, "Practical Guidelines for Interviewing, Selecting and Challenging Party-Appointed Arbitrators in International Commercial Arbitration", 14 *Arb Int* 395 (1998).

[31] DIS Rules section 2(2) DIS provides that, absent an agreement to the contrary, the chairman should be a lawyer.

10-40 What problems may arise where a tribunal is composed of non-lawyers is illustrated by a decision of the Italian Supreme Court in an action for the annulment of an award. The dispute concerned construction works and none of the arbitrators was legally trained. Therefore they decided to delegate to a lawyer, who had been appointed as an expert, to draw up the award since they considered themselves unable to do so. The Supreme Court annulled the award as it was not possible to delegate essential decision making powers.[32]

10-41 Adequate international experience of the arbitrators will facilitate an understanding of parties coming from different legal or cultural backgrounds. This in turn can lead to a greater acceptance of the tribunal and even the award by those parties. A party, which considers that an arbitrator has not given appropriate consideration to its presentation because it is not in conformity with the ordinary way of presentation in the arbitrator's country of origin, will consider itself treated unfairly. By contrast an awareness of the different legal traditions, as well as the different non-legal environments, will help to avoid such intercultural misunderstandings.

10-42 One further issue in international arbitration is the arbitrator's command of the language of the arbitration proceedings. An arbitrator should be able to follow the proceedings without the need for translation. The principal reason for this is to enable the arbitrator to understand the lawyers and the witnesses. Niceties and undertones will be lost in the translation which despite being accurate may therefore not give an accurate picture.

2.3 Requirements Imposed by the Parties

10-43 Parties can make specific qualifications or experience a condition for the appointment of potential arbitrators. This may be done through the wording in the arbitration clause, *e.g.*, the arbitrator must be a "commercial man".[33] Such required qualifications can also arise out of the chosen arbitration rules or the applicable arbitration law.[34] For example, some of the institutional rules require

---

[32] Corte di cassazione, 7 June 1989, *Sacheri v Robotto,* XVI YBCA 156 (1991). See also the German decision by the Bundesgerichtshof, 10 October 1991, XIX *YBCA* 200 (1994), where the court declared an arbitration clause contained in general conditions to be invalid since it would probably lead to the appointment of a non-lawyer, which would have effectively deprived a party of its right to have the general conditions scrutinised as to their validity.

[33] *Pando Compania Naviera SA v Filmo SAS* [1975] 1 QB 742.

[34] In some Arab countries the arbitrators must be Muslim to ensure that they have a knowledge of the Shari'a; see, *e.g.*, Saudi Arabia, Codes for the implementation of arbitration Chapter 1,

that the arbitrator be a member of the institution or appear on a list maintained by the institution or has been engaged in a specific area of trade.[35] Others require that the sole arbitrator or the chairman should be a lawyer.[36] If such an agreement exists and an arbitrator who does not have the necessary qualifications is appointed, the other party can either challenge the arbitrator or attack the award on the basis that the tribunal was not properly composed.[37]

10-44 Appointing authorities are bound by the parties' agreement on required qualifications. However, they are not bound by unilateral instructions of a party which did not fulfil its appointing obligations. Deviations from these instructions do not lead to an improperly composed tribunal which would justify a refusal of enforcement.[38] The same applies to the appointment of arbitrators who have been rejected by one of the parties during prior efforts to agree on an arbitrator. Appointing authorities may find themselves confronted with the situation that the most suitable nominees in their view have been rejected by one of the parties merely because they were suggested by the other party. Though there is no rule that these people may not be appointed their appointment should be avoided if other suitable arbitrators exist. A different approach may give rise to a greater unwillingness to co-operate and lead to challenge procedures in court.[39]

3. Participants in the Appointment Process

10-45 Party autonomy is the principal controller of the appointment process. Article 11(2) Model Law and most other arbitration laws[40] provide that the

---

Article 3; see Sanders, *Quo Vadis Arbitration?*, 229 *et seq*, with further limitations imposed by the national laws.

35 See, *e.g.*, GAFTA Arbitration Rules Form no 125 Rule 3:5.

36 See DIS Rules section 2(2); see also Article 13 Chinese Arbitration Act 1994 and Article 225 of the Code concerning the Organisation of Tribunal adopted by Chile in 1943.

37 Okekeifere, "The Parties' Rights against Dilatory or Unskilled Arbitrator", 15(2) *J Int'l Arb* 135 (1998).

38 See the decision by the Oberlandesgericht Dresden, 20 October 1998, 11 *Sch* 0004/98, *DIS-Materialien* VII Annex (2001) 41-171, where a German party tried to resist enforcement because the arbitrator appointed by the President of the Moscow Chamber of Commerce after the party's failure to make the required appointment could not speak German as requested by the party; see also Kröll, "Das neue deutsche Schiedsrecht vor staatlichen Gerichten: Entwicklungslinien und Tendenzen 1998-2000", 54 *NJW* 1173 (2001) 1177.

39 Bernstein's *Handbook*, 45 para 2-135.

40 See England, Arbitration Act sections 16(1), 18(1); US, FAA section 5; Netherlands, CCP Article 1027(1); Germany, ZPO section 1035(1); France, NCPC Article 1493; see also European Convention Article IV(1).

parties are generally free to agree on how the arbitration tribunal will be appointed. This can be done by including a special provision for the appointment of the tribunal into the arbitration agreement.[41] Alternatively, the parties can agree on an appointment procedure by submitting their dispute to arbitration rules which provide for the appointment of arbitrators. Furthermore, most national arbitration laws contain provisions dealing with those cases where the parties have not agreed on an appointment mechanism or the expected procedure did not work. These provisions have led national courts to decide that, despite the lack of specific agreements on the appointment process, arbitration agreements are valid.[42]

10-46 Parties, appointing authorities and state courts all have a distinct role to play in the appointment process. The procedure to be followed as well as the role of the different actors varies depending on whether a single or three member tribunal is to be appointed.

3.1. Role of the Parties

10-47 Appointment by the parties is invariably the best method of appointment. It ensures that the tribunal will be composed of persons who have the confidence of the parties. This increases the likelihood of co-operation during the proceedings as well as the voluntary enforcement of the award rendered. More importantly, as the parties are familiar with their case they are more likely to select appropriate arbitrators than an appointing authority. For these reasons arbitration agreements, and the various fall-back provisions in various arbitration rules and laws, generally give a strong role to the parties in the appointment process. In addition to the nomination of the party appointed arbitrators in a three member tribunal, often also the appointment of the chairman or a sole arbitrator is, in the first instance, submitted to the agreement of the parties.

10-48 Appointment by the parties, however, requires that the parties co-operate, in particular when they have to agree on an arbitrator. Practice shows that once a dispute has arisen even parties acting in good faith often have difficulties in

---

[41] This is quite common and recommended in some of the guides on drafting arbitration clauses; see, *e.g.*, Born, *International Commercial Arbitration*, 63 *et seq.*

[42] See, *e.g.*, Italy, Corte di appello Genoa, 3 February 1990, *Della Sanara Kustvaart - Bevrachting & Overslagbedrijf BV v Fallimento Cap Giovanni Coppola srl*, XVII YBCA 542 (1992); Germany, Oberlandesgericht Brandenburg, 12 February 2001, 8 SchH 1/01, unreported; for other examples see Fouchard Gaillard Goldman *on International Commercial Arbitration*, para 486.

agreeing anything. A perfectly suitable nomination may be rejected merely because it has been suggested by the other party. To avoid this and to improve the probability of an agreement between the parties some type of list procedure is often used.[43] One option is that each party draws up a list of arbitrators it considers suitable and who are acceptable to it; these lists are then exchanged and form the basis for discussion as to the sole or third arbitrator. A variant is for one party to propose a list of several potential arbitrators from which the other party will select or it must propose its own. Another version requires the parties to number persons from a list according to their preferences. The person with the lowest numbers will be appointed as an arbitrator.[44]

10-49 In this respect it is noteworthy that under most institutional rules the parties do not actually appoint the arbitrators but just nominate them for appointment by the institution. Though the institution will usually follow the nomination of the parties[45] it is by no means required to do so. This is clearly so under Article 7(1) LCIA Rules which provides that

> If the parties have agreed that any arbitrator is to be appointed by one or more of them or by any third person, that agreement shall be treated as an agreement to nominate an arbitrator for all purposes. Such nominee may only be appointed by the LCIA Court as arbitrator subject to his prior compliance with Article 5.3 [declaration of independence]. *The LCIA Court may refuse to appoint any such nominee if it determines that he is not suitable or independent or impartial.* [Emphasis added]

10-50 This limitation is particularly relevant in the context of a party appointed arbitrator where the institution is to ensure the independence and impartiality of the tribunal. It helps to protect the reputation of the institution and of the whole arbitration process which could be tarnished by the appointment of unsuitable or partial arbitrators. Where it is obvious that an arbitrator lacks the necessary qualification or impartiality or independence and will be open to challenge it is a

---

43 Such list procedures are also used if an agreement provides that the party appointed arbitrators have to agree on a chairman.

44 See Kröll, *Ergänzung und Anpassung von Verträgen durch Schiedsgerichte*, 290; see UNCITRAL Rules Article 6(3); for the use of a different type of list procedure to appoint the chairman in an arbitration between Qatar and Wintershall see Carver and Hossain, "An Arbitration Case Study: The Dispute that never was", 5(2) *ICSID Rev-FILJ* 311 (1990) 316. See partial award, 5 February 1988 and final award, 31 May 1988, *Wintershall AG v Government of Qatar*, 28 ILM 795 (1989).

45 Derains and Schwartz, *ICC Rules*, 143 *et seq.*

waste of resources to appoint this arbitrator and refer the other party to the challenge procedure.

3.2. Role of Appointing Authorities

10-51 Appointing authorities have an important role to play where an appointment by the parties is impossible because they cannot reach the necessary agreement or one party takes an obstructive role in the appointment procedure.[46] In these situations it is crucial that a default mechanism exists and ensures that despite a party's failure to co-operate the arbitration can nevertheless be constituted. Otherwise the whole arbitration process may be frustrated for lack of a tribunal. Therefore the arbitration agreement or the applicable arbitration rules and laws generally provide that the necessary appointments are made by an appointing authority if the parties fail to do so within a certain time.

10-52 However, the role of appointing authorities is not limited to that of a fall-back mechanism. In the light of the problems involved in reaching an agreement by the parties the appointment of the chairman or a sole arbitrator is often from the outset submitted to an appointing authority.[47] This may not only be faster but the appointing authority may also have a better overview about the potential arbitrators than the parties. It may possess a formal list or a database of potential arbitrators who it often knows from earlier arbitrations. Furthermore, no suitable arbitrator will be excluded just because he has been suggested by one party and rejected by the other and delays involved in party appointment may be prevented.

10-53 The parties are free to choose whichever appointing authority they consider appropriate. They can nominate an arbitration institution or trade association as appointing authority but can also entrust any other professional organisation, natural person or even state courts with the task. It is essential that the parties check in advance that the institution or body is willing and able to act as an appointing authority. Otherwise the refusal of the chosen authority to act can considerably delay the arbitration proceedings. In these cases the parties will either have to agree on a different appointing authority or apply to the courts for an appointment under the applicable arbitration law.

---

[46] This can be done either openly by not taking the necessary steps required, such as appointment of its own arbitrator. The delaying tactic may, however, be more subtle. Appointing arbitrators open to challenge or negotiating in bad faith on a joint nominee with no intention of reaching an agreement can delay the proceedings without appearing to be obstructive.

[47] See, *e.g.*, ICC Rules Article 8.

10-54 The selection of the appointing authority has a considerable impact on the type of arbitrators appointed and should therefore be made with care. Every organisation has its own preferences (*e.g.* common or civil lawyers, persons with expertise in the subject matter or in arbitration procedure, etc.), its own guidelines as to the factors to be taken into account and often also its own procedures for appointment.[48] Some institutions require that the arbitrators are chosen from a list or panel of arbitrators or are members of an association which may considerably limit the possible choices.[49] By contrast, the ICC takes a very liberal approach and just determines the nationality of the arbitrator while referring the actual selection to the relevant national committee.[50] Furthermore, it is important that the institution or person chosen has sufficient experience and an overview of the potential candidates. That is definitively the case with the leading arbitration institutions which have a considerable track record.[51]

10-55 An agreement by the parties on an appointing authority is of vital importance in *ad hoc* arbitration. Institutional rules generally entrust the administering institution with the task of the appointing authority failing an agreement by the parties to the contrary.[52] In *ad hoc* arbitration no administering institution is readily available which could act as appointing authority. Therefore the parties should always agree on an appointing authority, if they do not want to rely on the provisions in the national arbitration law.[53] Many arbitration institutions offer their services as an appointing authority for arbitrations not conducted under their rules,[54] *e.g.* the ICC and the LCIA.

---

[48] For a critical comment on the criteria applied see Nathan, "Well, why did you not get the right arbitrator?", 15(7) *Mealey's IAR* 24 (2000).

[49] See, *e.g.*, CIETAC Rules Article 24; GAFTA Arbitration Rules Form no 125 Rule 3:5.

[50] See ICC Rules Article 9(3) and (4); for a description of the ICC Procedure see Derains and Schwartz, *ICC Rules*, 141 *et seq.*

[51] It was this knowledge which enabled the ICC to find and appoint a suitably qualified arbitrator from one of the few countries where there was no Arthur Andersen office. See 10(4) *Am Rev Int Arb* 437 (1999).

[52] If the parties want to make such an agreement they must ensure that the changes made do not lead to frictions with the rest of the rules, which generally presuppose the existence of a particular appointing authority.

[53] National arbitration laws usually provide that if the parties have not agreed on an appointing authority the necessary appointments will be made by the courts, so that even in *ad hoc* arbitrations the lack of an agreement on an appointing authority does not prevent the constitution of a tribunal; in addition, arbitration rules for non-administered arbitration also contain provisions for the determination of an appointing authority; see, *e.g.*, UNCITRAL Rules Articles 6(2), 7(2)(b).

[54] See, *e.g.*, the special cost provisions in the ICC Rules Appendix III Article 3, and the LCIA Rules.

10-56 An appointing authority must ensure that the arbitrator appointed has the qualifications required by the parties. The relevant rules often set out other factors which the appointing authority should take into account. For example Article 9(1) ICC Rules provides

> In confirming or appointing arbitrators, the Court shall consider the prospective arbitrator's nationality, residence and other relationships with the countries of which the parties or the other arbitrators are nationals and the prospective arbitrator's availability and ability to conduct the arbitration in accordance with these Rules. The same shall apply where the Secretary General confirms arbitrators pursuant to Article 9(2).

10-57 Most of these factors relate to the independence and impartiality of the arbitrators and may trigger challenge proceedings. However, at the appointment or confirmation stage the institutions also take into consideration facts which would not justify a challenge but nevertheless may appear to favour one party, *e.g.* nationality of an arbitrator.[55]

3.3. Role of National Courts

10-58 The primary role of national courts in the appointment process in arbitration is that of a default mechanism. To ensure that the arbitration tribunal can be constituted, even where the parties have not agreed on any form of appointment procedure or the procedure provided for does not operate, most arbitration laws contain provisions which allow for appointment of the arbitrators by the courts.

10-59 The Model Law provides in Article 11(4)

> Where, under an appointment procedure agreed upon by the parties,
> (a) a party fails to act as required under such procedure, or
> (b) the parties, or two arbitrators, are unable to reach an agreement expected of them under such procedure, or
> (c) a third party, including an institution, fails to perform any function entrusted to it under such procedure,

---

[55] See, *e.g.*, LCIA Article 6; SCC Rules Article 16(8); UNCITRAL Rules Article 7(4); see also Model Law Article 11(5), dealing with appointments to be made by the courts. In the *Andersen Arbitration,* 10(4) *Am Rev Int'l Arb* 437 (1999), the Claimant insisted on having a sole arbitrator coming from one of the few countries where no Andersen member existed.

> any party may request the court or other authority specified in article 6 to take the necessary measure, unless the agreement on the appointment procedure provides other means for securing the appointment.

10-60 In addition, Article 11(3) Model Law, which deals with cases where the parties have not agreed on an appointment procedure, also provides for court appointment as a last resort.[56]

10-61 It is rare in international contracts to entrust the appointment of the arbitrators to a national court, as national courts often lack the necessary experience required for appointments in an international setting. For these cases, which are more common in domestic arbitration, the Swiss arbitration law provides in Article 179(3) that any court so chosen is under an obligation to act as an appointing authority. Most other arbitration laws do not contain such a provision and the courts have the discretion to accept the nomination as an appointing authority. In exercising its discretion a court should take into account the fall back provisions contained in the applicable arbitration law according to which a failure of the appointment procedure foreseen by the parties often leads to an appointment by the courts. In such cases it makes little sense that a judge or court chosen by the parties as appointing authority refuses to act and thereby forces a different court to make the appointment on the basis of the applicable arbitration law.[57]

10-62 Which national court has jurisdiction to make the appointment is determined by the relevant arbitration law. Most national laws contain special provisions as to jurisdiction for supportive matters. They usually make the existence of jurisdiction dependant on the place of arbitration either being in the country or not being yet determined or at least require that the proceedings must be based on the law of the country.[58] In Europe, Regulation 44/2001 and the Lugano Convention regulating jurisdiction within Europe are not applicable to international arbitration. All proceedings in relation to the appointment of an

---

56 See also Switzerland, PIL Article 179; France, NCPC Article 1493(2); United States, FAA section 5; Model Law Article 11(3) and (4).

57 Kröll, "Das neue deutsche Schiedsrecht vor staatlichen Gerichten: Entwicklungslinien und Tendenzen 1998-2000", 54 *NJW* 1173 (2001) 1178.

58 See, *e.g*, Germany, ZPO sections 1025, 1062; England, Arbitration Act sections 2, 105; France, NCPC Article 1493(2).

arbitrator are ancillary proceedings to an arbitration and are therefore covered by the arbitration exception contained in Article 1(2)(d).[59]

10-63 To avoid a denial of justice the Paris Court of Appeal in *National Iran Oil Company v State of Israel* has also made the necessary appointments in a case where the statutory requirements were not met but which had certain connections with France.[60] In the case arising out of a contract for the construction and maintenance of a pipeline the *ad hoc* arbitration agreement provided that each party was to appoint an arbitrator. These were to agree on a chairman which in the absence of an agreement was to be appointed by the Chairman of the ICC. Israel, however, did not appoint its own arbitrator and in 1996 the Paris Court of Appeal first rejected an application to appoint the arbitrator on Israel's behalf, since the jurisdictional requirements under Article 1493(2) NCPC were not met. When due to a "Manbar", a judgment declaring Iran to be an enemy of Israel, it became obvious that Iran could also not apply to the courts in Israel for appointment, the Paris Court of Appeal made the requested appointment. The required link to France was seen in the choice of the chairman of the ICC as appointing authority for the chairman.[61]

10-64 In making its appointment the national court is bound by any requirements as to the arbitrator's qualities agreed on by the parties. This is provided for in the Model Law where Article 11(5) states

> ... The court or other authority, in appointing an arbitrator, shall have due regard to any qualifications required of the arbitrator by the agreement of the parties and to such considerations as are likely to secure the appointment of an independent and impartial arbitrator and, in the case of a sole or third arbitrator, shall take into account as well the advisability of appointing an arbitrator of a nationality other than those of the parties.

---

59 ECJ, 25 July 1991, Case C 190/89, *Mark Rich & Co AG v Società Italiana Impianti PA* [1991] ECR I-3894; XVII YBCA 233 (1992); see also van Haersolte-van Hof, "The Arbitration Exception in the Brussels Convention: further comment", 18(1) *J Int'l Arb* 27 (2001); Beraudo, "The Arbitration Exception of the Brussels and Lugano Conventions: Jurisdiction, Recognition and Enforcement of Judgments", 18(1) *J Int'l Arb* 13 (2001).

60 Cour d'appel Paris, 29 March 2001, *National Iran Oil Company (NIOC) v State of Israel*, 17(6) Mealey's IAR A1 (2002) English translation and French original; 129 Clunet 498 (2002); see also the comment by Pinsolle, "Court Appointed Arbitrator: French Court Expands Jurisdiction to Avoid Denial of Justice", 17(6) *Mealey's IAR* 35 (2002).

61 See the critical comment on the decision by Cohen, 129 *Clunet* 501 (2002).

10-65 Comparable provisions can be found in a number of other national arbitration laws.[62] However, given the fact that arbitration is a creature of party autonomy courts should always give due regard to the parties intentions even where the applicable law does not expressly provide for it.

4. Procedures for Appointing Arbitrators

10-66 There is a fundamental difference in the arrangements for the appointment of arbitrators depending on whether there is to be one or three arbitrators. Whilst the basic principle of party autonomy prevails, the absence of agreement cannot be allowed to prevent or frustrate the arbitration. In any event it is necessary to ensure that there is fairness in the appointment process.

4.1. Appointment of a Sole Arbitrator

10-67 The appointment of a sole arbitrator is generally submitted to the agreement of the parties. Unless the parties have provided for a different appointment mechanism, this is the approach under most arbitration rules or laws.[63] A typical example is ICC Rules Article 8(3)

> Where the parties have agreed that the dispute shall be settled by a sole arbitrator, they may, by agreement, nominate the sole arbitrator for confirmation. If the parties fail to nominate a sole arbitrator within 30 days from the date when the Claimant's Request for Arbitration has been received by the other party, or within such additional time as may be allowed by the Secretariat, the sole arbitrator shall be appointed by the Court.[64]

10-68 This provision not only provides that the parties shall agree on a joint nominee but also provides that if no agreement can be reached the sole arbitrator is to be appointed by the ICC. It furthermore sets a time limit within which the parties shall agree on the sole arbitrator before the ICC will make an appointment. Such time limit is important to prevent one party delaying the constitution of the tribunal by negotiating in bad faith without any intention of reaching an agreement. The time limit can be extended by the ICC or by the

62 See, *e.g.*, England, Arbitration Act section 19; Egypt, Arbitration Law Article 17(3); Germany, ZPO section 1035(5).
63 See, *e.g.*, ICC Rules Article 8(3); DIS Rules section 14; AAA ICDR Rules Article 6; Model Law Article 11(3)(b); England, Arbitration Act section 16(3); Germany, ZPO section 1035(3).
64 See also WIPO Rules Article 16; DIS Rules section 14.

parties, if they want to continue their search for a joint nominee, and its expiry does not deprive the parties of the possibility to agree on an arbitrator but gives each party the right to rely on the default provisions if necessary.

10-69 Comparable procedures are provided for in other institutional rules. Differences exist in relation to the time limit after which the appointing authority can appoint the sole arbitrator. Under the WIPO Rules, for example, the institution can provide for a longer period of 45 days[65] while under GAFTA Rules only nine days are available.

10-70 A slightly different appointment procedure is provided for in the LCIA and SCC Rules. Under both sets of rules the appointment of the sole arbitrator is, from the outset, a matter for the institution. Article 16(5) SCC Rules provides that

> Where the dispute is to be decided by a sole arbitrator, the SCC Institute shall make the appointment, unless otherwise agreed by the parties.[66]

10-71 Similarly, Article 5(4) LCIA Rules provides that

> A sole arbitrator shall be appointed unless the parties have agreed in writing otherwise, or unless the LCIA Court determines that in view of all the circumstances of the case a three-member tribunal is appropriate.

10-72 Since the parties do not have to try to reach an agreement, but can leave it immediately to the institution, this procedure may be faster than the procedure in the ICC Rules. Furthermore, it avoids the problem of the most suitable arbitrators in the view of the institution having been rejected by one party during the negotiations on the mere fact that the names were suggested by the other party. This procedure may, however, deprive the parties of their influence on the appointment process even in cases where an agreement between the parties on a sole arbitrator may have been possible.

10-73 A more elaborate provision can be found in the UNCITRAL Rules which is in part due to the potential lack of an appointing authority. Therefore, the rules, in addition to providing a procedure to appoint the arbitrator, must also deal with the procedure of determining an appointing authority where it is required. Article 6 provides, in pertinent part

> 1. If a sole arbitrator is to be appointed, either party may propose to the other:

---

[65] See WIPO Rules Article 15(b).

[66] See also GAFTA Rule 3:1.

(a) The names of one or more persons, one of whom would serve as the sole arbitrator; and

(b) If no appointing authority has been agreed upon by the parties, the name or names of one or more institutions or persons, one of whom would serve as appointing authority.

2. If within 30 days after receipt by a party of a proposal made in accordance with paragraph 1 the parties have not reached agreement on the choice of a sole arbitrator, the sole arbitrator shall be appointed by the appointing authority agreed upon by the parties. If no appointing authority has been agreed upon by the parties, or if the appointing authority agreed upon refuses to act or fails to appoint the arbitrator within 60 days of the receipt of a party's request therefore, either party may request the Secretary-General of the Permanent Court of Arbitration at the Hague to designate an appointing authority.

10-74 According to established practice, an application to the Secretary-General should set out why the appointment of an appointing authority is needed and should be accompanied by the documents required under Article 8(1).[67] Eventually, further information as to potential arbitrators or appointing authorities will be required by the Secretary-General who also consults with other persons on an anonymous basis before nominating an appointing authority.[68]

10-75 Furthermore, UNCITRAL Rules also differ from other rules as they require the appointing authority to resort to a list procedure which strengthens the influence of the parties on the appointment process. Article 6(3) UNCITRAL Rules provides

> The appointing authority shall, at the request of one of the parties, appoint the sole arbitrator as promptly as possible. In making the appointment the appointing authority shall use the following list-procedure, unless both parties agree that the list-procedure should not be used or unless the appointing authority determines in its discretion that the use of the list-procedure is not appropriate for the case:
>
> (a) At the request of one of the parties the appointing authority shall communicate to both parties an identical list containing at least three names;
>
> (b) Within 15 days after the receipt of this list, each party may return the list to the appointing authority after having deleted the name or names to which

[67] The documents include copies of the notice of arbitration, the underlying agreement and the arbitration agreement if it is not contained in the underlying agreement.

[68] Redfern and Hunter, *International Commercial Arbitration*, para 4-33.

he objects and numbered the remaining names on the list in the order of his preference;

(c) After the expiration of the above period of time the appointing authority shall appoint the sole arbitrator from among the names approved on the lists returned to it and in accordance with the order of preference indicated by the parties;

(d) If for any reason the appointment cannot be made according to this procedure, the appointing authority may exercise its discretion in appointing the sole arbitrator.[69]

10-76 National arbitration laws generally contain fall back provisions which are similar to the solution under the ICC Rules: sole arbitrators are to be appointed by agreement of the parties or, should no agreement by reached, by the courts. For example, Article 11(3)(b) Model Law provides

> in an arbitration with a sole arbitrator, if the parties are unable to agree on the arbitrator, he shall be appointed, upon request of a party, by the court or other authority specified in article 6.[70]

10-77 Since the provision does not contain a time limit for an agreement on a sole arbitrator the question arises whether a party can immediately apply to the court if its suggestion of an arbitrator is turned down or must it engage in further negotiations. Pursuant to laws which contain a time limit, no further efforts to reach an agreement can be required once this time has expired.

10-78 A slightly different procedure is contained in the English Arbitration Act where, under section 16(3), the parties have to agree on an arbitrator within 28 days.[71] If no agreement can be reached and the parties have not provided for that contingency they can apply to the court to make the appointment. The court's powers, set out in Article 18(3), are

(a) to give directions as to the making of any necessary appointments;

(b) to direct that the tribunal shall be constituted by such appointments (or any one or more of them) as have been made;

---

[69] See also CPR Rules Rule 6.4 for Non-Administered Arbitration according to which, if the parties have not reached an agreement on the sole arbitrator within 30 days, the appointing authority submits a list of not less than five candidates which includes a brief statement of each candidate's qualifications. The parties will number the candidates in order of preference and notify any objections they have. The appointing authority will then appoint the candidate with the highest preference.

[70] See also Germany, ZPO section 1035(3).

[71] The courts have under section 79 the power to extend that period; Merkin, *Arbitration Act*, 51.

(c) to revoke any appointments already made;
(d) to make any necessary appointments itself.

10-79 In most cases the court will appoint the sole arbitrator itself as provided for under section 18(3)(d). It is, however, also conceivable that a court uses its power under section 18(3)(a) to give the parties directions to reach a settlement by the use of a list procedure and any other means.[72]

4.2. Appointment of a Three Member Tribunal

10-80 Three member tribunals are usually composed of two party appointed arbitrators and a chairman. While this basic structure can be found in nearly all arbitration rules and laws, differences exist as to the mechanics of the appointment process, in particular the procedure for the appointment of the chairman.

(a) Party appointed arbitrators

10-81 With parties from different legal and cultural backgrounds, the arbitration agreements often provide expressly that each party has a right to appoint an arbitrator. A good example is the arbitration clause contained in the contract for the construction of the Channel Tunnel. It stated that the "employer and the contractor shall each nominate one arbitrator."

10-82 Where the arbitration agreement does not contain such a provision the right for each party to appoint an arbitrator is generally granted by the applicable arbitration laws or rules. For example, Article 8(4) ICC Rules provides in the relevant part

> Where the dispute is to be referred to three arbitrators, each party shall nominate in the Request and the Answer respectively, one arbitrator for confirmation. If a party fails to nominate an arbitrator, the appointment shall be made by the Court. [...]

10-83 The provision is very specific as to when the party appointed arbitrator is to be named and provides what is to happen if this is not the case. How the appointment actually takes place is regulated in Article 7. Before the arbitrator nominated by a party is actually appointed by the ICC Court, he must sign a statement of independence which will then be transmitted to the other party for

---

[72] See Russell *on Arbitration*, para 4-062.

comments. On the basis of this information the ICC Court will make a decision for which no reasons are given.[73]

10-84 Comparable provisions providing for the nomination and a certain scrutiny of party appointed arbitrators can also be found in most other institutional rules. Though the institutions are not bound by any objections raised against the party nominated arbitrators, the role of this process should not be underestimated. Practice shows that institutions are more willing to refuse the confirmation of party nominated arbitrators for an alleged lack of independence than sustain challenges for the same reasons at a later stage.[74]

10-85 The appointment process for party appointed arbitrators in institutional rules differs from the procedure provided for under the UNCITRAL Rules and the arbitration laws. There the party appointed arbitrators are appointed directly by the parties without any control by an institution or the other side.[75] This does not mean that the party appointed arbitrators do not have to be independent or impartial. It only has the consequence that objections against an arbitrator must be raised in a separate challenge procedure and not during the appointment procedure.

10-86 To avoid a party misusing its appointing right and delaying the proceedings, this right must generally be exercised within a certain time limit. After this time the right to appoint is often transferred to an appointing authority or the courts. An appointment made after the expiry of the time limit by a defaulting party may only be valid if consented to by the other party.[76]

10-87 In making appointments for a defaulting party the appointing authority has to ensure that the arbitrator has the qualifications agreed on by the parties. It should also take into account any qualification requested by the defaulting party. However, a German court held that enforcement of an award cannot be resisted if

---

[73] For a detailed analysis of the procedure and examples of rejected party nominees see Calvo, "The Challenge of ICC Arbitrators", 15(4) *J Int'l Arb* 63 (1998) 67 *et seq.*

[74] See Bond, "The Experience of the ICC Court of Arbitration in the Selection and Confirmation/Appointment of Arbitrators", in ICC (ed), *Independence of Arbitrators*, 9, 12 which for the period of 1986-1988 reports a success rate of 72% for objections against a success rate for challenges of 9%; see also Craig Park Paulsson, *ICC Arbitration*, para 13-01.

[75] UNCITRAL Rules Article 7(1).

[76] Bayerisches Oberstes Landesgericht, 16 January 2002, 57 *Betriebs-Berater* 753 (2002).

the arbitrator does not possess the qualification asked for unilaterally by the defaulting party.[77]

10-88 A special provision dealing with the default of a party in the appointment procedure for a three member tribunal can be found in section 17 English Arbitration Act. This gives the opportunity for the party which has nominated an arbitrator to require its nominee to act as a sole arbitrator if the other party fails to appoint within the agreed time period. If this occurs the defaulting party can only challenge the appointment by applying to the court to set aside the award.

10-89 Awards of tribunals consisting of one party appointed arbitrator have been challenged on several occasions.[78] It was alleged that the appointment of a sole arbitrator by one party not only conflicts with the principle of neutrality of the tribunal, but also violates the parties' agreement on the composition of the arbitration tribunal. In cases where the parties expressly or by choosing the place of arbitration determine the applicable arbitration law, the provisions of that law become part of the parties agreement on the constitution of the arbitration tribunal.[79] Therefore, reliance on default provisions contained in the applicable arbitration rules or law cannot, in most countries, be invoked as a ground to resist enforcement on the basis of Article V(1)(d) New York Convention.[80]

---

[77] See Oberlandesgericht Dresden, 20 October 1998, 11 Sch 0004/98 *DIS-Materialien* VII Annex (2001) 41:171; the German party, after the expiry of the period for appointment, asked the institution to appoint as its arbitrator a person with German language skills. The arbitrator finally appointed did not have such skills. The Oberlandesgericht held that after the expiry of the time limit for appointment the institution had discretion to appoint the arbitrator and was not bound by any requests from the parties. The tribunal had thus been properly composed.

[78] See Schwebel and Lane, "Public Policy and Arbitral Procedure", *ICCA Congress series no 3*, 205; Szurski, "The constitution of the Arbitral Tribunal", van den Berg (ed), *ICCA Congress series no 9*, 331; Alvarez, "The Challenge of Arbitrators", 6 *Arb Int* 203 (1990); Calvo, "The Challenge of the ICC Arbitrators: theory and practice", 15(4) *J Int'l Arb* 63 (1998).

[79] See Supreme Court of Queensland, *Resort Condominium International Inc v Ray Balwell, Resort Condominium Pty Ltd*, XX YBCA 628 (1995); and India, Supreme Court, *Sumitomo Heavy Industries Ltd v ONGC Ltd (India)*, XXIVa YBCA 678 (1999).

[80] See, to that effect, Corte di cassazione, 20 January 1995, *Conceria G De Maio & F snc v EMAG AG*, XXI YBCA 602 (1996); Cour d'appel Paris, 20 January 1972, *Société Oromar v Société Commercial Matignon (SIMCOMA)*, Rev Arb 105 (1974); for a successful challenge see the German Bundesgerichtshof, 5 November 1970, *BGHZ* 54, 392; in a more recent decision, however, the court came to the opposite result: Bundesgerichtshof, 15 May 1986, *BGHZ* 98, 70, 73; 1 February 2001, 1 *RPS* 14 (2001) 16.

(b) Chairman or third arbitrator

10-90 The appointment of the third arbitrator, who acts as the chairman of the tribunal, is generally effected by an agreement of the parties, by selection of the party appointed arbitrators, or by an appointing authority. Each of these procedures can be found in practice and has its advantages.

10-91 Appointment of the chairman by the parties has the advantage of ensuring the greatest possible influence of the parties on the composition of the tribunal. For this reason it is often provided for in the arbitration agreement or in the rules of some institutions.[81] However, where an agreement of the parties is not possible, appointment will be in accordance with the applicable rules or law.

10-92 Many institutional rules entrust the appointment of the chairman directly to the institution, if the parties have not agreed otherwise. For example Article 8(4) ICC Rules provides

> The third arbitrator, who will act as chairman of the Arbitral Tribunal, shall be appointed by the Court, unless the parties have agreed upon another procedure for such appointment, in which case the nomination will be subject to confirmation pursuant to Article 9. Should such procedure not result in a nomination within the time limit fixed by the parties or the Court, the third arbitrator shall be appointed by the Court.[82]

10-93 The ICC Court will not consult with the party appointed arbitrators or with the parties who therefore do not have any influence on the selection of the chairman. To avoid such a result the parties often agree either in advance or after the dispute has arisen that the party appointed arbitrators should try to agree on a chairman.[83]

10-94 Other institutional rules[84] as well as the UNCITRAL Rules[85] submit the appointment of the chairman to the agreement of the party appointed arbitrators. This has the advantage of increasing the probability of a good working relationship within the tribunal and gives the parties at least an indirect influence on the appointment of the chairman. It is generally accepted that the two party

---

[81] See CIETAC Rules Article 24.

[82] Similar rules can be found in other institutional rules, *e.g.* the SCC Rules Article 17(4); GAFTA Rule 3:2(d).

[83] This happened, *e.g.*, in an ICC arbitration: Court of Appeal, *AT&T Corporation and another v Saudi Cable*, [2000] 2 Lloyd's Rep 127, 129.

[84] DIS Rules section 12(2); Geneva Rules Article 12(2); CPR Arbitration Rules Rule 5(2).

[85] Article 7; due to the lack of a permanent organisation which could act as an appointing authority, conferring the task on the other arbitrators is the most practical solution.

appointed arbitrators should consult with the parties who appointed them. Though they are not bound by any suggestions of the parties they should avoid appointing a chairman unacceptable to one of the parties.

10-95 Since the party appointed arbitrators may not be able to reach an agreement, a fall back procedure must be available. In institutional arbitration the appointment is then generally made by the institution. The UNCITRAL Rules provide in Article 7(3)

> If within 30 days after the appointment of the second arbitrator the two arbitrators have not agreed on the choice of the presiding arbitrator, the presiding arbitrator shall be appointed by an appointing authority in the same way as a sole arbitrator would be appointed under article 6.

10-96 Most arbitration laws also submit the appointment of the third arbitrator to the two party appointed arbitrators.[86] In case of a failure of the procedure, however, appointment is in general made by the national courts. Model Law Article 11(3)(a) provides that

> in an arbitration with three arbitrators, each party shall appoint one arbitrator, and the two party-appointed arbitrators should appoint the third arbitrator. If one party fails to appoint an arbitrator within thirty days of receipt of a request to do so from the other party, or if the two arbitrators fail to agree on the third arbitrator within thirty days of their appointment, then either party can request the competent national court to make the appointment.

5. Limits on the Parties Freedom to Determine the Appointment Process

10-97 Submitting the appointment process to party autonomy carries the danger that a stronger party can impose appointment procedures which are disadvantageous to the weaker party. These are not limited to the obvious cases where the tribunal is to be appointed by one party alone. This may be the case where, *e.g.* each party appoints one arbitrator and if they cannot agree on a chairman, one of the parties has the final choice. The composition of the tribunal may be influenced also by a requirement in the applicable rules that only

[86] See, *e.g.*, England, Arbitration Act section 15; Germany, ZPO section 1035; Italy, CCP article 810; France, NCPC Article 1444; Netherlands, CCP Article 1030; Switzerland, PIL Article 179 relating to International Arbitration; United States, FAA section 5.

members of a particular organisation can be appointed as arbitrators even in cases with non-members.[87]

10-98 Given the importance of the equality of the parties some national laws provide that appointment may be effected by the courts where the procedure agreed by the parties gives one party an unfair influence on the appointment of arbitrators. The German arbitration law provides in section 1034(2) ZPO

> If the arbitration agreement grants preponderant rights to one party with regard to the composition of the arbitration tribunal which place the other party at a disadvantage, that other party may request the court to appoint the arbitrator or arbitrators in deviation from the nomination made, or from the agreed nomination procedure. The request must be submitted at the latest within two weeks of the party becoming aware of the constitution of the arbitral tribunal. Section 1032 subs. 3 applies mutatis mutandis.

10-99 A similar provision can be found in Article 1028 Netherlands CCP. Since under both laws the appointment by the courts can only be requested within a short time period, a preponderant influence on the composition of the tribunal will not affect the validity of an award rendered. This may be different where the other side was not aware of the constitution of the tribunal and did not participate in the arbitration. In such cases the annulment of an award may be sought on the basis of an incorrectly constituted tribunal.[88]

10-100 These provisions gain a certain practical importance in multiparty proceedings.[89] In a three member tribunal one party may appoint an arbitrator, and the several parties on the other side have to agree on one arbitrator. This may be considered as a preponderant right with regard to the composition of the tribunal. In that case the appointment procedure foreseen by the parties would be replaced by appointment through the state courts. This would be in line with the special provisions dealing with appointment in multiparty situations provided in some arbitration rules.[90]

---

[87] See the German decision, Bundesgerichtshof, 19 December 1968, *BGHZ* 55, 255 where an arbitration clause providing for such an appointment was considered to be invalid; Lachmann, *Handbuch*, para 577.

[88] Van den Berg, van Delden and Snijders, *Netherlands Arbitration Law*, 39. See also Swiss Tribunal Fédéral, 12 January 1989, *GSA (Switzerland) v T Ltd (UK)*, XV YBCA 509 (1990).

[89] See Wiegand, "The UNCITRAL Model Law: New Draft Arbitration Acts in Germany and Sweden", 11 *Arb Int* 397 (1995) 400; Berger, *Das neue Recht der Schiedsgerichtsbarkeit* (RWS 1998), 27.

[90] See, *e.g.*, ICC Rules Article 10; LCIA Article 8; SCC Rules Article 16(3).

Chapter 11

IMPARTIALITY AND INDEPENDENCE OF ARBITRATORS

11-1 The juridical nature of the arbitration process imposes practical limits on the parties' freedom when choosing the arbitrators. This is because the tribunal exercises judicial functions and its award will have the same finality and binding effect as a judgment of a national court[1]. As the state lends its authority for the enforcement of the awards, it requires that the arbitration proceedings, as well as the composition of the tribunal, meet certain minimum standards which are considered to be indispensable characteristics of any fair trial.

11-2 The relationship between the parties and the arbitrator is normally based on a contract entered into after the appointment by which the arbitrator agrees to settle the dispute between the parties for a certain remuneration. In line with his special adjudicative function, the arbitrator has to be and remain independent and impartial and disclose all facts which may be relevant. A breach of any of these duties may result in the removal of the arbitrator and the annulment of the award. Whether the arbitrator may also be personally liable for damages depends on the degree of immunity afforded to him by the relevant laws.

11-3 This chapter deals with (1) the impartiality and independence of the arbitrator, (2) the duty of an arbitrator to disclose matters which may affect his impartiality and independence, and (3) the special role of the party appointed arbitrator.

[1] See generally Henry, *Le devoir d'indépendence de l'arbitrage*, (LGDJ 2001) 9 *et seq.*

1. The Arbitrator's Duty of Impartiality and Independence

11-4 It is a fundamental and universally accepted principle of international arbitration that arbitrators have to be impartial and independent of the parties and must remain so during the proceedings.[2] To ensure compliance with these requirements arbitrators usually have a duty to disclose all relevant facts. This also applies to party appointed arbitrators although in certain types of specialised or domestic arbitrations in some countries they may adopt a less objective role and represent their appointing party's interest.[3] In international arbitration this would require an agreement of the parties since the requirements of independence and impartiality follows from the judicial function of the tribunal.[4]

11-5 Both requirements are firmly established in most arbitration laws and rules and form part of the codes of ethics for arbitrators of the IBA[5] and the AAA.[6] Some rules clearly spell out that obligation. Article 5(2) LCIA Rules for example provides

> All arbitrators conducting an arbitration under these Rules shall be and remain at all times impartial and independent of the parties; and none shall act in the arbitration as advocates for any party. No arbitrator, whether before or after appointment, shall advise any party on the merits or outcome of the dispute.[7]

11-6 Others adopt a more indirect approach and make the lack of independence or impartiality a ground for challenge. Article 10(1) UNCITRAL Rules for example provides

---

2 Article 6 European Convention on Human Rights grants everyone the fundamental right to a fair hearing by an impartial tribunal in the determination of rights and liabilities; see also Article 10 Universal Declaration of Human Rights.

3 Such an approach prevails in domestic arbitration in the United States where the party appointed arbitrators are not expected to be neutral; see *e.g.*, *Sunkist Softdrinks v Sunkist Growers*, 10 F 3d 753 (11th Cir 1993); Smith, "The impartiality of the party-appointed arbitrators", 6 *Arb Int* 320 (1990) 321; for further examples of arbitrations involving state parties see Redfern and Hunter, *International Commercial Arbitration*, para 4-48.

4 Craig Park Paulsson, *ICC Arbitration*, para 12-04; Smith, "The impartiality of the party-appointed arbitrators", 6 *Arb Int* 320 (1990) 340.

5 Canon III.

6 Canon II.

7 Comparable provisions can be found in WIPO Rules Article 22(a); AAA ICDR Article 7(1); UNCITRAL Rules Article 9; see also IBA Rules of Ethics Rules 1 and 3-1.

> Any arbitrator may be challenged if circumstances exist that give rise to justifiable doubts as to the arbitrator's impartiality or independence.[8]

11-7 Few laws and rules, however, refer to only one of these requirements, *i.e.* independence[9] or impartiality.[10] In those cases the question arises whether it is a deliberate decision against imposing the missing requirement or due to other reasons. While the latter is the case for the omission of "impartiality" in Article 7(1) ICC Rules,[11] the reference to impartiality only in section 24 English Arbitration Act is the result of a decision against imposing the requirement of independence.[12] As a consequence both principles should be distinguished though in practice they are often used interchangeably.

11-8 The different arbitration rules and laws usually do not provide a clear definition of these terms or guidelines for their interpretation. An exception in this respect is the new Swedish arbitration law which contains in section 8 a list of instances where the required "impartiality" is deemed to be lacking. Certain guidelines as to the content of the concepts of "independence" and "impartiality" can also be found in Codes of Ethics and in the rules on the nationality of the sole arbitrator or the chairman.[13] Irrespective of these guidelines the vagueness of both concepts has led to divergent views as to their actual content.

11-9 In particular in the context of challenging an arbitrator or an award for lack of "independence" or "impartiality" courts have come to different conclusions as to whether arbitrators are subjected to the same requirements of "independence" and "impartiality" as judges. While the US Supreme Court held in 1968 in *Commonwealth Coatings v Continental Casualty*[14] that arbitrators

---

8 See also Model Law Article 12; Germany, ZPO section 1036(2); Russian Federation, LIA Article 12(2); Netherlands, CCP Article 1033(1).

9 See, *e.g.*, Switzerland, PIL Article 180(1); ICC Rules Article 7.

10 England, Arbitration Act section 24; Sweden, Arbitration Act section 8.

11 Derains and Schwartz, *ICC Rules,* 109; Calvo, "The Challenge of ICC Arbitrators", 15(4) *J Int'l Arb* 63 (1998) 64 *et seq*; the omission of "impartiality" under Swiss law, however, is seen by some authors as a recognition that it is inappropriate to require from a party appointed arbitrator the same degree of impartiality as is required from a state court; see Peter and Freymond in Berti (ed), *International Arbitration in Switzerland*, Article 180, para 10.

12 DAC Report, paras 102-4; see also *Laker Airways Inc v FLS Aerospace Ltd* [1999] 2 Lloyds Rep 45.

13 See also China, Arbitration Law Article 34 which lists grounds and examples for lack of independence or impartiality.

14 *Commonwealth Coatings Corp v Continental Casualty Co*, 393 US 145, 149 (1968); in later decisions of the Appellate Courts the same standard seems to have been applied with Judge Posner in *Merit Ins Co v Leatherby Ins Co*, 714 F 2d 673 (7th Cir 1983) cert denied 464 US 1009 (1983) on the basis of an alleged trade off between impartiality and choosing a judge even

should be submitted to stricter requirements than courts, since there is no appeal against their awards, the English Court of Appeal held in *AT&T v Saudi Cable*[15] that the same requirements apply to both.

11-10 Irrespective of whether in general the same standard should be applied, it is evident that both concepts cannot be interpreted in exactly the same way as for state judges.[16] This is so even where the arbitration law declares that an arbitrator can be challenged on the same grounds as a judge. Unlike judges, arbitrators are usually engaged in other occupations before, during and after the arbitration proceedings. They are appointed and paid for by the parties. Their special experience and reputation in a certain field is often one of the major reasons for their appointment though it may imply previous contacts with the parties. In particular, party appointed arbitrators may have a loose and special relationship with the appointing party or its lawyers. Frequently, lawyers are well acquainted with the arbitrators and it is on the basis of this knowledge, and past experience, that they are recommended for appointment as arbitrators. These factors and the necessity of making an informed selection must therefore be taken into account when interpreting the requirements of independence or impartiality.

1.1. The Concept of "Impartiality"

11-11 Impartiality requires that an arbitrator neither favours one party nor is predisposed as to the question in dispute.[17] In so far as this is a state of mind it is a fairly abstract and subjective standard which is hard to prove. Impartiality must be distinguished from neutrality as it is used in the AAA Code of Ethics, as this provides that in some types of arbitration party-appointed arbitrators do not have to be neutral.[18] This does not imply that those arbitrators can be biased. It only means that from the legal, social and cultural background they may be favourably

---

advocating a lesser standard; for the development in US law see Shore, "Disclosure and Impartiality: Arbitrator's Responsibility vis-à-vis Legal Standards", 57 *Dispute Resolution Journal* 32 (2002).

[15] *AT&T Corporation and another v Saudi Cable*, [2000] 2 Lloyd's Rep 127 (CA).

[16] UN Doc A/CN9/SR313, para 14 reproduced in Holtzmann and Neuhaus, *Model Law*, 104; see also Peter and Freymond, in Berti (ed), *International Arbitration in Switzerland*, Article 180, paras 10, 14.

[17] Redfern and Hunter, *International Commercial Arbitration*, para 4-51; Fouchard Gaillard Goldman *on International Commercial Arbitration*, paras 1033 *et seq*; Smith, "The Impartiality of the Party-Appointed Arbitrators", 6 *Arb Int* 320 (1990) 323.

[18] See AAA Code of Ethics, Canon VII; Carter, "Rights and Obligations of the Arbitrator", *Arbitration* 170 (1997); for the distinction between neutrality and impartiality see also Hanseatisches Oberlandesgericht Hamburg, 17 February 1989, XV *YBCA* 455 (1990) para 8.

disposed towards the appointing party which may even be necessary to fulfil the special functions of a party appointed arbitrator in an arbitration with parties from different countries. As long as this proximity is not allowed to dictate the outcome of the proceedings the so called lack of neutrality should not impair the impartiality.

11-12 The same applies in general to an arbitrator's nationality. Although there is a perception that there would be an implication of bias where a party shares the same nationality as an arbitrator, the mere fact of having identical nationalities should not, of itself, affect the arbitrator's impartiality. In fact, an arbitrator's nationality may play an important role as a kind of cultural interpreter and in the acceptance of a later award. That nationality is not itself a bias is evidenced in Article 11 Model Law:

> No person shall be precluded by reason of his nationality from acting as an arbitrator, unless otherwise agreed by the parties.

11-13 Nevertheless it is common practice and foreseen in most arbitration rules that a sole arbitrator or a chairman should be of a different nationality than either party.[19] The ICSID Convention even imposes the requirement that the majority of the arbitrators must be of a different nationality than the parties.[20] It is submitted that in such cases the exclusion of an arbitrator with the same nationality as either party is based more on the implied agreed qualifications of the arbitrator than on the basis of his perceived lack of impartiality.

11-14 Cases of actual partiality are rare. It is seldom that arbitrators accentuate their favour for one party in such a clear way as arose in an arbitration between Portuguese and Norwegian parties, where the arbitrator was overheard saying Portuguese people were liars.[21] In arbitration involving states more general political comments may become an issue as is evidenced by a well known example from the Iran-US Claims tribunal.[22] Iran called for the resignation of Judge Mangard from Sweden, one of the arbitrators from a third country. He

---

[19] See ICC Rules Article 9(5); LCIA Article 6(1); for the practice of the ICC Court in relation to the nationality of the arbitrator see Craig Park Paulsson, *ICC Arbitration*, para 13-05(iii); see also the arbitration proceedings in *Andersen Consulting v Arthur Andersen and Andersen Worldwide*, 10(4) Am Rev Int Arb 459 (1999) where the claimant insisted on the appointment of an arbitrator with a different nationality than any of the more than 140 parties involved so that the ICC had to look for a country where no member of Andersen Worldwide existed.

[20] Washington Convention, Article 39. See also ICSID Rules Rule 1.

[21] *Re The Owners of the Steamship "Catalina" and The Owners of the Motor Vessel "Norma"*, [1938] 61 Ll L Rep 360.

[22] For a full account of the incident see Khan, *The Iran-United States Claims Tribunal*, 65-77.

allegedly engaged in "unsound political propaganda" by accusing Iran "of condemning (sic) execution." The challenge was rejected by the President of the Supreme Court of the Netherlands, acting as an appointing authority, since Iran did not provide sufficient evidence that such a statement was made,[23] which in this context would probably have disqualified Judge Mangard.

11-15 A clear predisposition in relation to a dispute exists where the arbitrator has already expressed an opinion on the concrete legal question or has even acted as counsel for a party in the matter.[24] This must be distinguished from earlier publications dealing in an abstract way with the legal issue in question. Those publications do not impair the arbitrator's impartiality. In particular, party appointed arbitrators are sometimes chosen according to their perception or their expected attitude or open-mindedness to a particular argument or legal or scientific viewpoint. Given the subjective character of this concept which makes it hard to prove, the standard to be met is generally not actual impartiality but the appearance of impartiality.

11-16 The interviewing of arbitrators before appointment does not impair the impartiality of an arbitrator if properly conducted. It requires that the case is not discussed in detail and the arbitrator does not give a party advice on how to proceed and to frame its case. If the chairman is to be appointed by the two party appointed arbitrators impartiality is not impaired by *ex parte* contacts with the appointing party to receive views on the acceptability of potential nominees. Such behaviour is expressly provided for in Rule 5.2 IBA Rules of Ethics.[25] In international arbitration the task of a kind of cultural interpreter is desirable for the acceptance of an award and not a sign of partiality. However, the distinction is very subtle and transgressed if a party appointed arbitrator considers himself as the party's representative in the tribunal.

11-17 A strongly worded dissenting or concurring opinion rendered in a previous or preliminary award, by itself does not lead to sufficient doubts as to the impartiality of an arbitrator. It is part of the judicial task of the arbitrator to form an opinion on the relevant questions. A dissenting opinion cannot be

---

[23] In Re Judge Mangard, 1 *Iran-US CTR* 509, 516-518.

[24] Craig Park Paulsson, *ICC Arbitration*, para 13-03 with reference to the ICC practice where this issue is treated under the heading of "independence".

[25] See also Carter, "Rights and Obligations of the Arbitrator", 63 *Arbitration* 170 (1997) 172.

considered to be a sign of partiality, even if it reveals details of the tribunal's deliberations.[26] For a finding of partiality further indication must be present.

11-18 In an Australian case the insistence of the arbitrators on a cancellation fee which the claimant did not want to agree lead to the removal of the arbitrators for an appearance of bias. The New South Wales Supreme Court held that since the arbitrators went further than mere negotiation and tried to exert pressure on the parties, in particular the claimant, they lacked the necessary impartiality.[27]

1.2. The Concept of "Independence"

11-19 Independence requires that there should be no such actual or past dependant relationship between the parties and the arbitrators which may or at least appear to affect the arbitrator's freedom of judgment. While impartiality is needed to ensure that justice is done, independence is needed to ensure that justice is seen to be done.[28] In legal systems where either impartiality or independence is the relevant criterion the interpretation adopted incorporates most elements of both concepts.

11-20 In theory the required standard of independence should always be the same, although there are good reasons for institutions to adopt a stricter standard at the time of appointment of the arbitrators than at a later time when the issue is raised during challenge procedures. Given the disruptive effect every challenge has on an arbitration the potential for a late challenge should be minimised. Therefore a strict approach on the required independence is often adopted at the time of appointment. This leads more towards exclusion rather than leaving the risk of a subsequent challenge procedure. By contrast, if the independence of an arbitrator is challenged at a later stage in the arbitration a successful challenge may entail the retrial of considerable parts of the proceedings. This fact has to be

---

26 See the opinion by Sir Robert Jennings acting as Appointing Authority for the Iran-US Claims Tribunal in the challenge brought by the US against Judge Broms, 16(5) *Mealey's IAR* B1 (2001) B9.

27 See *ICT Pty Ltd v Sea Containers Ltd*, (2002) 17(3) Mealey's IAR B1; see also the English decision in *K/S Norjal A/S v Hyundai Heavy Industries Ltd* [1992] 1 QB 863, where such behaviour was considered to be misconduct.

28 There is, however, no internationally accepted definition of either terms which are often used interchangeably.

weighed against any possible appearance of dependence and may lead to a more pragmatic and lenient approach at that stage.[29]

11-21 Lack of independence is obvious where the arbitrator has a financial or other interest in the outcome of a case. It is a well accepted legal principle governing independent adjudication that no one should be a judge in his own cause.[30] Therefore major shareholders or directors of the parties are not suitable arbitrators. In this respect it is irrelevant whether or not there would be an actual threat of bias. By contrast, minor shareholdings the value of which will not be considerably affected by the outcome of an arbitration, may not necessarily lead to a lack of independence.[31]

11-22 Also disqualified as arbitrators are persons who have an important and actual relationship with either party such as being the party's usual lawyer. However in most cases the issue is less obvious and usually a question of degree depending on the time and the extent of the relationship with a party. A long-standing and continuing relationship with the arbitrator's law firm may cast doubts on the arbitrator's independence. By contrast if the law firm has only worked in a few completely unrelated matters for either party or an affiliate of the parties, that should in general not impair an arbitrator's independence.[32] In particular, with law firms growing or merging and the limited number of arbitration specialists it becomes less likely to find a suitable person where no connection whatsoever exists with either party.

11-23 A similar situation, however, relating to judges rather than arbitrators, was considered in the *Locabail* case[33] by the Court of Appeal in England. The case concerned a solicitor sitting as a deputy judge who discovered during the proceedings that his firm had acted in litigation against the ex-husband of one of

---

[29] For the approach taken by the ICC see Derains and Schwartz, *ICC Rules*, 113; for comparable considerations in the context of challenging a judge see *Locabail (UK) Ltd v Bayfields Properties* [2000] 1 All ER 65, 85 where it was held that the Law Society's conflict rules which probably would have prevented the solicitor judge from accepting the case were not sufficient to challenge him once the case has been going on for some time.

[30] For recent English case law on the principle see *Locabail (UK) Ltd v Bayfields Properties* [2000] 1 All ER 65; for the ICC practice in this respect Craig Park Paulsson, *ICC Arbitration*, para 13-05(iv).

[31] See Court of Appeal, 15 May 2000, *AT&T Corporation and another v Saudi Cable* [2000] 2 Lloyd's Rep 127 *et seq*, where owning 474 common shares was deemed sufficiently small and was not considered to have any impact on the impartiality of the arbitrator.

[32] But see for the restrictive ICC practice in that matter, Craig Park Paulsson, *ICC Arbitration*, para 13-05(v).

[33] *Locabail (UK) Ltd v Bayfields Properties* [2000] 1 All ER 65.

the parties. The court held that the pecuniary interests involved in the case were not of such nature to automatically disqualify the judge but that it had to be determined on the basis of the particular facts of the case whether there was a "real danger of bias". In the case the court denied such a danger since the judge's knowledge of the case involving the ex-husband was limited and the judge's interest in the fees earned by his law firm from that case tenuous and insubstantial.[34]

11-24 A borderline case in this respect may be the English practice to allow barristers who are appointed as arbitrators being in the same chamber as one of the parties counsel.[35] This issue has been widely discussed in light of the *Laker Airways* case,[36] in which the English court held that the fact that an arbitrator was from the same chambers as counsel for one of the parties did not give rise to justifiable doubts as to his impartiality or independence. This decision was specific to its facts. It is not the final word on this issue as the judge was not fully addressed on the issue as the complaining party did not attend the court.[37]

11-25 The English courts[38] decided differently in a case where a barrister was appointed as an expert on behalf of another barrister from his chambers and with whom he was also a very good friend. In reviewing the meaning of "independence" the court looked to see if there was "a relationship between the proposed expert and the party calling him which a reasonable observer might think was capable of affecting the views of the expert so as to make the expert unduly favourable to that party." The judge found that such a relationship did exist and held the barrister expert not to be independent. This test was closer to the test of impartiality than independence but the principle is clear. It should be extended to the independence and impartiality of an arbitrator from the same chambers or law firm of one of the parties or its counsel.

11-26 Arbitrators from law firms which are affiliated to or have an alliance with a firm representing one of the parties may also not be considered

[34] *Ibid*, 83-86; furthermore the Court of Appeal held that by not challenging the judge immediately after his disclosure any right to challenge him on the basis of these fact was waived.

[35] DAC Report, paras 102 *et seq*; Cour d'appel Paris, *KFTCIC v Kori Estero*, Rev Arb 568 (1992); see for the approach taken by the ICC to such cases Derains and Schwartz, *ICC Rules*, 116.

[36] *Laker Airways v FLS Aerospace* [1999] 2 Lloyd's Rep 45.

[37] Merjian, "Caveat Arbitor: Laker Airways and the Appointment of Barristers as Arbitrators in Cases involving Barrister-Advocates from the Same Chambers", 17(1) *J Int'l Arb* 31 (2000); Kendall, "Barristers Independence and Disclosure Revisited", 16 *Arb Int* 343 (2000).

[38] *Liverpool Roman Catholic Archdiocesean Trust v Goldberg* [2002] 4 All ER 950.

independent.[39] The same applies to arbitrators who have a close relationship to the lawyers of one side. In one arbitration in the United States in which the award had been rendered but not yet confirmed, the arbitrator was successfully challenged on the grounds of partiality for his behaviour during the arbitration. The presiding arbitrator was discovered to have spent two nights in the hotel room of a female lawyer representing the successful party in the arbitration.[40]

11-27 Where an arbitrator accepts repeat appointments from the same party, the other party may have concerns about his independence, fearing that the arbitrator's independence may be tainted by the wish to receive future appointments. Prior appointments by one party should not, in principle, be sufficient to cast doubts on the independence of an arbitrator unless there is a pattern of regular appointments by that particular party.[41] If in doubt, the arbitrator should consider disclosing to the parties his past connections and activities involving one or both of the parties. Thus, putting both parties on notice should they wish to raise any concerns or challenge the arbitrator at the outset. There is an active practising and academic community involved with international commercial arbitration, and arbitration practitioners and arbitrators regularly attend social events, seminars, study groups and lecture at events organised or sponsored by law firms. None of these events should in any way affect the independence of the arbitrator.[42]

11-28 Complex problems of independence can also arise if the same arbitrator is appointed for related matters. On the one hand this might save time and expense as the arbitrator is already familiar with the situation. On the other hand preconceived opinion may prevent the arbitrator from objectively evaluating the case of the party which has not been a party to the earlier arbitration proceedings.[43] No general rule can be stated as to how such matters would be resolved by arbitration institutions or state courts and it will very much depend on the relevant facts.

---

[39] *Mustang Enterprises, Inc v Plug-In Storage Systems, Inc*, 874 F Supp 881 (ND Ill 1995).

[40] Report on the Mission Insurance case in *The Wall Street Journal*, 14 February 1 1990.

[41] Hascher, "ICC Practice in Relation to the Appointment, Confirmation, Challenge and Replacement of Arbitrators", 6(2) *ICC Bulletin* 4 (1995) 7.

[42] See also the decision by the Cantonal Court Graubünden, 30 January 1996, *ASA Bulletin* 264 (1996) where it was held that arbitrator's membership in the same Rotary Club and in the board of an unrelated company as one of the parties did not justify a challenge for lack of impartiality.

[43] Cour d'appel Paris, 14 October 1994, *Ben Nasser et autre v BNP et Crédit Lyonnais*, Rev Arb 380 (1994) 386; see also Calvo, "The Challenge of ICC Arbitrators", 15(4) *J Int'l Arb* 63 (1998).

11-29 A special issue of independence arises in arbitrations where one of the parties is a state or a state entity and a person working in one way or another for the government is appointed. Although, in general, employees are considered to lack the necessary independence a different view is taken in relation to certain types of public officials and civil servants. In particular, judges, who are by their position required to be independent, or law professors are considered to be suitable party appointed arbitrators. The same may apply to directors of state controlled enterprises in arbitration against other state entities. In arbitrations with parties from developing countries an important factor to be taken into account in this respect is that apart from the functionaries there are often few trained and experienced jurists available who could serve as arbitrators.[44] A different standard may, however, apply if they are to be appointed as sole arbitrator or chairman of a tribunal.

2. Duty of Disclosure

11-30 To ensure compliance with the requirements of independence and impartiality, arbitrators are generally under a duty to disclose to the parties all facts which may be relevant in this respect. This duty is explicitly foreseen in most arbitration rules and laws.[45] Even where that is not the case, it follows from an implied term of the agreement between the parties and the arbitrator.[46] Each arbitrator is under an obligation to ensure a valid and fair resolution of a given dispute. This duty encompasses the duty to disclose all relevant facts which, when they become known, could lead to a successful challenge of the arbitrator or even the award with all the ensuing additional costs and delay incurred by the parties.

11-31 This disclosure obligation arises whenever a prospective arbitrator is approached for appointment and continues until the arbitration is terminated. Relevant facts and circumstances which may arise at a later stage, should therefore be disclosed by the arbitrator once he becomes aware of them.

[44] For the ICC practice see Craig Park Paulsson, *ICC Arbitration*, para 13-03.

[45] See, *e.g.*, Model Law Article 12; Sweden, Arbitration Act section 9; France, NCPC Article 1452; Netherlands, CCP Article 1034; UNCITRAL Rules Article 9; ICC Rules Article 7(2); DIS Rules section 16; LCIA Article 5(3); no provisions as to a duty to disclose are however contained in the English Arbitration Act and the Swiss PIL.

[46] See, *e.g.*, Swiss Tribunal Fédéral, 14 March 1985, *Société Z v L*, ATF 111 IA 72, 76; see also Peter and Freymond, in Berti (ed), *International Arbitration in Switzerland*, Article 180 para 23. For a different view in relation to English law see Eastwood, "A Real Danger of Confusion? The English Law Relating to Bias in Arbitrators", 17 *Arb Int* 287 (2001) 298-301.

Arbitrators should be mindful not only about their own conduct and business affairs, but also those with whom they are associated, during the arbitration process. This is because losing parties often look for a way to avoid the effects of an award against them. Attacking the independence and impartiality of the arbitrator is one such way.

11-32 In general, the duty extends to all information which could be relevant.[47] The big question is what information is relevant and what is sufficient to justify an objection to the arbitrator. Due to the different perceptions as to what facts may be relevant, some institutions prescribe in detail what types of information is required. Extensive guidelines can be found in Article 4.2 of the IBA Rules of Ethics for International Arbitrators. This provides that

> A prospective arbitrator should disclose:
>
> (a) any past or present business relationship, whether direct or indirect including prior appointment as arbitrator, with any party to the dispute, or any representative of a party, or any person known to be a potentially important witness in the arbitration. With regard to present relationships, the duty of disclosure applies irrespective of their magnitude, but with regard to the past relationship only if they were of more than a trivial nature in relation to the arbitrator's professional or business affairs. Non-disclosure of an indirect relationship unknown to a prospective arbitrator will not be a ground for disqualification unless it could have been ascertained by making reasonable enquiries;
>
> (b) the nature and duration of any substantial social relationships with any party or any person known to be likely to be an important witness in the arbitration;
>
> (c) the nature of any previous relationship with any fellow arbitrator (including prior joint service as an arbitrator);
>
> (d) the extent of any prior knowledge he may have of the dispute;
>
> (e) the extent of any commitments which may affect his availability to perform his duties as arbitrator as may be reasonably anticipated.

11-33 Disclosure factors are generally professional and personal contacts which the arbitrator has with either or both of the parties. Clearly, if the party arbitrator has advised, represented or worked with a party, even many years previously, this is likely to be considered relevant. In the case of a partner in a law firm this

[47] Hausmaninger, "Rights and Obligations of the Arbitrator with regard to the Parties and the Arbitral Institution - A Civil Law Viewpoint", in ICC (ed), *The Status of the Arbitrator*, 36, 38.

would include previous work undertaken by that firm for one of the parties.[48] Equally, if there is a personal relationship between the arbitrator and senior officers of a party. This would probably also include individuals who, although not close friends, meet regularly in social, political or business circles, *e.g.* investors in a common third business or in the same golf or bridge club.

11-34 Less clear is where a law firm has represented or advised a company within a multinational group where the company concerned and the party to the arbitration have little or no connection other than common ownership. It is even possible that the work done was prior to the company in question becoming part of the group. Equally, the fact that the proposed arbitrator knows and occasionally meets socially with, or is a member of the same club or other organization as, senior officers of one of the parties, should not automatically disqualify the arbitrator from accepting appointment. Whether such issues should be disclosed is always a matter of judgment for the arbitrator to be considered in each case.[49] The fact that the arbitrator might, many years previously, have been to school or university with, or even worked in the same company as, an officer of one of the parties is not of itself a fact (assuming he knows this fact) which needs to be disclosed. Even more concrete individual contacts, rather than friendships or substantive relationships, are also not automatically disclosable.

11-35 An interesting question is the extent to which the arbitrator should disclose his relationship with the law firm of the appointing party or the other party. This is a real issue as the arbitration community is relatively small and in many cases arbitrators are selected because they are known to the lawyers involved, either personally or by reputation. Frequently, well known arbitrators will have been involved in several arbitrations with the same lawyers; an arbitrator may have been appointed in another case by the lawyer representing the other party. A lawyer representing a party may previously have sat as an

---

48 The non-disclosure of the existence of a relationship between the arbitrator's law firm and a party has led in several cases to the annulment of an award; see Court of Appeal Cairo, 25 November 1998, Case No 42 of the 115th Judicial Year reported in 3 *Int ALR* N-80 (2000); see also the American decision in *Schmitz v Zilveti*, 20 F 3d 1043 (9th Cir 1994); *Sphere Drake Insurance Company Ltd v All American Insurance Co*, 17(6) Mealey's IAR C-1 (2002) (ND Ill). For the opposite view see the German Bundesgerichtshof, 4 March 1999, *ZIP* 859 (1999) with note Kröll, *EWiR* 1087 (1999); see also the appellate decision in *Beltz v Pankow*, 31 Cal App 4th 1503 (Cal App 1st Dist, 1995) where the same result was reached as the arbitrator had left the firm and was not even able to make a conflict check so that the non-disclosure could not create an appearance of bias.

49 See Oberlandesgericht Naumburg, 19 December 2001 which considered *inter alia* the common membership in a professional organization to be non disclosable. For an English commentary and summary, see 17(6) Mealeys IAR 27 (2002)

arbitrator together with the nominated arbitrator; the reason the arbitrator may have been selected could be because the lawyer was impressed by his judgment and approach when they were arbitrators together. Even where the individual arbitrators and counsel do not know one another, where the major international and national law firms are involved, there will invariably be contacts between the arbitrators and lawyers in their respective law firms. This is equally true of university professors who are often sought out as arbitrators. The fact that one of the lawyers was a student of the professor in years past is hardly likely to be a relevant factor; the student is more likely to remember the professor than the other way round.

11-36 Nevertheless, it will in the end be the arbitrator who decides what information is going to be disclosed.[50] Article 4.1 IBA Rules of Ethics provides that arbitrators should declare important factors which may cause justifiable doubts about the individual's independence.[51] In certain cases non-disclosure of facts has been considered to justify the challenge of an arbitrator.[52] However, facts which have been disclosed at the pre-appointment stage cannot be relied on at a later stage to challenge the arbitrator or the award. Parties have to raise their objections immediately or they are considered to have waived their right to rely on them.[53]

11-37 The suggested rule, when in doubt disclose, is not always appropriate. It may offer a party wishing to delay matters, or who is distrustful of the process, the opportunity to object, challenge the arbitrator and try to preserve the alleged conflict for a challenge to the award at a later stage. It is often considered that if the arbitrator felt it appropriate to disclose certain facts, there must be some relevance and likelihood of it affecting his judgment.

---

50 Carter,"Rights and Obligations of the Arbitrator", 63 *Arbitration* 170 (1997) 172; see also IBA Draft Joint Report on the Working Group on Standard Guidelines of Bias and Disclosure for International Commercial Arbitration 7 October 2002.

51 See for the ICC Practice in that regard, Derains and Schwartz, *ICC Rules,* 175 *et seq;* Eastwood, "A Real Danger of Confustion? The English Law Relating to Bias in Arbitrators", 17 *Arb Int* 287 (2001) 298.

52 See, *e.g.*, the US Supreme Court in *Commonwealth Coatings Corp v Continental Casualty Co*, 393 US 145 (1968); see also Tribunal de Grande Instance Paris, 12 May 1993, *Raoul Duval v V*, Rev Arb 411 (1996); confirmed by the Cour d'appel Paris, 12 October 1995, *Rev Arb* 324 (1999) and the Cour de cassation, 16 December 1997, unpublished, where the non-disclosure by an arbitrator of the fact that he will start working for one of the parties after the arbitration led to an action for liability against the arbitrator; see also the German decision of Oberlandesgericht Naumburg, 19 December 2001, 17(6) *Mealeys IAR* 27 (2002).

53 See, *e.g.*, Model Law Article 13(2), which sets a 15 days time limit for challenge of arbitrators.

11-38 Arbitrators should use common sense to disclose those factors which objectively could be relevant, rather than remote or distant factors. It is difficult to apply a uniform test acceptable to all cultural environments, since the approach to challenges also has an influence on the extent of the disclosure requirements. While the US approach, which is also favoured by the ICC, is to require disclosure of any past or present relationship with the parties and their lawyers, this idea is not acceptable in continental Europe.[54]

11-39 The duty to disclose also requires an arbitrator to make enquiries as to whether any relationships exist which have to be disclosed. He cannot just rely on his existing knowledge. The principle of reasonableness limits the extent of enquiries to be made by the arbitrator to find out potential conflicts and the resulting obligation to disclose those facts.[55] Arbitrators cannot, for example, be expected to extend their conflict check to their former law firms and to provide the parties with a complete and unexpurgated business biography.[56]

11-40 In practice a party appointed arbitrator may at first informally disclose all relevant information to the party approaching him. If the prospective appointing party considers the relations with either party not to be of such nature as to impair the arbitrator's independence or impartiality, the arbitrator should disclose the information in writing to the appointing authority, to the other party and the other arbitrators.

11-41 The form of disclosure to be used by the arbitrator depends on the applicable arbitration rules. To ensure compliance with this duty many institutions have a standard form which must be signed before appointment by the parties. For example, Article 7(2) ICC Rules provides:

> Before appointment or confirmation, a prospective arbitrator shall sign a statement of independence and disclose in writing to the Secretariat any facts or circumstances which might be of such a nature as to call into question the arbitrator's independence in the eyes of the parties. The Secretariat shall provide

---

[54] Hirsch, "May Arbitrators Know the Lawyers of the Parties?" *ASA Bulletin* 7 (1990) 7; and response by Bond, "The ICC Arbitrator's Statement of Independence: A Response to Prof Alain Hirsch", *ASA Bulletin* 226 (1990) 232; for the differences in approach see also Okekeifere, "Appointment and Challenge of Arbitrators under the UNCITRAL Model Law; Part II: Challenge", 3 *Int ALR* 13 (2000) 13 *et seq.*

[55] Carter, "Rights and Obligations of the Arbitrator", *Arbitration* 170 (1997) 172; Calvo, "The Challenge of ICC Arbitrators", 15(4) *J Int'l Arb* 63 (1998) 67.

[56] See US Supreme Court, *Commonwealth Coatings Corp v Continental Casualty*, 393 US 145, 151 *et seq*; Hoellering, "The Role of the Arbitrator: An AAA Perspective", in ICC (ed), *The Status of the Arbitrator*, 59, 62 *et seq.*

such information to the parties in writing and fix a time limit for any comments from them.[57]

11-42 The ICC Statement of Independence requires arbitrators to declare their willingness to act as an arbitrator and to check one of the two boxes beside the following two declarations:

❑ I am independent of each of the parties and intend to remain so; to the best of my knowledge, there are no facts or circumstances, past or present, that need be disclosed because they might be of such nature as to call into question my independence in the eyes of any of the parties.

OR

❑ I am independent of each of the parties and intend to remain so; however, in consideration of Article 7, paragraphs 2 & 3 of the ICC Rules of Arbitration, I wish to call your attention to the following facts or circumstances which I hereafter disclose because they might be of such a nature as to call into question my independence in the eyes of any of the parties.[58]

11-43 The duty of disclosure may in exceptional cases conflict with the duty of confidentiality owed to parties in a different arbitration. In such a case an arbitrator should decline appointment because the mere non-disclosure might justify a challenge if the facts are discovered at a later stage.[59]

11-44 The effects of a violation of the duty of disclosure and the sanctions involved depend to a large extent on the approach adopted to challenges of arbitrators by the relevant law. In England, for example, the Court of Appeal held in *AT&T Corporation v Saudi Cable*[60] that an inadvertent non-disclosure of a fact which might have affected the appointment process is not sufficient to lead to a "real danger of bias". Consequently the non-disclosure did not lead to a sanction.[61]

---

57 See similarly, AAA ICDR Rules Article 7(1); LCIA Article 5.3; SCC Rules Article 17(2).

58 Similar declarations are required by other major institutions.

59 See *Commonwealth Coatings Corp v Continental Casualty Co*, 393 US 145 (1968).

60 See *AT&T Corporation and another v Saudi Cable* [2000] 2 Lloyd's Rep 127 (CA); in the case the arbitrator had provided the parties and the ICC with a CV which due to a clerical mistake did not contain the information that the arbitrator was a non-executive director and a minimal shareholder of a company which was a competitor of one of the parties in the biding process which resulted in the contract giving rise to the dispute.

61 See also the decision to the same effect by the German Bundesgerichtshof, 4 September 1999, *ZIP* 859 (1999) with note Kröll, *EWiR* 1087 (1999). For an equivalent English decision see *Rental Trading Ltd v Gill & Duffus SA* [2000] 1 Lloyd's Rep 14.

11-45 However, it may be different in countries where the law allows a successful challenge of an arbitrator if there is "reasonable suspicion" or a threat of "an appearance" of lack of independence. For example, in *Commonwealth Coatings Corp v Continental Casualty Co*[62] an arbitrator had not disclosed business connections with one of the parties. Though the award was rendered unanimously and the court found no actual bias, the award was set aside due to due to the failure to disclose all facts which might create the appearance of bias.

11-46 In addition the non-disclosure of relevant facts may also result in an action for damages against the arbitrator. The Austrian Supreme Court, for example, held that the immunity granted to an arbitrator for his judicial task does not extend to a violation of the disclosure obligation for which an arbitrator may be liable for breach of a contractual duty.[63]

3. SPECIAL ROLE OF THE PARTY APPOINTED ARBITRATOR

11-47 In some specialised types of arbitration, as well as in domestic arbitration in some countries party appointed arbitrators take the role of the representatives of their appointing party. This is rare in international arbitration where party appointed arbitrators must be impartial and independent.[64] The various arbitration rules and laws as well as the codes of ethics do not distinguish between party appointed arbitrators and other arbitrators but generally extend the requirements of independence and impartiality to "every arbitrator".[65] Nevertheless party appointed arbitrators have a distinctive role to play which is important for the acceptance of arbitration as such as well as for the voluntary fulfilment of arbitration awards.

11-48 The party appointed arbitrator provides the appointing party with confidence that its case and arguments will be fully considered by the tribunal. This is particularly important in arbitrations where the parties come from

---

62 393 US 145 (1968).

63 Austrian Oberster Gerichtshof, 28 April 1998, *H GmbH v Hon*, RPS (2/1999) 7 (German Original), *Rev Arb* 392 (1999) (abstract in French); see also see also Tribunal de Grande Instance Paris, 12 May 1993, *Raoul Duval v V*, Rev Arb 411 (1996); confirmed by the Cour d'appel Paris, 12 October 1995, *Rev Arb* 324 (1999) and the Cour de cassation, 16 December 1997, unpublished, where non-disclosure by an arbitrator of the fact that he would start working for one of the parties after the arbitration led to an action for liability against the arbitrator.

64 Craig Park Paulsson, *ICC Arbitration*, para 12-04.

65 See, *e.g.*, ICC Rules Article 7(1); Introductory Note of the IBA's *Rules of Ethics for International Arbitrators*.

different cultural and legal backgrounds. In such cases a party may have the legitimate concern that due to its cultural and legal background the tribunal will not properly understand or appreciate its case and will not give sufficient weight to its arguments. By working as a cultural interpreter the party appointed arbitrator can and should help to ensure that the arguments will be properly appreciated and considered during the tribunal's deliberations.

11-49 The appointed arbitrator can do so in the internal deliberations of the tribunal by explaining certain arguments. He can also do so by directing questions during the hearing with the purpose of assisting the understanding by the tribunal where there may otherwise be some confusion. During the proceedings the arbitrator should ensure that procedural directions are drafted and conveyed in a form which takes account of the parties' predicaments. For example, a party from a developing country may not have the same facilities for expeditious communication and computerisation as is normally expected in a western industrialised country. This may also be a factor in determining how the arbitration proceedings should be organised and the collection of evidence.

11-50 This special role of the party appointed arbitrator justifies the different attitude towards their nationality; it is often expected that parties and their appointed arbitrator will be of the same nationality. Furthermore, this is evidenced by the fact that rules on ethics of arbitrators foresee that a party appointed arbitrator may discuss *ex parte* with the appointing party the acceptability of possible chairpersons.[66]

11-51 There is tension between ensuring that a party's case is properly understood and appreciated by the co-arbitrators and the requirement to stay independent and impartial. The slightest appearance of impropriety may destroy the confidence of the other members of the tribunal. It may in the worst cases lead to the removal of the arbitrator. It is therefore important that a party appointed arbitrator – with the exception of the appointment of the chairman - avoids all *ex parte* communications with his appointing party.

11-52 A problem may arise when one arbitrator has doubts as to the impartiality or independence of another arbitrator. One way to deal with this situation is for the other two arbitrators jointly to raise the issue with the third arbitrator. This can and should be done informally, as the right to challenge an

---

[66] See, *e.g.*, IBA Rules of Ethics Rule 5.2; AAA Code of Ethics Canon VII C; De Fina, "The Party Appointed Arbitrator in International Arbitrations - Role and Selection", 15 *Arb Int* 381 (1999) 383.

arbitrator is generally limited to the parties.[67] The LCIA Rules, however, theoretically allow for a formal request by the other two arbitrators to replace the arbitrator. An informal challenge could have various outcomes. It could clear the air and resolve the two arbitrators' concerns. It could also result in the challenged arbitrator resigning with the ensuing delay whilst a replacement is appointed. The party that appointed the arbitrator who resigns might decide to challenge the other two arbitrators, alleging bias on their part. This could effectively result in the disintegration of the whole arbitration. An alternative is for the two arbitrators and especially the chairman, to maintain their independence and render an award after all the evidence and arguments have been presented and considered. The key factor for the arbitration is to ensure that the ultimate award is enforceable.

---

67 See, *e.g.*, Derains and Schwartz, *ICC Rules*, 175.

Chapter 12

RIGHTS AND DUTIES OF ARBITRATORS AND PARTIES

12-1 Few arbitration laws and rules directly address the relationship between arbitrators and parties. Apart from the rules on liability and disclosure they primarily deal with the procedural aspects of arbitration. Some of those procedural duties of the arbitrator, however, can affect the status of the arbitrator and translate into obligations and rights towards the parties.

12-2 A fairly elaborate regulation of the arbitrator's duties can be found in the Code of Ethics prepared by the AAA[1] and the Rules of Ethics for International Arbitrators published by the IBA.[2] Both can be made part of the contract between the parties and the arbitrators but also give guidelines about the arbitrator's duties in cases where they are not agreed.

12-3 This chapter reviews (1) the contractual relationship between the parties and arbitrators, (2) the obligations the arbitrator owes to the parties, (3) the remuneration of arbitrators, (4) remedies and sanctions against arbitrators, and (5) immunity of arbitrators.

1. CONTRACTUAL RELATIONSHIP BETWEEN PARTIES AND ARBITRATOR

12-4 It is widely recognised that the relationship between the parties and the arbitrator is primarily based on contract.[3] The proposition to accord the arbitrator a status resulting directly from law and comprising rights and obligations assumed by the arbitrator in the public interest[4] has found little support. However, it is agreed that the special adjudicative function assumed by the arbitrator strongly influences the relationship between the parties and the arbitrator. There are a number of mandatory rules that are essential prerequisites of any dispute settlement system, private or public, which have a bearing on the duties of the arbitrator.[5]

12-5 The contract may be concluded expressly, as is primarily the case in *ad hoc* arbitration, where the parties and the arbitrator sign a separate document containing their respective rights and obligations. Often no such separate agreement will be signed. In those cases different views exist as to whether the

---

1 AAA, *Code of Ethics for Arbitrators in Commercial Disputes* (1977).

2 IBA, *Ethics for International Arbitrators* (1987).

3 See Clay, *L'arbitre*, 499 *et seq*; ICC (ed), "Final Report on the Status of the Arbitrator", 7(1) *ICC Bulletin* 27 (1996) 29; Lionnet, "The Arbitrator's Contract", 15 *Arb Int* 161 (1999) 162; see also the decision by the Austrian Oberster Gerichtshof, 28 April 1998, *H GmbH v Hon*, RPS 7 (2/1999) (German original), Rev Arb 392 (1999) (abstract in French).

4 See Mustill and Boyd, *Commercial Arbitration*, 220 *et seq*; Calavros, "Grundsätzliches zum Rechtsverhältnis zwischen Schiedsrichtern und Parteien nach griechischem Recht", *Festschrift Habscheid* 65 (1989) 75 *et seq.*

5 ICC (ed), "Final Report on the Status of the Arbitrator", 7(1) *ICC Bulletin* 27 (1996) 37 *et seq*; Fouchard Gaillard Goldman *on International Commercial Arbitration*, para 1104; Hausmaninger, "Rights and Obligations of the Arbitrator with Regard to the Parties and the Arbitral Institution- A Civil Law Viewpoint", in ICC (ed), *The Status of the Arbitrator*, 36, 37.

arbitrator becomes a party to the arbitration agreement[6] or whether a separate contract is concluded.[7] In the former case the exact terms of appointment are unclear. The parties may look to the applicable arbitration rules or the governing law, *i.e.* the law of the place of arbitration or the law governing the arbitration if it is different. In many such cases, arbitrators will present to the parties and seek their agreement to the arbitrator's own specific terms of appointment.[8]

12-6 The existence of a distinct contract between arbitrators and parties has the advantage of greater clarity since it separates the different functions of the arbitration agreement and the arbitrators' appointment. The conclusion of the contract usually coincides with the appointment of arbitrators. It is important to note that even though the power of appointment may lie with one party the contract is concluded with all parties involved. The appointing party is acting not only for itself but also as an agent for the other parties when concluding the contract of service with the arbitrators. The same applies if the arbitrators are appointed by an appointing authority, the courts or a party.[9]

12-7 Taking into account the impact of the arbitration agreement and the relevant rules determined by it on the content of the contract between the arbitrator and the parties the contractual relationship looks as follows:[10]

6 See, *e.g.*, *K/S Norjarl A/S v Hyundai Heavy Industries Co Ltd* [1991] 1 Lloyd's Rep 524, 536; *Compagnie Européenne de Céréales SA v Tradax Export SA* [1986] 2 Lloyd's Rep 301.

7 Fouchard, "Relationships between the Arbitrator and the Parties and the Arbitral Institution", in ICC (ed), *The Status of the Arbitrator*, 12 *et seq.*

8 See the Section on Appointment in Guidelines no 4 adopted by the Chartered Institute of Arbitrators, 66 *Arbitration* 167 (2000).

9 Lachmann, *Handbuch*, para 1747; Lionnet, "The Arbitrator's Contract", 15 *Arb Int* 161 (1999) 165 *et seq.*

10 See for a slightly different structure, Clay, *L'Arbitre*, 809.

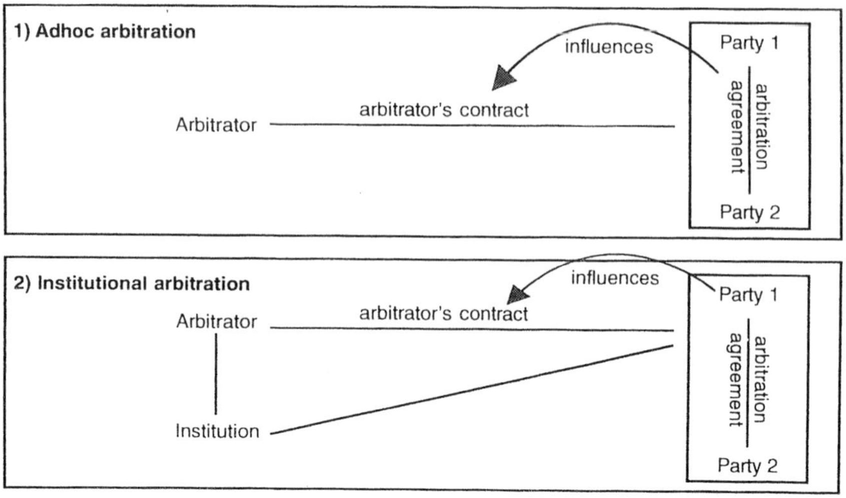

12-8 Under the terms of the contract the arbitrator agrees to settle the dispute between the parties in return for a certain remuneration. Different classifications are suggested for that contract which is either considered to be a contract of agency, a contract for the provision of services or a contract *sui generis.*[11] The law applicable to the contract can be agreed between the parties and the arbitrator.[12] If no such choice is made, as is invariably the case in practice, the applicable law has to be determined by conflict of laws rules. These usually refer to the law of the place which has the closest connection with the contract.

12-9 For the arbitrator's contract, there are several factors which could potentially determine the closest connection. The relevant factor may be the place of arbitration, the seat of the arbitration institution under the rules of which the arbitration is conducted, the domicile of the arbitrator or the law applicable to the arbitration procedure. The most convincing view is that the place of the arbitration should determine the applicable law though it may not always be fixed when the contract is concluded. In most cases hearings will take place there so that it qualifies as the principal place of performance for the arbitrator's

[11] For the different views see Clay, *L'arbitre*, 739 *et seq*; Fouchard Gaillard Goldman *on International Commercial Arbitration*, para 1113 *et seq*; Lachmann, *Handbuch*, para 1746.

[12] Lionnet, "The Arbitrator's Contract", 15 *Arb Int* 161 (1999) 169; Clay, *L'arbitre*, 745 *et seq*; ICC (ed), "Final Report on the Status of the Arbitrator", 7(1) *ICC Bulletin* 27 (1996) 29

function.[13] The seat of the institution may be irrelevant where the parties have chosen another place of arbitration. Relying on the law of the domicile of the arbitrators is impractical as it could lead to the odd result that the contract with the members of one tribunal will be submitted to different laws according to where each arbitrator lives.

2. Obligations of the Arbitrator Owed to the Parties

12-10 The duties of the arbitrator must either be derived from the contract itself or from provisions in the applicable rules or law. Though the law governing the arbitration primarily deals with procedural issues it is possible to see the procedural duties of an arbitrator as implied duties of the contract with the parties. Section 33(1) English Arbitration Act obliges the tribunal to

> a) act fairly and impartially as between the parties, giving each party a reasonable opportunity of putting his case and dealing with that of his opponent, and
>
> b) adopt procedures suitable to the circumstances of the particular case, avoiding unnecessary delay or expense, so as to provide a fair means for the resolution of the matters falling to be determined.

12-11 These procedural duties are not only owed to the state but also translate into the contract between each arbitrator and the parties. They result *inter alia* in a duty to avoid undue delay and to conduct the proceedings accordingly.[14]

2.1. Settle the Dispute between the Parties

12-12 The main obligation arising out of the contract between the parties and the arbitrator is to settle the dispute between the parties.[15] This includes in particular a duty to conduct the arbitration in such a way that it leads to a valid award not open to challenge. Each arbitrator has to take into consideration all issues which might threaten the validity of an award.[16]

---

[13] For a slightly different view (law governing to the arbitration), Austrian Oberster Gerichtshof, 28 April 1998, *H GmbH v Hon*, RPS 7 (2/1999), Rev Arb 392 (1999).

[14] For the influence of national laws on the obligations of the arbitrator see Fouchard, "Relationships between the Arbitrator and the Parties and the Arbitral Institution", in ICC (ed), *The Status of the Arbitrator*, 12, 18.

[15] ICC (ed.), "Final Report on the Status of the Arbitrator", 7(1) *ICC Bulletin* 27 (1996) 29.

[16] See ICC Rules Article 35; LCIA Article 32(2). See also Horvath, "The Duty of Tribunals to Render an Enforceable Award", 18(2) *J Int'l Arb* 135 (2001).

12-13 In this regard an arbitrator must make every effort properly to review all the issues raised by the parties and to determine all their differences. Even where issues seem unimportant or peripheral arbitrators must reach a conclusion and cover such issues in the award. Where arbitrators fail to determine a matter, they will not have completed their mission and the issue could be referred back to them by a court.[17] By corollary, arbitrators should not exceed their authority, either under the terms of the arbitration agreement, or their powers under the applicable rules or law. If arbitrators exceed their authority the consequent award can be set aside, [18] sent back to the arbitrators for review, [19] and it may be refused enforcement.[20]

12-14 In this respect the validity of an award in its country of origin must be distinguished from its enforceability in a different country. Though deniable, it is not one of the arbitrator's duties to ensure the enforceability of the award. He cannot know in which country the award has to be enforced and the requirements for enforcement may differ from country to country. For example, awards of interest on money due may be perfectly enforceable in western countries.[21] Similarly, other countries will not enforce an arbitration award which gives punitive damages.[22] In such a case, if a contractual duty exists to render an enforceable award and enforcement was anticipated in an Islamic country, the arbitrator would have to render an award without interest. Such duty would therefore have the curious effect of harming the party it wants to protect. The winning party may be better off with an award on interest enforceable at the place of arbitration and a number of other countries than without such an award.

---

17 See, *e.g.*, England, Arbitration Act section 68(3)(d).

18 See, *e.g.*, Model Law Article 34(2)(iii).

19 See, *e.g.*, England, Arbitration Act section 68(3)(a).

20 See, *e.g.*, New York Convention Article V(1)(c).

21 See Saleh, "The recognition and enforcement of foreign arbitral awards in the states of the Arab Middle East", in Lew (ed), *Contemporary Problems*, 340, 348; Gotonda, "Awarding Interests in International Arbitration", 90 *AJIL* 40 (1996) 47.

22 Enforcement may be problematic in Germany since the Bundesgerichtshof has held that the enforcement of foreign judgments awarding punitive damages is against public policy, see Bundesgerichtshof, 4 June 1992, 45 *NJW* 3096 (1992); Landgericht, Berlin, 35 *RIW* 988 (1989); whether this also applies to arbitration awards has not yet been decided; against such an extension Kühn, "RICO Claims in International Arbitration and their Recognition in Germany", 11(2) *J Int'l Arb* 37 (1994).

It is always possible that assets may become available in a country where the award can be enforced.[23]

2.2. Complete the Mandate

12-15 It follows from the contractual nature of the relationship that the arbitrator is not allowed to resign without good cause.[24] By accepting his appointment the arbitrator agrees to resolve the dispute between the parties. Provided that the parties do not settle their dispute that mission is only completed when the arbitrator renders an award. Any premature termination of the arbitrator's mandate could have serious repercussions on the arbitration and lead to considerable losses of time and money. Proceedings may have to be repeated and the delay involved in that may lead to additional damages. This is important to prevent delaying tactics.[25]

12-16 This contractual duty not to resign without good cause before an award is rendered is restated and clarified in a number of arbitration rules and laws. The ICC Rules state that by accepting appointment the "arbitrator undertakes to carry out his responsibilities."[26] Other rules make any voluntary resignation by the arbitrators subject to the consent or acceptance either of the arbitration institution or the parties.[27] Comparable statutory reinforcements of the contractual duty can be found also in some arbitration laws which require the permission of the courts for an arbitrator to resign without the parties' consent.[28] Those courts or arbitration institutions determine whether there is good cause for the arbitrator to

[23] A good example is provided by the decision in *Deutsche Schachtbau- und Tiefbohrgesellschaft mbH v Ras Al Khaimah National Oil Co et al* [1987] 2 Lloyd's Rep 246; XIII YBCA 522 (1988) where assets became available in England six years after the award had been rendered.

[24] Derains and Schwartz, *ICC Rules*, 128 for ICC arbitrations; Bernstein's *Handbook*, para 2-206 *et seq* for English Law; Lachmann, *Handbuch*, para 1968 *et seq* on German law; Hausmaninger, "Rights and Obligations of the Arbitrator with regard to the Parties and the Arbitral Institution - A Civil Law Viewpoint", in ICC (ed), *The Status of the Arbitrator*, 36, 39 *et seq.*

[25] That an arbitrator should not resign too hastily was discussed *in Laker Airways Inc v FLD Aerospace Ltd* [1999] 2 Lloyd's Rep 45, 48; see also the Australian case *Cleanae Pty Ltd v Australia and New Zealand Banking Group Ltd* [1999] VSCA 35 *et seq* where it was criticised that a judicial officer had acceded hastily to an unfounded disqualification application.

[26] Article 7(5).

[27] See, *e.g.*, Washington Convention, Article 56(3), ICSID Rules Rule 8(2); AAA ICDR Rules Article 10.

[28] Belgium, Judicial Code Article 1689; Netherlands, CCP Article 1029(2); see also Fouchard, "Relationships between the Arbitrator and the Parties and the Arbitral Institution", in ICC (ed), *The Status of the Arbitrator*, 12, 18; Solhchi, "The Validity of Truncated Tribunal Proceedings and Awards", 9 *Arb Int* 303 (1993) 313 classifies this as a of customary international law rule.

resign. This usually involves a comprehensive balancing of interests of the different parties concerned. Factors to be taken into a account include the stage of the proceedings, the possible delay caused by the resignation and the prospects of future cooperation with the arbitrator.

2.3. Stay Impartial and Independent

12-17 The arbitrator must be and stay independent and impartial. To this end, he should in general avoid *ex parte* communications with the parties which might create the appearance of partiality.[29] More important, he must not compromise himself and should disclose all relevant facts which might affect his independence or impartiality. This includes details of a pecuniary or proprietary interest[30] or a close relation to a party which may make the arbitrator "judge in his own cause".[31] This duty does not only exist at the appointment stage but continues throughout proceedings.

2.4. Conduct the Arbitration Fairly and Without Undue Delay

12-18 The arbitrator is bound to conduct the procedure in a fair manner, treat both parties equally and respect their right to be heard. What amounts to fairness is often discussed in subjective terms reflecting a party's position in a particular case. This generally reflects the frustration of a party that has not been successful in its particular submission. The best guideline that arbitrators can follow is to allow a party a reasonable amount of time to present its case and respond to the case of the other party. It will not be unreasonable to refuse many days of hearings, numerous witnesses or lengthy argument merely because one party demands it, in the interest of fairness. In every case the arbitrators should decide themselves what time and submissions are necessary to give the tribunal sufficient evidence to reach its conclusion. Equally important when an indulgence has been allowed, is to ensure the right to respond fully.

12-19 Most arbitration laws and rules now put considerable emphasis on the obligation to conduct the proceedings without undue delay. The duty to avoid

---

[29] Carter, "Rights and Obligations of the Arbitrator", 63 *Arbitration* 170 (1997) 172 *et seq*; Hausmaninger, "Rights and Obligations of the Arbitrator with regard to the Parties and the Arbitral Institution - A Civil Law Viewpoint", in ICC (ed), *The Status of the Arbitrator*, 36, 39.

[30] See *R v Bow Street Metropolitan Stipendiary Magistrates, ex parte Pinochet (No 2)* [1999] 2 WLR 272.

[31] See *Laker Airways v FLS Aerospace* [1999] 2 Lloyd's Rep 45.

any delay in the conduct of an arbitration should have a bearing at the appointment stage. The existing workload or other commitments can make it impossible for a prospective arbitrator to expeditiously discharge his functions in an arbitration. In an ideal world, arbitrators should in those cases either reject an appointment or at least disclose those facts to thc parties so that they can decide whether to appoint him or not.[32]

2.5. Keep the Arbitration Confidential

12-20 The arbitrator has to preserve the confidential and private nature of the proceedings. He is not allowed to communicate any details or names without the parties' consent.[33] This may not be easy where a case becomes a matter of public record. This duty of confidentiality is contained in some of the laws and rules.[34] The arbitrator's confidentiality is less controversial or uncertain than the general confidentiality binding the parties.[35]

3. Remuneration of Arbitrators

12-21 The principal right of an arbitrator, in return for his obligations, is to receive payment. The arbitrator provides a private dispute resolution service for the parties in accordance with an agreed procedure. In return for this service the arbitrator receives remuneration by way of fees.

---

[32] See Okekeifere, "The Parties's Rights Against Dilatory or Unskilled Arbitrator", 15(2) *J Int'l Arb* 130 (1998).

[33] For a list of the different duties see ICC (ed), "Final Report on the Status of the Arbitrator", 7(1) *ICC Bulletin* 27 (1996) 30.

[34] See, *e.g.*, LCIA Article 30(2); AAA ICDR Rules Article 34; Geneva, Rule 5; IBA Rules of Ethics Rule 9; see also Romania, Code of Civil Procedure Article 353 according to which an arbitrator may be liable for the disclosure of information about the arbitration without the consent of the parties.

[35] Under certain laws parties may, *e.g.*, be allowed to publish the award; on that see Swedish Supreme Court, 27 October 2000, *Bulgarian Foreign Trade Bank Ltd v AI Trade Finance Inc*, 15(11) Mealey's IAR B1 (2000); *Associated Electronic & Gas Insurance Services Ltd v European Reinsurance Company*, Zurich, [2003] HKPC II.

3.1. Bases for Remunerating Arbitrators

12-22 There are essentially two ways for calculating the arbitrator's fees. They may either be based on the time spent at a rate agreed between the parties and the arbitrator, or may depend on the amount in dispute.

12-23 Where the fees are based on the time expended the relevant rate may be directly agreed with the parties, as is the norm in *ad hoc* arbitration, or through the officials of the relevant institution, as in LCIA arbitrations. Time charges may be hourly or daily, and in the latter case it is important to define what is meant by a day. In addition the parties and the arbitrators may agree on cancellation or commitment fees. By accepting appointment or setting aside time for hearings arbitrators often forego the opportunity to accept other business for which they should be remunerated if hearings are cancelled.[36]

12-24 Time based fees have two disadvantages. First, rates can differ significantly even within the same three member tribunal. This will occur where the tribunal is comprised of different skills, *e.g.* an accountant, a surveyor, an engineer, a lawyer, or where the arbitrators are from different countries and the professional fee rates differ between these countries. The effect of such different remuneration arrangements can result in a lesser paid arbitrator feeling that more work should be done by the better paid arbitrator. Second, there will be a disparity in the fees to be paid because, inevitably, some arbitrators work more quickly than others. This makes it difficult for the parties to estimate the likely cost of the arbitration with any accuracy.

12-25 The second basis for arbitrators' remuneration is to make the fees dependent on the amount in dispute between the parties. This is known as an *ad valorem* basis of calculation and is best known by its use by the ICC. This system may not reflect the actual work done by the arbitrator but has the advantage of greater predictability. The parties and the arbitrators can evaluate the probable, or at least maximum, fees to be paid from the outset before making the decision to start an arbitration or to accept an appointment. Furthermore, calculation of fees on the basis of the amount in dispute makes sense economically by ensuring that the costs of the arbitration do not exceed a certain percentage of the amount in dispute.

---

[36] If no advance agreement on such fees has been reached arbitrators may have problems being remunerated for the time set aside; for related problems see decision by the New South Wales Supreme Court in *ICT Pty Ltd v Sea Containers Ltd*, 17(3) Mealey's IAR B 1 (2002). See also the English decision in *K/S Norjarl A/S v Hyundai Heavy Industries Ltd* [1992] 1 QB 863, [1991] All ER 211.

12-26 In some countries, such as Germany[37], there are guidelines as to the remuneration of an arbitrator on which the parties can agree or which apply in the absence of agreement. In general an agreement on the arbitrator's remuneration can be deduced from submitting the arbitration to certain rules. The different arbitration rules often provide for a means to fix the arbitrators' fees.

3.2. Fixing the Arbitrator's Remuneration

12-27 In institutional arbitration the fees to be paid are generally fixed by the institution. Accordingly, arbitrators do not have to negotiate their fees directly with the parties. The ICC and a number of other institutions have a schedule of fees attached to their rules which generally make the amount of the arbitrators' fees dependent on the value of the subject matter in dispute.[38] Some of these rules fix a range for the fees instead of a fixed amount to provide for a certain flexibility. This allows the institution to take into account the actual difficulties encountered in an arbitration without giving up the required predictability of costs. Other institutions, such as the ICDR or the LCIA rely on an hourly or daily rate which is fixed at the beginning of the arbitration.[39]

12-28 By contrast, in an *ad hoc* arbitration an agreement on the fees is necessary between the parties and essential between the parties and the arbitrators. The fees are usually negotiated when the full tribunal is appointed before the actual proceedings start. Where the contract does not contain any provision as to an arbitrator's fee it is a question of the law applicable to the contract of service that determines what fees have to be paid. Under most contract laws a reasonable fee has to be paid which is either to be fixed by the arbitrators, as under German law sections 315, 316 BGB, or to be determined by a neutral person or the court.[40]

12-29 If the agreed fees prove to be insufficient during the arbitration the arbitrators may approach the parties for an augmentation. An agreement must, however, be reached with all parties and it is not possible that only one party agrees to pay the higher fees. This could lead to an appearance of partiality or questionable independence. The arbitrators should not threaten the non-

[37] "Vereinbarung über die Vergütung der Schiedsrichter" (Agreement on the remuneration of arbitrators) developed by the German Bar Association in conjunction with the German Association of Judges which is based on the Statute on Attorney Fees (BRAGO).

[38] See, *e.g.*, ICC Rules; DIS Rules; CRCICA Rules, Appendix I.

[39] See LCIA Schedule of Arbitration Fees and Costs; AAA ICDR Rules Article 32.

[40] England, Arbitration Act section 28(2).

consenting party with any procedural disadvantages as that could be considered a lack of impartiality.[41]

12-30 Whether an arbitrator is entitled to fees for the services rendered, or even for future services if he is replaced during the proceedings, depends on the contract with the parties.[42] It may also depend on the reasons for his resignation or removal. Any unjustified resignation by the arbitrator may result in the loss of all claims for fees and could even give rise to claims for damages from him.[43] Resignations even with good cause will in general also result in the loss of any remuneration for future services. The English Arbitration Act gives an arbitrator who resigns the right to apply to court for a decision on his fees and expenses if there is no agreement with the parties.[44]

4. Remedies and Sanctions

12-31 What is the effect of the arbitrator having failed properly to fulfil his obligations? In many cases one of the parties will feel aggrieved that the arbitrators have failed them. This may be because the procedure followed by the tribunal was not exactly what that party wanted; or the arbitrators admitted or rejected evidence that one party considers it should not have had; or the arbitrators reached conclusions of law or fact, and made an award, which a party feels is manifestly wrong. However, none of these issues are necessarily wrong objectively nor do they show the arbitrator has in any way failed his mandate.

12-32 There are, however, situations where the arbitrator may have erred. For example, an arbitrator may not have disclosed all relevant facts which objectively could affect his independence or impartiality and which at a later stage lead to the arbitrator's removal or withdrawal; he may have objectively failed to adopt an appropriate procedure or have delayed the proceedings by sloppy case management; or he may not have applied the necessary care in rendering the award; or in extreme cases he may even have acted in bad faith.

---

41 See, *e.g., ICT Pty Ltd v Sea Containers Ltd*, 17(3) Mealey's IAR B1 (2002), where the arbitrators were removed for "appearance of bias" for their insistence on a cancellation fee which the claimant did not want to agree to pay.

42 This is provided for in the English Arbitration Act section 25(1)(a) and follows also from the principle of party autonomy.

43 Lachmann, *Handbuch*, para 1975.

44 Section 25(3)(b).

12-33 In general, the different arbitration laws and rules provide for remedies dealing with those situations. During the proceedings and before an award has been rendered the parties may have had the opportunity to challenge the arbitrator's decision or to seek the removal of the arbitrator for the non fulfilment of his duties. After that time any breach of a duty which is grave enough to be considered a serious error or irregularity may justify annulment of an award. Though these remedies are in most cases sufficient to prevent the breach of an arbitrator's duty resulting in an unfair outcome in the arbitration, they do not cover any losses incurred by the parties. Even if the arbitrator is removed from office early in the arbitration proceedings it will at least delay the proceedings. The parties may already have spent time and money for stages of the proceedings which have to be repeated. In such situations the question arises as to what is the remedy, if any, available to the parties.

4.1. Removal of the Arbitrator

12-34 Before an award has been rendered the normal remedy to sanction breaches of the arbitrator's duties is the removal of the arbitrator. Violations of obligations of a judicial nature generally result in a right to have an arbitrator removed. For example, a breach of the arbitrator's duty to be and stay independent and impartial, and to disclose the relevant facts, generally gives each party the right to apply to the competent institution or court to have the arbitrator removed. The same applies for violation of other duties such as the obligation to conduct the proceedings with the necessary care and diligence and to avoid undue delay. Furthermore the parties can always agree on the removal of an arbitrator if they are unhappy with the way the proceedings are conducted, even though the arbitrator has not breached a duty.[45]

4.2. Challenge of the Award

12-35 After the award has been rendered serious breaches of the arbitrator's duties may justify a challenge to the award to have it set aside or annulled, or be a ground to resist enforcement. The lack of independence and, in particular, the partiality of the arbitrator can fall under several of the widely recognised grounds for annulment. At least in extreme cases the tribunal may be considered to be constituted improperly, the procedure to be unfair for lack of due process, or the award to be contrary to public policy. Breaches of the duty to conduct the

---

[45] In this situation the parties may, however, be liable to pay the arbitrator's remuneration.

procedure in accordance with the rules agreed by the parties and with the necessary care, diligence and expedition may under certain circumstances also justify annulment of or refusal to enforce the award.

4.3. Action for Damages against the Arbitrator

12-36 In addition to the two other remedies which are aimed at ensuring that the arbitrator's violation of his duties does not affect the outcome, the question arises whether and to what extent the parties can also bring an action for damages against the arbitrator.

12-37 The issue of liability of the arbitrator reflects again the hybrid nature of arbitration. On the one hand the task of the arbitrator is based on a contract with the parties. Under contract law any breach of a contractual duty generally entails liability for the resulting damage. According to principles of professional liability, lawyers, valuers, architects or other experts are liable either on a contractual basis or in tort for negligence, for failing to exercise the necessary degree of care expected in the performance of their duties.[46]

12-38 On the other hand, in addition to his contractual duties the arbitrator is performing a judicial task. In most countries the law grants judges far-reaching immunity for all acts relating to their adjudicative function. The rationale of those rules is to protect the position and independence of the judiciary and the tasks they are performing. Furthermore, they are intended to preserve the finality of judgment. Claims for damages against the judges based on allegations that a party would have won the case if it had been properly decided would basically allow a party to re-litigate a dispute already decided with a *res judicata* effect.[47]

5. Immunity of Arbitrators[48]

12-39 Considerations underlying judicial immunity also apply to arbitrators, as "Courts and arbitrators are in the same business, namely the administration of

[46] While in civil law countries liability of arbitrators is primarily based on contract, in common law contracts it is based on tort; see Lew (ed), "The Indemnity of Arbitration"; Frank, "The Liability of International Arbitrators: A Comparative Analysis and Proposal for Qualified Immunity", 20 *NY L Sch J Int'l & Comp L* 1 (2000) 3 *et seq.*

[47] See Hausmaninger, "Civil Liability of Arbitrators - Comparative Analysis and Proposal for Reform", 7(4) *J Int'l Arb* 7 (1990) 12; Merkin, *Arbitration Act*, 73; Li, "Arbitral Immunity: A Profession Comes of Age", 64 *Arbitration* 53 (1998).

[48] See, *e.g.*, Lew (ed), *The Immunity of Arbitrators*.

justice."[49] It is for this reason that there is wide support in favour of limiting the liability of arbitrators. To allow unlimited actions against arbitrators would have a destabilising effect on arbitration in general.[50] It is feared that without immunity arbitrators could be harassed by actions of dissatisfied parties which might affect the arbitrator's independence in so far as the likelihood of being sued may influence the decision.[51] Furthermore, concerns have been voiced that without immunity from suit the number of available skilled arbitrators would diminish affecting arbitration in general.[52] However, arbitrators must have some liability for

> certain fundamental obligations implied into the contract between arbitrators and arbitrants. After all, arbitrators hold themselves out (some arbitrators canvass and seek appointments) as able to undertake certain types of arbitration and as having the requisite skill and expertise necessary for such disputes.[53]

12-40 There are different views as to whether the above reasons actually justify an exclusion of liability for arbitrators. In one of the leading English cases on the immunity of arbitrators, *Arenson v Casson Beckmann Rutley & Co*, Lord Kilbrandon, disagreeing with the majority, expressed the view that different principles govern the liability of judges and that of arbitrators. Arbitrators should be liable like any other professional person selected for his expertise and who pledges to exercise skill and care in the exercise of his duties. By contrast, the immunity of the judge is based on the fact that

> [t]he citizen does not select the judges in this system, nor does he remunerate them otherwise than as a contributor to the cost of government. The judge has no bargain with the parties before him. He pledges no skill. His duties are to the state: it is to the state that the superior judge at least promises that he will do justice between all parties, and behave to them as a judge should...
>
> Immunity is judged by the origin and character of appointment, not by the duties which the appointee has to perform, or his methods of performing them.[54]

---

[49] Donaldson J in *Bremer Schiffbau v South India Shipping Corp Ltd* [1981] AC 909, 921.

[50] Fouchard Gaillard Goldman *on International Commercial Arbitration*, para 1084.

[51] *Sutcliff v Thackrah* [1974] 1 All ER 859, 862; Domke, *Arbitration*, para 23-01.

[52] See Lord Salmon in *Arenson v Casson Beckman Rutley & Co* [1975] 3 All ER 901, 922 *et seq*; for a summary of the different arguments used for the extension of judicial immunity to arbitrators see Hausmaninger, "Civil Liability of Arbitrators - Comparative Analysis and Proposal for Reform," 7(4) *J Int'l Arb* 7 (1990) 11 *et seq.*

[53] Lew, "Introduction", in Lew (ed), *The Immunity of Arbitr*

[54] See Lord Kilbrandon, *Arenson v Casson Beckman Rutley & Co* [1975] 3 All ER 901, 918; against the equation of arbitrators and judges also Okekeifere, "The Parties's Rights Against

12-41 It is doubtful whether the existence of possible liability would prevent persons from accepting appointments as arbitrators. Arbitration has turned into a business with professionals who, either as part of their professional activities or on a full time basis, earn significant amounts as an arbitrator.[55] Arbitrators are no longer volunteers who are paid little for their services and who would be threatened by the prospects of liability. Insurance cover for negligence is also possible. On the other hand, it is argued that civil liability of arbitrators has a number of positive effects such as appeasing the injured party and increasing the quality of services rendered.[56]

12-42 Irrespective of whether these objections are well founded, arbitrators can not be held liable if the parties have accorded them immunity or such immunity is expressed in the national arbitration law or arbitration rules.

5.1. Contractual Limitations and the Different Arbitration Rules

12-43 Contractual limitations of the arbitrator's liability are rare in practice. This is in part due to the fact that often no express contract is concluded between the parties and the arbitrator. The forms recommended in the literature for such contracts, however, usually contain such a provision.[57] It seems at least doubtful if, in the absence of an express agreement, such an exclusion clause would be read or implied into the contract.[58]

12-44 The contractual limitation may also result from the chosen arbitration rules which often provide for a limitation of the arbitrator's liability. By

---

Dilatory or Unskilled Arbitrator", 15(2) *J Int'l Arb* 142 (1998); Li, "Arbitral Immunity: A Profession Comes of Age", 64 *Arbitration* 51 (1998) 54, footnote 49.

55 Li, *ibid*, 64 *Arbitration* 51 (1998).

56 *Ibid.*

57 See, *e.g.*, the form recommended by Lachmann, *Handbuch*, para 2260; see also the prosaic version suggested by Lord Kilbrandon in *Arenson v Casson Beckman Rutley & Co* [1977] AC 405, 431:

> I decline absolutely to accept the risk of having to defend a negligence suit, even though I be confident that I have not been negligent. I have no ambition, nor can I afford, to be a successful defendant, even in a leading case.

58 See Smith, "Contractual Obligations Owed by and to Arbitrators: Model Terms of Appointment", 8 *Arb Int* 7 (1992) 33, according to whom under English law no such term could be implied into the contract; but see the German decision of the Bundesgerichtshof, 6 October 1954, *BGHZ* 15, 12, 15, according to which a provision limiting the liability of an arbitrator is tacitly agreed if not explicitly excluded by the parties.

appointing arbitrators under the rules of those institutions such a provision becomes part of the contract between the parties and the arbitrator.

12-45 A complete exclusion of any liability is contained in Article 34 of the ICC Rules. It provides

> Neither the arbitrators, nor the Court and its members, nor the ICC and its employees, nor the ICC National Committees shall be liable to any person for any act or omission in connection with the arbitration.[59]

12-46 More limited provisions are contained in other arbitration rules such as the LCIA Rules which provide in Article 31(1)

> None of the LCIA, the LCIA Court (including its President, Vice-Presidents and individual members), the Registrar, any deputy Registrar, any arbitrator and any expert to the Arbitral Tribunal shall be liable to any party howsoever for any act or omission in connection with any arbitration conducted by reference to these Rules, save where the act or omission is shown by that party to constitute conscious and deliberate wrongdoing committed by the body or person alleged to be liable to that party.[60]

12-47 Whether such exclusions of liability are valid depends on the applicable national law. In particular the complete exclusion of liability under the ICC Rules may prove problematic in this respect. Despite this the ICC opted to have the widest possible exclusion in its Rules. The underlying idea was that the courts will only give effect to Article 34 to the extent that the liability can be validly excluded under the national law.[61] Under German law, for example, complete exclusions of liability are void and cannot be reduced to an acceptable standard of exclusion.[62]

5.2. The Position of the National Arbitration Laws

12-48 The approach adopted by the various national arbitration laws differs considerably. While some laws contain rules providing for immunity with few exceptions such as for fraud, others take the opposite approach and provide that

---

[59] See also NAI Rules Article 66.

[60] See similarly AAA ICDR Rules Article 35; WIPO Rules Article 77; DIS Rules section 44.

[61] Derains and Schwartz, *ICC Rules*, 352; Craig Park Paulsson, *ICC Arbitration*, para 22-06.

[62] BGB, section 309(7); Lachmann, *Handbuch*, para 1944; to this effect in relation to the limitation contained in other arbitration rules see Austrian Oberster Gerichtshof, 28 April 1998, *H GmbH v Hon*, RPS 7 (2/1999), Rev Arb 392 (1999).

arbitrators are liable for certain acts. A third category does not contain any provisions on the issue so that one has to rely on the general principles developed by the courts. The Model Law belongs to this last category. The drafters had doubts whether, in light of the widespread lack of regulation, a satisfactory solution to the problem of the liability of the arbitrator could be found.[63]

12-49 A typical example of the arbitration laws which provide for immunity is the English Arbitration Act 1996. Section 29 provides

> (1) An arbitrator is not liable for anything done or omitted in the discharge or purported discharge of his functions as arbitrator unless the act or omission is shown to have been in bad faith.
> (2) Subsection (1) applies to an employee or agent of an arbitrator as it applies to the arbitrator himself.
> (3) This Section does not affect any liability incurred by an arbitrator by reason of his resigning (but see section 25).

12-50 This provision is one of the few mandatory provisions of the Act, from which the parties cannot derogate.[64] Comparable rules can be found in a number of national laws, in particular in common law countries, even when adopting the Model Law.[65]

12-51 By contrast, in the Austrian Code of Civil Procedure instead of providing for immunity, the liability of an arbitrator is expressly stated. Article 584(2) provides

> An arbitrator who does not fulfil in time or at all the obligations assumed by his acceptance of office is liable to the parties for all the loss caused by his wrongful refusal or delay, without prejudice to the parties' rights to claim rescission of the arbitration agreement.[66]

---

[63] See First Secretariat Note para 70, A/CN9/207 (14 May 1981); First Working Group Report paras 51 *et seq*, A/CN9/216 (23 March 1982); reproduced in Holtzmann and Neuhaus, *Model Law*, 1148 *et seq.*

[64] Section 4; for the legal position before the Act entered into force see *Sutcliffe v Thackrah* [1974] AC 727; *Arenson v Casson Beckman Rutley & Co* [1977] AC 405; see also Redfern, "The Immunity of arbitrators", in ICC (ed), *The Status of the Arbitrator*, 121.

[65] See, *e.g.*, Australia, International Arbitration Act 1974 section 28; Pryles, "National Report Australia", in van den Berg and Sanders (eds), *ICCA Handbook*; New Zealand, Arbitration Act section 13; Bermuda, Arbitration Act section 34; for further examples see Sanders, *Quo Vadis Arbitration?*, 149.

[66] See similarly Spain, Arbitration Law Article 16(1) and Peru, General Arbitration Law Article 18(2).

12-52 The considerable differences which at first sight appear to result from these two markedly different approaches are in practice, however, mitigated by the limitations contained in both types of provisions.

12-53 The majority of arbitration laws still contain no provisions on arbitrators' liability. Where rules dealing with the immunity of judges exist these provisions are as such not applicable to arbitrators, since the latter do not assume a public office.[67] Nevertheless the underlying ideas are often held to be applicable also to arbitration. This has been the position in US law since the end of the nineteenth century. Already in 1884 a court in Massachusetts held

> An arbitrator is a quasi-judicial officer ... exercising judicial functions. There is as much reason in his case for protecting and insuring his impartiality, independence, and freedom from undue influence, as in the case of a judge or juror.[68]

12-54 Under French[69] and Canadian law[70] the courts have provided a certain amount of immunity from suit on the basis of equating the function of the arbitrator with that of a judge. The same result is achieved under German law where the courts base the restrictions of the arbitrator's liability on a contractual construction. The Federal Supreme Court has held that the parties implicitly agreed that the liability of an arbitrator should not go further than that of a judge. Despite the alleged contractual basis for such a limitation of liability the court made clear that a party cannot argue that it would never have agreed to such a limitation. The test applied is whether in general parties to an arbitration, acting reasonably, would have agreed to such a limitation.[71]

---

67 Frank, "The Liability of International Arbitrators: A Comparative Analysis and Proposal for Qualified Immunity", 20 *NY L Sch J Int'l & Comp L* 1 (2000) 23 *et seq*; Fouchard Gaillard Goldman *on International Commercial Arbitration*, para 1080 with further references.

68 *Hoosac Tunnel Dock & Elevator Co v O'Brian*, 137 Mass 424 (1884) 426.

69 Fouchard Gaillard Goldman *on International Commercial Arbitration*, para 1078 *et seq.*

70 *Sport Maska Inc v Zittrer* [1988] 1 SCR 564; Lalonde, "Canada", in van den Berg and Sanders (eds), *ICCA Handbook* (1993) 18. For other examples see Frank, "The Liability of International Arbitrators: a comparative analysis and proposal for qualified immunity", 20 *NY L Sch J Int'l & Comp L* 1 (2000) 36 *et seq.*

71 Bundesgerichtshof, 6 October 1954, *BGHZ* 15, 12, 15; Bundesgerichtshof, 19 November 1964, *BGHZ* 42, 313, 316. The 1998 reform law has not brought any changes. For a critical comment see Lachmann, *Handbuch*, paras 1932 *et seq.*

5.3. Scope and Limitations of the Liability of Arbitrators

12-55 The immunity provided for in the rules and laws is not unlimited. An arbitrator will be liable for any damages resulting from fraud, intentional misconduct or bad faith. These situations are excluded in the provisions of the national arbitration laws providing for immunity from suit. In other countries without such rules, such as Germany, these limitations on immunity follow from the fact that in such cases judges would also be liable.[72]

12-56 In some countries there is uncertainty as to the extent of immunity. In the US immunity was even extended to an arbitrator who fraudulently conspired with the attorneys of one party to induce the other arbitrators to join him in rendering an unjust award.[73] On the basis of this and several other decisions[74], as well as statutory provisions in some states, the United States are often referred to as a country providing for absolute immunity.[75] Other cases, however, have adopted a more limited concept of immunity.[76] It is uncertain whether in light of the international commercial arbitration practice arbitrators in the United States acting in bad faith would be able to avoid liability.

12-57 The relevance of limitation on the arbitrators' immunity depends on the interpretation of intentional misconduct and bad faith. A broad understanding of these concepts might include cases where an arbitrator accepted an appointment despite not being able to exercise his function in an expeditious manner due to other commitments or not having the necessary qualifications.[77] This lack of availability or qualification must in all cases be obvious and have been clear to the arbitrator when appointment was accepted.

12-58 Some liability may result from a premature withdrawal from the arbitration process, if the arbitrator cannot show good reason for his resignation.

---

[72] Only in the US the situation is not completely settled, since some courts granted absolute immunity from any civil liability; see, for a fairly recent example, *Austern v Chicago Bd Options Exchange, Inc* 898 F 2d 882 (2d Cir) cert denied 498 US 850 (1990).

[73] *Hoosac Tunnel Dock Elevator Co v O'Brian,* 137 Mass 424 (1884).

[74] See, *e.g.*, *Austern v Chicago Bd Options Exchange, Inc*, 898 F 2d 882 (2d Cir), cert denied, 498 US 850 (1990).

[75] Frank, "The Liability of International Arbitrators: A Comparative Analysis and Proposal for Qualified Immunity", 20 *NY L Sch J Int'l & Comp L* 1 (2000) 32.

[76] *Grane v Grane* 493 NE 2d 1112, 1118 (Ill App 1986); for views in the US literature supporting a limited liability see Hausmaninger, "Civil Liability of Arbitrators – Comparative Analysis and Proposal for Reform", 7(4) *J Int'l Arb* 7 (1990) 12.

[77] Okekeifere, "The Parties's Rights Against Dilatory or Unskilled Arbitrator", 15(2) *J Int'l Arb* 142 (1998).

A number of arbitration laws provide for the arbitrator's liability in such cases.[78] In other laws it follows from the fact that the immunity granted usually only covers acts done during arbitration proceedings or in discharge of the adjudicative function. Resignations do not fall within this category. In English law liability for resignation is excluded from the general immunity accorded to the arbitrator.[79] The arbitrator may either agree with the parties his liability arising out of resignation, or ask for a ruling of the court granting him relief from any liability.[80]

12-59 A violation of the duty to act with the necessary speed may give rise to liability in some situations.[81] Given the freedom of arbitrators to determine the procedure and organise the proceedings, an actionable breach of that duty will only exist in very few cases. Arbitrators are generally free to err in relation to the procedure adopted, as they are with the application of substantive law. An actionable breach may exist where the arbitrator does not act within the specified time having been asked by the institution or the court to do so, or refuses to act at all. The latter case is clearly not covered by the immunity for the discharge of the adjudicative functions, since no such function is exercised.[82] Difficulties may, however, arise in quantifying the damages inflicted through the conduct of the arbitrators. It is hard to evaluate damages incurred through delays based on a failure to conduct the arbitration proceedings in a speedy manner.

12-60 Where the failure to disclose relevant information gives rise to a successful challenge of the arbitrator or the award, this may not be covered by arbitrator's immunity. The French courts have on several occasions found arbitrators liable to compensate parties for losses incurred through a breach of the duty of disclosure. In the *Raoul Duval* case the chairman of the arbitration tribunal started working for one of the parties the day after the award was rendered without disclosing that fact to the parties. After the award was set aside on the ground of an unlawful constitution of the tribunal, Raoul Duval sued the arbitrator for the loss caused by his conduct. The court held that the arbitrator was liable on a contractual basis to pay damages for the fees paid to the

---

78 See Romania, CCP Article 353(a); Tunisia, Arbitration Code Article 11; see further Frank, "The Liability of International Arbitrators: a comparative analysis and proposal for qualified immunity", 20 *NY L Sch J Int'l & Comp L* 1 (2000) 12.

79 England, Arbitration Act section 29.

80 *Ibid*, section 25.

81 See the references at Hausmaninger, "Rights and Obligations of the Arbitrator with regard to the Parties and the Arbitral Institution - A Civil Law Viewpoint", in ICC (ed), *The Status of the Arbitrator*, 36, 42 *et seq.*

82 Merkin, *Arbitration Act*, 73.

arbitrators and the arbitration institution as well as costs incurred for the defence.[83]

12-61 Immunity also exists in respect of decisions relating to provisional measures by arbitrators. Under German law this has given rise to some controversy as the liability privilege for judges under section 839 BGB does not cover measures of provisional relief. The majority view does, however, consider interim relief to be covered by the exclusion of liability.[84]

5.4 Liability of Arbitration Institutions

12-62 Parties dissatisfied with the outcome or the conduct of the arbitration, have also tried to recover damages from the institution under whose rules the proceedings were conducted and which appointed the arbitrators. They usually base their claim on an alleged violation of duties arising out of the contract concluded between the institution and the parties when a request for arbitration was submitted. Through this contract the institution generally undertakes to perform certain functions in relation to the arbitration, such as a review of the *prima facie* existence of an arbitration agreement, the scrutiny of the award and in particular the appointment and removal of arbitrators.[85]

12-63 The issue of liability for appointments arises where problems result in delay or additional costs for the parties. This may be the case, for example, where an appointed arbitrator is successfully challenged by one party, due to information known to the institution, and after a new arbitrator is appointed certain parts of the proceedings have to be repeated. It is an open question whether in such a situation an appointing authority is liable for negligence in the appointment process of the arbitrator. The mere fact of a successful challenge as such will not be sufficient to justify any liability. The same applies if the chosen

---

[83] Tribunal de Grande Instance Paris, 12 May 1993, *Raoul Duval v V*, Rev Arb 411 (1996); confirmed by the Cour d'appel Paris, 12 October 1995, *Rev Arb* 324 (1999) and the Cour de cassation, 16 December 1997, unpublished; see also Austrian Oberster Gerichtshof, 28 April 1998, *H GmbH v Hon*, RPS 7 (2/1999), Rev Arb 392 (1999); Fouchard Gaillard Goldman *on International Commercial Arbitration*, para 1091 with further references; but see for a different view in the US Supreme Court of Minnesota, *L and H Airco, Inc v Rapistan Corp*, 446 NW 2d 372, 377.

[84] Raeschke-Kessler and Berger, *Recht und Praxis*, para 611; for a different view see Lachmann, *Handbuch*, para 1441.

[85] For a detailed analysis of the conclusion of the contract and the duties arising from it see Robine, "The Liability of Arbitrators and Arbitral Institutions in International Arbitrations under French Law", 5 *Arb Int* 323 (1989).

arbitrator proves incapable of handling the case where he lacks the necessary experience or knowledge or does not have sufficient time. These facts may indicate that the appointment was not made with the required care but for any liability to be established the appointing authority must have breached its obligations under the contract with the parties and failed in the duty of care owed to the parties. For this reason the arbitration institution should also not be liable where it rejects a challenge of an arbitrator which is later granted by the courts. Unless the institution acted in bad faith, it made an error of judgment which does not amount to a breach of contractual duty.

12-64 Given the fact that it is now common practice to require every potential arbitrator to file a declaration of independence, appointing an arbitrator without such a declaration may be considered to be such a breach.[86] An example of an even more obvious violation of duty by the appointing authority is the appointment of an arbitrator who does not possess the qualifications required by the parties.

12-65 In some countries the immunity accorded to arbitrators is extended to appointing authorities. In England, section 74 Arbitration Act expressly grants immunity to an institution on the appointment or nomination of an arbitrator for any act or omission of that arbitrator unless the failure or omission was in bad faith. This immunity is for both arbitration institutions and other organisations that offer services of an appointing authority.

12-66 The US courts have extended immunity to arbitration institutions. In *Austern v Chicago Board Options Exchange, Inc. (CBOE)* an award rendered by a tribunal acting under the rules of the CBOE had been vacated on the grounds that the composition of the tribunal was contrary to the rules of the CBOE and the claimant had not been informed about a hearing conducted *ex parte*. The claimant brought an action for damages against the CBOE on grounds of negligence in setting up the tribunal and a failure to provide adequate notice of a hearing. The Court of Appeal for the 2nd Circuit rejected the claim granting the CBOE immunity for all functions that are integrally related to the arbitration. The underlying rationale was that any liability for deficiencies in the arbitration process would serve to discourage CBOE to maintain its role as a commercial

---

[86] Raeschke-Kessler and Berger, *Recht und Praxis*, para 515.

sponsoring organisation of arbitration, a policy strongly encouraged by the Federal Arbitration Act.[87]

12-67 In addition, the rules of some of the major arbitration institutions now explicitly exclude the liability of the institution so that selection of their rules incorporates a contractual exclusion of liability clause. While the ICC Rules provide for a complete exclusion of liability[88], the rules of the other institutions often limit the exclusion. For example, WIPO Rules Article 77 provides

> Except in respect of deliberate wrongdoing, the arbitrator or arbitrators, WIPO and the Centre shall not be liable to a party for any act or omission in connection with the arbitration.[89]

12-68 Where no such provisions exist or the provision is considered to be invalid, arbitration institutions could be held liable for any damage arising out of a violation of their duties.[90] The basis for such a liability is the contract between the parties and the appointing authority which obliges the latter to make the appointment. Such liability arises independently of whether the appointing authority is paid to appoint the arbitrators. This may have an influence on the duty of care but does not exclude liability completely. Only judges or courts which make appointments within their ordinary function may be able to rely on privilege as to their liability in certain jurisdictions for judicial functions. Other appointing authorities cannot rely on such privilege. They are not exercising a judicial function but are fulfilling contractual duties which fall outside the ambit of such a privilege. This includes not only appointments made but also other tasks of arbitration institutions during the conduct of an arbitration such as fixing of the place of arbitration or any extension of time limits.[91]

12-69 Depending on the law applicable to the contract between the parties and the appointing authority the latter may be able to exclude or at least reduce

---

[87] *Austern v Chicago Bd Options Exchange, Inc*, 898 F 2d 882 (2d Cir), cert denied, 498 US 850 (1990); see also *Hawkins v National Association of Securities Dealers*, no 97-10383, 1998 WL 429434 (5th Cir, 1998); for other cases see Rubino-Samartano, *International Arbitration*, 369.

[88] ICC Rules Article 34.

[89] See also AAA ICDR Rules Article 35; LCIA Article 31; SCC Rules Article 42; DIS Rules section 44(2).

[90] See, *e.g.*, Cour d'appel de Paris, 15 September 1998, *Cubic Defense Systems, Inc (US) v International Chamber of Commerce (France)*, XXIVa YBCA 287 (1999) where, however, no liability existed since the ICC did not breach its duties.

[91] Raeschke-Kessler and Berger, *Recht und Praxis*, para 540 *et seq*; Cour d'Appel Paris, *Société Opinter France v Société Dacomex*, Rev Arb 87 (1986); Tribunal de Grande Instance Paris, *REDEC et G Pharaon v Uzinexport Import*, Rev Arb 97 (1989).

liability by showing that even if it had fulfilled its duties the damage would still have been incurred. For example, even where no declaration of independence was required by the appointing authority, there is a general acceptance that the arbitrator should disclose to the parties any facts which may affect his independence or impartiality. If the arbitrator fails to disclose relevant facts, the institution could argue that even if it had required a disclosure statement, it is likely the arbitrator would not have disclosed the facts giving rise to a challenge.

Chapter 13

CHALLENGE, REMOVAL AND REPLACEMENT OF ARBITRATORS

13-1 Once established, any arbitration tribunal remains in place until it has either rendered an award or the parties have settled their dispute. However, this is not always the case. An arbitrator's mandate may be terminated for various reasons before the allocated task has been fulfilled. For example, during the process an arbitrator's lack of impartiality and independence may become known; or an arbitrator may become incapable or refuse to act causing excessive delay. In such circumstances it should be possible for the parties to remedy the situation and have the arbitrator removed from office. Therefore, nearly all arbitration laws and rules contain procedures to challenge or seek the removal or replacement of an arbitrator. These provide a built-in insurance to safeguard the arbitration process.

13-2 The initiative for an early termination of the arbitrator's mandate may also come from within the tribunal. Arbitrators may wish to resign for various reasons which would not justify their removal.[1] This may be due to health or other personal reasons, but can also be an effort by a partisan arbitrator to delay the proceedings. In all such cases, irrespective of whether they concern a voluntary or a forced termination of the arbitrator's mandate, it should generally not be allowed to frustrate the arbitration proceedings.

13-3 For this reason it is essential that the applicable rules or laws must either provide for a replacement arbitrator to be appointed or, in cases of multi-member tribunals, allow the remaining arbitrators in some situations to render an award as a truncated tribunal.

13-4 This chapter considers with the various instances of a challenge or termination of the arbitrator's mandate and the replacement of an arbitrator. Specifically dealt with below are (1) challenging an arbitrator, (2) termination of the arbitrator's mandate, (3) replacement of arbitrators, and (4) truncated tribunals.

1. Challenge of an Arbitrator

13-5 Irrespective of any agreement of the parties arbitrators must generally meet certain minimum standards which follow from the *quasi* judicial function exercised by arbitration tribunals. It is one of the exigencies of a fair trial that the deciding body is impartial and independent.[2] Arbitrators who do not fulfil these requirements can generally be challenged by the parties under the applicable arbitration rules and laws. For example, Article 12(2) Model Law provides:

> An arbitrator may be challenged only if circumstances exist that give rise to justifiable doubts as to his impartiality or independence, or if he does not possess qualifications agreed to by the parties. A party may challenge an arbitrator appointed by him, or in whose appointment he has participated, only for reasons of which he becomes aware after the appointment has been made.

13-6 Like most other provisions dealing with challenge procedures Article 12(2) does not limit the right to challenge to arbitrators appointed by the other side or a neutral appointing authority. As expressly stated in some arbitration

---

[1] Whether the retiring arbitrator loses his right to remuneration or whether he is even liable for damages is a question for the applicable law or rules. See England, Arbitration Act section 25.

[2] See, *e.g.*, Universal Declaration of Human Rights Article 10; European Convention on Human Rights, 6 Article; Calvo, "The Challenge of ICC Arbitrators", 15(4) *J Int'l Arb* 63 (1998) 65.

rules parties may also challenge their own arbitrators under certain circumstances.[3]

13-7 Over the years the number of challenges of arbitrators has increased. In part this is due to the fact that parties are increasingly unwilling to accept biased arbitrators and frequently see partiality in an arbitrator appointed by the other side. The other main reason for this increase is that tactical challenges for dilatory purposes or procedural advantages have become more common.[4] As a consequence only a minority of challenges are successful, in particular in institutional arbitration where the arbitrator is scrutinised before being appointed.[5] A challenge to the arbitrator inevitably results in delays to the appointment process and the arbitration proceedings.

1.1. Grounds for Challenge

13-8 The grounds which justify a challenge differ depending on the rules and laws applicable. Since most of them recognise the lack of "qualifications agreed to by the parties" as a reason for challenge the whole process is *de facto* submitted to party autonomy. As the parties are free to agree on whatever qualifications they want they can agree on what reasons justify a challenge.

13-9 The most obvious grounds of challenge are the arbitrator's lack of impartiality or independence. These concepts are usually not defined in any of the arbitration rules and laws.[6] Certain guidelines as to the content can be found in the Codes of Ethics.[7] Nevertheless, in comparison to a detailed list of events

---

[3] See, *e.g.*, LCIA Article 10(3) and DIS Rules section 18(1) which only allow such a challenge if based on facts not known to the party at the time of appointment.

[4] See, *e.g.*, Redfern and Hunter, *International Commercial Arbitration*, para 4-59; Henry, "Les obligations d'indépendance et d'information de l'arbitre à la lumière de la jurisprudence récente", *Rev Arb* 193 (1999). In addition challenges may also be used to intimidate or warn the arbitrators, see Böckstiegel, "Practice of Various Arbitral Tribunals", *ICCA Congress series no 5*, 132.

[5] In the ICC context less than 10% of the challenges have been successful; see Craig, Park & Paulsson, *ICC Arbitration*, para 13-01; Calvo, "The Challenge of ICC Arbitrators", 15(4) *J Int'l Arb* 63 (1998) 71.

[6] A notable exception is section 8(a) of the Swedish Arbitration Law and Article 34 Chinese Arbitration law which contain lists of instances when impartiality is deemed to be lacking. See also Henry, Le devoir d'indépendence de l'arbitre, (LGDJ 2001).

[7] AAA, *Code of Ethics for Arbitrators in Commercial Disputes* (1977); IBA, *Ethics for International Arbitrators* (1987).

which would justify a challenge those general references to broad principles have the advantage of providing greater flexibility.

13-10 The majority of arbitration laws and rules recognise both the lack of independence and impartiality as justifiable reasons for a challenge.[8] Some laws, however, refer either to independence or to impartiality. For example, Article 180 Swiss PIL only mentions the lack of independence as a reason for challenge. Nevertheless it is generally accepted under Swiss law that a partial arbitrator can be challenged.[9]

13-11 By contrast section 24 English Arbitration Act dealing with the power of the court to remove arbitrator, only refers to the lack of impartiality.[10] Therefore independence is not considered to be a separate ground for removal of an arbitrator unless the lack of independence also gives rise as to justifiable doubts as to the arbitrator's impartiality. Section 24 provides that an arbitrator may also be removed if

> (b) ...he does not possess the qualifications required by the arbitration agreement
> (c) ... is physically or mentally incapable of conducting the proceedings or there are justifiable doubts as to his capacity to do so
> (d) ...he has refused or failed-
> (i) properly to conduct the proceedings, or
> (ii) to use all reasonable dispatch in conducting the proceedings or making an award, and that substantial injustice has been or will be caused to the applicant.

13-12 Article 11(1) ICC Rules gives a right to challenge an arbitrator "whether for lack of independence or otherwise." This provision appears to give an unlimited discretion to the ICC Court on a challenge to remove an arbitrator for whatever ground it deems appropriate.[11] Despite not being mentioned in the rules an arbitrator can also be challenged for his lack of impartiality. Other reasons

---

8 See, *e.g.*, Model Law Article 12(2); DIS Rules section 18(1).

9 For the drafting history and the interpretation of the requirement see Bucher, *Die neue internationale Schiedsgerichtsbarkeit in der Schweiz*, para 168 *et seq*; Peter and Freymond in Berti (ed), *International Arbitration in Switzerland*, Article 180 para 9 *et seq*.

10 The DAC report made clear that independence was deliberately left out as a ground for removal. The drafters feared that including independence as a separate ground might lead to "endless arguments" and that in some situations "parties desire their arbitrators to have familiarity with a specific field, rather than being entirely independent": paras 102, 103; the extensive list in section 24 is due to the fact that, contrary to most other laws and rules, the Act does not have a special provision for challenges but regulates all instances of removal of an arbitrator in one section.

11 Craig, Park & Paulsson, *ICC Arbitration*, para 13-05(i).

which have led to successful challenges are *inter alia* misconduct during the proceedings and the violation of the duty to disclose any connections with the parties in the required statement of independence.[12]

13-13 In general, however, the grounds for challenge are interpreted narrowly, in particular, if a considerable amount of time and resources have already been spent in the arbitration. There seem to be two different tests applied in the context of challenge proceedings: while in the majority of countries "justifiable doubts" as to the arbitrator's impartiality or independence are sufficient, [13] others, such as England[14] or the US[15], require that there is a "real danger" of a lack of impartiality. In most cases, however, both tests will probably lead to the same results.

13-14 A good description of the requirements to be met under the "justifiable doubt" standard can be found in a decision of 1995 by an appointing authority nominated by the Secretary General of the Permanent Court of Arbitration in an arbitration between two states under the UNCITRAL Rules.[16] The arbitrator challenged by the claimant was a government official of a third country who had been an advisor of that country in matters involving the claimant. The appointing authority, which finally rejected the challenge, defined the applicable standard in the following way.

> In sum, the test to be applied is that the doubts existing on the part of the claimant here must be 'justifiable' on some objective basis. Are they reasonable doubts as tested by the standard of a fair minded, rational, objective observer? Could that

---

12 Derains and Schwartz, *ICC Rules*, 175 *et seq*; Calvo, "The Challenge of ICC Arbitrators", 15(4) *J Int'l Arb* 63 (1998) 64.

13 See, *e.g.*, Model Law Article 12(2); Germany, ZPO section 1036(2); Switzerland, PIL Article 180(1)(c); South Africa, *Moch v Nedtravel (Pty) Ltd*, (1996) 3 SA 1; Australia, *R v Watson, ex parte Armstrong*, (1976) 136 CLR 248.

14 See *AT&T Corporation and another v Saudi Cable*, [2000] 2 Lloyd's Rep 127; *Laker Airways v FLS Aerospace* [1999] 2 Lloyd's Rep 45 which applied the "real danger" test though the English Arbitration Act uses "justifiable doubts"; for an overview of the English law see Gearing, "A Judge in his Own Cause?-Actual or Unconscious Bias of Arbitrators", 3 *Int ALR* 46 (2000); Eastwood, "A Real Danger of Confusion? The English Law Relating to Bias in Arbitrators", 17 *Arb Int* 287 (2001).

15 See, *e.g.*, *ANR Coal Co v Cogentrix of North Carolina, Inc*, 173 F 3d 493 (4th Cir 1999); for an extensive and critical discussion of the American case law see Shore, "Disclosure and Impartiality: An Arbitrators Responsibility vis-à-vis Legal Standards", 57(4) *Disp Res J* 34 (2002) 78 *et seq*; see also the Supreme Court of Bermuda in *Raydon Underwriting Management Company Ltd v Stockholm Re (Bermuda) Ltd (in Liquidation)*, 2 Int ALR N-55 (1999).

16 Challenge decision of 11 January 1995, XXII *YBCA* 227 (1997).

> observer say, on the basis of the facts as we know them, that the claimant has a reasonable apprehension of partiality on the part of the respondents' arbitrator?
>
> As to the level of knowledge and experience attributed to the 'reasonable', 'fair 1 bench mark as being the reaction of the well informed but disinterested commercial person assessing the matter without specific expertise but aware of the political background against which the matter arises and of the nature of a lawyer's professional services. In my opinion, therefore, there is no doubt whatsoever that it is in light of the standard of reasonableness that the matter must be judged. What is key to the disposition of the challenge is the assessment of the factual fabric that constitutes the background of the problem and has given rise to claimant's doubts....[17]

13-15 The stricter "real danger" test for challenges can be found in the English Court of Appeal's decision in the *AT&T v Saudi Cable* case.[18] The dispute arose out of an agreement concluded during a bidding process for a telecommunication project in Saudi Arabia under which the parties agreed to negotiate in good faith further related contracts. The arbitration was under ICC Rules and had its seat in London. One of the arbitrators, well known and respected, had provided the parties with his resumé and had signed the ICC Statement of Independence. Inadvertently the curriculum vitae did not contain the information that the arbitrator was a non-executive director and very small shareholder in Nortel, another telecommunications company involved in the bidding process. When this information came to light, two interim awards had already been issued by the tribunal in which it found that the agreement was legally binding and that AT&T breached its obligation to negotiate in good faith. Before the final award on damages was rendered AT&T challenged the chairman of the tribunal. The challenge was rejected by the ICC Court and AT&T was ordered to pay US$30,000,000 of damages to Saudi Cable. AT&T applied to the English courts to have the chairman removed and the award set aside on the grounds of unconscious bias and misconduct.

13-16 The Court of Appeal considered the issue from the viewpoint of actual bias rather than the appearance of bias. On the facts it held that there was no evidence that the arbitrator may be or was predisposed against AT&T. His directorship of Nortel was incidental to his professional life: he had very limited

---

[17] *Ibid*, paras 30-31.

[18] *AT&T Corporation and another v Saudi Cable* [2000] 2 Lloyd's Rep 127; for further examples from the English and US jurisprudence see Shore, "Disclosure and Impartiality: An Arbitrators Responsibility vis-à-vis Legal Standards", 57(4) *Disp Res J* 34 (2002).

involvement with the company, he did not attach importance to his directorship and his shareholding was insignificant. The arbitrator was a distinguished international lawyer and arbitrator, who was aware of his obligations of impartiality, he believed at all times that he was acting appropriately and nothing he had done or said during the proceedings had in any way shown bias of any kind.[19]

13-17 In relation to the issue of unconscious bias by an arbitrator the Court of Appeal endorsed a test developed by the House of Lords in *R v Gough*[20] for judges according to which

> ...the court should ask itself whether...there was a *real danger of bias* on the part of the relevant member of the tribunal in question, in the sense that he might unfairly regard (or have unfairly regarded) with favour, or disfavour, the case of a party to the issue under consideration by him.[21]

13-18 Despite the fact that the English Arbitration Act provides in section 24(1)(a) that an arbitrator may be removed if there are "justifiable doubts as to his impartiality", the real danger test was endorsed by the Court to be the relevant test under the Act.[22]

1.2. Limitation of the Right to Challenge

13-19 The importance attached to the independence and the impartiality of the tribunal connotes that parties cannot renounce their right to challenge arbitrators which do not fulfil these requirements in advance. Any such agreement would be contrary to public policy.[23] A German court in 1976 went as far as holding that the enforcement of an award rendered by arbitrators, the names of which were not divulged to the parties, would be contrary to public policy. It held that without such knowledge the parties could not exercise their fundamental right to

---

19 *Ibid*, 136.

20 [1993] AC 646, 670, *per* Lord Goff.

21 *AT&T Corporation and another v Saudi Cable*, [2000] 2 Lloyd's Rep 127, 135; the ICC Court of Arbitration, relying on the justifiable doubts test came to the same conclusion; for a different conclusion under the justifiable doubts test see, however, the 1968 decision of the US Supreme Court in *Commonwealth Coatings Corp v Continental Casualty Co*, 393 US 145 (1968).

22 *Laker Airways v FLS Aerospace* [1999] 2 Lloyd's Rep 45.

23 See Bezirksgericht, Affoltern am Albis, 26 May 1994, XXIII *YBCA* 754 (1998) paras 24-27; confirmed by the Court of Appeal in Zurich, 26 July 1995.

challenge.[24] Though it is doubtful whether today courts in Germany or elsewhere would still come to the same conclusion, it shows the importance attached to the right to challenge.

13-20 This does not imply that the right exists without limits and parties can initiate challenge proceedings at any time. To restrict the possibility of challenges being used for tactical and dilatory purposes most rules and laws submit the right to challenge an arbitrator to strict time limits. The challenge must generally be exercised within a very short period after the facts giving rise to the challenge become known. The period foreseen in the different arbitration rules and laws varies[25] but rarely exceeds the 30 days provided for under the ICC Rules.[26]

13-21 Parties cannot wait until the arbitration turns against them and then rely on a ground for challenge but must exercise their right immediately. Otherwise they are considered to have waived their objections. This is well evidenced by a recent decision of the Higher Regional Court in Cologne.[27] The chairman of an arbitration tribunal informed the parties that she had to take over a case from one of the partners of her law firm which involved a claim in a different matter by a third party against the claimant. Under the applicable arbitration rules challenges had to be made within two weeks after the relevant facts became known. Since it took the claimant four weeks to request the removal of the arbitrator, the court held that the ensuing challenge was inadmissible.

13-22 Considerations of waiver also underlie a second restriction on the right to challenge which can be found in various arbitration laws and rules, such as the DIS Rules which provide in section 18(1):

> An arbitrator may be challenged only if circumstances exist that give rise to justifiable doubts as to his impartiality or independence, or if he does not possess qualifications agreed to by the parties. A party may challenge an arbitrator

---

[24] Oberlandesgericht, Cologne, 10 June 1976, IV *YBCA* 258 (1979) para 6, German original published in 91 *Zeitschrift für Zivilprozess* (1978) 318, with note Kornblum, 323.

[25] The challenge must be raised within 15 days: UNCITRAL Rules Article 11(1); LCIA Article 10(4); SCC Rules Article 18(2); DIS Rules section 18(2); AAA ICDR Rules Article 8. See also Model Law Article 13(2). The challenge must be raised before the first or the next oral hearing under CIETAC Article 29.

[26] ICC Rules Article 11(2).

[27] Oberlandesgericht, Cologne, 14 September 2000, 9 *SchH* 30/00, unpublished.

nominated by him, or in whose nomination it has participated only for *reasons of which he becomes aware after the nomination has been made*. [emphasis added][28]

13-23 Parties who appoint their arbitrator despite knowing his lack of independence or impartiality are considered to have waived any objections to the arbitrator and any personal conflict hc may have in this respect.

13-24 Whether the same limitation applies to a party which knowing the incriminating facts did not object to an appointment made by the other side or an appointing authority is not as clear. The principle of etoppel might also justify an exclusion of the right to challenge in these cases. Irrespective of this the ICC allows challenges in such situations if they are raised within 30 days after the notification or the confirmation of an appointment.[29] In case of the Model Law the legislative history would support a different approach at least in cases of a joint appointment or where a party could veto any appointment. The Model Law contains an express reference to arbitrators "in whose appointments [the party] has participated", which is a purposeful deviation from the wording of the UNCITRAL Rules.[30]

1.3. Procedure for Challenge

13-25 The procedure for a challenge is submitted to party autonomy. Agreements between the parties on such a procedure are, however, very rare in practice. Therefore challenge proceedings are either governed by the rules provided for in the applicable arbitration rules or, if no such rules have been agreed on, by the provisions in the relevant arbitration laws.

(a) Provisions of the Arbitration Rules

13-26 In institutional arbitration the normal procedure for a challenge is by a reasoned submission sent to the institution, which will then solicit comments from the other party and the arbitration tribunal. If the parties cannot agree on the removal of the challenged arbitrator or the arbitrator does not resign voluntarily the institution will have to decide on the issue.[31] Differences exist primarily in

---

28 See also Model Law Article 12(2) and LCIA Article 10(3).

29 Derains and Schwartz, *ICC Rules*, 177.

30 Holtzmann and Neuhaus, *Model Law*, 390 *et seq*.

31 See, *e.g.*, ICC Rules Article 11; DIS Rules section 18(2); AAA ICDR Rules Articles 8, 9; CIETAC Rules Article 30; Zurich Chamber of Commerce Rules Article 16.

relation to the time within which such an application must be made and to whom the application must be sent. Under some rules, such as the LCIA Rules, the application must be sent directly to all parties involved and not only to the institution.[32]

13-27 Under the UNCITRAL Rules the application must be sent within 15 days directly to the parties and all members of the arbitration tribunal. If the parties cannot agree on the challenge or the arbitrator refuses to withdraw, Article 12 UNCITRAL Rules provides that the challenge will be determined:

> (a) When the initial appointment was made by an appointing authority, by that authority;
> (b) When the initial appointment was not made by an appointing authority, but an appointing authority has been previously designated, by that authority;
> (c) In all other cases, by the appointing authority to be designated in accordance with the procedure for designating an appointing authority as provided for in ....

13-28 If the arbitration institution or the appointing authority sustains the challenge the arbitrator in question will be removed. The decision of the institution or the appointing authority is final. Whether that also applies if the challenge is rejected, depends on the law applicable to the arbitration.

(b) Provisions of the Arbitration Laws

13-29 The Model Law allows an unsuccessful party in a challenge before an institution or appointing authority to continue its challenge in the courts. It provides in Article 13(3)

> If a challenge under any procedure agreed upon by the parties or under the procedure of paragraph (2) of this article is not successful, the challenging party may request, within thirty days after having received notice of the decision rejecting the challenge, the court or other authority specified in article 6 to decide on the challenge, which decision shall be subject to no appeal; while such a request is pending, the arbitral tribunal, including the challenged arbitrator, may continue the arbitral proceedings and make an award.

13-30 According to Article 13(1) the parties cannot deviate from that provision. The rationale for this approach is to avoid delays arising out of a challenged arbitrator conducting the proceedings and the risk of the award being set aside. To avoid the procedure being misused for dilatory tactics the law provides for a

---

32 LCIA Article 10(4).

short time limit, allows no appeal from the court's decision and gives the tribunal a discretion to continue the arbitration,[33] a discretion which is also exercised in practice.[34]

13-31 The extent of continuing challenges in the courts was an issue in the English decision in *AT&T v Saudi Cable*. On the basis of the provision in the ICC rules that any decision on a challenge by the ICC Court should be final, the judge at first instance considered himself bound by the decision of the ICC concerning any violation of the ICC Rules. However, this did not prevent him from determining whether the English rules on unconscious bias or misconduct had been violated. The Court of Appeal rejected that interpretation of the finality provision of the ICC and held that

> [t]he finality provision does not operate to exclude the English Court's jurisdiction under s. 23 of the 1950 Act [removal for misconduct]. Accordingly, Mr. Justice Longmore was entitled to consider whether there had been "misconduct" by breaching the terms of the arbitration agreement. When doing so the Court, if required to interpret the ICC rules, would naturally pay the closest attention to any interpretation of the ICC rules adopted by the ICC court, but the English Courts retain their jurisdiction to determine whether the ICC rules have been breached when entertaining an application to remove for alleged misconduct.[35]

13-32 However, under some arbitration laws, a party cannot generally continue the challenge proceedings in the court until the end of the arbitration proceedings.[36] If the parties have agreed upon a challenge procedure, any decision rendered in such procedure is considered to be final. A limited court control of the arbitrators' independence and impartiality is only possible at the post-award stage where it might justify annulment of the award.

---

33 Holtzmann and Neuhaus, *Model Law*, 407; see similarly England, Arbitration Act section 24(3).

34 See, *e.g.*, in Germany, the decision by the Oberlandesgericht Naumburg, 19 December 2001, 17(6) *Mealey's IAR* 27 (2002); see also Cour d'appel Paris, 24 February 1994, *Ministry of Public Works (Tunisia) v Société Bec Frères (France)*, XXII YBCA 682 (1997) para 14-20, Rev Arb 275 (1995) with note Gaudemet, 285), where the court found that the arbitrators were allowed to proceed with the arbitration and render an award while a challenge is pending, as this was not prohibited by the law applicable to the arbitration proceedings.

35 *AT&T Corporation and another v Saudi Cable* [2000] 2 Lloyd's Rep 127, 137.

36 For the position in France see Tribunal de Grande Instance Paris, 23 June 1988, *République de Guinée v MMR...et O...*, Rev Arb 657 (1988); Fouchard Gaillard Goldman *on International Commercial Arbitration*, para 872 *et seq*; for Switzerland, see Blessing, *Introduction to Arbitration*, para 524; Bucher, *Internationale Schiedsgerichtsbarkeit in der Schweiz*, para 175 *et seq*; see also Brazil, which deleted the provision of the Model Law providing for such a right when adopting the Model Law.

13-33 Irrespective of the above mentioned differences nearly all arbitration laws provide for challenge procedures if the parties have not agreed on a tailor-made challenge procedure. Otherwise the parties could be forced to continue arbitration proceedings without having any possibility at the pre-award stage to challenge the arbitrators even if they obviously lacked the necessary independence or impartiality. A typical example of those provisions is Article 13(2) Model Law which provides:

> Failing such agreement, a party who intends to challenge an arbitrator shall, within fifteen days after becoming aware of the constitution of the arbitral tribunal or after becoming aware of any circumstance referred to in article 12(2), send a written statement of the reasons for the challenge to the arbitral tribunal. Unless the challenged arbitrator withdraws from his office or the other party agrees to the challenge, the arbitral tribunal shall decide on the challenge.

13-34 Like a number of other national laws, the Model Law entrusts the tribunal with the task of deciding the challenges with the possibility to bring additional proceedings in the courts if the challenge is rejected.[37] Other laws, such as the English or the Belgian law, refer the decision from the outset to the courts.[38]

13-35 An exception is the Federal Arbitration Act which does not provide for any judicial review of an appointment at a pre-award stage.[39] Instead the parties' only option is to attack the award issued by the tribunal, where the lack of impartiality or independence is a reason for annulment or denial of enforcement. The disadvantages of this approach are obvious: the parties are required to continue the arbitration though one party has lost confidence in the impartiality of the tribunal and it is clear that the award will be challenged. In this respect it is

---

[37] See also Sweden, Arbitration Act section 10; Russian Federation, Arbitration Law Article 13(2); Germany, ZPO section 1037; but see the decision of the Egyptian Supreme Constitutional Court, 6 November 1999, Case no 84 of the 19th Judicial Year, 3 *Int ALR* N-80 (2000) which declared the referral of the decision to the arbitration tribunal to be unconstitutional

[38] England, Arbitration Act section 24; Switzerland, PIL Article 180(3); Belgium, Judicial Code Article 1691; Netherlands, CCP Article 1035; under Nigerian Law the challenge is decided by the appointing authority and if no authority has been designated by the Secretary General of the PCA; for other solutions adopted see Sanders, *Quo Vadis Arbitration?*, 106 *et seq.*

[39] *Availl, Inc v Ryder Sys, Inc* 110 F 3d 892, 895 (2d Cir 1997); *Folse v Richard Wolfe Med Insurance Corp* 56 F 3d 603, 605 (5th Cir 1995); *Certain Underwriters at Lloyd's, London et al v Continental Casualty Company (US)*, XXIII YBCA 1046 (1998) para 1-7 (Northern District of Illinois, Eastern Division, 7 August 1997); see also Veeder, "Laws and Court Decisions in Common Law Countries and the UNCITRAL Model Law", *ICCA Congress series no 5*, 140, 144.

interesting to note that though no separate challenge procedure exists the parties must put their objections to an arbitrator on the record to be able to attack the award at a later stage. If this is not done the parties may be considered to have waived their rights.[40]

1.4. Challenges after an Award has been Rendered

13-36 A slightly different situation arises when the facts which justify a challenge become known only a short time before the award is rendered or even after it has been rendered. Unless it is only a partial award the arbitrator's mandate is generally finished and he is *functus officio*. Therefore, it makes little sense or is no longer possible to initiate challenge procedures against the arbitrator.[41] Instead the parties must challenge the award and seek its annulment, either on the ground that the tribunal was not properly constituted, an incorrect procedure had been applied or that enforcement of the award would be contrary to public policy.[42]

13-37 In this context the question arises whether any connection between the arbitrator and the parties or their counsel which would have justified a challenge of the arbitrator before an award has been rendered also justifies the challenge of an award or whether a stricter standard has to be applied. The various national laws answer this question differently.

---

[40] See the decision in *The Island Territory of Curacao v Solitron Devices Inc*, 356 F Supp 1 (SDNY 1973).

[41] See, *e.g.*, the position under German law, where the Supreme Court jurisprudence consistently held that actions to challenge an arbitrator must be initiated before the final award has been rendered and are not admissible afterwards; Bundesgerichtshof, 4 March 1999, *ZIP* 859 (1999); see, to the same effect, France, Tribunal de Grande Instance Paris, 2 July 1990, *Annahold BV v L'Oréal*, Rev Arb 483 (1996); see also, in Switzerland, the decision of the Tribunal Fédéral, 14 March 1985, *Société Z v L*, ATF/BGE 111 IA 72, 74-78 .

[42] For the possible reasons to attack an award made by an allegedly partial arbitrator under Swiss law see Tribunal Fédéral, 12 January 1989, *G SA (Switzerland) v T Ltd (UK)*, XV YBCA 509 (1990) para 8. Regarding French law, see Cour d'appel Paris, 9 April 1992, *Société Annahold BV et al v L'Oreal*, Rev Arb 483 (1996), where the award was annulled since the applicant erred about the independence of the arbitrator who had not disclosed its links with the other party.

13-38 Under French[43], English[44] or Swiss[45] law the same test is applied irrespective of whether the lack of independence is used to challenge the arbitrator or whether it is used to challenge the award.

13-39 In contrast to that position under German law a different and stricter standard is applied. This was reiterated by the German Supreme Court.[46] There a party discovered after the award had been rendered that the law firm of the arbitrator it had appointed was advising the parent company of the other party. Since this had not been disclosed by the arbitrator the party requested the annulment of an award on the grounds of incorrect procedures used by the tribunal. The Supreme Court held that the challenge for an alleged lack of independence can only be brought before the award has been rendered. If the facts giving rise to doubts of the arbitrator's independence were only discovered after the award was made, they would only in cases of grave and obvious partiality or dependence justify annulment of the award. Since in the Supreme Court's view the facts did not reveal a grave case of partiality the award was upheld.

13-40 The application of a higher standard which required more or less proof of actual bias affecting the award was justified by considerations of legal certainty. It was held that the *res judicata* effect of the award should only be ignored in such extreme situations where the enforcement of an award would violate public policy but should prevail in all other cases.[47]

13-41 A violation of public policy was found to exist in an extreme case involving a contract for participation in an arms fair in Turkey. The contract was drafted by the Turkish claimant's lawyer and provided for arbitration in Turkey. It nominated the lawyer as the sole arbitrator and contained a clause according to which the sole arbitrator could not be removed under any circumstances. A

---

43 Cour d'appel Paris, 9 Avril 1992, *Société Annahold BV et al v L'Oreal*, Rev Arb 483 (1996); see also Henry, "Les obligations d'indépendance et d'information de l'arbitre à la lumière de la jurisprudence récente", *Rev Arb* 193 (1999)

44 *AT&T Corporation v Saudi Cable* [2000] 2 Lloyd's Rep 127.

45 Tribunal Fédéral, 14 Mars 1985, *Société Z v L*, ATF/BGE 111 IA 72, 74-78; Tribunal Fédéral, 18 August 1992, ATF 118 II 359, 361-362.

46 Bundesgerichtshof, 4 March 1999, *ZIP* 859 (1999) with note Kröll, *EWiR* 1087 (1999) which denied the existence of an exceptional case. For the opposite view in a comparable case, see Cairo Court of Appeal, 25 November 1998, Case No 42 of the 115th Judicial Year, reported in 3 *Int ALR* N-80 (2000).

47 In favour of showing actual bias see also Okekeifere, "Appointment and Challenge of Arbitrators under the UNCITRAL Model Law: Part II: Challenge", 3 *Int ALR* 13 (2000) 15.

contract penalty of Swiss Francs one million was to be paid to the arbitrator if this provision was violated. The arbitrator who by that time had also acted as a lawyer for the respondent, rendered an award in favour of the claimant which the respondent unsuccessfully challenged before the Turkish courts. The Swiss courts refused to enforce the award because the sole arbitrator lacked the necessary independence: he had drafted the agreement, represented the claimant and was effectively non-removable. This violated Swiss public policy.[48]

13-42 Courts are reluctant to set aside an award or refuse its enforcement for alleged bias of an arbitrator. A far-reaching decision was rendered by an Indian Court of Appeal where a high ranking official of one of the parties who was, however, not involved in the disputed transaction, was appointed as the sole arbitrator. The court held that as long as the arbitrator acted impartially and the appointment of an official of a party was not against the public policy of the place of arbitration, the enforcement of an award rendered by such an arbitrator would not be against Indian public policy. [49]

1.5. Exclusion of the Right to Challenge the Award

13-43 In general, there is no right to challenge an award on the basis of a lack of independence or impartiality of an arbitrator where those facts were known to the parties before the award was rendered. If parties do not make use of remedies available to them they can be considered to have waived their rights in relation to those facts. This was the position taken by the Supreme Court of Canada in 1966 when it stated:

> ... generally speaking, an award will not be set aside if the circumstances alleged to disqualify an arbitrator were known to both parties before the arbitration commenced and they proceeded without objection.[50]

13-44 This is also the case under the Model Law despite the fact that the requirements of independence and impartiality are mandatory requirements and according to Article 4, cannot be waived.[51] Otherwise the time limits for

---

[48] Bezirksgericht, Affoltern am Albis, 26 May 1994, XXIII *YBCA* 754 (1998) para 19; confirmed by the Court of Appeal in Zurich, 26 July 1995.

[49] *Transocean Shipping Agency (P) Ltd v Black Sea Shipping et al*, (1998) XXIII YBCA 713, para 11 (Court of Appeal, 14 January 1998).

[50] *Ghirardosi v Minister of Highways (BC)*, (1966) 56 DLR (2d) 469, 473; for further references see Redfern and Hunter, *International Commercial Arbitration*, para 4-70.

[51] For a contrary view, see Redfern and Hunter, *International Commercial Arbitration*, para 4-69.

challenges contained in the Model Law would be meaningless. A party could await the outcome of the proceedings and challenge the award on the basis of facts already known to it before the award was rendered.[52]

13-45 There is a tactical question of whether and when to challenge an arbitrator who is thought not to be independent or impartial. In many cases it may be preferable not to exercise the right to challenge. A party should always consider the effect of an unsuccessful challenge on its ongoing relationship with the tribunal and the attitude the challenged arbitrator may have towards the party.

13-46 Furthermore, a biased arbitrator will often be treated with suspicion by the rest of the tribunal, so that the chairman will be more prepared to listen to the other party appointed arbitrator. As a result the biased arbitrator may have little influence on the content of an award so that a challenge may actually not be necessary. It will then only lead to unnecessary delay since any challenge has the potential of causing disruption and delaying the rendering of an award. Furthermore, there is no guarantee that the party nominated replacement will be independent or impartial. It is also possible that the lack of independence or impartiality of the replacement may not be as obvious, and he may, by his personality and his status, be able to influence the outcome of the arbitration in a much stronger way than the originally appointed arbitrator.[53]

2. Termination of the Arbitrator's Mandate

13-47 An arbitrator's mandate can also be terminated by agreement. This is expressly provided for in an number of arbitration laws[54] and rules[55]. In any event, even without such a provision, it follows from the contractual basis of arbitration. As the parties are the masters of the arbitration they cannot be forced to continue an arbitration started with a tribunal they do not want.

---

[52] See, *e.g.*, Bundesgerichtshof, 1 February 2001 *RPS* 1 (2001) 16, 17(8) *Mealeys IAR* 34, where a party could not invoke an alleged lack of impartiality in proceedings for the enforcement of an award, as the facts on which such a defence was based were already known to the party before the award was rendered. In this case, the party appointed arbitrator, acting as a sole arbitrator under the applicable arbitration rules due to a failure of the German side to appoint its arbitrator, had been involved in discussing the claim on behalf of the other side.

[53] See also Craig, Park & Paulsson, *ICC Arbitration*, para 13-03 who suggest that it is best to challenge as infrequently as possible.

[54] See, *e.g.*, Model Law Article 14; England, Arbitration Act section 23(3)(4).

[55] See ICC Rules Article 12(1); see WIPO Rules Article 28.

13-48 In addition, under most laws and rules each party has the right to apply for a termination of an arbitrator's mandate and his replacement if the arbitrator is unable, prevented or fails to carry out his functions. While under some rules and laws this is considered to be just another reason for challenge within the special challenge procedure,[56] the Model Law treats it as a separate ground for termination which is submitted to a different procedure. Article 14(1) provides

> If an arbitrator becomes *de jure* or *de facto* unable to perform his functions or for other reasons fails to act without undue delay, his mandate terminates if he withdraws from his office or if the parties agree on the termination. Otherwise, if a controversy remains concerning any of these grounds, any party may request the court or other authority specified in article 6 to decide on the termination of the mandate, which decision shall be subject to no appeal.

13-49 Inability to perform his functions may arise if the arbitrator is seriously ill or dies or perhaps where due to political controls an arbitrator is physically or legally prevented from performing.[57] More problematic is to determine when "undue delay" has occurred or the arbitrator has failed "properly to conduct the proceedings" as stipulated in the English Arbitration Act. Once the proceedings have commenced it is very hard for the parties to agree on whether undue delay has occurred, in particular, if one of the parties is not interested in an expeditious rendering of the award.[58]

13-50 Depending on which courts have jurisdiction to remove an arbitrator in such a case an interested party should consider whether the proceedings for the removal of an arbitrator, in combination with the time for the appointment of a replacement arbitrator and the additional steps required, would delay the proceedings even more than keeping the arbitrator in place despite the delay.

13-51 It may prove valuable, in institutional arbitration, if the institution has a right of its own to remove an arbitrator for delay in exercising his functions. For example, ICC Rules Article 12(2) provides that:

---

56 See, *e.g.*, England, Arbitration Act section 24; ICC Rules Article 11(1).

57 An arbitrator may be legally prevented from performing his task where an antisuit-injuction has been addressed to him; see the description of a number of those cases by Kerr, "Concord and Conflict in International Arbitration", 13 *Arb Int* 121 (1997) 136-138; Nariman, "Finality in India: the Impossible Dream", 10 *Arb Int* 373 (1994).

58 Okekeifere, "The Parties's Rights Against Dilatory or Unskilled Arbitrator", 15(2) *J Int'l Arb* 136 (1998).

> An arbitrator shall also be replaced on the Court's own initiative when it decides that he is prevented *de jure* or *de facto* from fulfilling his functions, or that he is not fulfilling his functions in accordance with the Rules or within the prescribed time limits.

13-52 An arbitrator may also voluntarily tender his resignation and terminate his mandate, either in response to a challenge or for other reasons. Given the disruption caused by such a termination some arbitration laws and rules limit the right of an arbitrator to resign. Belgian Law, for example, requires a special authorisation by a court of first instance if an arbitrator wants to resign without the consent of the parties.[59] In most cases it is not in the parties' interest to force such an arbitrator to continue; it is better to replace him by another more co-operative arbitrator. In the light of the disruption caused by a voluntary resignation arbitrators should always be made aware of the effect on fees and the arbitrator's liability in contract as a result of such resignation. This should dissuade partisan arbitrators from resigning at any stage of the proceedings and thereby destabilising the arbitration process and creating delays.

3. Replacement of Arbitrators

13-53 Any successful challenge, the voluntary resignation of an arbitrator or other termination of the arbitrator's mandate before the award has been rendered, results in an incomplete tribunal. In these cases a new arbitrator has to be appointed if there was only one arbitrator or if the remaining arbitrators cannot or do not want to act as a truncated tribunal.

13-54 There are good reasons to submit the appointment of the replacement arbitrator to the same rules under which the original arbitrator was appointed. Such an approach is in line with the parties' intention as to the composition of the tribunal. For example, a replacement for a party appointed arbitrator should be by the same party to ensure that both parties have the same influence on the appointment of the tribunal which will finally render the award. If that arbitrator is appointed by a court or an appointing authority the party who originally appointed the replaced arbitrator may not have a person of their confidence in the tribunal. Relevant in this respect should be the agreed way of appointment for the

---

[59] Judicial Code Article 1689; provisions to the same effect can be found in Netherlands, CCP Article 1029(2). See also Article 12(1) ICC Rules; Solhchi, "The Validity of Truncated Tribunal Proceedings and Awards", 9 *Arb Int* 303 (1993) 313.

original arbitrator not how the arbitrator was actually appointed. Therefore a party who failed to make its appointment for the original tribunal should still have the right to appoint the replacement.

13-55 This approach is adopted in the Model Law which provides in Article 15:

> Where the mandate of an arbitrator terminates under article 13 or 14 or because of his withdrawal from office for any other reason or because of the revocation of his mandate by agreement of the parties or in any other case of termination of his mandate, a substitute arbitrator shall be appointed according to the rules that were applicable to the appointment of the arbitrator being replaced.[60]

13-56 The drawback of this approach is that it can easily be misused by a party for dilatory purposes. A party which has deliberately appointed a biased or unsuitable arbitrator may, after a successful challenge, do so again necessitating a second challenge with all its disruptive effects.

13-57 To limit this possibility a number of institutional arbitration rules give a certain discretion to the institution whether or not to apply the original appointment procedure for the replacement arbitrator. For example, Article 11(1) LCIA Rules, inspired by the slightly narrower Article 12(4) ICC Rules provides:

> In the event that the LCIA Court determines that any nominee is not suitable or independent or impartial or if an appointed arbitrator is to be replaced for any reason, the LCIA Court shall have a complete discretion to decide whether or not to follow the original nominating process.

13-58 A special provision for cases prone to misuse for dilatory purposes, which deviates from the original appointment procedure, is also contained in the ICSID Rules. Article 11.2 states:

> In addition to filling vacancies relating to arbitrators appointed by him, the Chairman of the Administrative Council shall appoint a person from the panel of Arbitrators:
> (a) to fill a vacancy caused by the resignation, without the consent of the Tribunal, of an arbitrator appointed by a party; or
> (b) at the request of either party, to fill any other vacancy, if no new appointment is made and accepted within 30 days of the notification of the vacancy by the Secretary-General.

[60] See also UNCITRAL Rules Article 11(2); DIS Rules Section 18(3).

13-59 Whenever a replacement arbitrator has been appointed the question arises to what extent the tribunal has to repeat parts of the proceedings. Before oral hearings have been held it is in general sufficient that the replacement arbitrator is given time to read the pleadings and the other documents exchanged. Furthermore, he should give his assent in written form to any procedural directions issued by the tribunal.

13-60 More problematic are replacements after evidence and legal arguments have been presented. In such a situation it is necessary to provide the replacement arbitrator with the same information as the other arbitrators and to give each party the opportunity to present its case adequately to the whole tribunal which is to render the award. This can be costly and time consuming. Where a transcript of the hearings exists it may be possible to have the arbitrator read the transcript. He can then decide which witnesses, if any, he wants to hear again or what additional questions he would like to ask the parties or the witnesses. If no transcript exists it is for the particular tribunal to decide which parts of the evidence, if any, should be repeated.

13-61 Although no general rule can be advanced on this point it is always to be borne in mind that each arbitrator has the right to participate in every part of the proceedings. Awards may be challenged for improper proceedings when that right is denied to a replacement arbitrator. This seems to be the position underlying the provisions dealing with this issue in the various arbitration rules. Most arbitration rules contain a provision according to which the tribunal, after an arbitrator has been replaced, has discretion on whether to repeat the hearings or any other actions. For example, Article 34 WIPO Rules provides

> Whenever a substitute arbitrator is appointed, the Tribunal shall, having regard to any observations of the parties, determine in its sole discretion whether all or part of any prior hearings are to be repeated.[61]

13-62 A more restrictive approach is adopted in the UNCITRAL Rules. This restricts the tribunal's discretion to the party appointed arbitrators. Article 14 provides

> If under Rules 13 to 15 the sole or presiding arbitrator is replaced, any hearings held previously shall be repeated unless otherwise agreed to by the parties. If any other arbitrator is replaced, such prior hearings may be repeated at the discretion of the Tribunal.

---

[61] See, similarly, ICC Rules Article 12(4).

13-63 It is noteworthy that the Iran-US Claims Tribunal altered this rule to allow the Tribunal discretion as to the repetition of hearings irrespective of the status of the arbitrator. This extended discretion was used when the question of rehearing arose in the Iran-US Claims Tribunal following the death of Judge Virally. There were eleven cases in which he had participated still pending. In most cases the new chairman considered the transcripts, notes of judge Virally and his assistant sufficient and only two cases were reheard.[62]

13-64 The Model Law, as well as most laws based on it, are silent on the issue. An exception is Egyptian law, where a provision was included to the effect that the removal of an arbitrator "shall entail considering the arbitral proceedings already conducted, including the Arbitral Award, null and void." The consequence of this approach is that all proceedings have to be repeated.[63] This rule will probably also override any discretion granted by the chosen arbitration rules.

13-65 By contrast the English Arbitration Act contains a more expansive provision dealing with the issue of rehearing. It is submitted to the parties' agreement and failing such agreement gives the tribunal a wide discretion as to whether parts of the proceedings have to be repeated. Section 27(4) provides

> The tribunal (when reconstituted) shall determine whether and if so to what extent the previous proceedings should stand.
> This does not affect any right of a party to challenge those proceedings on any ground which had arisen before the arbitrator ceased to hold office.[64]

13-66 A good illustration of how tribunals make use of their discretion is ICC Award No 6476. It was based on a rather extreme situation.[65] After the original tribunal had rendered a partial award on jurisdiction the respondent initiated unsuccessful challenge proceedings against the chairman which, despite being rejected, led to the resignation of the chairman. Upon further challenges by the defendant the new chairman, as well as the arbitrator appointed by the other party, also resigned. The respondent applied to the reconstituted tribunal to have all prior proceedings and rulings repeated. To avoid any further delay in the proceedings which were already ongoing for five years the tribunal decided to

---

[62] Baker and Davis, *UNCITRAL Rules*, 70-1.

[63] Article 19(4). See also, to the same effect, Oman, Arbitration Law Article 19(4).

[64] The Netherlands proceedings which are suspended until a replacement is appointed shall "continue from the stage they have reached": CPP Article 1030(3).

[65] 8(1) *ICC Bulletin* 59 (1997).

allow the proceedings to continue on the basis that it would review all prior proceedings and rulings and decide upon the application to repeat them in due course. In its final award the tribunal held that in its view

> ... the best and safest course is to review all prior proceedings and rulings of the Tribunal and to make such dispositions as it deems appropriate in the light of this review. This will exclude any possibility of the Defendant's attacking this award on the ground that it is based on prior proceedings and rulings by an improperly constituted tribunal.
>
> ...
>
> Upon reviewing the entire record of the case, the newly appointed members of the Tribunal have reached the conclusion that no proceedings need to be repeated for their benefit and that their study of the record, together with the additional submissions by the parties, has adequately informed them of what has transpired before. The Tribunal therefore concluded that no repetition of prior proceedings is necessary.
>
> ...
>
> The Tribunal's review, in the light of the submissions by both parties, leads it to conclude that all rulings by the Tribunal should be reaffirmed, except that the reasoning needs to be adjusted as indicated in the award.

4. TRUNCATED TRIBUNALS

13-67 Problems can occur where one arbitrator in a three person tribunal refuses to sign the award, take part in the arbitrators' deliberations or even the proceedings, or unilaterally withdraws from the tribunal.[66] A partisan arbitrator may also resign to prevent an award against the party appointing him, or to delay the proceedings. Where the refusal to co-operate comes shortly before an award is to be rendered the parties may have spent a considerable amount of money and time on the arbitration proceedings. To replace the unco-operative arbitrator and restart the proceedings is often not a realistic option. It would reward the unco-operative behaviour and the necessary rehearing of the case may be what the arbitrator intended.

---

[66] See the cases cited by Solhchi, "The Validity of Truncated Tribunal Proceedings and Awards", 9 *Arb Int* 303 (1993); Schwebel, "The Validity of an Arbitral Award rendered by an Truncated Tribunal", 6(2) *ICC Bulletin* 19 (1995); for a case where the arbitrator was apparently forced to abstain by the state party appointing him see Final Award of 16 October 1999 in *ad hoc* arbitration, *Himpurna California Energy Ltd v Republic of Indonesia*, XXV YBCA 186 (2000).

13-68 In these circumstances can the remaining two arbitrators proceed without the partisan arbitrator and render an award?[67] Such a procedure may be problematic in light of the fact that, in general, awards should be made by the whole tribunal. Though few laws contain provisions to that effect[68] the participation of all members of the tribunal in the making of an arbitration award is generally considered to be a fundamental part of due process.[69] It has been argued that the underlying rationale to ensure an equal representation of the parties in the tribunal, is affected where one of the party appointed arbitrator does not participate in part of the proceedings.[70] Furthermore it has been maintained that an award rendered by a truncated tribunal of two arbitrators is not in accordance with the agreement of the parties on a three member tribunal.[71]

13-69 These arguments do not lead to any conceptual problems in cases where a party appointed arbitrator, after the closing of the proceedings and the tribunal's deliberations, refuses to sign the award because he disagrees with its contents. The arbitrator had, during the proceedings and the ensuing deliberation, every opportunity to present his view and convince the other arbitrators of his opinion. Consequently, the party appointing him did have equal influence on the composition of the tribunal which in its deliberations decided on the award. The lack of an obstructive arbitrator's signature cannot be allowed to frustrate the arbitration. The appropriate way to express disagreement with the award may be to write a dissenting opinion. Therefore a number of laws and rules provide that in such cases the signature of the arbitrator is not required. By contrast it is considered sufficient that the award explains why the signature is lacking.[72]

13-70 In most cases, however, partisan arbitrators refuse to co-operate at an earlier stage, before the final deliberations or even before the closing of the proceedings. The failure of one arbitrator to participate in the final deliberations leading to the award or even part of the proceedings deprives him of any

---

67 The question also arises where the arbitrator dies, is successfully challenged or for other legitimate reasons prevented from participating in the proceedings. In those cases, the majority view is that, if no consent has already been given to an award, a replacement arbitrator should be appointed.

68 See, *e.g.*, Belgium, Judicial Code Article 1701(1).

69 Fouchard Gaillard Goldman *on International Commercial Arbitration*, para 1369.

70 See the account of the discussions involving awards by truncated tribunals in the framework of the Iran-US Claims Tribunal, Schwebel, *Three Salient Problems*, 251 *et seq.*

71 Szurski, "The Constitution of the Arbitral Tribunal", *ICCA Congress series no 9*, 331.

72 See, *e.g.*, Model Law Article 31(1); Belgium, Judicial Code Article 1701(4); Netherlands, CPP Article 1057(3); UNCITRAL Rules Article 34(4).

influence on the final award. The award is rendered only by the remaining two arbitrators.

13-71 This fact led the Cour d'appel de Paris in *ATC-CFCO v Comilog* to annul an award rendered by a truncated tribunal on the basis that the tribunal rendering the award was not properly constituted.[73] This case concerned the liability is for a collision of freight trains and the resulting damages. The arbitrator appointed by ATC-CFCO, the Congolese railroad authority, resigned after the draft award had been communicated to him by the president of the tribunal. ATC-CFCO applied to have the award set aside which was rendered by the remaining two arbitrators. The court considered it irrelevant whether the resignation had a dilatory or abusive character and whether the arbitrator by his behaviour breached a duty to complete his mandate. Emphasising the importance that the composition of the tribunal be consistent with the requirements of the arbitration agreement the court held

> ... that, contrary to the hypothesis advanced by Comilog, according to which the award remains valid because it is rendered by the tribunal chosen by the parties even if one of the arbitrators does not participate in the deliberation or refuses to sign the award, since by continuing to accept his mission he still may exercise his prerogatives, the award at issue has been rendered by an arbitral tribunal lacking one of its members and the composition of which no longer conformed to the agreement on which its jurisdictional power was based.[74]

13-72 A comparable view was taken by the Swiss Supreme Court in the *Milutinovic* case, albeit on the basis of the old Swiss arbitration law.[75] Irrespective of these decisions the prevailing view in international arbitration practice is that truncated tribunals should be allowed to proceed in such situations and to render an award, thus preventing an obstructive and partisan arbitrator from frustrating the whole arbitration.

13-73 This is well evidenced by a recent award in an *ad hoc* arbitration between *Hilmapura* and *Indonesia* where the Indonesian arbitrator, apparently under pressure from the state party appointing him, resigned at a late stage of the

---

[73] Cour d'appel Paris, 1 July 1997, *Agence Transcongolaise des Communications – Chemin de fer Congo Océan (ATC-CFCO) (Congo) v Compagnie Minière de l'Ogooue – Comilog SA (Gabon)*, XXIVa YBCA 281 (1999).

[74] *Ibid*, para 12.

[75] Tribunal Fédéral, *Ivan Milutinovic PIM v Deutsche Babcock AG*, reported in detail in Schwebel, "The Validity of an Arbitral Award rendered by an Truncated Tribunal", 6(2) *ICC Bulletin* 19 (1995) 22.

proceedings. Analysing the various precedents and dealing with the objection that a truncated tribunal is not properly constituted the remaining two arbitrators came to the conclusion that

> The weight of well established international authority makes clear that an arbitral tribunal has not only the right, but the obligation, to proceed when, without valid excuse, one of its members fails to act, withdraws or – although not the case here – purports to resign.
>
> ...
>
> The Arbitral Tribunal thus has no hesitation in finding that, in the circumstances of this arbitration, it has the power to proceed to fulfil its mandate and render an award, since Professor Priyatna's non participation is without valid excuse
>
> In reaching this finding, the Arbitral Tribunal notes that is was initially constituted in precise conformity with the will of the Parties as reflected in the Terms of Appointment, and that therefore Professor Priyatna's withdrawal prejudices not the constitution but the continued effective composition of the Arbitral Tribunal. As the International Court of Justice observed in it Advisory Opinion in Interpretation of Peace Treaties with Bulgaria, Hungary and Romania, and as highlighted by Judge Schwebel in his 1994 Goff Lecture, the distinction is fundamental.[76]

13-74 This reasoning shows that the doctrinal problems related to awards rendered by truncated tribunals can be overcome. In particular, where the resignation of an arbitrator requires the consent of the parties, the institution, the courts or the tribunal, the arbitrator's mandate is not terminated by his unilateral withdrawal. Therefore it can be argued that the tribunal is still formally constituted. This excludes at the same time any potential problems related to an even number of arbitrators and since no unanimity is required for an award the lack of consent by one arbitrator is also not a problem. The award by a truncated tribunal has the same support as a majority award, the only difference being that the party appointed arbitrator did not take part in the deliberations. Due process does not require that the third arbitrator actually takes part but only that he has an opportunity to do so.[77]

13-75 Various efforts to regulate the matter on an international level have not been successful. However, a number of the recently adopted rules and laws

---

[76] Final Award of 16 October 1999 in ad hoc arbitration, *Himpurna California Energy Ltd v Republic of Indonesia*, XXV YBCA 186 (2000) 194.

[77] Fouchard Gaillard Goldman *on International Commercial Arbitration*, para 1373.

provide for awards by truncated tribunals.[78] A fairly narrow provision can be found in the ICC Rules where the decision as to rendering such an award is taken by the ICC Court of Arbitration. Article 12(5) provides

> Subsequent to the closing of the proceedings, instead of replacing an arbitrator who has died or been removed by the Court pursuant to Articles 12(1) and 12(2), the Court may decide, when it considers it appropriate, that the remaining arbitrators shall continue the arbitration. In making such determination, the Court shall take into account the views of the remaining arbitrators and of the parties and such other matters that it considers appropriate in the circumstances, ...

13-76 The remaining arbitrators' right to proceed is limited to situations where a vacancy arises after the closing of the proceedings. By contrast the mere failure to participate without any formal resignation or vacancies arising at an earlier time will probably not give such a right.[79]

13-77 Broader provisions in other rules such as Article 35(a) WIPO Arbitration Rules. This provides:

> If an arbitrator on a three-person Tribunal, though duly notified and without good cause, fails to participate in the work of the Tribunal, the two other arbitrators shall, unless a party has made an application under Article 32, have the power in their sole discretion to continue the arbitration and to make any award, order or other decision, notwithstanding the failure of the third arbitrator to participate. In determining whether to continue the arbitration or to render any award, order or other decision without the participation of an arbitrator, the two other arbitrators shall take into account the stage of the arbitration, the reason, if any, expressed by the third arbitrator for such non-participation, and such other matters as they consider appropriate in the circumstances of the case.[80]

13-78 By submitting to arbitration under these rules the parties vest the tribunal with the power to render an award as a truncated tribunal subject to the third arbitrator having a fair opportunity to participate. This defeats any argument as to an improperly composed tribunal. The parties opted for that type of tribunal

---

78 See, *e.g.*, Sweden, Arbitration Act section 30(1); Germany, ZPO section 1052(2); Permanent Court of Arbitration Optional Rules 1993 Article 13(3); Permanent Court of Arbitration Optional Rules 1992 Article 13(3).

79 Derains and Schwartz, *ICC Rules*, 195 who suggest that in those cases the arbitrator has formally to be removed by the court first; Blessing, *Introduction to Arbitration*, para 153 *et seq*.

80 See also AAA ICDR Rules Article 11(1); LCIA Article 12(1).

irrespective of whether one considers the mandate of the non-participating arbitrator to be terminated or not.

13-79 In such cases only a very restrictive position of the applicable law concerning the equal representation of the parties in the deliberation can cause problems for awards by truncated tribunals. The majority of national laws, however, adopt a different approach allowing for such awards. The Swedish Act even contains an provision to that effect. Section 30 provides

> Where an arbitrator fails, without valid cause, to participate in the determination of an issue by the arbitral tribunal, such failure will not prevent the other arbitrators from ruling on the matter. Unless the parties have decided otherwise, the opinion agreed upon by the majority of the arbitrators participating in the determination shall prevail. If no majority is attained for any opinion, the opinion of the chairman shall prevail.[81]

13-80 In other countries, such as France[82] and the US[83], courts have interpreted the law in such a way which is in line with the majority position in international arbitration.[84] The reasons for that approach are well expressed in *Uiterwyk Corporation v Iran* decided by the Iran-US Claims Tribunal. In this case, after the Iranian Arbitrator had withdrawn from the deliberations, the other two members of Chamber One continued their deliberations and held

> [t]his is in accordance with the established practice of the Tribunal to continue its work and make awards despite the failure of one arbitrator to participate. The practice of the Tribunal in this respect is necessary to prevent disruption and frustration by one Member of the Tribunal's performance of its functions and is fully in accordance with recognized principles of international law.[85]

---

[81] See also Bermuda, International Conciliation and Arbitration Act 1993 section 30.

[82] Cour de cassation, 28 January 1981, *Industrija Motora Rakovica v Lynx Machinery Ltd*, Rev Arb 425 (1982); Cour d'appel Paris, 1 July 1997, *Agence Transcongolaise des Communications-Chemin de Fer Congo v La Compagnie Minière de l'Ogoove-Comelog SA*, XXIVa *YBCA* 281 (1999); Fouchard Gaillard Goldman *on International Commercial Arbitration*, para 1373.

[83] *Republic of Columbia v Cauca Company*, 23 S Ct 704, 190 US 524, 47 Led 1159 (S Ct, 1993). For other decisions see Domke, *Arbitration*, paras 22-04, 29-02.

[84] See Schwebel, *Three Salient Problems*, 296; Schwebel, 6(2) *ICC Bulletin* 19 (1995) 20 *et seq.*

[85] *Uiterwyk Corporation (et al) Claimants, and the Government of the Islamic Republic of Iran (et al)*, XIV YBCA 398 (1989) para 30; 19 Iran-US CTR 107.

13-81 The arbitrators in the *Milutinovic* case[86] even went a step further. The case concerned a dispute between the member of a consortium formed for the construction of a power station in Libya. The Consortium Agreement provided for ICC Arbitration in Zurich. After an exchange of written briefs and submissions and at the end of the examination of witnesses the claimant asked for the re-examination of some of the defendant's witnesses. The majority of the tribunal rejected that request which led to the resignation of the party appointed arbitrator. The other two arbitrators rendered a partial award. They decided that since the resignation had not been accepted by the ICC the unco-operative arbitrator was still considered to be a member of the Tribunal. Accordingly the Tribunal saw no problems as to its proper composition. Concerning its continuation of the deliberations the Tribunal held

> A decision of the Arbitral Tribunal to the contrary, *i.e.*, to present a request for the removal of Professor Jovanovic (either in Zurich or in Paris) and to re-start the proceedings with the eventual successor of Professor Jovanovic, would be contrary to the requirements of orderly and correct arbitration, providing to an arbitrator (or a party influencing him) the means to sabotage the correct coming to an end of an arbitral procedure and to extort from the opposed party the reopening of the proceedings. Such a possibility would neglect the demands of the solution of international commercial disputes and question the credibility of arbitration ...[87]

13-82 This decision was annulled by the Swiss Federal Tribunal. After accepting in a first round of proceedings that the behaviour of the remaining two arbitrators was justified, the Swiss Federal Court nevertheless annulled the award for a violation of fundamental rights. In its heavily criticised decision it held that due to the lack of participation by one arbitrator the tribunal was not properly composed when rendering the award. It has been doubted whether under the new Swiss law, Swiss courts would render the same decision.[88]

---

86 ICC case no 5017, *Ivan Milutinovic PIM v Deutsche Babcock AG*, reported in detail in Schwebel, "The Validity of an Arbitral Award rendered by an Truncated Tribunal", 6(2) *ICC Bulletin* 19 (1995) 22 *et seq.*

87 *Ibid*, 24. The tribunal, however, expressly limited its comments to cases where the oral hearing, including the taking of evidence, was done by the whole tribunal while declaring doubts whether the same approach could be taken before that stage.

88 *Ibid*, 27.

Chapter 14

DETERMINATION OF JURISDICTION

14-1 The jurisdiction of the tribunal is fundamental to the authority and decision making power of the arbitrators. Awards rendered without jurisdiction have no legitimacy. The absence of jurisdiction is one of the few recognised reasons for a court to set aside or refuse recognition and enforcement of an award. Accordingly, it is often necessary to resolve the issue of jurisdiction at an early stage.[1] The question may arise before an arbitration tribunal as well as before a state court.

---

[1] Gotanda, "An Efficient Method for Determining Jurisdiction in International Arbitrations", 40 *Columbia J Transnat'l L* 11 (2001), 15.

14-2 An arbitration tribunal faced with the issue of its own jurisdiction must first determine whether it is competent to deal with the specific jurisdictional question or whether it must be referred to the court. The question that follows is the form in which the decision should be made.

14-3 In national courts the tribunal's jurisdiction may become an issue at various stages. It could arise before the arbitration has even started, during the proceedings or after the award has been made. In the first case, where one party has begun court proceedings the court will be asked to decline jurisdiction in favour of arbitration, relying on Article II(3) New York Convention or an equivalent provision in the national law. The issue of jurisdiction may arise where a court is requested to act in support of arbitration, for example, to appoint an arbitrator, or where a party seeks a declaration as to the tribunal's jurisdiction.

14-4 When a court considers the validity of the arbitration agreement at the setting aside or enforcement stage of the arbitration, a question arises as to the effect of, and the extent to which the court may review, the decision of the arbitration tribunal on its own jurisdiction.

14-5 This chapter considers the determination of jurisdiction of the arbitration tribunal by (1) the tribunal itself, and (2) a national court.

1. Determination of Jurisdiction by Arbitration Tribunals

14-6 Before it can decide on the substantive issue in dispute an arbitration tribunal must ascertain that it has jurisdiction. This does not mean that arbitrators always have to make a full inquiry into all aspects of their jurisdiction. Generally, where both parties participate in the appointment of the tribunal and introduce their respective claims and counterclaims without reservations, jurisdiction will not be an issue. Where the tribunal is concerned about the scope of the arbitration agreement, and where there is no jurisdictional challenge, it may ask the parties to confirm the jurisdiction of the tribunal over the issue before it, which will give it jurisdiction if it did not exist before.

14-7 Many modern arbitration laws consider any participation in proceedings on the merits without challenging the jurisdiction of the tribunal as a submission to arbitration. For example, Article 16(2) Model Law provides that any objection to the jurisdiction of an arbitration tribunal has to be raised no later than the statement of defence.[2] After this time there is a deemed acceptance of the arbitration and a later challenge to jurisdiction would be estopped.[3]

14-8 An exception to this general rule is the question of objective arbitrability of a given dispute which is outside the reach of party autonomy. Irrespective of the wishes of the parties the tribunal should always verify the arbitrability of a dispute *ex officio* and should decline jurisdiction if the dispute is not arbitrable.[4]

14-9 A full inquiry into all aspects of the tribunal's jurisdiction is necessary when one party explicitly contests the jurisdiction or does not take any part in the proceedings. In these cases a decision on the jurisdiction of the tribunal is required.

14-10 Unlike the jurisdiction of state courts, the jurisdiction of an arbitration tribunal is not determined by the provisions of a single *lex fori*. Due to the hybrid character of arbitration it is based on a complex mixture of contractual and jurisdictional elements, *i.e.* the will of the parties as expressed in the arbitration agreement on the one hand, and the different laws applicable to the various aspects of the arbitration agreement on the other hand. As the interplay between the different possible applicable laws and the express terms of the arbitration agreement are often ambiguous, the question of the tribunal's jurisdiction is frequently a matter of dispute.[5]

14-11 Parties may also raise the jurisdiction issue for tactical reasons as it is an effective tool to delay proceedings. It is not always easy to identify when the jurisdictional challenge is made in good faith and where it is merely to delay the process.

14-12 To strengthen the jurisdiction of the arbitration tribunal and to minimise challenges being used to delay or derail arbitration proceedings most modern

---

2 See also England, Arbitration Act section 31; Germany, ZPO section 1040(2); Netherlands, CCP Article 1052(2).

3 To avoid any ambiguity some arbitration laws, such as the Belgian Judicial Code Article 1697(4), provide that the mere participation in the constitution of the tribunal is not deemed to be a submission to the jurisdiction of the tribunal; signing the Terms of Reference under ICC Rules Article 18, without objecting to the jurisdiction to the tribunal is, however, a form of arbitration agreement, either confirming the jurisdiction of the tribunal or accepting it formally.

4 See the reservation made for the plea of non-arbitrability in the Dutch arbitration law, Netherlands, CCP Article 1052(2). See also Berger, *International Economic Arbitration*, 352 *et seq*.

5 In 2000 approximately one third of ICC awards involved a jurisdictional challenge to the tribunal.

arbitration laws employ different techniques. The central element in those efforts is the recognition of the tribunal's authority to determine its own jurisdiction or competence, the so called "competence-competence" principle.

1.1. Competence-Competence

14-13 The doctrine of competence-competence overcomes the conceptual problems arising out of any decision by the arbitrator on his own jurisdiction.[6] Any decision by the tribunal that no valid arbitration agreement exists would include at the same time a corollary finding that the tribunal also lacked jurisdiction to decide on its own jurisdiction since there was no basis for such a jurisdiction.

14-14 This circuitous argument is particularly obvious when the tribunal concludes that the parties never agreed on arbitration. What then is the contractual basis for any jurisdiction of the arbitration tribunal? In such cases it is impossible to assume that the parties empowered the tribunal to determine its own jurisdiction. If the parties never agreed on arbitration how can they have empowered an arbitration tribunal to decide on its own jurisdiction? In this respect provisions in the different arbitration rules empowering tribunals to decide on their own jurisdiction are also of little help. To be applicable the parties must have agreed on them. If the parties never entered into an arbitration agreement they also never agreed on the arbitration rules. Although such problems arise primarily if the tribunal denies its jurisdiction they are inherent in any challenge. At the time when the tribunal has to determine whether it should decide on the challenge it does not usually know the outcome.

14-15 One possible solution would be to refer all questions on the tribunal's jurisdiction to the courts. A recalcitrant respondent could easily frustrate the parties' agreement to have their dispute decided by arbitration or at least create considerable delay by merely contesting the existence or validity of the

---

6 In addition, the so called "positive competence-competence" doctrine, if understood broadly, also has a bearing on whether courts can decide on the arbitrator's jurisdiction before the tribunal has itself dealt with the issue; for the different understandings of the doctrine of competence-competence see Park, "Determining Arbitral Jurisdiction: Allocation of Tasks between Courts and Arbitrators", 9 *ADRLJ* 19 (2000) 25 *et seq.*

arbitration agreement. This solution would seriously undermine arbitration as an effective means of private dispute resolution and deprive it of its attraction.[7]

14-16 The doctrine of competence-competence evolved to avoid these drawbacks. It is a legal fiction granting arbitration tribunals the power to rule on their own jurisdiction. To justify the assumption of these powers reference was first made in Article 36(6) Statute of the International Court of Justice (ICJ) allows the ICJ which to rule on its own jurisdiction. A comparable competence was recognised for arbitration tribunals in the European Convention. Article V(3) provides

> Subject to any subsequent judicial control provided for under the lex fori, the arbitrator whose jurisdiction is called in question shall be entitled to proceed with the arbitration, to rule on his own jurisdiction and to decide upon the existence or the validity of the arbitration agreement or of the contract of which the agreement forms part.

14-17 Since then the doctrine has found recognition in the ICSID Convention Article 41(1) and is now firmly established in most modern arbitration laws. The Model Law provides in Article 16(1)

> The arbitral tribunal may rule on its own jurisdiction, including any objections with respect to the existence or validity of the arbitration agreement. For that purpose, an arbitration clause which forms part of a contract shall be treated as an agreement independent of the other terms of the contract. A decision by the arbitral tribunal that the contract is null and void shall not entail *ipso jure* the invalidity of the arbitration clause.[8]

14-18 However, even if such provisions did not exist arbitration tribunals have traditionally assumed a right to rule on their own jurisdiction. A good example is the preliminary award on jurisdiction in *TOPCO v Libya*[9]. The dispute arose out

---

[7] Reisman, Craig, Park and Paulsson, *Commercial Arbitration*, 646; Holtzmann and Neuhaus, *Model Law*, 479.

[8] Similar provisions can also be found in non Model Law countries, *e.g.*, Switzerland, PIL Article 186; England, Arbitration Act section 30. An exception is the Chinese Law where the tribunal has no competence-competence but the decision on jurisdiction is either taken by the arbitration institution under the rules of which the arbitration takes place or by the courts.

[9] *Texaco Overseas Petroleum Company/California Asiatic Oil Company v The Government of the Libyan Arab Republic,* preliminary award on jurisdiction, 27 November 1975, French original in 104 Clunet 350 (1977), with introduction by Lalive, "Un grand arbitrage pétrolier entre un Gouvernement et deux sociétés privées étrangères", 104 *Clunet* 320 (1977). For excerpts in English see IV *YBCA* 176 (1979).

of the nationalisations of several Deeds of Concessions held by the US claimants. Since Libya did not appoint its arbitrator a sole arbitrator was appointed by the president of the ICJ. The Libyan Government did not take part in the arbitration but wrote a letter to the President of the ICJ contesting the appointment of the arbitrator. The sole arbitrator treated that letter as a challenge to his jurisdiction and dealt with the issue in a preliminary award. The arbitrator held that he did have the competence to determine his own jurisdiction. He based his decision primarily on

> ... a customary rule, which has the character of necessity, derived from the jurisdictional nature of the arbitration, confirmed by case law more than 100 years old and recognized unanimously by the writings of legal scholars.[10]

1.2. Separability and other Techniques to Strengthen Arbitrator's Jurisdiction

14-19 The doctrine of separability is another technique, recognised in arbitration rules and laws, which further strengthens the jurisdiction of the arbitrator. While competence-competence empowers the arbitration tribunal to decide on its own jurisdiction, separability affects the outcome of this decision. Any challenge to the main agreement does not affect the arbitration agreement: the tribunal can still decide on the validity of the main contract. [11] Without the doctrine of separability, a tribunal making use of its competence-competence would potentially be obliged to deny jurisdiction on the merits since the existence of the arbitration clause might be affected by the invalidity of the underlying contract.

14-20 Another technique in support of the jurisdiction of the arbitration tribunal found in national laws is to allow the tribunal to start or continue arbitration proceedings even though the jurisdiction of the tribunal is being challenged in the courts. For example, Article 8(2) Model Law provides

> Where an action referred to in paragraph (1) of this Article [action on the merits in front of a state court] has been brought, arbitral proceedings may nevertheless be

---

[10] *Ibid.*

[11] See also Fouchard Gaillard and Goldman *on International Commercial Arbitration*, para 416; Park, "Determining Arbitral Jurisdiction: Allocation of Tasks between Courts and Arbitrators", 9 *ADRLJ* 19 (2000) 27 *et seq.* While the Model Law deals with the two doctrines in one provision, Article 16(1) other laws deal with them in separate provisions: England, Arbitration Act sections 7 and 30; Sweden, Arbitration Act sections 2 and 3; Switzerland, PIL Articles 178(3) and 186.

commenced or continued, and an award may be made, while the issue is pending before the court.[12]

14-21 Whether arbitration tribunals should make use of such powers depends on the specific facts of the case. The effect of these provisions is that they are not required by the principle of *lis pendens* to stay the case or deny jurisdiction if an action has been brought in the courts.

14-22 The importance of this became evident in the decision of the Swiss Supreme Court in *Formento de Construcciones v Colon Container Terminal.*[13] The court held that under Swiss Law the principle of *lis pendens*, enshrined in Article 9 PIL, requires the tribunal to stay its proceedings if foreign court proceedings are pending and will lead within a reasonable time to a judgment which will be recognised in Switzerland. Since one of the parties had, prior to the commencement of the arbitration, initiated court proceedings in Panama the tribunal was required to stay the case unless it came to the conclusion that the resulting Panamanian judgment would not be recognised. As no such finding was made the tribunal lacked jurisdiction and the interim award assuming jurisdiction was annulled.[14]

1.3. Form of Decision on Jurisdiction

14-23 The form of the tribunal's decision on its jurisdiction depends on its outcome. Any decision denying jurisdiction should invariably be in the form of a final award so that it can be recognised under the New York Convention. By contrast, if jurisdiction is assumed the tribunal can either render a preliminary decision on jurisdiction or include its decision in the final award on the merits. In

---

[12] See also Sweden, Arbitration Act section 2; Germany, ZPO section 1032(3).

[13] Swiss Tribunal Fédéral, 14 May 2001, *Formento de Construcciones y Contratas SA v Colon Container Terminal SA*, Int ALR N-28 (2001). Proceedings challenging the validity of the arbitration agreement were ongoing in the Panamanian courts. An ICC tribunal, with its seat in Switzerland, was also asked to consider the validity and effect of the arbitration agreement. The Swiss Federal Tribunal held that the subsequently established arbitration tribunal should have stayed its proceedings pending a decision of the Supreme Court of Panama as the latter was first seized of the issue.

[14] See also the earlier decision by the Swiss Supreme Court, 19 December 1997, *Compañía de Minas Buenaventura SA v BRGM-Pérou SAS (formerly La-Source, Compagnie Minière SAS)*, XXIVa YBCA 727 (1999). For a criticism of the application of Article 9 PIL to arbitration see Perret, "Parallel Actions pending before an Arbitral Tribunal and a State Court: the Solution under Swiss Law", 16 *Arb Int* 333 (2000).

this respect the tribunal has full discretion which path to follow despite the underlying assumption in some arbitration rules and laws that on a challenge of jurisdiction a preliminary decision should be rendered.[15] In the absence of an agreement between the parties to the contrary the arbitration tribunal can include its decision on jurisdiction in the final award.[16]

14-24 The incorporation of the ruling on jurisdiction in the award on the merits is appropriate when both jurisdiction and merits turn on the same issues. In those cases it is artificial and impractical to render a preliminary decision on jurisdiction. Rendering a single award on jurisdiction and merits may also be appropriate where one party attempts to delay the proceedings. Preliminary decisions on jurisdiction are generally open to challenge either under express provisions to that effect[17] or under the general provisions dealing with challenges of an award.[18] Challenge proceedings before state courts may lead to considerable delay, in particular if they involve several instances. Inevitably, a recalcitrant party could initiate to challenge proceedings against each award, the preliminary award on jurisdiction and the final award on the merits.[19]

14-25 In practice, when jurisdiction is challenged arbitration tribunals often opt for rendering a preliminary decision on jurisdiction so that this issue is finally settled at an early stage.[20] Depending on the outcome the parties can either initiate court proceedings or concentrate on the merits of the case. If no challenge procedure is initiated within the period foreseen in the applicable arbitration law a preliminary award in favour of jurisdiction bars any later attack on the jurisdiction of the tribunal. Its *res judicata* effect also prevents parallel court

---

15 According to UNCITRAL Rules Article 21(4) a preliminary decision should be the rule; see also Switzerland, PIL Article 186(3); for the different forms the decision on jurisdiction may take see the Zurich Chamber of Commerce, Preliminary Award of 25 November 1994, XXII *YBCA* 211 (1997) 213 *et seq.*

16 See Cour de cassation, 8 March 1988, *SOFIDIF et al v Organization for Investment, Economic and Technical Assistance of Iran (OIETAI) and Atomic Energy Organization of Iran (AEOI)*, Rev Arb 482 (1989). In this case the terms of reference provided that the tribunal should deal with the objections to jurisdiction first. As the decisions on jurisdiction and the merits involved the same issues the tribunal decided it would render a final award dealing with both issues. The Cour de cassation upheld the award notwithstanding the terms of reference provision for a preliminary award on jurisdiction.

17 See, *e.g.*, Model Law Article 16(3); England, Arbitration Act section 30(2).

18 *E.g.*, under Swiss Law. See Bucher, *Die neue internationale Schiedsgerichtsbarkeit in der Schweitz*, para 133.

19 Reisman, Craig, Park and Paulsson, *International Commercial Arbitration*, 641.

20 *Ibid*, 643.

proceedings in the country where the award is rendered. Since such preliminary awards have to be recognised under the New York Convention this may also extend to other Member States of the Convention.

14-26 This is well evidenced by the decision of the Swiss Tribunal Fédéral in the *Westland Helicopters* case. Westland had entered into a joint venture with AOI, an international organization set up by four Arabian States. After three of the states withdrew from AOI Westland initiated arbitration proceedings against all four states for a breach of the joint venture agreement. Only Egypt participated in the proceedings and successfully attacked a preliminary award in which the arbitration tribunal assumed jurisdiction.[21] After an award on the merits had been rendered against the other states they tried to resist enforcement in Switzerland alleging a lack of jurisdiction of the tribunal. The Swiss court held that they were barred from raising that defence since the preliminary award was only annulled in relation to Egypt. For the other three states it was binding: they could not rely on the fact that they were not parties to the arbitration agreement.[22]

14-27 To minimise delay arising out of challenges to preliminary awards, some arbitration laws allow the proceedings on the merits to continue despite the court proceedings.[23] Furthermore, no appeal is possible against any court decision on the challenge.[24]

1.4. Review of Arbitrator's Decision by Courts

14-28 The tribunal's decision on its jurisdiction is open to a full review by the courts.[25] This is not the case for an award on the merits where review is limited to public policy issues. The reason for such a complete review is that it would be

---

[21] Preliminary award, 23 *ILM* 1071 (1984); annulment in Swiss Courts, XVI *YBCA* 174 (1991).

[22] Switzerland, Tribunal Fédéral, *ASA Bulletin* 174 (1994).

[23] Model Law Article 16(3); Germany, ZPO section 1040(3).

[24] See, *e.g.*, Model Law Article 16(3). However, see the deviation in the German law, ZPO section 1065(1).

[25] See, *e.g.*, England, Arbitration Act, section 67; Model Law Article 34(2)(a)(i); but see the decision of the Swiss Tribunal Fédéral, 17 August 1995, *Transport- en Handelsmaatschappij Vekoma BV v Maran Coal Company*, 8 ADRLJ 87 (1999) where there are indications that the standard of review concerning jurisdiction may be different depending on whether issues of law or of fact are at stake.

contrary to public policy to bind a party to a decision of a tribunal to which it never agreed.[26]

14-29 Under the old German law it was considered possible to give the arbitrator the power to make a more or less final decision on its jurisdiction.[27] The legal concept underlying this view was that the parties concluded a second arbitration agreement under which the arbitrator had the power to decide on the validity of the first. The effect was that the decision on jurisdiction, which would have been fully reviewable if only one arbitration agreement had been concluded, became a decision on the merits under the second arbitration agreement for which only a limited review existed. The new German law abolished this concept so that an arbitrator's decision on jurisdiction can be reviewed by the courts.[28]

14-30 Opinions expressed in the US Supreme Court in *First Options of Chicago Inc v Kaplan*[29] seem to adopt a comparable concept in American law. It concerned an action to vacate an award against the defendant who was the owner of a company which had entered into an agreement with First Options. In its award the arbitration tribunal had ruled that the arbitration agreement though only signed on behalf of the company also bound the owners personally. One of the issues which arose in the Supreme Court was the extent to which courts could review a decision of arbitrators concerning jurisdiction.

14-31 The court distinguished between ordinary arbitration agreements and those where the parties also submitted the issue of jurisdiction to the tribunal. While in the former case any decision of the arbitrator is fully reviewable, the Supreme Court held in relation to the second type of agreements:

> Just as the arbitrability of the merits of a dispute depends upon whether the parties agreed to arbitrate that dispute [references omitted], so the question who has the primary power to decide arbitrability' turns upon what the parties agreed about that matter. Did the parties agree to submit the arbitrability question itself to arbitration? If so, then the court's standard for reviewing the arbitrator's decision about that

---

[26] See, *e.g.*, Bundesgerichtshof, 9 March 1978, 39 *KTS* 227 (1978) 230; Oberlandesgericht Rostock, 22 November 2001, 1 *Sch* 3/2000. The standards for review of the decision on the merits and for review of the decision on jurisdiction are not so far apart, since violations of public policy can always be reviewed.

[27] See Bundesgerichtshof, 5 May 1977, *BGHZ* 68, 356, 366; Bundesgerichtshof, 6 June 1991, *WM* 1248 (1991). See also Schlosser, *Internationale Schiedsgerichtsbarkeit*, para 556 with further references; this view was, however, not uncontested.

[28] See Germany, ZPO section 1040(3); Lachmann, *Handbuch*, para 467 *et seq.*

[29] *First Options of Chicago v Manuel Kaplan et ux and MK Investment, Inc*, 115 SCt 1920 (1995).

> matter should not differ from the standard courts apply when they review any other matter that parties have agreed to arbitrate. [references omitted] That is to say, the court should give considerable leeway to the arbitrator, setting aside his or her decision only in certain narrow circumstances.[30]

14-32 This decision has been criticised and since the issue was dealt with only in the court's discussion it cannot be regarded as a binding precedent.[31] Ordinary arbitration agreements are in no way sufficient to grant arbitrators power to decide with binding effect on their jurisdiction. To assume the referral of such a wide reaching power at least a second and separate arbitration agreement would be required. Even then it seems doubtful whether the courts in most countries would recognise such a decision since it comes from the same arbitrator which under the first agreement could not decide with binding force on its jurisdiction.[32] In most countries the courts retain the last word on excluding their jurisdiction.[33]

2. Determination of Jurisdiction by a National Court

14-33 Courts may be asked at both the pre-award and post-award stages to deal with questions related to the jurisdiction of the arbitration tribunal. The most frequent situation is where one party brings a claim on the merits in the courts, and the other party asks for the court to stay its jurisdiction relying on an arbitration agreement. Some arbitration laws contain special provisions allowing the parties to apply to the courts for a declaration that an arbitrator has or lacks

---

[30] *Ibid*, 1943. The Supreme Court used "arbitrability" as referring to the tribunal's jurisdiction in general.

[31] Park, "The Arbitrability Dicta in First Options v Kaplan: What Sort of Kompetenz-Kompetenz Has Crossed the Atlantic?" 12 *Arb Int* 137 (1996) 143 *et seq*; Park, "Determining Arbitral Jurisdiction: Allocation of Tasks between Courts and Arbitrators", 9 *ADRLJ* 19 (2000) 22.

[32] In *Astro Valiente Compania Naviera SA v Pakistan Min of Food & Agriculture, "The Emmanuel Colocotronis"*, [1982] 1 All ER 823 the question whether a parent company was bound by an arbitration agreement entered into by a subsidiary in a loan contract was submitted by a second agreement to a separate arbitration tribunal; see also *LG Caltex Gas Co Ltd and Contigroup Companies Inc v China National Petroleum Co and China Petroleum Technology & Development Corp* [2001] EWCA Civ 788, 4 Int ALR N-23 (2002), where the Court of Appeal overruled the High Court which had assumed an *ad hoc* agreement to empower the tribunal to make a final decision on its jurisdiction, holding that such a second arbitration agreement should only be assumed if the parties explicitly said so. Otherwise, it is only a recognition of the tribunal's general power to decide on its own jurisdiction.

[33] Park, "Determining Arbitral Jurisdiction: Allocation of Tasks between Courts and Arbitrators", 9 *ADRLJ* 19 (2000) 29 *et seq*.

jurisdiction. Jurisdiction of the tribunal may also be an issue in court proceedings in support of arbitration, *e.g.* an application for the appointment of an arbitrator.

2.1. Actions on the Merits despite an Arbitration Agreement

14-34 The principle that a valid arbitration agreement requires courts to refer parties to arbitration is firmly established. It is a major prerequisite for the success of arbitration as an international dispute settlement mechanism. In addition to being provided for in Article II(3) New York Convention the principle can also be found in national arbitration laws. The Model Law, for example, provides in Article 8(1)

> A court before which an action is brought in a matter which is the subject of an arbitration agreement shall, if a party so requests not later than when submitting his first statement on the substance of the dispute, refer the parties to arbitration unless it finds that the agreement is null and void, inoperative or incapable of being performed.

14-35 Most national laws contain either identical or at least comparable provisions. They usually require that the arbitration agreement will be invoked or relied on by the defendant and that it is valid and can be effectively implemented, *i.e.* is not "null and void, inoperative or incapable of being performed." However, differences exist as to the standard of review and the action to be taken by the courts where there is a valid arbitration agreement

(a) Request for a stay of court proceedings in favour of arbitration

14-36 A common feature of all these national and international provisions is that the defendant in the court proceedings has to request a referral to arbitration. The courts are not obliged *ex officio* to stay their proceedings since each party is free to renounce its right to have a dispute decided by arbitration. By not invoking the arbitration agreement the defendant makes clear that it does not insist on its right to arbitration but tacitly accepts the plaintiff's choice of referring the dispute to the state courts.

14-37 National arbitration laws, and the Model Law often require that a referral of the case to arbitration must be requested before any steps relating to the merits of the case are taken.[34] Article VI(1) European Convention provides:

> A plea as to the jurisdiction of the court made before the court seized by either party to the arbitration agreement, on the basis of the fact that an arbitration agreement exists shall, under penalty of estoppel, be presented by the respondent before or at the same time as the presentation of his substantial defence, depending upon whether the law of the court seized regards this plea as one of procedure or of substance.

14-38 Even where the provisions of the national law are not so clear, courts have generally required the parties to raise the defence of an arbitration agreement.[35]

14-39 The relevant point in time for the request is usually the first plea on substance. As specifically relevant, provisions of the arbitration laws should supersede provisions in the general law of procedure according to which challenges to the court's jurisdiction must be raised at an earlier stage. The German supreme court held that this is so even when a court has set a shorter time limit for raising any defences.[36]

(b) "Null and void, inoperative or incapable of being performed"

14-40 The New York Convention, as well as the majority of arbitration laws, exempts national courts from referring a matter to arbitration if the court concludes that the arbitration agreement is "null and void, inoperative or incapable of being performed."[37] This phrase, however, was not discussed in any detail during the preparations of the New York Convention nor when national

---

[34] Model Law Article 8(1); Germany, ZPO section 1032(1); Belgium, Judicial Code Article 1679; England, Arbitration Act section 9(3); Switzerland, PIL Article 7.

[35] See, *e.g.*, the decisions in *Tracomin SA v Sudan Oil Seeds* [1983] 1 All ER 404.

[36] Bundesgerichtshof, 10 May 2001, with comment Kröll, 17(4) *Mealey's IAR* 25 (2002). See also the decision of 7 May 1996, *ABN Amro Bank Canada v Krupp Mak Maschinenbau GmbH and others*, 6 ADRLJ 37 (1997) 40.

[37] See, *e.g.*, Switzerland, PIL Article 7(b); Germany, ZPO section 1032(1); England, Arbitration Act section 9(4); Bermuda, Arbitration Act section 8; for a slightly different wording, but with the same meaning, see European Convention Articles V(1), VI(3) ("non-existent or null and void or had lapsed"); France, NCPC Article 1458 ("null and void"); Belgium, Judicial Code Article 1679(1) ("not valid or has terminated"); Netherlands, CCP section 1022(1) ("invalid"); US, FAA section 3 ("issue referable to arbitration").

provisions were drafted.[38] Courts have also not defined these terms; rather they usually limit themselves to determining whether an arbitration agreement is "null and void, inoperative or incapable of being performed".

14-41 In an arbitration friendly environment these terms should be interpreted narrowly. Furthermore, in the context of the New York Convention an autonomous interpretation should prevail which excludes national idiosyncrasies. Only such an autonomous interpretation can lead to the harmonisation intended by the Convention. However, it is not necessary to distinguish meticulously between the different grounds. Irrespective of the grounds on which a court bases its decision whether an agreement is "null and void, inoperative or incapable of being performed", the result will always be the same.

14-42 The words "null" and "void" have the same meaning, as evidenced by the use of a single word in the French and Spanish versions of the New York Convention. They refer to the cases where the arbitration agreement is affected by some invalidity right from the beginning. This would be the case, for example, if the arbitration agreement

- does not refer to a defined legal relationship;
- has not been validly agreed by the parties (due to lack of consent, misrepresentation or duress in relation to the arbitration agreement);
- refers the dispute to an uncertain or non-existent arbitration institution.[39]

14-43 In relation to the ambiguous reference to possible different or non-existent institutions, national courts have not easily reached a verdict of an agreement being null or void. Rather they have usually tried to give a workable meaning to these clauses. A good example is decision by the Kammergericht Berlin where the arbitration clause provided for arbitration under the rules of the "Central German Chamber of Commerce". Though there is no such institution the court considered the clause to be a valid reference to arbitration under the rules of the leading arbitration institution in Germany, the DIS.[40] Clauses were

---

[38] On the New York Convention see van den Berg, *New York Convention*, 156. For recent examples at the national level see the Reports on the new German and English laws which do not contain any information as to the possible meaning of the terms, apart from noting that they were already included in the old law.

[39] Germany, Bundesgerichtshof, 2 December 1982, *Wünsche Handelsgesellschaft v Coop S Maria srl*, XV YBCA 660 (1990).

[40] Kammergericht Berlin, 15 October 1999, [2000] *Int ALR* N-70; see also Cour de cassation, 14 December 1983, *Epoux Convert v Société Droga*, Rev Arb 483 (1984) 484 (Belgrade Chamber

only considered invalid where they were worded in such a way that two institutions could have been meant or no specific institution could readily be identified.[41]

14-44 Article IV(5) European Convention provides a solution for cases where the parties cannot agree an institution or it is not certain which of two possible institutions is chosen. In conjunction with Article IV(3) it refers to the chamber of commerce at the agreed place of arbitration, or the place where the respondent has its seat or habitual residence, provided such chamber of commerce has an arbitration function.[42]

14-45 The term "inoperative" refers to arbitration agreements which have not been invalid from the beginning but have since lost their effect. For example, termination or revocation of the agreement by the parties or the rendering of an award or judgment with *res judicata* effect in parallel proceedings. The arbitration agreement could also become inoperative where the applicable arbitration rules or law requires that the award has to be made within a certain time after which the arbitration tribunal loses its authority.

14-46 On a number of occasions parties have tried to argue that arbitration agreements are "inoperative" since they did not cover all the claims submitted or all parties concerned. Though such arguments have been successful in some cases[43] the general view is that this might create inconveniences but does not render arbitration agreements "inoperable".[44] The rationale underlying this view

---

of Commerce = Foreign Trade Arbitration Court at the Economic Chamber of Yugoslavia). See also Davis, "Pathological Clauses: Frédéric Eisemann's Still Vital Criteria", 7 *Arb Int* 365 (1991).

41 See Germany, Bundesgerichtshof, 2 December 1982, *Wünsche Handelsgesellschaft v Coop S Maria srl*, XV YBCA 660 (1990), Bayerisches Oberstes Landesgericht, 28 February 2000, 4 Z *SchH* 13/99, *RPS* 15 (1/2000). See also France, Cour d'appel de Versailles, 3 October 1991, *Ltd Capital Rice Co v SARL Michel Come*, Rev Arb 654 (1992); Lebanon, Cour de cassation, 27 April 1987, *Rev Arb* 723 (1988); Scotland, Court of Session (Outer House), 15 May 2001, *Bruce v Kordula and others*, 4 Int ALR N-6 (2002).

42 See, *e.g.*, the Hanseatisches Oberlandesgericht Hamburg, 15 November 1995, XXI *YBCA* 845 (1996), where the arbitration agreement provided for disputes to be referred to the "Arbitral Tribunal at the International Chamber of Commerce in Zurich". The Court held this to be invalid since it could mean ICC arbitration or Zurich Chamber of Commerce arbitration.

43 See, *e.g.*, the decision of the British Columbia Supreme Court, *Prince George (City) v McElhanney Engineering Services Ltd and Al Sims and Sons Ltd*, (1997) 6 ADRLJ 315 (BCSP 30 December 1994); further cases cited by van den Berg, *New York Convention*, 162 *et seq.*

44 See, *e.g.*, *Lonrho Ltd v Shell Petroleum Co Ltd et al* [1981] 2 All ER 456.

is explained in *Kaverit Steel. v Kone Corporation.* The Alberta Court of Appeal held

> In modern commercial disputes, it is almost inevitable that many parties will be involved and very unlikely that all parties will have an identical submission. The problem of multiple parties, which drove the decision of the chambers judge here, will exist in almost every case. There is no question that proliferation of litigation is a possibility. [...] In any event, the Convention cannot reasonably be taken as having abandoned any attempt at arbitration when this problem arises.[45]

14-47 Arbitration agreements are "incapable of being performed" where the arbitration cannot effectively be set in motion. Examples are agreements where the arbitrator appointed in the agreement refuses to act or cannot perform the function ascribed to him. The term also covers cases where arbitration is no longer possible at the agreed place of arbitration. In the aftermath of the Iranian Revolution US parties successfully refused to arbitrate under agreements providing for arbitration in Iran. US courts refused to enforce the obligation to arbitrate arising under those agreements since they considered it impossible to separate the choice of the place of arbitration from the rest of the clause.[46] Another example of arbitration agreements becoming inoperative resulted from the dissolution of East Berlin Arbitration Court attached to the Chamber of Foreign Trade of the GDR in the aftermath of the German unification.[47]

14-48 Different views exist as to whether the lack of sufficient funding will render arbitration agreements "incapable of being performed" or "inoperative". English courts have held that this is not the case unless the lack of funding is due

---

45 *Kaverit Steel and Crane Ltd et al v Kone Corporation et al*, (1994) XIV YBCA 643, 651 para 31 (Alberta Court of Appeal, 16 January 1992).

46 See *National Iranian Oil Co v Ashland Oil, Inc*, 817 F 2d 326 (5th Cir 1987).

47 Bundesgerichtshof, 20 January 1994, *BGHZ* 125, 7, 11 *et seq*; Bundesgerichtshof, 9 February 1995, *WM* 1198 (1995) 1201 *et seq*; see also Rechtbank van Koophandel, Brussels, 6 May 1993, *Pierreux NV (Belgium) v Transportmaschinen Handelshaus GmbH (Germany),* XXII YBCA 631 (1997). For a different view see Kirchner and Marriot, "International Arbitration in the Aftermath of Socialism - The Example of the Berlin Court of Arbitration", 10(1) *Int'l Arb* 5 (1991); also, in relation to the changes in Russia, see the decision of the Austrian Oberster Gerichtshof, 30 November 1994, XXII *YBCA* 628 (1997), considering the newly formed Court of Arbitration at the Chamber of Commerce and Industry of the Russian Federation to be the legitimate successor; see also Cour d'appel Paris, 25 March 1999, *SA Caviar Petrossian v Société OAO Vneshintorg*, 127 Clunet 66 (2000) note Kahn, where the parties had confirmed the jurisdiction of the tribunal.

to the breach of contract which is the issue in dispute.[48] The opposite view is taken by German courts, which have consistently held that the lack of funding renders an arbitration agreement "incapable of being performed." [49] Since no legal aid is available in arbitration proceedings the courts have held that it might result in a denial of justice to force a party which lacks the necessary funds to arbitrate. According to a recent decision of the Bundesgerichtshof that is so even where that party at an earlier stage has objected to court proceedings suggested by the other party.[50]

(c) Standard of review of arbitration agreement

14-49 It is an open question whether courts should engage in a complete review of the existence and validity of the arbitration clause at any time, regardless of whether the arbitration tribunal has already determined the issue. The other options are to defer review of the jurisdiction question until the post-award stage when either an appeal or challenge against the award is filed or enforcement is resisted. Alternatively they could limit it to a *prima facie* review until the arbitration tribunal has ruled on its own jurisdiction.

14-50 The advantage of a court dealing with the question of jurisdiction at an early stage is certainty. The parties do not have to wait for months or years for a final decision on the validity of the arbitration agreement. Furthermore, parties do not have to engage in arbitration proceedings which, in the end, may prove futile if the court dealing with the issue at a later stage denies the existence of a valid arbitration clause.

14-51 The disadvantage of this approach is that it provides the opportunity for a party to abuse court proceedings to delay and obstruct the arbitration. Though arbitrators are, according to modern laws, not required to stay the arbitration while court proceedings are pending,[51] in some cases they will feel it is necessary to do so.[52] Most arbitrators want to avoid a situation where, after considerable

---

48 See, *e.g.*, *Janos Paczy v Haendler & Natermann GmbH* [1981] 1 Lloyd's Rep 302 (CA); for further references see Russell *on Arbitration*, para 7-015.

49 Germany, Bundesgerichtshof, 30 January 1964, *BGHZ* 41, 104, 107 *et seq*; Bundesgerichtshof, 21 November 1968, *BGHZ* 51, 79, 82; Bundesgerichtshof, 10 April 1980, *BGHZ* 77, 65.

50 Bundesgerichtshof, 14 September 2000, 55 *Betriebs-Berater* 2330 (2000).

51 See, *e.g.*, Model Law Article 8(2) which provides that where court proceedings have been initiated, "arbitral proceedings may nevertheless be commenced or continued, and an award may be made, while the issue is pending before the court".

52 The Swiss Supreme Court has expressed the opinion that the first authority seized, court or arbitration tribunal, should decide the validity of the arbitration agreement and the other should

time and money has been spent, the court decides that there is no basis for jurisdiction.[53]

14-52 According to Article 6 Model Law, and comparable provisions in a number of modern arbitration laws,[54] appeals or challenges against awards, or actions for enforcement, can only be brought in certain designated courts. The idea behind these efforts to centralise all arbitration related disputes is to create specialised courts with experience and knowledge of international arbitration. These efforts would be rendered futile to a certain degree if each otherwise competent court were to rule on the validity and existence of an arbitration agreement whenever an action on the merits is brought before it. By contrast, if that review of the tribunal's jurisdiction is postponed until the post-award stage only the designated specialised courts will decide on the issue.

14-53 One drawback of the last solution is that a final decision on the jurisdiction of the tribunal may only be rendered after a considerable amount of time and money has been spent. In particular, if the courts are required to refer to arbitration those cases where the invalidity of the arbitration agreement is fairly obvious, a recalcitrant defendant may abuse the arbitration process to delay payment due and to exert pressure on a financially stressed party. This problem is considerably limited if the courts can at least review the *prima facie* existence of a valid arbitration agreement with a full review at the post award stage. In addition, the amount of time and money potentially wasted can be limited if the tribunal renders a partial award on its jurisdiction at an early stage. This award can be challenged in the courts before the arbitration proceedings on the merits continue.

14-54 The approaches adopted by international conventions and national laws follow all these possibilities. It is often unclear whether courts called upon to decide a dispute on the merits should at a pre-award stage only verify the *prima facie* existence and validity of the arbitration clause, or can engage in a complete review of the issue. This is less of a problem with rules which contain limits on

---

stay its proceedings until the issue was determined: 14 May 2001, *Formento de Construcciones y Contratos S A Y v Colon Container Terminal SA*, Int ALR N-28 (2001).

53 The German legislator, when adopting Article 8(2) Model Law, assumed that in most cases the arbitrator will stay the arbitration unless the obvious purpose of the court proceedings is to delay the proceedings, *BT-Drs* 13/5274, 38; see also Hußlein-Stich, *Das UNCITRAL-Modellgesetz über die internationale Handelsschiedsgerichtsbarkeit* (Carl Heymanns 1990), 50.

54 See, *e.g.*, Germany, ZPO section 1062; Sweden, Arbitration Act section 56; England, Arbitration Act 1996 section 105.

the extent of the pre-award review of the arbitration agreement by courts.[55] Most rules, however, do not contain such limits, but in line with Article 8 Model Law or Article II(3) New York Convention provide that a court must refer the parties to arbitration unless it finds that the arbitration agreement is "null and void, inoperative or incapable of being performed." This wording seems to imply that the courts can engage in a full trial of the existence, validity and effectiveness of the arbitration agreement. However, in some jurisdictions a restrictive interpretation has been given to this provision.

14-55 One of the more restrictive provisions relating to pre-award court review is Article 1458 French Code of Civil Procedure:

> If a dispute pending before an arbitral tribunal on the basis of an arbitration agreement is brought before a state court, it shall declare itself incompetent. If the dispute is not yet before an arbitral tribunal, the state court shall also declare itself incompetent, unless the arbitration agreement is manifestly null and void. In neither case may the state court declare itself incompetent at its own motion.

14-56 The French Cour de cassation has interpreted this provision strictly. If arbitration proceedings were already pending, courts cannot even engage in a review of the *prima facie* existence of a valid arbitration agreement if the defendant in an action on the merits challenged the jurisdiction.[56] For the cases where the dispute is not yet pending before an arbitration tribunal, the Cour de cassation adopted a very strict standard as to when an arbitration agreement can be considered to be "manifestly null and void", thereby limiting the possibility of state courts assuming jurisdiction.[57]

14-57 An express restriction against the review of the existence of an arbitration agreement, except on a *prima facie* level, is also provided for in the European Convention. Article VI(3) provides

> Where either party to an arbitration agreement has initiated arbitration proceedings before any resort is had to a court, courts of Contracting States subsequently asked to deal with the same subject-matter between the same parties or with the question

---

55 See, *e.g.*, European Convention Article VI(3) or France, NCPC Article 1458.

56 Cour de cassation, 10 May 1995, *Coprodag v Dame Bohin*, Rev Arb 617 (1995), with note Gaillard (manifest nullity does not justify a declaration that the tribunal has no jurisdiction).

57 Cour de cassation, 21 May 1997, *Renault v V 2000 (formerly Jaguar France)*, Rev Arb 537 (1997) with note Gaillard; see also the decision in Cour de cassation, 26 June 2001, *American Bureau of Shipping* reported by Gaillard, "The Negative Effect of Competence-Competence", 17(1) *Mealey's* IAR 27 (2002).

> whether the arbitration agreement was non-existent or null and void or had lapsed, shall stay their ruling on the arbitrator's jurisdiction until the arbitral award is made, *unless they have good and substantial reasons to the contrary*. [Emphasis added.]

14-58 A "good and substantial reason" exists if there is obviously no valid arbitration agreement. This will be in exceptional circumstances and not in every case where the jurisdiction of the court is challenged. Article VI(3) presupposes that the arbitration proceedings have already been initiated but says nothing about the situation when this is not the case.

14-59 Under Swiss law the degree of court review on the existence of a valid arbitration clause raised as a defence against the court's jurisdiction depends on the seat of the arbitration tribunal. Article 7(b) Swiss PIL provides that a court shall decline jurisdiction unless it finds "that the arbitration agreement is null and void, inoperative or incapable of being performed." This seems to imply a full review of the existence of a valid arbitration clause. Nevertheless the Swiss Federal Court has decided that where the tribunal has its seat in Switzerland the courts should limit themselves to verifying the *prima facie* existence of a valid arbitration agreement. A full review should only take place at the post-award stage irrespective of whether or not arbitration proceedings have already been initiated.[58] If the tribunal has its seat outside Switzerland the Swiss courts in an action on the merits before them can fully review the existence of a valid arbitration clause when their jurisdiction is challenged. The reason for this is that a post-award review of the arbitrator's jurisdiction in setting aside procedures is not possible.

14-60 A limited review of the arbitrator's jurisdiction at the pre-award stage is also favoured in some of the countries which adopted the Model Law. For example, in Canada the Ontario Court of Justice in *Rio Algom v Sammi Steel* held that courts are limited to deciding whether the arbitration clause is "null and void, inoperative or incapable of being performed" while questions on the scope of the

---

[58] Tribunal Fédéral, 16 January 1995, *Compagnie de Navigation et de Transports SA v MSC Mediterranean Shipping Company SA*, 121 III ATF/BGE 38, English summary in *ASA Bulletin* 488 (1996); Tribunal Fédéral, 29 April 1996, *Fondation M v Banque X,* ATF 122 III 139, *ASA Bulletin* 527 (1996) 530 *et seq*, note Mayer 364; but see the decision of the Tribunal Fédéral, 14 May 2001, in *Formento de Construcciones y Contratas SA v Colon Container Terminal SA*, Int ALR N-28 [2001], where the court decided that there is no basis for the proposition that an arbitration tribunal should have priority in deciding on its jurisdiction.

arbitration agreement, its interpretation and whether a certain dispute is covered by it should be decided by the arbitration tribunal.[59]

14-61 By contrast other Model Law countries interpret Article 8 or the provisions based on it to allow for a full review of the existence of a valid arbitration agreement.[60] This is in line with the drafting history of the Model Law. The drafters rejected the proposal to add the term "manifestly" before "null and void" since this would have limited the court to a *prima facie* finding. It was, however, felt that a full review would be more appropriate[61]

14-62 In Germany this right is not affected by the limitation contained in section 1032(2) ZPO, according to which the special actions for the determination of the arbitration tribunal's jurisdiction can only be initiated until the tribunal is constituted.[62] The legislative materials make clear that this limitation only relates to the special action and not actions on the merits where the arbitration defences are invoked.[63]

14-63 Similarly, in England, the Arbitration Act 1996 section 32 allows only a limited right to apply to the courts for a determination of a preliminary point of jurisdiction. The limitation does not affect the right of the courts under section 9 to stay proceedings on the merits. Though courts when facing a contested application for a stay of proceedings under Section 9 have referred the parties to arbitration for a full trial of the existence and validity of the arbitration agreement they are by no means obliged to do so. Section 6.2 of the Civil Procedure Rules Practice Direction 49G, which regulates what courts have to do when a stay is

---

[59] *Rio Algom Ltd v Sammi Steel Co Ltd*, XVIII YBCA 166 (1993) 170 *et seq* (Ontario Court of Justice, 1 March 1991); *ABN Amro Bank Canada v Krupp Mak Maschinenbau GmbH and others*, 7 May 1996, 6 ADRLJ 37 (1997) (trial court not obliged to decide on validity of arbitration agreement and should not do so if issue relates also to merits); see also *Pacific International Lines (Pte) Ltd v Tsinlien Metals and Minerals Co Ltd*, XVIII YBCA 180 (1993) 185 *et seq* (Hong Kong Supreme Court, 30 July 1992), allowing only a *prima facie* review in cases where the appointment of an arbitrator is sought.

[60] This is the position under the new Spanish law, see Fröhlingsdorf, "Neue Entwicklungen im spanischen Schiedsverfahrensrecht", 1 *RPS* 2 (2001); the same applies for New Zealand see District Court of Auckland, *Clarence Holdings Ltd v Prendos Ltd* [2000] DC Reg 404.

[61] See Holtzmann and Neuhaus, *Model Law*, 303.

[62] Section 1032(2) provides "Prior to the constitution of the arbitral tribunal, an application may be made to the court to determine whether or not arbitration is admissible."

[63] See *BT-Drs* 13/5274, 38.

required and the validity and scope of the arbitration agreement are in issue, provides that "the Court may determine that question."[64]

14-64 In the United States courts have interpreted the almost identical Article II(3) New York Convention in a way which allows for a full review of the existence of a valid arbitration agreement. This is also true if the issue is raised as a defence in an action on the merits in state courts.[65]

(d) "Referral" to arbitration

14-65 Considerable differences exist as to what is required from the courts if the defendant invokes a valid arbitration agreement. According to the New York Convention, the Model Law and a number of national laws the courts, have to "refer the parties to arbitration."[66] Other arbitration laws require the courts to decline jurisdiction[67], while under German law courts have to declare themselves as not having jurisdiction.[68] Common law countries traditionally require the courts to "stay the proceedings."[69]

14-66 These differences are more the result of national traditions than of a different approach to arbitration. For example, English courts which "only" have to stay their jurisdiction and are not obliged "to refer the parties to arbitration" go as far as issuing anti-suit injunctions to enforce arbitration agreements.[70] Furthermore, even where the law requires the courts to "refer the parties to arbitration" they do, in general, just stay or dismiss their own proceedings. Contrary to the express statutory provisions courts do not issue directives imposing arbitration on the parties.[71] It is rarely practicable to compel the parties to participate in an arbitration.[72] Often a referral may not even be possible since

64 For case law and the various options open to an English Court when faced with a dispute as to the validity of an arbitration clause see Merkin, *Arbitration Act*, 38.

65 This is even more so when a party applies to compel arbitration; see *Sandvik AB v Advent International Corp*, 15(7) Mealey's IAR 4 (2000), XXVI YBCA 961 (2001) 968 (3rd Cir).

66 See also Russian Federation, Arbitration Law Article 8.

67 See, *e.g.*, France, NCPC Article 1458; Switzerland, PIL Article 7; Netherlands, CCP Article 1022; Belgium, Judicial Code Article 1679.

68 Germany, ZPO section 1032.

69 See England, Arbitration Act section 9; US, FAA section 3.

70 See, *e.g.*, *Aggeliki Charis Compania Maritima SA v Pagnan SpA (The Angelic Grace)* [1995] 1 *Lloyd's Rep* 87; *XL Insurance Ltd v Owens Corning* [2000] 2 Lloyd's Rep 500.

71 Van den Berg, *New York Convention*, 129 *et seq.*

72 See the special action available in US, FAA section 4.

no arbitration tribunal has yet been constituted to which the case could be referred.

14-67 While under all laws the court proceedings must be halted when a valid arbitration clause is invoked, differences exist as to the status of the court proceedings. Under German law the proceedings are terminated by the court's procedural judgment declaring itself incompetent. Consequently the court has to engage in a full review of the validity of the arbitration clause. The report explaining the new law justifies this deviation from the Model Law with the need for legal certainty as to the status of the courts proceedings.[73]

14-68 A different solution exists in countries where the law requires the court only to stay the action. The court proceedings are not terminated but merely halted until a decision of the arbitration tribunal. The court proceedings may then revive. Apart from the different standards of review of the validity of the arbitration agreement these differences have little practical impact. The termination of the court proceedings does not prevent the courts from intervening at a later stage in support of the arbitration, or the review or enforcement of the final award.

2.2. Special Actions to Determine Jurisdiction

14-69 Some national laws expressly provide for special proceedings on preliminary points of jurisdiction. German and English law, for example, give the parties the right to apply to the courts for a preliminary ruling on the issue while US law allows for actions compelling arbitration.

14-70 Under German law such an application to the courts for a decision on the admissibility of arbitration proceedings can only be made before the tribunal has been constituted.[74] However, no consent by the other party is required. Parties have made use of this special procedure with a view to preventing the other side from starting arbitration proceedings.[75]

---

[73] *BT-Drs* 13/5274, 38.

[74] Germany, ZPO section 1032(2).

[75] See, *e.g.*, Oberlandesgericht Hamm, 10 February 1999, *RPS* 2/1999, Supplement 11 *Betriebsberater* 38/1999, 10, note Bredow.

14-71 In England applications can be made even after the tribunal has been constituted. However, they have to meet strict requirements as a party may only seek an interim court ruling if the application is made

> (a)...with the agreement in writing of all the other parties to the proceedings, or ...
> (b)...with the permission of the tribunal and the court is satisfied-
> (i) that the determination of the question is likely to produce substantial savings in costs,
> (ii) that the application was made without delay, and
> (iii) that there is good reason why the matter should be decided by the court.76

14-72 In the light of these requirements the scope of application of this special procedure is fairly limited. One of the few situations where the requirements may be fulfilled and a tribunal might consider submitting the question of its jurisdiction to the court is, when it is likely that any decision the tribunal on its jurisdiction will be challenged, so that court proceedings are inevitable.

14-73 In the US a party to an arbitration agreement can apply to the courts under sections 4, 206 or 303 Federal Arbitration Act for an order to compel the other party to proceed to arbitration. To decide whether such an order should be granted the courts will have to determine the validity of the arbitration agreement.[77] In these actions it is obvious that the court must engage in a full review of the existence and validity of an arbitration agreement before it can order a party to go to arbitration.

14-74 In the majority of arbitration laws no special court proceedings for a declaration as to the non-existence or invalidity of the arbitration agreement is possible. As a consequence no declaratory relief can be sought. This is particularly apparent in countries where the arbitration law includes provisions like Article 5 Model Law. This provides that on all issues in relation to arbitration, courts only have the powers set out in the arbitration law. Parties have to wait until the tribunal has either rendered a preliminary award on jurisdiction or until the final award is rendered to ask the courts to review the tribunal's decision.

---

[76] England, Arbitration Act Section 32(2); for the exceptional character of the remedy see also the DAC Report, para 141, 147; Merkin, *Arbitration Act*, 79.

[77] On the issues to be decided by the court see *Prima Paint Corp v Flood & Conklin Mfg Co*, 388 US 395, 403-404 (1967) (Section 4); *Sedco, Inc v Petroleos Mexicanos Nat'l Oil Corp*, 767 F 2d 1140, 1145 (5th Cir 1985) (Section 206); see also Roth, Wulff and Cooper, *The Alternative Dispute Resolution Practice Guide* (Lawyers Cooperative Publishing 1998), para 6-1.

2.3. Actions in Support of Arbitration

14-75 Questions on the validity of arbitration agreements also arise in actions in support of arbitration. Refusing to cooperate in the appointment of a tribunal is often based on a party's view that there is no valid arbitration agreement. In court proceedings for the appointment of an arbitrator the defaulting party will invariably invoke the invalidity of the arbitration agreement and ask the court not to appoint the arbitrator.

14-76 Whether, and if so according to which standard, courts will review the arbitrators' jurisdiction in such cases is regulated in certain national arbitration laws. Where the lack of a valid agreement must be "manifest" the provision only allows for a *prima facie* review of the existence of an arbitration agreement.[78] For example, section 18 Swedish Arbitration Act provides

> Where a party has requested that the District Court appoint an arbitrator pursuant to section 12, third paragraph or sections 14 or 17, the Court may reject the request on the grounds that the arbitration is not legally permissible only where such is manifest.

14-77 A similar provision is found in the French domestic arbitration law.[79] To what extent this provision also applies to international arbitrations is disputed. The most convincing view is that the courts at that stage can review the *prima facie* existence of a valid arbitration agreement but not whether such an agreement is adequate for the purpose of constituting the tribunal.[80]

14-78 However, even without such an express provision courts have examined the existence and validity of arbitration agreements in actions for appointment of arbitrators when it was challenged by one of the parties.[81] It appears that the courts in this respect will engage in a full review of the existence and validity of

---

[78] The same standard of review is provided for under Swiss Arbitration Law, PIL Article 179(3); see Peter and Legler, in Berti (ed), *International Arbitration in Switzerland*, Article 179 para 35.

[79] Article 1444(3) Code of Civil Procedure provides

> If the arbitration clause is manifestly null and void or insufficient to constitute an arbitration tribunal, the President shall so determine and declare that there is no basis for appointment.

[80] Fouchard Gaillard Goldman *on International Commercial Arbitration*, paras 851-855.

[81] See, *e.g.*, Supreme Court of India, 4 April 200, *Wellington Associates Ltd v Kirit Mehta*, Int ALR N-52 (2000); Germany, Bayerisches Oberstes Landesgericht, 4 June 1999, *Betriebs-Berater* 1785 (1999); Bayerisches Oberstes Landesgericht, 28 February 2000, *RPS* (2/2000) 19, *DIS Materialien* VII (2001) 37.

the arbitration clause.[82] They adopt the same standard of review as applied in proceedings on the merits where the defendant, alleging the existence of a valid arbitration agreement, challenges the jurisdiction of the court. However, in proceedings in support of arbitration there is less need to engage in a full review. Unlike in proceedings on the merits the decision will have no *res judicata* effect which could exclude further proceedings in the court.

14-79 The Bavarian Higher Regional Court went further and raised the issue of the tribunal's jurisdiction on its own volition when asked to appoint an arbitrator in a case involving the arbitration clause of the German Football Association. It provided for all disputes arising between any member and the association to be resolved by an arbitration tribunal set up in advance by the association.[83] The Football Association started arbitration against one of their members claiming damages arising in connection with a sale of land by that member. The member applied to the courts for the appointment of new arbitrators since the claimant had a prevailing influence on the composition of the tribunal. The court denied this application since it found that the dispute at issue was not covered by the arbitration clause. This point had not been raised by the respondent who only wanted the composition of the tribunal changed.

14-80 Such an attitude does interfere too much with the autonomy of the parties. Unless the invalidity of an arbitration agreement is based on a lack of arbitrability courts should not deal with the lack of jurisdiction question on their own volition. Even if at the time of the court action, the underlying dispute is not covered by the arbitration agreement there is still the possibility that the parties may nevertheless submit the dispute to arbitration. Any steps on the merits taken by a party can be considered to be a submission to arbitration.

---

[82] See for Germany, Lachmann, *Handbuch*, para 570 *et seq* with further references. To the same effect, see the decision of the Supreme Court of India, *Wellington Associates Ltd v Kirit Mehta*, Int ALR N-52 (2000).

[83] Bayerisches Oberstes Landesgericht, 15 December 1999, *RPS* 16 (2/2000), VII *DIS Materialien* 49 (2001).

Chapter 15

Arbitration and the Courts

15-1 By entering into an arbitration agreement parties express their intention that all disputes between them be referred to and settled by arbitration. This choice at the same time manifests a decision against dispute resolution by the competent state courts. With the acceptance of party autonomy the level of court intervention has significantly diminished over the years. The general trend is towards limiting court intervention to those cases where it is either necessary to support the arbitration process or required by public policy considerations.

15-2 Judicial and effectively state respect for the parties' agreement to arbitrate means that no court proceedings on the merits of the dispute can be brought before courts and that all disputes covered by that agreement are referred to arbitration. There are, however, some situations where court intervention and assistance is needed. For example, courts may be asked to assist with the appointment or removal of arbitrators, and the collection of evidence. They may also be asked to order supporting or protective measures where the arbitrators lack coercive power. Ultimately, state courts have to give effect to and enforce the arbitration award if it is not complied with voluntarily.

15-3 In addition to their supportive function, courts may also intervene to guarantee that the minimum requirements of procedural fairness are fulfilled and exercise a supervisory function. The courts may remove an arbitrator for his lack of impartiality or may annul an award based on unfair procedures.

15-4 This chapter describes the (1) general approach that has developed and which now prevails on court intervention, and (2) specific areas of court involvement during the arbitration process.[1]

1. General Approach to Court Involvement

15-5 In most countries the attitude taken towards arbitration as a voluntary dispute resolution mechanism and to court intervention in arbitration has changed considerably over the last century. Courts have moved from strong scepticism resulting in extensive judicial intervention in the arbitration process or the non-enforcement of arbitration agreements to a position in favour of arbitration giving priority to party autonomy and eschewing intervention.

15-6 English law provides a good example of this evolution. Early English arbitration law developed devices to make arbitration agreements enforceable which received statutory recognition in the Arbitration Act 1698.[2] In return, however, the courts retained a large degree of control over the arbitration process. This is evidenced in particular by the notorious special case stated

---

1 Interventions which may have a supervisory character for one party have a supportive character for the other. Enforcement of awards, for example, has a supportive function in so far as the state is lending its coercive powers to the arbitration but at the same time the reasons to resist enforcement allow for a certain supervision of the proceedings.

2 Section 1 allowed the parties to agree to make their submission of an existing dispute to arbitration into a "rule of court", so that any breach of the agreement was considered to be a contempt of court and was subject to fines. For a description of arbitration in the pre-1854 Act see the reprint of a letter from Francis Russell Esq (author of Russell *on Arbitration*) to Lord Brougham & Vaux in 13 *Arb Int* 253 (1997); see also Samuel, "Arbitration Statutes in England and the US", 8 *ADRLJ* 2 (1999) 5-7.

procedure which was introduced by Section 4 1854 Common Law Procedure Act and was retained and developed in the Arbitration Act 1950. It vested the court with the power to require referral of any question of law it thought ought to be decided by it.[3] Essentially it allowed for an effective appeal on any relevant point of law. This case stated procedure could not be excluded.[4]

15-7 In light of strong international criticism the special case procedure was significantly curtailed by the Arbitration Act 1979.[5] In particular parties were allowed to exclude the procedure in advance or, in cases concerning shipping, commodity and insurance, after the dispute had arisen. As a consequence any agreement of the parties on institutional rules, which contained a waiver of the right to judicial recourse, such as the ICC or LCIA rules, led to an exclusion of the case stated procedure.[6]

15-8 The Arbitration Act 1979 provided further that when the parties were silent on the question of appeal, as is the case in the vast majority of cases, an appeal was only possible with permission of the court. The House of Lords in *Pioneer Shipping v BTP Tioxide (The "Nema")*[7] and *Antaios Compania Naviera SA v Salen Rederierna AB (The "Antaios")*[8] set down strict guidelines as to the exercise of this discretion which clearly show the change in approach to court intervention. The judges distinguished between one-off cases and other cases which involve regularly recurring legal problems. In one-off cases court permission would only be granted if it could be shown that the arbitrators were "obviously wrong" while for regularly recurring issues it was sufficient if the decision by the arbitrator was "probably wrong".[9] In dealing with section 3 of the 1979 Act Lord Diplock held that it

> ...gives effect to a reversal of public policy in relation to arbitration as it had been expounded more than half a century before in *Czarnikow v Roth, Schmidt & Co.*

---

3 Arbitration Act 1950 section 21.

4 See *Czarnikow v Roth Schmidt and Co* [1922] 2 KB 478; Samuel, "Arbitration Statutes in England and the US", 8 ADRLJ 2 (1999) 19-20.

5 For a summary of the criticism see also the "Mustill Report", 6 *Arb Int* 3 (1990) paras 17-22.

6 Provisions like Article 13(1) ICC Rules 1988 excluding any right of recourse were considered to be such an exclusion agreement; see *Arab African Energy Corp Ltd v Olieprodukten Nederland BV* [1983] 2 Lloyd's Rep 419.

7 [1982] AC 724; [1981] 2 Lloyd's Rep 239.

8 [1985] AC 191; [1984] 2 Lloyd's Rep 235.

9 In matters of public importance, such as EC law, leave to appeal should be granted if the arbitrator was "arguably wrong"; see *Bulk Oil (Zug) AG v Sun International Ltd and Sun Oil Trading Co,* [1983] 2 Lloyd's Rep 587.

> Exclusion agreements, which oust the statutory jurisdiction of the High Court to supervise the way in which arbitrators apply the law in reaching their decision in individual cases are recognized as being no longer contrary to public policy"[10]

15-9 The House of Lords decision was based on a clear "parliamentary intention to give effect to the turn of the tide in favour of the finality in arbitral awards" when deciding between the two conflicting principles of finality and meticulous legal accuracy.[11]

15-10 The Arbitration Act 1996 finally completely abolished the special case stated procedure. It allows appeal on questions of English law in very limited circumstances. Furthermore, powers which were originally reserved for the courts, for example in the area of the administration of evidence, were transferred to the arbitration tribunal.[12] As a result under English law "courts nowadays generally only intervene in order to support rather than displace the arbitral process."[13]

15-11 Although the special case procedure was primarily an English peculiarity a comparable development towards lesser court intervention has taken place in most other countries. Supervisory court intervention has the potential of seriously disrupting the arbitration process and impeding the parties' quest for a speedy dispute resolution. It is a common feature of recent arbitration legislation to limit the scope for court intervention. The effect has been that tribunals are given wider powers by statute and can be given further powers by the parties. The traditional authority of the courts has been limited in some cases completely excluded or at least made dependent on agreement by the parties.

15-12 This approach is illustrated by Article 5 Model Law which states that "no court shall intervene except where so provided in this Law."[14] This general rule

---

[10] [1981] 2 Lloyd's Rep 239, 246.

[11] *Ibid*, 243; see also *Antaios Compania Naviera SA v Salen Rederierna AB ("The Antaios")*, [1984] 2 Lloyd's Rep 235, 237.

[12] See, *e.g.*, the courts' powers under the Arbitration Act 1950 section 12, transferred to tribunals according to section 38(4) and (5) Arbitration Act; see Merkin, *Arbitration Act*, 89.

[13] DAC Report, para 22.

[14] Article 5. Also in Hong Kong, Arbitration Ordinance section 34(C); Germany, ZPO section 1026, where the law, in sections 1032(2), 1034(2) and 1050, however, provides for additional types of court intervention; Russian Federation, Arbitration Law Article 5; India, Arbitration and Conciliation Ordinance 1996 section 5.

excluding court intervention where not explicitly permitted is also followed in national arbitration laws which are not based on the Model Law.[15]

15-13 Court intervention is normally possible only in two situations: where expressly provided for in the arbitration law, or where the issue is not covered by the law. In the latter situation court intervention may be possible as a default mechanism for the support of the arbitration proceedings. For example, the Model Law addresses the issue of interim measures by the tribunal without providing for a power of the courts to enforce the measures granted. Nevertheless it is widely accepted that courts can enforce interim measures since the regulation in the Model Law only extends to the granting of those measures while their enforcement is not regulated.[16] In some cases it may be difficult to determine whether a particular issue is regulated by the arbitration law. On the whole the approach will increase certainty for the parties, since once an issue is governed by the relevant arbitration law it is no longer possible to rely on general residual powers claimed by the courts.[17]

15-14 In addition to limiting court intervention, the laws often include features with the intention of minimising the disruption that may be caused by a judicial intervention. Modern laws provide a very limited or no right of appeal against court decisions rendered in the context of arbitration. Under the Model Law[18] decisions relating to the appointment or challenge of arbitrators or concerning the arbitrator's decision on his jurisdiction cannot be appealed.[19] These restrictions prevent court proceedings in support of the arbitration becoming a case on its own.

---

15 See England, Arbitration Act section 1(c); see also the decision by the Austrian Oberster Gerichtshof, 4 December 1994, 4 OB 1542/94, XXII *YBCA* 263 (1997).

16 Holtzmann and Neuhaus, *Model Law*, 218 with a list of issues not covered by the Model Law.

17 Chukwumerije, "Judicial Supervision of Commercial Arbitration: The English Arbitration Act of 1996", 15 *Arb Int* 171 (1999) 176. A famous example for a residual power not foreseen in the relevant English arbitration legislation was the decision of the House of Lords in *Channel Tunnel Group v Balfour Beatty* [1993] AC 334.

18 Model Law Articles 11(5), 13(3), 14(1), and 16(3).

19 The same applies to a similar or even greater extent for a number of national arbitration laws in Model Law countries as well as other countries. See, *e.g.*, Germany, ZPO section 1064 which contains even further restrictions; for limitations on the grounds which can be invoked in an appeal against a decision recognising an award see Bundesgerichtshof, 15 July 1999, *BGHZ* 142, 204, 205-6; see also Kröll, "Das neue deutsche Schiedsrecht vor staatlichen Gerichten: Entwicklungslinien und Tendenzen", *DIS-Materialien* VII, 65, 70; France, NCPC Article 1457. In England, appeals against decisions usually require leave for appeal. See, *e.g.*, Arbitration Act sections 17(4), 18(5), 21(6), 24(6), 25(5), 32(5), 42(2), 44(7), 67(4), 68(4), and 69(8).

15-15 Another feature to limit court intervention is to, give jurisdiction to a higher court in the legal system in respect of issues relating to arbitration rather than a court of first instance.[20] Furthermore, arbitration laws often provide that the arbitration proceedings may be commenced or continued while an action in court is pending. According to Article 13(3) Model Law, for example, a challenge of an arbitrator in the courts does not prevent the arbitration tribunal from continuing the proceedings and rendering an award.[21] This is to prevent court interventions being used solely as a delaying tactic.

15-16 In most arbitration laws court intervention is at least to a certain extent dependent on the connection a case has with that particular country. Under the Model Law and a number of other modern laws the granting of supportive measures, such as appointment of arbitrators, as well as the exercise of a supervisory task, such as the annulment of awards, is dependent on the place of arbitration being located in that country.[22] Other relevant factors for court intervention can be nationality of the parties, the law governing the arbitration and domicile or place of business of the parties.[23]

15-17 A tendency to make court intervention dependent on the existing connections with the country can also be found in case law. Judges have frequently seen the strength of the connections with a country as an important factor in the exercise of their discretion to intervene.[24] The fewer the connections with the forum the lesser the inclination of a national court to intervene. For example, what interest has an English court to intervene in an arbitration in

---

[20] See, *e.g.*, Germany, ZPO section 1062; France, NCPC Article 1486 (appeal and setting aside procedure).

[21] Holtzmann and Neuhaus, *Model Law*, 407; further examples from the Model Law which can be found in a comparable way in other laws are Article 8(2) (actions on the merits in state courts); and Article 16(3) (appeal against an interim award on jurisdiction).

[22] See Model Law Article 1(2); Germany, ZPO section 1025(1); Switzerland, PIL Article 176(1); England, Arbitration Act section 2; Netherlands, CCP Article 1073(1). See also the interpretation given to the relevant provisions of Indian law by the Delhi High Court, 5 July 2000, *Marriot International Inc v Ansal Hotels Ltd*, 4 Int ALR N-19 (2001), which held that interim relief could only be granted in relation to arbitration proceedings with their seat in India.

[23] Under German Law, ZPO section 1025(3) the intervention of courts in cases where the seat has not yet been determined depends on the habitual residence of at least one of the parties in Germany; see also Netherlands, CPP Article 1073(2).

[24] See *Bank Mellat v Helliniki Techniki SA* [1984] QB 291 (CA).

France between a German and a Swiss party when the dispute has no connection to England?[25]

15-18 The previous Belgian law went a step further: it restricted Belgian interest to where a Belgian party or someone carrying on business in Belgium was involved. Specifically, it expressly excluded the possibility for an action for annulment of an award rendered in Belgium if neither the parties nor the dispute had any connection to Belgium.[26] Today the place of arbitration is considered generally to be a sufficient connecting factor.

15-19 Another factor which influences the exercise of discretion in court intervention is the type of measures requested. Are the measures sought available under most laws or are they based more on the character and peculiarities of local procedural law? In the latter case courts have been more reluctant to make use of their powers as this may have conflicted with the parties expectations. [27] When selecting the place of arbitration few parties actually look to the particularities of local law. The choice is mainly based on considerations such as practical convenience and neutrality of the venue, its acceptability to both parties and issues of enforceability. Only where it is clear that the parties have actually made an informed choice based on the particularities of the local law, should the local court make use of its powers of intervention. In all other cases courts should eschew becoming involved in accordance with the general practice of arbitration and the legitimate expectations of the parties.

---

[25] The supervisory powers granted by the Arbitration Act depend on the seat of arbitration being in England while some supportive powers may also be exercised if the seat is outside of England. In those cases the connection to England is an important issue in the decision whether or not to exercise the given powers.

[26] Belgium, old Code Judiciaire Article 1717, recently revised in light of the benefits which may arise out of court intervention. See also Switzerland, PIL Article 192(1) according to which the parties can exclude the possibility of challenging an award if none of them has is domicile in Switzerland; the same provision can be found in Sweden, Arbitration Act 1999 section 51; for the benefits of courts supervision see Park, "Control Mechanisms in the Development of a Modern Lex Mercatoria", in Carbonneau (ed), *Lex Mercatoria*, 145 *et seq.*

[27] See, *e.g.*, *Bank Mellat v Helleniki Techniki SA* [1984] QB 291 *et seq*, where the power to order security for costs was not exercised since it was an international arbitration under ICC Rules; this is even more so when the place of arbitration is in a different country; see *ContiChem PG v Parsons Shipping Co Ltd*, 229 F 3d 426 (2d Cir 11 Oct 2000): The US Court of Appeals for the Second Circuit affirmed a district court holding that a New York rule providing for pre-arbitration attachment (order pursuant 9 USC section 1 *et seq* and NY CPLR 7502(c)) is limited to domestic arbitrations and that it cannot be used to provide provisional measures in aid of a maritime arbitration in London arising from an alleged breach of charter party. See also 12 *WAMR* 20 (2001).

15-20 There are many stages, throughout the arbitration process, for parties to seek the intervention and support of the court. At each stage, the court must take account of party autonomy, the help or supervision sought and the mandatory law of the jurisdiction. Above all, the court must remember its intervention should not violate the parties' expressed intention to submit their disputes to arbitration.

2. Specific Areas of Court Involvements

2.1. Proceedings Concerning Validity of the Arbitration Agreement

15-21 A party may initiate court proceedings in an attempt to avoid arbitration proceedings either because it prefers or believes the courts will be to its advantage, or because it genuinely challenges the validity of the arbitration agreement. A crucial element in ensuring that arbitration proceedings can take place without court intervention is the obligation for courts not to hear actions on the merits. In all states party to the New York Convention there is a mandatory obligation, under public international law, for national courts to stay their proceedings and refer matters to the arbitration system selected by the parties.[28]

15-22 Differences exist concerning as to what extent the courts can at the pre-award stage review the existence of a valid arbitration agreement. The greatest limitations on court intervention at that stage is in the French law. There the arbitrator has a right of first decision and any court review is deferred to the post award stage. The majority of arbitration laws as well as the international conventions, however, do not go as far but allow at least a review of the *prima facie* existence of an arbitration agreement or even a complete review.

15-23 In addition some arbitration laws provide for a specific action to determine preliminary points of jurisdiction.[29] The narrow limits under which these rights exist prevent important issues from being decided by the courts contrary to the parties' agreement. The advantages of having an early and binding decision on the arbitrator's jurisdiction by a competent court counterbalance the intrusion on the competence of the arbitrator.

---

[28] New York Convention Article II(3).

[29] See, *e.g.*, England, Arbitration Act section 32; Germany, ZPO section 1032(2).

2.2. Anti-suit Injunctions

15-24 Closely related to the issue of jurisdiction are "anti-suit injunctions". These are national court orders used, especially in common law countries, either to protect the jurisdiction of the arbitration tribunal or to prevent the tribunal from assuming jurisdiction. Through such an injunction, operating *in personam* against the party to the action, a party can be ordered not to pursue court proceedings initiated in breach of an arbitration agreement.[30] By corollary, a party may be ordered not to take any further steps in arbitration if the court has decided that the arbitration agreement is invalid or ineffective.[31] Both types of orders are found in practice but they are granted only in limited circumstances.

(a) Injunctions restraining arbitration proceedings

15-25 Injunctions restraining the further conduct of arbitration proceedings are in general only granted where it is absolutely clear that the arbitration proceedings have been wrongly brought.[32] By contrast, these measures should not be granted where it is simply more convenient to hear the case in court, for example, because third parties can be joined or the tribunal does not have the power to dispose of all issues in dispute. In such cases the parties are bound by their arbitration agreement and a court should not interfere with it.[33]

15-26 These injunctions can be directed against the parties alone. They may, however, also be directed against the arbitrators, if the court granting the injunction has personal jurisdiction over them. They are then enjoined from hearing the case.[34] Parties or arbitrators continuing the proceedings despite an

---

[30] See, *e.g.*, the recent US decision *Smith Enron Cogeneration Limited Partnership, Inc et al v Smith Cogeneration International, Inc*, XXV YBCA 1088 (2000) para 30 *et seq* (2d Cir).

[31] See, *e.g.*, the injunctions granted by the Indonesian courts in connection with the arbitration proceedings in *Himpurna California Energy Ltd (Bermuda) v Republic of Indonesia*, XXV *YBCA* 11 (2000) 18 *et seq*; a motion for such an injunction was denied in the Dutch Courts see President Arrondissementsrechtbank, The Hague, 21 September 1999, *Republic of Indonesia v Himpurna California Energy Ltd*, XXV YBCA 469 (2000) para 8 *et seq*.

[32] Russell *on Arbitration*, para 7-024.

[33] See *Industry Chimiche Italia Centrale v Alexander G Tsavliris and Sons Maritime Co (The "Choko Star")* [1987] 1 Lloyd's Rep 508; but see *Nordin v Nutri/System Inc*, 897 F 2d 339 (8th Cir 1990). For other examples of US decisions restraining arbitration proceedings see Born, *International Commercial Arbitration*, 406.

[34] According to Russell *on Arbitration*, para 7-024 in the majority of cases the injunction is directed against the parties as well as against the arbitrators. See, *e.g.*, the unsuccessful application in Arrondissementsrechtbank, The Hague, 21 September 1999, *Republic of Indonesia v Himpurna California Energy Ltd (Bermuda) et al*, XXV YBCA 469 (2000).

award rendered in these proceedings will probably be unenforceable at least in the country where the injunction was granted.

15-27 In particular, Indian and Pakistani parties have been successful in convincing their courts to grant injunctions restraining arbitration proceedings.[35] These injunctions were not only granted in order to restrain arbitration proceedings but also to order a party not to continue enforcement of an award. That was the case in *ONGC v Western* where a tribunal having its seat in London had issued an award in favour of a US party. Since the arbitrators applied Indian law the Indian party started proceedings in India to have the award set aside and applied for an injunction ordering the American party not to enforce the award in the US. The Indian Supreme Court granted the injunction.[36]

(b) Injunctions restraining parallel court proceedings

15-28 More frequent are injunctions intended to prevent or restrain proceedings in courts in breach of an arbitration agreement. As their aim is to enforce an agreement between the parties, the courts are more willing to grant these measures. Such injunctions are typical where there are concurrent court proceedings in another country. These proceedings could frustrate the ongoing arbitration: they absorb resources in time and expense and lead to re-litigating the same issue. A judgment rendered may prevent the enforcement of the final award of the tribunal, if its findings are irreconcilable with the award.

15-29 The position taken on this issue by the English Courts can be found in the judgment of the Court of Appeal in *Aggeliki Charis Compania Maritima v*

---

[35] See the description of a number of those cases by Sir Michael Kerr, "Concord and Conflict in International Arbitration", 13 *Arb Int* 121 (1997) 136; Nariman, "Finality in India: the Impossible Dream", 10 *Arb Int* 373 (1994); for an account of the various injunctions issued against foreign investors in the *Hub-WAPDA* and the *Himpurna-Indonesia* arbitration see Cornell and Handley, "Himpurna and Hub: International Arbitration in Developing Countries", 15(9) *Mealey's IAR* 39 (2000); see also Canadian decision by Cour d'appel Quebec, 29 November 1999, *Lac D'Amiante du Canada LTÈE et 2858-0702 Québec Inc v Lac D'Amiante Québec LTÈE,* Int ALR N-6 (2000), where an injunction was granted to prevent a party from pursuing a counterclaim in arbitration for which it already had started court proceedings; see also the US decision in *General Electric Co v Deutz AG*, 13(10) Mealey's IAR C1 (1998).

[36] *Oil & Natural Gas Commission Ltd* v *Western Company of North America*, (1987) All India Rep SC 674. On this case see also the divergent views of Deshpande, "Jurisdiction Over 'Foreign' and 'Domestic' Awards in the New York Convention, 1958", 7 *Arb Int* 123 (1991); Tupman, "Staying Enforcement of Arbitral Awards under the New York Convention", 3 *Arb Int* 209 (1987).

Pagnan (The Angelic Grace). In explaining the general approach to be adopted the court held that

> where an injunction is sought to restrain a party from proceeding in a foreign Court in breach of an arbitration agreement governed by English law, the English Courts feel no diffidence in granting the injunction, provided that it is sought promptly and before the foreign proceedings are too far advanced. ... The justification for the grant of the injunction in either case is without it the plaintiff will be deprived of its contractual rights in a situation in which damages are manifestly an inadequate remedy. The jurisdiction is, of course, discretionary and is not exercised as a matter of course ...[37]

15-30 The court made it clear that, unlike in other types of anti-suit injunctions based on considerations of *forum non conveniens,* it would not use its discretion sparingly. The foreign action is contrary to an agreement of the parties and would deprive the applicant of its contractual right to arbitrate.[38] Where an English court has jurisdiction over the defendant the requirements for an anti-suit injunction are therefore that a valid arbitration agreement exists, an application is made without undue delay[39], the foreign action is not well advanced and there is no other good reason why the injunction should not be granted.[40]

15-31 A similar approach prevails in Australia[41] while in the US a slightly stricter test for antisuit injunctions against foreign proceedings exists. It is set out in *BHP Petroleum v Baer* where the court compelled the defendant to arbitrate in

---

[37] *Aggeliki Charis Compania Maritima SA v Pagnan SpA (The Angelic Grace),* [1995] 1 Lloyd's Rep 87, 96; see already *Pena Copper Mines Ltd v Rio Tinto Co Ltd,* (1911) 105 LT 846; see also *Shell International Petroleum Co Ltd v Coral Oil Co Ltd* [1999] 1 Lloyd's Rep 72; *XL Insurance Ltd v Owens Corning,* [2000] 2 Lloyd's Rep 500; for further references see Spenser Underhill and Valentin, "Restraining Foreign Proceedings Pursued in Breach of an Agreement to Arbitrate in England", 2 *Int ALR* 151 (1999).

[38] *The Angelic Grace,* [1995] 1 Lloyd's Rep 87, 96.

[39] For an example of unreasonable delay see *Toepfer International GmbH v Molino Boschi Srl,* [1996] 1 Lloyd's Rep 510 where it took the applicant seven years after the foreign proceedings were started; see also *Schiffahrtsgesellschaft Detlev van Appen GmbH v Voest Alpine Intertrading GmbH ("The Jay Bola")* [1997] 2 Lloyd's Rep 279 (CA) where the applicant was burdened with the cost resulting from its delay but obtained the required injunction.

[40] Spenser Underhill and Valentin, "Restraining Foreign Proceedings Pursued in Breach of an Agreement to Arbitrate in England", 2 *Int ALR* 151 (1999) 155; see also Mustill and Boyd, *2001 Companion,* 215-216; for an overview what might constitute such a good cause see Pengelley, "Judicial comity and Angelic Grace", 8 *ADRLJ* 195 (1999) 200 *et seq.*

[41] See the decision by the New South Wales Supreme Court in *CSR Ltd v NZI,* (1994) 36 NSWLR 138; Pengelley, "Judicial comity and angelic grace", 8 *ADRLJ* 195 (1999) 205 *et seq.*

Texas and issued an injunction restraining him from pursuing proceedings in Ecuador. The court referred to the test applicable for antisuit-injunctions in support of court proceedings and considered it to be relevant also for injunctions in support of arbitration. It held

> that an injunction barring a foreign action was proper if the simultaneous prosecution of an action would result in 'inequitable hardship' and 'tend to frustrate and delay the speedy and efficient determination of the cause.' .... The focus of the inquiry is whether there exists a need to prevent vexatious or oppressive litigation.
> In light of the strong federal policy favouring arbitration, the court finds that plaintiffs would be irreparably harmed if Baer were permitted to continue litigating in Ecuador while the same claims were being arbitrated. Therefore, the court grants plaintiffs' application for injunction.[42] [References omitted.]

15-32 The relevant standard to be met under the US approach is "irreparable harm". Furthermore in deciding whether to grant the requested injunction the stage of the foreign proceedings is an issue, as well as the expectation of the parties to litigate in that particular court. While there is little case law on such international cases courts have been more willing to issue injunctions restraining proceedings in state court.[43]

15-33 Enforcement of anti-suit injunctions may pose problems. Although supposed to work *in personam,* foreign courts, in particular in civil law countries, have considered anti-suit injunctions to be an unacceptable intrusion on their jurisdiction.[44] Unless the addressee of the injunction has assets in the issuing state which could be attached for any breach of the court's order, enforcement is often not possible.[45] Within the EU there is a prevailing view that antisuit injunction

---

42 *BHP Petroleum (Americas) Inc et al v Walter F Baer Reinhold,* no H-97-879, XXIII YBCA 945 (1998); 12(5) *Mealey's IAR* I-1 (1997), (USDC, Southern District of Texas, Houston Division, 28 April 1997); see also *Wal-Mart Stores, Inc v PT Multipolar Corp et al,* XXV YBCA 1085 (2000) 1086 (9th Cir 1999); see description of the test in Born, *International Commercial Arbitration in the US,* 406.

43 See, *e.g.*, *Mc Mahon v Shearson/American Express Inc* 709 F Supp 369, 374 (SDNY 1989); see also Born, *International Commercial Arbitration in the US,* 407.

44 See, *e.g.*, Oberlandesgericht Düsseldorf, 10 January 1996, *IPRax* 245 (1997) which already refused to serve a judgment containing an anti-suit injunction relying on the public policy exception under the Hague Service convention.

45 See the example referred to by Spenser Underhill and Valentin, "Restraining Foreign Proceedings Pursued in Breach of an Agreement to Arbitrate in England", 2 *Int ALR* 151 (1999) 153.

should not be granted to restrain court proceedings within another Member State.[46]

2.3. The Role of the Court before the Tribunal is Established

15-34 It is not uncommon that once a dispute has arisen immediate protective action is required and it would be commercially damaging to wait until the arbitration tribunal has been constituted. Evidence may have to be preserved[47] or rights of a party protected from irreparable harm. In such cases "if the parties and the arbitral process need protection there is nowhere to turn but the national Court."[48] Since the arbitration tribunal is not yet in existence the parties cannot turn to it to request those measures. It is not possible to turn to the agreed arbitration institution for such measures.[49]

15-35 As a consequence most national laws and the Model Law, provide that the courts have the right to grant interim relief and that an application for such relief is compatible with the existence of an arbitration agreement. In exercising their discretion under those rules courts should take account of the non-availability of other forms of interim relief. National court intervention in such cases is not disruptive, but rather beneficial to the arbitration proceedings.[50] Therefore, as long as the requested measures cannot be postponed and do not pre-empt the decision on the merits, courts should not feel restricted by the arbitration agreement to exercise their powers. Where the measures granted would effectively determine the dispute a less interventionist approach should be adopted.

---

46 England takes a different view.

47 See, *e.g.*, the factual background in the US decision: *In the Matter of the Application of Deiulemar Compagnia Di Navigazione Spa for the Perpetuation of Evidence*, 198 F 3d 473, XXV YBCA 443 (2000) (4th Cir 1999) where an expert was allowed to inspect the engine of a vessel which was about to be repaired.

48 See Lord Mustill in *Coppée-Lavalin SA/NV v Ken Ren Chemicals and Fertilizers Ltd* [1994] 2 Lloyd's Rep 109, 116.

49 For an effort to overcome this situation in the WIPO context see the project of "WIPO Emergency Relief Rules" described by Blessing, introduction in Berti (ed), *International Arbitration in Switzerland*, paras 887- 890.

50 Derains and Schwartz, *ICC Rules*, 272.

2.4. Proceedings in relation to the Composition of the Arbitration Tribunal

15-36 Courts have an important role to play in the composition of the tribunal, either as a fall back appointing authority or during challenge procedures. The former is the case if the parties cannot agree on the arbitrator or where the prescribed appointment mechanism does not work. The Model Law[51] and most national laws provide that in such a situation the arbitrators are to be appointed by the courts.[52] In such situations court intervention is necessary to make the agreement to arbitrate workable.

15-37 The use of the court's supervisory powers in connection with challenges to arbitrators is also important even though it will seriously disrupt the arbitration proceedings. This is obvious in the case of a successful challenge when it may be necessary to review all issues from the beginning. However, even an unsuccessful challenge will have a disruptive effect as it may bring the proceedings on the merits to a halt and hamper the relationship between the parties and the tribunal. To discourage parties from using challenge procedures as a means of delaying the arbitration proceedings courts are generally reluctant to make use of their powers to remove an arbitrator.[53]

2.5. Court Involvement during the Arbitration Proceedings

15-38 During the arbitration proceedings issues may arise where the tribunal lacks the necessary coercive powers to conduct the arbitration in an appropriate way, protect the rights of the parties or preserve existing evidence. Therefore the Model Law, as well as many national laws, provide for several types of court intervention. These include granting assistance in the taking of evidence, interim relief, extension of time limits, or determining preliminary points of law.

(a) Governing principles

15-39 Most laws give the courts considerable discretion on whether to grant the supportive measures requested. In exercising that discretion different considerations apply depending on the type and nature of the measure requested.

---

[51] Article 11(3)(4).

[52] See, *e.g.*, England, Arbitration Act section 18; Switzerland, PIL article 179(2).

[53] See, *e.g.*, the decision by the English Court of Appeal in *AT&T Corporation and another v Saudi Cable*, [2000] 2 *Lloyd's Rep* 127; Shore, "Disclosure and Impartiality: An Arbitrator's Responsibility vis-à-vis Legal Standards", 57(4) *Disp Res J* 34 (2002).

Despite differences in national laws it is possible to classify the different forms of court intervention to one of three categories:

- the ordering of purely procedural steps which cannot be ordered or enforced by the arbitrators;
- orders for maintaining the *status quo*; and
- measures to ensure that the award has the intended practical effect and can be enforced.[54]

15-40 The first type of measures does not involve any encroachment on the merits of the dispute. It just supplements missing powers of the tribunal. By contrast measures of the second type, such as money or asset blocking orders, may call for an assessment of the claim. As this involves some trespassing on the arbitrator's territory, courts are and should be more hesitant to grant such orders. An even stronger potential for such encroachment is involved in measures of the third type such as interlocutory injunctions. To order such measures the

> court will often find it necessary to consider whether a particular state of affairs which the arbitrators are being asked to create or declare (for example whether one party is obliged to do a certain act or abstain from doing another) is likely in the event to be created or declared by the award, in order to decide whether it is just to order holding relief in the shape of an injunction; and the intrusion will of course be even greater where the interim measure takes the shape of an order that the party shall perform in advance of an award the very obligation the existence of which the arbitrators are in the course of deciding.[55][references omitted]

15-41 Orders of the third type, *i.e.* to ensure the award has its intended effect, should therefore generally be reserved for the tribunal. This is especially the case if the measure is more a national peculiarity rather than an internationally available remedy in arbitration.

(b) Assistance in the taking of evidence

15-42 The consensual nature of arbitration and the resulting lack of coercive powers sometimes limits the tribunal's options in taking evidence. In general it cannot force witnesses to appear at a hearing or answer questions, or order third parties to produce documents. For those and comparable measures arbitration tribunals therefore have to rely on court support.

---

[54] Lord Mustill in *Coppée Lavalin v Ken Ren* [1994] 2 Lloyd's Rep 109.

[55] *Ibid.*

15-43 This power is set out in Article 27 Model Law which provides

> The arbitral tribunal or a party with the approval of the arbitral tribunal may request from a competent court of this State assistance in taking evidence. The court may execute the request within its competence and according to its rules on taking evidence.[56]

15-44 Since such assistance in taking evidence clearly belongs to the first category of supportive measures, courts have in general been willing to make use of their powers in aid of arbitration.[57] The threat of unwanted intrusion into the arbitration is minimised by the fact that the request for support in general must come from the tribunal itself or at least with its approval.

(c) Interim relief

15-45 In general the right of the courts to grant interim relief is not limited to the pre-constitution phase but also extends to the time after the tribunal has been constituted. There are a number of measures which an arbitration tribunal cannot take but which are from time to time necessary to make the arbitration agreement effective. The most obvious are attachments and injunctions affecting third parties, which can normally be granted effectively only by state courts.

15-46 However, courts are hesitant to use their powers, especially where the interim relief requested is identical to the relief requested in the arbitration.[58] The courts are very reluctant to effectively remove the matter from the arbitrators, contrary to the parties' agreement. This applies in particular where the provisional measures requested can also be granted by the arbitration tribunal.[59]

---

[56] See also Germany, ZPO section 1050; England, Arbitration Act sections 43, 44.

[57] The refusal by US courts to order pre-trial discovery in aid of foreign arbitration is not based on the exercise of an existing discretion. It is based on the fact that section 1781 US Judicial Code is not applicable to arbitration; see *National Broadcasting Co v Bear Sterns & Co*, XXIVa YBCA 884 (1999) (2d Cir); *The Republic of Kazakhstan v Biedermann International*, XXV YBCA 641 (2000) (5th Cir); Rivkin and Legum, "Attempts to Use Section 1782 to Obtain US Discovery in Aid of Foreign Arbitrations", 14 *Arb Int* 213 (1998).

[58] See, *e.g.*, the decision of the House of Lord in *Channel Tunnel Group Ltd v Balfour Beatty Ltd* [1993] AC 334 and the minority judgment of Lord Mustill in *Coppée-Lavalin SA/NV v Ken Ren Chemicals and Fertilizers Ltd* [1994] 2 Lloyd's Rep 109, 123.

[59] See, *e.g.*, the decision by the Hong Kong Court of First Instance in *Leviathan Shipping Co Ltd v Sky Sailing Overseas Ltd* [1998] 4 HKC 347, (1998) 1 *Int ALR* N-114 where an *ex parte* Mareva injunction and an order to provide security for the release of a ship were set aside since the tribunal had been appointed and could have ordered the measures.

The situation may, however, be different in the countries where interim relief by courts exists as a matter of right and is not at the courts discretion.[60]

(d) Extension of time limits

15-47 By choosing particular rules parties often agree on time limits for starting the arbitration, the appointment of arbitrators or the rendering of an award. If the required action has not been taken within the agreed time limit the whole arbitration agreement may become ineffective and there will be no forum in which the parties' disputes can be determined. To overcome this situation the question arises whether the national courts have the power to vary or grant an extension of those time limits.

15-48 Most laws, including the Model Law, do not give such powers to the courts. Quite the opposite: Article 5 Model Law and comparable rules provide that courts can only intervene in an arbitration to the extent provided for in the law. Unless expressly allowed, no variations or extensions of time can be granted by state courts.

15-49 By contrast, some arbitration laws provide for the extension of time limits by the courts. For example under English law the courts can grant extensions of time for the commencement of proceedings[61], the time during which an award has to be made[62] and all other time limits agreed by the parties.[63] While the first power belongs to the mandatory provisions of the Arbitration Act, the parties can exclude the other two by agreement. These powers do not extend to statutory time limits outside the Arbitration Act and an application can only be made after any available arbitration process for obtaining an extension has been exhausted.

15-50 To limit the possible interference with the arbitration the granting of extensions under all provisions is subject to restrictive conditions. For example, time limits for commencement of arbitration proceedings can only be extended by the English courts if they are satisfied

> (a) that the circumstances are such as were outside the reasonable contemplation of the parties when they agreed the provision in question, and that it would be just to extend the time, or

---

[60] See, *e.g.*, Germany, ZPO sections 916 *et seq.*

[61] England, Arbitration Act section 12.

[62] *Ibid,* section 50.

[63] *Ibid,* section 79.

(b) that the conduct of one party makes it unjust to hold the other party to the strict terms of the provision in question.[64]

15-51 The extension of all other time limits is dependent on the court considering that substantial injustice would otherwise be done.[65] This is also the case if the application is made by the tribunal, but in such circumstances, there is less need for a restrictive interpretation of the provision. If the application comes from the tribunal any extension granted by the courts has, in effect, the character of filling a gap or extending the arbitration tribunal's powers.

15-52 Under French law, the courts can extend the period of time during which the arbitrators have to render their award before their mandate expires.[66] In particular in *ad hoc* arbitration the power is often used.[67] The six month period provided for in French law is very short and the parties can often not agree on an extension, so that recourse to the courts is necessary. The application has to be made before the time has expired but the decision may be rendered afterwards.[68] The courts have also used their powers in relation to international arbitrations having their seats in France even when they were not submitted to French law.[69]

(e) Preliminary determination of question of law

15-53 In general it is for the arbitration tribunal to determine all questions of fact and law. Some cases will turn on questions of law which are of general interest. This may be the case when the question arises frequently or involves issues of public policy. Alternatively, the question of law may involve issues of public policy and an appeal is likely whatever the tribunal decides. In such cases there may be an advantage in seeking a court ruling at an early stage.

15-54 The English Arbitration Act provides a possibility either for the parties or the arbitration tribunal to refer that question of law for a preliminary decision to the courts. A court does not need to accept the case unless it is satisfied that the question of law "substantially affects the rights of one or more of the parties" and that there is likely to be a substantial saving in costs by the court determining

---

64 Arbitration Act section 12(3).

65 Sections 50(3), 79(3).

66 NCPC Article 1456(2).

67 Grandjean, "La durée de la mission des arbitres", *Rev Arb* 39 (1991) Fn 15.

68 Tribunal de Grande Instance Paris, 21 May 1984, Rev Arb 165 (1985) 165.

69 See Tribunal de Grande Instance Paris, 3 April 1985, *Application des gaz v Wonder Corp of America,* Rev Arb 170 (1985); see also Fouchard Gaillard Goldman on *International Commercial Arbitration*, para 1387.

the question. Furthermore, if the substantive dispute is governed by a law other than English law[70], or if the parties agree that the award can be made without reasons, then there is no right to ask the English courts to determine the question of law.[71]

15-55 The Model Law and most laws do not contain comparable provisions.[72] Given the principle of party autonomy the parties should, however, be allowed to agree on having preliminary questions of law decided by the competent state court. Whether the same applies also for referral by the arbitration tribunal without the parties' consent is an open question. Any such referral of a preliminary question of law to the state courts defeats the parties' intention to have their disputes solely decided by the arbitration tribunal. A referral by the arbitration tribunal may streamline the arbitration process and result in an enforceable award where a question of law which may otherwise give rise to an appeal has already been decided at a preliminary stage.

2.6. The Role of the Court Involvement after the Award has been rendered: Challenge, Appeals and Enforcement

15-56 After the award has been rendered the courts may become involved when a party challenges or lodges an appeal against the award, or seeks to enforce it.[73] The courts in which this relief is sought will invariably be different. A challenge or appeal will be in the courts of the country of the place of arbitration. Enforcement proceedings will be either where the respondent is resident or has its principal place of business, or where it has money or other assets against which the award can be enforced.

15-57 The increasingly favourable climate for arbitration has led to arbitration awards being considered final and binding and to a pro-enforcement policy over the last twenty years. Challenge proceedings are generally based on an excess of jurisdiction of the tribunal or some procedural irregularity which has prevented a fair procedure. In some countries the previously existing possibilities to appeal

---

70 See also *Reliance Industries Ltd and Amor v Enron Oil and Gas India Ltd* [2002] 1 All ER (Comm) 59.

71 England, Arbitration Act section 45. See similarly Hong Kong, Ordinance Section 23(4); New Zealand, Arbitration Act section 4; Singapore, International Arbitration Act 1994 Article 29.

72 This is, *e.g.*, the case of German law, Swiss law, French law and Swedish law.

73 In addition, courts may be requested to order post award attachments to ensure that the award can be enforced.

against awards on points of law have largely been abolished.[74] Generally grounds for appeal are interpreted in a restrictive manner. The same applies for the limited grounds to resist enforcement under the New York Convention or national laws.

[74] See in particular England, where the right to appeal in section 69 is submitted to considerable limitations.

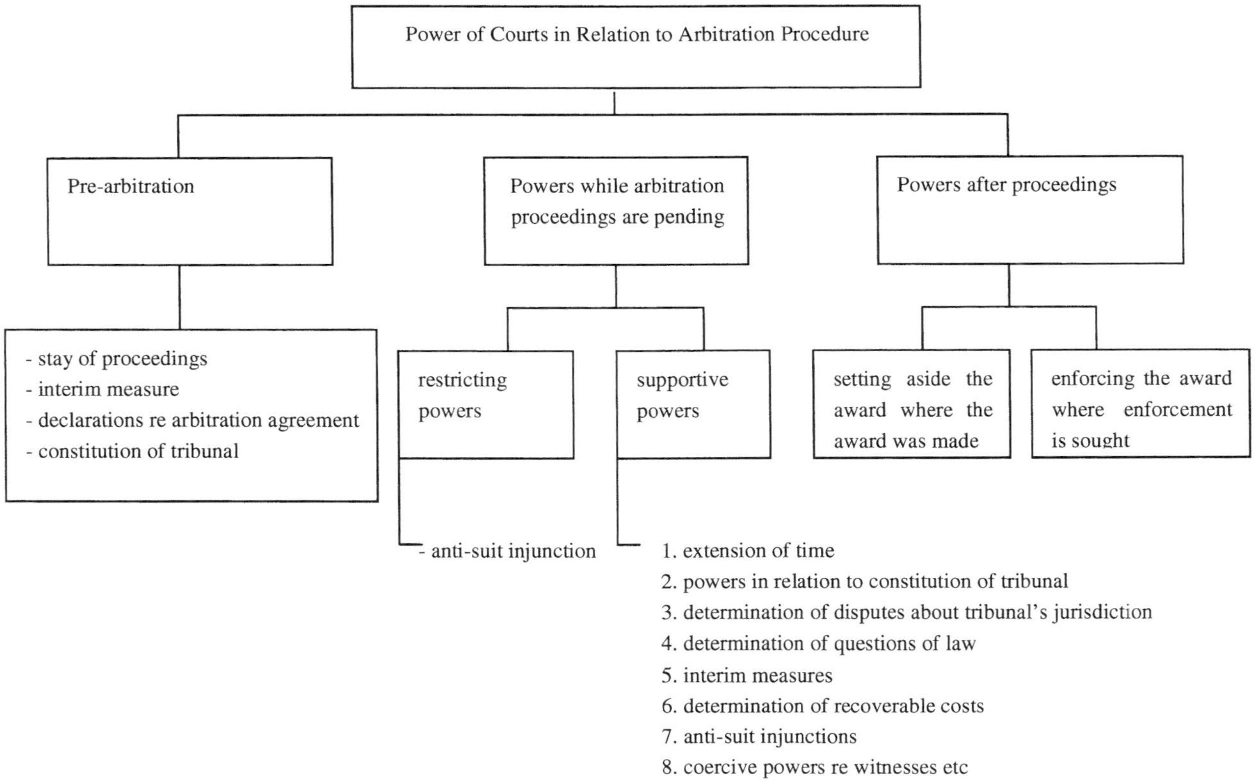
Power of Courts in Relation to Arbitration Procedure
Pre-arbitration
Powers while arbitration proceedings are pending
Powers after proceedings
- stay of proceedings
- interim measure
- declarations re arbitration agreement
- constitution of tribunal
restricting powers
supportive powers
setting aside the award where the award was made
enforcing the award where enforcement is sought
- anti-suit injunction
1. extension of time
2. powers in relation to constitution of tribunal
3. determination of disputes about tribunal's jurisdiction
4. determination of questions of law
5. interim measures
6. determination of recoverable costs
7. anti-suit injunctions
8. coercive powers re witnesses etc

Chapter 16

MULTIPARTY AND MULTICONTRACT ARBITRATION

16-1 There is a general tendency to presume that arbitration involves only two parties. Whilst this may be the norm it is not always the case. Increasingly arbitrations involve more than two parties.[1] Multiparty contract structures are a common feature in international business transactions.

16-2 In these situations most disputes involve more than two parties. There are situations where an arbitration between two parties will have an impact also on other parties. Since different disputes often arise out of one event and are therefore based on the same facts, it may be desirable to have them all decided in one set of arbitration proceedings. This has the advantage of enabling the dispute

[1] There were more than two parties in 20.4% of ICC cases in 1995. In 2001 the percentage increased to 30%; see also Platte, "When Should an Arbitrator Join Cases?", 18 *Arb Int* 67 (2002) who reports that more than 50% of the LCIA cases involve more than two parties.

to be resolved in one single procedure taking account of all issues and the interests of all parties affected and can save considerable costs and time. Evidence would be presented once in an all encompassing way which gives the tribunal a complete understanding of the facts and issues in dispute.[2] In addition, the parties would only have to pay for one arbitration tribunal. Even more important, such proceedings have the effect of avoiding conflicting decisions which may arise out of separate arbitration proceedings.[3]

16-3 Multiparty arbitration is also fraught with considerable problems. In particular, it is essential to show that the parties have actually consented to this type of arbitration and that they are treated equally since the lack of consent as well as any unequal treatment of the parties are grounds of resisting enforcement under the New York Convention.

16-4 One can distinguish two types of situations which may result in multiparty arbitration: a single contract with several parties, such as joint venture or consortia agreements, and a web of related or interdependent contracts between different parties. In the former scenario the problems relate primarily to ensuring equal treatment in the organisation of the proceedings, in particular, in the composition of the tribunal. In the multicontract - multiparty situation those problems are preceded by the question whether it is possible to consolidate the different disputes into one multiparty arbitration or allow the joinder of a third party. This is primarily a question of consent.[4]

16-5 Consolidation of different arbitration proceedings may arise also in a bi-party multicontract situation. The same parties may have entered into a number of contracts all providing for arbitration. In particular, where these contracts are part of a single venture it may be advisable to settle all disputes between the

---

2 For a more detailed list of the advantages see Leboulanger, "Multi-Contract Arbitration", 13(4) *J Int'l Arb* 43 (1996) 62 *et seq.*

3 See, *e.g.*, the conflicting decisions in the "Vimeira" cases *Interbulk Limited v Aiden Shipping Company Ltd (The Vimeira),* [1983] 2 Lloyd's Rep 424; [1984] 2 Lloyd's Rep 66; Veeder, "Multi-party disputes: Consolidation under English Law. The Vimeira - a sad forensic fable", 2 *Arb Int* 310 (1986); for a detailed discussion on maritime arbitrations see Yang, "Multi-party maritime arbitrations", 4 *ADRLJ* 30 (1995). See also the conflicting awards in *CME Czech Republic v Czech Republic* and *Lauder v Czech Republic* available at <www.cme.cz/doc10/en/00.htm>.

4 Consent is also an issue where a party seeks to look through the bi-party contract to include another party who is clearly involved. This is typically the case where a contract has been performed by someone other than the contract party, *e.g.* a subsidiary, parent or other group company, or through an agency arrangement.

parties in one arbitration, instead of having several separate arbitration proceedings. This facilitates set-off, may save time and is generally cheaper than a number of separate arbitrations.

16-6 This chapter considers (1) multiparty arbitrations arising out of a single contract, (2) multiparty arbitrations arising out of separate contracts, including joinder of third parties and consolidation of separate disputes and arbitrations, (3) consolidation of different arbitrations between the same parties, (4) guidelines as to appropriateness of multiparty arbitrations, and (5) problems of enforcing awards where parties have been joined or arbitrations consolidated.

1. Multiparty Arbitration Arising out of a Single Contract

16-7 Contracts with more than two parties exist in all fields of business. Probably the most prominent field of application is business entities where companies or partnerships have more than two shareholders or partners. Other examples can be found in the construction industry or in the finance sector where contracts of consortia and private finance initiatives play an important role. The sheer size of the projects, the required expertise and considerations of risk management often mandate that several companies join forces to bid for a project, to finance it or enter into loan agreements.

1.1. Consent to Multiparty Arbitration

16-8 In all these situations the parties are bound to each other through a single contract with a single arbitration clause. When agreeing on the arbitration clause the parties must or should have been aware that in the event of a dispute it may entail multiparty arbitration.[5] To this extent consent to multiparty arbitrations can be assumed.

16-9 However, the ICC Court has held that under a standard ICC clause contained in a multiparty consortium agreement such consent is limited to the case where two sides are involved each comprising several parties. By contrast

---

[5] Stippel, "International Multiparty Arbitration: The Role of Party Autonomy", 7 *Am Rev Int Arb* 51 (1996) 54; Platte, "When Should an Arbitrator Join Cases?", 18 *Arb Int* 67 (2002) 70. This was also confirmed by the French Cour de cassation, 7 January 1992, *Siemens AG/BKMI Industrianlagen GmbH v Dutco Construction Company*, XVIII YBCA 140 (1993), which considered the consent given before the dispute had arisen to be invalid; see also the note by Jarrosson, 119 *Clunet* 726 (1992) 729.

cases covering cross claims by one respondent against another respondent are not considered to be covered by such a consent.[6]

16-10 Problems of consent may also arise when a party that has not signed the arbitration agreement is made a party to the arbitration on the basis that the arbitration agreement is also binding on it. In light of the doctrine of competence-competence, the arbitration tribunal can decide whether or not a multiparty arbitration is covered by the arbitration agreement.

1.2. Equal Treatment in the Appointment of Arbitrators

16-11 A prime area of concern is the composition of the tribunal. This is reflected by the fact that the rules or laws which contain special provisions on multiparty arbitration usually address this issue.[7] The appointment of a three member tribunal has proven to be the most problematic.[8] In a two party situation equal treatment of the parties is promoted by giving each party the right to appoint its own arbitrator and to agree, if they can, on the chairman.

16-12 In a multiparty arbitration considerable problems arise. To give every party involved the right to appoint its own arbitrator is not workable. It could lead to tribunals of an impractical size frustrating the whole purpose of the arbitration. Even more important it may be unfair to the side with fewer parties, which would have less influence on the composition of the tribunal.[9]

16-13 It is equally problematic to allow all claimants and all respondents to appoint an equal number of arbitrators irrespective of how many parties there may be. The fact that several parties are named as respondents does not mean that that they have identical interests or will co-ordinate their defence. Bringing a claim against several parties may just be a matter of convenience or tactics for the claimant. In such a situation it might be unfair to give the claimant the right

---

[6] Devolvé, "Final Report on Multi-Party Arbitrations", 6(1) *ICC Bulletin* 26 (1995) 34.

[7] See, *e.g.*, the adaptations suggested by the Permanent Court of Arbitration for multiparty arbitrations taking part under the PCA's Optional Rules for Arbitrations Involving International Organizations and States, XXII *YBCA* 338 (1997).

[8] The appointment of a sole arbitrator is generally either made by agreement of the parties involved or by an appointing authority so that equal treatment is ensured.

[9] See Berger, *International Economic Arbitration,* 314. For example, in a partnership one partner may bring a claim that the common behaviour of the other three partners violates the partnership contract. If each partner could appoint its own arbitrator there would be a tribunal with three arbitrators appointed from the respondents while the claimant would have appointed only one.

to appoint its own arbitrator while obliging the respondents to agree on one arbitrator despite their opposing interests.

16-14 This consideration was the basis of the *Dutco* decision of the French Cour de cassation.[10] The case arose out of a contract for the construction of a plant. The contract contained an arbitration clause for proceedings in accordance with the ICC Rules by three arbitrators appointed under those rules. *Dutco* brought claims against the two other members of the consortium, Siemens and BKMI and nominated one arbitrator. According to its practice at that time the ICC required Siemens and BKMI as the two respondents to nominate an arbitrator jointly, which they refused to do. Upon threats by the ICC to appoint an arbitrator on their behalf, Siemens and BKMI nominated an arbitrator jointly but reserved their right to challenge the regularity of the appointment procedure. The tribunal in an interim award confirmed the regularity of the appointment.

16-15 In the ensuing challenge proceedings the Cour de cassation annulled the award because of the inherent unfairness of the claimant having a greater influence on the composition of the tribunal than the two respondents. It stated that "the principle of the equality of the parties in the appointment of arbitrators is a matter of public order (ordre public) which can be waived only after the dispute has arisen". Consequently it was considered to be irrelevant whether the parties when entering into the arbitration agreement could anticipate such an appointment procedure or even agreed to it.[11]

16-16 As a result of the *Dutco* decision, a number of the major international arbitration institutions adopted specific provisions to deal with the issue of appointment of arbitrators in a multiparty situation. They usually try to ensure equal treatment of the parties by submitting the appointment of the whole arbitration tribunal to the institution if the parties cannot agree on a joint nominee. For example, Article 10 ICC Rules provides

> (1) Where there are multiple parties, whether as Claimant or as Respondent, and where the dispute is to be referred to three arbitrators, the multiple Claimants, jointly, and the multiple Respondents, jointly, shall nominate an arbitrator for confirmation pursuant to Article 9.
>
> (2) In the absence of such a joint nomination and where all parties are unable to agree to a method for the constitution of the Arbitral Tribunal, the Court may

---

[10] Cour de cassation, 7 January 1992, *Siemens AG/BKMI Industrieanlagen GmbH v Dutco Construction Company*, XVII YBCA 140 (1993) original in French, 119 Clunet 712 (1992).

[11] *Ibid*, 141.

appoint each member of the Arbitral Tribunal and shall designate one of them to act as chairman. In such case, the Court shall be at liberty to choose any person it regards as suitable to act as arbitrator, applying Article 9 when it considers this appropriate.[12]

16-17 This is also the solution adopted by most of the special multiparty arbitration clauses used or suggested in practice. For example, the arbitration clause in the Consortium Agreement of the Scandinavian Airlines System concluded between the Danish, Norwegian and the Swedish Airline corporations provides for the three arbitrators to be appointed by the Presidents of the Supreme Courts of the three countries, one each.[13]

16-18 The downside of this solution is that it deprives the parties of one major advantage of arbitration, *i.e.*, the possibility of appointing arbitrators in whom they have confidence. Concerns have been raised that such a procedure may conflict with the agreement of the parties. Where the arbitration agreement provides for appointment by the parties without taking into account the multiparty situation, as is often the case with standard arbitration agreements, an appointment by an appointing authority appears to be contrary to this agreement.[14]

16-19 These concerns are not justified. The perceived conflict does not exist. By agreeing to arbitrate under the rules of an institution providing for a special appointment procedure in a multiparty situation this procedure becomes part of the parties' agreement. This is particularly clear in Article 8(2) LCIA Rules according to which in a multiparty situation "the Arbitration Agreement shall be treated for all purposes as a written agreement by the parties for the appointment of the Arbitral Tribunal by the LCIA Court." By agreeing to LCIA arbitration, parties have agreed to the appointment procedure in Article 8.[15]

---

[12] See similarly, *e.g.*, LCIA Article 8; AAA ICDR Rules Article 6; DIS Rules section 13.

[13] See Sanders, *Quo Vadis Arbitration?*, 211. For a list of other multiparty clauses see Devolvé, "Final Report on Multi-Party Arbitrations", 6(1) *ICC Bulletin* 26 (1995) 42 *et seq*; Wetter "Six multi-party arbitration clauses", in ICC (ed), *Multiparty Arbitration*, 115 *et seq.*

[14] Redfern and Hunter, *International Commercial Arbitration*, para 3-71; Devolvé, "Final Repot on Multi-Party Arbitration", 6(1) *ICC Bulletin* 26 (1995) 40; Raeschke-Kessler and Berger, *Recht und Praxis*, para 779; Jaeger, *Die Umsetzung des Uncitral-Modellgesetzes über die Internationale Handelsschiedsgerichtsbarkeit im Zuge der nationalen Reformen* (Lang 2001), 119.

[15] See also Gravel, "Multiparty Arbitration and Multiple Arbitrations", 7(2) *ICC Bulletin* 45 (1996) 47.

16-20 Where, despite the *Dutco* principles, the parties wish to exclude the multiparty appointment procedures provided for in the chosen rules their intent should be clearly expressed. References in boilerplate arbitration clauses to appointment of the arbitration tribunal "by the parties" should not be considered special agreements excluding the multiparty provisions of the chosen rules. This would require express wording, *i.e.* an agreement that in a multiparty situation each "side" can appoint one arbitrator on whom the parties belonging to this "side" must agree.[16]

16-21 The most detailed provision on appointment in multiparty cases is contained in Article 18 WIPO Arbitration Rules. This provides

> (a) Where
> (i) three arbitrators are to be appointed,
> (ii) the parties have not agreed on a procedure of appointment, and
> (iii) the Request for Arbitration names more than one claimant, the claimants shall make a joint appointment of an arbitrator in their Request for Arbitration. The appointment of the second arbitrator and the presiding arbitrator shall, subject to paragraph (b) of this Article, take place in accordance with Article 17(b), (c) or (d), as the case may be.
> (b) Where
> (i) three arbitrators are to be appointed,
> (ii) the parties have agreed on a procedure of appointment, and
> (iii) the Request for Arbitration names more than one respondent, the respondents shall jointly appoint an arbitrator. If, for whatever reason, the respondents do not make a joint appointment of an arbitrator within 30 days after receiving the Request for Arbitration, any appointment of the arbitrator previously made by the claimant or claimants shall be considered void and two arbitrators shall be appointed by the Center. The two arbitrators thus appointed shall, within 30 days after the appointment of the second arbitrator, appoint a third arbitrator, who shall be the presiding arbitrator.
> (c) Where
> (i) three arbitrators are to be appointed,
> (ii) the parties have agreed upon a procedure of appointment, and
> (iii) the Request for Arbitration names more than one claimant or more than one respondent, paragraphs (a) and (b) of this Article shall, notwithstanding Article 15(a), apply irrespective of any contractual provisions in the Arbitration

---

[16] Even appointment under such a clause agreed on before the dispute has arisen could violate public policy if the parties are not given equal influence on the composition of the tribunal.

> Agreement with respect to the procedures of appointment, unless those provisions have excluded the application of this Article."

16-22 The distinction in approach between several claimants and several respondents is sensible.[17] Each claimant can always decide whether it wants to bring its claim alone or in conjunction with other claimants; no such choice exists for the respondents. Since the decision to join forces with other claimants is taken after the dispute has arisen the obligation to agree with the other claimants on a joint arbitrator is not a violation of the *Dutco* rule. The distinction furthermore makes it impossible for the claimant to deprive a single respondent of its right to appoint its own arbitrator by just adding an additional claimant.[18]

16-23 Another approach is adopted in the Vienna Arbitration Rules. According to Article 10, where claims are brought against different respondents they can decide whether they want to have the dispute determined by a sole arbitrator or three arbitrators. If they opt for a three member tribunal they are then obliged to appoint a joint arbitrator which, failing an agreement, will be appointed by the institution. The rules give the defendants the right to ensure equality in enforcement by opting for a sole arbitrator.

16-24 No similar provisions for the appointment of the tribunal in multiparty situations are contained in the older arbitration rules such as the UNCITRAL Rules. The same is true for most arbitration laws including the Model Law.

16-25 For this reason the German legislature when adopting the Model Law added a special provision dealing with situations when one party has a stronger influence on the composition of the arbitration tribunal.

16-26 Although not specifically intended to deal with multiparty situations it might be applicable.[19] Section 1034(2) ZPO provides

> If the arbitration agreement grants preponderant rights to one party with regard to the composition of the arbitral tribunal which place the other party at a disadvantage, that other party may request the court to appoint the arbitrator or

---

17 The same distinction can be found in the DIS Rules section 13.

18 This is the case if the whole tribunal is always appointed by the institution.

19 For such a view in relation to the German Law see Schlosser, "Bald neues Recht der Schiedsgerichtsbarkeit in Deutschland?", *RIW* 723 (1994); see also for the Dutch Law, van den Berg, "The ICC Arbitration Rules and Appointment of Arbitrators in Cases Involving Multiple Defendants", in Plantey, Böckstiegel and Bredow (eds), *Festschrift für Ottoarndt Glossner*, (Recht und Wirtschaft 1994), 19, 31.

arbitrators in deviation from the nomination made, or from the agreed nomination procedure. The request must be submitted at the latest within two weeks of the party becoming aware of the constitution of the arbitral tribunal. Section 1032 subs. 3 applies *mutatis mutandis.*[20]

16-27 It is unclear how a tribunal is to be appointed when neither the applicable law nor the chosen rules contain a special provision. It seems doubtful whether the provision in the arbitration agreement or arbitration rules that each party appoint one arbitrator can be interpreted in a way that each "party" means each "side". However, earlier case law in a number of countries shows that courts may not have the same understanding of the principle of equality of parties as the French Cour de cassation in *Dutco.*[21] There are court decisions which decide otherwise and apparently consider the equality of parties to be a principle from which they can derogate in advance before the dispute has arisen.[22]

16-28 This can be justified if the multiparty situation arises out of the extension of an arbitration clause to other members of the same group of companies. The close ties existing between the different members of the group can justify an obligation for those parties to agree on a single arbitrator. In those cases, the selection of arbitrators has rarely been a problem in practice.

---

[20] A comparable rule can be found in the Netherlands CCP where Article 1028 provides

> If the arbitration agreement gives one of the parties a privileged position with regard to the appointment of the arbitrator or arbitrators, the other party may, despite the method of appointment laid down in that agreement, request the President of the District Court within one month after the commencement of the arbitration to appoint the arbitrator or arbitrators. The other party shall be given an opportunity to be heard. The provisions of article 1027(4) shall apply accordingly.

[21] The Paris Court of Appeal for example came to a different conclusion than the Cour de cassation; see Seppala and Gogek, "Multi-party arbitration under ICC rules", *Int Fin L Rev* 32 (1989).

[22] Kammergericht Berlin, 2 January 1966, *KTS* 100 (1966), 102; see also the decisions of the Court de justice, Geneva, 26 November 1982, affirmed by the Tribunal Fédéral, 16 May 1983, *Arab Republic of Egypt v Westland Helicopters Ltd*, ASA Bulletin 203 (1984) which upheld the former ICC practice of requesting each side to appoint a joint arbitrator dispite the criticism by Egypt that this gave Westland a preponderant influence on the composition of the tribunal; see Poudret, "Arbitrage multipartite et droit Suisse", *ASA Bulletin* 8 (1991); Berger, *International Economic Arbitration*, 319; Platte, "When Should an Arbitrator Join Cases?", 18 *Arb Int* 67 (2002) 76 with further references. The Vienna Chamber of Commerce even provides, in its new rules, for a type of appointment procedure comparable to the one in *Dutco*; see Austrian Federal Economic Chamber Arbitration Rules 2001 Article 10; see also the introduction by Melis, XXVI *YBCA* 446 (2001) 448.

16-29 A multiparty situation may result from the joinder of a party after the tribunal has been established. As joinder requires agreement of the parties one can presume this agreement extends to all aspects of the arbitration, including the tribunal as composed. If there is no such agreement, joinder is impossible, even if all of them are parties to the same arbitration clause. This issue arose in ICC case no 5625 where the respondent wanted to join another company which had signed the arbitration agreement. The tribunal rejected the application for a joinder.[23] While the tribunal based its reasoning primarily on procedural issues relating to the naming of the parties in the request for arbitration, the crucial point it would seem is that the third party never agreed to that type of arbitration. Although it must have been aware of the possibility of multiparty arbitration its consent to the arbitration clause cannot be interpreted as a waiver of its right to be involved in the composition of the arbitration tribunal.

1.3. Other Issues

16-30 Even after the appointment of arbitrators, considerable problems may arise during the proceedings. This is especially the case where the parties on one side have opposing interests or have raised cross-claims.[24] It must be determined in which order the parties' submissions have to be presented. Do the several claimants or respondents have to submit their briefs all at the same time or can some of them be allowed additional time to answer allegations of their co-parties? An alternative would be to allow split submissions to deal with separate parts of the claim. There is no ideal solution to these problems. A tailor-made solution can only be found in party autonomy, confirmed in a specific written instrument, such as the terms of reference in an ICC arbitration or in the procedural directions issued by the tribunal.

16-31 The allocation of time at the hearings for each party to present its case must be determined. Does each party have the same amount of time or must equality be guaranteed between the claimants and respondents different sides? Must each side first answer the other side and then deal separately with different parties respective claims, or must all be presented at once? How can delay, which may result from the involvement of several parties be avoided? What happens if

---

[23] ICC case no 5625 in Jarvin Derains Arnaldez, *ICC Awards 1986 – 1990*, 484; for a different view see de Boisesson, *Le droit français de l'arbitrage*, 534 *et seq.*

[24] For a summary of the issues which arise in multiparty situations see Wetter, "Overview of the issues of multiparty arbitration", in ICC (ed), *Multiparty Arbitration, 9 et seq.*

one respondent brings a claim against another respondent? How are the costs of the arbitration allocated between the parties?

16-32 It is rare that parties provide for such issues in the arbitration agreement. It is also virtually impossible to set out general rules on how to deal with these issues apart from thc guiding principle that the procedure adopted must ensure equal treatment for all the parties.[25] The arbitration tribunal must regulate these issues and much will depend on the particular facts.[26]

16-33 An additional issue can arise in the context of company law where a number of disputes may affect all shareholders irrespective of whether or not they were parties to the relevant proceedings. For example, decisions of a shareholders meeting can sensibly only be annulled in relation to all shareholders and not only to those which participate in the annulment proceedings. Consequently national company laws often extend the effects of the relevant court decision to shareholders which were not parties to the proceedings. Whether these provisions are also applicable to arbitration awards, and if so under what conditions, or whether their non applicability even makes the arbitration agreement inoperable, may depend on the organisation of the arbitration proceedings and the applicable law. In some countries even if there is an arbitration agreement in the companies' bylaws or shareholder agreements, it may not be possible to arbitrate these company law disputes or at least require particular contractual provision.[27] In other countries their referral to arbitration

---

[25] Devolvé, "Final Report on Multi-Party Arbitrations", 6(1) *ICC Bulletin* 26 (1995) 38.

[26] A successful example of multiparty arbitration was *Andersen Consulting v Arthur Andersen and Andersen Worldwide*, where the dispute involving 140 parties was settled within two and a half years, 10 *Am Rev Int Arb* 437 (1999) 442; for another account of a complex multiparty arbitration involving 17 parties see Medalie, "The Libyan Producers Agreement Arbitration – Developing Innovative Procedures in a Complex Multiparty Arbitration", 7(2) *J Int'l Arb* 7 (1990).

[27] Bundesgerichtshof, 29 March 1996, BGHZ 132, 278; the controversial judgment has led to an abundant literature discussing its effect on German arbitration law. For a correct interpretation of the misleadingly worded decision, allegedly dealing with the arbitrability of such disputes, see Schmidt, "Schiedklauseln und Schiedsverfahren im Gesellschaftsrecht als prozessuale Legitmationsprobleme - Ein Beitrag zur Verzahnung von Gesellschafts- und Prozessrecht", 56 *Betriebs-Berater* 1857 (2001) 1858. For an overview of the suggested clauses and a workable Model clause see Zilles, *Schiedsgerichtsbarkeit im Gesellschaftsrecht,* 43 *et seq.*

may not be a problem despite the extension of the effects of the award to other shareholders.[28]

2. MULTIPARTY ARBITRATIONS ARISING OUT OF SEPARATE OR A SERIES OF CONTRACTS

16-34 In a typical construction and engineering contractual situation there will often be separate contracts between employer and main contractor, main contractor and sub-contractor, employer and supplier, supplier and sub-contractor. When a dispute arises between two of these parties there will be no direct contractual links to the other contracts. Each contract will have its own arbitration clause.

16-35 If disputes arise between an employer and a main contractor and which primarily relate to the work carried out by a sub-contractor, the main contractor may have an interest in these disputes being resolved in a single arbitration to which the sub-contractor is a party or which is binding on him.[29] Otherwise the main contractor faces the risk of exposure should the tribunals come to different conclusions. For example, a tribunal in an arbitration with the employer may find that the work carried out does not meet the contractual standard and hold it liable, but in the ensuing proceedings against the sub-contractor to recover damages for defective work, the second tribunal could reach a different conclusion. By corollary, a tribunal could decide on a longer extension of time than a second tribunal.

16-36 The interest in having an arbitration with all parties concerned is not only limited to the main contractor. A sub-contractor who may be bound by the outcome of the arbitration between the employer and the main contractor may therefore want to participate in that arbitration. The employer may also be interested in having a second solvent party against which to enforce the award.[30]

---

28 Austrian Oberster Gerichtshof, 10 December 1998, *RdW* 206 (1999) = *ecolex* 106 (1999); for an English report of the case see Reiner, "Some Recent Austrian Court Decisions in the Field of Arbitration", 17(2) *J Int'l Arb* 85 (2000).

29 For such a situation see *Abu Dhabi Gas Liquefaction Co Ltd v Eastern Bechtel Corp* [1982] 2 Lloyd's Rep 425; *Lafarge Redlands Aggregates Ltd v Shephard Hill Civil Engineering Ltd,* [2000] 1 WLR 1621.

30 Level, "Joinder of Proceedings, Intervention of Third Parties and additional Claims and Counterclaims", 7(2) *ICC Bulletin* 36 (1996) 39.

16-37 The problem in such a situation is that due to the consensual nature of arbitration in general an agreement to arbitrate between all parties is required.[31] Once a dispute has arisen it is rare that all parties will agree on a single multiparty arbitration. There will usually be at least one party who sees advantages in separate proceedings.[32]

16-38 Whether a party can be compelled to participate in a single multiparty arbitration depends on the provisions in the various contracts, the chosen arbitration rules and the applicable law. They may allow joinder of a party or provide for consolidation of different arbitration proceedings. Consolidation means that several arbitrations which are pending or initiated are united into a single set of proceedings before the same tribunal. Joinder is when a third party who is not a party to the arbitration agreement is joined as a party to the arbitration proceedings.

2.1. Joinder and Intervention of Third Parties

16-39 Joinder of third parties or their intervention in the proceedings is a well known feature in litigation in state courts. For reasons of efficient administration of justice national court rules allow the joinder of third parties, irrespective of whether all parties concerned agree. The only requirement is, in general, that such joinder is necessary for reasons of procedural economy and the effective administration of justice, since the cases involve the same issues and are closely related. The power to compel the parties to participate in those proceedings stems from the national court's sovereign power.

16-40 The situation is completely different in arbitration. Since the jurisdiction of the tribunal is based on the agreement of the parties the idea of statutory joinder or intervention appears to be in conflict with this basic principle of arbitration. With rare exceptions the arbitration laws consider this principle of party autonomy to be so important as to outweigh any considerations of procedural efficacy. Consequently, very few laws contain provisions which allow for a joinder or intervention against the will of any of the parties concerned. Generally joinder is only possible if all parties involved consent.

---

[31] Devolvé, "Final Report on Multi-Party Arbitrations", 6(1) *ICC Bulletin* 26 (1995) 27; Level, "Joinder of Proceedings, Intervention of Third Parties and additional Claims and Counterclaims", (7(2) *ICC Bulletin* 36 (1996) 37.

[32] Platte, "When Should an Arbitrator Join Cases?", 18 *Arb Int* 67 (2002) 71.

16-41 It is not sufficient that the parties to an arbitration agreement have, either in the agreement itself or otherwise, agreed for a third party to be joined if that party does not agree to such a joinder. Furthermore, a third party wishing to intervene in arbitration proceedings cannot do so without the consent of all parties to the arbitration.

16-42 In both situations it is not necessary that the parties consent at the time the request is made. Such consent may be given at an earlier stage in the contract itself, for example by agreeing to arbitration under one of the few arbitration rules which allow for joinder or the intervention of third parties. The consequence is that none of the parties can object when a third party wants to join with the consent of another party.

16-43 For example, Article 22(1)(h) LCIA rules provides

> (1) Unless the parties at any time agree otherwise in writing, the Arbitral Tribunal shall have the power, on the application of any party or of its own motion, but in either case only after giving the parties a reasonable opportunity to state their views;
>
> ...
>
> (h) to allow, only upon the application of a party, one or more third persons to be joined in the arbitration as a party provided any such third person and the applicant party have consented thereto in writing, and thereafter to make a single final award, or separate awards, in respect of all parties so implicated in the arbitration.

16-44 It is noteworthy that Article 22(1)(h) requires the consent of the third party to be joined as well as of the party applying for a joinder.[33] It has a much narrower scope than the provisions providing for joinder and intervention in court proceedings which do not require such consent. Its only effect is that the second party to the arbitration agreement does not have to expressly consent to the joinder. It has done so by agreeing to the LCIA Rules. The decision whether to allow a joinder is taken by the tribunal which has discretion in this respect.

16-45 A narrower provision can be found in Rule 18 of the Arbitration Rules of the Geneva Chamber of Commerce and Industry (CCIG) which provides

> (1) If a respondent intends to cause a third party to participate in the arbitration, it shall so state in its answer and shall state the reasons for such participation. The respondent shall deliver to the CCIG an additional copy of its answer.

---

[33] This does not, however, cover the eventuality of joining a third party in relation to a counterclaim.

(2) The CCIG shall send the answer to the third party whose participation is sought, the provisions of Articles 8 and 9 being applicable by analogy.
(3) Upon receipt of the third party's answer, the CCIG shall decide on the participation of the third party in the already pending proceeding, taking into account all of the circumstances. If the CCIG accepts the participation of the third party, it shall proceed with the formation of the arbitral tribunal in accordance with Article 17; if it does not accept the participation, it shall proceed according to Article 12.
(4) The decision of the CCIG regarding the participation of third parties shall not prejudice the decision of the arbitrators on the same subject. Regardless of the decision of the arbitrators on such participation, the formation of the arbitral tribunal cannot be challenged.

16-46 This provision only allows for a joinder of a third party by the respondent. The rationale is that the claimant initiated the proceedings and could have named any party it wanted as a respondent from the outset. Furthermore, the request for a joinder must already be contained in the reply to the statement of claim. At a later stage joinder is only possible with the consent of all parties concerned.[34] It is noteworthy that it is the institution which decides first on the participation of a third party, however, without prejudice to the decision of the arbitration tribunal. The tribunal will have the final say on a joinder or intervention.

16-47 Due to the inherent conflict between the consensual nature of arbitration and a statutory joinder not based on consent, the different arbitration laws in general do not contain provisions dealing with the joinder of third parties or their intervention. The drafters of the Model Law saw no need to include a specific provision.[35] The underlying rationale was that either the parties agree on a joinder so that no further regulation is necessary or there will be no joinder.

16-48 A special provision dealing with the issue of a joinder can be found in the Netherlands CCP, Article 1045

(1) At the written request of a third party who has an interest in the outcome of the arbitral proceedings, the arbitral tribunal may permit such party to join the proceedings, or to intervene therein. The arbitral tribunal shall send without delay a copy of the request to the parties.

---

34 For a detailed analysis see Imhoos, "The 1992 Geneva Chamber of Commerce and Industry Arbitration Rules under Scrutiny", 9(4) *J Int'l Arb* 121 (1992) 132.
35 Holtzmann and Neuhaus, *Model Law*, 311-312.

(2) A party who claims to be indemnified by a third party may serve a notice of joinder on such a party. A copy of the notice shall be sent without delay to the arbitral tribunal and the other party.
(3) The joinder, intervention or joinder for the claim of indemnity may only be permitted by the arbitral tribunal, having heard the parties, if the third party accedes by agreement in writing between him and the parties to the arbitration agreement.
(4) On the grant of a request for joinder, intervention, or joinder for the claim of indemnity, the third party becomes a party to the arbitral proceedings. Unless the parties have agreed thereon, the arbitral tribunal shall determine the further conduct of the proceedings.

16-49 It is important to note that Article 1045(3) requires the consent of all parties for a joinder to be possible, so that despite all criticism it is not comparable to the provisions allowing for a joinder in proceedings in the state courts.[36] The decision whether to allow the joinder or not if all parties agree is taken by the arbitration tribunal.

2.2. Consolidation of Different Arbitrations

16-50 Consolidation of different arbitration proceedings also requires the consent of the parties. The only difference with joinder is that with consolidation all parties have submitted to arbitration arising from different contracts. The issue is whether these arbitrations can be consolidated into one set of proceedings to avoid inconsistent results.

(a) Arbitration agreement

16-51 The easiest way to facilitate consolidation is an agreement by the parties or a special provision in the arbitration clause. Such agreements are rare in practice.[37] They are difficult to draft since they have to anticipate the possible disputes that may arise between the parties concerned.[38] It is not surprising that none of the leading arbitration institutions has officially recommended a multiparty arbitration clause providing for consolidation.

---

36 Van den Berg, van Delden and Snijders, *Netherlands Arbitration Law*, 69.

37 One of the few examples where the parties agreed on consolidation after the dispute had arisen is ICC case no 6719, Arnaldez Derains Hascher, *ICC Awards 1991-1995*, 567 *et seq.*

38 Redfern and Hunter, *International Commercial Arbitration*, para 3-80; Berger, *International Economic Arbitration*, 296; Leboulanger, "Multi-Contract Arbitration", 13(4) *J Int'l Arb* 43 (1996) 72 *et seq.*

16-52 The clauses discussed usually are based on broad notions such as "related dispute"[39] which are complicated in practice. This leads to questions of what constitutes the necessary connection: must it be a legal or economic, direct or indirect, strong or weak connection? Furthermore it is not sufficient that the arbitration clause in one contract allows for a consolidation but the clauses of all contracts involved must do so. Only then can there be consent of all parties affected by the consolidation.

16-53 An example of the problems encountered in drafting arbitration clauses allowing for the consolidation of separate arbitration proceedings between different parties is provided by the decision of the House of Lords in *Lafarge Redland v Shepard Hill.*[40] The case arose out of the construction of a road. The main contract between the respondent and the employer contained a standard ICE arbitration clause. According to the standard dispute resolution clause contained in the subcontract all disputes in connection with the subcontract were to be finally settled by arbitration. Where those disputes also related to disputes under the main contract the main contractor had the right to

> require that any such dispute under this subcontract shall be dealt with jointly with the dispute under the main contract in accordance with the provisions of clause 66 thereof. In connection with such joint dispute the sub-contractor shall be bound in like manner as the contractor by any decision of the engineer or any award by an arbitrator.

16-54 When the subcontractor declared its intention to initiate arbitration proceedings the general contractor gave notice under this provision. Respondent applied to the court to challenge the validity of the notices given. In interpreting the procedure anticipated under the clause, for which the parties submitted four different suggestions, the Court of Appeal concluded that a tripartite arbitration proceeding was envisaged. The problem involved in this interpretation and clearly seen by the Court of Appeal was that the employer under its contract with the general contractor could not be forced to take part in this proceeding since the arbitration clause did not contain such an obligation.

---

[39] See, *e.g.*, the clause discussed by the ICC working group on multiparty arbitration, Annex II to ICC Doc 420/276, which however was not approved officially by the ICC; see also the other clauses listed in the final report on Multiparty Arbitration, *ICC Bulletin* 26 (1995) 42 *et seq.*

[40] *Lafarge Redlands Aggregates Ltd v Shephard Hill Civil Engineering Ltd,* [2000] 1 WLR 1621; for another example see the decision by the Privy Council in *The Bay Hotel and Resort Ltd v Cavalier Construction Co Ltd,* [2001] UKPC 34, 17(1) Mealey's IAR B-1 (2002), B-7 *et seq.*

16-55 This interpretation was upheld by the majority in the House of Lords. The two dissenting judges rejected this interpretation and one including joint hearings. It interpreted the clause in such a way as to "request the contractor to represent the interest of the sub-contractor in the proceedings before the engineer and the arbitrator under the main contract." If the contractor does so in the observance of good faith the sub-contractor is bound by the results.

16-56 It may be possible to interpret less explicit arbitration clauses as permissive of consolidation of proceedings. If all contracts concluded in connection with a single economic venture between the different parties involved contain identically worded arbitration clauses this may be an indication of consent to consolidation. The same may apply when the heads of agreement of a specific project contains an arbitration clause to which the different contracts concluded in the execution of this heads of agreement refer. In both situations the mere fact of an identical wording in itself is not conclusive.[41]

16-57 The question of multiparty arbitration on the basis of different arbitration clauses became an issue in the *Andersen* arbitration arising out of the dissolution of the Andersen Organisation.[42] It consisted of Andersen Worldwide, the umbrella entity based in Geneva responsible for co-ordinating the activities of all member firms, and more than 140 member firms located around the world which constituted the Andersen Consulting and Arthur Andersen business units of the Andersen Organisation. When Andersen Consulting initiated arbitration proceedings against Andersen Worldwide and Arthur Andersen to be relieved of its contractual obligation to pay hundreds of millions of dollars in transfer payments annually, the respondents challenged the jurisdiction of the sole arbitrator. They relied on the fact that though the member firm parties' contract was supposed to be based on a standard form contract, the arbitration clauses differed since many of the member firms had not yet updated their particular contracts to include the most recently approved arbitration clause. While earlier forms did not provide for ICC arbitration, or at least not when the place of

---

41 See Devolvé, "Final Report on Multi-Party Arbitrations", 6(1) *ICC Bulletin* 26 (1995) 32; Nicklisch, "Multi-Party Arbitration and Dispute Resolution in Major Industrial Projects", 11(4) *J Int'l Arb* 57 (1994) 60; but see also ICC case no 5989, XV *YBCA* 74 (1990), where a slightly different wording of arbitration clauses in the main agreement and the purchase contract concluded thereunder were not considered to be an obstacle to consolidation.

42 For a more detailed analysis of the various problems involved in this arbitration see the contributions by Ostrager, Thomas, and Smit in 10 *Am Rev Int'l Arb* 437 *et seq* (1999).

arbitration was in Switzerland, the most recent version of the arbitration clause on which the claimants relied provided for ICC arbitration.[43]

16-58 In an interim award the sole arbitrator assumed jurisdiction basing his decision on an intention of the parties to be bound by a single arbitration clause. Principles of good faith prevented the respondents from relying on the differences in wording. The respondents applied to the Swiss supreme court to have the award set aside. The supreme court rejected this application and confirmed the award on jurisdiction. It based its decision on principles of agency, incorporation by reference, waiver, estoppel and good faith which taken together led it to conclude that the whole dispute should be resolved in a single arbitration despite the existence of at least three types of differently worded arbitration clauses. The court held that on the basis of the mentioned theories the most recent arbitration clause was binding on all parties. Interesting in this respect is that the court found the doctrines to be applicable not on the basis of a particular national law but as "general principles of law."

16-59 In general, however, differences in such substantial matters as the chosen seat or the applicable law usually exclude consolidation.[44] Even where all contracts involved are concluded within the framework of the same venture between the various parties involved, the arbitration tribunal has to verify its jurisdiction in relation to each party and to each issue. It cannot assume a global jurisdiction for all contracts concluded for that venture.

16-60 This is well illustrated by a decision of the French Cour d'appel de Versailles following the break up of the Iranian-French nuclear co-operation in the aftermath of the Iranian Revolution.[45] The various French claimants had based their application on two arbitration clauses contained in different contracts. The clauses differed as one provided for the seat of arbitration in France and the application of French law, while the other was silent on these issues. The arbitration tribunal assumed jurisdiction at least in relation to some of the parties involved and rendered an award in a unified arbitration. On an application by the Iranian party, the French court annulled the award. It rejected the view that the tribunal could assume jurisdiction over parties or claims not covered by a specific

---

[43] The various versions of the arbitration clauses can be found in the judgment of the Swiss Supreme Court, 10 *Am Rev Int'l Arb* 459 (1999) 461 *et seq.*

[44] Platte, "When Should an Arbitrator Join Cases?", 18 *Arb Int* 67 (2002) 72.

[45] Cour d'appel Versailles, 7 March 1990, *OIAETI et Sofidif v Cogema et al*, Rev Arb 326 (1991) with note Loquin.

arbitration clause on the basis of a general will of all parties in a project to submit to arbitration.[46]

16-61 In all these cases the question of whether consolidation is possible depends in the end on an interpretation of the various arbitration agreements. It is therefore up to the arbitration tribunal to decide whether or not to consolidate since the issue falls within its competence-competence.

(b) Arbitration rules

16-62 Consent to consolidation can also arise from the chosen arbitration rules. Some rules contain special provisions for consolidation under certain circumstances.[47] A good example is Article 11 CEPANI Rules

> When several contracts containing the CEPANI arbitration clause give rise to disputes that are closely related or indivisible, the Appointments Committee or the Chairman of CEPANI is empowered to order the joinder of the arbitration proceedings.
>
> This decision shall be taken either at the request of the Arbitral Tribunal, or, prior to any other issue, at the request of the parties or the most diligent party, or even on CEPANI's own motion.
>
> Where the request is granted, the Appointments Committee or the Chairman of CEPANI shall appoint the Arbitral Tribunal that shall decide the disputes that were joined. If necessary, it shall increase the number of arbitrators to a maximum of five.
>
> The Appointments Committee or the Chairman of CEPANI shall make its decision after having summoned the parties, and, if need be, the arbitrators who have already been appointed.
>
> They may not order the joinder of disputes in which an interim award, or an award on admissibility or on the merits of the claim, has already been rendered.

16-63 The first sentence clarifies that consolidation is only possible if all contracts contain a CEPANI arbitration clause. Only then can all parties involved be assumed to have consented to a consolidation. These clauses need not be identical. However, if one contract contains a different (*e.g.* institutional or *ad hoc*) clause those parties can resist consolidation if the latter is not provided for

---

[46] *Ibid*, 337-338.

[47] See also Society of Maritime Arbitrators (NY) Arbitration Rules, section 2. Commented on by Bulow, "The Revised Arbitration Rules of the Society of Maritime Arbitrators", 12(1) *J Int'l Arb* 87 (1995).

by the applicable arbitration law. Furthermore, it is the institution which decides on the consolidation of separate proceedings and not the tribunal.

16-64 A slightly different procedure can be found in the Zurich Arbitration Rules. For each arbitration in a multiparty situation the same three member tribunal is appointed. The arbitrators can then decide whether or not to consolidate the different arbitrations. Article 13 provides

> If there are several claimants or several respondents, or if the respondent, within the deadline for the answer, files a claim with the Zurich Chamber of Commerce, against a third party based on an arbitration clause valid according to Article 2 subs. 2 an identical three-men Arbitral Tribunal is appointed according to Article 12 subs. 3 for the first and all other arbitrations.
>
> The Arbitral Tribunal may conduct the arbitrations separately, or consolidate them, partly or altogether.

16-65 Although not as clear as the CEPANI rule, the Zurich rule requires that all contracts concerned contain an arbitration clause in favour of the Zurich Chamber of Commerce as this could be interpreted as consent to that type of procedure. However, it is doubtful whether the mere reference to a set of arbitration rules which contain comparable provisions on consolidation or joinder can be seen as a consent of the parties to multiparty arbitration.[48] The decision on consolidation is split between the institution, which decides on the appointment of an identical tribunal, and the tribunal which decides whether or not to consolidate the proceedings.[49]

(c) Arbitration laws

16-66 If no agreement exists between the parties, consolidation can only be based on the law governing the arbitration. However, given that consolidation of arbitration proceedings without the consent of the parties seems to be contrary to the fundamental principle of party autonomy, very few arbitration laws provide for statutory consolidation. In general, if provisions on consolidation are contained at all, they usually require the consent of all parties involved.

16-67 This is apparent in the provision of the English Arbitration Act dealing with consolidation and concurrent hearings. Section 35 provides

> (1) The parties are free to agree

---

48 Berger, *International Economic Arbitration*, 308 *et seq.*

49 See also JCAA Commercial Arbitration Rules Rule 41.

> (a) that the arbitral proceedings shall be consolidated with other arbitral proceedings, or
> (b) that concurrent hearings shall be held, on such terms as may be agreed.
> (2) Unless the parties agree to confer such power on the tribunal, the tribunal has no power to order consolidation of proceedings or concurrent hearings.[50]

16-68 Although the Model Law does not deal with the issue at all,[51] a number of countries, when adopting the Model Law, included provisions on consolidation. Like the English provision, these rules generally require that all parties concerned agree to consolidation or concurrent hearings. Then the courts or the arbitration tribunal have the powers necessary to overcome difficulties in appointing the arbitrators and organising the proceedings. For example, the International Commercial Arbitration Act of British Columbia provides in section 27(2)

> Where the parties to 2 or more arbitration agreements have agreed, in their respective arbitration agreements or otherwise, to consolidate the arbitrations arising out of those arbitration agreements, the Supreme Court may, on application by one party with the consent of all the other parties to those arbitration agreements, do one or more of the following:
> (a) order the arbitrations to be consolidated on terms the court considers just and necessary;
> (b) where all parties cannot agree on an arbitral tribunal for the consolidated arbitration, appoint an arbitral tribunal in accordance with section 11 (8);
> (c) where all parties cannot agree on any other matter necessary to conduct the consolidated arbitration, make any other order it considers necessary.[52]

16-69 Similar provisions can be found in a number of state arbitration statutes in the US.[53] In Australia[54] the powers are not conferred on the courts but on the

---

[50] Similar provisions can be found in Canada, British Columbia Commercial Arbitration Act section 21; US, Florida International Arbitration Act section 684(12).

[51] For the reasons see First Working Group Report A/CN9/216, para 37.

[52] See also Ontario, International Commercial Arbitration Act section 7; Alberta, Arbitration Act section 8(4)(5).

[53] California International Arbitration and Conciliation Act, sections 1297.272 and 273; Texas, CCP sections 172-173; Oregon, Mediation and Arbitration Act 36.506(2); Ohio, International Arbitration Act section 2712.52; North Carolina, Act on Commercial Arbitration section 1-567.57.

[54] International Arbitration Act section 24.

arbitration tribunal.[55] Sometimes distinctions are made between arbitrations pending before the same tribunal and those pending before different tribunals and under some laws the provisions are limited to arbitrations between the same parties.[56]

16-70 Since these rules require an agreement of the parties for consolidation they are not really legislative solutions comparable to these applicable in litigation where typically no consent of the parties is required. Such a rule is, however, contained in the Netherlands Arbitration Law. Article 1046 provides

> (1) If arbitral proceedings have been commenced before an arbitral tribunal in the Netherlands concerning a subject matter which is connected with the subject matter of arbitral proceedings commenced before another arbitral tribunal in the Netherlands, any of the parties may, unless the parties have agreed otherwise, request the President of the District Court in Amsterdam to order a consolidation of the proceedings.
> (2) The President may wholly or partially grant or refuse the request, after he has given all parties and the arbitrators an opportunity to be heard. His decision shall be communicated in writing to all parties and the arbitral tribunals involved.
> (3) If the President orders consolidation in full, the parties shall in consultation with each other appoint one arbitrator or an uneven number of arbitrators and determine the procedural rules which shall apply to the consolidated proceedings. If, within the period of time prescribed by the President, the parties have not reached agreement on the above, the President shall, at the request of any party, appoint the arbitrator or arbitrators and, if necessary, determine the procedural rules which shall apply to the consolidated proceedings. The President shall determine the remuneration for the work already carried out by the arbitrators whose mandate is terminated by reason of the full consolidation.
> (4) If the President orders partial consolidation, he shall decide which disputes shall be consolidated. The President shall, if the parties fail to agree within the period of time prescribed by him, at the request of any party, appoint the arbitrator or arbitrators and determine which rules shall apply to the consolidated proceedings. In this event the arbitral tribunals before which arbitrations have already been commenced shall suspend those arbitrations. The award of the arbitral tribunal appointed for the consolidated arbitration shall be communicated in writing to the

---

55 See also New Zealand, Arbitration Act 1996 section 2 (Second Schedule) where an appeal can be brought in the state courts if the tribunal or the tribunals do not consolidate the proceedings; for a detailed analysis of the differences see Sanders, *Quo Vadis Arbitration?*, 215 *et seq.*

56 Bermuda, Arbitration Act 1986 section 9 (for domestic arbitration which also applies to international arbitrations, if parties contract out of the Model Law).

other arbitral tribunals involved. Upon receipt of this award, these arbitral tribunals shall continue the arbitrations commenced before them and decide in accordance with the award rendered in the consolidated proceedings.

16-71 The Dutch construction industry was the driving force behind the inclusion of this rule and is also the main user of the provision. On average three requests for consolidation are made per year and are usually granted.[57] In these cases it is not the arbitration tribunal that orders consolidation but the courts.

16-72 Comparable provisions exist in the arbitration laws for domestic arbitration in Hong Kong[58] and in the various Australian States and Territories.[59] Furthermore Article 1126 NAFTA contains a special provision allowing for consolidation of different arbitration proceedings.[60]

16-73 In addition, there is significant opinion in Switzerland which suggests that consolidation of arbitrations can be allowed under Article 185 PIL which provides for court assistance in arbitration.[61]

16-74 It is hard to reconcile these provisions with the principle of party autonomy which lies at the heart of commercial arbitration. Few parties will be aware of those provisions when selecting the place of arbitration so that the determination of the place can hardly be seen as a consent to consolidation. There is concern that parties may have to engage in arbitrations with other parties with whom they never contracted. Furthermore, due to the involvement of multiple

---

57 Van Haersolte van Hof, "Consolidation under the English Arbitration Act 1996: A View from the Netherlands", 13 *Arb Int* 427 (1997) 428 who reports initiatives taken by the construction industry to replace the system of court-ordered consolidation by a system of institution-ordered consolidation.

58 Hong Kong Arbitration Ordinance section 6B; for applications of the provision see High Court of Hong Kong, 12 September 1986, *Shui On Construction Co Ltd v Moon Yik Co Ltd et al*, XIV YBCA 215 (1989); Veeder, "Consolidation: More News from the Front-Line - The Second Shui On Case", 3 *Arb Int* 262 (1987).

59 Section 26 of the various "Uniform Arbitration Acts"; see, *e.g.*, the Queensland Commercial Arbitration Act 1990; a detailed discussion of the provision, its legislative history and application can be found in de Fina, "Consolidation of Arbitration Proceedings in Australia", 4 *Int ALR* 164 (2001).

60 Under the provision, when an investor applies for consolidation a special tribunal is set up to deal with the request and consolidation may be ordered without the consent of all parties involved.

61 See, *e.g.*, Lalive, Poudret and Reymond, *L'arbitrage Interne et International en Suisse*, Article 185 no 7; Berti (ed), *International Arbitration in Switzerland*, Art 185, para 12. See similarly Leboulanger, "Multi-Contract Arbitration", 13(4) *J Int'l Arb* 43 (1996) 61 who suggests that in France courts may be allowed to consolidate *ad hoc* arbitrations under Article 1493 NCPC.

parties these proceedings may differ considerably from what was agreed.[62] Whether the perceived advantages of consolidation justify such an intrusion on party autonomy seems questionable.[63] The possibility of the parties excluding consolidation does not overcome this difficulty. Since few parties are aware of this possibility of consolidation they would have to agree an exclusion after the dispute has arisen. At that time it will be hard to agree as the parties will have different views concerning conflicting awards and delay of proceedings.

16-75 One other factor against consolidation without consent is confidentiality. A party may be willing to reveal its documents to a party with whom it contracted but not to a third party joining an arbitration, in particular, if that third party is its competitor or has some adverse interests.[64]

16-76 These objections are reflected in the practice of arbitration tribunals and state courts. In the vast majority of cases consolidation was only effected if agreed by the parties or when a special provision allowed for consolidation in arbitration.[65] A certain reservation must, however, be made with regard to the US practice. Although the Federal Arbitration Act does not contain a rule providing for consolidation, some US courts have done so relying on Rule 42(a) of the Federal Rules of Civil Procedure providing for consolidation in litigation.

16-77 In 1975 the Court of Appeal for the Second Circuit in *Compania Espanola de Petroleos SA v Nereus Shipping SA* dealing with a contract of affreightment for which a guarantee was given, consolidated the arbitrations between the shipowner and the guarantor and between the shipowner and the charterer. In rejecting the respondent's objection to consolidation the court held

> We agree that Fed. R. Civ P., Rules 42 (a) and 81 (a) (3), are applicable. Moreover, we think the liberal purpose of the Federal Arbitration Act clearly requires that this

---

[62] If in both arbitration proceedings tribunals have already been appointed disputes may arise as to which arbitrator remains in place, if any.

[63] Critical also Berger, *International Economic Arbitration*, 301 *et seq*; Jarvin, "Consolidated Arbitrations, the New York Arbitration Convention and the Dutch Arbitration Act 1986 - a Critique of Dr van den Berg", 3 *Arb Int* 254 (1987).

[64] *Oxford Shipping Company Limited v Nippon Yusen Kaisha (The Eastern Saga)* [1984] 2 Lloyd's Rep 373; Leboulanger, "Multi-Contract Arbitration", 13(4) *J Int'l Arb* 43 (1996) 65 *et seq*; Collins, "Privacy and Confidentiality in Arbitration Proceedings", 11 *Arb Int* 321 (1995).

[65] Compare also Kaplan and Morgan, "Hong Kong Law", *ICCA Handbook* (1999) 18, reporting that section 6B Arbitration Ordinance, which allows for court ordered consolidation in domestic cases, is rarely used.

> act be interpreted so as to permit and even encourage the consolidation of arbitration proceedings in proper cases, such as the one before us.[66]

16-78 This ruling followed by some district courts[67] has been rejected by several courts of appeal which required the parties' consent for consolidation.[68] In 1993 the Court of Appeal for the Second Circuit in *Government of the United Kingdom of Great Britain v Boeing Co*[69] abandoned its earlier ruling and denied the applicability of Rule 42(a) to arbitration agreements. In dealing with the arguments of the plaintiff the court stated

> The United Kingdom also makes much of the inefficiencies and possible inconsistent determinations that may result if the United Kingdom/Boeing and United Kingdom/Textron arbitrations are allowed to proceed separately. Although these may be valid concerns to the United Kingdom, they do not provide us with the authority to reform the private contracts which underlie this dispute. If contracting parties wish to have all disputes that arise from the same factual situation arbitrated in a single proceeding, they can simply provide for consolidated arbitration in the arbitration clauses to which they are a party.

(d) Other possible consolidation solutions

16-79 In the light of the difficulties concerning consolidation and joinder it is not surprising that practice has searched for other solutions to the problems of multiparty arbitration. One way that the threat of conflicting decisions can be minimised is by appointing the same arbitrators in the different arbitrations. This requires the different arbitration agreements to provide that the same arbitrators should be appointed in all arbitrations relating to contracts concluded for the same purpose.[70] This is a practical, not a legal consolidation. Even when such arbitration agreements do not exist courts have expressed their willingness to appoint the same arbitrators for different arbitrations arising out of contracts

---

66 527 F 2d 966, 968-970, 974-976.

67 *Sidermar SpA v Antco Shipping Co Ltd and New England Petroleum Corp*, (SDNY 1977) cited by van den Berg, *New York Convention*, 164; for further cases see Schwartz, "Multiparty Disputes and Consolidated Arbitration: An Oxymoron or the Solution to a Continuing Dilemma?", *Case W J Int'l L* 341 (1990) 347 *et seq.*

68 See *Weyershaeuser Co v Western Seas Shipping Co* 743 F 2d 635 (9th Cir 1984); *De E Webb Constr v Richardson Hosp Autho,* 823 F 2d 145, 150 (5th Cir 1987); *Protective Life Ins Corp v Lincoln Nat'l Life Ins Corp* 873, F 2d 281, 282 (11th Cir 1989); *American Centennial Ins Co v National Casualty Co*, 951 F2 d 107, 108 (6th Cir 1991).

69 998 F 2d 68 (2d Cir 1993).

70 This is the solution adopted by Zurich Chamber of Commerce Arbitration Rules Article 13.

concluded for a common purpose. Lord Denning, regretting that the court could not order a consolidation of the arbitrations, stated in the *Adgas* case

> It seems to me that there is ample power in the court to appoint in arbitration the same arbitrator. It seems to me highly desirable that this should be done so as to avoid inconsistent findings.[71]

16-80 This approach was also adopted in Iran-US Claims Tribunal where the President of the Tribunal could refer cases involving the same preliminary or main issue which were pending before different Chambers to the same Chamber.[72] However, this solution might face considerable difficulties where the arbitrators are not appointed by the same appointing authority but by the parties. Conflicting decisions will primarily concern the party which is involved in both arbitrations. Other parties may give more weight to their right to nominate or appoint an arbitrator in whom they have confidence than the risk of conflicting decisions. A person appointed by a party in one arbitration may not enjoy the trust of the party in the other arbitration. In many cases a party may intentionally and legitimately decide to appoint a different arbitrator in the related case. If not provided in the arbitration agreement none of the parties could be forced to appoint an arbitrator who would also be suitable for the other arbitration.[73]

16-81 Another possible way forward is to hold concurrent hearings for the connected parts of the proceedings. Some arbitration rules, for example, the LMAA rules provide for concurrent hearings, and even regulate the admissibility of evidence used in one set of proceedings in other proceedings.[74]

---

[71] *Abu Dhabi Gas Liquefaction Co Ltd v Eastern Bechtel Corp* [1982] 2 Lloyd's Rep 425, 427.

[72] Presidential Order no 1, 19 October 1981, no 5(a); see also Devolvé, "Final Report on Multi-Party Arbitrations", 6(1) *ICC Bulletin* 26 (1995) 36.

[73] For further problems with appointing the same tribunal relating to impartiality and preconceptions see Level, "Joinder of Proceedings, Intervention of Third Parties and additional Claims and Counterclaims", 7(2) *ICC Bulletin* 36 (1996) 43 *et seq*; Gravel, "Multiparty Arbitration and Multiple Arbitrations", 7(2) *ICC Bulletin* 45 (1996) 49 *et seq.*

[74] See Article 14(b) which grants the tribunal the following powers to avoid unnecessary delay or expense

> Where two or more arbitrations appear to raise common issues of fact or law, the tribunals may direct that the two or more arbitrations shall be heard concurrently. Where such an order is made, the tribunals may give such directions as the interests of fairness, economy and expedition require including:
> (i) that the documents disclosed by the parties in one arbitration shall be made available to the parties to the other arbitration upon such conditions as the tribunals may determine;

16-82 The Supreme Court of New South Wales in *Aerospatiale v Elspan et al.*[75] even considered extending this approach to cases where the arbitration proceedings were concurrent to court proceedings. To avoid conflicting decisions in the parallel proceedings the court assumed that under Part 72 of the Supreme Court Rules it could in the court proceedings

> appoint a person, agreed as an arbitrator in respect of some issues in dispute between particular parties, as referee to hear and report to the court upon associated matters in dispute between the same parties, and additional parties. The court also has a power to fix the hearing of that reference at the same time as the arbitration (Part 72 r2 and r8). Equally it has a power to give directions to regarding the conduct of an arbitration within the purview of the Commercial Arbitration Act 1984 (Sect. 47). That includes a power to direct when the arbitration is to be heard.[76]

16-83 Another solution which is found in practice is to stay one set of proceedings until the other has been terminated.[77] That allows the tribunal in the second arbitration at least to take into account the solution reached in the first set of proceedings. However, this has the disadvantages of considerably delaying any resolution of the dispute in the second set of proceedings and breaching the privacy and confidentiality of the arbitration process.[78]

16-84 A particular solution for multiparty situations is followed in the commodity trade with only one arbitration for a string or chain contract. Goods are often sold to a purchaser who then passes them on down a line of intermediaries until it reaches the final recipient to whom the goods are physically delivered. In such a situation disputes as to the quality of the goods do not have to be arbitrated up the chain in a number of arbitrations. Rather, the recipient of the goods can bring the arbitration against the original seller, and the result will bind all other parties. This prevents conflicting awards within the

---

(ii) that the evidence given in one arbitration shall be received and admitted in the other arbitration, subject to all parties being given a reasonable opportunity to comment upon it and subject to such other conditions as the tribunals may determine.

See also GAFTA Arbitration Rules Form no 125 Rule 7:2.

75 *Aerospatiale Holdings Australia Pty Ltd et al v Elspan International Pty Ltd (Hong Kong),* XIX YBCA 635 (1994), no 55053/92 (Supreme Court of New South Wales, 14 August 1992).

76 *Ibid*, 640, para 13.

77 See the decision of the US Supreme Court in *Volt Information Sciences, Inc v Board of trustees of Leland Stanford Junior University*, 109 S Ct 1248 (1989), in XV *YBCA* 131 (1990), where however, such an option was expressly provided for in the applicable Californian statute.

78 See, for a rejection of a stay, ICC case no 6610, XIX *YBCA* 162 (1994).

chain and saves money and time.[79] The same approach can be found in certain maritime arbitrations concerning the charter and the different sub-charters of a vessel which is allegedly not fit for purpose.[80]

16-85 While all these solutions are geared towards synchronising the different arbitrations, some national courts have come to the conclusion that arbitration agreements are inoperative in such multiparty situations.[81] Accordingly, such disputes are to be decided in the state courts where joinder and consolidation is possible. The argument is that the parties by inserting an arbitration clause in their contract opted for a final and complete solution of the ensuing disputes through arbitration. In multiparty situations a second set of arbitration proceedings may be necessary so the arbitration clause is not able to provide the final solution, and this renders the arbitration agreement inoperative. This argument misinterprets the notion of "inoperative" under Article II(3) New York Convention and the parties' intention, and has found little support in the courts.[82]

3. Consolidation of Different Arbitrations Between the Same Parties

16-86 At first sight the problems of whether a consolidation of separate proceedings between the same parties in multicontract situations is possible seems to be comparable to those in multiparty situations. However, considerable differences exist.

16-87 Most of the objections raised against consolidation of arbitrations arising out of separate contracts involving different parties are not totally relevant to consolidation of arbitrations in a two-party context. Issues of confidentiality do not arise, nor are parties forced into arbitrations with third parties with whom

---

[79] See, *e.g.*, GAFTA Arbitration Rules Form no 125 Rule 7:1 which foresees such a procedure for disputes on quality and conditions if the contracts in a string of contracts contain materially identical terms; Bernstein's *Handbook*, para 3-97 – 3-99.

[80] Bernstein's *Handbook*, para 4-87 – 4-89.

[81] See, *e.g.*, British Columbia Supreme Court, *Prince George (City) v McElhanney Engineering Services Ltd and Al Sims and Sons Ltd*, 6 *ADRLJ* 315 (1997); see also the cases cited by van den Berg, *New York Convention*, 162 *et seq.*

[82] See, *e.g.*, the rejection of such an interpretation by the Supreme Court of India, *Svenska Handelsbanken et al v Indian Charge Chrome Ltd et al*, XXI YBCA 557 (1996), 557 para 19 (24 January 1994); Alberta Court of Appeal, 16 January 1992, *Kaverit Steel and Crane Ltd et al v Kone Corporation et al*, XIX YBCA 643, 643 (1994).

they may not have entered into arbitration agreements.[83] Also the problems involving appointment of arbitrators are greatly reduced. Both parties can still appoint an arbitrator of their choice and are only restricted in so far as they cannot appoint different arbitrators for each arbitration – though there are situations where parties do not wish to appoint the same arbitrator for the two arbitrations. Furthermore, the procedure adopted by the arbitration tribunal in consolidated two-party arbitrations may be closer to the procedure actually foreseen by the parties than it is in consolidated multiparty arbitration.[84]

16-88 In the light of these differences consolidation in bi-party, multicontract situations pose fewer problems. They are provided for in some arbitration rules. Article 4(6) ICC Rules allows, in limited circumstances, consolidation on the request of one party.

> When a party submits a Request in connection with a legal relationship in respect of which arbitration proceedings between the same parties are already pending under these Rules, the Court may, at the request of a party, decide to include the claims contained in the Request in the pending proceedings provided that the Terms of Reference have not been signed or approved by the Court. Once the Terms of Reference have been signed or approved by the Court, claims may only be included in the pending proceedings subject to the provisions of Article 19. [85]

16-89 Whether an arbitration clause in one contract also covered disputes arising under a closely related but separate contract was an issue in ICC case no 5989.[86] The dispute concerned a series of contracts in connection with the reorganisation of a fuel distribution network. The claimant had concluded with the first respondent, a state organisation, a Basic Agreement under which the relevant contracts should be concluded. The agreement contained an arbitration clause and provided *inter alia* that the respondent had the right to purchase any equipment imported into the country upon termination of any of the more specific contracts. When the first contract was terminated the second respondent,

---

[83] See *Aerospatiale Holdings Australia Pty Ltd et al v Elspan International Pty Ltd (Hong Kong)*, XIX YBCA 635 (1994) 640, no 55053/92 (Supreme Court of New South Wales, Common Law Division, 14 August 1992).

[84] Leboulanger, "Multi-Contract Arbitration", 13(4) *J Int'l Arb* 43 (1996) 64 *et seq*.

[85] Similar provisions can be found in the rules of other institutions; see *e.g.*, Geneva Rule 16; Zurich Article 14.

[86] ICC case no 5989, XV *YBCA* 77 (1990); see also the decision of the Singapore High Court in *Mancon (BVI) Investment Holding Co Ltd v Henry Holdings SEA (Pte) Ltd*, [2000] 3 SLR 220 analysed by Dharmananda and Kiat, "The Great Bind: Joinder of Issue and Parties in Arbitration Proceedings", 16(2) *Mealey's IAR* 43 (2001).

due to an internal reorganisation, took over the functions of the first respondent and entered into a purchase agreement with the claimant which also provided for arbitration. When disputes arose relating to the purchase agreement, as well as the Basic Agreement, the claimant initiated arbitration proceedings against both respondents. The second respondent contested jurisdiction since it did not consider itself bound by the arbitration clause in the Basic Agreement. The tribunal held that the second respondent was the successor of the first respondent and therefore bound by the arbitration clause in the Basic Agreement. On the issue of hearing all disputes in one arbitration the tribunal said

> It is beyond doubt that the parties intended to have their disputes settled by arbitration, that both the arbitration clauses and the parties are identical and that the claims are connected in such a manner that in the context of an international arbitration we must find that their joint examination - apart from allowing a better understanding of the facts of the case - is admissible in the light of the intention of the parties, as expressed in the arbitration clauses. In fact, the Purchase Contract has been concluded 'in application of Article 4.3 of the Basic Agreement' and it refers in regard to the price of the purchase, to annex B 3 of the Basic Agreement.[87]

16-90 Where a party is seeking consolidation in an ICC arbitration it should request this at the outset from the ICC court. However, this does not prevent a tribunal from deciding a consolidation request. Consolidation can only take place after that by agreement of all the parties.

4. Guidelines as to the Appropriateness of Multiparty Arbitration

16-91 Where multiparty arbitration is legally possible and requested by one of the parties or potential parties the question arises whether the arbitration tribunal or the competent institution or court should make use of their power to allow for it. Although each case will turn on its specific facts certain guidelines can be given.

16-92 A multiparty arbitration is desirable and should be ordered if:

- It serves procedural economy, *i.e.* it saves time and money.
- It reduces the risk of inconsistent awards.
- It is fair and equitable in order to facilitate fact-finding and the comprehensive presentation of legal and factual positions.

---

87 ICC case no 5989, XV *YBCA* 77 (1990) 78, para 5.

- It is appropriate for purposes of privacy and confidentiality.
- The parties involved can have equal influence on the composition of the tribunal or if the selection of arbitrators is left to an appointing authority.

16-93 By corollary, multiparty arbitration should not be ordered if:

- Two arbitration tribunals have been constituted.[88]
- One of the parties wishes to appoint different arbitrators for the different arbitrations.
- It is apparent from the outset that the parties will not co-operate and will use every possible means to disrupt and delay the multiparty arbitration.
- The award will be vulnerable to challenges and anti-enforcement actions.

5. Problems of Enforcing Awards in Multiparty Arbitration

16-94 There is a real issue whether an arbitration award rendered in multiparty proceedings can be enforced. Under the New York Convention there are three fundamentals for enforcement. First, the parties must have agreed to submit their differences to arbitration. Second, the arbitrators must not have exceeded their authority. Third, the conduct of the arbitration must be fair.

16-95 Where the agreement is between two parties, they are the legitimate parties to the arbitration. If a third party is joined, or another dispute or arbitration is consolidated to the first arbitration, this may violate the fundamental agreement between the two parties to submit *their* disputes to arbitration.

16-96 Whether the award against or in favour of the third party joined to the arbitration, or involving the party or parties to the consolidated arbitration, can be enforced, will depend on whether there was agreement of all the parties concerned to the joinder or consolidation.[89] If the parties have all agreed on the joinder or consolidation, the award should be enforceable. However, where a tribunal, an institution, appointing authority or a national court has authority to order joinder or consolidation the issue is far from clear.

---

[88] Stipanowich, "The Search for Workable Solutions", 72 *Iowa L Rev* 513 (1987).

[89] See Privy Council, *The Bay Hotel and Resort Ltd v Cavalier Construction Co Ltd,* 17(1) Mealey's IAR B-1 (2002), B-7 *et seq.*

16-97 It is doubtful whether an award arising out of consolidated arbitration proceedings would be enforceable under the New York Convention. The expansion of multinational arbitrations has not undermined the fundamentals of party autonomy and the New York Convention. The most obvious basis for refusal to enforce an award would be the absence of an appropriate arbitration agreement between the parties.

16-98 Article IV(1) New York Convention requires, as a precondition for enforcement, that the arbitration agreement be filed with the court; this will show who the parties were to the arbitration agreement. The New York Convention allows a court to refuse enforcement of an award if a party was unable to present its case,[90] or the composition of the tribunal or the procedures were not as agreed.[91] To overcome this situation, tribunals and institutions should encourage the parties to record their agreement to joinder or consolidation. This can be in the terms of reference or in some other document, or the tribunal can record it in the procedural directions or other early procedural decisions.

16-99 Arbitrators must always be careful to ensure that they treat all the parties equally. In reaching conclusions in a dispute between two parties, the tribunal should not be influenced by extraneous evidence to the dispute from a third party, especially if one party has not been able, or has refused or failed, to refute or respond to claims on the basis that the third party is not properly a party to the arbitration. The tribunal's jurisdiction is properly prescribed by the terms of the agreement to arbitrate and must not make decisions or consider issues outside that scope. If the tribunal does go beyond its authority it could provide a basis for a court to refuse enforcement of the award under Article V(1)(c) New York Convention.

---

[90] Article V(1)(b).

[91] Article V(1)(d); for divergent views on this issue see Jarvin, "Consolidated Arbitrations, the New York Arbitration Convention and the Dutch Arbitration Act 1986 - a Critique of Dr van den Berg", 3 *Arb Int* 254 (1987); van den Berg, "Consolidated Arbitrations, the New York Arbitration Convention and the Dutch Arbitration Act 1986 - A Replique to Mr Jarvin", 3 *Arb Int* 257 (1987).

Chapter 17

DETERMINATION OF APPLICABLE LAW

17-1 The answer to every dispute may be found initially in the contract itself. What did the parties intend, what did they agree and what did they expect? Many disputes can be resolved without reference to any law or rules, and arbitrators need consider only the purpose of the contract and whether it has been attained, *e.g.*, questions of quality or conformity of goods, delivery or performance under the contract. The arbitration tribunal must determine what the parties intended and give effect to their intention.[1]

17-2 However, where there are issues which depend on an applicable legal or non-legal standard, the arbitration tribunal should determine what that law or standard is and apply it to determine the dispute.

17-3 The determination of the applicable substantive law is a critical issue in international arbitration. It has a legal, practical and psychological influence on every arbitration. Nothing is more important in any international arbitration than knowing the legal or other standards to apply to measure the rights and obligations of the parties. This is an independent exercise in the dispute resolution process for resolving the dispute itself.

17-4 There is a complex relationship between the parties' choice of arbitration as the mechanism for resolving their disputes, the overriding authority of party autonomy in the arbitration process and the methods of determining the applicable law that arbitrators must apply. As international arbitration has an independent, non-national and transnational character varying from case to case, so too the applicable laws and the choice of law methodologies also differ in every case. The existence of the arbitration in every instance is the result of the exercise of party autonomy. The choice of law process should reflect that same party autonomy.

17-5 There are various options available to an arbitration tribunal as to the law or rules to apply: national, non-national, or even international; legal, non-legal, or contractual. The first question for the arbitrators is how to determine this selection. What are the essential criteria for such a choice? Does the subjective view of the arbitrators prevail over the expressed will of the parties? In the absence of an express choice by the parties, is there some objective standard to be used by international arbitrators to determine the applicable law in a contractual dispute between parties from different countries? Should the choice of law process be determined on the basis of traditional national criteria or are there international or non-national criteria to be applied in the international or non-national arena?

17-6 In practical terms the first issue is always to see what the parties have chosen. As party autonomy is universally accepted as a connecting factor in private international law, a choice of law by the parties will avoid argument as to

---

[1] Lew, *Applicable Law*, para 439.

the law to apply to the issue in dispute, thus making any determination of the applicable law by the arbitrators unnecessary. However surprising, the applicable law is often not decided by the parties in advance and is left to be determined by the arbitrators.[2]

17-7 This chapter describes how in practice arbitration tribunals determine the legal or other standard to be applied to international commercial disputes and the extent to which conflict of laws rules are relied on. It considers separately (1) the application of the law chosen by the parties, (2) the independent determination of the applicable law by arbitrators in the absence of any choice by the parties, and suggests (3) a three-step method.

1. CHOICE OF LAW BY THE PARTIES – PARTY AUTONOMY

1.1. Party Autonomy in Context

17-8 All modern arbitration laws recognise party autonomy, *i.e.* parties are free to determine the substantive law or rules applicable to the merits of the dispute to be resolved by arbitration.[3] Party autonomy provides contracting parties with a mechanism of avoiding the application of an unfavourable or inappropriate law to an international dispute. This choice is and should be binding on the arbitration tribunal. This is also confirmed in most arbitration rules.[4]

17-9 Traditionally national law was the only basis for party autonomy and determined the conditions and limits within which it could be exercised. Party autonomy in international contracts has been well recognised and developed in

---

2 According to the statistics of the ICC approximately 20% of arbitrations do not have an express choice of law in the contract. In 1998 82.1% of cases, in 1999 82%, in 2000 77% and in 2001 78% included an express choice of law.

3 See Model Law Article 28(1); Belgium, Judicial Code Article 1700; Brazil, Arbitration Law Article 2; England, Arbitration Act section 46(1); France, NCPC Article 1496; Germany, ZPO section 1051(1); India, Arbitration Ordinance 1996, section 28(1)(b); Netherlands, CCP Article 1054(2); Russian Federation, International Arbitration Law 1993 Article 28; Switzerland, PIL Article 187(1).

4 See UNCITRAL Rules Article 33; AAA ICDR Article 28(1); ICC Article 17(1); LCIA Article 22(3); DIS section 23(1); CCI of the Russian Federation, section 13(1); NAI, Article 46; Stockholm Institute Article 24(1); Vienna Article 16(1); WIPO Article 59(1); Zurich Article 4.

national laws for many years.[5] Some authorities recognised party autonomy as having a legislative character between the parties, so that their agreement was effectively the making of private law by the parties.[6] In the context of international commercial arbitration, the right of parties to determine the law applicable to the merits of their dispute is undisputed.[7] This principle was confirmed in an International Law Institute resolution relating to international arbitration involving state parties in September 1989 [8] and has also been adopted in many international conventions relating to contracts or arbitration.[9]

17-10 Due to the universal acceptance of party autonomy in most developed legal systems and its origin in the express or determinable intention of the parties, it is now recognised that party autonomy operates as a right in itself. The rule has a special transnational or universal character and has binding effect because it has been agreed to and adopted by the parties. Unquestionably, party autonomy is the most prominent and widely accepted international conflict of laws rule. These national conflict of laws systems recognise that contracting parties do express their view as to the law to govern their contractual relations, and the national laws have no reason to ignore and very limited rights to interfere with the expressed will of the parties.

---

5 See Rabel, *The Conflict of Laws. A Comparative Study*, Vol I (2d ed, Drobnig 1958), 90.

6 See Wolff, *Private International Law* (Oxford 1950), 414.

7 See Lew, *Applicable Law*, para 441; Born, *International Commercial Arbitration*, 543. See similarly Berger, *International Economic Arbitration*, 480-481 and 556; Derains and Schwartz, *ICC Rules*, 217; Fouchard Gaillard Goldman *on International Commercial Arbitration*, para 1434; Redfern and Hunter, *International Commercial Arbitration*, para 2-24. Note, however, that Mustill and Boyd, *Commercial Arbitration*, 27 and Craig Park and Paulson, *1998 ICC Rules*, 101-102, suggest there remain some limits to the absolute freedom of choice of law.

8 XVI *YBCA* 236 (1991) 238. Article 6 states

> The parties have full autonomy to determine the procedural and substantive rules and principles that are to apply in the arbitration. In particular, (1) a different source may be chosen for the rules and principles applicable to each issue that arises and (2) these rules and principles may be derived from different national legal systems as well as from non-national sources such as principles of international law, general principles of law, and the usages of international commerce.

9 See, *e.g.*, Articles 1, 6 United Nations (Vienna) Convention on Contracts for the International Sale of Goods (1980); Article 2 Hague Convention on the Law Applicable to International Sale of Goods (1955); Article 3 Uniform Law on the International Sale of Goods (1964); Article 2 EC (Rome) Convention on the Law Applicable to Contractual Obligations (1980). See also, indirectly, in Article V(1)(a) New York Convention; categorically in Article VII European Convention; Article 42 Washington Convention.

1.2. Express or Implied Choice of Law

17-11 Choice of law by the parties is common in international commercial agreements. It is generally accepted for simple and logical reasons as it provides certainty, predictability and uniformity. It is part of the normal contractual process whereby parties try to regulate all or most issues between them and to avoid uncertainty in the future. A clear choice of the applicable substantive law removes a possible issue for dispute and allows the parties to control the scope of contractual interpretation and application.

17-12 A further and important reason for a choice of law by the parties is to avoid the risk of unexpected decisions by the arbitrators. Arbitrators do not have their own substantive law or conflict of laws system. By applying the law chosen by the parties, the tribunal is alleviated from the difficult task of determining the applicable law and can give effect to the expectations of the parties.

17-13 The intention of the parties as to the applicable law or rules may be express or implied. The former will normally be in the written contract or either in written or oral submissions before the arbitrators. Implied choice will be found in words or acts which manifest the intention and expectation of the parties that a particular law governs their relations. The parties' choice, express or implied, must be demonstrated with reasonable certainty by the terms of the contract or the circumstances of the case.[10]

17-14 Where there is an express choice of law, the parties' intention will generally be clear and easy to identify. This is not always so where the choice is implied, and where the tribunal will presume an agreement of the parties through the circumstances of the case, the parties' actions, the surrounding facts and other objective factors. This may include various elements including the language used in the contractual documentation and the parties' relationship.

17-15 It was for many years presumed that because parties selected a particular place of arbitration there was an implied choice that the law of that place should apply to the substance of the dispute. While there are cases where national courts[11] and arbitration tribunals[12] have considered that the chosen place of

---

[10] A reference to seller's general terms and conditions which contain a choice of law clause is sufficient; Award in ICC case no 5865, *Panamanian company v Finnish company*, 125 Clunet 1008 (1998).

[11] See, *e.g.*, Oberlandesgericht Hamm, 15 November 1994, *Slovenian company, formerly Yugoslav State enterprise v Agent (Germany)*, RIW 681 (1995), XXII YBCA 707 (1997); choice of Zurich as seat may imply choice of law of canton of Zurich.

arbitration is an implied choice of the law of that place, this is no longer an absolute presumption. It is irrational and inaccurate.[13] Today it is no more than another general connecting factor which may be of relevance in the circumstances of the particular case.[14] It has been stated that

> An agreement to refer disputes to arbitration in a particular country may carry with it, and is capable of carrying with it, an implication of inference that the parties have further agreed that the law governing the contract (as well as the law governing the arbitration procedure) is to be the law of that country. But I cannot agree that this is a necessary or irresistible inference or implication.[15]

17-16 Arbitrators have found there to be an implied choice of the applicable law where the parties argue their case on the basis of the same law, even though they have not expressly agreed on its application.[16]

17-17 The choice of applicable law made by the parties is generally understood to be a choice of substantive law. This can be seen in a number of arbitration awards.[17] Thus reference to the choice of law rules of the chosen legal system,

---

[12] See Friendly Arbitration (Hamburg) award, 29 December 1998, XXIVa *YBCA* 13 (1999), para 6: choice of seat implies choice of *lex arbitri* and choice of substantive law.

[13] See Lew, *Applicable Law*, paras 170-193, 184-208.

[14] In a 1976 ICC award made in Paris, arbitrators considered the applicable law could be implied from the determination of the seat of arbitration: ICC case no 2735, 104 *Clunet* 947 (1977). By contrast, in a 1988 ICC award, made in London, the tribunal held that the choice of England as the place of arbitration and English as the language of the contract, did not manifest the parties' intention that English law should apply to the contract: ICC case no 5717 (1988), 1(2) *ICC Bulletin* 22 (1990). See also ICC case no 7177 (1993), 7(1) *ICC Bulletin* 89 (1996).

[15] *Compagnie d'Armement Maritime v Compagnie Tunisienne de Navigation* [1971] AC 572, 588, *per* Lord Morris of Borth y Guest. *Star Shipping AS v China National Foreign Trade Transportation Corp (The STAR TEXAS)* [1993] 2 Lloyd's Rep 445 (CA); It is suggested that the presumption, though weakened, is still an influencing factor in England even after the Arbitration Act 1996: *Russell on Arbitration*, 69 *et seq*; see also *PPG Industries Inc v Pilkington plc and Libbey-Owens-Ford Co*, 825 F Supp 1465 (D Ariz 1993); ICC case no 2735 (1976), *Yugoslavian seller v US purchaser*, 104 Clunet 947 (1977). *Contra*: Hof van Beroep Brussels 15 October 1992, *Haegens Bouw BV (Netherlands) v Theuma Deurenindustrie NV (Belgium)*, Tijdschrift voor Arbitrage 38 (1993) 38 *et seq*; original in Dutch, English translation in XVIII YBCA 612 (1993).

[16] See, *e.g.*, ICC case no 1434, *Multinational group A v State B*, 103 Clunet 978 (1976). See also Award in ICSID case no ARB/87/3, *Asian Agricultural Products Ltd (AAPL) v Democratic Socialist Republic of Sri Lanka*, XVII YBCA 106 (1992).

[17] See, *e.g.*, the pre-Model Law Award in ICC case no 1455 (1967), III *YBCA* 212 (1978); and Partial award in ICC case no 5073 (1986), *US exporter v Argentine distributor*, XIII YBCA 53 (1988).

i.e. renvoi, is excluded. This position has been endorsed by legal scholars[18] and international contract law codification.[19] It has also been confirmed by Article 28(1) Model Law

> Any designation of the law or legal system of a given State shall be construed, unless otherwise expressed, as directly referring to the substantive law of that State and not to its conflict of laws rules.[20]

1.3. Scope and Subject Matter of the Parties' Choice of Law

17-18 It is widely accepted that parties may choose a system of substantive law to regulate their contractual relationship. They may also choose more amorphous bodies of law, such as general principles of law, transnational law or international commercial law, *i.e. lex mercatoria.* The parties may also authorise the arbitrators to act as *amiables compositeurs* or to apply some other non-legal standard.

17-19 Parties also may, and sometimes do, in the spirit of compromise in the context of their agreement, select a moveable or changing body of rules to apply. For example, a floating choice of law clause may provide that one system of law applies assuming an agreed jurisdiction, but some other law if proceedings are brought in another jurisdiction. This may be relevant where arbitrators are authorised to determine the dispute on the basis of a non-national or international legal standard, even though the contract is expressly governed by another national law. Similarly where there is a "saving clause" providing for the application of law A or law B, but giving preference to the law that saves the claim.[21] Such clauses are common in bills of lading.[22]

---

18 This is reflected in all leading private international textbooks. See, *e.g.*, Batiffol and Lagarde, *Droit international privé*, Vol I (8th ed, 1993) para 311; Dicey and Morris, *Conflict of Laws* (13th ed, Sweet and Maxwell 1999) Chapter 4, 65-79; Kegel & Schurig, *Internationales Privatrecht* (8th ed, Beck 2000) §10; Scoles and Hay, *Conflict of Laws* (3rd ed, West 2000), 3 II B.

19 See Article 15 EC Rome Convention on the Law Applicable to Contractual Obligations. But see US Restatement 2d Conflict of Laws (1971) §8(2)-(3).

20 See similarly England Arbitration Act section 46(2) and SCC Rules Article 24(2).

21 See, *e.g.*, *Astro Venturoso Compania Naviera v Hellenic Shipyards SA (The Mariannina)* [1983] 1 Lloyd's Rep 12; *Star Shipping AS v China National Foreign Trade Transportation Corp (The STAR TEXAS)*, [1993] 2 Lloyd's Rep 445 (CA): the floating choice of law was deemed invalid.

22 Floating choice of law clauses have been upheld, *e.g.*, in the US: *Bremen & Zapata Off-Shore Co*, 407 US 1 (1972); England: *Black Clawson Int'l Ltd v Papierwerke Waldhof Aschaffenburg AG*, [1981] 2 Lloyd's Rep 446, *Star Shipping AS v China National Foreign Trade*

17-20 Parties can also choose different laws to govern different aspects of their relationship.[23] This doctrine of *dépeçage* is accepted in international commercial arbitration[24] and was confirmed by a resolution of the International Law Institute adopted in Athens in 1979, with particular regard to contracts between a state and a foreign private person.[25] It is also endorsed by various arbitration rules which refer to laws in plural form.[26]

17-21 When expressing their choice, parties should always state their intentions clearly. This will invariably be the case where a national law is chosen or some other clearly identified body of law or rules. The problem for arbitrators is more difficult if the choice is unclear or the rules chosen are not easily identifiable.

1.4. Limitations to Party Autonomy

17-22 The extent to which parties are free to choose any law or rules has always been an issue. Courts are constrained by their national conflict of laws rules. International tribunals have no national conflict of laws rules. The question is whether a tribunal must always apply the law chosen by the parties or is it

---

Transportation Corp (The Star Texas) [1993] 2 Lloyd's Rep 445; and in Austria: Oberster Gerichtshof, 20 October 1993 and 23 February 1998, *Kajo-Erzeugnisse Essenzen GmbH (Austria) v DO Zdravilisce Radenska (Slovenia)*, XXIVa YBCA 919 (1999).

23 This should not be confused with a provision providing that principles common to several specified legal systems will govern a given contract. See, *e.g.*, clause 68 of the Channel Tunnel contract, cited in *Channel Tunnel Group v Balfour Beatty Ltd* [1993] 1 All ER 664, 673:

> common principles of English and French law, and in the absence of such common principles by such principles of international trade law as have been applied by national and international tribunals.

The same method was also used in ICC case no 5163, unpublished but cited in Gaillard, 10 *ICSID Rev – FILJ L J* 225 (1995).

24 *Saudi Arabia v Arabian American Oil Co (ARAMCO)*, 27 ILR 117 (1963) 166 where the tribunal held that

> since the Parties themselves declared that the Concession was not to be governed by a single law, the Tribunal can justifiably split the contract into parts, to be governed by several laws.

25 Institut de Droit International, *Table of Adopted Resolutions* (1957-1991), 332, 333 (1992). See also Gertz, "The Selection of Choice of Law Provisions in International Commercial Arbitration: A Case for Contractual Dépeçage", 12 *NW J Int'l L & Bus* 163 (1991).

26 See AAA ICDR Article 28(1); LCIA Article 22(3); CAMCA Rules (1996) Article 30. *Cf* Zurich Chamber of Commerce Award in case no 273/95 of 31 May 1996, *Raw material processor (Hungary) and Processing group (Argentina) v Raw material seller (Russia)*, XXIII YBCA 128 (1998), where the tribunal found that there was no case for *dépeçage*.

constrained by limitations either in the law of the place of arbitration or by some other controlling factor?

17-23 An international arbitration tribunal should not seek to substitute its own choice of law for that of the parties where there is an express clear and unambiguous choice of law. It has been suggested that there are situations which allow arbitrators to apply law other than that chosen by the parties.[27] These are largely considered to be unsatisfactory.[28] For instance there is no justification for refusing to apply the chosen law because

- it is incomplete.[29] The fact that parties may agree contract terms which are insufficient, or that the chosen law does not deal with a specific issue does not entitle arbitrators to ignore express terms agreed.
- it is surprising in the circumstances of the contractual relationship.[30] It is not for arbitrators to decide that a choice is inappropriate or that a reasonable businessman would not have made that choice.
- the choice was unconscionable or unfair. This cannot be the basis for ignoring any term in an international contract.

17-24 In some cases arbitrators are entitled to, and may even have to strictly apply relevant trade usages independently of the provisions of the law chosen by the parties. In fact trade usages add a layer of regulation of the relationship in question rather than defeat a choice of law by the parties.[31].

17-25 Not all issues in dispute may be governed by the same chosen law. Typically this will be the situation where the additional issue before the tribunal arises from a separate but related contract governed by another law, or is of a

---

[27] See, *e.g.*, Pommier, "La résolution du conflit de lois en matière contractuelle en présence d'une élection de droit; le rôle de l'arbitre", 119 *Clunet* 5 (1992).

[28] See the classification in Fouchard Gaillard Goldman *on International Commercial Arbitration*, paras 1511-1528 (unsatisfactory theories) and 1529-1536 (legitimate restrictions).

[29] *Ibid*, paras 1512. See the most extreme example of this approach: *In the Matter of an Arbitration Between Petroleum Dev (Trucial Coast) Ltd and the Seikh of Abu Dhabi*, 1 ICLQ (1952) 154 and 247. See also Award in ICSID case no ARB/84/3, 20 May 1992, *SPP (Middle East) Ltd, Southern Pacific Properties Ltd v Arab Republic of Egypt, Egyptian General Company for Tourism and Hotels (EGOTH) (The Pyramids)*, 32 ILM 933; XIX YBCA 51 (1994).

[30] ICC case no 1581 (1971) and ICC case no 1422 (1966), 101 *Clunet* 887 (1974).

[31] See Fouchard Gaillard Goldman *on International Commercial Arbitration*, paras 1513-1514. See also ICC case no 3896, 30 April 1982, *Framatome SA v Atomic Energy Organisation of Iran (AEOI)*, 111 Clunet 58 (1984). The problem can be avoided if one adopts a strict concept of trade usages as practices followed in a particular business sector. Once the parties have made a choice of law, it should not be excluded or amended.

non-contractual nature.[32] In any event the extent of the application of the law chosen cannot be greater than the scope intended by the parties.

17-26 However, there are situations where it may be appropriate for the tribunal to select and apply a law different to that chosen by the parties. This is where there is relevant mandatory law and where there are clear implications of international public policy.

(a) Mandatory rules

17-27 The effect of national mandatory rules is more complicated.[33] Mandatory rules limit the parties' choice and must be applied to certain situations. These rules define themselves.[34] A national court will normally apply its mandatory laws whatever the applicable substantive law it applies to the issues before it.[35] There can be little argument that arbitrators must apply the mandatory rules of the law chosen by the parties, subject only to compliance with international public policy.[36] However, as international arbitrators have no national forum, all national mandatory rules are "foreign" to them. Other than that of the chosen applicable law, there is no mandatory law for international arbitration.

17-28 Mandatory rules can displace or restrict party autonomy in certain situations. In particular

> Arbitrators have [shown] hesitation in applying international mandatory rules not belonging to the proper law of the contract. However, there are sufficient examples of cases where arbitrators have allowed *lois de police* to displace the proper law of the contract as chosen by the parties, adopting the position that arbitrators are also

[32] For some legal issues, such as property rights, many private international law systems do not give effect to any choice of law, and in other issues, such as tortious liability, the parties may choose the law only after the dispute has arisen.

[33] Blessing, "Mandatory Rules of Law versus Party Autonomy in International Arbitration", 14(4) *J Int'l Arb* 23 (1997); Voser, "Mandatory Rules of Law as a Limitation on the Law Applicable in International Commercial Arbitration", 7 *Am Rev Int'l Arb* 319 (1996); Seraglini, *Lois de police et justice arbitrale internationale* (Dalloz 2001).

[34] Mayer, "Les lois de police étrangères", 108 *Clunet* 277 (1981)

[35] The issue whether national courts must apply foreign mandatory rules raises problems. For example, while all states ratified the part of the Rome Convention which gives effect to the mandatory rule of the forum, several states, including the United Kingdom and Germany, made a reservation to Article 7(1) which intended to give the same effect to foreign mandatory rules.

[36] See, *e.g.*, ICC case no 8385 (1995), 124 *Clunet* 1061 (1997), application of RICO as mandatory rule of the chosen New York law.

ready to set limits on the scope of the proper law even if by so doing they do not strictly abide by the parties' will.[37]

17-29 This may happen where these rules have a direct impact on the performance of the contract.[38] Even when applying the Rome Convention a tribunal with its seat in an EU Member State does not have to apply the mandatory law of another country with which the contract has some connection.[39] Mandatory rules may have to be applied in cases where failure to do so may be inconsistent with international public policy, *e.g.* where an element of illegality or immorality is asserted.

17-30 What mandatory law should international arbitrators apply? This could be the law of the place of arbitration or the place where the contract was to be performed, or the law of the place of enforcement. There is no basis for a tribunal to ignore the express choice of the parties because it determines that there is a contrary mandatory rule in one of these national laws.

17-31 Mandatory rules were applied in the *OTV and Hilmarton* case.[40] OTV, a French company, had engaged Hilmarton, an English company, to provide legal and tax advice, and to co-ordinate administrative matters with a view to obtaining and performing a contract relating to a sewage processing system in Algiers. The contract was governed by Swiss law. A dispute arose concerning payment of the agreed commissions and the sole arbitrator sitting in Geneva considered that, as the claimant essentially gathered confidential information, surveyed and observed and also used its influence on the Algerian authorities, the claimant's mission was contrary to Algerian law, which prohibits the use of intermediaries. He declared the contract void on the grounds that it contravened an Algerian mandatory rule and indirectly *bonos mores* within the meaning of Article 20(1)

---

[37] See Grigera Naón, *Choice-of-law Problems*, 74; Grigera Naón, "Choice-of-law Problems in International Commercial Arbitration", 289 *RCADI* 8 (2001) 200 *et seq*, 296 *et seq*.

[38] Award in ICC case no 1399 (1967), *Mexican licensee v French licensor*, unpublished, see Lew, *Applicable Law*, para 422, 550-52.

[39] Article 7(1). See similarly, Swiss PIL Article 19. See in ICC award no 6379, 1990, *Principal (Italy) v Distributor (Belgium)*, XVII YBCA 212 (1992), where neither Rome Convention nor foreign mandatory rules were considered applicable. In Swiss Tribunal Fédéral, 30 December 1994, *State agency A and State owned bank B v Consultant X (Panama)*, XXI YBCA 172 (1996), it was held that observance of foreign mandatory rules will be essential only if the non-observance will result in a violation of public policy. See also Hochstrasser, "Choice of Law and "Foreign" Mandatory Rules in International Arbitration", 11(1) *J Int'l Arb* 57 (1994); Fouchard Gaillard Goldman *on International Commercial Arbitration*, para 1519 with further references.

[40] Award in ICC case no 5622 (1988), XIX *YBCA* 112 (1994).

of the Swiss Code of Obligations. This was thus a clear application of the mandatory rules approach, under which the arbitrator felt entitled to give effect to the mandatory rules of a law other than that governing the contract. The award was set aside by the Court of Justice of the canton of Geneva, on the grounds that it was arbitrary. The Court held that, unlike corruption, the use of intermediaries did not offend Swiss law, which was applicable to the merits of the case.[41]

(b) International public policy

17-32 International public policy or *ordre public international* provides one limited basis on which arbitrators can exclude the application of the law chosen by the parties. This is because its effect would be to contravene some fundamental standard reflected in the public policy being applied. Every legal system, national and international, has certain immutable moral and ethical standards that cannot generally be ignored or avoided by a different choice of law. Public policy reflects:

> ... the fundamental economic, legal, moral, political, religious and social standards of every state or extra-national community. Naturally public policy differs according to the character and structure of the state or community to which it appertains, and covers those principles and standards which are so sacrosanct as to require their maintenance at all costs and without exception.[42]

17-33 Public policy can be national, regional, international or transnational. The real issue is to determine the nature and content of public policy relevant to the arbitration process. What may be a relevant public policy in one forum or system may not apply elsewhere. Identifying the various public policies may sometimes be clear and evident; in other cases it may be controversial. While the existence and the content of national and regional[43] public policy may be

---

[41] *Hilmarton v OTV*, 17 November 1989, XIX YBCA 214 (1994). The decision was upheld by the Swiss Federal Tribunal on 17 April 1990, *OTV v Hilmarton*, 1993 Rev Arb 315, for an English translation see XIX *YBCA* 214 (1994).

[42] Lew, *Applicable Law* 532. This definition was endorsed by the International Law Association Committee on International Commercial Arbitration in "Final Report on Public Policy as a Bar to Enforcement of Arbitral Awards" (London 2000), 5 (Report) or 344 (proceedings). See also Racine, *L'arbitrage commercial international et l'ordre public*, paras 628 *et seq.*

[43] There is, for example, European (EC) public policy. See Awards in ICC case no 7315 (1992), *ICC Bulletin*, Special Supplement, International Commercial Arbitration in Europe 42, 44 (1994) and ICC case no 7181 (1992), *Software designer v Bank/Secondary Software designer et al*, 6(1) ICC Bulletin 55 (1995), XXI YBCA 99 (1996), regarding EC antitrust law. See also *Eco Swiss China Time Ltd (Hong Kong) v Benetton International NV (Netherlands)*, Gerechtshof The Hague, 28 March 1996; Hoge Raad, 21 March 1997, 207 Ned Jur 1059 (1998) with note

identifiable, the existence of an international and transnational public policy is controversial as is its effect on international arbitration.[44]

17-34 Issues of international public policy are complex and relevant at various stages in the international arbitration process. Their relevance will be determined by both national courts and the arbitration tribunal. A national court will have to consider the effect of its own international public policy when considering the recognition and enforcement of the arbitration agreement or the award. This will cover whether specific issues are arbitrable, *i.e.* capable of settlement by arbitration[45] and whether the substance of the award contradicts a fundamental standard of the enforcing court.[46]

17-35 An arbitration tribunal may have to consider the effects of international public policy at different stages of the proceedings. This includes when deciding whether to give full or limited effect to the law chosen by the parties or which is otherwise applicable, if jurisdiction, *i.e.* arbitrability, is contested, or where the factual or substantive issues are alleged to be contrary to fundamental international standards.

17-36 Examples of international public policy include not seeking to bribe or corrupt government officials,[47] arrangements to smuggle goods in to or out of a particular country[48], assembling a mercenary army to support an insurrection against a legitimate government, agreements to transport children intended for slavery or under age labour, or to transport and smuggle individuals into another

---

Snijders, 1084. Also ECJ, 1 June 1999, C-126/97, *Eco Swiss Time Ltd v Benetton International NV*, 14(6) Mealey's IAR B-1(1999), XXIVa YBCA 629 (1999). It was found that Article 85 (now 81) EC Treaty is part of the public policy of the EC and hence of each member state.

44 Lalive, "Transnational (or Truly International) Public Policy and International Arbitration", Sanders (ed), *ICCA Congress series no 3,* 258, 312-317.

45 See, *e.g.*, New York Convention V(2)(a), II(1).

46 See, *e.g.*, New York Convention Article V(2)(b).

47 See, *e.g.*, *Westacre Investments Inc v Jugoimport-SPDR Holding Co Ltd and Others* [1999] 2 Lloyd's Rep 65; [2000] QB 288 (CA); Cour d'appel Paris, 30 September 1993, *European Gas Turbines SA v Westman International Ltd*, Rev Arb 359 (1994), XX YBCA 198 (1995); ICC case no 6248 (1990), XIX YBCA 124 (1994); ICC case no 5622 (1998), Rev Arb 327 (1993), English translation in XIX YBCA 105 (1994); Iran-US Claims Tribunal award in case no 48 (255-48-3), 19 September 1986, *American Bell International Inc v The Islamic Republic of Iran, Ministry of Defense, Ministry of Post, Telegraph and Telephone of the Islamic Republic of Iran and The Telecommunications Company of Iran*, XII YBCA 292 (1987).

48 See, *e.g.*, *Soleimany v Soleimany* [1998] 3 WLR 811, [1999] QB 785 (CA); Lalive, "Transnational (or Truly International) Public Policy and International Arbitration", Sanders (ed), *ICCA Congress series no 3*, 258-318, para 84.

country, supplying armaments to a terrorist organisation[49], and the supply of illicit drugs. Contracts which have these activities as their object will often be illegal and unenforceable under the laws of many countries but to circumvent the application of such laws parties may expressly submit their contract to some other law that would validate the contract, or authorise the tribunal to determine any dispute on the basis of the contract terms or as *amiables compositeurs*. Where arbitration proceedings are brought to enforce rights under these types of contract, arbitrators would probably be constrained by international public policy not to enforce and give effect to the contract.

17-37 It is rare that contracts for a purpose which is contrary to international public policy will be an issue in international arbitration. Such issue may just not be arbitrable, legally or practically. As with mandatory law, national public policy is rarely directly relevant for application in most international arbitrations.

2. Choice of Law by the Tribunal – Arbitrator's Autonomy

17-38 When parties have made no choice of law in respect of the merits of the dispute and occasionally even if they have made a choice,[50] international arbitrators are faced with conflict of laws problems and the need to determine the law or the rules according to which the dispute can be decided. Arbitration tribunals "view choice-of-law issues from a pragmatic and result-oriented standpoint militating in favour of analysing their choice-of-law determinations from a functional perspective."[51] In this regard it is essential that the tribunal's choice does not defeat reasonable expectations of the parties as expressed in their agreement.

17-39 A tribunal is assisted in determining the applicable law. For example, the parties may have made a partial choice of law, solutions may be offered by the

[49] *National Oil Corporation v Libyan Sun Oil Company*, 733 F Supp 800-822 (D Ct Delaware, 1990). See also Swiss Federal Tribunal decision of 20 November 1985, reported in 271 *Neue Zürcher Zeitung* 34 (21 November 1985).

[50] At least in theory, choice of law by the parties does not eliminate conflict of laws problems as the choice may not cover all issues. See also Grigera Naón, "Choice-of-law Problems in International Commercial Arbitration", 289 *RCADI* 9 (2001) 37.

[51] Grigera Naón, "Choice-of-law Problems in International Commercial Arbitration", 289 *RCADI* 9 (2001) 28-9.

contract itself, the circumstances of the case and the submissions of the parties[52] or the law or rules governing the arbitration may offer a conflict of laws rule. Arbitrators determine the applicable law indirectly using conflict of laws rules (*voie indirecte*) or directly, applying the law they consider appropriate (*voie directe*).

2.1. The Relevance of Conflict of Laws Rules

17-40 In the absence of a choice of law by the parties, the power of the arbitration tribunal to determine the rules to apply to the merits of the dispute can be considered an extension of the principle of party autonomy. This is on the basis that the tribunal acts as an agent of the parties and has a delegated authority to determine the law governing the issues in dispute. This power and authority is both implied in the general submission of disputes to arbitration, and in the law or rules governing the arbitration. Consequently, the tribunal should try to determine the intent of parties with regard to the applicable law.

17-41 Traditionally, the choice of law process constitutes an attempt to localise a legal issue, *i.e.* to link a contractual arrangement with a national legal system to govern the legal relationship between the parties. Consequently the traditional conflict of laws rules in general provide for the application of a certain national law.

17-42 By contrast modern conflict of laws rules for international arbitration recognise that it is often inappropriate to localise legal issues arising out of an international contract. In international commercial arbitration there is no need to localise legal issues, as many transactions and legal relationships have contacts with several jurisdictions and are truly international or denationalised. It has also been suggested that law is merely a non-mandatory model for the arbitrator and there may be no obligation on the arbitrator to apply it.[53] Hence, in some cases it is appropriate for arbitrators to find some international or non-national rule or

---

[52] See, *e.g.*, ICC award no 10533 (2000), ICC award 10452 (2001), both unpublished but cited in Grigera Naón, "Choice-of-law Problems in International Commercial Arbitration", 289 *RCADI* 9 (2001) 36, footnote 8.

[53] See Mayer, "Reflections on the International Arbitrator's Duty to Apply the Law – The 2000 Freshfields Lecture", 17 *Arb Int* 235 (2001) 237-240.

practice appropriate to the question in issue rather than apply a conventional national law.[54]

17-43 Often international tribunals have to make a positive choice of the national law to be applied. How should this choice of applicable substantive law be made? As there is no mandatory conflict of laws rules directly applicable to international commercial arbitration, arbitrators are free to select the conflict of laws system or rules which they consider appropriate. In recent years many laws have incorporated conflict of laws rules for international arbitration.[55] However, these conflict of laws rules are permissive; they can be and are applied where arbitrators consider them appropriate.

17-44 In selecting the applicable substantive law, the parties usually are guided by considerations such as compromise, and the neutrality and sophistication of a legal system. Parties are not concerned with the state's interest in applying its law to the dispute. Hence, the tribunal choosing the applicable law or rules should not begin an analysis by considering the state's interest and refer automatically to national conflict rules, which codify state policies with regard to choice of law questions. Since international arbitrators owe a duty to the parties rather than the sovereign, they need not implement or follow state policies; the parties' intent is the arbitrator's criteria.[56] Consequently, the tribunal's determination of the applicable law can be based on an analysis of the substantive rules rather than on the application of conflict of laws rules.

17-45 This same conclusion may be reached by examining the aim of national conflict rules. A sovereign has no interest in binding an international arbitration tribunal to its conflict rules. Even if there are conflict of laws rules in the arbitration laws, these provide a tool that the arbitrators may use rather than an obligation to apply them. Thus in choosing the substantive rules, the tribunal should consider the national legal systems relevant to the contractual relationship out of which the dispute arises, as well as any relevant non-national rules. The tribunal's choice should be made on the basis of the adequacy, completeness and appropriateness of a set of rules, rather than their source. International arbitrators whose mandate is based on the parties' agreement are not bound by the choice of

[54] See Lew, *Applicable Law*, para 443-45, 582-583.

[55] See, *e.g.*, Model Law Article 28(2); England, Arbitration Act section 46(3); Germany, ZPO section 1051(2); Switzerland, PIL Article 187(1).

[56] Danilowicz, "The Choice of Applicable Law in International Arbitration", 9 *Hastings Int'l & Comp L Rev* 235 (1986) 284.

law rules of any specific country. They may choose the conflict of laws rules which they prefer.

17-46 This approach is recognised by Article 28(2) Model Law which provides:

> Failing any designation by the parties, the arbitral tribunal shall apply the law determined by the conflict of laws rules which it considers applicable.[57]

17-47 There is no requirement to apply the choice of law rules of the place of arbitration. This freedom of conflict of laws system originates from Article VII European Convention[58] and has been adopted in many arbitration laws and rules.[59] Some national arbitration laws authorise the arbitrators directly to apply the rules they deem applicable without any reference to conflict of laws rules.[60] The same principles may be found in most modern arbitration rules.[61]

17-48 Accordingly, there are two ways international arbitration tribunals determine the applicable substantive law

- *Indirectly*, applying conflict of laws rules, or
- *Directly*, applying the law which appears to be most appropriate or has the closest connection with the dispute.

---

57 This provision may be considered a non-determinative conflict or a pre-conflict rule of the place of arbitration.

58 Article VII(1) provides in pertinent part:

> ... Failing any indication by the parties as to the applicable law, the arbitrators shall apply the proper law under the rule of conflict that the arbitrators deem applicable.

This rule was also contained in the 1975 ICC Rules Article 13(3).

59 See, *e.g.*, England, Arbitration Act section 46(3); UNCITRAL Rules Article 33(1).

60 See, *e.g.*, France, NCPC Article 1496 ("in accordance with the rules of the law he considers appropriate"); India, Arbitration Ordinance 1996 section 28(1)(b)(iii) ("apply the rules of law it considers to be appropriate given all the circumstances surrounding the dispute"); Netherlands, CCP Article 1054(2) ("in accordance with the rules of law which it considers appropriate"). By contrast, German and Swiss law require the tribunal to apply the law with which it has the closest connection to the issue in dispute: see Germany, ZPO section 1051(2); Switzerland, PIL Article 187(1).

61 See AAA ICDR Article 28(1); ICC Article 17(1); LCIA Article 22(3); DIS section 23(2); CCI of the Russian Federation section 13(1); NAI Article 46; Stockholm Article 24(1); WIPO Article 59(1). AAA ICDR, ICC, LCIA, NAI, Stockholm, and WIPO do not make any express reference to conflict of laws opting for *voie directe*, *i.e.* allowing the tribunal to directly apply the law they consider appropriate.

2.2. Indirect Determination of Substantive Law via Conflict of Laws Rules

17-49 Arbitration laws or rules which contain special conflict of laws rules for the indirect determination of applicable law assist the tribunal in determining this substantive law. Most of them generally opt for the determination via conflict of laws rules which the tribunal considers appropriate.[62]

17-50 International arbitration practice may guide tribunals in deciding which conflict of laws are appropriate. In fact arbitration tribunals have applied various different conflict of laws systems including

- conflict rules of the place of arbitration
- conflict rules most closely connected with the subject matter of the proceedings
- conflict rules the tribunal considers appropriate
- converging conflict of laws rules
- general principles of conflict of laws.[63]

(a) Conflict rules of the place of arbitration

17-51 The traditional view, following the jurisdictional theory, is that the conflict rules of the place or seat of arbitration should apply.[64] This solution was recommended by the International Law Institute in 1957 and 1959[65] and it is reflected in arbitration laws opting for a territorial approach. In its modern illustration it can be found in the special conflict of laws rule which despite its applicability to international arbitration it is a conflict of laws rule of the place of arbitration.

---

62 See, *e.g.*, Model Law Article 28(3); England, Arbitration Act section 46(3); European Convention Article VII; UNCITRAL Rules Article 33(1); Vienna Rules Article 16(1).

63 Other conflict of laws systems which have been suggested are those of the country from where the sole arbitrator or chairman of the tribunal comes, the state which would have had jurisdiction in the absence of an arbitration agreement, and the country where the award is to be enforced. These theories have had no support in law or practice.

64 See, *e.g.*, Mann, "Lex Facit Arbitrum", in Sanders (ed), *Liber Amicorum Martin Domke*, 167.

65 47 II *AnnIDI* 394 (1957) and 48 II *AnnIDI* 264 (1959). For a critical assessment of this solution see Lew, *Applicable Law*, paras 226-244. See also Fouchard Gaillard Goldman *on International Commercial Arbitration*, paras 1541-1543.

17-52 Conflict of laws rules of the place of arbitration are applied by international arbitrators in many systems.[66] However, it is today generally considered illogical to apply this rule absolutely as frequently the choice of place is accidental and is not made by the parties or the arbitrators.

17-53 This approach is based on two incorrect assumptions: (i) that an arbitration tribunal exercises the same function as a national court,[67] and (ii) that national conflict of laws rules apply not only to judicial but also to international arbitration proceedings in the particular jurisdiction. However, the status and functions of an international arbitration tribunal differ fundamentally from those of a judge. "The arbitrator draws his power from the arbitration clause and does not, in any manner, render justice in the name of a given state, whether the state of the seat [of the arbitration] or any other state."[68] Whilst this statement remains correct, in recent years many national laws, including the Model Law, have enacted conflict of laws rules specifically for application by an international tribunal. These rules are intended to assist arbitrators in these countries, rather than bind them absolutely in their task of determining the applicable law.

17-54 Significant connection between the place of arbitration and the dispute may justify the application of the conflict of laws rules of the place of arbitration. However this is not an absolute rule. The purpose of conflict rules is to delimit and regulate the scope of the state's legislative competence. This purpose is not advanced by requiring an international tribunal, which is not an organ of the state, to apply national conflict of laws rules.[69] Moreover, the application of the

---

66 See, *e.g.*, Award in ICC case no 5460 of 1987, *Austrian franchisor v South African franchisee*, XIII YBCA 104 (1988); Interim award in ICC case no 6149 of 1990, *Seller (Korea) v Buyer (Jordan)*, XX YBCA 41 (1995). This was also the case in the Götaverken arbitration: Cour d'appel Paris, 21 February 21 1980, *General National Maritime Transport Company Libya, as legal successor of Libyan General Maritime Transport Organization v AB Götaverken*, 107 Clunet 660 (1980), VI YBCA 221 (1981). See also Foreign Trade Commission of the USSR Chamber of Commerce and Industry, Moscow, Award of 6 October 1977, V *YBCA* 20 (1980); Arbitration Court of the Czechoslovakian Chamber of Commerce, Prague, Award of 9 January 1975, II *YBCA* 143 (1976).

67 See Mann, "Lex Facit Arbitrum", in Sanders (ed), *Liber Amicorum Martin Domke*, 167.

68 Lalive, "Les règles du conflit de lois appliquées au fond du litigé par l'arbitre international siegean en Suisse", *Rev Arb* 155 (1976) 159. Translation of the extract by Danilowicz, 9 *Hastings Int'l & Comp L Rev* 235 (1986) 260-1.

69 Danilowicz, 9 *Hastings Int'l & Comp L Rev* 235 (1986) 261.

conflict of laws rules of the place may lead to the application of some law which the parties would never have intended.[70]

17-55 Currently, in the absence of a choice of law by the parties, only the Zurich Arbitration Rules refers the tribunal to Swiss conflict of laws rules but even that is limited to where the laws of the parties would lead to different substantive conclusions.[71] Most modern laws and rules abandoned all references to the forum or the place of arbitration with regard to the choice of applicable law[72] and have replaced it with a special conflict of laws rule for international arbitration.[73] The application of the choice of laws rules of the place of arbitration has been confirmed by many awards.[74]

(b) Conflict rules most closely connected with the subject matter

17-56 Under the influence of US conflict of laws some arbitrators apply the conflict rules of the state most closely connected with the dispute. This approach has been followed by arbitration tribunals.[75]

17-57 This theory ignores the autonomy of the arbitration process. By applying the conflict rules of that state most closely related to the dispute, an arbitrator relinquishes the power to determine the applicable law to the state. In doing so,

---

[70] Wortmann, "Choice of Law by Arbitrators: The Applicable Conflict of Laws System", 14 *Arb Int* 97 (1998) 106-7.

[71] Article 4 provides

> If the parties have not chosen an applicable law, the Arbitral Tribunal decides the case according to the law applicable according to the rules of the Private International Law Statute.
>
> If however, the application of the PIL at the seat, domicile or habitual residence of all parties leads similarly to a different result, the case must be decided accordingly on motion of one of the parties.

[72] See, *e.g.*, Netherlands CCP Article 1054, Switzerland PIL Article 187(1); Italy CCP Article 834. See also Maniruzzaman, "Conflict of Laws Issues in International Arbitration: Practice and Trends", 9 *Arb Int* 371 (1993).

[73] See, *e.g.*, Model Law Article 28(2); England, Arbitration Act section 46(3); France, NCPC Article 1496; India, Arbitration Ordinance 1996 section 28(1)(b)(iii); Netherlands CCP Article 1054(2); Germany, ZPO section 1051(2); Switzerland PIL Article 187(1).

[74] See, *e.g.*, Award in ICC case no 1412, 1971, *Indian cement company v Pakistani bank*, I YBCA 128 (1976); Award in ICC case no 2730, 1982, *Yugoslav companies v Dutch and Swiss group companies*, 111 Clunet 914 (1984); Award in ICC case no 6527, 1991, XVIII *YBCA* 44 (1993); Award in ICC case no 8385, 1995, *US company v Belgian company*, 124 Clunet 1061 (1997).

[75] Award in ICC case no 1422, 1966, 101 *Clunet* 884 (1974); ICC case no 4434 of 1982, 110 *Clunet* 889 (1983); ICC case no 3742 of 1983, 111 *Clunet* 910 (1984); ICC case no 6149 of 1990, *seller (Korea) v buyer (Jordan),* XX YBCA 41 (1995) paras 38-41.

the arbitrator furthers the state's interests and policies, as expressed in its conflict rules. Typically, disputes submitted to international arbitration are commercial, with parties from diverse jurisdictions. When commercial matters are involved, there is no justification for an international tribunal, appointed by the parties and not representing a state, to further or apply the state's interests embodied in its conflict rules.[76]

(c) Conflict rules the tribunal considers appropriate

17-58 Dissatisfaction with the perceived obligation that arbitration tribunals should apply a national conflict of laws rule, and the increasing acceptance of the non-national character of international arbitration, influenced the choice of law provisions in the European Convention. This allowed the tribunal the freedom to find an "applicable" conflict rule. Article VII(1) provided, in pertinent part:

> Failing any indication by the parties as to the applicable law, the arbitrators shall apply the proper law under the rule of conflict that the arbitrators deem applicable.[77]

17-59 There is no assistance in any of these texts as to what is meant by "applicable" or "appropriate". This is left to the discretion of arbitrators, to be decided on the facts and circumstances in each arbitration. At that time, for logical and conservative reasons, a conflict of laws rule was considered necessary. It would explain the arbitrator's reasons and rationale for the law chosen. However, it left arbitrators free to select a conflict rule from a national conflict system, a relevant international convention, academic writing, or even a rule which the arbitrators for good or esoteric reasons considered appropriate.[78]

17-60 This method of determining the applicable law was discussed by the Cour de cassation in *Pabalk Ticaret Ltd Sirketi v Norsolor SA,*[79] a few English cases,[80] and several ICC awards.[81]

---

[76] See Danilowicz, 9 *Hastings Int'l & Comp L Rev* 235 (1986) 264; Wortmann, "Choice of Law by Arbitrators: The Applicable Conflict of Laws System", 14(2) *Arb Int* 97 (1998) discusses the concept and makes references to awards in his section III(d) and IV.

[77] Article 13(3) ICC Arbitration Rules 1975 (now superseded by 1998 ICC Arbitration Rules: see Article 17(1)) contained an identical provision just changing the word "applicable" to "appropriate". This language was then followed in Article 33(1) UNCITRAL Rules and Article 28(2) Model Law.

[78] See Lew, Applicable Law, paras 291, 296 and 449.

[79] Cour de cassation, 9 October 1984, 112 *Clunet* 679 (1985); English translation in 24 *ILM* 360 (1985), XI *YBCA* 484 (1986) para 11.

[80] *Channel Tunnel Group Ltd and another v Balfour Beatty Construction Ltd and others* [1992] WLR 741 (CA); *Deutsche Schachtbau-und Tiefbohrgesellschaft mbH v Ras Al Khaimah*

(d) Cumulative application of relevant conflict of laws rules

17-61 This approach involves simultaneously applying conflict of laws rules of the legal systems connected with the dispute. The fact that the rules differ is of little consequence, provided that they lead to the same result.[82] If they do not, the tribunal has to select the conflict rule it considers "the most appropriate."

17-62 International arbitration tribunals have often adopted this approach to avoid choosing any single system of conflict rules.[83] When the conflict rules of all the jurisdictions related to the dispute point to the same substantive law there is a "false conflict" situation,[84] and it is not necessary to determine the applicable law. If satisfied that all conflict rules lead to the same conclusion, the arbitrator may proceed to apply the substantive law directly. [85]

17-63 For the arbitrator to apply the cumulative-application approach the conflict rules involved need not be identical.[86] For example, a false conflict could exist even if one of the jurisdictions adheres to the law of the place where the

---

National Oil Co and Shell International Petroleum Co Ltd [1987] 2 Lloyd's Rep 246; [1987] 2 All ER 769 (CA).

81 See, *e.g.*, ICC Case no 7319 (1992), XXIVa *YBCA* 141 (1999); ICC case no 6527 (1991), XVIII *YBCA* 44 (1993); ICC case no 4237 (1984), X *YBCA* 52 (1985).

82 Derains, "L'application cumulative par l'arbitre des systèmes de conflit des lois interessés au litigé", *Rev Arb* 99 (1972) 105.

83 See, *e.g.*, ICC case no 3043, 1978, *South African company v German company*, 106 Clunet 1000 (1979); ICC case no 4996, 1985, *French agent v Italian principal*, 113 Clunet 1131 (1986); Interim award in ICC case no 5314, 1988, *US Manufacturer v Italian Licensor*, 4 ICC Bulletin 70 (October 1993), XX YBCA 35 (1995); ICC case no 6281, 1989, *Egyptian buyer v Yugoslav seller*, XV YBCA 96 (1990); ICC case no 6283, 1990, *Belgian agent v US principal*, XVII YBCA 178 (1992); ICC case no 6149, 1990, *Korean seller v Jordanian buyer*, XX YBCA 41 (1995); ICC case no 7250, 1992, *U.S. distributor v Dutch producer*, 7(1) ICC Bulletin 92 (1996); Partial award in ICC case no 7319, 1992, *French Manufacturer v Irish Distributor*, 5(2) ICC Bulletin 56 (1994), XXIVa, YBCA 141 (1999); Stockholm Arbitration Institution Interim award, 17 July 1992 and final award, 13 July 1993, *Swedish Licensor/buyer v Chinese Manufacturer*, XXII YBCA 197 (1997).

84 See, *e.g.*, Grigera Naón, "Choice-of-Law Problems in International Commercial Arbitration", 289 *RCAD* 9 (2001), 244 *et seq;* Scoles and Hay, *Conflict of Laws* (3d ed, West 2000), §§3-1 – 3-2; Morris, on *The Conflict of Laws* (Sweet and Maxwell 2000), 559-561; Kegel and Schurig, *Internationales Privatrecht* (8th ed, Beck 2000) 312.

85 See, *e.g.*, ICC case no 953, 1956, III *YBCA* 214 (1978); ICC case no 1990, III *YBCA* 217 (1978).

86 In fact the situation became easier with the harmonisation of national choice of law rules for international contracts, see, *e.g.*, Article 4(1) Rome Convention which provided for application of the closest connection or the proper law.

contract was made and the other to the law of the place of performance, if the contract was concluded and was to be performed in the same place.[87]

17-64 The advantage of the cumulative application approach is that it satisfies the parties and ensures that the award will be recognised in all related jurisdictions.[88] Moreover, by detaching the arbitration from any particular national legal system, the cumulative application approach recognises the international or transactional nature of the contractual relationship, and seeks a non-national but predictable and well balanced outcome.[89] However, the inherent limits of the cumulative method are evident where the various conflict of laws systems connected with the dispute lead to different results.

(e) General principles of conflict of laws rules

17-65 According to this approach, arbitrators do not limit their analysis to the conflict of laws rules of the jurisdictions connected with the dispute. Instead, through a comparative analysis of all conflict systems, they attempt to establish the existence of universally recognised principles of conflict of laws. In some cases general principles of law may be articulated in scholarly writing and formal or informal codification of law.[90]

17-66 In appropriate cases tribunals have applied these general principles of conflict of laws.[91] The general principles approach has a significant advantage over the cumulative application of conflict rules as the tribunal does not have to determine the jurisdictions to which the dispute is related. However, the general principles approach is limited because with the exception of a few basic rules, few conflict rules are recognised universally.

---

87 ICC case no 3043, 1978, 106 *Clunet* 1000 (1979).

88 Derains, "L'application cumulative par l'arbitre des systèmes de conflit des lois interessés au litigé", *Rev Arb* 99 (1972) 121; Lew, *Applicable Law*, 335-341; Lew, "The Law Applicable to the Form and Substance of the Arbitration Clause", *ICCA Congress series no 9*, 114.

89 Although seen as an innovative approach to conflict of laws in international arbitration since the early 1970's, the cumulative-application approach was introduced in conflict of laws in 1930. See Fränkel, "Der Irrgarten des internationalen Privatrechts", 4 *RabelsZ* 239 (1930); Rabel, "Das Problem der Qualifikation", 5 *RabelsZ* 241 (1931).

90 *E.g.* the International Encyclopaedia of Comparative law; or instruments developed by international intergovernmental organisations or private organisations; American Law Institute Restatement 2d Conflict of Laws and ILA Resolutions.

91 See, *e.g.*, Award in ICC case no 1512, I *YBCA* 128 (1976); Award in ICC cases nos 2096 (1972) and 2585 (1977) cited by Craig, Park and Paulsson *ICC Arbitration*, 326, notes 26 and 27; Lew, *Applicable Law*, paras 283-6, 327-335.

2.3. Direct Determination of Substantive Law

17-67 Direct determination allows a tribunal to select the applicable substantive law or rules relevant for the particular case without reference to any conflict of laws rules. This method is confirmed in a number of modern arbitration laws[92] and recently adopted arbitration rules.[93]

17-68 There are two expressions of direct determination of substantive law. *Voie directe* may be unlimited, allowing the tribunal to apply any appropriate rules or standards, or may be limited to national laws, contractual agreements and trade usages.

(a) Unlimited voie directe

17-69 Modern national laws which have adopted the direct application approach include France and the Netherlands[94] and certain countries which have adapted their application of the Model Law.[95] For example Article 1496 French Code of Civil Procedure provides that in the absence of an express choice of law, arbitrators

> shall resolve the dispute in accordance with the rules of law he or she considers appropriate.

17-70 The more recent international arbitration rules expressly allow arbitrators to apply the rules of law or other standards the tribunal considers appropriate. Article 17(1) ICC Rules contains an unambiguous endorsement of a direct application approach. It provides

---

[92] See, *e.g.*, France, NCPC Article 1496; Germany, ZPO section 1051(2); India, Arbitration Act section 28(1)(b)(iii); Netherlands, CCP Article 1054(2); Switzerland, PIL Article 187(1).

[93] See, *e.g.*, AAA ICDR Article 28(1); ICC Rules Article 17(1); LCIA Article 22(3); NAI Rules Article 46; SCC Rules Article 24(1); WIPO Rules Article 59(1).

[94] See Netherlands, CCP Article 1054(2) which provides the tribunal shall make its award in accordance with the rules of law which it considers appropriate.

[95] See, *e.g.*, Canada, Ontario International Commercial Arbitration Act 1990 Article 6 (which expressly deviates from Article 28(2) Model Law); British Columbia International Commercial Arbitration Act 1986 Article 28(3); India, Arbitration Ordinance 1996 section 28(1)(b)(iii); Kenya, Arbitration Act 1995 Article 29(3).

> In the absence of any such agreement [with regard to the rules of law to be applied by the Arbitral Tribunal], the Arbitral Tribunal shall apply the rules of law which it determines to be appropriate.[96]

17-71 Article 22(3) LCIA Rules provides similarly

> If and to the extent that the Arbitral Tribunal determines that the parties have made no such choice [of law(s) or rules of law], the Arbitral Tribunal shall apply the law(s) or rules of law which it considers appropriate.[97]

17-72 This rule recognised what arbitrators do in practice. It may be considered a tailor-made choice of law process or conflict of laws rule, with a flexible connecting factor, specific for international arbitration. Arbitrators apply the substantive law or rules, or non-legal standard they consider appropriate in the particular circumstances of the case.[98] What remains unclear, objectively, is the meaning of "appropriate" in these laws and rules.

17-73 "Appropriate" has a broad meaning and can be applied in a wider sense. Accordingly, a national system may be appropriate because it is highly developed and sophisticated and suitable for the contract or dispute in question, although it is not closely connected to the dispute. A national system of law or a set of legal or non-legal rules which are directly or closely connected with the transaction and the dispute will normally also be appropriate to be applied to determine the substance of the dispute. Ultimately this autonomous arbitration conflict of laws rule facilitates a wider acceptance and application of international legal[99] and non-legal standards which are relevant to the resolution of disputes in international arbitration.

17-74 The principle of direct application of national law is in effect akin to the doctrine of the proper law. Accordingly, in an ICC award[100] the tribunal held that Korean law should apply, because "the Agreement is for an important part to be

---

[96] See Craig, Park and Paulsson, *ICC Arbitration*, 329; Derains and Schwartz, *ICC Rules,* 221-224 with further references.

[97] The wording of Article 28(1) AAA ICDR is identical. Many arbitration rules follow this trend: WIPO Rules Article 59(a); CAMCA Rules Article 30(1); AIA Rules Article 17(2); NAI Rules Article 46; SCC Institute Article 24(1).

[98] Fouchard Gaillard Goldman *on International Commercial Arbitration*, paras 1552-3 with further references.

[99] A tribunal directly applied the *lex mercatoria* in ICC case no 3540, 1980, *French enterprise v Yugoslav subcontractor*, 108 Clunet 914 (1981); English text in VII YBCA 124 (1982).

[100] ICC case no 4132, *Italian company v Korean company*, 110 Clunet 891 (1983); for an English translation, see X YBCA 44 (1985).

performed within the territory of the Republic of Korea". In this and other awards in which the direct application of national law is employed, the direct choice method simply has the effect of dispensing with the need to give reasons for the selection of the choice of law rule or connecting factor used by the arbitrators in determining the applicable law.

(b) Limited voie directe

17-75 There are a number of national laws which provide a direct choice of law rule for application by the tribunal.[101] For example, Swiss PIL provides that in the absence of any choice of law by the parties the tribunal

> Shall decide the dispute ... according to the rules of law with which the case has the closest connection.

17-76 This provision allows the tribunal to apply national or non-national rules provided it considers that the rules have the closest connection to the transaction. In practice there is no difference between this rule and the unlimited *voie directe* of the French law.

17-77 However, German law is more restrictive and controlling. It limits the choice by the tribunal to national law. Rules of non-national origin cannot be applied. Section 1051(2) ZPO provides

> Failing any designation by the parties the arbitral tribunal shall apply the law of the state with which the subject-matter of the proceedings is most closely connected.[102]

3. THREE-STEP METHOD

17-78 The determination of the applicable law in international commercial arbitration is a choice of law process and operates in a three step method. Whilst the issues are frequently complicated and depend on the facts and circumstances of each case, so that only a casuistic approach is adequate the questions that require an answer in each step are as follows:

---

[101] See, *e.g.*, Italy, CCP Article 834 (1994); Mexico, Commercial Code Article 1445 (1993); Switzerland, PIL Article 187. It is noteworthy that Germany, ZPO section 1051(2) and Egypt Law no 27 1994 both amended the Model Law to follow this formula.

[102] See similarly DIS rules section 23(2); Italy CCP Article 834(1); Tunisia Arbitration Code 1993 Article 75(2).

- Is there a choice of law by the parties? In the affirmative, does it cover the entire dispute before the tribunal? Is there any contradiction with mandatory rules or public policy? In any event, is it possible to solve the dispute by relying exclusively on the contract?
- In the absence of choice of law by the parties, is it possible to determine the applicable law or non legal standard without reference to conflict of laws? Is that an appropriate law or non legal standard for this particular dispute?
- If it is necessary to employ conflict of laws rules, which conflict of laws rules should we apply? Is there a conflict of laws system most closely connected with the dispute? Is it possible to apply cumulatively all relevant conflict of laws systems? Is it possible to apply generally accepted conflict of laws rules?

Chapter 18

APPLICABLE SUBSTANTIVE LAW

18-1 Having chosen the applicable legal or non-legal system or standard to apply, arbitrators must proceed to find and apply the specific legal or other rules to the factual situation. The determination of the applicable law prescribes the ambit of argument as to liability and rights of the parties in a given situation. Accordingly the tribunal must identify the content of the rules and decide how they can be applied.

18-2 The application of a national substantive law, an international legal standard or a non-legal standard by the tribunal is more complicated than the application of national law by the courts. Arbitrators may have little or no connection with or access to the applicable national law, unlike the national judges who normally apply the law they have been trained in for years.

18-3 This is not a defect in the international arbitration system. Rather it is a characteristic and inevitable facet of the process where there are several national and international factors all of which influence the applicable law and standard to be applied. International arbitration deals preponderantly with disputes arising from international commercial transactions while national courts deal predominately with national cases for which national law and state interests are relevant.

18-4 When selecting the standard or rule to apply, arbitrators can and should, wherever possible, internationalise or denationalise the dispute. If there is an international convention or some other international instrument relevant to the dispute, it can be applied in preference to a national law. Accepted trade standards should be applied in preference to the rules of national law.[1] Similarly, where possible a dispute should be resolved by resorting to the customs and usages of the particular trade or industry.

18-5 This chapter discusses how an arbitration tribunal, having determined the applicable law or non-legal standard, finds and applies the relevant specific rules to this dispute. It considers (1) the principles relating to proof and interpretation of the applicable law or other standards, (2) the application of national law rules, (3) the international and transnational legal standards that can be applied, and (4) the non-legal substantive rules and standards, including arbitrators deciding as *amiable compositeurs* or ex *aequo et bono*.

1. Proof of Applicable Law

18-6 In the majority of cases arbitrators are able to resolve the dispute between the parties solely on the facts and the terms of the contract.[2] In these cases the tribunal will decide on the balance of evidence, the relevant facts, what has occurred and what is necessary under the agreement between the parties.

---

1 Lew, *Applicable Law*, paras 443, 582-3.

2 Alvarez, "To What Extent Do Arbitrators in International Cases Disregard the Bag and Baggage of National Systems?", *ICCA Congress series no 8*, 139, 140.

There is no need for arbitrators to apply any law or rules to determine the issues.[3] Only if the tribunal is unable to resolve the dispute on the facts and contract terms does the applicable law become relevant.

18-7 Where the tribunal has concluded that a national or international law, or some non-legal standard is applicable for the determination of the dispute, the tribunal has then to ascertain and may also have to interpret the content of the applicable law or rules.

1.1. Proof of Law or Non-Legal Standard

18-8 How should the tribunal find the applicable rules it is to apply? It is not uncommon that the applicable substantive law is foreign to the arbitrators and to the parties' lawyers. The content of this law must become known to the tribunal so that it can be applied as appropriate. This is equally applicable to non-legal standards.

18-9 Before national courts there are two basic approaches to proof of foreign law. These originate from the long-standing "law/fact" distinction regarding foreign law.[4] This distinction is further enhanced by the adversarial or inquisitorial conduct of proceedings. In an adversarial system the presumption is that the parties must make representations with regard to the applicable law. In inquisitorial proceedings it is for the judges to decide on which issues they want to gather evidence. Irrespective of the doctrinal debate and the impact of the adversarial or inquisitorial systems in international arbitration, a combination of both methods is employed in order to acquire knowledge of the applicable law.[5]

---

[3] See, *e.g.*, Japan Commercial Arbitration Association award, 30 November 1976, *US company v Japanese company*, IV YBCA 213 (1979) (quality standards); Iran-US Claims Tribunal award in case no 18 (260-18-1), 13 October 1986, *PepsiCo Inc v The Government of the Islamic Republic of Iran and others*, XII YBCA 253 (1987) (calculation of interest).

[4] See the discussion in Fentiman, *Pleading and Proof of Foreign Law* (Oxford University Press 1998), 3-6, 21, 70-77, 286-315.

[5] This follows from the emerging convergence of arbitration procedures. See, in that sense, Hascher, "Principes et pratique de procédure dans l'arbitrage commercial international", 282 *RCADI* 51 (2000) 87 *et seq*; Lowenfeld, "International Arbitration as Omelette: What Goes into the Mix", in Frommel and Rider (eds), *Conflicting Legal Cultures*, 19, 24-26; Lazareff, "International Arbitration: Towards a Common Procedural Approach", in Frommel and Rider (eds), *id*, 31 *et seq* who argues that, although unification or procedural methods has become fashionable, it is not an absolute virtue.

18-10 Generally speaking most civil law systems treat foreign law as law; it is presumed the court knows the law. Most common law systems treat foreign law as fact; evidence must be brought to the court as with all facts. This doctrinal position creates presumptions but practice often adopts a more liberal approach. What is important is to provide access for the tribunal to the content of the applicable foreign law. Within these basic approaches there is a spectrum of national court positions.

18-11 In those systems where foreign law is "law" the ultimate burden of ascertaining foreign law lies with the court. It has discretion as to the means of ascertaining foreign law. The court may research the law itself or ask the parties for assistance in ascertaining foreign law. This may be done by expert reports from neutral, appropriately qualified scholars, or practising lawyers. Frequently the parties' counsel may make submissions as to foreign law, taking the court through the relevant texts. Ultimately the court will review and determine the issue itself.[6]

18-12 The usual method of determining law as a fact is proof by written expert opinion ("*amicus* brief" or "*Gutachten*") of foreign lawyers, though the parties may request the court to conduct the necessary research.[7] In England and Spain although foreign law is to be proved as fact, expert reports and oral evidence are the usual methods.[8] In the United States, a party who intends to raise an issue concerning the law of a foreign country is required to give reasonable written notice. The court, in determining foreign law, may consider any relevant material or source, including testimony, whether or not submitted by a party or admissible under the Federal Rules of Evidence. The court's determination is treated as a ruling on a question of law.[9]

18-13 The situation in international arbitration is different. There are no "forum" procedural requirements to follow. Rather, the composition of the

---

6 See, *e.g.*, Hartwieg, "Pleading Actions and Defences under Foreign Law", in Fletcher, Mistelis and Cremona (eds), *Foundations and Perspectives of International Trade Law* (Sweet and Maxwell 2001), 173, 180, paras 12-010 and 12-012 with further references. See also ZPO section 293.

7 See Hartwieg, *ibid*, 177, para 12-009. See also Dicey and Morris *Conflict of Laws* (13th ed, Sweet and Maxwell 2000), 221-225, paras 9-001 – 9-012.

8 See Lew and Shore, "International Commercial Arbitration: Harmonising Cultural Differences" 54-Aug *Disp Resol J* 33 (1999) 36-7.

9 Fed R Civ P 44.1.

tribunal and the attitude of the arbitrators, often influenced by their own legal background, is a crucial factor. Equally there is no "foreign" law.

18-14 Most institutional or *ad hoc* arbitration rules are silent on this issue. The tribunal has considerable flexibility for proving the substantive law. The concept that the tribunal knows the law is not a firm rule in arbitration proceedings.[10] Hence, arbitrators have discretion to decide how to ascertain foreign law.[11]

18-15 There are various approaches as to how the law should be ascertained by an international arbitration tribunal.

18-16 One option is to follow a strict civil law inquisitorial procedure. This leaves the task of ascertaining the applicable rules to the tribunal. This option anticipates research undertaken by the arbitrators or expert opinions on the applicable law or rules. In practice arbitrators will rarely wish to undertake lengthy research into the applicable law. They would prefer some help from the parties. Considerations of expense may also deter parties from wanting tribunals to undertake such research.

18-17 In many cases, where influenced by common law procedures, the parties plead and seek to prove the applicable substantive law rules. This process relies on testimony and examination of expert witnesses. Cross-examination of expert witnesses is not particularly useful in resolving the content of the applicable law. There will normally be at least two different opinions for each legal issue, and often the tribunal will be reluctant to choose the testimony of one legal expert over that of another.

18-18 A third and preferred option is a hybrid procedure, fixed for each arbitration and drawing on both the inquisitorial and adversarial systems. The parties make full legal argument, in writing and orally, about the applicable rules. They may support this with legal materials and independent export reports. The tribunal may request further specific details about the applicable law. It will, however, decide itself what the specific applicable rules are rather than rely on any expert. This approach leaves considerable discretion to the tribunal and is increasingly the norm in international arbitration.

---

[10] Derains, "Observations", *Rev Arb* 709-711 (1998) 711. See also Tackaberry, "*Jura Novit Curia - But not in Arbitration*", paper delivered at *the Millennium Conference of the Chartered Institute of Arbitrators*, November 1999.

[11] Lew and Shore, 54-Aug *Dispute Resol J* 33 (1999) 37.

18-19 This approach reflects a neutral and international expectation that the applicable law or rules must be ascertained and applied. It recognises that in international arbitration there is no domestic, forum or foreign law. There is only the applicable law for the particular case.

1.2. Interpretation

18-20 How should an arbitration tribunal interpret and understand the applicable substantive rule or law once this law has been determined?[12]

18-21 There is little published case law to show how international tribunals have addressed this issue. It is arguable that if the parties have chosen or the tribunal has determined the applicable substantive law this should be applied and interpreted by the tribunal in the way in which it would have been applied by national judges applying that law.[13] The arbitrators should look at the legislative texts, case law, scholarly writings and other sources in the legal system in question.

18-22 While the arbitrators should look at the methods of interpretation of the chosen substantive law, the process of interpretation should be free from doctrinal formalism. International tribunals should take account of the fact that they are dealing with an international dispute and should interpret national law rules to reflect international practice and to give effect to the parties' intentions. Many arbitrators are from jurisdictions different to the applicable law and may have difficulty interpreting the law in accordance with that legal system itself. Although the applicable substantive law should be interpreted in its context tribunals have employed international standards in interpreting domestic or uniform law.[14]

---

[12] In ICC case no 7639 (1994), *Sponsor (Qatar) v Contractor (Italy)*, XXIII YBCA 66 (1998) the parties were in agreement as to the applicable law; however, its interpretation was disputed. The published report offers no guidance as to how the tribunal decided the issue of interpretation.

[13] To that effect, the Romanian Law No 105 of 22 September 1992 on the Settlement of Private International Law Relations, Chapter VIII, Article 80(a): "The law applicable to the essence of the contract (...) is in particular applicable to: (a) the interpretation of its juridical nature and of the clauses it contains". See also Supreme Court of India, 7 October 1993, *Renusagar Power Co Ltd v General Electric Co*, 8(12) Mealey's IAR A-1 (1993), XX YBCA 681 (1995), para 42.

[14] See, *e.g.*, International Court of Arbitration of the Federal Chamber of Commerce of Vienna, award no 4318 and award no 4366, 15 June 1994, *RIW* 690 (1995), *Clunet* 1055 (1995) where the UNIDROIT Principles were used for the interpretation of international uniform law and the

2. Application of National Law

18-23 Determination of the applicable substantive law will often itself resolve many issues. That is why in many cases the tribunal will decide the applicable law as an interim issue. However, other particular issues may arise including

- What is the ambit of the applicable national law?
- Can more than one national law apply?
- Is the law applicable that at the time of the agreement or the time of the dispute?

2.1. Ambit of National Law

18-24 The determination that a national law shall apply encompasses all rules of that law with the hierarchy of sources as valid in that system. This will include references to statutes, case law, scholarly writings and customs, with the authority they are vested with in that legal system.

18-25 Problems may arise if reference is made to the law of a federal state with no further specification. Although it may be preferable for a reference to be made to Swiss law,[15] rather than a specified canton's law, a reference to US law may well be problematic. An express choice of the Swiss Federal Code of Obligations was held by arbitrators to be a comprehensive choice of Swiss law.

> ... as there is no indication for the Parties' intention to separate or to limit the applicable law, this choice of law clause has to be interpreted in a more comprehensive sense comprising the entirety of the Swiss substantive law. This extended interpretation also corresponds with the Terms of Reference on which this Arbitration is based where the Parties, more generally, agreed that *'Swiss Law is applicable to their dispute'*. ...
>
> Even if the clause was based on the intention to limit the applicable law, the reference to the CO automatically comprises the Introductory Provisions of the Swiss Civil Code (...) not only because the CO is the fifth part of the Civil Code but also because the Introductory Provisions include certain general rules like the principle of 'good faith' (Art. 2 CC) or the general rules of evidence (Art. 8 CC)

ICC award no 8128, 1995, *Clunet* 1024 (1996) where the UNIDROIT Principles were used for the interpretation of CISG.

[15] See Knapp, "Le droit suisse est applicable au présent contrat", in *Etudes de droit international en l'honneur de Pierre Lalive* (1993), 81. It is argued that with regard to public law a reference to federal law is most appropriate.

> which apply to the CO as well and which cannot be excluded by the Parties by stipulation ... [16] [footnotes omitted].

18-26 Often the combination of state and federal law will ensure that no gaps are left unfilled. In one case the arbitrator stated

> ... The parties agreed that the contract should be governed by the Laws of the State of Michigan and thus that the remedies for breach given by those Laws should be available and, likewise, where those laws required or necessitated the application of the Laws of the United States (as for instance, in the arbitration clause) then Federal Law should apply.[17]

18-27 A general reference to US law would normally call upon the arbitrators to determine which state's law governs the contract. This will be asserted by determining the parties' intentions. If the parties' intention is not clear the matter is entirely at the discretion of the arbitrators. In *Filanto SpA v Chilewich International Corp*[18] it was considered that a convention, *e.g.* the Convention on the International Sale of Goods, which the US has ratified may reflect federal principles better than the common denominator of state laws.[19]

18-28 Similarly a vague reference to "British law" will need to be specified by the arbitrators as a reference to English or Scottish or Northern Ireland law. British law as such is very limited to either constitutional law or law harmonised by the European Community. As a general rule, an express choice of British law will be interpreted as a choice of English law.[20]

18-29 A reference to the "the law of the Members States of the European Union" will be valid if there is such law harmonised by the EU. As private law harmonisation in the EU is sporadic arbitrators may have to fill gaps by reference

---

16 ICC case no 6248 (1990), XIX *YBCA* 124 (1994), paras 3-5 [emphasis added].

17 ICC case no 7453 (1994), *Agent (US) v Principal (Germany) and Managing director of principal (Germany)*, XXII YBCA 107 (1997), para 29.

18 789 F Supp 1229 (SDNY 1992), XVIII YBCA 530 (1993).

19 *Ibid*, para 30 in *YBCA* report.

20 See, *e.g.*, *Vimar Seguros y Reaseguros SA v M/V Sky Reefer, her Engines etc et al*, 115 S Ct 2322, 132 L Ed 2d 462, XXI YBCA 773 (1996), (US Supreme Court, 19 June 1995), para 20, where reference to British law was understood as a reference to English COGSA. See also, *e.g.*, *Hirji Mulji and Others Appellants v Cheong Yue Steamship Company Ltd* [1926] AC 497 (PC); *Casillo Grani v Napier Shipping Co (The 'World Ares')*, [1984] 2 Lloyd's Rep 481 (QBD).

to the law of a member state as a supplementary source of law for a particular dispute.[21]

18-30 What is clear is that arbitrators have wide discretion in determining the substantive national law rules to apply in any given case. This discretion is steered by the parties' choice and intentions as well as common sense.

18-31 The *Shari'ah* can also qualify as national law although it is, in principle, a set of religious rules. It consists of the *Quran*, the *Sunnah* (the sayings and practices of Muhammad), the *Ijma* (consensus among recognised Islamic religious authorities) and *Qiyas* (*per analogiam*, inference by precedent). It is a source of national substantive law in several jurisdictions[22] and in some countries it is allegedly the principal source of law.[23] Its effect on international commercial arbitration is limited, as normally it does not apply to commercial transactions.[24] Many of the jurisdictions that accept *Shari'ah* as a source of law have adopted civil and commercial codes, ratified the New York Convention and accepted arbitration laws based on the Model Law.[25] The *Shari'ah* remains relevant for transactions for which it is the only source of law, and for issues of probative value of evidentiary means.

---

[21] See, *e.g.*, ICC case no 7319 (1992), *Manufacturer (France) v Distributor (Ireland)*, XXIV YBCA 141 (1999).

[22] It is applied, *e.g.*, in Saudi Arabia, United Arab Emirates, Kuwait, Oman, Bahrain, Syria, Yemen, Iraq, Iran, Egypt, Tunisia, Sudan, Morocco, Algeria, Pakistan, Bangladesh, Malaysia, Indonesia, Uzbekistan, and Azerbaijan. In some jurisdictions it is the law applicable to all legal issues involving Muslims; in other jurisdictions it only applies for personal status cases. In Saudi Arabia the *Shari'ah* applies to all legal issues.

[23] The constitutional provisions of, *e.g.*, Egypt, Qatar and Yemen, which declare *Shari'ah* a principal source of law should be read with caution. In most cases they merely acknowledge *Shari'ah* as a source of law; national courts often interpret *Shari'ah* in a liberal manner.

[24] See, however, CRCICA award, 30 July 1990, case no 13/1989, *North American Company represented by a local agent v an African agricultural bank*, in Mohie Eldin I Alam Eldin, *Arbitral Awards of the Cairo Regional Centre* (2d edition, Kluwer 1999) 13 (international sale of goods); CRCICA award, 17 July 1995, case no 52/1994, *Two African companies v an African government body*, in: Mohie Eldin I Alam Eldin, *Ibid*, 73 (administrative contract); ICC case no 6363 (1991), XVII *YBCA* 186 (1992) (assignment and procurement).

[25] For general principles of *Shari'ah* see Abdul Hamid El Ahdab, *Arbitration with the Arab Countries* (2d ed, Kluwer 1999); Abdul Hamid El-Ahdab, "General Introduction on Arbitration in Arab Countries", *Intl Handbook on Comm Arb*, Suppl 15 - August (1993) 15 *et seq*; Nathan, "Who is Afraid of *Shari'a*? - Islamic Law and International Commercial Arbitration", 59 *Arbitration* 125 (1993); Redfern and Hunter, *International Commercial Arbitration* paras 2-47 - 2-50.

2.2. Application of Several Laws or Standards

18-32 Frequently, rather than select and apply one national law, parties or arbitrators choose or apply different laws to govern different aspects of their relationship. This may be simply that the parties have chosen one law to govern the overall formation and interpretation of the content, but another law to govern certain aspects of performance. Further, even where parties agree one law, the parties may claim (*e.g.* punitive damages) and arbitrators may apply some other law which they conclude applies separately to the chosen law.

18-33 This selection of separate laws was allowed, for instance, in the *Aramco* arbitration[26] where the tribunal ruled

> since the parties themselves declared the concession was not to be governed by a single law, the tribunal can justifiably split the contract into parts, to be governed by several laws.[27]

18-34 The acceptance of several laws applying in international commercial arbitration was confirmed by a resolution of the International Law Institute adopted in Athens in 1979, particularly for contracts between a state and a foreign private person.[28] It is also endorsed by various arbitration rules which refer to laws in plural form[29] as well as by the Model Law.[30] In that sense, substantive law codifications, such as Article 6 CISG, anticipate different laws being applied, by allowing parties to exclude the application of the CISG or derogate from or vary the effect of any of its provisions.

18-35 Equally parties may agree to either general principles of law or some other non-legal standard to apply to their contract. In the *Channel Tunnel* contract the parties chose the concurrent application of principles common to English and French laws and in the absence of such common principles, the general principles of international trade law as have been applied by national and

---

26 *Saudi Arabia v Arabian American Oil Co (ARAMCO)*, 27 ILR 117 (1963).

27 *Ibid*, 166. Dépeçage was deemed inappropriate in Zurich Chamber of Commerce award in case no 273/95, 31 May 1996, *Raw material processor (Hungary) and Processing group (Argentina) v Raw material seller (Russian Federation)*, XXIII *YBCA* 128 (1998).

28 Institut de Droit International, *Table of Adopted Resolutions (1957-1991)*, 332, 333 (1992) (in French). See further Gertz, "The Selection of Choice of Law Provisions in International Commercial Arbitration: A Case for Contractual Dépeçage", 12 *NW J Int'l L & Bus* 163 (1991).

29 See AAA ICDR Article 28(1); LCIA Article 22(3); SCC Rules Article 24.

30 Model Law Article 28. See also Broches, "Commentary on the UNCITRAL Model Law", in Paulsson (ed), *Int'l Handbook on Comm Arb*, Suppl 11 January (Kluwer 1990) 11, Article 28, paras 15-16.

international tribunals.[31] Similarly, parties may agree a national law to govern the contract, a specific INCOTERM to govern the terms of delivery, passing of risk, insurance obligations, *etc* and an industry standard to apply to certain aspects of performance, *e.g.* special accounting principles to apply to the special purpose accounts for buy out or earn out arrangements.

2.3. Stabilised Law: the Inter-Temporal Problem

18-36 It is not unusual, especially at times of economic, social, or political evolution of a particular state, that the law changes. For instance, new laws were adapted in and significant changes were made to the laws of many eastern European and CIS countries in the 1990s and the early 21st century. Indeed, in most countries law is ever changing. It is a matter of inter-temporal conflict of laws[32] to decide whether the law at the time the agreement was concluded or at the time of the dispute applies. As a general rule the law is applied as it stands at the time when it is being applied, except where the parties have agreed otherwise or where there is some clear law or treaty obligation.[33]

18-37 Parties may agree themselves that the law at the time of the agreement shall apply. This is known as a stabilisation clause which effectively freezes the content of the applicable law as between the parties to a particular point in time. Agreements of this kind stop any unilateral change of essential variables defined in the clause. Such variables include the applicable tax regime, import and export regulations, currency exchange regulations, investment legislation, etc.[34]

18-38 Stabilisation clauses are predominantly employed in contracts which involve a state party, especially as state parties usually insist on their own laws to apply. This is particularly the case in long term contracts where one party seeks to maintain in existence a legal system or laws irrespective of social, political and economic changes. The aim is to prevent the state changing its law in order to

---

[31] Clause 68 of the Channel Tunnel contract was cited in *Channel Tunnel Group v Balfour Beatty Ltd* [1993] 1 All ER 664.

[32] See Grodecki, "Intertemporal Conflict of Laws", Chapter 8 in Vol 3 *International Encyclopedia of Comparative Law* (Mohr and Martinus Nijhoff, 1976).

[33] This is found in the foreign investment laws of emerging countries to encourage investments from abroad. See, *e.g.* Republic of Kazakhstan, Law no 266-XIII of 27 December 1994 Concerning Foreign Investments.

[34] Jarvin, "ICC: Disputes Prevention Methods", in *28th ICC Congress Stockholm 17 June 1984*, 1(4) *J Int'l Arb* 355 (1984).

alter the terms of the contract to which it is a party.[35] On the other hand if a state wants to treat the other party unfairly, a stabilisation clause might not be effective since the state can enact legislation avoiding or prohibiting stabilisation clauses. Whilst controversial because they aim to preclude a government from using its legislative powers, stabilisation clauses have been confirmed in many international arbitrations.[36] By contrast there is no established case law for national courts, as stabilisation clauses are usually found in contracts that also contain an arbitration clause.

18-39 A stabilisation clause is not a guaranteed protection from laws which change or withdraw rights of a contract party. The *AMINOIL* award[37] illustrates the fluctuations that can occur in a geographical area and an economic sector of production that can upset the contractual equilibrium. The dispute concerned a concession agreement between Kuwait and the American Independent Oil Company (AMINOIL) entered into in 1948 when Kuwait was still under British control. The concession was to last for sixty years. It was a typical concession agreement then current in the oil industry: the oil company fixed the prices and paid an annual royalty. An additional agreement, concluded in 1961 when Kuwait achieved independence, included both a stabilisation clause and a provision for renegotiation in pursuance of which a draft agreement was reached in 1973.

18-40 In the *AMINOIL* arbitration the tribunal denied the effect of the stabilisation clause in two circumstances. First, if the state embarks on a programme of economic reform, the stabilisation clause will not make the contract immune to legislative changes. It may, however, be judicially possible to devise a clause which excludes these legislative changes, provided it is for "a relatively limited period". Secondly, though the case did not involve the application of the *clausula rebus sic stantibus* principle, the tribunal recognised

---

35 *Sapphire Int'l Petroleum Ltd v National Iranian Oil Co*, 15 March 1963, 35 ILR 136 (1967).

36 See, *e.g.*, *Texaco Overseas Petroleum Co v Libyan Arab Republic*, 19 January 1977, IV YBCA 177 (1980); *Government of the State of Kuwait v American Independent Oil Co (AMINOIL)*, 24 March 1982, IX YBCA 71 (1984); ICSID case no ARB/77/1, *AGIP SpA v Government of the People's Republic of Congo*, 30 November 1979, VIII YBCA 133 (1983); ICSID Case no ARB/83/2, *Liberian Eastern Timber Co v Government of the Republic of Liberia*, 31 March 1986, XIII YBCA 35 (1988).

37 *Kuwait v American Independent Oil Co (AMINOIL)*, 24 March 1982, IX YBCA 71 (1984). Economic and political fluctuations are also discussed in the *Lena Goldfields* arbitration. See Veeder, "The Lena Goldfields Arbitration: The Historical Roots of Three Ideas", 47 *ICLQ* 747 (1998).

that there could be a change in the nature of the contract itself "brought about by time and the acquiescence or conduct of the parties."[38] If this occurs, the alteration of the contract cannot be fettered by the stabilisation clause.

3. Substantive International and Transnational Rules

18-41 Instead of choosing a national law, parties may choose or the arbitrators may decide to apply non-national, international and transnational substantive rules or standards.[39] The departure from national law as the source of standards for international commercial relations has emerged by a combination of factors, such as discontent in the international business community with the law and lawyers, and efforts to evade the application of the conflict of laws altogether. Accordingly, arbitrators can and do apply non-national substantive rules, the *lex mercatoria* or transnational law and other substantive rules of non-national origin.

18-42 There is substantial academic literature on the existence, content, sources and scope of the non-national and non-legal substantive rules which may be applicable for international commercial transactions.[40] The diversity of

---

[38] See the reference in the full version of Aminoil, in 21 *ILM* 976 (1982) 1065, para 26.

[39] For examples of the application of transnational rules see ICC award no 6500 (1992), 119 *Clunet* 1015 (1992); ICC award no 8385 (1995), 124 *Clunet* 1061 (1997); Paris Arbitration Chamber, 8 March 1996, *Agent (Austria) v Principal (Egypt)*, XXII YBCA 28 (1997); Cour de cassation, 9 October 1984, *Pabalk Ticaret Limited Sirketi v Norsolor SA*, 112 Clunet 679 (1985), English translation in 24 ILM 360 (1985); Corte di cassazione, 9 May 1996, no 4342 ; Corte di appello Bari, 2 November 1993, no 811, *Société Arabe des Engrais Phosphates et Azotes (SAEPA) and Société Industrielle d'Acide Phosphorique et d'Engrais (SIAPE) v Gemanco srl*, XXII *YBCA* 737 (1997).

[40] See, *e.g.*, Schmitthoff, "International Business law: A New Law Merchant", 2 *Current Law and Social Problems* 129 (1961); Langen, *Transnational Commercial Law* (Sijthoff & Noordhoff 1973); Bonell, "Das autonome Recht des Welthandels", 42 *RabelsZ* 485 (1978); Schmitthoff, *Commercial Law in a Changing Economic Climate* (2d ed, Sweet & Maxwell 1981); Ole Lando, "The Lex Mercatoria in International Commercial Arbitration", 34 *ICLQ* 747 (1985); Lord Mustill, "The New Lex Mercatoria – the First Twenty-five Years", in Bos & Brownlie (ed), *Liber Amicorum for Lord Wilberforce* (Oxford 1987), 149 and 2 *Arb Int* 86 (1988); Dezalay and Garth, *Dealing in Virtue*; Teubner (ed), *Global Law Without a State* (Aldershot 1997); Berger, "The New Law Merchant and the Global Market Place: A 21st Century View of Transnational Commercial Law", *IntALR* 91-102 (2000); Mistelis, "Regulatory Aspects: Globalization, Harmonization, Legal Transplants and Law Reform", 34(3) *The International Lawyer* 1055 (Fall 2000); Mistelis, "Is Harmonisation a Necessary Evil? The Future of Harmonisation and New Sources of International Trade Law", in Fletcher, Mistelis and Cremona (eds), *Foundations and Perspectives of International Trade Law* (Sweet and Maxwell 2001), 1.

approaches tends to undermine the intention of applying a commercial law that is relatively universal and under which international trade usage will control the determination of a dispute.[41] It is probably more accurate to state that there are a variety of international commercial laws rather than a universal system.[42] However, it is clear that the resolution of many issues would benefit from a tribunal's taking into account recognised commercial principles, especially when the applicable substantive national law does not provide clear guidance.

18-43 Supplementing the applicable substantive law with international (transnational) commercial law is, of course, a much less difficult choice on the part of a tribunal than seeking to displace the applicable law altogether, which could be an invitation to an enforcement challenge. Where it is possible for international commercial law to be applied as substantive law, a tribunal should do so. The English Court of Appeal has upheld a Swiss arbitration award where the arbitrators applied "internationally accepted principles of law governing contractual relations"[43] because the application of those principles was valid under the system where the award was made.

18-44 The gradual shift from a national substantive law to the application of international commercial law is heralded by the use of the expression *"rules of law"* that can be found in modern arbitration laws and rules. It appears that the new term was first used in an arbitration law in Article 1496 of the New French Code of Civil Procedure.[44] This provision allows the parties or the arbitrators to choose transnational rules or the *lex mercatoria*.[45]

18-45 Article 28 Model Law uses the same term, albeit only in connection with the choice of law by the parties. Arguably, failing a designation of rules of law by the parties, the arbitration tribunal may only apply the "*law*" which it considers applicable. The drafters of the Model Law considered *"rules of law"* as

---

41 Goode, "Usage and Its Reception in Transnational Commercial Law", 46 *ICLQ* 35 (1997).

42 See the discussion in van Houtte, *The Law of International Trade* (Sweet and Maxwell 1995), para 1-35.

43 *Deutsche Schachtbau- und Tiefbohrgesellschaft mbH v R'As al-Khaimah National Oil Co* [1987] 3 WLR 1023.

44 The expression "rules of law" is used similarly in Netherlands CCP Article 1054 and Swiss PIL, Article 187.

45 See Fouchard, "L'arbitrage international en France après le décret du 12 Mai 1981", 109 Clunet 374 (1982) para 39; de Boisséson, *Le droit français de l'arbitrage*, para 661, 591.

national law of a State; national laws of different States; rules embodied in a convention or a similar legal text elaborated on the international level...[46]

3.1. Notion of Lex Mercatoria and Transnational Law

18-46 There is extensive doctrinal debate about the meaning, existence, content and application of the *lex mercatoria* and/or transnational rules. In attempts to define *lex mercatoria*[47] and transnational rules several expressions have been used, such as "transnational commercial law", "general principles of international

---

[46] UNCITRAL Doc A/CN 9/245, para 94, Art XIX(1). See also Holtzmann and Neuhaus, *Model Law*, 766-767. For the drafters of the Model Law rules of law did not include "general legal principles" or "*lex mercatoria*". This attitude has now changed and it is generally accepted that "rules of law" are included in the definition of *lex mercatoria*.

[47] See Aguilar Alvarez, "To What Extent Do Arbitrators in International Cases Disregard the Bag and Baggage of National Systems?", *ICCA Congress series no 8*, 139-156; Baron, "Do the UNIDROIT Principles Form a New Lex Mercatoria?", 15 *Arb Int* 115 (1999); Berger, *The Creeping Codification of Lex mercatoria*; Berger, "The New Law Merchant and the Global Market Place - A 21st Century View of Transnational Commercial Law", in Berger (ed), *The Practice of Transnational Law* (Kluwer 2000); Carbonneau (ed), *Lex Mercatoria and Arbitration*; De Ly, *International Business Law and Lex Mercatoria* (North-Holland 1992); Freeman, "Lex mercatoria: its emergence and acceptance as a legal basis for the resolution of international disputes", IX *ADRLJ* 289 (1997); Goldman "The applicable law: general principles of law", in Lew (ed), *Contemporary Problems*, 113; Goldman, "Le lex mercatoria dans les contrats et l'arbitrage internationaux; realites et perspectives", 106 *Clunet* 475 (1979); Goldman, "Lex Mercatoria" 3 *Forum Internationale* 194 (1983); Goldstáin, "Reflections on the Structure of the Modern International Trade", in Šarčević (ed), *International Contracts and Conflict of Laws* (Aspen 1990), 14-35; Hunter, "Publication of Arbitration Awards and Lex Mercatoria", 54 *Arbitration* 55 (1988); Lando, "The Lex Mercatoria in International Commercial Arbitration", 34 *ICLQ* 747 (1985); Langen, *Transnational Commercial Law* (Sijthoff & Noordhoff 1973); Lowenfeld, "Lex Mercatoria: An Arbitrator's View" 6 *Arb Int* 133 (1990); Maniruzzaman, "The Lex Mercatoria and International Contracts: A Challenge for International Commercial Arbitration", 14 *Am U Int'l L Rev* 657 (1999); Mayer, "Mandatory rules of laws in international arbitration", 2 *Arb Int* 274 (1986); Mustill, "Contemporary Problems in International Commercial Arbitration: A Response" 17 *Int'l Bus Law* 161 (1989); Mustill, "The New Lex Mercatoria – the First Twenty-five Years" in Bos & Brownlie (ed), *Liber Amicorum for Lord Wilberforce* (Oxford 1987), 149 and 2 *Arb Int* 86 (1988); Nottage, "The Vicissitudes of Transnational Commercial Arbitration and the Lex Mercatoria: A View from the Periphery", 16 *Arb Int* 53 (2000); Paulsson, "Le lex mercatoria dans l'arbitrage CCI", *Rev Arb* 55 (1990); Rivkin, "Enforceability of Arbitral Awards based on Lex Mercatoria", 9 *Arb Int* 67 (1993); Schutze, "The Precedential Effect of Arbitration Decisions", 11(3) *J Int Arb* 69 (1994); Stein, *Lex mercatoria - Realität und Theorie* (Klostermann 1995); Stoecker, "The Lex Mercatoria": To What Extent does it Exist?" 7(1) *J Int Arb* 101 (1990); Wilkinson "The New Lex Mercatoria – Reality or Academic Fantasy?" 12(2) *J Int Arb* 103 (1995).

commercial law", "principles common to several legal systems"[48] and "international trade usages".[49] By choosing *lex mercatoria* the parties or the arbitrators may avoid the technicalities of national legal systems.

18-47 The lex mercatoria is created by and for the participants in international trade and applied by arbitrators to settle international trade disputes. The rules of the lex mercatoria are founded on usages developed in international trade, standard clauses and contracts, uniform laws, general principles of law and international instruments. Trade usages are undeniably important in international trade and often included in standard contracts or standard clauses. They are often drawn up by the commercial organisation of a business sector and are used by the members of that sector (e.g. FIDIC, GAFTA, ICC). Goldman offered the following definition of lex mercatoria

> Lex mercatoria would thus, irrespective of its origin and the nature of these sources, be the *law proper to international economic [commercial] relations*. One would encompass not only transnational customary law, whether it is codified or not (and in the latter case revealed and clarified by arbitral awards) but also law of an interstate, or indeed State, which relates to international trade. Thus, for example, the successive Hague (1954) and Vienna (1980) Conventions Establishing Uniform Laws for the International Sale of Goods would be part of lex mercatoria. This would also be the case with respect to national legislation whose specific and exclusive object is international trade. ... The same applies to rules specific to international trade established by national case law, such as for example, the French notions of the autonomy of parties, the general validity of international arbitration agreements, and the capacity of state and of public entities to bind themselves by such agreements.[50] [Emphasis in the original]

18-48 The above definition actually describes the multi-faceted sources of international trade law as it considers both national statutes, international agreements, contractual clauses, trade usages, customary law, general principles

---

[48] Rivkin, "Enforceability of Arbitral Awards Based on Lex Mercatoria", 9 *Arb Int* 67 (1993) 72 *et seq*, who makes references to various clauses.

[49] On the terminology see Fouchard Gaillard Goldman *on International Commercial Arbitration*, para 1446, 805-6.

[50] Goldman, "The Applicable Law: General Principles of Law", in Lew (ed), *Contemporary Problems*, 113. This wide view was always expressed by Schmitthoff (ed), *The Sources of the Law of International Trade* (International Association of Legal Science 1964) and Schmitthoff, "The Law of International Trade", in *Commercial Law in a Changing Economic Climate* (2d ed, Sweet & Maxwell 1981), 18-33. It is comparable to the definition offered by Jessup in his seminal work *Transnational Law* (Yale University Press 1956).

of law and codes of conduct. Consequently, this definition "resides solely in the *object* of its constituent elements". It does not consider equally "its *origin* and its *customary*, and thus *spontaneous* nature"[51] nor does it highlight the conclusive role of the business community.

18-49 Despite the uncertainty as to the content of *lex mercatoria* many compilations of laws have recognised its influence on international practice. For example, the Convention on the International Sale of Goods (CISG) and the UNIDROIT Principles are said to be the product or even source of *lex mercatoria*.[52]

3.2. Method and Content of Lex Mercatoria in International Arbitration Practice

18-50 There is a substantial body of arbitration case law which acknowledges or applies the *lex mercatoria*.[53] The International Law Association adopted a resolution at its 1992 Conference in Cairo, according to which arbitration awards "based on transnational rules (general principles of law, principles common to several jurisdictions, international law, usages of trade, etc) rather than a particular national law" are enforceable

- if the parties have agreed that the arbitrator may apply transnational rules, or
- if the parties have remained silent concerning the applicable law.[54]

18-51 Decisions of national courts have confirmed the principles of the resolution and the application of *lex mercatoria*.[55]

---

[51] Goldman, in Lew (ed), *Contemporary Problems*, 114.

[52] See Weinberg, "Equity in International Arbitration: How Fair is 'Fair'? A Study of Lex Mercatoria and Amiable Composition", 12 *Boston U Int'l L J* 227 (1994) 230. See also Berger (ed), *The Practice of Transnational Law* (Kluwer 2000).

[53] See Lew, *Applicable Law*, paras 366-372, 465-474; Berger, "The New Law Merchant and the Global Market Place - A 21st Century View of Transnational Commercial Law", in Berger, *The Practice of Transnational Law*, 3(4) *IntALR* 91 (2000).

[54] See International Law Association Committee on International Commercial Arbitration, "The Applicability of Transnational Rules in International Commercial Arbitration", ILA Report of the 64th Conference, Queensland, Australia (1991). See also Bowden, "Transnational Rules in International Commercial Arbitration", ICC Publication No 480/4 (1993), 247.

[55] See Rivkin, 9 *Arb Int* 67 (1993). See also *Deutsche Schachtbau- und Tiefbohrgesellschaft mbH v R'As al Khaimah National Oil Co* [1987] 3 WLR 1023; YBCA XIII (1988), 522 (CA and HL); Cour de cassation, 22 October 1991, No. 1354, *Compania Valenciana de Cementos Portland SA*

18-52 With regard to the question how to identify *lex mercatoria* and transnational rules the tribunal should take into account the dynamic character of such rules; there is no definitive list of general principles of international commercial law.[56] Therefore the tribunal will need to ascertain at a first stage whether there is an appropriate trade usage or relevant rule in an international commercial law codification.

18-53 The arbitration tribunal should look at the choice of law clause itself. A vague reference to general principles of law or international commercial usages rather than specific rules or a specific codification will normally be a sufficient choice for the application of *lex mercatoria* rules by the tribunal.[57]

18-54 The parties often include clauses which make express reference to general or common principles of law.[58] This is a negative choice of law, the parties having excluded certain obvious laws by their failure to select them. In this situation arbitrators apply, wherever possible, the law or rules common to the parties, or the general principles of law common to both parties. This can operate when such principles common in national laws exist.[59] Other clauses refer to

v Primary Coal Inc, Rev crit dip 113 (1992), with note by Oppetit, 114, 119 *Clunet* 177 (1992) with note by Goldman, 178; Rev Arb 457 (1992), with note by Lagarde, 458; (in English) XVIII YBCA 137 (1993); Cour de cassation, 9 December 1981, *Fougerolle v Banque du Proche-Orient*, 109 *Clunet* 935 (1982); Tribunal de grande instance Paris, 4 March 1981, *Société Norsolor v Société Pabalk Ticaret Sirketi,* 108 *Clunet* 836 (1981).

56 Berger, *The Creeping Codification of Lex Mercatoria*, 218 *et seq* (1999).

57 See Award in ICC Case no 3540, 3 October 1980, *French enterprise v Yugoslav subcontractor,* 108 Clunet 914 (1981), with commentary by Derains, 921, VII YBCA 124 (1982); Cour de cassation, 9 December 1981, *Fougerolle v Banque du Proche-Orient*, 109 *Clunet* 935 (1982); Tribunal de grande instance Paris, 4 March 1981, *Société Norsolor v Société Pabalk Ticaret Sirketi,* 108 *Clunet* 836 (1981).

58 See Rubino-Sammartano, "Le 'tronc commun' des lois nationales en présence (réflexions sur le droit applicable par l'arbitre international)", *Rev Arb* 133 (1987); Ancel, "The Tronc Commun Doctrine: Logics and Experience in International Arbitration", 7(3) *J Int Arb* 65 (1990).

59 See the *Channel Tunnel* case, [1993] 1 All ER 664. The three Libyan nationalisation oil arbitrations involved an identical choice of law clause: "This concession shall be governed by and interpreted in accordance with the principles of law of Libya common to the principles of international law, and in the absence of such common principles, then by and in accordance with the general principles as may have been applied by international tribunals." *Texaco Overseas Petroleum Co v The Government of Libyan Arab Republic*, 17 ILM 3 (1978); *Libyan American Oil Co v The Government of Libyan Arab Republic*, VI YBCA 89 (1981); *British Petroleum Co Ltd v The Government of Libyan Arab Republic*, V YBCA 158 (1980). Another tribunal applied the same method interpreting Egyptian law as conforming with the principle exemplified in Art 42(1) ICSID: *(The Pyramids Case) SPP (Middle East) v The Arab Republic of Egypt*, IX YBCA 111 (1984). See *Banque Arabe et Internationale d'Investissements et al v Inter-Arab Investment*

rules of international origin and vary in formulation.[60] In any event, the tribunal should either (or cumulatively) request submissions by the parties as to what they consider "common" or "general" principles. Comparative law is also of paramount importance in determining transnational rules.

18-55 International conventions, such as the CISG[61] and international arbitration case law are also instrumental in determining the content of the *lex mercatoria.*

18-56 Professor Ole Lando[62] and Lord Mustill[63] compiled lists of principles or sources that could comprise the *lex mercatoria.* These two scholars have reached different conclusions. In any event these various sources have been considered in arbitration awards as constituting general principles and have often been quoted by legal scholars and used to support the *lex mercatoria.*[64]

Guarantee Corporation, 17 November 1994, XXI YBCA 13 (1996), where common legal principles prevailing in member countries of IAIGC and recognised principles of international law were chosen as applicable law; ICC Award no 6378, 1991, 120 *Clunet* 1018 (1993) ("principles of law applicable in Western Europe").

60 See, *e.g.*, ICC Award no 5333 ("generally recognised principles of international commercial law"), unpublished, cited in Fouchard Gaillard Goldman *on International Commercial Arbitration*, para 1457, note 163.

61 A number of awards use the CISG as a means of determining international trade usages and lex mercatoria: award in ICC case no 5713 (1989), XV *YBCA* 70 (1990); Interim Award in ICC case no 6149 (1990), *Korean seller v Jordanian buyer*, XX YBCA 41 (1995); award in ICC case no 7331 (1994), *Yugoslav seller v Italian buyer*, 122 Clunet 1001 (1995). Other awards use the CISG in order to support the position of a domestic law: award in ICC case no 6281 (1989), *Egyptian buyer v Yugoslav seller*, XV YBCA 96 (1990); Zurich Chamber of Commerce award in case no 273/95 of 31 May 1996, *Raw material processor (Hungary) and Processing group (Argentina) v Raw material seller (Russian Federation)*, XXIII YBCA 128 (1998). On the application of CISG as applicable law see award in ICC case no 7153, *Austrian party v Yugoslav* party, 119 *Clunet* 1006 (1992); Award in ICC case no 8324 (1995), 123 *Clunet* 1019 (1996); award in ICC case no 8128 (1995), 123 *Clunet* 1024 (1996). See also De Ly, "La pratique de l'arbitrage commercial internationale et la vente internationale", 3(4) *RDAI/IBLJ* 465 (2001).

62 Lando, "The Lex Mercatoria and International Commercial Arbitration"' 34 ICLQ 747 (1985). See also Lando, "The Law Applicable to the Merits of the Dispute, in Sarčević (ed), *Essays*, 129.

63 Mustill, "The New Lex Mercatoria – the First Twenty-five Years" in Bos & Brownlie (eds), *Liber Amicorum for Lord Wilberforce* (Oxford 1987), 149-183 and 2 *Arb Int* 86 (1988).

64 See, *e.g.*, Kahn, "Les principes généraux du droit devant les arbitres du commerce international", 116 *Clunet* 305 (1989) 325; Berger, *International Economic Arbitration*, 543-554 (with further references); Lowenfeld, "Lex Mercatoria: An Arbitrator's View", in Carbonneau (ed), *Lex Mercatoria and Arbitration*, 71; see also <www.tldb.de> and <www.unilex.info>.

18-57 These various principles[65] that have been applied by international tribunals include:

- Contracts should be enforced according to their terms: *Pacta sunt servanda,*[66] unless there is a significant change of circumstances, *rebus sic stantibus.*[67]
- Unfair and unconscionable contracts and clauses should not be enforced.[68]
- There may be a doctrine of *culpa in contrahendo*[69] according to which liability may be assumed for contractual negotiations.
- A contract should be performed in good faith.[70]
- A contract designed to achieve an illegal object[71] or obtained by bribes or other dishonest means is void, or at least unenforceable.[72]

---

[65] For the purpose of this discussion the principles are drawn from the article of Lord Mustill, "The New Lex Mercatoria – the First Twenty-five Years" in Bos & Brownlie (eds), *Liber Amicorum for Lord Wilberforce* (Oxford 1987), 149-183 and 2 *Arb Int* 86 (1988).

[66] See, *e.g.*, award in ICC case no 5485 (1987), *Bermudan company v Spanish company*, XIV YBCA 156 (1989); award in ICC case no 3540 (1980), *French contractor v Yugoslav sub-contractor*, VII YBCA 124 (1982); award in ICC case no 2321 (1974), *Two Israeli companies v The Government of an African State*, I YBCA 133 (1976); ICSID Award in case no ARB/81/1, *Amco Asia Corp v Republic of Indonesia*, 21 ILM 1022 (1985), 134; *Sapphire* Award, ILR 136 (1967).

[67] See interim awards and final award of 1983, 1984 and 1986 in ICC case no 4145, *Establishment of Middle East country v South Asian construction company*, 112 Clunet 985 (1985), XII YBCA 97 (1987); Iran-US Claims Tribunal award in Case no 59 (191-59-1), 25 September 1985, *Questech, Inc v The Ministry of National Defence of the Islamic Republic of Iran*, XI YBCA 283 (1986); *Ad hoc* award of July 6 1983, *Hungarian State enterprise v Jugoslavenski naftovod (Yugoslav Crude Oil Pipeline)*, IX YBCA 69 (1984). See also Berger, *International Economic Arbitration*, note 350, 548.

[68] This principle can be found in many civil law systems but are of limited use in common law. See, however, UCC Sect 2-302. In most cases public policy would bar the enforceability of unfair and unconscionable clauses.

[69] See Iran - US Claims Tribunal, award in case no 149 (53-149-1), 10 June 1983, *Mark Dallal v Islamic Republic of Iran and Bank Mellat*, IX YBCA 264 (1984); Berger, *International Economic Arbitration*, note 336, 545.

[70] See, *e.g.*, award in ICC case no 3131 (1979), *Pabalk Ticaret Sirketi SA (Turkey) v Norsolor SA*, *Rev Arb* 1983, 525, 531; IX *YBCA* 109 (1984). See also Tribunal de grande instance Paris, 4 March 1981, *Norsolor SA (France) v Pabalk Ticaret Sirketi SA (Turkey)*, Rev Arb 465 (1983), note Goldman, 379; Cour d'appel of Paris, 15 December 1981 and 19 November 1982, *Rev Arb* 1983, 470; Cour de cassation, 9 October 1984, 25 *ILM* 360 (1985).

[71] See award in ICC case no 2730 (1982), *Two Yugoslav companies v Dutch and Swiss group companies*, 111 Clunet 914 (1984) 920.

- A State entity cannot evade its obligations by asserting that the agreement is unenforceable for want of procedural formalities to which the entity is subject.[73]
- Parties should negotiate in good faith to overcome unforeseen difficulties in the performance of a contract, even if the contract contains no revision clause.[74]
- "Gold clause" agreements are valid and enforceable.[75] In some cases either a gold clause or a "hardship" revision clause may be implied.[76]
- One party is entitled to treat itself as discharged from its obligations if the other has committed a substantial breach.[77]
- No party can be allowed by its own act to bring about a non-performance of a condition precedent to its own obligation.[78]
- A tribunal is not bound by the characterisation of the contract ascribed to it by the parties.[79]
- Damages for breach of contract are limited to the foreseeable consequences of the breach and include loss actually suffered and loss of profit.[80]

---

72 See, *e.g.*, award in ICC case no 110 (1963), *Mr X, Buenos Aires v Company A*, 10 Arb Int 282 (1994), XXI YBCA 47 (1996).

73 See, *e.g.*, AAA award, 24 August, 1978, *Revere Copper & Brass Inc v OPIC*, 17 ILM 1321 (1978) 1322; *Texaco Overseas Petroleum Co v The Government of Libyan Arab Republic*, 17 ILM 3 (1978) 19.

74 See award in ICC case no 2291 (1975), 103 *Clunet* 989 (1976); award in ICC case no 6219 117 *Clunet* 1047 (1990); award in ICC case no 5953, 117 *Clunet* 1056 (1990); award in ICC case no 8365 (1996), *Spanish bank v German bank*, 124 Clunet 1078 (1997).

75 See award in ICC case no 1512 (1971), I *YBCA* 128 (1976); award in ICC case no 1990, 101 *Clunet* 897 (1974); award in ICC case no 2748, 102 *Clunet* 925 (1975); award in ICC case no 2291, 103 *Clunet* 989 (1976).

76 See Berger, *International Economic Arbitration*, note 340, 546 and Mustill, supra note 63, note 95.

77 See, *e.g.*, award in ICC case no 3540 (1980), *French enterprise v Yugoslav subcontractor*, VII *YBCA* 124 (1982); award in ICC case no 2583, 103 *Clunet* 950 (1976).

78 See, *e.g.*, award in ICC case no 2521, 103 *Clunet* 997 (1976); award in ICC case no 6294, 118 *Clunet* 1050 (1991); Final award in ICC case no 4629 (1989), *Contractor (European Country) and Contractor (Middle Eastern Country) v Owner (Middle Eastern Country)*, XVIII *YBCA* 11 (1993). The principle is that the claimant is not entitled to sue because he has not performed his own part of the agreement; the Latin maxim is *exceptio non adimpleti contractus*.

79 See Fouchard Gaillard Goldman *on International Commercial Arbitration*, para 1477, 827-8.

- A party which has suffered a breach of contract must take reasonable steps to mitigate its loss.[81]
- Damages for non-delivery are calculated by reference to the market price of the goods and the price at which the buyer purchased equivalent in replacement goods.[82]
- A party must act in a diligent and practical manner to safeguard its own interests[83] and to avoid being considered as having waived its rights.[84]
- Contract terms should be construed on the presumption that they are effective.[85]

18-58 The determination of transnational rules for resolving disputes is a dynamic process and cannot be reduced to a definitive list of rules. A number of open-ended codifications[86] constitute a creeping codification of *lex mercatoria*. In most cases such lists complement each other[87] and have found statutory

---

80 See, *e.g.*, award in ICC case no 1526 (1968), *Belgian party v African state*, 101 Clunet 915 (1974); *Amco* arbitration, 24 *ILM* 1036 (1985), 114 *Clunet* 155 (1987).

81 See, *e.g.*, award in ICC case no 2478, 102 *Clunet* 925 (1974); award in ICC case no 4761, *Italian consortium v Libyan company*, 114 Clunet 1012 (1987); award in ICC case no 5514 (1990), *French company v Government committed to the provision of financing*, 119 Clunet 1022 (1992) 1024; award in ICC case no 6840 (1991), *Egyptian seller v Senegalese buyer*, 119 Clunet 1030 (1992), 1034.

82 See CISG Articles 75-76.

83 See award in ICC case no 2520, *Two Czechoslovak companies v Italian company*, 103 Clunet 992 (1976).

84 See award in ICC case no 3344, 108 *Clunet* 978 (1982); award in ICC case no 3243, 108 *Clunet* 968 (1982); award in ICC case no 2250, 102 *Clunet* 992 (1976).

85 See, *e.g.*, award in ICC case no 1434 (1975), 102 *Clunet* 982 (1976); award in ICC case no 3380 (1980), *Italian company v Syrian company*, VII *YBCA* 116 (1982); award in ICC case no 8331 (1996), 125 *Clunet* 1041 (1998).

86 See, *e.g.*, CISG, the INCOTERMS, the UNIDROIT Principles of International Commercial Contracts 1994; the Principles of European Contract Law 1995-1999 in Lando/Beale (eds), *Principles of European Contract Law, Parts I and II Combined and Revised* (Kluwer 2000); the CENTRAL List of Principles, Rules and Standards of the Lex Mercatoria 1996, in CENTRAL (ed), *Transnational Law in Commercial Legal Practice* (Quadis Publishing 1999), 146 *et seq.* This CENTRAL Publication contains also the texts of the UNIDROIT Principles and The Principles of European Contract Law.

87 See, in addition to the *lex mercatoria* principles listed, other principles in Berger, *International Economic Arbitration*, 544-553 and Fouchard Gaillard Goldman *on International Commercial Arbitration*, paras 1459-1499, 818-834. The additional principles include: prohibition of unjust enrichment; *volenti non fit iniuria*; *favor negotii*; obligation to inform the other party promptly of any difficulties arising during the course of the contract; the buyer loses the right to rely on a lack of conformity of the goods, if he does not give notice to the seller within reasonable time;

approval in national laws. This evolving body of principles is a useful tool to both arbitrators and the business community. Increasingly it represents and is used as the appropriate law or source of substantive rules to be applied in international arbitrations to determine disputes according to the parties' needs and wishes.[88]

3.3. Principles of International Business

18-59 There have been various developments of internationally accepted principles and standards for direct application by arbitrators. Best known among these, and which have been applied by arbitrators, are the ICC INCOTERMS 2000 and Uniform Customs and Practice for Documentary Credits, UNIDROIT Principles and the CISG.

(a) INCOTERMS 2000 and Uniform Customs and Practice for Documentary Credits

18-60 INCOTERMS 2000[89] are the most commonly used international trade terms and are published with the endorsement of the ICC. First issued in 1923 with a survey on the interpretation of 6 trade terms in 13 countries, by 1953 the INCOTERMS expanded their coverage to provide a uniform interpretation of 10 trade terms in 18 countries. The INCOTERMS 2000 confirm the common measure of practice around those trade terms.

18-61 The INCOTERMS, *e.g.*, FOB, CIF, Ex Works, have achieved such a wide recognition that their meanings stand alone without any need for legal interpretation. There have been many awards in which tribunals have directly applied the INCOTERMS to the facts of the case referring only to the ICC booklet rather than to the otherwise applicable law. INCOTERMS are invoked as

---

apparent authority, agency by estoppel; presumption of competence of the contracting party; contracts should be construed *contra proferentem*; *lex specialis derogat legi generali*; *falsa demonstratio non nocet*; principle of piercing the corporate veil; application of the usages and customs of the particular branch of trade, etc.

88 Freeman, "Lex mercatoria: its emergence and acceptance as a legal basis for the resolution of international disputes", IX *ADRLJ* 289 (1997) 300.

89 Ramberg, *Guide to ICC Incoterms 2000* (ICC publication no 620, 1999).

a relevant trade usage: as a direct result of choice by the parties or indirectly by implication of the otherwise applicable law.[90]

18-62 This is equally the case with the ICC Uniform Customs and Practice for Documentary Credits (UCP 500) which is a codification of customs and practices used voluntarily by most banks.[91] Nearly all arrangements for documentary credits around the world are made subject to the terms of this instrument. UCP may be used as directly applicable rules to determine, for instance, compliance of documents with the terms of documentary credits or decide matters of assurance for payment.[92]

(b) UNIDROIT Principles

18-63 The UNIDROIT Principles represent a modern approach to international trade law.[93] They are increasingly being used in international contract practice and dispute resolution.[94]

---

[90] See, *e.g.*, ICC case no 7645 (1995), *Supplier (Slovakia) v Buyer (Korea)*, 11(2) ICC Bulletin 34 (2000), XXVI YBCA 130 (2001) (INCOTERMS were introduced via CISG Article 9 which binds the parties to any relevant trade usage; relevant term: CFR); Paris Arbitration Chamber award in case no 9392/9426, 16 January 1998, *Buyer (Netherlands) v Seller (Asian country)*, XXVI YBCA 13 (2001) (relevant term: FOB); CRCICA award, 21 December 1995, case no 24/1995, *African government body v European poultry company*, in Alam Eldin (ed), *Arbitral Awards of the Cairo Regional Centre for International Commercial Arbitration* (Kluwer 2000) 45.

[91] ICC Uniform Customs and Practice for Documentary Credits (UCP 500), ICC publication no 500/2 (2002).

[92] See, *e.g.*, ICC case no 7645 (1995), *Supplier (Slovakia) v Buyer (Korea)*, 11(2) ICC Bulletin 34 (2000), XXVI YBCA 130 (2001) (compliance of documents and impact of delay of shipment); Iran-US Claims Tribunal award in case 187 (342-187-3) 18 December 1997, *Gordon Williams v Islamic Republic of Iran, Bank Sepah and Bank Mellat*, XIV YBCA 34 (1989) (claim under letter of credit and evidence of demand for payment of letter of credit); CRCICA award, 31 December 1989, case no 14/1989, *European company v African government authority*, in Alam Eldin (ed), *Arbitral Awards of the Cairo Regional Centre for International Commercial Arbitration* (Kluwer 2000), 17-22 (failure to open documentary credit).

[93] See, *e.g.*, Bonell, "The UNIDROIT Principles of International Commercial Contracts - Nature, Purposes & First Experiences in Practice", <http://www.unidroit.org/english/principles/pr-exper.html>; Bonell, "The UNIDROIT Principles in Practice - The Experience of the First Two Years", in <http://www.cisg.law.pace.edu/cisg/biblio/pr-exper.html>, 27 *Uniform L Rev* 34 (1997); Garro, "The Contribution of the UNIDROIT Principles to the Advancement of International Commercial Arbitration", 3 *Tul J Int'l & Comp L* 93 (1994); Vagts, "Arbitration and the UNIDROIT Principles", in: *Contratacion internacional, Comentarios a los Principios sobre los Contratos Internationales del Unidroit*, (Universidad Nacional Autonoma de Mexico-1998) 265-277 <http://www.cisg.law.pace.edu/cisg/biblio/vagts.html>; Van Houtte, UNIDROIT

18-64 The ambit of the Principles is not restricted to a particular kind of transaction but covers the general part of contract law.[95] The aim is simply to reflect existing international contract law. The decisive criterion in their preparation was not just which rule had been adopted by the majority of countries, but also which of the rules under consideration had the most persuasive value and/or appeared to be particularly well suited for cross-border transactions. Hence, they are not subject to compromises which often dominate international legislative efforts.

18-65 The UNIDROIT Principles aim to avoid, or at least considerably reduce, the uncertainty accompanying the use of the *lex mercatoria*.[96] According to paragraph 3 of the Preamble, the Principles

> may be applied when the parties have agreed that their contract shall be governed by "general principles of law", the lex mercatoria or the like.

18-66 If the international business community and arbitrators recognise the Principles, they will be part of the *lex mercatoria*. In actual practice, an increasing number of cases are being reported in which the Principles have been applied as the applicable law to govern international sales contracts.[97] In two

---

Principles of International Commercial Contracts 11 *Arb Int* 373 (1995). On 27 April 2001 ICC and UNIDROIT organised jointly a symposium on the Use of the UNIDROIT Principles in International Commercial Arbitration.

94 Similar to the UNIDROIT Principles, but not so widely used, are the Principles of European Contract Law. This is a restatement of rules of contract law common to all European jurisdictions. See Beale and Lando, *Principles of European Contract Law*, Kluwer 1999. See also the commentary at <http://www.cisg.law.pace.edu/cisg/text/peclintro.html> The Principles of European Contract Law also provide a useful set of contractual rules which may be adopted by parties or be inferred by a tribunal for the interpretation of contractual provisions.

95 See Bridge, *The International Sale of Goods: Law and Practice* (Oxford University Press 1999), 54 *et seq*.

96 Comment 4(b) in the Preamble. See also *UNIDROIT Principles for International Commercial Contracts: A New Lex Mercatoria* (ICC Publication 490/1, 1995).

97 There are more than 20 reported awards. See, *e.g.*, award in ICC case no 8331 (1996), 125 *Clunet* 1041 (1998); Milan Court of Arbitration award no 1795, 1 December 1996, *Uniform L Rev* 602 (1997); International Arbitration Centre for the CCI of the Russian Federation award no 116, 20 January 1997, cited in Bonell, *An International Restatement of Contract Law* (2d ed, Transnational Publishers 1997), 252. One ICC award denies application of the Principles: ICC case no 8873, 125 *Clunet* 1017 (1998). See also ICC Bulletin 2002 Special Supplement *UNIDROIT Principles of International Commercial Contracts* and 12(2) ICC Bulletin for extracts and discussion of awards. Many awards are also available at <www.unilex.info>.

other cases the UNIDROIT Principles were applied without an express reference to them by the parties.[98]

18-67 The UNIDROIT Principles have also been used in international arbitration proceedings as a means of interpreting domestic law[99] or as a means of interpreting international uniform law.[100] Hence, they have been and may further be applied in situations not expressly contemplated in the preamble.

---

[98] See ICC award no 9797, 28 July 2000, *Andersen Consulting v Arthur Andersen and Andersen Worldwide Société Coopérative,* 15(8) Mealey's IAR A1 (2000) and Bonell, "A `Global´ Arbitration Decided on the Basis of the UNIDROIT Principles: *In re Andersen Consulting Business Unit Member Firms v Arthur Andersen Business Unit Member Firms and Andersen Worldwide Société Coopérative*", 17 *Arb Int* 249 (2001). See award in ICC case no 8502, 1996, 10(2) *ICC Bulletin* 72 (1999). The contract between a Vietnamese exporter and French and Dutch buyers was for the supply of rice. The contract did not contain a choice of law clause. The Tribunal decided to base its award on "trade usages and generally accepted principles of international trade" and to refer "in particular to the 1980 Vienna Convention or to the Principles of International Commercial Contracts enacted by UNIDROIT, *as evidencing admitted practices under international trade law*" [emphasis added]. The individual provisions it then referred to were Articles 76 CISG and 7.4.6 (*Proof of harm by current price*) of the Principles. Another award was rendered in an *ad hoc* Arbitration held in Buenos Aires, award of 10 December 1997, *Uniform Law Review* 178 (1998). The contract was for the sale of shares (between shareholders of an Argentine company and a Chilean company). The contract did not contain a choice of law clause and the parties authorised the tribunal to act as *amiables compositeurs.* Notwithstanding the fact that both parties had based their claims on specific provisions of Argentine law, the tribunal decided to apply the UNIDROIT Principles. It held that the Principles constituted "*usages of international trade reflecting the solutions of different legal systems and of international contract practice*" [emphasis added], and that as such, according to the Model Law, Article 28(4), they should prevail over any domestic law. The individual provisions of the Principles applied to the merits of the case were Articles 3.12 (*Confirmation*), 3.14 (*Notice of avoidance*) and 4.6 (*Contra proferentem* rule).

[99] See, *e.g.*, Court of Arbitration, Berlin, 1990, award in case SG 126/90, *Am J Comp L* 657 (1992) 665; ICC case no 8240, 28 *Law & Policy in Int'l Bus* 943 (1997) 982; ICC case no 8540, *Uniform L Rev* 600 (1997); ICC case no 8486, 125 *Clunet* 1047 (1998); Zurich Chamber of Commerce award 25 November 1994, XXII YBCA 211 (1997); Court of Arbitration of the Economic Chamber in Prague award 17 December 1996, *Uniform L Rev* 604 (1997).

[100] See, *e.g.*, International Court of Arbitration of the Federal Chamber of Commerce in Vienna, 15 June 1994, awards in cases SCH 4318 and SCH 4366, *RIW* 690 (1995), 122 *Clunet* 1055 (1995); ICC award no 8128 (1995), 123 *Clunet* 1024 (1996). See also, the judgment of the Supreme Court of Venezuela, 9 October 1997 (interpretation of the Inter-American Convention on Commercial Arbitration), *Uniform L Rev* 176 (1998). See also Article 14 Model Contract for the International Commercial Sale of Perishable Goods (UNCTAD/WTO 1999).

(c) Convention on the International Sale of Goods

18-68 The United Nations Convention on Contracts for the International Sale of Goods (CISG) was adopted at an international conference in Vienna in 1980.[101] It came into force on 1 January 1988. Drafted in a permissive way so that parties may opt out and/or make use of trade usages, it is currently estimated that two thirds of the world trade is conducted under the CISG.[102]

18-69 The CISG provides a code for direct application in cases of international sale of goods. The effect will be, with increasing numbers of countries adopting the CISG, that the rules it contains will be accepted in more and more countries.[103]

18-70 The CISG rules have been applied by many arbitration tribunals in disputes involving international sale of goods.[104]

3.4. Public International and Supranational Law

18-71 Public international law rules are also applicable to the rights of private parties and may be applied by international arbitration tribunals. This body of rules may be appropriate and useful to explain and determine concepts and notions unknown in national law or that are more developed in international law.[105] These rules may regulate the particular situation whether by recognising

---

[101] See <www.uncitral.org>.

[102] See to that effect <www.cisg.law.pace.edu>.

[103] See, *e.g.*, ICC case no 8817 (1997), *Agent (Spain) v Principal (Denmark)*, XXV YBCA 355 (2000) (this case was relating to agency and it was held by the tribunal that principles of CISG would be applicable). All major trade nations, except Japan and the UK, have ratified the convention. The main collection of awards and cases on the CISG, <www.cisg.law.pace.edu> lists almost 1000 cases and awards. More than 80 awards are reported on that site, including awards from ICC, Iran-US Claims Tribunal, CIETAC, SCC, Hungary, Germany, Russian Federation, and Vienna.

[104] See, *e.g.*, Hamburg Chamber of Commerce award, 4 September 1996, *Buyer (Liechtenstein) v Seller (Germany)*, XXII YBCA 51 (1997); ICC case no 7645 (1995), *Supplier (Slovakia) v Buyer (Korea)*, 11(2) ICC Bulletin 34 (2000), XXVI YBCA 130 (2001) (CISG prevails over national law applicable to contract); *Medical Marketing Inc v Internazionale Medico Scientifica SRL*, XXV YBCA 517 (2000) (US District Court, Eastern District of Louisiana); CIETAC, September 1994, *Xiamen Trade v Lian Zhong*, <http://cisgw3.law.pace.edu/cases/940900c1.html>; Arbitration Court of the Chamber of Commerce and Industry of Budapest, 25 May 1999, arbitration Vb 97142, <http://cisgw3.law.pace.edu/cases/990525h1.html>; See also the SCC award, 5 June 1998, *Beijing Light Automobile Co v Connell*, <http://cisgw3.law.pace.edu/cases/980605s5.html>.

[105] Lew, *Applicable Law*, para 444, 583.

rights (*e.g.*, the granting of an exclusive concession with one investor beneficiary) or by regulating specific situations (*e.g.*, the setting of standards for environmental protection in a particular area which may impact on construction or navigation). It is not a valid excuse to avoid their application, to argue that one of the parties is not a sovereign or that the national law of the state party contains a contrary rule. Parties expect these public international law rules to apply and protect their interests.

18-72 The traditional division between national law and public international law is no longer as strict as in the *Serbian Loans* case.[106] In the last decades public and private international law have grown closer together.[107] Consequently, although public international law is primarily concerned with relations between states, it may be applicable to commercial contracts, in particular, where one of the parties is a state entity. In 1962 an English judge stated

> Thus, it may be, though perhaps it would be unusual, that the parties could validly agree that a part, or the whole, of their legal relations should be decided by the arbitral tribunal on the basis of a foreign system of law, or perhaps on the basis of principles of international law;[108]

18-73 In fact public international law is increasingly relevant to all kinds of commercial transactions. In some cases an embargo, which is a public international law act, may affect private commercial transactions.[109] Over the years public international law has been applied in several ICC[110] or *ad hoc*

---

[106] The *Serbian Loans* case, PCIJ Series A, No 20, 41: "Any contract which is not a contract between states acting in their capacity as subjects of international law, is based on the municipal law of some country."

[107] See Spanogle, "The Arrival of Private International Law", 25 *Geo Wash J Int'l L & Eco* 477 (1991); Steinhardt, "The Privatization of Public Law", 25 *Geo Wash J Int'l L & Eco* 523 (1991).

[108] *Orion Compania Espanola de Seguros v Belfort Maatschappoj voor Algemene Verzerkringen* [1962] 2 Lloyd's Rep 257, 264 (*per* Megaw J).

[109] See, *e.g.*, Corte di appello Genoa 7 May 1994, *Fincantieri - Cantieri Navali Italiani SpA and Oto Melara SpA (Italy) v Ministry of Defence, Armament and Supply Directorate of Iraq and Republic of Iraq*, 4(3) *Riv Arb* 505 (1994) = (in English) XXI *YBCA* 594 (1996). AAA ICDR award of 24 August 1978, *Revere Copper and Brass, Inc v Overseas Private Investment Corporation*, 17 ILM 1321 (1978) (investment guarantee, nationalisation); *Ad hoc* Award of 24 May 1982, *Govt of the State of Kuwait v The American Independent Oil company (AMINOIL)*, 21 ILM 976 (1982); *Westland Helicopters Ltd v Arab Organsiation for Industrialisation* [1994] 2 Lloyd's Rep 608, [1995] QB 282 QBD.

[110] See, *e.g.*, Award in ICC Case no 1512, 1971, I *YBCA* 129 (1976). Interim award in ICC case no 7263 of 1994, *Ministry of Defence (Country X) v Contractor (US)*, XXII YBCA 92 (1997); Award in ICC case no 3493, 16 February 1983, *SPP (Middle East) Ltd (Hong Kong) and*

international commercial arbitrations.[111] ICSID as a matter of mandate deals with public international law.[112] More recently WTO has developed public international law which is relevant to commercial transactions.

18-74 In the field of international investments the problem is expressly dealt with in Article 42(1) ICSID Convention.

> The Tribunal shall decide a dispute in accordance with such rules of law as may be agreed by the parties. In the absence of such agreement, the Tribunal shall apply the law of the Contracting State party of the dispute (including its rules on the conflict of laws) and such rules of international law as may be applicable.

18-75 Whilst Article 42 only applies to investment agreements and disputes to which the ICSID Convention applies, there is no reason why this solution should be limited to a particular category of state contracts.

18-76 Further, there are some situations where, by virtue of an agreement between the parties, supranational law, such as the law of the European Union and NAFTA, may be applicable to relations between the parties. Supranational law possesses an innate supremacy and applies in national legal systems directly without a prior ratification act. Arbitrators should apply supranational law where it is applicable and relevant to the dispute before them. Supranational law may also be applicable in the form of, and because of its nature as, mandatory provisions, for example Article 81 and 82 EC Treaty.[113]

Southern Pacific Properties Ltd (Hong Kong) v Arab Republic of Egypt and The Egyptian General Company for Tourism and Hotels ("EGOTH"), IX YBCA 111 (1984).

[111] Award of 15 March 1967, 35 *ILR* 136 (1967).

[112] See, *e.g.*, ICSID tribunal decision on objections to jurisdiction, 24 May 1999, *Ceskoslovenska Obchodni Banka, AS v The Slovak Republic*, 14(1) ICSID Review FILJ 250 (1999); ICSID case no ARB/93/1, award of 21 February 1997, *American Manufacturing & Trading, Inc v Republic of Zaire*, 12(4) Mealey's IAR A-1 (1997); ICSID, November 30 1979, *AGIP Company SpA (Italy) v Government of the Popular Republic of the Congo*, 21 ILM 726 (1982).

[113] See awards in ICC case no 7315 (1992) and ICC case no 7181 (1992) regarding EC antitrust law in *ICC Bulletin, Special Supp, International Commercial Arbitration in Europe* 42 (1994) 44, 6(1) *ICC Bulletin* 55 (1995). See also *Eco Swiss China Time Ltd v Benetton International NV*, Gerechtshof, 28 March 1996; Hoge Raad, 21 March 1997, *Ned Jur* 207 *Ned Jur* 1059 (1998), with note Snijders, 1084. Also ECJ, *Eco Swiss Time Ltd v Benetton International NV*, C-126/97, 1 June 1999.

4. NON-LEGAL STANDARDS

18-77 Many disputes can be resolved without the application of rules of substantive law. Instead, arbitrators may rely exclusively on the contract between the parties and the facts proven. In such cases, the tribunal's decision may depend solely on an interpretation of the parties' contract.[114] On occasions, the language or indeed the terms of the contract may provide an adequate basis for a solution to the dispute.[115] Thus the tribunal stated in one case

> Insofar as the questions in dispute are regulated by the parties in their contract and this contractual regulation does not contravene the mandatory rules of the two laws in question, it is permitted to resolve them on the basis of the contract. This applies in the present case to the validity, execution, rescission or adaptation to the circumstances of the contract.[116]

18-78 In many instances, the terms of a contract will not provide a solution for all the disputed issues because certain aspects of the parties' relationship may have been omitted from the contract, either deliberately or accidentally, *e.g.*, interest rate for late payment, right to withhold tax payments, termination arrangements including, in particular, the notice period. Moreover, a dispute might involve a question which is non-contractual in nature.[117]

18-79 Where interpretation of the contract does not provide a solution for all the issues in the arbitration, the tribunal could resort to external sources of interpretation, such as general customs and trade usages, as well as customs and practices between the parties.[118]

4.1. Contract Itself

18-80 Most arbitration laws and rules state clearly that in all cases, regardless of the applicable law, the tribunal should determine the case in accordance with the contract within the context of the commercial environment of the parties.

---

[114] Sanders, "Trends in the Field of International Commercial Arbitration", 145 *RCADI* 207 (1975-II) 264; Lew, *Applicable Law*, paras 373-4, 493-94.

[115] Ehrenhaft, "Effective International Commercial Arbitration", 9 *Law & Pol'y Int'l Bus* 1191 (1977) 1212.

[116] Award in ICC case no 1990 (1972), III *YBCA* 217 (1978).

[117] *Ibid.*

[118] Ehrenhaft, "*Effective International Commercial Arbitration*", 9 *Law & Pol'y Int'l Bus* 1191 (1977), 1212.

This includes taking account of relevant trade usages or the normal trading understanding of the parties as illustrated by their past dealings. Essentially these non-legal and non-national standards prevail over the otherwise applicable legal rules. For example, Article 28(4) of the Model Law provides

> In all cases, the arbitral tribunal shall decide in accordance with the terms of the contract and shall take into account the usages of the trade applicable to the transaction.[119]

18-81 This fully accords with what happens in practice. The meaning and application of the contract terms is one area where international commercial arbitrators are most inclined to free themselves of national laws, and apply general principles of law and the contract terms themselves. Effectively a tribunal will seek to apply the terms when determining the respective rights and obligations of the parties.[120]

18-82 In many cases the tribunal need only determine what the parties intended and what they understood at the time of contracting by the terms used in the contract. This can be achieved by resorting either to an objective or a subjective interpretation.[121] To determine what the parties intended, the arbitrators may look at the written documents, memoranda, letters and the contract itself, together with the parties' performance of the contract up to the time of the dispute.

18-83 Whatever the nature or object of a commercial agreement, it is implied that the parties will do all they can to fully and effectively perform their obligations under the contract. By corollary it is equally implied that the parties will do nothing to sabotage or render impossible performance of the contract. These commercial principles are enhanced by the "principle of effectiveness" in the interpretation of international commercial contracts. This requires that when two different interpretations of the terms of a contract are possible, the interpretation preferred is that which gives effect to these terms.[122]

18-84 International arbitration case law recognises the existence of a number of principles concerning the interpretation of contracts. The most general principle

---

[119] See also UNCITRAL Rules Article 33(3); HKIAC Rules Article 33(3); ICC Rules Article 17(2) and AAA ICDR Article 28(2).

[120] ICC case no 1434, 103 *Clunet* 982 (1976).

[121] Lew, *Applicable Law*, para 384, 501-504. See also CISG Article 8(1) and (2) and UNIDROIT Principles Articles 4(1) and 4(2).

[122] Kahn, "L'interprétation des contrats internationaux", 108 *Clunet* 5 (1981). See also ICC case no 7920 (1993), XXIII *YBCA* 80 (1998).

is that the contract should be interpreted in good faith.[123] This principle has nothing to do with the characterisation of the parties' conduct; it merely requires that a literal interpretation should not prevail over an interpretation reflecting the parties' intentions.[124] In 1955 Cassin pointed out that "the fundamental principle of good faith … entails searching for the common intention of … the parties."[125] There is no principle that silence should be interpreted as acquiescence.[126]

18-85 When arbitrators use the contract itself to determine a dispute, in principle, clauses should be interpreted *contra proferentem*, *i.e.* against the party that drafted it. Hence it is in the interest of the party drafting contractual terms to do so in a clear way and without any ambiguities.[127]

4.2. Amiable Composition and Ex Aequo et Bono

18-86 Except where some other criteria is expressly stated by the parties, a tribunal must determine the issue between the parties taking account of the contract terms, trade usages and the applicable law. One such exception is where the parties agree the tribunal should determine the issues in accordance with its view of what is right and fair in the circumstances.

18-87 This type of flexible, non-legal standard is generally referred to as *amiable composition* or arbitrators deciding *ex aequo et bono*. There is one prerequisite to this rule: the parties must have expressly authorised the tribunal to act in this way. Almost all the laws and rules which contain such authority are in similar terms. For example, Article 28(3) Model Law provides:

---

[123] ICC case no 2291 (1975), 103 *Clunet* 989 (1976).

[124] See, *e.g.*, ICC case no 3460 (1980), 108 *Clunet* 939 (1981). CRCICA award 24 September 1996 case no 64/1995, *An African tourism company v Another African tourism company*, Alam Eldin, *Arbitral Awards of the Cairo Regional Centre*, 175. See also UNIDROIT Principles Articles 4(1) and 4(2)

[125] Award of 10 June 1955, *Royal Hellenic Government v HM British Government*, 22 ILR 820 (1955), 5 ICLQ 471 (1956), Rev Arb 15 (1956), 45 Rev crit dip 278 (1956) 279.

[126] See, *e.g.*, Bundesgerichtshof, 9 March 1978, *Wertpapier-Mitteilungen* 1978 573 *et seq*, IV *YBCA* 264 (1979); *Tradax Internacional SA v Cerrahogullari TAS* [1981] 3 All ER 344; *Halki Shipping Corp v Sopex Oils Ltd*, [1999] 2 WLR 726 (CA); XXIII *YBCA* 802 (1998), para 70. See also Fouchard Gaillard Goldman *on International Commercial Arbitration*, para 1473 with further references.

[127] ICC case no 2795 (1977), IV *YBCA* 210 (1979); ICC case no 3460 (1980), 108 *Clunet* 939 (1981); award 26 April 1993 of the Society of Maritime Arbitrators, NY, in case *Nordic American Shipping A/S v Bayoil Inc*, XX *YBCA* 126 (1995), 131. See also Article 4.6 UNIDROIT Principles.

The arbitral tribunal shall decide *ex aequo et bono* or as *amiable compositeur* only if the parties have expressly authorized it to do so.

18-88 In principle, when parties authorise the arbitrators to act as *amiables compositeurs* or *ex aequo et bono*, they allow them to depart from the constraints of any particular national system.[128] They have to decide according to fairness and common sense principles; they can ignore any applicable law rules but arguably not the contract between the parties. Nevertheless, the arbitration tribunal's powers to find a fair and equitable solution to the dispute may be limited by relevant mandatory procedural and substantive rules.

18-89 *Amiable composition* is a concept developed originally in France and subsequently in other civil law countries.[129] The notion was developed with the aim of restoring harmony between the parties and to achieving a new workable legal relationship between them.[130]

18-90 The power to decide *ex aequo et bono* was adopted by the Permanent Court of International Justice[131] as an exception to the sources of law normally relied upon by the Court. Subsequently, it has been included in the statute of the International Court of Justice.[132] The expression can be traced back to Roman Law, meaning "in justice and fairness", "according to what is just and good" or "according to equity and conscience."[133] A judgment made *ex aequo et bono* is based on considerations of fairness, not of existing law. Such decisions are made *praeter legem* or *contra legem* (against the law), not *intra legem* (within the law).

18-91 A review of available literature and published arbitration decisions provide a number of useful guidelines as to how an international tribunal acting *as amiables compositeurs* or *ex aequo et bono* should decide issues:[134]

---

[128] The terms are used interchangeably. ICC Rules Article 13(4); Model Law Article 28(3); Netherlands Article 1054(3); Switzerland PIL Article 187(2); DIS section 23(3). See however, the discussion in Fouchard Gaillard Goldman *on International Commercial Arbitration*, para 1502.

[129] Born, *International Commercial Arbitration in the US*, 557. Loquin, *L'amiable composition.*

[130] David, *Arbitration in International Trade*, 334-335.

[131] Article 38(4) Statute of the PCIJ, as amended by the Protocol of 14 September 1929.

[132] Article 38(2) Statute of the International Court of Justice reads "This provision shall not prejudice the power of the Court to decide a case *ex aequo et bono*, if the parties agree thereto".

[133] Black's Law Dictionary (6th ed, West 1990), 557; see also Mayer, "Reflections on the International Arbitrator's Duty to Apply the Law", 17 *Arb Int* 235 (2001), 241 *et seq.*

[134] According to Aguilar Alvarez, "To What Extent Do Arbitrators in International Cases Disregard the Bag and Baggage of National Systems?" *ICCA Congress series no 8*, 139, 141. See also see

- Where parties refer to both *amiable composition* and a national law in their agreement, arbitrators may depart from the application of the said national law, if its application would produce an unfair result.[135]
- Arbitrators acting as *amiables compositeurs* need not research the proper law of the contract.[136]
- Arbitrators acting as *amiables compositeurs* are not required to apply general principles of international law or any other form of non-national rule.[137]
- To the extent that ignorance of rules of international public policy may lead to the setting aside of the award under the New York Convention, arbitrators should observe such rules even when they act as *amiables compositeurs.*[138]
- A reference to amiable composition does not excuse the arbitrator from respecting rules of due process.[139]

18-92 There is uncertainty whether when exercising the powers of the *amiable composition* arbitrators may alter the bargain of the parties without breaching their own mandate.[140] On the other hand, arbitrators have often ventured to

---

Loquin, *L'amiable composition*, and Loquin, "L'amiable composition dans le Décret du 14 mai 1980 rélatif à l'arbitrage", *Rev Arb* 651 (1980); Yu, "Amiable Composition–A Learning Curve", 17(1) *J Int'l Arb* 79 (2000).

135 ICC case no 5118, *Italian party v Tunisian parties*, 114 Clunet 1027 (1987); *ad hoc* award, *Mechema Ltd v SA Mines, Minerais et Métaux*, VII YBCA 77 (1982); ICC case no 2139, 102 *Clunet* 929 (1975); ICC case no 2216, 102 *Clunet* 917 (1975); ICC case no 2879, *Collection of ICC Awards 1974-1985*, 353.

136 *E.g.*, ICC case no 3267, *Mexican company v Belgian company*, VII YBCA 96 (1982).

137 ICC case no 3267, VII *YBCA* 96 (1982); ICC case no 3742, 111 *Clunet* 910 (1984). However, arbitrators often do, of their own volition, refer to some form of transnational or non national rule: ICC case no 3327, *French company v African state*, 109 Clunet 971 (1982); ICC case no 3267, VII *YBCA* 96 (1982). More controversial is the opinion of some arbitral tribunals: ICC case no 1850, 100 Clunet (1973); ICC case no 3540, *Collection of ICC Awards 1974-1985*, 110; ICC case no 5103, 115 *Clunet* 1213 (1988). See also Fouchard Gaillard Goldman *on International Commercial Arbitration*, para 1505, 838.

138 See, *e.g.*, ICC case no 4265, *Egyptian company v Dutch company*, 111 Clunet 922 (1984); ICC case no 6503, *French company v Spanish company*, 122 Clunet 1022 (1995), 1024.

139 In ICC case no 3327, 109 *Clunet* 971 (1982), the arbitrators founded their refusal to reject written memoranda submitted out of time on the arbitrators' status as amiables compositeurs. See further Fouchard Gaillard Goldman *on International Commercial Arbitration*, para 1638.

140 "An arbitrator who smoothes the corners of a contract which seem to him too sharp is not complying with his mandate (...)" (Mustill, "The New Lex Mercatoria: The First Twenty-Five

"moderate" what they considered to be unfair contractual provisions,[141] and even ignored certain clauses of the contract because they could lead to unfair or inequitable treatment.[142]

18-93 This implies that *amiables compositeurs* must comply with the provisions of the contract, even if that would lead to an inequitable result.

18-94 Generally speaking, civil law jurisdictions have no difficulty in accepting *amiable composition* together with arbitration according to the rules of law. Both types of arbitration are well known. In countries adhering to the common law concept, it may be doubted whether arbitrators can be authorised to *decide ex aequo et bono*. Thus in most cases of historical value, common law countries adopting the Model Law did not exclude the possibility of authorising arbitrators to decide as amiables compositeurs. This applies to Australia, Bermuda, Canada, common law provinces and territories, Hong Kong and Scotland. England with section 46(1)(b) Arbitration Act arguably also allows for *amiable composition*.[143] In the US, States adopting the Model Law as a rule maintain the possibility of Article 28(3) to authorise arbitrators to decide *ex aequo et bono*.[144]

18-95 In China Article 53 CIETAC Rules provides that

> the arbitration tribunal shall independently and impartially make its arbitration award in accordance with the facts of the case, the law and the terms of the contracts, international practices and the principle of fairness and reasonableness.

18-96 This provision is in accordance with the Chinese tradition that the tribunal may decide the case as *amiables compositeurs*, even if the parties have not authorised it to act so. Parties desiring to prevent a CIETAC tribunal from rendering an award as *amiables compositeurs* must make an express provision to

---

Years", *Liber Amicorum for Lord Wilberforce*, 103). See also award in ICC case no 3938 (1982), *French buyer v Dutch seller*, 111 Clunet 926 (1984).

141 116 *Clunet* 1100 (1989); 105 *Clunet* 975 (1978); 106 *Clunet* 977 (1979); 109 *Clunet* 971 (1982); 109 *Clunet* 978 (1982); 107 *Clunet* 961 (1980).

142 See the discussion in Fouchard Gaillard Goldman *on International Commercial Arbitration*, para 1507, 839-41.

143 See Redfern and Hunter, *International Commercial Arbitration*, para 2-73, 128. See also the discussion in Yu, "Amiable Composition–A Learning Curve", 17(1) *J Int Arb* 79 (2000).

144 See, *e.g.*, California section 1297(284), Florida section 684(17), North Carolina section 1-567(58), Ohio section 2712(54) and Oregon section 36(508) under 4.

that effect in the arbitration agreement, though it is unclear whether Article 53 is regarded as peremptory such that the parties could not exclude it.[145]

4.3. Technical Standards and Quality Arbitration[146]

18-97 In commodity and technical standard arbitration cases, an award can only be based on the terms of the contract and generally established technical standards. In these kinds of arbitration the arbitrators will often be specialists in the commodity or technology involved and frequently the arbitration will be held under the auspices of specialist institution.

18-98 Where a contract for the sale of goods is based on a sample or technical specifications, the question for the arbitrators will be whether or not the goods delivered are of the same quality as the sample or in conformity with the specifications. Similarly where a contract is for the sale of a particular commodity or a specified quality or grade, the tribunal need determine only the grade or quality the contracts required and the grade or quality of goods actually delivered. The two findings will be compared. This is a factual, not a legal question.

18-99 Similarly though far more difficult to resolve is a technical standard arbitration. The conformity of computer software or a machine to the agreed specification is a task of comparison. Arbitrators will need to determine the capacity or output or speed promised and what in fact is the capacity or output or speed of the actual machine or software delivered, and if it is not achieving the contractual standard, for what reason.

---

[145] See Yan, "The New Arbitration Rules of the China International Economic Trade and Arbitration Commission", 11 *Arb Int* 183 (1995); Houzhi, "Is There an Expanding Culture that Favors Combining Arbitration with Conciliation or Other ADR Procedures?" *ICCA Congress series no 8,* 101 (1998).

[146] See Lew, *Applicable Law*, para 383, 499-501; Covo, "Commodities, Arbitrations and Equitable Considerations", 9 *Arb Int* 57 (1993); Kirby Johnson, *International Commodity Arbitration.*

Chapter 19

ARBITRATION AND EUROPEAN LAW

19-1 The significance of European integration and the importance of European law is evidenced in all areas of law including arbitration. Arbitration tribunals, as well as courts performing a supportive or supervisory role, have to deal increasingly with legal rules of a European origin. A number of questions arise in this context. They relate to the application of primary and secondary law, as found in the treaties, as well as to all other sources of European law including international conventions concluded within the framework of the European Union. The European Court of Justice (ECJ) has on several occasions been asked to clarify certain aspects of the relationship between arbitration and various aspects of European law.

19-2 This chapter concentrates on (1) the reference of questions for preliminary ruling to the ECJ, (2) the application and ramifications of the competition law provisions in the European Community Treaty within the context of arbitration, (3) the application of other provisions of European law by arbitration tribunals, and (4) the relationship between arbitration and the schemes of judicial cooperation embodied in the Brussels Convention and its successor, Regulation 44/2001 of 22 December 2000.

1. References to the ECJ for Preliminary Rulings

19-3 Courts in the different Member States of the EU apply European law as part of their national law.[1] The same obligation exists for arbitration tribunals. If the law applicable to the contract is the law of a Member State arbitration tribunals shall apply the relevant provisions of European law unless they are empowered to decided *ex aequo et bono* or as *amiables compositeurs*.[2]

19-4 To ensure a uniform interpretation and application of those European provisions within the Member States, national courts have the opportunity or the obligation to submit disputed questions to the ECJ for a preliminary ruling. Article 234 (ex[3] Article 177) European Community (EC) Treaty provides

> The Court of Justice shall have jurisdiction to give preliminary rulings concerning
> a) the interpretation of the Treaty;
> b) the validity and interpretation of acts of the institutions of the Community and of the ECB;
> c) the interpretation of the statutes of bodies established by an act of the Council, where those statutes so provide.

---

1 For the various types of European legislation, its application by the courts and its relation to the national law see Weatherill and Beaumont, *EU Law* (3rd ed, Penguin 1999), Chapters 5, 11, 12.

2 ECJ, 23 March 1982, Case 102/81, *Nordsee Deutsche Hochseefischerei GmbH v Reederei Mond Hochseefischerei Nordstern AG & Co KG and Reederei Friedrich Busse Hochseefischerei Nordstern AG & Co KG,* [1982] *ECR* 1095, 1111, para 14; Mustill and Boyd, *2001 Companion*, 80; Weitbrecht and Fabis, "Gemeinschaftsrechtliche Anforderungen an die gerichtliche Kontrolle von Schiedsgerichtsentscheidungen", 8 *EWS* 1 (1997).

3 The numbering of Articles of the European Community Treaty (formerly EEC Treaty of Rome, 1957) changed following a consolidation of the text in 1997 under the Amsterdam Treaty.

> Where such a question is raised before any court or tribunal of a Member State, that court or tribunal may, if it considers that a decision on the question is necessary to enable it to give judgment, request the ECJ to give a ruling on the issue.
> Where any such question is raised in a case pending before a court or tribunal of a Member State, against whose decision there is no judicial remedy under national law, that court or tribunal shall bring the matter before the Court of Justice.

19-5 An arbitration tribunal is a private forum not attached to a national legal system, irrespective of where it has its seat. Although it may be subject to the ultimate authority of the local national law and required to apply European law, the question whether an arbitration tribunal is "a court or tribunal" in the terms of Article 234 has been the subject of considerable debate. In *Vassen v Beambtenfonds* the ECJ extended the right to refer questions for a preliminary ruling to arbitration tribunals operating on a statutory basis.[4] It based its decision on the fact that the arbitration tribunal in question, the *Scheidsgerecht van het Beambtenfonds voor het Mijnbedrijf* (arbitration court of the miners' pension fund) was foreseen by and organised according to the law as the mandatory dispute settlement mechanism: it had to apply the law in the same way as ordinary courts, and its members were appointed by the minister responsible for mining.

19-6 In *Nordsee v Reederei Mond*[5] the question was whether non-statutory arbitration tribunals based on an agreement by the parties could also submit relevant questions to the ECJ for preliminary ruling. The dispute concerned a contract by which the parties agreed to pool aid received from the then EEC for the building of six ships. A share of 1/13 of the aid received was to be allocated to each of the ships actually built irrespective of whether any aid was granted for the particular ship. After European Community officials had doubted the validity of the pooling contract the respondent refused to pay the claimant its share from the aid. The claimant started arbitration proceedings in which the crucial question was the legality of the pooling contract by reference to the EEC provision under which the aid was granted. In the light of that the arbitrator referred several

---

[4] ECJ, 30 June 1966, Case 61/65, *Vassen-Göbbels v Vorstand des Beambtenfonds voor het Minjnbedrijf*, [1966] ECR 583, 601 *et seq*; confirmed in ECJ, 27 April 1994, Case 393/92, *Municipality of Almelo v NV Energiebedrijf Ijsselmij*, [1994] ECR I 1477.

[5] ECJ, 23 March 1982, Case 102/81, *Nordsee Deutsche Hochseefischerei GmbH v Reederei Mond Hochseefischerei Nordstern AG & Co KG and Reederei Friedrich Busse Hochseefischerei Nordstern AG & Co KG*, [1982] ECR 1095; for a detailed discussion of the case see Erauw, "Reference by arbitrators to the European Court of Justice for Preliminary Rulings", in CEPANI (ed), *Arbitration and European Law*, 101-140.

questions as to the interpretation of those provisions to the ECJ under Article 177 including whether an arbitrator could make references under Article 177, (now EC Treaty Article 234).

19-7 The ECJ held that though there are a number of similarities between the activities of an arbitration tribunal and a state court the former could not be considered to be a "court or a tribunal of a Member State". The link between arbitration and the organisation of legal remedies through the courts was not considered to be sufficiently close. Neither were the parties forced to have their disputes resolved by arbitration nor were the public authorities involved in that decision or could they intervene automatically in the proceedings.[6]

19-8 The ECJ, however, made clear that the result of this ruling is not that the arbitrators are free to ignore EC Law but rather that

> ...Community law must be observed in its entirety throughout the territory of all the Member States; parties to a contract are not, therefore, free to create exceptions to it. ...attention must be drawn to the fact that if questions of Community law are raised in an arbitration resorted to by agreement, the ordinary courts may be called upon to examine them either in the context of their collaboration with arbitration tribunals, in particular in order to assist them in certain procedural matters or to interpret the law applicable, or in the course of a review of an arbitration award ... and which they may be required to effect in case of an appeal or objection, in proceedings for leave to issue execution or by any other method of recourse available under the relevant national legislation.[7]

19-9 As a result of the *Nordsee v Reederei Mond* decision arbitration tribunals which require guidance on issues of European law are in a difficult position. Indeed, despite their doubts about the application of EC law, arbitration tribunals cannot directly refer questions to the ECJ for a preliminary ruling. Instead they are required to decide the issue themselves with the risk of misinterpreting European law. However, state courts are required by the ECJ to examine the application of the EC Treaty by an arbitration tribunal in proceedings for the review or enforcement of an award. Consequently a misapplication, for example,

---

[6] Case 102/81, [1982] *ECR* 1095, 1110, paras 11 *et seq*; approved in ECJ, 1 June 1999, Case 126/97, *Eco Swiss China Time Ltd v Benetton International NV*, [1999] ECR I 3055, 3092, para 34.

[7] Case 102/81, [1982] *ECR* 1095, 1110, para 14.

of Article 81 EC Treaty by the arbitration tribunal may open up the award to challenge proceedings or attack in enforcement proceedings.[8]

19-10 Unlike arbitration tribunals, the courts in enforcement and annulment proceedings can submit the relevant question of European law to the ECJ for a preliminary ruling. As a result, instead of having the relevant question decided by the ECJ at an early stage such decision is deferred to the post award stage. In the event that the ECJ comes to a different conclusion than the arbitration tribunal a considerable amount of time and resources may have been wasted.

19-11 A different and less technical interpretation of the notion "court or tribunal of a Member State" has been supported in the literature.[9] This relies on the function performed by arbitration tribunals which it claimed justified granting arbitrators the right to refer questions of European law to the ECJ for a preliminary ruling.

19-12 This approach appears *prima facie* to be more in line with the general developments taking place since the ECJ decision in 1982. The importance of European law for contractual relationships between private parties has increased considerably with a growing number of regulations and directives affecting core issues of contract law.[10] As a consequence the likelihood that questions of European law are relevant in arbitration has risen. In addition, the attitude towards arbitration has changed in the Member States as well as within the European Institutions.[11] For example, the European Development Fund has its

---

[8] See, *e.g.*, the enforcement proceedings in *Eco Swiss v Benetton* where the ECJ held that the enforcement of an award which violated Article 81 would be contrary to public policy, ECJ, 1 June 1999, Case 126/97, *Eco Swiss China Time Ltd v Benetton International NV*, [1999] ECR I 3055, 3091, para 32 *et seq*; the Hoge Raad in enforcement proceedings referred the case to the ECJ for a preliminary ruling, Hoge Raad, 21 March 1997, XXIII *YBCA* 180 (1998); see also the challenge proceedings in *Bulk Oil (Zug) AG v Sun International Ltd and Sun Oil Trading Co*, [1986] 2 All ER 744, where the High Court referred the relevant question to the ECJ.

[9] Schmitthoff, "Arbitration and EEC Law", 24 *CMLRev* 143 (1987) 153; Bebr, "Arbitration Tribunals and Article 177 of the EEC Treaty", 22 *CMLRev* 489 (1985) 497 *et seq*; Hill, *International commercial disputes* (2d ed, LLP 1998), para 24-3-3.

[10] See, *e.g.*, Directives 86/653 EEC (self-employed commercial agent), 2000/31 EC (Electronic Commerce), 93/13 EEC (unfair terms in consumer contracts) and various directives for consumer protection. See further the various regulations in the context of competition law affecting *inter alia* distribution, purchasing, franchising and research and development contracts. See also Weatherill, "The Role of the European Community", in Fletcher, Mistelis and Cremona (eds), *Foundations and Perspectives of International Trade Law* (Sweet & Maxwell 2001), 43.

[11] The Commission has promoted the use of ADR including arbitration, in particular in consumer contracts; see, *e.g.*, Commission Recommendation 98/257 EC of 30 March 1998 on the

own procedural rules on conciliation and arbitration for works, supply of goods and services financed by the European Development Fund.[12] The importance and resort to arbitration by parties has been recognised by the favourable attitudes of the arbitration laws in most European countries.[13] It is considered an important alternative to litigation which should be treated equally and given the necessary support. The mere fact that the parties intentionally step out of the court system is generally not considered to justify the refusal to grant the required court support necessary for the effective conduct of an arbitration.

19-13 Despite all those developments the ECJ has in 1999, in *Eco Swiss v Benetton,* endorsed its earlier interpretation of the notion "court or tribunal of a Member State". Irrespective of the changes there are still a number of reasons which justify the exclusion of arbitration tribunals from the ambit of Article 234.

19-14 First, the question would be which tribunals could refer questions to the ECJ. Article 234 EC refers to "courts of member states". Does that only cover arbitration tribunals which have their seat within a member state? What if the parties were from outside the EU, but the arbitration has its seat within the EU, or the tribunal had its seat outside the EU, but one or more of the parties was from a member state?

19-15 Second, if one considers an arbitration tribunal to be a "court or tribunal" in the sense of Article 234 EC it must probably be considered as one "against whose decision there is no judicial remedy" since there is generally no appeal against arbitration awards. Hence tribunals would not only have the right to submit questions to the ECJ but would also have the obligation to do so. Preliminary references could be misused to bring arbitration proceedings to a halt and delay the rendering of an award. Any request for a preliminary ruling from the ECJ would seriously disrupt the arbitration proceedings as it usually takes more than a year before the questions are answered during which time the arbitration proceedings would be moribund. Any referral of a question destroys

---

principles applicable to the bodies responsible for the out-of-court settlement of consumer disputes, *Official Journal* 1998 L 115, 31 *et seq.* See also the Commission Green Paper on alternative dispute resolution in civil and commercial law, 19 April 2002, *COM* 196 (2002).

12 Council Decision of 16 December 1991, 92/97/EC.

13 Member States such as for example Netherlands, France, England, Italy, and Greece. Germany Scotland, Ireland, Sweden, Belgium have enacted more liberal arbitration laws since 1982.

the confidentiality of the arbitration proceedings as with the request the dispute will be in the public domain.[14]

19-16 Third, the *Nordsee v Reederei Mond* decision only concerned direct references of questions of European law to the ECJ by the arbitration tribunal itself. It did not exclude indirect submissions where the question is first submitted to a court which in turn submits it then to the ECJ pursuant to Article 234. In arbitration proceedings governed by English law such an indirect referral does not pose any problems. Section 45 Arbitration Act 1996 explicitly provides that under certain conditions a question of law can be referred to the courts for a preliminary ruling. This provision also covers EC law. Once a question of EC law has been submitted to the English court by the arbitration tribunal this court could refer it to the ECJ.[15]

19-17 In arbitration proceedings that have their seat in a different Member State the arbitration law of which does not contain a provision comparable to section 45 Arbitration Act 1996 the legal situation is less obvious. It might be possible for the arbitration tribunal to refer the question to the courts under the general provisions providing for court assistance. Another possibility to finally arrive at a reference of the question to the ECJ might be to couch it in a proforma request for any other measure which in turn would require a preliminary ruling on the relevant question.[16]

19-18 Further, and perhaps most significantly, parties by selecting arbitration as a dispute settlement mechanism have opted out of the court system. This right is recognised by all legal systems and the New York Convention. There is no reason to make an exception for a question of EC law. One should remember that most European laws are permissive, even if they aim at harmonisation of the law of Member States. If arbitrators make a mistake in law there is no recourse; it is one of the risks of arbitration which parties gladly and knowingly accept. This is the same for EC law. The only limitation to this argument is mandatory EC law, *e.g.*, anti-trust law. This can be rectified at a challenge on enforcement.

---

[14] See the objections against a direct submission for a preliminary ruling by Erauw, "Reference by arbitrators to the European Court of Justice for Preliminary Rulings", in CEPANI (ed), *Arbitration and European Law*, 101, 128 *et seq*; Berger, *International Economic Arbitration*, 455 *et seq*.

[15] *Ibid*, 132 *et seq*.

[16] For that and further examples see Hill, *International commercial disputes* (2d ed, LLP 1998), para 24-3-4.

2. Application of European Competition Law by Arbitrators

19-19 Allegations of competition law infringements are a common feature in international arbitration. Parties which do not fulfil their contractual obligations may rely on competition law in an attempt to avoid the legal consequence of non-performance of their contractual obligations. The legal sanction for contracts infringing competition law is usually for the contract to be deemed void. This is also the case with the relevant provisions of EC competition law, Articles 81 and 82 EC Treaty (ex Articles 85 and 86).

19-20 Under Article 81 agreements which have as the purpose or effect "the prevention restriction or distortion of competition within the common market" are prohibited. They are void and have no legal or binding effect.[17] This covers agreements to fix prices or alter trading conditions, to limit or control production or markets or to make contracts conditional on supplementary obligations which are unrelated to the principal contract. However, exemption from these prohibitions may be possible where the benefits outweigh the restrictions on competition.[18] Except where there is a "block" exemption for specific types of agreement, exemption can only be granted by the EC Commission.[19] Accordingly, it is the EC Commission which has the principal authority to enforce the competition rules in the Treaty.

19-21 The same applies for Article 82, which prohibits the abuse of a dominant position. Though fines for such an abuse may only be imposed by the Commission the courts may be called to determine whether a certain conduct or clauses in an agreement amount to an abuse and are therefore void or even give rise to claims for damages.

19-22 In the context of arbitration Articles 81 and 82 raise questions as to:

- the arbitrability of disputes involving their alleged violation;
- the obligation of the tribunal to apply them *ex officio*; and

---

17 Article 81(2).

18 Article 81(3).

19 Regulation 17/62, OJ 13 of 21 Feb 1962, 204/62. From 1 May 2004 onwards the system will be replaced by that established by the successor Regulation 1/03. Exemptions will no longer be granted individually by the Commission but the exception contained in Article 81(3) will be directly applicable. For an extensive review of the White Paper preceding the new Regulation and the suggested changes see, *e.g.* Jones and Sufrin, *EC Competition Law* (Oxford University Press 2001), Chapter 16.

- their influence in the appeal and enforcement stage.[20]

19-23 Although these issues have been the object of numerous decisions and awards an authoritative ruling by the ECJ only exists for the third question which was dealt with in *Eco Swiss v Benetton* in 1999.

2.1. The ECJ Decision in ECO Swiss v Benetton[21]

19-24 The dispute concerned a premature termination of a licensing agreement by Benetton, the licensor. In 1993 an arbitration tribunal sitting in the Netherlands held in a "Partial Final Award" that compensation had to be paid to Eco Swiss for the wrongful termination by Benetton. As the parties could not agree on the amount of the compensation this was fixed in a final award in June 1995. In July 1995 Benetton lodged an action for the annulment of the award alleging violation of public policy by virtue of the nullity of the licensing agreement under Article 81 EC Treaty, a point not raised in the arbitration proceedings. Under Article 1064(3) Netherlands Code of Civil Procedure an appeal has to be lodged within three months after the award is deposited with the Registry of the District Court. As the general obligation to pay compensation was already determined in the partial final award of 1993 against which no appeal was lodged the question arose whether the courts were prevented by the time limit in Article 1064(3) to examine whether the awards were contrary to Article 81 EC Treaty. The *Hoge Raad* referred several questions concerning the relationship of Article 81 EC Treaty and arbitration to the ECJ.[22]

19-25 The ECJ held that in the light of its importance for the functioning of an internal market, Article 81 is a mandatory provision of public policy character. Accordingly, the ECJ held that the misapplication of Article 81 by the arbitration tribunal justifies annulment of the award under the national laws as well as a refusal of enforcement under the New York Convention. This applies irrespective of the fact that in the particular Member State the violation of national provisions of competition law is generally not considered to be an infringement of public policy.

---

[20] For a detailed discussion of some of the issues see Weigand, "Evading EC-Competition Law by Resorting to arbitration", 9 *Arb Int* 249 (1993).

[21] ECJ, 1 June 1999, Case C-126/97, *Eco Swiss China Time Ltd v Benetton International NV*, [1999] ECR I 3055.

[22] Hoge Raad, 21 March 1997, *Eco Swiss China Time Ltd v Benetton International NV*, XXIII YBCA 180 (1998).

19-26 The ECJ further held that despite its public policy character Article 81

> ...does not require a national court to refrain from applying domestic rules of procedure according to which an interim arbitration award which is in the nature of a final award and in respect of which no application for annulment has been made within the prescribed time-limit acquires the force of res judicata and may no longer be called in question by a subsequent arbitration award, even if it is necessary in order to examine, in proceedings for annulment of a subsequent arbitration award, whether an agreement which the interim award held to be valid in law is nevertheless void under Art. 85 of the Treaty.[23]

19-27 Accordingly, actions for annulment of an award based on an alleged violation of Article 81 can only be brought within the time period foreseen by the national arbitration law. The principle of legal certainty embedded in those time limits and the ensuing *res judicata* effect justify this limitation of the right to have the application of Article 81 by the arbitration tribunal reviewed. As long as the national provisions dealing with the review of arbitration awards do not make the exercise of rights conferred by EC law excessively difficult or virtually impossible, the standard of review required by EC law is met.

19-28 The *Eco-Swiss* judgment has clarified a number of issues concerning the application of Article 81 in the context of arbitration.

- First, it has made clear that the non-application or the misapplication of Articles 81 and 82 may give rise to the public policy defence in enforcement proceedings.
- Second, the ECJ has stated unambiguously that this does not affect time limits and other restrictions which limit the possible control of the award for purposes of legal certainty.
- Third, it follows from the judgment that disputes concerning alleged infringements of Article 81 are arbitrable.

2.2. Arbitrability of Competition Law Disputes

19-29 The arbitrability of disputes involving the application of Articles 81 and 82 (previously Articles 85 and 86) has been seriously doubted in a number of cases at least until the mid 1990s. Arbitration tribunals as well as national courts have held that these questions could either not be considered at all or that the

---

[23] ECJ, *Eco Swiss China Time Ltd v Benetton International NV*, XXIVa YBCA 629 (1999) 630.

authority of the arbitration tribunal was limited to those cases where finally a violation of the provisions was denied. By contrast when the arbitrators were convinced that there was a violation of Articles 81 or 82 it was considered that the disputes ceased to be arbitrable, since the arbitrators could not effectively sanction any infringement.[24]

19-30 These objections were to a certain extent based on the importance of Articles 81 and 82 for the market structure in the EU. It was felt that due to the public policy character of both articles their application should be left to the public authorities. The main argument against the arbitrability of competition law disputes, however, as the Commission's exclusive powers in relation to granting individual exemptions under Article 81(3) and to imposing fines.[25]

19-31 With its recognition of the arbitrability of competition law disputes in *Eco Swiss* the ECJ has made clear that the exclusive powers of the Commission do not exclude the arbitrability of the dispute. This recognises the necessary distinction between the public sanctions and the private sanctions following an infringement of EC competition law. It is uncontested that disputes as to whether public sanctions in the form of fines should be imposed are not arbitrable. Nor can an arbitration tribunal grant an individual exemption under Article 81(3).[26]

19-32 By contrast, arbitration tribunals can determine what consequences infringements of Articles 81 or 82 have on contractual or non-contractual relationships between the parties. For infringements of the prohibitions contained in Article 81(1) voidness follows directly from Article 81(2), while additional consequences such as the entitlement to damages or restitution are based on the relevant provisions of the applicable law. In relation to these private law consequences the Commission has no power to determine the respective rights of

---

[24] See, *e.g.*, Tribunale Bologna, 18 July 1987, *Coveme SpA (Italy) v CFI - Compagnie Française des Isolants SA (France)*, XVII YBCA 534 (1992); ICC case no 6106 reproduced in Verbist, "The Application of European Community Law in ICC Arbitrations", *ICC Bulletin Special Supplement* 34 (1994) summarising the position under French and Italian law; the award formed the basis of the annulment action in Switzerland, Tribunal Fédéral, 28 April 1992, XVIII *YBCA* 143 (1993); Sornarajah, *The Settlement of Foreign Investment Disputes* (Kluwer 2000), 178.

[25] See Regulation 17/62, OJ 13 of 21 Feb 1962, 204/62. According to the new Regulation 1/03 the exemptions in Article 81(3) are of direct application, which can be determined by national authorities and courts. The right to order fines, however, will rest exclusively with the Commission.

[26] It may, however, determine that a certain agreement is covered by a block exemption and is therefore not prohibited. Notwithstanding, such determination may be overturned by the Commission at any time.

the parties and there is no reason to justify a restriction on the arbitrability of those disputes.

19-33 The lack of exclusive powers is also an indication that the public policy character of the provisions does not require them to be taken out of the purview of arbitration. The *Eco Swiss* judgment is based on the assumption that the public policy character may impose certain minimum requirements on the review of arbitration awards. However, it does not affect the arbitrability of disputes involving infringements of EC competition law. This position is maintained now in most countries within the EU.[27]

2.3. Effect of Concurrent Investigations by the Commission

19-34 The general power of the tribunal to deal with issues of European competition law raises an additional question. How should a tribunal proceed when the issue of whether an agreement relevant to the arbitration is in violation of EC competition law is being investigated by the Commission? Should the proceedings be stayed until a decision has been rendered by the Commission? Or should the tribunal proceed with the arbitration to avoid the delay which will necessarily follow from such an investigation?[28] The answer depends on the particular facts and the relevant circumstances.

19-35 In general, the Commission is better equipped than an arbitration tribunal to determine whether or not an agreement is in breach of Article 81 or 82. It has broad investigative powers granted under Regulation 17/62 and its successor Regulation which ensure access to the relevant documents and materials. It also has a staff of experienced lawyers and economists with an understanding of

---

[27] See, *e.g.*, in France: Cour d'appel Paris, 19 May 1993, *Rev Arb* 645 (1993); in Italy: Corte di Appello, Bologna, 21 December 1991, *SpA Coveme (Italy) v CFI - Compagnie Française des Isolants SA (France)*, XVIII YBCA 422 (1993); ICC case no 7181, XXI *YBCA* 99 (1996) 105; ICC case no 7146, XXVI *YBCA* 121 (2001) 123; ICC case no 8423, XXVI *YBCA* 153 (2001) 155. See also the non-EU decisions of the Swiss Tribunal Fédéral, 28 April 1992, *V SpA v G SA*, XVIII YBCA 143 (1993) 148 (French Original, ATF 118 II 193); 13 November 1998, *X SA et al v Z SA*, XXV YBCA 511 (2000) 513; and the award rendered by a tribunal sitting in Geneva in ICC case no 4604, X *YBCA* 973 (1985) 973 *et seq*, French original in Jarvin, Derains and Arnaldez, *ICC Awards 1986-1990*, 545.

[28] This was the approach taken by an ICC arbitrator in a case reported by Blessing, "Introduction to Arbitration – Swiss and International Perspectives", in Berti, Honsell, Vogt and Schnyder, *International Arbitration in Switzerland*, para 734; for a case where the Commission awaited the outcome of the arbitration see ICC case no 7181, 6(1) *ICC Bull* 55 (1995) 56.

competition law and the economic issues within the EU. Accordingly, the argument is that the tribunal should stay the proceedings where the investigation has already been going on for some time and a decision can be expected in the near future. Where this is not the case the arbitrator has to consider the risk of a misapplication of Articles 81 or 82 and the ensuing violation of public policy against the potentially resulting delay.

19-36 In balancing the various interests it should be taken into account that the parties opted for arbitration with the knowledge that there will generally be no appeal possible. Parties understand the risks of a tribunal making an error in law and accept this as a business risk. Arbitrators should not easily avoid decision making in favour of the Commission and in opposition to the parties' intent. By leaving or referring the issue to the Commission a tribunal reneges on its authority or responsibility, even with the risk that the Commission may decide differently. Equally the Commission could take many months or years to conclude its investigation and there is no certainty it will decide differently to the tribunal. Only in very rare circumstances will the risk of a wrong decision on European competition law justify the stay of proceedings pending a decision from the Commission.[29]

19-37 Comparable considerations are relevant for the question of whether a tribunal should seek the advice of the Commission in relation to the application of competition law even where no investigations are pending. Since there is no obligation to seek the advice of the Commission (or any other regulatory body) the tribunal should not, in principle, do so. This would again, not only be a negation of authority and responsibility, but would also breach the parties' confidentiality. This approach is well evidenced by ICC case no 7146 where the tribunal refused to seek the Commission's advice holding that in light of a

> quasi-decisional impact on the issues ...[t]he Arbitral Tribunal would not fulfil its task if it preliminary and entirely entrusted the task to settle the issues of community law to the EC Commission.[30]

---

[29] One such situation occurs if an investigation has been ongoing for some time before the arbitration was commenced and a decision by the Commission is imminent.

[30] ICC case no 7146, XXVI *YBCA* 121 (2001) para 10-11.

2.4. Ex officio Application of Competition Laws by Tribunal

19-38 The public policy character of Articles 81 and 82 raises the question whether arbitrators are under an obligation to apply those provisions *ex officio, i.e.*, of its own volition. This question may arise in two different situations.

19-39 The first formed the basis of the *Eco Swiss* decision where the law applicable to the contract was the law of a Member state which includes Articles 81 and 82, but where none of the parties invoked the provisions. No clear position was taken by the ECJ concerning the question whether an arbitration tribunal in such a situation should invoke or apply Articles 81 and 82 of its own volition. In the underlying arbitration proceedings the defendant had not invoked the invalidity of the licensing agreement. This, according to the *Hoge Raad*, prevented the arbitrators from dealing with the issue of invalidity of the agreement for an infringement of Article 81. In its view the arbitrators would have gone beyond the ambit of the dispute and thereby their mandate if they had decided on the validity of the agreement.[31]

19-40 It is undisputed that arbitration tribunals can neither deal with disputes not submitted to them nor can their award go beyond the relief requested by the parties. The excess of jurisdiction constitutes a ground to challenge the award and refuse enforcement under the various national laws, as well as under Article V(1)(c) New York Convention. This does not, however, preclude a tribunal from raising Article 81(2) of its own volition if the facts presented by the parties point to a violation of competition law even if this is not raised by the parties. Any claim not to have breached a contract includes as a preliminary issue the very existence of a valid contract. Insofar as the application of Article 81(2) to those cases would not violate the principle of *ultra petita*, it is a matter of applicable law.[32] The classification of Article 81 as being a provision of public policy suggests its automatic application:[33] it is a feature of public policy that it is not left to the disposition of the parties.[34] Otherwise parties may use arbitration to

---

[31] Hoge Raad, 21 March 1997, XXIII *YBCA* 180 (1998) 190.

[32] See, for the relationship between "ultra petita" and the application of non-pleaded law by the Court, Swiss Tribunal Fédéral, 30 December 1994, *State agency A and State owned bank B v Consultant X (Panama)*, XXI YBCA 172 (1996) 173-176.

[33] Failure to apply the provision *ex officio* does not amount to a violation of public policy; see Swiss Tribunal Fédéral, 13 November 1998, *X SA et al v Z SA*, XXV YBCA 511 (2000) 513-516.

[34] See ICC case no 7181, XXI *YBCA* 99 (1996) 105; ICC case no 8423, XXVI *YBCA* 153 (2001) 155; ICC case no 7539, 123 *Clunet* 1030 (1996); *cf* Spiegel, "Note to the ECJ's *Eco Swiss v Benetton* decision", *EuZW* 568 (1999), 569.

evade the application of EC competition law which would severely undermine the trust in arbitration by national laws.

19-41 However, difficulties may arise where the tribunal raises the issue and the parties are agreed that the competition laws do not apply and are not infringed. In such a case the tribunal could be accused of exceeding its authority if it reached a determination on some basis, legal or otherwise, which neither party argued or accepted and had in fact rejected. A tribunal should treat this issue with great care as it is not the arbitrators' role to police EC competition law or to decide issues not within its jurisdiction or expressly allowed by the parties.

19-42 In the second situation the place of arbitration is not in a Member State nor is the law applicable to the merits that of a Member State. Nevertheless one of the parties relies on Articles 81 or 82. In such a situation the question arises whether an arbitration tribunal should also apply the provisions for their mandatory character though they do not form part of the applicable law. Arbitration tribunals and courts have adopted different solutions in practice. These span from a strict non-application of Articles 81 or 82, to their application whenever the facts fall within the extraterritorial reach of the provisions.[35] There is also an intermediate position which only applies Articles 81 and 82 if the award is probably going to be enforced within an EU Member State.[36]

19-43 At least when the award is likely to be enforced within a Member State there are a number of arguments why the tribunal should apply Articles 81 and 82. As a result of the *Eco Swiss* decision awards which are contrary to the prohibitions contained in European competition law may not be enforceable within a Member State. National courts are required to refuse enforcement of such award on the basis of the public policy exception, which also exists under the New York Convention.

---

35 See, *e.g.*, ICC case no 7673, 6(1) *ICC Bull* 57 (1995) 58 where the tribunal applied EC competition law despite the fact that the underlying contract was governed by Swiss law; this seems to be the predominant opinion in Switzerland, see Blessing, "Introduction to Arbitration – Swiss and International Perspectives", in Berti, Honsell, Vogt and Schnyder, *International Arbitration in Switzerland*, paras 735 *et seq*.

36 For a detailed discussion of the cases see Lazareff, "Mandatory Extraterritorial Application of National Law", 11 *Arb Int* 137 (1995) 137 *et seq*; for the Swiss approach to that issue see Blessing, "Introduction to Arbitration – Swiss and International Perspectives", in Berti, Honsell, Vogt and Schnyder, *International Arbitration in Switzerland*, para 730 *et seq*.

2.5. Arbitration in the Area of Merger Control

19-44 Arbitration has also found its way into the area of merger control. According to Merger Regulation 4064/89[37] intended mergers which may affect competition have to be notified to the Commission which then decides whether the proposal raises competition concerns. It is common that after consultation with the Commission and to enable the merger to be approved, the parties are required to give certain undertakings to dispel concerns that trade within the EU will be restricted by the merger. One possible undertaking recently required, is to provide for arbitration to determine complaints by third parties about specific rights and access to technology or markets following the merger.

19-45 This was required in the proposed acquisition by BskyB of 24% of the German KirchPayTV. The Commission was concerned that Kirch's technology should be available to third parties in the EU. Accordingly, the Commission required BSkyB and KirchPayTV to agree that any dispute with a third party concerning market access or rights to use the technology would be referred to arbitration. The parties further agreed that the tribunal would determine these issues taking into account any prior decisions by other arbitrators, courts or regulatory bodies in relation to the relevant undertakings, and that this did not in any way affect the power of the Commission to take direct action. The proposal accepted by the Commission provided for arbitration under the DIS Rules before a three member tribunal.[38] This was a one-off occurrence but the mechanism could be used again by the Commission in an appropriate case.[39]

3. Application of Other Provisions of EC Law

19-46 Both primary and secondary EC law form part of the national legal orders of the EC Member States. Consequently, as confirmed in the *Nordsee* case,[40] arbitration tribunals have to apply these provisions, whenever a dispute is

---

[37] OJ L 395, 30 December 1989, 1; as amended by Regulation (EC) No 1310/97, OJ L 180, 9 July 1997, 1.

[38] See the decision of 21 March 2000, CELEX database, doc no 300J0037.

[39] Interestingly, this arbitration would not be based on an arbitration agreement between the parties but on a unilateral offer to submit disputes to arbitration. This practice is also known in the area of investment protection.

[40] ECJ, 23 March 1982, Case 102/81, *Nordsee Deutsche Hochseefischerei GmbH v Reederei Mond Hochseefischerei Nordstern AG & Co KG and Reederei Friedrich* Busse *Hochseefischerei Nordstern AG & Co KG,* [1982] ECR 1095.

governed by the law of a member state. A recent decision of the ECJ,[41] however, raises the question whether in addition to Articles 81 and 82 further provisions of secondary EC law also require application in cases governed by the law of a non-member state.

19-47 The case concerned the contract by which Ingmar GB Ltd. was appointed as Eaton's commercial agent in the UK. The contract provided that Californian law would be applicable to the contract. When the contract was terminated Ingmar brought proceedings in the UK seeking *inter alia* compensation for damage suffered as a result of the termination of its agreement with Eaton relying on Regulation 17 English Commercial Agents (Council Directive) Regulation 1993 on self-employed commercial agents.[42] The High Court rejected the claim on the basis that due to the parties' choice of Californian law the English Regulation was not applicable. On appeal the Court of Appeal submitted to the ECJ the question whether the rules contained in Directive 86/653/EEC were applicable despite the choice of a different law by the parties when the commercial agent carries out its activity within a Member State.

19-48 The ECJ, relying on the purpose of the Directive to protect commercial agents and to ensure the freedom of establishment and undistorted competition through a harmonisation of the applicable law, came to the conclusion that the provisions of the directive are mandatory. It held that

> ... it is essential for the Community legal order that a principal established in a non-member country, ... cannot evade those provisions by the simple expedient of a choice-of-law clause. The purpose served by the provisions in question requires that they be applied where the situation is closely connected with the Community, in particular where the commercial agent carries on his activity in the territory of a Member State, irrespective of the law by which the parties intended the contract to be governed[43]

19-49 How this decision will influence the application of provisions based on the commercial agent Directive or other comparable Directives by arbitration tribunals is not yet clear. There are considerable differences between the

---

41 ECJ, 9 November 2000, Case no 381 98, *Ingmar GB Ltd v Eaton Leonard Technologies Inc*, [2001] 1 All ER (EC) 57, para 25.

42 Implementing Council Directive 86/653/EEC of 18 December 1986 on the coordination of the laws of the Member States relating to self-employed commercial agents, OJ 1986 L 382, 17.

43 ECJ, 9 November 2000, Case no 381/98, *Ingmar GB Ltd v Eaton Leonard Technologies Inc*, [2001] 1 All ER (EC) 57, para 25.

application of mandatory provisions by a court or by a tribunal. In international litigation a court in a Member State must apply the mandatory provisions of the forum despite the parties' choice of a different law. By contrast for an arbitration tribunal the application of those mandatory rules would constitute an application of mandatory rules of a third country, a concept highly disputed in international litigation.[44] The mere fact that an arbitration tribunal has its seat in a Member State does not make it part of the judicial system of that state in the sense that all rules of that state would be considered to be "national rules of the arbitration tribunal."

19-50 The non-application of EC mandatory rules by an arbitration tribunal having its seat in a Member State may result in the award being challenged. If the courts consider that the rules are part of the international public policy of that country their non-application would justify the annulment of the award under the public policy exception contained in the various arbitration laws. It seems that there is agreement that arbitrators must apply the mandatory rules of the law chosen by the parties, subject only to compliance with international public policy.

4. Arbitration and the Judicial Cooperation within the European Union

19-51 From the early stages of European integration it was clear that the objectives of a common market required a close judicial cooperation and the mutual recognition of judgments. Therefore Article 293 (formerly Article 220) called on Member States to enter into negotiations with each other for the

> simplification of formalities governing the reciprocal recognition and enforcement of judgments of courts or tribunals and of arbitration awards.

---

[44] *E.g.*, several states have made a reservation to Article 7(2) Rome Convention on the law applicable to contracts which allows for the application of mandatory rules of a third country.

4.1. The Legal Framework of Judicial Cooperation: Brussels Convention and Regulation 44/2001

19-52 The Brussels Convention[45] entered into between Member States came into force on 1 February 1973. Its purpose was to foster intra-community trade by avoiding jurisdictional conflicts as widely as possible. It contains an elaborate system of jurisdictional rules for the courts in different Member States and requires the courts to recognise judgments rendered in another Member State. Despite its inclusion in Article 220 EC Treaty, arbitration was expressly excluded from the ambit of the Brussels Convention.[46] The Member States were of the opinion that the existing international conventions, in particular the New York Convention, provided a sufficient framework to ensure the proper and effective development of arbitration.[47] This exclusion has given rise to a number of problems concerning the relation of arbitration to different rules of the Brussels Convention.

19-53 These problems have not been resolved by Regulation 44/2001 on jurisdiction and the recognition and enforcement of judgments in civil and commercial matters[48] which entered into force in March 2002 and replaced the Brussels Convention.[49] Despite certain amendments in other areas the arbitration exception remains.

4.2. The Arbitration Exception and its Relevance

19-54 Article 1(2)(d) Regulation 44/2001[50] provides that the Regulation does not apply to arbitration. The official reports to the Brussels Convention[51] made

---

45 Brussels Convention on Jurisdiction and the Enforcement of Judgments in Civil and Commercial Matters, 27 September 1968. For a consolidated version see *Official Journal* C 27 (28 January 1998).

46 See Brussels Convention Article 1(2)(4).

47 Jenard Report, *Official Journal* C 59 (1979) 1m 13.

48 *Official Journal* L 12 (2001); the aim of the Regulation rendered by the Council on 22 December 2000 on the basis of Articles 61(2) and 67(1) is to include the provisions of the Brussels Convention in a legal instrument of the Community which is binding, directly applicable and facilitates future amendments.

49 According to EC Treaty Article 69, Denmark, the United Kingdom and Ireland are not bound by the powers granted to the EC by the Amsterdam Treaty which form the basis of the Regulation 44/2001. While the United Kingdom and Ireland have declared that they want to take part in the adoption of the Regulation, no such declaration exists from Denmark, where the Brussels Convention remains applicable.

50 Previously Article 1(2)(4) Brussels Convention.

clear that this exception not only covers arbitration proceedings as such, but also court proceedings ancillary to arbitration such as

> ... for example the appointment or dismissal of arbitrators, the fixing of the place of arbitration, the extension of the time limit for making awards ... A judgment determining whether an arbitration agreement is valid or not, or, because it is invalid, ordering the parties not to continue the arbitration proceedings, is not covered by the 1968 Convention.[52]

19-55 The exact scope of the arbitration exception is far from clear and has given rise to a number of questions of considerable practical importance. This has a direct influence on the jurisdiction of the courts called in support of arbitration proceedings. If the required measures fall within the ambit of the Regulation national courts have to base their jurisdiction on the heads of jurisdiction contained in the Regulation; they cannot rely on the often wider heads of jurisdiction under their national law.

19-56 The scope of the arbitration exclusion is relevant for two reasons.[53] First, it determines whether proceedings brought at the place of arbitration or in other Member States in support of the arbitration may have to be stayed by virtue of the *lis pendens* provisions in Articles 27 and 28 Regulation 44/2001. This will not be the case if either those proceedings or the proceedings brought in breach of the arbitration agreement fall within the arbitration exclusion and are therefore

---

51 The original Brussels Convention and all amendments made during the various accessions of new Member States have been accompanied by an official report, which are important tools for interpreting the Convention.

52 See Schlosser, "Report on the convention of October 1978 on the Accession of the Kingdom of Denmark, Ireland and the United Kingdom of Great Britain and Northern Ireland to the Convention on Jurisdiction and Enforcement of Judgments in Civil and Commercial matters and to the Protocol on its Interpretation by the Court of Justice", *Official Journal* C 59 (5 March 1979) 71, 93, para 64; see also ECJ, 25 July 1991, Case no 190/89, *Marc Rich & Co AG v Società Italiana Impianti SpA*, [1991] ECR I 3855, 3901, para 18.

53 For the potential implications of these issues see Kaye, "The Judgments Convention and Arbitration: Mutual Spheres of Influence", 7 *Arb Int* 289 (1991); Kaye, "The EEC and Arbitration: The Unsettled Wake of the Atlantic Emperor", 9 *Arb Int* 27 (1993); Thomas, "The Arbitration Exclusion in the Brussels Convention 1968: An English Perspective", 7(2) *J Int'l Arb* 43 (1990); Audit, "Arbitration and the Brussels Convention", 9 *Arb Int* 1 (1993); Beraudo, "The Arbitration Exception of the Brussels and Lugano Conventions: Jurisdiction, Recognition and Enforcement of Judgments", 18(1) *J Int'l Arb* 13 (2001); van Haersolte - van Hof, "The arbitration exception in the Brussels Convention: further comments", 18(1) *J Int'l Arb* 27 (2001); for further references see Hill, *International Commercial Disputes* (2d ed, LLP 1998), paras 3-3-17 *et seq*; Kropholler, *Europäisches Zivilprozeßrecht* (7th ed, Verlag Recht und Wirtschaft 2002) Art. 1, paras 40 *et seq*.

not covered by the Regulation. Secondly, the scope of the arbitration exclusion may also be relevant for the question whether judgments rendered in breach of the arbitration agreement have to be recognised or enforced in other Member States under Regulation 44/2001. Only if those judgments are not covered by Article 1(2)(d) can they benefit from the facilitated recognition and enforcement under Title III of the Regulation 44/2001.

4.3. The ECJ Decisions in the Marc Rich and Van Uden Cases

19-57 The ECJ judgment in *Marc Rich v Impianti*[54] arose out of proceedings for the appointment of an arbitrator and dealt with the question whether the exception of Article 1(2) no 4 Brussels Convention also applies if one party contested the validity of the arbitration clause. The parties had entered into a contract for the sale of crude oil by an exchange of faxes the last of which contained an arbitration clause providing for arbitration in England. When the oil was loaded a dispute arose as to its quality and the Swiss buyer claimed damages. The Italian respondent initiated proceedings in Italy for a declaration of non-liability. The Swiss claimant contested the jurisdiction of the Italian courts due to the arbitration clause, and started arbitration proceedings in England. As the respondent refused to participate in the arbitration the claimant applied to the High Court for appointment of the tribunal. In contesting the jurisdiction of the High Court the Italian respondent alleged that the Brussels Convention applied to the case and that by virtue of the *lis pendens* provision the case should be tried in Italy. It argued that the arbitration exception did not apply to the proceedings in the High Court as the existence and validity of the arbitration clause was contested and became therefore a preliminary issue in the proceedings. Upon referral of several questions by the English Court of Appeal, the ECJ held that in

> ...order to determine whether a dispute falls within the scope of the Convention, reference must be made solely to the subject-matter of the dispute. If, by virtue of its subject-matter, such as the appointment of an arbitrator, a dispute falls outside the scope of the Convention, the existence of a preliminary issue which the court must resolve in order to determine the dispute cannot, whatever that issue may be, justify application of the Convention.
>
> It would also be contrary to the principle of legal certainty, which is one of the objectives pursued by the Convention for the applicability of the exclusion laid

[54] ECJ, 25 July 1991, Case no 190/89, *Marc Rich & Co AG v Società Italiana Impianti PA*, [1991] ECR I 3855.

> down in Article 1(4) of the Convention to vary according to the existence or otherwise of a preliminary issue, which might be raised at any time by the parties. Consequently, the reply must be that Article 1(4) of the Convention must be interpreted as meaning that the exclusion provided for therein extends to litigation pending before a national court concerning the appointment of the arbitrator, even if the existence or validity of an arbitration agreement is a preliminary issue in that litigation. [References omitted][55]

19-58 The consequence of this decision was that the *lis pendens* provisions of the Convention did not apply and the English Court retained jurisdiction. This required it to form a view on the validity of the arbitration agreement, the very question which was pending before the Italian courts.

19-59 In *Van Uden v Deco-Line*[56], the ECJ had to decide whether provisional measures granted in support of arbitration proceedings fell within the arbitration exception. The parties had entered into a charter agreement by which the Dutch claimant made available cargo space to the German defendant. When the defendant failed to pay certain invoices the claimant started arbitration proceedings in the Netherlands according to the arbitration clause contained in the contract. Furthermore, alleging serious cash flow difficulties the claimant applied to the Rotterdam court for an interim payment order for parts of the outstanding debts. The respondent disputed the jurisdiction of the Dutch courts and alleged that the action could only be brought in Germany where it was domiciled. As the Rotterdam court based its jurisdiction in part on Article 24 Brussels Convention (now Article 31 Regulation 44/2001) the question arose whether the application of the Brussels Convention was excluded by virtue of the arbitration exception in Article 1(2) No 4. The ECJ held that

> ...it must be noted in that regard that provisional measures are not in principle ancillary to arbitration proceedings but are ordered in parallel to such proceedings and are intended as measures of support. They concern not arbitration as such but the protection of a wide variety of rights. Their place in the scope of the Convention is thus determined not by their own nature but by the nature of the rights which they serve to protect. [References omitted][57]

---

[55] *Ibid,* ECR I 3855, 3903, para 26 *et seq.*

[56] ECJ, 17 November 1998, Case no C-291/95, *Van Uden Maritime BV trading as Van Uden Africa Line v Kommanditgesellschaft in Firma Deco-Line*, [1998] ECR 1 7091, 7133, para 33 *et seq.*

[57] *Ibid* 3903, para 26 *et seq.*

19-60 It must therefore be concluded that where, as in the case in the main proceedings, the subject-matter of an application for provisional measures relates to a question falling within the scope of the Regulation 44/2001, the Regulation is applicable. Accordingly, Article 31 may confer jurisdiction on the court hearing that application even where arbitration proceedings have already been, or may be, commenced on the substance of the dispute.[58] As a consequence, the Dutch court had jurisdiction under Article 24 Brussels Convention, now 31 Regulation 44/2001, to grant the interim relief requested by the claimant.

4.4. Consequences of these Decisions

19-61 The *Marc Rich* and *Van Uden* judgments have clarified when proceedings in state courts fall within the arbitration exception of Regulation 44/2001. The decisive criterion in this respect is the subject matter lying at the heart of the proceedings. If that is *ancillary* to the arbitration Regulation 44/2001 is not applicable.

19-62 It follows that all court proceedings which are required to support or facilitate the actual arbitration are covered by the arbitration exception, provided they do not protect other rights. In addition to the appointment of arbitrators and the other supportive measures listed in the official reports[59], it also includes the taking of evidence by the courts and court orders for security for costs. By contrast proceedings for the enforcement of undertakings given in fulfilment of such orders are covered by Regulation 44/2001 as their subject matter is not an issue for the arbitration.[60] Also within the scope of the arbitration exception are all proceedings for the revocation, amendment, challenge, recognition and enforcement of arbitration awards. This should also be the case where a judgment based on the award rather than the award is to be enforced,[61] *i.e.*, double exequatur.

---

[58] For the distinction made between "ancillary proceedings" and "parallel proceedings" see van Haersolte van Hof, "The arbitration exception in the Brussels Convention: further comments", 18(1) *J Int'l Arb* 27 (2001) 28-31.

[59] See, *e.g.*, Schlosser Report, *Official Journal* C 59 (5 March 1979) 71, para 48.

[60] *Lexmar Corporation and Steamship Mutual Underwriting Association (Bermuda) Ltd v Nordisk Skibsrederforening and Northern Tankers (Cyprus) Ltd* [1997] 1 Lloyd's Rep 289.

[61] *Arab Business Consortium International Finance & Investment Co v Banque Franco-Tunisienne* [1996] 1 Lloyd's Rep 485, 488 *et seq*; for the possible identical contents of the award and the exequatur judgment see also Italy, Corte di cassazione, 13 March 1991, no 2846, *Fratellli Damiano v August Topfer & Co*, XVII YBCA 559 (1992) 560.

19-63 The ECJ decisions have largely settled the legal situation concerning proceedings in direct support of arbitration. However, they have not resolved two other situations where the scope of the arbitration exclusion plays a role: (a) proceedings aimed at preventing a breach of an arbitration agreement, and (b) proceedings brought in breach of an arbitration agreement.

(a) Proceedings directed at preventing a breach of the arbitration agreement

19-64 In some countries, such as England, parties who want to prevent the other party from starting court proceedings in breach of an arbitration agreement can apply to the courts for anti-suit injunctions. Through such injunctions, which work *in personam*, parties are ordered not to take any steps in foreign proceedings. However, anti-suit injunctions have been criticised for violating the basic principles of Regulation 44/2001, as well as the comity that each court determines its own jurisdiction.[62] English courts have granted anti-suit injunctions in relation to proceedings brought in a different Member State.[63]

19-65 In *Toepfer International v Molino Boschi*[64] the English court considered anti-suit injunctions not to be covered by the arbitration exception. The court held that they were more directed to stopping foreign proceedings than to initiating arbitration proceedings.[65] Nevertheless the court did not consider itself bound to deny jurisdiction in favour of proceedings brought earlier in a different Member State. In its view the proceedings for an anti-suit injunction concerned a different cause of action than the challenge to jurisdiction brought in the proceedings in breach of the arbitration agreement.

---

[62] This view prevails in civil law countries; see, *e.g.*, Kropholler, Art 21, para 19; see also van Houtte, "May Court Judgments that disregard Arbitration Clauses and Award be Enforced und the Brussels and Lugano Conventions?", 13 *Arb Int* 85 (1997) 91-92.

[63] See, *e.g.*, *Aggeliki Charis Compania Maritima SA v Pagnan SpA (The «Angelic Grace»)* [1995] 1 *Lloyd's Rep* 87; *Navigation Maritime Bulgare v Rustal Trading Ltd*, [2002] 1 Lloyd's Rep 106 *et seq*; however, in December 2001, the House of Lords referred the question of whether an antisuit injunction to prevent proceedings before an English employment tribunal is compatible with the Brussels Convention to the ECJ, see *Turner v Grovit and Others* [2001] UKHL 65. Arguably, as the case submitted to the ECJ does not concern arbitration but jurisdiction of the employment tribunal, injunctions to protect an arbitration agreement may still be granted.

[64] *Toepfer International GmbH v Molino Boschi Srl* [1996] 1 Lloyd's Rep 510.

[65] *Ibid*, 513; however, see Kropholler, Europäisches Zivilprozeßrecht, (7 ed, Verlag Recht und Wirtschaft 2002), Art 1, para 44, who does not consider anti-suit injunctions to be in accordance with the Brussels Convention.

19-66 On the basis of the *Marc Rich* and the *Van Uden* decisions it would seem that anti-suit injunctions in support of arbitration are covered by the arbitration exception. Though directed to stop court proceedings the only purpose of an anti-suit injunction is to enforce the arbitration agreement. For that reason there are strong arguments that anti-suit injunction should be considered proceedings ancillary to arbitration.[66]

19-67 Instead of or in addition to an anti-suit injunction, parties could try to enforce their arbitration agreement by applying for a declaration that a valid agreement exists. *Marc Rich*, for example, sought such a declaration in the Italian courts as well as in the ensuing English proceedings.[67] Such a declaration may have a *res judicata* effect preventing proceedings in breach of the arbitration agreement in a different court. Even when a request for such a declaration is broadly phrased it cannot be convincingly argued that the subject matter does not fall within the exception in Article 1(2)(d) Regulation 44/2001.[68] Such reasoning is also supported by the statement of Advocate-General Darmon that "a dispute as to the existence of an arbitration agreement falls outside the scope of the Convention."[69]

(b) Proceedings in breach of the arbitration agreement

19-68 Most decisions rendered in connection with the arbitration exception have focused primarily on proceedings brought in support of an arbitration. The question whether court proceedings brought in breach of the arbitration agreement are covered by Regulation 44/2001 has not been addressed.

---

66 See *Toepfer International GmbH v Société Cargill France* [1997] 2 Lloyd's Rep 98; *Toepfer International GmbH v Société Cargill France* [1998] 1 Lloyd's Rep 379; *Navigation Maritime Bulgare v Rustal Trading Ltd* , [2002] 1 Lloyd's Rep 106 *et seq*; Hill, *International commercial disputes* (2d ed, LLP 1998), para 3-3-26.

67 Corte di cassazione, 25 January 1991, no 749, *Marc Rich & Co AG v Italimpianti*, XVII YBCA 554 (1992); *Marc Rich & Co AG v Società Italiana Impianti SpA (The "Atlantic Emperor") (No 2)*, [1992] 1 Lloyd's Rep 624 (CA).

68 But see in relation to the predecessor, Article 1(2)(4) of the Brussels Convention, Diamond in *Partenreederei M/S «Heidberg» and Vega Reederei Friedrich Dauber v Grosvenor Grain and Feed Co Ltd, Union Nationale des Cooperatives Agricoles de Cereales and Assurances Mutuelles Agricoles (" The Heidberg")* [1994] 2 Lloyd's Rep 287, 303. See also to this effect *Union de Remorquage et de Sauvetage SA v Lake Avery Inc (The "Lake Avery")* [1997] 1 Lloyd's Rep 540.

69 ECJ, 25 July 1991, Case no 190/89, *Marc Rich & Co AG v Società Italiana Impianti SpA*, [1991] ECR I 3855, 3876 para 35; see also Hascher, "Recognition and Enforcement of Judgements on the Existence and Validity of an Arbitration Clause under the Brussels Convention", 13 *Arb Int* 33 (1997) 39.

19-69 The issue arose during the negotiations for the accession to the Brussels Convention of Denmark, Ireland and the United Kingdom but the Member States could not reach agreement. The United Kingdom supported a wide interpretation of the arbitration exception according to which it includes all disputes covered by arbitration clauses which are considered to be valid in a Member State.[70] The consequences would be that proceedings brought in breach of an arbitration agreement could neither trigger the *lis pendens* provision nor could judgments rendered in such proceedings be recognised and enforced under the Brussels Convention.[71] The majority of Member States gave the exception a narrower meaning not excluding all proceedings brought in breach of an arbitration agreement from the scope of the Brussels Convention. The question remains unresolved by Regulation 44/2001.

19-70 Of considerable practical importance is whether judgments arising out of such proceedings are recognised and enforced under Regulation 44/2001. According to Regulation 44/2001 courts are obliged to recognise and enforce judgments rendered in a different Member States unless one of the limited grounds of refusal listed in Article 34 exists.[72] The basis upon which the court assumed jurisdiction in general does not matter. A lack of jurisdiction according to the enforcing court's view is not one of the reasons upon which recognition or enforcement can be denied. It is assumed that the other court applied the Regulation 44/2001 correctly.

19-71 In consequence, judgments rendered in breach of the arbitration agreement have to be recognised and enforced unless they are either excluded from the scope of Regulation 44/2001 by virtue of Article 1(2)(b), or the breach

---

[70] See Schlosser, "Report on the Convention of October 1978 on the Accession of the Kingdom of Denmark, Ireland and the United Kingdom of Great Britain and Northern Ireland to the Convention on Jurisdiction and Enforcement of Judgments in Civil and Commercial matters and to the Protocol on its Interpretation by the Court of Justice", *Official Journal* C 59 (5 March 1970) 71, 92 para 61; see also Gaudemet-Tallon, *Les Conventions de Bruxelles et de Lugano*, (2d Paris 1996), 39; Audit, "Arbitration and the Brussels Convention", 9 *Arb Int* 1 (1993) 11 *et seq*, and 22; van Haersolte van Hof, "The arbitration exception in the Brussels Convention: further comments", 18(1) *J Int'l Arb* 27 (2001) 33.

[71] See *Jenard Report*, 43 where the author states: "It follows from Article 1 that Title III cannot be invoked for the recognition and enforcement of judgments given on matters excluded from the scope of the Convention."

[72] Article 34 provides that a judgment shall not be recognised in various circumstances: if it is contrary to public policy or irreconcilable with an earlier judgment given in a dispute between the same parties in the Member State in which recognition is sought; where it was given in default of appearance; or if the defendant did not have sufficient time to arrange its defence.

of the arbitration agreement triggers one of the reasons to resist recognition. A recognition of those judgments would prevent, or at least seriously hamper, all proceedings in direct or indirect support of the arbitration as well as the arbitration proceedings themselves. Those proceedings require the existence of a valid arbitration agreement. To that extent they conflict with the express or at least implied finding of the judgment that no valid arbitration agreement exists. Furthermore, rulings as to the merits of the case contained in the judgment will have *res judicata* effect and make the arbitration proceedings obsolete.

19-72 Whether judgments rendered in breach of an arbitration agreement had to be recognised under the Brussels Convention was raised by the English Court of Appeal in proceedings following the ECJ decision in *Marc Rich*. Marc Rich had not only contested the jurisdiction of the court where the declaration of non-liability was sought but initiated proceedings before the Italian Corte di cassazione for a declaration that the Italian courts lacked jurisdiction. The Italian Corte di cassazione rendered a judgment that no arbitration agreement existed.[73] If that judgment was recognised under Article 26 Brussels Convention it would have barred all other English proceedings in this matter based on the contrary assumption that an arbitration agreement existed. In particular the new proceedings initiated by Marc Rich for a declaration that an arbitration agreement actually existed would not have been posible. The Court of Appeal, after declaring that no clear guidance could be drawn from the decision of the ECJ, did not answer the question. It preferred to base its judgment on the fact that by that time Marc Rich had taken steps in the Italian proceedings which could be seen as a submission to jurisdiction.[74]

19-73 The question had to be addressed by an English judge in *The Heidberg*.[75] Cargo owners had started proceedings in France for damages incurred through the collision of vessels. At about the same time the ship owners, who contested the jurisdiction of the French courts, started proceedings in England seeking a declaration that an arbitration clause was incorporated into the bill of lading. The French court declared itself competent denying the existence of an arbitration clause. The English judge then had to decide whether he was bound by this

---

[73] Corte di cassazione, 25 January 1991, no 749, *Marc Rich & Co AG v Italimpianti*, XVII YBCA 554 (1992) 557 *et seq.*

[74] *Marc Rich & Co AG v Società Italiana Impianti SpA (The "Atlantic Emperor") (No 2)* [1992] 1 Lloyd's Rep 624, 632 *et seq.*

[75] *Partenreederei M/S «Heidberg» et al v Grosvenor Grain and Feed Co Ltd et al (The "Heidberg")* [1994] 2 Lloyd's Rep 287.

decision under the Brussels Convention. He considered it to be primarily a question of policy and saw stronger arguments in favour of including such judgments in the Convention as a binding decision of one court could prevent conflicting judgments on the same issue.[76] The decision has received a mixed reception with criticism going as far as considering it "palpably wrong."[77]

4.5. The Effect of Regulation 44/2001 Depends on the Nature of the Issue in Dispute

19-74 There remains considerable uncertainty as to the scope of the arbitration exception. In the light of the ECJ decisions one should distinguish between two types of proceedings. First there seems to be no reason why proceedings for the declaration that no arbitration agreement exists should be treated differently than proceedings in which a declaration as to the existence of an arbitration agreement is sought. These issues fall within the arbitration exception and the recognition of a judgment and enforcement could not be based on Regulation 44/2001.[78]

19-75 The second situation is where the question as to the existence and validity of an arbitration agreement arises as an incidental issue in an action for substantive relief or a declaration of non-liability. A judgment rendered in such proceedings does not fall within the arbitration exception and can benefit from the facilitated recognition and enforcement under Regulation 44/2001.[79] Despite criticism that such a solution would undermine arbitration as a method of dispute settlement[80] it is in line with the objectives of Regulation 44/2001 to facilitate the free movement of judgments within the European Union. The alternative is that a party could exclude recognition of a judgment under Regulation 44/2001 by the allegation that an arbitration agreement exists.

---

[76] *Ibid*, 300 *et seq*; see in this regard the German decision by the Oberlandesgericht Celle, 8 December 1976, *RIW* 131 (1977).

[77] Mayss and Reed, *European Business Litigation* (Dartmouth 1998), 374 *et seq*.

[78] Hascher, "Recognition and Enforcement of Judgements on the Existence and Validity of an Arbitration Clause under the Brussels Convention", 13 *Arb Int* 33 (1997) 40.

[79] See also the Evrigenis and Kerameus Report, *Official Journal* C 298/10 (1986) para 35 which suggests that "... the verification as an incidental question of an arbitration agreement which is cited by a litigant in order to contest the jurisdiction of the court before which he is being sued pursuant to the Convention, must be considered as falling within its scope"; Hascher, "Recognition and Enforcement of Judgements on the Existence and Validity of an Arbitration Clause under the Brussels Convention", 13 *Arb Int* 33 (1997) 53.

[80] Hill, *International commercial disputes* (2d ed, LLP 1998), para 3-3-33.

19-76 Furthermore, a party can rely on the breach of an arbitration agreement to resist recognition and enforcement of a judgment under Regulation 44/2001 despite the fact that in general the jurisdiction of the court rendering a judgment cannot be scrutinised.[81] Before an award has been rendered the only conceivable ground for resisting enforcement could be a violation of public policy. It has been argued that Article II also contains an implied obligation not to enforce a judgment rendered in breach of an arbitration agreement considered to be valid by the enforcing court.[82] According to Article 71, the Regulation is not to interfere with obligations of the Member States arising under different treaties. This may provide a possible basis to argue the prevalence of obligations under the New York Convention.

19-77 The situation may be different when an award has been rendered which comes to a different conclusion than the judgment. In those cases Article 34 No 3 Regulation 44/2001 may present a ground to resist recognition and enforcement of the judgment. An enforcement order issued for an award is a pre-existing judgment in the sense of Article 34 No 3. Even if no such order has been issued the award, though not being a judgment in the proper sense, should be sufficient to justify a refusal of recognition and enforcement. Under the national arbitration laws awards are given the same effect as judgment and the New York Convention contains an obligation to recognise and enforce foreign awards. The rationale underlying Article 34 is applicable also to arbitration awards.[83]

---

[81] It cannot, however, be argued that to refuse enforcement in reliance of an arbitration clause is a question of the scope of the Regulation which was mentioned in Article 37 as a reason to resist enforcement and not a question of jurisdiction, which would not have been reviewable; see Beraudo, "The Arbitration Exception of the Brussels and Lugano Conventions: Jurisdiction, Recognition and Enforcement of Judgments", 18(1) *J Int'l Arb* 13 (2001) 24. Although some of the other areas excluded from the scope of the Convention are mentioned, a different view as to the existence of an arbitration agreement is not listed in Article 27.

[82] Van Houtte, "May Courts Judgements that Disregard Arbitration Clauses and Awards be Enforced under the Brussels and Lugano Conventions?", 13 *Arb Int* 85 (1997) 88.

[83] *Ibid*, 90.

Chapter 20

COMMENCEMENT OF ARBITRATION

20-1 The commencement of arbitration proceedings is a significant step in every arbitration. It evidences the existence of a dispute between the parties and the decision of one of them to refer it to arbitration in accordance with their agreement. Commencing the arbitration may only be, or start out as, a tactic in the ongoing negotiations between the parties where one of them wishes to illustrate its resolve and strength of feeling towards enforcing and protecting its rights.[1]

20-2 However, the real significance is the legal consequences attached to the commencement of the arbitration. Most important is the fact that it stops the limitation periods from running which otherwise, if exceeded, would limit or preclude the exercise of rights.

20-3 In the light of these consequences, when is the arbitration deemed to have been formally commenced? What must be done to commence the arbitration and what information, if any, must be presented or exchanged

1 In this respect this action is the same as commencing proceedings according to the relevant procedure in the national courts.

between the parties? Is it sufficient that notice of the dispute and a request for arbitration has been sent to the other side? Or does arbitration only begin when all arbitrators have been appointed? To answer these questions one needs to look first at the applicable arbitration law and rules. In institutional arbitration, the rules of the relevant institution will determine how the arbitration is started.

20-4 Beyond those more legal consequences attached to the commencement the initial phase of the arbitration may also have a bearing on the future conduct of the arbitration. Careful planning of the future proceedings can avoid unnecessary delays and increase the level of satisfaction with the proceedings since both parties know what to expect from the outset.

20-5 This chapter deals in particular with the (1) the legal consequences of commencement, (2) the effect on the time limits for bringing claims in an arbitration, and (3) the requirements for commencement under different laws and rules.

1. Legal Consequences

20-6 The commencement of an arbitration may have a number of legal consequences, procedural or substantive. For example, once an arbitration has been started it may not be easy to stop: the claimant may no longer be in a position to withdraw from the arbitration without the consent of other parties involved. They may have an interest in having a dispute judicially determined to avoid it being resubmitted at a later stage in some other forum.[2] If nothing else the respondent may wish the claimant to compensate it for any costs it has incurred in responding to the commencement of the arbitration.

20-7 The commencement of arbitration can also be relevant for the standard of care to be applied. The substantive law of some countries imposes special duties of care on the respondent once an action has been started in court or arbitration. In Germany, for example, a respondent is subjected to a stricter liability once an action has been commenced.[3]

20-8 Commencement of an arbitration may also be relevant to the accrual of interest on the amount claimed. Arbitrators have taken the date considered to be

---

[2] This could be possible if a unilateral withdrawal was permissible. See Domke, *Arbitration,* para 14-01.

[3] Germany, BGB sections 286 and 287.

the date of commencement of arbitration, as the date from which interest on the sums awarded accrues.[4] Such position is expressly foreseen in the substantive law of some countries.[5]

20-9 Perhaps the most important legal consequence is the effect the commencement of arbitration proceedings has on the expiry of time limits. Under most laws the start of court proceedings stops the running of prescription periods and other time limits.[6] That effect is generally also extended to arbitration proceedings which replace actions in courts. Therefore the timely initiation of such proceedings may be crucial for the enforcement of any claim or right.

2. Time Limits

20-10 Time limits may be imposed by law or they may be of a contractual nature. Their generally accepted purpose is to provide legal certainty. A party should be able to rely on the fact that after the expiry of a given time no further cause of action will arise out of a certain event. Furthermore, time limits are to ensure that claims are made whilst the event giving rise to a dispute is relatively fresh and sufficient evidence available. Memories and recollections fade over time, witnesses may die, move to other jobs or other countries, and documentary or other evidence may disappear.[7]

20-11 The expiry of time limits can have different effects on the claims as well as on the arbitration proceedings:

- it can bar the claim so that it is no longer capable of being enforced. The arbitrator may still rule on the claim but must render an award against the claimant since its claim is statute barred;
- it can bar the remedy due to the time limit by agreement with the parties. In those cases the claim remains valid and enforceable but enforcement cannot be effected by means of arbitration. If a claimant wishes to assert

---

4 Fouchard Gaillard Goldmann *on International Commercial Arbitration*, para 1217.

5 See, *e.g.*, BGB section 291 which provides that interest must be paid from commencement onwards. See also BGB section 989; the position is similar in English law where interest starts to accrue when proceedings are commenced unless otherwise agreed by the parties.

6 See, *e.g.*, Belgium, Civil Code Article 2246; France, Civil Code Article 2244; Germany, BGB section 204; Netherlands, Civil Code Article 3:316.

7 Hondius, "Modern developments in Extinctive Prescription/Limitation of Actions" in Kerameus (ed), *General Reports presented to the XIVth , International Congress Academy of Comparative Law* (Kluwer & Sakkoulas, 1995), 89-119; Mustill and Boyd, *Commercial Arbitration*, 201.

its rights it must be done in the state courts since the arbitrator lacks jurisdiction;

- time limits may have both effects, i.e. bar both the remedy and the claim.[8]

20-12 As already indicated, in many legal systems the running of limitation periods stop when arbitration proceedings are started. It is noteworthy that the inclusion of an express provision to this effect in the Model Law was rejected. It was feared that such a rule might be outside the field of arbitration and conflict with existing rules on prescription.[9] Equally, it could be said to be self evident and if any national law provides differently it should do so expressly.

2.1. Contractual Time Limits

20-13 Contractual time limits are fairly common, in particular in commodity and maritime arbitration.[10] A number of standard form contracts or arbitration rules of specialised institutions in the field, such as GAFTA and FOSFA,[11] contain time limits.

20-14 Another prominent example, with considerable practical importance, was clause 67 of the FIDIC Red Book which has become, in a slightly amended form, Article 20 of the various new versions of FIDIC Rules. It provided that a party dissatisfied with the decision of an engineer had to give notice of its intention to commence arbitration within 70 days. Though the clause did not explicitly provide for what was to happen if no notice had been given it was understood to have the effect of barring recourse to arbitration as well as to courts.[12]

20-15 Contractual time limits may also be individually agreed by the parties. The interpretation of these contractual time limits can cause difficulty as the effect of a failure to meet the time limits is not always clear. Theoretically parties

---

8 Mustill and Boyd, *Commercial Arbitration*, 193 *et seq.*

9 Holtzmann & Neuhaus, *Model Law*, 610 *et seq.*

10 Mustill and Boyd, *Commercial Arbitration*, 200 *et seq*; Smid, "The Expedited Procedure in Maritime and Commodity Arbitrations", 10(4) *J Int'l Arb* 59 (1993); see also Domke, *Arbitration*, para 15-01.

11 See, *e.g.*, the FOSFA Rules of Arbitration and Appeal where Rule 2(b) requires the claimant to appoint its arbitrator within a certain time.

12 See Seppala, "The Pre-Arbitral Procedure for the Settlement of Disputes in the FIDIC (Civil Engineering) Conditions of Contract", 3 *ICLR* 315 (1985-1986) 330; left open by Corbet, *FIDIC 4th- A practical legal Guide* (Sweet and Maxwell 1991), 449; for the English ICE conditions see *Harbour and General Works Ltd v The Environmental Agency* [2000] ADRLJ 125.

can limit the effect of such clauses to exclude the right to arbitrate after the period has expired.[13] For such an interpretation given the exceptional character of these clauses clear language or strong evidence would be required. In all other cases the expiry of the time limit bars the claim not only in arbitration but also in court proceedings.[14]

20-16 The expiry of a time limit contained in an arbitration clause does not render the clause inoperable in the sense of Article II(3) New York Convention. Accordingly courts are not barred from assuming jurisdiction in this situation.[15]

20-17 Some clauses provide that the time limits start to run following a breakdown in negotiations. It can be difficult to determine exactly when such a breakdown occurs. When negotiations are finally considered to be unsuccessful will be open to discussion between the parties. In a case before the Swiss Federal Tribunal, *Transport- en Handelsmaatschappij "Vekoma" BV v Maran Coal Corporation,* the charter-party contained a time limit running thirty days from the time it was agreed that negotiations were unsuccessful. A dispute arose as to the quality of the goods shipped. After some negotiations Maran sent a letter to the respondent substantiating its claims and setting a deadline by which Vekoma should have settled the claims. In the event of failure to do so the initiation of arbitration proceedings was threatened. Though Vekoma did not reply within the deadline mentioned in that letter no immediate action was taken. Rather Maran waited three months after the expiry of the deadline before a reminder of the outstanding claim was sent. Upon reply that no obligations were outstanding, Maran started arbitration proceedings. Contrary to the finding of the arbitrator in an action for the annulment of the award the Swiss court considered the set deadline to be the relevant date for starting the time limit irrespective of whether the other party answers or not, or the party makes another offer later.[16]

20-18 Under certain circumstances a party may be prevented from relying on a contractual time limit. By its conduct it may have created the appearance that it

---

13 See, *e.g.*, the contractual clause in *Transport- en Handelsmaatschappij "Vekoma" BV v Maran Coal Corporation* [1999] ADRLJ 87.

14 See for the US law on that effect Domke, *Arbitration*, para 15-01.

15 Such an interpretation of this type of arbitration clauses was rejected by the Italian Supreme Court in *Rocco Giuseppe e Figli snc v Armadora San Francisco SA*, X YBCA 446 (1985).

16 [1999] ADRLJ 87. It may be necessary to raise a limitation defence in the arbitration proceedings. For this see the Indian decision by the Bombay High Court in *Toepfer International Asia Pte Ltd (Singapore) v Thopaz Ispat Ltd (Punjab, India)*, 4(5) Int ALR N-34 (2001).

will not rely on the time limit, which can lead to issues of waiver and estoppel. However, mere negotiations are in general not sufficient to lead to those consequences. A party must therefore either agree an extension with the other side beforehand or start arbitration proceedings despite any ongoing negotiations to safeguard its rights.

20-19 The arbitration tribunal may be granted the power to extend contractual time limits, either by express agreement of the parties or the applicable arbitration rules. For example, the FOSFA Rules of Arbitration and Appeal accord such a right to the arbitrator.[17] This shows clearly that the arbitrator must also be empowered to decide whether the time limit requirements have been fulfilled.

20-20 The English Arbitration Act vests a power to grant an extension of contractual time limits in the courts. Section 12 provides

> (1) Where an arbitration agreement to refer future disputes to arbitration provides that a claim shall be barred, or the claimant's right extinguished, unless the claimant takes within a time fixed by the agreement some step-
>
> (a) to begin arbitral proceedings, or
>
> (b) to begin other dispute resolution procedures which must be exhausted before arbitral proceedings can be begun,
>
> the court may by order extend the time for taking that step.

20-21 The considerations to be met before such an extension is granted are fairly high. A party must have been hindered by some justifiable reason from starting the arbitration in time, as a mere mistake in interpreting the requirement is not sufficient.[18] Further, the intended respondent must have been responsible for the untimely commencement of the arbitration. This is the case where it has led the claimant to believe, during settlement negotiations, that it would not invoke the time limit.[19] Furthermore, an extension presupposes that all reliefs

---

[17] See Rule 2(b); see also GAFTA 125 Rule 2:7 *Ets Soulex & Cie v International Trade and Development Co Ltd* [1979] 2 Lloyd's Rep 122; for further case law see Mustill and Boyd, *Commercial Arbitration*, 209 *et seq*; see also Hong Kong, Arbitration Ordinance section 2GD.

[18] *Cathiship SA v Allansons Ltd, "The Catherine Helen"* [1998] 2 Lloyd's Rep 638; *Grimaldi Compagnia di Navigazione SpA v Sekihyo Lines Ltd* [1998] 2 Lloyd's Rep 638; *Harbour and General Works Ltd v The Environmental Agency* [2000] ADRLJ 125; *Thyssen Inc v Calypso Shipping Corporation SA* [2000] 2 Lloyd's Rep 243, 248; see also Hong Kong, Arbitration Ordinance section 2GD(5).

[19] Merkin, *Arbitration Act*, 44.

available in arbitration have been exhausted.[20] It is, however, difficult to see courts making use of that power to extend time limits if such an extension has been denied by the arbitral tribunal.[21]

20-22 If the parties have agreed very short time limits the question may arise whether they are valid or violate public policy. In general these clauses have been upheld by the courts on the simple basis that they were agreed to by the parties.[22]

2.2. Statutory Time Limits

20-23 Statutory time limits usually apply to arbitration in the same way as they apply to litigation. That is explicitly provided for in some laws, such as section 13 Arbitration Act 1996,[23] but also applies in most other laws which do not contain such a provision. Statutory time limits are usually much longer and in most cases they are calculated in years and not months or days. Contrary to contractual time limits, in principle, statutory time limits can not be extended by an arbitration tribunal or the courts. The provisions granting such a power are generally limited to contractual time limits.[24] The length of a given time limit varies from country to country and depends on the nature of the claim. For contractual claims in some countries the limitation period is three years while in other countries it can be as long as six years. Thus it may be decisive which law is applicable. A further problem arises when the issue of time limits is considered to be part of the substantive law in some legal systems and is considered to be part of the procedural law in others.[25]

---

[20] England, Arbitration Act Section 12(2).

[21] DAC Report, para 74.

[22] See Mustill and Boyd, *Commercial Arbitration*, 201 with references to the English law in this respect.

[23] See also China, Arbitration Law Article 74.

[24] See, *e.g.*, England, Arbitration Act section 12; see also Hondius, "Modern developments in Extinctive Prescription/Limitation of Actions", in Kerameus (ed), *General Reports presented to the XIVth , International Congress Academy of Comparative Law* (Kluwer and Sakkoulas 1995), 17.

[25] *Ibid*, Hondius, 23. Historically common law countries consider statutory limitations to be a matter of procedure while civil law systems consider it a matter of substance. Dicey & Morris, *The Conflict of Laws*, (12th ed, Sweet & Maxwell, 1993), chapter 7 paras 7-040 – 7-048; Ailes, "Substance and Procedure in the Conflict of Laws", 39 *Michigan L Rev* 392; Cook, "Substance and Procedure in the Conflict of Laws" 42 *Yale L J* 333. See also *Huber v Steiner* (1835) 2 Bing NC 202, CP 1835; *McKain v R W Miller & Co (South Australia) Pty Ltd* (1991) 104 ALR 257, and Contracts (Applicable Law) Act 1990 Sch 1, Article 10(1)(d).

20-24 The relevant law establishing the time limit also defines what actions must be taken to stop the time from running. Most, if not all, laws usually consider the commencement of arbitration proceedings to be sufficient to stop the time running.[26] The procedural steps required for the commencement of arbitration may differ from country to country. This issue is not governed by the law applicable to the contract but by the law governing the procedure.

2.3. *Date of Commencement*

20-25 The parties can agree when arbitration proceedings are considered to have been commenced and what steps are necessary to effectively commence proceedings. This is expressly provided for in Article 21 Model Law according to which the date of commencement only becomes relevant if no other time has been agreed by the parties. Similar provisions can be found in most laws based on the Model Law[27] as well as other arbitration laws such as the English Arbitration Act section 14(1) which provides

> The parties are free to agree when arbitral proceedings are to be regarded as commenced for the purposes of this Part and for the purposes of the Limitation Acts.[28]

20-26 Even where no such express provision can be found in the applicable arbitration law party autonomy should prevail. This is obvious in connection with contractual time limits. It is reasonable and normal that the parties who agreed the time limit can also determine what is sufficient to fulfil it, irrespective of whether according to the law governing the arbitration it would have commenced at an earlier stage.

20-27 The situation is slightly different when it comes to statutory time limits or other legal issues related to the commencement of arbitration. At first sight it seems to be sensible to allow the law governing the arbitration to regulate the requirements which have to be met for a commencement of an arbitration. However, in these cases too there are strong arguments in favour of party autonomy prevailing. Imposing additional requirements for the commencement of arbitration has the same effect as providing for a shorter contractual time limit.

---

[26] See, *e.g.*, Switzerland, Obligations Law Article 135(2); Germany BGB section 204(1) no 11.

[27] Germany, ZPO section 1044; India, Arbitration and Conciliation Act 1996 section 21; Russian Federation, Arbitration Law Article 21.

[28] See also Sweden, Arbitration Act section 19; Netherlands, CCP Article 1025(3).

To fulfil the additional requirements a claimant has to take action earlier. By contrast the relaxation of requirements have the same effect as a renouncement of the defence of limitation.

20-28 If the parties have not agreed expressly on when the arbitration is considered to be commenced the steps required for the initiation of the proceedings are governed by the chosen arbitration rules and the law governing the arbitration. These may differ considerably as to the time when the proceedings are deemed to have been commenced. An extreme case are ICSID arbitrations where the arbitration is deemed to have been commenced when the "Secretary-General notifies the parties that all arbitrators have accepted their appointment."[29] In *ad hoc* arbitration,[30] as well as under most national arbitration laws, the receipt of the initiating document by the respondent is the relevant date for valid commencement of the arbitration. For example, Article 21 Model Law provides

> Unless otherwise agreed by the parties, the arbitral proceedings in respect of a particular dispute commence on the date on which a request for that dispute to be referred to arbitration is received by the respondent.[31]

20-29 The provision takes account of the fact that there may be no institution involved on which the initiating documents could be served. Problems arise, however, if the claimants cannot serve the document on the defendant either because its address is not known or for any other reason. The UNCITRAL Rules provide for this contingency in Article 2(1)

> For the purposes of these Rules, any notice, including a notification, communication or proposal, is deemed to have been received if it is physically delivered to the addressee or if it is delivered at his habitual residence, place of business or mailing address, or, if none of these can be found after making reasonable inquiry, then at the addressees last-known residence or place of business. Notice shall be deemed to have been received on the day it is so delivered.

---

29 See ICSID Arbitration Rules Rule 6(1); see also Brazil, Arbitration Law Article 19 according to which the procedure is commenced when the appointment is accepted by the tribunal.

30 See UNCITRAL Rules Article 3(2); under Netherlands, CCP Article 1024, arbitration will start upon the conclusion of the submission agreement.

31 Germany, ZPO section 1044; India, Arbitration and Conciliation Act 1996 section 21; Russian Federation, Arbitration Law Article 21; Sweden, Arbitration Law Article 19; see also England, Arbitration Act section 14(4) where the request to appoint an arbitrator must be served; the same applies for Switzerland, PIL Article 181.

20-30 To avoid these problems institutional rules usually provide that the relevant date for the commencement of arbitration is the date the institution receives the initiating document.[32] This is the position under the ICC Rules[33] and the LCIA Rules.[34] The rules and laws, however, differ as to what is required as an initiating document: a mere notice of arbitration or a more detailed request for arbitration. The claimant should be careful to ensure that the notice of arbitration or request for arbitration is properly drafted and served in accordance with the requirements of the relevant rules or law. In addition, in institutional arbitrations the requisite registration fee must be included to commence the proceedings.

2.4. Fulfillment of Pre-Arbitration Procedures

20-31 Increasingly parties include multi-tiered dispute clauses in their contracts. Parties are obliged to engage in the agreed mandatory alternative dispute resolution procedures, such as mediation, before arbitration can be started. In particular, in the construction industry disputes are often submitted to the engineer or some other third person before arbitration can be initiated by a party. Before the parties have gone unsuccessfully through this preliminary procedure it may not be possible to start an arbitration.[35]

20-32 Where dispute resolution clauses are not clearly drafted, describing the various dispute resolution stages and preconditions with specific timetables, before arbitration proceedings can be commenced, confusion and delay can easily occur. It may well be that the pre-arbitration procedures are only optional so that their non-fulfilment does not bar the bringing of a claim in arbitration.[36] In particular in connection with clauses requiring efforts to settle the case amicably it has been held that these should not be applied to oblige the parties to engage in

---

[32] Certain exceptions are the institutions which apply the UNCITRAL Rules such as the Cairo Regional Centre or the Hong Kong International Arbitration Centre where according to Article 3(2) UNCITRAL Rules service on the respondent is the relevant date for commencement.

[33] Article 14(2).

[34] Article 1(1); see also AAA ICDR Rules Article 2(2); DIS Rules Article 6; ICAC Rules Article 14; NAI Rules Article 6; Stockholm Institute Rules Article 5; WIPO Rules Article 7; under the CIETAC Rules Article 13 it is the issuance of the Notice of Arbitration by the Institution which is relevant.

[35] See, *e.g.*, ICC Award no 6535 in Arnaldez, Derains and Hascher, *ICC Awards* 1991-1995, 495; Russell *on Arbitration*, para 5-021 *et seq.*

[36] See, *e.g.*, Interim Award of 17 July 1992, Stockholm Chamber of Commerce, XXII *YBCA* (1997) 197 *et seq.*

fruitless negotiations where it is clear that no settlement will be reached and the time limit may expire.[37]

3. Documents for Initiating the Arbitration Process

3.1. Different Types of Documents and Requirements

20-33 The parties are free to determine the content of the initiating document either directly or by submitting their arbitration to a set of arbitration rules. In other cases the applicable arbitration law will often contain provisions as to what information should be included in the initiating document. Regardless of which rules or law is applicable the initiating document must inform the other parties unambiguously that a specific dispute is being referred to arbitration. The respondent should be given sufficient information to make an informed choice on whether or not to arbitrate the dispute. Therefore, he must be able to determine the nature of the dispute and not merely that there is a dispute.[38]

20-34 A notice of arbitration can be limited to a brief reference to the claim and the relief sought. Its main purpose is to inform the respondent that arbitration proceedings have been started and a claim will be submitted. A full statement of claim with sufficient details will only be required at a later stage, after the tribunal has been appointed and in accordance with the directions of the tribunal. Generally, where a request for arbitration is necessary much more detail will be required. It must contain descriptive information concerning the nature and the circumstances of the contractual arrangement, the alleged breaches and the relief sought. The advantage of a more detailed request is that necessary decisions for the future conduct of the arbitration, such as the fixing of the place of arbitration, the appointment of arbitrators, the procedure to be followed, any relevant advance on costs, may be taken on an informed basis and on the specific needs of

---

[37] ICC case no 8445, XXVI *YBCA* 167 (2001) 168-169; Award of 4 May 1999 in *ad hoc* arbitration, *Himpurna California Energy Ltd v PT Perusahaan Listruik Negara*, XXV YBCA 13 (2000) 27; see also ICC case no 6149, XX *YBCA* 41 (1995) 48.

[38] For cases where the notice was considered not to fulfil the necessary minimum see the American decisions cited in Domke, *Arbitration*, para 14-01.

the case. In some situations an additional round of exchange of statements may be saved.[39]

20-35 By contrast a short notice of arbitration has the advantage that an arbitration can be started at an earlier stage when the claimant may not be able to fulfil certain requirements of a detailed statement of claim.[40] Furthermore, in cases where settlement negotiations are still pending and the primary purpose of the notice of arbitration is to prevent the passing of a time limit it may be premature to set out the claim in any detail.

20-36 Beyond those minimum prerequisites, the content required by the arbitration rules and laws differ. In general one can distinguish between those rules and laws which require a more detailed request for arbitration and those which consider a mere "notice" of arbitration sufficient to initiate the proceedings.[41] For the "notice" usually a brief reference to the claim and the relief sought is sufficient which does nothing more than just inform the party about the initiation of arbitration proceedings and the nature of the dispute. A full statement of the claim and supporting documents and evidence will then have to be submitted at a later stage, often after the constitution of the arbitration tribunal.

20-37 This is the position under the UNCITRAL Rules where Article 3(3) describes the required content of the notice of arbitration, necessary for the commencement of an arbitration

> 3. The notice of arbitration shall include the following:
> (a) A demand that the dispute be referred to arbitration;
> (b) The names and addresses of the parties;
> (c) A reference to the arbitration clause or the separate arbitration agreement that is invoked;
> (d) A reference to the contract out of or in relation to which the dispute arises;
> (e) The general nature of the claim and an indication of the amount involved, if any;

---

39 Derains and Schwartz, *ICC Rules*, 47; for the differences between notice of arbitration and request for arbitration see also Craig, Park & Paulsson, *ICC Arbitration,* para 10-04.

40 See van Hof, Commentary on the UNCITRAL Arbitration Rules, 29; Kreindler, "Speedier arbitration as a response to changes in world trade: a necessary goal or a threat to the expectations of the parties", in Benjamin Davis (ed), *Improving International Arbitration*, 180, 183.

41 The terminology used differs and often both terms are used interchangeably so that the drafters of the Model Law considered it irrelevant what name was given to the initiating document, Seventh Secretariat Note, A/CN9/264, Article 21, para 2.

(f) The relief or remedy sought;

(g) A proposal as to the number of arbitrators (*i.e.* one or three), if the parties have not previously agreed thereon.[42]

20-38 In the notice of arbitration a reference to the general nature of the claim is sufficient while according to Article 3(4) a statement of claim is only an optional element. It can be submitted within a period specified by the arbitration tribunal, as provided for in Article 18.[43]

20-39 By contrast Article 4(3) ICC Rules expressly requires the Request for Arbitration to contain "a description of the nature and circumstances of the dispute giving rise to the claims" and "a statement of the relief sought, including, to the extent possible, an indication of any amount(s) claimed."[44]

20-40 The different arbitration laws often do not specify at all what should be contained in the initiating document. For example, Article 21 Model Law provides that the arbitration proceedings for a particular dispute commence when a "request for that dispute to be referred to arbitration is received by respondent."[45] By including the qualification as to a "particular" dispute the drafters wanted to make sure that the request identified the claim with sufficient specificity since vague requests for arbitration could not commence arbitration proceedings.[46]

20-41 A notice of arbitration is also considered sufficient in England under section 14 Arbitration Act 1996, but it has to be accompanied by a request to the respondent to take the steps required from him for the appointment of an arbitrator in the specific case.[47] In most cases where such a specific request was missing the English Courts have, however, interpreted the requirement liberally taking account of the business practices which often rely on short documents. They have considered a notice sufficient, if it was clear that the claimant intended

---

42 See also CRCICA Rules Rule 1(b), which adopts the UNCITRAL Rules.

43 This is also the position under the Model Law, though the initiating document is called "request for arbitration". See Model Law Article 23.

44 Derains and Schwartz, *A Guide to ICC Rules*, 47 *et seq*. For comparable provisions see LCIA Article 1; AAA ICDR Arbitration Rules Article 2(3).

45 For identical provisions see Germany, ZPO section 1044; India, Arbitration and Conciliation Act 1996 section 21; Russia, Arbitration Law Article 21.

46 Fourth Working Group Report, A/CN9/245, para 27; Holtzmann & Neuhaus, *Model Law*, 612.

47 See also Sweden, Arbitration Act section 19 according to which the claimant has to nominate its arbitrator within the request; Switzerland, PIL Article 181. A notice of arbitration is also sufficient in the Netherlands, CCP Article 1025.

to commence an arbitration and that actions by the respondent for an appointment were required.[48]

20-42 As a consequence of this wide reaching freedom of the parties all types of initiation documents are used in practice. Some are very long and set out the case in great detail; others are very short, limited to the absolute minimum required for their validity. These differences often reflect pragmatic or tactical considerations. Some claimants prefer to give the required information at a late stage to give as little time as possible to the defendant to prepare its case. By contrast, claimants which consider their case to be very strong often opt for the opposite approach. In setting out their case and the available evidence in sufficient detail they may be able to convince the other side not to defend the case but to reach a settlement. Parties often only realise the weakness of their own case after having seen the case of the other side.

3.2. Service of Documents and Receipt

20-43 In international arbitration parties are generally free to agree how the initiating document should be served. Though few arbitration laws actually provide for this it follows from the principle of party autonomy and is recognised at least implicitly.[49] Commercial contracts often set out how the service of documents is to be effected providing typically the use of registered mail to a certain address for the attention of a certain person. In ICC arbitration, for example, the secretariat is responsible for sending the request for arbitration to the respondent.[50]

20-44 In the absence of such an agreement most arbitration rules contain provisions dealing with the service of documents. They are usually more flexible than the rules governing service of documents in court proceedings and allow more or less for service by any effective means which ensures that the respondent

---

48 *Allianz Versicherungs- Aktiengesellschaft v Fortuna Co Inc, "The Baltic Universal"* [1999] 1 Lloyds Rep 497; *Seabridge Shipping AB v AC Orsleff's Efef's A/S* [1999] 2 Lloyd's Rep 685; Russell *on Arbitration*, para 5-029; for a different view see *Vosnoc Ltd v Transglobal Projects Ltd* [1998] 1 Lloyd's Rep 711.

49 For a clear recognition see in particular England, Arbitration Act section 71(1); for an implicit recognition see Model Law Article 3(1); Germany, ZPO section 1028; Russia, Arbitration Law Article 3.

50 ICC Article 4(5); the secretariat sends the documents by courier to ensure recorded delivery.

is informed about the arbitration.[51] This also includes e-mail as expressly mentioned in the LCIA Rules.[52] To avoid problems resulting from change of address it is sufficient to serve the notice or request of arbitration by mail to the addressee's last known principal residence or place of business.[53]

20-45 In a number of countries special procedures of service are foreseen if no actual service can be effected. Examples of such fictitious service are the French *signification au parquet*[54] or service of documents under Article 3 Nr. 1 of the Russian Law for International Court for Commercial Arbitration. While service under those rules may be sufficient for domestic arbitration they may give rise to problems in international arbitration. For example, a German court refused enforcement of an award for a violation of public policy where the service was made according to the above mentioned Russian rule and the respondent only learned about the arbitration after the period to apply for annulment of the award in Russia had expired.[55]

20-46 The date of receipt of the request for arbitration has two important functions. First, it often marks the commencement of the arbitration with all the consequences attached to it as described above.[56] Secondly, the time for answering to the request usually starts to run from the date of receipt.

3.3. Failure to Comply with Requirements

20-47 In the majority of cases parties comply with the requirements for the commencement of arbitration. However, this is not always the case. The notice or request may not contain the necessary information, is drafted in a wrong language, is not supplied in sufficient copies or, in institutional arbitration the

---

[51] Domke, *Arbitration*, para 14-2; Russell, *on Arbitration*, para 5-033.

[52] LCIA Article 4(1); for the ICC see Craig, Park & Paulsson, *ICC Arbitration,* para 10-04, fn 22; Derains and Schwartz, *ICC Rules*, 50.

[53] See, *e.g.*, England, Arbitration Act section 76(4); LCIA Article 4(2); ICC Rules Article 3(2); Russell *on Arbitration*, para 5-034.

[54] NCPC Article 683 *et seq*, which is, however, only possible where the respondent has his residence abroad.

[55] Bayerisches Oberstes Landesgericht, 16 March 2000, 4 *Z Sch* 50/99. See also Greek Court of Appeal Patras, Decision no 426 (1982), XIV *YBCA* 636 (1989) where it was held that neither Greek public policy nor Article V(1)(a) would have any difficulty with service of documents or a notice in compliance with the law governing the arbitration, in this case the law of Czechoslovakia.

[56] See, *e.g.*, Model Law Article 21; Germany, ZPO section 1042.

registration fee is not attached.[57] What happens in such cases? Few problems arise if the failure can be remedied within the relevant time limit. The situation can be different if no remedial action is taken before the time limit expires.

20-48 There are no provisions in the different arbitration rules or laws dealing specifically with this issue. In such a case it can be argued that the arbitration was not validly commenced before the expiry of the time limit and therefore the claims are barred. Many rules and laws contain provisions that objections to the tribunal's jurisdictions or failures to comply with procedural rules must be raised before any further steps in the arbitration are taken.[58] It may be possible to extend the application of that provision to the issue of incorrect commencement so that any objections raised at a later time will not lead to a barred claim.[59] In cases where the insufficiency of the initiating document is raised at an early stage no such rules exist. Under ICC Rules the general practice seems to be that as long as the other side has been informed about the initiation of a claim non-fulfilment of additional requirements will not prevent the valid commencement of an arbitration. The missing parts can be remedied at a later stage and the time limit is fulfilled.[60]

20-49 Under some laws an action started in courts instead of arbitration is considered to be sufficient to stop the expiry of time limits.[61] English law adopts a different position to prevent claimants from initiating proceedings whenever it is convenient for them to stop the expiry of time limits.[62] A claimant who has doubts about the validity of an arbitration clause should therefore initiate arbitration proceedings as well as court proceedings to stop the time limit from expiring. However, this may entail the danger that the initiation of proceedings before the courts is considered to be a waiver of the right to arbitrate.

---

[57] See LCIA Article 1(1)(f) and ICC Rules Articles 3(1) and 4(4).

[58] See, *e.g.*, Model Law Article 16(2); England, Arbitration Act Article 31; Switzerland, PIL Article 186(2); Germany, ZPO section 1040(2); LCIA Article 23(2); ICC Rules Article 33.

[59] Russell *on Arbitration*, para 5-025.

[60] See Final Award ICC case no 6784 (1990), 8(1) *ICC Bulletin* 53 (1997); Interim Award ICC case no 6228 (1990), 8(1) *ICC Bulletin* 53 (1997); Derains and Schwartz, *A Guide to ICC Rules*, 57; for a comparable approach under other rules see Fouchard Gaillard Goldmann *on International Commercial Arbitration*, para 1215.

[61] That was, *e.g.*, the case in Germany before 1 January 2002, when BGB section 212(2) required that the arbitration had to be brought within six months after the court had denied jurisdiction.

[62] *Thyssen Inc v Calypso Shipping Corporation SA* [2000] 2 Lloyd's Rep 243, 246.

Chapter 21

ARBITRATION PROCEDURE

21-1 In some languages the word for "arbitrator" is the same as the word used for "referee" or "umpire" in sporting events. For instance, in German the word "*Schiedsrichter*", and in Greek the work "*διαιτητής*", denote either referee or arbitrator. In real life referees rarely make the rules of the game; they only ensure that certain rules or principles are applied and they have on occasion decision-making power. The teams and their performance determine the game and its outcome.

21-2 This chapter examines the core of arbitration proceedings from a theoretical and a practical perspective. The issue is who controls the procedure and what minimal standards have to be complied with? Most arbitration laws provide a set of rules which may be used to regulate arbitration proceedings. Occasionally such rules are mandatory or express public policy. Furthermore, the internationalisation and harmonisation of international arbitration has resulted in the formulation of international rules for the regulation of arbitration procedure.

21-3 Parties are free to agree generally the procedure and, in any event, the arbitration tribunal has the power to fix the procedure and determine procedural issues. The distinction between procedural and substantive issues is not always clear. *Procedural issues* are technical matters relating to the organisation and conduct of proceedings. *Substantive issues* are matters which influence the outcome of the case.[1] The relevance is that they may be governed by different laws. The English Arbitration Act offers a statutory classification of procedural issues. Section 34(1) English Arbitration Act provides that procedural issues include

> (a) when and where any part of the proceedings is to be held;
> (b) the language or languages to be used in the proceedings and whether translations of any relevant documents are to be supplied;
> (c) whether any and if so what form of written statements of claim and defence are to be used, when these should be supplied and the extent to which such statements can be later amended;
> (d) whether any and if so which documents or classes of documents should be disclosed between and produced by the parties and at what stage;
> (e) whether any and if so what questions should be put to and answered by the respective parties and when and in what form this should be done;
> (f) ...
> (g) whether and to what extent the tribunal should itself take the initiative in ascertaining the facts and the law;
> (h) whether and to what extent there should be oral or written evidence or submissions.

---

1 See Karrer, "Freedom of an arbitral tribunal to conduct the proceedings" 10(1) *ICC Bulletin* 14 (1999) 16.

21-4 This chapter examines (1) the power of the parties and the tribunal to fix the arbitration procedure, (2) procedural directions and terms of reference, (3) the planning of international arbitration proceedings, with focus on the format of the hearings and submissions, (4) legal or other representation of parties, (5) default proceedings and (6) expedited procedures.

1. Fixing the Arbitration Procedure

21-5 The law or rules governing the arbitration procedure is determined by looking to the intent of the parties. While this autonomy is widely recognised in arbitration theory and practice, in some recent arbitration statutes it is not without limitations. The same limitations apply also when it is the tribunal that fixes the procedure.

1.1. Party Agreement

21-6 It is universally accepted that whatever law governs the arbitration party autonomy plays a significant role in determining the conduct of proceedings. This is evidenced by Article V(1)(d) New York Convention which provides that an award may be refused recognition if the "procedure was not in accordance with the agreement of the parties, or, failing such agreement, was not in accordance with the law of the country where the arbitration took place."[2]

21-7 Although the arbitration tribunal performs a judicial function, rules of national civil procedure are invariably unsuitable and irrelevant for international arbitration.[3] For this reason most national laws contain provisions for the procedures to be adopted in international arbitration which deviate from the rules to be applied by national courts. These provisions allow wide freedom to the parties and the arbitration tribunal to determine the procedure to be followed.

21-8 This is reflected in Model Law Article 19

> (1) Subject to the provisions of this Law, the parties are free to agree on the procedure to be followed by the arbitral tribunal in conducting the proceedings.
> (2) Failing such agreement, the arbitral tribunal may, subject to the provisions of this Law, conduct the arbitration in such manner as it considers appropriate. The

---

2 See similarly European Convention Article IX(1)(d) and Inter-American Convention Articles 2 and 3.

3 This is true despite the fact that international arbitration proceedings have become increasingly judicialised. See Oppetit, "Philosophie de l'arbitrage commercial international", 120 *Clunet* 811 (1993) 818.

power conferred upon the arbitral tribunal includes the power to determine the admissibility, relevance, materiality and weight of any evidence.

21-9 The phrase "subject to" does not really restrict party autonomy. There are few rules in the Model Law relating to procedure which are of mandatory nature as they uphold principles of due process.[4] The same applies to the arbitration laws that have adopted the Model Law[5] and many other arbitration laws.[6]

21-10 Parties may decide to exercise their autonomy by including specific procedural rules in their arbitration agreement or by reference to institutional rules.[7] In institutional arbitration the reference will normally be to the rules of the chosen institution. In *ad hoc* arbitration reference is often made to the UNCITRAL Rules. However, these arbitration rules are generally silent on the specific procedures to be followed; they give arbitrators power to fix the procedure in the absence of the parties' agreement.

21-11 Parties do occasionally choose national rules of civil procedure to be followed in arbitration. Unless the chosen law contains specific provisions for international arbitration such a choice is unwise as national civil procedure rules are normally designed for domestic litigation before state courts, not for the arbitration of international cases. Arbitration requires a greater degree of flexibility.

1.2. Arbitrators Fixing the Procedure

21-12 Where parties have not agreed, and under most institutional rules, the tribunal will decide the procedure to be adopted. Such procedure, while it may have general common characteristics, will be adapted to the specifics of the case and will be distinct for each arbitration. In fixing the procedure the tribunal must be fair and reasonable.[8]

---

4 See Hong-Lin Yu and Molife, "The Impact of National Law Elements on International Commercial Arbitration", 4(1) *Int ALR* 17 (2001).

5 See, *e.g.*, Germany, ZPO section 1042(4); Russian Federation, Arbitration Law Article 19.

6 See, *e.g.*, Belgium, Judicial Code Article 1693; Brazil, Arbitration Law Article 21; England, Arbitration Act section 34(1); France, NCPC Article 1494; Netherlands, CCP Article 1036; Switzerland, PIL Article 182(1).

7 See, *e.g.*, Brazil, Arbitration Law Article 21; England, Arbitration Act section 4(3); Switzerland, PIL Article 182(2).

8 A good example can be seen in section 5a of the 2002 Rules and Principles of the Arbitration Court attached to the Economic Chamber of Czech Republic which provides:

21-13 The tribunal should seek the parties' agreement on the procedure to follow. However, frequently parties cannot agree on procedural issues once a dispute has arisen. In practice, once the tribunal has been constituted and the arbitration started, it will often be for the tribunal to fix the proceedings as it considers appropriate.[9]

1.3. Limitations to Procedure Adopted

21-14 Limitations on the autonomy of the parties and the tribunal to regulate the procedure may result from the mandatory provisions of the law of the place of arbitration.[10] These mandatory rules of the place of arbitration define the outer boundaries within which parties and arbitrators may operate. The limitations imposed by these mandatory provisions may vary from country to country and have changed over the years.

21-15 Before the latest wave of arbitration reform it was of considerable importance which law governed the arbitration proceedings. Various national laws imposed different limitations on the arbitration process, provided for

---

> The arbitrators shall be free to proceed in the proceedings in a manner they consider appropriate always ensuring the equal treatment of the parties and providing all parties with an equal opportunity to exercise their rights with the aim of ascertaining, without unnecessary formalities, all the facts of the dispute necessary for its resolution.

9 The issue of whether the party autonomy in determining procedure ceases with the establishment of the tribunal was debated in the UNCITRAL Working Group which discussed the Model Law. The Working Group suggested that the autonomy of parties is continuous. However, as a matter of practice, once arbitration has started, the proceedings are fixed by the arbitrators. See Sanders, "Chapter 12: Arbitration", in Cappelletti (ed), *IECL Vol XVI: Civil Procedure* (Mohr Siebeck and Martinus Nijhoff 1996), para 157, 102-3.

10 For a comprehensive discussion of the various models representing the territoriality versus autonomy debate and the importance of mandatory rules of the place of arbitration see Park, "The Lex Loci Arbitri and International Commercial Arbitration", *ICLQ* 31 (1983); Goode, "The Role of the *Lex Loci Arbitri* in International Commercial Arbitration", 17 *Arb Int* 19 (2001). See also *Union of India v McDonnell Douglas*, [1993] 2 Lloyd's Rep 48; XIX YBCA 235 (1994); *Dubai Islamic Bank PJSC v Paymentech Merchant Services Inc* [2001] 1 Lloyd's Rep. 65 (QBD). See also the recent debate: Nakamura, "The Place of Arbitration - Its Fictitious Nature and Lex Arbitri", 15(10) *Mealey's IAR* 23 (2000); Rubins, "The Arbitral Seat is No Fiction: A Brief Reply to Tatsuya Nakamura's Commentary, 'The Place of Arbitration - Its Fictitious Nature and Lex Arbitri'", 16(1) *Mealey's IAR* 23 (2001); Pinsolle, "Parties to An International Arbitration With the Seat in France are at Full Liberty to Organise the Procedure as They See Fit: A Reply to the Article By Noah Rubins", 16(3) *Mealey's IAR* 30 (2001); Nakamura, "The Fictitious Nature of the Place of Arbitrations May not Be Denied", 16(5) *Mealey's IAR* (2001).

considerable court intervention and control, and required the tribunal to apply rules of national procedure unsuitable for arbitration.

21-16 In modern arbitration laws, however, the limitations imposed by mandatory rules are restricted to those considered necessary to guarantee that the parties have the opportunity to present their case and answer the case against them. This is generally known as due process and is a fundamental element of international arbitration. Apart from these few minimum requirements, the so called "*Magna Carta of arbitration*",[11] all other procedural provisions are usually of a non-mandatory character and can be derogated from by the parties and the tribunal.

21-17 This duty of due process is described in various ways. Article 18 Model Law provides that "parties shall be treated with equality and each party shall be given a *full opportunity* to present his case".[12] Belgian Law provides that the "tribunal shall give each party *an opportunity* of substantiating his claims and of presenting his case."[13] English law mandates that each party must be given "a *reasonable* opportunity of putting its case and dealing with that of its opponent."[14] The Model Law requiring a "full opportunity" opts for greater rigidity in controlling proceedings than other systems which empower the tribunal to exercise flexibility to prevent parties abusing the process.

21-18 The universally accepted principle that parties should be allowed to respond to the allegations of the other side[15] is known as the *"principle of*

---

[11] See Holtzmann and Neuhaus, *Model Law*, 550.

[12] [Emphasis added].

[13] [Emphasis added], Belgium Judicial Code Article 1694(1).

[14] [Emphasis added], England Arbitration Act section 33(1)(a).

[15] See Model Law Articles 23(1), 24(1)(3), 25 and 26(2); Belgium, Judicial Code Articles 1683, 1693, 1694; Brazil, Arbitration Law Articles 19-22; China, Arbitration Law Articles 21-29, 39-48; England, Arbitration Act sections 14, 33-45; France, NCPC Articles 1460-1461, 1467-1468; Germany, ZPO sections 1042-1050; Hong Kong, Arbitration Ordinance sections 2GA-2GG and Model Law provisions; Netherlands, CCP Articles 1036-1042; Switzerland, PIL Articles 181-185; US, FAA section 7. See also GAFTA Rule 4. Under the Model Law where the claimant sets out its claim and relief sought the respondent shall state its defence to the claim: Article 23(1); a party may request a hearing: Article 24(1); all statements, documents or other information supplied to the tribunal by one party must be communicated to the other party. The tribunal is also required to communicate to the parties any expert report or evidentiary document on which the award may rely: Article 24(3); default proceedings may only be carried on when the defaulting party cannot justify its default. Documents and submissions still have to be communicated to the defaulting party: Articles 24(3) and 25; a party may challenge an expert appointed by the tribunal at a hearing: Article 26(2).

contradiction". Accordingly, all arguments and evidence invoked by a party must be communicated to the other party who must be given an opportunity to answer them.[16] In practice it is not always necessary to grant absolute equality in quantitative terms to both parties. Often one party needs less time and less evidence to prove its case or rebut the case against it.

2. Terms of Reference and Procedural Directions

2.1. Need for Planning

21-19 At the beginning of the arbitration, the tribunal will often arrange a meeting with the parties to discuss and fix the format and schedule for the proceedings. In the absence of an agreement the tribunal will fix the format and schedule for the arbitration.[17] This may include the different steps or phases of the proceedings and set out dates for the completion of each step. Assuming that they are realistic in the time planning a useful timetable to guide them through the proceedings can be made.

21-20 Essentially it is necessary to determine what has to be done for the conduct of the arbitration. Generally this will include:

- Schedule for the service of written submissions, claims, counter-claims and defences. The form and structure of written submissions, and whether they include witness evidence and documents.
- Any specific evidentiary rules.
- Representation of parties in the hearings and the entire proceedings.
- Whether the tribunal may decide specific issues with orders or interim awards.
- Arrangements for documentary disclosure, if any.
- Arrangements for communications between the parties and the tribunal.
- How interim procedural issues are to be resolved, *e.g.*, requests for extensions of time.

---

[16] The principle is known as *"audi alteram partem"*. See Van Houtte, "Conduct of Arbitral Proceedings", in Šarčević (ed), *Essays*, 113, 126.

[17] See, *e.g.*, Model Law Articles 19(2); Belgium, Judicial Code Article 1693(1); England, Arbitration Act sections 33 and 34; France, NCPC Article 1494; Switzerland, PIL Article 182(2); ICC Rules Article 15(1); LCIA Article 14(2); UNCITRAL Rules Article 15(1).

- Appointment of a secretary to carry on purely administrative tasks for the tribunal.

21-21 UNCITRAL published the *Notes on Organizing Arbitral Proceedings*[18] to assist parties and arbitrators in determining procedural matters in international commercial arbitration.[19] These can be followed in appropriate circumstances. While there is no reliable data as to how often the UNCITRAL Notes have been used in practice,[20] they undoubtedly provide a useful guide for the preparation and running of arbitration proceedings.

21-22 A number of arbitration rules require the parties and the tribunal to establish terms of reference or procedural directions at an early stage of the proceedings. The purpose is to prescribe the ambit of the arbitration and the issues to be determined.[21]

2.2. Terms of Reference

21-23 Terms of reference are an essential element of ICC arbitration and a pre-requisite to the commencement of the substantive process.[22] The main function of the ICC terms of reference is to fix the subject matter of the arbitration. This is to stop the parties from continually changing the content and nature of their claims.[23] The obligation to draw up the terms of reference is placed on the tribunal "on the basis of documents or in the presence of the parties and in the light of their most recent submissions". The terms of reference should include

(a) the full names and descriptions of the parties;

---

18 UN Doc V 96-84935. See also XXII *YBCA* 448 (1997).

19 See discussion on the UNCITRAL Notes on Organising Arbitral Proceedings in van den Berg (ed), *ICCA Congress Series no 7*, 172 – 195.

20 See, however, the first NAFTA award – Annex 1: Decision Regarding the Place of Arbitration in *Ad hoc* arbitration, 28 November 1997, *Ethyl Corporation v The Government of Canada*, XXIVa YBCA 211 (1999).

21 The terms of reference consist of a document which is signed by the parties and the arbitration tribunal.

22 The original purpose of the terms of reference was to overcome the French legal rule at the time that an agreement to arbitrate future disputes was invalid. By listing the issues in dispute in the terms of reference, which were agreed by the parties, there was a submission agreement of an existing dispute ("*compromis*") which was valid. See Derains and Schwartz, *ICC Rules*, 228; Craig, Park and Paulsson, *ICC Arbitration*, 273-4.

23 ICC Rules Article 19 provides that after the terms of reference "no party shall make new claims or counterclaims which fall outside the limits of the Terms of Reference unless it has been authorized to do so by the Arbitral Tribunal, which shall consider the nature of such new claims or counterclaims, the stage of the arbitration and other relevant circumstances."

(b) the addresses of the parties to which notifications and communications arising in the course of the arbitration may be made;
(c) a summary of the parties' respective claims and of the relief sought by each party with an indication to the extent possible of the amounts claimed or counterclaimed;
(d) unless the Arbitral Tribunal considers it inappropriate, a list of issues to be determined;
(e) the full names, descriptions and addresses of the arbitrators;
(f) the place of the arbitration; and
(g) particulars of the applicable procedural rules and, if such is the case, reference to the power conferred upon the Arbitral Tribunal to act as *amiable compositeur* or to decide *ex aequo et bono*.[24]

21-24 The ICC Rules require the tribunal and the parties to agree and sign the terms of reference within two months of the appointment of the tribunal.[25] The effect of the parties' signature is to make the terms of reference an agreement between the parties with its own legal consequences. They may well qualify as a submission to arbitration.[26] Terms of reference may also modify the arbitration agreement, *e.g.*, agreeing one rather than three arbitrators or extending jurisdiction to other contracts than the one in which the arbitration agreement exists. If a party refuses to agree or sign the terms of reference the tribunal will sign it and send it for approval to the ICC Court.[27] In these cases or when all parties refuse to sign the terms of reference, the document will be merely a record of the tribunal. In any event terms of reference cannot be reviewed by courts.[28]

21-25 An intriguing complication stems from the fact that arbitrators also sign the terms of reference. Consequently, it has been argued, the terms of reference are binding not only on the parties, but also on the arbitrators, who must comply with the parties' intentions. The Paris Court of Appeal applied this principle

---

[24] ICC Rules Article 18(1).

[25] ICC Rules Article 18(2).

[26] See Cour d'appel Paris, 19 March 1987, *Kis France v ABS*, Rev Arb 498 (1987); Cour d'appel Paris, 12 January 1988, *Replor SA v Ploemeloise de financement, de participation, d'investissement SARL*, Rev Arb 691 (1988). This will, however, only be the case where there is no challenge to the jurisdiction of the tribunal. Where one party is challenging jurisdiction it will either refuse to sign the terms of reference or do so only in respect of the tribunal deciding the jurisdictional challenge.

[27] ICC Rules Article 18(3). See also CEPANI Rules Article 24(2).

[28] See, however, Supreme Court of Argentina, 24 October 1995, *Compania Naviera Perez SACFIMFA v Ecofisa SA*, 11(2) Mealey's IAR 9 (1996).

when it set aside an award in which the issue of jurisdiction had been addressed together with the merits of the dispute, though the terms of reference signed by the parties required the arbitrators to rule on their own jurisdiction in a separate award.[29] This decision was overruled by the Cour de cassation[30] which held that in international arbitration there may be a duty on the arbitrators relating to the procedure to be followed. This can include an obligation to make separate awards concerning jurisdiction and the substance of the dispute, provided that this is unambiguously expressed in the terms of reference. This decision redefines the extent to which the terms of reference bind the tribunal.

21-26 The concept and practice of terms of reference are also found in the rules of other arbitration institutions.[31] CEPANI is the only other arbitration institution which opted for a detailed list of issues to be agreed in the context of terms of reference. The list of issues includes

> ....
>
> c) a brief statement of the parties' claims; ...
>
> d) the subject of the arbitration, a description of the circumstances of the case and a definition of the contentious issues; ...
>
> e) the duties of the arbitrator and the questions on which he must decide; ...
>
> ...
>
> h) any other particulars deemed useful by the arbitrator.[32]

21-27 It has been argued that agreeing terms of reference complicates and delays the proceedings without providing any actual benefit.[33] There are, however, three distinct advantages of terms of reference.[34]

- First, terms of reference assist the tribunal and the parties to summarise the claims, counterclaims and defences which sometimes are not clearly

---

[29] See Cour d'appel Paris, 19 December 1986, *OIAETI v SOFIDIF*, Rev Arb 359 (1987) and note Gaillard, Rev Arb 275 (1987).

[30] Cour de cassation, 8 March 1988, *SOFIDIF v OIAETI*, Rev Arb 481 (1989).

[31] See CEPANI Article 24; AIA Article 24; JCAA Article 15; Euro-Arab Chamber of Commerce Article 23(7). A different concept of terms of reference is often used with regard to the appointment of an expert by the Tribunal. See, *e.g.*, UNCITRAL 27(1); EDF Article 28(1); CMI 11(4); Iran-US Claims Tribunal 27(1); MIGA 43(c); NAI 31(1); and WIPO 55(a).

[32] CEPANI Rules Article 2(1).

[33] See Smit, "The Future of International Commercial Arbitration: A Single Transnational Institution?", 25 *Columbia J Transnat'l L* 9 (1986) 21.

[34] See Craig, Park and Paulsson, *ICC Arbitration*, 273-293; Bond, "ICC Terms of Reference Rules Saves Time and Money While Promoting Common Understanding", 6(8) *Mealey's IAR* 33 (1991); Fouchard Gaillard Goldman *on International Commercial Arbitration*, paras 1231-1234.

expressed in the first submissions of the parties.[35] The terms of reference set the limits of the dispute and may reduce the risk of the award being set aside by holding that the arbitrators' brief is confined within these limits.[36]

- Second, terms of reference create a useful framework and focus of consideration and enable the parties to express their views on a number of issues from the outset of the proceedings. They do not limit the discretion of the tribunal regarding the conduct of proceedings.
- Third, terms of reference as a procedural task bring the parties together at the outset of the proceedings. In the event that a party refused to participate in the drawing of the terms, the validity of the subsequent award is not affected.[37]

2.3. Procedural Directions

21-28 The planning of proceedings in the form of procedural directions is quite a common practice in continental type arbitrations. As a matter of practice international arbitration tribunals increasingly manage the disputes actively by preparing procedural directions. A procedural timetable may take the form of a provisional or final procedural order.[38]

21-29 Procedural directions, and in particular a procedural timetable, assist the tribunal in the management of the case and can impose discipline on parties which refuse to co-operate or employ delaying tactics. They are often issued in the form of a procedural order so that they can be amended by the tribunal when it is deemed necessary.

21-30 Procedural directions are normally binding on the parties[39] but are not enforceable or subject to review by the courts.[40] Only rarely are courts at the

---

35 Frequently the effect of terms of reference is to assist the parties to reach a settlement.

36 See Cour de cassation, 6 March 1996, *Farhat Trading Co v Daewoo*, Rev Arb 69 (1997).

37 See Cour d'appel Paris, 28 June 1991, *KFTCIC v Icori Estero*, Rev Arb 568 (1992).

38 See, *e.g.*, the First NAFTA award – Award on Jurisdiction in *Ad hoc* arbitration, 24 June 1998, *Ethyl Corporation v The Government of Canada*, XXIVa YBCA 211 (1999).

39 See, *e.g.*, England, Arbitration Act section 40(2)(a).

40 See, *e.g.*, Pryles, "Interlocutory Orders and Convention Awards: The case of *Resort Condominiums v Bolwell*", 10 *Arb Int* 385 (1994) 392; Austrian Supreme Court, 12 April 1994, *Dipl Ing Peter L v Dr Andreas R et al*, 4 Obester Gerichtshof 1542/94, and comment by Melis, in XXII *YBCA* 264 (1997); Tribunal de Grande Instance Paris, 21 May 1997, *Cubic Defense System v Chambre de Commerce Internationale*, Rev Arb 417 (1997). Hjerner, "On partial awards, orders and other decisions in arbitral proceedings, in particular with respect to

place of arbitration empowered to assist with the enforcement of procedural directions.[41] It will be for the tribunal to decide what action can be taken if a party fails to comply with procedural directions.

21-31 UNCITRAL Notes on Organising Arbitral Proceedings list issues that parties and tribunals may wish to consider. In particular, depending on the volume and kind of documents relevant to each arbitration, it may be helpful to consider whether practical arrangements on details such as the following should be made:

- Whether the submissions will be made as paper documents or by electronic means (*e.g.* CD-ROM), or both;
- The number of copies in which each document is to be submitted;
- A system for numbering documents and items of evidence, and a method for marking them, including by tabs;
- The form of references to documents (*e.g.* by the heading and the number assigned to the document or its date);
- Paragraph numbering in written submissions, in order to facilitate precise references to parts of a text.[42]

3. Procedural Issues

21-32 The procedural issues to be determined may include (1) whether the proceedings will be conducted in an inquisitorial or adversarial style; (2) the timetable and arrangements for written submission and hearings, including issues of place and language; and (3) additional powers the tribunal may have to decide interim issues and to make interim/partial awards.

arbitration in Sweden", *Yearbook of the Stockholm Arbitration Institute* 31 (1984); Swiss Tribunal Fédéral, 2 July 1997, *L Ltd Gibraltar v The Foreign Trade Association of the Republic of U*, 3 ASA Bulletin 494 (1997) 498; See also Jarvin, "To What Extent Are Procedural Decisions of Arbitrators Subject to Court Review?", van den Berg (ed), *ICCA Congress series no 9*, 366-382.

[41] The 1991 Alberta Arbitration Act expressly refers to procedural direction in the title of Article 25 and gives power to local courts to enforce procedural directions; see also England, Arbitration Act section 41(5).

[42] UNCITRAL Notes para 42 with further references.

3.1. Inquisitorial or Adversarial Proceedings?

21-33 It is a continental European tradition that a court takes the initiative in directing the ascertainment of the facts and the law. For that purpose it may conduct its own examination of witnesses. Litigation in common law countries is, on the other hand, traditionally adversarial.[43] In adversarial proceedings the principle is that the parties arrive at the truth by each leading evidence, and then testing that evidence through cross-examination of the relevant witnesses.

21-34 While these characteristics are pertinent in court procedures, arbitration proceedings are more flexible. The parties and the tribunal may agree to conduct proceedings in an adversarial or an inquisitorial way,[44] or in a hybrid[45] manner. Often a blend of inquisitorial and adversarial procedure is the best solution. Even where an inquisitorial procedure is followed, it is important that the matters which are to form the basis of the tribunal's decision should be made available for examination and critical analysis by the parties. It is desirable for the tribunal to make use of its general experience and expertise in making its decisions, but where it intends to rely on specific points, these should be put to the parties for examination and comment.[46]

21-35 A harmonising approach would allow a tribunal to permit cross-examination to proceed before the tribunal members put their questions to a witness. This does not prevent a tribunal from, in civil law fashion, exploring matters at length that one or both parties had not viewed as central to their argument. At the same time, this sequence permits the parties to present the case that they think should be advanced, without undue intervention from the tribunal.

---

43 The case management system introduced with the 1999 Civil Procedure Rules in England is a clear indication that a traditional adversarial procedure is moving towards a mild inquisitorial system. This is also the case with recent reforms in the United States and Japan.

44 See Tateishi, "Inquisitorial Approach in Dispute Resolution", 44 *Wave Length Bulletin of the Japanese Shipping Exchange* 8 (March 2002).

45 Such an approach was taken in the Iran-US Claims Tribunal. See Holtzmann, "Fact-finding by the Iran-United States Claims Tribunal", in Lillich (ed), *Fact-Finding before International Tribunals*, 101 *et seq.*

46 There are not many reported cases where an award was challenged because the tribunal based its award on arguments not discussed by the parties. Such a process can be seen as excess of the tribunal's authority. Nevertheless, authority exists to support the proposition that any issue that is inextricably tied up with the merits of the underlying dispute may properly be decided by the arbitrator. See *Dighello v Busconi*, 673 F Supp 85, 87 (D Conn 1987), *aff'd mem* 849 F 2d 1467 (2d Cir 1988).

21-36 The choice of the place of arbitration normally has no impact on the style of proceedings. It is the selection of lawyers and arbitrators and their background which may influence the way the proceedings are conducted.[47]

21-37 The choice of institution should not be a determinative factor as to the nature of the proceedings either. In an award made in the Zurich Chamber of Commerce an interesting distinction was made

> As the Arbitral Tribunal pointed out at the Hearing of 9 January 1996, the question of jurisdiction is under the inquisitorial system and outside the ambit of the adversarial system which is normally followed on the merits of the case. Accordingly, the Arbitral Tribunal is not limited to the allegations of facts presented to it by the parties. It is on the contrary perfectly proper for an arbitral tribunal to go out on its own and find facts which establish its own jurisdiction.[48]

21-38 English Arbitration Act section 34(2)(g) provides that in the absence of agreement it is for the tribunal to decide "whether and to what extent the tribunal should itself take the initiative in ascertaining the facts and the law."

21-39 A survey indicates that only a few arbitration laws favour conduct of proceedings in adversarial[49] or inquisitorial[50] manner. In any event, it appears that the provisions that favour adversarial or inquisitorial proceedings are not mandatory. Most other laws empower the tribunal to determine the proceedings with regard to ascertaining the facts and the law. Many laws allow for a mixed system.[51] The tribunal should not be bound by any rules applicable in local court proceedings.[52]

---

[47] See Redfern and Hunter, *International Commercial Arbitration*, para 6-12, with references to two unpublished cases (*Oranzio de Nora Impianti Elettrochimici v The Government of Kuwait* and ICC Case no 1776).

[48] See award in case no 273/95, 31 May 1996, *Raw material processor (Hungary) and Processing group (Argentina) v Raw material seller (Russian Federation)*, XXIII YBCA 128 (1998).

[49] Brazil, Arbitration Law Article 21(2). But see Article 8 regarding arbitration agreement and Article 22(1) regarding evidence where the arbitration tribunal can ascertain facts and law in an inquisitorial manner; Portugal, Law no 31/86 Article 16(1).

[50] Austria, CCP Article 587(1); Iraq, Law of Civil Procedure Article 267; New Zealand, Arbitration Act 1996 section 3(1)(a) of the Second Schedule (optional rules); Singapore, International Arbitration Act 1994 Article 12(3); Japan, Draft Arbitration Law Article 27(1).

[51] See, *e.g.*, Model Law Articles 18 and 23; England, Arbitration Act section 34(2)(g) (at the discretion of the tribunal); France, NCPC Article 1460; Switzerland, PIL Article 182(2).

[52] See, *e.g.*, France, NCPC Article 1460.

3.2. Timetable, Written Submissions, and Hearings

(a) Timetable

21-40 The tribunal will normally establish in a separate document a timetable which it intends to follow for the conduct of the arbitration.[53] In preparing the timetable the tribunal must take into account the complexity and the circumstances of the case, the anticipated amount of evidence to be produced and presented, as well as suggestions of the parties and their counsel. In appropriate circumstances the timetable can always be amended.

(b) Hearings or documents only?

21-41 Parties may agree in the arbitration clause how they want the proceedings to be conducted, *i.e.*, orally only, documents only, or mixed. In most cases it is advisable to make such a determination in the light of the actual dispute, ideally in consultation with the tribunal. Some degree of flexibility should be maintained throughout the proceedings, For instance, if the parties decide for a documents only process, they should be able to change the choice to a mixed arbitration by agreement.

21-42 The opportunity of the parties to present their arguments orally is a fundamental element of the proceedings in both the common and civil law litigation systems. In principle and in the absence of an agreement to the contrary, a hearing should be held in most arbitration proceedings.[54] Consequently most arbitration laws[55] and rules[56] require the tribunal to hear the parties, unless the parties have expressly waived that right. However, in France

---

[53] See, *e.g.*, ICC Rules Article 18(4).

[54] See Wilbeforce, "Written Briefs and Oral Advocacy", 5 *Arb Int* 348 (1989); Borris, "Common Law and Civil Law: Fundamental Differences and Their Impact on Arbitration" 2 *ADRLJ* 92 (1995) 95.

[55] Unlike arbitration rules, only a few arbitration laws have specific provisions. See, *e.g.*, Model Law Article 24; China, Arbitration Law Article 39; England, Arbitration Act section 33; France, NCPC Article 1494; Germany, ZPO section 1047; Netherlands, CCP Article 1039; Sweden, Arbitration Act section 24; Switzerland, PIL Article 182.

[56] See, *e.g.*, UNCITRAL Rules Article 15(2); AAA ICDR Articles 16, 20; CIETAC Articles 6, 32; CEPANI Article 25; DIS Section 28; Iran-US Claims Tribunal Article 15(2); ICC Articles 20, 21; LCIA Article 19(1); LMAA Term 14; ICAC Rule 27 (hearing only); NAI Article 26; SIAC Rule 22; Stockholm Institute Article 25; Vienna Article 14(1); WIPO Article 53.

arbitration tribunals can decide to dispense with hearings and reach their decisions on the basis of the parties' written submissions.[57]

21-43 Arbitration proceedings conducted orally only can be attractive to settle very simple issues. The tribunal may require a meeting as soon as the argumentation becomes sophisticated or documentary evidence has to be submitted in support of the claim or the response to it.[58]

21-44 An arbitration without hearings, a documents only arbitration, can also be attractive in some cases. It will save time and money, including travel and extensive legal costs. Therefore documents are practically suited to disputes between parties from different parts of the world where the amount at issue is relatively small. The main pitfall of a documents-only arbitration is that one party may not be in a position to develop its case properly and the arbitrators will not be able to ask simple clarifying questions. However, clarification questions submitted in writing will almost invariably be possible.

21-45 A *mixed arbitration* may well combine the best of both documents only and oral proceedings. The choice of an oral only or a mixed arbitration is an issue which touches upon the cultural differences of the parties and the arbitrators. Common law lawyers are more accustomed than civil law lawyers to extensive oral argument. Civil lawyers attach much greater importance on written submissions.

21-46 The arbitration tribunal in deciding these matters will normally estimate the necessary (minimum) length of the hearings, whether they will be continuous or arranged in instalments, and the format of the hearings. Before the hearing some tribunals will give the parties a fixed time during which to present their case. This will include both witness statements and oral submissions.

21-47 Where a hearing is held minutes of the hearing are often taken. Minutes will normally include indication of the place, date and names of the parties and their representatives attending, the names of the arbitrators and interpreters and other participants of the hearing. Most importantly they will contain a precise description of the proceedings during the hearing and will also bear the signature of the arbitrators.[59] Another way of recording the content of the hearing is by tape-recording or production of a full transcript of the session. Advanced

---

[57] See Fouchard Gaillard Goldman *on International Commercial Arbitration*, 706, para 1296.

[58] See van Houtte, "Conduct of Arbitral Proceedings", in Šarčević (ed), *Essays*, 113, 117.

[59] See, *e.g.*, Economic Chamber of Czech Republic Arbitration Court Rules and Principles 2002 section 30.

technology, such as voice recognition software, facilitates the production of full records of the hearings which can prove invaluable to the parties and the tribunal.

(c) Written submissions

21-48 Comprehensive written submissions are a well-established feature of the international arbitration process. This is, however, an area where different cultures in the conduct of proceedings clash.[60] The civil law idea that all important issues be fully expressed and elaborated in writing is increasingly the norm in international arbitration. These submissions should tell the story, explain the facts and state the legal positions and contentions of the parties. They should all be produced before the hearing.

21-49 The Model Law sets down the accepted international standard for written submissions. Article 2 provides

> Within the period of time agreed by the parties or determined by the arbitral tribunal, the claimant shall state the facts supporting his claim, the points at issue and the relief or remedy sought, and the respondent shall state his defence in respect of these particulars, unless the parties have otherwise agreed as to the required elements of such statements. The parties may submit with their statements all documents they consider to be relevant or may add a reference to the documents or other evidence they will submit.

21-50 This follows a continental style of proceedings, according to which parties make representations as to the facts, not as to the law. It is usual practice though that parties will also make submissions as to the law supporting their claim or defence. Most modern arbitration systems rely on a "ping pong" type exchange of (written) arguments with numerous exhibits. It is essential that the tribunal communicates clearly to the parties its expectations for a certain type of written submission.

21-51 In practice the full written submissions of the parties are normally prepared at an early stage of the proceedings. As a matter of emerging harmonised international arbitration practice these submissions normally include:

- the facts supporting their claim, or defence or counter-claim;
- legal issues in dispute;
- the relief or remedy sought;

---

60 See Lew and Shore, "International Commercial Arbitration: Harmonising Cultural Differences", 54-Aug *Disp Resol J* 33 (1999).

- contentions about the grounds for jurisdiction of the arbitration tribunal;
- submissions concerning the law governing the arbitration and the law applicable to the substance of the dispute;
- the legal argument;
- detailed specification of amounts of damages claimed; and
- requests for the reimbursement of arbitration expenses and counsel fees.

21-52 A claimant who is confident about his case and wishes to avoid unreasonable delays should present all relevant facts and documents at the first stage of proceedings. Failure to do so may give the respondent an opportunity to delay the proceedings. A party that raises new facts at a later stage of proceedings without reasonable ground and delays the process may be penalised and forced to bear the additional costs caused as a result.[61]

21-53 In ICC proceedings several written submissions are made prior to the terms of reference, *e.g.*, request for arbitration, answer, counterclaim, answer to counterclaim.[62] These early written statements have considerable importance and will have an impact on the drafting of the terms of reference and the composition of the arbitration tribunal. Initial written submissions are of lesser importance under the UNCITRAL Rules.[63]

21-54 There are few differences between the rules on the required written submissions. Under LCIA Rules, after the parties have delivered the Request for Arbitration and Answer, written submissions consisting of a statement of case, statement of defence, and statement of reply follow each other within certain time limits. The written submissions should be accompanied by all essential documents on which the party concerned relies and by any other relevant samples or exhibits.[64]

21-55 AAA ICDR Rules provide for the exchange of initial statements of claim and defence,[65] to be followed by additional written statements should the tribunal so decide.[66]

---

[61] Van Houtte, "Conduct of Arbitral Proceedings", in Šarčević (ed), *Essays*, 113, 121.

[62] See ICC Rules Articles 4 and 5.

[63] See UNCITRAL Rules Articles 18 and 19.

[64] LCIA Article 15(6). The WIPO Rules take a similar approach with regard to statement of claim (Article 41) and statement of defence and further written statements (Article 42).

[65] AAA ICDR Rules Article 2.

[66] AAA ICDR Rules Article 17(1).

21-56 ICSID Rules use the American terms memorial and counter-memorial[67], to be followed, if necessary, by a reply and a rejoinder.[68] The memorial shall contain a statement of the relevant facts, a statement of law and a submission. The counter-memorial, the reply and the rejoinder shall respond to the statements and submissions made in the memorial and add any additional facts, statement of law or submissions of the respondent.[69]

21-57 Written submissions are normally exchanged sequentially, *i.e.* first the claimant and the respondent answers. If there is a counterclaim, the respondent would normally submit its counterclaim at the same time as the response to the claimant's claim and that document will then be called "answer and counterclaim" or "defence and counterclaim". The claimant will then submit the reply to the respondent's counterclaim and sometimes may also be allowed to submit a rejoinder to the respondents' response.[70] It is exceptional, but sometimes useful, that the arbitration tribunal requires the parties to make their written submissions simultaneously. This can help to expedite the proceedings.

(d) Place(s) of hearing

21-58 The place where the hearings are to be held or where the evidence of witnesses is to be taken is important. It may be the seat of arbitration or another place. This must be determined by agreement between the parties or, failing such agreement, by the arbitration tribunal.

21-59 It is common practice that the arbitration tribunal may, for reasons of convenience, hold hearings at locations other than the place of arbitration without changing the seat of arbitration. Indeed, the choice of seat of arbitration does not normally impose any obligation on the arbitration tribunal to have all hearings and evidence gathering meetings at this very place. Most arbitration laws[71] and

---

67 On the terminology see Redfern and Hunter, *International Commercial Arbitration,* para 6-56.

68 ICSID Rules Article 31.

69 ICSID Rules Article 31(3).

70 See Redfern and Hunter, *International Commercial Arbitration,* para 6-55.

71 See, *e.g.*, Model Law Article 20(1). See similar formulations in Belgium, Judicial Code Article 1693(2); England, Arbitration Act section 53 (impliedly); Germany, ZPO section 1043(2); Netherlands, CCP Article 1037(3).

rules[72] authorise the tribunal to hold hearings in other places then the seat of the arbitration.

(e) Language of hearing

21-60 Arbitration proceedings may be conducted in any language convenient for the parties and the tribunal. This is not necessarily the language at the seat of arbitration. The parties are free to agree the language of proceedings.[73] The freedom of parties to choose the language of arbitration and, failing that, the power of the tribunal to determine that language is reflected in all major institutional rules.[74] The choice of the parties may be contained in the arbitration clause or in the terms of reference. The language of the arbitration agreement can also account for an implied choice of language.[75] The language of the substantive contract and used in the initial documents of arbitration may be another presumption for an implied choice of language. If the parties cannot agree on the language of proceedings, then the arbitration tribunal has to determine the language which is most appropriate for the proceedings, considering also the convenience of the parties.

21-61 The language of the arbitration should be used, in principle, for all written and oral submissions and for the award. Generally documentary evidence submitted in its original language should be accompanied by a translation into the language of the arbitration. To the extent that the parties include voluminous exhibits, arbitration tribunals may accept documents in the original language, thus restricting the translation of documents provided the parties and the tribunal are conversant with those languages. Parties are naturally entitled to express themselves in their native language, provided they arrange for interpretation in the language of proceedings at their own expense.[76]

21-62 It is convenient but not necessary that the proceedings are conducted in one language and that the arbitrators have a degree of fluency in that language. In

---

[72] See, *e.g.*, UNCITRAL Rules Article 16(2) and (3); AAA ICDR Article 13(2); DIS section 21(2); ICC Article 14(2) and (3); LCIA Article 16(2); ICAC section 7(2) and (3) (only within the territory of Russian Federation); NAI Article 22; Vienna Article 1(3); WIPO Article 39(b).

[73] See, *e.g.*, Model Law Article 22(1) and Holtzmann and Neuhaus, *Model Law*, 628-630.

[74] See, *e.g.*, UNCITRAL Rules Article 17; AAA ICDR Rules Article 14; CIETAC Article 75; CEPANI Articles 12, 22; DIS sections 6(3) and 22; Iran-US Claims Tribunal Article 17; ICC Article 16; LCIA Article 17; MIGA Article 29; ICAC Rule 10; NAI Article 40; SIAC Rule 20; Stockholm Institute Article 23; Vienna Article 6; WIPO Article 40; Zurich Article 22.

[75] See AAA ICDR Article 14.

[76] See UNCITRAL Report, *ILM* 1343 (1985).

fact the IBA Rules of Ethics for International Arbitrators require knowledge of the language of the arbitration and provide in Article 2(2)

> A prospective arbitrator shall accept an appointment only if he is fully satisfied that he is competent to determine the issues in dispute, and has an adequate knowledge of the language of the arbitration.

21-63 The language of the arbitration may impose a moral obligation on the arbitrators and a *de facto* restriction concerning the selection of arbitrators and the selection of the lawyers representing the parties.

(f) Notices and time limits

21-64 Tribunals will invariably fix time limits for the submission of written pleadings. Time limits set be the tribunal should be seen as "target time limits"[77] rather than deadlines; they should be extended when it is reasonable and fair to do so. When deciding whether to admit late submissions a tribunal should consider the circumstances of the cases, the need for equality and fairness, the possibility of prejudice to the other party and the requirements for orderly conduct of proceedings.[78] An unreasonable rejection of a late submission may be in breach of due process. Some institutional rules provide for time limits to reply to the request for arbitration. They often opt for a 30 days time limit[79], less often for a 45 days[80] time limit. Almost all institutional rules provide for the possibility of extending the time limit[81], when justified, and only few provide for the possibility of shortening the time limit[82], when it is appropriate to expedite the proceedings.

3.3. Power of Tribunal to Decide Procedural Issues

21-65 It is generally accepted that the arbitration tribunal has the power to decide interim procedural issues, such as the extension of time and requests for document production. In practice tribunals often request the parties to agree that

---

77 See Redfern and Hunter, *International Commercial Arbitration*, para 6-57.

78 See Holtzmann, "Fact-finding by the Iran-United States Claims Tribunal", in Lillich (ed), *Fact-Finding before International Tribunals*, 101, III-1.

79 See, *e.g.*, LCIA Article 15; CAMCA Article 19; CIETAC Article 19; SIAC Rule 18.

80 See, *e.g.*, UNCITRAL Rules Article 23; SIAC Article 18(5); AAA ICDR Rules Article 17(2). In all the mentioned rules 45 days are deemed as the maximum period unless otherwise agreed.

81 See, *e.g.*, ICC Article 5; LCIA Articles 4, 15; UNCITRAL Rules Articles 22; Geneva Rule 6, CAMCA Article 19; Vienna Article 8; CEPANI Article 15; AIA Article 10; NAI Article 3; SIAC Article 18(5); AAA ICDR Article 4, 17.

82 See, *e.g.*, ICC Article 32; Geneva Article 31.

the chairman shall have the power to act alone in relation to procedural issues, unless one of the parties expressly requests all three arbitrators to be involved.[83] This is essential in cases where the co-arbitrators are elusive, and when the matter is urgent, when, for instance, the requested extended period is to expire before the tribunal can have an opportunity to confer.

4. Representation of Parties

21-66 In almost all international arbitrations parties are represented by legal counsel of their choice. While in court proceedings parties are normally represented by local qualified counsel, in international arbitration the parties may select counsel on the basis of their experience. There are no restrictions on the choice of lawyers or even the lawyers being qualified. Parties can choose lawyers in whom they have confidence even though they are not qualified in the law of the place of arbitration or the applicable law.

21-67 Few arbitration rules expressly allow for representation by non-lawyers.[84] There are some institutions where lawyers may not attend without the permission of the tribunal.[85] There are also cases where it may be more appropriate for parties to be represented by non-lawyers, *e.g.*, engineers, accountants. In such cases parties will invariably have legal assistance within the representative team.

21-68 There were some jurisdictions which precluded foreign lawyers from representing parties in arbitration. These included Malaysia, Singapore and Japan. This has changed.

21-69 In Malaysia the Supreme Court ruled in 1989 that foreign lawyers may represent parties in arbitration proceedings held in Malaysia.[86]

---

83 Hunter, "The Procedural Powers of Arbitrators under the English Act", 13 *Arb Int* 345 (1997) 357. See also, *e.g.*, England, Arbitration Act section 34(3).

84 See UNCITRAL Rules Article 4; AAA ICDR Article 12; ICC Article 21(4); LCIA Article 18; LMAA Third Schedule 14; NAI Article 21; WIPO Article 13. The silence of the other rules should not be read as tacit exclusion of non-lawyers. Tateishi, "Recent Japanese Case Law in Relation to International Arbitration", 17(4) *J Int'l Arb* 63 (2000) 66; Rivkin, "Keeping Lawyers out of International Arbitrations", *Int'l Fin L Rev* 11 (1990).

85 See LME Rules Article 8(1). See also *Henry Bath & Son Ltd v Birgby Products* [1962] 1 Lloyds Rep 389 (QBD).

86 *Government of Malaysia v Zublin - Muhibbah Joint Venture, consisting of Ed Zublin AG and Muhibbah Engineering Sdn Bhd*, XVI YBCA 166 (1991) (Supreme Court, 2 January 1990). The

21-70 In Singapore, the Legal Profession (Amendment No 2) Act 1991 overturned the High Court decision in *Turner Pte Ltd v Builders Federal*[87] that ruled against foreign lawyers appearing in arbitration proceedings.[88] Singapore was fairly rapid in curing the defect by enacting the Model Law and amending the Legal Profession Act. As a result foreign lawyers can represent parties provided they have local legal representation for matters involving Singapore law.

21-71 Recently, the Supreme Court of California held that a New York lawyer cannot represent a party in arbitration proceedings held in California. The court held that representing a party in arbitration is legal practice which, in the State of California, is reserved for members of the California Bar. The implication was that the counsel was unable to recover his fee when he failed a claim for it.[89] The court, fortunately, made an express exception from its rule with regard to international arbitration.

21-72 The English Arbitration Act in section 36 takes a liberal approach

> Unless otherwise agreed by the parties, a party to arbitral proceedings may be represented in the proceedings by a lawyer or other person chosen by him.

21-73 It seems that this is the approach taken in all modern arbitration laws, either as a result of legislation or case law.[90] In Japan, rule 4 of the new rules of

---

High Court decision is published in 2 *Current Law Journal* 112 (July 1990). The Supreme Court stated:

> Having heard submissions from ... parties, and ... from the Bar Council, I gave a decision ... that a person representing a party in an arbitration proceeding need not be an advocate and solicitor within the meaning of the Legal Profession Act 1976; and that the said Act has no application to an arbitration proceeding in West Malaysia.

87 *Turner (East Asia) Pte Ltd (Singapore) v Builders Federal (Hong Kong) Ltd (Hong Kong) and Josef Gartner & Co (FR Germany)*, (1988) 5(3) J Int'l Arb 139; (1988) 3(4) Mealey's IAR 6-9 and C1-C26; (1989) XIV YBCA 224 (High Court of Singapore 30 March 1988).

88 The High Court of Singapore, although it acknowledged that the Legal Profession Act has no application to arbitration proceedings, ruled that representation of the respondents by a New York firm would contravene sections of the Act in its 1988 version. See the critical discussion in Lowenfeld, "Singapore and the Local Bar: Aberration or Ill Omen?", 5(3) *J Int'l Arb* 71 (1988); Rivkin, "Restrictions on Foreign Counsel in International Arbitrations", XVI *YBCA* 402 (1991).

89 *Birbrower, Montabano, Condon & Frank v The Superior Court of Santa Clara County*, 1998 Cal Lexis 2; 1998 WL 1346 (Cal 1/5/98).

90 In France see Cour de cassation, 19 June 1979, *SARL Primor v Société d'exploitation industrielle de Bétaigne*, Rev Arb 487 (1979). See also Rivkin, "Restrictions on Foreign Counsel in International Arbitration" XVI *YBCA* 402 (1991). The survey identified in the early 1990s Singapore, Turkey, Japan, Portugal and Yugoslavia as arbitration venues which do not

the JCAA omit the reference to *bengoshi*, thus allowing foreign lawyers as counsel to arbitration in Japan[91] and following international standards. Article 21 Arbitration Rules of the Singapore International Arbitration Centre follows the same trend.

21-74 A final point with regard to legal representation relates to the existence of power to represent a party and the proof of such power. The tribunal or arbitration institution may require proof of such authority at an early stage. Article 21(4) ICC Rules requires "duly authorised representatives". Article 18(2) LCIA Rules gives a right to the tribunal to require proof of the authority of the representatives. The tribunal has discretion as to when and what form of proof of authority may be requested.[92] A number of rules or institutions require the parties to communicate directly with the tribunal in writing to confirm the appointment of their representatives.[93] In practice many tribunals require the lawyers to provide a power of attorney confirming their authority to represent the client.

5. Default Proceedings

21-75 There is a general assumption that all parties will co-operate in arbitration proceedings. However, there are cases where one party, normally the respondent, will refuse or just ignore the arbitration. In these circumstances the defaulting party may undermine or, at least, slow down the proceedings. The effect of a defaulting party raises practical questions for both the tribunal and the other party as it may have implications on the enforceability of the award.

21-76 Default of appearance is not unknown in court proceedings. However, in litigation, courts possess coercive power and can proceed without the participation of one party ("*ex parte*"). International arbitration by contrast is based on the agreement of parties to submit their disputes to arbitration and default of appearance raises due process concerns.[94] The question is whether and

allow for foreign legal counsels. In almost all these countries the practice or the law has changed.

91 See Stevens, "Japan Commercial Arbitration Rules Revisited", 9(3) *Arb Int* 317 (1993); Stevens, "Foreign Lawyer Advocacy in International Arbitrations in Japan", 2 *JCAA Newsletter* 1 (1997). See also Nakamura, "Continuing Misconceptions of International Commercial Arbitration in Japan", 18(6) *J Int'l Arb* 641 (2001) 642-3.

92 SIAC Article 21 vests the tribunal with similar discretion.

93 See, *e.g.*, ICSID Rules Article 18(1); UNCITRAL Rules Article 4; WIPO Article 13(a).

94 See, *e.g.*, New York Convention Article V(1)(b).

in what circumstances a tribunal can make a default award.[95] Hence, it is essential that the tribunal has the power to proceed if one of the parties fails to appear. Most recent arbitration laws[96] and rules[97] have dealt with default proceedings in an unequivocal support of the arbitration proceedings.

21-77 It is essential that tribunals intending to make use of their power to render a default award exercise maximum care and specify the circumstances in the text of the award.[98] Such a practise will disarm a party who will try to resist enforcement of any award rendered.

5.1. Forms of Default

21-78 There are four circumstances which can be classified as failure to participate in the proceedings:

- When a party refuses to take any part in the proceedings because the tribunal allegedly lacks jurisdiction.[99]
- When a party refuses to reply to communications from the tribunal or to comply with procedural directions, such as submissions of pleadings, or production of documents.[100]
- When a party does not notify any unwillingness to participate, but creates such an unreasonable delay which could be treated as having abandoned its right to present its case.[101]

---

95 For a comparison of default awards and default judgments see Steyn, "Remedies Against the Reluctant Respondent: The Position Under English Law", 5(3) *Arb Int* 294 (1989).

96 See, *e.g.*, Model Law Article 25; Canada, Act to Amend CC and CCP in Respect of Arbitration Article 944(5); China, Arbitration Law Article 42; Colombia, Law 315 of 1996 Article 22; Czech Republic, Arbitration Act 1994 Article 21; England, Arbitration Act section 41; Germany, ZPO section 1048; Hungary, Act LXXI 1994 section 35; Japan, Draft Arbitration Law Article 26; Netherlands, CCP Article 1040; US, FAA Section 4. France, NCPC contains no specific provision.

97 See, *e.g.*, UNCITRAL Rules Article 28; WIPO Article 56; MIGA Rules Article 49; IACAC Article 28; AAA ICDR Article 23; CIETAC Article 42; DIS Section 30; JCAA Article 28; NAI Article 36. See also Tunik, "Default Proceedings in International Commercial Arbitration", 1(2) *IntALR* 86 (1998).

98 See van den Berg (ed), *ICCA Congress Series no 5.*

99 See, *e.g.*, Award on Re-opening, *ad hoc* arbitration, August 1974, *British Petroleum Company (Libya) Ltd v The Government of the Libyan Arab Republic*, 53 ILR 297 (1979), V YBCA 158 (1980).

100 See, *e.g.*, Model Law Article 25(a) and (b). For a commentary see Holtzmann and Neuhaus, *Model Law*, 698-701 and legislative history, 701-716.

- When a party disrupts the hearing so that it becomes impossible to conduct it in an orderly manner.[102]

5.2. Proceedings in the Absence of one or more Parties

21-79 The clear intention in the laws or rules relating to default of appearance is to allow arbitrators to continue proceedings and render an award or to dismiss the proceedings, if it is the claimant who defaults. This power is essential in order to safeguard the effectiveness of international commercial arbitration.

21-80 A default procedure, however, is subject to two conditions. First, the parties should not have agreed upon excluding default proceedings or provided for special protection in case of default. Second, the provision can only operate, if the tribunal is of the opinion that the party which failed to take part in the proceedings does not have a "sufficient cause"[103] for its absence.[104]

21-81 Default of claimant and default of respondent should be treated differently. The Model Law covers four different scenarios and differentiates between claimant and respondent in only two of them.

- Under Article 25(a) where a claimant initiated arbitration proceedings but fails to communicate the statement of claim, the tribunal could terminate the proceedings and order the claimant to pay costs. An order for termination should not be automatic. The tribunal must warn the claimant, at least once, normally twice, before terminating the proceedings. A question remains whether the tribunal should dismiss the proceedings "with" or "without prejudice", *i.e.*, having determined or not determined the substantive issues.[105]

---

101 It is worth noting that arbitration tribunals are normally very liberal with deadlines as they want to avoid unfair hearing allegations. See Redfern and Hunter, *International Commercial Arbitration,* 337, para 6-109. See also Irish Supreme Court, 11 July 1989, *SH Ltd v Grangeford Structures Ltd,* 5(2) Mealey's IAR B1-5 (1990). See also ICSID Convention Article 45(2). On the application of this rule by ICSID tribunals see, *e.g.*, ICSID case no ARB/83/2, 31 March 1986, *Liberian Eastern Timber Corp v The Government of the Republic of Liberia,* 26 ILM 647 (1987), XIII YBCA 35 (1988).

102 Redfern and Hunter, *International Commercial Arbitration,* paras 6-108 and 6-109.

103 This phrase was debated extensively in the drafting of the Model Law. See Holtzmann and Neuhaus, *Model Law,* 698-716.

104 Van Houtte, "Conduct of Arbitral Proceedings", in Šarčević (ed), *Essays,* 113, 122.

105 For example, in ICC award in case no 6998 (1994), *Hotel and Hotel v Joint Venture Co and Joint Venture Co,* XXI YBCA 54 (1996) para 83, the tribunal held that "without prejudice" refers to future rights but not to rights prior to the hearing date.

- Under Article 25(b) where a respondent fails to communicate the statement of defence in time, the tribunal will invariably admit late submissions. The problem is normally where the respondent does not make any submissions and ignores the tribunal's communications. In such case, under Article 25(b) the tribunal has the power to continue the proceedings *ex parte* and make a binding award.[106] The failure of the respondent to react to the claim should not be treated as an admission of the claimant's allegations. The tribunal will have to gather evidence and critically assess the claimant's submissions; it should determine the issues, not merely take arguments from one party.[107] The tribunal will also have to ensure that the defaulting party has been notified in an appropriate manner, normally by registered letter.
- Where the claimant or the respondent fails to appear at a hearing or in the entire proceedings,[108] without sufficient cause, under Article 25(c) the tribunal may continue the proceedings and render an award on the basis of evidence before it.
- Where the claimant or the respondent fails to produce documentary evidence, the tribunal pursuant to Article 27 can request a court to compel the party to submit this evidence, or the tribunal may continue the proceedings and render an award on the basis of the evidence before it.

21-82 If a party fails to comply with a tribunal's directions, under certain laws and rules the tribunal is entitled to issue a peremptory order,[109] and failing

---

[106] See also England Arbitration Act section 41(4)

> If without showing sufficient cause a party-
>
> (a) fails to attend or be represented at an oral hearing of which due notice was given, or
>
> (b) where matters are to be dealt with in writing, fails after due notice to submit written evidence or make written submissions, the tribunal may continue the proceedings in the absence of that party or, as the case may be, without any written evidence or submissions on his behalf, and may make an award on the basis of the evidence before it.

[107] See England, Arbitration Act section 33 and DAC Report, February 1996, para 208. See also ICSID Article 45(1). See ICC case law to the same effect, *e.g.*, ICC award no 6670 (1992), *Financial institution based in France v Two companies*, 119 Clunet 1010 (1992); ICC award no 7153 (1992), *Austrian party v Yugoslav party*, 119 Clunet 1005 (1992); ICC award no 7701 (1994), 8(2) *ICC Bulletin* 66 (1997).

[108] The ICC Rules were modified in 1998 to reflect the fact that a party can default throughout the whole proceedings or at "any stage thereof." See Derains and Schwartz, *ICC Rules*, 102.

[109] See, *e.g.*, England, Arbitration Act section 41(5):

> If without showing sufficient cause a party fails to comply with any order or directions of the tribunal, the tribunal may make a peremptory order to the same effect, prescribing such time for compliance with it as the tribunal considers appropriate.

compliance with such order it is entitled after notice to the party in default to proceed *ex parte*.[110] The tribunal should carry on with a hearing *ex parte*, examine whether it has jurisdiction, assess the situation, and determine the issues in dispute.[111] It is also important to give notice to the defaulting party for every stage of the proceedings. Whatever the circumstances the tribunal must at all times act impartially and fairly between the parties.

21-83 On the balance of interests and in the interest of justice it is essential that international commercial arbitration does not accommodate delaying and bad faith driven tactics. The power of a tribunal to make a default award pays service to the effectiveness of international commercial arbitration.[112] The tribunal cannot allow the proceedings to drag on indefinitely if one of the parties is not actively participating in the process. In any event, there must be evidence that the defaulting party was summoned in an adequate manner and with reasonable notice. Therefore notices should preferably be made by means which provide proof of receipt and it may even be advisable for the tribunal to repeat the notification shortly before the hearing and other notable dates in the proceedings. All principles of due process must have been regarded. If that is the case then the default award should be enforceable.[113]

6. Expedited Procedures

21-84 The development of arbitration world-wide and the emergence of formalism in procedure have slowed down arbitration proceedings significantly. To overcome this problem expedited procedures or fast-track arbitrations have been introduced. Historically, swift arbitrations are not a novelty. Quality, commodity and some motor insurance arbitrations are numerically significant but legally indifferent. Modern fast arbitration concerns international commercial

[110] *Bremer Vulkan v South India Shipping* [1981] AC 904, 987 E-F.

[111] See Redfern and Hunter, *International Commercial Arbitration*, para 6-110.

[112] See Hanotiau, "Default Procedure", in *International Commercial Arbitration, Procedure and Evidence* (Kluwer 1985); Wenger, "Säumnis und Säumnisfolgen im internationalen Schiedsverfahren", in Reymond and Bucher (eds), *Recueil des travaux suisses sur l'arbitrage international*, 245 (Schulthess 1984).

[113] See, *e.g.*, Landgericht Bremen, 8 June 1967, *IPRspr* 1966-1967 no 283, II *YBCA* 234 (1977); High Court of the Hong Kong Special Administrative Region, Court of First Instance, 19 January 1998; *Ng Fung Hong Ltd v ABC*, 13(2) Mealey's IAR D-1 (1998); Court of Appeal Tokyo (2d Civ Sect) 14 March 1963, I *YBCA* 194 (1976); Singapore High Court, 29 September 1995 *Hainan Machinery Import and Export Corporation (PR China) v Donald & McArthy Pte Ltd (Singapore)*, [1996] 1 Singapore L Rep 34, (1997) XXII YBCA 771.

arbitrations with often complex and challenging legal issues which cannot wait too long to be resolved.

21-85 Expedited proceedings, in which parties agree to shorten the time limits that would otherwise apply, can be found in a number of institutions either explicitly[114] or as an expression of party autonomy. Where parties agree on a procedural timetable with stringent deadlines the arbitration may be referred to as fast-track.[115]

21-86 The widely publicised *Panhandle* case is an example of ICC fast-track arbitration. The parties had agreed that in the event of a dispute, certain issues were to be resolved by the arbitration tribunal within two months of the request for arbitration. These issues concerned the determination of the price in a long-term gas supply contract between Canada and the United States. It took nine weeks for the arbitration proceedings and the award to be rendered by the tribunal.[116]

21-87 The development of fast-track or expedited arbitration is welcome and may contribute to the appeal of arbitration to potential users who have been reluctant because of costs and time spent. However, fast-tract or expedited proceedings can only be used for issues which are capable of being resolved in

---

[114] See, *e.g.*, WIPO Expedited Rules 1994; Stockholm Institute Rules for Expedited Arbitrations 1995; CAMCA Arbitration Rules 1996 Article 39; Venice Arbitration Court Rules 1998 Article 39; JCAA Arbitration Rules 1996 Articles 52-61; Korean Commercial Arbitration Board Rules 1989/1993 Articles 57-61; Geneva Rules Article 31. See also "Chapter 2: Accelerating the procedures: the parties" with contributions by Werner, Freyer, Bond and Derains in Davis (ed), *Improving International Arbitration*, 99-120.

[115] See, *e.g.*, ICA Rules 1998 Article 43; LMAA Terms 1997/2002, FALCA Rules (Third Schedule of LMAA Terms).

[116] See Rovine, "International Fast-Track Arbitration - Part I: An Overview", 5 *WAMR* 165 (1994); ICC Final award in cases no 7385 (1992) and no 7402 (1992), XVIII *YBCA* 68 (1993). See also Davis, "Fast-Track Arbitration and Fast-Tracking Your Arbitration", 9(4) *Int'l Arb* 14 (1992); Davis (ed), *Improving International Arbitration*; Müller, "Fast-Track Arbitration: Meeting the Demands of the Next Millennium", 15(3) *J Int'l Arb* 5 (1998) with a comparative table. See also the special issue - 10(4) *J Int'l Arb* (1993) with papers by Davis, Lagacé, Volkovitsc, "When Doctrines Meet - Fast –Track Arbitration and the ICC Experience", *ibid*, 69; Silverman, "The Fast-Track Arbitration of the International Chamber of Commerce - The User's Point of View", *ibid*, 113; Smid, "The Expedited Procedure in Maritime and Commodity Arbitrations", *ibid*, 59; Tschanz, "The Chamber of Commerce and Industry of Geneva's Arbitration Rules and their Expedited Procedure", *ibid*, 51; Mustill, "Comments on Fast-Track Arbitration", *ibid*, 121.

such a manner. Price and quality determination are good examples. Sports disputes can also be resolved within a few days.[117]

21-88 Fast-track proceedings may compromise due process or equality of parties.[118] The parties (in particular, the respondent) must have enough time to prepare their cases. Another consideration for fast-track arbitration is to chose a place of arbitration where the local courts can be of assistance in hearing applications to extend time limits.[119]

21-89 In all fast-track arbitrations the tribunal plays a significant role in ensuring that arbitration will be efficient and as rapid as possible. Setting short deadlines may be counterproductive if the parties and their counsel do not co-operate. However, active case management and adequate organisation may contribute to a speedy resolution.[120]

21-90 The NAI Rules have also introduced a unique "summary proceedings mechanism"[121] modelled after the Netherlands Code of Civil Procedure summary proceedings (*kort geding*).[122] The summary proceedings of NAI[123] are automatically available to parties that have agreed on the application of the NAI Rules and the place of arbitration is in the Netherlands, provided that the parties have made a separate agreement to that effect. This mechanism offers a variety of practical and strategic advantages, including the availability of a broad range of reliefs, an extremely expedited process (normally between a few days and few weeks) and reduced legal costs. Further pursuant to Article 1051(3) Netherlands CCP decisions rendered in the context of summary proceedings are classified as awards in the context of the New York Convention.

---

117 See, *e.g.*, Paulsson, "Arbitration of International Sports Disputes", 9 *Arb Int* 359 (1993) 360; Rochat, "Tribunal arbitral du sport: quelle procédure pour quel litige?", in *Arbitration of Sports-Related Disputes: A Collection of Reports and Materials*, delivered at the Swiss Arbitration Association - Court of Arbitration for Sport Conference Held in Lausanne on January 16, 1998, 11 *ASA Special Series* (1998).

118 See Schwartz, "Reconciling Speed with Justice in International Arbitration", in Davis (ed), *Improving International Arbitration*, 44.

119 See Fouchard Gaillard Goldman *on International Commercial Arbitration*, paras 1248 and 1387.

120 See, *e.g.*, Karrer, Lazareff, Caldwell, and Rubino Sammartano, "Chapter 5; Accelerating the procedure: the arbitrator", in Davis (ed), *Improving International Arbitration*, 135. See also Smit, "Fast-Track Arbitration", 2(2) *Am Rev Int Arb* 138 (1991).

121 See NAI Rules Articles 37, 42a-42o.

122 See Netherlands, CCP Article 289 and the reference to this provision in Article 1051.

123 See King and van Leeuwen, "Summary Arbitral Proceedings: A Powerful New Mechanism in NAI Arbitrations", 15(3) *Mealey's IAR* 59 (2000).

21-91 The 1998 NAI Rules establish two alternatives for the use of summary proceedings.

- The first is *an ancillary procedure* that can be used where an arbitration on the merits has been commenced and the tribunal has been constituted.[124] The ancillary procedure can commence at any stage of thc proceedings before an existing tribunal, provided that a party files a request[125] for summary proceedings seeking an immediate provisional measure.[126]
- The second and more interesting alternative is *the stand-alone procedure* which can be invoked where the proceedings have not commenced and the tribunal has not been constituted.[127] Section 4A NAI Rules allows the commencement of summary arbitration proceedings by a party in cases where no arbitration on the merits has been filed, or where such arbitration has been filed but the tribunal has not yet been constituted.[128] The procedures established in Section 4A are designed with speed in mind. The procedure is left to the discretion of the tribunal and typically consists of oral argument by counsel. Parties may produce evidence as they see fit.

---

124 NAI Rules Article 37(6) and (7).
125 NAI Rules Article 37(2).
126 NAI Rules Article 37(1).
127 NAI Rules Articles 42a-42o.
128 NAI Rules Article 42a, in general, and relationship with Article 37 on procedure.

Chapter 22

TAKING EVIDENCE IN INTERNATIONAL ARBITRATION

22-1 In the presentation of every case, parties develop and present factual scenarios which form the basis for their contentions. The claim or defence, and the remedies sought, depend on the existence of certain facts. If the facts vary, the result may not be the same. The establishment of the facts is therefore essential in any arbitration.

22-2 Often arbitrators are told that the facts are not in real dispute. However, the story changes as the two parties present their arguments and contentions. Sometimes, it is like ships passing in the night, rather than colliding head on. This should not really be surprising because the facts are the real basis of the dispute and each party identifies them subjectively. The law and the money involved follow quickly behind.

22-3 The facts on which a party bases its case are often tactically determined. Time is spent deciding what documents should be presented. What information should be withheld unless asked for? Should experts be relied upon? Which witnesses should be presented? What questions should be posed and in what terms? Even issues of the applicable legal rules and the remedies sought are often carefully selected to comply with the facts as claimed.

22-4 Taking and presentation of evidence to the tribunal is one of the key issues of international commercial arbitration. Evidence is crucial to the determination of disputed issues of fact and disputed issues of opinion (presented by experts). In addition, in some legal systems, foreign law must be proven as if it were fact. Establishing the facts and clarifying disputed issues of opinion is essential in assisting the tribunal to reach a decision. Accordingly, many cases are decided on the facts or their interpretation. Historically, at least in England, one of the main reasons for the development of arbitration is that parties wanted more flexibility with respect to taking and presenting evidence.[1]

22-5 International arbitration laws and rules typically contain few specific rules on taking evidence. Hardly any of these rules are mandatory. The 1999 IBA Rules for Taking Evidence in International Commercial Arbitration are not directly applicable; they are optional and have to be adopted. This leaves wide flexibility and discretion to the arbitrators. The procedure for taking evidence depends largely on the nationality, training and legal background, and experience of the arbitrators.[2]

---

1 Veeder, "Evidential Rules in International Commercial Arbitration: From the Tower of London to the New 1999 IBA Rules", 65 *Arbitration* 291 (1999) 292-3.

2 The differences between common and civil law procedures as to the taking of evidence are discussed in Wetter, "The Conduct of the Arbitration", 2(2) *J Int'l Arb* 7 (1985); Marriott, "Evidence in International Arbitration", 5 *Arb Int* 280 (1989); Rubino-Sammartano, "Rules of

22-6 This chapter considers these issues and looks at (1) the lack of sources and the emerging uniform evidentiary rules, including general principles and practices, relating to the taking and presentation of evidence in international commercial arbitration, (2) the major evidentiary means, *i.e.* documents, witnesses, expert evidence, site or subject matter inspections, and (3) the assistance of national courts

1. LIMITED SOURCES AND EMERGING UNIFORM PRACTICES

1.1. Taking Evidence in Common and Civil Law Procedures and in International Commercial Arbitration

22-7 There are considerable differences between common and civil law procedures in relation to the taking of evidence. While such differences are amplified in the context of litigation they are not as significant in international commercial arbitration.

22-8 Often a mixture of the common law and civil law systems of taking evidence is applied or even transplanted in international commercial arbitration. It is, for example, a traditionally continental European idea that a tribunal will take initiative in directing the ascertainment of the facts and the law, including examining of witnesses. Litigation (and often arbitration) in the common law countries is, on the other hand, traditionally adversarial: the principle is that the parties arrive at the truth by each leading evidence and each then testing the evidence led by the other through cross-examination of the relevant witnesses. Certain departures from each system can be seen as, for instance, in England the new Civil Procedure Rules call for more case management by the courts and several civil law legal systems reassure the parties that adversarial procedures are always available.

Evidence in International Arbitration – A Need for Discipline and Harmonization", 3(2) *J Int'l Arb* 87 (1986); Dieryck, "Procédure et moyens de preuve dans l'arbitrage commercial international", *Rev Arb* 267 (1988); "Thorens, L'arbitre international au point de rencontre des traditions du droit civil et de la common law – Deux problèmes liés, l'un à la communication des pièces et l'autre à l'audition des témoins", in *Etudes de droit international en l'honneur de Pierre Lalive* (1993), 693; Paulsson, "Overview of Methods of Presenting Evidence in Different Legal Systems", *ICCA Congress series no 7*, 112.

22-9 Further, in common law court proceedings, experts and witnesses are summoned by the parties; they are examined and cross-examined by the parties' counsel with the judge only asking additional questions. In civil law court proceedings the aim is to find the "objective truth". Therefore witnesses and experts are summoned by the courts, questioned by the judges in the first place with the parties' counsel only asking additional questions. Experts and witness are reimbursed by the courts as to their expenses for their appearance in court and experts receive a fee for their opinion from the courts.

22-10 While it is uncontroversial to state that each arbitration is unique and has its own procedure for presenting the case, it may be daring to go further and identify standard procedures for the taking of evidence.[3] At least the emerging practice for taking of evidence in international commercial arbitration comprises elements of both civil and common law type procedures,[4] other legal systems, and practices specially appropriate for an international process.

22-11 When procedural disputes arise between parties from common and civil law countries, and where they are represented by counsel from those legal systems, the disputes are rarely derivative of the different legal backgrounds. In fact such disputes normally arise because of the different tactical evaluation of the case.[5] Legal representatives of disputing parties in international commercial arbitration will invariably take a flexible approach; the ultimate goal is to convince the tribunal of their position and to disarm the other side.

22-12 Rigid distinctions that exist between civil law and common law approaches are not imposed upon international commercial arbitration. As a general rule in international arbitration written presentations are extensive and are the principal means of introducing evidence. Disclosure of documents (rather

---

[3] See Friedland, "A Standard Procedure for Presenting Evidence in International Arbitration", 11(4) *Mealey's IAR* 4 (1996). See also Hascher, "Principes et pratique de procedure dans l'arbitrage commercial international", 279 *RCADI* 51 (1999) 87 *et seq.*

[4] See, *e.g.*, Friedland, "Combining Civil Law and Common Law Elements in the Presentation of Evidence in International Commercial Arbitration", 12(9) *Mealey's IAR* 25 (1997); Borris, "The Reconciliation of Conflicts Between Common Law and Civil Law Principles in the Arbitration Process", in Frommel and Rider (eds), *Conflicting Legal Cultures*, 1; Lazareff, "International Arbitration: Towards a Common Procedural Approach", in Frommel and Rider (eds), *ibid*, 31; Lowenfeld, "International Arbitration as an Omelette: What Goes into the Mix", in Frommel and Rider (eds), *ibid*, 19; Elsing and Townsend, "Bridging the Common Law-Civil Law Divide in Arbitration", 18 *Arb Int* 59 (2002).

[5] Friedland, "A Standard Procedure for Presenting Evidence in International Arbitration", 11(4) *Mealey's IAR* 4 (1996).

than discovery common law style) takes place only under order of the arbitration tribunal. Such converging practices are now accepted in international arbitration practice as an acceptable non-national or transnational standard, irrespective of their legal background.

22-13 A formal attempt to reconcile differences between common and civil law approaches and to develop an internationally acceptable standard was made in the 1999 IBA Rules of Evidence.[6] They provide mechanisms for the presentation of documents, witnesses of fact, expert witnesses and inspections, as well as for the conduct of evidentiary hearings. The Rules are designed to be used in conjunction with, and adopted together with, institutional or *ad hoc* arbitration rules.[7]

1.2. General Principles

22-14 Despite the differences in various legal cultures and laws, there are some general principles pertaining to the taking of evidence in international commercial arbitration. These relate to (a) the application of the principle of party autonomy; (b) the determination of the relevant applicable law or rules of law; (c) the availability of evidentiary means and the allocation of burden of proof; (d) the methods for presenting of evidence; (e) the probative value of the various evidentiary means; and (f) the need for evidentiary hearings.

---

6 The Rules are available at <www.ibanet.org/pdf/rules-of-evid-2.pdf>. See also, *e.g.*, Rivkin, "International Bar Association IBA Rules on the Taking of Evidence in International Commercial Arbitration", XXIVa *YBCA* 408 (1999); Veeder, "Evidential Rules in International Commercial Arbitration: From the Tower of London to the New 1999 IBA Rules", 65 *Arbitration* 291 (1999); Bühler and Dorgan, "Witness Testimony Pursuant to the 1999 IBA Rules of Evidence in International Commercial Arbitration", 17(1) *J Int'l Arb* 3 (2000); Peppard, "New International Evidence Rules Advance Arbitration Process" 73-March *Wisconsin Lawyer* 18 (2000); Raeschke-Kessler, "The Production of Documents in International Arbitration – A Commentary on Article 3 of the New IBA Rules of Evidence", 18(4) *Arb Int* 411 (2002) and Darwazeh, "Document Discovery and the IBA Rules on Evidence: A Practitioners View", 5 *Int ALR* 101 (2002).

7 The Rules were prepared by a working party of the Section on Business Law of the International Bar Association. The 1999 Rules of Evidence replaced the 1983 IBA Supplementary Rules Governing the Presentation and Reception of Evidence in International Commercial Arbitration. The new Rules reflect procedures in use in many different legal systems, and they may be particularly useful when the parties come from different legal cultures.

(a) Party autonomy and tribunal's flexibility

22-15 Most modern arbitration laws recognise that procedural flexibility is one of the paramount considerations in international commercial arbitration. This principle extends to the taking of evidence, the admissibility of evidentiary means and the probative value the tribunal attaches to them.

22-16 Unless otherwise agreed by the parties, the tribunal has the power to determine the rules relating to evidence. The wording of Model Law Article 19 is unambiguous

> (1) Subject to the provisions of this Law, the parties are free to agree on the procedure to be followed by the arbitral tribunal in conducting the proceedings.
> (2) Failing such agreement, the arbitral tribunal may, subject to the provisions of this Law, conduct the arbitration in such manner as it considers appropriate. The power conferred upon the arbitral tribunal includes the *power to determine the admissibility, relevance, materiality and weight of any evidence*." [Emphasis added]

22-17 This is provided for in other laws as well.[8] Under the English Arbitration Act, where the parties do not agree to dispense with the strict rules of evidence in their arbitration agreement, the arbitration tribunal may decide

> (f) whether to apply strict rules of evidence (or any other rules) as to the admissibility, relevance or weight of any material (oral, written or other) sought to be tendered on any matters of fact or opinion, and the time, manner and form in which such material should be exchanged and presented.[9]

22-18 Party autonomy and flexibility are limited by public policy considerations[10] and the mandatory rules at the place of arbitration, if any. These limits, which are also reflected in Article V New York Convention, should be observed if the tribunal wishes to render an enforceable award.

---

[8] See, *e.g.*, Brazil, Arbitration Law Article 21; China, Arbitration Law Articles 43-47; England, Arbitration Act sections 33-34; France, NCPC Article 1460; Netherlands, CCP Articles 1036, 1039; Switzerland, PIL Articles 182, 184.

[9] Section 34(2)(f). See also the discussion in Veeder, "Evidential Rules in International Commercial Arbitration: From the Tower of London to the New 1999 IBA Rules", 65 *Arbitration* 291 (1999) 294-5.

[10] See Schwebel and Lahne, "Public Policy and Arbitral Procedure", *ICCA Congress Series 3*, 205, 219.

22-19 Similar provisions can be found in most arbitration laws: in determining the rules of evidence the tribunal must ensure that the parties are treated with equality and that each party is given an opportunity of presenting his case.[11]

22-20 Modern arbitration rules also confirm this principle of due process; it is expected that parties give notice of the evidence on which they wish to rely on.[12]

(b) Applicable law issues

22-21 In general the taking of evidence is considered to be a procedural matter governed by the law applicable to the arbitration. Some issues, such as parol evidence rule or burden of proof lie in the greyzone between substance and procedure; in some systems they will be governed not by the law governing the arbitration but the law applicable to the merits of the case.[13]

22-22 There is, however, a trend clearly embedded in modern arbitration laws pursuant to which evidence is to be taken in accordance with agreed rules or principles, irrespective of whether such rules are present or even conform with local law. This is most notably recorded in England,[14] France,[15] the Netherlands,[16] and Switzerland,[17] as well as in the Model Law.[18] These modern provisions require no compliance with a pre-determined system of law, unless the parties have chosen one.[19]

---

[11] See, *e.g.*, Model Law Articles 18, 34, 36; Belgium, Judicial Code Article 1694; Netherlands, CCP Article 1039; Switzerland, PIL Article 182.

[12] See, *e.g.*, AAA ICDR Articles 19, 20; CIETAC Articles 38, 41; DIS sections 26, 27; ICC Articles 15, 20; Korea Rules Article 41; LCIA Articles 14, 20-22; ICAC paragraph 34; NAI Article 27; Stockholm Institute Article 26; UNCITRAL Rules Article 24-25; Vienna Article 14; WIPO Article 48; Zurich Articles 35, 43, 44.

[13] See, to that effect, *Oriental Commercial & Shipping Ltd and others v Rosseel NV*, (1992) XVII YBCA 696 (SDNY 1991); *Rosseel NV v Oriental Commercial Shipping and others*, (1991) XVI YBCA 615 (QBD). See also Reymond, 10 *Arb Int* 317 (1994) 325; Veeder, "Evidence: The Practitioner in International Commercial Arbitration", 1 *International Law FORUM* 228 (1999).

[14] England, Arbitration Act section 34(1) and 34(2)(f).

[15] France, NCPC Article 1460.

[16] Netherlands, CCP Article 1036, but see also Article 1039.

[17] Switzerland, PIL Article 182(2).

[18] Model Law, Article 19.

[19] See the discussion in Patocchi and Meakin, "Procedure and the Taking of Evidence in International Commercial Arbitration – The Interaction of Civil Law and Common Law Procedures", 7 *RDAI/IBLJ* 884 (1996) 888.

22-23 There is a threefold rationale underlying the modern approach evidenced in the above mentioned systems. First, there is no obvious reason why the rules of evidence applicable in court proceedings at the place of arbitration should be applicable to international arbitrations. Secondly, allowing the parties and their counsel in co-operation with the arbitration tribunal to incrementally develop a set of rules which are suitable for the case at hand, has the advantage of satisfying the parties' needs and expectations and promoting equality.[20] Finally, this approach has the added benefit of bridging cultural gaps by agreeing to a hybrid framework.

22-24 As a result of the liberal approach the tribunal may refer to an existing national or transnational set of rules, such as the UNCITRAL Notes on Organising Arbitral Proceedings[21] or the IBA Rules of Evidence.[22] Parties and arbitration tribunals may adopt the IBA Rules of Evidence, in whole or in part, or they may vary them or use them as guidelines in developing their own procedures. If parties wish to adopt the IBA Rules of Evidence they should provide for it in the arbitration agreement.

(c) Burden and standard of proof

22-25 In modern international arbitration practice tribunals require each party to prove the facts upon which it relies.[23] An exception may be made in relation to a proposition that is so obvious that proof is not required.[24] A rule to that effect was not included in the Model Law since the Commission accepted that certain aspects of the burden of proof may be regarded as issues of substantive rather than procedural law which are subject to Article 28. Generally the burden of proof raises an issue of characterisation, as in civil law jurisdictions it is deemed to be an issue of substantive law while in common law jurisdictions it is considered to be a procedural issue.[25] Moreover, such a provision was seen as

---

20 *Ibid*, 889.

21 In particular, paras 48-83; The Notes are available at <www.uncitral.org>.

22 See <www.ibanet.org/pdf/rules-of-evid-2.pdf>.

23 The principle is widely accepted but rarely codified. See, *e.g.*, Malta, Arbitration Act 1996 section 35(1): "Each party shall have the burden of proving facts relied on to support his claim or defence". See also Sandifer, *Evidence before International Tribunals*, 127.

24 See Redfern, Reymond, Reiner, Hanotiau, Eveleigh, Menzies, and Philip, "The Standard and Burden of Proof in International Arbitration", 10 *Arb Int* 317 (1994); von Mehren, "Burden of Proof in International Arbitration", *ICCA Congress Series 7*, 123.

25 See Patocchi and Meakin, "Procedure and the Taking of Evidence in International Commercial Arbitration – The Interaction of Civil Law and Common Law Procedures", 7 *RDAI/IBLJ* 884

unnecessarily interfering with the general principle of Article 19; its status as a generally recognised principle was also acknowledged.[26]

22-26 The standard of proof is more problematic. In effect it not only may be a matter of substantive law, but it can also reflect subjective standards ("inner conviction") of arbitrators.

22-27 The pragmatic and flexible approach in relation to the burden and standard of proof is reflected in many arbitration rules.[27] There are no specific rules; the arbitrators must be satisfied that the parties' allegations are proven.

(d) Methods of presenting evidence

22-28 In international arbitration, the practice of submitting memoranda accompanied by supporting documents is so established as to be unremarkable.[28] This practice marks a departure from the traditional common law concept of introducing and receiving documents into evidence. Evidence is allowed in written form or orally; normally oral evidence is accompanied by a full transcript or written summary.

(e) Admission and probative value

22-29 It is generally assumed that the admissibility of evidence is a matter of procedure and hence subject to the law governing the arbitration and/or any other transnational rules the tribunal or the parties may wish to consider. Arbitration tribunals will admit almost any evidence submitted to them in support of parties' position, they retain significant discretion in the assessment and the weighing of the evidence.[29] Accordingly even hearsay evidence will be admitted.[30]

(1996) 889. See also Ferrari, "Burden of Proof Under the United Nations Convention on Contracts for International Sale of Goods (CISG)", 5 *RDAI/IBLJ* 665 (2000)

26 See Berger, *International Economic Arbitration*, 446 and UN Doc A/40/17, para 328 and UN Doc A/CN9/SR331, paras 20, 29 (statements of the Swiss, German and Finnish delegates).

27 See, *e.g.*, UNCITRAL Rules Article 25(6); ICC Rules Article 20; NAI Rules Article 27; Stockholm Institute Article 26; WIPO Article 48; Zurich Rules Article 44.

28 Friedland, "A Standard Procedure for Presenting Evidence in International Arbitration", 11(4) *Mealey's IAR* 4 (1996).

29 See, *e.g.*, Model Law Article 19(2); England, Arbitration Act section 34(2)(f); Switzerland, PIL Article 182(2). See also ICSID Rules 34(1): "The Tribunal shall be the judge of the admissibility of any evidence adduced and of its probative value."

30 See, *e.g.*, AAA ICDR Award of 4 January 1980, case no 1310-0417-78, *American steamship company v Thai transportation enterprise*, VIII YBCA 166 (1983).

Admissibility has nothing to do with the relevance and probative value of evidence, *i.e.* the logical relationships between oral and written statements and facts.

22-30 Arbitration tribunals are quite often active in guiding the parties as to what they require, or expect, by way of evidentiary material.[31] This can be of great assistance to the parties' representatives in the preparation of their cases, particularly where the arbitration tribunal has made its views known at a sufficiently early stage.[32]

22-31 IBA Rules of Evidence Article 9 offer a welcome regulation of issues of admissibility and assessment of evidence. It provides

1. The Arbitral Tribunal shall determine the admissibility, relevance, materiality and weight of evidence. [...]
3. The Arbitral Tribunal may, where appropriate, make necessary arrangements to permit evidence to be considered subject to suitable confidentiality protection.

22-32 Grounds for exclusion of evidence, irrespective of relevance, include unreliability, public policy considerations (*e.g.* privileged material) or even a *ratione personae* consideration, such as the incompetence of a young child to appear as a witness. Inadmissible evidence cannot be received by the court whatever its relevance, value or weight.

22-33 The weight given to the evidence of the parties (or other persons having a direct interest in the outcome) will be assessed according to the effectiveness with which that evidence may be tested.[33] A decision of the United States District Court for the Southern District of New York illustrates the problem. The court, in upholding the arbitrators' decision, said

---

[31] See Holtzmann, "Fact-finding by the Iran-US Claims Tribunal", in Lillich (ed), *Fact-Finding before International Tribunals*, 106 *et seq.*

[32] See Hunter, "The Procedural Powers of Arbitrators under the English 1996 Act", 13 *Arb Int* 345 (1997) 353-4.

[33] Saleh, "Reflections on Admissibility of Evidence: Interrelation between Domestic Law and International Arbitration", 15 *Arb Int* 141 (1999) 142-3. See also Roth, "Consequences and Prevention of False Evidence Under the English Arbitration Act 1996: A Comparative Perspective", 13 *Arb Int* 391 (1997).

arbitrators, like courts, may weigh the probative value of the testimony against the risk of wasting time, prolonging hearings, and confusing issues... Arbitrators are charged with the duty of determining the relevance of evidence.[34]

22-34 Article 9(2) IBA Rules offers guidance in relation to the admissibility and probative value of evidence. In particular, this provision deals with evidence that may be excluded at a request of the party or the tribunal's own motion because of

a) a lack of sufficient relevance or materiality;
b) the legal impediment or privilege under the legal or ethical rules determined by the Arbitral Tribunal to be applicable;
c) an unreasonable burden to produce the requested evidence;
d) the loss or destruction of the document that has been reasonably shown to have occurred;
e) the grounds of commercial or technical confidentiality that the Arbitral Tribunal determines to be compelling;
f) the grounds of special political or institutional sensitivity (including evidence that has been classified as secret by a government or a public international institution) that the Arbitral Tribunal determines to be compelling; or
g) considerations of fairness or equality of the Parties that the Arbitral Tribunal determines to be compelling.

(f) Hearings

22-35 Evidentiary hearings, as other hearing during the arbitration, are not, strictly speaking necessary. Indeed, under some institutional rules, a party must request the tribunal for a hearing, if it wants to be heard orally.[35] In most international arbitrations hearings do take place.

22-36 UNCITRAL Notes have listed several issues that parties and tribunals may wish to consider in determining whether and how they should organise evidentiary hearings.[36] These issues include:

- Whether to hold hearings and whether to have one or several sets of hearings;

---

[34] *Iron Ore Company of Canada v Argonaut Shipping, Inc*, XII YBCA 173 (1987) (SDNY, 1985). The related arbitration award is published in the *Award Service of the Society of Maritime Arbitrators, Inc*, no 2065, and extracted in XI *YBCA* 197 (1986).

[35] See, *e.g.*, LCIA Article 19; WIPO Rules Article 53. See also UNCITRAL Rules Article 15(2).

[36] UNCITRAL Notes paras 74-85.

- Setting dates for hearings;
- Whether there should be a limit on the aggregate amount of time each party will have for oral arguments and questioning witnesses;
- The order in which the parties will present their arguments and evidence;
- Length of hearings;
- Arrangements for a record of the hearing.

22-37 Article 8 IBA Rules contains a detailed "soft regulation" on evidentiary hearings. Perhaps, the most important element of the provision is that the arbitration tribunal has complete control of the evidentiary hearing, hence subscribing to an "inquisitorial" or "case management" style. It also includes rules about the organisation of the hearing.

2. Evidentiary Means

22-38 There are four different groups of evidentiary means in international commercial arbitration:

- Documents;
- Witness testimony of third parties provided by the parties to the dispute;
- Experts, appointed by the parties or the arbitration tribunal; and
- Site or subject matter inspections.

2.1. Documents

22-39 Documents are normally an integral part of arbitration. All arbitrations begin with documents. The written submission of parties (also called pleadings, memorials, or memoranda) and the documents attached to them in support of claims and defences are essential to the process. Although hearings serve the purpose of clarifying and highlighting important aspects of the case, the permanent nature of documents makes them of central importance.

22-40 Documentary evidence includes letters, faxes or emails exchanged between the parties, contractual instruments, protocols, minutes of meetings, records of discussions or phone calls; financial instruments, account records, warehouse records, dock receipts, bills of lading, certificates of quality, licences. More controversial, but increasingly acceptable as documents are CD, audio and visual recordings, floppy disks and hard disks.

22-41 IBA Rules of Evidence Article 1 offers a permissive definition

> "Document" means a writing of any kind, whether recorded on paper, electronic means, audio or visual recordings or any other mechanical or electronic means of storing or recording information.

22-42 This definition confirms the importance of writing and written proof in the taking of evidence. Written evidence is often deemed stronger and more credible, as a matter of form; it is recorded on a durable medium. The IBA Rules definition effectively treats as documents written witness statements or affidavits. Oral evidence is slowly being transformed to a more or less written form of evidence.[37]

22-43 There are a number of critical issues relating to documentary evidence:

- When should a party submit documents?
- Are all documents admissible?
- Is discovery allowed? If yes, to what extent?
- What if the documents are not in the language of arbitration?
- What if the parties are unable to submit original documents?

(a) Admissibility and timing

22-44 In general, arbitration tribunals will read whatever the parties wish to put forward, even over the objections of the other party. They approach the task of evaluating evidence more by assessing the weight to be given to it, rather than its admissibility.[38]

22-45 The admissibility of evidence is generally left to the discretion of the tribunal.[39] There are no fixed rules. When determining the admissibility of documents, the tribunal's authority is detached from the rule of law in other

---

[37] Berger, *International Economic Arbitration*, 427.

[38] See Sandifer, *Evidence before International Tribunals*, 203. See also Hunter, "The Procedural Powers of Arbitrators under the English 1996 Act", 13 *Arb Int* (1997) 352-3. See also, regarding documents "without prejudice", *K/S A/S Bill Biakh and K/S A/S Bill Biali v Hyundai Corp* [1988] 1 Lloyd's Rep 187.

[39] AAA ICDR Rules Article 20(6).

respects, except for the principles of legal privilege, including those involving the confidentiality of communication between lawyers and clients.[40]

22-46 Article 3(1) IBA Rules of Evidence reflects the modern practice of rejecting the strict application of admissibility and expressly requires each party to submit all relevant documents. All documents produced are protected by confidentiality.[41]

22-47 Pursuant to IBA Rules Article 9(4), if a party fails to produce any document, the tribunal *may* infer that such documents would be adverse to the interests of that party. It provides

> If a Party fails without satisfactory explanation to produce any document requested in a Request to Produce to which it has not objected in due time or fails to produce any document ordered to be produced by the Arbitral Tribunal, the Arbitral Tribunal may infer that such document would be adverse to the interests of that Party.

(b) Production of documents and discovery

22-48 It is often essential that several documents are made available during the arbitration. Where a party does not produce a document requested voluntarily, the tribunal may be asked to order production of the documents sought.[42] Parties may be ordered by the tribunal to produce documents, including many of their own internal documents, to the other party during the course of the arbitration. Generally, such production will only be given for specifically identified and relevant documents. The tribunal will generally not allow fishing expeditions for documents or information which may be useful.

22-49 Discovery is an integral part of common law procedure and has been described as a powerful instrument of justice,[43] if it is employed with discretion.[44]

---

40 Saleh, "Reflections on Admissibility of Evidence: Interrelation between Domestic Law and International Arbitration", 15 *Arb Int* 141 (1999) 158.

41 Article 3(12) IBA Rules:

> All documents produced by a Party pursuant to the IBA Rules of Evidence (or by a non-Party pursuant to Article 3:8) shall be kept confidential by the Arbitral Tribunal and by the other Parties, and they shall be used only in connection with the arbitration. The Arbitral Tribunal may issue orders to set forth the terms of this confidentiality. This requirement is without prejudice to all other obligations of confidentiality in arbitration.

42 IBA Rules Article 1.

43 See Mustill and Boyd, *Commercial Arbitration*, 324.

English discovery never extended to the wider ranging pre-trial procedures applied in the US.[45] In civil law proceedings, parties' lawyers generally produce those documents upon which they seek to rely. Although the concept of compulsory disclosure of documents exists in civil law systems, its implementation is quite limited.[46]

22-50 An attempt to bridge the differences in document production was made in UNCITRAL Rules Article 24(2) and (3). They state

> 2. The arbitral tribunal may, if it considers it appropriate, require a party to deliver to the tribunal and to the other party, within such a period of time as the arbitral tribunal shall decide, a summary of the documents and other evidence which that party intends to present in support of the facts in issue set out in his statement of claim or statement of defence.
> 3. At any time during the arbitral proceedings the arbitral tribunal may require the parties to produce documents, exhibits or other evidence within such a period of time as the tribunal shall determine.[47]

22-51 In principle, discovery as understood in the common law systems does not have a place in international commercial arbitration. Parties rely on the documents in their possession and there is no obligation to produce copies of internal and confidential documents merely because requested by the opposing party. In practice document production may be ordered by a tribunal but generally this is limited to specific and identified documents or categories of documents, which are directly relevant to the issues in the arbitration.

22-52 This is reflected in most arbitration rules which grant the tribunal the power to order production of documents.[48] ICC Article 20(5) provides

> At any time during the proceedings, the Arbitral Tribunal may summon any party to provide additional evidence.

---

44 *Ibid*, 325, list as disadvantages that discovery is time-consuming and expensive.

45 See Sutton, "Discovery and Production of Evidence in Arbitral Proceedings – the US and England distinguished", *ICC Publication no 440/8* (1990), 61.

46 See, *e.g.*, France, NCPC Article 1460(3), which is applicable unless the parties agree otherwise under Article 1495.

47 This solution has been criticised as being heavily slanted towards continental European practice. See Reisman, Craig, Park and Paulsson, *International Commercial Arbitration*, 888-9.

48 See, *e.g.*, UNCITRAL Rules Article 24(3); AAA ICDR Article 19(3); LCIA Articles 22(1)(e) and 15(6); LMAA rule 12(b) and 3rd Schedule para 3; ICAC Articles 15, 19, 22 and 34; NAI Article 28; Stockholm Institute Articles 21, 26; WIPO Article 48; Zurich Article 42.

22-53 Most rules, however, do not address the issue of the form that the request for the production of documents should take. Such order may take the form of an interim or partial award[49] or a procedural order. An award is normally enforceable under the New York Convention.

22-54 There is consensus in international arbitration that specifically identified documents may be ordered if the need is established, but whole categories of documents will not be ordered. Exceptions to the latter rule may arise where, for example, the parties' agreement provides for a right to audit.[50] According to an expert report submitted to an ICC tribunal, a tribunal may request the production of specific categories of documents. Such specific categories include minutes of the board of directors' meetings of one party referring to the transaction in question, all internal memoranda dealing with a particular corporate decision, correspondence with a specified third party, reports of meetings on a specified subject and complaints about a specific matter received from third parties.[51]

22-55 The IBA Rules of Evidence dealt with production of documents both in the 1983 and in the 1999 edition. The new Article 3 (2) provides that a party may submit to the tribunal a request to produce which must contain

> (a) (*i*) a description of a requested document sufficient to identify it, or (*ii*) a description in sufficient detail ... of a narrow and specific requested *category of documents* that are reasonably believed to exist;
> (b) a description of how the documents requested are relevant and material to the outcome of the case; and
> (c) a statement that the documents requested are not in the possession, custody or control of the requesting Party, ... [emphasis added].

22-56 The tribunal has discretion to decide whether to order the production of documents or categories of documents.[52] The Rules provide that a tribunal may exclude from production any documents for reasons listed in Article 9(2).

---

49 See, *e.g.*, AAA ICDR Article 21; WIPO Article 46.

50 See Friedland, "A Standard Procedure for Presenting Evidence in International Arbitration", 11(4) *Mealey's IAR* 4 (1996).

51 The letter of the expert is mentioned in Bond, "Recent Interesting Issues and their Resolution in International Arbitration", *presentation at the Japan Commercial Arbitration Association, 22-24 November 2000 - Osaka/Tokyo*, 30-31. See also Derains and Schwartz, *ICC Rules*, 261-2.

52 See also Hascher, "Principes et pratique de procedure dans l'arbitrage commercial international", 279 *RCADI* 51 (1999) 87-93 with further references.

22-57 The real problem is documents in the possession of third parties. Arbitrators have no authority over parties other than those involved directly in the arbitration. Article 3(8) IBA Rules provides

> If a Party wishes to obtain the production of documents from a person or organization who is not a Party to the arbitration and from whom the Party cannot obtain the documents on its own, the Party may ... ask it to take whatever steps are legally available to obtain the requested documents. The Party shall identify the documents in sufficient detail and state why such documents are relevant and material to the outcome of the case. The ... Tribunal shall decide on this request and shall take the necessary steps if in its discretion it determines that the documents would be relevant and material.

22-58 There is no recognised enforcement mechanism for procedural orders of an arbitration tribunal. There are two recent cases[53] which distinguish between enforcing partial awards under the New York Convention and documentary production orders. Partial awards are enforceable, but orders for production of documents are not normally enforceable.[54] Further, contractual rights to documents production are also enforceable.[55]

(c) Copies and translations

22-59 Tribunals expect to receive either original documents or authorised copies. The IBA Rules reflect established practice in Article 3(11) which states

> If copies are submitted or produced, they must conform fully to the originals. At the request of the Arbitral Tribunal, any original must be presented for inspection.

22-60 In the event that the document is in a language with which the members of the tribunal are not familiar, a translation into the language of the arbitration will invariably be required.

---

53 See *Publicis v True North Communications Inc*, 206 F 3d 725 (7th Cir, 2000) and *Resort Condominiums International Inc v Bolwell and another*, (1993) 118 ALR 655, (1994) 9(4) Mealey's IAR A1; (1995) XX YBCA 628 (Supreme Court of Queensland).

54 See however Hong Kong, Arbitration Ordinance, Section 2GG(1) according to which decisions of a tribunal are enforceable in the same way as a decision of a state court.

55 Webster, "Obtaining Documents from Adverse Parties in International Arbitration", 17 *Arb Int* 41 (2001) 42-43, 55-58.

2.2. Witnesses[56]

22-61 Witness testimony is a principal form of fact-finding. The question arises whether parties are always entitled to call and examine witnesses irrespective of the circumstances and the nature of the dispute. The short answer must be negative; it has been argued that the use of too many and irrelevant witnesses can often undermine the cost-effectiveness of arbitration. This is particularly true where the witness evidence is oral and the parties and their witnesses are based in various jurisdictions, frequently different from the seat of arbitration.[57]

22-62 The tribunal invariably has control over the procedure in relation to witnesses giving oral evidence[58] ensuring, in any event, the equal treatment of the parties.[59] A refusal to hear the testimony of a witness is unlikely to be the sole ground for the setting aside of the award.[60]

22-63 As a matter of emerging practice written witness testimonies are submitted to or exchanged with the other party and the tribunal within agreed periods of time. This may well expedite proceedings, especially if the tribunal decides to limit the (direct) oral examination of witnesses to particular issues.

(a) Admissibility issues

22-64 The practice in international arbitration is to admit evidence liberally leaving it to the arbitrators to assess its weight.[61] Often the admissibility of a witness or a witness testimony is decided by the tribunal only after the hearing.[62] These considerations apply to witness evidence; but as witness testimony at a hearing can be time-consuming, arbitrators are often inclined to exercise their

---

[56] For a definition of witness see Hascher, "Principes et pratique de procedure dans l'arbitrage commercial international", 279 *RCADI* 51 (1999) 93-101.

[57] Lew, "Achieving the Potential of Effective Arbitration", 65 *Arbitration* 282 (1999) 288.

[58] See Berger, *International Economic Arbitration*, 439 and IBA Rules Article 4. See also Griffin, "Recent Trends in the Conduct of International Arbitration – Discovery Procedures and Witness Hearings", 17(2) *J Int'l Arb* 19 (2000) 26-29.

[59] See New York Convention Article V and UN Doc A/CN9/264, para 6.

[60] See, Cour d'appel Paris, 15 March 1984, *Soubaigne v Limmareds Skogar*, Rev Arb 285 (1985); *Dalmia Dairy Industries v National Bank of Pakistan* [1978] 2 Lloyd's Rep 223, 270 (CA).

[61] See Hunter, "Modern Trends in the Presentation of Evidence in International Commercial Arbitration", 3 *Am Rev Int Arb* 204 (1992) 211.

[62] See, *e.g.*, Iran-US Claims Tribunal Partial Award in Case no 381 (375-381-1) of 6 July 1988, *Uiterwyk Corporation and others v The Government of the Islamic Republic of Iran and others*, XIV YBCA 398 (1989) paras 24-5.

power to exclude testimony if a witness' evidence is manifestly irrelevant, immaterial, or repetitious.[63]

22-65 In international arbitration any person, including parties and their legal representatives, are generally permitted to testify as a witness.[64] This practice is consistent with the rules applied in some legal systems, particularly of the common law tradition, where there is no bar against a party appearing as a witness.[65] However, a bar against a party (or a party's legal representative) appearing as a witness does exist in some legal systems, for example, in France and Germany.[66] This rule is still applied, on occasion, in international arbitration.[67] The modern permissive practice is reflected in IBA Rules Article 4(2)

> Any person may present evidence as a witness, including a Party or a Party's officer, employee or other representative.

(b) Written witness statements

22-66 There is no established international arbitration practice relating to written witness statements. In some cases, witness statements are submitted with the parties' written submissions; in other cases after the parties' submissions are submitted. Some tribunals require witness statements as a pre-condition to any oral testimony by witnesses. IBA Rules Article 4(4) authorises an arbitration tribunal to order each party to submit written statements by each witness on whose testimony it relies. This practice is welcome because it helps to expedite hearings and proceedings.[68]

---

63 See Bühler and Dorgan, "Witness Testimony Pursuant to the 1999 IBA Rules of Evidence in International Commercial Arbitration", 17(1) *J Int'l Arb* 3 (2000) 29.

64 *Ibid*, 7. See also Huleatt-James and Hunter, "The Laws and Rules Applicable to Evidence in International Commercial Arbitrations, and Some Issues Relating to Their Determination and Application", 63 *Arbitration* 270 (1997) 277; Melis, "Presentation of Documentary Evidence and Witnesses", *ICCA Congress Series no 5*, 512.

65 See, *e.g.*, US Federal Rules of Evidence 601.

66 See, *e.g.*, France, NCPC Article 199. This rule may violate due process, as interpreted by the European Court of Human Rights in *Dombo Beheer BV v Pays Bas*, 27 October 1993, Série A, 274. See also Bühler and Dorgan, "Witness Testimony Pursuant to the 1999 IBA Rules of Evidence in International Commercial Arbitration", 17(1) *J Int'l Arb* 3 (2000) 8-10.

67 See Bühler and Dorgan, *ibid*, 17(1) *J Int'l Arb* 3 (2000) 7-8 with further references.

68 Friedland, "A Standard Procedure for Presenting Evidence in International Arbitration", 11(4) *Mealey's IAR* 4 (1996).

22-67 Many arbitration rules make no express reference to witness evidence. According to LCIA Rules Article 20.3 the initiative for the submission of written witness statements is in the hands of the parties,[69] subject to any order otherwise made by the arbitration tribunal.

22-68 Further, IBA Rules Article 4(6) provides that the parties may submit revised or additional witness statements to respond to matters contained in another party's witness statements. These are sometimes called "rebuttal statements". IBA Rules Article 4(5) provides that written witness statements should contain

a. the full name and address of the witness, his or her present and past relationship (if any) with any of the Parties, and a description of his or her background, qualifications, training and experience, if such a description may be relevant and material to the dispute or to the contents of the statement;
b. a full and detailed description of the facts, and the source of the witness's information as to those facts, sufficient to serve as that witness's evidence in the matter in dispute;
c. an affirmation of the truth of the statement; and
d. the signature of the witness and its date and place.

(c) Procedure for hearing witness evidence

22-69 Arbitration tribunals are free to determine whether, how, where and when witnesses may be examined.[70] The parties and the tribunal will normally agree on a pattern of procedure for the examination of witnesses. Such procedure will often contain elements of different legal traditions. Hence, it is desirable and established practice, that the tribunal will organise evidentiary hearings and will issue a procedural order setting out the way in which examination of witnesses will take place.[71]

22-70 Such a procedural order may include who will examine whom, in which order, on which subject matter, in which language, who will appoint interpreters, who will keep minutes and how. Quite often, the names of witnesses will have been identified and will be included in the order. A procedural order with such

---

69 See also AAA ICDR Article 20(5); UNCITRAL Article 25(5); WIPO Article 54(d).

70 See, *e.g.*, Model Law Article 19(2); Brazil, Arbitration Law Article 22; England, Arbitration Act sections 34(2)(f) and 38(5); Netherlands, CCP Article 1041(1); Switzerland, PIL Article 182(2); US, FAA section 7.

71 A way of organising hearing of witnesses is by witness conferencing. See Peter, "Witness Conferencing", 18 *Arb Int* 47 (2002).

content will ensure that the hearing runs smoothly and that no party or counsel is taken by surprise. It will also accommodate different legal cultures by creating an acceptable common ground.[72]

22-71 Whilst normally it is up to the parties to decide what witnesses they wish to present, arbitration tribunals may refuse to hear some or all witnesses orally.[73] Article 15(2) UNCITRAL Rules, however, provides that the tribunal shall hold hearings for the presentation of evidence by witnesses, if either party so requests.

22-72 It is the parties' responsibility to present their witnesses.[74] This implies that the party advances or reimburses the costs that the witness incurs for the purpose of attending the hearing which would then become part of the arbitration costs.[75] Under some national laws, a party may seek the assistance of local courts to obtain the appearance of a witness who is unwilling to testify.[76]

22-73 Different legal systems impose various restrictions on the contact between the parties' lawyers with witnesses. In international arbitration practice there are no clear rules and lawyers do generally work with witnesses in advance of their giving evidence. IBA Rules Article 4(3) records this practice according to which parties' counsel may contact witness in preparation of the hearing

> It shall not be improper for a Party, its officers, employees, legal advisors or other representatives to interview its witnesses or potential witnesses.

22-74 Logistics of the evidentiary hearing such as language and interpretation as well as record of the testimony are normally dealt with in the procedural order that deals with evidentiary matters. How translation is arranged depends on the circumstances of the case; in most cases the parties will make the arrangements.

---

[72] See Patocchi and Meakin, "Procedure and the Taking of Evidence in International Commercial Arbitration – The Interaction of Civil Law and Common Law Procedures", 7 *RDAI/IBLJ* 884 (1996) 893-4; Marriott, "Evidence in International Arbitration", 5 *Arb Int* 290 (1989) 284.

[73] See, *e.g.*, IBA Rules Article 8(1); ICC Article 20(3); LCIA Article 20(2).

[74] See Bühler and Dorgan, "Witness Testimony Pursuant to the 1999 IBA Rules of Evidence in International Commercial Arbitration", 17(1) *J Int'l Arb* 3 (2000) 19-20 with further references.

[75] *Ibid*, 19. See also Bühler, "Costs in ICC Arbitration; A Practitioner's View", 3 *Am Rev Int Arb* 116 (1992) 138 *et seq.*

[76] See, *e.g.*, Model Law Article 27; England, Arbitration Act section 43; Switzerland, PIL Article 184(2); US, FAA section 7.

Testimonies are often tape-recorded and transcripts are produced when necessary.[77]

(d) Examination of witnesses

22-75 Generally, witnesses who have presented a witness statement will, at the hearing, be examined or cross-examined first by counsel for the opponent party. However, in international arbitration, cross-examination is a delicate issue and an area of stark contrast between the civil and common law traditions.

22-76 Civil lawyers often consider cross-examination an area of discomfort where English or American approaches or techniques are adopted as part of the arbitration procedure. Even the most polite and articulate cross-examiner may have difficulties to strike the right cultural balance before a tribunal composed of arbitrators from different backgrounds, *e.g.*, one common lawyer, one civil lawyer and one from Islamic law background.

22-77 Although cross-examination may have the appearance of an aggressive technique of attacking witness, it is not without merit. It is often an unstated assumption that witness statements are party-generated. Therefore the point of cross-examination is to challenge the direct evidence in the witness statement and to adduce additional facts from the witness, which may assist the tribunal in understanding the contemporaneous documents and determining which of those documents may be more reliable than others.[78]

22-78 The effort to harmonise these differences should involve, and in the hands of many tribunals does involve, a procedure whereby the cross-examiners are encouraged to make only their most important points by application of strict time limits. Despite time constraints, a skilful lawyer can challenge credibility and expose significant problems in a witness statement that will cause a tribunal to treat that statement with great caution. In practice questions by lawyers not trained in the common law tradition are frequently quite effective before an international tribunal.[79]

---

[77] See Bühler and Dorgan, "Witness Testimony Pursuant to the 1999 IBA Rules of Evidence in International Commercial Arbitration", 17(1) *J Int'l Arb* 3 (2000) 21-23 with further references.

[78] Lew and Shore, "International Commercial Arbitration: Harmonising Cultural Differences", 54-Aug *Disp Resol J* 33 (1999) 34.

[79] *Ibid*, 34-5.

22-79 As a general rule availability and intensity of cross-examination is at the discretion of the arbitration tribunal. The hybrid of cross-examination that one may experience in international commercial arbitration will normally be "both civil and uncommon".[80]

2.3. Expert Evidence

22-80 In some instances an arbitration tribunal may be assisted by expert evidence provided either by an expert witness or an expert report. Expert evidence normally assists the tribunal in forming an opinion in relation to technical matters of specialist knowledge, *e.g.*, quality of goods or quantification of damages.

22-81 Expert evidence differs from expert determination. In an expert determination, the expert makes the final determination based on his own knowledge even having heard arguments from the parties. The expert in arbitration merely assists the tribunal to determine relevant issues, but the decision is ultimately the tribunal's own.

22-82 There are two main categories of expert evidence. The expert may be appointed by the tribunal or by the parties. Both should be independent, will have to produce a report,[81] and be available for examination at an oral hearing.

22-83 Different approaches concerning the adducing of expert evidence have been recorded in the context of litigation. Traditionally, in England each party appoints an expert; the experts are cross-examined by the opposing party. The new Civil Procedure Rules encourage the use of single joint experts and seek to foster the neutrality of experts. In the US, however, there appears to be less of an interest in encouraging the use of court-appointed experts. Civil law lawyers are much more familiar with the principle and practice of the court-appointed or tribunal-appointed expert. It appears that there is already a narrowing of the

---

80 Friedland, "A Standard Procedure for Presenting Evidence in International Arbitration", 11(4) *Mealey's IAR* 4 (1996).

81 According to the IBA Rules Article 1, *Expert Report* means a written statement by a Tribunal-Appointed Expert or a Party-Appointed Expert submitted pursuant to the IBA Rules of Evidence.

English common law approach and the continental European tradition, with the American common law approach standing somewhat outside the circle.[82]

22-84 Towards an internationally accepted procedure, there can be little argument that arbitration tribunals should explore the possibility of appointing an expert answerable to the tribunal. Fairness, however, requires that the parties are provided with the opportunity to comment on a report produced by an expert. Alternatively, a less inexpensive approach, suggests that initially each party appoints an expert, who is treated as an expert witness and then the tribunal appoints a third expert.[83]

22-85 Arbitration tribunals will normally determine issues of expert evidence in agreement with the parties in a procedural order addressing evidentiary matters. The critical issue will normally be the brief of an expert witness which will set out all relevant terms and identify the issue(s) on which the expert report is sought.

(a) Tribunal appointed experts

22-86 A "*Tribunal-Appointed Expert*" is a person or organisation appointed by the arbitration tribunal in order to report to it on specific issues determined by the arbitration tribunal.[84]

22-87 Tribunal appointed *experts* are preferred in many legal systems.[85] Article 26 Model Law provides that unless the parties agree otherwise, the tribunal

a. may appoint one or more experts to report to it on specific issues to be determined by the arbitral tribunal
b. may require a party to give the expert any relevant information or to produce, or to provide access to, any relevant documents, goods or other property for his inspection.

---

82 Lew and Shore, "International Commercial Arbitration: Harmonising Cultural Differences", 54-Aug *Disp Resol J* 33 (1999) 36. See also Hascher, "Principes et pratique de procedure dans l'arbitrage commercial international", 279 *RCADI* 51 (1999) 101-107 with further references.

83 See, *e.g.*, WIPO Rules Article 55(c).

84 IBA Rules Article 1.

85 See, *e.g.*, Belgium, Judicial Code 1696(1); England, Arbitration Act section 37; Malta, Arbitration Act section 39; Netherlands, CCP Article 1042; Saudi Arabia, Arbitration Regulation section 33; Tunisia, Arbitration Code Article 71; as well as all Model Law jurisdictions.

2. Unless otherwise agreed by the parties, if a party so requests or if the arbitral tribunal considers it necessary, the expert shall, after delivery of his written or oral report, participate in a hearing where the parties have the opportunity to put questions to him and to present expert witnesses in order to testify on the points at issue.

22-88 Article 6 IBA Rules of Evidence offers a comprehensive set of rules relating to tribunal appointed experts. Accordingly, in pertinent part:

- The tribunal, in consultation with the parties, may appoint one or more independent experts to report to it on specific issues designated by the tribunal. The tribunal will also establish the terms of reference for any expert report after having consulted with the Parties.
- The expert must submit to the tribunal and to the parties a statement of his or her independence before accepting an appointment.
- The expert may request a party to provide any relevant and material information or to provide access to any relevant documents, goods, samples, property or site for inspection. The expert must record in the report any non-compliance by a party and shall describe its effects on the determination of the specific issue.
- The expert must report in writing to the tribunal describing in the report the method, evidence and information used in arriving at the conclusions.
- The tribunal must send a copy of such report to the parties and who will have an opportunity to respond.
- The expert must be present at an evidentiary hearing and may be questioned by the tribunal and the parties.
- Any expert report made by a tribunal appointed expert and its conclusions will be assessed by the arbitration tribunal.
- The fees and expenses of a tribunal appointed expert, will be funded in a manner determined by the tribunal, and will form part of the costs of the arbitration.

(b) Party appointed experts

22-89 *Party-Appointed Expert* means an expert witness presented by a party.[86] Arbitration laws allow party appointed experts as a matter of party autonomy.

[86] IBA Rules Article 1.

This is justified as parties' lawyers will normally be unable to assess the quality of an expert report. Moreover, for most technical scientific issues there will invariably be a different academic view. Party appointed experts assist each party in the preparation of evidentiary hearings and putting their case forward.

22-90 Article 5 IBA Rules makes provisions for party appointed experts and their reports:

- A party may rely on a party appointed expert as a means of evidence on specific issues. Such an expert must submit a written report.
- The expert report must contain the name and address of the expert and his present and past relationship with any of the parties and a description of his background, qualifications, training and experience; a statement of the facts on which he is basing his expert opinions and conclusions; his expert opinions and conclusions, including a description of the method, evidence and information used in arriving at the conclusions; an affirmation of the truth of the Expert Report; and the signature of the Party-Appointed Expert and its date and place.
- The tribunal may order the party appointed experts who submitted reports to attend a meeting. At such a meeting the experts must attempt to reach agreement on those issues on which they had differences of opinion and they must record in writing issues on which they reach agreement.
- Each party appointed expert must appear for testimony at an evidentiary hearing, unless the parties agree otherwise and the tribunal accepts this. If an expert does not appear without a good reason at a hearing, the tribunal must disregard his or her report unless the tribunal determines otherwise.

(c) Institutional rules

22-91 Most arbitration rules provide for experts in similar terms as the national laws and the IBA Rules. Accordingly, the tribunal may appoint experts, unless otherwise agreed by the parties.[87] Only NAI Rules deal expressly with both party appointed[88] and tribunal appointed experts.[89]

---

87 See, *e.g.*, UNCITRAL Rules Article 27; AAA ICDR Article 22; CIETAC Articles 39-41; ICC Article 204; LCIA Article 21; ICAC 34(1); NAI Article 30-31; Stockholm Institute Article 27; Vienna Article 14(3); WIPO Article 55; Zurich Article 41.

88 NAI Article 30.

89 NAI Article 31.

22-92 As a general rule an expert must be independent and not an advocate for the parties. The primary duty owed by a party-appointed expert is to the tribunal. This is confirmed by case law[90] and relevant professional bodies.[91]

2.4. Site or Subject Matter Inspections

22-93 An arbitration tribunal has discretion to order a site or subject matter inspection,[92] unless the parties have expressly excluded such power. Parties have to be informed well in advance of the exact time and date of inspection and will also have to tolerate inspections in their premises. Site or subject matter inspections are more common in construction, engineering and mining disputes where the tribunal can, for example, form a view of the state of affairs[93] or evaluate a property.[94]

22-94 Article 7 IBA Rules provide for on site inspection

> ... the Arbitral Tribunal may, at the request of a Party or on its own motion, inspect or require the inspection by a Tribunal-Appointed Expert of any site, property, machinery or any other goods or process, or documents, as it deems appropriate. ...[95]

3. ASSISTANCE OF NATIONAL COURTS

22-95 As discussed above arbitration tribunals have considerable power in relation to the taking of evidence. This authority comes from the arbitration agreement, relevant arbitration rules[96] or laws. As tribunals do not have coercive

---

[90] See, *e.g.*, *National Justice Compania Naviera SA v Prudential Assurance Co, The IkarianReefer* [1993] 2 Lloyd's Rep 68, 81-82.

[91] See, *e.g.*, Academy of Experts Code <www.academy-experts.org/codeofpractice.htm> of June 2001, last visited in December 2002.

[92] See LCIA Article 22(1)(d); JCAA Rule 34; NAI Article 34; WIPO Article 50, Zurich Article 40.

[93] See, *e.g.*, Cour d'appel Paris, 24 February 1994, *Ministry of Public Works (Tunisia) v Société Bec Frères (France)*, Rev Arb 275 (1995), XXII YBCA 682 (1997).

[94] See, *e.g.*, Iran-US Claims Tribunal, Award in Case no 316 (566-316-2), 14 July 1995, *Protiva v The Government of the Islamic Republic of Iran*, XXI YBCA 321 (1996).

[95] The UNCITRAL Notes on Organising Arbitral Proceedings provide further guidance in relation to the arrangement of a site inspection; see paras 57-58. See to that effect Bulgaria, Arbitration Law Article 31(1).

[96] See, *e.g.*, AAA ICDR Articles 16, 19, 20, 22; CAMCA Articles 22, 24-25; CIETAC Articles 38-41; DIS sections 26, 27, 30; Geneva Articles 25-28; ICC Article 20; Korea Article 41; LCIA

power, there are instances where court assistance may be required for collection of evidence.

22-96 Various national laws contain provisions that allow tribunals and parties to seek the court's assistance in obtaining evidence in arbitrations.[97] This may be evidence both within and outside the jurisdiction of the courts of the place of arbitration. This is reflected in Article 27 Model Law

> The arbitral tribunal or a party with the approval of the arbitral tribunal may request from a competent court of this State assistance in taking evidence. The court may execute the request within its competence and according to its rules on taking evidence.[98] [Emphasis added]

22-97 This power generally applies in respect of factual evidence. However, in some jurisdictions it can extend to expert evidence. For example, a tribunal with its seat in the Netherlands[99] can ask the Dutch courts to obtain foreign legal information under the European Convention on Information on Foreign Law (1968). This power is of little practical relevance as the tribunal will either possess such knowledge or will be assisted by experts or the parties' counsel.[100]

22-98 Often an arbitration tribunal is concerned with evidence which is outside the jurisdiction of the courts at the place of arbitration. Proceedings may be delayed for as much as six months or one year by requests for taking evidence outside the place of arbitration.[101] As the place of arbitration is often chosen because of its neutrality, evidence will normally be "located" outside of that place. However, it will be essential for the tribunal to have access to such evidence in order to ascertain the relevant facts.

Articles 20-22; ICAC paragraph 34; NAI Articles 27-33; SIAC 22-25; Stockholm Articles 25-27; UNCITRAL Rules Article 24-25, 27; Vienna Article 15, 20; WIPO Articles 48-56; Zurich Articles 43, 44.

97 See, *e.g.*, Belgium, Articles 1693-1694; Brazil, Articles 21-22; China, Articles 43-48; England, Arbitration Act sections 33-34; France, NCPC Articles 1460-1461, 1467; Germany, ZPO sections 1042, 1049-1050; Hong Kong, sections 2GA-2GG and Model Law provisions; Netherlands, CCP Articles 1036, 1039-1044; Switzerland, PIL Articles 182, 184-185; US, FAA section 7.

98 For a commentary see Calavros, *Das UNCITRAL Modellgesetz über die internationale Handelsschiedsgerichtsbarkeit* (Bielefeld 1988), 121.

99 See Netherlands, CCP Article 1044.

100 Berger, *International Economic Arbitration*, 452.

101 The statement was made by Holtzmann in UN Doc A/CN9/SR325, para 66.

22-99 By referring to the competent court of this State Article 27 Model Law appears to be limited to the taking of evidence in the country adopting the Model Law.[102] A strict interpretation of Article 27 would imply that if evidence is "located" in several different Model Law countries then the tribunal or the interested party should make requests in each country in order to gather all related "foreign" evidence. The issue arises as to whether or not an arbitration tribunal with a place of arbitration outside a Model Law country could temporarily move to that country to overcome this difficulty.[103] Such a move would be dependant inevitably on whether the courts accept that the place of arbitration is within their jurisdiction. This is doubtful, except in very occasional circumstances.[104]

22-100 In implementing Article 27 German ZPO Section 1050 adopted a more permissive wording

> The ... tribunal or a party with the approval of the ... tribunal may request from a court assistance in taking evidence or performance of other judicial acts which the ... tribunal is not empowered to carry out. ... The arbitrators are entitled to participate in any judicial taking of evidence and to ask questions. [Emphasis added]

22-101 "The performance of other judicial acts" may well include requests for judicial assistance abroad in, for example, the examination of a witness who is outside the jurisdiction of the court. This could be obtained by consular authorities.[105]

22-102 The English courts will assist parties to foreign arbitrations to obtain evidence situated within their jurisdiction. This is expressed in sections 43 and 44 of the English Arbitration Act and they apply to foreign arbitrations by virtue of section 2(3)

> The powers conferred by the following Sections apply even if the seat of the arbitration is outside England and Wales or Northern Ireland or no seat has been designated or determined-

---

[102] See Holtzmann and Neuhaus, *Model Law*, 738; van Houtte, "Conduct of Arbitral Proceedings", in Šarčević (ed), *Essays*, 113, 126.

[103] This was suggested by Spenser-Underhill and Valentin, "Securing Evidence for Foreign Arbitrations", *Int ALR* 205 (1998) in the context of the English Arbitration Act 1996.

[104] *Ibid.*

[105] Similarly in Switzerland in accordance with Article 184(2).

> section 43 (securing the attendance of witnesses), and
>
> section 44 (court powers exercisable in support of arbitral proceedings) but the court may refuse to exercise any such power if, in the opinion of the court, the fact that the seat of the arbitration is outside England … makes it inappropriate to do so.[106]

22-103 In fact section 43 covers both witness testimony and production of documents. The Act does not specify when it may be "inappropriate to do so". While several factors have been suggested,[107] the English courts will normally consider it inappropriate to make an order if the courts having jurisdiction over the arbitration had sufficient powers to grant the parties the same or similar relief.

22-104 In the United States the courts will also assist in the taking of evidence in arbitrations outside the US. This follows section 28 US Judicial Code which provides in pertinent part

> The district court of the district in which a person resides or is found may order him to give his testimony or statement or produce a document or other for use in a proceeding in a foreign or international tribunal. The order may be made pursuant to a letter rogatory issued, or request made, by a foreign or international tribunal or upon the application of any interested person …

22-105 This is well illustrated in two cases where the District Court of the Southern District of New York made the judicial assistance under section 1782 dependant on whether the parties had exhausted the procedures for obtaining evidence prescribed in the rules applicable to the arbitration.[108] Consequently, for a section 1782 application to be successful, it must be in accordance with the rules or law governing the arbitration, and after the remedies of the law governing the arbitration have been exhausted, i.e. an order was first obtained from the court in the jurisdiction where the arbitration is taking place.

---

[106] In *Commerce & Industries Co of Canada and another v Certain Underwriters at Lloyds of London* [2002] 2 All ER (Comm) 204, the court exercised their discretion rejecting the claimants' application to have evidence taken from two witnesses in England as they failed to satisfy the court that it was appropriate in the circumstances.

[107] See Spenser Underhill and Valentin, "Securing Evidence for Foreign Arbitrations", 1 *Int ALR* 205 (1998) 208.

[108] *In Re Application of Technostroyexport*, 853 F Supp 695 (SDNY 1994); *In Re Application of Medway Power Limited*, 985 F Supp 402 (SDNY 1997).

22-106 A complication was caused by the Court of Appeal for the Second Circuit in NBC v Bear Stearns.109 The case arose out of an ICC arbitration in Paris between a Mexican claimant, Azteca, and NBC, which had obtained leave ex parte to serve six document subpoenas in accordance with section 1782 of the US Judicial Code against various financial institutions, none of which were parties to the ICC arbitration. Azteca and the institutions succeeded in quashing the subpoenas. One reading of the case is that parties in a foreign arbitration will not gain access to an American style discovery through use of section 1782.[110]

[109] See *National Broadcasting Company Inc v Bear Stearn & Co Inc* 165 F 3d 184 (2d Cir 1999); Comments, *ibid, 205-7.*

[110] Rivkin and Legum, "Attempts to Use Section 1782 to Obtain US Discovery in Aid of Foreign Arbitration", 14 *Arb Int* 213 (1998) 226.

Chapter 23

INTERIM AND CONSERVATORY MEASURES

23-1 Interim or conservatory measures, also referred to as provisional measures, are an important remedy and tool in international litigation and arbitration. The relief sought in the principal action is frequently insufficient to protect effectively the rights or interest of the alleged innocent party. Due to the time gap between commencement of the proceedings and the substantive hearing, the subject-matter or necessary evidence may disappear; by the time the final relief is to be granted irreparable and non-compensatory harm may occur. One party may frustrate the rights of the other party and make enforcement impossible by dissipating or placing beyond reach assets or the subject-matter in issue.

23-2 In these situations one of the parties may seek to protect its rights or property by some appropriate interim measures. As stated by the European Court of Justice, interim measures are "intended to preserve a factual or legal situation so as to safeguard rights the recognition of which is sought from the court having jurisdiction as to the substance of the case."[1] The effect of such measures is to distribute the risk for the duration of the main action between the parties, shifting it from the party applying for the interim measures to the other party.[2]

23-3 Interim measures take various forms, are understood and applied differently and may encompass different concepts in different legal systems. What interim measures are appropriate in international commercial arbitration is determined according to the specific facts of each dispute and the arbitrators' subjective perception of the risks involved. These measures may also be influenced by the relevant national legal systems involved in each arbitration.

23-4 Interim measures are granted only in limited circumstances as they can be determinative of the dispute and may be hard or even impossible to repair. They can also be abused as an offensive weapon to exert pressure on the other side.[3] In this respect it makes no difference to the parties whether the interim or conservatory measures are ordered, and whether the underlying dispute will be determined, by a national court or an international arbitration tribunal. What does matter are the criteria according to which interim measures may be granted.

---

[1] *Van Uden Maritime BV, trading as Van Uden Africa Line v Kommanditgesellschaft in Firma Deco-Line* [1998] ECR I 7091, 7133 para 37.

[2] Besson, *Arbitrage International et Measures Provisoires*, 23 para 8; UNCITRAL Secretariat Report, "Analytical Commentary on Draft Text of a Model Law on Commercial Arbitration", UN Doc A/CN.9/264, published in Holtzmann & Neuhaus, *Model Law*, 542.

[3] See further Bötsch, "The Problem of Provisional Remedies in International Commercial Arbitration", in Bötsch (ed), *Provisional Remedies*, 4; Lew, "Commentary on Interim and Conservatory Measures in ICC Arbitration Cases", 11(1) *ICC Bulletin* 23 (2000).

23-5 A number of specific questions determine whether the interim measures are sought from a national court or an arbitration tribunal. The first fundamental issue is which forum is competent to order provisional measures: the arbitration tribunal, the state courts or both? Only rarely is this regulated in the arbitration agreement. Furthermore, whenever the applicable arbitration law or rules provide for provisional measures by an arbitration tribunal the procedure, types of measures and in particular their enforcement may be an issue. This issue has been on the agenda of UNCITRAL's Working Group on Arbitration since 1999.[4] Two draft articles are proposed; they provide for the enforcement of interim measures along similar lines to enforcement of awards, with specific grounds for refusal taking into account the particularities of interim relief.[5]

23-6 This chapter reviews (1) the circumstances in which interim and conservatory measures can be ordered by an arbitration tribunal, (2) how such orders are enforced, (3) when such interim measures can be ordered by courts in support of arbitration, and (4) the concurrent powers of the courts and arbitrators, *i.e.* which forum has principal responsibility for this type of relief.

1. Grant of Interim Measures by Arbitration Tribunals

23-7 Has an arbitration tribunal the power to order the interim measure sought? This will depend on the rules and law governing the arbitration and the arbitrators' authority. What conditions must be satisfied if the tribunal is to order the interim measure sought? These conditions depend on the rules relevant to the grant of such relief, and will differ from case to case, depending on the contract terms, the circumstances of the case, the make up of the tribunal and the governing law.

1.1. General Power to Order Interim Measures

23-8 Generally, the power to order interim relief depends on the authority of the tribunal as agreed by the parties. This may be done expressly in the arbitration agreement or by the choice of arbitration rules which allow arbitrators

---

4 See *Official Records of the General Assembly, Fifty fourth session,* Supplement no 17, UN Doc A/54,17, para 371 *et seq.*

5 See the proposals discussed by the Working Group, 7-11 October 2002, UN Doc A/CN9/523.

to order such relief. In many cases the power to order interim relief is implied by the applicable arbitration law, provided the parties have not excluded it.[6]

23-9 The power to order interim relief is generally classified as a matter of procedure and therefore governed primarily by the law governing the arbitration.[7] This is generally the law of the place of arbitration,[8] though a number of tribunals have not referred to any law when deciding on their power to order interim relief.[9] In addition regard may also be taken of the law of the place where the interim measure is to be enforced.

(a) The changing approach

23-10 For many years in a number of jurisdictions an arbitration tribunal did not have the power to order interim measures, or at least such powers were limited. This was a power vested in the courts only.[10] The reasons for this restrictive approach were twofold. Historically, national courts were assertive of their jurisdiction over disputing parties before reaching a conclusion on the merits; this was considered an exclusive sovereign power. More significantly were the practical problems of one party only (*ex parte*) applications, the time inevitably taken to bring the tribunal together, and the need for enforcement powers on the part of the forum making the order. [11]

23-11 Even today some laws do not allow arbitrators to make such orders. For example, Article 818 Italian Code of Civil Procedure provides

> The arbitrators may not grant attachments or other interim measures of protection.[12]

---

6 See Besson, *Arbitrage International et Measures Provisoires*, 92 *et seq.*

7 *Ibid*, 81 *et seq*; Born, *International Commercial Arbitration*, 922.

8 See, *e.g.*, ICC case no 7895, *ICC Bulletin* 64 (2000) 65; ICC case no 8113, *ICC Bulletin* 65 (2000) 67; ICC case no 8786, ICC Bulletin 81 (2000) 82 *et seq.*

9 See, *e.g.*, ICC case no 8894 (1997), *ICC Bulletin* 94 (2000) 97; see also Lew, "Commentary on Interim and Conservatory Measures in ICC Arbitration Cases", 11(1) *ICC Bulletin* 23 (2000) 26.

10 See, *e.g.*, Switzerland: Article 26 Swiss Concordat on Arbitration (replaced by PIL Article 183 concerning international arbitration); Greece, CCP Article 889 now replaced, with respect to international arbitration, by the International Commercial Arbitration Act 2735 of 1999.

11 This was, *e.g.*, the case in Germany, see Bundesgerichtshof, 22 May 1957, ZZP 427 (1958); Landgericht Frankfurt, 26 July 1982, 36 *NJW* 761 (1983); Kühn, "Vorläufiger Rechtsschutz und Schiedsgerichtsbarkeit", *Jahrbuch für die Praxis der Schiedsgerichtsbarkeit* 47 (1987) 48.

12 See China, Arbitration Law Article 68: the Arbitration Commission must refer any request for interim relief to the courts; see also Quebec, Arbitration Law Article 940(4). For further references see Lew, "Commentary on Interim and Conservatory Measures in ICC Arbitration

23-12 Similarly Article 753 Argentine Code of Civil Procedure provides

> Arbitrators cannot order compulsory measures or measures leading to enforcement. They must request them from the judge who will lend the support of his jurisdictional powers for the most swift and effective carrying out of the arbitral proceedings.

23-13 In the majority of modern laws a different approach prevails. In the absence of public policy issues which require the authority to order interim measures to be reserved for the national courts, these laws either expressly grant arbitration tribunals the power to order interim relief, or at least allow the parties to confer such powers on the tribunal. This is a recognition of party autonomy and also the greater authority of arbitrators in international arbitration.

23-14 It is now widely recognised that the arbitration tribunal will often be the best forum to determine the appropriateness of specific interim measures for each case.[13] If the tribunal has already been established and the proceedings have started, the arbitrators would be more familiar with the legal and factual details of the case than a judge who is not going to determine the real issues between the parties. The tribunal is in a good position to evaluate the chances of success in the substantive dispute and to decide the impact the interim measures may have on the case and whether they should be granted. Furthermore, the tribunal will also be in a good position to distinguish interim measures applications which have been brought for dilatory, tactical or offensive purposes rather than in pursuit of a legitimate interest.[14]

(b) Arbitrators' authority under national laws

23-15 While these considerations have led to a wide recognition of the tribunal's power to order interim relief, the various national laws differ considerably as to the extent and the requirements for such powers. In general one can distinguish three different approaches. First, arbitration laws where the law itself vests the arbitrator with a broad power to order interim relief, subject to

---

Cases", 11(1) *ICC Bulletin* 23 (2000) 24; Rubino-Samartano, *International Arbitration*, 620 *et seq*.

13 According to a study conducted by the AAA there is a widely felt uncertainty as to the availability of interim relief from arbitration tribunals which results in the limited number of requests. See Naimark and Keer, "Analysis of UNCITRAL Questionnaires on Interim Relief", 16(3) *Mealey's IAR* (2001). See, *e.g.*, the Canadian decision, *Quintette Coal Limited v Nippon Steel Corporation,* [1989] 1 WWR 120, 132 (BC Supreme Court).

14 Berger, *International Economic Arbitration*, 348.

any agreement to the contrary by the parties. Second, laws which grant the power to order certain types of interim relief but require party agreement for all other types. Third, laws where an agreement by the parties is required for the tribunal to order interim relief as no powers are implied by law.

23-16 The first approach is adopted in the Model Law Article 17 provides

> Unless otherwise agreed by the parties, the arbitration tribunal may, at the request of a party, order any party to take such interim measure of protection as the arbitration tribunal may consider necessary in respect of the subject-matter of the dispute. The arbitration tribunal may require any party to provide appropriate security in connection with such measure.

23-17 This gives the tribunal a general power to order provisional measures. It is not limited to certain measures and depends on the tribunal's evaluation of whether these measures are necessary and appropriate in the particular circumstances. A certain restriction may result from the fact that it must be a measure "in respect of the subject matter of the dispute."[15]

23-18 A similarly broad authority is allowed by various national laws based on the Model Law[16] and a number of arbitration laws not based on the Model Law. For example, Article 183(1) Swiss PIL provides

> Unless the parties have agreed otherwise, the arbitral tribunal may, at the request of a party, order provisional or protective measures.

23-19 The powers conferred by Article 183(1) PIL are wider than those under the Model Law as the phrase "subject matter of the dispute" is omitted.[17]

23-20 The second approach can be found in the English Arbitration Act. Unless otherwise agreed by the parties, the law only allows certain types of interim relief. In addition to empowering the arbitration tribunal to order security for costs, Section 38 provides, in pertinent part that

> (4) The tribunal may give directions in relation to any property which is the subject of the proceedings or as to which any question arises in the proceedings, and which is owned by or is in the possession of a party to the proceedings-

---

15 See further Redfern and Hunter, *International Commercial Arbitration*, para 7-22.

16 See, *e.g.*, Canada, Arbitration Act Article 17; Germany, ZPO section 1041; Egypt, Arbitration Act Article 24; Greece, International Commercial Arbitration Act 2735 of 1998 Article 17.

17 See also Belgium, Judicial Code Article 1696.

(a) for the inspection, photographing, preservation, custody or detention of the property by the tribunal, an expert or a party, or

(b) ordering that samples be taken from, or any observation be made of or experiment conducted upon, the property.

...

(6) The tribunal may give directions to a party for the preservation for the purposes of the proceedings of any evidence in his custody or control.

23-21 For all other types of interim relief the agreement of the parties is required.[18] Since, according to section 48 Arbitration Act, the parties can also determine the remedies available in the main proceedings, the powers of the tribunal concerning interim relief depend significantly on the parties' will.[19]

23-22 The third approach can be found in arbitration laws which do not provide for interim relief to be granted by arbitrators, such as the US, French or Belgian laws. While under these laws no power to order interim relief is implied, they do at least recognise conferral of powers on the tribunal by the parties.[20]

(c) International arbitration rules

23-23 The parties may also confer the power on arbitrators to grant provisional measures by choosing arbitration rules. Most leading international arbitration rules contain provisions for the granting of provisional measures. However, these rules differ considerably in their approach and ambit.

23-24 Some rules set out in detail what specific measures a tribunal can order. LCIA Rules contain a detailed provision on security for costs, general rules and an overriding authority to grant interim relief. Article 25(1) provides

The Arbitral Tribunal shall have the power, unless otherwise agreed by the parties in writing, on the application of any party:

---

18 Section 39(1) provides that the "parties are free to agree that the tribunal shall have power to order on a provisional basis any relief which it would have power to grant in a final award".

19 See the DAC-Report, para 201, according to which freezing orders (Mareva injunctions) and search orders (Anton Pillar orders) should not be covered by that provision but generally left to the courts; Merkin, Arbitration Act, 93; Russell on Arbitration, para 6-020; for a different view see Besson, *Arbitrage International et Measures Provisoires*, 108 *et seq.*

20 For US law see Born, *International Commercial Arbitration*, 924 *et seq*; for French law see Buchman, "France", in Bötsch (ed), *Provisional Remedies*, 253, 257; for Belgian law see de Mishaegen, "Belgium", in Bötsch (ed), *Provisional Remedies*, 77, 83 *et seq*; see also Besson, *Arbitrage International et Measures Provisoires*, 104.

(a) to order any Respondent party to a claim or counterclaim to provide security for all or part of the amount in dispute, by way of deposit or bank guarantee or in any other manner and upon such terms as the Arbitral Tribunal considers appropriate. Such terms may include the provision by the claiming or counterclaiming party of a cross-indemnity, itself secured in such manner as the Arbitral Tribunal considers appropriate, for any costs or losses incurred by such Respondent in providing security. The amount of any costs and losses payable under such cross-indemnity may be determined by the Arbitral Tribunal in one or more awards;
(b) to order the preservation, storage, sale or other disposal of any property or thing under the control of any party and relating to the subject matter of the arbitration; and
(c) to order on a provisional basis, subject to final determination in an award, any relief which the Arbitral Tribunal would have power to grant in an award, including a provisional order for the payment of money or the disposition of property as between any parties.[21]

23-25 Other arbitration rules contain a general empowerment with special rules for certain issues, such as protecting the subject-matter or relevant evidence in the dispute. For example, Article 26 UNCITRAL Rules provides

1. At the request of either party, the arbitral tribunal may take any interim measures it deems necessary in respect of the subject-matter of the dispute, including measures for the conservation of the goods forming the subject-matter in dispute, such as ordering their deposit with a third person or the sale of perishable goods.
2. Such interim measures may be established in the form of an interim award. The arbitral tribunal shall be entitled to require security for the costs of such measures.

23-26 The arbitrators' authority is limited in that the interim measures must be "in respect of the subject matter of the dispute."[22] Protective measures not dealing directly with the subject matter are not covered. It seems that the provision is primarily directed to the preservation and the sale of goods but does not cover measures necessary to prevent the dissipation of assets.[23]

---

[21] See also Stockholm Institute Article 31, which only provides for ordering specific performance.

[22] See also DIS section 20; NAI Article 38.

[23] Redfern, "Arbitration and the Courts: Interim Measures of Protection - Is the Tide About to Turn?", 30 *Texas Int'l Law J* 72 (1995) 80; Marchac, "Interim Measures in International Commercial Arbitration under the ICC, AAA, LCIA and UNCITRAL Rules", 10 *Am Rev Int'l Arb* 123 (2000) 128.

23-27 Such measures should, however, be covered by the broader provision in the ICC Rules which empowers the tribunal to grant any type of interim or conservatory measure it considers appropriate in the circumstances of the case. Article 23 provides

> Unless the parties have otherwise agreed, as soon as the file has been transmitted to it, the Arbitral Tribunal may, at the request of a party, order any interim or conservatory measure it deems appropriate. The Arbitral Tribunal may make the granting of any such measure subject to appropriate security being furnished by the requesting party. Any such measure shall take the form of an order, giving reasons, or of an Award, as the Arbitral Tribunal considers appropriate.[24]

23-28 By contrast, a serious limitation on the arbitrators' power to order interim relief exists in the CIETAC Rules. Article 23 provides only for granting of provisional measures by courts. This obligation is not limited to the phase before the constitution of the arbitration tribunal and the rules contain no other provision dealing with interim measures. A tribunal cannot order any type of interim relief as an application from one of the parties would be transferred by CIETAC to the local courts.

23-29 Arbitration tribunals under the ICSID Convention are restricted to recommendations instead of orders.[25] Given the possibility to draw negative inferences from non-compliance and the economic pressure exerted by the World Bank as the sponsoring institution, in practice such recommendations often have the same effect as orders.

(d) Implied authority of arbitrators

23-30 Where the governing law and the applicable rules neither grant the arbitrators the power to order interim relief, nor expressly exclude them, the question arises whether the tribunal has an inherent power to do so. Such a power was assumed by several tribunals under the 1988 ICC Rules which did not contain any express power.[26] The underlying rationale for this view is that by the arbitration agreement the parties give the tribunal the powers necessary to settle their dispute. This also includes the power to order any measure of provisional

---

24 Similar provisions can be found, *e.g.*, in WIPO Article 46; AAA ICDR Article 21.

25 Article 47. For further details see Lörcher, *Neue Verfahren*, 352 *et seq.*

26 ICC case no 7589, *ICC Bulletin* 60 (2000) 61; ICC case no 7210, *ICC Bulletin* 49 (2000) 50 *et seq*; Craig, Park & Paulsson, *ICC Arbitration*, para 26-05; Yesilirmak, "Interim and Conservatory Measures in ICC Arbitral Practice", 11(1) *ICC Bulletin* 31 (2000) 32; for other case law see Born, International Commercial Arbitration, 924 *et seq.*

relief which is necessary to safeguard the rights of the parties and the efficiency of the tribunal's decision making.[27]

(e) Inherent limits of the arbitrators' powers

23-31 Important limits to the arbitrators' powers to order interim measures arise directly from the consensual nature of their authority. A tribunal cannot order acts to be done or omitted by third parties who are not parties to the arbitration. Any such measures which may be available to state courts cannot be granted by an arbitration tribunal.[28] Unless specifically agreed by the parties, a tribunal lacks the power to enforce its measures and cannot impose penalties for non-compliance.[29]

23-32 A third limitation to interim relief by tribunals arises from the fact that it can only be effectively granted once the tribunal has been set up. Very often, however, measures are needed before that time and it is impossible or at least impractical to wait until the tribunal has been constituted. In institutional arbitration a conceivable solution could be to turn to the institution for interim relief but at present most institutions do not grant measures of interim relief.

23-33 There is, however, a WIPO initiative to provide for interim relief before the tribunal has been constituted.[30] The "WIPO Emergency Relief Rules" are applicable only if agreed upon by the parties. In their present format they provide for two types of procedure - one with the participation of both parties, one *ex parte* - both of which are initiated by a "Request for Relief". The decision will be taken by one of the "stand-by arbitrators" drawn from WIPO's list of arbitrators.[31]

---

[27] Berger, *International Economic Arbitration*, 331 *et seq*; Mendez, "Arbitrage international et mesures conservatoires", *Rev Arb* 51 (1985) 56; critical Besson, *Arbitrage International et Measures Provisoires*, 99 *et seq*.

[28] Lew, "Commentary on Interim and Conservatory Measures in ICC Arbitration Cases", 11(1) *ICC Bulletin* 23 (2000) 25 with further references; Craig, Park & Paulsson, *ICC Arbitration*, para 26-05; Russell *on Arbitration*, para 6-131; Born, *International Commercial Arbitration*, 925; Besson, *Arbitrage International et Measures Provisoires*, 68 *et seq*; see also ICC case no 9324, *ICC Bulletin* 103 (2000) 104.

[29] Besson, *Arbitrage International et Measures Provisoires*, 57 *et seq*.

[30] The ICC Pre-Arbitral Referee Procedure also allows for interim relief before the tribunal has been constituted. Since their entry into force on 1 January 1990, the Rules have not been widely used. In 2001, only two applications were made. See 13(1) *ICC Bulletin* 14 (2002).

[31] See for details Blessing, *Introduction to Arbitration*, para 887 *et seq*.

1.2. Interim Measures which Arbitration Tribunals May Order

23-34 Under most laws and rules party autonomy generally determines the types of measures the arbitration tribunal can order. This is well illustrated by section 39(1) English Arbitration Act which stipulates that the parties may give the tribunal all powers it has in the main action.[32] Subject to the mandatory law of the place of arbitration, the types of interim measures available are not limited to those which could be granted by the state courts at the place of arbitration.[33] An arbitration tribunal with its seat in Germany, for example, may be empowered to order an English type freezing order blocking the assets of one of the parties while a German court cannot make such an order.[34]

23-35 The various types of interim measure which can be granted under the various laws and rules can be classified under five general headings:[35]

- Measures for the preservation of evidence;
- Measures to regulate and stabilise relations between the parties during the proceedings;
- Measures to secure the enforcement of the award;
- Measures to provide security for costs;
- Orders for interim payments.

(a) Measures for the preservation of evidence

23-36 Evidence crucial for the determination of the substantive issues may need to be preserved or taken at an early stage of the proceedings. An example is where the quality of goods must be determined before the goods are either sold or

---

32 See also Netherlands, CCP Article 1051(1).

33 Marchac, "Interim Measures in International Commercial Arbitration under the ICC, AAA, LCIA and UNCITRAL Rules", 10 *Am Rev Int'l Arb* 123 (2000) 128; for a different view see *Bocotra Construction Pte Ltd and Others v The Attorney-General of Singapore*, (1996) 5 ADRLJ 312 (Singapore Court of Appeal).

34 Berger, *International Economic Arbitration*, 341; Bandel, *Einstweiliger Rechtsschutz im Schiedsverfahren*, 162 *et seq*. In such a case enforcement of the measures may be problematic. It may be that the courts do not enforce such a measure at all or only in a modified way known to the procedural law of the enforcing state; see Raeschke-Kessler and Berger, *Recht und Praxis*, para 597.

35 The classification has no influence on the requirements to be met. A number of measures, such as, *e.g.*, orders not to sell the property in dispute, might qualify for two categories, since they do not only regulate the relations between the parties for the time of proceedings but also ensure enforcement of the final award.

perish, or where a crucial witness is terminally ill. Where entitlement to the results of a research and development contract are at stake, or where the sale and purchase agreement which provides for the buy out or purchase price to be calculated according to the financial results of the company, the relevant data, or financial and accounting papers, may need to be preserved.

23-37 It is undisputed that tribunals can take appropriate measures to preserve evidence under most laws or rules.[36] Some of them even allow such measures either under a general rule or in a special provision.[37] Even when express references are lacking these measures will generally be admissible as they usually concern the subject matter of the dispute as required by the narrower provisions of the arbitration rules.

(b) Measures to regulate and stabilise

23-38 It is often necessary to regulate the relationship between the parties for the duration of the arbitration. It is widely accepted that the tribunal can order a relief which directly affects the physical subject matter of the dispute. The sale of perishable goods at market price or orders for their storage and maintenance is expressly regulated in a number of rules.[38] This allows for quality, contract terms, liability and final remedies to be determined at a later date.

23-39 Measures which do not directly deal with the property in dispute, but rather order a party to stop or to continue doing certain action pending the award, are more problematic. Such measures may be necessary where damages would not be sufficient to fully compensate a party for the loss it would suffer during the proceedings if the other party were allowed to continue its action or non-action. For example, the refusal of a sub-contractor in a large construction project to continue its part of the work due to a dispute may bring the whole enterprise to a halt, cause enormous damage, and even undermine the commercial viability of the project.[39] Similar problems may arise where the right of a licensee to use intellectual property rights is the subject of the arbitration.[40] By the time the final

---

[36] Redfern and Hunter, *International Commercial Arbitration*, para 7-11; see also Craig, Park &. Paulsson, *ICC Arbitration*, para 26-05

[37] See, *e.g.*, England, Arbitration Act section 38(4), AAA ICDR Article 21.

[38] UNCITRAL Rules Article 26(1); CPR Rules Rule 13; LCIA Article 25(1)(b).

[39] See, *e.g.*, *Channel Tunnel Group Ltd v Balfour Beatty Construction Ltd* [1993] AC 334.

[40] See, *e.g.*, *Resort Condominiums International Inc v Ray Bolwell and others*, (1995) XX YBCA 628 (Supreme Court of Queensland, 29 October 1993).

award is issued the applicant may already have long been forced out of the market if an interim injunction is not granted.

23-40 Some injunctive measures can be ordered by arbitrators under the Model Law and the UNCITRAL Rules: both texts refer to "measures...in respect of the subject matter of the dispute". This has been narrowly interpreted by some authors to include only measures dealing with the preservation of the property in dispute. There is uncertainty whether injunctions or orders to refrain from ceasing work or to stop using intellectual property rights are outside the powers of the tribunal. If the tribunal is so limited, then all it can do is issue non-binding recommendations to influence the parties' conduct in a certain way.[41]

23-41 This seems unreasonable in light of the overall authority of the tribunal and the intent of these instruments. As long as the interim measure is closely connected with the matter in dispute it is for the tribunal to decide what is necessary and justified. This would appear to be the situation for all arbitrations held under one of the more permissive arbitration rules.[42] Tribunals under the ICC Rules have ordered parties to stop selling the goods of the other side,[43] to continue executing a long term contract pending the award,[44] to pay money into an escrow account or to deposit shares in a trust and not remove them without a further order of the tribunal or agreement by the parties.[45]

(c) Measures to secure enforcement

23-42 Whilst arbitration is ongoing a party could try to frustrate its purpose or the effectiveness of the final award by transferring assets beyond the reach of the other party or the tribunal. Where one party is concerned that this may occur, it could seek the sequestration of the property in dispute, or the attachment of a party's assets. Furthermore, the financial situation of one party might give

---

41 Redfern, "Arbitration and the Courts: Interim Measures of Protection-Is the Tide About to Turn?", 30 *Texas Int'l L J* 72 (1995) 80; Marchac, "Interim Measures in International Commercial Arbitration under the ICC, AAA, LCIA and UNCITRAL Rules", 10 *Am Rev Int Arb* 123 (2000) 128; Redfern and Hunter, *International Commercial Arbitration*, para 7-26.

42 See Craig, Park & Paulsson, *ICC Arbitration*, para 26-05; Lew, "Commentary on Interim and Conservatory Measures in ICC Arbitration Cases", 11(1) *ICC Bulletin* 23 (2000) 29.

43 ICC case no 7895, 11(1) *ICC Bulletin* 64 (2000) 65.

44 ICC case no 6503, 122 *Clunet* 1022 (1995).

45 ICC case no 8879, *ICC Bulletin* 84 (2000) 89 *et seq*; further examples Lew, "Commentary on Interim and Conservatory Measures in ICC Arbitration Cases", 11(1) *ICC Bulletin* 23 (2000) 29; Yesilirmak, "Interim and Conservatory Measures in ICC Arbitral Practice", 11(1) *ICC Bulletin* 31 (2000) 33.

reasonable doubts that it will still be able to fulfil any of its pecuniary obligations ordered in the award. In such a case it may be necessary to provide adequate security in the form of a bank deposit or guarantee.

23-43 Some arbitration rules refer to these types of measures. For example, Article 38(1) NAI Rules provides

> At the request of one of the parties, the arbitral tribunal may order the other party to provide security or to have security provided in favour of the requesting party, in a form to be determined by the arbitral tribunal, for the claim or counterclaim, as the case may be, as well as for costs relating to the arbitration which are deemed to be required by the arbitral tribunal.[46]

23-44 Even where these specific types of measures are not expressly provided for in the applicable rules, the general power to grant interim relief under most laws and rules also covers measures intended to provide security for the enforcement of the final award.[47] However, a tribunal will only provide such measures if the money in dispute is specific and the right to it is a subject of the arbitration. No funds should be blocked merely because one party claims damages for such amount from the other party.

23-45 The same applies in relation to orders dealing directly with the property in dispute, such as a prohibition to sell shares in a company where ownership of the shares is in dispute. Such measures are often allowed under arbitration laws and rules, which refer to measures in relation to the subject matter in dispute.[48] It is under the UNCITRAL Rules that Iran-US Claims Tribunal has ordered measures forbidding the sale of the goods in dispute.[49]

23-46 The situation is, however, different in relation to orders which are not limited to the property in dispute. This applies, in particular, to orders relating to pre-award attachments. The power to order such measures may in some cases be

---

[46] See also LCIA Article 25(1)(a); CEPANI Rules Article 17(1); for an order to provide a bank guarantee in the amount of USD 6,500,000 granted under the NAI rules see NAI, Interim Award of 21 December 1996, case no 1694, *American Producer v German Construction Company*, XXIII YBCA 97 (1998).

[47] See ICC case no 8113, 11(1) *ICC Bulletin* 65 (2000) 67 and ICC case no 8223, 11(1) *ICC Bulletin* 71 (2000) 73, where it was assumed that such a power existed but the arbitrators found that the prerequisites for granting relief did not exist.

[48] See Model Law Article 17, UNCITRAL Rules Article 26.

[49] See, *e.g.*, Iran-US Claims Tribunal, case no 11875 (ITM 27-11875-1), *The Government of the United States of America, on behalf and for the benefit of Shipside Packing Company Inc v The Islamic Republic of Iran (Ministry of Roads and Transportation)*, IX YBCA 297 (1984).

excluded by the relevant law. For example, the Belgian Judicial Code, Article 1696(1) provides

> Without prejudice to Article 1679(2) [right to apply to the courts], the arbitral tribunal may, at the request of a party, order provisional or protective measures, with the exception of an attachment order.

23-47 Even where no exclusion exists attachment orders are often considered to be outside the powers of the tribunal for different reasons. First, they are directed at assets which are not the subject matter in dispute in a narrow sense but are merely needed to secure enforcement of the award. On a narrow interpretation, some of the arbitration rules do not extend to attachment orders.[50] This interpretation ignores the needs of international arbitration and is out of line with the general pro-arbitration trend recorded in many countries. The mere fact that the measure is needed in connection with a matter in dispute should be sufficient to bring a measure within the powers provided for in the Model Law.

23-48 Accordingly, under German law, where Section 1041 ZPO follows Article 17 Model Law, a wide interpretation is endorsed by the legislative materials. These provide that an arbitration tribunal has the same powers in relation to provisional measures as a state court, including orders for attachment.[51] This argument is unnecessary if the arbitration is under ICC or other rules which grant the arbitration tribunal the power to order *any* provisional measures it deems appropriate.

23-49 The second objection against the tribunal's power to order attachment relates primarily to the coercive powers necessary for any kind of enforcement. Under French doctrine orders for attachment are considered to be part of the enforcement process, which clearly falls within the exclusive jurisdiction of the state courts.[52] However, enforcement of an award and measures at a pre-award stage intended to secure that enforcement have to be clearly distinguished. The lack of finality of those conservatory measures make it obvious that they are not an early step towards enforcement.

23-50 The main objections against attachments or freezing orders relate to the coercive character of these measures. The effect of an order of attachment is considered to infringe upon the rights of the parties, a power reserved for state

---

[50] Redfern and Hunter, *International Commercial Arbitration*, para 7-33.

[51] BT-Drs 13/5274, 45.

[52] Fouchard Gaillard Goldman *on International Commercial Arbitration*, para 1334 *et seq*.

courts.[53] However, the effect of attachment orders differs from country to country. Under some laws orders of the tribunal may result directly in an attachment and no further action is required. In other countries a second act of enforcement is required as the ordering of a measure by a tribunal does not include the use of state force or authority. For example, under German law the mere ordering of an attachment does not entail any direct intrusion on the parties' rights; the order of attachment requires an additional act of enforcement. The order can be granted by a tribunal but the actual attachment is reserved for the courts.[54]

23-51 A given factual or legal position and the future enforcement of an award may not only be protected by attachment orders affecting the property but also by other remedies which operate against the parties to the arbitration. In this respect most of the arguments against attachment orders are inapplicable as they primarily relate to the effect on the property of such orders. It is therefore widely accepted that a tribunal can grant English style freezing orders which require a person not to dispose of its assets or to transfer them abroad.[55]

(d) Measures intended to provide security for costs

23-52 Costs in international arbitration may be considerable. A successful party is generally entitled to be reimbursed for the costs of the arbitration and its legal fees. The respondent against whom the proceedings were brought has an interest in ensuring that at least part of the fees incurred will be recoverable. To this end several arbitration rules contain provisions empowering the tribunal to grant security for costs. For example, Article 25(2) LCIA Rules provides

> The Arbitral Tribunal shall have the power, upon the application of a party, to order any claiming or counterclaiming party to provide security for the legal or other costs of any other party by way of deposit or bank guarantee or in any other manner and upon such terms as the Arbitral Tribunal considers appropriate. Such terms may include the provision by that other party of a cross-indemnity, itself secured in such manner as the Arbitral Tribunal considers appropriate, for any costs and losses incurred by such Claimant or Counterclaimant in providing security. The amount of any costs and losses payable under such cross-indemnity may be determined by the

---

53 Berger, *International Economic Arbitration*, 341 with further references in Fn 878.

54 See Bandel, *Einstweiliger Rechtsschutz im Schiedsverfahren*, 138 *et seq*; see also ICC case no 8118, 11(1) *ICC Bulletin* 69 (2000) 70 where such a power was assumed but not exercised; for a different view see ICC case no 7589, 11(1) *ICC Bulletin* 60 (2000).

55 Berger, *International Economic Arbitration*, 341.

Arbitral Tribunal in one or more awards. In the event that a claiming or counterclaiming party does not comply with any order to provide security, the Arbitral Tribunal may stay that party's claims or counterclaims or dismiss them in an award.[56]

23-53 Similar rules can be found in some arbitration laws.[57] In these cases the tribunal's power to order security for costs is beyond doubt. However, even where no such express provisions exist, tribunals can grant such orders under their general power to grant interim relief. For example, Article 23(1) ICC Rules, is considered to constitute a valid basis for orders for security of costs.[58]

23-54 On what conditions should the tribunal exercise this power?[59] There are few cases where arbitrators have ordered security for costs. This may be an indication that tribunals are reluctant to exercise this power.[60] One reason is the strong view that orders for security for costs are not appropriate in arbitration.[61] There are good arguments that a higher standard should be applied than in court proceedings. Arbitration generally requires that the respondent agreed to arbitrate with the claimant. Furthermore the burden placed on the claimant by the obligation to pay an advance on costs under the institutional rules or to the arbitrators in respect of their fees is considered to be a sufficient safeguard to exclude any abusive and extravagant claims. Since the lack of sufficient funds is often due to the actions or contractual non-performance of the respondent it is

---

56 See also NAI Article 38; WIPO Article 46(b) and CEPANI Article 17.

57 England, Arbitration Act section 38(3); Hong Kong Arbitration Ordinance Section 2GB(1)(a); Singapore, International Arbitration Act section 12(1).

58 Craig, Park & Paulsson, *ICC Arbitration*, para 26-05 *iv*; see also ICC case no 7489, 120 *Clunet* 1078 (1993), where the tribunal considered the power to order security for costs to be part of its inherent powers even under the old rules. But see *McKensey v Hewitt*, (2002) 17(3) Mealey's IAR C-1, C-2 (New South Wales Supreme Court, 11 March 2002).

59 See the "Guidelines for Arbitrators on how to Approach an Application for Security for Costs", issued by the Chartered Institute of Arbitrators, 63 *Arbitration* 166 (1997); for guidelines applicable to arbitrations in Hong Kong see Soo, "Securing Costs in Hong Kong Arbitration", 3 *Int ALR* 25 (2000); for Singapore see Hsu, "Orders for security for Costs and International Arbitration in Singapore", 3 *Int ALR* 108 (2000) 111 *et seq*; for England see Fitzpatrick, "Security for Costs under the Arbitration Act 1996", 1 *Int ALR* 139 (1998).

60 See ICC case no 8670, 11(1) *ICC Bulletin* 77 (2000) 77 *et seq*; ICC case no 8223, 11(1) *ICC Bulletin* 71 (2000) 73.

61 For a case where security for costs was granted by the courts see *Coppeé SA v Ken-Ren Chemicals and Fertilisers*, [1994] 2 WLR 631, where the House of Lords ordered the Kenyan claimant to post security for costs in an ICC arbitration. The criticism that followed was a factor for the transfer of the power to order security from the courts to the arbitration tribunal in the Arbitration Act 1996. See DAC Report, para 193.

feared that in those cases parties may abuse requests for additional security to prevent underfunded claimants from pursuing their rights.[62] The fact that the claimant is domiciled in a different country should not be sufficient in itself to justify the granting of security for cost.[63]

(e) Orders for interim payments

23-55 In many commercial transactions one of the parties depends on payments due under a contract to preserve its cash flow. This is often the case with construction and building contracts. The problem with such interim payments is that one party is granted in part, though on a provisional basis, what it requests in the main action.[64] It needs to receive those payments to survive and remain in business. For this reason it may be possible for arbitrators to order such payments, leaving the parties' respective rights to be resolved in the final award. Section 39(2) Arbitration Act explicitly allows parties to empower the tribunal to make

> (a) a provisional order for the payment of money or the disposition of property as between the parties, or
>
> (b) an order to make an interim payment on account of the costs of the arbitration.

23-56 Even without such national legislation or arbitration rule empowerment, ICC tribunals have assumed a power to grant this type of measure.[65]

1.3. Prerequisites for the Grant of Interim Measures

23-57 The majority of rules governing interim relief by tribunals have a limited content. They generally only provide that the tribunal can order interim measures it considers "necessary" or "deems appropriate" and perhaps further specify the type of measures which can be granted. No further specifications are contained as

---

62 Craig,Park & Paulsson, *ICC Arbitration*, para 26-05 *iv*.

63 This is provided for in Hong Kong, Arbitration Ordinance section 2GB(3).

64 A comparable problem with an interim measure granting the relief requested in the main action arises in the context of sport arbitration, where athletes banned for doping apply for a starting permission. See Oberlandesgericht Frankfurt, 5 April 2001, 24 *Sch* 1/01, unpublished. The court enforced an interim order of the arbitration panel of the German Athletics Association granting Dieter Baumann the right to start in the German Indoor Championship.

65 ICC case no 7544, 11(1) *ICC Bulletin* 56 (2000) 56 *et seq.*

to the circumstances and conditions under which such measures can and should be granted.

23-58 Views as to the conditions for issuing interim measures by an arbitration tribunal differ considerably. This is evidenced by the discussion in Germany in connection with section 1041(1) ZPO which provides that tribunals can grant interim measures of protection the tribunal may consider necessary.[66] Since the rule is silent as to any further requirements, it has been concluded that the only substantive requirement is that the tribunal considers the measure necessary.[67] It has also been suggested that in relation to the question of whether or not interim relief should be granted, the tribunal should apply sections 916 *et seq* ZPO which govern interim relief by German courts and set up additional requirements, such as urgency and a good arguable case on the merits.[68]

23-59 The same divergence of approaches can also be found in relation to other laws and international arbitration practice. An instructive illustration of relying on the provisions regulating interim relief by the courts is provided by a decision of a tribunal under NAI rules. The case arose out of a construction contract between a US manufacturer and a German construction company.[69] The American claimant, relying on alleged financial difficulties of the respondent requested from the tribunal to order the respondent to provide security of 200 million Dutch Guilders. The tribunal held

> Wide discretion in deciding whether to grant a request for provisional relief is afforded to Judges and Arbitrators by Dutch law. Nonetheless, the Tribunal's review of the relevant jurisprudence, in light of the parties' submissions, reveals that there are three criteria that should be considered .... in adjudicating the Request for Security.
>
> First, ... there must be an urgent need for the requested relief ... Second, an arbitral tribunal has discretion to grant a provisional remedy so long as it is clear that the underlying claim is not groundless on the merits. Finally, assuming that the first two requirements are met, Dutch law requires the Tribunal to undertake a balancing of the interests with respect to the requested relief .... the factors to be considered in this balancing include the strength of the claimant's case on the merits and the likelihood that the claimant will suffer substantial harm if the relief is not granted.

---

[66] This is identical to Model Law Article 17.

[67] See Bandel, *Einstweiliger Rechtsschutz im Schiedsverfahren*, 32-34.

[68] See Schütze, *Schiedsgericht und Schiedsverfahren* (3rd ed, Beck 1999), para 237.

[69] NAI case no 1694, *American Producer v German Construction Co*, XXIII YBCA 97 (1998).

23-60 In this case the tribunal referred to the provisions dealing with court ordered interim relief when deciding on the conditions under which interim relief should be granted.[70] There are, however, a number of other decisions where the tribunals have not made any reference to the provisions of a national law but just relied on the provisions of the chosen rules.[71]

23-61 International arbitration practice suggests there are at least two widely agreed substantive requirements for the granting of interim relief by arbitration tribunals: no pre-judgment of the case, and the threat of irreparable or substantial harm which cannot be compensated for by damages.[72]

23-62 By contrast, the requirement of a good arguable case on the merits, which is considered in some laws to be a prerequisite for interim relief in support of court proceedings, has received mixed reactions. This is due to the fact that unlike court proceedings, where the judge granting interim relief will frequently be different from the judge dealing with the merits of the case, in arbitration the same tribunal will deal with both issues. To avoid any appearance of pre-judgment arbitrators are invariably reluctant to express their views on the merits before they have considered at least a significant amount of the evidence presented by the parties.[73] For this reason the merits of the case rarely play any direct role in determining whether or not interim relief is granted.[74]

23-63 A party requesting a provisional measure can seek to persuade the tribunal with whatever evidence the tribunal considers sufficient that the relief sought should be granted. It does not have to rely on the special means for proving such matters prescribed in court proceedings.[75] The specific evidence

---

[70] See also ICC case no 7544, 11(1) *ICC Bulletin* 58 (2000) 58 *et seq*, where Articles 809 and 873 of the French NCPC were considered to be "helpful as a pointer to and an example of the general principles to be exercised in dealing with such applications."

[71] See Lew, "Commentary on Interim and Conservatory Measures in ICC Arbitration Cases", 11(1) *ICC Bulletin* 23 (2000) 26.

[72] See ICC case no 8113, 11(1) *ICC Bulletin 65* (2000) 67.

[73] For the arbitrator's dilemma see Lew, "Commentary on Interim and Conservatory Measures in ICC Arbitration Cases", 11(1) *ICC Bulletin* 23 (2000) 25; but see also Yesilirmak, "Interim and Conservatory Measures in ICC Arbitral Practice", 11(1) *ICC Bulletin* 31 (2000) 34.

[74] But see award in Summary Arbitral Proceedings in NAI case 2212, 28 July 1999, XXVI *YBCA* 198 (2001) 204 *et seq*, where the presentation of a *prima facie* case by the applicant was held to be an accepted requirement for interim relief; see also the draft Article 17(3)(e), discussed by the UNCITRAL Working Group on Arbitration, UN Doc A/CN0/523, which requires "a substantial possibility that the requesting party will succeed on the merits" for interim relief to be granted.

[75] Berger, *International Economic Arbitration*, 336.

required will vary from case to case; it will depend on the measures sought, the substantive issues in dispute, the particular circumstances of the case, the place of arbitration and the approach of the arbitrators.

23-64 The requirement of not prejudging the substantive issues in a case connotes that measures granted should not cover what is requested in the main proceedings.[76] The Iran-US Claims Tribunal refused to order a transfer of the goods in dispute to a warehouse of the respondent's choice since this would have been tantamount to the final relief requested by the respondent in its counterclaim.[77] However, there are cases where the interim measures sought are so intricately bound to the ultimate effectiveness of the final award that if all other conditions are satisfied the tribunal will make orders for the relief sought.[78]

23-65 The interim measures must be necessary to grant effective protection for the relief sought in the main proceedings, and to prevent irreparable harm to one of the parties. In this respect "irreparable" must be understood in an economic, not a literal, sense. It must take account of the fact that it may not always be possible to compensate for actual losses suffered or sullied business reputation through damages. What degree of urgency is required depends on the impact the provisional measure sought would have on the right of the other party. The tribunal in every case must seek to balance the conflicting interests involved.[79] In this balancing process, undertakings of a party not to carry out certain actions or the possibility of giving security may play a considerable role in influencing the arbitrators' decision.[80]

1.4. Procedure for Applications for Interim Measures

23-66 There are three fundamental procedural issues for all tribunals granting interim measures of protection:

---

[76] ICC case no 8113, 11(1) *ICC Bulletin* 65 (2000) 67.

[77] Iran-US Claims Tribunal, *Behring International, Inc v Iranian Air Force*, 8 Iran-US CTR 44; see van Hof, *Commentary on the UNCITRAL Arbitration Rules*, 179 *et seq* with further references.

[78] *E.g.*, where the relief requested is to stop the transfer of shares to a third party pending the tribunal's decision on the merits and the transfer takes place, it will irretrievably give control of a company to another party and damages will not be an adequate remedy.

[79] For the requirement of necessity under Swiss Law see ICC case no 8786, 11(1) *ICC Bulletin* 81 (2000) 83; Berger, *International Economic Arbitration*, 336.

[80] See, *e.g.*, the ICC case no 7544, 11(1) *ICC Bulletin* 56 (2000) 59 *et seq.*

- the relief must be requested by a party;
- the tribunal must have jurisdiction over the parties; and
- the tribunal must ensure that the parties' right to be heard is respected.

(a) Measures must be requested by a party

23-67 Generally provisional measures can be granted only if requested by a party. Most provisions empowering the tribunal to order interim relief make that power dependent on a request of a party.[81] An exception to this general rule are the ICSID Arbitration Rules which allow the tribunal to recommend orders on its own initiative.[82]

(b) The tribunal must have jurisdiction

23-68 The arbitration tribunal must at least have *prime facie* jurisdiction in the main action.[83] Otherwise it also lacks jurisdiction to order the interim relief. The mere existence of a challenge to the jurisdiction of a tribunal does not prevent a tribunal from ordering interim relief. If the tribunal considers that there is at least some basis for its jurisdiction it can order the required measures.[84]

(c) The tribunal must hear both parties

23-69 National courts often grant provisional measures *ex parte, i.e.*, on application from one party and without hearing the other party. This occurs when the measures are urgent or intended to prevent the dissipation of assets. It may be impossible or counterproductive to inform the other party about the pending attachment or restraining order since this might allow it to take action that would

---

81 See, *e.g.*, Model Law Article 17; Switzerland, PIL Article 183(1); Netherlands, CCP Article 1051(1); Germany, ZPO section 1041(1); see also Bandel, *Einstweiliger Rechtsschutz im Schiedsverfahren*, 82.

82 Rule 39(3) reads:

> The tribunal may also recommend provisional measures on its own initiative or recommend measures other than those specified in a request. It may at any time modify or revoke its recommendations.

83 Bandel, *Einstweiliger Rechtsschutz im Schiedsverfahren*, 86 *et seq*; see also ICC case no 8113, 11(1) *ICC Bulletin* 65 (2000) 69.

84 See, *e.g.*, ICSID tribunal in *Holiday Inns v Morocco*, reported by Lalive, "The First 'World Bank' Arbitration (Holiday Inns v Morocco) – Some Legal Problems", 51 *BYBIL* 123 (1980) 136 *et seq*; see also Lörcher, *Neue Verfahren*, 354 *et seq* and UN Convention of the Law of the Sea Article 290(1).

negate the effectiveness of the order. In these cases the applicant's right to effective protection is considered to outweigh the defendant's right to be heard which is postponed to the appeal stage.

23-70 In international arbitration the availability of *ex parte* interim relief by a tribunal is controversial. In general, the issue can only really arise once the tribunal has already been constituted.[85] It is usually not possible to constitute the tribunal without informing the other party. In addition, the constitution of the tribunal can take so much time that assets may have disappeared or vital evidence have been destroyed before measures could be ordered by the tribunal.

23-71 Even where a tribunal has already been constituted the granting of interim relief by the tribunal in the absence of one party is often considered inappropriate. Some arbitration rules and laws require that both parties should be heard. For example, the ICSID Rules provide that a tribunal should

> only recommend provisional measures, or modify or revoke its recommendations, after giving each party the opportunity to be heard.[86]

23-72 Most laws and rules are silent on this issue. Nevertheless it is widely held that unlike court proceedings the right to be heard prevents the tribunal from ordering interim relief *ex parte*.[87] This is because the right to be heard and the observance of the rules of natural justice are fundamental to arbitration.[88] The major difference to proceedings in an ordinary court, which seems to justify different treatment in arbitration, is the non-existence of a right to appeal from a decision of a tribunal.[89]

23-73 Given the interlocutory nature of provisional measures the tribunal always has the opportunity to lift the measures ordered, without a formal appeal procedure and at its own discretion. There are no obstacles to hearing the party against whom provisional measures are ordered in the presence of the other party in an informal way and at any time. It can therefore be argued that in exceptional

---

[85] It is conceivable to empower the institution to grant interim relief before the tribunal is constituted which is then reviewed by the tribunal.

[86] See also UN Convention on the Law of the Sea Article 290(3).

[87] See Stalev, "Interim Measures of Protection in the Context of Arbitration" in van den Berg (ed), *International Arbitration in a Changing World* (Kluwer 1994), 111; in relation to German Law, Scheef, *Der einstweilige Rechtsschutz*, 35-37; in relation to Hong Kong, *Charteryard Industrial Ltd v The Incorporated Owners of Bo Fung Gardens* [1998] 4 HKC 171.

[88] New York Convention Article V(1)(c); van den Berg, *New York Convention*, 306.

[89] Scheef, *Der einstweilige Rechtsschutz*, 37.

cases a tribunal can proceed in the absence of a party, as long as it hears the other party once the measure has been granted.[90]

1.5. Form of and Security for Orders for Interim Measures

23-74 The form which provisional measures may take can have an important bearing not only on their enforceability but also on a number of other issues. Likely forms for such measures may be a recommendation, a more or less informal procedural order, or an interim award.

23-75 Recommendations have played little role in practice outside the ICSID framework, where they are the only form of interim relief unless the parties have agreed on binding measures.[91] The reason for this limited relevance is not that tribunals lack the power to make recommendations,[92] but rather that recommendations can only be effective within a framework where there is sufficient extralegal pressure to make them persuasive. While this is the case within ICSID, interim measures in other systems have usually taken either the form of an order or of an award.

23-76 Interim measures in the form of an award have advantages. Greater formality may have a positive effect in persuading a party to comply with the award. An interim award may be challenged or resisted when enforcement is sought. It will also be submitted to formalities, most notably the requirement for a reasoned decision. This will inevitably take additional time, especially with a three-person tribunal. In ICC arbitration, all awards have to be approved by the Court and any non-observance may be grounds for an annulment.[93] While an interim award can only be reversed through a new final award, procedural orders are usually submitted to less formality and can be reversed easily by the tribunal but cannot be reviewed by courts but cannot be reviewed by courts.

---

90 For such a view in the context of the WIPO Rules see Blessing, "The conduct of Arbitral Proceedings under the Rules of the Arbitration Institutions: The WIPO Rules in a comparative practice", in *WIPO/ASA Conference on Rules for Institutional Arbitration and Mediation*, Geneva 1995, 41, 54; Lörcher, *Neue Verfahren*, 362; in relation to German law Lachmann, *Handbuch*, para 1440; in relation to English Law Scheef, *Der einstweilige Rechtsschutz*, 61.

91 Washington Convention Article 47.

92 See Bandel, *Einstweiliger Rechtsschutz im Schiedsverfahren*, 39 *et seq.*

93 See the decision of the Cour d'appel Paris, 1 July 1999, *Braspetro Oil v GMRA*, 14(9) Mealey's IAR D1 (1999) D3, where the violation of that rule was held to justify annulment of an award; the Tribunal having "labelled" the award a procedural order.

23-77 It is rare for the arbitration laws to prescribe a certain form for interim relief. A notable exception is the Netherlands CCP which provides in relation to summary arbitral proceedings in Article 1051(3)

> A decision rendered in summary arbitral proceedings shall be regarded as an arbitral award ....

23-78 The Model Law, as well as most other laws, are silent as to the form provisional measures may take. The same applies to a number of arbitration rules.[94] The UNCITRAL Rules provide that interim measures may be granted in the form of an interim award without imposing a particular form.[95] In these cases it should be for the tribunal to decide the form of the interim relief.

23-79 This is the solution adopted in Article 23(1) ICC Rules which leaves the form of interim measures to the discretion of the tribunal. ICC arbitrators can grant provisional relief either in the form of a reasoned order or of an award.[96] Both forms have been used in practice depending on the circumstances of the case.[97]

23-80 Like state courts, arbitration tribunals have the power to make provisional measures dependent on the provision of any type of security by the applicant. This power, which is provided for in some of the more recent laws and rules,[98] is intended to facilitate the granting of interim relief. By ordering security the tribunal can effectively protect the interest of the parties against whom the measures are directed. The tribunal retains jurisdiction to determine any claim of damages by the party against whom unjustified measures were ordered.[99]

23-81 In England the arbitrator may, like a judge, require a cross undertaking in damages, with financial guarantees, to be available to pay compensation if the interim measures are found to have been unjustified and to have caused damage to the party against which they were ordered.

---

94 See, *e.g.*, DIS section 20; LCIA Article 25; CPR Rules for non administered arbitration Rule 13.

95 UNCITRAL Rules Article 26(2); see also AAA ICDR Article 21(2).

96 Before the 1998 Rules were adopted a Working Party recommended that interim measures should be issued in form of an order to avoid the formalities connected with an award. See Final Report on Interim and Partial Awards, *ICC Bulletin* 26 (1990) 29.

97 See ICC case no 3540, VII *YBCA* 124 (1982); for orders see *ICC Bulletin* 76 (1993); for further cases see Yesilirmak, "Interim and Conservatory Measures in ICC Arbitral Practice", 11(1) *ICC Bulletin* 31 (2000) Fn 6.

98 See Model Law Article 17; Germany, ZPO section 1041(1); Switzerland, PIL Article 183(3); ICC Article 23(1); LCIA Article 25(1)(2).

99 *E.g.*, Germany, ZPO section 1041(4).

2. ENFORCEMENT OF INTERIM MEASURES ORDERED BY ARBITRATION TRIBUNALS

23-82 Arbitration tribunals in general lack the state courts' powers to enforce their orders over the parties or their property.[100] Furthermore penalties for non-compliance are only possible if the parties have either agreed on them or they are specifically allowed by the applicable law.[101] In all other cases the intervention of state courts is necessary for the enforcement of such measures.

23-83 The lack of coercive powers is at least partly compensated by the persuasive powers of the tribunal. It can draw negative inferences from non-compliance with its orders or take that into account when deciding on the cost of an arbitration. Therefore provisional measures ordered by the tribunal are invariably complied with voluntarily.[102] In some cases tribunals order informal interim measures the enforcement of which is not intended.[103]

2.1. National Laws to Assist Enforcement of Interim Measures

23-84 Where enforcement is necessary it has to be effected by state courts. In the past problems of enforcement have been one of the major arguments against provisional measures ordered by arbitration tribunals. National enforcement provisions were normally interpreted to apply only to final awards so that the provisional character excluded any interim measure from enforcement under those rules.[104] To deal with this problem some modern recent arbitration laws

---

[100] But see the rare cases where the parties have put in advance certain amounts or property at the disposal of the tribunal, *e.g.*, in the context of the Algier Accords establishing the Iran-US Claims Tribunal, which can authorize payment from a bank account at its disposal.

[101] See, however, Netherlands, CCP Article 1056 which provides:

> The arbitral tribunal has the power to impose a penalty for non-compliance in cases where the court has such power.

[102] Bond, "The nature of conservatory and provisional measures", in ICC (ed), *Conservatory and Provisional Measures*, 8, 16; Berger, *International Economic Arbitration*, 334; Craig, Park & Paulsson, *ICC Arbitration*, para 26.05; for the possible means of indirect enforcement see also Karrer, "Interim Measures Issued by Arbitral Tribunals and the Courts: Less Theory, Please", *ICCA Congress series no 10*, 102-104.

[103] Raeschke-Kessler and Berger, *Recht und Praxis*, para 609 *et seq*; see, *e.g.*, ICC case no 3896, X *YBCA* 47 (1985), where the tribunal denied the requested declaration but stated in its partial award that the parties should refrain from any action affecting the *status quo*.

[104] Bundesgerichtshof, 22 May 1957, *ZZP* 427 (1958); see also Besson, *Arbitrage International et Measures Provisoires*, para 494 *et seq*.

contain special provisions regulating the enforcement of provisional measures ordered by tribunals. For example, German ZPO section 1041(2) provides

> The court may, at the request of a party, permit enforcement of a measure … unless application for a corresponding interim measure has already been made to a court. It may recast such an order if necessary for the purpose of enforcing the measure.

23-85 A comparable provision can be found in Article 183(2) Swiss PIL which provides that where the parties do not comply voluntarily with the relief ordered "the arbitral tribunal may request the assistance of the competent court." Similarly, section 42(1) English Arbitration Act provides

> Unless otherwise agreed by the parties, the court may make an order requiring a party to comply with a peremptory order made by the tribunal.[105]

23-86 While English law requires that the interim relief is ordered in the form of a peremptory order to be enforced by the courts this is not the case under the Hong Kong Arbitration Ordinance. Following recent amendments to the law[106] the courts can now, under section 2GG Arbitration Ordinance, give effect to and enforce interlocutory orders and directions of a tribunal.[107] Furthermore this power was originally intended for but is not limited to arbitrations with their seat in Hong Kong but also covers tribunals sitting outside the PRC and Hong Kong.[108] However, the courts are unlikely to enforce an order which is not permitted in their own jurisdiction.[109]

---

[105] Russell *on Arbitration*, para 6-130, doubts whether these powers could be used to enforce provisional measures.

[106] Arbitration (Amendment) Ordinance no 2 of 2000.

[107] Section 2GG provides:

> (1) An award, order or direction made or given in or in relation to arbitration proceedings by an arbitral tribunal is enforceable in the same way as a judgment, order or direction of the Court that has the same effect, but only with the leave of the Court or a judge of the Court. If that leave is given, the Court or judge may enter judgment in terms of the award, order or direction.
>
> (2) Notwithstanding anything in this Ordinance, this section applies to an award, order and direction made or given whether in or outside Hong Kong.

[108] See Morgan, "Enforcement of Chinese Arbitral Awards Complete Once More – But with a Difference", 30 *HRLJ* 375 (2000) 379.

[109] *Ibid.* See also *Bocotra Construction Pte Ltd v Attorney-General of Singapore* [1995] 2 SLR 523.

23-87 No comparable provision can be found in the Model Law. A provision in an earlier draft was deleted as the question was considered too controversial and was left to the national laws.[110]

2.2. Applying the Rules for Enforcing Awards to Enforce Orders for Interim Measures

23-88 Some laws provide for the enforcement of interim measures. In general these rules are limited to interim measures ordered by tribunals which have their seat in the country of the enforcing court. Where the tribunal has its seat in a different country these rules do not apply; nor do they cover the enforcement of interim measures abroad. In such cases enforcement depends on the rules governing the enforcement of awards in the place where enforcement is sought.

23-89 In these cases it is still contested whether and to what extent enforcement is possible. The only legal basis is through the recognition and enforcement of awards. The first question is whether the interlocutory nature of interim measures precludes the application of the rules dealing with the enforcement of awards.[111] If this is not the case, the issue is whether these rules only apply to interim measures in the form of a preliminary award or also to those in the form of an order.

23-90 The answer to the first question depends on the perception of interim measures. The classical approach is to consider whether these measures are a final decision on the question or whether the issues are still to be determined in the final award. From this viewpoint interim measures do not finally and in a binding fashion dispose of claims brought by the parties; they have an interim function only. This is the prevailing view on interim measures ordered under Article 17 Model Law, independently of whether these measures are granted in the form of an interim award or as a procedural order.[112] This view also prevails under the New York Convention and most arbitration laws.[113]

---

[110] See UN Doc A/CN9/245, Article XIV para 72; for the earlier draft see UN Doc. A/CN9/WGII/WP40, Article XIV.

[111] One has to distinguish interim measures from partial final awards, which in practice are sometimes referred to as "interim awards"; see Di Pietro and Platte, *Enforcement of International Arbitration Awards*, 34.

[112] Berger, *International Economic Arbitration*, 343.

[113] Craig, Park & Paulsson, *ICC Arbitration*, para 26-05 *iii*; Raeschke-Kessler and Berger, *Recht und Praxis*, para 606.

23-91 This position was illustrated by the Supreme Court of Queensland in *Resort Condominiums v Bolwell.*[114] The parties had concluded a licensing agreement for the use of know-how and trademarks in relation to time-sharing. The claimant initiated arbitration proceedings in the US and the arbitrator in an interim award ordered the respondent to refrain from certain actions, in particular using the know-how and trademark covered by the licensing agreement. When the claimant wanted to enforce this interim award the question arose whether it was a final award in the sense of the New York Convention or section 8 of the relevant Arbitration Act. The court denied that it was a final decision and held

> It does not appear that the Act or Convention contemplates any type of 'award' or 'order' of an arbitrator, other than an award which determines at least all or some of the matters referred to the arbitrator for decision. The applicant can derive no comfort from Sect. 8(1) of the Act which states that '... a foreign award is binding by virtue of this Act for all purposes on the parties to the arbitration agreement in pursuance of which it was made', with no word 'final' appearing therein, as it does for example in Sect. 28 of the Queensland Act. Whilst it is true that a valid interlocutory order is in one sense 'binding' on the parties to the arbitration agreement at least until it is varied or discharged by the tribunal which made it ... An interlocutory order which may be rescinded, suspended, varied or reopened by the tribunal which pronounced it, is not 'final' and binding on the parties ....[115]

23-92 However, interim measures can also be seen as a final and enforceable award on certain substantive interim claims on which the parties have agreed.[116] The prevailing view in US case law is that such interim measures constitute an award open to confirmation and enforcement as well as vacation under sections 9 and 10 Federal Arbitration Act.[117]

23-93 The policy underlying this approach was expressed in *Yasuda Fire & Marine Insurance v Continental Casualty.*[118] The tribunal made an interim order for security obliging the claimant in the action to open an interim letter of credit. After the respondent applied for confirmation of this interim order the claimant

---

[114] *Resort Condominiums International, Inc v Ray Bolwell and others*, XX YBCA 628 (1995) (Supreme Court of Queensland, 29 October 1993).

[115] *Ibid*, para 32; for a commentary on the case see Pryles, "Interlocutory Orders and Convention Awards: the Case of Resort Condominium v Bolwell", 10 *Arb Int* 385 (1994).

[116] Schlosser, *Das Recht der internationalen privaten Schiedsgerichtsbarkeit*, para 776.

[117] Carbonneau, *Arbitration*, 601; Born, *International Commercial Arbitration*, 972 *et seq.*

[118] *Yasuda Fire & Marine Insurance Co of Europe v Continental Casualty Co*, 37 F3d 345 (7th Cir, 1994).

asked for its release. Before coming to the point whether a release was justified the court had first to consider whether the order constituted an award in the sense of sections 9 and 10 FAA. The court referred to an earlier decision where an interim order to pay the money in dispute into an escrow account was a final order "that can be reviewed for confirmation and enforcement by districts courts under the FAA."[119] In the *Yasuda Fire* case the Court stated

> The arbitration panel in this case ordered Yasuda to post an interim letter of credit in order to protect a possible final award in favour of CAN. ... Because this relief protects CAN's interests, CAN has the right to confirm the order in the district court, which it has done. Analogously, Yasuda should have the right to attack this relief. The interim relief represents a "temporary equitable order .... calculated to preserve assets...needed to make a potential final award more meaningful." ... we find that an interim letter of credit constitutes an "award" under section 10 and that the district court had jurisdiction to consider Yasuda's Petition to Vacate.[120]

23-94 The *Yasuda Fire* case can be distinguished on its specific facts and the nature of the interim measure ordered. In any event, US practice is still the minority view, in particular, in relation to the enforcement of interim measures under the New York Convention which applies to final and binding awards. Provisional or interim measures are not final.

2.3. Development of International Rules to Enforce Orders for Interim Measures

23-95 The enforcement of interim measures ordered by an arbitration tribunal in one country by the courts of another country continues to be an intractable problem. Despite some national laws seeking to assist with enforcement of interim measures either with express provisions or with practical court support, the real problem is the absence of an international convention to regulate the enforcement of interim or conservatory measures ordered by a tribunal which has its seat in another country.

23-96 National laws do not provide for the enforcement of interim measures granted in arbitration outside their jurisdiction. This leaves some scope for

---

[119] *Pacific Reinsurance v Ohio Reinsurance*, 935 F2d 1019 (9th Cir, 1991).

[120] *Ibid*, 348. See also *Sperry International Trade v Government of Israel*, 532 F Supp 901 (SDNY 1982) where the order by the tribunal to pay the proceeds of a standby letter of credit into an escrow account was held to be an enforceable award under the New York Convention; *Banco de Seguros del Estado v Mutual Marine Offices Inc*, 17(8) Mealey's IAR 15 (2002); for further examples see Craig, Park & Paulsson, *ICC Arbitration*, para 26-05 *iii*.

international harmonisation by an international instrument. National courts should give effect, to interim or conservatory measures ordered by a competent and properly constituted arbitration tribunal, subject only to international public policy. This will enhance the sovereignty of the national court and the international standing of the local law.

2.4. Enforcement of Interim Measures Ordered after Hearing only the Party Seeking the Order

23-97 Where enforcement of an interim measure is possible an additional question arises: must the party against whom the order is made be heard before an enforcing order is made? Such a requirement may deprive interim measures of their effectiveness. A party which is to be heard before interim measures can be enforced may have sufficient time to frustrate these measures. In such a situation it may be advisable for a party to go directly to the state courts for the interim measures, provided this option is available. Their interim relief may be granted and enforced *ex parte*, having heard only one party.

23-98 To ensure the efficiency of interim measures by tribunals German law provides for enforcement proceedings involving only one party where necessary. Section 1063(3) ZPO provides

> The presiding judge of the civil court senate (Zivilsenat) may issue, without prior hearing of the party opposing the application, an order to the effect that, until a decision on the request has been reached, the applicant may pursue enforcement of the award or enforce the interim measure of protection of the arbitration court pursuant to section 1041. In the case of an award, enforcement of the award may not go beyond measures of protection. The party opposing the application may prevent enforcement by providing as security an amount corresponding to the amount that may be enforced by the applicant.

23-99 This provision offers the possibility of obtaining effective interim relief from the tribunal which prevents a party from frustrating an order before it becomes effective. To grant minimum protection for the unheard party it is fair that it be heard as soon as possible after the enforcing order has been issued. At that time the order can be confirmed, removed or varied by the court. Furthermore the judge when faced with an application to enforce interim measures without reference to the respondent party should require that security is provided for eventual damage claims arising from this enforcement.

3. PROVISIONAL MEASURES ORDERED BY COURTS IN SUPPORT OF ARBITRATION

23-100 Despite the power of tribunals to order interim and conservatory measures in practice parties often apply to state courts for interim measures. There are many reasons: the tribunal may not yet have been composed or it may lack the required power; urgent relief may be required and the tribunal cannot be constituted quickly; an application without the involvement of the respondent may be essential to prevent avoidance of the relief sought; effective authority may be required from a national court within whose jurisdiction the party against whom the relief is sought is resident; the public nature of the interim measures procedure in national courts may assist the position of the party seeking the relief.[121] There are also situations where the applicant for interim measures may go to the courts with the aim to disrupt or undermine the arbitration proceedings. Not all these reasons, or the facts in each case, will justify resorting to national courts, but tactical as well as practical factors invariably influence the way cases are conducted.

3.1. Effect of the Arbitration Agreement

23-101 Following the New York Convention and the Model Law, most national laws require their courts to refer a dispute to arbitration if a valid arbitration clause exists. Despite this almost universally accepted rule, courts may order interim measures; such an action is not an exercise of excessive jurisdiction by the court or a negation of the arbitration clause. This is categorically stated in Article VI(4) European Convention

> A request for interim measures or measures of conservation addressed to a judicial authority shall not be deemed incompatible with the arbitration agreement, or regarded as a submission of the substance of the case to the court.[122]

23-102 Similar provisions can be found in a number of arbitration laws. For example, Article 9 Model Law provides that

> It is not incompatible with an arbitration agreement for a party to request, before or during arbitral proceedings, from a court an interim measure of protection and for a court to grant such measure.[123]

---

[121] See, for a summary of situations when court intervention may be beneficial, Goswami, "Interim Relief: The Role of the Courts", *ICCA Congress series no 10*, 113.

[122] On the application of the European Convention see, *e.g.*, Audiencia Provincial Cadiz, 12 June 1991, *Bahia Industrial SA v Eintacar-Eimar SA*, XVIII YBCA 616 (1993).

23-103 Dutch law even goes a step further. It not only allows for ordinary interim measures but also for summary proceedings. Article 1022(2) Netherlands CCP provides

> An arbitration agreement shall not preclude a party from requesting a court to grant interim measures of protection, or from applying to the President of the District Court for a decision in summary proceedings ... In the latter case the President shall decide the case in accordance with the provisions of article 1051.

23-104 Frequently the arbitration agreement makes clear that it is not intended to prevent a party seeking interim measures from a national court. This may be in the arbitration clause itself or in the arbitration rules applicable. The right to submit to the courts may be general, *i.e.*, at any time during the arbitration proceedings, or limited to the time before the tribunal is constituted. The former is the case with the UNCITRAL Rules which provide in Article 26(3)

> A request for interim measures addressed by any party to a judicial authority shall not be deemed incompatible with the agreement to arbitrate, or as a waiver of that agreement.[124]

23-105 The narrower view distinguishes between measures requested before the file has been transferred to the tribunal and those requested thereafter. The right to resort to a court after the tribunal has been established may be restricted. For example, Article 23(2) ICC Rules provides in its pertinent part

> Before the file is transmitted to the Arbitral Tribunal, and *in appropriate circumstances even thereafter,* the parties may apply to any competent judicial authority for interim or conservatory measures. [Emphasis added]

23-106 Similarly, Article 25(3) LCIA Rules provides

> The power of the Arbitral Tribunal under Article 25.1 shall not prejudice howsoever any party's right to apply to any state court or other judicial authority for interim or conservatory measures before the formation of the Arbitral Tribunal and, *in exceptional cases, thereafter.* [Emphasis added]

---

[123] See also Greece, International Commercial Arbitration Act 1999 Article 9; Germany, ZPO section 1033; India, Arbitration and Conciliation Act section 9; see also *Trade Fortune Inc v Amalgamated Mill Supplies Ltd*, (1995) XX YBCA 277 (British Columbia Supreme Court, 25 February 1994); *Katran Shipping Co Ltd v Kenven Transportation Ltd*, (1993) XVIII YBCA 175 (Supreme Court of Hong Kong, 29 June 1992).

[124] See also AAA ICDR Rules Article 21(3); DIS Rules section 20(2); CRCICA Rules 26(3).

23-107 The description of when parties may resort to the courts after the tribunal is established in the ICC and LCIA Rules makes clear that the authority of the tribunal for interim relief takes precedence over national courts. The Rules provide the tribunal with the power to grant various types of interim measures. The right to apply to a state court is limited to "appropriate circumstances" and "exceptional cases"

23-108 What are "appropriate circumstances" and "exceptional cases" depends on the facts of the particular case. It is important to note that the Rules presume that generally interim relief should be granted by the tribunal, at least once the file has been transferred to it.[125]

23-109 Even in cases where neither the applicable arbitration rules nor the relevant law contain express provisions for interim measures by the courts, judges have in most cases asserted such a power and have assumed a concurrent jurisdiction of state courts and arbitration tribunals in relation to interim measures. For example, the French Cour de cassation has consistently held that the existence of an arbitration agreement does not prevent the courts from ordering statutory investigative measures under Article 145 NCPC.[126]

23-110 In some jurisdictions, such as India, it is doubtful whether the power of the courts to order interim relief also extends to arbitration tribunals having their seat in a different country or whether it is limited to arbitrations having their seat in India. While Article 9 Model Law, on which the Indian law is based, provides for court ordered interim relief irrespective of the seat of arbitration the Indian provision is not equivalent in this regard. Though there are also good reasons to allow interim relief in connection with arbitrations having their seat in a different country there are a number of court decisions where it was decided differently.[127]

23-111 There was uncertainty as to the availability of interim relief by courts in the US. Article 8 FAA[128] expressly empowers courts to grant provisional

---

125 Derains and Schwartz, *ICC Rules*, 276.

126 See Cour de cassation, 20 december 1982, *SCI Le Panorama v Société immobilière et mobilière du Tertre (SIMT)*, Rev Arb 233 (1986); see further Fouchard Gaillard Goldman *on International Commercial Arbitration*, para 1332; see also Pretura of Verona, 22 April 1985, *Pama Industrie SpA v Shultz Steel Company / Banca Nazionale del Lavoro*, XII YBCA 494 (1987); Corte di cassazione 7 August 1992, *Attika Shipping Company v Bluemar SA*, XIX YBCA 680 (1994).

127 Goswami, "Interim Relief: The Role of the Courts", *ICCA Congress series no 10*, 116.

128 "If the basis of jurisdiction be a cause of action otherwise justiciable in admiralty, then, notwithstanding anything herein to the contrary the party claiming to be aggrieved may begin

measures in maritime disputes in the form of the seizure of a vessel. However, as there is no other provision dealing with interim measures it was argued that the right for a court to grant such measures was limited to maritime arbitration and that in all other types of arbitration the courts are obliged to refer the case to arbitration.[129] This is no longer the accepted view. US courts can order provisional matters in support of arbitration in all areas of law. The Third Circuit Court of Appeals in *Blumenthal v Merrill Lynch* held[130]

> the pro-arbitration policies reflected in the ...Supreme Court decisions are furthered, not weakened, by a rule permitting a district court to preserve the meaningfulness of the arbitration through a preliminary injunction. Arbitration can become a "hollow formality" if parties are able to alter irreversibly the status quo before the arbitrators are able to render a decision in the dispute. A district court must ensure that the parties get what they bargained for- a meaningful arbitration of the dispute. ....[131]

23-112 This explains why national courts retain their authority even when neither the arbitration agreement nor the applicable rules or laws expressly allow for court ordered interim measures. The underlying rationale of the national courts' obligation to stay proceedings in favour of arbitration is to protect arbitration from unwanted court interference and to ensure the effectiveness of arbitration agreements. There are, however, situations where court ordered provisional measures are necessary to ensure effective arbitration proceedings.

23-113 In practice provisional measures are often needed before the arbitration has started and when the tribunal has yet to be constituted. In such situations it would be against the purpose of Article II(3) New York Convention and other comparable rules to oblige a court to decline jurisdiction for ordering provisional

---

his proceeding hereunder by libel and seizure of the vessel or other property of the other party according to the usual course of admiralty proceedings, and the court shall then have jurisdiction to direct the parties to proceed with the arbitration and shall retain jurisdiction to enter its decree upon the award."

[129] *McCreary Tire & Rubber Co v Seat SpA*, 501 F2d 1032 (3d Cir, 1974); *Cooper v Ateliers de la Motobecane SA*, 456 NY 2d 728 (NY CA, 1982); for further cases see Wagoner, "Interim Relief in International Arbitration: Enforcement is a Substantial Problem" 51 Oct *Disp Resol J* 68 (1996) 70 *et seq.*

[130] *Blumenthal v Merrill Lynch, Pierce, Fenner & Smith Inc*, 910 F2d 1049 (2d Cir 1990); it seems that also the Court of Appeal for the 3d Circuit which decided McCreary now follows this view, see *Ortho Pharmaceutical Corp v Amgen Inc*, 882 F.2d 806 (3d Cir, 1989).

[131] See also *Daye Nonferrous Metals Company (China) v Trafigura Beheer BV (Netherlands)*, XXIII YBCA 984 (1998) (USDC SDNY, 2 July 1997). For further examples see Born, *International Commercial Arbitration*, 936 *et seq.*

measures.[132] Furthermore, even after the tribunal has been constituted provisional measures by state courts may be useful and necessary to support an arbitration, in particular in cases where time is of the essence and property at risk of dissipation or destruction. Due to the standing organisation of state courts, and the direct enforceability of court ordered interim measures, they are in general quicker and more effective than measures ordered by tribunals which in some cases may have to be declared enforceable by state courts.[133]

23-114 Parties can agree to preclude a national court from granting interim measures. The extent to which the powers of national courts can be excluded varies as, in many situations, the courts will not allow their overriding protective powers to be excluded. However, the rules as to the concurrent jurisdiction of arbitration tribunals and state courts generally do not have a mandatory character. Therefore the courts have no jurisdiction to grant provisional measures in an arbitration under the ICSID Convention, if no right to apply to the national court is reserved.[134]

23-115 The ICC pre-arbitration *reférée* procedure can also be seen as an exclusion of court jurisdiction.[135] A limited restriction which only relates to orders for security for costs can be found in the LCIA Rules.[136] The parties, by opting for arbitration under those rules, make those restrictions part of their agreement. These types of limitation should be respected by the courts.

23-116 Court ordered interim relief may also be excluded in the arbitration agreement itself. In *Mantovani v Caparelli SpA*[137] for example, the arbitration clause provided that neither party "shall bring any action or other legal proceedings against the other of them in respect of any such dispute until such dispute shall first have been heard and determined by the arbitrators." The English Court of Appeal interpreted this clause to cover any type of interim relief and held that the request for interim relief directed to the Italian courts by one of the parties was a breach of the arbitration agreement which in principle gave rise to an action for damages.

---

132 Fouchard Gaillard Goldman *on International Commercial Arbitration*, para 1307 *et seq.*

133 Lachmann, *Handbuch*, para 1464; the general existence of a power by the courts to order interim relief does not mean that the court should make use of that power.

134 Article 26.

135 Fouchard Gaillard Goldman *on International Commercial Arbitration*, para 1321.

136 Article 25(3).

137 [1980] 1 Lloyd's Rep 375.

23-117 Hence, the general reference often found in arbitration clauses, that disputes shall be decided by arbitration to the exclusion of all court proceedings should not be sufficient to exclude court jurisdictions to grant provisional measures.[138]

3.2. No Waiver of the Right to Arbitrate

23-118 An application to state courts for interim relief should not be considered a waiver of the right to arbitrate. This is clearly stated in some arbitration laws and rules.[139] It follows also from the provisions which declare court ordered interim relief to be compatible with the existence of an arbitration agreement. Even where the applicable rules or law are silent, an application to the courts for interim relief cannot be considered to be a waiver of the right to arbitration but may sometimes be necessary to protect such right.[140]

23-119 However, the situation is different where the requested relief goes beyond mere conservatory measures and includes damages. In such cases the applications may be considered to be in violation of the arbitration agreement and a waiver of the right to arbitrate.[141]

4. CONCURRENT POWERS OF STATE COURTS AND ARBITRATION TRIBUNALS

23-120 As the existence of an arbitration agreement does not exclude the court's jurisdiction to order interim measures a question arises as to the relationship between the jurisdictions of state courts and the arbitration tribunal. Are both jurisdictions concurrent in a way that a party has a free choice when seeking interim measures? Or is the tribunal the primary forum in which interim relief in international arbitration should be sought, the court's role being subsidiary and supportive?

23-121 There are arguments to support both positions. On the one hand, any restriction on the court's power to order interim measures opens up a new area of

---

[138] For such an interpretation see English Commercial Court in *Re Q's Estate* [1999] 1 Lloyd's Rep 931, 935; see also Wessel and North Cohen, "In tune with Mantovani: the 'Novel' case of damages for Breach of an arbitration agreeement", 4 *Int ALR* 65 (2001) 68.

[139] See, *e.g.*, European Convention Article VI(4); UNCITRAL Rules Article 26(3).

[140] See, *e.g.*, ICC case no 6566, 11(1) *ICC Bulletin* 48 (2000).

[141] See ICC case no 5896, 11(1) *ICC Bulletin* 37 (2000).

potential dispute as to whether the requirements for court ordered interim measures are actually met. Vague concepts such as "urgency" are prone to different views and entail an unwanted degree of uncertainty. Furthermore in court proceedings interim measures may be available as of right while tribunals in general have a discretion.[142] There are strong arguments in favour of making interim measures ordered by the tribunal the primary means of interim relief and to restrict the jurisdiction of the courts to cases where for some reason effective protection cannot be granted by the tribunal. To give state courts an unlimited power to grant interim relief may frustrate the parties agreement to have disputes determined by arbitration.

23-122 In many cases interim measures may have a considerable effect on the outcome of the main proceedings. Some authors suggest that interim measures often actually decide the dispute.[143] There is a risk that a court ordered interim measure will take the dispute out of the hands of the tribunal. The pressure exerted by the seizure of a bank account or the arrest of a vessel will often force a party with limited financial funds into a settlement which it would not have accepted without such an order and without the merits of the dispute being properly aired. In such a situation the tribunal will not have the opportunity to deal with the dispute as was originally agreed by the parties. Furthermore a party may find itself entangled in an dispute over the granting of interim measures in a foreign court. The pressure exerted by the costs involved may be amplified by the publicity engendered in those court proceedings which would destroy the privacy of the arbitration process. This could be a forceful argument for settlement. The arguments against interim measures ordered by courts are even stronger in cases where the provisional measures required are of the same kind as the order which is ultimately sought from the arbitrators. In these situations the court ordering of the interim measures may actually interfere with the arbitration.[144]

23-123 The Model Law is silent on this point. Article 9 does not contain any restrictions as to the powers of the courts to grant interim measures. The drafting history makes it clear that this is not the result of a positive decision in favour of equality of both types of interim measures. The drafters considered the issue to

---

142 See the official report in connection with the German Arbitration Law, BT-Drs 13/5274, 39.

143 Bötsch, "The Problem of Provisional Remedies in International Commercial Arbitration", in Bötsch (ed), *Provisional Remedies*, 4 *et seq.*

144 See *Channel Tunnel Group Ltd v Balfour Beatty Construction Ltd*, [1993] AC 334, 367-368.

be so controversial that it should be regulated by the different national laws.[145] These differ considerably in that matter.

23-124 In Germany adoption of Article 9 Model Law containing no restrictions on courts jurisdiction is a clear decision in favour of true concurrent jurisdiction. It is stated that the jurisdiction of the state courts exists in its own right and does not depend on the non-availability of interim relief from the tribunal.[146] On the contrary, German courts are bound to grant interim relief once the requirements set out in the relevant provisions of the ZPO are met and some authors go as far as to consider provisional measures by courts to be the primary form of interim relief.[147]

23-125 A true concurrent jurisdiction between courts and arbitration tribunals is also assumed in Switzerland.[148]

23-126 Other arbitration laws submit interim measures by courts to a number of additional requirements which give a subsidiary character to court ordered measures. Often the power of the courts is limited to cases of urgency, or to cases where the tribunal has not been established, or is for any other reason prevented from making those measures.[149] For example, section 44 English Arbitration Act grants courts the general right to order certain types of provisional measures but provides

> (3) If the case is one of urgency, the court may, on the application of a party or proposed party to the arbitration proceedings, make such orders as it thinks necessary for the purpose of preserving evidence or assets.
> (4) If the case is not one of urgency, the court shall act only on the application of a party to the arbitral proceedings (upon notice to the other parties and to the tribunal)

---

[145] See Holtzmann & Neuhaus, *Model Law*, 531; for an overview of different approaches see Schäfer "New Solutions for Interim Measures of Protection in International Commercial Arbitration: English, German and Hong Kong Law compared", 2 *EJCL* 2.

[146] BT-Drs 13/5274 38 *et seq*; Lachmann, *Handbuch*, paras 1401 *et seq.*

[147] Lachmann, *Handbuch*, paras 1463 *et seq.*

[148] See Berti, in Berti (ed), *International Arbitration in Switzerland*, Article 183 para 5; for further references see Besson, *Arbitrage International et Measures Provisoires*, 192.

[149] See, *e.g.*, the interpretation given to section 2GC(6) Hong Kong Arbitration Ordinance by the court in *Leviathan Shipping Co Ltd v Sky Sailing Overseas Ltd* [1998] 4 HKC 347, 1 *Int ALR* N-114 (1998) according to which a court should not make use of its powers to order interim relief if arbitration proceedings are pending and the relief can be ordered by the tribunal; in favour of such a restriction also Bond, "The nature of conservatory and provisional measures", in ICC (ed), *Conservatory and Provisional Measures*, 18.

> made with the permission of the tribunal or the agreement in writing of the other parties.
> (5) In any case the court shall act only if or to the extent that the arbitral tribunal, and any arbitral or other institution or person vested by the parties with power in that regard, has no power or is unable for the time being to act effectively.[150]

23-127 National laws relating to the concurrent jurisdiction of state courts and arbitration tribunals are not mandatory. The choice of institutional rules which limit the right of a party to apply for interim measures from the courts will prevail over any provision of the law governing the arbitration which allows the courts an unlimited power to order interim measures.[151]

23-128 State courts do, and should, act cautiously before granting interim measures in cases where the parties have agreed on arbitration. This is well illustrated by the *Channel Tunnel* decision of the House of Lords.[152] The respondent in this case was one of the sub-contractors employed in the construction of the Channel Tunnel. A dispute arose as to the amount payable for the cooling system and the respondent threatened to suspend all works. Although the contract provided for arbitration in Brussels the claimant applied to the English courts for an interim injunction to restrain the respondent from suspending all work. The House of Lords came to the conclusion that it had jurisdiction to issue the required injunction but refrained from doing so as

> [t]here is always a tension when the Court is asked to order, by way of interim relief in support of an arbitration, a remedy of the same kind as will ultimately be sought from the arbitrators: between, on the one hand, the need for the Court to make a tentative assessment of the merits in order to decide whether the plaintiff's claim is strong enough to merit protection, and on the other hand the duty of the Court to respect the choice of tribunal which both parties have made, and not to take out of the hands of the arbitrators (or other decision-makers) a power of decision which the parties have entrusted to them alone.[153]

23-129 State courts are even more reluctant when the arbitration and the parties have little connection with the state concerned and the seat of the arbitration is

---

[150] See also Ohio, Code of International Commercial Arbitration, section 2712.36.
[151] LCIA Article 25(3).
[152] *Channel Tunnel Group Ltd v Balfour Beatty Construction Ltd*, [1993] AC 334.
[153] *Ibid*, 367-368.

outside that state.[154] In some countries, such as India, the power to grant interim relief in aid of arbitration is even limited to arbitration proceedings having their seat in the country.[155]

23-130 The parties' choice of arbitration is also relevant insofar as measures ordered by the tribunal should always prevail where they are in conflict with measures ordered by state courts. Ultimately arbitrators should have the final word and be allowed to overrule, release or vary interim measures ordered by state courts.[156]

---

[154] Bond, "The nature of conservatory and provisional measures", in ICC (ed), *Conservatory and Provisional Measures*, 12 *et seq*; see also *HSBC Bank USA v National Equity Corp*, 719 NYS 2d 20 (2001).

[155] See *Mariott International Inc v Ansal Hotels Limited*, (2001) XXVI YBCA 788 (Delhi High Court) where it was held that due to the seat of arbitration being in Malaysia the Indian courts could not grant the requested relief, neither on the basis of section 9 Indian Arbitration Act which only applies to arbitrations with their seat in India nor on the basis of an inherent power. See also *Contichem v Parsons Shipping*, 229 F3d, 462 (2d Cir, 2000) where a pre-arbitration attachment in the US for arbitration in London was denied.

[156] Fouchard Gaillard Goldman *on International Commercial Arbitration*, para 1330; for a different view see Berger, *International Economic Arbitration*, 347; Di Pietro and Platte, *Enforcement of international awards*, 43; ICC case no 4998, 113 *Clunet* 1139 (1986) which was, however, decided on the basis of the old Swiss law which prohibited interim relief by arbitrators in general.

Chapter 24

ARBITRATION AWARD

24-1 The arbitration award is the instrument recording the tribunal's decision provisionally or finally determining claims of the parties. The award may concern legal or factual differences between the parties, may involve interpretation of contract terms or determining the respective rights and obligations of the parties under the contract. It may also deal with preliminary but substantive issues, such as jurisdiction of the tribunal, applicable law and limitation of actions. There are also many issues where the tribunal will be asked to rule on issues concerning procedure, the conduct of the arbitration and other preliminary and non-substantive matters. There are several legal consequences associated with the rendering of the various types of awards. For example, after the final award is issued, the tribunal's authority expires and the tribunal can do no more in respect of the parties' differences. Further, the award is generally final and binding and has *res judicata* effect between the parties, *i.e.* no claim can be brought in respect of the same matter.

24-2 This chapter examines (1) various decisions of the arbitration tribunal, (2) types of awards, (3) making of award, (4) content of an award, (5) reliefs ordered (6) correction and interpretation of awards, (7) confidentiality and publication of awards, and (8) termination of proceedings without an award.

1. Decisions of the Arbitration Tribunal

24-3 Arbitration tribunals make many decisions during the arbitration process. While all awards are decisions of the tribunal not all decisions are awards.[1] The term "decision" is generic and refers to the result of any conclusion or resolution reached after consideration[2] while an "award" is a decision affecting the rights between the parties and which is generally capable of being enforced, for instance, under the New York Convention.

24-4 There is no universally acceptable definition of an "award". In particular, in the context of the Model Law Article 2 all suggested definitions were rejected as were proposals to deal with the issue in other articles. One of the most controversial matters was whether decisions of the tribunal in respect of procedural issues could be classified as awards.[3] In most cases, an award marks

---

[1] See, *e.g.*, UNCITRAL Rules Article 31(1).

[2] *Concise Oxford Dictionary* (10th ed, Oxford University Press 1999), 371.

[3] See Holtzmann and Neuhaus, *Model Law*, 153-154 and 867-868. See also UN Doc A/CN9/246, paras 129 and 192. According to para 192:

the determination of a specific issue or the end of the proceedings[4]. Except on very limited grounds the decision is final between the parties and cannot be challenged.

24-5 Several decisions of the tribunal aim at organising the procedure, relate to technical and procedural matters and are rendered without any formality or reasoning. Such decisions are characterised as procedural orders. Procedural orders do not decide the dispute; they simply make arrangements for the proceedings,[5] *e.g. a* procedural order, may fix the hearing at a place different from the seat of arbitration, order or refuse to order disclosure of documents, set deadlines for the submission of documents, or indicate to the parties the issues on which the tribunal would like to hear arguments.[6]

24-6 Procedural orders generally cannot be challenged.[7] However, occasionally procedural decisions may go beyond the scope of traditional procedural orders and may effectively be deemed to be awards. In such cases courts will have to decide whether the classification by the tribunal of a procedural decision as an order is conclusive or whether the court may reclassify it as an award and, hence, review it. Two significant court decisions have addressed the issue.

24-7 In *Braspetro Oil Services Company v The Management and Implementation Authority of the Great Man-Made River Project* ("Brasoil"),[8] the dispute concerned a 1986 construction contract between Brasoil and GMRA. In May 1995 a tribunal rendered a partial award on the merits against Brasoil. During the stage of quantification of damages by the tribunal GMRA submitted documents which Brasoil believed to have been fraudulently withheld at the

---

> ... award means a final award which disposes of all issues submitted to the arbitral tribunal and any other decision of the arbitral tribunal which finally determine [sic!] any question of substance or the question of its competence or any other question of procedure but, in the latter case, only if the arbitral tribunal terms its decision award.

The definition was rejected mainly due to the inclusion of issues of procedure.

4 Sanders, *IECL*, Vol XVI, Chapter 12, para 178.

5 See Swiss Federal Tribunal, 17 May 1990, *BGE* 109 Ia 85, *ASA Bulletin* 1990, 286, 288. See also Berger, *International Economic Arbitration*, 592.

6 See also the comprehensive list in Jarvin, "To What Extent Are Procedural Decisions of Arbitrators Subject to Court Review?", *ICCA Congress Series no 9*, 366, 369-370.

7 *Ibid*, 372 *et seq*.

8 Decision of the Cour d'appel Paris, 1 July 1999, 14(8) Mealey's IAR G1 (1999), XXIVa YBCA 296 (1999). See also commentary by Reed, "Court of Appeal of Paris Breaks New Ground by Annulling ICC 'Procedural Order' in Brasoil Arbitration Case", 14(8) *Mealey's IAR* 24 (1999).

merit stage. Then, in October 1997, Brasoil filed a request for the reconsideration of the first award on the basis of newly discovered facts. GMRA answered that the request was inadmissible but also filed a 500 pages long submission addressing the merits of the fraud claim. Brasoil filed a two page response challenging GMRA's answer on the ground that it went beyond the issue of admissibility. The tribunal scheduled a one day hearing on the issue of admissibility in principle of the request for reconsideration of the award. The parties were invited to state their views. GMRA did so, but Brasoil protested that it did not come prepared to discuss the merits of the fraud allegation. In its "procedural order" of 14 May 1998, the tribunal, after citing that both parties had had the opportunity to present their positions, rejected the request for reconsideration because Brasoil had failed to prove fraud.

24-8 The Paris Court of Appeal annulled the order on two independent grounds. First it held that the "procedural order" was effectively an award because it settled a substantive issue between the parties; as an award it should have been submitted for scrutiny to the ICC Court and by failing to do so the tribunal had violated the terms of its mandate. Second, the court held that the tribunal had violated Brasoil's rights of due process. Each of the grounds was itself sufficient to annul the "award".

24-9 It is significant that the court totally ignored the classification of the tribunal's decision as a "procedural order". The decision[9] expressly states that the terms used by the tribunal or the parties do not affect the qualification of a decision as an "award". In pertinent part the Court of Appeal held

> The qualification of [a decision as an] award does not depend on the terms used by the arbitrators or by the parties. ... the arbitral tribunal rendered the 'order' of 14 May 1998, by which, after a lengthy examination of the parties' positions, it declared that the request could not be granted ... This reasoned decision ... by which the arbitrators ... solved, in a final manner, the dispute between the parties concerning the admissibility of Brasoil's request for a review ... appears to be an exercise of its jurisdictional power by the arbitral tribunal.... notwithstanding its qualification as an 'order', the decision of 14 May 1998, which did not concern the evidence-taking in the arbitration, is thus indeed an award. ... [10]

---

[9] XXIVa *YBCA* 296 (1999).

[10] *Ibid*, 297-8.

24-10 In *Publicis Communication & Publicis SA v True North Communications Inc*[11] the parties had engaged in a joint venture between 1989 and 1997. They had agreed to arbitrate all disputes before the LCIA under UNCITRAL Rules. Publicis refused to turn over certain tax records and True North filed for arbitration. A three member tribunal was appointed, held a hearing and issued an "order" signed by one arbitrator "for and on behalf of the Arbitrators" according to which Publicis had to turn over tax information to True North. Publicis did not comply with the order and True North filed suit in federal district court to confirm the order.

24-11 Both the district court and the Court of Appeals for the Seventh Circuit upheld the order and enforced the award under the New York Convention. In determining the classification of the decision neither the "form defences" (*i.e.* the award had be signed by one arbitrator only) nor the qualification used by the tribunal ("order") were decisive. The Court of Appeals analysed the effect of the tribunal's order and held that the order was final as it resolved the entire issue before the panel. As a consequence it was considered to be enforceable under the New York Convention.

24-12 Hence the main criterion for the classification of a decision of an arbitration tribunal lies in its function and its effect rather than the form or qualification the tribunal has ascribed to it. Any decision which finally resolves a substantive issue affecting the rights and obligations of the parties is an award.

24-13 There are several essential characteristics that distinguish an award from other decisions of an arbitration tribunal. An award:

- concludes the dispute as to the specific issue determined in the award so that it has *res judicata* effect between the parties; if it is a final award, it terminates the tribunal's jurisdiction;
- disposes of parties' respective claims;
- may be confirmed by recognition and enforcement;
- may be challenged in the courts of the place of arbitration.

---

11 206 F 3d 725, XXV YBCA 1152 (2000) (7th Cir, 14 March 2000). See also "Arbitrators' Order Was Final, 7th Circuit Rules", 15(4) *Mealey's IAR* 4 (2000), 11 *WAMR* 144 (2000).

2. TYPES OF AWARD

24-14 The main types of awards are final, interim, partial, default, and award on agreed terms. UNCITRAL Rules state unambiguously in Article 32(1) that the tribunal in addition to making a final award "shall be entitled to make interim, interlocutory, or partial awards".

24-15 Article 2(iii) ICC Rules refers to interim, final and partial awards without attempting any definition. Similar provisions can be found in other arbitration rules and laws[12] However, what constitutes a final, partial, or interim award is rarely defined in laws or rules. As a consequence the terminology is often not used consistently, in particular, in relation to interim and partial awards. A tribunal would normally know whether to render an interim or a final partial award.

2.1. Final Award

24-16 The term final award is used to denote two different situations. First, it refers to an award which marks the end of the proceedings and settles all claims between the parties.[13] This is the way the term is used in the Model law where Article 32(1) states that "the arbitral proceedings are terminated by the final award". When a final award is made the authority of the tribunal ends; the arbitrators become *functus officio*.[14]

24-17 Second, the term "final" is used to describe awards which only settle certain severable parts of the dispute with a binding effect on the parties.[15] An award is final in this sense if it produces *res judicata* effect between the parties and can be challenged or enforced without necessarily terminating the complete arbitration proceedings.[16]

---

12 See, *e.g.*, CIETAC Article 57; Netherlands, CCP Article 1049.

13 See Sanders, "Arbitration", *IECL*, Vol XVI, Chapter 12, para 178.

14 For the origin of the term *functus officio* see Bauer, "Once a Catchy Phrase, Always Immutable Law. The Origins and Destiny of Three Famous Mantras: Functus Officio, Once on Demurrage, Always on Demurrage, Manifest Disregard of the Law", 11(4) *J Int'l Arb* 41 (1994) 41.

15 This is particularly clear, *e.g.*, in the Netherlands, CCP Article 1049, which provides for "final awards" and "partial final awards".

16 See Berger, *International Economic Arbitration*, 589.

24-18 It follows that a final award may put an end to a part of the dispute or the entire proceedings.[17] An award which is classified as final and binding may be subject to challenge procedure at the courts of the place of arbitration or may be enforced anywhere in the world. The presumption is that awards are enforceable.

2.2. Partial Award

24-19 Parts of the claims submitted to the tribunal may be appropriate for resolution at an earlier stage while other issues require further submissions and assessment. The partial award may be a precondition to deciding whether the arbitration should continue to a further stage, *e.g.*, if there is an issue whether a claim is statute barred. The parties can agree that the tribunal determines a specific issue by rendering a partial award. Such partial award will be a ruling, for example, on issues of jurisdiction,[18] applicable law,[19] or liability[20] or quantification of damages. In the absence of an agreement the tribunal may still render a partial award if it considers that it is appropriate in the circumstances of the case. [21]

24-20 Article 26(7) LCIA Rules provides that

> The Arbitral Tribunal may make separate awards on different issues at different times. Such awards shall have the same status and effect as any other award ...

24-21 This is the approach taken in most arbitration rules[22] and several national arbitration laws[23] which expressly provide for the freedom of an arbitration

---

[17] See, *e.g.*, Geneva CCI, 7 March 1996, *L Ltd v The Foreign Trade Association of the Republic of U*, ASA Bulletin 494 (1997); England, Arbitration Act section 58(1); Netherlands, CCP Article 1049.

[18] See, *e.g.*, partial award in ICC case no 4402 (1983), *Bahamian company and Luxemburg company v French company and another French company*, IX YBCA 138 (1984).

[19] See, *e.g.*, partial award in ICC case no 8113 (1995), XXV YBCA 323 (2000).

[20] See, *e.g.*, partial award of 5 February 1988 in *ad hoc* arbitration, *Wintershall AG et al v Government of Qatar*, 28 ILM 798 (1989), XV YBCA 30 (1990).

[21] See, ICC case no 3790 (1983), *French contractor v Libyan employer*, 110 Clunet 910 (1983), XI YBCA 119 (1986); ICC case no 5073 (1986), *US exporter v Argentine distributor*, XIII YBCA 53 (1988); and partial award in *Wintershall AG v Government of Qatar*, XV YBCA 30 (1990).

[22] See, *e.g.*, UNCITRAL Rules Article 32(1); CIETAC Article 57; ICC Article 2(iii); LCIA Article 26(7); AAA ICDR Article 27(7); Stockholm Institute Article 34.

[23] See, *e.g.*, Belgium, Judicial Code Article 1699; England, Arbitration Act section 47; Netherlands, CCP Article 1049; Sweden, Arbitration Law Article 29; Switzerland, PIL Article 188.

tribunal to render partial awards. If the parties give specific enough directions, failure of the tribunal to follow them may lead to the annulment of the final award.[24] Hence, the parties will have to exclude expressly the possibility of partial awards if they do not favour a step-by-step procedure.[25]

24-22 No arbitration law or rules, however, define a partial award. For the avoidance of confusion, a partial award must be contrasted with a final award which resolves all the issues in the arbitration.[26] Indeed, if a partial award is made, it terminates the proceedings in respect of the specific issues decided, it is partial in the context of the overall dispute referred to arbitration. A partial award is final and is subject to the means of recourse every arbitration law makes applicable to final awards.

24-23 While it is often desirable to adopt a step-by-step approach so that the tribunal decides on specific issues one by one, it is inevitable that it could lead to delay in the proceedings. Provided that partial awards may be challenged it is not unlikely that in the process of an arbitration where several partial awards are issued during the process, several challenge procedures may be pending before courts. If the parties, however, are co-operative partial awards may be an incentive for settlement of the dispute during the arbitration.

2.3. Interim Award

24-24 According to the working group preparing the Model Law an interim or interlocutory or provisional award is an award which does not definitively determine an issue before the tribunal.[27] This definition is in line with the general meaning of the term "interim" as opposed to "final". However, the definition was not adopted in the final text of the Model Law. One of the reasons was that in practice the term "interim award" is often used interchangeably with that of "partial awards".[28] Actually the majority of so called interim awards are partial

---

[24] See, *e.g.*, Cour d'appel Paris, 19 December 1986, *OIAETI v Sofidif*, Rev Arb 359 (1987); Cour de cassation, 8 March 1988, *Sofidif v OIAETI*, Rev Arb 481 (1989); English translation in 3(3) Mealey's IAR B1 (1988).

[25] Even if the parties have excluded the possibility of partial awards, the tribunal may render an interim award on jurisdiction or a preliminary award on the law applicable to the merits of the dispute. See Sanders, "Arbitration", *IECL*, Vol XVI, Chapter 12, paras 186-188.

[26] See Fouchard Gaillard Goldman *on International Commercial Arbitration*, para 1360, 740.

[27] See Holtzmann and Neuhaus, *Model Law*, 867.

[28] See Redfern and Hunter, *International Commercial Arbitration*, para 8-34.

awards in the sense that they often contain final determinations of separate issues such as jurisdiction, damages or even questions of applicable law.[29] For reasons of clarity the term interim award should be limited to those awards which do not settle a separate part of the proceedings finally.[30]

24-25 A typical example of an interim award which does not determine an issue finally would be an award making orders for interim relief. This is expressly provided for in Article 26(2) UNCITRAL Rules which states that interim relief can be ordered in the form of an interim award.[31]

24-26 Different views exist as to the enforceability of interim awards under the New York Convention. Some courts have enforced them like any other awards.[32] Provisions such as Article 2 (1)(c) Indian Arbitration Act which state that interim awards are awards seem to support this view. It also seems to be in line with the terminology of interim award.

24-27 The prevailing position, at least in relation to interim awards dealing with interim relief, is expressed in a decision of the Supreme Court of Queensland, Australia. The court held that an interim award is not enforceable under the New York Convention or Australian law. It stated that

> ... the 'Interim Arbitration Order and Award' made by the arbitrator ... is not an 'arbitral award' within the meaning of the Convention nor a 'foreign award' ... It does not take on that character simply because it is said to be so. ... .[33]

---

[29] See, *e.g.*, Interim award of 26 September 1999 in *ad hoc* arbitration, *Himpurna California Energy Ltd v Republic of Indonesia*, XXV YBCA 109 (2000); in fact although called "interim award" the award of 26 September has the appearance and the content of partial final award; ICC interim awards in case no 4145 of 1983 and 1984, *Establishment of Middle East country X v South Asian construction company*, XII YBCA 97 (1987).

[30] See, *e.g.*, Netherlands, CCP Article 1049 which distinguishes between a final, a partial final and an interim award which implies that the later is not final.

[31] See also AAA ICDR Article 21(2).

[32] *Yasuda Fire & Marine Insurance Co of Europe v Continental Casualty Co*, 37 F 3d 345 (7th Cir 1994); for further cases to this effect see Carbonneau, *Arbitration*, 601; Born, *International Commercial Arbitration*, 972 *et seq.*

[33] See *Resort Condominiums International Inc (USA) v Ray Bolwell and Resort Condominiums (Australasia) Pty Ltd (Australia)*, (1994) 9(4) Mealey's IAR A1, (1995) XX YBCA 628, 641 (Queensland Supreme Court, 29 October 1993). In fact the court equating "interim awards" with "partial final awards" had to deny that the measure ordered was an interim award despite the clear wording of "order". See, to the same effect, Colombian Corte Suprema de Justicia, 26 January and 1 March 1999, *Merck & Co Inc (USA) et al v Technoquimicas SA (Colombia)*, XXVI YBCA 755 (2001).

24-28 In line with this the Austrian Supreme Court held that, unlike a partial award, an interim award (*Zwischenschiedsspruch*) cannot be challenged independently from the final award. The Court also noted the confusion in the terminology.[34] As they do not finally determine issues interim awards cannot be challenged nor can they be enforced.

2.4. Award on Agreed Terms

24-29 An award on agreed terms (or consent award) is a ruling of the tribunal which incorporates a settlement that the parties have reached during the arbitration. Several arbitration laws[35] and rules[36] recognise awards on agreed terms. According to some arbitration rules a tribunal may issue an order or may render an award incorporating the parties' settlement.[37] Arguably tribunals always have this discretion even if not expressly provided in the rules.

24-30 ICC Rules mandate that the tribunal record the settlement agreement if so requested by the parties. Article 26 provides

> If the parties reach a settlement after the file has been transmitted to the Arbitral Tribunal in accordance with Article 13, the settlement *shall* be recorded in the form of an Award made by consent of the parties if so requested by the parties and the Arbitral Tribunal agrees to do so. [Emphasis added].

24-31 The Model Law[38], scholarly opinion[39] and the limited case law[40] support the conclusion that an award on agreed terms is enforceable under the New York Convention.

---

34 See Oberster Gerichtshof, 25 June 1992, XXII YBCA 619 (1997).

35 See, *e.g.*, Model Law Article 30; Singapore, Arbitration Law Article 18; Germany, ZPO sections 1053, 1054. For an application of section 1054 see Bundesgerichtshof, 2 November 2000, 54 *NJW* 373 (2001), English summary in 5 *Int ALR* N-12 (2002). See also Mankowski, "Der Schiedsspruch mit vereinbartem Wortlaut", *ZZP* 37 (2001).

36 See, *e.g.*, LCIA Article 26(8), Stockholm Institute Article 32(5).

37 See, *e.g.*, UNCITRAL Rules Article 34(1); ICSID Rules Article 43.

38 Model Law Articles 30 and 31.

39 See Lörcher, "Enforceability of Agreed Awards in Foreign Jurisdictions", 17 *Arb Int* 275 (2001); Fouchard Gaillard Goldman *on International Commercial Arbitration*, para 1366; De Boisséson, *Le droit français de l'arbitrage*, 808-9; Kreindler, "Settlement Agreements and Arbitration in the Context of the ICC Rules", 9(2) *ICC Bulletin* 22 (1998).

40 But see *United States v Sperry Corporation et al*, 493 US 52, 110 S Ct 387, 107 L Ed 2d 290 (28 November 1989). This case recognised an award on agreed terms rendered by the Iran-US

2.5. Default Award

24-32 A default award is an award made by the tribunal in proceedings where one party fails to make an appearance. Default proceedings are acceptable in modern arbitration systems provided that each party is given an opportunity to present its case and to reply to the arguments of the other party. Consequently, if there is evidence that copies of all notices and submissions were sent to the other party in time and by recorded delivery and the defaulting party simply refuses to participate the award will survive a challenge and would be enforceable.[41]

2.6. Additional Award

24-33 An additional award is normally available so that the tribunal can address issues which it failed to determine during the arbitration proceedings. Arbitration rules[42] provide for the eventuality of the tribunal having to render an additional award. According to most rules a tribunal must render the additional award within a certain time limit, normally 30 days.[43]

24-34 Some national laws also allow for additional awards.[44] It is possible that the law imposes restrictions as to which matters may be dealt with in an additional award. Typically they may address the issue of costs.[45] Additional awards are final and may be challenged and/or enforced in the normal ways.

Claims Tribunal relying on Article 34(1) of its Rules which corresponds to UNCITRAL Rules Article 34(1).

41 See, *e.g.*, Cour d'appel Paris, 24 March 1995, *Bin Saud Bin Abdel Aziz v Crédit Industriel et Commercial de Paris*, Rev Arb 259 (1996); *Anhui Provincial Import and Export Corp (PR China) v Hart Enterprises International Inc (USA)*, 11(5) Mealey's IAR E1 (1996); *Harris Adacom Corp (USA) v Perkom Sdn Bhd (Malaysia)*, (1997) XXII YBCA 753 (High Court of Malaysia, 10 December 1993); *Agromet Motorimport Ltd (Poland) v Maulden Engineering Co Ltd (UK)*, [1985] 2 All E R 436 (QBD). But see *Victrix SS Co v Salen Dry Cargo AB*, 825 F 2d 709 (2d Cir 1987) where a default award against a bankrupt party was not enforced because payment of the award from the debtor's estate would conflict with a US public policy of giving effect to a Swedish bankruptcy proceedings for the equitable distribution of the estate's assets. See also Style and Reid, "The Challenge of Unopposed Arbitrations", 16 *Arb Int* 219 (2000).

42 See, *e.g.*, UNCITRAL Rules Article 37; AAA ICDR Article 30; CIETAC Article 62; LCIA Article 27(3); NAI Article 53; SIAC Rule 29; Stockholm Institute Rule 31.

43 *Ibid.* See also Vollmer and Bedford, "Post-Award Proceedings", 15(1) *J Int'l Arb* 37 (1998) with further references; Sanders, *IECL*, Vol XVI, Chapter 12, para 196.

44 See, *e.g.*, Model Law Article 33; England, Arbitration Act section 57.

45 See, *e.g.*, Israel, Arbitration Law 1974 section 22; Malaysia, Arbitration Act 2000 Article 19(4).

3. Making of an Award

24-35 The award must be made by the tribunal.[46] There is little uniformity as to how awards are made. The award is normally the result of deliberations of the tribunal but these are not communicated to the parties.[47] Effectively awards are the result of a unanimous or majority vote while occasionally dissenting or concurring opinions may be included in the award. Arbitration rules require the notification of the award to the parties while in some countries the award still needs to be registered or deposited with national courts.

3.1. Time Limits

24-36 It is generally expected that awards are made promptly.[48] However, the majority of arbitration laws do not set time limits for the making of the award. They normally leave it to the discretion of the tribunal to determine the appropriate time for the rendering of an award.[49]

24-37 This is the approach adopted for example in the Model Law. The drafters considered the issue and it was suggested that setting time limits would have the effect of avoiding delay in arbitration. The counterargument was that no time limit could be fixed for all types of cases and therefore a mechanism for the extension of time limits should also be put in place. Moreover no agreement could be reached as to what the legal consequences would be on the expiry of a statutory or party agreed time limit.[50]

24-38 Very few arbitration laws set a default time limit for the making of an award.[51] In these cases awards rendered after the time limits have expired may be

---

[46] See, *e.g.*, Italy, Corte di cassazione, 7 June 1989, *Sacheri v Robotto*, XVI YBCA 156 (1991). In this case the Corte di cassazione annulled an award in a construction arbitration because it was not drafted by the arbitrators, none of whom was legally trained, but by a lawyer who has been appointed as an expert to draw up the award.

[47] See Fouchard Gaillard Goldman on *International Commercial Arbitration*, para 1374 with further references. This confidentiality may be suspended when an award is challenged: Reilly, "The Court's Power to Invade the Arbitrators' Deliberation Chamber", 9(3) *J Int'l Arb* 27 (1992); Bredin, "Le secret du délibéré arbitral", in *Etudes offertes à Pierre Bellet* (LITEC 1991), 71.

[48] For an express statement of this expectation see, *e.g.*, AAA ICDR Article 27(1).

[49] See, *e.g.*, Netherlands, CCP Article 1049.

[50] See Holtzmann and Neuhaus, *Model Law*, 442 and 443, para 74.

[51] See, *e.g.*, Brazil, Arbitration Law Article 23 which sets a default time-limit, *i.e.*, unless otherwise agreed by the parties, of six months from the date of commencement of arbitration

challenged as, for example, provided in the Article 829(4) Italian Code of Civil Procedure. A number of arbitration laws contain provisions for the extension of such limits to be granted by state courts[52] or by mutual consent of the parties and the arbitrators.[53]

24-39 Time limits for the making of an award can also be found in some arbitration rules. Time limits when adopted in arbitration rules range from 60 days after the closure of the proceedings[54], six months from the adoption of Terms of Reference,[55] to nine months from the date on which the tribunal has been formed.[56] When rules provide for a time limit they invariably also provide for a mechanism for its extension.

24-40 Where time limits are set by the parties or the relevant arbitration rules they must be observed and the tribunal should also consider extension of the time limit if necessary. Indeed the tribunal should balance the need for an expedited resolution of the dispute with the requirement to give each party a good opportunity to present their case and to respond to the arguments of the other party. Otherwise the award may be challenged.[57] Time limits set by the parties or the arbitration rules should be seen as targets for the tribunal.[58]

3.2. Majority or Unanimity

24-41 It is established practice that a tribunal with more than one member may decide by majority or by unanimous decision. While unanimity is desirable it cannot always be achieved. Majority decisions are a legitimate result of

---

proceedings or from the date of the substitution of an arbitrator. See also Italy, CCP Article 820 (domestic arbitration) which sets a time limit for making the award of one hundred and eighty days after the acceptance of the appointment by the last arbitrator.

52 See, *e.g.*, England, Arbitration Act section 50.

53 See Brazil, Arbitration Law Article 23 sole paragraph. See also NAI Article 43.

54 See, *e.g.*, ICSID Rules rule 46 (an extension of further thirty days may be given). LMAA Terms Rule 20 states that the award should normally be available within six weeks from the close of proceedings.

55 See, *e.g.*, ICC Article 24. Stockholm Institute Article 33 which provides for six months from the date when the case was referred to the arbitration tribunal.

56 See, *e.g.*, CIETAC Article 52; WIPO Article 63 provides for close of proceedings within nine months of the delivery of the statement of defence or the establishment of the tribunal, whichever event occurs later, and an additional three months for the delivery of the award.

57 See the discussion on an unsuccessful challenge in Kautz and Kreindler, "Agreed Deadlines and the Setting Aside of Arbitral Awards", 15 *ASA Bulletin* 576 (1997).

58 See Redfern and Hunter, *International Commercial Arbitration*, para 8-62.

deliberation among the members of the tribunal and satisfy due process expectations of the parties. The general practice is reflected in Article 29 Model Law

> In arbitral proceedings with more than one arbitrator, any decision of the arbitral tribunal shall be made, unless otherwise agreed by the parties, by a majority of all its members.

24-42 Some laws simply opt for majority decisions,[59] others for a majority decision unless otherwise agreed by the parties[60] and many laws provide for the possibility of a casting vote by the chairman.[61]

24-43 Similar distinctions can be found in arbitration rules which allow for majority decisions,[62] unless otherwise agreed by the parties,[63] chairman's decision for procedural matters[64] or any matters.[65]

24-44 There is substantial case law of the Iran-US Claims Tribunal which highlights some of the problems of majority votes. In cases where one arbitrator either refuses to participate in deliberations or takes positions which in the eyes of the other two arbitrators are unreasonable, the other arbitrator would normally have no choice but to accept the position the chairman takes or in the case of the chairman a position which seems more reasonable so as to avoid infinite arguments in deliberations. This has been in some instances recorded in the award.[66]

---

59 See, *e.g*. Brazil, Arbitration Law Article 24(1); China, Arbitration Law Article 53 1st sentence; France, NCPC Article 1470; England, Arbitration Act section 52(3).

60 See, *e.g*., Model Law Article 29; Belgium, Judicial Code Article 1701(2); Germany, ZPO section 1052(2); Netherlands, CCP Article 1057(1); Switzerland, PIL Article 189(2).

61 See, *e.g*., Belgium, Judicial Code Article 1701(2); Brazil, Arbitration Law Article 24(1); China, Arbitration Law Article 53, 3rd sentence; Switzerland, PIL Article 189(2).

62 See, *e.g*., UNCITRAL Rules Article 31(1); AAA ICDR Article 26(1) ICSID Rules rule 47(2) and (3); CIETAC Article 54(1); ICC Article 25(1); LCIA Article 26(1); ICAC paragraph 39(2); NAI Article 49(1); Stockholm Institute Article 32(1); Vienna Article 18(2).

63 See, *e.g*., WIPO Article 61.

64 See, *e.g*., UNCITRAL Rules Article 31(2); AAA ICDR Article 26(2).

65 See, *e.g*., CIETAC Article 54(2); ICC Article 25(1); LCIA Article 26(3); ICAC paragraph 39(2); WIPO Article 61.

66 See, *e.g*., Holtzmann's opinion in the 14 June 1983 award of the Iran-US Claims Tribunal, *Economy Forms Corp v Iran*, Award no 55-165-1, 3 Iran-US CTR 42, 55. See also Schwebel, "The Majority Vote of an International Arbitral Tribunal", in Dominicé, Patry and Reymond (eds), *Études de Droit International en l'honneur de Pierre Lalive* (Helbing & Lichtenhahn 1993), 671.

3.3. Dissenting and Concurring Opinions

24-45 An arbitrator who disagrees with the majority of the tribunal may wish to express his opinion in the award or an annex to it. A concurring opinion is the opinion of an arbitrator who agrees with the majority of the tribunal as far as the dispositive part of the award is concerned but disagrees with the reasoning.[67] A dissenting opinion is an opinion which disagrees both with the result and the reasoning. Dissenting opinions may cause problems in that they may reveal the content of the deliberations.[68] However, an ICC working group in 1991 could not identify any national laws that impose specific consequences for breach of this obligation by an arbitrator.[69]

24-46 A dissenting opinion is often expressed by a refusal to sign an award. Dissenting opinions do not generally form part of the award;[70] they are not frequent in international commercial arbitration.[71]

24-47 Few laws expressly permit dissenting or concurring opinions and their provisions vary.[72] During the discussions for the drafting of the Model Law it was suggested that a provision be included to allow for dissenting opinion, but it did not have much support.[73] Arguably, even in laws where no express reference is made to dissenting opinions, they may still be delivered by arbitrators.[74]

---

[67] See, *e.g.*, separate opinion of Sir Gerald Fitzmaurice in the *Aminoil* arbitration, 21 ILM 976 (1982). See also the practice of the ICJ on separate opinions in Article 57 of the ICJ Statute.

[68] See the discussion in Redfern and Hunter, *International Commercial Arbitration*, paras 8-69 - 8-71.

[69] See "Final Report of the Working Party on Dissenting Opinions", 1 *ICC Bulletin* 32 (1991) and the discussion in Redfern and Hunter, *International Commercial Arbitration*, para 8-71. On the usefulness of dissenting opinions see Fouchard Gaillard Goldman *on International Commercial Arbitration*, paras 1399-1401.

[70] See, *e.g.*, Swiss Federal Tribunal, 11 May 1992, *D v A*, ASA Bulletin 381 (1992) 386.

[71] See Redfern and Hunter, *International Commercial Arbitration*, para 8-70.

[72] See, *e.g.*, Brazil, Arbitration Law Article 24(2); China, Arbitration Law Article 53; Washington Convention Article 48(4).

[73] See Holtzmann and Neuhaus, *Model Law*, 837 and 856. However, several jurisdictions added a provision on dissenting opinions when adopting the Model Law. See, *e.g.*, Bulgaria, Arbitration Law Article 39(1); Quebec, CCP Article 945.

[74] See, *e.g.*, Levy, "Dissenting Opinions in International Arbitration in Switzerland", 5 *Arb Int* 35 (1989); Werner, "Dissenting Opinions – Beyond Fears", 9(4) *J Int'l Arb* 23 (1992). See also *Ad hoc* award, 29 December 1993, *Icori Estero SpA v Kuwait Foreign Trading Contracting & Investment Co*, 9(12) Mealey's IAR A1 (1994); Interim Award in ICC case no 3879, 5 March 1985, *Westland Helicopters Ltd v Arab Organization for Industrialization*, 112 Clunet 232 (1985), English translation in XI YBCA 127 (1986).

24-48 The UNCITRAL Rules do not contain any provision for dissenting opinions. However, the Iran-US Claims Tribunal amended the UNCITRAL Rules to allow dissenting and concurring opinions.[75] Such opinions are frequently produced by the Tribunal. Some other arbitration rules also provide for dissenting opinions.[76]

24-49 While dissenting or concurring opinions do not form part of the award, they are normally made available as a matter of practice. It is essential that while arbitrators are allowed to express their minority opinions they do not do so in a way which would form effectively the basis for challenge proceedings or a basis for resisting enforcement.[77] It is equally essential to allow the parties to know that the tribunal did not reach a unanimous decision. Common sense and feelings of justice should prevail when arbitrators decide to express a minority opinion.[78]

3.4. Notification and Deposit

24-50 Once the award is made it must be communicated to the parties. Some national legal systems require the registration or deposit of awards with national courts, normally on payment of an appropriate fee.[79] In other countries registration is optional and serves the purpose of recognition by the courts.[80] Where the requirement of deposit is mandatory the parties must do so; where it is optional it may well function as a pressure for the unsuccessful party.

24-51 Most laws and rules contain provisions for the notification of the award to the parties. Notification is essential, so that parties can request the correction or interpretation of the award if necessary, and challenge of the award can be made. The time period within which a party may request correction or

---

75 Article 32 Iran-US Claims Tribunal Rules provides that "any arbitrator may request that his dissenting vote or his dissenting vote and the reasons therefore be recorded."

76 See, *e.g.*, ICSID Rules rule 47(3); Stockholm Institute Article 32(4); NAI Article 48(4) allows dissenting or concurring opinions only in international arbitration.

77 See, *e.g.*, the 23 pages long dissenting opinion of J Handl, 11 September 2001, in the UNCITRAL arbitration proceedings, *CME Czech Republic BV v The Czech Republic*, available at <www.mfcr.cz/scripts/hpe/default.asp> (last visited December 2002).

78 See further Mosk and Ginsburg, "Dissenting Opinions in International Arbitration", 15(4) *Mealey's IAR* 26 (2000).

79 See, e.g., Belgium, Judicial Code Article 1702(2); France, NCPC Article 1477; Italy, CCP Article 825; Japan, CCP Article 799(2).

80 One of the ways of enforcing an award in England is by registering it as a judgment under Part III of the Practice Direction made under CPR 49G.

interpretation, or challenge the award normally runs from the date of communication of the award to the parties.[81]

24-52 Laws[82] or rules[83] which provide for notification do not normally set a time for it to happen. It is generally stated that this should happen promptly and is often conditional on payment of costs.[84] Often the successful party will try to obtain a copy of the award as soon as possible so that it can communicate it to the unsuccessful party. Communication will be in the way which is common in the particular form of arbitration, or is normal between the parties or in the particular region or sector. Such communication will be invariably by recorded delivery.

4. Content and Form of Award

24-53 The structure, form and detail of the award will depend on the legal style of the draftsman, the composition of the tribunal and the applicable laws and rules. Awards may be long and detailed, resembling a hybrid of common law style court judgments and continental European treatises or may be concise and cryptic, like judgments of the French Cour de cassation. Often the chosen arbitration rules or the applicable law dictate a certain minimum content and impose certain form requirements. They vary considerably as to the detail in which requirements for the validity of an award are described. A fairly short list can be found in Article 31 Model Law which requires that the award

- is in writing and signed;
- states the reasons upon which it is based;
- states the date and the place of arbitration; and
- is delivered to each party.[85]

---

81 See Bundesgerichtshof, 20 September 2001, 54 *NJW* 3787 (2001) which held that the time limit for challenging an award did only start to run when the award was properly served on a party despite the admission of the party that it had received the award earlier.

82 See, *e.g.*, Model Law Article 31(4); Belgium, Judicial Code Article 1702(1); Brazil, Article 29; England, Arbitration Act section 55; Netherlands, CCP Article 1058; Switzerland, PIL Article 190(1).

83 See, *e.g.*, UNCITRAL Rules Article 32(6); AAA ICDR Article 27(5); ICC Article 28(1); LCIA Article 26(5); ICAC para 40; NAI Article 50; WIPO Article 62(f).

84 See, *e.g*, ICSID Rules rule 48(1); ICC Article 28(1); LCIA Article 26(5); England Arbitration Act section 56.

85 See also the laconic UNCITRAL Rules Article 32.

24-54 More detailed lists can be found in other laws and rules.[86] Generally, the fact that the award is imperfect as to form does not impede its finality.[87] An award will normally be in the language of the arbitration and mandatory requirements of the law governing the arbitration must be observed.

4.1. Content of Award

24-55 The principal content of the award should record the claims and defences of the parties, the tribunal's conclusions on these issues and the main reasons for the determination reached. A typical award in international commercial arbitration will invariably contain:

- The procedural background detailing the substantive submissions of the parties, and the evidence on which they have relied;
- The basis for the jurisdiction of tribunal;
- Factual background to the arbitration, including relationship between the parties, their respective businesses and the essential terms of their agreement;
- Nature of the dispute and the respective positions of the parties;
- Issues for determination by the tribunal;
- Reliefs sought by the parties;
- Tribunal's analysis and conclusions on each of the issues listed;
- Award of the tribunal with declaration and order, decisions on damages, interest and costs.

4.2. In Writing and Signed

24-56 These two form requirements for an award are often combined either expressly or impliedly. For example, Article 31(1) Model Law provides that an

---

[86] See the detailed list of requirements in ICSID Rules rule 47; see also China, Arbitration Law Article 54.

[87] See, *e.g.*, *Fradella v Petricca*, 183 F 3d 17 (1st Cir, 7 July 1999). This cases relates to a securities arbitration where the award was imperfect as to form. The issue was that the signatures were put next to a passage which made no reference to Massaschussetts law, which governed the arbitration, but to New York law. The award was valid and binding as of the date of signature rather than the date of correction.

award shall be made in writing and be signed by the tribunal.[88] By contrast Article 1473 French Code of Civil Procedure states that the award shall by signed thus implying or assuming that it must be in writing.[89] New York Convention also implies in Article IV that the award be in writing.

24-57 While many arbitration rules requirc that the award be in writing and signed,[90] others make no express reference to the signature[91] or writing requirement.[92] It is generally not necessary that the signatures of all arbitrators are contained in a single document. It is possible that they sign identical copies of the same document.[93]

24-58 There are different approaches in laws and rules as to whether all arbitrators should sign the award, or only the majority of them, or occasionally only the presiding arbitrator. Generally, if one party-appointed arbitrator refuses to sign the award the signature of the remaining arbitrators is sufficient, provided that the reason for the missing signature is stated.[94] Some laws require the signature of the presiding arbitrator only.[95] A third group of laws requires the signature of all arbitrators who voted for the award.[96] A final group of laws has no specific provisions.[97]

24-59 Similar differences also appear in arbitration rules. Several rules expect the majority of arbitrators to sign the award with reasons stated for non-signature;[98] other rules require all arbitrators to sign the award;[99] a third group of

---

88 See, *e.g.*, Belgium, Judicial Code Article 1701; Brazil, Arbitration Law Article 24; England, Arbitration Act section 52(3); Netherlands, CCP Article 1057.

89 See also Switzerland, PIL Article 189(2).

90 See, *e.g.*, UNCITRAL Rules Article 32(2) and (4); CRCICA Article 32(2) and (4); GAFTA Rule 9:1; LCIA Article 26(1) and 26(4); ICAC paragraphs 40(1) and 41(1); NAI Articles 48(2) and 49(1); Vienna Article 18; WIPO Article 62; Zurich Article 47; ICSID Rules rule 47.

91 See, *e.g.*, AAA ICDR Article 27.

92 See, e.g., CIETAC Article 56; LMAA Rule 20; Stockholm Institute Article 32(1).

93 Oberlandesgericht Frankfurt am Main, 6 September 2001, 3 Sch 2/00, unreported.

94 See, *e.g.*, Model Law Article 31(1); France, NCPC Article 1473; Germany, ZPO Article 1054(1); Netherlands, CCP Article 1057(3).

95 See, *e.g.*; Switzerland, PIL Article 189(2).

96 See, *e.g.*, Belgium, Judicial Code Article 1701(4); Brazil, Arbitration Law Article 24(1); China, Arbitration Law Article 53; England, Arbitration Act section 52(3); Switzerland, PIL Article 189(2).

97 It is noteworthy that the English Arbitration Act leaves the issue to party autonomy and provides default rules in the absence of an agreement by the parties.

98 See, *e.g.*, UNCITRAL Rules Article 32(4); CRCICA Article 32(4); LCIA Article 26(4); Stockholm Institute Article 32(1); Vienna Article 18.

rules requires all arbitrators to sign, however the signature of the chairman alone may be sufficient.[100] Finally another group of rules requires the signature of all arbitrators who have voted for the award.[101]

24-60 If national laws or arbitration rules were to require that all arbitrators sign the award, this would enable a dissenting arbitrator to undermine the arbitration by refusing to sign the award. In general, the signature of the presiding arbitrator will be required.[102]

4.3. Place and Date

24-61 Where the award is made may be relevant for the nationality of the award which affects the jurisdiction for challenge proceedings and the relevant enforcement regime. Consequently the arbitration rules and laws often require that the place of arbitration should be stated. Unless otherwise agreed an award shall be deemed to have been made at the stated place of the arbitration.[103]

24-62 The place of signing the award has to be distinguished from the place where the award is made. The act of signing an award is an expression of agreement with its contents and an act of endorsement. As often arbitrators have their domiciles in different places or countries the award may be signed at different localities. An award does not normally need to be signed at the place of arbitration. The place of signature should not be deemed the place where the award was made.[104] This is supported by arbitration laws[105] and rules.[106] If an

---

[99] See, *e.g.*, Zurich Article 47 (maximum requirement), signature of the presiding arbitrator suffices.

[100] See, *e.g.*, CIETAC Article 56; GAFTA Rule 9:1; ICC Article 25(1); LCIA Article 26(4); ICAC paragraph 39(2); Stockholm Institute Article 32(3); WIPO Article 62(4); Zurich Article 47.

[101] See, *e.g.*, ICSID Rules rule 47(2).

[102] See Sanders, "Arbitration", *IECL*, Vol XVI, Chapter 12, para 179.

[103] See, *e.g.*, UNCITRAL Rules Article 32(4); AAA ICDR Article 27(3); ICC Article 25; LCIA Article 26(1); Model Law Article 31(3).

[104] See, however, *Hiscox v Outhwaite* [1991] 3 WLR 292 (HL). In this case which was decided before the English Arbitration Act 1996, the arbitration took place in London. The sole arbitrator who had moved to France to take up residence signed the award in Paris. This was stated in the award. The court considered that the award was made in Paris and hence was a foreign award pursuant New York Convention. Section 53 English Arbitration Act deals with the issue created by *Hiscox v Outhwaite* by stating:

> Unless otherwise agreed by the parties, where the seat of the arbitration is in England and Wales or Northern Ireland, any award in the proceedings shall be treated as made there, regardless of where it was signed, despatched or delivered to any of the parties.

award does not state the place of arbitration it would require a fact-finding procedure to determine where the award was made.[107] Under the New York Convention it suffices to establish that the award was not made in the country where enforcement is sought.

24-63 The date of the award is important, *inter alia*, for the running of statutory time limits for the challenge of the award[108] and for determining when the award begins having *res judicata* effect.[109]

4.4. Reasons

24-64 Different attitudes exist as to whether an arbitration award should contain the reasons on which the decision is made. It is often suggested that the requirement to give reasons is imposed by the due process considerations as expressed, for instance, in the European Convention of Human Rights[110] or the UK Human Rights Act.[111] It is unclear whether the statement of reasons is a formal requirement, arguably invoked by human rights consideration, or a matter of content of the award. Article 31(2) Model Law reflects the modern common denominator in providing

---

105 See, *e.g.*, Model Law Article 31(3); Belgium, Judicial Code Article 1701(5)(d) and (e) according to which it is required that the award states both the place of arbitration and the place where the award was made; England, Arbitration Act sections 52(5) and 53; Germany, ZPO section 1054(3); Italy, CCP Article 828.

106 See, *e.g.*, AAA ICDR Article 27(3); ICC Article 25(3); LCIA Article 26(1); NAI Article 49(2); WIPO Article 62(b).

107 On the process of determining the place of arbitration in such circumstances see Oberlandesgericht Düsseldorf, 23 February 2000, *EWiR* 795 (2000), English summary in 4 *Int ALR* N-25 (2001); Oberlandesgericht Stuttgart, 4 June 2002, 1 Sch 22/01, unreported.

108 See, *e.g.*, Model Law Article 34(3); China, Arbitration Law Article 59; England, Arbitration Act section 70(3); France, CCP Article 1486.

109 See, *e.g.*, France, NCPC Article 1476 and CIETAC Rules Article 56(4).

110 See, *e.g.*, *Van de Hurk v Netherlands* [1994] 18 EHRR 481, para 61; *Hiro Balani v Spain* [1995] 90 EHRR 566, para 27. Reasoning is essential but may be limited: *Garcia Ruiz v Spain* [2001] 31 EHRR 589, para 23. None of these cases is an arbitration case.

111 See *North Range Shipping Ltd v Seatrans Shipping Corporation* [2002] 2 Lloyd's Rep 1 (CA). In *North Range* the appeal was on the ground that the English court did not give reasons when refusing an application under section 69 Arbitration Act (appeal on a point of law). See also Godwin, "Arbitration and Reasons: The North Range Decision", 5 *Int ALR* 109 (2002) 111-2.

> The award *shall* state the reasons upon which it is based, unless the parties have agreed that no reasons are to be given or the award is an award on agreed terms ... [Emphasis added.]

24-65 There are four main groups of legislative attitudes in relation to reasons of an award:

- under some laws reasons are always required;[112]
- under other laws reasons are required unless otherwise agreed by the parties or it is an award on agreed terms,[113]
- in a third group of laws reasons are required unless the award is on the condition or quality of goods[114] and
- a fourth set of laws has no specific provisions as to the reasons of the award.[115]

24-66 Arbitration rules take two different approaches: either reasons are always required[116] or reasons are required unless otherwise agreed by the parties.[117]

24-67 Under the LMAA Rules, provided that the parties agree to dispense with reasons, a tribunal may issue an award together with a document which does not form part of the award but which gives, on a confidential basis, an outline of the reasons for the tribunal's decision. Such reasons are referred to as "privileged reasons".[118] The document containing privileged reasons may not be relied upon or referred to by either party in any proceedings relating to the award.[119]

24-68 In most cases a reasoned award is made. In systems where reasons are an essential requirement this is regarded as a rule of international or transnational

---

[112] See, *e.g.*, Belgium, Judicial Code Article 1701(6); Brazil, Arbitration Law Article 26(II); France, NCPC Article 1471; Russian Federation, Arbitration Law Article 31(2).
[113] See, *e.g.*, Model Law Article 31(2); China, Arbitration Law Article 54; England, Arbitration Act section 52(4); Switzerland, PIL Article 189(2).
[114] See, *e.g.*, Netherlands, Article 1057(e).
[115] See, *e.g.*, US, FAA; the situation is different for US states which have enacted the Model Law. English law required no reasons prior to the 1979 Arbitration Act and this was also the case in India prior to the 1996 Arbitration Law.
[116] See, *e.g.*, CIETAC Article 55; ICC Article 25(2); ICAC paragraph 41(1); NAI Article 49(2)(e); Stockholm Institute Article 32(1); Zurich Article 47; ICSID Rules rule 47(1)(i).
[117] See, *e.g.*, UNCITRAL Rules Article 32(3); AAA ICDR Article 27(2); CRCICA Article 32(3); LCIA Article 26(1); LMAA rule 22(b); Vienna Article 18(1); WIPO Article 62(c).
[118] LMAA rule 22(c).
[119] LMAA rule 22(d).

public policy.[120] The question, however, arises as to whether an award may be challenged only for complete lack of reasoning or also for insufficient reasoning. To the extent that none of the laws requiring a statement of reasons on which the award is based is specific as to the extent of reasoning, only total lack of reasons should lead to setting aside.[121] In other words reasoning is required but need not be detailed.

24-69 There are no specific guidelines as to how specific and detailed reasons should be. In some cases, such as quality arbitrations, it will be almost impossible to express any reasons.[122] As a matter of emerging practice, awards in international commercial arbitration contain reasons but these are normally expressed in concise terms and in a manner which is adequate for the type of arbitration. What is required is a reasoning of the decision not a legal treatise of the issue at stake.[123] An arbitration decision without reasons would seem arbitrary.[124]

5. Reliefs Ordered

5.1. Remedies

24-70 A wide range of remedies are available to arbitrators. The prevailing view is that every remedy that is available in litigation should be available in arbitration as well.[125] The issue as to the classification of remedies as procedural or substantive will determine whether the relevant applicable law is the law governing the arbitration or the law applicable to the merits. In any event arbitrators should be careful not to exceed their mandate.[126]

---

120 While the German Bundesgerichtshof, 18 January 1990, III ZR 269/88. XVII *YBCA* 503 (1992) held that an award without reasons does not violate public policy, the Italian Corte di cassazione, 3 April 1987, *SpA Abati Legnami (Italy) v Fritz Häupl*, XVII YBCA 529 (1992) refused enforcement of an award because the reasons given were insufficient and illogical.

121 See Sanders, "Arbitration", *IECL*, Vol XVI, Chapter 12, para 181.

122 See Bingham, "Reasons and Reasons for Reasons: Differences between a Court Judgment and an Arbitral Award, 4 *Arb Int* 141 (1988) 145.

123 Redfern and Hunter, *International Commercial Arbitration*, para 8-58, 392.

124 Delvolvé, "Essai sur la motivation des sentences arbitrales", *Rev Arb* 149 (1989) 165.

125 See, *e.g.*, Schlosser, "Right and Remedy in Common Law Arbitration and in German Arbitration Law", 4(1) *J Int'l Arb* 27 (1987).

126 *Ibid*, 40, and New York Convention Article V(1)(c).

24-71 Remedies which may be the subject matter of an arbitration award include:

- Specific performance;
- Damages / monetary compensation;
- Declaratory relief
- Gap-filling and contract adaptation;[127]
- Punitive damages and exemplary damages.
- Restitution;[128]
- Rectification;[129]
- Injunctive relief.[130]

(a) Specific performance

24-72 Specific performance is a widely accepted remedy in civil law countries, less so in common law systems. In international arbitration various tribunals have ordered specific performance and their decisions have been upheld by state courts also in common law countries.[131] There are, however, a number of decisions, in particular, in arbitrations involving states but also between private parties, where specific performance has been refused as inappropriate in the proceedings.[132] It has been argued that ordering specific performance would be

---

[127] See, *e.g.*, Kröll, *Ergänzung und Anpassung von Verträgen durch Schiedsgerichte* (Carl Heymanns 1998); Berger, "Power of Arbitrators to Fill Gaps and Revise Contracts to Make Sense", in Fletcher, Mistelis and Cremona (eds), *Foundations and Perspectives of International Trade Law* (Sweet and Maxwell 2001), 269.

[128] See, *e.g.*, England, Arbitration Act section 48(5)(a); See also Bonell, "A 'Global' Arbitration Decided on the Basis of the UNIDROIT Principles" 17 *Arb Int* 249 (2001) 257-8.

[129] See, *e.g.*, Redfern and Hunter, *International Commercial Arbitration*, para 8-14.

[130] See, *e.g.*, ICC Rules Article 23; UNCITRAL Rules Article 26.

[131] But see *e.g. In re Staklinski,* 180 NYS 2d 20 (NY App. Div. 1958), *aff'd,* 160 NE 2d (NY 1959); for further US cases see Elder, "The Case Against Arbitral Awards of Specific Performance in Transnational Commercial Disputes", 13 *Arb Int* 1 (1997) 13 *et seq*; for a rare case where specific performance was ordered against a state see *Texas Overseas Petroleum Co/California Asiatic Oil Co v Government of the Libyan Arab Republic,* 17 ILM 1 (1978) 36.

[132] Specific performance was deemed an inappropriate remedy in, *e.g.*, ICSID Final award, 31 March 1986 and Interim award, 24 October 1984, *Liberian Eastern Timber Corporation ("LETCO") v The Government of the Republic of Liberia,* 26 ILM 647 (1987), XIII YBCA 35 (1988); Zurich arbitration award in case no 273/95, 31 May 1996, *raw material processor (Hungary) and processing Group (Argentina) v raw material seller (Russian Federation),* XXIII YBCA 128 (1998); ICC award no 8032 (1995), XXI *YBCA* 113 (1996).

contrary to the well balanced fabric of the New York Convention, which provides for as little involvement as possible of the courts of the place of performance. The efforts necessary for enforcing awards rendering specific performance would put too high an obligation on the enforcing courts.[133]

(b) Damages

24-73 An award of monetary compensation (damages) is the "natural" remedy in international commercial arbitration.[134] A tribunal will normally order a party to pay a sum of money in a given currency. The sum is either a debt owed by one party to the other or compensation for defective or non-performance or a breach of contract, or a combination of those.

24-74 While the award of damages is so common as to be unremarkable the award of punitive damages has been controversial.[135] Punitive damages are normally awarded to punish and deter; they are an exceptional and extreme measure, permitted only, for example, in cases of fraud or substantial malice. Punitive damages or exemplary damages are known in some common law jurisdictions but are virtually unknown in civil law or Islamic law systems.[136]

24-75 Punitive damages have been awarded by arbitration tribunals, in particular, in the United States where either the law governing the arbitration or the arbitration agreement provided for multiple or punitive damages.[137] There is, however, a strong public policy restricting the right of arbitrators to award them.[138] Consequently, awards with punitive damages may not be enforced as a matter of public policy under Article V(2)(b) New York Convention.[139] Tribunals

---

[133] See Elder, "The Case Against Arbitral Awards of Specific Performance in Transnational Commercial Disputes", 13 *Arb Int* 1 (1997).

[134] See Ortscheidt, *La reparation du dommage dans l'arbitrage commercial international* (Dalloz 2001) with further references.

[135] See, *e.g.*, Pedrick Sullivan, "The Scope of Modern Arbitral Awards", 62 *Tulane L Rev* 1113 (1988) 1125 *et seq*; Farnsworth, "Punitive Damages in Arbitration", 7 *Arb Int* 3 (1991); Gotanda, "Awarding Punitive Damages in International Commercial Arbitrations in the Wake of Mastrobuono v Shearson Lehman Hutton Inc", 38 *Harvard Int'l L J* 59 (1997).

[136] Gotanda, *ibid*, 65-67.

[137] See, *e.g.*, *Willoughby Roofing & Supply Co v Kajima International Inc*, 776 F2d 269 (11th Cir, 1985); *Mitsubishi v Soler Chrysler-Plymouth Inc,* 473 US 614 (1985); *Mastrobuono v Shearson Lehman Hutton Inc,* 115 S Ct 1212 (1995).

[138] See, *e.g.*, *Garrity v Lyle Stuaryt Inc,* 40 NY 2d 35, 353 NE 2d 793 (1976).

[139] See, *e.g.*, Supreme Court Tokyo, 11 July 1997, reported in Tateishi, "Recent Japanese Case Law in Relation to International Arbitration", 17(4) *J Int'l Arb* 63 (2000) 71-72.

will be reluctant to award punitive damages even in cases where the parties have empowered them to do so.

(c) Declaratory order

24-76 A tribunal may be asked to make a declaratory award or an award which contains a declaration about the rights of the parties. This may happen as a matter of the law governing the arbitration proceedings[140] or as a result of an agreement of the parties.[141] A declaratory award may be useful for further negotiations or adaptation of contracts in long-term or relational contracts.

(d) Gap-filling and contract adaptation

24-77 Often arbitrators have an ultimate task to fill gaps or revise the contract which parties entered into long before the dispute has arisen. Adaptation and amendment of contracts by arbitrators in international commercial disputes has been of paramount importance and widely debated.[142] The main question relating to that issue is whether the arbitrators have the power to fill gap in the contracts or adapt it to the changed circumstances. This may be conferred upon the tribunal by the arbitration agreement. Some laws also provide for such power expressly or impliedly.[143]

5.2. Decision on Costs

24-78 There is little data available on the issue of costs awarded in international commercial arbitration cases but the issue has attracted considerable scholarly discussion.[144] In the absence of an agreement to the contrary the tribunal's power

---

[140] See, *e.g.*, England, Arbitration Act section 48(3).

[141] See, *e.g.*, *Saudi Arabia v Arabian American Oil Company (Aramco)*, 27 ILR 117 (1963) 145. As no party wished to jeopardise their business relationship the tribunal was asked to make a declaration that the agreement was breached without claiming any damages.

[142] See, *e.g.*, Kröll, *Ergänzung und Anpassung von Verträgen durch Schiedsgerichte*; Berger, "Power of Arbitrators to Fill Gaps and Revise Contracts to Make Sense", in Fletcher, Mistelis and Cremona (eds), *Foundations and Perspectives of International Trade Law* (Sweet and Maxwell 2001), 269.

[143] See, *e.g.*, Model Law Article 7(2); Bulgaria, Arbitration Act 1988/1993 Article 1(2); Netherlands, CCP Article 1020(3); Sweden, Arbitration Act Article 1(2); CEPANI Rules Article 6(1); see also Kröll, *ibid*, 305, who concludes that the English and the German arbitration laws also provide for the power of the tribunal to fill gaps and adapt the contract.

[144] See, *e.g*, Gotanda, "Awarding Costs and Attorney Fees in International Commercial Arbitrations", 21 *Michigan J Int'l L* 1 (1999); O'Reilly, *Costs in Arbitration Proceedings* (LLP

to decide on the allocation of costs is widely recognised in arbitration laws and rules.[145] This also applies to tribunals which deny their jurisdiction.[146]

24-79 An arbitration tribunal may wish to deal with the scope of costs at a preliminary hearing. This would avoid any dispute over the extent of the jurisdiction of the tribunal to award costs at the end of the proceedings. Inevitably, the authority of the tribunal to award costs is always subject to the agreement of the parties at any time.[147]

24-80 Costs related to arbitration can be divided into two main groups: arbitration costs and legal costs. Arbitration costs include the arbitrators' fees,[148] expenses connected with the hearings (*e.g.* hiring venue, translators' fees), fees and expenses of any experts appointed by the tribunal and the administrative expenses of the arbitration institution, if the arbitration is an institutional one. In institutional arbitration, the institution is responsible for obtaining an advance from the parties in respect of these fees and expenses.[149] In most cases, the schedules with fee tables do not form part of the institutional rules, and they can be amended by the institution more easily and more frequently than the rules.

24-81 In the absence of an agreement by the parties, the tribunal has discretion to apportion these costs as it sees fit.[150] Some rules, however, like CIETAC Article 59, limit the power of tribunals to apportion costs.[151]

1995); Wilson, "Saving Costs in International Arbitration", 6 *Arb Int* 151 (1990); Wetter and Priem, "Costs and their Allocation in International Commercial Arbitrations", 2 *Am Rev Int'l Arb* 249 (1991); Gurry, "Fees and Costs", 6(10) *WAMR* 227 (1995); Buehler, "Correction and Interpretation of Awards and Advances on Costs", *ICC Bulletin - Supplement* 53 (1997); Smith, "Costs in International Commercial Arbitration", 56(4) *Disp Resol J* 30 (2001) with assessment of laws and rules and practical proposals.

[145] See, *e.g.*, ICC Article 31(3); LCIA Article 28; AAA ICDR Article 31; UNCITRAL Rules Article 40.

[146] Bundesgerichtshof, 6 June 2002, *W GmbH v A Ltd*, 1 Schieds VZ 39 (2003) 40

[147] Smith, "Costs in International Commercial Arbitration", 56(4) *Disp Resol J* 30 (2001) 33.

[148] See Gotanda, Setting Arbitrators' Fees: An International Survey, 33 *Vanderbilt J Transnat'l L* 779 (2000) with further references.

[149] See, *e.g.*, ICC Rules Article 31.

[150] See, *e.g.*, in Switzerland: Vaud Cantonal Tribunal, 16 February 1993, *Brega v Techint*, ASA Bull 57 (1995) 62; in the United States: *Compagnie des Bauxites de Guinée v Hammersmills Inc*, 1992 WL 122712, XVIII YBCA 566 (1993) (DDC 1992).

[151] Article 59 provides:

> The arbitration tribunal has the power to decide in the arbitral award that the losing party shall pay the winning party as compensation a proportion of the expenses reasonably

24-82 An emerging trend can be recorded for the arbitration tribunal to order the losing party to pay all or the substantial part of the costs of the arbitration. This tradition is widely accepted and can be seen, for example, in England[152] in France[153] and Switzerland.[154] The other emerging trend in allocating costs between the parties is to take into account their attitude during the proceedings.[155] This development is significant, as when delaying tactics are employed proceedings may get very lengthy and expensive.[156]

24-83 A substantive part of the arbitration costs consists of the arbitrators' fees. In *ad hoc* arbitration, arbitrators negotiate their hourly fee with the parties before their appointment. In institutional arbitration, institutions approach the matter differently. For instance, the LCIA sets out a recommended range of hourly rates which may only be deviated from in exceptional circumstances.[157] The ICC calculates the arbitrators' fees proportionally to the sum in dispute (*ad valorem method*). It is also possible to have arbitrators paid on a *fixed fee* basis.[158]

---

incurred by the winning party in dealing with the case. The amount of such compensation shall not in any case exceed 10% of the total amount awarded to the winning party.

152 See, *e.g.*, England, Arbitration Act section 61 and *Channel Island Ferries Ltd v Cenargo Navigation Ltd (The Rozel)*, [1994] 2 Lloyd's Rep 161, (1994) ASA Bulletin 439.

153 See, *e.g.*, ICC Award 6962 (1992), *Swiss seller v Romanian buyer*, XIX YBCA 184 (1994).

154 See, *e.g.*, ICC Award 7419 (1995), *European Company B SA v North African Company S SA*, ASA Bulletin 535 (1995).

155 See, *e.g.*, ICC Award 8486 (1996), *Dutch party v Turkish party*, 125 *Clunet* 1047 (1998).

156 See Schneider, "Lean Arbitration: Cost Control and Efficiency Through Progressive Identification of Issues and Separate Pricing of Arbitration Services", 10(2) *Arb Int* 119 (1994). See also ICC Award 3879 (1993), *Westland Helicopters Ltd v Arab Organisation for Industrialisation*, unpublished, cited in *ASA Bulletin* 404 (1994). The tribunal awarded costs of £18 million against the losing party. The losing party delayed the proceedings which lasted 13 years. In an ICSID arbitration, which followed an ICC arbitration, the tribunal awarded over $5 million compensation for legal and expert fees on top of damages: ICSID case no ARB/84/3, *Southern Pacific Properties (Middle East) Ltd v Arab Republic of Egypt*, 32 ILM 933 (1993), corrected at 32 ILM 1470 (1993), XIX YBCA 51 (1994).

157 LCIA Schedule of Fees and Costs (effective 10 May 2002). Previously the LCIA had a fixed minimum and maximum daily rate.

158 On the methods of assessing fees see Redfern and Hunter, *International Commercial Arbitration*, paras 4-106 to 4-109 and 4-111 to 4-114. The German Federal Court, however, has annulled an award for violation of public policy in a case where the arbitrators have fixed their own fees. See Bundesgerichtshof, *BGHZ* 142, 204, 206-7, *NJW* 2974 (1999). It seems that this is not the final determination of the issue in Germany. See also the discussion in Kröll, "Das neue Schiedsrecht vor staatlichen Gerichten: Entwicklungslinien und Tendenzen", *NJW* 1173 (2001) 1184.

24-84 Legal costs normally include the cost for legal representation in the arbitration proceedings as well as the expenses of the legal teams for preparing the case and advising the parties.[159]

24-85 In litigation before the English High Court, as a general rule, the legal costs of the prevailing party are paid by the losing party, in addition to any sum to be paid pursuant to the judgment on the merits. If not agreed, the amount of the costs is normally determined in a "taxation" or "detailed assessment".[160] The principle that the losing party pays the prevailing party's legal costs is generally recognised in Europe. In many countries, however, there is rarely a separate or specialist hearing relating to this matter. Instead, the question of liability for legal costs is addressed together with the merits by the trial judge. The trial judge will estimate what he or she believes the costs of the prevailing party should have amounted to, and, subject to the parties' arguments, normally there will be no further adjudication on this matter. The concept of "loser pays" is generally foreign to US lawyers.[161]

24-86 The harmonised practice that is emerging in international commercial arbitration in relation to costs is similar to the position in many civil law jurisdictions, where recovery of costs is permitted under the applicable law or rules. While the losing party is expected to bear the costs of the other party,[162] there is generally no separate award relating to this matter, and no "taxation" process. Instead, the tribunal assess the legal costs incurred by the prevailing party and make a provision for these costs in the final award.[163] There are, however, cases where the fundamental decision on costs was made in the award while the amount was fixed in a separate award.[164] In any event, in allocating legal costs the arbitration tribunal will take into account any prior agreement between the parties as well as their behaviour during the proceedings.

---

[159] See Gotanda, "Awarding Costs and Attorneys' Fees in International Commercial Arbitrations", 21 *Michigan J Int'l L* 1 (1999) with further references.

[160] See Civil Procedure Rules Part 47.

[161] See Lew and Shore, "International Commercial Arbitration: Harmonising Cultural Differences", 54-Aug *Disp Resol J* 33 (1999) 38.

[162] See, *e.g.*, AAA ICDR Article 31(d), LCIA Article 28(4), NAI Article 60, SIAC Rule 30(3) and UNCITRAL Rules Articles 38(e) and 40(2).

[163] See Lew and Shore, "International Commercial Arbitration: Harmonising Cultural Differences", 54 *Disp Resol J* 33 (1999) 38.

[164] Oberlandesgericht Stuttgart, 4 June 2002, *W GmbH v A Ltd*, 1 Sch 22/01.

5.3. Interest

24-87 There is no consensus on the method of awarding interest in international commercial arbitration.[165] If money is claimed, interest is sought to be added. Arbitrators invariably accept this request and add interest to the substantive amount awarded. The tribunal will have to determine:

- whether the debtor is liable to pay interest;[166]
- the rate of interest to apply;[167]
- the starting point from which interest has to be paid; [168] and
- whether interest should be compounded and if so from what date?[169]

24-88 A tribunal will determine these questions by looking at national laws (which vary considerably), contractual interests and interest as a matter of damages.[170] Where there is no agreement, arbitrators should look at the law governing the arbitration or the arbitration rules which apply. Interest (and its rate) is not specifically covered by any arbitration rules. It is always advisable that the parties provide in their agreement the rate of interest payable on money due or other payments.

24-89 Several Islamic countries do not allow interest as part of the award. This is the case for countries having legal systems based on Shari'a. Shari'a expressly prohibits the taking of interest or (riba). Some countries, like Egypt, have

---

165 See Gotanda, "Awarding Interest in International Arbitration", 90 *Am J Int'l L* 40 (1996) 62; Lew, "Interest on Money Awards in International Arbitration", in Cranston (ed), *Making Commercial Law – Essays in Honour of Roy Goode* (Clarendon Press 1997), 543, 568; Hunter and Triebel, "Awarding Interest in International Arbitration: Some Observations Based on a Comparative Study of the Laws of England and Germany", 6(1) *J Int'l Arb* 7 (1989).

166 There is a general presumption that the debtor is liable for payment of interest.

167 See the discussion in Lew, "Interest on Money Awards in International Arbitration", in Cranston (ed), *Making Commercial Law – Essays in Honour of Roy Goode* (Clarendon Press 1997), 543, 565-8 where the suggestions made by Gotanda are discussed.

168 There is a general presumption that interest runs from the day of default.

169 There is a general presumption that interest accrues at a rate corresponding to that of a commonly used saving vehicle in the currency in which payment is to be made and is to be compounded quarterly. See also Gotanda, "Awarding Interest in International Arbitration", 90 *Am J Int'l L* 40 (1996) 42 *et seq.*

170 See Lew, "Interest on Money Awards in International Arbitration", in Cranston (ed), *Making Commercial Law – Essays in Honour of Roy Goode* (Clarendon Press 1997), 543, 545-560 with comparative analysis.

departed from this rule of Shari'a and allow for interest.[171] A tribunal which expects its award may be enforced in an Islamic country will make a separate award on interest which may be enforced in other countries where assets of the debtor may be located. In this way the award on interest does not tarnish the award on the merits.

6. CORRECTION AND INTERPRETATION OF AWARD

24-90 It is sometimes necessary to correct obvious clerical, typographical or computing errors in an award or to clarify some ambiguity. The ICC scrutiny process of the draft aims to reduce the need for corrections or interpretation.[172] Nevertheless correction or interpretation of awards may be undertaken by the tribunal also under the ICC Rules.[173]

6.1. Correction

24-91 Generally arbitration laws and rules provide for the possibility of correction of awards.[174] The Model Law, for example, provides for correction of the award within 30 days of its receipt by the party requesting the correction. Such correction may only concern corrections of "errors in computation, any clerical or typographical errors or any errors of similar nature".[175] The Model Law further empowers the tribunal to correct the award on its own initiative, within the same time period.

24-92 The correction of an award is normally made by the tribunal.[176] The tribunal's power is, however, limited to correcting the errors and not altering the

---

171 See Lew, *ibid*, 550-1. See also Gotanda, "Awarding Interest in International Arbitration", 90 *Am J Int'l L* 40 (1996) 47-50 with comparative remarks.

172 ICC Rules Article 27 provides that tribunals *must* submit draft awards to the ICC Court, which may lay down modifications of form and draw the tribunal's attention to points of substance.

173 See ICC Article 29. See also Daly, "Correction and Interpretation of Arbitral Awards under the ICC Rules of Arbitration", 15(1) *ICC Bulletin* 61 (2002); and the appendix "Extracts from ICC Addenda and Decisions on the Correction and Interpretation of Arbitral Awards", 15(1) *ICC Bulletin* 72 (2002).

174 See, *e.g.*, Model Law Article 33; China, Arbitration Law Article 56; England, Arbitration Act section 57; France, NCPC Article 1475; Netherlands, CCP Article 1060; US, FAA section 11.

175 Model Law Article 33.

176 But see US, FAA section 11 according to which the correction is made by the court. However, most states have adopted legislation similar to the Uniform Arbitration Act which in addition to

content of the award. For example, it cannot change the amount awarded if it has misinterpreted an underlying expert opinion or other facts. This would not be a correction in the sense of the Model Law but a second award for which the tribunal lacks jurisdiction.[177]

24-93 Arbitration rules also provide for correction or modification of the award by the tribunal.[178] For example, the replacement of a period with a comma could change a sum of money from thousands into millions.[179] Other corrections may relate to the calculation of costs, where one party instead of 50% is in fact ordered to pay 100% of the costs.[180] In some instances issues of substance may be interwoven with typographical or clerical matters. This may be the case when the application for correction of awards may relate to the calculation of interest but also the tribunal's reasoning in the respect.[181]

24-94 It is essential that arbitration rules actually provide for correction of awards, as after the award is rendered the tribunal's mandate terminates.[182] The reference in the rules to the possibility of correction of awards can be interpreted as a legal basis for the extension of the scope of the arbitrators' duty by agreement of the parties.[183]

6.2. Interpretation

24-95 Interpretation of an award is justified only when the ruling, rather than the discussion of facts and arguments, is expressed in vague terms[184] or where there is ambiguity as to how the award should be executed.[185]

---

section 13 (similar to FAA section 11) contains section 9 which provides for correction or modification of the award by the arbitrators.

[177] See Oberlandesgericht Stuttgart, 20 December 2001, 1 Sch 13/0,1 unreported. In this case the second award was annulled for a lack of jurisdiction. But see also the ICC practice, *e.g.*, ICC Addendum in case 9391, 15(1) *ICC Bulletin* 76-7(2002).

[178] See, *e.g.*, UNCITRAL Rules Article 36; AAA ICDR Article 30; CIETAC Article 61; ICC Article 29; LCIA Article 27; LMAA rule 25; ICAC paragraph 42; NAI Article 52; Stockholm Institute Article 37; WIPO Article 66.

[179] See, *e.g.*, ICC Addendum to case no 10386, 15(1) *ICC Bulletin* 86 (2002).

[180] See, *e.g.*, ICC Addendum to case no 9391, 15(1) *ICC Bulletin* 76 (2002).

[181] See, *e.g.*, ICC Addendum to case no 9908, 15(1) *ICC Bulletin* 77 (2002).

[182] See Smit, "Correcting Arbitral Mistakes", 10 *Am Rev Int'l Arb* 225 (1999) with discussion of *Hyle v Doctor's Associates Inc*, 198 F3d 368 (2d Cir 1999).

[183] See Sanders, "Arbitration", *IECL*, Vol XVI, Chapter 12, para 197.

[184] Fouchard Gaillard Goldman *on International Commercial Arbitration*, 776.

24-96 Unlike correction, interpretation of the award is not normally permitted under most arbitration laws. Indeed interpretation was included in Article 33 Model Law only after considerable debate. It is allowed if so agreed by the parties and with notice given to the other party. The interpretation should relate to a specific point or part of the award. In the light of this provision interpretation is a clarification of a specific part of the award.[186] Only few non-Model Law countries provide for interpretation of awards.[187]

24-97 Arbitration rules more often provide for the interpretation of awards at the request of either party within a certain period of time from the communication of the award to the parties.[188] Tribunals should reject any request which goes beyond the interpretation of the award; provisions in arbitration rules for the interpretation of awards are not meant to empower the tribunal to change the substance of their ruling.[189] Admissible requests include, for example, interpretation related to the time period and the geographical extent of royalty payments,[190] or clarifying which claims were disposed of and which are left for the tribunal in parallel proceedings.[191]

24-98 The reluctance in allowing interpretation of the award is a defence mechanism so that the parties do not effectively re-open the case after the award has been made.[192] Hence, clarification will normally be made even where the laws or rules make no express provision to that effect,[193] but extensive revisions of the award will not be made unless deemed essential and the parties have expressly agreed so.

---

185 See Daly, "Correction and Interpretation of Arbitral Awards under the ICC Rules of Arbitration", 15(1) *ICC Bulletin* 61 (2002) 63-4.

186 See Holtzmann and Neuhaus, *Model Law*, 890-91.

187 See, *e.g.*, France, NCPC Article 1475 (applicable to domestic arbitration); Brazil, Arbitration Law Article 30(2).

188 See, *e.g.*, UNCITRAL Rules Article 35; AAA ICDR Article 30; ICC Article 29, see also Daly, "Correction and Interpretation of Arbitral Awards under the ICC Rules of Arbitration", 15(1) *ICC Bulletin* 61 (2002), 70-1; LMAA rule 25; ICAC paragraph 42; Stockholm Institute Article 37; ICSID Rules Chapter VII and in particular rule 51.

189 See, *e.g.*, ICC case no 8810, 15(1) *ICC Bulletin* 72 (2002).

190 See, *e.g.*, ICC Addendum in case no 10189, 15(1) *ICC Bulletin* 81 (2002).

191 See, *e.g.*, ICC Addendum in case no 10172, 15(1) *ICC Bulletin* 79 (2002).

192 Iran-US Claims Tribunal which arbitrates under the UNCITRAL Rules does not grant a request for interpretation.

193 See, *e.g.*, *ad hoc* arbitration in *Wintershall AG v Government of Qatar*, 5 February 1988 and 31 May 1988, XV YBCA 30 (1990); the final award interpreted the partial award.

7. Confidentiality and Publication of Awards

24-99 Confidentiality is often considered to be one of the main advantages of international commercial arbitration.[194] Unlike court decisions which are in the public domain and are regularly published and used as precedents, arbitration proceedings normally remain confidential. The rule is that no publication takes place if one party objects to it. However, publication of awards generally serves important purposes: published arbitration awards may be used as precedents[195] and contribute directly or indirectly to the development of arbitration, may inspire confidence in the arbitration process and most certainly assists scholars and practitioners to study the topic by being a practical and influential source of information. For this last purpose publication of awards without references to the names of the parties or other information that may identify them suffices.

24-100 Confidentiality has not always been an issue in several countries. For example, until the early 1990s no-one in England ever thought that arbitration was really "confidential", as distinct from "private".[196]

24-101 In general arbitration laws do not contain provisions concerning confidentiality or publication of awards.[197] The Model Law Working Group refrained from inserting a provision on publication of awards. Indeed it was observed

> It may be doubted whether the Model Law should deal with the question whether an award may be published. Although it is controversial since there are good reasons

---

[194] See also Paulsson and Rawding, "The Trouble with Confidentiality", 11 *Arb Int* 303 (1995); Collins, "Privacy and Confidentiality in Arbitration Proceedings", 11 *Arb Int* 321 (1995); Smit, "Confidentiality in Arbitration", 11 *Arb Int* 337 (1995); Neill, "Confidentiality in Arbitration", 12 *Arb Int* 287 (1996); Rogers and Miller, "Non-Confidential Arbitration Proceedings", 12 *Arb Int* 319 (1996); Fortier, "The Occasional Unwarranted Assumption of Confidentiality", 15 *Arb Int* 131 (1999); Leahy and Bianchi, "The Changing Face of International Arbitration", 17(4) *J Int'l Arb* 19 (2000); Bagner, "Confidentiality – A Fundamental Principle in International Commercial Arbitration?", 18(2) *J Int'l Arb* 243 (2001); Oakley-White, "Confidentiality revisited: Is International Arbitration Losing one of its Major Benefits?", 1 *Int ALR* 29 (2003).

[195] See, *e.g.*, Berger, "The International Arbitrators' Application of Precedents", 9(4) *J Int'l Arb* 5 (1992) 19 *et seq.*

[196] The *Lena Goldfields* case was heard in public in 1930 and the award printed in a daily newspaper. See Award of 2 September 1930, *Lena Goldfields Ltd v USSR*, substantially reproduced in *The Times*, 3 September 1930 and 36 *Cornell Law Quarterly* 31 (1950-51). Further, as late as the 1970s maritime awards were posted on the floor of the Baltic Exchange if the debtor did not pay.

[197] See, *e.g.*, China, Arbitration Law Article 40 which reserves confidentiality only to the hearings; France, NCPC Article 1469 provides that the deliberations are secret.

for and against such publication, the decision may be left to the parties or the arbitration rules chosen by them.[198]

24-102 Unlike laws, most rules contain specific provisions about confidentiality or the publication of awards. They state that awards may be made public only with thc consent of both parties.[199]

24-103 There is a body of case law which confirms confidentiality unless otherwise agreed by the parties.[200] The Paris Court of Appeal has criticised a claimant who sought bizarrely to challenge in France an award rendered in Paris. The Court pointed out that by initiating challenge proceedings the confidentiality of the award may be breached.[201]

24-104 In practice many awards are published without the consent of the parties[202] and without reference to their names. Since the 1980s a new tendency may be observed: ICC makes awards available for research purposes and abstracts are often published without disclosure of the names of the parties in *Clunet* and the *ICCA Yearbook of Commercial Arbitration* or the *ICC Bulletin*.[203]

---

198 See UNCITRAL Secretariat's note A/CN9/207 and Holtzmann and Neuhaus, *Model Law*, 845, para 95.

199 See, *e.g.*, UNCITRAL Rules Article 32(5); AAA ICDR Article 34; CRCICA Article 37bis; LCIA Article 30; LMAA rule 26; NAI Article 55; Vienna Article 18(10); WIPO Articles 73-76; IBA Rules of Ethics rule 9 which relates to confidentiality of deliberations; AAA ICDR Rules of Ethics for Arbitrators in Commercial Disputes canon VI.

200 See 11 *Arb Int* (1995), for expert reports by Bond and Lew, 273 and 283, respectively, in the case of *Esso Australia Resources Ltd and others v The Hon Sidney James Plowman, The Minister for Energy and Minerals and others*, (1995) 183 CLR 10, (1995) 11 Arb Int 235. See also Swedish Supreme Court, 27 October 2000, *Bulgarian Foreign Trade Bank Limited v AI Trade Finance Inc,* 13 WTAM 147 (2001), XXVI YBCA 291 (2001); *Associated Electric & Gas Insurance Services Ltd v European Reinsurance Company of Zurich* [2003] UKPC 11 (PC, 29 January 2003).

201 *Ibid*, Cour d'appel Paris, 18 February 1986, *Aïta* v *Ojjeh,* Rev Arb 583 (1986).

202 See also the new trend in *Andersen* arbitration, 10(4) *Am Rev Int'l Arb* 437 (1999) where the parties wanted to keep their dispute publicly known, and the awards in *CME Czech Republic BV v Czech Republic* and *Lauder v Czech Republic*, voluntarily published by one of the parties in <www.mfcr.cz/scripts/hpe/default.asp> (last visited December 2002).

203 It also started in 1990 with a volumes of collected awards. See Jarvin and Derains, *Collection of ICC Awards 1974-1985*; Jarvin, Derains and Arnaldez, *Collection of ICC Awards 1986-1990*; Arnaldez, Derains and Hascher, *Collection of ICC Awards 1991-1995*. Similar collections have been published with awards of the Cairo Regional Centre for International Arbitration, the Stockholm Chamber of Commerce and other institutions. *Mealey's International Commercial Arbitration Report* also publishes arbitration awards.

All awards of the Iran-US Claims Tribunal are officially published,[204] and many ICSID awards are published especially after the reform of the ICSID Rules in 1984.[205]

8. Termination of Proceedings without Award

24-105 Not all arbitration proceedings terminate with an award. Termination of proceedings without award is rarely regulated in arbitration laws other than Article 32 Model Law which states

> 1. The arbitral proceedings are terminated by the final award or by an order of the arbitral tribunal in accordance with paragraph (2) of this article.
> 2. The arbitral tribunal shall issue an order for the termination of the arbitral proceedings when:
>   a. the claimant withdraws his claim, unless the respondent objects thereto and the arbitral tribunal recognizes a legitimate interest on his part in obtaining a final settlement of the dispute;
>   b. the parties agree on the termination of the proceedings
>   c. the arbitral tribunal finds that the continuation of the proceedings has for any other reason become unnecessary or impossible. …

24-106 Similarly arbitration rules rarely contain references about termination of the proceedings without an award.[206]

---

[204] See *Iran-US Claims Tribunal Reports*; the awards are also available at WESTLAW.

[205] See <www.worldbank.org/icsid>.

[206] See, *e.g.*, UNCITRAL Rules Article 34; AAA ICDR Article 29; CRCICA Article 34; ICAC paragraph 45; WIPO Article 65.

Chapter 25

CHALLENGES TO AWARD

25-1 There are few grounds on which a party can seek to avoid an award. If dissatisfied with an award and unwilling to voluntarily accept its effect, an unsuccessful party has three options. It can

- appeal against the award, if this is permitted under the applicable law or the arbitration rules;
- challenge the award in the courts of the place where the award was made;
- wait until the successful party initiates enforcement proceedings before a court at which stage it can seek to resist enforcement.

25-2 In the third case the initiative is in the hands of the successful party while in the first two cases the initiative lies with the unsuccessful party. In either case it is the unsuccessful party that invokes the grounds for challenging the validity of an award.[1] In the third case the forum selection is a matter for the successful party while in the first two cases the forum is normally the place where the award was made.[2]

25-3 Parties may provide for an appeal or a second instance in the arbitration agreement.[3] This is rare in commercial arbitrations but is used in GAFTA commodity arbitrations.[4] A party has a right to appeal to a Board of Appeal[5] within no more than 30 days after the award was made.[6] An appeal invariably involves a new hearing and the Board of Appeal may confirm, amend or set aside the award.[7] An appeal may be withdrawn at any time.[8]

25-4 After the award has been made a party may apply to the courts in the place of arbitration to set it aside.[9] The grounds laid down for challenging an award are often comparable with the grounds referred to in the New York Convention for the purposes of refusing enforcement. It may also be possible, under some systems, to appeal the award in very limited circumstances.

25-5 While public scrutiny of the arbitration is inevitable at the time when recognition of the award is sought, it is less evident why the courts at the seat of arbitration should monitor an award prior to enforcement.[10] This is effectively a struggle between finality and fairness. It is understood that review of awards by the courts at the seat of arbitration promotes efficiency in international arbitration

---

1 See David, *Arbitration in International Trade*, 362; Šarčević, "The Setting Aside and Enforcement of Arbitral Awards under the UNCITRAL Model Law", in Šarčević (ed), *Essays*, 177.

2 Austrian Oberster Gerichtshof, 22 October 2001, 1 Ob 236/01, *ZfRV* 197 (2002) with note Hoyer. But see, *e.g.*, *Hitachi Ltd et al (Japan) v Mitsui & Co (Germany) and Rupali Polyester (Pakistan)*, XXV YBCA 486 (2000), (Supreme Court of Pakistan, 10 June 1998).

3 See, *e.g.*, Netherlands, CCP Article 1050(1); Argentina, CCP Article 763; Peru, Decree no 25935 of 1992 Article 54(2).

4 But see also Court of Arbitration for Sports Ad Hoc Rules Article 20(c)(iii).

5 Consisting of three members of the Association if the award was made by a sole arbitrator or five members if the award was made by a three member tribunal. See further GAFTA rule 11.

6 See GAFTA rule 10(1).

7 The appeal procedure is provided in GAFTA Rule 12. Appeal awards are regulated by GAFTA rule 15.

8 GAFTA rule 13.

9 Other terms used include "challenge", "annul", "recourse", or "review" the award. These terms are used interchangeably. See, *e.g.*, Model Law Article 34 ("recourse" and "set aside"); Switzerland, PIL Article 190 ("setting aside"); and US, FAA section 10 ("vacation").

10 See Park, "Why Courts Review Arbitral Awards", in Briner, Fortier, Berger and Bredow (eds), *Law of International Business and Dispute Settlement in the 21st Century – Liber Amicorum Karl-Heinz Böckstiegel* (Carl Heymanns 2001), 595.

by enhancing the trust of the parties in the process.[11] Most laws provide for challenge of the award at the place where it was made, while parties may modify in the arbitration agreement the extent to which such challenge proceedings are available to their arbitration.

25-6 This chapter examines (1) the requirements for the challenge of an award, (2) the grounds for setting aside, (3) the appeal on a matter of law, (4) legal and practical consequences of a claim for the challenge to an award, and (5) the contractual modification (waiver or exclusion) of the right to challenge an award.

1. Requirements for Challenge

25-7 A challenge procedure is a guarantee that state courts may review the award if a party has a good reason to be dissatisfied or aggrieved with the arbitration and the way in which the award was rendered.[12] This guarantee inspires the confidence of the parties in the arbitration process. The possibility of challenging awards at the place of arbitration has been heralded as a "bulwark against corruption, arbitrariness and bias."[13]

25-8 Challenge is the only remedy a party has against an award in the courts of the place where the award was made; enforcement may still be resisted in other courts. A challenge cannot and should not amount to a review of the merits of the award. Otherwise the principle of finality would be violated.[14] The court may set aside the award in part or in its entirety but cannot alter its content.

25-9 A challenge aims either at modifying, or more often at nullifying, the award in the jurisdiction where the award was made. The effect of a successful challenge will be to preclude enforcement of the award at the place of arbitration or elsewhere under the New York Convention. However, in some limited

---

[11] *Ibid*, 595 *et seq*.

[12] See Berger, *Arbitration Interactive*, paras 15-28 - 15-32; Redfern and Hunter, *International Commercial Arbitration*, paras 9-03 – 9-06.

[13] Kerr, "Arbitration and the Courts: The UNCITRAL Model Law", 34 *ICLQ* 1 (1985) 15. See also Craig, "Uses and Abuses of Appeal from Awards", 4 *Arb Int* 174 (1988) 198-202.

[14] See the dictum *per* Leggat J in *Arab African Energy Corporation Ltd v Olieprodukten Nederland BV* [1984] 2 Lloyd's Rep 419, 424 (QBD). See similarly *Fertilizer Corp of India v IDI Mgt*, 517 F Supp 948, 957-8 (SD Ohio 1981); Swiss Federal Tribunal, 8 January 1995, *Inter-Maritime Management SA v Russin and Vecchi*, 10(9) Mealey's IAR D1 (1995), XXII YBCA 789 (1997).

instances, even where an award has been set aside it may still be enforced outside the seat of arbitration.[15]

1.1. Legal Bases for Challenge

25-10 All national arbitration laws and international instruments regulating arbitration contain certain provisions for the challenge of awards.[16] Normally they provide for an action to set aside the award.[17]

25-11 International conventions make reference to setting aside of awards but contain no substantive rules relating to challenge, such as grounds and time limits within which it may be raised.[18]

25-12 However, because it establishes a specific and autonomous regime the ICSID Convention provides for the challenge of awards. Article 52 gives either party the right to challenge within 120 days after the date on which the award was rendered on one or more of the exhaustive list of grounds. It also includes specific substantive and procedural rules dealing with the challenge of the awards.

25-13 It is arguable whether parties can by agreement modify the scope of judicial review in respect of awards and whether it would be possible for them to confer jurisdiction on courts to review an award on its merits.[19] Ultimately the

---

[15] This could be the case where the award was set aside for violation of public policy of the court; see, *e.g.*, European Convention Article IX; see also Sanders, "Arbitration", *IECL*, Vol XVI, Chapter 12, para 229 (there are no reported cases about this option); or where an enforcing state has not accepted New York Convention Article V(1)(e) which states that a court may refuse enforcement if an award has not yet become binding on the parties or has been set aside or suspended; see, *e.g.*, Cour d'appel Paris, 29 December 1991, *Hilmarton Ltd v Omnium de Traitement et de Valorisation*, Rev Arb 300 (1993), XIX YBCA 655 (1994).

[16] See, *e.g.*, Model Law Article 34; Belgium, Judicial Code Articles 1704-1707; Brazil, Arbitration Law Articles 32-33; China, Arbitration Law Articles 58-61; England, Arbitration Act sections 67-71; France, NCPC Articles 1481-1491, 1504-6; Hong Kong, Arbitration Ordinance sections 23, 25 and Model Law provisions; Netherlands, CCP Articles 1064-1068; Switzerland, PIL Articles 190-1; US, FAA sections 10-12, 207. See also New York Convention Articles V(1)(e) and VI; European Convention Article IX; Inter-American Convention Articles 5(1)(e) and 6.

[17] Terminology may differ; see, *e.g.*, Model Law Article 34 (recourse and set aside); Swiss, PIL Article 190 (setting aside); and US, FAA section 10 (vacation).

[18] See New York Convention Articles V(1)(e) and VI; European Convention Article IX; Inter-American Convention Articles 5(1)(e) and 6.

[19] See Drahozal, "Standards for Judicial Review of Arbitral Awards in the United States: Mandatory Rules or Default Rules?", 16(9) *Mealey's IAR* 27 (2001); Cullinan, "Contracting for an Expanded Scope of Judicial Review in Arbitration Agreements", 51 *Vanderbilt L Rev* 395

question is whether arbitration laws dealing with grounds for challenge of awards are mandatory or default rules.[20] In some US cases it was held that parties cannot by agreement expand the grounds for judicial review of awards.[21] In other cases it was held that parties can contractually limit the grounds for court review of awards.[22] Consequently, various US Courts of Appeals are not in agreement so the matter will eventually be decided by the US Supreme Court. It appears, however, that parties can make agreements to set standards for the review of awards.

1.2. National Courts

25-14 Parties who wish to challenge an award should first exhaust possibilities for review of the award by the tribunal that rendered it[23] or the institution within which the award was made.[24] This includes seeking correction and interpretation of the award as appropriate.

25-15 Challenges must be filed with a court which has jurisdiction to hear the application. This is normally the court at the seat of arbitration.[25] This is the position adopted in the Model Law[26] and the majority of arbitration laws.[27] Applications made to courts, outside the place of arbitration are generally

(1998); Holstein, "Co-Opting the Federal Judiciary: Contractual Expansion of Judicial Review of Arbitral Awards", 12(11) *WAMR* 276 (2001); Montgomery, "Expanded Judicial Review of Commercial Arbitration *Awards* for the Best of Both Worlds: Lapine Technology Corp v Kyocera Corp", 68 *U Cin L Rev* 529 (2000).

20 Smit, "Contractual Modification of the Scope of Judicial Review of Arbitral Awards", 8 *Am Rev Int'l Arb* 147 (1997) and "Postscript", 8 *Am Rev Int'l Arb* 273 (1997). See also Drahozal, "Standards for Judicial Review of Arbitral Awards in the United States: Mandatory Rules or Default Rules?", 16(9) *Mealey's IAR* 27 (2001).

21 See, *e.g.*, *Bowen v Amoco Pipeline Co*, 2001 US App LEXIS 13867 (10th Cir, 20 June 2001); *Roadway Package System Inc v Kayser*, 2001 US App LEXIS 11846 (3d Cir, 7 June 2001). For a critical discussion which highlights the misgivings of the latter case see Drahozal, *ibid*, 16(9) *Mealey's IAR* 27 (2001).

22 See, *LaPine Technology Corp v Kyocera Corp*, 130 F 3d 884, 889 (9th Cir, 1997); *Gateway Technologies Inc v MCI Telecommunications Corp*, 64 F 3d 993, 997 (5th Cir, 1995).

23 See, *e.g.*, England, Arbitration Act section 70(2).

24 See, *e.g.*, GAFTA rule 12(6); ICSID Rules Article 50, 52, 55.

25 Unless otherwise agreed by the parties. It has been suggested that it is unnecessary and unhelpful to exercise this freedom to choose another court. See Redfern and Hunter, *International Commercial Arbitration*, para 9-45 and footnotes 36-38.

26 See Model Law Articles 34, 1 and 6.

27 See, *e.g.*, Brazil, Arbitration Law Article 33; China, Arbitration Law Article 58; England, Arbitration Act sections 67-71, and 1; France, NCPC Articles 1486, 1505; Netherlands, CCP Article 1064; Switzerland, PIL Article 191. See also New York Convention Article V(1)(e).

rejected.[28] There are, however, a few cases where the courts have assumed jurisdiction to hear challenges of awards rendered abroad on the basis that the law of this state was applicable to the merits.[29]

25-16 For the purposes of refusing enforcement, Article V(1)(e) New York Convention assumes that an award may be challenged "by a competent authority of the country in which, or under the laws of which, that award was made." Accordingly, an award may be challenged in a country under the law[30] of which it is actually made or is deemed to have been made.[31] This article can be interpreted in a negative fashion as limiting the courts in which an award may be challenged[32] or may be seen in a positive fashion as manifesting the potential for challenging an award in a place other than the place of arbitration.[33] In this respect it is noteworthy that national courts are reluctant to allow foreign courts to consider challenges to awards made within their jurisdiction.[34]

---

[28] But see Austrian Oberster Gerichtshof, 22 October 2001, 1 Ob 236/01, *ZfRV* 197 (2002) with note Hoyer. The court discussed the issue of whether an award made in China could be challenged in Austria on the grounds of Austrian law or New York Convention; the court found that it lacked jurisdiction.

[29] See, *e.g.*, *Hitachi Ltd et al (Japan) v Mitsui & Co (Germany) and Rupali Polyester (Pakistan)*, (2000) XXV YBCA 486 (Supreme Court of Pakistan, 10 June 1998): the award was made in England but it was challenged in respect of the arbitrators' alleged misconduct in Pakistan; the proper law of the contract was Pakistani law; the arbitration governed by ICC Rules and English law. See also, in relation to the pre-1996 Indian Arbitration and Conciliation Act which enacted the Model Law, Nariman, "Finality in India: The Impossible Dream", 10 *Arb Int* 373 (1994).

[30] This is the law governing the arbitration procedure, not the merits of the arbitration, save for a few states, such as Pakistan. For the orthodox view see, *e.g.*, Belgium, Court of Appeals Brussels, 14 October 1980, *SA Mines, Minérais et Métaux v Mechema, Ltd*, VII YBCA 316 (1982); France, Cour de cassation, 25 May 1983, *Maatschappij voor Industriële Research en Ontwikkeling BV v Henri Liévremont and M Cominassi*, XII YBCA 480 (1987); Germany, Bundesgerichtshof, 12 February 1976, II YBCA 242 (1977); India, *Oil and Natural Gas Commission v The Western Company of North America*, (1988) XIII YBCA 473 (Supreme Court, 16 January 1987); Spain, Tribunal Supremo, 24 March 1982, *Cominco France SA v Soguiber SL*, VIII YBCA 408 (1983); South Africa, Supreme Court, 27 August 1985, *Laconian Maritime Enterprises Ltd v Agromar Lineas Ltd*, XIV YBCA 693 (1989).

[31] *Yusuf Ahmed Alghanim & Sons WLL v Toys "R" Us Inc*, 126 F3d 15 (2d Cir 1997), 21, cert denied (1998).

[32] See, *e.g.*, *International Standard Electric Corp v Bridas sociedad anonima petrolera industrial y commercial*, 745 F Supp 172, 177-8 (SDNY 1990).

[33] See, *e.g.*, India, *National Thermal Power Corporation v The Singer Company*, (1992) 7(6) Mealey's IAR C1, (1993) XVIII YBCA 403 (Supreme Court). There was a challenge application in India concerning an award made in London. The Supreme Court assumed jurisdiction for the challenge on the grounds that the contract was governed by Indian law. This case was decided under the old Indian Arbitration Act.

[34] See, *e.g.*, *Union of India v McDonnell Douglas Corp* [1993] 2 Lloyd's Rep 48.

25-17 ICSID awards cannot be challenged in the courts of the place where the award was made. Pursuant to rule 52 ICSID Arbitration Rules, when a party files an application for the annulment of an award, an *ad hoc* committee will be appointed by the Chairman of the ICSID Administrative Council to decide on the matter thus excluding jurisdiction of any national court.[35] The ICSID autonomous regime has been used often and with success.[36]

25-18 In limited situations an award may not be challenged. An example is the concept of anational awards,[37] *i.e.* awards not connected with any national courts or laws.[38] While anational or transnational awards are a rarity, they exist both in theory and in practice.[39] For example, the Swiss Federal Tribunal held in 1992 that arbitrations between international organisations and private entities can be isolated from Swiss law even if the seat of the arbitration is in Switzerland.[40] Similarly, the Paris Court of Appeal rejected an action to challenge an award on

---

[35] Where such a challenge is successful the dispute may be submitted to a new tribunal which will render a new award. See ICSID Rules Article 55.

[36] The first challenge concerned the award in ICSID, case no ARB/81/2, *Klöckner et al v Cameroon and SOCAME,* X YBCA 71 (1985). The award was annulled, XI *YBCA* 162 (1986). The second challenge was directed against the award in ICSID, *Amco v Indonesia*, 1(1) Mealey's IAR 601 (1986). After annulment of the award, XII *YBCA* 129 (1987), 25 *ILM* 1441 (1986), both parties resubmitted the dispute. The third challenge concerned the award in ICSID, *MINE v Guinea*, XIV YBCA 89 (1989). After the award was annulled in part, XVI *YBCA* 40 (1991), the parties reached an amicable settlement of their dispute. A fourth challenge was directed against the award in ICSID, case no ARB/84/3, *SPP v Egypt*, 32 ILM 933 (1993), XIX YBCA 51 (1994). The parties reached a settlement. In ICSID, case no ARB/99/3, *Philippe Gruslin v Malaysia*, 5 ICSID Reports 483, also reported in Helgeson and Lauterpacht (eds), *Reports of Cases Decided under ICSID*, the annulment proceedings were discontinued with an order on 2 April 2002, for lack of payment of advances pursuant to Administrative and Financial Regulation 14(3)(d). In ICSID, case no ARB/9/3, *Compañía de Aguas del Aconquija SA & Vivendi Universal v Argentine Republic*, forthcoming 6 ICSID Reports, the award was in part annulled for a manifest disregard of the tribunals' power. The tribunal did not address certain issues which it should have dealt with due to a misperception as to its jurisdiction.

[37] Rensmann, "Anational Arbitration Awards – Legal Phenomenon or Academic Phantom", 15(2) *J Int'l Arb* 37 (1998); van den Berg, *New York Convention*, 28-51.

[38] See, *e.g.*, Paulsson, "Arbitration Unbound: Award Detached From the Law of its Country of Origin", 30 *ICLQ* 358 (1981); Goldman, "Les conflits de lois dans l'arbitrage international de droit privé", 109 *RCADI* 380 (1963).

[39] See, *e.g.*, Schmitthoff, "Finality of arbitral awards and judicial review", in Lew (ed), *Contemporary Problems*, 230, 231-2.

[40] See, *e.g.*, Switzerland, Tribunal Fédéral, 21 December 1992, *Groupement Fougerolle & Consorts v CERN*, BGE 118I b, 562, 568, Rev Arb 175 (1994).

the ground that no national law had been applied, despite the fact that France was the place of arbitration, the arbitration not having been submitted to French law.[41]

25-19 Potential anational awards may be seen in sports arbitration (where for instance Lausanne is always the seat for arbitrations in the context of Olympic Games) and online arbitration where the seat may be nominal or fictional.[42] Where a seat has been nominated, the courts at the nominated seat will have to entertain a challenge action despite the lack of territorial nexus.[43]

25-20 Another problem can be seen in relation to multi-national awards. Awards are deemed to be made in a particular place by normally applying the rules of that place. As different criteria exist in various countries granting nationality to an arbitration and an award it is possible that an arbitration may have dual or multiple nationality.[44] Each court will have the right to decide whether the award is made within its jurisdiction.

25-21 Once the seat and the nationality of the award have been determined, challenges will be brought to the competent authority, normally a court of higher instance.[45] For example, an award made in an arbitration with its seat in England must be challenged in the English High Court, in Switzerland in the Swiss Supreme Court (Tribunal Federal);[46] in France challenges are heard by the relevant court of appeal.[47]

---

41 Cour d'appel Paris, 21 February 1980, *General National Maritime Transport Company (GMTC) Libya, as legal successor of Libyan General Maritime Transport Organization (GMTO) v AB Götaverken*, VI YBCA 221 (1981). French law has since changed. According to NCPC Article 1495, applicable procedural rules no longer need to comply in all aspects with French procedural rules for an award to be regarded as French.

42 Kaufmann-Kohler, "Identifying and Applying the Law Governing the Arbitration Procedure – The Role of the Law of the Place of Arbitration", *ICCA Congress Series no 9*, 336.

43 *Ibid*, 348. Award no 5P 427/2000 made by the Cour d'arbitrage du sport has been unsuccessfully challenged in Switzerland; while the Swiss courts assumed jurisdiction they held that there were no grounds for the award to be set aside. See Swiss Tribunal Fédéral, *Raducan v IOC*, 4 December 2000, ATF 119 II 271, reported in Kaufmann-Kohler, *Arbitration at the Olympics*, 80.

44 Van Houtte, "International Arbitration and National Adjudication", in Voskuil and Wade (eds), *Hague-Zagreb Essays on the Law of International Trade* (Kluwer 1983), 325. See also Šarčević, "The Setting Aside and Enforcement of Arbitral Awards under the UNCITRAL Model Law", in Šarčević (ed), *Essays*, 176, 180, and 178-180 for an overview of various criteria for the granting of nationality.

45 The competent court is designated in Model Law Article 6.

46 See Switzerland, PIL Article 191.

47 See France, NCPC Article 1486. This is also the case in Germany, ZPO section 1062(1)(4).

25-22 The court designated has exclusive jurisdiction and no other court of the state will assume jurisdiction to hear the challenge. In Croatia the Constitutional Court rejected two complaints aimed at challenging awards despite allegations that there was an issue of constitutionality. The court held that the challenge procedure before the competent court should be followed and that this is the only way to have an award set aside.[48]

1.3. Time Limits

25-23 Time is of the essence in relation to the challenge of awards. Following the international tendency favouring finality of awards, challenges should be considered by the competent court as soon as possible after the award is made. As a matter of fairness time limits start to run from the time the award was deposited or is notified to the party wishing to challenge it. These time limits must be observed. Failure to do so may bar a challenge to the award.

25-24 Most national laws require the challenge to be launched within weeks rather than months after the time limits have started to run. Periods for bringing a claim to set aside an award may be as short as 28 days,[49] often three months[50] and occasionally as long as six months.[51]

25-25 Article 34(3) Model Law sets a time limit of three months from notification of the award to the party wishing to challenge it

> An application for setting aside *may* not be made after three months have elapsed from the date on which the party making that application had received the award or, if a request had been made under article 33, from the date on which that request had been disposed of by the arbitral tribunal. [Emphasis added]

25-26 The word "may" indicates that there is some discretion afforded to a court which would decide to hear a case after the expiration of the time limit. This use of language in Article 34 is justified: an action for challenge is the only recourse the unsuccessful party has in the country where the award was made; it

---

[48] Constitutional Complaint in case U 410/95 and Constitutional Complaint in case U 488/96. See Triva, "Arbitration and Public Policy: Constitutional Complaint as Means for Setting Aside Arbitral Awards", 7 *Croat Arbit Yearb* 115 (2000) 137-139.

[49] See, *e.g.*, England, Arbitration Act section 70(3); France, NCPC Articles 1486, 1505.

[50] See, *e.g.*, Belgium, Judicial Code Article 1707(3); Brazil, Arbitration Law Article 33(1); Netherlands, CCP Article 1064(3); US, FAA section 12.

[51] See China, Arbitration Law Article 59.

also manifests confidence that the courts will exercise their discretion wisely. It is unlikely that courts will allow challenges after the expiration of time limits given the pro-finality of awards policy in most countries. Further, the Model Law Working Party rejected a proposal to make the three month period of time subject to contrary agreement of the parties.[52]

25-27 The 28 days time limit under English law runs from the date of the award or if there has been any internal arbitration process of review or appeal, from the date when the applicant was notified of the result of that process.[53] The English courts considered this time limit in light of the finality of awards. It held that the party looking to challenge an award out of time must satisfy the court that there is a reasonable excuse for extending the limit.[54]

25-28 In the US section 12 FAA provides a maximum time limit of three months for a motion to vacate an award, after the award is filed or delivered.[55]

25-29 Chinese Arbitration Law provides for one of the longest time limits of six months from the date of receipt of the award.[56] The competent court, however, must decide within two months of the filing of a challenge application.[57]

25-30 Unless a partial award can be challenged only in conjunction with the final award, as is the case in Switzerland,[58] the time limit for initiating the challenge procedure runs for each award separately.[59] For example, in the *Eco Swiss v Benetton* case, the tribunal first rendered an award determining general liability and then a second award determining the quantum of damages. When Benetton tried to challenge the second award alleging violation of EC competition law, the Hoge Raad considered this action to be time barred since the

---

52 UNCITRAL Report, UN Doc A/40/17, para 304. See also Holtzmann and Neuhaus, *Model Law*, 919, 1003.

53 England, Arbitration Act section 70(3).

54 In *Aoot Kalmnoft v Glencore International AG and Another* [2002] 1 All ER 76 the request for an extension of the time limit to challenge the award (14 weeks after the expiration of the 28 day time limit) was rejected.

55 The period of three months is also available by most state arbitration laws. See Redfern and Hunter, *International Commercial Arbitration*, para 9-46.

56 China, Arbitration Law Article 59.

57 China, Arbitration Law Article 60.

58 Except for issues of jurisdiction or the constitution of the tribunal.

59 The Municipal Court Budapest, 5 P 22-301/2002/5, 5 *Int ALR* N-52 (2002) held that at the setting aside stage there is no difference between final award, partial award or interim award in respect of the obligation to produce a reasoned award.

defence related to the award on general liability for which the time limit for challenge had already expired.[60]

2. Grounds for Setting Aside

25-31 A party challenging an award must prove one of the exclusively listed grounds in the arbitration laws or international conventions. Laws containing specific provisions as to the burden and standard of proof require that the party seeking challenge furnishes proof of the particular grounds invoked.[61] Some grounds may be raised by the party but, on the basis of the legislative language, also may be invoked by the court. Such reasons are normally that the subject matter of dispute is not capable of settlement by arbitration or violates public policy.[62]

25-32 There are several grounds on which a challenge of an award may be based.[63] These grounds often mirror the grounds listed in Article V New York Convention. Indeed this was the legislative intent in Article 34(2) Model Law. Some linguistic amendments were however introduced.[64]

2.1. Natural Justice and Legality

25-33 The grounds listed in Article 34 Model Law unequivocally suggest that judicial review in the context of an application to challenge an award can only be based on natural justice and legality grounds. There can be no review on the

---

60 Netherlands, Hoge Raad, 21 March 1997, XXIII *YBCA* 180 (1998); this approach was held to be in conformity with EC Competition Law: ECJ, Case C-126/97, 1 June 1999, *Eco Swiss China Time Ltd v Benetton International NV*, [1999] ECR I 3055. See also Oberlandesgericht Stuttgart, 4 June 2002, 1 Sch 22/01, *W GmbH v A Ltd*, unreported.

61 See, *e.g.*, Model Law Article 34(2)(a); China, Arbitration Law Article 58; Germany, ZPO section 1059(2)(1).

62 See, *e.g.*, Model Law Article 34(2)(b); Germany, ZPO section 1059(2)(2).

63 One classification of the grounds for challenge distinguishes between lack of jurisdiction (*e.g.*, validity of arbitration agreement, constitution of tribunal, scope of arbitration agreement, arbitrability of matters submitted to arbitration) and other grounds (*e.g.*, substantive grounds). See Redfern and Hunter, *International Commercial Arbitration*, paras 9-13 – 9-17.

64 See Šarčević, "The Setting Aside and Enforcement of Arbitral Awards under the UNCITRAL Model Law", in Šarčević (ed), *Essays*, 176, 186-7. See Holtzmann and Neuhaus, *Model Law*, 915-917. The Commission, by deleting the reference to the "law applicable to them", eliminated the choice-of-law rule as "too simplistic and not accepted in all legal systems". See further UN Doc A/CN9/233 paras 141 and 149 and UN Doc A/CN9/233 para 149; UN Doc A/CN9/246 para 135.

merits.[65] Due process and legality are preconditions of arbitration. The Model Law and national arbitration laws contain these requirements; their breach may amount to a challenge of the award.[66] All these grounds, irrespective of how general or specific, are in full conformity with the grounds for resisting enforcement referred to in Article V New York Convention. Matters of natural justice or legality are often matters of jurisdiction or matters of procedure. They should not, under any circumstances, be used by courts to review an award on its merits or for increased judicial intervention in arbitration proceedings.[67] The policy behind provisions on challenge is to make it more difficult to challenge an award.

25-34 *Absence or invalidity of the arbitration agreement.*[68] An arbitration award made in the absence of an arbitration agreement or submission of parties can be set aside.[69] When a tribunal rules that it has no jurisdiction, its decision can be challenged with an application to set aside relying on the grounds available in the relevant law but not on the basis that the tribunal has erroneously denied its jurisdiction.[70]

25-35 *Irregularity in the constitution or the appointment of the arbitration tribunal.*[71] A tribunal must be constituted in accordance with the agreement of the

65 See the classification introduced by Schmitthoff, "Finality of arbitral awards and judicial review", in Lew (ed), *Contemporary Problems*, 230, 232-236.

66 See, *e.g.*, Model Law Article 34(2); Belgium, Judicial Code Article 1704(2)(a)-(g); Brazil, Arbitration Law Articles 32; China, Arbitration Law Article 58; England, Arbitration Act sections 67-68; France, NCPC Article 1504; Netherlands, CCP Article 1065; Switzerland, PIL Article 190(2); US, FAA sections 10, 207.

67 See, *e.g.*, *Petroships Pte Ltd v Petec Trading and Investment Co and others* [2001] 2 Lloyd's Rep 348, 351, *per* Creswell J; *Weldon Plants v Commissioner for New Towns* [2000] BLR 490, 503, *per* Judge Humphrey Lloyd QC.

68 See, *e.g.*, Model Law Article 34(2)(a)(i). This ground can also be found in Article V(1)(a) and in Article II New York Convention.

69 See, *e.g.*, *Hussman (Europe) Ltd v Al Ameen Development & Trade Co* [2000] 2 Lloyd's Rep 83, where a disappointed claimant succeeded in setting aside the award because the respondent was not a signatory to the arbitration agreement, but merely a successor legal entity. But see *Athletic Union of Constantinople v National Basketball Association and others* [2002] 1 All ER (Comm) 70 where the respondents' conduct in the arbitration gave an appearance of consent, and *Astra SA Insurance and Reinsurance Co v Sphere Drake Insurance Ltd and others* [2000] 2 Lloyd's Rep 550 where a succession by a party to a contract entailed automatic succession to the arbitration agreement. See also Shackleton, "Challenging arbitration award: Part I Jurisdiction", *New L J* 1746 (2002).

70 Bundesgerichtshof, 6 June 2002. The court concluded that none of the grounds mentioned in section 1059(2) ZPO were fulfilled. Effectively an award denying jurisdiction can not be challenged in Germany, 1 *SchiedsVZ* 39 (2003).

71 See, *e.g.*, Model Law Article 34(2)(a)(iv). See also New York Convention Article V(1)(d).

parties and failing such agreement in accordance with the law governing the arbitration. A truncated tribunal may be irregularly composed.[72] There are different views as to whether this ground may be used to challenge an award for the alleged bias of an arbitrator.[73]

25-36 *Procedural irregularity*[74] amounts to *violation of the principle of fairness.* Various legal systems apply different standards of fairness.[75] It is essential that certain minimum standards are observed and that arbitration proceedings are conducted fairly.[76] Failure to disclose documents may not amount to a serious irregularity justifying challenge of an award.[77] Undoubtedly proper notice of the appointment of arbitrators or notice of the arbitration proceedings are expressions of fairness; so is also the opportunity of each party to present its case and respond to the case put forward by the other party.[78] To the extent that the principle of fairness is upheld tribunals have jurisdiction to determine procedure and change their mind about it.[79]

25-37 The prevailing view is that a procedural irregularity or defect alone will not invalidate an award. The test is that of a significant injustice so that the tribunal would have decided otherwise had the tribunal not made a mistake.[80] Similarly assessment of evidence is in the discretion of the tribunal and can rarely amount to a ground for challenge of an award.[81]

---

[72] See, *e.g.*, Cour d'appel Paris, 1 July 1997, *ATC-CFCO (Congo) v COMILOG (Gabon)*, XXIVa YBCA 281 (1999), Int ALR N-47 (1999) with note Schwartz. The award was set aside on the grounds that the tribunal which rendered the award was irregularly constituted as one arbitrator did not take part in the proceedings.

[73] See Cour d'appel Paris, 2 July 1992, *Sté Raoul Duval v Sté Merkuria Sucden*, Rev Arb 411 (1996) in favour of a challenge; *contra*, see Bundesgerichtshof, 4 March 1999, BGHZ 141, 90, Kröll, "Die Ablehnung eines Schiedsrichters nach deutschem Recht", 116 *ZZP* 123 (2003).

[74] See Shackleton, "Challenging arbitration award: Part II – Procedural Irregularity", *New L J* 1816 (2002) for English case law.

[75] *E.g.*, in the US, lack of oral hearing may be seen as a breach of due process and a ground to set aside the award: *Parsons & Whittemore Overseas Co v Societe Generale de L'Industrie du Papier*, 508 F 2d 969 (2d Cir 1974).

[76] See also Liebscher, "Global Developments: Fair Trial and Challenge of Awards in International Arbitration", 6 *Croat Arbit Yearb* 83 (1999) for a further comparative survey.

[77] See, *e.g.*, *Profilati Italia srl v Painewebber Inc* [2001] 1 Lloyd's Rep 715 (QBD).

[78] See, *e.g.*, Model Law Article 34(2)(a)(ii). See also New York Convention Article V(1)(b).

[79] See, *e.g.*, *Charles M Willie & Co (Shipping) Ltd v Ocean Laser Shipping Ltd* [1999] 1 Lloyd's Rep 225, 248.

[80] See, *e.g.*, *Gannet Shipping Ltd v Eastrade Commodities Inc* [2002] 1 All ER (Comm) 297, 304.

[81] See, *e.g.*, *Ranko Group v Antarctic Maritime SA*, 16 June 1999 (QBD *per* Toulson J), unreported: tribunal's refusal to order production of documents no ground to challenge the

25-38 *Arbitration tribunal exceeded its jurisdiction or failed to respect the agreement of the parties.*[82] Here the tribunal had jurisdiction but either exceeded its power by deciding issues not submitted to it or failed to deal with all matters referred to it. Normally the issues decided in the award which fall under the scope of the reference to arbitration will survive an eventual challenge of the award for issues not covered. An award which fails to deal with all issues may be characterised as incomplete, but it is not as such challengeable.[83]

25-39 Although it is expected that the award addresses all issues raised the tribunal may exercise its discretion not to deal with issues which are insignificant or immaterial and need not explain in detail how its conclusions were reached.[84]

25-40 *The award or the proceedings from which it stems is contrary to the public policy of the court.*[85] There may be a violation of public policy of the court either because the matter is not capable of settlement by arbitration[86] or because the award *per se* is contrary to the public policy of the court where challenge is sought.[87] The test of public policy compliance would normally be a national test in light of the international public policy at the place of arbitration.[88] Occasionally it may be a transnational test where the court assesses the compliance of the award with internationally accepted standards of public policy. For example, transnational public policy rules may require that the award be challenged if it has been induced or affected by bribery, corruption or fraud.

award; *Brandeis Brokers Ltd v Black and others* [2001] 2 Lloyd's Rep 359: tribunal has discretion to permit call and cross-examination claimant's employees as a witness; *Bulfracht (Cyprus) Ltd v Boneset Shipping Co Ltd ("The Pamphilos")*, 7 November 2002 (QBD *per* Colman J), unreported: an error in the assessment of evidence is "an ordinary incident of the arbitral process" and not a ground to challenge the award. See also Shackleton, "Challenging arbitration award: Part II – Procedural Irregularity", *New L J* 1816 (2002).

82 See, *e.g.*, Model Law Article 34(2)(a)(ii). See also New York Convention Article V(1)(c)

83 See van den Berg, *New York Convention*, 318.

84 See *Hussman (Europe) Ltd v Al Ameen Development & Trade Co* [2000] 2 Lloyd's Rep 83, 97 (*per* Thomas J); see also Shackleton, "Challenging arbitration award: Part II – Procedural Irregularity", *New L J* 1816 (2002) 1817.

85 See, *e.g.*, Model Law Article 34(2)(b). See also New York Convention Article V(2).

86 See, *e.g.*, Model Law Article 34(2)(b)(i). See also New York Convention Article V(2)(a).

87 See, *e.g.*, Model Law Article 34(2)(b)(ii). See also New York Convention Article V(2)(b).

88 See, *e.g.*, *Deutsche Schachtbau-und Tiefbohrgesellschaft mbH* v *R'as Al Khaimah National Oil Co (UAE) and Shell International Co Ltd (UK)* [1987] 2 Lloyd's Rep 246, [1987] 2 All ER 769, (1988) XIII YBCA 522, 530, 534.

2.2. Other Grounds under National Laws

25-41 Other grounds are introduced under various national laws. These may be formal grounds such as the expiration of specific time limits, or substantive grounds relating to the application of law by the tribunal. The former rules are unproblematic to the extent that they do not lead to substantive injustice. The latter grounds raise concerns as they may amount to an appeal on merits.

25-42 *Award made after the expiration of certain time limit.* An award may be challenged if it was made after the expiration of time limits agreed by the parties or provided for in the applicable rules or law.[89] The Paris Court of Appeal rejected the argument that the award could be challenged as it was rendered later than the three months time limit set in the arbitration agreement. The court found no ground to apply French NCPC Article 1502(1).[90]

25-43 *Award with contradictory decisions.* This ground can be found in Article 25(2)(j) European Uniform Law on Arbitration.[91] It has been implemented in Article 1704(2)(j) Belgian Judicial Code Article.[92] Similar provisions can be found in other arbitration laws.[93]

25-44 *Control of the merits of the case - often appeal on a point of law.* Generally court control of the merits of the award is exceptional in civil law countries, though it is rarely stated expressly.[94] In most common law jurisdictions there is a risk of court control on the merits in the exceptional cases where there is an appeal on a question of law.

25-45 An internal appeal procedure is also available under ICSID Arbitration Rules. Rule 50 provides that a party may apply to the Secretary General for a

---

[89] See, *e.g.*, Italy, CCP Article 829(4); Spain, Arbitration Law 1988 Article 45(3); Switzerland, Concordat 1969 Article 36(g), however, no such provision is contained in the Swiss PIL.

[90] See, *e.g.*, Cour d'appel Paris, 24 February 1994, *Ministry of Public Works (Tunisia) v Société Bec Frères (France)*, XXII YBCA 682 (1997), original in Rev Arb 275 (1995). The Tunisian Ministry appealed against the leave for enforcement granted by the Court of First Instance in Paris. Its appeal was rejected. The argument that the arbitration agreement had expired in accordance with Tunisian law was also rejected on the facts without reference to NCPC Article 1502(1).

[91] Also known as the Strasbourg Arbitration Convention of 20 January 1966.

[92] It provides that an award may be set aside "if the award contains conflicting provisions." Belgium is the only country to have ratified the Uniform Law.

[93] See also, *e.g.*, Argentina, CCP 1981 Article 761; Poland, CCP 1964 Article 712(1)(4).

[94] The Quebec Law of 30 October 1986 amending the Civil Code and the Code of Civil Procedure in matters of arbitration Article 946(2) provides that the "court cannot ... examine the merits" ("le tribunal ... ne peut examiner le fond du différend).

revision or annulment of the award. Relevant grounds include that the tribunal was not properly constituted; the tribunal manifestly exceeded its powers; there was corruption on the part of one arbitrator; there was a serious departure from a fundamental rule of procedure; and the award failed to state the reasons on which it is based.[95]

3. APPEAL ON A QUESTION OF LAW

25-46 While appeal on the merits exists in a few civil law systems[96] it is rare, even in domestic arbitration. In international arbitration it is assumed that an appeal to the courts has been excluded by the arbitration agreement or arbitration rules to which it refers.[97]

25-47 In some common law jurisdictions it is possible to appeal due to the tribunal failing to apply the applicable law properly or at all. This is the case in English law where an appeal on a question of law may be allowed in exceptional circumstances.

25-48 Under section 69 English Arbitration Act an application for permission to appeal is made before the court can look into the matter.[98] For permission to appeal to be granted the court will need to be satisfied that the determination of the question of law will substantially affect the rights of one or more of the parties. The question must be one which the tribunal was asked to determine, and, on the basis of the tribunal's findings of fact the tribunal's decision on the law is obviously wrong, or the question is one of general public importance and the decision of the tribunal is at least open to serious doubt.[99] The policy argument is that despite the agreement of the parties to resolve the matter by arbitration, it is fair in all the circumstances for the court to determine the question.

---

95 ICSID Rules Article 50(1)(iii).

96 France, NCPC Article 1483. See also Portugal, Law no 31/86 Articles 29 and 27(3). See also Sanders, "Arbitration", *IECL*, Vol XVI, Chapter 12, para 225 for other national examples.

97 France, NCPC Articles 1502 and 1504.

98 See England, Arbitration Act section 69. See also Diamond and Veeder, "The New English Arbitration Act 1996: Challenging an English Award before the English Courts", 8 *Am Rev Int'l Arb* 47 (1997); Saville, "The Arbitration Act 1996", *Lloyd's MCLQ* 502 (1997), 509; Shackleton, "Challenging arbitration award: Part III – Appeals on Questions of Law", *New L J* 1834 (2002).

99 See, *e.g.*, *Pioneer Shipping Ltd v BTP Tioxide ("The Nema")* [1982] AC 724, (1981) VI YBCA 155 (HL).

25-49 For example, in English law findings of arbitrators on the facts are conclusive and final but their ruling on the law may be subject to judicial review, provided there is no agreement of the parties to the contrary, and the conditions imposed by section 69 are satisfied. The question must be one of English law, otherwise no leave to appeal will be granted.[100] A court must be persuaded that it is "just and proper" to intervene despite the parties' choice to arbitrate rather than litigate.[101] One of the main problems is to decide what is a question of law; some issues may be interwoven with questions of fact or procedure.[102] The right to appeal under English law "ignores modern international arbitration practice and is out of line with the Model Law."[103]

25-50 In the United States[104] an award may be set aside in the event of manifest disregard of the law.[105] This ground is used in limited circumstances: manifest disregard is not as such sufficient; it is also necessary that the court finds that had the law been applied properly the result would have been different. Misinterpretation of the law is generally not a ground to set aside an award.[106] Accordingly, the test is not whether the law has been applied correctly but if the correct application would have led to a different outcome. The issue is not whether the law was correctly applied but whether the parties' expectations were frustrated by the manifest disregard of the law.

---

[100] See *Reliance Industries Ltd v Enron Oil & Gas India Ltd* [2002] 1 All ER (Comm) 59 (QBD): the leave to appeal was not granted as the questions were relating to Indian law, not English law.

[101] See England, Arbitration Act section 69(3).

[102] See *Fence Gate Ltd v NEL Construction Ltd*, (2001) 82 Con LR 41, 56, *per* Judge Thornton QC.

[103] See Shackleton, "Challenging arbitration award: Part III – Appeals on Questions of Law", *New L J* 1834 (2002) 1835.

[104] Bowman Routledge, "On the Importance of Institutions: Review of Arbitral Awards for Legal Errors", 19(2) *J Int'l Arb* 81 (2002) 82-88 with extensive references to US case law.

[105] See, *e.g.*, *Wilko v Swan*, 346 US 427, 436-437 (1953); *Merrill Lynch, Pierce, Fenner & Smith, Inc v Bobker*, 808 F 2d 930 (2d Cir 1986); *Yusuf Ahmed Alghanim & Sons v Toys "R" Us Inc*, 126 F 3d 15, 23, XXIII YBCA 1058 (1998) (2d Cir 1997); *Brandeis Intsel Ltd v Calabrian Chemicals Corp*, 656 F Supp 160, XIII YBCA 543 (1988) 544-548, 552 (SDNY 1987); see also the domestic employment arbitration case *Halligan v Jaffray*, 148 F 3d 197 (1998) and Holtzmann, "US National Report – Part IV: Recent Developments in Arbitration Law and Practice", in van den Berg (ed), *ICCA Handbook*, 57-59.

[106] See, *e.g.*, Singapore, *John Holland Pty Ltd v Toyo Engineering Corp*, 16(4) *Mealey's IAR* 12 (2001) 14, where the court held that it will require more than an error of law and fact (or both) to set aside an award.

4. Consequences of Challenge Claims

25-51 A court hearing a request for a challenge to an award has a number of options. It may reject the challenge and uphold the award, or it may accept the challenge and annul the award in whole or in part. A successful challenge may nullify the award at the place of arbitration. A court may also remit the case to the arbitration tribunal.

4.1. Court Rejects Challenges and Upholds Award

25-52 Although there is no statistical data it is generally accepted that most challenges are unsuccessful. When a state court rejects a challenge, the award is confirmed and its national and international recognition is inevitable. The award has legal effect subject only to rare cases where the international public policy of the court of enforcement is affected.

4.2. Court Accepts Challenge

25-53 When a court accepts the challenge the award is annulled or vacated and is not enforceable in the country in which it was made. It will usually be unenforceable in other countries although it may occasionally be enforceable in some countries.[107] Challenge may nullify the award in its entirety or in part.[108]

25-54 After the award has been set aside the main question is whether the parties are still bound by the arbitration agreement or whether the ousted jurisdiction of state courts is revived. If a court decided that the arbitration agreement is invalid the parties are no longer bound by it. If, however, the award has been challenged on any procedural, jurisdictional or substantive grounds the situation is different. In such circumstances the question is whether or not a new arbitration can be started.

---

[107] This is the case, *e.g.*, in the US and France. See, *e.g.*, *Chromalloy Gas Turbine Corp v Arab Republic of Egypt*, 939 F Supp 907 (DDC 1996); France, Cour de cassation, 10 June 1997, *Omnium de Traitement et de Valorisation v Hilmarton*, XXII YBCA 696 (1997); France, Cour de cassation, 23 March 1994, *Omnium de Traitement et de Valorisation v Hilmarton*, XX YBCA 663 (1995); France, Cour de cassation, 9 October 1984, *Pabalk Ticaret Ltd Sirketi (Turkey) v Norsolor SA (France)*, XI YBCA 484 (1986).

[108] See, *e.g.*, *Richard A Davis v Prudential Securities Inc*, 59 F 3d 1186 (11th Cir 1995), where the award was affirmed in part, vacated in part and remanded.

25-55 Several arbitration laws deal with this issue but suggest different solutions. Under Article 1485 French NCPC a court dealing with a request for challenge of a domestic award may only decide issues within the limits of the arbitration unless the parties agree to the contrary.[109] Under the Swiss Concordat Article 40(4) the tribunal must re-hear the issues unless the parties object on the basis that the arbitrators participated in the previous proceedings. Article 1067 Netherlands CCP stipulates the contrary

> Unless the parties have agreed otherwise, as soon as a decision setting aside the award has become final, the jurisdiction of the court shall revive.

25-56 The Model Law is silent on this issue. It only suggests in Article 34(4) that the state court may remit the case to the arbitration tribunal.[110] Some jurisdictions enacting the Model Law have taken positions in support of arbitration. German law unequivocally provides in section 1059(5)

> Setting aside the arbitral award shall, in the absence of any indication to the contrary, result in the arbitration agreement becoming operative again in respect of the subject-matter of the dispute.

25-57 In North Carolina, it is stated that where an award has been successfully challenged, the court "*shall* not engage in de novo review of the subject matter" of the dispute which formed the basis of the arbitration proceedings. The court may order a re-hearing by the arbitration tribunal.[111]

25-58 Article 830(2) Italian CCP takes a different position. It empowers the court of appeal when upholding a challenge to decide on the merits or to remand the case to the instructing judge if the decision on the merits requires the taking of further evidence.

25-59 Section 71 English Arbitration Act is a comprehensive rule on the consequences of a challenge or appeal of the award. There are several scenarios:

- If the award is varied, the variation has effect as part of the tribunal's award;

---

[109] This provision is not applicable to international arbitration: see France, NCPC Article 1507. The distinction between domestic and international arbitration is also made in Tunisia, Arbitration Code 1993. In domestic arbitration the court *shall* on the request of the parties settle the dispute: Article 44(2). In international arbitration the state court *may* do so: Article 78(5).

[110] See also China, Arbitration Law Article 61.

[111] North Carolina, Act on International Commercial Arbitration section I.567.64. This is also the position adopted by the US, Uniform Arbitration Act section 12(c).

- If the award is remitted to the tribunal, in whole or in part, for reconsideration, the tribunal *shall* make a fresh award in respect of the matters remitted;
- If the award is set aside or declared to be of no effect, in whole or in part, the court *may* annul any provision requiring an award before legal proceedings can be brought.

25-60 Finally, in Islamic arbitration, if the award is set aside, a court may re-examine the substantive issues at the request of a party. If the award is upheld the decision of the court is akin to enforcement of the award.[112]

25-61 If an award is set aside for reasons other than invalidity of the arbitration agreement, the agreement would survive the award and the parties would still be bound to have their disputes settled by arbitration.[113] Often it will be a case of remission of the matter or it may be a new arbitration before a new tribunal.

4.3. Remission

25-62 In some common law jurisdictions a court may remit the case to the arbitrators.[114] This may happen where an appeal on a question of law is allowed or when the arbitration procedure is challenged in the courts.[115] Under the English Arbitration Act the annulment of the award[116] is seen as a drastic remedy and is only justified when remission cannot produce the required results.[117]

25-63 Article 61 China Arbitration Law 1994 also provides for remission as an appropriate result of a successful application for the setting aside of an award, subject to the discretion of courts. It states

---

[112] See El-Ahdab, *Arab Arbitration*, 53.

[113] See, *e.g.*, Netherlands, CCP Article 1067, according to which jurisdiction of courts will be revived, unless parties agree otherwise.

[114] See, *e.g.*, Bermuda, Arbitration Act 1986 section 29; Hong Kong, Arbitration Ordinance section 23; Ireland, Arbitration Act 1954 as amended by the Arbitration (International and Commercial) Act (1998) section 36; Malaysia, Arbitration Act section 23; Sri Lanka, Arbitration Act no 11 of 1995 section 36.

[115] See, *e.g.*, England, Arbitration Act section 68(3)(a). See also the discussion in Mustill and Boyd, *Commercial Arbitration*, 546-570; *The Vimeira* [1985] 2 Lloyd's Rep 377, 400.

[116] See, *e.g.*, England, Arbitration Act section 69(7)(c); US, Uniform Arbitration Act section 12(c).

[117] See England, Arbitration Act sections 68(3) and 69(7)(d). See also *Ascot Commodities NV (Switzerland) v Olam International Ltd (Singapore)*, (2002) Int ALR N-20 (8 November 2001), where a GAFTA award was, despite procedural irregularity sufficient to set aside the award, directed back for rehearing with fresh submissions from both parties.

> If the People's Court that has accepted an application for setting aside an arbitration award considers that re-arbitration can be carried out by the arbitration tribunal, it shall notify the tribunal that it should re-arbitrate the dispute within a certain time limit and shall rule to stay the setting aside procedure. If the arbitration tribunal refuses to re-arbitrate the dispute, the People's Court shall rule to resume the setting aside procedure.

25-64 The concept of remission is relatively new in most civil law countries.[118] Remission is now codified in the Model Law. Article 34(4) provides

> The court, when asked to set aside an award, may, where appropriate and so requested by a party, suspend the setting aside proceedings for a period of time determined by it in order to give the arbitral tribunal an opportunity to resume the arbitral proceedings or to take such other action as in the arbitral tribunal's opinion will eliminate the grounds for setting aside.

25-65 The Model Law provision appears to be less supportive of remission than English law. However, it may be that the Model Law will develop in practice similarly to English law. Generally, remission is a main remedy in common law jurisdictions; it is of lesser significance in Model Law jurisdictions.

5. Waiver of the Right to Challenge an Award

25-66 A party may waive or exclude the right to challenge the award. Waiver may be by conduct once an irregularity has occurred. Exclusion or waiver may be agreed and/or may occasionally be provided for in arbitration laws or rules.

5.1. Exclusion

25-67 In principle, court control over an arbitration award in challenge proceedings cannot be excluded. Such exclusion could be considered a violation of public policy unless the applicable arbitration law expressly permits the exclusion.[119] This principle is laid down in a number of civil law arbitration statutes.[120]

25-68 Article 192 Swiss PIL is an exception to the rule: where all the parties to an arbitration in Switzerland are not Swiss they can by express agreement

---

118 In many civil law countries remission was introduced with the enactment of the Model Law.

119 See Sanders, "Arbitration", *IECL*, Vol XVI, Chapter 12, para 247.

120 See, *e.g.*, Austria, CCP section 598(1).

exclude the right to challenge. Foreign parties who have subjected their arbitration to Swiss law have not used the option of Article 192.[121]

25-69 The 1983 "Storme amendment" in 1985 to Belgian arbitration law aimed at establishing Belgium as a "paradise for international arbitration".[122] The law made it impossible where all the parties to the arbitration were non-Belgian to bring an annulment action in Belgium of an award made in Belgium. Article 1717(4) Belgian Judicial Code from 1985 provided

> The Belgian Court can take cognizance of an application to set aside only if at least one of the parties to the dispute decided in the arbitral award is either a physical person having Belgian nationality or residing in Belgium, or a legal person formed in Belgium or having a branch ... or some seat of operation ... there.

25-70 This provision was amended in 1998[123] in new Article 1717(2) which spells out clearly the principle of party autonomy in a manner similar to that of Swiss law. It does not automatically exclude the challenge of an award made in an international arbitration with seat in Belgium or under Belgian law

> The parties may, by an express statement in the arbitration agreement or by a subsequent agreement, exclude any application to set aside the arbitral award where none of the parties is either an individual of Belgian nationality or residing in Belgium, or a legal person having its head office or a branch there.[124]

25-71 Even if an arbitration law allows the parties to exclude the right to challenge an award normally it is advisable not to do so.

5.2. Waiver

25-72 Contrary to exclusion, waiver is a general principle, known under various names, such as estoppel or the principle of *venire contra factum proprium.*[125]

---

[121] See, *e.g.*, Poudret, "Challenge and Enforcement of Arbitral Awards in Switzerland", 4 *Arb Int* 278 (1988) 282-3; Bucher and Tschanz, *International arbitration in Switzerland*, paras 290 *et seq*; Park, "Judicial Controls in the Arbitral Process", 5 *Arb Int* 230 (1989) 232-3, 256.

[122] See, *e.g.*, Storme, "Belgium: A paradise for international commercial arbitration", *International Business Lawyer* 294 (1986); Vanderelst, "Increasing the Appeal of Belgium as an International Arbitration Forum? – the Belgian Law of March 27, 1985 Concerning the Annulment of Awards", 3(2) *J Int'l Arb* 77 (1986).

[123] And entered into force in 1999.

[124] See, for the Belgian reform, Demeyere, "1998 Amendments to Belgian Arbitration Law: An Overview", 15 *Arb Int* 295 (1999) 307-9; Verbist, "Reform of the Belgian Arbitration law (The law of 19 May 1998)", *RDAI/IBLJ* 843 (1998).

[125] That is, no person may act in contradiction with its own previous conduct without consequences.

While the principle of waiver is accepted there are no specific references in the provisions of national arbitration laws dealing with waiver of the right to challenge an award. Several national laws contain provisions concerning waiver of the right to challenge either in the context of not contesting the invalidity of arbitration agreement or challenging arbitrators.[126]

25-73 Few arbitration laws contain specific rules on waiver of the right to challenge an award.[127] The English Arbitration Act refers to the loss of right to object and to challenge an arbitration award. Section 73(1) provides in pertinent part

> (1) If a party to arbitral proceedings takes part, or continues to take part, in the proceedings without making ... any objection-
>
> (a) that the tribunal lacks substantive jurisdiction,
>
> (b) that the proceedings have been improperly conducted,
>
> (c) that there has been a failure to comply with the arbitration agreement or with any provision of [the Act], or
>
> (d) that there has been any other irregularity affecting the tribunal or the proceedings,
>
> he may not raise that objection later, before the tribunal or the court, unless he shows that, at the time he took part or continued to take part in the proceedings, he did not know and could not with reasonable diligence have discovered the grounds for the objection.

25-74 Furthermore, a party trying to base its challenge on lack of jurisdiction must have objected to the tribunal's decision establishing its jurisdiction on a timely basis.[128]

25-75 "Objection" in section 73 is to be construed narrowly.[129] It has been interpreted to mean the particular facts and circumstances which form the grounds for challenging the arbitration proceedings and possibly the award.

25-76 Similarly, Article 33 ICC Rules provides that a party which proceeds with the arbitration without raising its objection to a failure to comply with any provisions of the ICC rules, or any other rules applicable to the proceedings, or to

---

[126] See, *e.g.*, Model Law Article 16(2); Netherlands, CCP Article 1027.

[127] See, *e.g.*, Model Law Article 4; Belgium, Judicial Code Article 1704(4).

[128] See England, Arbitration Act section 73(2).

[129] See, *e.g.*, *Athletic Union of Constantinople (AEK) v National Basketball Association*, 2001 WL 825340 (QBD), [2002] 1 Lloyd's Rep 305, [2002] 1 All ER (Comm) 70.

the conduct of the proceedings, shall be deemed to have waived its right to object. All major arbitration rules contain similar provisions.[130]

25-77 These provisions record the clear dilemma that parties have when there is a ground to challenge jurisdiction or something the tribunal has done in the course of the arbitration. A party should always record an objection in case it wishes, at a later stage, to challenge the award. Failure to do so runs the risk of waiver of the particular irregularity. There may even be an issue whether the party should continue to participate in the arbitration, but refusing or failing to do so and allowing the tribunal to make an award in default of a party is a dangerous tactic.

[130] See, *e.g.*, UNCITRAL Rules Article 30; AAA ICDR Article 25; CRCICA Article 30; ICSID Rules Article 27; LCIA Article 32(1); NAI Article 63; WIPO Article 58.

Chapter 26

RECOGNITION AND ENFORCEMENT OF FOREIGN ARBITRATION AWARDS

26-1 The recognition and enforcement of awards is of paramount importance for the success of arbitration in the international arena. This is well evidenced by the fact that the enforceability of awards world wide is considered one of the primary advantages of arbitration. Unless parties can be sure that at the end of arbitration proceedings they will be able to enforce the award, if not complied with voluntarily, an award in their favour will be only a pyrrhic victory. Further, the high degree of voluntary compliance is due to there being an effective system for the enforcement of awards in case of non-compliance.

26-2 There is an international policy favouring enforcement of awards.[1] With exceptions, it is increasingly rare to find "horror stories" of non enforcement in published cases.[2] Indeed, according to one report,[3] as of 1996 more than 95% of cases where enforcement was sought the awards were enforced by the courts. In another survey the figure for voluntary enforcement or enforcement by state courts is 98%.[4] This is the result of harmonisation of the rules relating to recognition and enforcement in, and the extensive acceptance by so many states of, the New York Convention.[5]

---

1 See, *e.g.*, Lamm and Hellbeck, "The Enforcement of Foreign Arbitral Awards under the New York Convention: Recent Developments", 5 *Int ALR* 137 (2002) 138.

2 See Reed, "Experience of Practical Problems of Enforcement", *ICCA Congress Series no 9*, 557. It is also noted that only 2 out of 556 cases (reported in the Yearbook of Commercial Arbitration) successfully resisted enforcement.

3 Van den Berg, "The New York Convention: Its Intended Effects, Its Interpretation, Salient Problem Areas", in Blessing (ed), *The New York Convention of 1958*, ASA Special Series no 9 (1996) 25.

4 Kerr, "Concord and Conflict in International Arbitration", *Arb Int* 121 (1997) 129.

5 See de Boisséson, "Enforcement in Action: Harmonization Versus Unification", *ICCA Congress Series no 9*, 593.

26-3 In limited instances it may be possible to enforce an award by exercising direct or indirect commercial or other pressures.[6] Examples can be seen in the practice of GAFTA where the Rules provide that if a party refuses to comply with a GAFTA arbitration award, the Council of the Association may circulate a notice informing the members of the Association about the refusal to abide by the award.[7]

26-4 In all other instances the enforcement of arbitration awards not complied with voluntarily is largely outside the sphere of the arbitration tribunal. Although the tribunal may make every effort to render an enforceable award (as is mandated by some arbitration rules[8]), the recognition and enforcement of awards is in the coercive power of the courts. Most arbitration rules provide that the parties by submitting their dispute to arbitration undertake to carry out the award without delay.[9] However, neither the tribunal nor the arbitration institutions have any means to secure enforcement.

26-5 As a consequence, at the recognition and enforcement stage, arbitration and the parties often leave the private sphere in which they were operating. The successful party requests the assistance of national courts in the same way as the unsuccessful party may seek the courts' assistance to resist enforcement. Recognition and enforcement of foreign awards may be essential in practical terms especially when the compulsive power of state courts is required for the performance of the award by the unsuccessful party (award debtor). If the award debtor does not comply with the award there can be no enforcement without recourse to a state power which would normally be exercised by the courts.

26-6 Theoretically recognition and enforcement are important as they provide official recognition of the arbitration process and confirm its product. A private act is being empowered by a public act, a judgment of a state court.

26-7 For the purposes of recognition and enforcement one has to distinguish between foreign awards and domestic awards. While the enforcement of domestic awards is solely regulated by the national arbitration laws, foreign awards are primarily enforced under the New York Convention. In general there are no great differences between the enforcement regimes for national and

---

6 See, *e.g.*, Redfern and Hunter, *International Commercial Arbitration*, para 10-04.

7 GAFTA Rules Article 23(1).

8 See, *e.g.*, ICC Rules Article 35 and LCIA Article 32(2).

9 See, *e.g.*, UNCITRAL Rules Article 32(2); AAA ICDR Article 27(1); CRCICA Article 32(2); ICC Article 28(6); LCIA Article 26(9); ICAC paragraph 44; NAI Article 51; Stockholm Institute Article 36; WIPO Article 64.

international awards. The Model law and some other laws actually adopted a unified system for the enforcement of foreign and domestic awards.

26-8 This chapter reviews (1) the distinction between recognition and enforcement, (2) the regime for the enforcement of domestic awards, (3) regimes for recognition and enforcement of foreign awards, (4) the sphere of application of the New York Convention, (5) the prerequisites for applications to have a foreign award enforced, (6) the grounds to refuse enforcement and (7) an analysis of different approaches.

1. Distinction between Recognition and Enforcement

26-9 In most cases the enforcement of awards assumes their recognition and the two terms appear as if they were intertwined. This is partly so because the New York Convention and other relevant provisions refer to "recognition and enforcement."[10] Generally, when an award is enforced it is also recognised. There may, however, be instances where an award is recognised but not enforced.[11] As a consequence a distinction may be made between recognition and enforcement.[12]

26-10 Recognition is the national court proceedings which amount to a judicial decision, often called an exequatur. In many cases these proceedings are not full-fledged, but summary proceedings confirming the award. The exequatur acknowledges the existence of the arbitration and recognises the decision of the tribunal. Recognition has been described as a defensive process which acts as a shield.[13]

26-11 Recognition may be useful when the unsuccessful party initiates court proceedings for any or all of the issues dealt with in the arbitration award. Recognition of the award will prevent court proceedings from being held in respect of decided matters. Recognition may be useful for tax or financial

[10] However, the Geneva Convention 1927 refers to recognition or enforcement in Article IV. Distinctions are made also, *e.g.*, in the English Arbitration Act sections 101 and 102. See also Redfern and Hunter, *International Commercial Arbitration*, para 10-09.

[11] See, *e.g.*, *Mark Dallal v Bank Mellat* [1986] QB 411, (1986) XI YBCA 547, 553, where an Iran-US Claims Tribunal award was recognised but not enforced.

[12] See, *e.g.*, Taniguchi, "Enforcement in Action: Theoretical and Practical Problems", *ICCA Congress Series no 9*, 589.

[13] Redfern and Hunter, *International Commercial Arbitration*, paras 10-10, 10-12.

reasons; a party may wish to have the award recognised so that there is evidence of a debt or receivables.

26-12 Enforcement is normally a judicial process which either follows or is simultaneous to recognition and gives effect to the mandate of the award.[14] Enforcement may function as a sword[15] in that the successful party requests the assistance of the court to enforce the award by exercising its power and applying legal sanctions should the other party fail or refuse to comply voluntarily. The type of sanctions available will vary from country to country and may include seizure of the award debtor's property, freezing of bank accounts or even custodial sentences in extreme cases.

2. The Regime for the Enforcement of Domestic Awards

26-13 The national provisions for the enforcement of domestic awards are of considerable importance to international arbitration. Often awards arising out of international arbitration proceedings are actually enforced under the regime for domestic awards. Though each state is generally free to determine which awards it considers to be domestic, the relevant criterion is normally the place of arbitration. As a consequence, recognition and enforcement of award rendered within a country is usually governed by the provisions on domestic awards irrespective of the national or international character of the underlying arbitration.[16]

26-14 The national legislature is generally free to regulate the recognition and enforcement of domestic awards. There are no international conventions imposing a minimum standard as exist for foreign awards. In general, however, national arbitration laws have adopted a pro-enforcement approach also for domestic awards. The relevant provisions normally stipulate that domestic awards should be recognised and enforced like a judgment subject to very few

---

14 See Taniguchi, "Enforcement in Action: Theoretical and Practical Problems", *ICCA Congress Series no 9*, 589.

15 Redfern and Hunter, *International Commercial Arbitration*, para 10-12.

16 Only in countries such as France, where the relevant criterion for distinguishing the different enforcement regimes is the implications of the interests of international commerce (NCPC Article 1492 and Title VI), will the rule on enforcement of domestic awards play no role for international arbitrations.

reasons allowing refusal.[17] In fact, domestic awards are often recognised automatically so that any decision on recognition has only declaratory character. In these cases proceedings are only necessary for the enforcement of the award.

26-15 Apart from this difference the provisions on recognition and enforcement often mirror those for foreign awards. Certain differences may exist in relation to the formal requirements to be submitted for recognition and enforcement. The laws sometimes impose more lenient requirements for domestic than for foreign awards. This is, for example, the case under German law where section 1064(1) ZPO requires for the enforcement only the submission of a copy of the award. [18]

26-16 There are also slight deviations in relations to the grounds upon which recognition and enforcement can be refused. Provisions for domestic awards may be more lenient. For example, in the Netherlands enforcement can only be resisted for public policy reasons.[19] Often they are also stricter. For example under Italian law, domestic awards may be challenged because they were rendered after the expiry of the relevant time limit, or the award does not state reasons or does not indicate the seat of arbitration.[20] No such ground exists with respect to the enforcement of a foreign award. [21]

26-17 Where recognition and enforcement of a domestic award is refused this may automatically lead to the setting aside of the award.[22] This is the logical consequence of the fact that the grounds for refusing recognition and enforcement are often identical to those justifying a challenge and the same courts have jurisdiction for challenge and enforcement proceedings.

26-18 Despite these differences the regime for the enforcement of domestic awards is in general largely comparable to that of foreign awards. At least in Contracting States of the New York Convention this is often the position as

---

[17] See, *e.g.*, England, Arbitration Act section 66; India, Arbitration Act section 36; China, Arbitration Law Articles 62-3 and Civil Procedure Law Article 217; Netherlands, CCP Articles 1062-3.

[18] In fact the courts are divided as to what extent these more lenient provisions are also applicable to the enforcement of foreign awards; see Kröll, "Recognition and Enforcement of Foreign Arbitral Awards in Germany", 5 *Int ALR* 160 (2002) 160-161.

[19] See, *e.g.*, Netherlands, CCP Article 1063 which limits the grounds basically to public policy.

[20] Italy, CCP Articles 829 and 823.

[21] See also the various grounds which exist in England to challenge an award and which may also be raised in proceedings to have an award declared enforceable: Arbitration Act sections 67 *et seq*.

[22] See Germany, ZPO section 1060; England, Arbitration Act section 66.

Article III stipulates an obligation that provisions for the enforcement of foreign awards may not be substantially stricter than those for national awards.

3. Recognition and Enforcement of Foreign Awards

26-19 One might assume that a foreign state would be more willing to recognise and enforce a court judgment of another state than an award made by private arbitrators whose authority is derived from an agreement of the parties. However, in reality it is far easier to enforce an arbitration award than a foreign judgment. This is due to the uniqueness of the New York Convention and its dual rationale to make the enforcement of foreign awards simpler and harmonise the national rules on enforcement. In contrast, there is no comparable international instrument on the enforcement of foreign judgments. While several regional and bilateral conventions exist, the complex web of conventions does not cover many jurisdictions; most notably the US is not party to any multilateral agreement on the enforcement of foreign judgments.

26-20 The New York Convention constitutes the backbone of the international regime for the enforcement of foreign awards. In addition, a number of other international conventions[23] and bilateral treaties provide for the enforcement of foreign awards. Frequently these public international law obligations are supplemented by autonomous provisions of the national arbitration law which provide for the enforcement of foreign awards.

3.1. The New York Convention

26-21 *The 1958 New York Convention*[24] is one of the most widely accepted international conventions and a major improvement of the regime created by the 1927 Geneva Convention.[25] It significantly simplified the enforcement of foreign awards and harmonised the national rules for the enforcement of foreign awards.

---

[23] See, *e.g.*, Giardina, "The Practical Application of Multilateral Conventions", *ICCA Congress Series no 9*, 440.

[24] Published in 330 *UNTS* 38 (1959), no 4739. The text is also available in <www.uncitral.org>.

[25] The 1927 Geneva Convention, 92 *LNTS* 302 (1929-1930), is now only of historic interest. The Convention was an early attempt to deal with enforcement of awards. One of the problematic provisions was the requirement that the award had become final in the country in which it was made, Article I(d). This led to the problem known as "double exequatur": the award had to be recognised at the courts of the country where it was made before a second exequatur could be obtained in the enforcing state. Another problematic provision was Article I(e) requiring that the award not be contrary to the public policy or the principles of law of the enforcing state.

The New York Convention has received praise as the "pillar on which the edifice of international arbitration rests"[26] and also for being the "most effective instance of international legislation in the history of commercial law."[27] The number of countries party to the New York Convention has increased dramatically within the last twenty-five years. The number of state parties stood at 133 in January 2003, ranging from Albania to Zimbabwe.[28] Consequently, the number of parties seeking enforcement under its terms has also increased.

26-22 Article III New York Convention is unambiguous in providing that "each contracting state shall recognise arbitration awards as binding and enforce them in accordance with the rules of procedure of the territory where the award is relied on." In addition Article III mandates that a foreign award must be enforceable without unnecessary inconvenience or excessive fees, and the conditions[29] must not be more onerous than those for domestic awards.

3.2. Other Multilateral Conventions

26-23 *The 1961 European Convention*[30] deals with the enforcement of foreign awards indirectly. Indeed the Convention only sought to supplement the New York Convention.[31] As pointed out in an Italian case the European Convention does not repeal, but merely restricts the grounds to refuse enforcement of awards to those provided for in the New York Convention.[32] It provides that an award set aside at the seat of arbitration may be recognised by the courts of states applying the Convention.[33] The relevant provisions have been used in few cases.[34] In fact

---

[26] Wetter, "The Present Status of the International Court of Arbitration in the ICC: An Appraisal", 1 *Am Rev Int'l Arb* 91 (1990).

[27] Mustill, "Arbitration: History and Background", 6(2) *J Int'l Arb* 43 (1989) 49.

[28] For a complete list of ratifications see <www.uncitral.org/english/status/status-e.htm>. See also van den Berg, *New York Convention*; Blessing (ed), *The New York Convention of 1958*, A Collection of Reports and Materials Delivered at the ASA Conference Held in Zurich on 2 February 1996, ASA Special Series no 9 (1996); Di Pietro & Platte, *Enforcement of International Arbitration Awards*.

[29] Set out in New York Convention Article IV.

[30] Published in 484 *UNTS* 364 (1963-64) no 704.

[31] See Fouchard Gaillard Goldman *on International Commercial Arbitration*, para 1714.

[32] See Italy, Corte di Appello Florence, 22 October 1976, *Tradax Export SA v Carapelli SpA*, III YBCA 279 (1978).

[33] European Convention Article IX(1) provides that the setting aside of an award covered by the Convention at the seat of arbitration shall only constitute a ground for the refusal of recognition or enforcement in another Contracting State where such setting aside took place in a State in which, or under the law of which, the award has been made for one of the reasons listed in New York Convention Article V(1)(a) – V(1)(d).

it is not the grounds for refusing enforcement which are restricted but the impact of a decision to set aside an award in the country of origin.[35]

26-24 *The 1965 Washington Convention*[36] ratified by more than 130 countries, provides its own enforcement procedures in Articles 53 and 54. Pursuant to these procedures each party must comply with the terms of the award[37] while each member state is under a public international law obligation to recognised an award rendered pursuant to the Convention and enforce the pecuniary obligations imposed by the award, as if it were a final judgment of the court in that state.[38] However, awards made under the ICSID Additional Facility but not under the Washington Convention can only be enforced under the New York Convention.

26-25 *The 1972 Moscow Convention* promulgated by the Council for Mutual Economic Assistance is no longer used as most of its member states have either withdrawn their membership[39] or ceased to exist.[40] Although the Convention is still in force in relation to a few countries, the Secretariat under which it operates has ceased to function. According to the Moscow Convention arbitration awards are to be enforced voluntarily[41] and failing that as if they were court judgments of the enforcing state.[42] The grounds on which enforcement may be resisted[43] are modelled after the New York Convention.

26-26 *The 1975 Inter-American Convention on International Commercial Arbitration (Panama Convention)*[44] is a regional convention ratified by more than 15 South American states and the US. According to the House Report of the Judiciary Committee accompanying the bill implementing the Panama Convention in the US as part of the Federal Arbitration Act, the Panama

---

34 See, *e.g.*, Austria, Oberster Gerichtshof, 20 October 1993, *Radenska v Kajo*, XX YBCA 1051 (1995); Spain, Tribunal Supremo, 27 February 1991, *Nobulk Cargo Services Ltd v Compañía Española de Laminación SA*, XXI YBCA 678 (1996).

35 See Fouchard Gaillard Goldman *on International Commercial Arbitration*, para 1715 with further references.

36 Published in 575 *UNTS* 160 (1966), no 8359. See also <www.worldbank.org/icsid>.

37 See Washington Convention Article 53(1).

38 See Washington Convention Article 54(1).

39 See, *e.g.*, Poland, Hungary and the Czech Republic.

40 *E.g.*, the German Democratic Republic.

41 Moscow Convention Article IV(1).

42 Moscow Convention Article IV(2).

43 Moscow Convention Article V.

44 Published in 14 *ILM* 336 (1975).

Convention and the New York Convention "are intended to achieve the same results, and their key provisions adopt the same standards."[45]

26-27 *The 1987 Amman Arab Convention on Commercial Arbitration* provides that awards made under the auspices of the Arab Centre for Commercial Arbitration may only be refused enforcement by the supreme courts of Contracting States where the award violates the public policy of the enforcing state.[46]

3.3. Bilateral Conventions

26-28 In addition to the multilateral conventions there are many bilateral conventions[47] dealing with the enforcement of awards rendered in another contracting state. The first recorded example of a reference to arbitration awards in a bilateral convention appears to be the Treaty between the Grand-Duchy of Baden and the Canton of Aargau (28 September 1867).[48] Such bilateral conventions work normally on the basis of reciprocity. They are often conventions of judicial assistance and their general subject matter and title may be a treaty of commerce, friendship and navigation. Conflicts between such bilateral and multilateral conventions are normally easily resolved.[49] Bilateral conventions have been useful in the past but may have an adverse effect on the harmonisation and uniformity achieved by the New York Convention. However, some more recent bilateral conventions refer to the New York Convention in respect of enforcement so that there is no real danger of disunification.

3.4. National Laws and Model Laws

26-29 National arbitration laws also normally contain provisions relating to the enforcement of foreign awards. Few provide a truly autonomous national regime deviating more than marginally from that of the New York Convention. One example is France where the setting aside of an award in its country of origin does not constitute a ground for refusing enforcement.

---

45 See *101st Cong, 2d Sess, 5 HR Rep* (1990) 101, reprinted in *US Code Congress & Administration News* (1990) 675, 678.

46 Amman Convention Article 35.

47 See, *e.g.*, Matscher, "Experience with Bilateral Treaties", *ICCA Congress Series no 9*, 452.

48 *Ibid.*

49 See, *e.g.*, Fouchard Gaillard Goldman *on International Commercial Arbitration*, paras 216-235.

26-30 Others usually incorporate verbatim the text of the relevant international conventions and add procedural rules of national implementation or merely provide that enforcement of foreign awards will be governed by the New York Convention.[50]

26-31 Article 36 Model Law, which lists the grounds on which a state court may refuse enforcement of an award, mirrors Article V New York Convention. Most importantly there is no reciprocity requirement;[51] the conditions are intended as maximum standards encouraging states to adopt even less onerous conditions.[52]

26-32 The OHADA[53] Uniform Arbitration Act also contains rules for the enforcement of awards. A party wishing to rely on an award must establish the existence of the award on the same conditions as in the New York Convention.[54] The recognition and enforcement of an award shall be refused where it is manifestly contrary to international public policy of the member states.[55] A judicial decision refusing enforcement of the award can only be set aside by the Common Court of Justice and Arbitration.[56] A judicial decision granting the enforcement of an award is not subject to any recourse.[57]

3.5. Relationship between the Different Regimes: Article VII New York Convention

26-33 The New York Convention sets minimum formal requirements for the enforcement of awards and maximum standards on which enforcement may be refused. It does not prevent the contracting states from restricting the grounds for refusal enumerated in Article V New York Convention and thereby create a more favourable law for enforcement. Accordingly, Article VII provides that the party

---

[50] See, *e.g.*, Belgium, Judicial Code Articles 1710-1723; Brazil, Arbitration Law Articles 34-40; China Arbitration Law Articles 62-64, 71-17 and Civil Procedure Law Articles 217 and 270; England, Arbitration Act sections 66, 99-104; France, NCPC Articles 1498-1503; Germany, ZPO sections 1061, 1064; India, Arbitration Act sections 36, 44-60; Netherlands, CCP Articles 1062-1063 and 1075-1076; Switzerland, PIL Article 194; US, FAA sections 201-208, 301-307.

[51] See Model Law Article 35(1).

[52] See Model Law Article 35(2)***.

[53] Organisation for the Harmonisation of Business Law in Africa. See also <www.ohada.com>; Mayer, *OHADA: Droit de l'arbitrage* (Bruyant 2002), 221 *et seq.*

[54] See OHADA Uniform Arbitration Act Article 31 and New York Convention Article IV.

[55] See OHADA Uniform Arbitration Act Article 31.

[56] This is an institution under the auspices of OHADA.

[57] See OHADA Uniform Arbitration Act Article 32.

that wants to uphold the award may rely on any more favourable right to enforcement. Examples of more favourable regimes on enforcement may be found in multi-lateral conventions, bilateral treaties and autonomous national laws on enforcement.[58]

26-34 Different views exist as to the application of Article VII. One view suggests that Article VII allows the parties a choice between different regimes but not "cherry picking" between the various regimes.[59] Another view is that Article VII allows the parties to rely on more favourable provisions even where enforcement is sought under the New York Convention.[60] This second view is in accordance with the undisputed pro-enforcement policy in the Convention and allows for its co-existence with the more favourable provisions in national laws or international instruments.

26-35 More favourable provisions exist in particular in relation to awards set aside in their country of origin. In France,[61] for example, this is not recognised as a separate ground to refuse enforcement. The European Convention also has limited this ground of refusal.[62]

26-36 Despite its wording, only the party seeking enforcement may rely on Article VII New York Convention. The aim of the Convention is to facilitate enforcement of awards by allowing only a limited number of exceptions to enforcement. If the respondent was allowed to seek a basis for enforcement more favourable to him the minimum standard of the Convention could be circumvented easily.

4. Sphere of Application of New York Convention

26-37 The sphere of application of the New York Convention in relation to recognition and enforcement is defined in Article I. Generally the Convention applies to all foreign awards as defined in Article I(2). According to Article I(3) the contracting states may however declare certain reservations.

---

[58] See, *e.g.*, Article IX European Convention, France, NCPC 1502, Netherlands, CCP Article 1076.

[59] See, *e.g.*, van den Berg, *New York Convention*, 119; more recently, van den Berg, "The Application of New York Convention by Courts", *ICCA Congress series no 9*, 25, 33-4.

[60] See, *e.g.*, Di Pietro and Platte, Enforcement of International Arbitration Awards, 171-2.

[61] France, NCPC Article 1502. See also France, Cour de cassation, 23 March 1994, *Hilmarton v Omnium de Traitement et de Valorisation (OTV)*, XX YBCA 663 (1995).

[62] Article IX European Convention.

4.1. Meaning of Foreign Award

(a) Award

26-38 The New York Convention relates only to awards but offers no definition of an award.[63] Only decisions of a tribunal which determine finally a specific issue and have *res judicata* effect may be enforced. They may be jurisdictional decisions,[64] and will normally be final decisions. *Arbitrato irrituale* decisions as well as price appraisals and expert determinations cannot be enforced as awards.[65] Procedural or other orders rendered by a tribunal although binding are not enforceable under the New York Convention unless they can be functionally characterised as awards.[66] The New York Convention does not specifically refer to interim awards or orders. Many institutional rules give arbitrators power to grant interim relief but these decisions are rarely final awards.

26-39 In *Resort Condominiums International Inc v Bolwell*[67] the Supreme Court of Queensland had to consider whether an interim award was enforceable in Australia. The applicants had obtained an "Interim Arbitration Order and Award" in the US ordering the respondent not to operate or enter into any agreements relating to a time-share contract until a final award was issued. The applicant applied to have the interim award enforced in Australia. The Supreme Court of Queensland refused enforcement. It held that, though it would be unduly restrictive to apply the New York Convention only to final awards terminating the whole proceedings, to fall within the ambit of the Convention a decision "must determine finally at least some of the matters in dispute before the parties."[68] The mere fact that the decision was called an "Interim Arbitration Order and Award" did not imply it takes "on that character simply because it is said to be so."[69] The finality of the award, partial or otherwise, therefore seems to

---

63 Article I(2) provides that "arbitral awards" shall include not only awards made by arbitrators appointed for each case but also those made by permanent arbitral bodies to which the parties have submitted.

64 See, *e.g.*, Di Pietro and Platte, *Enforcement of International Arbitration Awards*, 31-56.

65 See van den Berg, *New York Convention*, 44-51; Kröll, "Recognition and Enforcement of Foreign Arbitral Awards in Germany", 5 *Int ALR* 160 (2002) 164.

66 See, *e.g.*, *Publicis Communication and Publicis SA v True North Communications Inc*, 206 F 3d 725, XXV YBCA 1152 (2000) (7th Cir, 14 March 2000).

67 XX *YBCA* 628 (1995).

68 *Ibid*, 641, para 37. In the decision the court used the term "interim award" to describe a partial final award in the sense of the terminology used here. Consequently it came to the conclusion that "interim awards" (partial final awards) are enforceable under the Convention but that the award for interim relief did not constitute such an "interim award" (partial final award).

69 XX *YBCA* 628 (1995) 642, para 40.

have been the determining factor as to whether the award should be upheld by the courts.

26-40 Despite US cases to the contrary and support in the literature,[70] the prevailing position in practice is that finality is the defining factor. This has prompted the UNCITRAL Working Group on Arbitration to discuss the inclusion of rules for enforcement of interim awards into the Model Law. These rules it is suggested should follow as closely as possible the provisions of the New York Convention.

(b) Foreign

26-41 An award is foreign if it is considered "non domestic" by the enforcing court. The Convention employs two criteria to determine when awards are foreign. This characterization may be the result of a territorial criterion or a functional criterion.

26-42 The territorial criterion is codified in the first sentence of Article I(1) New York Convention according to which the Convention applies to

> ... awards made in the territory of a State other than the State where the recognition and enforcement of such awards are sought, and arising out of differences between persons, whether physical or legal.

26-43 It is irrelevant whether the subject matter of the arbitration is international, or the law applied is a foreign one, or what nationality the parties are.[71] The "location" of the arbitration is the dominant criterion. This is a predictable and certain way of establishing the scope of the Convention.

26-44 Award "made in the territory other than the state" where enforcement is sought can normally be easily ascertained. The award is made in the country of the legal seat of arbitration, not the place of the hearings or the place where the award was signed.[72] However, failing an indication in the award, it is ultimately for the enforcing court to determine whether the award was made within or outside its jurisdiction.

---

[70] See, *e.g.*, van den Berg, "The Application of the New York Convention by the Courts", *ICCA Congress Series no 9,* 25, 28-29. The UNCITRAL Working Group is working on the adoption of provisions dealing with the enforceability of provisional measures granted by the tribunal. See UN Document A/CN.9/523 of 11 November 2002, paras 78-80.

[71] See, *e.g.*, van den Berg, *New York Convention*, 15-19.

[72] See England, Arbitration Act section 100(2)(b) which effectively overruled *Hiscox v Outhwaite* [1991] 3 All ER 641.

26-45 The last sentence of Article I(1), however, qualifies the territorial criterion. It states that the Convention will also apply to

> ... arbitral awards not considered as domestic awards in the State where their recognition and enforcement are sought.

26-46 This sentence affords the contracting states a great deal of autonomy to broaden the scope of application of the Convention. Although this functional criterion may be criticised as less certain it has the advantage of allowing ratifying states discretion to decide which awards may be enforced under the Convention, in addition to awards rendered outside their territory or jurisdiction. For instance, under this functional criterion state courts may enforce anational awards[73] or awards which, although rendered within their territorial jurisdiction are deemed foreign. To the extent that there is no Convention definition of non domestic awards it is for the state courts to decide.

26-47 The rationale underlying this unspecified reference is well expressed by the US Court of Appeal for the Second Circuit in *Bergesen v Joseph Muller.*[74] It also offers a useful and contemporary definition of non-domestic awards

> The definition appears to have been left out deliberately in order to cover as wide a variety of eligible awards as possible, while permitting the enforcing authority to supply its own definition of 'non-domestic' in conformity with its own national law. Omitting the definition made it easier for those States championing the territorial concept to ratify the Convention while at the same time making the Convention more palatable in those States which espoused the view that the nationality of the award was to be determined by the law governing the arbitral procedure. We adopt the view that awards 'not considered as domestic' denotes awards which are subject to the Convention not because made abroad, but because made within the legal framework of another country, *e.g.*, pronounced in accordance with foreign law or involving parties domiciled or having their principal place of business outside the enforcing jurisdiction.[75]

26-48 The US implementation of the New York Convention in section 202 FAA departs from the Convention and specifies that an award

---

[73] See, *e.g.*, van den Berg, *New York Convention*, 28-43; van den Berg, "The Application of the New York Convention by the Courts", *ICCA Congress Series no 9*, 25, 27-28.

[74] See *Sigval Bergesen v Joseph Muller AG*, 701 F 2d 928, IX YBCA 487 (1984) (2d Cir, 1983), affirming 548 F Supp 650 (SDNY 1982).

[75] *Ibid*, IX YBCA 487 (1984) 492. See also to the same effect *Yusuf Ahmed Alghanim & Sons WLL v Toys "R" Us Inc*, 126 F 3d 15, XXIII YBCA 1057 (1998) (2d Cir, 1997).

> ... arising out of such a [commercial] relationship which is entirely between citizens of the United States shall be deemed not to fall under the Convention unless that relationship involves property located abroad, envisages performance or enforcement abroad, or has some other reasonable relation with one or more foreign states.

26-49 Section 202 not only incorporates the commercial reservation in the implementing Act but also adds a further requirement. Only awards arising out of disputes with an international element will be enforced under the Convention. While this may be legitimate it is uncertain how US courts will determine whether a legal relationship has a "reasonable" connection with one or more foreign states.

4.2. Reservations

26-50 To facilitate the widest possible ratification Article I(3) New York Convention allows contracting states to make two reservations: that the Convention applies only on the basis of reciprocity, *i.e.* only to arbitration awards made in another contracting state, and to awards rendered in commercial matters.

(a) Reciprocity

26-51 The reciprocity reservation was introduced as some contracting states did not subscribe to the principle of universality,[76] *i.e.* they were not willing for the Convention to apply to all awards irrespective of where they were made and only wished to recognise awards made in the jurisdiction of another contracting state.[77] More than half of the contracting states have used the reciprocity reservation.[78] Consequently, the reciprocity reservation should be taken into account when choosing the place of arbitration.

---

[76] See, *e.g.*, van den Berg, *New York Convention*, 12-15

[77] See, *e.g.*, the implementation in US, FAA section 201. See also Born, *International Commercial Arbitration*, 730 *et seq* for a review of case law.

[78] In 2002 some 70 states had done so. As most of the major international trade nations have ratified the Convention some states have withdrawn this reservation. See, *e.g.*, the withdrawal by Austria in 1988, by the Swiss Federal Council on 23 April 1993 and by Germany on 31 August 1998. Also, in some states such as France where the national law is more favourable than the New York Convention the reciprocity reservation has effectively no application.

(b) Commercial matters

26-52 More than 40 states have used the "commercial" reservation. The US has reflected it in its implementing act.[79] The rationale for this reservation was to enable states which only allow arbitration of commercial disputes to ratify the convention albeit with limited scope. There is no Convention concept of what is commercial: this is determined by the law of the enforcing court.[80]

26-53 The High Court of India held that consulting services by a company promoting a commercial deal should not be regarded as a commercial transaction. This decision was rightly reversed by the Supreme Court which suggested that the expression commercial should be construed widely having regards to the manifold activities which are integral to contemporary international trade.[81]

26-54 This approach of wide teleological interpretation was not followed by the Tunisian Cour de cassation.[82] It held that a contract between a company and two architects for the drawing up of an urbanisation plan for a resort in Tunisia could not be classified as commercial under Tunisian law.

26-55 A uniform concept of "commercial" should be adopted for international trade and international commercial arbitration. The Model Law offers a wide and permissive definition[83]

5. Pre-requisites for Enforcement

5.1. Jurisdiction of the Enforcement Court

26-56 Applications to have foreign awards declared enforceable require the court to have jurisdiction over the respondent. In general the existence of assets within a country is sufficient to establish jurisdiction for enforcement actions. The award creditor will have to investigate where assets of the unsuccessful party are located and where enforcement proceedings will be simpler.

---

79 See US, FAA section 202.

80 See van den Berg, *New York Convention*, 51-54, 54.

81 India, *RM Investment & Trading Co Pvt Ltd v Boeing Company*, [1994] 1 Supreme Court Journal 657, (1997) XXII YBCA 710 (Supreme Court, 10 February 1994).

82 Tunisia, Cour de cassation, 10 November 1993, *Société d'Investissement Kal v Taieb Haddad and Hans Barett*, XXIII YBCA 770 (1998).

83 Model Law Article 1(1)**.

26-57 Unlike challenge proceedings, which can only be held at the place of arbitration, enforcement proceedings are possible more or less everywhere assets are located. This fact that enforcement is possible and effective wherever the award debtor has assets, allows for forum shopping. Such discretion in relation to choosing a forum for enforcement proceedings is generally welcome. In the US, however, courts have exercised their discretion not to enforce an award where they considered that they were not the appropriate forum (*forum non conveniens*) normally due for lack of personal jurisdiction.[84]

5.2. Required Documents

26-58 Article IV New York Convention imposes minimum formal conditions. The rationale is to make the formal requirements for enforcement as simple as possible. Article IV prevails over stricter national law in respect of foreign awards. The party seeking recognition or enforcement must submit to the court

- an authenticated award or certified copy and, if necessary, translations and
- the original or a copy of the arbitration agreement and, if necessary, translations.

26-59 An authenticated award or a certified copy is essential as it is evidence of the entitlement of the party seeking enforcement. The fact that Article IV requires additionally the submission of the arbitration agreement referred to in Article II does not imply any obligation on the party seeking enforcement to establish the formal validity of the arbitration agreements.[85] In an English decision the court held that the presentation of a *prima facie* valid arbitration agreement is required. This shifts the burden of proof to the respondent wishing to resist enforcement.[86]

---

[84] See, *e.g.*, *Monegasque de Reassurances SAM (Monde Re) v NAK Naftogaz of Ukraine and State of Ukraine* (2d Cir, 15 November 2002): the award was made is Moscow, Ukraine was the natural forum for enforcement; the state of Ukraine invoked the Foreign Sovereign Immunity Act. See also *Base Metal Trading Ltd v OJSC "Novokuznetsky Aluminium Factory"*, 6 March 2002, XXVII YBCA 902 (2002) (4th Cir, 6 March 2002); *Glencore Grain Rotterdam BV v Shivnath Rai Harnarain Co*, 284 F 3d 1114, XXVII YBCA 922 (2002) (9th Cir, 2002); *Dardana Ltd v Yuganskneftegaz*, 2003 WL 122257 (2d Cir, 2003).

[85] See Di Pietro and Platte, *Enforcement of International Arbitration Awards*, 125 van den Berg, *New York Convention*, 250.

[86] See, *e.g.*, *Dardana Ltd v Yukos Oil Co* and *Petroalliance Services Co Ltd v Same*, [2002] 2 Lloyd's Rep 326 (CA). But see the less orthodox Norway, Hålogaland Court of Appeal, 16 August 1999, *Charterer (Norway) v Shipowner (Russian Federation)*, XXVII YBCA 519 (2002) where enforcement was refused due to lack of an arbitration agreement; the

26-60 The submission of the two documents may be at the same time as the application for enforcement. If this is not the case it can be rectified by subsequent submission of the arbitration agreement and such "delay" cannot be a ground to deny enforcement.[87]

26-61 The required authentication refers generally to the signing of the award by the tribunal and that the document is genuine. Certification is an assurance that the submitted documents are a true copy of the original. The Convention is silent as to how this certification should be effected, in terms of form or legal requirements. As a general rule it is the law of the place of enforcement which stipulates how the award should be authenticated and certified, *e.g.*, by a notary, consular or judicial authorities of the place where the award was made.

26-62 The few reported cases suggest that the enforcing courts have taken a rather liberal attitude in respect of authentication and certification.[88] This is evidenced by a decision of the German Federal Court.[89] The arbitration proceedings were based on an undertaking to arbitrate contained in the Treaty of Friendship between Germany and Poland so that it was impossible to submit a copy of an arbitration agreement. The respondent alleged that the copy of the award submitted was not duly certified. The Federal Court considered Article IV to be a rule establishing a standard of proof. As long as the authenticity of the award was not challenged the non-fulfilment of the form requirements does not constitute a ground to refuse enforcement. International conventions regarding the recognition of international documents for civil procedure may also be of use.[90]

26-63 The party seeking enforcement also must produce a translation of the award and the agreement if they are in a language other than the official language of the court in which enforcement is sought. The translation must be certified by

correspondence was contained in emails and the court held that under New York Convention the party had not submitted a valid arbitration clause for enforcement. In several Spanish cases it was held that a letter of confirmation not signed by the buyer is not a valid arbitration agreement: Tribunal Supremo, 16 September 1996, *Actival International SA v Conservas El Pilas SA*, XXVII YBCA 528 (2002); Tribunal Supremo, 7 July 1998, *Union de Cooperativas Agricolas Epis Centre (France) v Agricersa SL (Spain)*, XXVII YBCA 546 (2002).

[87] See, *e.g.*, Austria, Oberster Gerichtshof, 17 November 1965, *German party v Austrian party*, 3 Ob 128/65; 9 ZfRV 123 (1968), I YBCA 182 (1976); *Imperial Ethiopian Government v Baruch Foster Corporation*, 535 F 2d 334, II YBCA 252 (1977) (5th Cir 1976).

[88] See, *e.g.*, van den Berg, *New York Convention*, 250-258.

[89] Bundesgerichtshof, 17 August 2000, 53 *NJW* 3650 (2001) 3651.

[90] See, *e.g.*, the Hague Convention Abolishing the Requirement of Legalisation of Foreign Public Documents, 5 October 1961.

an official translator or by a diplomatic or consular authority. Courts normally accept a translation made in the country where the award was made or in the country where enforcement is sought.[91]

26-64 It is important to note that no permission for enforcement is needed in the country where the award was made. This was different under the 1927 Geneva Convention which required that the award had become final in the country in which the award was made.[92] Under the New York Convention it is sufficient that the award is "binding" in the country of origin.[93]

6. GROUNDS TO REFUSE ENFORCEMENT

26-65 The obligation on a national court to recognise and enforce arbitration awards as provided in Article III New York Convention is subject to limited exceptions. Recognition and enforcement may be refused *only* if the party against whom enforcement is sought can show that one of the exclusive grounds[94] for refusal enumerated in Article V(1) New York Convention has occurred. The court may refuse enforcement *ex officio* if the award violates that state's public policy.[95]

26-66 All grounds for refusal of enforcement must be construed *narrowly*; they are exceptions to the general rule that foreign awards must be recognised and enforced. The Convention sets *maximum* standards so that Contracting States cannot adopt legislation which adds grounds for resisting recognition and enforcement. Except for the public policy defence the second look at the award during the enforcement stage is confined to the procedural issues listed in Article V(1). A re-examination of the merits of the award is not allowed by the Convention.

---

[91] See also the discussion in van den Berg, *New York Convention*, 258-262.

[92] As a proof for the finality many courts required a leave for enforcement (exequatur) of a court in the country of origin. As another leave for enforcement was needed in the country of enforcement the party seeking enforcement needed a "double exequatur". See also footnote 19 above and accompanying text as well as Craig, "Some Trends and Developments in the Laws and Practice of International Commercial Arbitration", 30 *Texas Int'l L J* 1 (1995) 9.

[93] New York Convention Article V(1)(e).

[94] See, *e.g.*, *Parsons and Whittemore Overseas Co, Inc v Société générale de l'industrie du papier (RAKTA)*, 508 F 2d 969 (2d Cir, 1974). See also van den Berg, *New York Convention*, 265.

[95] New York Convention Article V(2)(a) and V(2)(b).

26-67 Finally, it is important to stress the permissive language in Articles V(1) and V(2). A court *may* but is not obliged to refuse enforcement if one of the exceptions is satisfied.

26-68 Accordingly, even if one of the grounds listed which would justify refusal of enforcement is proven by the resisting party, the court has a residual discretion to enforce the award. This has been eloquently stated by the Hong Kong Supreme Court in a 1994 decision which confirmed that

> ... the grounds of opposition are not to be inflexibly applied. The residual discretion enables the enforcing Court to achieve a just result in all the circumstances.[96]

26-69 In some countries, however, the "may" in Article V is interpreted as a "shall" leaving no discretion to the courts if one of the grounds to refuse enforcement exists.[97]

26-70 The first group of exceptions "further the loser's right to a fair arbitration."[98] These are set out exhaustively in Article V(1) New York Convention and grant to national courts the discretion to reject or annul an award tainted with procedural irregularity. The courts even have the discretion to partially enforce an award if the decisions on matters submitted to arbitration can be separated from those not so submitted.[99]

6.1. Invalidity of Arbitration Agreement

26-71 Article V(1)(a) effectively provides two different defences to enforcement: incapacity of a party and invalidity of the arbitration agreement. A court may refuse enforcement if it is shown proof that

> The parties to the agreement referred to in Article II were, under the law applicable to them, *under some incapacity*, or *the said agreement is not valid* under the law to which the parties have subjected it or, failing any indication thereon, under the law of the country where the award was made. [Emphasis added.]

---

96 See Hong Kong, Supreme Court, 13 July 1994, *China Nanhai Oil Joint Service Corp v Gee Tai Holdings Co Ltd*, (1995) XX YBCA 671, 677.

97 See, *e.g.*, Germany, Bundesgerichtshof, 2 November 2000, ZIP 2270 (2000) 2271.

98 Park, "Duty and Discretion in International Law", 93 *Am J Int'l L* 805 (1999) 810.

99 New York Convention Article V(1)(c).

(a) Incapacity

26-72 One type of incapacity relates to arbitrations involving a state party which invokes the defence of sovereign immunity (though this may be more a question of subjective arbitrability). Sovereign immunity is restricted to cases in which a state acts in its governmental capacity (*acta iure imperii*). It is not applicable if the state participates in commercial life (*acta iure gestionis*).[100] Further a state may always waive its immunity. This has been clearly stipulated by the Italian Supreme Court (quoting the arbitration tribunal) in a case dealing with enforcement

> ... we consider that, under the law applicable to international commerce, which necessarily governs the arbitration clause in the present case, legal persons of public law may, unless the parties have explicitly agreed otherwise, undoubtedly agree to arbitration, independent of domestic prohibitions, by expressing their consent and sharing, in the international marketplace, the conditions common to all operators.[101]

26-73 This Italian decision is arguably the most advanced position in this area and the concept of international capacity contemplated is particularly suitable for international commercial disputes. Despite this modern view state parties may still in certain parts of the world be successful in resisting enforcement by invoking the lack of capacity to enter into an arbitration agreement.[102]

26-74 The capacity of a party to enter into an arbitration agreement may also be restricted by the necessity of special permissions for foreign trade transactions[103] or the lack of authority of the person signing the arbitration agreement.[104]

---

[100] See Tunisia, Court of First Instance of Tunis, 22 March 1976, *Société Tunisienne d'Electricité et de Gaz (STEG) v Société Entrepose (France)*, III YBCA 283 (1978). According to the case which did not deal with enforcement directly, prohibitions in national law in respect of the capacity of state bodies to refer disputes to arbitration should not apply in the case of international commercial arbitration.

[101] See Italy, Corte di cassazione, 9 March 1996, no 4342, *Société Arabe des Engrais Phosphates et Azotes - SAEPA (Tunisia) and Société Industrielle d'Acide Phosphorique et d'Engrais - SIAPE (Tunisia) v Gemanco srl (Italy)*, XXII YBCA 737 (1997) 742.

[102] An example of an extremely conservative case can be seen in a case before the Syrian Administrative Tribunal Damascus, 31 March 1988, *Fougerolle SA v Ministry of Defence of the Syrian Arab Republic*, XV YBCA 515 (1990). The Administrative Tribunal found that the ICC awards were "non-existent" because the Syrian Council of State had not advised on the arbitration clause. Enforcement was, therefore, refused.

[103] See, *e.g.*, Bundesgerichtshof, 23 April 1998, XXIVb *YBCA* 928 (1999) where a Yugoslav party lacked the necessary export trade license and therefore could not validly enter into an arbitration agreement with a foreign party.

[104] See, *e.g.*, ICC case no 6850, XXIII *YBCA* 37 (1998); Court of Cassation Dubai, 25 June 1994, 1 *Int ALR* N-62 (1998), where the person agreeing on the arbitration clause was acting under a

(b) Invalidity

26-75 The defence of the invalidity of the arbitration agreement has given rise to considerable case law. Enforcement has been refused where the arbitration agreement was ambiguous,[105] or not validly assigned.[106] While it is obvious that substantive validity must be determined according to the law chosen by the parties or, in the absence of a choice by the law of the place of arbitration, different views exist as to the relevant form requirements.

26-76 There is support for the view which considers that the reference in Article V(1)(a) to "the agreement referred to in Article II" requires that formal validity, which is often inseparably linked to the question of consent, be determined on the basis of Article II.[107] Reliance on more favourable national form requirements is excluded where recognition is sought under the New York Convention.[108] It can then only be relied upon where enforcement is sought under a more favourable national regime.[109]

26-77 The alternative view is that formal validity is governed by the law chosen by the parties or the law of the place of arbitration. The reference to Article II is considered a superfluous additional description of the arbitration agreement. This has the advantage that form requirements which are more lenient than Article II can be taken into account within the framework of the Convention. Article II is only considered to be a maximum standard above which the national legislator

power of attorney which according to the view of the Court did not cover the submission to arbitration; for an unsuccessful reliance on this ground see Corte di cassazione, 23 April 1997, *Dalmine SpA v M & M Sheet Metal Forming Machinery AG*, XXIVa YBCA 709 (1999); Spain, Tribunal Supremo, 17 February 1998, *Union de Cooperativas Agricolas Epis Centre (France) v La Palentina SA (Spain)*, XXVII YBCA 533(2002); see also Greece, Areios Pagos, decision no 88 of 14 December 1977, *Agrimpex SA v J F Braun & Sons Inc*, IV YBCA 269 (1979): enforcement was refused due to lack of written power of attorney to conclude the arbitration agreement.

105 Corte di Appello Florence, 27 January 1988, *Eastern Mediterranean Maritime Ltd v SpA Cerealtoscana*, XV YBCA 496 (1990).

106 District Court Moscow, 21 April 1997, *IMP Group (Cyprus) Ltd v Aeroimp*, XXIII YBCA 745 (1998).

107 See, *e.g.*, *Harry L Reynolds Jr v International Amateur Athletic Federation*, XXI YBCA 715 (1996): no written agreement in the meaning of the New York Convention.

108 See, *e.g.*, Oberlandesgericht Schleswig, *RIW* 706 (2000); Turkey, Supreme Court of Appeals, 8 April 1999, *Ozsoy Tarim Sanayi Ve Ticaret Ltd (Izmir) v All Foods SA (Buenos Aires)*, 4 Int ALR N-33 (2001): arbitration agreement contained in unsigned NAFTA contract does not meet the New York Convention writing requirement; the award was refused enforcement.

109 This view, however, seems to unduly limit the application of Article VII New York Convention.

cannot go.[110] This difference in views has considerable influence on the validity of arbitration agreements contained in letters of confirmation.[111] They will not be formally valid under Article II but are valid under many national laws.

26-78 Generally under the national regimes for enforcement of awards no such difficulties exist, since they all lack a similar reference to Article II. Therefore, when the validity of the arbitration is an issue, it might be easier to rely on national rules rather than enforcing under the Convention.[112] If the Convention is to be relied on a dynamic interpretation of its provisions should be adopted.[113]

(c) More favourable other provisions

26-79 Under Article 1076 Dutch Arbitration Law, the respondent may only rely on the invalidity of the arbitration agreement or on a failure in the composition of the tribunal if the party who invokes this ground as a defence to enforcement has raised a respective plea in the arbitration proceedings.

6.2. Violation of Due Process

26-80 According to Article V(1)(b) recognition and enforcement of the award may also be refused if the party resisting enforcement furnishes proof that he

> ... was *not given proper notice* of the appointment of the arbitrator or of the arbitration proceedings or was otherwise *unable to present his case.* [Emphasis added.]

---

[110] See Di Pietro and Platte, *Enforcing International Arbitration Awards*, 143; Kröll, "Recognition and Enforcement of Foreign Arbitral Awards in Germany", 5 *Int ALR* 160 (2002) 166; Fouchard Gaillard Goldman *on International Commercial Arbitration*, para 271; Oberlandesgericht Dresden, 12 January 1999, 11 Sch 6/98, unreported.

[111] See, *e.g*, Oberlandesgericht Rostock, 22 November 2001, 1 Sch 3/2000, unreported, note Kröll, 5 *Int ALR* N-31 (2002): award refused enforcement because no existence of arbitration agreement was demonstrated, the only document was a letter of confirmation of one party. See also Tribunal Supremo, 16 September 1996, *Actival International SA v Conservas El Pilas SA*, XXVII YBCA 528 (2002); Tribunal Supremo, 7 July 1998, *Union de Cooperativas Agricolas Epis Centre (France) v Agricersa SL (Spain)*, XXVII YBCA 546 (2002).

[112] See, *e.g.*, Gerechtshof The Hague, 4 August 1993, *Owerri Commercial Inc v Dielle Srl*, XIX YBCA 703 (1994) where enforcement was based on the Dutch regime rather than on the New York Convention.

[113] In this way, *e.g.*, modern electronic communications will be accommodated and the problem of invalidity of an arbitration agreement because of use of e-mail as in Norway, Hålogaland Court of Appeal, 16 August 1999, XXVII YBCA 519 (2002), will be avoided.

26-81 This is a due process defence and the paragraph particularly contemplates the right to be heard. The rationale of this defence is to ensure that certain standards of fairness are observed by the arbitration tribunal. Article V(1)(b) provides for two dimensions in relation to fairness of proceedings. First, a proper notice must be given; second, each party must be able to present his case. The Convention is not specific enough as to the benchmark of fairness; apparently observance of standards set by the law chosen by the parties to govern the arbitration, or alternatively by the law at the place of arbitration, would suffice.[114] However the view that Article V(1)(b) is a genuinely international rule is also convincing.[115] Ultimately the question of violation of due process is a matter of fact which the parties will have to prove.

26-82 This ground to refuse enforcement may overlap with the international public policy defence of Article V(2)(b). This is so because fairness and observance of due process are often seen as international public policy of many states. However, according to Article V(2)(b) the only relevant public policy is that of the enforcing state.

(a) Proper notice

26-83 Proper notice always must be given. This covers lack of notice or where notice of proceedings was received after the award had been rendered. Such cases are rare.[116] Short time notices do not normally violate the requirement of proper notice as they are typical in certain industry and trade sectors.[117]

26-84 The most important issue is whether the notice was timely and appropriate.[118] This is a matter of fact and several of the formal requirements will

---

[114] See van den Berg, *New York Convention*, 298, with reference to case law in footnote 186.

[115] See, *e.g.*, Fouchard, *L'arbitrage*, para 526.

[116] See, *e.g.*, *Sesotris SAE v Transportes Navales*, 727 F Supp 737, XVI YBCA 640 (1991) (District Court, D Mass, 1989); Bayerisches Oberlandesgericht, 16 March 2000, RPS 2/2000, Beilage 12 zu Heft 50 *BetriebsBerater* 15 (2000), where the enforcement of a Russian award was refused because the respondent was actually only informed about the proceedings after the award was rendered as service was constructive rather than real.

[117] See, *e.g.*, Switzerland, Obergericht Basel, 3 June 1971, *Dutch seller v Swiss buyer*, IV YBCA 309 (1978).

[118] In Corte di Appello Naples, 18 May 1982, *Bauer & Grobmann OHG v Fratello Cerrone Alfredo e Raffaele*, X YBCA 461 (1985), the award was refused enforcement because one month's notice was deemed inadequate: the respondent's area had been hit by an earthquake. In *Guangdong New Technology Import & Export Corp Jiangmen Branch (PR China) v Chiu Shing Trading as BC Property & Trading Co*, (1993) XVIII YBCA 385 (Supreme Court Hong Kong, 23 August 1991), the award was recognised despite late notice because the party was not prejudiced.

be invoked by national laws. However, often a more liberal interpretation of national law requirements is needed. In a case before the Mexican Court of Appeal it was held that the Mexican law requirement was waived since the parties opted for arbitration. The award is enforceable since the parties complied with the requirements set by the applicable arbitration rules.[119] In order to avoid the objection that no letter was received important communications should be made by registered mail or courier with return receipt.

26-85 Not only must notice of proceedings be proper, but also other notices, such as disclosure of the names of arbitrators. In an exceptional case, the German Court of Appeal in Cologne refused to enforce an award made under the Arbitration Rules of the Copenhagen Committee for Grain and Food Stuff Trade which allowed non-disclosure of the arbitrators' names.[120]

(b) Unable to present his case

26-86 This defence has been clearly defined in a decision of the US Court of Appeal for the Seventh Circuit. The Court held that this defence

> ... basically corresponds to the due process defense that a party was not given the opportunity to be heard "at a meaningful time and in a meaningful manner" ... Therefore, an arbitral award should be denied or vacated if the party challenging the award proves that he was not given a meaningful opportunity to be heard as our due process jurisprudence defines it ... It is clear that an arbitrator must provide a fundamentally fair hearing ... A fundamentally fair hearing is one that 'meets "the minimal requirements of fairness"- adequate notice, a hearing on the evidence, and an impartial decision by the arbitrator'.[121] [References omitted]

26-87 Standards of fairness have been discussed in other US cases.[122] Normally reference is given to the national law standards of impartiality and independence of the tribunal. Some national laws afford parties a full opportunity[123] to present their case; other laws afford a reasonable opportunity.[124]

---

[119] See Mexico, Tribunal Superior de Justicia, 1 August 1977, *Malden Mills Inc (USA) v Hilaturas Lourdes SA (Mexico)*, IV YBCA 302 (1979).

[120] See Oberlandesgericht Cologne, 10 June 1976, IV YBCA 258 (1979).

[121] See *Generica Limited v Pharmaceuticals Basics Inc*, XXIII YBCA 1076 (1998) 1078-9 (7th Cir, 1997).

[122] See, *e.g.*, *Parsons and Whittemore Overseas Co, Inc v Société générale de l'industrie du papier (RAKTA)*, 508 F 2d 969, I YBCA 205 (1976) (2d Cir, 1974).

[123] See, *e.g.*, Model Law Article 18.

[124] See, *e.g.*, England, Arbitration Act section 33(1)(a).

26-88 Specific issues which can amount to a ground for challenge of an award include the fact that a party has not been able to participate in the taking of evidence or in discovery proceedings,[125] that a party had been denied the right to introduce certain evidence,[126] or to comment on an expert's report submitted to the tribunal[127] or that the standards of adversarial proceedings adopted by the tribunal deprived a party of its fundamental right to defence.[128] However, it is only required that the tribunal gives the parties the opportunity to present their case. Whether the party actually makes use of it or not, and in which way, does not generally affect the enforceability of the award.[129]

26-89 It is essential that there is a duty on the parties to raise an objection promptly. This implies that objection should be raised during the arbitration first if the relevant facts are known to the party objecting. Otherwise the party may be estopped from raising the objection before the enforcing court as this undermines the purpose of the New York Convention.[130]

6.3. Arbitrators have Acted Beyond their Jurisdiction

26-90 Recognition and enforcement of the award may be refused, under Article V(1)(c), if the award deals with a

> *difference not contemplated by or not falling within* the terms of the submission to arbitration, or it contains *decisions on matters beyond the scope* of the submission to arbitration, provided that, if the decisions on matters submitted to arbitration can be separated from those not so submitted, that part of the award which contains

[125] See, *e.g.*, *Polytek Engineering Co Ltd v Hebei Import and Export Corp*, (1998) XXII YBCA 666 (High Court Hong Kong, 16 January 1998).

[126] See, *e.g.*, US, *Iran Aircraft Industries v AVCO Corporation*, 980 F 2d 141, XVIII YBCA 596 (1993) (2d Cir, 1992); *Laminoirs-Trefileries-Cableries de Lens SA v Southwire Co*, 484 F Supp 1063 (ND Ga 1980): award nevertheless recognised.

[127] See, *e.g.*, *Paklito Investment Ltd v Klockner East Asia Ltd*, (1994) XIX YBCA 654 (Supreme Court of Hong Kong, 15 January 1993).

[128] See, *e.g.*, Germany, Oberlandesgericht Hamburg, 3 April 1975, *US firm v German firm*, II YBCA 241 (1977). In Bundesgerichtshof, 18 January 1990, XVII *YBCA* 503 (1992) the award was recognised despite the fact that the tribunal did not consider all arguments.

[129] See Oberlandesgericht Hamburg, 30 June 1998, 6 Sch 3/98, unreported; *Fitzroy Engineering Ltd v Flame Engineering Ltd*, 1994 US Dist LEXIS 17781 (ND Ill, 2 December 1994); Hong Kong, *Sam Ming Forestry Economic Co v Lam Pun Hing*, (2000) 15(1) Mealey's IAR 12 (HCHK): the award was enforced even though the beneficiary did not participate in the proceedings.

[130] See, *e.g.*, *Société Nationale pour la Recherche, la Production, le Transport, la Transformation et la Commercialisation des Hydrocarbures (Sonatrach) (Algeria) v Shaheen National Resources Inc (USA)*, 585 F Supp 57, X YBCA 540 (1985) (SDNY 1983).

decisions on matters submitted to arbitration may be recognized and enforced. [Emphasis added.]

26-91 While the presumption is that the tribunal acted within its powers,[131] this provision covers two different issues. First, the case where the tribunal rendered a decision outside its jurisdiction or without jurisdiction (*extra petita*), and second, where the tribunal has exceeded its jurisdiction (*ultra petita*). In either case it is assumed there is an arbitration agreement which in principle confers jurisdiction on the tribunal, albeit not in respect of matters decided by it. This ground may cover the non enforcement of the award or a severable part of it.

(a) Extra petita

26-92 This defence has rarely been successfully invoked. The defence covers cases where the tribunal has decided matters outside the jurisdiction conferred upon it by the parties. This may be the case, for example, when the tribunal awards consequential damages while the contract between the parties expressly excluded this type of damages.[132] This is also the case when the tribunal awards remedies not specified in the contract despite the objection of one party.[133]

(b) Ultra petita

26-93 This defence has also rarely been successfully invoked; there is a strong presumption that arbitrators have not exceeded their authority. Courts have looked beyond the wording of the claims submitted to establish whether tribunals awarded more than requested. In this instance the Convention wishes to safeguard the part of the award which has not been tainted by the *ultra petita* objection. In an Italian case the court held that only the part of the award which is consistent with the mandate of the tribunal is enforceable but not the remaining part of the award which exceeded the tribunal's of jurisdiction.[134]

---

[131] See, *e.g.*, *Sojuznefteexport (SNE) v Joc Oil Ltd,* (1990) XV YBCA 384 (Court of Appeal of Bermuda, 7 July 1989).

[132] See, *e.g.*, *Fertilizer Corporation of India v IDI Management*, 517 F Supp 948, VII YBCA 382 (1982) (SD Ohio, 1981). The Court found the justification of the award of damages colourful and satisfactory and confirmed the award. See also *The Ministry of Defense and Support for the Armed Forces of The Islamic Republic of Iran v Cubic Defense Systems Inc (US)*, 29 F 2d 1168, XXIVa YBCA 875 (1999) (SD Cal 1998).

[133] See, *e.g.*, *In the Matter of the Arbitration between Millicom International v Motorola Inc and Proempres Panama SA*, 2002 WL 472042, XXVII YBCA 948 (2002) (SDNY 28 March 2002).

[134] See Italy, Corte di Appello Trento, 14 January 1981, *General Organisation of Commerce and Industrialisation of Cereals of the Arab Republic of Syria v SpA Simer*, VIII YBCA 352 (1983).

6.4. Irregular Procedure or Composition of Tribunal

26-94 Article V(1)(d) introduces two grounds on which enforcement may be refused. It establishes the supremacy of party autonomy over the law of the place of arbitration and allows a national court to refuse recognition and enforcement where

> The *composition of the arbitral authority* or the *arbitral procedure* was not in accordance with the agreement of the parties, or, failing such agreement, was not in accordance with the law of the country where the arbitration took place. [Emphasis added.]

26-95 Article V(1)(d) has rarely been invoked before courts. One notable exception is a decision of the Supreme Court of Hong Kong. The dispute was whether the composition of the tribunal was in accordance with the agreement of the parties.[135] The arbitrators were supposed to be on the Beijing list while they were on the Shenzhen list. The court rejected the request to refuse enforcement as the arbitrators were on CIETAC list and the parties had agreed to CIETAC arbitration. Further the court held that as the objection was not raised during the arbitration the party was estopped from raising this ground at the enforcement stage.[136]

26-96 In another unsuccessful attempt to invoke this defence, a party argued that the arbitrators had acted as *amiables compositeurs*. The Belgian court held that this was not the case and enforced the award.[137]

26-97 In another case an award was refused enforcement because the proceedings were bifurcated into liability and damages phases contrary to the

---

135 See *Al Haddad Bros Enterprises Inc v MS Agapi*, 635 F Supp 205 (D Del, 1986), aff'd (3d Cir, 1987): award enforced despite the fact that it was made by a sole arbitrator rather than three arbitrators as provided in the arbitration agreement. In Corte di Appello Florence, 13 April 1978, *Rederi Aktiebolaget Sally v Termarea srl*, IV YBCA 294 (1979), the award was refused enforcement because the award was made by two arbitrators while the arbitration agreement provided for three arbitrators.

136 See *China Nanhai Oil Joint Service Corp v Gee Tai Holdings Co Ltd*, (1995) XX YBCA 671 (Hong Kong Supreme Court, 13 July 1994). See also Oberlandesgericht Dresden, 20 October 1998, 11 Sch 4/98, unreported, where the court refused an application to resist enforcement of a Russian award. The background was relating to the appointment of an arbitrator by the Russian Chamber of Commerce as the German party failed to appoint an arbitrator within the time limit. The German Court held that the fact that the arbitrator did not speak German, as the German party had requested, did not amount to an irregular composition of the tribunal.

137 See Belgium, Cour d'appel Brussels, 24 January 1997, *Inter-Arab Investment Guarantee Corporation v Banque Arabe et Internationale d'Investissements*, XXII YBCA 643 (1997).

applicable arbitration rules.[138] Further, a number of court decisions confirm the view that if the procedure adopted by the tribunal conforms with the applicable arbitration rules or with the law governing the arbitration there can be no ground to refuse enforcement.[139]

6.5. Award is Not Binding, or Has Been Suspended or Set Aside

26-98 The fifth ground to refuse recognition and enforcement is, under Article V(1)(e), where the award

> has *not yet become binding* on the parties or *has been set aside or suspended* by a competent authority of the country in which, or under the law of which, that award was made. [Emphasis added.]

26-99 This provision has been criticised as it allows for "local standards of enforcement."[140] It has been omitted by some national laws.[141] Here again there are two separate reasons: the award is not yet "binding", and the award has been set aside or suspended.

(a) Not binding

26-100 The drafters of the Convention intentionally chose the expression "not binding" and not the word "final" (as was the case with the 1927 Convention). The reason was simply to avoid the problem of the party seeking enforcement having to request leave for enforcement by the courts at the place of arbitration.[142]

26-101 However, the meaning of the term "binding" has generated debate. The main issue is whether the term "binding" is an autonomous term or is subject to national law determination. As the drafters of the New York Convention wanted

---

[138] See Appelationsgericht Basel, 6 September 1968, *Swiss Corp X AG v German firm Y*, I YBCA 200 (1976); the Hamburg Commodity Association Arbitration Rules were applicable.

[139] See, *e.g.*, *Industrial Risk Insurers and Barnard & Burk Group Inc and Barnard and Burk Engineers and Constructors Inc v MAN Gutehoffnungshütte GmbH*, 141 F 3d 1434, XXIVa YBCA 819 (1999) (11th Cir 1998): no irregularity of procedure as the AAA Rules were complied with; Oberlandesgericht Hamburg, *Charterer v Shipowner*, XXV YBCA 714 (2000): lack of reasons in the award or absence of oral hearing no procedural irregularity.

[140] See, *e.g.*, Paulsson, "The Case for Disregarding LSAS (Local Standard Annulments) Under the New York Convention", 7 *Am Rev Int'l Arb* 99 (1996); van den Berg, *New York Convention*, 355.

[141] See, *e.g.*, France, NCPC Article 1502.

[142] See van den Berg, *New York Convention*, 333-337.

to depart from the national characterisation envisaged by the Geneva Convention an autonomous interpretation of "binding" is preferred.

26-102 An award can be binding notwithstanding the fact that some additional formalities are required to make it enforceable where it was made.[143] Consequently an award may not be refused enforcement because, *inter alia*,[144] formal time limits imposed by the law of the place of arbitration have not yet expired, or confirmation of the award is required in court at the place of arbitration and this has not yet been given,[145] or the award needs to be deposited with the court at the place of arbitration.[146] Further, if the award is not subject to a genuine appeal on the merits to a second arbitration tribunal or court, it must be considered "binding."[147] Partial awards are binding and hence enforceable.

(b) Award set aside or suspended

26-103 If the party resisting enforcement has successfully applied for a suspension or setting aside of the award the enforcement court may adjourn its decision.[148] To the extent that the New York Convention does not harmonise the rules on which challenge of awards may be effected the local standard for annulment of awards has been referred to as the "anathema of local particularities."[149]

26-104 The enforcing court has discretion to enforce the award despite the fact that it was successfully challenged at the place of arbitration. Awards annulled at the place of arbitration have been enforced in the US, France and Austria.

---

[143] See, *e.g.*, Australia, *Resort Condominiums International Inc v Ray Bolwell and Resort Condominiums Pty Ltd*, (1994) 9(4) Mealey's IAR A1, (1995) XX YBCA 628 (Supreme Court Queensland, 29 October 1993).

[144] *Ibid*, 337-346.

[145] See, *e.g.*, *Fertilizer Corporation of India v IDI Management*, 517 F Supp 948, VII YBCA 382 (1982) (SD Ohio 1981).

[146] See, *e.g.*, France, Cour d'appel Paris, 10 May 1971, *Compagnie de Saint Gobain-Pont à Mousson v The Fertilizer Corporation of India Ltd*, I YBCA 184 (1976).

[147] Van den Berg, *New York Convention*, 342; Redfern and Hunter, *International Commercial Arbitration*, para 10-40.

[148] New York Convention Article VI.

[149] Paulsson, "The Case for Disregarding LSAS (Local Standard Annulments) Under the New York Convention", 7 *Am Rev Int'l Arb* 99 (1996).

(c) More favourable provisions

26-105 Pursuant to Article IX European Convention the annulment of the award in the country of origin is a ground to refuse enforcement only if the award was annulled for one of the reasons listed in Article V(1)(a)–(d) New York Convention. Accordingly, an annulment because the award contravenes the public policy of the country of origin does not hinder enforcement in another contracting state.[150]

26-106 French courts are by law under an obligation to enforce a foreign award even if it was set aside in the country of origin. The nullification of the award is not recognised as a ground to refuse enforcement.[151] Courts in Austria[152] and the US[153] have also recognised awards set aside at the place of arbitration.

26-107 In *Hilmarton* the dispute dealt with a consultancy fee payable by a French firm (OTV) to an English firm (Hilmarton) in relation to a contract in Algeria. The award was made in 1988 in Switzerland and held that the payment was not due as the use of intermediaries was prohibited in Algeria in respect of public contracts, although Algerian law was not chosen by the parties. It was alleged that corrupt practices were involved, possibly violating international public policy in Algeria and Switzerland. The award was successfully challenged in Switzerland in 1990[154] but was recognised by the Court of Appeal in Paris and the Cour de cassation in 1994.[155] A second award was rendered in Geneva in 1992 and this was initially recognised in France in 1995 by the Versailles Court of Appeal.[156] The Cour de cassation, however, reversed the judgment of the

150 *Ibid.*

151 France, NCPC Article 1502. See also France, Cour de cassation, 23 March 1994, *Hilmarton v Omnium de Traitement et de Valorisation (OTV)*, XX YBCA 663 (1995).

152 Austria, Oberster Gerichtshof, 20 October 1993 / 23 February 1998, *Kajo-Erzeugnisse Essenzen GmbH (Austria) v DO Zdravilisce Radenska (Slovenia)*, XXIVa YBCA 919 (1999). The Court applied the European Convention as more favourable law.

153 See, *e.g.*, *Chromalloy Aeroservices Inc (US) v The Arab Republic of Egypt*, 939 F Supp 907, XXII YBCA 1001 (1997) (DDC 1996).

154 Switzerland, Tribunal Fédéral, 17 April 1990, *Omnium de Traitement et de Valorisation (OTV) v Hilmarton (UK)*, Rev Arb 315 (1993), with note Heuzé, "La morale, l'arbitre et le juge", 179; Rivista dell'Arbitrato 735 (1992), with note Giardina, "Norme imperative contro le intermediazioni nei contratti ed arbitrato internazionale", 784. English text in XIX YBCA 214 (1994).

155 France, Cour de cassation, 23 March 1994, *Hilmarton v Omnium de Traitement et de Valorisation (OTV)*, XX YBCA 663 (1995).

156 France, Cour d'appel Versailles, 29 June 1995, *Omnium de Traitement et de Valorisation (OTV) v Hilmarton*, XXI YBCA 524 (1996).

Court of Appeal in Versailles as it violated the *res judicata* of the recognised first award.[157] The second award was enforced in England.[158]

26-108 An award made and set aside in Egypt was enforced in the US. In *Chromalloy* the dispute relating to the procurement of a military equipment contract between a US firm and the Egyptian state was decided by a tribunal in Cairo in 1994.[159] Chromalloy was the successful party and sought enforcement in the US before the District Court for the District of Columbia. Before the US court could decide the matter the award was challenged successfully at the Cairo Court of Appeal.[160] Despite the challenge the US court recognised the award.[161] This award was also enforced in France by the Paris Court of Appeal.[162] Chromalloy has not been followed by other US courts.[163]

26-109 Similarly an award made and challenged in Slovenia was enforceable in Austria,[164] and an award made in Austria but partly set aside there was enforceable in France.[165]

26-110 The discretion exercised by courts in recognising and enforcing awards set aside at the place of arbitration has been welcomed by many writers[166] and

---

[157] France, Cour de cassation, 10 June 1997, *Omnium de Traitement et de Valorisation (OTV) v Hilmarton*, XXII YBCA 696 (1997).

[158] *Hilmarton v Omnium de Traitement et de Valorisation (OTV)*, (1999) 14(6) Mealey's IAR A1, (1999) XXIVa YBCA 777 (QBD, 24 March 1999).

[159] Reported in 11(8) *Mealey's IAR* C1 (1996).

[160] Egypt, Court of Appeal Cairo, 5 December 1995, *Ministry of Defense of the Republic of Egypt v Chromalloy Aeroservices Inc*, XXIVa YBCA 265 (1999).

[161] US, *Chromalloy Aeroservices Inc (US) v The Arab Republic of Egypt*, 939 F Supp 907 XXII YBCA 1001 (1997) (DDC, 1996).

[162] France, Cour d'appel Paris, 14 January 1997, *The Arab Republic of Egypt v Chromalloy Aeroservices Inc (US)*, 12(4) Mealey's IAR B1 (1997).

[163] See *Baker Marine (Nigeria) Ltd v Chevron (Nigeria) Ltd*, 191 F 3d 194 (2d Cir 1999) where the Court of Appeal for the Second Circuit refused to enforce two awards set aside by a Nigerian court. Similarly the District Court for the Southern District of New York following Baker Marine refused to enforce an award set aside in Italy: *Martin Spier v Calzaturifico Tecnica SpA*, 71 F 2d 279, 14(11) Mealey's IAR E1 (1999) (SDNY, 1999). See also the discussion in Gaillard and Edelstein, "Baker Marine and Spier Strike A Blow to the Enforceability in the United States of Awards Set Aside at the Seat", 3 *Int ALR* 37 (2000).

[164] Austria, Oberster Gerichtshof, 20 October 1993 / 23 February 1998, *Kajo-Erzeugnisse Essenzen GmbH (Austria) v DO Zdravilisce Radenska (Slovenia)*, XXIVa YBCA 919 (1999).

[165] See France, Cour de cassation, 9 October 1984, *Pabalk Ticaret Limited Sirketi (Turkey) v Norsolor SA (France)*, 24 ILM 360 (1985) with introductory note by Gaillard, XI YBCA 486 (1984).

[166] See, *e.g.*, Chan, "The Enforceability of Annulled Foreign Awards in the United States: A Critique of Chromalloy", 17 *Boston U Int'l L J* 141 (1999); Gaillard, "Enforcement of Awards Set Aside in the Country of Origin: The French Experience", *ICCA Congress Series no 9*, 505;

criticised by others.[167] In any event the practice is justified as a matter of Article VII New York Convention and more favourable positions in national law or international conventions. The problem can only be eliminated by establishing international standards for annulment of awards.

6.6. Violation of Public Policy of Country of Enforcement

26-111 Article V(2) of the New York Convention provides further grounds on which recognition and enforcement of an award may be resisted. Both grounds listed in sub-paragraphs (a) and (b) fall under the heading public policy defence. In relation to this paragraph the court may *ex officio* raise the issue of public policy; no request of a party is necessary. Article V(2) provides that

> Recognition and enforcement of an arbitral award may also be refused if the competent authority in the country where recognition and enforcement is sought finds that:
> (a) The subject matter of the difference is not capable of settlement by arbitration under the law of that country; or
> (b) The recognition or enforcement of the award would be contrary to the public policy of that country.

26-112 The two aspects of public policy[168] envisaged relate to whether the subject matter of the dispute is capable of settlement by arbitration in the enforcing state (arbitrability) and whether the recognition and enforcement of the award would violate the international public policy of the enforcing state. There are as many shades of international public policy as there are national attitudes towards arbitration.

Paulsson, "The Case for Disregarding LSAS (Local Standard Annulments) Under the New York Convention", 7 *Am Rev Int'l Arb* 99 (1996); Paulsson, "May or Must Under the New York Convention An Exercise in Syntax and Linguistics", 14 *Arb Int* 227 (1998); Petrochilos, "Enforcing Awards Annulled in the State of Origin under New York Convention:", 48 *ICLQ* 856 (1999); Rivkin, "The Enforcement of Awards Nullified in the Country of Origin; The American Experience", *ICCA Congress Series no 9*, 528.

[167] See, *e.g.*, Bajons, "Enforcing Annulled Arbitral Awards – A Comparative View", 7 *Croat Arbit Yearb* 55 (2000); Giarding, "The International Recognition and Enforcement of Arbitral Awards Nullified in the Country of Origin", in Briner, Fortier, Berger and Bredow (eds), *Law of International Business and Dispute Settlement in the 21st Century, Liber Amicorum Karl-Heinz Böckstiegel* (2000), 205; Rogers, "The Enforcement of Awards Nullified in the Country of Origin", *ICCA Congress Series no 9*, 548; Schwartz, "A Comment on Chromalloy: Hilmarton à l'americaine", 14(2) *J Int'l Arb* 125 (1997).

[168] See, *e.g.*, Racine, *L'arbitrage commercial international et l'ordre public* (LGDJ, 1999).

(a) Arbitrability

26-113 A national court may refuse recognition and enforcement if the subject matter cannot be settled by arbitration on its own territory. The concept of arbitrability has expanded considerably in recent decades as a consequence of a general policy favouring arbitration. Consequently, in countries with a wide concept of arbitrability, such as the US, the courts have repeatedly noted this policy.[169] Ultimately they exercise their discretion not to refuse enforcement of awards on ground of non-arbitrability under the law of the US, if the case has an international element.[170] There are very few cases in which enforcement of an award has been refused for lack of arbitrability of the underlying dispute.[171]

(b) Enforcement violates public policy

26-114 Public policy "is never argued at all but where other points fail."[172] This ground to resist enforcement, as all other grounds in Article V, must be construed narrowly. In fact, only violation of the enforcement state's public policy with respect to international relations (international public policy or *ordre public international*) is a valid defence.[173] This defence is only available "where the enforcement would violate the forum state's most basic notions of morality and

---

[169] See, *e.g.*, *SONATRACH (Algeria) v Distrigas Corp*, XX YBCA 795 (1995) (D Mass 1987).

[170] See, *e.g.*, *Parsons & Whittemore Overseas Co v Societe Generale de l'Industrie du Papier*, 508 F 2d 969 (2d Cir, 1974); as there no US national interest, the award was enforced.

[171] See, *e.g.*, Belgium, Cour de cassation, 28 June 1979, *Audi-NSU Auto Union AG v Adelin Petit & Cie (Belgium)*, V YBCA 257 (1980). The case was not arbitrable under Belgian law as at the time of the case there was an exclusive jurisdiction of Belgian courts in respect of unilateral termination of concessions for exclusive distributorships for an indefinite time. US, *BV Bureau Wijsmuller v United States of America*, III YBCA 290 (1978) (SDNY, 1976), a case related to the US Public Vessels Act which rendered several disputes non-arbitrable. Italy, Corte di cassazione, 12 May 1977, *Sherk Enterprises AG v Société des Grandes Marques*, IV YBCA 286 (1979) where trade marks disputes were deemed non arbitrable and the award was refused enforcement.

[172] *Richardson v Melish* (1824) 2 Bing 229, 252, *per* Borrough J.

[173] Distinctions between domestic and international public policy have been recorded, *e.g.*, in Bundesgerichtshof, 18 January 1990, XVII *YBCA* 503 (1992), where the court held that New York Convention Article V(2)(b) requires violation of international public policy; and *General Electric Co (US) v Renusagar Power Co (India)*, (1990) XV YBCA 465 (High Court Bombay, 21 October 1988). References to international public policy are made in all laws which have been influenced by the French NCPC Articles 1498 and 1502. Followers of this model include Portugal, Algeria, and Lebanon. See also, *e.g.*, Tunisia, Arbitration Code 1993 Articles 78(2)(II) and 81(II); 1992 Romania, Law on Settlement of Private International Law Disputes Articles 168(2) and 174; US, FAA sections 201 (incorporation of New York Convention) and 301 (incorporation of the Panama Convention) and *Sherk v Alberto Curver*, 417 US 506 (1974) which distinguishes between domestic and international public policy.

justice."[174] The public policy exception set out in Article V(2)(b) is an acknowledgment "of the right of the State and its courts to exercise ultimate control over the arbitral process."[175]

26-115 It is difficult, if not impossible, to define the concept of public policy. In 1853 the House of Lords identified the public policy notion as "that principle of law which holds that no subject can lawfully do that which has a tendency to be injurious to the public, or against the public good."[176] In the context of enforcement of foreign awards it has been just as difficult to define public policy. The Court of Appeal in *DST v Rakoil* observed that

> Considerations of public policy can never be exhaustively defined, but they should be approached with extreme caution. ... It has to be shown that there is some element of illegality or that the enforcement of the award would be clearly injurious to the public good or, possibly, that enforcement would be wholly offensive to the ordinary reasonable and fully informed member of the public on whose behalf the powers of the state are exercised.[177]

26-116 In a case in India where a party sought enforcement of an ICC award the Supreme Court observed that the concept of public policy was incapable of precise definition. It did confirm that

> Public policy connotes some matter which concerns the public good and the public interest. The concept of what is for the public good or in the public interest or what is injurious or harmful to the public good or public interest has varied from time to time.[178]

26-117 In 2000 and 2002 the International Law Association Committee on International Commercial Arbitration published a report and a resolution on

---

[174] See, *e.g.*, *Parsons and Whittemore Overseas Co, Inc v Société générale de l'industrie du papier (RAKTA)*, 508 F 2d 969, 974 (2d Cir, 1974). Hwang and Chan, "Enforcement and Setting Aside of International Arbitral Awards – The perspective of Common Law Countries", *ICCA Congress series no 10*, 145, 156.

[175] See ILA Committee on International Commercial Arbitration, *Public Policy as a Bar to the Enforcement of International Arbitral Awards*, London Conference Report (2000), 2. See also Mistelis, "Keeping the Unruly Horse in Control or Public Policy as a Bar to the Enforcement of Foreign Arbitral Awards", 2(4) *International Law FORUM du droit international* 248 (2000). The final Report of the ILA Committee was presented at the 2002 New Delhi conference and published in the 2002 Proceedings and at <www.ila-hq.org>.

[176] See *Egerton v Brownlow* (1853) 4 HLC 1.

[177] See *Deutsche Schachtbau-und Tiefbohrgesellscaft mbH v Ras Al Khaimah National Oil Company* [1987] 2 Lloyd's Rep 246, 254.

[178] See *Renusagar Power Co Ltd v General Electric Co,* (1995) XX YBCA 681, para 24.

public policy as a bar to the enforcement of foreign arbitration awards.[179] The report offers a guidance for the classification of public policy grounds as procedural or substantive. Accordingly, possible procedural public policy grounds include[180] fraud in the composition of the tribunal; breach of natural justice; lack of impartiality; lack of reasons in the award; manifest disregard of the law; manifest disregard of the facts; annulment at place of arbitration. The report further lists as substantive public policy grounds[181] mandatory rules / *lois de police*; fundamental principles of law; actions contrary to good morals; and national interests / foreign relations. This classification although it has merit may not be universally accepted as it emerges from case law in a limited number of countries. Further, public policy has by its very nature, a dynamic character, so that any classification may crystallise public policy only at a certain period of time.

26-118 Widely accepted examples of violations of international public policy include biased arbitrators, lack of reasons in the award, serious irregularities in the arbitration procedure, allegations of illegality,[182] corruption or fraud,[183] the award of punitive damages[184] and the breach of competition law.[185] It is generally rare that an award is successfully refused enforcement in a state because of violation of its international public policy.

26-119 One of the more intriguing cases to arise under the public policy defence in England is the case of *Soleimany v Soleimany*. An agreement was entered into

---

[179] ILA Committee on International Commercial Arbitration, *Public Policy as a Bar to the Enforcement of International Arbitral Awards*, London Conference Report (2000). The final Report of the ILA Committee was presented at the 2002 New Delhi conference and published in the 2002 Proceedings and at <www.ila-hq.org>.

[180] See *ibid*, ILA London Conference Report (2000), 24-30.

[181] *Ibid*, 17-24.

[182] See, *e.g.*, *Soleimany v Soleimany* [1998] 3 WLR 811, [1999] QB 785 (CA); Lalive, "Transnational (or Truly International) Public Policy and International Arbitration", *ICCA Congress series no 3*, 258-318, para 84.

[183] See, *e.g.*, *Westacre Investments Inc v Jugoimport-SPDR Holding Co Ltd And Others* [1999] 2 Lloyd's Rep 65 (CA), [2000] QB 288 CA; Cour d'appel, Paris 30 September 1993, *European Gas Turbines SA v Westman International Ltd,* Rev Arb 359 (1994), XX *YBCA* 198 (1995).

[184] See, *e.g.*, Japan, Supreme Court, 11 July 1997, 5(o) *Heisei* 1762, 51 *Minshu* 2573, 1624 *Hanrei Jiho* 90, 958 *Hanrei Times* 93.

[185] See Hoge Raad, 21 March 1997, *Eco Swiss China Time Ltd (Hong Kong) v Benetton International NV (Netherlands)*, Ned Jur 207 1059 (1998); European Court of Justice, C-126/97, 1 June 1999, *Eco Swiss Time Ltd v Benetton International NV*, [1999] 2 All ER (Comm) 44, [1999] ECR I-3055. It was held that ex Article 85 (now 81) EC Treaty is part of the public policy of the EC and hence of each member state.

between a father and son, of Iranian Jewish origin, concerning valuable Persian carpets exported from Iran. The son had gone over to Iran to free a consignment of carpets that had been seized by the Iranian customs authorities. The export of the carpets was in contravention of the Iranian revenue and export controls laws. This was not disputed. The carpets were sold by the father in England and a dispute arose about the division of the proceeds of sale. When efforts at mediation failed the parties agreed to go to arbitration before the Beth Din (Court of Chief Rabbi, in London). The tribunal applied Jewish law and found in favour of the son. The award acknowledged the illegality of smuggling the carpets out of Iran but this was held not to undermine the contractual rights of the parties. The award ordered a payment by the father to the son. When the father refused to voluntarily comply with the award, the son sought enforcement in the English courts. The father argued that the illegality of the arrangement rendered the award unenforceable in England as it was contrary to public policy.

26-120 Although this case does not stem from a traditional international commercial arbitration it is illustrative of the approach taken by the English courts when questions of illegality are raised. It is the first ever case which refused enforcement of an award because of public policy considerations. The facts of the case highlight the illegality issue. The Court of Appeal confirmed that the English courts exercise control over enforcement proceedings of arbitration awards. It held

> where public policy is involved, the interposition of an arbitration award does not isolate the successful party's claim from the illegality which gave rise to it.[186]

26-121 The court ultimately held that the agreement was illegal and as such it was contrary to public policy to enforce such an English award. The court also concluded that it would also not enforce "a contract governed by the law of a foreign and friendly state, or which requires performance in such a country, if performance is illegal by the law of that country."[187] Smuggling is not an activity which the English courts would uphold even in a case where the governing law took a more relaxed view of the illegality.

26-122 This case was, in effect, a domestic matter as both father and son were resident in England where the contract was made, and English law was the putative applicable law but for their choice of the rabbinic courts to decide the issue. It is not clear if the outcome would have been different if the Court of

---

[186] *Soleimany v Soleimany* [1998] 3 WLR 811, [1999] QB 785 (CA), [1999] 3 All ER 847, 859.
[187] *Ibid*, 861.

Appeal had been deliberating on the enforcement of an award made outside England and where at least one of the parties was not resident nor carried on its business in England.

26-123 In *Westacre Investments Inc*[188] a foreign award was at issue. The parties had entered into an agreement, governed by Swiss law, for the sale of military equipment to Kuwait. The respondent repudiated the agreement and Westacre instituted an ICC arbitration in Switzerland. The respondent submitted that the contract was void as it involved Westacre having to bribe various Kuwaiti officials. The arbitrators rejected these allegations and made an award in favour of Westacre. After the Swiss Federal Court refused to set aside the award Westacre sought enforcement of the award against the respondent in England. The enforcement was challenged by the respondent on the grounds that the contract was essentially one for the purchase of personal influence and was therefore contrary to public policy in England. Alternatively, they sought to reopen the factual basis of the case alleging it had been obtained by perjury as the underlying agreement was in fact only used as a means to pay bribes through Westacre to a third party. These submissions were rejected by the Judge as grounds for challenging the enforcement of the award and the appellants took their claim to the Court of Appeal.

26-124 Waller LJ summarised the decision in the earlier case of *Lemenda*[189] in four main categories namely

> (1) there are some rules of public policy which if infringed will lead to non-enforcement by the English Court whatever their proper law and wherever their place of performance, but others are based on considerations which are purely domestic;
> (2) contracts for the purchase of influence are not of the former category; thus
> (3) contracts for the purchase of personal influence, if to be performed in England, would not be enforced as contrary to English domestic public policy; and
> (4) where such a contract is to be performed abroad, it is only if performance would be contrary to the domestic public policy of that country also, that the English court would not enforce it.[190]

---

188 See *Westacre Investments Inc v Jugoimport-SDPR Holding Co Ltd and Others* [1999] 3 All ER 864.

189 See *Lemenda Trading Co Ltd v African Middle East Petroleum Co Ltd* [1988] 1 All ER 513 (QBD).

190 See *Westacre Investments Inc v Jugoimport-SDPR Holding Co Ltd and Others* [1999] 3 All ER 864, 876.

26-125 The Court of Appeal held that the award should be enforced. Although the underlying contract which involved the purchase of personal influence would have been contrary to the public policy of Kuwait, its enforcement was not contrary to the public policy of Switzerland. The parties had chosen Swiss law as the governing law and the arbitration was also held in Switzerland. There were, therefore, no international public policy objections that could be raised in England to prevent the enforcement of the award. The arbitrators had dealt with the alleged illegality and it was not now for the English courts to look behind the reasons for such a decision unless fresh and compelling evidence was available.

26-126 The international trend emerging from courts throughout the world is to take a robust view of the application of the New York Convention.[191] It has been largely applied to ensure that the foreign award is enforced and this seems to be consistent. Only in very limited circumstances will an award be refused enforcement. In Hilmarton, for example, it was held that the court was not adjudicating the underlying legality of the contract but merely had to decide whether the award was enforceable in England. The court did not think it was relevant that English law may have reached a different outcome in the arbitration award, noting

> the reason for the result is that Swiss law is different from English law, and the parties chose Swiss law and Swiss arbitration. If anything, this consideration dictates (as a matter of policy of the upholding of international arbitration awards) that the award should be enforced.

adding that

> it would of course be quite wrong for this court to entertain any attempt to go behind this explicit and vital finding of fact.[192]

26-127 The Supreme Court of Korea also gave a narrow interpretation to the public policy principle in *Adviso NV (Netherlands Antilles) v Korea Overseas Construction Corp.*[193] The ICC award rendered in Zurich was granted in favour of Adviso under a know-how licence concerning a sewage treatment plant.[194] Adviso then sought enforcement of the award which the Korean Court of Appeal granted. The decision was appealed and the Supreme Court confirmed the earlier decision. The court accepted that Article V(2) gave the competent court power to

---

[191] See, *e.g.*, *Omnium de Traitement et de Valorisation SA v Hilmarton Ltd*, [1999] 2 All ER (Comm) 146.
[192] *Ibid*, 148 and 149.
[193] XXI YBCA 612 (1996).
[194] For the full decision see final award in ICC case no 6363 (1991), XVII *YBCA* 186 (1992).

refuse enforcement of a foreign award if the award would be contrary to the public policy of that country. The court stated

> The basic tenet of this provision is to protect the fundamental moral beliefs and social order of the country where recognition and enforcement is sought from being harmed...[195]

26-128 The Supreme Court felt, however, that regard should be given to international public order as well as domestic concerns. The exception in Article V(2) must therefore be interpreted narrowly. The mere fact that the particular foreign legal rules applied in an arbitration award violated mandatory provisions of Korean law did not of itself constitute a valid reason to refuse enforcement.

> Only when the concrete outcome of recognising such an award is contrary to the good morality and other social order of Korea, will its recognition and enforcement be refused.[196]

26-129 In a Swiss decision the court acknowledged that the Swiss public policy defence had a more restricted application when foreign arbitral awards were being considered. It noted

> From a formal point of view, we find that a procedural defect in the course of the foreign arbitration does not lead necessarily to refusing enforcement even if the same defect would have resulted in the annulment of a Swiss award (with the obvious exception of the violation of fundamental principles of our legal system, which would contrast in an unbearable manner with our feeling of justice)...[197]

26-130 Violation of regional public policy was found in the case of *Eco Swiss China Time Ltd v Benetton International NV.*[198] The Dutch Court of Appeal decided that Article 81 EC Treaty was a provision of public policy within the meaning of Article 1065(e) of The Netherlands CCP. The ECJ in its decision confirmed that Article 81 "constitutes a fundamental provision which is essential to the accomplishment of the tasks entrusted to the Community"[199] and for the proper functioning of the internal market. The ECJ concluded that

---

195 XXI YBCA 612 (1996) 615, para 9.

196 *Ibid.*

197 See Camera di Esecuzione e Fallimenti Canton Tessin, 19 June 1990, *K S AG v CC SA*, XX YBCA 762 (1995).

198 ECJ, 1 June 1999, C-126/97, [1999] 2 All ER (Comm) 44, [1999] ECR I-3055.

199 *Ibid*, [1999] ECR I-3055, para 36.

> the provisions of Article 81 EC may be regarded as a matter of public policy within the meaning of the New York Convention.[200]

26-131 The Hong Kong Special administrative region (SAR) Court enforced a mainland China arbitration award. A CIETAC tribunal had made an award in favour of Sunlink. An *ex parte* order was made by the Court granting leave to the claimant to enforce the award. Judge Burrell in the High Court of Hong Kong SAR did not find that there were any special grounds into which the case fell and held that the award should be enforced. In that case he referred to the recent decision in *Hebei*[201] case. The Hong Kong Court of Final Appeal confirmed that there must be compelling reasons before an award can be set aside in accordance with the public policy provisions of the New York Convention. The court said

> that the reasons must be so extreme that the award falls to be cursed by bell, book and candle. But the reasons must go beyond the minimum which would satisfy setting aside a domestic judgement or award.[202]

26-132 All these cases illustrate how the courts make a distinction between the rules they may have applied in a domestic situation and those taken into account when enforcing a foreign award. A different standard being imposed on foreign as opposed to domestic awards. This distinction is expressed in the New French Code of Civil Procedure where it permits an international arbitration award to be set aside "if the recognition or execution is contrary to international public policy (*ordre public international*)."[203]

26-133 In an unreported decision of 30 September 1999 the *Oberlandesgericht* Bremen had to consider whether to enforce an arbitration award issued by the Istanbul Chamber of Commerce.[204] The dispute arose between two shareholders of the same company under a shareholders agreement. The respondent had tried to obtain a declaration of inadmissibility from the courts in Turkey. The respondent had also applied to have the award set aside on the grounds that the case had been decided before the court had ruled on the admissibility of arbitration. This application succeeded and a further arbitration was held at the Istanbul Chamber of Commerce which again found in favour of the applicant. The applicant sought recognition and a declaration of enforceability of this award

[200] *Ibid*, para 39.

[201] See *Hebei Import & Export Corp v Polytek Engineering Co. Ltd* [1999] 1 HKLRD 552.

[202] *Ibid.*

[203] France, Decree Law no 81-500 of 12 May 1981 Article 1502(5).

[204] Oberlandesgericht Bremen, 2 Sch 4/99, 30 September 1999, unreported, see Kröll, 4(4) *Int ALR* N26-27 (2001).

in Germany under section 1061(1) Code of Civil Procedure in accordance with the New York Convention. The respondent challenged this request on a number of grounds including public policy.

26-134 The court rejected the argument that the award was contrary to public policy because the respondent had not been heard. The fact that the tribunal had not granted some of the respondent's motions to take evidence not produced in the first arbitration did not of itself constitute a breach of public policy. The court felt it was clear from the award that the panel had considered the motions to produce evidence. The refusal to grant the motions would only amount to

> an infringement of the *ordre public* if it is shown that the evidence could have caused the case to be decided differently.

26-135 The court did not find a violation of the international *ordre public* even though the award did not expressly state why the tribunal had judged the respondent defences against the claim to be insufficient. The court acknowledged that it would be contrary to the principles of German internal *ordre public* for a tribunal to merely state that it had considered all the facts without giving any detailed reasoning. The court distinguished this from the international *ordre public* which would only be violated if the foreign decision was contrary to the German procedural law to such an extent that the result could not be fair or constitutional

> because it contains substantial errors touching upon the very foundation of public and economic life.[205]

26-136 This very much echoes the US District Court's decision of 25 June 1999 where it concluded that enforcement of an arbitration award could only be found contrary to public policy if "it would violate our most basic notions of morality and justice."[206] Only in very extreme cases will the foreign award be set-aside on public policy considerations.

26-137 The *Cour Superieure de Justice* of Luxembourg had to consider a case involving allegations of fraudulent inducement. At the enforcement stage the public policy principle was raised as a defence by the loosing parties.[207] The dispute involved an investment in a plot in Marbella which was subject to receiving the appropriate building certificates. Payment under the contract was

---

[205] *Ibid.*

[206] See *Seven Seas Shipping (UK) Ltd v Tondo Limitada*, XXV YBCA 987 (2000) 989.

[207] See *Kersa Holding Company Luxembourg v Infancourtage and Famajuk Invesment and Isny*, XXI YBCA 617 (1996) 625, para 22.

by way of instalments. Financing for the project was not secured and the three respondent companies did not pay the contract price. Arbitration was commenced by Kersa. The arbitrators sitting in Brussels found against Kersa and the respondents sought enforcement of the award in Luxembourg which was granted by the Court of First Instance. Kersa appealed the decision relying on Article V(2)b of the New York Convention, among other grounds. Kersa submitted that it would be

> undoubtedly contrary to international public policy to execute a contract obtained by fraudulent manoeuvres and swindling.

26-138 The Court confirmed that it could only determine whether the enforcement of the Belgian award was of such a nature as to affect the public policy of Luxembourg

> a principle which is generally called 'attenuated public policy.'[208]

26-139 Thus the reference is to that country's international public policy. The *Cour Superieure de Justice* of Luxembourg continued to define this concept as being

> all that is considered 'as essential to the moral, political or economic order' and which *per se* must necessarily exclude the enforcement of an award incompatible with the public policy of that State where it is being invoked.[209]

26-140 When the court is considering whether to enforce an arbitral award it must do so on the basis of the fundamental convictions of the applicable law of international relationships. The court accepted that a contract based on fraud would not be enforceable in Luxembourg but did not find any evidence in this case of fraudulent representations.

7. Analysis of Different Approaches

26-141 The scope and extent of the enforcement provision of the New York Convention have been felt all over the world. The interpretation given to the exceptions to enforcement tends to vary from country to country. Courts have not always adopted a consistent approach to the enforcement of foreign awards despite the fact that they apply the same rules as courts in other countries. This is especially true when the public policy principle set out in Article V(2) is raised.

---

[208] *Ibid.*

[209] *Ibid,* 625, para 23.

26-142 It is this ongoing quest for uniformity in the application of the New York Convention balanced against the national courts discretion to set aside an award on public policy grounds that makes this a topical and pervasive issue. It highlights the tension between the international obligations to enforce an arbitration award and the interest of national courts to maintain certain standards, in particular not lending their support to fraudulent or criminal agreements.

26-143 The majority of the cases acknowledge that an award will only be set aside on overriding international public policy concerns. There is still, however, a certain latitude given to national courts to determine on a case by case basis the circumstances when an award cannot be enforced because of international public policy concerns. Furthermore, there is little guidance on the enforceability of interim awards even though it is anticipated that

> as international arbitration expands into new and complex areas such as intellectual property and environmental disputes, the need for interim measures of relief will accelerate.[210]

26-144 While Article V(1) New York Convention places significant emphasis on party autonomy and the ability to be able to settle their disputes as they choose, the public policy restriction in Article V(2) does place a significant limitation on that autonomy. Public policy is a key issue in international arbitration as

> each state has its own rules, which may be different from those of other States. At the same time public policy shifts with time, reflecting the changing values of society.[211]

26-145 The finality of awards is of paramount importance in international commercial arbitration. There is a recognised international policy in favour of enforcing awards.[212] This ensures a certain degree of certainty and predictability in the international arbitration process essential to international trade. The reluctance to refuse to enforce an award is especially obvious where the illegality or other grounds for challenging an award has already been considered by the tribunal in its award. It is also clear that many national courts apply a concept of international public policy which is usually more restrictive than its domestic public policy. Indeed national courts have acknowledged that although there may

---

[210] Wagoner, "Interim Relief in International Arbitration: Enforcement is a Substantial Problem", 51-Oct *Disp Resol J* 68 (1996) 72.

[211] Yu, "The Impact of National Law Elements on International Commercial Arbitration", 4(1) *Int ALR* 17 (2001) 19.

[212] See, *e.g.*, Lamm and Hellbeck, "The Enforcement of Foreign Arbitral Awards Under the New York Convention: Recent Developments", 5 *Int ALR* 137 (2002) 138.

be some inconsistency in the domestic rules or procedures applied in arbitration that in itself is not enough to refuse enforcement under international public policy.

26-146 Furthermore, in cases of criminal or illegal activities, consideration must be given to whose international public policy is relevant. Is it just the law of the country where enforcement is being sought or does it also include the law of the place of performance? It appears due regard will be given to the international public policy of the place where the award is being enforced,[213] but also to that of the governing law. Less emphasis seems to be placed on the law of the place of performance.[214]

26-147 The arguments in favour of upholding foreign awards are self apparent ensuring as they do a high degree of certainty in international trade. However, it would clearly be wrong if by carefully drafting an arbitration clause and choosing its governing law parties could by-pass fundamental and mandatory laws of an otherwise relevant foreign country. It is clear from a review of even a small number of cases that there is an uneasy tension between international public policy and considerations of domestic public policy. As has been aptly pointed out

> to expect court enforcement of arbitration agreements and awards without any encroachments of national legal particularities would be a logical impossibility, like both having and eating the proverbial cake.[215]

---

[213] See *Soleimany v Soleimany,* [1998] 3 WLR 811, [1999] QB 785 (CA).

[214] See *Westacre Investments Inc v Jugoimport-SPDR Holding Co Ltd and Others,* [1999] 2 Lloyd's Rep 65 (CA), [2000] QB 288 CA; *Omnium de Traitement et de Valorisation SA v Hilmarton Ltd,* [1999] 2 All ER (Comm) 146.

[215] Park, "Judicial Controls in the Arbitral Process", 5 *Arb Int* 230 (1989) 251.

Chapter 27

ARBITRATION WITH GOVERNMENT AND STATE OWNED ENTITIES

27-1 States and state owned entities are major participants in national and international business transactions. This is equally true for socialist and former socialist countries, such as China or Russia, and market economies, such as the European Union. Often, the state is the largest consumer in the market.[1]

27-2 States enter into contracts for the purchase or the supply of goods or services, just as any other private entity would do. The state may either contract directly through a ministry or an agency of the state. Or it may use special purpose companies and other legal or formal entities which it controls directly or indirectly. These entities may be owned by the state, *i.e.*, nominally any profit belongs to the state, which in turn is liable for its losses; alternatively, whilst the entity may be legally independent of the state, the government may control the

[1] Reich, *International Public Procurement Law* (Kluwer 1999), 1; Sornarajah, *The Settlement of Foreign Investment Disputes*, 86.

appointment of senior officers, its commercial policy, its finances and actual business activity.[2]

27-3 Frequently, contracts entered into by states or state entities contain an arbitration clause, in particular where they involve private parties from a different country. The state is not willing to submit to a foreign court, and the foreign investor is not prepared to accept the jurisdiction of courts of the state party where it may not get a fair trial.[3]

27-4 Transactions involving states and state entities raise special questions relating to sovereign immunity. This chapter looks at specific questions relating to the involvement of states and state entities in arbitration: (1) Can a state party validly enter into an arbitration agreement? (2) Who becomes a party to the arbitration agreement when a state owned entity with a separate legal personality rather than the state is charged with the implementation of the contract? Is it the state or only the separate entity? And which property is amenable for enforcement? (3) To what extent does sovereignty entitle a state party to immunity from jurisdiction and enforcement? Finally, (4) are there any other grounds for resisting enforcement of an award?

1. Subjective Arbitrability: States and Arbitration Agreements

27-5 Private parties are generally free to decide whether they want their disputes to be decided by state courts or by arbitration tribunals. This is not always the case for states and state entities. It is not uncommon to find laws which restrict the capacity of states or state entities to enter into an arbitration agreement. In France, *e.g.*, Article 2060 Civil Code provides that disputes concerning public entities cannot be referred to arbitration, unless the public entity is specifically authorised to do so. While in France such restrictions do not extend to international arbitration[4] this is not the case for many other countries with similar restrictions.[5] In Saudi Arabia, Iran and Syria, *e.g.*, the state or the

2 For the forms of state ownership and involvement see Nedjar, "Tendances actuelles du droit international des immunités des Etats", 124 *Clunet* 59 (1997) 86.

3 Langkeit, *Staatenimmunität und Schiedsgerichtsbarkeit*, 25 *et seq.*

4 See Cour de cassation, 2 May 1966, *Trésor Public v Galakis*, 93 Clunet 648 (1966); Cour d appel Paris, 10 April 1957, *Myrtoon Steam Ship v Agent judiciaire du Trésor*, 85 Clunet 1002 (1958); but see the restrictive interpretation of Article 809 Lebanese CCP in Lebanese Conseil d'Etat, 17 July 2001, *Etat Libanais v Société FTML* and *Etat Libanais v Libancell*, Rev Arb 855 (2001): permission to submit to arbitration in international commercial contracts did exclude BOT contracts and concessions.

5 See Reymond, "Souveraineté de l'Etat et participation à l'arbitrage", *Rev Arb* 517 (1985) 527.

state entity must obtain approval from the relevant authorities before it can enter into an arbitration agreement.[6]

27-6 These provisions are frequently treated under the heading of "capacity" of the state to enter into an arbitration agreement.[7] Since the issue of capacity of a party is usually governed by the law applicable to it, it follows that the law of the state party determines its capacity. However, properly classified, it is less an issue of capacity and more one of subjective arbitrability for which different conflict of laws considerations are applicable.[8]

27-7 Restrictions on the capacity of a party to enter into arbitration agreements aim to protect the party itself. By contrast, the restrictions on the state's entitlement to enter into arbitration agreements are based on policy considerations. To a certain extent most of these restrictions are influenced by the old concept that it is against sovereign dignity to submit to any type of dispute resolution system not controlled by the state itself. These restrictions are the expression of a deep rooted distrust of arbitration in countries which historically considered arbitration to be a dispute settlement favouring parties from industrialised countries.[9]

27-8 Lack of subjective arbitrability to enter into an arbitration agreement, makes the agreement void. Therefore private parties should verify that no such restrictions exist when they enter into an arbitration agreement with a state party. It is generally recommended to include an express reference in the arbitration agreement that the state party has complied with all necessary procedures.[10]

27-9 This is not necessary in cases falling within the ambit of the European Convention. The Convention confirms the right of legal persons of public law to

---

6 See for Saudi Arabia: Redfern and Hunter, *International Commercial Arbitration*, para 3-18; Iran: Jafarian and Rezaeian, "The New Law on International Commercial Arbitration in Iran", 15(3) *J Int'l Arb* 31 (1998); Gharavi, "The 1997 Iranian International Commercial Arbitration Law: The UNCITRAL Model Law à L'Iranienne", 15 *Arb Int* 85 (1999); Syria: Sarkis, "L'autorisation d'arbitrage, obstacle au recours à l'arbitrage des enterprises du secteur public en Syrie", *Rev Arb* 97 (1998).

7 Redfern and Hunter, *International Commercial Arbitration*, para 3-20.

8 Fouchard Gaillard Goldman *on International Commercial Arbitration*, para 539; Hanotiau, "The Law Applicable to Arbitrability", *ICCA Congress series no 9*, 146, 147 *et seq.*

9 Sornarajah, *The Settlement of Foreign Investment Disputes*, 110; see also Paulsson, "Third World Participation in International Investment Arbitration", 3 *ICSID Rev-FILJ* 1 (1987) 19, who considers that such a view was justified in the early 1950s.

10 Redfern and Hunter, *International Commercial Arbitration*, para 3-18.

enter into arbitration agreements subject to any reservations declared by a signatory state.[11]

27-10 Only Belgium has used this reservation and has limited the ability to enter into arbitration agreements to the state itself. In all cases falling under the European Convention Article II supersedes all national restrictions on the rights of states or state entities to enter into arbitration agreements.[12]

27-11 A different provision, but with the same effect, can also be found in the Swiss PIL. Since Swiss law cannot directly regulate the rights of foreign public entities to enter into an arbitration agreement, Article 177(2) only excludes the possibility of relying on restrictions contained in the national law of the state party. It provides

> If a party to the arbitration agreement is a state or an enterprise or organization controlled by it, it cannot rely on its own law in order to contest its capacity to be a party to an arbitration or the arbitrability of a dispute covered by the arbitration agreement.

27-12 By contrast, the Model Law and most other national arbitration laws do not contain such a provision.[13] Therefore it is not surprising that arbitration tribunals and courts have had to address this issue on several occasions. In general, they have concluded that in an international context state parties cannot rely on their own law to invalidate an arbitration agreement they entered into freely.[14] The arguments used to achieve this result, however, differ.

27-13 This general trend and a summary of the different approaches can be found in the *Benteler* award of 1983. In this case a dispute arose out of a contract between Belgian and German companies for the restructuring of a Belgian company. Benteler initiated arbitration proceedings against the Belgian state relying on an elaborate arbitration clause contained in the contract. Belgium

---

[11] Article II.

[12] Hascher, "European Convention", XX *YBCA* 1006 (1995) 1016.

[13] However, a number of countries adopting the Model Law such as Egypt, Bulgaria and Tunisia, included a provision allowing state or public entities to enter into arbitration agreements; see Sanders, "Unity and Diversity in the Adoption of the Model Law", 11 *Arb Int* 1 (1995) 12.

[14] See, *e.g.*, award of April 1982 in *ad hoc* arbitration, *Company Z and others v State Organization ABC* , VIII YBCA 94 (1983) 109; for a summary of case law see Fouchard Gaillard Goldman *on International Commercial Arbitration*, paras 542 *et seq.* Often it is the State party who attempts to rely on the lack of subjective arbitrability. But private parties have also tried to avoid the effects of the arbitration agreement by invoking similar provisions; see, *e.g.*, the decision of the Corte di cassazione, 9 May 1996, *Société Arabe des Engrais Phosphates et Azotes - SAEPA v Gemanco srl*, XXII YBCA 737 (1997).

contested the jurisdiction of the arbitrators relying on the since abandoned Article 1676(2) Judicial Code, according to which it could not validly submit to arbitration except by virtue of a special empowerment in a treaty. On the basis of Article II(2) European Convention, the tribunal concluded that Belgium could not rely on restrictions in its national law to preclude a valid submission to arbitration. It considered this rule to be a general principle of international arbitration which was achieved in practice in various ways including:

- Limiting the prohibition against the state agreeing to submit to arbitration to national (domestic) cases only; [15]
- Submitting the capacity of the state to enter into an arbitration agreement to the law of the contract and not to the law of the state party;[16] and
- Holding that any state which entered into an arbitration agreement would violate international public policy if it later invoked its internal law to avoid the arbitration agreement;[17] and
- Allowing an arbitrator to disregard that type of restriction as the state would be acting against its earlier behaviour, *contra factum proprium*.[18]

27-14 Three of these approaches stem from the presumption that in general the law of the state party is relevant but its effects have to be remedied. According to the fourth the issue is regulated by a different law, the law of the contract.

27-15 A fifth approach, based on the classification of the problem as one of subjective arbitrability, is now probably already the prevailing view. According to this view, the issue of subjective arbitrability is governed by a substantive rule of international arbitration and not by the law of the state party. This rule requires state parties to honour the arbitration agreement precluding them from relying on national restrictions to avoid the effects of arbitration agreements it

---

[15] See Cour d'appel Paris, 10 April 1957, *Myrtoon Steam Ship v Agent Judiciaire du Trésor*, 85 Clunet 1002 (1958) with note Goldman; Cour d'appel Paris, 24 February 1994, *Ministry of Public Works (Tunisia) v Société Bec Frères (France)*, XXII YBCA 682 (1997) para 5-10, French original in Rev Arb 275 (1995) with note Gaudemet, 285.

[16] See Cour de cassation, 14 April 1964, *ONIC v Capitaine du SS San Carlo*, 92 Clunet 646 (1965).

[17] Cour d'appel Paris, 17 December 1991, *Gatoil v National Iranian Oil Co*, Rev Arb 281 (1993), English translation in 7(7) *Mealey's IAR* B1 (1991).

[18] *Benteler v Belgium*, Rev Arb 339 (1989) 345 *et seq*; see also ICC case no 6474, XXIV *YBCA* 279 (2000) 282 *et seq*, which dealt with an unusual variation of the subjective arbitrability defence: the state party in that case did not try to rely on its internal law, but on the fact that the territory it represented was not internationally recognised. Consequently, it claimed that it would go against transnational public policy if it was allowed to conclude valid arbitration agreements or participate in arbitration proceedings.

has concluded.[19] The rule is derived from international arbitration practice[20] and the provisions in the various laws and conventions. In particular, while the European Convention expressly provides for the subjective arbitrability of state parties, the ICSID Convention is based on the premise that a state party that has agreed to arbitrate is bound by its promise.

2. Existence and Interpretation of the Arbitration Agreement

27-16 The involvement of a state party may raise problems in relation to the existence and interpretation of arbitration agreements. States often use a number of separate entities for their activities; they may be subdivisions of the state's organisational structure or have separate legal personality. In the former case the question can arise whether the person who agreed on arbitration had the power to bind the state. If the state entity has its own legal personality it may be difficult to determine whether an arbitration agreement also binds the state which has not signed the agreement.

27-17 In practice contracts entered into by state entities often require government approval. A question which frequently arises is whether a contract containing an arbitration clause will bind the state party though it has not signed it? By corollary, where the state has signed the arbitration clause the question is whether the entity implementing the contract is bound by the arbitration agreement?

2.1. Power of the Acting Person to Bind the State

27-18 The individual who signed the arbitration agreement on behalf of the state may not be entitled to do so under the law of that state. This risk exists, in particular, if agreements are not entered into by the head of the state or the government, but by persons of a lower rank who head a governmental subdivision charged with implementation of a contract. It has been suggested that in such a case the party is acting without authority. Hence no valid arbitration

---

19 Fouchard Gaillard Goldman *on International Commercial Arbitration*, 541 *et seq*; Hanotiau, "The Law Applicable to Arbitrability", *ICCA Congress series no 9*, 146 149 *et seq*; see also Paulsson, "May a State Invoke its Internal Law to Repudiate Consent to International Commercial Arbitration?", 2 *Arb Int* 90 (1986).

20 For criticism of the practice and the rule see Sornarajah, *The Settlement of Foreign Investment Disputes*, 104 *et seq*.

agreement exists which could be considered as an express waiver of immunity.[21] The preferred view, however, is to regard the arbitration agreement as valid as long as the official who entered into the arbitration agreement had apparent authority to do so.[22]

2.2. Binding Effect of an Arbitration Agreement Signed by a State Entity on the State

27-19 Often parties contracting with a state entity will seek to include the state itself in the arbitration proceedings although the state has not signed the arbitration agreement. Usually this will be because the state entity has insufficient funds to meet the claim, those funds may not be as easily accessible as the assets of the state, or a set-off option may only exist in relation to the state itself.[23] There may also be a coercive element of causing embarrassment by involving a government or a state as a party.

27-20 The principal argument for involving the state at the outset is that the state entity did not have a separate legal personality but was merely a subdivision of the state administration. Thus, under well established principles of state responsibility, the entity may have no power to bind the state in any way. By making the state, and not the state entity, a party to the arbitration agreement this possibility is eliminated. Frequently, however, the state entity has its own legal personality so that it and not the state becomes party to the arbitration agreement. In those cases a state which has not signed the arbitration agreement can only be made a party if it can be shown that the state nevertheless submitted to arbitration or cannot rely on the separate legal personality of its state owned entity.

27-21 This situation is comparable to that arising in the context of groups of companies. There is a strong argument to extend the rules governing the group of companies issue to arbitration agreements entered into by state entities.[24] One could also argue that even stricter rules should be applicable. Companies as private parties are subject to the jurisdiction of the courts. For them the effect of entering into an arbitration agreement is limited to selecting a forum which decides the case. By contrast states enjoy sovereign immunity and may not be

---

[21] Sornarajah, "Problems of Applying the Restrictive Theory of Sovereign Immunity", 31 *ICLQ* 661 (1982) 685.

[22] Hill, *International commercial disputes*, para 2-3-22.

[23] See US Supreme Court, *National City Bank* v *Banco para el Comercio Exterior de Cuba*, 462 US 611 (1983).

[24] Fouchard Gaillard Goldman *on International Commercial Arbitration*, para 509.

amenable to the jurisdiction of any court if they do not submit expressly to it. In this respect consent to arbitration has a much broader effect for states: it is not only the selection of a private forum but also a waiver of sovereign immunity.

27-22 Irrespective of whether a stricter approach should be taken, the mere fact that the state is the owner of the entity and exercises a certain control over it is not sufficient to justify an extension of the arbitration agreement. It follows from the separate legal personality of the entity that additional requirements must be fulfilled before the state can be considered to be bound by the arbitration agreement.[25] The rule must be to respect the legal separation between state and the state entity with a presumption that when a state has not signed an arbitration agreement, the entity which signed it should be regarded as the sole party to the arbitration. Prior or subsequent approval by state representatives are in general insufficient to make the state a party to an arbitration agreement.

27-23 Those principles underlie Article 7 Institute of International Law 1989 Resolution. This provides

> Agreement by a state enterprise to arbitrate does not in itself imply consent by the State to be a party to the arbitration.[26]

27-24 These rules can be derived from the decision of the Swiss and French courts in two famous cases dealing with state contracts. The Pyramids arbitration arose out the construction of a hotel complex near the Pyramids. In September 1974 SPP, a Hong Kong based developer, entered into a framework contract with Egypt and the state owned Egyptian Tourist Organisation (EGOTH). Under this agreement SPP and EGOTH formed a joint venture for the construction of the hotel, while Egypt would provide the necessary title to the land. The joint venture agreement concluded three months later between SPP and EGOTH provided for arbitration under the ICC rules and contained on its last page a statement "Approved, agreed and ratified by the Minister of Tourism", accompanied by the minister's signature and an official stamp. After the cancellation of the project SPP started arbitration proceedings against EGOTH and Egypt. Egypt objected to the jurisdiction of the tribunal, primarily on the ground that it had not agreed to the arbitration clause contained in the joint venture agreement. The arbitrators assumed jurisdiction and found that

---

[25] See, *e.g.*, Cour de cassation, 15 July 1999, *Dumez GTM v Etat irakien et autres*, Clunet 45 (2000) 46 with note Cosnard; and Cour d'appel Rouen, 20 June 1996, *Société Bec Frères v Office des céréales de Tunisie*, Rev Arb 263 (1997) with note Gaillard.

[26] Resolution on Arbitration between States, State Enterprises or State Entities, and Foreign Enterprises, adopted in Santiago de Compostela, 12 September 1989, XVI *YBCA* 236 (1991).

> by contractually undertaking a number of obligations under the December Agreement [joint venture agreement], the government became a party to it and engaged its responsibility with respect to the performance of the said obligations. ... By so doing, the Government necessarily extended its Agreement to the mechanism provided for the settlement of disputes.... We accept the principle that acceptance of an arbitration clause should be clear and unequivocal: However, in the December Agreement we see no element of ambiguity. The Government, in becoming a party to that agreement, could not have reasonably doubted that it would be bound by the arbitration clause contained in it.[27]

27-25 The tribunal rendered an award in favour of SPP ordering Egypt to pay a very substantial amount to SPP. Egypt applied to the French courts for annulment of the award. The Court of Appeal of Paris vacated the award[28] and upon appeal by SPP the Cour de cassation upheld that decision. The French courts decided that the terms "Approved, agreed and ratified" had to be interpreted in the light of the Egyptian legislation and the declarations by EGOTH and SPP, both of which foresaw an approval of EGOTH's obligations by the Minister for Tourism. The court held that the ratification did not constitute an agreement of the Ministry to become a party to the joint venture agreement. It was only the approval given by the minister in his capacity as EGOTH's supervisory authority and the minister's responsibility to approve all tourism related constructions.

27-26 The *Westland* case arose out of a joint venture between the English company, Westland Helicopters, and the Arab Organization for Industrialization (AOI), a supranational organization set up in 1975 by the Arab Republic of Egypt, the Kingdom of Saudi Arabia, the United Arab Emirates and Qatar to promote their defence industry. In the aftermath of the peace agreement between Egypt and Israel and the consequent intended dissolution of AOI by the three other states, disputes arose between the parties. Westland started arbitration against AOI and all four states on the basis of an arbitration clause contained in the shareholders agreement concluded between Westland and AOI for the setting up of a joint venture company. Egypt denied being bound by the arbitration agreement and the three other states did not participate at all in the arbitration.

27-27 The arbitration tribunal rendered an interim award on jurisdiction. It held that the legal personality accorded to AOI was not conclusive in itself on the question whether the states were bound by any obligations entered into by AOI,

---

[27] Award of 11 March 1983, IX *YBCA* 111 (1984) 115, para 46; 22 *ILM* 752 (1983).

[28] Cour d'appel Paris, *The Arab Republic of Egypt* v *Southern Pacific Properties Ltd and Southern Pacific Properties (Middle East) Ltd*, 23 ILM 1048 (1984).

including the arbitration agreement. In the tribunal's view the question had to be determined by examining the founding documents of AOI. These did not contain any rules for the exclusion of liability of the state. Furthermore, due to the supranational character of AOI, national rules providing for such an exclusion were not applicable. The tribunal decided that the states were bound by the arbitration agreement entered into by AOI

> [i]n the absence of any provision expressly or impliedly excluding the liability of the 4 States, this liability subsists since, as a general rule, those who engage in transactions of an economic nature are deemed liable for the obligations which flow therefrom. In default by the 4 States of formal exclusion of their liability, third parties which have contracted with AOI could legitimately count on their liability.[29]

27-28 Furthermore, the arbitrators invoked principles of equity which in their view justified an inclusion of the four states to avoid a denial of justice in the specific circumstances of the case. In this respect the tribunal held

> Equity, in common with the principles of international law, allows the corporate veil to be lifted, in order to protect third parties against an abuse which would be to their detriment[30]

27-29 Egypt brought an action for annulment in the Swiss courts. The Tribunal Fédéral annulled the award in relation to Egypt for lack of jurisdiction. The Tribunal Fédéral first rejected the basic assumption underlying the award that by accepting responsibility for the obligation contracted by AOI the states were also bound by the arbitration clause. The court held that

> [a]n arbitration clause cannot be opposed to a party which did not sign it unless this party is nevertheless bound by the signature of an entity or a third party empowered to act on behalf of the first party, on the basis of an act granting to that entity or third party the power to refer a dispute to arbitration.[31]

27-30 The court then went on to determine the independent legal personality of AOI and concluded

> AOI's autonomy rules out the possibility that its contracts with third parties, and more particularly the arbitration clause signed by it, may be considered as contracts concluded by a representative or an agency, *i.e.*, binding on the founding States.

---

29 ICC case no 3879 (1984), *Westland Helicopters Ltd v Arab Organization for Industrialization and others*, 23 ILM 1071 (1984) 1084.

30 *Ibid*, 1087. See also ICJ, 5 February 1970, *Re Barcelona Traction* (reference in the award).

31 Tribunal Fédéral, 19 July 1988, *Westland Helicopters (UK) v The Arab Republic of Egypt, The Arab Organization for Industrialization and The Arab British Helicopter Company*, XVI YBCA 174 (1991) 180.

The predominant roles played by these States in AOI and the fact that AOI's highest authority is a committee consisting of ministers cannot affect AOI's independence and legal personality, nor can it lead to the conclusion that AOI bound the founding States when dealing with third parties.[32]

27-31 Furthermore both the Geneva Court of Appeal and the Tribunal Fédéral also rejected the equity argument, *i.e.*, subjective fairness, reasoning that

> [t]he arbitrators erroneously resorted to equity in order to sustain their point of view. Equity cannot be applied in this case. There is no denial of justice since Westland is free to initiate court proceedings against Egypt in the Egyptian courts.[33]

27-32 The same rules apply if the problem arises at the enforcement stage. In general national courts have rejected applications by private parties to attach the property of a state owned entity with a separate legal personality when made in an effort to enforce an award against the state. Unless the separate entity has only been set up to avoid enforcement or the state has intervened in the daily course of business courts have respected the separate legal personality of state owned entities.[34]

27-33 This approach is illustrated in the US decision in *S & Davis International Inc v The Republic of Yemen.*[35] The case arose out of a contract to purchase wheat between the US claimant and the state owned General Corporation for Foreign Trade and Grains of Yemen. Upon instruction by the Yemen Ministry of Supply and Trade, General Corporation terminated the contract and was ordered to pay damages by a GAFTA arbitration tribunal. S & Davis International sought enforcement of the award in the US against the Republic of Yemen.

27-34 The court held that the ministerial intervention in the day to day business which had the effect of terminating the contract was sufficient to establish the principal-agent relationship; the Republic of Yemen could be made defendant of the action. In general, separate legal entities established by the state, such as

---

[32] *Ibid,* 181.

[33] Cour de Justice Geneva, 3 November 1987, XVI *YBCA* 174 (1991) 180. As the award was only annulled in relation to Egypt, the arbitration continued against the other three states. After a substantial award in favour of Westland was rendered, the state parties started annulment proceedings in the Swiss courts alleging lack of jurisdiction. The action was dismissed as, under Swiss law, any reliance on those grounds was precluded by the existence of an interim award on jurisdiction; see Tribunal Fédéral, 19 April 1994, 3 *ASA Bulletin* 404 (1994).

[34] Cour de cassation, 15 July 1999, *Dumez GTM v Etat irakien et autres*, 127 Clunet 45 (2000) 46 with note Cosnard; Cour d'appel Rouen, 20 June 1996, *Société Bec Frères v Office des céréales de Tunisie*, Rev Arb 263 (1997) with note Gaillard.

[35] 218 F 3d 1292, XXVI *YBCA* 978 (2001) 980 (11 Cir, 2000).

General Corporation, should be treated as separate and independent entities. However, the

> presumption of separate legal status may be overcome in two ways, (1) where a corporate entity is so extensively controlled by its owner that a relationship of principal and agent is created or (2) where recognition of the instrumentality as an entity separate from the state 'would work fraud or injustice.' [36] [References omitted]

3. SOVEREIGN IMMUNITY

27-35 The doctrine of sovereign immunity is a well established principle of international law, based on comity and the equality of states. Its rationale is to promote the functioning of all governments by protecting states from the burden of defending litigation abroad.[37] Over centuries foreign states were considered to enjoy absolute immunity from jurisdiction and measures of execution in courts other than their own. Actions against state parties could only be brought with their express consent which was also required for any measure of execution.

27-36 In the twentieth century the growing involvement of states in commercial activities led to a progressive erosion of the absolute immunity doctrine. Most countries now follow a restrictive immunity doctrine. This is reflected in international conventions such as the European Convention on State Immunity[38] and the Draft Articles on Jurisdictional Immunity, prepared by the International Law Commission[39], as well as in national codifications such as the US Foreign Sovereign Immunity Act or the English State Immunity Act.[40]

27-37 Some countries still adhere to the doctrine of absolute immunity.[41] However, reflecting the changes which have taken place the Swiss Federal

---

36 *Ibid*, 980 para 5.

37 Brownlie, *Principles of Public International Law* (5th ed, OUP 1998), 329; Shaw, *International Law* (4th ed, CUP 1997), 496; Daillier/Pellet, *Droit International Public* (6th ed, LGDJ 1999), para 289; Oparil, "Waiver of Sovereign Immunity in the United States and Great Britain by an Arbitration Agreement", 3(4) *J Int'l Arb* 61 (1986) 61; for the different bases see Langkeit, *Staatenimmunität und Schiedsgerichtsbarkeit*, 30.

38 Council of Europe, 16 May 1972, 11 *ILM* 470 (1972).

39 26 *ILM* 625 (1987); see also Lowe, "The International Law Commission's Draft Articles on the Jurisdictional Immunities of States and their Property: The Commercial Contract Exception", *Columbia J Transn'l L* 657 (1989).

40 For an overview see Fox, "States and the Undertaking to Arbitrate", 37 *ICLQ* 1 (1988) 11.

41 For a list of states and general developments see Brownlie, *Principles of Public International Law* (5th ed, OUP 1998), 331 *et seq*.

Supreme Court considered the theory of restrictive immunity to have the status of a trade usage.[42] It is based on the idea that once a state enters the market place and acts like a private party there is no more justification for allowing the state to avoid the economic consequences of its actions. This was pertinently described by Lord Mustill in the House of Lords in *Kuwait Airways v Iraqi Airways*

> where a sovereign chooses to doff his robes and descend into the market place he must take the rough with the smooth, and having condescended to engage in mundane commercial activities he must also condescend to submit himself to an adjudication in a foreign court on whether he has in the course of those activities undertaken obligations which he has failed to fulfil.[43]

27-38 Therefore a distinction is drawn between those acts of a private and commercial nature (*acta jure gestionis*) and state activities which are public (*acta jure imperii*). Only in relation to its sovereign activities may the state reasonably expect to be immune from legal proceedings in a foreign court while no immunity exists for activities of a purely commercial and private nature. Furthermore, under the doctrine of restrictive immunity the concept of waiver of immunity has been extended. It is no longer necessary that a state expressly waives its immunity after the dispute has arisen; waiver can be obtained in advance.[44] Despite a general acceptance of these basic principles, considerable differences exist as to the scope of these two exceptions from immunity in different national laws. This is particularly true for the issue of immunity from execution where the exceptions are generally much narrower.[45]

3.1. Immunity from Jurisdiction

27-39 The defence of immunity from jurisdiction has been raised in arbitration as well as in national courts acting in support of arbitration. Concerning the jurisdiction of the arbitration tribunal, the private nature of arbitration raises the question whether the doctrine of sovereign immunity applies at all. It is primarily directed against the exercise of a sovereign power of one state over another state.

---

[42] See Swiss Tribunal Fédéral, 19 June 1980, *Socialist People's Libyan Arab Republic Jamahiriya v Libyan American Oil Company (LIAMCO) (US)*, VI YBCA 151 (1981) 152.

[43] *Kuwait Airways Corporation v Iraqi Airways Co*, [1995] 1 WLR 1147, 1171, (HL).

[44] Brownlie, *Principles of Public International Law* (5th ed, OUP 1998), 343 *et seq*; Shaw, *International Law* (4th ed, CUP 1997), 516 *et seq.*

[45] Hill, *International Commercial Disputes*, para 2-3-13; critical to this distinction in the field of arbitration, Bernini and van den Berg, "The Enforcement of Arbitral Awards against a State: the Problem of Immunity from Execution", in Lew (ed), *Contemporary Problems*, 359, 363.

27-40 Irrespective of this issue, the existence of a valid arbitration agreement prevents successful reliance on sovereign immunity by the state. The arbitration agreement is generally considered to be at least an implied waiver of immunity in relation to the arbitration tribunal itself.[46] If the state agrees to arbitration it cannot at a later stage invoke its sovereign immunity to resist the jurisdiction of the tribunal and thereby defeat the agreement it entered into. Such behaviour would violate general principles of law and good faith which are expressed in the principle of estoppel. This is clear in the international instruments and is also recognised by international practice.[47]

27-41 Much more problematic is the question whether, and which, courts have jurisdiction to grant measures in support of the arbitration proceedings. Specifically has a state which has signed an arbitration agreement providing for arbitration in London also submitted to the jurisdiction of the English courts to appoint an arbitrator or to set aside an award? If the non-state party applies for recognition and enforcement of the award in a third country, does it make a difference whether the underlying contract is a civil and commercial matter or one which relates to a sovereign arbitration?

27-42 If one considers the arbitration agreement to be a waiver of immunity the answers to all these questions depend on its interpretation. The extent of this waiver is determined by the actual or imputed will of the parties. Only in very exceptional circumstances can it be assumed that the waiver is limited to the proceedings before the arbitration tribunal. In all other cases the waiver could also cover the court proceedings necessary for a proper and efficient conduct of an arbitration. If no court assistance was possible for reasons of sovereign immunity the state could easily circumvent any agreement to arbitrate. By not participating in the appointment it could prevent the establishment of the tribunal and frustrate the arbitration proceedings.[48] It is difficult to imagine a commercial

---

46 Langkeit, *Staatenimmunität und Schiedsgerichtsbarkeit*, 63 *et seq*; Wetter, "Pleas of Sovereign Immunity and Acts of Sovereignty before International Tribunals", 2(1) *J Int'l Arb* 7 (1985); Reymond, "Souveraineté de l'Etat et Participation à l'Arbitrage", *Rev Arb* 517 (1985); *Libyan American Oil Company ("LIAMCO") v Socialist People's Libyan Arab Jamahirya*, 482 F Supp 1175 (DDC 1980).

47 ICC case no 2321, I *YBCA* 133 (1976) 135; Delaume, "Sovereign Immunity and Transnational Arbitration", 3 *Arb Int* 28 (1987) 30; Langkeit, *Staatenimmunität und Schiedsgerichtsbarkeit*, 56 *et seq*.

48 See Tribunal de Grande Instance Paris, 10 January 1996, *National Iranian Oil Co v Israel*, ASA Bulletin 319 (1996), English text in 11(2) *Mealey's IAR* B5 (1996); Tribunal de Grande Instance Paris, 20 October 1997, *Boulois v UNESCO*, Rev Arb 575 (1997); confirmed by the Cour d'appel Paris as cited in Fouchard Gaillard Goldman *on International Commercial Arbitration*, 645.

party entering into such a contract. On the other hand, taking into account the importance attached to sovereign immunity, it is questionable whether by entering into an arbitration agreement a state party intends to waive its immunity for proceedings everywhere in the world.

27-43 The relevant rules differ in relation to the scope of the waiver attached to an arbitration agreement. A fairly narrow view is contained in Article 12(1) European Convention on State Immunity of 1972. This provides

> Where a Contracting State has agreed in writing to submit to arbitration a dispute which has arisen or may arise out of a civil or commercial matter, that State may not claim immunity from the jurisdiction of a court of another Contracting State on the territory or according to the law of which the arbitration has taken or will take place in proceedings relating to:
>
> a the validity or interpretation of the arbitration agreement
>
> b the arbitration procedure
>
> c the setting aside of the award,
>
> unless the arbitration agreement otherwise provides.

27-44 This provision contains two limitations. First, it applies only to civil and commercial matters. These matters are in most cases already covered by the second exception from immunity, *i.e.* the acts of a commercial nature exception, so that the State could not invoke its immunity even without the existence of an arbitration clause. By contrast, measures in support of arbitrations dealing with sovereign actions will not be covered. Second, the waiver of immunity does not extend to all court proceedings associated with an arbitration. It covers only the three specified types of proceedings which do not extend to actions for the recognition and enforcement of awards.

27-45 Under the English State Immunity Act arbitration agreements provide a more extensive waiver of immunity in relation to court proceedings in support of arbitration. Section 9 provides

> Where a State has agreed in writing to submit a dispute which has arisen, or may arise, to arbitration, the State is not immune as respects proceedings in the courts of the United Kingdom which relate to arbitration.

27-46 This wording implies that by submitting to arbitration, anywhere in the world, a state cannot invoke its sovereign immunity in the English courts in any matter relating to that arbitration irrespective of any connection between the arbitration and England.[49] It is difficult to assume an implied waiver in such cases and certain authors favour a more restrictive interpretation of section 9, requiring at least some sort of connection between England and the arbitration, *e.g.*, the place of arbitration, chosen law or some other factor.[50] In the majority of cases a certain connection will be required by the ordinary rules on jurisdiction in England to establish personal jurisdiction over the state party since the State Immunity Act only deals with the issue of immunity. However, there may be cases where no such connection exists and the state which agreed to arbitrate in a third country may under a wide interpretation of section 9 nevertheless be considered to have waived its sovereign immunity before the English courts.

27-47 A more restrictive interpretation of Section 9 would be in line with the relevant provision of the US Foreign Sovereign Immunities Act 1978. This requires some connection of the arbitration with the United States before considering the state party to have waived its immunity in the US courts. Section 1605 (a) (6) provides in pertinent part

> a) A foreign state shall not be immune from the jurisdiction of courts of the United States or of the States in any case
>
> ...
>
> 6) in which the action is brought, either to enforce an agreement made by the foreign state with or for the benefit of a private party to submit to arbitration all or any differences which have arisen or which may arise between the parties with respect to a defined legal relationship, whether contractual or not concerning a subject matter capable of settlement by arbitration under the law of the United States, or to confirm an award made pursuant to such an agreement to arbitrate, if (A) the arbitration takes place in the United States (B) the agreement or award is or may be governed by a treaty or other international agreement in force for the United States calling for the recognition and enforcement of arbitral awards, (C) the underlying claim, save for the agreement to arbitrate, could have been brought in a United States court under this section or section 1607, or (D) paragraph (1) of this subsection is otherwise applicable [waiver of immunity]...

27-48 In applying this provision US courts have consistently denied a waiver of immunity if the state submitted to arbitration in a different country and no other

49 Mann, "The State Immunity Act 1978", 50 *BYblL* 43 (1979) 58.

50 Oparil, "Waiver of Sovereign Immunity in the United States and Great Britain by an Arbitration Agreement", 3(4) *J Int'l Arb* 61 (1986) 72 *et seq*; in favour of such an interpretation also Fox, "States and the Undertaking to Arbitrate", 37 *ICLQ* 1 (1988) 14.

substantial connection to the United States existed.[51] In *LIAMCO v Libya* the court also assumed jurisdiction for cases where the parties left it to the arbitrators to determine the place of arbitration. The court concluded that Libya had also by implication waived its sovereign immunity in relation to US courts. It stated

> Libya agreed to this provision: Although the United States was not named, consent to have a dispute arbitrated where the arbitrators might determine is consent to have it arbitrated in the United States.[52]

27-49 Furthermore, in countries which have not codified the issue of sovereign immunity courts and commentators have consistently considered arbitration agreements to be a waiver of immunity for court proceedings in support of arbitration. This includes France, Switzerland and Sweden.[53]

27-50 In practice, sovereign immunity has been raised primarily as a defence in proceedings to recognise and declare foreign awards enforceable. State parties have argued that such proceedings are already part of the execution of an award for which the immunity was not waived by the arbitration agreement. This is in line with the European Convention on State Immunity 1972: despite references to court proceedings, where the existence of an arbitration agreement excludes any reliance on sovereign immunity, proceedings for the recognition and enforcement of foreign awards are not included. Some courts also considered those decisions to be part of the enforcement proceedings.

27-51 The Paris Court of Appeal in *SOABI v Sénégal*, for example, did not consider proceedings to declare an ICSID award enforceable to be covered by the waiver of immunity contained in the arbitration clause.[54] The Cour de cassation came to a different conclusion holding that

> A foreign State which has consented to arbitration has thereby agreed that the award may be rendered enforceable which, as such, does not constitute a measure

---

[51] See, *e.g.*, *Verlinden BV v Central Bank of Nigeria*, 488 F Supp 1284 (SDNY 1980); *Ohntrup v Firearms Center, Inc*, 516 F Supp 1281 (ED Pa 1981).

[52] *Libyan American Oil Company ("LIAMCO") v Socialist People's Libyan Arab Jamahirya*, 482 F Supp 1175, 1178 (DDC 1980); for a detailed analysis of the FSIA provisions see Burrows and Newman, *The Practice of International Litigation* (2d ed, Kluwer 2000), I-31 *et seq*, V-40 *et seq*.

[53] *Société Européenne d'Etudes et d'Entreprises (SEEE) v République socialist fédérale de Yougoslavie*, 24 ILM 345 (1985) 349, affirmed by the Cour de cassation; for an overview of national laws see Langkeit, *Staatenimmunität und Schiedsgerichtsbarkeit*, 163 *et seq.*

[54] Cour d'appel Paris, *Société ouest-africaine de bétons industriels (SOABI) v Sénégal*, 29 ILM 1341 (1990).

of execution that might raise issues pertaining to the immunity from execution of the State concerned.[55]

27-52 This position clearly prevails in practice.[56] It finds support in Articles 54 and 55 ICSID Convention which clearly distinguish between a declaration of enforceability and measures of execution. A state party can only rely on sovereign immunity against execution under Article 55. The arbitration agreement is considered to be a waiver of immunity for actions to recognise the award and have it declared enforceable. The same applies to the US FSIA. Measures of execution are governed by section 1610 FSIA and are only possible in limited circumstances. By contrast actions to 'confirm an award' are governed by section 1605 (a) (6) according to which the existence of an arbitration agreement having the necessary connections with the US is sufficient to waive the defence of immunity.[57]

3.2. Immunity from Execution

27-53 The fact that a state cannot claim immunity from jurisdiction does not necessarily mean that the state is not immune from the actual execution of the award. In most laws the exceptions to immunity from execution are narrower than the exceptions to immunity from jurisdiction. Measures of execution are generally considered to be a "more intensive interference with the right of a state" so that prestige plays an even greater role in this context.[58] In addition there is often the fear that generous execution of awards will prevent foreign states from contracting since their property will be amenable to measures of execution.[59]

---

[55] Cour de cassation, *Société ouest-africaine de bétons industriels (SOABI) v Sénégal*, 30 ILM 1167 (1991) 1169.

[56] See, *e.g.*, US, *Ipitrade International SA v Federal Republic of Nigeria*, 465 F Supp 824 (DDC 1978); Belgium, Cour d'appel Bruxelles, 10 March 1993, 123 *Clunet* 444 (1993); for an overview of case law see Langkeit, *Staatenimmunität und Schiedsgerichtsbarkeit*, 131 *et seq*; Delaume, "Sovereign Immunity and Transnational Arbitration", 3 *Arb Int* 28 (1987).

[57] Bernini and van den Berg, "The Enforcement of Arbitral Awards against a State: the Problem of Immunity from Execution", in Lew (ed), *Contemporary Problems*, 359.

[58] Böckstiegel, *Arbitration and State Enterprises* (Deventer 1984), 50; see also Germany, Bundesverfassungsgericht, 13 December 1977, *BVerfGE* 46, 342, 367; 65 *ILR* 146 (1984).

[59] Bernini and van den Berg, "The Enforcement of Arbitral Awards against a State: the Problem of Immunity from Execution", in Lew (ed), *Contemporary Problems*, 359, 360 *et seq.*

(a) Waiver of immunity

27-54 Contrary to the position concerning immunity from jurisdiction, arbitration agreements are not in themselves considered to be a waiver of immunity from execution. Until recently only few authors have voiced support for such an interpretation of the arbitration agreement though there might be good reason to do so.[60] By entering into an arbitration agreement the parties are considered to have undertaken an obligation to honour the ensuing award.

27-55 Article 54 ICSID Convention provides that by entering into an arbitration agreement the state also undertakes to honour the award. Therefore the principle of *pacta sunt servanda* should prevent a state from relying on its sovereign immunity to avoid commitments entered into freely and intentionally. Furthermore, it is not very convincing to assume that non-state private parties, which often have the same bargaining power as the state party involved, would enter into agreements which allow the state party to avoid enforcement of unfavourable awards by being able to invoke its immunity. Commercial parties in general do not contract for potentially pyrrhic victories.

27-56 Such theory of a double waiver contained in an ordinary arbitration clause has until recently found little support in the national laws and relevant case law. The ICSID Convention, for example, despite setting out an obligation to honour the award, allows immunity from execution.[61]

27-57 The English State Immunity Act makes clear that the submission to jurisdiction does not automatically include a submission for enforcement purposes. Section 13(3) provides that the principle of immunity from enforcement as set out in subsection 2

> ... does not prevent the giving of any relief or the issue of any process with the written consent of the State concerned; and any such consent (which may be contained in a prior agreement) may be expressed so as to apply to a limited extent or generally; but a provision merely submitting to the jurisdiction of the courts is not to be regarded as a consent for the purposes of this subsection.

27-58 Though the last sentence only refers to submission to the jurisdiction of the courts, the principle is also applied to arbitration agreements which are not

---

[60] *Ibid*, 363; Langkeit, *Staatenimmunität und Schiedsgerichtsbarkeit*, 220 *et seq.*

[61] Article 55 Washington Convention.

considered to be sufficient to constitute a submission for the purpose of enforcement.[62]

27-59 There are decisions which appear at first sight to support the view that a waiver of immunity from jurisdiction always includes a waiver of immunity from execution. The Swiss Federal Court held that as the powers of execution directly derive from powers of jurisdiction, there would be no reason for Swiss courts to treat immunity from execution differently from immunity from enforcement.[63] The decision however concerned commercial property which was in fact the crucial issue.[64] Therefore despite that broad statement, under Swiss law an arbitration agreement can still not be considered to be a waiver of immunity from execution if it does not say so explicitly.

27-60 The decision of the French Cour de cassation in *Creighton v Qatar* has given support for a double waiver of immunity. The court saw the submission to ICC arbitration as a waiver of immunity from execution. It based its argument primarily on the obligation in Article 24 ICC Rules 1988 (now Article 28) to carry out the resulting award and to waive any right to appeal. This was considered sufficient to assume an implied waiver of immunity from execution.[65] Given the fact that a number of other arbitration rules contain similar provisions as to the waiver of any rights, the decision might lead to a general exclusion of the defence of immunity from execution.

27-61 It is doubtful whether other countries will follow that decision. Consequently at present a more or less express waiver of immunity from execution is required and highly recommended in state contracts.[66] The model clause suggested by ICSID reads

---

62 See Fox, "States and the Undertaking to Arbitrate", 37 *ICLQ* 1 (1988) 14.

63 See Tribunal Fédéral, 10 February 1960, *United Arab Republic v Mrs X*, 88 Clunet 458 (1961); Lalive, "Swiss Law and Practice in Relation to Measures of Execution against Property of a Foreign State", 10 *NYIL* 153 (1979).

64 Swiss Tribunal Fédéral, 20 July 1979, *Arab Republic of Egypt v Cinetelevision International*, 65 ILR 425 (1984) 430. See, similarly, Landgericht Frankfurt, 2 December 1975, 65 *ILR* 131 (1984) 135.

65 Cour de cassation, 6 July 2000, *Creighton Limited v Ministry of Finance and Ministry of Municipal Affairs and Agriculture of the State of Qatar*, 15(9) Mealey's IAR A-1 (2000); for indications of such a change in French case law see Cour d'appel Rouen, 20 June 1996, *Société Bec Frères v Office des Céréales de Tunisie*, Rev Arb 263 (1997).

66 Delaume, "How to draft an ICSID Arbitration Clause", 7 *ICSID Rev-FILJ* 168 (1992) 194 has called such a waiver "a matter of elementary prudence".

> The Host State hereby waives any right of sovereign immunity as to it and its property in respect of the enforcement and execution of any award rendered by an Arbitral Tribunal constituted pursuant to this agreement.[67]

27-62 Terms in an agreement such as waiver of "whatever defences it may have of sovereign immunity for itself or its property" have, however, also been considered sufficient to allow measures of execution to be taken by the English courts.[68] These waivers in international loan agreements are fairly common where the lender has a strong bargaining power.

27-63 However, in the US even such an express waiver would probably not make property held and used exclusively for sovereign activities amenable for execution. The US FSIA limits all execution to property used for commercial purposes. Section 1610(a), which regulates the exceptions from the general principle in section 1609 FSIA, provided that property of a foreign state is immune from execution. This only relates to property "used for a commercial activity in the United States."[69] Consequently under the FISA a state could resist execution of an award in property held for commercial purposes by virtue of its sovereign immunity, even where it had waived its immunity.[70]

27-64 By contrast, under most other laws on sovereign immunity, including English and Canadian law, the European Convention on State Immunity and International Law Commission's Draft articles,[71] such an express waiver would make property held and used for *acta iure imperii* amenable for execution.[72] The

---

[67] Doc ICSID/5/Rev 2, Clause 15; for further examples see Schreuer, "Commentary on the ICSID Convention", 14 *ICSID Rev-FILJ* 17 (1999) 150.

[68] *A Co Ltd v Republic of X*, [1990] 2 Lloyd's Rep 520. But see the decision of the Cour d'appel Paris in Noga v. Russian Federation reported in Kröll, "Neuere Entwicklungen im französischen Recht der Vollstreckung in das Vermögen ausländischer Staaten - Vorbild oder Irrweg?", 22 *IPRax* 439 (2002) 441, where an explicit waiver of immunity from execution was considered not to extent to diplomatic immunity so that the embassy's bank account was not amenable for execution.

[69] Henkin, Pugh, Schachter and Smit, *International Law Cases and Materials* (3rd ed West 1993), 1178.

[70] The positive effects of a waiver of immunity are primarily limited to court proceedings, where they exclude the additional requirement that the property against which enforcement of the award is sought was used for the same commercial activity out of which the claim arose. By virtue of section 1610(a)(6), this condition is of no relevance for arbitration.

[71] Draft Articles on Responsibility of States for internationally wrongful acts, UN Doc A/CN4/ L602/Rev1, 26 July 2001 adopted by the General Assembly on 28 January 2002, A/Res/56/83. See <www.un.org/law/ilc/convents.htm>.

[72] See, *e.g.*, Canada, State Immunity Act, section 11(1)(a); for an analysis see Schreuer, "Commentary on the ICSID Convention", 14 *ICSID Rev-FILJ* 117 (1999) 145 *et seq*.

same applies in a number of countries where the law of sovereign immunity is based on case law.

(b) Commercial activity

27-65 In practice, the "commercial activity or purpose exception" is more important than the "waiver exception". This can be found in the law on sovereign immunity in most countries and the relevant international instruments.[73] Considerable differences exist as to the extent of the exception.

27-66 A narrow interpretation can be found in the International Law Institute's Draft Articles on Jurisdictional Immunities of States and their Property 1991. This provides in pertinent part of Article 18

> 1. No measure of constraint, such as attachment, arrest and execution, against property of a State may be taken in connection with a proceeding before a court of another State unless and except to the extent that:
>
> ...
>
> (b) the State has allocated or earmarked property for the satisfaction of the claim which is the object of that proceeding; or
>
> (c) the property is specifically in use or intended for use by the State for other than government non-commercial purposes and is in the territory of the State of the forum and has a connection with the claim which is the object of the proceeding or with the agency or instrumentality against which the proceedings was directed.[74]

27-67 A similar limitation relating to the commercial property claims can also be found in the leading French decision on the issue, *Eurodif v Iran.*[75]

27-68 Following the Iranian revolution, Iran abandoned its participation in the Eurodif nuclear fuel enrichment project and ceased to make payments due under a shareholder purchase agreement. Eurodif and the other participants in the project started an ICC arbitration against Iran. In addition they obtained a conservatory attachment from the Tribunal de Commerce of Paris authorising the seizure of a debt owed by one of the participants to Iran under a loan agreement.

---

[73] By contrast, the European Convention on State Immunity of 1972 did not contain a general exception based on the commercial purpose of a given property, but required a special declaration to this effect by the Contracting States.

[74] However, an arbitration agreement might be considered a valid waiver of immunity from execution under Article 18(a)(ii).

[75] Cour de cassation, 14 March 1984, *Eurodif v Islamic Republic of Iran*, 23 ILM 1062 (1984).

After the Cour d'appel had lifted the seizure declaring Iran to be immune, the Cour de cassation reversed the decision and declared as a general rule that no immunity existed whenever the seised asset had been allocated to economic or commercial activity governed by private law. The prevailing view is that the existence of a nexus between the property singled out for execution and the underlying claim is still a necessary prerequisite for any execution in France. However, since the decision of the Cour de cassation in *Creighton v Qatar*,[76] parties may benefit from the waiver exception.

27-69 There are good arguments against imposing this type of restriction on the execution in property held for commercial purposes. It is hard to think of a justification why a claimant who finds assets of the state party in France and which are connected to the transaction can enforce its award against those assets. Whereas an equally deserving claimant is barred from enforcement against those assets even though used for commercial activities by the state but have no such connection to the particular claim.[77]

27-70 The limitation to commercial property which has some connection to the underlying claim can be a serious restriction on the ability to enforce an award against a state. Often obligations of the state party to pay for goods or services, or to pay its share of a joint venture, only arise at a later stage of the contractual relationship. If the state has not yet assigned certain property for use in that transaction, there may be no sufficient property with a connection to the underlying claim for enforcement. In addition to the serious limitation on the assets available for execution, in particular in investment contracts, those assets may be located in the state itself which further aggravates any execution.

---

[76] Cour de cassation, 6 July 2000, *Societé Creighton Ltd v Ministre des Finances de l'Etat du Qatar et ministre des Affaires municipal et de l'agriculture du Gouvernement de l'Etat du Qatar*, 127 Clunet 1054 (2000) with note Pingel-Lenuzza; see also Meyer-Fabre, "Enforcement of Arbitral Awards against Sovereign States, a New Milestone: Signing the ICC Arbitration Clause Entails Waiver of Immunity from Execution Held French Court of Cassation in Creighton v Qatar, July 6, 2000", 15(9) *Mealey's IAR* 48 (2000); Gaillard and Edelstein, "Recent Developments in State Immunity from Execution in France: Creighton v Qatar", 15(10) *Mealey's IAR* 49 (2000); Turck, "French and US Courts Define Limits of Sovereign Immunity in Execution and Enforcement of Arbitral Awards", 17 *Arb Int* 327 (2001); note Kaplan/Cuniberti, *JCP-La Semaine Juridique Édition Générale* 763 (2001).

[77] Paulsson, "Foreign Sovereign Immunity From Jurisdiction, French Case law Revisited", 19 *Int'l Lawyer* 277 (1985) 282-285; As a consequence, the requirement formerly contained in the US FSIA that enforcement of an award could only affect property used for the same commercial activity was replaced by a provision allowing for enforcement against property used in any commercial activity within the US.

27-71 No such special nexus between the property in question and the underlying claim is required by US law or the law of other common law countries such as England, Canada or Australia.[78] They all include a special provision for the execution of awards, which omits the nexus requirement which exists for courts. Section 1610(a)(6) FSIA for example provides

> The property in the United States of a foreign state, as defined in section 1603(a) of this chapter, used for a commercial activity in the United States, shall not be immune from attachment in aid of execution, or from execution, upon a judgment entered by a court of the United States or of a State after the effective date of this Act, if
>
> ...
>
> 6) the judgment is based on an order confirming an arbitral award rendered against the foreign state, provided that attachment in aid of execution, or execution, would be inconsistent with any provision of the arbitral agreement.

27-72 In most cases a certain nexus between the claim or the arbitration and the United States may be required by the general rules on personal jurisdiction. It has been made clear by the US courts that the FSIA only regulates subject matter jurisdiction. Personal jurisdiction by contrast must be established under the ordinary rules of jurisdiction as in any other action between private parties. These rules on personal jurisdiction in general require a certain link between the defendant state and the US.[79]

27-73 Under Swiss law the execution of an award requires a certain nexus with Switzerland beyond the mere existence of property against which the execution is sought. The case law is often based on the premise that the arbitration agreement contains an implied waiver of immunity from execution. Therefore the nexus must be between the arbitration and Switzerland and not between the underlying claim and the property in question. According to the *LIAMCO* decision of the Swiss Tribunal Fédéral the fact that the seat of the arbitration tribunal was in Switzerland was not sufficient to justify execution in Switzerland. In that instance the seat had not been determined by the parties but by the tribunal.[80]

---

[78] See, *e.g.*, US, FSIA, section 1610 (a)(6); England, State Immunity Act, section 13(4); Australia, Foreign States Immunity Act 1985 section 32; Canada, State Immunity Act of 1982 section 11(1)(b).

[79] See *Monegasque de Rassurances SAM v NAK Naftogaz of Ukraine*, 311 F 3d 488 (2d Cir, 15 November 2002).

[80] Swiss Tribunal Fédéral, 19 June 1980, *Socialist People's Libyan Arab Jamahiriya v LIAMCO*, 20 ILM 151 (1981).

27-74 In Italy the traditional position that measures of execution against states are subject to executive control has been declared unconstitutional by the Corte di cassazione as it would prevent execution against property of a state used for commercial purposes.[81]

27-75 Under all these laws and international instruments two closely related questions are posed: what constitutes "property for commercial use" or "of commercial origin" and by which means and by whom the nature of property has to be proven?

27-76 It is recognised that the nature of the property is determined according to the national law of the state where enforcement is sought. The English State Immunity Act defines commercial purpose in vague terms in section 17(1). According to section 13(5) the burden of proof that the property is covered by that definition can be shifted to the private party by a certificate of the head of the State's diplomatic mission in the United Kingdom stating that the property is not intended for use for commercial purposes.[82] The burden to prove the opposite is fairly high as is illustrated by the House of Lords' decision in *Alcom v Republic of Colombia*.[83] It related to a bank account held for the Colombian embassy on which the non-state party had applied for a garnishee order. The House of Lords held

> Unless it can be shown by the judgment creditor who is seeking to attach the credit balance by garnishee proceedings that the bank account was earmarked by the foreign State solely (save for *de minimis* exceptions) for being drawn on to settle liabilities incurred in commercial transactions, as for example by issuing documentary credits in payment of the price of goods sold to the state, it cannot in my view, be sensibly brought within the crucial words of the exception for which section 13(4) provides.[84]

27-77 Comparable decisions as to bank accounts held by an embassy have been rendered in various other countries where the courts even considered those accounts to profit from the special protection accorded to property used for diplomatic purposes.[85] In Germany the Federal Constitutional Court even held

---

81 Corte di cassazione, 2 July 1992, 33 *ILM* 593 (1994).

82 See also the Australian Foreign States Immunities Act of 1985 which contains a comparable definition in section 32(2)(a). However, according to section 41, a certificate of the head of state's mission has only evidential weight and is not decisive.

83 *Alcom Ltd v Republic of Colombia*, [1994] AC 580.

84 *Ibid*, 604.

85 See further Schreuer, "Commentary on the ICSID Convention", 14 *ICSID Rev-FILJ* 46 (1999) 139 *et seq*.

that any enquiry into the use of the funds in an embassy's bank account would be a violation of the state's immunity from execution. It considered it to be a customary rule of international law that embassy bank accounts are immune from execution without the consent of the state.[86] As a consequence execution on those bank accounts is generally only possible if immunity from execution and diplomatic immunity have been expressly waived.

27-78 Special treatment is often accorded to bank accounts held by a foreign national bank. In England and the US for example the relevant statutes more or less exclude any execution against the funds held by a foreign central bank.[87]

27-79 By contrast, other types of bank accounts, in particular those held by state entities, have been the object of execution measures. Particularly far reaching is a decision of the German Federal Constitutional Court which upheld attachment orders worth nearly US$200 million against bank accounts held by the National Iranian Oil Company (NIOC). NIOC's invoked immunity from execution as the credit balances were to be used after their transfer to Iran to fund the state budget. The court rejected that argument as under German law the credit balances, at least until their referral to the Iranian central bank, belonged to the state's financial assets which are not considered to be public matters. The court held that

> [t]he law of general immunity of states does not prevent the forum state from ordering security measures as regards claims from credit balances that are located in accounts with banks in the forum state and that are earmarked for transfer to an account maintained by a foreign state with its central bank to meet its state budget, since the forum may classify these credit balances as assets that do not serve sovereign purposes of the foreign state at the time of the beginning of the security measure.[88]

27-80 US courts have classified registration fees and taxes due from ships flying the Liberian flag to be revenues for the support and maintenance of government functions and granted immunity.[89]

---

86 Bundesverfassungsgericht, 13 December 1977, *BVerfGE* 46, 342, 364; 65 *ILR* 146 (1984).

87 See State Immunity Act section 14(4), Hill, *International Commercial Disputes*, para 2-3-61; US, FSIA section 1611(b)(1).

88 Bundesverfassungsgericht, 12 April 1983, 22 *ILM* 1279 (1983) 1305 *et seq*; see also, in this decision, the references to court decisions in other countries dealing with the same issue.

89 See *Liberian Eastern Timber Corp (LETCO) v The Government of the Republic of Liberia*, (SDNY, 12 December 1986), 2 ICSID Reports 385, 388 *et seq*, affirmed by the Court of Appeals, 19 May 1987 (unpublished). The same applies to corporate income taxes owed by

27-81 In general, those rules on immunity from execution are also applicable for interim relief intended to preserve assets for execution. English courts have therefore refused to grant a freezing order where a later execution would not be possible for reasons of immunity.[90]

4. Reasons to Resist Enforcement of Awards

27-82 Apart from the issue of immunity from enforcement the involvement of a state party can also raise special issues concerning the grounds for refusal of enforcement mentioned in the New York Convention. Article V(2)(a) New York Convention provides, as a ground for refusal of enforcement, the lack of objective arbitrability.

27-83 In *LIAMCO v Libya* the District Court for the District of Columbia held that the act of state doctrine, which prevents courts from reviewing acts of foreign governments done within their territories, forbade the enforcement of an award calling for compensation for the nationalisation of LIAMCO's assets in Libya.[91] To avoid such results section 15 was included into the Federal Arbitration Act which now provides

> Enforcement of arbitral awards, agreements, confirmation of arbitral awards and execution upon judgments based on orders confirming such awards shall not be refused on the basis of the Act of State doctrine.

---

airlines see *LNC Investment Inc v Republic of Nicaragua*, 15(8) Mealey's IAR 18-20 (2000) (SDNY).

90 See *Arab Banking Corporation v International Tin Council*, 77 ILR 1 (1986).

91 *Libyan American Oil Company ("LIAMCO") v Socialist People's Libyan Arab Jamahirya*, 482 F Supp 1175 (DDC 1980).

Chapter 28

ARBITRATION OF INVESTMENT DISPUTES

28-1 Foreign investment is increasingly an integral part of the world economy. In developing countries, major infrastructure projects and the exploitation of natural resources often require financing by and technical know-how of private foreign investors. Even in developed countries the share of foreign investment in the GNP is significant.[1]

28-2 The investment may be considerable which may need years for the investor to recover. In developing countries foreign investment often relates to core components of the national economy. These factors make foreign investment particularly vulnerable to possible interference by the host state. While clear cut nationalisations are rare there are a number of other measures of a lower threshold which may affect foreign investment, such as currency restrictions preventing repatriation of profits, prohibitions on price increases, tax increases or new taxes and environmental legislation.

28-3 To create a favourable climate for foreign investment, and to protect their own citizens, states have entered into large numbers of bilateral and multilateral treaties. International organisations have been established and have engaged in promoting international or regional treaties and conventions providing a stable framework for investment in an effort to create a worldwide standard for the treatment of foreign investment. Although this effort has finally failed, there are a number of regional or bilateral treaties which aim to promote and protect foreign investment, including the Lomé Agreements, North American Free Trade Agreement, and the Energy Charter Treaty.

28-4 In order to encourage foreign investment some countries have implemented specific investment laws to provide the necessary legal certainty sought by investors. Investment protection legislation can be found in nearly all the Commonwealth of Independent States and most developing countries.

28-5 In these efforts to promote and protect investment the issue of dispute resolution has been of crucial importance. Investors usually have little faith in the courts of the host country. With sensitive infrastructure projects investors are concerned they may not be able to protect their investments. On the other hand states are rarely willing to submit to foreign courts.[2]

---

1 See UNCTAD Book of Statistics. Online version at <http://stats.unctad.org/public/eng/TableViewer/Wdsview/dispviewp.asp?ReportID=60>.

2 Wälde, "Investment Arbitration Under the Energy Charter Treaty – From Dispute Settlement to Treaty Implementation", 12 *Arb Int* 429 (1996) 431 *et seq*; Lörcher, *Neue Verfahren der Internationalen Streiterledigung in Wirtschaftssachen*, 156; Turner, "Investment Protection

28-6 For these reasons arbitration has played a prominent role in the settlement of investment disputes. *Ad hoc* arbitration proceedings in the aftermath of the expropriation of oil concessions have greatly contributed to developing and shaping the laws on investor protection. Most of the international conventions provide for arbitration as the preferred method of dispute settlement. In general they either provide for *ad hoc* arbitration under the UNCITRAL Rules or under the rules of an acceptable arbitration institution, *e.g.* ICC, SCC and in particular ICSID.[3] In addition, some treaties, such as NAFTA, also devise their own arbitration system to take account of the particular circumstances.

28-7 This chapter provides an overview of (1) the special features of investment disputes, (2) dispute settlement under national investment laws, (3) dispute resolution systems in bilateral investment treaties, (4) NAFTA, (5) the Energy Charter Treaty, (6) ICSID as the natural forum for investor-state disputes and the conduct of arbitration proceedings under the ICSID Convention and Arbitration Rules, and (7) the ICSID Additional Facility Rules.

1. Special Features of Investment Disputes Arbitration

28-8 Investment disputes differ in several respects from ordinary commercial disputes. Frequently the amount in dispute is remarkable and the issues may have considerable political implications. Disagreements often concern the objectives of the investment, the repatriation of revenues and the ultimate control and benefit of the investment. The investment may relate to vital infrastructure the completion of which is of significant importance for the national economy. The outcome of the dispute may also affect the general investment climate in a country. In addition, one party is a state vested with sovereign powers, which is nevertheless in need of foreign investment and is bound by international instruments.

28-9 These factors influence the conduct of the arbitration in various respects. In the composition of the tribunal the nationality of the arbitrators may become a more important issue than in ordinary commercial arbitrations. Concerning the

---

through Arbitration: The Dispute Resolution Provisions of the Energy Charter Treaty", 1 *Int ALR* 166 (1998) 167.

3 For an overview see Parra, "Provisions on the Settlement of Investment Disputes in Modern Investment Laws, Bilateral Investment Treaties and Multilateral Instruments", 12 *ICSID Rev-FILJ* 287 (1997).

applicable substantive and procedural laws there is a much stronger tendency to delocalise and apply principles of international law. Investment disputes can have a greater impact on parties other than those involved and thus may be more in the public domain. Investment disputes may relate to legislation which not only affects a specific investor but a complete class of investors, the relationship between the host state and the investor's home state.

28-10 Recognising these diverse interests in the proceedings between *Methanex Corporation v United States* the tribunal under NAFTA Chapter 11 allowed the submission of *amicus curia* briefs by non parties.[4] It considered that in the absence of an express prohibition the decision on whether to allow such briefs fell within the tribunal's procedural powers in accordance with Article 15(1) UNCITRAL Rules. In exercising its discretion the tribunal took into account several factors, in particular the public interest in the case. This greater public interest is also evidenced by the policy adopted in relation to the publication of awards which is much more liberal than in commercial arbitration.[5]

28-11 The greatest difference to commercial arbitrations is the source of the tribunal's power. Commercial arbitrations require an arbitration agreement between the parties. By contrast, in investment disputes arbitration may also be possible without such an arbitration agreement in the ordinary sense. National legislation or treaties may give each party the right to initiate arbitration proceedings against the other.[6] There may even be no contractual relationship between the parties at all which has led to labelling investment arbitration "arbitration without privity."[7]

---

4 4 *Int ALR* N-3 (2001).

5 On the publication of NAFTA awards see Eklund, "A Primer on the Arbitration of NAFTA Chapter Eleven Investor-State Disputes", 11(4) *J Int'l Arb* 135 (1994) 156; on the publication of ICSID awards see Washington Convention Rule 48(4).

6 For the avoidance of potential problems arising out of this different source of authority, NAFTA Article 1121 and Energy Charter Treaty Article 26(5) require a special consent by the investor; they further specify that this consent in conjunction with that of the state, as expressed in the treaty provisions, shall be deemed to satisfy the arbitration agreement requirement.

7 See Paulsson, "Arbitration Without Privity", 10 *ICSID Rev-FILJ* 232 (1995); Werner, "Arbitration of Investment Disputes: The First NAFTA Award - Introductory comments on the Ethyl Corporation case", 16(3) *J Int'l Arb* 139 (1999); see, *e.g.*, ICSID, case ARB/97/3, Award of 21 November 2000, *Companía de Aguas del Aconquija, SA & Compagnie Générale des Eaux (now Vivendi Universal) v Argentine Republic*, 40 ILM 426 (2001).

28-12 Investment arbitrations are frequently based on provisions in national investment protection laws or international treaties by which the state agrees generally to arbitrate investment disputes. These provisions constitute a unilateral standing offer to the public to submit to arbitration with any party fulfilling the requirements. The offer is accepted by the investor when it initiates arbitration proceedings against the state.[8] Until that time the investor is not bound to arbitrate and the state cannot initiate proceedings against the investor.

28-13 Disputes on jurisdiction are often not about interpreting a contract between the parties. Rather the tribunal will interpret the statutes, treaties and conventions, to see whether the dispute falls within the ambit of the state's obligation to arbitrate in these instruments. Consequently, the nationality of the investor is often an issue of the utmost importance, since the offer to arbitrate may only extend to nationals of certain countries. Investments are frequently done by local special purpose companies to meet requirements of local participation and consortia are structured in a way to allow maximum profits and tax advantages. When a dispute arises it may be necessary to determine who is the actual investor: the local company, its direct shareholders or someone further down the line of ownership and control.

2. National Investment Laws

28-14 Many states have adopted investment protection laws. Their objective is to provide an investor friendly environment and attract foreign investment by guaranteeing certain minimum standards, including national treatment, no discrimination and no expropriation without fair compensation. These national laws usually provide for arbitration as a means of dispute settlement.[9]

---

[8] Cremades, "Arbitration in Investment Treaties: Public Offer of Arbitration in Investment Protection Treaties", in Briner, Fortier, Berger and Bredow (eds), *Liber Amicorum Böckstiegel*, 156 *et seq*; for a detailed analysis of the differences see Wälde, "Investment Arbitration Under the Energy Charter Treaty – From Dispute Settlement to Treaty Implementation", 12 *Arb Int* 429 (1996) 434 *et seq*.

[9] The Report of the Executive Directors of the World Bank accompanying the 1965 ICSID Convention refers in para 24 to the provisions in national investment legislation as one possible way to submit to the jurisdiction of the Centre. For an overview of provisions found in national investment laws see Parra, "Provisions on the Settlement of Investment Disputes in Modern Investment Laws, Bilateral Investment Treaties and Multilateral Instruments", 12 *ICSID Rev-FILJ* 287 (1997) 314.

28-15 Unlike bilateral or multilateral treaties, the provisions contained in national investment protection laws generally extend to all foreign investors. Such provisions may in effect contain an open offer to arbitrate disputes with the foreign investor. Nevertheless states have in several cases challenged the jurisdiction of tribunals in arbitration proceedings initiated on the basis of investment protection laws.

28-16 An example is provided by the *SPP v Republic of Egypt* arbitration arising out of an abandoned project to construct a hotel complex near the pyramids. It is one of the first cases where a party tried to initiate arbitration on the basis of a provision in a national investment law. After an ICC award rendered in SPPs favour had been annulled for lack of an arbitration agreement with Egypt by the French courts,[10] SPP successfully initiated ICSID arbitration proceedings relying on Article 8 Egyptian Investment Law (Law no 43 of 1974) which provided

> Investment disputes in respect of the implementation of the provisions of this Law shall/are to be settled in a manner to be agreed upon with the investor, or within the framework of the agreements in force between the Arab Republic of Egypt and the investor's home country, or within the framework of the Convention for the Settlement of Investment Disputes between the State and the nationals of other countries to which Egypt has adhered ... where it applies.

28-17 Egypt objected to the jurisdiction of the tribunal for three reasons which were all rejected by the tribunal.[11] First, it submitted that the claimants had not consented to ICSID's jurisdiction since it first initiated ICC proceedings. The tribunal held that by sending a request for arbitration and an earlier letter to the minister the investor consented to ICSID arbitration. It was not barred by either Article 26 ICSID Convention, according to which submission to ICSID excludes all other remedies, or any other principle of international law such as estoppel.[12]

28-18 Second, Egypt denied the applicability of Law no 43, since the approval for the Pyramids project had been withdrawn before the arbitration proceedings were initiated. Egypt alleged that Law no 43 only covered an investment for

---

[10] Cour d'appel Paris, 12 July 1984, X *YBCA* 113 (1985); confirmed by the Cour de cassation, 6 January 1987, XIII *YBCA* 152 (1988); for an account of the case see Delaume, "The Pyramids Stand - The Pharaohs Can Rest in Peace", 8 *ICSID Rev-FILJ* 231 (1993).

[11] See the two awards on jurisdiction, 27 November 1985 and 14 April 1988, *Southern Pacific Properties Ltd (Middle East) et al v Arab Republic of Egypt*, XVI YBCA 16 (1991).

[12] *Ibid*, award on jurisdiction of 27 November 1985, paras 7-13.

which an approval existed. The tribunal held that the relevant point was whether the investment when made was covered by Law no 43 not whether an approval had subsequently been withdrawn. In the tribunal's view the withdrawal was invalid.[13] It further held that the dispute was covered by Law no 43 since the withdrawal of the permission constituted a violation of the protection granted under the investment law.

28-19 Third, Egypt argued that even if Law no 43 was applicable, Article 8 would not suffice to establish Egypt's consent to ICSID's jurisdiction. The tribunal rejected that contention. It held that despite the alleged difference between the Arab version and the English and French versions of Article 8 its language was sufficiently clear and broad to create a binding offer for arbitration which covered the case in issue.[14]

28-20 In dealing generally with the interpretation of dispute settlement provisions in national investment laws the tribunal made clear that it was not bound by the interpretation of the provisions submitted by the state party which drafted them. These provisions are governed by the principles of statutory interpretation which may be influenced by the rules of interpretation of treaty law; this is particularly true where the provisions of the national laws relate to obligations under international treaties.[15]

28-21 Comparable objections, as to scope of the offers contained in the dispute settlement provisions of national laws, their general applicability and the effect of withdrawals, have been raised in other arbitrations.[16] In particular, to allow a state to withdraw an offer to arbitrate contained in an investment law after an investment has been made would deprive the investor of its basic protection. Therefore the time when the investment is made should usually be relevant for determining whether it enjoys the benefits of a national protection law.

---

[13] *Ibid*, paras 14-21.

[14] *Ibid*, paras 21-24; award on jurisdiction, 27 November 1985, paras 43-69.

[15] *Ibid*, paras 33-37.

[16] Comparable objections were raised in *Gaith Pharaon v Republic of Tunisia* - an ICSID arbitration based on Tunisian investment law - which was, however, settled before the tribunal could deal with them; see Paulsson, "Arbitration Without Privity", 10 *ICSID Rev-FILJ* 232 (1995) 235. See also ICSID, Decision on Jurisdiction, 24 December 1996, *Tradex Hellas SA v Republic of Albania*, 14 ICSID Rev-FILJ 161 (1999) where the main issue was the retroactive application of law.

3. BILATERAL INVESTMENT TREATIES

28-22 Bilateral Investment Treaties (BITs) have proliferated over the last three decades and are an effective and well used mechanism to guarantee protection of foreign investments.[17] In addition to substantive rules they usually contain dispute resolution provisions for certain defined categories of investments, invariably providing for arbitration. The scope and the content of these clauses differ considerably, depending on the states involved and their respective bargaining power. In the majority of cases they constitute a unilateral offer by the state involved to all investors from the other state party to settle disputes by arbitration. Some, however, only contain declarations of intent to make such offers in the future.[18] Some BITs provisions cover all types of disputes under a very wide definition of investment; others only cover certain types of disputes, for example, those relating to expropriation or specific types of investment.[19] Often the exhaustion of local remedies is made a prerequisite for the right to arbitration.

28-23 Differences not only exist in the scope of investor protection provided in each BIT, but the type of arbitration provided for will also vary. Frequently the clauses provide for ICSID arbitration, or give the investor a choice between ICSID and other institutions such as the ICC, the AAA or the SCC. Often arbitration is the final stage in a multi-tier dispute resolution clause, providing first for negotiations or other diplomatic efforts to settle the dispute amicably.[20]

28-24 There have been numerous arbitration proceedings, which are based on provisions in BITs.[21] In a recent case a party successfully invoked a BIT despite an exclusive jurisdiction clause for the main claim. In *Vivendi Universal v*

---

17 See Obadia, "L'evolution de l'activité du CIRDI", *Rev Arb* 633 (2001), according to whom there were approximately 2000 bilateral investment treaties in the beginning of 2001.

18 Cremades, "Arbitration in Investment Treaties: Public Offer of Arbitration in Investment Protection Treaties", in Briner, Fortier, Berger and Bredow (eds), *Liber Amicorum Böckstiegel*, 159 *et seq.*

19 Paulsson, "Arbitration Without Privity", 10 *ICSID Rev-FILJ* 232 (1995) 236 *et seq.*

20 See Blessing, *Introduction to Arbitration*, para 332; for an overview see Parra, "Provisions on the Settlement of Investment Disputes in Modern Investment Laws, Bilateral Investment Treaties and Multilateral Instruments", 12 *ICSID Rev-FILJ* 287 (1997) 322 *et seq.*

21 See, *e.g.*, *Asian Agricultural Products Ltd v Republic of Sri Lanka,* 6 ICSID Rev-FILJ 526 (1991), 30 ILM 577 (1991); XVII YBCA 106 (1992); *Joseph Charles Lemire v Ukraine,* 15 ICSID Rev-FILJ 528 (2000).

Argentine Republic,[22] the French investor had entered into a concession contract with Tucumán, a province of Argentina. The contract did not make any reference to the BIT between Argentina and France. It provided that disputes relating to the interpretation and application of the contract should be submitted to the exclusive jurisdiction of the administrative courts in Tucumán. Vivendi started ICSID proceedings against the Republic of Argentina, which had neither been a party to the concession nor participated in the negotiations. Vivendi alleged that the actions of the Tucumán authorities constituted a breach by Argentina of the provisions in the relevant BIT, according to which investors are guaranteed fair and equitable treatment and prohibited expropriation. Vivendi argued that for this reason its claims against Argentina were covered by Article 8 BIT providing for ICSID arbitration. The tribunal assumed jurisdiction stating the need to distinguish between contractual claims against Tucumán and the claims for breach of the BIT brought by the investor against Argentina. The latter were not affected by the exclusive jurisdiction clause in the Concession Contract but could be referred to arbitration under the ICSID Convention.[23]

28-25 In *Ceskoslovenska Obchodni Banka AS v The Slovak Republic*[24] the relevant treaty had never entered into force but the parties had provided in their agreement that it should be governed by the treaty. The tribunal considered this sufficient to establish its jurisdiction as the parties had made the article part of their contract.[25] BITs have given foreign investors the possibility of relying on dispute resolution options that best suit their needs. Many investments made by a subsidiary of a global corporation will now fall under at least one BIT.[26]

---

22 ICSID, *Companía de Aguas del Aconquija, SA & Compagnie Générale des Eaux (now Vivendi) v Argentine Republic*, ARB/97/3, 21 November 2000, 40 ILM 426 (2001); see also the preliminary decision on jurisdiction in *Lanco International Inc.v The Argentine Republic*, ARB/97/6, 8 December 1998, 40 ILM 457 (2001).

23 *Ibid*, 435 *et seq*. The decision on jurisdiction was confirmed in the annulment proceedings.

24 ICSID, Decision on Objections to Jurisdiction, 24 May 1999, *Ceskoslovenska Obchodni Banka, AS (Czech Republic) v The Slovak Republic*, XXIVa YBCA 44 (1999); 14 ICSID Rev-FILJ 250 (1999); Decision on further and partial objection to jurisdiction, 1 December 2000, 15 ICSID Rev-FILJ 542 (2000).

25 *Ibid*, 57-60.

26 See the two *ad hoc* Lauder arbitrations *CME Czech Republic BV v Czech Republic* and *Lauder v Czech Republic* available at <*www.cme.cz/doc10/en/oo.htm*>.

4. The North American Free Trade Agreement

28-26 The North American Free Trade Agreement (NAFTA) was entered into in 1993 by the United States, Canada and Mexico to provide for a widely liberalised common market between the three countries. In addition to a general encouragement to settle disputes by arbitration or other means of alternative dispute resolution NAFTA contains dispute settlement mechanisms in three different chapters, the most relevant of which is Chapter 11. It deals with investments and has three parts: Part A sets out the substantive obligations of the contracting states; Part B provides a dispute settlement mechanism; and Part C defines the significant terms used in the Chapter.[27]

28-27 According to Part A the three contracting states guarantee certain standards of treatment, *i.e.* national or most favoured nation treatment, whichever is better, freedom from performance requirements, the right to control the investment through senior management of whatever nationality, the right to repatriate profits without restrictions, certain conditions of expropriation and information requirements.[28] Any dispute arising out of an alleged violation of any of these duties in relation to an investment, as defined in Article 1139, is to be settled under the provisions of Part B.

28-28 According to the non-mandatory provisions of Article 1118 the disputing parties shall first try to settle any disputes amicably. If such an attempt fails the investor from a state party to NAFTA can proceed to arbitration on giving a 90 days notice of an intention to submit a claim and provided that six months have elapsed since the events giving rise to the claim.[29] The investor has the choice to initiate arbitration under the ICSID Convention, the ICSID Additional Facility

---

[27] For a detailed analysis of Chapter 11 see Eklund, "A Primer on the Arbitration of NAFTA Chapter Eleven Investor-State Disputes", 11(4) *J Int Arb* 135 (1994); Horlick and Marti, "NAFTA Chapter 11B - A Private Right of Action to Enforce Market Access through Investments", 14(1) *J Int Arb* 43 (1997); Alvarez, "Arbitration Under the North American Free Trade Agreement", 16 *Arb Int* 393 (2000); see also Trakman, "Arbitrating Investment Disputes Under the NAFTA", 18(4) *J Int Arb* 385 (2001) dealing with a hypothetical case under NAFTA on the "expropriation" of a salmon farm by a tax raise intended to protect the environment.

[28] *Ibid*, 137-140.

[29] Articles 1119, 1120(1), which are intended to give the state the opportunity to reconsider the alleged violation, essentially a cooling off period; see Trakman, "Arbitrating Investment Disputes Under the NAFTA", 18(4) *J Int'l Arb* 385 (2001) 397; in the *ad hoc* arbitration, *Ethyl Corporation v The Government of Canada*, 38 ILM 708 (1999) the tribunal waived the six month period.

Rules or as an *ad hoc* arbitration under UNCITRAL Rules.[30] According to Article 1121 the investor when doing so has to submit to arbitration under NAFTA to ensure that any adverse award is also binding on him and to waive the right to continue the same claim before other courts or tribunals.[31]

28-29 Unless otherwise agreed by the parties the tribunal will consist of three arbitrators, one to be appointed by each party. While the proceedings will generally be governed by the relevant ICSID or UNCITRAL Rules there are several peculiar features of NAFTA arbitrations. The first is the right to demand consolidation if a controversial state measure affects several investors under Article 1126 NAFTA. In particular the state party should be protected from having to defend numerous arbitrations for the same measures with the threat of conflicting awards. Therefore the state or investor may ask the Secretary General to establish a "super-tribunal" under UNCITRAL Rules to hear all claims in a single arbitration.[32]

28-30 The second special feature of Chapter 11B arbitrations is that questions of the interpretation of NAFTA must, upon the request of one party, be transferred to the Commission. It must render in writing within 60 days an interpretation binding on the arbitration tribunal. The Commission has not yet been called on to exercise this role but it did issue a note on the interpretation of certain Chapter 11 provisions.[33]

28-31 The investor's right to initiate arbitration proceedings under Chapter 11 NAFTA has generated substantial case law already. This is largely due to the fact that the requirements relevant to reaching the threshold of Chapter 11B, in particular the notions of "investment" and "measure" are defined and interpreted very broadly. According to the definition in Article 1139[34] "investment" only excludes financial rights arising out of contracts of sale and services but covers a

---

[30] Article 1120; in certain cases ICSID or ICSID Additional Facility arbitration may not be available since the dispute does not fall within the ambit of these rules; see Alvarez, "Arbitration Under the North American Free Trade Agreement", 16 *Arb Int* 393 (2000) 404.

[31] Alvarez, *ibid*, 408.

[32] For details see Eklund, "A Primer on the Arbitration of NAFTA Chapter Eleven Investor-State Disputes", 11(4) *J Int'l Arb* 135 (1994) 149.

[33] See Notes of Interpretation of Certain Chapter 11 Provisions, NAFTA Free Trade Commision, 31 July 2001 at <www.dfait-maeci.gc.ca/tna-nac/NAFTA-Interpr-en.asp>.

[34] For the text of the provision see <www.sice.oas.org/trad/nafta/naftatce.asp> or 32 *ILM* 289 (1993).

number of issues which go beyond the classical definition of investment. "Measures" which might give rise to the right to arbitration include, *inter alia*, legislative actions but also court decisions. It is, however, important that the investor claims a violation of an obligation under Chapter 11. A claim for breach of an investment contract as such is not sufficient if it does not at the same time constitute a violation of Chapter 11.[35]

28-32 The jurisdiction of a tribunal established under Chapter 11B had to be considered in *Ethyl Corporation v Canada,*[36] one of the first arbitrations under NAFTA. It arose out of a legislative ban by Canada of certain fuel additives produced by Ethyl. Canada challenged the jurisdiction of the tribunal. The tribunal rejected the objections since at the time of the decision the legislation had been enacted and therefore constituted a "measure" in the sense of Chapter 11 and the cooling off period had expired. Furthermore, it held that there was no need to give a restrictive application to the relevant provision of Chapter 11B the interpretation of which is governed by Articles 31 and 32 of the Vienna Convention on the Law of Treaties.

28-33 The right to initiate arbitration proceedings may be lost when the investor pursues its rights by other means of dispute settlement. In *Waste Management v United Mexican States*[37] the Municipality of Acapulco de Juárez in Mexico granted a concession to a wholly owned subsidiary of the US claimant to run a public waste management service. The claimant submitted the waiver required by Article 1121 NAFTA but added a qualification that it did not extend to proceedings based on other sources of law. The tribunal held by majority that though the waiver fulfilled the formal requirements of Article 1121 it was not valid. Since Waste Management had initiated arbitration proceedings against the Municipality of Acapulco de Juárez for the payment of its services and proceedings against the guarantor bank, it had shown that it did not want to abdicate its rights as required by Article 1121.[38]

---

35 ICSID, 1 November 1999, *Robert Azinian, Kenneth Davitian & Ellen Bacca v The United Mexican States*, 14 ICSID Rev-FILJ 538 (1999).

36 See the decision on the place of arbitration and the award on jurisdiction, XXIVa *YBCA* 211 (1999); however, the case was settled before an award on the merits was rendered.

37 *Waste Management, Inc v United Mexican States*, 15 ICSID Rev-FILJ 211 (2000).

38 *Ibid*, 231-239; in a dissenting opinion the US arbitrator appointed by claimant rejected this view since in his opinion the proceedings concerned other issues not covered by Chapter 11.

5. THE ENERGY CHARTER TREATY[39]

28-34 The Energy Charter Treaty was entered into in 1994 by 49 countries from Western, Central and Eastern Europe, Japan and Australia.[40] Its objective is to provide a legal framework for a continuing cooperation between the Contracting States in the energy sector, in particular to create a level playing field for investment in the eastern European energy sector.[41] Part III sets out the provisions for the promotion, protection and treatment of investments in the energy sector. These include a non discriminatory and national or most favoured nation treatment of investments, the removal of barriers and restrictions such as domestic content requirements, compensation for harm to the investment through state actions and prompt, adequate and effective compensation in the event of expropriation. The Treaty essentially provides the same type of investment protection available to foreign investors from other industries.[42]

28-35 Part V contains the rather innovative regime for dispute settlement; creating a direct investor/state obligation of compulsory arbitration. According to Article 26(2) an investor from a Contracting State alleging a violation of treaty obligations has the right to bring a direct claim against the state (a) in the courts or administrative tribunals of the host state, or (b) in line with a pre-agreed dispute settlement procedure, or (c) in arbitration proceedings. The investor is not bound by earlier contractual commitments when making its choice. It may opt for arbitration even though the contract with the state included a forum selection clause in favour of the host state's court or a different type of arbitration.[43] An investor opting for arbitration can choose between arbitration under the ICSID

---

39 For a detailed account see Wälde, "Investment Arbitration Under the Energy Charter Treaty – From Dispute Settlement to Treaty Implementation", 12 *Arb Int* 429 (1996); Turner, "Investment Protection through Arbitration: The Dispute Resolution Provisions of the Energy Charter Treaty", 1 *Int ALR* 166 (1998).

40 The ECT came into force on 16 April 1998 and there are now 51 signatories. <www.encharter.org>.

41 See Wälde (ed), *European Energy Charter Treaty: An East-West Gateway for Investment & Trade?* (Graham & Trotman, 1996).

42 Energy investment, given its political and economic importance, was often excluded from BITs; see Elshihabi, "The Difficulty Behind Securing Sector-Specific Investment Establishment Rights: The case of the Energy Charter", 35 *Int Lawyer* 137 (2001).

43 Paulsson, "Arbitration Without Privity", 10 *ICSID Rev-FILJ* 232 (1995) 249; contra: Wälde, "Investment Arbitration Under the Energy Charter Treaty – From Dispute Settlement to Treaty Implementation", 12 *Arb Int* 429 (1996) 445.

Rules, the ICSID Additional Facility Rules, the SCC Rules or *ad hoc* under UNCITRAL Rules.

28-36 Unlike NAFTA, the Energy Charter Treaty contains few amendments to the arbitration proceedings under the chosen rules. It only provides that the tribunal has to decide the case on the basis of the treaty itself and applicable rules and principles of international law. There have been no cases decided under the Treaty although one case was filed under ICSID and subsequently settled.[44]

28-37 The Energy Charter Treaty does not contain a special enforcement regime. Therefore with the exception of arbitration under ICSID rules, enforcement has to be based on the New York Convention. However, if a contracting state refuses to enforce or comply with an award such non-compliance amounts to a breach of the Treaty for which interstate arbitration under Article 27 is possible.

6. Arbitration Proceedings under the ICSID Convention

28-38 ICSID was established by the 1965 Washington Convention on the Settlement of Investment Disputes Between States and Nationals of the Other States.[45] The purpose of the Convention, prepared under the auspices of the World Bank, was to provide a special forum for the settlement of investment disputes in order to encourage foreign investment and world development.[46] In 1978 ICSID created the "Additional Facility" to cover cases which fall outside the ambit of the ICSID Convention, in particular where one of the parties is not from a Contracting State.

28-39 To date over 130 states have ratified the ICSID Convention and over 100 disputes have been referred to ICSID arbitration.[47] Of more significance is the scale of investment covered by ICSID clauses. In addition to arbitration agreements in favour of ICSID in investment contracts numerous bilateral and multilateral investment protection treaties and national investment laws now

---

[44] *AES Summit Generator Ltd v Republic of Hungary*, Arb/01/4 at <www.worldbank.org/icsid/cases/cases.htm>.

[45] Text reproduced in 4 *ILM* 532 (1965).

[46] See generally Schreuer, *The ICSID Convention: A Commentary* (CUP 2001).

[47] A list of the cases filed can be found at <http://www.worldbank.org/icsid/cases/cases.htm>.

provide for arbitration under ICSID or the Additional Facility.[48] As a consequence there has been a constant increase in the number of cases filed per year.

28-40 ICSID arbitration is an example of delocalised arbitration proceedings governed solely by international rules and not submitted to the provisions of any one national arbitration law.[49] In particular, an ICSID award is not submitted to the scrutiny of national courts for annulment or enforcement. The only means of redress is the delocalised internal ICSID annulment procedure and a facilitated procedure for the recognition and declaration of enforceability by ICSID.

28-41 ICSID arbitration by definition involves a state party and so the rules are based on the assumption that no state can invoke its sovereign immunity in order to challenge the jurisdiction of the tribunal. Submission to ICSID arbitration is considered to be a waiver of sovereign immunity for questions of jurisdiction including *exequatur* proceedings.[50] By contrast, Article 55 makes clear that such waiver does not extend to issues of execution where the national rules are relevant and are not affected by the ICSID rules.

28-42 If no special reservation is made, the existence of a valid ICSID arbitration clause, according to Article 26, excludes any other means of legal recourse to enforce claims, including interim relief. The parties may agree that an ICSID arbitration can only be brought after the means of recourse against a decision available under national law have been exhausted. However, such clauses have been rare in practice. National courts as well as other arbitration

---

[48] There are around 1500 different Bilateral and Multilateral Investment agreements which refer disputes to ICSID; see Obadia, "L'evolution de l'activité du CIRDI", *Rev Arb* 633 (2001); Parra, "Provisions on the Settlement of Investment Disputes in Modern Investment Laws, Bilateral Investment Treaties and Multilateral Instruments", 12 *ICSID Rev-FILJ* 287 (1997); Schreuer, "Commentary on the ICSID Convention", 11 *ICSID Rev-FILJ* (1996) 318; see also Cremades, "Arbitration in Investment Treaties: Public Offer of Arbitration in Investment Protection Treaties", in Briner, Fortier, Berger and Bredow (eds), *Liber Amicorum Böckstiegel*, 161.

[49] Broches, "Convention on the Settlement of Investment Disputes between States and Nationals of other States of 1965 - Explanatory Notes and Survey of its Application", XVIII *YBCA* 627 (1993) 629; Parra, "Provisions on the Settlement of Investment Disputes in Modern Investment Laws, Bilateral Investment Treaties and Multilateral Instruments", 12 *ICSID Rev-FILJ* 287 (1997) 301 *et seq*; Schreuer, "Commentary on the ICSID Convention", 11 *ICSID Rev-FILJ* (1996) 318; Cremades, *Ibid*, 149; Arnoldt, *Praxis des Welthandelsübereinkommens*, 169.

[50] Delaume, "Sovereign Immunity and Transnational Arbitration", 3 *Arb Int* 28 (1987) 32; Arnoldt, *Ibid*, 170.

tribunals have enforced this exclusivity and generally denied jurisdiction when proceedings where started before them.[51] Under Article 27 diplomatic protection by the investor's country of origin is excluded by the arbitration clause.

6.1. The Scope of the ICSID Convention

28-43 It is of considerable practical importance whether a dispute can be referred to arbitration under the ICSID Convention. The scope of the Convention is defined in Article 25(1)

> The jurisdiction of the Centre shall extend to any legal dispute arising directly out of an investment, between a Contracting State (or any constituent subdivision or agency of a Contracting State designated to the Centre by that State) and a national of another Contracting State, which the parties to the dispute consent in writing to submit to the Centre. When the parties have given their consent, no party may withdraw its consent unilaterally.

28-44 Consequently, investment disputes fall within the ambit of the ICSID Convention if the following four requirements are met:

- it must be a legal dispute;
- the parties must have agreed to submit their dispute to ICSID;
- the dispute must be between a Contracting State or its subdivisions and a foreign investor from another Contracting State;
- it must arise directly out of an investment.

28-45 The first requirement is fulfilled whenever there is a dispute about legal rights.[52] The other three requirements have been relied upon by states to challenge the jurisdiction of tribunals formed under the ICSID Rules. Some states have also made use of their right under Article 25(4) to limit their consent to ICSID to a certain category of investment disputes.

---

[51] For the exceptional cases where jurisdiction was assumed despite the existence of ICSID arbitration clause, see Broches, "Convention on the Settlement of Investment Disputes, XVIII *YBCA* 627 (1993) 647, paras 49 *et seq.*

[52] ICSID, Decision of 11 July 1997 on Objections to Jurisdiction and award of 9 March 1998 in case no ARB/96/3, *Fedax NV v Republic of Venezuela*, XXIVa YBCA 23 (1999) 24, paras 1-2, 37 ILM 1378 (1998); ICSID, Decision of the Tribunal on Objections to Jurisdiction, 24 May 1999, *Ceskoslovenska Obchodni Banka, AS (Czech Republic) v The Slovak Republic*, XXIVa YBCA 44 (1999) 60, para 46; 14 ICSID Rev-FILJ 250 (1999).

(a) Consent to arbitration

28-46 ICSID arbitrations require that all parties concerned have agreed to submit to ICSID arbitration. The mere ratification of the ICSID Convention is not in itself consent to arbitration by a state. As the Preamble of the Convention clearly sets out, ratification does not oblige the state to submit a given dispute to arbitration. It serves only to make the state party to the ICSID Convention but does not grant jurisdiction to an ICSID tribunal.[53]

28-47 The necessary consent may be contained in an arbitration agreement concluded between the state and the investor within the framework of the investment contracts or after the dispute has arisen.[54] It is, however, by no means necessary that the consent is contained in a single document or documents exchanged at the conclusion of the investment. Often the contract underlying the investment is not even concluded between the state and the investor but between the investor and a separate private entity incorporated in the state of investment.[55]

28-48 The state in practice often declares its consent to ICSID arbitration in its investment legislation or in BITs. The standing offer by the state to arbitrate may be accepted at any time, including after the dispute has arisen. It is sufficient for an acceptance that an investor files a request for arbitration or invokes the provisions in a letter written to government officials.[56]

---

53 For the required "double consent" to the ICSID Convention and the arbitration agreement see Cremades, "Arbitration in Investment Treaties: Public Offer of Arbitration in Investment Protection Treaties", in Briner, Fortier, Berger and Bredow (eds), *Liber Amicorum Böckstiegel*, 152 *et seq*.

54 For one of the rare cases where a state agreed under strong pressure from the investor's home state (delaying a loan of the Inter-American Development Bank) to ICSID arbitration after the dispute had arisen see the award of 17 February 2000, *Compania del Desarrollo de Santa Elena, SA v Republic of Costa Rica*, , 15 ICSID Rev-FILJ 169 (2000).

55 In *SPP v Egypt, e.g.*, the investment contract was concluded between SPP and the Egyptian General Organization for Tourism and Hotels, a public entity with separate legal personality under the Ministry of Tourism.

56 ICSID, Decision on jurisdiction, 27 November 1985, South Pacific Properties (Middle East) Ltd *and South Pacific Properties Ltd (Hong Kong) v The Arab Republic of Egypt*, XVI YBCA 19 (1991), and ICSID, Decision of 14 April 1988, XVI YBCA 28 (1991); *Asian Agricultural Products Ltd (AAPL) v Republic of Sri Lanka*, 30 ILM 580 (1991); XVII YBCA 106 (1992); *Tradex Hellas SA v Republic of Albania*, Decision on Jurisdiction, 24 December 1996, 14 ICSID Rev-FILJ 161 (1999) 187; *Ceskoslovenska Obchodni Banka, AS (Czech Republic) v The Slovak Republic*, Decision of the Tribunal on Objections to Jurisdiction, 24 May 1999, XXIVa YBCA 44 (1999) 54; for other cases see Broches, "Convention on the Settlement of Investment Disputes", XVIII *YBCA* 627 (1993) 643, paras 36 *et seq*; out of the 44 cases pending in 2001

28-49 Once an arbitration agreement has been concluded, no party can unilaterally revoke its effect. Although this follows from general contract law and is clearly provided for in Article 25(1), the issue arose in *Alcoa v Jamaica.*[57] Shortly before it changed its legislation relating to the production of bauxite and the imposition of a production levy, Jamaica informed ICSID that it had withdrawn certain classes of disputes from the ICSID Convention. On the basis of that declaration, Jamaica contested the jurisdiction of the tribunal. The tribunal held that Jamaica had consented to arbitration in the investment agreement with *Alcoa* and could not unilaterally withdraw from that agreement. Jamaica's declaration could only be effective for future agreements.

(b) Requirements as to the parties involved

28-50 For the Convention to be applicable, one of the parties to the dispute must be a Contracting State or a "constituent subdivision or agency" which has been registered with the Centre. The registration, however, has primarily an evidentiary purpose in order to avoid doubts on whether a state entity can be a party to ICSID arbitration. Therefore, the lack of formal registration does not prevent an entity becoming an eligible party if it has been made clear that it is a constituent subdivision or agency of a Contracting State.[58]

28-51 The other party must be a national of another Contracting State.[59] This requirement must be fulfilled with regard to a natural person, both at the time of the conclusion of the arbitration agreement and at the time of the application for arbitration. For a legal entity, it is sufficient that it has the nationality of another Contracting State only at the time that they entered into the arbitration agreement. It is also not necessary that the legal entity is a privately owned

---

nearly two third were based on consent either in national laws, bilateral or multilateral treaties; see Obadia, "L'evolution de l'activité du CIRDI", *Rev Arb* 633 (2001).

[57] *Alcoa Minerals of Jamaica v Government of Jamaica*, IV YBCA 206 (1979) 207 *et seq.*

[58] See the jurisdictional decision in *Manufacturers Hanover Trust Company v Arab Republic of Egypt and General Authority for Investment and the Free Zones*, (ARB/89/1), unpublished, Annual Report 1991, 7; for a different view see *Cable Television of Nevis Ltd and Cable Television of Nevis Holding, Ltd v The Federation of St Christopher (St Kitts) and Nevis*, 18 ICSID Rev-FILJ 329 (1998) 345, where the tribunal declined jurisdiction because the state was not a party to the contract containing the arbitration clause and the subdivision which signed the contract had not been registered with ICSID.

[59] See ICSID Convention Article 25(2).

company; partly or wholly state owned companies also are covered. The nature of its activities is relevant. They must be private and commercial.[60]

28-52 Article 25(2)(b) states that a legal entity with the nationality of the host state may under certain circumstances be considered as a "national of a different Contracting State". This takes into account the fact that foreign investors are often required to channel their investment through locally incorporated companies. The parties may agree that in these circumstances the local legal entity may be given the status of a "national of a different Contracting State" so that ICSID procedures are available. In *Amco v Indonesia* the tribunal held that it was not necessary to expressly give this status to the local company. It was sufficient for the state party to know that the local company was owned by an investor from a different Contracting State.[61]

28-53 Often the local company is not controlled directly by the foreign investor but is at the end of a pyramid of control. Questions as to the nationality of the controlling party may arise if certain parts of the pyramid are not nationals of Contracting States. In *Amco v Indonesia* the tribunal considered the direct parent company to be the relevant party which had to have the nationality of another Contracting State.[62] In *SOABI v Senegal* the local company was a 100% subsidiary of a Panamanian company which was in turn controlled by Belgian interests. Though Panama was not a contracting state the tribunal rejected the challenge to its jurisdiction.

28-54 It held that the purpose of the final clause of Article 25(2)(b) was to allow the foreign investor access to arbitration despite being required to carry out the investment through locally incorporated companies. In this respect it was irrelevant whether the investor was a direct shareholder of the local company or channelled its investment through intermediary companies, exercising the same control over the local company. Therefore the tribunal considered the party at the top of the pyramid of control to be relevant in determining whether an investor

---

60 See ICSID, 24 May 1999, *Ceskoslovenska Obchodni Banka, AS (Czech Republic) v The Slovak Republic,* Decision on Objections to Jurisdiction, XXIVa YBCA 44 (1999) 48; 14 ICSID Rev-FILJ 250 (1999).

61 ICSID, *Amco Asia Corp and others v Republic of Indonesia*, Decision on Jurisdiction, 23 ILM 351 (1984) 359 *et seq.*

62 *Ibid*, 362 *et seq.*

from a Contracting State was involved.[63] The tribunal in *Vacuum Salt v Ghana* confirmed that foreign control within the context of Article 25(2)(b) does not require or infer a particular percentage of share ownership. Each case must be looked at on the facts of the particular dispute. "There is no "formula". It stands to reason, of course, that 100 percent foreign ownership almost certainly would result in foreign control... and that a total absence of foreign shareholding would virtually preclude the existence of such control."[64] The question of how much control is enough is not always easy to answer and is of paramount importance for a large company seeking to commence a claim through one or more of its subsidiaries against a host state.

28-55 It is not possible to bring a claim within the ambit of the Convention by assigning it to a party from a Contracting State which would fulfil the requirements of Article 25. This would violate the basic principle that arbitration requires the consent of both parties and would defeat the carefully structured system of jurisdiction under the ICSID Convention.[65]

(c) Investment

28-56 An "investment" within the scope of Article 25 is not defined in the ICSID Convention. The draftsmen wanted to leave it primarily to the parties to decide what constituted an investment.[66] An arbitration clause providing for ICSID arbitration is an implied agreement that their "investment" falls under Article 25. The same applies to the unilateral offers to arbitrate contained in the various investment protection laws and investment treaties. They extend the ICSID arbitration option to all types of investment covered by the relevant legal instrument. As a consequence the wide definitions of investment contained, for example, in NAFTA or the Energy Charter Treaty are indirectly also relevant for

---

[63] ICSID, Decision on Jurisdiction, *Société Ouest Africaine des Bétons Industriels v Republic of Senegal*, 6 ICSID Rev-FILJ 217 (1991) 225, paras 35 *et seq.*

[64] *Vacuum Salt Production Limited v Government of the Republic of Ghana*, 4 ICSID Reports 320 (1997) 346 para 43; see further Amerasinghe, "Jurisdiction Ratione Personae Under the Convention on the Settlement of Investment Disputes between States and Nationals of Other States", *BYBIL* 227 (1971-75) 264-265.

[65] ICSID, 15 March 2002, ARB/00/02, *Mihaly International Corporation v Democratic Socialist Republic of Sri Lanka*, 17(7) Mealey's IAR A1 (2002) A2.

[66] Shihata, "Towards a Greater Depoliticization of Investment Disputes: The Role of ICSID and MIGA", 1 *ICSID Rev-FILJ* 1(1986) 5; see also ICSID, Decision on Objections to Jurisdiction, 24 May 1999, *Ceskoslovenska Obchodni Banka, AS (Czech Republic) v The Slovak Republic*, XXIVa YBCA 44 (1999) 61.

the determination of what constitutes an investment for the purposes of Article 25.

28-57 In *Ceskoslovenska Obchodni Banka, AS (Czech Republic) v The Slovak Republic*[67] the tribunal stated that while the consent given by the parties is an important element in determining whether a dispute qualifies as an investment under the Convention it is not conclusive. The tribunal confirmed that

> The concept of an investment as spelled out in ... [Article 25] is objective in nature in that the parties may agree on a more precise or restrictive definition of their acceptance of the Centre's jurisdiction, but they may not choose to submit disputes to the Centre that are not related to an investment. A two-fold test must therefore be applied in determining whether this Tribunal has the competence to consider the merits of the claim: whether the dispute arises out of an investment within the meaning of the Convention and, if so, whether the dispute relates to an investment as defined in the parties' consent to ICSID arbitration, in their reference to the BIT and the pertinent definitions contained in Art. 1 of the BIT.[68]

28-58 In dealing with the objective notion of "investment" under the Convention the Tribunal held

> ... that investment as a concept should be interpreted broadly because the drafters of the Convention did not impose any restrictions on its meaning. Support for a liberal interpretation of the question whether a particular transaction constitutes an investment is also found in the first paragraph of the Preamble to the Convention, which declares that 'the Contracting States [are] considering the need for international cooperation for economic development, and the role of private international investment therein'. This language permits an inference that an international transaction which contributes to cooperation designed to promote the economic development of a Contracting State may be deemed to be an investment as that term is understood in the Convention.[69]

28-59 These proceedings arose out of a series of contracts concluded for the privatisation of claimant. Non performing loan portfolio assets were to be transferred to two "Collection Companies" which had to pay for the transfer. The necessary funds for the payment were to be provided by a loan by claimant to the

---

[67] *Ibid*, XXIVa YBCA 44 (1999); 14 ICSID Rev-FILJ 250 (1999).

[68] ICSID, Decision on Objections to Jurisdiction, 24 May 1999, *Ceskoslovenska Obchodni Banka, AS (Czech Republic) v The Slovak Republic*, XXIVa YBCA 44 (1999) 62 para 53.

[69] *Ibid*, 61, para 49.

two companies; security for its repayment was given by the two states. The dispute concerned the alleged non-fulfilment of the obligation to cover the losses of the Slovak Collection Company by the Slovak Republic. The tribunal came to the conclusion that, considering the whole contractual framework the allegedly breached undertaking constituted an investment by claimant in the sense of Article 25. In determining whether the undertaking would qualify as an investment the tribunal took into account the whole contractual relationship, in particular the loan agreement. Taken together with a number of other obligations it served to ensure a further presence of the claimant in the Slovak Republic and therefore constituted an investment in the Slovakian territory.

28-60 Another case dealing with the interpretation of investment was *Fedax v Republic of Venezuela.*[70] It concerned promissory notes issued by Venezuela in the acknowledgement of a debt for services rendered by a Venezuelan corporation. These notes had been assigned to Fedax, a company from the Dutch Antilles, which initiated ICSID proceedings when a dispute arose in connection with the repayment of the notes. Venezuela objected to the jurisdiction of the tribunal contending that the promissory notes did not constitute an investment within the meaning of Article 25(1) ICSID Convention. It argued that an investment required the "laying out of money or property in business ventures, so that it might produce a revenue or income."

28-61 The tribunal, after analysing the drafting history of the Convention and subsequent case law, rejected the objections.[71] It held that Article 25(1) covers direct and indirect foreign investments. The tribunal then held that the notes as such were not excluded from the Convention so that the definition given to the term investment by the parties was relevant. The tribunal looked to Article 1 of the BIT between the Netherlands and Venezuela on which the investor had relied when initiating the arbitration. Since the Treaty covered "every kind of assets" the tribunal was of the view that the promissory notes fell within the scope of the ICSID Convention.

28-62 To what extent pre-investment expenditures made in the process of preparing an investment fall within the ambit of the Convention became an issue

---

70 ICSID, Decision, 11 July 1997, on Objections to Jurisdiction and award, 9 March 1998, case no ARB/96/3, *Fedax NV v Republic of Venezuela*, 37 ILM 1378 (1998), XXIVa YBCA 23 (1999).

71 The tribunal held the meaning of investment under Article 25 to be wider than the meaning under the MIGA Convention, Article 12.

in *Mihaly International v Sri Lanka*.[72] The dispute arose out of a Build Operate and Transfer (BOT) project for the construction of a power plant in Sri Lanka. At the end of the bidding process, a letter of intent was issued to the claimant that further negotiations would be made exclusively with it for a certain period. This was followed by two further documents extending the time period and recording the agreements reached so far. When the project was dropped the claimant initiated arbitration proceedings for the expenses made in preparation of the project from the time of the letter of intent.

28-63 On the specific circumstances the tribunal held that the costs incurred did not constitute an investment in the sense of Article 25 ICSID Convention. Sri Lanka had consistently made it clear that the documents exchanged did not create any obligation to enter into a contract for the construction of the power plant. The tribunal concluded that the costs of the preliminary phase were prior to authorisation for an investment.[73] The tribunal made clear that without the insistence on the non-binding character of the documents the result may have been different and that a successful negotiation might have brought the pre-investment costs under the umbrella of the investment protection.[74]

6.2. Specifics of ICSID Arbitration Proceedings

28-64 ICSID arbitration proceedings are in many respects similar to other types of institutional arbitration. They are governed by the ICSID Convention and the ICSID Arbitration Rules in force at the time of the parties' consent to arbitration.[75] No national law is applicable to the proceedings which has led many legal authorities to consider ICSID arbitration as an object of delocalised arbitration. If the procedural rules found in the Convention and the arbitration

---

[72] ICSID, 15 March 2002, ARB/00/02, *Mihaly International Corporation v Democratic Socialist Republic of Sri Lanka*, 17(7) Mealey's IAR A1 (2002).

[73] See Award in *Metalclad Corporation v United Mexican States,* 5 ICSID Reports 209 (2002) para 125 where expenditure made pre-investment was also deemed not to be included as part of the investment.

[74] ICSID, 15 March 2002, ARB/00/02, *Mihaly International Corporation v Democratic Socialist Republic of Sri Lanka*, 17(7) Mealey's IAR A1 (2002) A6.

[75] ICSID Convention Article 44.

rules do not provide for a certain problem, the tribunal has a residual power to decide that issue in a manner which it deems appropriate.[76]

28-65 The relevant ICSID provisions contain a number of special rules which concern the composition of the tribunal, the proceedings, the tribunal's powers generally and the power to grant interim relief as well as substantive rules of law.

(a) Composition of the arbitration tribunal

28-66 The parties are free to agree the number of arbitrators. In the absence of an agreement a three member tribunal will decide the case; one arbitrator appointed by each party and the two party appointed arbitrators together agree on the chairman.[77] The parties are not bound to appoint people from the panel of arbitrators maintained by ICSID but they must comply with Article 39, according to which the majority of arbitrators must have a different nationality from those of the parties. The effect of this provision is that only if the parties appoint all members of the tribunal together can they appoint arbitrators of their nationality. In this respect the ICSID Convention differs from the rules of other institutions which only require that the chairman or sole arbitrator is a neutral national.[78]

28-67 If the arbitrators have not been appointed within 90 days after sending the notification, or within any period agreed by the parties, their appointment can be made by ICSID from members of its panel who should not be of the same nationality as any of the parties. [79] To minimise the threat of annulment proceedings, ICSID recommends that the tribunal asks the parties to confirm that it has been properly constituted.[80]

---

[76] Broches, "Convention on the Settlement of Investment Disputes", XVIII *YBCA* 627 (1993) 676, para 136; Schreuer, "Commentary on the ICSID Convention", 12 *ICSID Rev-FILJ* 365 (1997) 404.

[77] Washington Convention Article 37(2)(b); ICSID Rules Rule 2.

[78] Parra, "Provisions on the Settlement of Investment Disputes in Modern Investment Laws, Bilateral Investment Treaties and Multilateral Instruments", 12 *ICSID Rev-FILJ* 287 (1997) 308.

[79] This was the case in ICSID, *Ceskoslovenska Obchodni Banka, AS (Czech Republic) v The Slovak Republic*, XXIVa YBCA 44 (1999), 14 ICSID Rev-FILJ 250 (1999), where the chairman was appointed under Article 38; and *Tradex Hellas SA v Republic of Albania*, 14 ICSID Rev-FILJ 161 (1999), where the chairman and the arbitrator for defendant also had to be appointed by ICSID

[80] Broches, "Convention on the Settlement of Investment Disputes", XVIII *YBCA* 627 (1993) 663, para 101.

28-68 Article 14 requires that the arbitrators should be people of high moral standards and qualifications and that they can be relied upon to render an independent judgment. The notion of independent judgment relates to the independence of the appointing party as well as to the impartiality of the arbitrators.[81] The parties may challenge any arbitrator who does not fulfil these requirements. A decision on any challenge is taken by the other members of the tribunal or, if they cannot agree (or a sole arbitrator has been appointed) by ICSID.[82]

(b) Proceedings before the arbitration tribunal

28-69 Proceedings are initiated by the request for arbitration which must contain information concerning the issues in dispute, the identity of the parties and their consent to arbitration. The request has to be lodged with the Secretary General. To avoid any misuse of ICSID, the Secretary General may refuse to register the request if, on the basis of the information provided, the dispute is manifestly outside the jurisdiction of the Centre.[83]

28-70 The ICSID Rules provide for two distinct phases of the proceedings: written proceedings followed by oral proceedings. After the constitution of the tribunal, the chairman or sole arbitrator should hold a pre-hearing conference to agree the form of the proceedings. Objections to the jurisdiction of the tribunal must be raised as early as possible and no later than the time fixed for the counter-memorial or the rejoinder, if they relate to a counterclaim. As the tribunal may ascertain its jurisdiction at any stage of the proceedings on its own motion, the consequences of a late filing are not serious.[84] Objections to jurisdiction will in general be dealt with in an interim procedure while the proceedings on the merits are stayed.

28-71 According to Rule 21(2) ICSID Arbitration Rules, on the request by one party a pre-hearing conference may be held to reach an amicable settlement.

---

[81] Broches, *ibid*, 638, para 20.

[82] Washington Convention Article 58.

[83] *Ibid*, Article 36(3).

[84] Schreuer, "Commentary on the ICSID Convention", 12 *ICSID Rev-FILJ* 365 (1997) 383.

(c) Powers of the arbitration tribunal

28-72 The arbitration tribunal can decide on its own jurisdiction. The registration of a request for arbitration by the Secretary General does not influence the decision of the tribunal. Even if the Secretary General finds that *prima facie* an arbitration agreement exists, the tribunal can come to the opposite conclusion.[85] The tribunal at its discretion can either decide on its jurisdiction as a preliminary question or join it to the decision on the merits. It is a question of procedural economy. In general it makes little sense to enter into an expensive and time consuming trial on the merits if the tribunal's jurisdiction has not been authoritatively determined. Therefore most tribunals have dealt with objections to jurisdiction in a preliminary decision. There may, however, be cases where questions of jurisdiction cannot be separated from the merits.[86]

28-73 A preliminary decision finding jurisdiction, however, does not of itself constitute an award for the purposes of Rule 50 or 52 ICSID Rules which could be the object of a separate action for annulment. In *SPP v Egypt* the acting Secretary General rejected a request for annulment by Egypt against a decision in favour of jurisdiction. He referred Egypt to the annulment procedure against the final award to raise its objections to jurisdiction.[87] Without doubt the non-availability of immediate relief against such a preliminary decision in favour of jurisdiction will speed up the rendering of an award on the merits. It is not necessary to wait for the results of a lengthy annulment procedure.[88]

---

[85] ICSID, Decision on jurisdiction, *Holiday Inns S A and others v Morocco*, 1 ICSID Reports 655 (1993); ICSID, *AMT v Zaire*, award 21 February 1997, 36 ILM 1542 (1997); Schreuer, "Commentary on the ICSID Convention", 12 *ICSID Rev-FILJ* 365 (1997) 374.

[86] See ICSID, Decision on Jurisdiction, 1 August 1984, *Société Ouest Africaine des Bétons Industriels v Republic of Senegal*, 2 ICSID Reports 180 (1994) 189 where out of the two objections raised against jurisdiction one was dealt with in a preliminary decision while the other was joined to the merits; for a similar approach see ICSID, Decision on Jurisdiction, 25 September 1983, *Amco Asia Corp and others v Republic of Indonesia*, 23 ILM 351 (1984); *Tradex Hellas SA v Republic of Albania*, Decision on Jurisdiction, 24 December 1996, 14 ICSID Rev-FILJ 161 (1999).

[87] See ICSID, award of 20 May 1992, *South Pacific Properties (Middle East) Ltd and South Pacific Properties Ltd (Hong Kong) v The Arab Republic of Egypt*, 3 ICSID Reports 193 (1995) 2; see also Schreuer, "Commentary on the ICSID Convention", 13 *ICSID Rev-FILJ* 478 (1998) 540 *et seq*, paras 64 *et seq*.

[88] Hirsch, *The Arbitration Mechanism of ICSID*, 46; Schreuer, "Commentary on the ICSID Convention", 12 *ICSID Rev-FILJ* 365 (1997) 380. Whether this solution is more in line with procedural economy than the approach taken in most other types of arbitration where preliminary awards on jurisdiction can be appealed separately, seems to be at least questionable.

28-74 The internal annulment proceedings are the only way to control the decision of the arbitration tribunal. Following Article 53(1) it cannot be controlled in domestic courts. As an annulment under Article 52(1)(b) is only possible if the tribunal "manifestly exceeded it powers" the standard of control in this respect is more lenient than it would be in front of a national court. In a national court, any excess of jurisdiction would justify an appeal or refusal to recognise the award under the New York Convention. The question arose in the annulment proceedings in the case between *Klöckner v Cameroon.* The tribunal left open the question whether the first tribunal actually had jurisdiction as that tribunal's decision was at least tenable and did not constitute a manifest excess of powers.[89] Annulment proceedings for manifest excess of powers must also be available for awards denying the existence of jurisdiction.[90]

28-75 The tribunal can engage in default proceedings if one party does not take part in the arbitration. Default is not considered to be an admission of the other party's claim. By contrast, Rule 42(4) ICSID Rules requires the tribunal to examine its jurisdiction and, provided that it has jurisdiction, decide whether the submissions are well founded in both law and fact. It may require the party not in default to present evidence as to any issues relevant for the decision.

(d) Provisional measures

28-76 In ICSID arbitrations interim relief can only be granted by the tribunal. Without an agreement to the contrary no party can apply to a state court for interim measures of protection.[91] In the aftermath of the *Atlantic Triton* arbitration, where interim relief was granted by the French courts,[92] the Centre

---

If at a later stage it is determined that the arbitration tribunal had no jurisdiction, all proceedings on the merits would have been futile.

89 ICSID, Decision on Annulment, 3 May 1985, *Klöckner Industrie-Anlagen GmbH and others v United Republic of Cameroon and Société Camerounaise des Engrais*, 1 ICSID Rev-FILJ 89 (1986) 93 *et seq.*

90 Schreuer, "Commentary on the ICSID Convention",12 *ICSID Rev-FILJ* 365 (1997) 378.

91 ICSID Convention Article 26.

92 See Cour de cassation, 18 November 1986, *Atlantic Triton Company v Republic of Guinea and Soguipeche*, XII YBCA 184 (1987): the court confirmed an attachment order for three Guinean ships in favour of Atlantic Triton; it held that the arbitration clause in favour of ICSID did not exclude the jurisdiction of French courts to grant interim relief. A different view was taken by Swiss and Belgian courts in comparable situations; see Delaume, "Sovereign Immunity and Transnational Arbitration", 3 *Arb Int* 28 (1987) 36; *Atlantic Triton Company v People's Revolutionary Republic of Guinea*, 3 ICSID 13 (1995).

clarified in its arbitration rules that the parties cannot apply for interim relief in the state courts unless agreed between the parties. Rule 39(5) ICSID Rules now provides

> Nothing in this Rule shall prevent the parties provided they have so stipulated in the agreement recording their consent, from requesting any judicial or other authority to order provisional measures, prior to the institution of the proceeding, or during the proceeding, for the preservation of their respective rights and interests.

28-77 State parties will generally refuse to submit expressly to the jurisdiction of the courts of third countries for interim relief.

28-78 The power of a tribunal to grant interim relief is limited. According to Article 47 it cannot order measures but merely recommend them.[93] Though the failure to accept those recommendations can be taken into account in the final award the limited experience with this type of non binding interim relief does not allow a final evaluation of its effectiveness. In *AGIP v Congo* the tribunal's recommendation to assemble the financial reports of the nationalised subsidiary and keep them available for presentation was not followed by the respondent.[94] By contrast in *Mine v Guinea* the claimant followed the recommendation and did not pursue its actions in court.[95] Given the possibility of the tribunal drawing negative inferences from non-compliance and the economic pressure exerted by the World Bank as sponsoring institution, these recommendations have often *de facto* the same effect as orders.[96]

---

[93] Article 47 ICSID Convention provides

> Except as the parties otherwise agree, the Tribunal may, if it considers that the circumstances so require, recommend any provisional measures which should be taken to preserve the respective rights of either party.

An earlier draft allowing further reaching powers met strong opposition and was rejected; for the drafting history see Schreuer, "Commentary on the ICSID Convention", 12 *ICSID Rev-FILJ* 365 (1997) 206, 212 para 3; a tribunal may also order interim relief under Article 47 Additional Facility Rules, upon the request of a party.

[94] See ICSID, *AGIP Company v Popular Republic of the Congo*, 21 ILM 726 (1982) 731, para 42.

[95] ICSID, *Maritime International Nominees Establishment v Republic of Guinea*, XIV YBCA 82 (1989); see also Broches, "Convention on the Settlement of Investment Disputes", XVIII *YBCA* 627 (1993) 678, paras 144 *et seq*; ICSID, Decision on Objections to Jurisdiction, 24 May 1999, *Ceskoslovenska Obchodni Banka, AS (Czech Republic) v The Slovak Republic*, XXIVa YBCA 44 (1999); 14 ICSID Rev-FILJ 250 (1999) (Suspension of bankruptcy proceedings).

[96] Lörcher, *Neue Verfahren der Internationalen Streiterledigung in Wirtschaftssachen*, 353 *et seq.*

28-79 The third peculiar feature of interim relief within the ICSID framework is the power of the tribunal to recommend measures on its own initiative.[97] This also includes the power to recommend measures which differ from those requested by the parties as was, for example, the case in the *Holiday Inn v Morocco* case.[98]

28-80 The prerequisites under which interim relief can be granted are not specified in the Convention or the Rules. They state only that measures can be granted if the tribunal "considers that the circumstances so require." The case law and the *travaux préparatoires* reveal that measures will only be granted where the question cannot await the outcome of the award on the merits.[99] All parties involved must be heard before the recommendation is issued.[100]

(e) Applicable law

28-81 The law applicable to the substance of the case can be chosen by the parties. Such choice does not have to be express or even in a specific form if the tribunal finds clear evidence of the parties' agreement on law.[101] Since Article 42(1) refers to the "rules of law as may be agreed by the parties" the parties may also choose a non-national law, such as *lex mercatoria* or international law.[102] Article 42(3) provides that the parties can also empower the tribunal to decide *ex aequo et bono*. This can either be done in the arbitration clause or during the proceedings as was the case in *Benvenuti & Bonfant v Congo.*[103]

---

[97] ICSID Rules Rule 39(3) provides

> The tribunal may also recommend provisional measures on its own initiative or recommend measures other than those specified in a request. It may at any time modify or revoke its recommendations.

[98] See Lalive, "The First 'World Bank' Arbitration (Holiday Inns v Morocco) – Some Legal Problems", 51 *BYBIL* 123 (1980) 136 *et seq*. None of the actual proceedings in this case have been made public; see 1 ICSID Reports 645 (1995) for an account of the case.

[99] Schreuer, "Commentary on the ICSID Convention", 12 *ICSID Rev-FILJ* 365 (1997) 206, 217, para 14 *et seq*.

[100] ICSID Arbitration Rules Rule 39(4).

[101] See, *e.g.*, *Compania del Desarrollo de Santa Elena, SA v Republic of Costa Rica*, 17 February 2000, 15 ICSID Rev-FILJ 169 (2000) 190, where allegations of such an agreement were rejected by the tribunal.

[102] Broches, "Convention on the Settlement of Investment Disputes", XVIII *YBCA* 627 (1993) 667, para 113.

[103] ICSID, *Benvenuti & Bonfant Sarl v Government of the People's Republic of the Congo,* 21 ILM 740 and 1478 (1982).

28-82 In the absence of an express choice of law by the parties, the tribunal has to apply the law of the state party, including the relevant conflict of laws rules, and "such rules of international law as may be applicable". This reflects the general presumption that a state will not submit to foreign national law. By corollary it is presumed the private party will be concerned about unilateral and unfavourable changes of the law by the state party, if the law of the latter is applicable. To accommodate these concerns it is usually the law of the state party which applies, with the results of such application to be tested against the rules of international law. If international law is violated by the application of the host state's national law, the national law will not be applied.

28-83 The question of the applicable law has been addressed in several cases and by *ad hoc* committees during annulment actions.[104] The relationship between the law of the host state and the rules of international law was explored in detail by the *ad hoc* committee constituted for the annulment action in the *Amco v Indonesia* arbitration. The Committee held that

> [t]he law of the host State is, in principle, the law to be applied in resolving the dispute. At the same time, applicable norms of international law must be complied with since every award has to be recognized, and pecuniary obligations imposed by such award enforced, by every Contracting State of the Convention (Article 54(1), Convention). Moreover, the national State of the investor is precluded from exercising its normal right of diplomatic protection during the pendency of the proceedings and even after such proceedings, in respect of a Contracting State which complies with the award (Article 27, Convention). The thrust of Article 54(1) and of Article 27 of the Convention makes sense only under the supposition that the award involved is not violative of applicable principles and rules of international law.
>
> The above view on the supplemental and corrective role of international law in relation to the law of the host State as substantive applicable law, is shared in case law .... and in literature ...., and finds support as well in the drafting history of the Convention ....[105]

---

[104] The application of rules other than those chosen by the parties or determined according to Article 42(1) or an unauthorised decision *ex aequo et bono* constitute a manifest excess of power which can be the basis for an annulment under Article 52(1)(b); see Schreuer, "Commentary on the ICSID Convention", 12 *ICSID Rev-FILJ* 365 (1997) 406 *et seq.*

[105] ICSID, Decision on Annulment, 16 May 1986, *Amco Asia Corp and others v Republic of Indonesia,* 25 ILM 1441 (1986) 1446, para 21; see also the Decision of the *ad hoc* Committee in

28-84 In *Asia Agricultural Products v Sri Lanka* the tribunal came to the conclusion that the law applicable to the merits was the BIT on the basis of which the arbitration proceedings were initiated. It based its findings on the submissions of the parties which it considered to be an *ex post* selection of the applicable law since both parties had referred to the provisions of this treaty.[106]

(f) ICSID awards

28-85 Awards can be rendered by the majority of the tribunal. Every arbitrator has the right to have an individual opinion, agreeing or dissenting, attached to the award. Article 48(3) requires that the award has to address every issue presented to the tribunal with reasons given. Several *ad hoc* committees considered the ambit of this requirement, the non-fulfilment of which constitutes a reason for annulment in accordance with Article 52(1)(e).

28-86 The effects of the awards are regulated in Article 53(1)

> The award shall be binding on the parties and shall not be subject to any appeal or to any other remedy except those provided for in this Convention. Each party shall abide by and comply with the terms of the award except to the extent that enforcement shall have been stayed pursuant to the relevant provisions of this Convention.

28-87 The binding nature of the arbitration award, which prevents a party from re-litigating the same issue in a different court, is inherent in the concept of arbitration. In this respect Article 53(1) has primarily a declaratory and clarifying function. Distinctive features of ICSID arbitration follow from the other two parts of Article 53(1). The obligation to comply with the award is, as far as the State is concerned, an international treaty obligation; for the non-state party it is an obligation arising under the arbitration agreement. Therefore non-compliance with an award is a breach not only of a contractual duty to the investor but also of an international commitment in relation to all other

---

ICSID, Decision on Annulment, 3 May 1985, *Klöckner Industrie-Anlagen GmbH and others v United Republic of Cameroon and Société Camerounaise des Engrais*, 1 ICSID Rev-FILJ 89 (1986) 112, para 69 which explains the dual role of the general principles: complementary and corrective.

[106] ICSID, *Asian Agricultural Products Ltd v Republic of Sri Lanka*, 27 June 1990, 6 ICSID Rev-FILJ 526 (1991) 533 *et seq*; in the dissenting arbitrator's view the parties had not really agreed on the applicable law and the second sentence of Article 42(1) should have been applied, with Sri Lankan law including the BIT, as primary source.

Contracting States, including the home state of the investor. The duty to comply with the award is not affected by the possibility of a state party seeking to resist enforcement by relying on its sovereign immunity under Article 55.

6.3. Remedies against Awards

28-88 The most distinctive feature of ICSID arbitration is the self-contained and exhaustive nature of its review procedures. Unlike other arbitration regimes, control is exercised by internal procedures rather than by the courts. Remedies against the award are limited to those provided for in the Convention and do not include court involvement. The Convention provides for rectification of minor clerical errors (Article 49(2)), interpretation (Article 50), revision (Article 51), and annulment (Article 52) of the award.

(a) Rectification, interpretation and revision

28-89 Rectification, interpretation and revision are not remedies in a true sense as they do not require the referral of a dispute to a different decision making body. The ICSID Convention provides that rectification can only be granted from the original tribunal. The two other requests, interpretation and revision, should preferably be handled by the original tribunal which is in the best position to grant those remedies. If that tribunal is for any reason no longer available, then requests for interpretation and revision can be referred to a new tribunal, constituted in accordance with the procedure adopted for the original tribunal. In both cases enforcement of the award can be stayed while a decision is pending and the application for revision leading to an automatic preliminary stay.

28-90 Rectification of clerical, arithmetical or similar errors, as well as decisions on omitted issues, can be requested from the tribunal by any party within 45 days of the award being rendered. According to Rule 49 the request has to be directed to the Secretary General and must state in detail what error should be rectified or what question has been omitted. Rectification may not be used to modify the award and the other side must be heard before the remedy is granted.[107] The decisions become part of the award which for the purposes of

[107] In the appeal against AMCO II award (unpublished) the *ad hoc* Committee annulled the rectification of the award because the tribunal had not given the respondent the opportunity to present its views properly. Indonesia had submitted its objections to the jurisdiction of the tribunal and reserved the right to submit its observations on the merits. The tribunal never set a

time limits is considered to be rendered on the day of the rectification or completion.

28-91 A revision of the award is only possible if a fact which could decisively affect the award was only discovered after the award was made and the lack of knowledge is not based on negligence. A request for revision can, however, only be brought within three years after the award has been rendered and it should be made within 90 days after the fact was discovered. No time limits exist for requests for interpretation. In practice these remedies have not played a major role, with only one application for revision made to date.[108]

(b) Annulment proceedings

28-92 The annulment proceedings under Article 52 are a distinct feature of ICSID arbitrations. Under all other arbitration regimes, the review of an award in challenge proceedings is effected by state courts, in general those of the place of arbitration. Article 52 provides for internal control through a so-called *ad hoc* committee. This internal ICSID control of the award is intended to avoid protracted and long lasting proceedings in state courts. Furthermore, it takes account of the special factual situation in state contracts. The state party would not want to submit to the jurisdiction of a different state and the private party may not trust the courts of the host state.

28-93 Up to December 2002 annulment proceedings have been instituted in seven cases, two of which settled or were discontinued before a decision.[109] In

---

time limit for submissions but dealt with the request for rectification in a summary fashion; for a commentary on this decision see Broches, "Convention on the Settlement of Investment Disputes", XVIII *YBCA* 627 (1993) 693; for a more recent example of a rectification see *Compania del Desarrollo de Santa Elena, SA v Republic of Costa Rica*, 17 February 2000, 15 ICSID Rev-FILJ 169 (2000) 205.

[108] Schreuer, in "Commentary on the ICSID Convention", 14 *ICSID Rev-FILJ* 493 (1999) 495 *et seq*, refers to the Democratic Republic of Congo's application for revision of the ICSID award of 21 February 1997, *AMT v Zaire*, 36 ILM 1531 (1997).

[109] In *SPP v Egypt* a settlement was reached, while in ICSID, case no ARB/99/3, *Philippe Gruslin v Malaysia*, 5 ICSID Reports 183 (2002) also Helgeson and Lauterpacht (eds), *Reports of Cases Decided under ICSID*, the proceedings were terminated by an order for discontinuance on 2 April 2002 for non-payment of the advances pursuant to Administrative and Financial Regulation 14(3)(d); the annulment application was dismissed in *Wena Hotels Ltd v Egypt* Annulment decision of 5 February 2002, ICSID case no ARB/98/4 unpublished see <www.worldbank.org/icsid/cases/conclude.htm>; see Annulment of 21 March 2001 in ICSID, case no ARB/97/3, 21 November 2000, *Compañía de Aguas del Aconquija SA and Vivendi*

three cases the awards or at least parts of it were annulled. In *Mine v Guinea* the partial annulment of the award led to an agreement between the parties.[110] In *Klöckner v Cameroon*[111] and *Amco v Indonesia*[112], the annulment of the award resulted in a second set of arbitration proceedings in front of newly constituted tribunals. The awards rendered by those second tribunals were challenged again by the parties, but without success.[113] The strict standards applied by the first *ad hoc* committees in *Klöckner v Cameroon* and *Amco v Indonesia* have raised criticism as to whether the annulment proceedings were not turned into a means of reviewing the awards on the merits.[114]

28-94 Irrespective of whether the criticism is justified and of the control actually exercised, all *ad hoc* committees have emphasised the fact that the annulment proceedings are not supposed to be an appeal. They are limited to controlling the legitimacy of the decision making process.

28-95 The right to have the award controlled in annulment proceedings cannot completely be waived in advance. Not all grounds which justify an annulment primarily protect the interest of the parties. Some of them, for example the impartiality of the arbitrator, also serve to protect the integrity of the arbitration process as such and are therefore not at the disposition of the parties. The parties are still obliged to raise the grounds of challenge as early as possible. A party which knowingly fails to challenge a serious procedural irregularity before the tribunal may be barred by Rule 27 from seeking annulment on that basis.[115]

28-96 The grounds for an annulment are exhaustively listed in ICSID Convention Article 52(1)

Universal v Argentine Republic, 40 ILM 426 (2001), publication announced in 42 *ILM* 2003 and forthcoming 6 ICSID Reports; for an overview of the recent applications for annulment see Gaillard, "Chronique des sentences arbitrales", 129 *Clunet* 189 (2002).

[110] XVI YBCA 40 (1991).

[111] XI YBCA 162 (1986).

[112] XII YBCA 129 (1987); 25 ILM 1141 (1986).

[113] For a summary of those cases, see Schreuer, "Commentary on the ICSID Convention", 13 *ICSID Rev-FILJ* 478 (1998) 524, paras 21 *et seq.*

[114] See the summary of the discussion by Schreuer, *ibid*, 13 *ICSID Rev-FILJ* 478 (1998) 529, paras 36 *et seq*; Arnoldt, *Praxis des Welthandelsübereinkommens*, 225 *et seq.*

[115] For an analysis of the entire waiver mechanism see Schreuer, "Commentary on the ICSID Convention", 13 *ICSID Rev-FILJ 478 (*1998) 534 paras 51 *et seq.*

Either party may request annulment of the award by an application in writing addressed to the Secretary-General on one or more of the following grounds:

(a) that the Tribunal was not properly constituted;

(b) that the Tribunal has manifestly exceeded its powers;

(c) that there was corruption on the part of a member of the Tribunal;

(d) that there has been a serious departure from a fundamental rule of procedure; or

(e) that the award has failed to state the reasons on which it is based.

28-97 Most of the grounds mentioned are also found in the provisions for control of awards contained in other arbitration regimes. The grounds mentioned in Article 52 are, however, narrower in that not every excess of power or departure from a rule of procedure is sufficient to annul an award. By contrast the ICSID Convention requires a qualified form, or a manifest excess of powers. Furthermore, violation of public policy is not mentioned as a separate ground for annulment. Proper constitution of the tribunal and corruption of an arbitrator have been of no practical importance to date. The ICSID secretariat manages the appointment process carefully and the arbitrators appointed are usually of such quality that these grounds do not arise.

i. Excess of powers (Article 52(1)(b))

28-98 An excess of power exists if the tribunal lacks jurisdiction either because the dispute is not covered by the arbitration agreement or the other requirements of Article 25 are not met. Any tribunal which has not been authorised by the parties exceeds its powers if it renders an award.[116] The same applies if the award goes beyond what the parties have requested. The *ad hoc* committee in *Vivendi Universal v Argentine Republic*[117] also considered the failure to exercise existing jurisdiction to be a manifest excess of power; annulling the award on the merits in part.

28-99 An excess of power may also exist when the tribunal disregards the applicable law. The provisions on the applicable law are essential elements of the

---

[116] Broches, "Convention on the Settlement of Investment Disputes", XVIII *YBCA* 627 (1993) 689, paras 180 *et seq*; Schreuer, "Commentary on the ICSID Convention", 13 *ICSID Rev-FILJ* 478 (1998) 565 paras 147 *et seq.*

[117] ICSID, *Companía de Aguas del Aconquija, SA and Vivendi Universal (formerly Compagnie Générale des Eaux v Argentine Republic*, ARB/97/3, paras 86 *et seq.*

parties' agreement to arbitrate and constitute important parameters for the tribunal's activity. Tribunals which base their award on a law other than that applicable under Article 42 or even decide *ex aequo et bono* without being authorised to do so manifestly exceed their powers.[118]

28-100 Annulment proceedings based on allegations of the non-application of the applicable law are more problematic. The dividing line between non-application and wrong application is thin and easily transgressed.[119] An incorrect application of a law often consists in the non-application of a single rule of that law which should have been applied. Therefore, to control whether single rules of the applicable law have been applied may have the potential of turning the annulment proceedings into an appeal on the merits.[120]

28-101 In *Klöckner v Cameroon*, the first case which came up for annulment, the tribunal determined that Cameroon law was applicable to the case. In relation to the relevant duty of disclosure it held that

> ... the principle according to which a person who engages in close contractual relations, based on confidence, must deal with his partner in a frank, loyal and candid manner is a basic principle of French civil law, as is indeed the case under other national codes we know of ...[121]

28-102 The *ad hoc* committee annulled the award on the basis that the tribunal did not ascertain the principle, but just postulated its existence without any reference to legislative texts, judgments or scholarly opinions. In its view the reasoning of the award made it impossible to derive whether or not the postulated

---

[118] ICSID, *Maritime International Nominees Establishment (MINE) v Government of Guinea*, ICSID Rev-FILJ 95 (1990) 104, para 5-03; Schreuer, "Commentary on the ICSID Convention", 13 *ICSID Rev-FILJ* 478 (1998) 574, paras 167 *et seq.*

[119] Arnoldt, *Praxis des Welthandelsübereinkommens*, 187.

[120] In this respect the annulment of the first award in *Amco v Indonesia* for an alleged non-application gave rise to concern. The non-application was derived from the fact that in the light of a provision of Indonesian law according to which only registered investment could be counted the tribunal had overstated the claimant's investment by 250%; see ICSID, Decision on Annulment, 16 May 1986, *Amco Asia Corp and others v Republic of Indonesia,* 25 ILM 1441 (1986) 1449, paras 92 *et seq.*

[121] ICSID, Final Award, *Klöckner Industrie-Anlagen GmbH and others v United Republic of Cameroon and Société Camerounaise des Engrais*, X YBCA 71 (1985); see Paulsson, "The ICSID *Klöckner v Cameroon* Award: The Duties of Partners in North-South Economic Development Agreements", 2(1) *J Int'l Arb* 145 (1984) 157, 2 ICSID Reports 3 (1994).

principle of French law came from positive French law but bears every appearance of

> ... a simple reference to equity, to the 'universal' principles of justice and loyalty, such as those which would be invoked by amiables compositeurs ...In conclusion, it must be recognized that, by reasoning as it has done, that is to say by limiting itself to postulating the existence of a principle, without either proving its existence or attempting to identify the rules which form the context of the principle in question, the arbitration tribunal did not apply 'the law of the Contracting State'.[122]

28-103 Later *ad hoc* committees have adopted more lenient standards as to the required substantiation of the legal sources.[123] In particular, it has to be kept in mind that not every reference to "equitable principles" implies that the tribunal has decided *ex aequo et bono.* These principles are often part of the applicable law.[124] If the annulment proceedings are not to be turned into a review on the merits the requirement that only a manifest excess of power justifies annulment must be taken seriously. Manifest does not refer to the gravity of the excess but to the ease with which its perceived.[125] An excess of power is manifest if it can be discerned with little effort and without deeper analysis.[126]

ii. Serious departure from a fundamental rule of procedure (Article 52(1)(d))

28-104 A double qualification is required for annulments based on the departure from a rule of procedure. Not only has the departure to be serious but it must also be a "fundamental" rule of procedure, *i.e.* rules of natural justice such as the right

---

[122] Decision on Annulment, *Klöckner Industrie-Anlagen GmbH and others v United Republic of Cameroon and Société Camerounaise des Engrais*, 1 ICSID Rev-FILJ 90 (1986) 114, paras 77, 79.

[123] See, *e.g.*, ICSID, Decision on Annulment, *Maritime International Nominees Establishment (MINE) v Government of Guinea*, 5 ICSID Rev-FILJ 95 (1990), para 6-50 where the *ad hoc* Committee did not consider it a reason for annulment that the tribunal instead of referring to the applicable provision of Guinea law constantly referred to the nearly identical provision of French law on which the Guinean law was based; see Schreuer, "Commentary on the ICSID Convention", 13 *ICSID Rev-FILJ* 478 (1998) 585, paras 190 *et seq.*

[124] ICSID, Decision on Annulment, 16 May 1986, *Amco Asia Corp and others v Republic of Indonesia,* 25 ILM 1441 (1986) 1446, para 26; Schreuer, "Commentary on the ICSID Convention", 13 *ICSID Rev-FILJ* 478 (1998) para 206.

[125] Schreuer, "Commentary on the ICSID Convention", 13 *ICSID Rev-FILJ* 478 (1998) 561, paras 138 *et seq.*

[126] Feldmann, "The Annulment Proceedings and the Finality of ICSID Arbitral Awards", 2 *ICSID Rev-FILJ* 85 (1987) 100 *et seq.*

to be heard, equal treatment of the parties and impartiality of the arbitrators. The *ad hoc* committee in *Mine v Guinea* held that the notion of "serious departure" entailed quantitative as well as qualitative elements. It required a substantial departure of the kind which deprived the party of the protection or benefits the rule was intended to provide.[127]

28-105 Article 52(1)(d) was successfully invoked by Indonesia in the annulment proceedings against the rectification of the second *Amco v Indonesia* award. Indonesia had previously contested the jurisdiction of the tribunal and reserved its right to present arguments on the issue as to whether the rectification required by Amco was not in reality a modification of the award. The tribunal rectified the contract without taking note of Indonesia's reservation and without giving it a chance to present its arguments on that point. The *ad hoc* committee held this to be a serious violation of Article 49(4); giving a party a right to be heard before an award is rectified was considered to be a fundamental rule of procedure. It annulled the rectification of the award. [128]

iii. Failure to state reasons (Article 52 (1)(e))

28-106 A failure to state the reasons for the award has been invoked by the applicants in all published annulment decisions. Besides the complete absence of reasons it covers cases where the reasons given contradict each other and the award cannot be based on the reasoning of the remaining parts.[129] The alleged failure to state reasons usually only relates to certain questions. *Ad hoc* committees have often adopted a very generous standard and supplied reasons themselves if they considered the result to be correct but not sufficiently reasoned.[130]

---

[127] ICSID, Decision on Annulment, *Maritime International Nominees Establishment (MINE) v Government of Guinea*, 5 ICSID Rev-FILJ 95 (1990) 104, paras 5-05 *et seq.*

[128] For a summary of this decision, see Broches, "Convention on the Settlement of Investment Disputes", XVIII *YBCA* 627 (1993) 693, paras 194 *et seq.*

[129] See ICSID, Decision on Annulment, *Klöckner Industrie-Anlagen GmbH and others v United Republic of Cameroon and Société Camerounaise des Engrais*, 1 ICSID Rev-FILJ 90 (1986) 125 para 116.

[130] See *Amco Asia Corp and others v Republic of Indonesia,* Decision on Annulment, 16 May 1986, 25 ILM 1441 (1986) 1452 para 58 *et seq* (Indonesia was found responsible for acts of army and police personnel); see also Schreuer, "Commentary on the ICSID Convention", 13 *ICSID Rev-FILJ* 478 (1998) 623 paras 276 *et seq.*

28-107 The extent to which reasons that are not considered to be sufficient can also justify annulment under Article 52(1)(e) is a controversial issue. Different views exist as to what is required under Article 48(3). The *ad hoc* committee in *Klöckner v Cameroon*, followed in *Amco v Indonesia*, required the reasons to be sufficiently relevant that is, reasonably sustainable and capable of providing a basis for the decision.[131] Such an investigation into the adequacy of the reasons entails the danger of a review on the merits.[132] To avoid a review on the merits, the more lenient standard adopted by the *ad hoc* committee in *Mine v Guinea* seems preferable. It was of the opinion that

> ... the requirement that an award has to be motivated implies that it must enable the reader to follow the reasoning of the Tribunal on points of fact and law. It implies that, and only that. The adequacy of the reasoning is not an appropriate standard of review under paragraph (1)(e), because it almost inevitably draws an ad hoc Committee into an examination of the substance of the tribunal's decision, in disregard of the exclusion of the remedy of appeal by Article 53 of the Convention. A Committee might be tempted to annul an award because that examination disclosed a manifestly incorrect application of the law, which, however, is not a ground for annulment.
>
> In the Committee's view, the requirement to state reasons is satisfied as long as the award enables one to follow the tribunal's reasoning from Point A to Point B and eventually to its conclusion, even if it had made an error of fact or of law. This minimum requirement is in particular not satisfied by either contradictory or frivolous reasons.[133]

28-108 In addition to the duty to state reasons Article 48(3) also obliges the tribunal to deal with all questions submitted to it. Whether a violation of that duty can be subsumed under Article 52(1)(e) is uncertain. Opponents of such an

---

[131] ICSID, Decision on Annulment, *Klöckner Industrie-Anlagen GmbH and others v United Republic of Cameroon and Société Camerounaise des Engrais*, 1 ICSID Rev-FILJ 90 (1986) 126 para 120; in ICSID, Decision on Annulment, 16 May 1986, *Amco Asia Corp and others v Republic of Indonesia*, 25 ILM 1441 (1986) 1450 para 43 the reasons had to be "sufficiently pertinent".

[132] Arnoldt, *Praxis des Welthandelsübereinkommens*, 189; Feldmann, The Annulment Proceedings and the Finality of ICSID Arbitral Awards, 2 *ICSID Rev-FILJ* 85 (1987) 93 *et seq.*

[133] ICSID, Decision on Annulment, *Maritime International Nominees Establishment (MINE) v Government of Guinea*, 5 ICSID Rev-FILJ 95 (1990) 105, paras 5-08 *et seq*; see also the Decision on Annulment in ICSID, *Companía de Aguas del Aconquija, SA and Vivendi Universal (formerly Compagnie Générale des Eaux) v Argentine Republic*, ARB/97/3, paras 64 *et seq.*

inclusion rely on the fact that Article 52(1)(e) only refers to the duty to state reasons, while Article 49 contains a special procedure for cases where the tribunal has not dealt with all questions submitted to it.[134] The prevailing view adopted by the different *ad hoc* committees is that the failure to deal with crucial and decisive arguments submitted to the tribunal can also justify annulment under Article 52(1)(e). This is the case, for example, where the questions not dealt with in the award will influence other parts of the award so that only an annulment is appropriate.[135]

iv. Annulment process

28-109 Applications for annulment must be made in writing to the Secretary General who verifies their *prima facie* admissibility before registering them. An application must be made within 120 days after the award is rendered and must contain the grounds on which it is based. If the request is based on an alleged corruption of the arbitrator the time only starts to run after the corruption has been discovered, within the limit of three years. The three member *ad hoc* committee is appointed by the Chairman of the Administrative Council and the parties. None of its members should have the same nationality as the parties or the arbitrators of the original tribunal or should have been appointed to the panel of arbitrators by either the state party or the home state of the private party.[136] These requirements are stricter than those for the original tribunal and should safeguard maximum objectivity. Upon application by either party the enforcement of the award shall be provisionally stayed until the committee has ruled on a stay of enforcement pending its decision.

28-110 Proceedings before the *ad hoc* committee are conducted according to the same rules as for the original proceedings. If the *ad hoc* committee finds that a ground for annulment exists it has discretion whether or not to annul the entire

---

134 Feldmann, "The Annulment Proceedings and the Finality of ICSID Arbitral Awards", 2 *ICSID Rev-FILJ* 85 (1987) 105 *et seq*; Niggemann, "Das Washingtoner Weltbankübereinkommen von 1965 – Das Nichtigkeitsverfahren im Ad-Hoc-Komitee", 4 *Jahrbuch für die Praxis der Schiedsgerichtsbarkeit* 115 (1990).

135 ICSID, Decision on Annulment, 16 May 1986, *Amco Asia Corp and others v Republic of Indonesia*, 25 ILM 1441 (1986) 1448, para 32; ICSID, Decision on Annulment, *Maritime International Nominees Establishment (MINE) v Government of Guinea*, 5 ICSID Rev-FILJ 95 (1990) 106, para 5-13; see also Broches, "Convention on the Settlement of Investment Disputes", XVIII *YBCA* 627 (1993) 695, paras 201 *et seq.*

136 ICSID Convention Article 52(3).

award or the incriminated parts of it.[137] It cannot modify the award nor substitute its decision for that of the tribunal. Upon annulment of the award the dispute will be submitted to a new tribunal constituted in the same way as the original one. It is not bound by the reasoning of the *ad hoc* committee[138] and its award may be subject to annulment proceedings, as has happened in both cases where a second award was rendered.[139]

6.4. Recognition and Enforcement

28-111 ICSID awards are subject to a special regime for recognition and enforcement contained in Article 54 of the Convention.[140] All Contracting States are required to recognise the award and enforce its pecuniary obligations as if it were a final judgment of the court of the state. This obligation exists independently from whether or not the state in question or its nationals were a party to the proceedings. While the obligation to recognise awards is not limited to any form of award the facilitated enforcement procedure only covers the pecuniary obligations. Orders for specific performance or other non pecuniary obligations must be enforced under the New York Convention or the law of the state of enforcement.[141]

28-112 Contrary to these systems review is not possible under the special procedure foreseen by the ICSID Convention. Article 54 does not contain any grounds upon which recognition and enforcement can be denied. Those grounds can only be raised within the framework of an annulment procedure. If this is not done, it is sufficient for a party seeking recognition and enforcement to furnish a copy of the award certified by the Secretary General to the competent authority as named by the state. The task of the Secretary General is limited to ascertaining

---

[137] ICSID, Decision on Annulment, *Maritime International Nominees Establishment (MINE) v Government of Guinea*, 5 *ICSID Rev-FILJ* 95 (1990) 103, paras 4-09 *et seq*; Schreuer, "Commentary on the ICSID Convention", 13 *ICSID Rev-FILJ* 478 (1998) 660, paras 362 *et seq*; a different view was taken by the *ad hoc* Committee, Decision on Annulment, *Klöckner Industrie-Anlagen GmbH and others v United Republic of Cameroon and Société Camerounaise des Engrais*, , 1 *ICSID Rev-FILJ* 90 (1986) 144, para 179.

[138] Schreuer, "Commentary on the ICSID Convention", 13 *ICSID Rev-FILJ* 478 (1998) 518 *et seq.*

[139] *Ibid.*

[140] This provision is modelled after Article 192 EEC (now Article 256 EC Treaty). See Schreuer, "Commentary on the ICSID Convention", 14 *ICSID Rev-FILJ* 71 (1999) 75.

[141] Schreuer, "Commentary on the ICSID Convention", 14 *ICSID Rev-FILJ* 46 (1999) 100.

the authenticity of the award and verifying that no intervening stay of enforcement exists.[142]

28-113 The relevant authority is also not allowed to grant an *exequatur* with certain restrictions. An *exequatur* granted by the French Tribunal de grande instance Paris which contained a limiting condition that no measures of execution should be taken without prior authorization by the court[143] was successfully appealed before the Cour d'appel Paris. It held

> The judge at first instance, acting on a request pursuant to Article 54 of the Convention of Washington could not therefore, without exceeding his competence, become involved in the second stage, that of execution, to which the question of the immunity from execution of foreign States relates.
> Consequently that part of the order of 23 December 1980 of the President of the Tribunal de grande instance of Paris which is the object of this appeal must be deleted.[144]

28-114 Article 54 requires the Contracting States to give ICSID awards the same status as final judgments of a local court and to enforce them in the same manner. It does not demand a preferential treatment of awards. Therefore a state party can resist execution of an award by invoking its sovereign immunity if that defence would also exist in relation to a domestic judgment. This is specifically stated in Article 55 according to which the ICSID Convention does not affect the national rules on sovereign immunity from enforcement.

28-115 The second means to ensure the award is enforced is via diplomatic protection through the investor's home state. Article 27(1) provides that the right to diplomatic protection revives if a state does not comply with its obligation to enforce the award. The obligation does not only exist towards the investor party, but also towards the other Contracting States. By not complying with the award, for example, by relying on sovereign immunity from execution, a state violates its international treaty obligation so that an action could be brought to the ICJ under Article 64. Other means of diplomatic protection may be negotiations or set offs against claims which the debtor state may have against the investor's

---

142 Delaume, "Sovereign Immunity and Transnational Arbitration", 3 *Arb Int* 28 (1987) 34.

143 See Tribunal de grande instance Paris, 13 January 1981, *Benvenuti et Bonfant SARL v Gouvernement de la Republique du Congo*, 108 Clunet 365 (1981) and Cour d'appel Paris, 23 December 1980, 108 *Clunet* 843 (1981).

144 Cour d'appel Paris, 26 June 1981, 1 ICSID Reports 369 (1993) 371.

home state. As with all other types of diplomatic protection usually the exhaustion of all legal remedies to secure enforcement in the host state is required.

28-116 In practice most awards are performed voluntarily as generally a cost/benefit analysis is in favour of compliance. The damage to the international reputation of the state following from non-compliance and the effect that can have on further investment is, in most cases, greater than the amounts to be paid under the award. In the past the Secretary General of ICSID has officially communicated with recalcitrant parties and reminded them of their obligation.[145]

7. Arbitration under ICSID Additional Facility Rules

28-117 The Additional Facility and its arbitration rules were created in 1978 to provide for dispute settlement facilities under the auspices of the World Bank for disputes between a state and a foreign party which are not covered by the ICSID Convention.[146] According to Article 2(a) Additional Facility Rules jurisdiction requires that either the state or the private party's state of origin is a Contracting States to the ICSID Convention. It is not required that the dispute arises out of an investment in the sense of the ICSID Convention but it must involve a transaction which by the intention of the parties, its duration or importance goes beyond an ordinary commercial contract.[147] The practical importance of the Additional Facility has increased considerably with NAFTA, the Energy Charter Treaty, and a number of BITs referring to its dispute settlement proceedings.[148]

28-118 Arbitration under the Additional Facility Rules are more akin to other institutional arbitrations than ICSID Convention arbitration. Accordingly, awards made under the Additional Facility Rules may be subject to challenge in the courts of the place of arbitration as the self-contained and exhaustive review system of the ICSID Convention is not applicable.[149] Awards rendered under the

---

[145] Schreuer, "Commentary on the ICSID Convention", 14 *ICSID Rev-FILJ* 46 (1999) 62.

[146] For the historical background see Broches, *Selected Essays – World Bank, ICSID, and Other Subjects of Public and Private International Law* (Martinus Nijhoff 1995) 249.

[147] Additional Facility Rules Article 4(3).

[148] See, *e.g.*, ICSID, *Joseph Charles Lemire v Ukraine*, 15 ICSID Rev-FILJ 528 (2000), where the dispute arose under a BIT between the US and Ukraine.

[149] See, *e.g.*, the partial annulment by the Supreme Court of British Columbia, 2001 *BCSC* 664, of an award rendered in NAFTA proceedings, ICSID, *United States of Mexico v Metalclad*

Additional Facility Rules do not benefit from the facilitated recognition and enforcement under the ICSID Convention; they have to be enforced under the New York Convention.

28-119 The rapid development and establishment of investment arbitration has influenced international commercial arbitration practice as well. The autonomous and delocalised nature of public international law arbitrations has enhanced the status of institutional and *ad hoc* arbitrations. Essentially there is little difference to the overall structures, procedures and effectiveness, except for the problem of enforcement against sovereign entities. What is clear is that the characteristics of investment arbitrations are seen in commercial arbitrations and vice versa.

Corporation, 40 ILM 36 (2001); also reported in Gaillard, "Chronique des sentences arbitrales", 129 *Clunet* 189 (2002) 190 *et seq*.

ABBREVIATED BIBLIOGRAPHY

This list contains arbitration books only which have been used in abbreviated form in the text. Other bibliographical references to general books, articles and other publications are made in full in the footnotes.

Abdelgawad, *Arbitrage et Droit de la Concurrence*	Walid Abdelgawad, *Arbitrage et Droit de la Concurrence. Contribution à l'étude des rapports entre ordre spontané et ordre organisé* (LGDJ 2001).
Bandel, *Einstweiliger Rechtsschutz im Schiedsverfahren*	Stefan Bandel, *Einstweiliger Rechtsschutz im Schiedsverfahren - Zulässigkeit und Wirkungen schiedsrichterlicher und gerichtlicher einstsweiliger Maßnahmen gemäß den Bestimmungen des SchiedsVfG* (Beck, 2000)
Berger, *Arbitration Interactive*	Klaus Peter Berger, *Arbitration Interactive* (Peter Lang 2002)
Berger, *Creeping Codification of Lex mercatoria*	Klaus Peter Berger, *The Creeping Codification of Lex mercatoria* (Kluwer 1999)
Berger, *International Economic Arbitration*	Klaus Peter Berger, *International Economic Arbitration* (Kluwer 1993)
Bernard, *L'arbitrage voluntaire*	A Bernard, *L'arbitrage volontaire en droit privé* (Bruylant 1937)
Bernstein's *Handbook*	Ronald Bernstein, John Tackaberry, Arthur L. Marriott and Derek Wood (eds), *Handbook of Arbitration Practice* (3rd ed, Sweet & Maxwell, 1997)
Berti (ed), *International Arbitration in Switzerland*	Stephen V Berti (ed), *International Arbitration in Switzerland: An Introduction to and a Commentary on Articles 176-194 of the Swiss Private International Law Statute* (Kluwer Law International, Helbing & Lichtenhahn 2000)
Besson, *Arbitrage*	Sébastien Besson, *Arbitrage International et*

International et Measures Provisoires	*Measures Provisoires* (1st ed, Schulthess 1998)
Blessing, *Introduction to Arbitration*	Marc Blessing, *Introduction to Arbitration - Swiss and International Perspectives* (Helbing & Lichtenhahn 1999)
Born, *Arbitration Agreements*	Gary Born, *International Arbitration and Forum Selection Agreements: Planning Drafting and Enforcing* (Kluwer Law International 1999)
Born, *International Commercial Arbitration*	Gary Born, *International Commercial Arbitration Commentary and Materials* (2d ed, Transnational Publishers / Kluwer Law International 2001)
Born, *International Commercial Arbitration in the US*	Gary Born, *International Commercial Arbitration in the US - Commentary and Materials* (Kluwer 1994)
Bötsch (ed), *Provisional Remedies*	Axel Bötsch (ed), *Provisional Remedies in International Commercial Arbitration – A Practitioner Handbook* (De Gruyter 1994)
Brower and Brueschke, *Iran-United States Claims Tribunal*	Charles N Brower and Jason D Brueschke, *The Iran-United States Claims Tribunal* (Kluwer 1998)
Bucher and Tschanz, *International Arbitration in Switzerland*	Andreas Bucher and Pierre-Yves Tschanz, *International Arbitration in Switzerland* (Helbing & Lichtenhahn 1989)
Bucher, *Arbitrage International en Suisse*	Andreas Bucher, *Le nouvel arbitrage international en Suisse* (Helbing & Lichtenhahn 1988)
Bucher, *Die neue internationale Schiedsgerichtsbarkeit in der Schweitz*	Andreas Bucher, *Die neue internationale Schiedsgerichtsbarkeit in der Schweitz* (Helbing & Lichtenhahn 1989)
Carbonneau (ed), *Lex*	Thomas Carbonneau (ed), *Lex Mercatoria and*

Mercatoria and Arbitration — *Arbitration: a Discussion of the New Law Merchant* (2d revised ed, Kluwer and Juris Publishing 1998)

Carbonneau, *Arbitration* — Thomas E Carbonneau, *Cases and materials on the law and practice of arbitration* (2d edition, Juris Publishing 2000)

CEPANI (ed), *Arbitration and European Law* — CEPANI (ed), *Arbitration and European Law* (Bruylant 1997)

Craig Park Paulsson, *1998 ICC Rules* — W Lawrence Craig, William W Park, Jan Paulsson, *Annotated Guide to the 1998 ICC Arbitration Rules with Commentary* (Oceana 1998)

Craig Park Paulsson, *ICC Arbitration* — W Lawrence Craig, William W Park, Jan Paulsson, *International Chamber of Commerce Arbitration* (3rd ed, Oceana 2000)

David, *Arbitration in international trade* — René David, *Arbitration in international trade* (Kluwer Law and Taxation1985)

David, *L'arbitrage* — René David, *L'arbitrage dans le commerce international* (1982)

Davis (ed), *Improving International Arbitration* — Benjamin Davis (ed), *Improving International Arbitration: The Need for Speed and Trust, Liber Amicorum Michel Gaudet* (ICC 1998)

de Boisséson, *Le droit français de l'arbitrage* — Matthieu de Boisséson, *Le droit français de l'arbitrage interne et international* (2d edition, JLN Joly 1990)

Derains and Schwartz, *ICC Rules* — Yves Derains, Eric A Schwartz, *A Guide to the New ICC Rules of Arbitration* (Kluwer 1998)

Dezalay and Garth, *Dealing in Virtue* — Yves Dezalay and Bryant Garth, *Dealing in Virtue - International Commercial Arbitration and the Construction of a Transnational Legal Order* (University of Chicago Press 1996)

Di Pietro and Platte, *Enforcement of International Arbitration Awards*	Domenico Di Pietro and Martin Platte, *Enforcement of International Arbitration Awards* (Cameron May, 2001)
Domke, *Arbitration*	Martin Domke, *The Law and Practice of Commercial Arbitration* (Chicago 1968 with Supplement 1974)
El Ahdab, *Arbitration with the Arab Countries*	Abdul Hamid El Ahdab, *Arbitration with the Arab Countries (*Kluwer 1998)
Fouchard Gaillard Goldman *on International Commercial Arbitration*	Emmanuel Gaillard and John Savage (eds), Fouchard Gaillard Goldman *on International Commercial Arbitration* (Kluwer 1999)
Fouchard, *L'arbitrage*	Philippe Fouchard, *L'arbitrage commercial international* (Dalloz 1965)
Friedland, *Arbitration Clauses*	Paul Friedland, *Arbitration Clauses for International Contracts* (Juris Publishing 2000).
Frommel and Rider (eds), *Conflicting Legal Cultures*	Stefan N Frommel and Barry A Rider (eds), *Conflicting Legal Cultures in Commercial Arbitration* (Kluwer 1999)
Grigera Naón, *Choice-of-law Problems*	Horacio Grigera Naón, *Choice-of-law Problems in International Commercial Arbitration* (Mohr 1992)
Helgeson and Lauterpacht (eds), *Reports of Cases Decided under ICSID*	Edward Helgeson and Elihu Lauterpacht (eds), *Reports of Cases Decided under the Convention on the Settlement of Investment Disputes between States and Nationals of Other States 1965* (Cambridge University Press 2002)
Hill, *International commercial disputes*	Jonathan Hill, *The Law Relating to International Commercial Disputes* (2d ed, LLP 1998)
Hirsch, *The Arbitration Mechanism of ICSID*	Moshe Hirsch, *The Arbitration Mechanism of the International Centre for the Settlement of Investment Disputes* (Martinus Nijhoff 1993)

Holtzmann and Neuhaus, *Model Law*	Howard Holtzmann and Joseph Neuhaus, *A Guide To The UNCITRAL Model Law On International Commercial Arbitration: Legislative History* (Kluwer 1989)
Hunter, Marriott and Veeder (eds), *Internationalization of International Arbitration*	Martin Hunter, Arthur Marriott and V V Veeder (eds), *The Internationalization of International Arbitration* (Kluwer 1995)
ICC (ed), *60 Years of ICC Arbitration*	International Chamber of Commerce, *60 Years of ICC Arbitration – A Look at the* Future (ICC 1984)
ICC (ed), *Conservatory and Provisional Measures*	ICC (ed), *Conservatory and Provisional Measures* (ICC 1993)
ICC (ed), *Independence of Arbitrators*	ICC (ed), *The Arbitral Process and the Independence of Arbitrators* (ICC 1991)
ICC (ed), *International Commercial Arbitration in Latin America*	ICC (ed), *International Commercial Arbitration in Latin America, ICC Bulletin,* Special Supplement (Paris 1997)
ICC (ed), *Multiparty Arbitration*	ICC (ed), *Multiparty Arbitration, Views from International Arbitration Specialists* (ICC 1991)
ICC (ed), *The Status of the Arbitrator*	ICC (ed), *The Status of the Arbitrator, ICC Bulletin Special Supplement* (ICC 1995)
ICCA Congress series no 1	Pieter Sanders (ed), *ICCA Congress series no 1, New Trends in the Development of International Commercial Arbitration and the Role of Arbitral and other Institutions* (Kluwer 1983)
ICCA Congress series no 2	Pieter Sanders (ed), *ICCA Congress series no 2, UNCITRAL's Project for a Model Law on International Commercial Arbitration* (Kluwer 1984)
ICCA Congress series no 3	Pieter Sanders (ed), *ICCA Congress series no 3, Comparative Arbitration Practice and Public Policy in Arbitration* (Kluwer1987)

ICCA Congress series no 4 — Pieter Sanders (ed), *ICCA Congress series no 4, Arbitration in Settlement of International Disputes involving the Far East and Arbitration in Combined Transportation* (Kluwer 1989)

ICCA Congress series no 5 — Albert Jan van den Berg (ed), *ICCA Congress series no 5, Preventing Delay and Disruption of Arbitration - Effective Proceedings in Construction Cases* (Kluwer 1991)

ICCA Congress series no 6 — Albert Jan van den Berg (ed), *ICCA Congress series no 6, International Arbitration in a Changing World* (Kluwer 1994)

ICCA Congress series no 7 — Albert Jan van den Berg (ed), *ICCA Congress series no 7, Planning Efficient Arbitration Proceedings The Law Applicable in International Arbitration* (Kluwer 1996)

ICCA Congress Series no 8 — Albert Jan van den Berg (ed), *ICCA Congress Series no 8, International Dispute Resolution: Towards an International Arbitration Culture* (Kluwer 1998)

ICCA Congress series no 9 — Albert Jan van den Berg (ed), *ICCA Congress series no 9, Improving the Efficiency of Arbitration and Awards: 40 Years of Application of the New York Convention* (Kluwer 1999)

ICCA Congress Series no 10 — Albert Jan van den Berg (ed), *ICCA Congress Series no 10, International Arbitration and National Courts: The Never Ending Story* (Kluwer 2001)

IECL — Konrad Zweigert and Ulrich Drobnig (eds), *International Encyclopaedia of Comparative Law* (Martinus Nijhoff 1982 *et seq*)

Jarrosson, *La notion d'arbitrage* — Charles Jarrosson, *La notion d'arbitrage* (LGDJ 1987)

Jarvin Derains Arnaldez, *ICC Awards 1986-1990*	Sigvard Jarvin, Yves Derains, Jean Jacques Arnaldez, *Collection of ICC Arbitral Awards, 1986-1990* (Kluwer Law and Taxation Publishers 1994)
Johnson, *Commodity Arbitration*	Derek Kirby Johnson, *International Commodity Arbitration* (LLP 1991)
Kaplan, *Hong Kong and China Arbitration*	Neil Kaplan, Jill Spruce and Michael Moser, *Hong Kong and China Arbitration: Cases and Materials* (Butterworths Asia 1994)
Kassis, *Problèmes de base*	Antoine Kassis, *Problèmes de base de l'arbitrage en droit comparé et droit international* (LGDJ 1987)
Katsch and Rivkin, *Online Dispute Resolution.*	Ethan Katsch and Janet Rifkin, *Online Dispute Resolution. Conflict Resolution in Cyberspace* (Jossey Bass 2001)
Kaufmann-Kohler, *Arbitration at the Olympics*	Gabrielle Kaufmann-Kohler, *Arbitration at the Olympics* (Kluwer 2001)
Khan, *The Iran-United States Claims Tribunal*	Rahmatullah Khan, *The Iran-United States Claims Tribunal: Controversies, Cases, and Contribution* (Martinus Nijhoff 1990)
Klein, *L'arbitrage en droit international privé*	Frédéric-Edouard Klein, *Considerations sur l'arbitrage en droit international privé* (Heilbing & Lichtenhahn 1955)
Koussoulis, *Main Issues on Arbitration*	Stellios Koussoulis, *Main Issues on Arbitration. B - Theory* (in Greeek, Ant Sakkoulas Publishers 1996)
Kröll, *Ergänzung und Anpassung von Verträgen durch Schiedsgerichte*	Stefan Kröll, *Ergänzung und Anpassung von Verträgen durch Schiedsgerichte* (Heymanns 1998)
Lachmann, *Handbuch*	Jens Peter Lachmann, *Handbuch für die Schiedsgerichtspraxis* (2d edition, Otto Schmidt Verlag 2002)

Lalive, Poudret and Reymond, *L'arbitrage Interne et International en Suisse*	Pierre Lalive, Jean-François Poudret and Claude Reymond, *Le Droit de L'arbitrage Interne et International en Suisse* (Payot 1989)
Langkeit, *Staatenimmunität und Schiedsgerichtsbarkeit*	Jochen Langkeit, *Staatenimmunität und Schiedsgerichtsbarkeit* (Recht und Wirtschaft 1989)
Lazic, *Insolvency Proceedings*	Vesna Lazic, *Insolvency Proceedings and Commercial Arbitration* (Kluwer 1998)
Lew (ed), *Immunity*	Julian D M Lew (ed), *Immunity of Arbitrators* (LLP 1990)
Lew (ed), *Contemporary Problems*	Julian D M Lew (ed), *Contemporary Problems in International Arbitration* (CCLS 1986)
Lew, *Applicable Law*	Julian D M Lew, *Applicable Law in International Commercial Arbitration* (Oceana 1978)
Lillich & Brower (eds.), *International Arbitration*	Richard B Lillich & Charles N Brower (eds), *International Arbitration in the 21st Century: Towards Judicialization and Uniformity?* (Transnational Publishers 1994)
Lillich (ed), *Fact-Finding before International Tribunals*	Richard B Lillich (ed), *Fact-Finding before International Tribunals* (Transnational Publishers 1991)
Lillich (ed), *The Iran-United States Claims Tribunal 1981-83*	Richard B Lillich (ed), *The Iran-United States Claims Tribunal 1981-83* (The University Press of Virginia 1984)
Loquin, *L'amiable composition*	Eric Loquin, *L'amiable composition en droit comparé et international. Contribution à l'étude du non droit dans l'arbitrage international* (Litec 1980)
Lörcher, *Neue Verfahren*	Torsten Lörcher, *Neue Verfahren der internationalen Streiterledigung in*

Wirtschaftssachen (Lang 2001)

Merkin, *Arbitration Act*	R M Merkin, *Arbitration Act – An Annotated Guide* (2d ed, LLP 2000)
Mohie Eldin I Alam Eldin, *Arbitral Awards of the Cairo Regional Centre*	Mohie Eldin I Alam Eldin, *Arbitral Awards of the Cairo Regional Centre for International Commercial Arbitration* (Kluwer 1999)
Mustill and Boyd, *2001 Companion*	Michael J Mustill and Stewart C Boyd, *Commercial Arbitration 2001 Companion* (2d ed, Butterworths 2001)
Mustill and Boyd, *Commercial Arbitration*	Michael J Mustill and Stewart C Boyd, *Commercial Arbitration* (2d ed, Butterworths, 1989)
Park, *International Forum Selection*	William W Park, *International Forum Selection* (Kluwer 1995)
Racine, *L'Arbitrage Commercial International et l'Ordre Public*	Jean-Baptiste Racine, *L'Arbitrage Commercial International et l'Ordre Public* (LGDJ 1999)
Raeschke-Kessler and Berger, *Recht und Praxis*	Hilmar Raeschke-Kessler and Klaus Peter Berger, *Recht und Praxis des Schiedsverfahrens* (3rd ed, RWS Kommunikationsforum 1999)
Recueil de Travaux Suisses	*Recueil de Travaux Suisses sur L'arbitrage International* (Schulthess Verlag 1984)
Redfern and Hunter, *International Commercial Arbitration*	Alan Redfern and Martin Hunter, *Law and Practice of International Commercial Arbitration* (3rd ed, Sweet & Maxwell 1999)
Reisman Craig Park Paulsson, *International Commercial Arbitration*	W Michael Reisman, W Laurence Craig, William W Park and Jan Paulsson, *International Commercial Arbitration* (Foundation Press 1997)
Robert, *L'arbitrage*	Jean Robert, *L'arbitrage - droit interne, droit international prive* (6th ed, Dalloz 1993)

Rubellin-Devichi, *L'arbitrage: nature juridique*	Jacqueline Rubellin-Devichi, *L'arbitrage: nature juridique: droit interne et droit international privé* (LGDP 1965)
Rubino-Sammartano, *International Arbitration*	Mauro Rubino-Sammartano, *International Arbitration Law* (2d ed, Kluwer 2001)
Rule, *Online Dispute Resolution*	Colin Rule, *Online Dispute Resolution for Business* (Jossey Bass 2002)
Russell *on Arbitration*	Russell *on Arbitration*, 21 edition, edited by David St Sutton, John Kendall, Judith Gill (Sweet & Maxwell 1997)
Samuel, *Jurisdictional Problems*	Adam Samuel, *Jurisdictional Problems in International Commercial Arbitration: A Study of Belgian, Dutch, English, French, Swedish, U.S., and West German Law* (Schulthess 1989)
Sanders (ed), *International Commercial Arbitration.*	Pieter Sanders (ed), *International Commercial Arbitration* (UIA 1965)
Sanders (ed), *Liber Amicorum Martin Domke*	Pieter Sanders (ed) *International Arbitration – Liber Amicorum Martin Domke* (1967)
Sanders, *Quo Vadis Arbitration?*	Pieter Sanders, *Quo Vadis Arbitration? Sixty Years of Arbitration Practice* (Kluwer 1999)
Sandifer, *Evidence before International Tribunals*	Durward Sandifer, *Evidence before International Tribunals* (University of Virginia Press 1975)
Sarčević (ed), *Essays*	Petar Sarčević (ed), *Essays on International Commercial Arbitration* (Martinus Nijhoff 1989)
SCC, *Arbitration in Sweden*	Stockholm Chamber of Commerce (ed), *Arbitration in Sweden* (2d ed, Stockholm Chamber of Commerce 1984)
Scheef, *Der einstweilige Rechtsschutz*	Hans Claudius Scheef, *Der einstweilige Rechtsschutz und die Stellung der Schiedsrichter*

	bei dem Abschluss von Schiedsvergleichen nach deutschem und englischem Schiedsverfahrensrecht (Lang 2001)
Schlosser, *Internationale Schiedsgerichtsbarkeit*	Peter Schlosser, *Das Recht der internationalen privaten Schiedsgerichtsbarkeit (*2d ed, Mohr 1989)
Schreuer, *ICSID Commentary*	Christoph Schreuer, *The ICSID Convention – A Commentary* (CUP 2001)
Schwebel, *Three Salient Problems*	Stephen Schwebel, *International Arbitration: Three Salient Problems* (Grotius 1987)
Simpson, Thacher & Bartlett (eds), *International Arbitration Rules*	Simpson, Thacher & Bartlett (eds), *Comparison of International Arbitration Rules* (2d ed, Juris Publishing 2002)
Sornarajah, *The Settlement of Foreign Investment Disputes*	M Sornarajah, *The Settlement of Foreign Investment Disputes* (Kluwer 2000)
Stipanowich & Kneckell, *Commercial Arbitration*	Thomas Stipanowich & Peter Kneckell, *Commercial Arbitration At Its Best* (CPRI & ABA 2001)
Tweeddale and Tweeddale, *Arbitration Law*	Andrew Tweeddale and Karen Tweeddale, *A Practical Approach to Arbitration Law* (Blackstone 1999)
van den Berg (ed), *ICCA Handbook*	Albert Jan van den Berg (ed), *ICCA Handbook on Commercial Arbitration* (Kluwer 1984)
van den Berg, *New York Convention*	Albert Jan van den Berg, *The New York Arbitration Convention of 1958. Towards a Uniform Judicial Interpretation* (Kluwer Law and Taxation 1981)
van den Berg, van Delden, Snijders, *Netherlands Arbitration Law* ed),	Albert Jan van den Berg, Robert van Delden, Henricus Joseph Snijders, *Netherlands Arbitration Law* (Kluwer Law and Taxation 1993)

van Hof, *Commentary on the UNCITRAL Arbitration Rules*	Jacomijn J van Hof, *Commentary on the UNCITRAL Arbitration Rules- The Application by the Iran-US Claims Tribunal* (Kluwer1991)
Westberg, *Case Law of the Iran-United States Claims Tribunal*	John A Westberg, *International Transactions and Claims involving Government Parties: Case Law of the Iran-United States Claims Tribunal* (International Law Institute 1991)
Zilles, *Schiedsgerichtsbarkeit Gesellschaftsrecht*	Stephan Zilles, *Schiedsgerichtsbarkeit im Gesellschaftsrecht* (Luchterhand 2002)

TABLE OF INTERNATIONAL CONVENTIONS AND INSTRUMENTS
All references are to paragraph numbers

TABLE OF ARBITRATION RULES
All references are to paragraph numbers

TABLE OF NATIONAL LAWS

All references are to paragraph numbers

TABLE OF ARBITRATION AWARDS

All references are to paragraph numbers

Awards are organised chronologically; institutions alphabetically

***Ad hoc* arbitrations**

Award of 2 September 1930, *Lena Goldfields Ltd v USSR,* The Times, 3 September 1930, 36 Cornell Law Quarterly 31 (1950-51)
 - 24-100

Award of 10 June 1955, *Royal Hellenic Government v HM British Government,* 22 ILR 820 (1995), 5 ICLQ 471 (1956), 45 Rev crit dip 278 (1956)
 - 18-84

Award of 15 March 1963, *Sapphire Int'l Petroleum Ltd v National Iranian Oil Co,* 35 ILR 136 (1967)
18-38

Saudi Arabia v Arabian American Oil Co (ARAMCO), 27 ILR 117 (1963)
 - 17-20, 18-33, 24-76

Award on reopening of 1 August 1974, *British Petroleum Company (Libya) Ltd v The Government of the Libyan Arab Republic,* 53 ILR 297 (1979), V YBCA 158 (1980)
 - 18-54, 21-78

Texaco Overseas Petroleum Co v Libyan Arab Republic, 19 January 1977, IV YBCA 177 (1979)
 - 18-38, 18-54

Texaco Overseas Petroleum Company / California Asiatic Oil Company v The Government of the Libyan Arab Republic, Preliminary Award on jurisdiction, 27 November 1975, 104 Clunet 350 (1977), IV *YBCA* 176 (1979), 17 ILM 1 (1978)
 - 14-18, 24-72

Award of 12 April 1977, *Libyan American Oil Company (LIAMCO) v Government of the Libyan Arab Republic,* 10 ILM 1 (1981)
 - 18-54

Award of 3 November 1977, *Mechema Ltd v SA Mines, Minerais et Metaux,* VII YBCA 77 (1982)
 - 18-91

Award of 24 March 1982, *Government of the State of Kuwait v American Independent Oil Co (AMINOIL),* IX YBCA 71 (1984), 21 ILM 976 (1982)
 - 18-38, 18-39, 18-73

Award of April 1982, *Company Z and others v State Organization ABC,* VIII YBCA 94 (1983)
 - 9-90, 27-12

Award of 6 July 1983, *Hungarian State enterprise v Jugoslavenski naftovod,* IX YBCA 69 (1984)
 - 18-57

Interim Award of 18 November 1983, *Erick Benteler KG and Helmut Benteler KG (both FR Germany) v Belgian State and SA ABC (Belgium),* Journal des Tribunaux 230 (1984), X YBCA 37 (1985), Rev Arb 339 (1989)
 - 4-23

Partial Award of 5 February 1988, *Wintershall AG et al v Government of Qatar,* 28 ILM 798 (1989), XV YBCA 30 (1990)
 - 10-48, 24-19, 24-98

Award of 15 September 1989, *E v Z, ICA Z and Société M,* ASA Bulletin 270 (1990)
 - 7-51

Award of 1991, ASA Bulletin 202 (1992)
7-51

Award of 29 December 1993, *Icori Estero Spa v Kuwait Foreign Trading Contracting & Investment Co,* 9(12) Mealey's IAR A1 (1994)
 - 24-47

ICSID

Iran-US Claims Tribunal

Table of National and International Court Decisions

All references are to paragraph numbers

Court decisions from common law systems are organised alphabetically; decisions from civil law countries are organised chronologically.

Argentina

Supreme Court, 24 October 1995, *Compania Naviera Perez SACFIMFA v Ecofisa SA*, 11 Mealey's IAR 9 (1996)
21-24

Australia

Aerospatiale Holdings Australia Pty Ltd et al v Elspan International Pty Ltd, (1994) XIX YBCA 635, no 55053/92 (Supreme Court of New South Wales, Common Law Division, 14 August 1992)
16-82, 16-87

Cleanae Pty Ltd v Australia and New Zealand Banking Group Ltd [1999] VSCA 35
12-15

CSR Ltd v NZI, (1994) 36 NSWLR 138 (New South Wales Supreme Court)
15-31

Esso Australia Resources Ltd and others v The Hon Sidney James Plowman, The Minister for Energy and Minerals and others, 10 Commonwealth Law Reports 183 (1995)
1-27, 24-103

Hi-Fert Pty Ltd and Cargill Fertilizer Inc v Kiukiang Maritime Carriers and Western Bulk Carriers Ltd, (1999) 159 ALR 142, 12(7) Mealey's IAR C-1 (1997), Int ALR N-17 (2000), XXIII YBCA 606 (1998) (Federal Court of Australia)
5-37, 7-61, 10-28

ICT Pty Ltd v Sea Containers Ltd, 17(3) Mealey's IAR B1 (2002) (New South Wales Supreme Court)
11-18, 12-29

McKain v R W Miller & Co (South Australia) Pty Ltd (1991) 104 ALR 257
20-23

McKensey v Hewitt, 17(3) Mealey's IAR C-1 (2002) (New South Wales Supreme Court 11 March 2002)
23-53

Multiplex Construction Pty Ltd v Suscindy Management Pty Ltd [2000] NSWSC 484
7-94

R v Watson, ex parte Armstrong, (1976) 136 CLR 248
13-13

Resort Condominiums International Inc v Ray Bolwell and Resort Condominiums Pty Ltd, 9(4) Mealey's IAR A1 (1994) XX YBCA 628 (1995) (Supreme Court Queensland, 29 October 1993)
10-89, 22-58, 23-39, 23-91, 24-27, 26-39, 26-102

Austria

Oberster Gerichtshof, 17 November 1965, *German party v Austrian party*, 3 Ob 128/65, 9 ZfRV 123 (1968), I YBCA 182 (1976)
- 26-60

Oberster Gerichtshof, 17 November 1971, I YBCA 183 (1976)
6-36, 7-19

China

Subject Index

All references are to paragraph numbers